FEMINIST FRONTIERS

NINTH EDITION

Verta Taylor

Nancy Whittier

Leila J. Rupp

FEMINIST FRONTIERS, NINTH EDITION

Published by McGraw-Hill, a business unit of The McGraw-Hill Companies, Inc., 1221 Avenue of the Americas, New York, NY 10020. Copyright © 2012 by The McGraw-Hill Companies, Inc. All rights reserved. Previous editions © 2009, 2007 and 2004. Printed in the United States of America. No part of this publication may be reproduced or distributed in any form or by any means, or stored in a database or retrieval system, without the prior written consent of The McGraw-Hill Companies, Inc., including, but not limited to, in any network or other electronic storage or transmission, or broadcast for distance learning.

Some ancillaries, including electronic and print components, may not be available to customers outside the United States.

This book is printed on acid-free paper

2 3 4 5 6 7 8 9 0 DOC/DOC 1 0 9 8 7 6 5 4 3 2

ISBN 978-0-07-802662-1
MHID 0-07-802662-8

Vice President & Editor-in-Chief: *Michael Ryan*
Vice President & Director Specialized Publishing: *Janice M. Roerig-Blong*
Editorial Director: *William Glass*
Senior Sponsoring Editor: *Debra B. Hash*
Director of Marketing and Sales: *Jennifer J. Lewis*
Senior Project Manager: *Lisa A. Bruflodt*
Design Coordinator: *Margarite Reynolds*

Cover Designer: *Studio Montage, St. Louis, Missouri*
Cover Image: © *Ginger Green*
Buyer: *Kara Kudronowicz*
Media Project Manager: *Sridevi Palani*
Compositor: *MPS Limited, a Macmillan Company*
Typeface: 9/11 *Palatino*
Printer: *R. R. Donnelley*

Cover
About the artist: Ginger Green

I grew up in Indianapolis where I attended John Herron School of Art and Design. My family led me to the Florida Keys, where my style originated. I call it urban island folk with a Caribbean flair. It's characterized by its whimsical look and vibrant colors, inspired by the sun, sand, and surf of island living.

If you would like to contact me, e-mail me at: artbyginger@aol.com

All credits appearing on page or at the end of the book are considered to be an extension of the copyright page.

Library of Congress Cataloging-in-Publication Data

Feminist frontiers / [edited by] Verta Taylor, Nancy Whittier, Leila J. Rupp. — 9th ed.
    p. cm.
  ISBN 978-0-07-802662-1 (alk. paper)
  1. Feminism—United States. 2. Women—United States. 3. Sex role—United States. 4. Women—Cross-cultural studies. I. Taylor, Verta A. II. Rupp, Leila J., 1950- III. Whittier, Nancy, 1966-
HQ1426.F472 2012
305.420973—dc23
                                                              2011023216

www.mhhe.com/taylorff9e

In memory of our mothers,
who in different ways raised us all to be strong women

Alice Taylor Houston
(1926–2008)

Sally Anne Kennedy
(1933–2007)

Sidney Stanton Rupp
(1912–1995)

VERTA TAYLOR is Professor and Chair of the Department of Sociology and affiliated faculty member in Feminist Studies at the University of California, Santa Barbara. She teaches courses on gender and sexuality, feminism, and social movements and has won numerous teaching awards, including the Ohio State University Distinguished Teaching Award, a Multicultural Teaching Award, an Outstanding Faculty Award from the Office of Gay, Lesbian, and Bisexual Student Services, and a University Distinguished Diversity Enhancement Award.

Taylor is the coauthor, with Leila J. Rupp, of *Drag Queens at the 801 Cabaret,* which won the 2005 book award from the Sex and Gender Section of the American Sociological Association, author of *Rock-a-by Baby: Feminism, Self-Help, and Postpartum Depression*; and coauthor with Leila J. Rupp of *Survival in the Doldrums: The American Women's Rights Movement, 1945 to the 1960s.* In addition, she has published numerous articles in scholarly journals and edited volumes.

In recognition of her lifetime of scholarship on women, Professor Taylor was the 2011 Recipient of the American Sociological Association's Jessie Bernard Award, and she has been honored by Sociologists for Women in Society (SWS) with its Mentoring Award and Feminist Lecturership Award. In 2008, she also received the John D. McCarthy Lifetime Achievement Award for her scholarship on social movements, and, the Simon and Gagnon Award for her career of scholarship in sexualities.

NANCY WHITTIER is Professor and former chair of the Department of Sociology at Smith College. She teaches courses on gender, social movements, queer politics, and research methods. She was a Fellow at the Center for Advanced Study in the Behavioral Sciences in 2010–2011. She is the author of *The Politics of Child Sexual Abuse: Emotion, Social Movements, and the State,* which received the 2010 Charles Tilly Award for Best Book Published in Collective Behavior and Social Movements from the American Sociological Association Section on Collective Behavior and Social Movements; *Feminist Generations: The Persistence of the Radical Women's Movement*; and co-editor of *Social Movements: Identity, Culture, and the State.* Her work on the women's movement, activism against child sexual abuse, social movement culture and collective identity and activist generations has appeared in numerous scholarly collections and journals.

LEILA J. RUPP is Professor of Feminist Studies and Associate Dean of Social Sciences at the University of California, Santa Barbara, where she holds affiliated appointments in the Departments of History and Sociology. A historian by training, she teaches introductory women's studies and courses on sexuality and women's movements. She received an Academic Senate Distinguished Teaching Award in 2008 and while teaching at Ohio State University won the Ohio State University Distinguished Teaching Award, a Multicultural Teaching Award, and an outstanding teaching award from the Ohio Academy of History. She also won awards at both Ohio State and the University of California for her contributions to gay, lesbian, bisexual, transgender, and queer students. She is the author of *Mobilizing Women for War: German and American Propaganda, 1939–1945, Worlds of Women: The Making of an International Women's Movement, A Desired Past: A Short History of Same-Sex Love in America, Sapphistries: A Global History of Love between Women,* and coauthor, with Verta Taylor, of *Survival in the Doldrums: The American Women's Rights Movement, 1945 to the 1960s* and *Drag Queens at the 801 Cabaret,* which won the 2005 book award from the Sex and Gender Section of the American Sociological Association. In addition, she has published numerous articles in journals and edited collections.

PREFACE

The first edition of *Feminist Frontiers* was conceived in the late 1970s at a time when many women inside and outside academia were beginning to recognize and challenge male domination. At the time of its publication, only a handful of books and anthologies written for classroom use presented a feminist perspective on women's lives.

The evolution of this book through nine editions reflects both the success of the women's movement and the incredible development of feminist scholarship over the past decades. Women's studies courses have blossomed and spread to campuses in even the most conservative regions of the country. Feminist scholars have, in the meantime, refined and enlarged our understanding of how gender inequality operates and how it intersects with other systems of domination based on race, ethnicity, class, sexuality, nationality, and ability. There is no doubt that the situation of women has changed since the publication of the first edition of *Feminist Frontiers*. Gender inequality has not, however, disappeared.

We write this preface to the ninth edition of *Feminist Frontiers* with pride and excitement. We are proud to be part of the continuing women's movement; and we are excited about the burgeoning knowledge about how gender is connected to class, race, ethnicity, sexuality, and other differences and how forces of globalization in the contemporary world shape the experiences of women. We feel fortunate to be writing, teaching, and learning at a time when feminist thought and research are flourishing and deepening, despite the challenges we face both nationally and globally. It is, simultaneously, a time to enjoy the bounty of feminist scholarship and to sow new feminist seeds.

In this edition of *Feminist Frontiers*, we highlight the impact of new technologies on women's lives and women's activism. The Internet is everywhere, shaping the way we present ourselves, communicate with each other, learn about the world, meet people, locate resources, organize, work, and engage in activism. Recognizing the pervasiveness of these new ways of being in the world, this ninth edition offers ten selections that focus on or include an analysis of online interactions or that originally appeared on the Internet.

We developed *Feminist Frontiers* for use as the major—or supplementary—text in courses on women's studies, gender studies, or the sociology of women or gender. Because this book offers a general framework for analyzing women, society, and culture, it can also be used as a supplementary text in introductory sociology classes and in courses on social problems, comparative studies, and American studies.

Although we have retained some of the articles from previous editions of *Feminist Frontiers*— particularly writings that have become feminist classics—the book has been updated to include more recent scholarship. We have added nineteen new selections and one heavily revised article. For the first time, we have eliminated the boxed inserts, allowing more in-depth coverage of a range of topics. We have continued to select readings that emphasize the diversity of women's experiences and the intersections of gender with race, ethnicity, class, sexuality, nationality, and ability. As in previous editions, the introductions to each section contain focused summaries of the readings and their relationship to each other, as well as discussion questions for each reading.

ORGANIZATION

Feminist Frontiers is organized into four major parts, each introduced by a sociological and feminist analysis. **Part One: Introduction** begins with a section representing the diversity of women's experiences and gender systems. That is followed by a section titled "Theoretical Perspectives," which presents social constructionist and intersectional theoretical approaches to gender. **Part Two: Gender, Culture, and Socialization** has two sections, "Representation, Language, and Culture" and "Socialization." **Part Three: Social Organization of Gender** has five sections, providing readings on work and the economy, families, sexualities, bodies, and violence. **Part Four: Social Change** includes articles on global politics and the state and on social protest and feminist movements.

CRITERIA FOR SELECTION

As we set about selecting articles for this edition, we found an abundance of excellent pieces. We used the following criteria for choosing what to include:

- We wanted each selection to be engagingly written and accessible in style and language to readers from different disciplinary backgrounds.
- As a testament to the tremendous growth in the depth and complexity of feminist scholarship, we sought selections exploring a wide range of theoretical and substantive issues.
- We wanted this anthology to reflect a diversity of racial, ethnic, class, sexual, and cultural experiences.
- Given the increasingly powerful forces of globalization in our contemporary world, we looked for articles that attend to the processes of globalization.
- We sought to capture the cross-disciplinary nature of gender research. We looked for articles that explored the impact of new technologies on the lives of women (and men).

CHANGES IN THE NINTH EDITION

The ninth edition contains nineteen new articles and one selection that has been heavily revised., representing the most current scholarship and public debates and expanding our coverage of issues important to feminist scholarship. We have deleted dated pieces while retaining readings that are classic in the field.

Central topics that continue to receive coverage in this edition include social constructionist theories of gender; feminist intersectionality theory; gendered and raced beauty standards; racialized gender socialization; gender, race, and ethnicity in the workplace; marriage and family issues; diverse sexualities; body issues; reproductive rights; violence against women; globalization; women and welfare; women's movements; and queer politics.

Additions to the text focus on new technologies and their impact on women's lives and experiences. These articles include **danah boyd** on "Sexing the Internet," **Sophia DeMasi** on online dating, **France Winddance Twine** on the use of the Internet to find surrogate mothers, **N. Tatiana Masters** on men's antirape Web sites, **Marisa D'Mello** on Indian women technology professionals, **Anita Harris** on young women's use of the Internet and social networking sites, and **Moya Bailey** and **Alexis Pauline Gumbs** on young black women's use of the internet. In addition, both **Jennifer Klein** and **Eileen Boris**'s article on home care and **Laurie Essig** and **Lyn Owens**'s on marriage originally appeared online. Other new additions include articles on such topics as disability oppression, gendered borderlands, gender on the Internet, heteronormativity in children's films, gender in children's clothing, racialized gender in the work of home care, the disadvantages of marriage, online dating, hooking up, girls kissing, transgender people at work and in intimate interactions, the politics of surrogate motherhood, girls' violence, men's online antirape activism, welfare mothers and constructions of motherhood, the gendering of information technology work in India, globalized militarization, young women's use of online cultures, and young black feminists' online activism.

NEW READINGS IN THE NINTH EDITION

Every section has been updated with new selections. Section 1 ends with an article by **Eli Clare** on his attempt to climb Mount Adams despite his cerebral palsy, an experience that leads to a consideration of disability oppression. This section also restores the full version of **Audre Lorde**'s classic piece "The Master's Tools Will Never Dismantle the Master's House." Section 2 adds a piece by **Denise Segura** and **Patricia Zavella** on the gendered borderlands of spaces between and within the United States and Mexico.

Section 3, "Representation, Language, and Culture," adds **danah boyd**'s reflections on the consequences of required identity markers on the Internet. Two added articles in Section 4, on socialization, provide new perspectives: **Karin Martin** and **Emily Kazyak** analyze the messages on romance and sexuality in films marketed to children, and **Catherine Newman** tells the story of her son who loves the color pink.

In Section 5, "Work," **Jennifer Klein** and **Eileen Boris** contribute an article about the work of home care and the efforts of poorly paid home care workers to organize to improve the conditions of their labor. Section 6, "Families," adds a consideration of the arguments against marriage.

Four new pieces appear in Section 7, "Sexualities." **Sophie DeMasi** looks at online dating, **Elizabeth Armstrong, Laura Hamilton,** and **Paula England** consider the advantages and disadvantages of hooking up and relationships for college women, **Leila Rupp** and **Verta Taylor** ask what is going on when young presumably straight women kiss and make out with other women, and **Kristin Schilt** and **Laurel Westbrook** compare the reactions of women and men to transgender people at work and in intimate relations. Section 8, "Bodies," offers **France Winddance Twine**'s analysis of the race, class, and global dynamics of gestational surrogacy. Section 9, "Violence Against Women," adds **Laurie Schaffner**'s article on girls' violence and **N. Tatiana Masters**'s analysis of men's antirape activism and the construction of masculinity on antirape Web sites.

Section 10, "Global Politics and the State," includes new articles on poor women's resistance to the labeling of women on welfare as bad mothers (**Karen McCormack**) the impact of gender on Indian women working in information technology (**Marisa D'Mello**), and the consequences of and means of resisting globalized militarization (**Gwyn Kirk**).

Section 11 offers a revised and updated consideration of the history and continuity of the U.S. women's movement (**Alison Dahl Crossley, Verta Taylor, Nancy Whittier,** and **Cynthia Fabrizio Pelak**) and new articles by **Anita Harris** on the political possibilities of young women's engagement with online cultures and **Moya Bailey** and **Alexis Pauline Gumbs** on young black women's online research and activism.

CONNECTIONS AMONG SECTIONS

Many of the articles in *Feminist Frontiers* make connections to topics covered in different sections, a sign of the multiple intersections of women's studies. For example, the concept of intersectionality, illustrated in the diverse and complex experiences covered in Section 1 and outlined in the theoretical articles in Section 2, can be traced through **Kimberlé Crenshaw**'s classic article on violence against women of color in Section 9 and **Andrea Smith**'s consideration of reproductive politics in the context of race, class, and ability. That we cannot talk about gender without acknowledging the ways that it is raced and classed is central to **Pierrette Hondagneu-Sotelo**'s article on Latina domestics, **Jennifer Klein** and **Eileen Boris**'s on home care workers, **Hung Cam Thai**'s on Vietnamese marriages, **Becky Wangsgaard Thompson**'s on eating disorders, **France Winddance Twine**'s on surrogacy, **Karen McCormack**'s on women on welfare, **Marisa D'Mello**'s on Indian women technology professionals, and **Lila Abu-Lughod**'s on Muslim women.

Likewise, global forces appear throughout the volume, not just in the section on global politics: in **Denise Segura** and **Patrticia Zavella**'s and **R. W. Connell**'s theoretical articles in Section 2, **Yen Le Espiritu**'s analysis of cross-national socialization practices in Section 4, the pieces on Korean manicurists and Latina domestics in Section 5, the article on Vietnamese marriages in Section 6, the consideration of African genital cutting in light of cosmetic labial surgery in the United States and global gestational surrogacy in Section 8, **Grace Chang**'s article on Asian women workers fighting globalization, the piece on Indian women in the global software economy, **Gwyn Kirk** on globalized militarization and reflections on Muslim women in light of the "war on terror" in Section 10, and the overview of women's movements in Section 11.

Other issues, too, cross sections. Transsexuality, transgenderism, and intersexuality appear in **Paula Gunn Allen**'s reflections on being Native American, **Suzanne Kessler**'s consideration of surgery on intersexed infants, **Susan Stryker**'s article, **Kristin Schilt**'s and **Laurel Westbrook**'s article on transgender people, and **Cathy Cohen**'s article on queer politics. Other connections across sections focus on work, bodies, disability, beauty, youth, motherhood, and migration.

SUPPLEMENTS

Companion Web site

The *Feminist Frontiers* Web site proves general information about the book and offers separate areas for students and instructors.

For the Student
The "Student side" of the site is organized to correspond to the eleven sections of the text. There are practice test questions, an annotated list of Web links, and a link to Census 2000 updates.

For the Instructor
Instructor's Manual: The Instructor's Manual is organized to correspond to each section of the text. It offers learning objectives, discussion questions, summaries of the key points of the section introductions and readings, suggestions for assignments and exercises, and an annotated list of Web links.

Test Bank: The Test Bank offers multiple-choice, short answer, and essay questions on the section introductions and individual readings.

Visit the companion Web site at:
www.mhhe.com/taylor9e

ACKNOWLEDGMENTS

We gratefully acknowledge the support, skill, and help of many people. We extend thanks to the authors of the articles, not only for writing the selected pieces but also for allowing us to reprint them here. At McGraw-Hill, we thank Nikki Weissman, Debra Hash, Joynn Kilburg, Lisa Bruflodt, and Wendy Langerud for their support, and attention to detail and Sheryl Rose for her expert copyediting. We thank Ruma Khurana for her skillful management of the production process. We also thank Fred Courtright for his services as permissions editor. We thank Shannon Weber for her excellent work on the Instructor's Manual and other supplements for this edition. Nicole Raeburn provided research assistance and revisions of the Test Bank for earlier editions of the book, and Lisa Leitz put her charisma as a teacher to use in developing a previous version of the Web site. We continue to benefit from the work of Kegan Allee on an earlier edition. In addition, we are grateful to Eileen Boris and Laury Oaks for sharing with us their experiences teaching the previous edition and suggesting potential articles. Finally, we express our appreciation to students in our classes on the sociology of women, sex and gender, queer studies, and women's studies at Smith College and the University of California, Santa Barbara. They have contributed to the development of this anthology by their thoughtful responses to potential articles.

We are also grateful for the comments of the following scholars who served as reviewers in the development of *Feminist Frontiers*:

Samantha Elliott Briggs, The University of Alabama
Diane M. Hodge, Radford University
Alice Julier, Chatham University, University of Pittsburg
Maura Kelly, University of Connecticut
Neal King, Virginia Tech
Natalie M. Peluso, University of Connecticut

We continue to be grateful to Laurel Richardson, who, together with Verta Taylor, initiated the first edition of *Feminist Frontiers*. Special thanks go to Kate Weigand, who provided feedback and insight into the collection's organization and offered consistent encouragement and companionship. Jonah, Eva, and Isaac Weigand-Whittier are a constant source of inspiration as we seek to reconstruct gender. To them and to the students and colleagues who have touched our lives positively, we express our gratitude.

Verta Taylor
Nancy Whittier
Leila J. Rupp

CONTENTS

PART ONE

INTRODUCTION

What is gender? Our gender affects how we think about ourselves, the ways we interact with each other, the kinds of relationships we form, and our positions in our communities. As an element of social relationships, gender operates at multiple levels to categorize and distinguish people. But gender is also about social institutions that distribute power, resources, and status among various groups of women and men. Gender also interacts with race, class, ethnicity, and sexuality. In other words, gender means different things, and has different consequences for status and power, depending on race, class, ethnicity, and sexuality.

What does it mean to be a woman? Thinking about women's experiences is a complicated task because women have as many differences from each other as commonalities. On the one hand, women everywhere suffer from restrictions, oppression, and discrimination because they are living in patriarchal societies. Yet gender is not the sole influence on any woman's life. Race, ethnicity, class, sexuality, age, nation, region, and religion shape women's experiences. Moreover, these differences intersect with each other. For example, Asian-American women of various ages, sexual orientations, classes, and ethnic and national origins have different experiences.

The experience of being a woman is quite different for distinct groups of women. For a white, upper-class, heterosexual, American woman, for example, femininity might entail being economically dependent on her husband, maintaining a delicate and refined physical appearance, and achieving social influence through child-raising and volunteer work. Womanhood for a middle-class African-American woman might mean providing financial support for her children, holding influential and respected positions within her church and community, yet being stereotyped by the dominant white culture as sexually promiscuous or unintelligent. For a Mexican immigrant to the United States, femininity might mean being a good mother—which, as Denise Segura and Patricia Zavella suggest in Section 2, may mean working long hours at low pay in order to support her children.

The experiences of men are similarly varied. Although men benefit from power and privilege over women, some groups of men also exercise power over other men, while other groups of men are excluded from economic or political influence due to their race, class, nationality, or sexual identity. To understand the position of a particular man, in other words, we must consider his gender, race, class, sexuality, age, and so forth, in order to understand the particular advantages and disadvantages he faces.

In short, gender is defined in various ways for different groups. Gender definitions bring with them a distinct set of restrictions and disadvantages for members in each group, as well as privileges and sources of power or resistance. The task for you as students, and for scholars of gender, is to recognize patterns of male dominance while simultaneously recognizing variations.

As if matters were not complex enough, individuals also have unique constellations of experiences. Each of us has our own story to tell. Each of us has multiple alliances and identifications with groups that shift through time and social context. The religious identity of childhood may be shunted aside during young adulthood, for example, only to be reclaimed in later years. Self-definitions as heterosexual may give way later in life to new identities as lesbian or bisexual. As biracial or bicultural or mixed-religion daughters, we might identify with the heritage of either parent or both. In addition, we have different degrees of allegiance to the gender standards of our particular groups. Some of us adopt prescriptions about masculinity or femininity wholeheartedly, others reject those prescriptions, and still others adopt some aspects of socially approved gender standards and reject others. Some of us identify strongly with the category—woman or man—to which we are assigned, while others identify as transgendered and seek either to identify with the other gender category or to construct an alternate gender identity. Although social forces such as sexism, racism, heterosexism, and class inequality shape our biographies, it is as individuals that we experience and make sense of our lives.

The task of feminist scholarship, and of this volume, is to illuminate the social and structural roots of our gendered experiences while simultaneously recognizing the complicated and unique factors that shape our lives. Feminist research builds upon and links two levels of analysis: structure and biography. The structural level looks at social institutions and cultural practices that create and sustain gender inequalities, and it links those inequalities to other systems of oppression, such as racism, ageism, and homophobia. The biographical level honors each individual's expression of her own experience. It pays attention to how individuals represent themselves and recognizes personal voice. As a result, we can learn how difference and commonality are structurally rooted and personally experienced. We can see how larger social forces affect our own and others' lives.

Feminist research is not just about analyzing the ways that social structures shape and restrict the lives of women. Of course, it is important to document the inequalities faced by various groups of women and to examine the ways that women have been oppressed and victimized based on gender. Experiences such as discrimination in hiring and pay, sexual violence, and legal subordination, for example, are undeniably central to gender. Yet feminist scholarship also emphasizes the sources of power that women find: how they define themselves, influence their social contexts, and resist the restrictions that they face. The articles in this volume view women not as passive victims of patriarchal social structures, but as actors who exercise control over their own lives, find pleasure and fulfillment, and resist social constraints.

Further, feminist research is not just about documenting women's experiences. It is about recognizing the ways that gender shapes the lives of both women and men and analyzing a broad system of gender. The gender system affects not only the lives of individuals but the organization of other institutions in the larger society. By documenting

the influence of social structures on gender and highlighting individuals' complex mixture of domination, resistance, and complicity, feminist scholarship leads us to rethink the structural changes necessary to meet the needs of actual women and men.

Feminist theory and scholarship on gender, then, face a broad set of questions. Approaches to answering these questions vary enormously; we hope that you will recognize disagreement and debate, as well as cooperation, in the readings that follow. There are, however, some shared assumptions that run through the selections in this book.

First, feminist scholars view gender as pervasive, as part of every feature of social life and individual identity. It is impossible, therefore, to analyze any part of social life as if it were gender neutral. As a result, feminist scholars challenge the male bias hidden under claims of scientific objectivity in academic research. As you read these essays and those in other classes, ask yourself how the social conditions and practices of doing research reinforce or challenge gender inequities.

Second, feminist researchers understand systems of oppression as interlocking. Race, class, ethnicity, sexuality, and other systems of domination affect how one experiences gender. Therefore, although gender is a basic fact of social life, women and men in different positions in society experience their gender and the power or oppression that results from it differently. Just as feminist researchers challenge knowledge claims about "people" based on research on men, they question knowledge about "women" based on research on white, middle-class women.

Third, feminist scholars experiment with new ways of doing research, rethinking the relationship between the researcher and the researched. The scientific method of research assumes that there is a separation between the scholar and the subjects of research and that this separation is necessary to produce "objective" and "valid" research. Feminist researchers challenge this tenet. Treating women as "objects" of research contravenes feminist goals of equality by elevating the researcher's agenda and perspective above those of the researched. One of the major questions of feminist thought is how to do research that empowers both the researcher and the researched. How do we create social research practices in which researcher and researched collaborate in the process of interpreting the world? For some, the solution has been to write about their own lives; some acknowledge directly how their own biases affect their work; others study groups of which they are a part; still others do "participatory" or "action" research in which the researcher and the researched determine together the topics, methods, goals, and political action to follow from the project, so that the scholar is a participant in the project, but not its leader.

These are not only theoretical concerns; they are important ethical questions. What right does a scholar have to write about another person's life? How should we write about the lives of those who are different from ourselves? How can we use the skills and privileges of academic practice to diminish social inequality?

We invite you to engage in reading, thinking about, and doing feminist research. We hope that you will consider some of the central questions that run through this book. What are the commonalities and differences among women or among men? What, if anything, do women or men of different classes, races, or sexualities share in common? We hope that you will reflect on the complicated balance between oppression and resistance, between the pervasive influence of society and the ways that individuals and groups define themselves and carve out meaningful lives. We encourage you to discuss your ideas, to debate the issues this volume raises with your friends and classmates, to agree or disagree with the authors here, and to come to your own conclusions. We hope, too, that through this engagement you will consider how gender has shaped your life and how gender intersects with the other systems of inequality that affect you. We hope as well that you will share your understandings with others, becoming a researcher yourself and a theorist of your own and others' lives so that you might help empower us all and transform society.

SECTION 1

Diversity and Difference

Gender shapes women's and men's lives in complex ways, and scholars are interested in understanding these experiences in ways that can contribute to positive social change. Women everywhere face male dominance in various manifestations. Yet differences among women arise from factors such as race, ethnicity, class, sexual orientation, age, geographic region, and religion. Further, not all men possess the same advantages or social power. Men of subordinate racial or ethnic groups, social classes, or sexual orientations may have power relative to women in their own group but be subordinate in some ways to other men and to women in more powerful groups.

The readings in this section discuss points of similarity and difference among women and among men. Although these readings give only a sampling of the varied and rich experiences of women and men, they begin to illustrate the vast range of meanings that gender has for women and men in different groups. These readings also provide some key analytical frameworks and concepts for understanding the tension between the significance of gender as a category by which people are grouped and the ways that gender is shaped by other forms of inequality and social distinctions.

The readings in this section examine the distinctions among women's experiences by showing how race, ethnicity, and age shape the lives of specific groups of women. The first reading in this section, Kimberly Springer's "Being the Bridge: A Solitary Black Woman's Position in the Women's Studies Classroom," tackles the similarities and differences among women directly. Recounting her experiences as a

women's studies student and campus activist, Springer shows how being a black woman in a predominantly white feminist context pushed her to serve as a "bridge between cultures, races, and theories." For Springer, activism includes teaching and writing about black feminism and working to bring black feminists together outside of academia as well. What does Springer's experience suggest about how connections and coalitions among different groups of women might occur? Why are these connections important, and how are they limited? For Springer, activism and academic work are inextricably linked. Do you agree with her that scholarly study of gender must be linked to activism for social change? Why or why not?

Peggy McIntosh adds to Springer's analysis by focusing on the often-unrecognized ways that white women benefit from their racial category. In a classic piece, "White Privilege: Unpacking the Invisible Knapsack," McIntosh discusses the taken-for-granted systems and practices that privilege white women over women of color. She argues that much of what white women take for granted in daily life is in fact a result of their dominant social status. Documenting her own white privilege helps her understand how she benefits from this system and shows that racism cannot change through individual attitudes alone, but requires change in social institutions. How does her list of benefits from white privilege change your understanding of racism? How does it change your understanding of gender inequality, or of the degree to which women of different races share oppression in common? Can you think of other advantages to add to her list? If you are a member of another privileged group, can you construct a list of the benefits you receive by virtue of your gender, class, sexual orientation, religion, or nationality? If you are a member of a subordinated group, can you list some of the ways you are disadvantaged? Most readers will have some statuses that grant them privilege (such as white skin, male gender, heterosexuality, U.S. nationality, youth, or Christian religion) and some statuses that disadvantage them (such as nonwhite skin, female gender, lesbian or gay or bisexual sexual orientation, non-U.S. nationality, age, or non-Christian religion). In what ways do the forms of privilege and disadvantage that you possess interact?

Paula Gunn Allen suggests that assumptions about what it means to be a woman in Anglo-European culture do not hold in American Indian cultures. In "Where I Come from Is Like This," she draws on her bicultural experiences to explore the contradictions between the images of women embedded in Anglo and American Indian culture. The images of American Indian women she grew up with are ones of "practicality, strength, reasonableness, intelligence, wit, and competence," in contrast to Anglo-American ideas about women as "passive and weak." Again, we see the difficulty of generalizing about women's experiences. What are the assumptions about women that are part of your own culture?

Audre Lorde, in "The Master's Tools Will Never Dismantle the Master's House," also emphasizes the difficulties of accurately analyzing how systems of oppression affect people's lives. Lorde argues in this classic piece, excerpted here, that feminists must critically examine their own use of dominant concepts. She suggests that academic knowledge is based in an institution that historically has excluded women and people of color, and she asks whether academic knowledge can undermine the inequalities on which it is based. Do you think that the "regular" methods of scholarship and science are adequate to the task of understanding the diversity among women and the

complexity of the gender system? Are the "master's tools" able to challenge social inequality? Will new tools be necessary? What might they be? Lorde argues that encouraging women to talk to each other at the points of their differences promotes growth, creativity, and social change. Do these conversations across differences happen on your campus?

In the final selection in this section, "The Mountain," Eli Clare writes about how disability and societal attitudes about it affect his experience of his own body. The metaphor of the mountain serves as a way to look at how the American emphasis on individual struggle and triumph is magnified when it's applied to disabled people, who are celebrated for "overcoming disability," what Clare calls being a "supercrip." When disabled people are caught between the model of the supercrip, social and physical barriers, and the danger of others' pity or institutionalization, Clare shows, the emotional consequences are intense. Ultimately, he seeks to understand her own body as "home," with his unique experiences of bodily ability and impairment as well as childhood abuse and rural white working-class culture.

Why do you think Clare uses socially stigmatized words like "gimp" and "crip"? What does he mean by the "lure of overcoming"? Can you think of other examples in which people want to overcome their social or bodily categories? For Clare, being queer, a tomboy as a child and genderqueer as an adult, shapes his experience of his body and how others respond to her. Think about cultural images of disabled people. How does gender affect these depictions? How do these depictions reflect the idealization of the "supercrip"? Think about your own experiences of your body—your abilities and impairments, your physical experiences, and how others respond to your body. How are these experiences similar to and different from Clare's? How do "place and community and culture" affect your own sense of yourself, your body, and what Clare calls "home"?

Being the Bridge: A Solitary Black Woman's Position in the Women's Studies Classroom as a Feminist Student and Professor

First published in 2002

Gloria Anzaldúa's autograph in my copy of *This Bridge Called My Back* reads, *"Para Kim, que te vaya bien con tus estudios. contigo, Gloria E. Anzaldúa 10.2.91."* I doubt she knew the significant role her words and *This Bridge* would play in my development as an activist, a student of women's studies, and a professor. *Bridge* not only introduced me to the feminism of Asian-American, Latina, and Native American women, but on a basic level this text showed me the possibility of even *being* a Black feminist.[1] However, this particular bridge could only take me so far and from that point on I began to create, if you will, an expansion. The bridge I envision is like one in movies featuring rainforests and uncharted jungles: rickety ol' planks strung together with rope that looks like it's seen many hardships. But the bridge *exists;* someone took the time to build it and it awaits use, as well as reinforcement for those who will follow. Through awareness, activism, and scholarship, I hope to reinforce the bridge by replacing a few well-worn planks with constructive criticism of Black feminism's past, as well as self-critique of my own Black feminist praxis.

In this essay, I recall demands from white peers in the classroom that I *be* the bridge over which they cross from being racist to interrogating their own privilege and my refusal to do so. I also gingerly step onto the bridge I now provide as a scholar-activist in my academic work. Through these experiences I reflect upon *Bridge*'s impact on my life, my relationship to Black feminism, and my understanding of coalition-building. Feelings of wonderment, rage, isolation, and transformation within *Bridge* were guideposts for the socialization I underwent from an assimilated, working-class girl into a Black feminist woman. Call them stages of Black feminist development.

Feminism, as theorized in *Bridge,* was a guide mapping many potential directions for my analysis of the complexity of Black feminism. With this personal narrative I demonstrate the continuing existence of Black feminist activism from Black women active in the 1970s (Kate Rushin, Beverly Smith, Barbara Smith, Beverly Guy-Sheftall, Audre Lorde), many still active today. I oppose a media-generated image of a second-wave/third-wave fracture and speculate on the possibilities for an intergenerational Black feminist theory. Rather than competing with the Black feminists who came before me, as much predominately white third-wave feminist literature attests, I see myself as the bridge between my fore mothers and future Black feminists. Feminists must do coalition work on many levels simultaneously: connect with those outside the groups we choose to call home and examine our internal politics to determine what keeps us separated and reinventing the wheel.

BLACK GIRLHOOD AND INCIPIENT FEMINISM

There are perils to growing up Black and female in the United States, but there are also unimaginable joys and triumphs. Watching my young second-cousin, Skylar, grow up, I'm simultaneously filled with pride and trepidation. Her mother reminds me of my own mother: the best mother possible, trying to raise a healthy, whole African-American girl in a society that devalues her based on her race and gender. I try to assist, reminding Skylar how smart, beautiful, and truly bold she is through creative feminist gifts and encouraging words. However, there is only so much I can do to protect her from the racist, sexist, heterosexist attitudes that will eventually try to shape her into someone other than who she was meant to be. I often compose letters and practice conversations I'd like to have when she is old enough to comprehend my meaning.

> Dear Skylar Jade,
>
> What's up, Skydee-dy-dee? Are you keeping Mama busy with your activities and questions and just all-around brilliance? I remember the time we tried to go see a holiday light festival. You were in the backseat all strapped in, asking me why we couldn't, after all, go. I'd left my wallet at home and explained the situation. You asked for the 3rd or 4th time and I lost my patience and, with a heavy sigh, said, "BECAUSE, Sky, I don't have any money on me." From the backseat I heard this preteen (though you were only 5) sucking of teeth and an exasperated "I was just ASKING." That, my dear, was what Alice Walker and other women in our family would call acting "womanish," but I had to laugh because you were so SASSY. I hope you remain secure in who you are—a complex almost-young-woman who'll keep questioning until satisfied with the answers. Enclosed is a copy of Toni Morrison's *The Bluest Eye* Call me when you've read it. Kisses. Love, Cousin Kim

Part of the message I received growing up was "Each one, teach one." I try to apply this edict as I reach back to younger Black girls who have yet to figure out that feminism is not a "white girls' thing" or a "bad word"; to help young girls and women see that female empowerment is not a crotch-grabbing "video-ho" and that we can, in fact, say, "Sister, that is fucked-up behavior." As my dear friend, another Kimberly, says, we need to bring our whole selves to the table, not just the newly sexually-empowered parts. I want to offer my Black feminist experiences as just one of many options to get them through the times when the news media, popular culture, and even some of their peers try to tell them that they're not intelligent and beautiful because they don't fit the dominant norms of beauty or that they are not keeping it real unless they are singing about some man paying the bills.

Preparing to graduate in the spring of 1992, I sat trying to decide what protest message to write on my mortar board. Among the sea of Greek letters and accolades for years spent partying, I wanted my cap to reflect my growing Black feminist consciousness. Not that I hadn't

gotten my apolitical groove on to Public Enemy a number of times, but my years at the University of Michigan were my own flashpoint. Onto the television came another round of bulletins about the L.A. rebellion. A reporter asked a teenaged African-American girl a typically inane mainstream question: "What does the verdict in the Rodney King trial say to you?" I could feel my young sister's anguish as she choked out between tears, "It makes me feel like they think we don't matter at all." I knew then what to write on my mortarboard ("Burn, Hollywood, Burn"), but it was hard to see through my own tears as I felt similar feelings of worthlessness and defiance all at once. I think of that girl when I contemplate the shock of waking up from a deep assimilated sleep and into the cold reality of social injustice. How could I help her and others cross the icy waters of degradation threatening to overtake us all every time a bullet rips through the flesh of another sister or brother?

IDENTITY POLITICS/IDENTIFYING POLITICALLY

What does it mean that a white man, a gay white man, introduced me to feminism? Is my feminism any less legitimate than that of my classmate who came to feminism following years of sexual abuse at her father's hands? Is it any less legitimate than that of my friend whose lesbian mother raised her with feminist principles, as if *Free to Be You and Me* were the sugar on every child's morning cereal?

My resident advisor, Jim, taught me many things that year. He taught me what it meant to think critically about power and privilege. He taught me what it meant to have my first real bona fide crush on a gay man and opt instead for being a dear friend. He also suggested that I take Introduction to Women's Studies during my first year. He led this horse to water, but he didn't have to make me drink. I partook of every reading, required and suggested, that I could get my hands on. Finally, there was something, or rather many "someones," who could explain just what the hell it was I felt as I learned about Black women's history for the first time, who all the powerful Black figures were in Boogie Down Productions' song "You Must Learn," why someone would want to spell *woman* "womyn," and the import of my senior high/junior college paper on *Bowers v. Hardwick*.

For me this mixing of cultures and political allegiances meant that, early on, I had an abiding belief in building coalitions across identities. It sounds clichéd, but I really could not see how one could harbor prejudices toward entire groups of people if one had experienced discrimination and also entered into intimate relationships with people different from one's self. I'm sure the label "sell-out" was tossed at my back, but I was too busy, thrilled by the activism and camaraderie, to notice. As an activist in anti-racist work, defending suburban Detroit clinics with reproductive rights organizations, studying social movements, I encountered people with differing political priorities. While it was never easy to negotiate all the demands and a few friendships fell by the wayside, I never regret trying to bridge the externally-imposed divides between my political interests. In those interests for women's, lesbian/gay, and people of color's rights, I had my own hands-on practicum in how power and privilege circulate to positively and negatively impact movement outcomes.

Just when I was discovering what each aspect of my identity had to do with the others, postmodern theorists (mostly white, European men) tried to suck *all* the damn air out of the room and tell me there was no "I." I was also discovering how my powerlessness and privilege lived side-by-side, making for a very confused, angry, but oddly exhilarated young woman. In my Intro to Women's Studies course, one of the *Bridge* essays I elected to read was the dialogue between Beverly and Barbara Smith. Not having a sister myself, I could only read in awe: two Black feminists in the same family? They captured precisely the conflict I felt while taking advantage of my educational privilege for eight months of the year, then going "home" to my family and Black community during holidays:

> There are ways we act when Black people are together that white women will never see in a largely white context. Now, I don't think this is about acting white in a white context. It's about one, a lack of inspiration. Because the way you act with Black people is because they inspire the behavior. And I do mean inspire. And the other thing is that when you are in a white context, you think "Well, why bother? Why waste your time?" If what you're trying to do is get things across and communicate and what-have-you, *you talk in your second language.* (119, my emphasis)

Barely passing French my first year, I became bilingual in my Blackness and my feminist inclinations. What I had yet to learn was how to defend myself in this new language, this new land where different parts of me fought to lay claim to my time and energy. The Black Student Union protest or drive to a Clinic Defense in suburban Detroit? The United Coalition Against Racism meeting or the Take Back the Night March? Like the 1970s Black feminists I would later study, I was torn between two lovers and, surely, feeling like a fool. I straddled the fence of my identity and burned out quickly trying to bring an anti-sexist analysis to my "race work" and an anti-racist sensibility to my "gender work." Not surprisingly, these two branches never met. It was like trying to keep two lovers from finding out about one another, but secretly wanting them to meet, fall in love, and forget all about me. Bringing an anti-heterosexist perspective to either aspect of my activism was, needless to say, an even rougher battle as I tried to be pro-lesbian/gay/bi rights and *still* get a date with one of the SNAGs (Sensitive New Age Guys) on campus. Was I being naive in thinking that, unlike Rushin in her "Bridge Poem," I would somehow be exempt from translating for everyone who selected which parts of me they wanted to encounter?

Inside the classroom a different battle was only just beginning. I tried to defend myself in my women's studies classes where I was "The Only One." The only Black woman, the only one who knew the importance of talking about hair and its racial and gender implications for Black women. The only one who thought, "You must be kidding" when professors at one of the most prestigious universities in the country spoke of being ghettoized. Tell it to the folks in Cabrini Green. The only one who cringed and slouched over self-consciously when a white professor declared, "Black women don't have body image issues. There's just a different aesthetic in the Black Community." Did you hear that, hips? You're just a different *aesthetic.* Yeah. Right. Donna Kate Rushin's poem rang in my ears: "Sick of being the sole Black friend to 34 individual white people." Sick of being the sole person in the room unimpressed when professors tokenized bell hooks on their otherwise all-white feminist theory syllabi.

The struggles with white feminists were not only with professors, but with teaching assistants of the next generation of feminist activism too. The TA for a required course interrogated me, "Well, 100-level students will want to know. *Are* you a feminist?" It made me angry that all the replies I could think of were not mine. Not the historically logical answer: "*Hell,* no, I'm not a feminist! Do I look like Sojourner Truth, waiting for some Northern suffragist to turn her back on me? I ain't no fool." That would be too "angry Black woman" and I might not pass the interview to facilitate the 100-level women's studies class, which I needed to fulfill my major. I opted for "Throw Her off the

Scent Answer #2": "No, I'm not a feminist. I'm a *womanist*." While appeasing my Birkenstock-wearing, cultural-feminist TA, it did nothing for me but give me a reprieve from committing myself to feminism or to non-Black status in the eyes of some of my friends and relatives. Still, I felt so good and authentic that I went out and bought my *own* pair of Birkenstocks—militantly **black** ones.

I kept those broke-down sandals as a memento of what I saw as a simpler time in my feminist trajectory. It was easier in undergraduate school for me to parrot the lines of my real and imagined mentors on the need for socialist revolution, Black liberation, and patriarchy's downfall. It wasn't that I didn't believe those things but just that I didn't think about them much. It was much easier to take these principles as my own, rather than wrestle with my inner-life contradictions: my middle-class aspirations, my vast amount of book-learning, a decreasing belief in god, the ability to get instantly weepy at a strong rendition of the gospel hymn "Goin' up' a Yonder," the desire for a throw-down revolution Che Guevara–style, and a penchant for a Black Panther in a black leather coat.

IN THE BELLY OF THE FEMINIST BEAST

In the face of all that confusion I went to graduate school. Thinking I'd find out who I was and what I wanted to be, or at least buy myself a little more time, I applied to and was accepted into a doctoral program in women's studies. It seemed like a logical next step, building on my undergraduate major in women's studies and sociology. I could continue finding ways to remain politically active because I would still be a student—or so I thought.

The program I chose was, at the time, one of two offering a Ph.D. in women's studies. I assumed that it was a feminist program—after all, what else would a women's studies program be? Not until I began studying social movements and organizations did I understand it in the context of the institutionalization and professionalization of an area founded by activists. I entered a women's studies program in which most faculty and students *studied* women, but not necessarily tried to investigate or apply feminism.[2] This was, in fact, a double-sided realization: slight dismay that I could no longer assume that women's studies equaled feminist studies, but a determination to focus on feminist theory in my own work.

After another Black woman left the program for one more suited to her interests and sanity, I was once again the only Black woman in the program.[3] In addition to my status as the only Black woman, I also encountered many students who hadn't majored in or taken women's studies courses as undergraduates. This lack of training had significant consequences on my intellectual and activist outlook. It baffled me that a few women's studies graduate students in my classes professed to do women's studies, but flushed at the thought of having to enter a classroom and talk about feminist perspectives on film, religion, science, politics, or any number of other topics. Soon I learned that many of the women opting for a certificate in women's studies, wasting valuable class time in my feminist theory course with asinine debates about standard vacuum cleaners versus Dustbusters, merely added the certificate to their resume in the hopes of landing a scarce teaching position in their respective fields. That's when I decided that there's meeting women where they are and there's leaving their asses by the side of the road (or at a very nice rest stop) if you've got places to go.

IT'S A LOVE/HATE THANG

Recently three constellations saved me from chewing through the rope I was holding. My academic research, a few students, and a posse of Black, Asian-American, Latina, and white feminist friends were, and still are, my bridge between women's studies and feminism, between academic professionalization and activism. That's what the hyphen in scholar-activist means to me: I can still think critically, write, and teach about ideas of social justice, democracy, and equality, while encouraging students and myself to participate in direct action that makes those ideas practical tools for living.

Part of my struggle as a scholar-activist is my research on 1970s Black feminist organizations. I read about several organizations, searched them out to join up, but found that they'd all disbanded around the time I was saving my allowance for candy and *Archie* comic books. So I decided to discover what happened to these organizations and, more important, how they did it in the first place. How did they get a group of Black women together in the same room for something besides planning Women's Day at church or getting their hair done, which for a long time was my limited experience of women's organizing activities? Over the course of twelve years, several hundred, if not thousands, of Black feminists laid the groundwork for Black feminist activism and the expansion of what we call feminist issues (including, but not limited to, the right to *have* children and informed consent about sterilization as valid reproductive rights). Black feminists in at least five organizations in Boston, New York, Chicago, and San Francisco participated in consciousness-raising groups with white women and in groups of only Black women where they started to believe that they were not crazy for being Black *and* feminist.

Though these groups ceased meeting by the early 1980s, they left a legacy inspiring me to document their existence. Kitchen Table Press pinned a button stating, "Black Feminism *LIVES!*" to every copy of the reprinted Combahee River Collective Statement! This feminism lives in me as I read and re-read feminist-of-color writings and as I try to relay to my students the excitement and danger of a time in women's movement history that I wasn't around for either.

As an instructor on social movements, I struggle to teach about identity politics. Some postmodernists view identity politics as essentialist, reinforcing ideas of how marginalized people "naturally" are. Well, in some ways essentialism is *essential.* As the Smith sisters and the Combahee River Collective note, there once was, and still is, value in *identifying politically* with people who look like you. Yet as Bernice Johnson Reagon points out, this does not mean we don't ever open the door to the place we call home. In fact, it often behooves us to collectively tear the roof off our ideas of home and invite others in to see what we can make of the future.

As much as I complain about students' lack of historical context or wish I could just uncritically enjoy my *Entertainment Weekly,* I wouldn't trade in my feminism for anything in the world. Every time I experience a student having that "click" of how to think critically about discrimination and social change, I have that same spark of recognition all over again. We are still working on a bridge to somewhere exciting, dangerous, and new.

Incredibly enough, I've seen a few frat boys experience that click while some young sisters try to get over on me, Sister/Teacher, because, after all, "You know what it's like to be the only Black woman in a classroom of white folks *and* not have done the classwork because of last night's Kappa step show." At that moment Black feminist organizations' lessons come back to haunt me: do not assume that because someone looks like you, they share your political and personal objectives; I return to the idea of identity politics and remind myself there is much intragroup coalition work to be done. Moreover, I must be aware of how my own internal identity politics can impede internal critique and connections with the Black woman I hope to be and with other Black women.

One way I sought to make the exchange between activism and scholarship was to help organize a Black Feminist Salon while living in Atlanta. Unfortunately for me, I was moving away soon after the group formed, but it filled me with hope and pride that we could get several sisters to sit in a room and share what it means to be Black and feminist, lesbian, straight, and bisexual. Living about a thousand miles away from the Salon is disappointing, but just getting it together lets me know I can build community wherever I go. Whether that community is with other Black women or with feminist women and men in my predominately white mountain town, the bridges I've learned to build are internal and transport well.

There is so much work to be done around gender that I will not be left to my leisure even if I live miles away from a critical mass of Black sisters and brothers. The work heterosexual Black feminists need to do in conjunction with our Black lesbian and gay counterparts around homophobia in Black communities is unending. The dialogues that Black women of all sexual orientations need to open up with one another about sexuality and competition and "diva-dissing" could fill hours of conversation and anthologies yet to be conceived. Continuing to push for a redefined Black masculinity that does not replicate patriarchy's worst tendencies is a project just beginning in academia and the street.

Feminism, specifically third-world feminism, has been a bridge, a lifeline, and even an extension of my being. Yet sometimes I wonder how much longer I can continue being a bridge between cultures, races, and theories. As a member of the Black Feminist Salon in Atlanta said, "I consider it my activism whenever I leave the house." This is a lifetime of work. Social change is a process. I will often be afraid inside and outside spaces I call home. Perhaps I can persuade myself to look forward to the challenges and growth that will come as I continue crossing the bridge built by *This Bridge Called My Back* twenty years ago.

What Donna Kate Rushin calls for is not throwing in the towel because we're sick of white folks and everyone else who looks to Black women to be political Mammys. Instead, she affirms the work we need to do internally as well as externally to continue waging battles that have yet to be fought. Rushin's determined words warrant repeating: "The bridge I must be/Is the bridge to my own power/I must translate/My own fears/Mediate/My own weaknesses/I must be the bridge to nowhere/But my true self/And then I will be useful." Amen, sistah Kate, amen!

NOTES

The author thanks AnaLouise Keating and Kimberly Wallace-Sanders for their extensive sisterly comments.

1. Equally critical in my personal-political Black feminist development was *Home Girls,* another Kitchen Table publication.

2. By the time I graduated from the program in 1999, I perceived students' greater dedication to critically engaging feminism.

3. The next year, sister Francis Wood came to the program, bringing heat and light.

READING 2   **Peggy McIntosh**

White Privilege: Unpacking the Invisible Knapsack
First published in 1988

Through work to bring materials and perspectives from Women's Studies into the rest of the curriculum, I have often noticed men's unwillingness to grant that they are overprivileged in the curriculum, even though they may grant that women are disadvantaged. Denials that amount to taboos surround the subject of advantages that men gain from women's disadvantages. These denials protect male privilege from being fully recognized, acknowledged, lessened, or ended.

Thinking through unacknowledged male privilege as a phenomenon with a life of its own, I realized that since hierarchies in our society are interlocking, there was most likely a phenomenon of white privilege that was similarly denied and protected, but alive and real in its effects. As a white person, I realized I had been taught about racism as something that puts others at a disadvantage, but had been taught not to see one of its corollary aspects, white privilege, which puts me at an advantage.

I think whites are carefully taught not to recognize white privilege, as males are taught not to recognize male privilege. So I have begun in an untutored way to ask what it is like to have white privilege. This paper is a partial record of my personal observations and not a scholarly analysis. It is based on my daily experiences within my particular circumstances.

I have come to see white privilege as an invisible package of unearned assets that I can count on cashing in each day, but about which I was "meant" to remain oblivious. White privilege is like an invisible weightless knapsack of special provisions, assurances, tools, maps, guides, codebooks, passports, visas, clothes, compass, emergency gear, and blank checks.

Since I have had trouble facing white privilege, and describing its results in my life, I saw parallels here with men's reluctance to acknowledge male privilege. Only rarely will a man go beyond acknowledging that women are disadvantaged to acknowledging that men have unearned advantage, or that unearned privilege has not been good for men's development as human beings, or for society's development, or that privilege systems might ever be challenged and *changed*.

I will review here several types or layers of denial that I see at work protecting, and preventing awareness about, entrenched male privilege. Then I will draw parallels, from my own experience, with the denials that veil the facts of white privilege. Finally, I will list forty-six ordinary and daily ways in which I experience having white privilege, by contrast with my African-American colleagues in the same building. This list is not intended to be generalizable. Others can make their own lists from within their own life circumstances.

Writing this paper has been difficult, despite warm receptions for the talks on which it is based.[1] For describing white privilege makes one newly accountable. As we in Women's Studies work to reveal male privilege and ask men to give up some of their power so one who writes about having white privilege must ask, "Having described it, what will I do to lessen or end it."

The denial of men's overprivileged state takes many forms in discussions of curriculum change work. Some claim that men must be central in the curriculum because they have done most of what is important or distinctive in life or in civilization. Some recognize sexism in the curriculum but deny that it makes male students seem unduly important in life. Others agree that certain *individual* thinkers are male-oriented but deny that there is any *systemic* tendency in disciplinary frameworks or epistemology to over-empower men as a group. Those men who do grant that male privilege takes institutionalized and embedded forms are still likely to deny that male hegemony has opened doors for them personally. Virtually all men deny that male overreward alone can explain men's centrality in all the inner sanctums of our most powerful institutions. Moreover, those few who will acknowledge that male privilege systems have over-empowered them usually end up doubting that we could dismantle these privilege systems. They may say they will work to improve women's status, in the society or in the university, but they can't or won't support the idea of lessening men's. In curricular terms, this is the point at which they say that they regret they cannot use any of the interesting new scholarship on women because the syllabus is full. When the talk turns to giving men less cultural room, even the most thoughtful and fair-minded of the men I know will tend to reflect, or fall back on, conservative assumptions about the inevitability of present gender relations and distributions of power, calling on precedent or sociobiology and psychobiology to demonstrate that male domination is natural and follows inevitably from evolutionary pressures. Others resort to arguments from "experience" or religion or social responsibility or wishing and dreaming.

After I realized, through faculty development work in Women's Studies, the extent to which men work from a base of unacknowledged privilege, I understood that much of their oppressiveness was unconscious. Then I remembered the frequent charges from women of color that white women whom they encounter are oppressive. I began to understand why we are justly seen as oppressive, even when we don't see ourselves that way. At the very least, obliviousness of one's privileged state can make a person or group irritating to be with. I began to count the ways in which I enjoy unearned skin privilege and have been conditioned into oblivion about its existence, unable to see that it put me "ahead" in any way, or put my people ahead, overrewarding us and yet also paradoxically damaging us, or that it could or should be changed.

My schooling gave me no training in seeing myself as an oppressor, as an unfairly advantaged person, or as a participant in a damaged culture. I was taught to see myself as an individual whose moral state depended on her individual moral will. At school, we were not taught about slavery in any depth; we were not taught to see slaveholders as damaged people. Slaves were seen as the only group at risk of being dehumanized. My schooling followed the pattern which Elizabeth Minnich has pointed out: whites are taught to think of their lives as morally neutral, normative, and average, and also ideal, so that when we work to benefit others, this is seen as work that will allow "them" to be more like "us." I think many of us know how obnoxious this attitude can be in men.

After frustration with men who would not recognize male privilege, I decided to try to work on myself at least by identifying some of the daily effects of white privilege in my life. It is crude work, at this stage, but I will give here a list of special circumstances and conditions I experience that I did not earn but that I have been made to feel are mine by birth, by citizenship, and by virtue of being a conscientious law-abiding "normal" person of goodwill. I have chosen those conditions that I think in my case *attach somewhat more to skin-color privilege* than to class, religion, ethnic status, or geographical location, though these other privileging factors are intricately intertwined. As far as I can see, my African-American co-workers, friends, and acquaintances with whom I come into daily or frequent contact in this particular time, place, and line of work cannot count on most of these conditions.

1. I can, if I wish, arrange to be in the company of people of my race most of the time.
2. I can avoid spending time with people whom I was trained to mistrust and who have learned to mistrust my kind or me.
3. If I should need to move, I can be pretty sure of renting or purchasing housing in an area which I can afford and in which I would want to live.
4. I can be reasonably sure that my neighbors in such a location will be neutral or pleasant to me.
5. I can go shopping alone most of the time, fairly well assured that I will not be followed or harassed by store detectives.
6. I can turn on the television or open to the front page of the paper and see people of my race widely and positively represented.

7. When I am told about our national heritage or about "civilization," I am shown that people of my color made it what it is.

8. I can be sure that my children will be given curricular materials that testify to the existence of their race.

9. If I want to, I can be pretty sure of finding a publisher for this piece on white privilege.

10. I can be fairly sure of having my voice heard in a group in which I am the only member of my race.

11. I can be casual about whether or not to listen to another woman's voice in a group in which she is the only member of her race.

12. I can go into a bookshop and count on finding the writing of my race represented, into a supermarket and find the staple foods that fit with my cultural traditions, into a hairdresser's shop and find someone who can deal with my hair.

13. Whether I use checks, credit cards, or cash, I can count on my skin color not to work against the appearance that I am financially reliable.

14. I could arrange to protect our young children most of the time from people who might not like them.

15. I did not have to educate our children to be aware of systemic racism for their own daily physical protection.

16. I can be pretty sure that my children's teachers and employers will tolerate them if they fit school and workplace norms; my chief worries about them do not concern others' attitudes toward their race.

17. I can talk with my mouth full and not have people put this down to my color.

18. I can swear, or dress in secondhand clothes, or not answer letters, without having people attribute these choices to the bad morals, the poverty, or the illiteracy of my race.

19. I can speak in public to a powerful male group without putting my race on trial.

20. I can do well in a challenging situation without being called a credit to my race.

21. I am never asked to speak for all the people of my racial group.

22. I can remain oblivious to the language and customs of persons of color who constitute the world's majority without feeling in my culture any penalty for such oblivion.

23. I can criticize our government and talk about how much I fear its policies and behavior without being seen as a cultural outsider.

24. I can be reasonably sure that if I ask to talk to "the person in charge," I will be facing a person of my race.

25. If a traffic cop pulls me over or if the IRS audits my tax return, I can be sure I haven't been singled out because of my race.

26. I can easily buy posters, postcards, picture books, greeting cards, dolls, toys, and children's magazines featuring people of my race.

27. I can go home from most meetings of organizations I belong to feeling somewhat tied in, rather than isolated, out of place, outnumbered, unheard, held at a distance, or feared.

28. I can be pretty sure that an argument with a colleague of another race is more likely to jeopardize her chances for advancement than to jeopardize mine.

29. I can be fairly sure that if I argue for the promotion of a person of another race, or a program centering on race, this is not likely to cost me heavily within my present setting, even if my colleagues disagree with me.

30. If I declare there is a racial issue at hand, or there isn't a racial issue at hand, my race will lend me more credibility for either position than a person of color will have.

31. I can choose to ignore developments in minority writing and minority activist programs, or disparage them, or learn from them, but in any case, I can find ways to be more or less protected from negative consequences of any of these choices.

32. My culture gives me little fear about ignoring the perspectives and powers of people of other races.

33. I am not made acutely aware that my shape, bearing, or body odor will be taken as a reflection on my race.

34. I can worry about racism without being seen as self-interested or self-seeking.

35. I can take a job with an affirmative action employer without having my co-workers on the job suspect that I got it because of my race.

36. If my day, week, or year is going badly, I need not ask of each negative episode or situation whether it has racial overtones.

37. I can be pretty sure of finding people who would be willing to talk with me and advise me about my next steps, professionally.

38. I can think over many options, social, political, imaginative, or professional, without asking whether a person of my race would be accepted or allowed to do what I want to do.

39. I can be late to a meeting without having the lateness reflect on my race.
40. I can choose public accommodation without fearing that people of my race cannot get in or will be mistreated in the places I have chosen.
41. I can be sure that if I need legal or medical help, my race will not work against me.
42. I can arrange my activities so that I will never have to experience feelings of rejection owing to my race.
43. If I have low credibility as a leader, I can be sure that my race is not the problem.
44. I can easily find academic courses and institutions that give attention only to people of my race.
45. I can expect figurative language and imagery in all of the arts to testify to experiences of my race.
46. I can choose blemish cover or bandages in "flesh" color and have them more or less match my skin.

I repeatedly forgot each of the realizations on this list until I wrote it down. For me, white privilege has turned out to be an elusive and fugitive subject. The pressure to avoid it is great, for in facing it I must give up the myth of meritocracy. If these things are true, this is not such a free country; one's life is not what one makes it; many doors open for certain people through no virtues of their own. These perceptions mean also that my moral condition is not what I had been led to believe. The appearance of being a good citizen rather than a troublemaker comes in large part from having all sorts of doors open automatically because of my color.

A further paralysis of nerve comes from literary silence protecting privilege. My clearest memories of finding such analysis are in Lillian Smith's unparalleled *Killers of the Dream*, and Margaret Andersen's review of Karen and Mamie Fields' *Lemon Swamp*. Smith, for example, wrote about walking toward black children on the street and knowing they would step into the gutter; Andersen contrasted the pleasure that she, as a white child, took on summer driving trips to the south with Karen Fields' memories of driving in a closed car stocked with all necessities lest, in stopping, her black family should suffer "insult, or worse." Adrienne Rich also recognizes and writes about daily experiences of privilege, but in my observation, white women's writing in this area is far more often on systemic racism than on our daily lives as light-skinned women.[2]

In unpacking this invisible knapsack of white privilege, I have listed conditions of daily experience that I once took for granted, as neutral, normal, and universally available to everybody, just as I once thought of a male-focused curriculum as the neutral or accurate account that can speak for all. Nor did I think of any of these perquisites as bad for the holder. I now think that we need a more finely differentiated taxonomy of privilege, for some of these varieties are only what one would want for everyone in a just society, and others give license to be ignorant, oblivious, arrogant, and destructive. Before proposing some more finely tuned categorization, I will make some observations about the general effects of these conditions on my life and expectations.

In this potpourri of examples, some privileges make me feel at home in the world. Others allow me to escape penalties or dangers that others suffer. Through some, I escape fear, anxiety, insult, injury, or a sense of not being welcome, not being real. Some keep me from having to hide, to be in disguise, to feel sick or crazy, to negotiate each transaction from the position of being an outsider or, within my group, a person who is suspected of having too close links with a dominant culture. Most keep me from having to be angry.

I see a pattern running through the matrix of white privilege, a pattern of assumptions that were passed on to me as a white person. There was one main piece of cultural turf; it was my own turf, and I was among those who could control the turf. I could measure up to the cultural standards and take advantage of the many options I saw around me to make what the culture would call a success of my life. *My skin color was an asset for any move I was educated to want to make.* I could think of myself as "belonging" in major ways and of making social systems work for me. I could freely disparage, fear, neglect, or be oblivious to anything outside of the dominant cultural forms. Being of the main culture, I could also criticize it fairly freely. My life was reflected back to me frequently enough so that I felt, with regard to my race, if not to my sex, like one of the real people.

Whether through the curriculum or in the newspaper, the television, the economic system, or the general look of people in the streets, I received daily signals and indications that my people counted and that others *either didn't exist or must be trying, not very successfully, to be like people of my race.* I was given cultural permission not to hear voices of people of other races or a tepid cultural tolerance for hearing or acting on such voices. I was also raised not to suffer seriously from anything that darker-skinned people might say about my group, "protected," though perhaps I should more accurately say *prohibited,* through the habits of my economic class and social group, from living in racially mixed groups or being reflective about interactions between people of differing races.

In proportion as my racial group was being made confident, comfortable, and oblivious, other groups were likely being made unconfident, uncomfortable, and alienated. Whiteness protected me from many kinds of hostility, distress, and violence, which I was being subtly trained to visit in turn upon people of color.

For this reason, the word "privilege" now seems to me misleading. Its connotations are too positive to fit the conditions and behaviors which "privilege systems" produce. We usually think of privilege as being a favored state, whether earned or conferred by birth or luck. School graduates are reminded they are privileged and urged to use their (enviable) assets well. The word "privilege" carries the connotation of being something everyone must want. Yet some of the conditions I have described here work to systemically over-empower certain groups. Such privilege simply *confers dominance,* gives permission to control, because of one's race or sex. The kind of privilege that gives license to some people to be, at best, thoughtless and, at worst, murderous should not continue to be referred to as a desirable attribute. Such "privilege" may be widely desired without being in any way beneficial to the whole society.

Moreover, though "privilege" may confer power, it does not confer moral strength. Those who do not depend on conferred dominance have traits and qualities that may never develop in those who do. Just as Women's Studies courses indicate that women survive their political circumstances to lead lives that hold the human race together, so "underprivileged" people of color who are the world's majority have survived their oppression and lived survivors' lives from which the white global minority can and must learn. In some groups, those dominated have actually become strong through *not* having all of these unearned advantages, and this gives them a great deal to teach the others. Members of so-called privileged groups can seem foolish, ridiculous, infantile, or dangerous by contrast.

I want, then, to distinguish between earned strength and unearned power conferred systemically. Power from unearned privilege can look like strength when it is, in fact, permission to escape or to dominate. But not all of the privileges on my list are inevitably damaging. Some, like the expectation that neighbors will be decent to you, or that your race will not count against you in court, should be the norm in a just society and should be considered as the entitlement of everyone. Others, like the privilege not to listen to less powerful people, distort the humanity of the holders as well as the ignored groups. Still others, like finding one's staple foods everywhere, may be a function of being a member of a numerical majority in the population. Others have to do with not having to labor under pervasive negative stereotyping and mythology.

We might at least start by distinguishing between positive advantages that we can work to spread, to the point where they are not advantages at all but simply part of the normal civic and social fabric, and negative types of advantage that unless rejected will always reinforce our present hierarchies. For example, the positive "privilege" of belonging, the feeling that one belongs within the human circle, as Native Americans say, fosters development and should not be seen as privilege for a few. It is, let us say, an entitlement that none of us should have to earn; ideally it is an *unearned entitlement.* At present, since only a few have it, it is an *unearned advantage* for them. The negative "privilege" that gave me cultural permission not to take darker-skinned others seriously can be seen as arbitrarily conferred dominance and should not be desirable for anyone. This paper results from a process of coming to see that some of the power that I originally saw as attendant on being a human being in the United States consisted in *unearned advantage* and *conferred dominance,* as well as other kinds of special circumstance not universally taken for granted.

In writing this paper I have also realized that white identity and status (as well as class identity and status) give me considerable power to choose whether to broach this subject and its trouble. I can pretty well decide whether to disappear and avoid and not listen and escape the dislike I may engender in other people through this essay, or interrupt, answer, interpret, preach, correct, criticize, and control to some extent what goes on in reaction to it. Being white, I am given considerable power to escape many kinds of danger or penalty as well as to choose which risks I want to take.

There is an analogy here, once again, with Women's Studies. Our male colleagues do not have a great deal to lose in supporting Women's Studies, but they do not have a great deal to lose if they oppose it either. They simply have the power to decide whether to commit themselves to more equitable distributions of power. They will probably feel few penalties whatever choice they make; they do not seem, in any obvious short-term sense, the ones at risk, though they and we are all at risk because of the behaviors that have been rewarded in them.

Through Women's Studies work I have met very few men who are truly distressed about systemic, unearned male advantage and conferred dominance. And so one question for me and others like me is whether we will be like them, or whether we will get truly distressed, even outraged, about unearned race advantage and conferred dominance and if so, what we will do to lessen them. In any case, we need to do more work in identifying how they actually affect our daily lives. We need more down-to-earth writing by people about these taboo subjects. We need more understanding of the ways in which white "privilege" damages white people, for these are not the same ways in which it damages the victimized. Skewed white psyches are an inseparable part of the picture, though I do not want to confuse the kinds of damage done to the holders of special assets and to those who suffer the deficits. Many, perhaps most, of our white students in the United States think that racism doesn't affect them because they are not people of color; they do not see "whiteness" as a racial identity. Many men likewise think that Women's Studies does not bear on their own existences because they are not female; they do not see themselves as having gendered identities. Insisting on the universal "effects" of "privilege" systems, then, becomes one of our chief tasks, and being more explicit about the *particular* effects in particular contexts is another. Men need to join us in this work.

In addition, since race and sex are not the only advantaging systems at work, we need to similarly examine the daily experience of having age advantage, or ethnic advantage, or physical ability, or advantage related to nationality, religion, or sexual orientation. Professor Marnie Evans suggested to me that in many ways the list I made also applies directly to heterosexual privilege. This is a still more taboo subject than race privilege: the daily ways in which heterosexual privilege makes some persons comfortable or powerful, providing supports, assets, approvals, and rewards to those who live or expect to live in heterosexual

pairs. Unpacking that content is still more difficult, owing to the deeper embeddedness of heterosexual advantage and dominance and stricter taboos surrounding these.

But to start such an analysis I would put this observation from my own experience: The fact that I live under the same roof with a man triggers all kinds of societal assumptions about my worth, politics, life, and values and triggers a host of unearned advantages and powers. After recasting many elements from the original list I would add further observations like these:

1. My children do not have to answer questions about why I live with my partner (my husband).
2. I have no difficulty finding neighborhoods where people approve of our household.
3. Our children are given texts and classes that implicitly support our kind of family unit and do not turn them against my choice of domestic partnership.
4. I can travel alone or with my husband without expecting embarrassment or hostility in those who deal with us.
5. Most people I meet will see my marital arrangements as an asset to my life or as a favorable comment on my likability, my competence, or my mental health.
6. I can talk about the social events of a weekend without fearing most listeners' reactions.
7. I will feel welcomed and "normal" in the usual walks of public life, institutional and social.
8. In many contexts, I am seen as "all right" in daily work on women because I do not live chiefly with women.

Difficulties and dangers surrounding the task of finding parallels are many. Since racism, sexism, and heterosexism are not the same, the advantages associated with them should not be seen as the same. In addition, it is hard to isolate aspects of unearned advantage that derive chiefly from social class, economic class, race, religion, region, sex, or ethnic identity. The oppressions are both distinct and interlocking, as the Combahee River Collective statement of 1977 continues to remind us eloquently.[3]

One factor seems clear about all of the interlocking oppressions. They take both active forms that we can see and embedded forms that members of the dominant group are taught not to see. In my class and place, I did not see myself as racist because I was taught to recognize racism only in individual acts of meanness by members of my group, never in invisible systems conferring racial dominance on my group from birth. Likewise, we are taught to think that sexism or heterosexism is carried on only through intentional, individual acts of discrimination, meanness, or cruelty, rather than in invisible systems conferring unsought dominance on certain groups. Disapproving of the systems won't be enough to change them. I was taught to think that racism could end if white individuals changed their attitudes; many men think sexism can be ended by individual changes in daily behavior toward women. But a man's sex provides advantage for him whether or not he approves of the way in which dominance has been conferred on his group. A "white" skin in the United States opens many doors for whites whether or not we approve of the way dominance has been conferred on us. Individual acts can palliate, but cannot end, these problems. To redesign social systems, we need first to acknowledge their colossal unseen dimensions. The silences and denials surrounding privilege are the key political tool here. They keep the thinking about equality or equity incomplete, protecting unearned advantage and conferred dominance by making these taboo subjects. Most talk by whites about equal opportunity seems to me now to be about equal opportunity to try to get into a position of dominance while denying that *systems* of dominance exist.

Obliviousness about white advantage, like obliviousness about male advantage, is kept strongly inculturated in the United States so as to maintain the myth of meritocracy, the myth that democratic choice is equally available to all. Keeping most people unaware that freedom of confident action is there for just a small number of people props up those in power and serves to keep power in the hands of the same groups that have most of it already. Though systemic change takes many decades, there are pressing questions for me and I imagine for some others like me if we raise our daily consciousness on the perquisites of being light-skinned. What will we do with such knowledge? As we know from watching men, it is an open question whether we will choose to use unearned advantage to weaken invisible privilege systems and whether we will use any of our arbitrarily awarded power to try to reconstruct power systems on a broader base.

ACKNOWLEDGMENTS

I have appreciated commentary on this paper from the Working Papers Committee of the Wellesley College Center for Research on Women, from members of the Dodge seminar, and from many individuals, including Margaret Andersen, Sorel Berman, Joanne Braxton, Johnnella Butler, Sandra Dickerson, Marnie Evans, Beverly Guy-Sheftall, Sandra Harding, Eleanor Hinton Hoytt, Pauline Houston, Paul Lauter, Joyce Miller, Mary Norris, Gloria Oden, Beverly Smith, and John Walter.

NOTES

1. This paper was presented at the Virginia Women's Studies Association conference in Richmond in April 1986, and the American Educational Research Association conference in Boston in October 1986, and discussed with two groups of participants in the Dodge seminars for Secondary School Teachers in New York and Boston in the spring of 1987.
2. Andersen, Margaret, "Race and the Social Science Curriculum: A Teaching and Learning Discussion," *Radical Teacher*, November 1984, pp. 17–20. Smith, Lillian, *Killers of the Dream*, New York: W. W. Norton, 1949.
3. "A Black Feminist Statement," The Combahee River Collective, pp. 13–22 in G. Hull, P. Scott, B. Smith, Eds., *All the Women Are White, All the Blacks Are Men, but Some of Us Are Brave: Black Women's Studies*, Old Westbury, NY: The Feminist Press, 1982.

Where I Come from Is Like This

First published in 1986

I

Modern American Indian women, like their non-Indian sisters, are deeply engaged in the struggle to redefine themselves. In their struggle they must reconcile traditional tribal definitions of women with industrial and postindustrial non-Indian definitions. Yet while these definitions seem to be more or less mutually exclusive, Indian women must somehow harmonize and integrate both in their own lives.

An American Indian woman is primarily defined by her tribal identity. In her eyes, her destiny is necessarily that of her people, and her sense of herself as a woman is first and foremost prescribed by her tribe. The definitions of woman's roles are as diverse as tribal cultures in the Americas. In some she is devalued, in others she wields considerable power. In some she is a familial/clan adjunct, in some she is as close to autonomous as her economic circumstances and psychological traits permit. But in no tribal definitions is she perceived in the same way as are women in western industrial and postindustrial cultures.

In the West, few images of women form part of the cultural mythos, and these are largely sexually charged. Among Christians, the madonna is the female prototype, and she is portrayed as essentially passive: her contribution is simply that of birthing. Little else is attributed to her and she certainly possesses few of the characteristics that are attributed to mythic figures among Indian tribes. This image is countered (rather than balanced) by the witch/goddess/whore characteristics designed to reinforce cultural beliefs about women, as well as western adversarial and dualistic perceptions of reality.

The tribes see women variously, but they do not question the power of femininity. Sometimes they see women as fearful, sometimes peaceful, sometimes omnipotent and omniscient, but they never portray women as mindless, helpless, simple, or oppressed. And while the women in a given tribe, clan, or band may be all these things, the individual woman is provided with a variety of images of women from the interconnected supernatural, natural, and social worlds she lives in.

As a half-breed American Indian woman, I cast about in my mind for negative images of Indian women, and I find none that are directed to Indian women alone. The negative images I do have are of Indians in general and in fact are more often of males than of females. All these images come to me from non-Indian sources, and they are always balanced by a positive image. My ideas of womanhood, passed on largely by my mother and grandmothers, Laguna Pueblo women, are about practicality, strength, reasonableness, intelligence, wit, and competence. I also remember vividly the women who came to my father's store, the women who held me and sang to me, the women at Feast Day, at Grab Days, the women in the kitchen of my Cubero home, the women I grew up with; none of them appeared weak or helpless, none of them presented herself tentatively. I remember a certain reserve on those lovely brown faces; I remember the direct gaze of eyes framed by bright-colored shawls draped over their heads and cascading down their backs. I remember the clean cotton dresses and carefully pressed hand-embroidered aprons they always wore; I remember laughter and good food, especially the sweet bread and the oven bread they gave us. Nowhere in my mind is there a foolish woman, a dumb woman, a vain woman, or a plastic woman, though the Indian women I have known have shown a wide range of personal style and demeanor.

My memory includes the Navajo woman who was badly beaten by her Sioux husband; but I also remember that my grandmother abandoned her Sioux husband long ago. I recall the stories about the Laguna woman beaten regularly by her husband in the presence of her children so that the children would not believe in the strength and power of femininity. And I remember the women who drank, who got into fights with other women and with the men, and who often won those battles. I have memories of tired women, partying women, stubborn women, sullen women, amicable women, selfish women, shy women, and aggressive women. Most of all I remember the women who laugh and scold and sit uncomplaining in the long sun on feast days and who cook wonderful food on wood stoves, in beehive mud ovens, and over open fires outdoors.

Among the images of women that come to me from various tribes as well as my own are White Buffalo Woman, who came to the Lakota long ago and brought them the religion of the Sacred Pipe, which they still practice; Tinotzin the goddess, who came to Juan Diego to remind him that she still walked the hills of her people and sent him with her message, her demand, and her proof to the Catholic bishop in the city nearby. And from Laguna I take the images of Yellow Woman, Coyote Woman, Grandmother Spider (Spider Old Woman), who brought the light, who gave us weaving and medicine, who gave us life. Among the Keres she is known as Thought Woman, who created us all and who keeps us in creation even now. I remember Iyatiku, Earth Woman, Corn Woman, who guides and counsels the people to peace and who welcomes us home when we cast off this coil of flesh as huskers cast off the leaves that wrap the corn. I remember Iyatiku's sister, Sun Woman, who held metals and cattle, pigs and sheep, highways and engines and so many things in her bundle, who went away to the east saying that one day she would return.

II

Since the coming of the Anglo-Europeans beginning in the fifteenth century, the fragile web of identity that long held tribal people secure has gradually been weakened and torn. But the oral tradition has prevented the complete destruction of the web, the ultimate disruption of tribal ways. The oral tradition is vital; it heals itself and the tribal web by adapting to the flow of the present while never relinquishing its connection to the past. Its adaptability has always been required, as many generations have experienced.

Certainly the modern American Indian woman bears slight resemblance to her forebears—at least on superficial examination—but she is still a tribal woman in her deepest being. Her tribal sense of relationship to all that is continues to flourish. And though she is at times beset by her knowledge of the enormous gap between the life she lives and the life she was raised to live, and while she adapts her mind and being to the circumstances of her present life, she does so in tribal ways, mending the tears in the web of being from which she takes her existence as she goes.

My mother told me stories all the time, though I often did not recognize them as that. My mother told me stories about cooking and childbearing; she told me stories about menstruation and pregnancy; she told me stories about gods and heroes, about fairies and elves, about goddesses and spirits; she told me stories about the land and the sky, about cats and dogs, about snakes and spiders; she told me stories about climbing trees and exploring the mesas; she told me stories about going to dances and getting married; she told me stories about dressing and undressing, about sleeping and waking; she told me stories about herself, about her mother, about her grandmother. She told me stories about grieving and laughing, about thinking and doing; she told me stories about school and about people; about darning and mending; she told me stories about turquoise and about gold; she told me European stories and Laguna stories; she told me Catholic stories and Presbyterian stories; she told me city stories and country stories; she told me political stories and religious stories. She told me stories about living and stories about dying. And in all of those stories she told me who I was, who I was supposed to be, whom I came from, and who would follow me. In this way she taught me the meaning of the words she said, that all life is a circle and everything has a place within it. That's what she said and what she showed me in the things she did and the way she lived.

Of course, through my formal, white, Christian education, I discovered that other people had stories of their own—about women, about Indians, about fact, about reality—and I was amazed by a number of startling suppositions that others made about tribal customs and beliefs. According to the un-Indian, non-Indian view, for instance, Indians barred menstruating women from ceremonies and indeed segregated them from the rest of the people, consigning them to some space specially designed for them. This showed that Indians considered menstruating women unclean and not fit to enjoy the company of decent (nonmenstruating) people, that is, men. I was surprised and confused to hear this because my mother had taught me that white people had strange attitudes toward menstruation: they thought something was bad about it, that it meant you were sick, cursed, sinful, and weak and that you had to be very careful during that time. She taught me that menstruation was a normal occurrence, that I could go swimming or hiking or whatever else I wanted to do during my period. She actively scorned women who took to their beds, who were incapacitated by cramps, who "got the blues."

As I struggled to reconcile these very contradictory interpretations of American Indians' traditional beliefs concerning menstruation, I realized that the menstrual taboos were about power, not about sin or filth. My conclusion was later borne out by some tribes' own explanations, which, as you may well imagine, came as quite a relief to me.

The truth of the matter as many Indians see it is that women who are at the peak of their fecundity are believed to possess power that throws male power totally out of kilter. They emit such force that, in their presence, any male-owned or -dominated ritual or sacred object cannot do its usual task. For instance, the Lakota say that a menstruating woman anywhere near a yuwipi man, who is a special sort of psychic, spirit-empowered healer, for a day or so before he is to do his ceremony will effectively disempower him. Conversely, among many if not most tribes, important ceremonies cannot be held without the presence of women. Sometimes the ritual woman who empowers the ceremony must be unmarried and virginal so that the power she channels is unalloyed, unweakened by sexual arousal and penetration by a male. Other ceremonies require tumescent women, others the presence of mature women who have borne children, and still others depend for empowerment on postmenopausal women. Women may be segregated from the company of the whole band or village on certain occasions, but on certain occasions men are also segregated. In short, each ritual depends on a certain balance of power, and the positions of women within the phases of womanhood are used by tribal people to empower certain rites. This does not derive from a male-dominant view; it is not a ritual observance imposed on women by men. It derives from a tribal view of reality that distinguishes tribal people from feudal and industrial people.

Among the tribes, the occult power of women, inextricably bound to our hormonal life, is thought to be very great; many hold that we possess innately the blood-given power to kill—with a glance, with a step, or with a judicious mixing of menstrual blood into somebody's soup. Medicine women among the Pomo of California cannot practice until they are sufficiently mature; when they are immature, their power is diffuse and is likely to interfere with their practice until time and experience have it under control. So women of the tribes are not especially inclined to see themselves as poor helpless victims of male domination. Even in those tribes where something akin to male domination was present, women are perceived as powerful, socially, physically, and metaphysically. In times past, as in times present, women carried enormous burdens with aplomb. We were far indeed from the "weaker sex," the designation that white aristocratic sisters unhappily earned for us all.

I remember my mother moving furniture all over the house when she wanted it changed. She didn't wait for my father to come home and help—she just went ahead and moved the piano, a huge upright from the old days, the couch, the refrigerator. Nobody had told her she was too weak to do such things. In imitation of her, I would delight in loading trucks at my father's store with cases of pop or fifty-pound sacks of flour. Even when I was quite small I could do it, and it gave me a belief in my own physical strength that advancing middle age can't quite erase. My mother used to tell me about the Acoma Pueblo women she had seen as a child carrying huge ollas (water pots) on their heads as they wound their way up the tortuous stairwell carved into the face of the "Sky City" mesa, a feat I tried to imitate with books and tin buckets. ("Sky City" is the term used by the Chamber of Commerce for the mother village of Acoma, which is situated atop a high sandstone table mountain.) I was never very successful, but even the attempt reminded me that I was supposed to be strong and balanced to be a proper girl.

Of course, my mother's Laguna people are Keres Indian, reputed to be the last extreme mother-right people on earth. So it is no wonder that I got notably nonwhite notions about the natural strength and prowess of women. Indeed, it is only when I am trying to get non-Indian approval, recognition, or acknowledgment that my "weak sister" emotional and intellectual ploys get the better of my tribal woman's good sense. At such times I forget that I just moved the piano or just wrote a competent paper or just completed a financial transaction satisfactorily or have supported myself and my children for most of my adult life.

Nor is my contradictory behavior atypical. Most Indian women I know are in the same bicultural bind: we vacillate between being dependent and strong, self-reliant and powerless, strongly motivated and hopelessly insecure. We resolve the dilemma in various ways: some of us party all the time; some of us drink to excess; some of us travel and move around a lot; some of us land good jobs and then quit them; some of us engage in violent exchanges; some of us blow our brains out. We act in these destructive ways because we suffer from the societal conflicts caused by having to identify with two hopelessly opposed cultural definitions of women. Through this destructive dissonance we are unhappy prey to the self-disparagement common to, indeed demanded of, Indians living in the United States today. Our situation is caused by the exigencies of a history of invasion, conquest, and colonization whose searing marks are probably ineradicable. A popular bumper sticker on many Indian cars proclaims: "If You're Indian You're In," to which I always find myself adding under my breath, "Trouble."

III

No Indian can grow to any age without being informed that her people were "savages" who interfered with the march of progress pursued by respectable, loving, civilized white people. We are the villains of the scenario when we are mentioned at all. We are absent from much of white history except when we are calmly, rationally, succinctly, and systematically dehumanized. On the few occasions we are noticed in any way other than as howling, blood-thirsty beings, we are acclaimed for our noble quaintness. In this definition, we are exotic curios. Our ancient arts and customs are used to draw tourist money to state coffers, into the pocketbooks and bank accounts of scholars, and into support of the American-in-Disneyland promoters' dream.

As a Roman Catholic child I was treated to bloody tales of how the savage Indians martyred the hapless priests and missionaries who went among them in an attempt to lead them to the one true path. By the time I was through high school I had the idea that Indians were people who had benefited mightily from the advanced knowledge and superior morality of the Anglo-Europeans. At least I had, perforce, that idea to lay beside the other one that derived from my daily experience of Indian life, an idea less dehumanizing and more accurate because it came from my mother and the other Indian people who raised me. That idea was that Indians are a people who don't tell lies, who care for their children and their old people. You never see an Indian orphan, they said. You always know when you're old that someone will take care of you— one of your children will. Then they'd list the old folks who were being taken care of by this child or that. No child is ever considered illegitimate among the Indians, they said. If a girl gets pregnant, the baby is still part of the family, and the mother is too. That's what they said, and they showed me real people who lived according to those principles.

Of course the ravages of colonization have taken their toll; there are orphans in Indian country now, and abandoned, brutalized old folks; there are even illegitimate children, though the very concept still strikes me as absurd. There are battered children and neglected children, and there are battered wives and women who have been raped by Indian men. Proximity to the "civilizing" effects of white Christians has not improved the moral quality of life in Indian country, though each group, Indian and white, explains the situation differently. Nor is there much yet in the oral tradition that can enable us to adapt to these inhuman changes. But a force is growing in that direction, and it is helping Indian women reclaim their lives. Their power, their sense of direction and of self will soon be visible. It is the force of the women who speak and work and write, and it is formidable.

Through all the centuries of war and death and cultural and psychic destruction have endured the women who raise the children and tend the fires, who pass along the tales and the traditions, who weep and bury the dead, who are the dead, and who never forget. There are always the women, who make pots and weave baskets, who fashion clothes and cheer their children on at pow wow, who make fry bread and piki bread, and corn soup and chili stew, who dance and sing and remember and hold within their hearts the dream of their ancient peoples—that one day the woman who thinks will speak to us again, and everywhere there will be peace. Meanwhile we tell the stories and write the books and trade tales of anger and woe and stories of fun and scandal and laugh over all manner of things that happen every day. We watch and we wait.

My great-grandmother told my mother: Never forget you are Indian. And my mother told me the same thing. This, then, is how I have gone about remembering, so that my children will remember too.

The Master's Tools Will Never Dismantle the Master's House

First published in 1984

I agreed to take part in a New York University Institute for the Humanities conference a year ago, with the understanding that I would be commenting upon papers dealing with the role of difference within the lives of american [*sic*] women: difference of race, sexuality, class, and age. The absence of these considerations weakens any feminist discussion of the personal and the political.

It is a particular academic arrogance to assume any discussion of feminist theory without examining our many differences, and without a significant input from poor women, Black and Third World women, and lesbians. And yet, I stand here as a Black lesbian feminist, having been invited to comment within the only panel at this conference where the input of Black feminists and lesbians is represented. What this says about the vision of this conference is sad, in a country where racism, sexism, and homophobia are inseparable. To read this program is to assume that lesbian and Black women have nothing to say about existentialism, the erotic, women's culture and silence, developing feminist theory, or heterosexuality and power. And what does it mean in personal and political terms when even the two Black women who did present here were literally found at the last hour? What does it mean when the tools of a racist patriarchy are used to examine the fruits of that same patriarchy? It means that only the most narrow perimeters of change are possible and allowable.

The absence of any consideration of lesbian consciousness or the consciousness of Third World women leaves a serious gap within this conference and within the papers presented here. For example, in a paper on material relationships between women, I was conscious of an either/or model of nurturing which totally dismissed my knowledge as a Black lesbian. In this paper there was no examination of mutuality between women, no systems of shared support, no interdependence as exists between lesbians and women-identified women. Yet it is only in the patriarchal model of nurturance that women "who attempt to emancipate themselves pay perhaps too high a price for the results," as this paper states.

For women, the need and desire to nurture each other is not pathological but redemptive, and it is within that knowledge that our real power is rediscovered. It is this real connection which is so feared by a patriarchal world. Only within a patriarchal structure is maternity the only social power open to women.

Interdependency between women is the way to a freedom which allows the *I* to *be*, not in order to be used, but in order to be creative. This is a difference between the passive *be* and the active *being*.

Advocating the mere tolerance of difference between women is the grossest reformism. It is a total denial of the creative function of difference in our lives. Difference must be not merely tolerated, but seen as a fund of necessary polarities between which our creativity can spark like a dialectic. Only then does the necessity for interdependency become unthreatening. Only within that interdependency of different strengths, acknowledged and equal, can the power to seek new ways of being in the world generate, as well as the courage and sustenance to act where there are no charters.

Within the interdependence of mutual (nondominant) differences lies that security which enables us to descend into the chaos of knowledge and return with true visions of our future, along with the concomitant power to effect those changes which can bring that future into being. Difference is that raw and powerful connection from which our personal power is forged.

As women, we have been taught either to ignore our differences or to view them as causes for separation and suspicion rather than as forces for change. Without community there is no liberation, only the most vulnerable and temporary armistice between an individual and her oppression. But community must not mean a shedding of our differences, nor the pathetic pretense that these differences do not exist.

Those of us who stand outside the circle of this society's definition of acceptable women; those of us who have been forged in the crucibles of difference—those of us who are poor, who are lesbians, who are Black, who are older—know that *survival is not an academic skill.* It is learning how to stand alone, unpopular and sometimes reviled, and how to make common cause with those others identified as outside the structures in order to define and seek a world in which we can all flourish. It is learning how to take our differences and make them strengths. *For the master's tools will never dismantle the master's house.* They may allow us temporarily to beat him at his own game, but they will never enable us to bring about genuine change. And this fact is threatening only to those women who still define the master's house as their only source of support.

Poor women and women of Color know there is a difference between the daily manifestations of marital slavery and prostitution because it is our daughters who line 42nd Street. If white american [sic] feminist theory need not deal with the differences between us, and the resulting difference in our oppressions, then how do you deal with the fact that the women who clean your houses and tend your children while you attend conferences on feminist theory are, for the most part, poor women and women of Color? What is the theory behind racist feminism?

In a world of possibility for us all, our personal visions help lay the groundwork for political action. The failure of academic feminists to recognize difference as a crucial strength is a failure to reach beyond the first patriarchal lesson. In our world, divide and conquer must become define and empower.

Why weren't other women of Color found to participate in this conference? Why were two phone calls to me considered a consultation? Am I the only possible source of names of Black feminists? And although the Black panelist's paper ends on an important and powerful connection of love between women, what about interracial cooperation between feminists who don't love each other?

In academic feminist circles, the answer to these questions is often, "We did not know who to ask." But that is the same evasion of responsibility, the same cop-out, that keeps Black women's art out of women's exhibitions, Black women's work out of most feminist publications except for the occasional "Special Third World Women's Issue," and Black women's texts off your reading lists. But as Adrienne Rich pointed out in a recent talk, white feminists have educated themselves about such an enormous amount over the past ten years, how come you haven't also educated yourselves about Black women and the differences between us—white and Black—when it is key to our survival as a movement?

Women of today are still being called upon to stretch across the gap of male ignorance and to educate men as to our existence and our needs. This is an old and primary tool of all oppressors to keep the oppressed occupied with the master's concerns. Now we hear that it is the task of women of Color to educate white women—in the face of tremendous resistance—as to our existence, our differences, our relative roles in our joint survival. This is a diversion of energies and a tragic repetition of racist patriarchal thought.

Simone de Beauvoir once said: "It is in the knowledge of the genuine conditions of our lives that we must draw our strength to live and our reasons for acting."

Racism and homophobia are real conditions of all our lives in this place and time. *I urge each one of us here to reach down into that deep place of knowledge inside herself and touch that terror and loathing of any difference that lives there. See whose face it wears.* Then the personal as the political can begin to illuminate all our choices.

The Mountain

First published in 1999

I: A METAPHOR

The mountain as metaphor looms large in the lives of marginalized people, people whose bones get crushed in the grind of capitalism, patriarchy, white supremacy. How many of us have struggled up the mountain, measured ourselves against it, failed up there, lived in its shadow? We've hit our heads on glass ceilings, tried to climb the class ladder, lost fights against assimilation, scrambled toward that phantom called normality.

We hear from the summit that the world is grand from up there, that we live down here at the bottom because we are lazy, stupid, weak, and ugly. We decide to climb that mountain, or make a pact that our children will climb it. The climbing turns out to be unimaginably difficult. We are afraid; every time we look ahead we can find nothing remotely familiar or comfortable. We lose the trail. Our wheelchairs get stuck. We speak the wrong languages with the wrong accents, wear the wrong clothes, carry our bodies the wrong ways, ask the wrong questions, love the wrong people. And it's goddamn lonely up there on the mountain. We decide to stop climbing and build a new house right where we are. Or we decide to climb back down to the people we love, where the food, the clothes, the dirt, the sidewalk, the steaming asphalt under our feet, our crutches, all feel right. Or we find the path again, decide to continue climbing only to have the very people who told us how wonderful life is at the summit booby-trap the trail. They burn the bridge over the impassable canyon. They redraw our topo maps so that we end up walking in circles. They send their goons—those working-class and poor people they employ as their official brutes—to push us over the edge. Maybe we get to the summit, but probably not. And the price we pay is huge.

Up there on the mountain, we confront the external forces, the power brokers who benefit so much from the status quo and their privileged position at the very summit. But just as vividly, we come face-to-face with our own bodies, all that we cherish and despise, all that lies imbedded there. This I know because I have caught myself lurching up the mountain.

II: A SUPERCRIP STORY

I am a gimp, a crip, disabled with cerebral palsy. The story of me lurching up the mountain begins not on the mountain, but with one of the dominant images of disabled people, the supercrip. A boy without hands bats .486 on his Little League team. A blind man hikes the Appalachian Trail from end to end. An adolescent girl with Down's syndrome learns to drive and has a boyfriend. A guy with one leg runs across Canada. The nondisabled world is saturated with these stories: stories about gimps who engage in activities as grand as walking 2,500 miles or as mundane as learning to drive. They focus on disabled people "overcoming" our disabilities. They reinforce the superiority of the nondisabled body and mind. They turn individual disabled people, who are simply leading their lives, into symbols of inspiration.

Supercrip stories never focus on the conditions that make it so difficult for people with Down's to have romantic partners, for blind people to have adventures, for disabled kids to play sports. I don't mean medical conditions. I mean material, social, legal conditions. I mean lack of access, lack of employment, lack of education, lack of personal attendant services. I mean stereotypes and attitudes. I mean oppression. The dominant story about disability should be about ableism, not the inspirational supercrip crap, the believe-it-or-not disability story.

I've been a supercrip in the mind's eye of nondis-abled people more than once. Running cross-country and track in high school, I came in dead last in more races than I care to count. My tense, wiry body, right foot wandering out to the side as I grew tired, pushed against the miles, the stopwatch, the final back stretch, the last muddy hill. Sometimes I was lapped by the front runners in races as short as the mile. Sometimes I trailed everyone on a cross-country course by two, three, four minutes. I ran because I loved to run, and yet after every race, strangers came to thank me, cry over me, tell me what an inspiration I was. To them, I was not just another hopelessly slow, tenacious high school athlete, but supercrip, tragic brave girl with CP, courageous cripple. It sucked. The slogan on one of my favorite t-shirts, black cotton inked with big fluorescent pink letters, one word per line, reads PISS ON PITY.

Me lurching up the mountain is another kind of supercrip story, a story about internalizing supercrip-dom, about becoming supercrip in my own mind's eye, a story about climbing Mount Adams last summer with my friend Adrianne. We had been planning this trip for years. Adrianne spent her childhood roaming New Hampshire's White Mountains and wanted to take me to her favorite haunts. Six times in six years, we set the trip up, and every time something fell through at the last minute. Finally, last summer every-thing stayed in place.

I love the mountains almost as much as I love the ocean, not a soft, romantic kind of love, but a deep down rumble in my bones. When Adrianne pulled out her trail guides and topo maps and asked me to choose one of the mountains we'd climb, I looked for a big mountain, for a long, hard hike, for a trail that would take us well above treeline. I picked Mount Adams. I think I asked Adrianne, "Can I handle this trail?" meaning, "Will I have to clamber across deep gulches on narrow log bridges without hand railings to get to the top of this mountain?" Without a moment's hesita-tion, she said, "No problem."

I have walked from Los Angeles to Washington, D.C., on a peace walk; backpacked solo in the southern Appalachians, along Lake Superior, on the beaches at Point Reyes; slogged my way over Cottonwood Pass and down South Manitou's dunes. Learning to walk took me longer than most kids—certainly most non-disabled kids. I was two and a half before I figured out how to stand on my own two feet, drop my heels to the ground, balance my weight on the whole long flat of each foot. I wore orthopedic shoes—clunky, unbend-ing monsters—for several years, but never had to suf-fer through physical therapy or surgery. Today, I can and often do walk unending miles for the pure joy of walking. In the disability community I am called a walkie, someone who doesn't use a wheelchair, who walks rather than rolls. Adrianne and I have been hik-ing buddies for years. I never questioned her judg-ment. Of course, I could handle Mount Adams.

The night before our hike, it rained. In the morning we thought we might have to postpone. The weather reports from the summit still looked uncertain, but by 10 a.m. the clouds started to lift, later than we had planned to begin but still okay. The first mile of trail snaked through steep jumbles of rock, leaving me breathing hard, sweat drenching my cotton t-shirt, dripping into my eyes. I love this pull and stretch, quads and calves, lungs and heart, straining.

The trail divides and divides again, steeper and rockier now, moving not around but over piles of craggy granite, mossy and a bit slick from the night's rain. I start having to watch where I put my feet. Bal-ance has always been somewhat of a problem for me, my right foot less steady than my left. On uncertain ground, each step becomes a studied move, especially when my weight is balanced on my right foot. I take the trail slowly, bringing both feet together, solid on one stone, before leaning into my next step. This assures my balance, but I lose all the momentum gained from swinging into a step, touching ground, pushing off again in the same moment. There is no rhythm to my stop-and-go clamber. I know that going down will be worse, gravity underscoring my lack of balance. I watch Adrianne ahead of me hop from one rock to the next up this tumble trail of granite. I know that she's breathing hard, that this is no easy climb, but also that each step isn't a strategic game for her. I start getting scared as the trail steepens, then steepens again, the rocks not letting up. I can't think of how I will ever come down this mountain. Fear sets up a rumble right along-side the love in my bones. I keep climbing. Adrianne starts waiting for me every 50 yards or so. I finally tell her I'm scared.

She's never hiked this trail before so can't tell me if this is as steep as it gets. We study the topo map, do a time check. We have many hours of daylight ahead of us, but we're both thinking about how much time it might take me to climb down, using my hands and butt when I can't trust my feet. I want to continue up to treeline, the pines shorter and shorter, grown twisted and withered, giving way to scrub brush, then to lichen-covered granite, up to the sun-drenched cap where the mountains all tumble out toward the hazy blue horizon. I want to so badly, but fear rumbles next to love next to real lived physical limitations, and so we decide to turn around. I cry, maybe for the first time, over something I want to do, had many reasons to believe I could, but really can't. I cry hard, then get up and follow Adrianne back down the mountain. It's hard and slow, and I use my hands and butt often and wish I could use gravity as Adrianne does to bounce from one flat spot to another, down this jumbled pile of rocks.

I thought a lot coming down Mount Adams. Thought about bitterness. For as long as I can remember, I have avoided certain questions. Would I have been a good runner if I didn't have CP? Could I have been a surgeon or pianist, a dancer or gymnast? Tempting questions that have no answers. I refuse to enter the territory marked *bitterness*. I wondered about a friend who calls herself one of the last of the polio tribe, born just before the polio vaccine's discovery. Does she ever ask what her life might look like had she been born five years later? On a topo map, bitterness would be outlined in red.

I thought about the model of disability that separates impairment from disability. Disability theorist Michael Oliver defines impairment as "lacking part of or all of a limb, or having a defective limb, organism or mechanism of the body."[1] I lack a fair amount of fine motor control. My hands shake. I can't play a piano, place my hands gently on a keyboard, or type even 15 words a minute. Whole paragraphs never cascade from my fingertips. My longhand is a slow scrawl. I have trouble picking up small objects, putting them down. Dicing onions with a sharp knife puts my hands at risk. A food processor is not a yuppie kitchen luxury in my house, but an adaptive device. My gross motor skills are better but not great. I can walk mile after mile, run and jump and skip and hop, but don't expect me to walk a balance beam. A tightrope would be murder; boulder hopping and rock climbing, not much better. I am not asking for pity. I am telling you about impairment.

Oliver defines disability as "the disadvantage or restriction of activity caused by a contemporary social organisation which takes no or little account of people who have physical [and/or cognitive/developmental/mental] impairments and thus excludes them from the mainstream of society."[2] I write slowly enough that cashiers get impatient as I sign my name to checks,

stop talking to me, turn to my companions, hand them my receipts. I have failed timed tests, important tests, because teachers wouldn't allow me extra time to finish the sheer physical act of writing, wouldn't allow me to use a typewriter. I have been turned away from jobs because my potential employer believed my slow, slurred speech meant I was stupid. Everywhere I go people stare at me, in restaurants as I eat, in grocery stores as I fish coins out of my pocket to pay the cashier, in parks as I play with my dog. I am not asking for pity. I am telling you about disability.

In large part, disability oppression is about access. Simply being on Mount Adams, halfway up Air Line Trail, represents a whole lot of access. When access is measured by curb cuts, ramps, and whether they are kept clear of snow and ice in the winter; by the width of doors and height of counters; by the presence or absence of Braille, closed captions, ASL, and TDDs; my not being able to climb all the way to the very top of Mount Adams stops being about disability. I decided that turning around before reaching the summit was more about impairment than disability.

But even as I formed the thought, I could feel my resistance to it. To neatly divide disability from impairment doesn't feel right. My experience of living with CP has been so shaped by ableism—or to use Oliver's language, my experience of impairment has been so shaped by disability—that I have trouble separating the two. I understand the difference between failing a test because some stupid school rule won't give me more time and failing to summit Mount Adams because it's too steep and slippery for my feet. The first failure centers on a socially constructed limitation, the second on a physical one.

At the same time, both center on my body. The faster I try to write, the more my pen slides out of control, muscles spasm, then contract trying to stop the tremors, my shoulder and upper arm growing painfully tight. Even though this socially constructed limitation has a simple solution—access to a typewriter, computer, tape recorder, or person to take dictation—I experience the problem on a very physical level. In the case of the bodily limitation, my experience is similarly physical. My feet simply don't know the necessary balance. I lurch along from one rock to the next, catching myself repeatedly as I start to fall, quads quickly sore from exertion, tension, lack of momentum. These physical experiences, one caused by a social construction, the other by a bodily limitation, translate directly into frustration, making me want to crumple the test I can't finish, hurl the rocks I can't climb. This frustration knows no neat theoretical divide between disability and impairment. Neither does disappointment nor embarrassment. On good days, I can separate the anger I turn inward at my body from the anger that needs to be turned outward, directed at the daily ableist shit, but there is nothing simple or neat about kindling the latter while transforming the former. I decided that Oliver's model of disability makes theoretical and political sense but misses important emotional realities.

I thought of my nondisabled friends who don't care for camping, hiking, or backpacking. They would never spend a vacation sweat-drenched and breathing hard halfway up a mountain. I started to list their names, told Adrianne what I was doing. She reminded me of other friends who enjoy easy day hikes on smooth, well-maintained trails. Many of them would never even attempt the tumbled trail of rock I climbed for an hour and a half before turning around. We added their names to my list. It turned into a long roster. I decided that if part of what happened to me up there was about impairment, another part was about desire, my desire to climb mountains.

I thought about supercrips. Some of us—the boy who bats .486, the man who through-hikes the A.T.—accomplish something truly extraordinary and become supercrips. Others of us—the teenager with Down's who has a boyfriend, the kid with CP who runs track and cross-country—lead entirely ordinary lives and still become supercrips. Nothing about having a boyfriend or running cross-country is particularly noteworthy. Bat .486 or have a boyfriend, it doesn't matter; either way we are astonishing. In the creation of supercrip stories, nondisabled people don't celebrate any particular achievement, however extraordinary or mundane. Rather, these stories rely upon the perception that disability and achievement contradict each other and that any disabled person who overcomes this contradiction is heroic.

To believe that achievement contradicts disability is to pair helplessness with disability, a pairing for which crips pay an awful price. The nondisabled world locks us away in nursing homes. It deprives us the resources to live independently.[3] It physically and sexually abuses us in astoundingly high numbers.[4] It refuses to give us jobs because even when a workplace is accessible, the speech impediment, the limp, the ventilator, the seeing-eye dog are read as signs of inability.[5] The price is incredibly high.

And here, supercrip turns complicated. On the other side of super-cripdom lies pity, tragedy, and the nursing home. Disabled people know this, and in our process of knowing, some of us internalize the crap. We make supercrip our own, particularly the type that pushes into the extraordinary, cracks into our physical limitations. We use supercripdom as a shield, a protection, as if this individual internalization could defend us against disability oppression.

I climbed Mount Adams for an hour and a half scared, not sure I'd ever be able to climb down, knowing that on the next rock my balance could give out, and yet I climbed. Climbed surely because I wanted the summit, because of the love rumbling in my bones. But climbed also because I wanted to say, "Yes, I have CP, but see. See, watch me. I can climb mountains too." I wanted to prove myself once again. I wanted to overcome my CP.

Overcoming has a powerful grip. Back home, my friends told me, "But you can walk any of us under the table." My sister, a serious mountain climber who spends many a weekend high up in the North Cascades, told me, "I bet with the right gear and enough practice you *could* climb Mount Adams." A woman who doesn't know me told Adrianne, "Tell your friend not to give up. She can do anything she wants. She just has to want it hard enough." I told myself as Adrianne and I started talking about another trip to the Whites, "If I used a walking stick, and we picked a dry day and a different trail, maybe I could make it up to the top of Adams." I never once heard, "You made the right choice when you turned around." The mountain just won't let go.

III: HOME

I will never find home on the mountain. This I know. Rather home starts here in my body, in all that lies imbedded beneath my skin. My disabled body: born prematurely in the backwoods of Oregon, I was first diagnosed as "mentally retarded," and then later as having CP. I grew up to the words *cripple, retard, monkey, defect*, took all the staring into me and learned to shut it out.

My body violated: early on my father started raping me, physically abusing me in ways that can only be described as torture, and sharing my body with other people, mostly men, who did the same. I abandoned that body, decided to be a hermit, to be done with humans, to live among the trees, with the salmon, to ride the south wind bareback.

My white body: the only person of color in my hometown was an African-American boy, adopted by a white family. I grew up to persistent rumors of a lynching tree way back in the hills, of the sheriff running people out of the county. For a long time after moving to the city, college scholarship in hand, all I could do was gawk at the multitude of humans: homeless people, their shopping carts and bedrolls, Black people, Chinese people, Chicanos, drag queens and punks, vets down on Portland's Burnside Avenue, white men in their wool suits, limos shined to sparkle. I watched them all, sucking in the thick weave of Spanish, Cantonese, street talk, English. This is how I became aware of my whiteness.

My queer body: I spent my childhood, a tomboy not sure of my girlness, queer without a name for my queerness. I cut firewood on clearcuts, swam in the river, ran the beaches at Battle Rock and Cape Blanco. When I found dykes, fell in love for the first time, came into a political queer community, I felt as if I had found home again.

The body as home, but only if it is understood that bodies are never singular, but rather haunted, strengthened, underscored by countless other bodies. My alcoholic, Libertarian father and his father, the gravedigger, from whom my father learned his violence. I still dream about them sometimes, ugly dreams that leave me panting with fear in the middle of the night. One day I will be done with them. The white, working-class loggers, fishermen, and ranchers I grew up among: Les Smith, John Black, Walt Maya. Their ways of dressing, moving, talking helped shape my sense of self. Today when I hear queer activists say the word *redneck* like a cuss word, I think of those men, backs of their necks turning red in the summertime from long days of work outside, felling trees, pulling fishnets, baling hay. I think of my butchness, grounded there, overlaid by a queer, urban sensibility. A body of white, rural, working-class values. I still feel an allegiance to this body, even as I reject the virulent racism, the unexamined destruction of forest and river. How could I possibly call my body home without the bodies of trees that repeatedly provided me refuge? Without queer bodies? Without crip bodies? Without transgendered and transsexual bodies? Without the history of disabled people who worked as freaks in the freak show, displaying their bodies: Charles Stratton posed as General Tom Thumb, Hiriam and Barney Davis billed as the "Wild Men from Borneo"? The answer is simple. I couldn't.

The body as home, but only if it is understood that place and community and culture burrow deep into our bones. My earliest and most enduring sense of place is in the backwoods of Oregon, where I grew up but no longer live, in a logging and fishing town of a thousand that hangs on to the most western edge of the continental United States. To the west stretches the Pacific Ocean; to the east the Siskiyou Mountains rise, not tall enough to be mountains but too steep to be hills. Portland is a seven-hour drive north; San Francisco, a twelve-hour drive south. Home for me is marked by Douglas fir and chinook salmon, south wind whipping the ocean into a fury of waves and surf. Marked by the aching knowledge of environmental destruction, the sad truth of that town founded on the genocide of Native peoples, the Tuni and Coquille, Talkemas and Latgawas. In writing about the backwoods and the rural, white, working-class culture found there, I am not being nostalgic, reaching backward toward a re-creation of the past, Rather I am reaching toward my bones. When I write about losing that place, about living in exile, I am putting words to a loss which also grasps at my bones.

The body as home, but only if it is understood that language too lives under the skin. I think of the words *crip, queer, freak, redneck*. None of these are easy words. They mark the jagged edge between self-hatred and pride, the chasm between how the dominant culture views marginalized peoples and how we view ourselves, the razor between finding home, finding our bodies, and living in exile, living on the metaphoric mountain. Whatever our relationships with these words—whether we embrace them or hate them, feel them draw blood as they hit our skin or find them entirely fitting, refuse to say them or simply feel uncomfortable in their presence—we deal with their power every day. I hear these words all the time. They are whispered in the mirror as I dress to go out, as I straighten my tie and shrug into my suit jacket; on the streets as folks gawk at my trembling hands, stare trying to figure out whether I'm a woman or man; in half the rhetoric I hear from environmentalists and queer activists, rhetoric where rural working-class people get cast as clods and bigots. At the same time, I use some, but not all, of these words to call out my pride, to strengthen my resistance, to place myself within community. *Crip, queer, freak, redneck* burrowed into my body.

The body as home, but only if it is understood that bodies can be stolen, fed lies and poison, torn away from us. They rise up around me—bodies stolen by hunger, war, breast cancer, AIDS, rape; the daily grind of factory, sweatshop, cannery, sawmill; the lynching rope; the freezing streets; the nursing home and prison. African-American drag performer Leonard/Lynn Vines, walking through his Baltimore neighborhood, called a "drag queen faggot bitch" and shot six times. Matt Sheppard—gay, white, young—tied to a fence post in Wyoming and beaten to death. Some bodies are taken for good; other bodies live on, numb, abandoned, full of self-hate. Both have been stolen. Disabled people cast as supercrips and tragedies; lesbian/gay/bisexual/trans people told over and over again that we are twisted and unnatural; poor people made responsible for their own poverty. Stereotypes and lies lodge in our bodies as surely as bullets. They live and fester there, stealing the body.

The body as home, but only if it is understood that the stolen body can be reclaimed. The bodies irrevocably taken from us: we can memorialize them in quilts, granite walls, candlelight vigils; remember and mourn them; use their deaths to strengthen our will. And as for the lies and false images, we need to name them, transform them, create something entirely new in their place, something that comes close and finally true to the bone, entering our bodies as liberation, joy, fury, hope, a will to refigure the world. The body as home.

The mountain will never be home, and still I have to remember it grips me. Supercrip lives inside my body, ready and willing to push the physical limitations, to try the "extraordinary," because down at the base of the mountain waits a nursing home. I hang on to a vision. Someday after the revolution, disabled people will live ordinary lives, neither heroic nor tragic. *Crip, queer, freak, redneck* will be mere words describing human difference. Supercrip will be dead; the nursing home, burnt down; the metaphoric mountain, collapsed in volcanic splendor. Post-revolution I expect there will still be literal mountains I want to climb and can't, but I'll be able to say without doubt, without hesitation, "Let's turn around here. This one is too steep, too slippery for my feet."

NOTES

1. Quoted in Hevey, David, *The Creatures Time Forgot: Photography and Disability Imagery* (London: Routledge, 1992), p. 9.
2. Quoted in Hevey, p. 9.
3. Russell, Marta. *Beyond Ramps* (Monroe, Maine: Common Courage Press, 1998), pp. 96–108.
4. Sobsey, Dick, *Violence and Abuse in the Lives of People with Disabilities* (Baltimore: Paul H. Brookes Publishing, 1994), p. 68.
5. Shapiro, Joseph, *No Pity: People with Disabilities Forging a New Civil Rights Movement* (New York: Times Books, 1994), pp. 27–29.

SECTION 2

Theoretical Perspectives

Theory is simply an effort to understand and explain the social world. Theories of gender are attempts to outline the major processes and social structures that give rise to the differences and inequalities between women and men and to analyze how these gender inequalities are connected to other major inequalities of race, class, sexuality, and nationality. You may notice as you read some of these selections that the language of theory is a bit different from some other forms of writing. Some of these readings may seem "harder" to you. In fact, the language in some of them *is* more complex as the authors attempt to make sense of abstract and complicated social processes. We hope that you will not be intimidated by this. Every student is smart enough to understand "theory," and the effort you put into reading these works will be rewarded in two ways: You will grasp the fascinating and provocative ideas the authors put forward, and you will gain a sense of your own competence. We are all theorists of gender, after all, whether we construct our theories in formal academic language or in everyday discussions with friends.

One important distinction in feminist theory is between *sex,* or the biological characteristics of men and women, and *gender,* or the social statuses and meanings assigned to women and men. Gender is one of the most important social distinctions. Societies define men and women as separate and distinct categories, and gender- or sex-based stratification is ubiquitous. Even our physical bodies (what might be considered an aspect of *sex,* or biology) are shaped and interpreted through societies' focus on differ-

ences between women and men. For example, men are widely considered to be stronger than women, despite the fact that men's physical strength is also affected by social practices such as weight-training or manual labor. Women are considered to be biologically "softer" and more delicate than men, but these characteristics are produced in part by social practices such as clothing, hairstyle, and the shaving of body hair. Although there are undeniably physical or biological attributes that differ between women and men (including, but not limited to, reproductive organs), the distinction between biological sex and social gender is far from clear-cut.

Another central tenet of feminist theory about gender is *intersectionality*—the recognition that gender is inextricably entwined with race, class, sexuality, nationality, and other major distinctions. We cannot think about gender in the abstract, apart from other distinctions, because gender takes different forms for different groups. The ways that gender inequality manifests itself in the lives of women from different racial group are not just quantitatively distinct—that is, it's not just that some groups are more disadvantaged than others. The manifestations of gender inequality are qualitatively distinct—the particular expectations and forms of subordination are different. Feminist scholars seek to understand how societies construct gender and how it affects individual identities, the ways people interact with each other, the ways social institutions are organized, and inequality.

Explanations of gender inequality fall into two basic schools of thought: the essentialist and the social constructionist. The *essentialist* position holds that the behaviors of men and women are rooted in biological and genetic factors, including differences in hormonal patterns, physical size, aggressiveness, the propensity to "bond" with members of the same sex, and the capacity to bear children. For the essentialist, the sexual division of labor in human societies is rooted in the sexual determination that is found in all species, from ants to deer to primates. Viewing such differences as a natural outgrowth of human evolution, essentialists contend that sex-based differences in responsibilities and the natural superiority of the male are inevitable, functional, and necessary for the survival of the species.

The second school of thought, the *social constructionist*, bases its position on a growing body of historical and anthropological research that points to wide variations in gender behavior and in the sexual division of labor among human societies throughout history. Social constructionists contend that the diversity of cultural understandings of gender is too great to be explained by biological factors. Instead, they argue, male dominance appears to be inevitable only because cultural ideas and beliefs have arisen to justify and perpetuate sex-based stratification systems that entitle men to greater power, prestige, and wealth than women. While such ideologies do not cause gender inequality, they certainly justify it as natural.

Gender is simultaneously socially constructed—"made up," artificial, created by people out of quite flimsy bases—and very real in its ramifications for individuals and for society as a whole. The task of theorists of gender is to explain this contradiction and the means by which gender becomes "real." The readings in this section present various approaches to understanding gender and its construction. In "'Night to His Day': The Social Construction of Gender," Judith Lorber outlines a social constructionist approach. She defines gender as a social institution that rests on the "socially constructed statuses" of "man" and "woman." Even the apparently dimorphic physical characteristics of the two sexes, Lorber argues, are socially interpreted and emphasized. How does the social institution of gender create *sameness* among members of each gender and *difference* between women and men? How

are the genders ranked in a hierarchy that privileges men over women?

In "The Medical Construction of Gender," Suzanne Kessler illustrates the powerful role medicine plays in the social construction of the categories of male and female. Kessler challenges the notion that the biological distinctions between women and men are natural rather than subject to social construction. Drawing on interviews with medical experts who have had clinical experience managing babies born with genitals that are neither clearly male nor clearly female, Kessler discusses the standard practices used by the medical establishment to define the gender of intersexed infants. The primary consideration in physicians' gender assignments and corrective surgery is the ability to construct correctly formed genitals, not the other potential gender markers such as chromosomes, hormones, or psychological factors. Kessler argues that the view that gender consists of two mutually exclusive types—female and male—is created by these medical practices, despite biological evidence of greater natural variation in actual gender markers. Do you agree with the medical view that gender must be assigned immediately, decisively, and irreversibly when an intersexed child is born? What role, if any, do you think social factors should play in making decisions about gender identity? What does Kessler's article suggest about the relationship between biological differences and societal gender systems?

Susan Stryker examines the relationship between sex and gender further in "Transgender Feminism: Queering the Woman Question." Defining "transgender phenomena" as "anything that disrupts or denaturalizes normative gender" and exposes the processes that produce the illusion of gender as natural, Stryker asks how thinking about transgender changes the way we think about feminism. She suggests that transgender helps us think about how bodies are used to justify inequality. Stryker recounts her own experiences with various forms of oppression to illustrate that transgender experiences can shed light on a range of other important social phenomena, from gender and sexual discrimination, to the controlling role of medicine, to state surveillance, to violence and hate crimes. Further, she suggests, transgender issues are a key connection between feminism and "queer politics" because they focus our attention on the relationships between gender, bodies, and sexuality.

In her conclusion, Stryker argues that "how we live in our bodies is a vital source of knowledge for us all." How is your own embodied experience shaped by the demands of sex and gender? How is this experience affected by the degree to which you conform to what "women" or "men" are supposed to be like? Stryker suggests that it is hard but important to imagine a future in which justice has prevailed. What are the "claims of justice" that transgender issues make upon us? Can you imagine what a world in which those transformations had occurred would be like?

In "Theorizing Difference from Multiracial Feminism," Maxine Baca Zinn and Bonnie Thornton Dill develop a model of how race, class, and gender are related to one another. In this model, race and other "differences" among women are central to the task of understanding gender. Arguing that these different forms of inequality intersect with one another in a "matrix of domination" (Hill Collins), Baca Zinn and Dill discuss how experiences of gender vary according to race and class. Their multiracial feminist perspective is relevant to the experiences of women and men of all races, because, they contend, categories of dominance and power are constructed in relationship to subordinate categories. As race, class, and gender intersect, they create both oppression and opportunity for various groups of people. Multiracial feminism is not simply a theory of inequality and oppression, however. Baca Zinn and Dill argue that individuals exercise their own agency, resisting the social structures that attempt to restrict them and finding ways to live satisfying lives.

Can you apply the multiracial feminist perspective to some of the readings from Section 1, "Diversity and Difference"? Which of the readings take a multiracial feminist perspective, and what would that perspective add to the readings that do not? Can you analyze a currently relevant topic on your own campus or in your own community using a multiracial feminist perspective? How is this perspective different from other points of view on that topic? As you read the remaining selections in this volume, consider the ways in which they are informed by a multiracial feminist perspective.

In "Gender in the Borderlands," Denise Segura and Patricia Zavella apply a multiracial feminist perspective to "borderlands" between nations, between categories of social inequality, between cultures. They focus on the U.S.-Mexican border and examine borders in terms of economies and states, ideologies about women and migrants, and how women themselves organize their daily lives or work for social change. Understanding borderlands is important, as women are entering the low-wage labor force in both countries in increasing numbers and are migrating more often within Mexico and from Mexico to the United States. The identity that characterizes women at the borderlands—what Segura and Zavella call "subjective transnationalism"—is hybrid and shifting.

Segura and Zavella write, "When women become the center of analysis, questions change and previously-held assumptions become subjects of inquiry." What are some of the changes in assumption and questions that they discuss in the selection? Think about recent debates about migration to the United States. How are women migrants represented? Can you think of examples in which, as Segura and Zavella say, "Their reproductive bodies are represented as hostile and foreign, threatening the social safety net and thus the well-being of the nation"? Think about the representation of different groups of migrants, such as Somalis, Cambodians, or other common groups in your region. How are these groups represented similarly or differently from the Mexican migrants Segura and Zevella analyze? The concept of borderlands can apply to many different borders. What categories or locations do you fall between, if any? How does this "in-between-ness" shape your life?

R. W. Connell follows Segura and Zavella's concern with how transnationalism and gender affect each other. Focusing specifically on the forms of masculinity that characterize global capitalism, Connell argues in "Masculinities and Globalization" that masculinity is defined in different ways in different contexts and time periods. In contrast to theorists who see masculinity as having one single definition, Connell emphasizes how different versions of masculinity exist in relation to each other. In this view, some kinds of masculinity, which she calls "hegemonic masculinity," characterize more powerful men, and other kinds of masculinity characterize subordinated men. Although masculinities are constructed in specific contexts, Connell emphasizes that they are linked to a global gender order. This global gender order specifies divisions of labor among nations and individuals (through production, work, and trade), creates power relations between women and men and among different nations, structures emotions, and represents gender through culture.

Connell outlines the prevailing masculinities during three major global time periods: conquest and settlement, empire, and postcolonial or neoliberal. What does she see as the major forms of masculinity during each period? Connell also notes local variations on "transnational business masculinity." Look at articles or pictures in a newspaper for examples of transnational business masculinity, and consider the extent to which they represent a Western model. How are the masculinities that prevail in your own community shaped by global forces? What possibilities for social change in the gender order does Connell identify, and what does she see as barriers to those changes?

As you consider the various ways of thinking about gender presented in these articles, with which do you agree? As you read the selections in the rest of the book, consider the questions raised here about what gender is; how extensively women share commonalities of oppression or experience; how gender intersects with other forms of inequality such as race, class, or nationality; and how gender is part of our cultural systems of meaning and our institutions and social structures.

READING 6 *Judith Lorber*

"Night to His Day": The Social Construction of Gender
First published in 1993

Talking about gender for most people is the equivalent of fish talking about water. Gender is so much the routine ground of everyday activities that questioning its taken-for-granted assumptions and presuppositions is like thinking about whether the sun will come up.[1] Gender is so pervasive that in our society we assume it is bred into our genes. Most people find it hard to believe that gender is constantly created and recreated out of human interaction, out of social life, and is the texture and order of that social life. Yet gender, like culture, is a human production that depends on everyone constantly "doing gender" (West and Zimmerman 1987).

And everyone "does gender" without thinking about it. Today, on the subway, I saw a well-dressed man with a year-old child in a stroller. Yesterday, on a bus, I saw a man with a tiny baby in a carrier on his chest. Seeing men taking care of small children in public is increasingly common—at least in New York City. But both men were quite obviously stared at—and smiled at, approvingly. Everyone was doing gender—the men who were changing the role of fathers and the other passengers, who were applauding them silently. But there was more gendering going on that probably fewer people noticed. The baby was wearing a white crocheted cap and white clothes. You couldn't tell if it was a boy or a girl. The child in the stroller was wearing a dark blue T-shirt and dark print pants. As they started to leave the train, the father put a Yankee baseball cap on the child's head. Ah, a boy, I thought. Then I noticed the gleam of tiny earrings in the child's ears, and as they got off, I saw the little flowered sneakers and lace-trimmed socks. Not a boy after all. Gender done.

Gender is such a familiar part of daily life that it usually takes a deliberate disruption of our expectations of how women and men are supposed to act to pay attention to how it is produced. Gender signs and signals are so ubiquitous that we usually fail to note them—unless they are missing or ambiguous. Then we are uncomfortable until we have successfully placed the other person in a gender status; otherwise, we feel socially dislocated. In our society, in addition to man and woman, the status can be *transvestite* (a person who dresses in opposite-gender clothes) and *transsexual* (a person who has had sex-change surgery). Transvestites and transsexuals carefully construct their gender status by dressing, speaking, walking, gesturing in the ways prescribed for women or men—whichever they want to be taken for—and so does any "normal" person.

For the individual, gender construction starts with assignment to a sex category on the basis of what the genitalia look like at birth.[2] Then babies are dressed or adorned in a way that displays the category because parents don't want to be constantly asked whether their baby is a girl or a boy. A sex category becomes a gender status through naming, dress, and the use of other gender markers. Once a child's gender is evident, others treat those in one gender differently from those in the other, and the children respond to the different treatment by feeling different and behaving differently. As soon as they can talk, they start to refer to themselves as members of their gender. Sex doesn't come into play again until puberty, but by that time, sexual feelings and desires and practices have been shaped by gendered norms and expectations. Adolescent boys and girls approach and avoid each other in an elaborately scripted and gendered mating dance. Parenting is gendered, with different expectations for mothers and for fathers, and people of different genders work at different kinds of jobs. The work adults do, as mothers and fathers and as low-level workers and high-level bosses, shapes women's and men's life experiences, and these experiences produce different feelings, consciousness, relationships, skills—ways of being that we call feminine or masculine.[3] All of these processes constitute the social construction of gender.

Gendered roles change—today fathers are taking care of little children, girls and boys are wearing unisex clothing and getting the same education, women and men are working at the same jobs. Although many traditional social groups are quite strict about maintaining gender differences, in other social groups they seem to be blurring. Then why the one-year-old's earrings? Why is it still so important to mark a child as a girl or a boy, to make sure she is not taken for a boy or he for a girl? What would happen if they were? They would, quite literally, have changed places in their social world.

To explain why gendering is done from birth, constantly and by everyone, we have to look not only at the way individuals experience gender but at gender as a social institution. As a social institution, gender is one of the major ways that human beings organize their lives. Human society depends on a predictable division of labor, a designated allocation of scarce goods, assigned responsibility for children and others who cannot care for themselves, common values and their systematic transmission to new members, legitimate leadership, music, art, stories, games, and other symbolic productions. One way of choosing people for the different tasks of society is on the basis of their talents, motivations, and competence—their demonstrated achievements. The other way is on the basis of gender, race, ethnicity—ascribed membership in a category of people. Although societies vary in the extent to which they use one or the other of these ways of allocating people to work and to carry out other responsibilities, every society uses gender and age grades. Every society classifies people as "girl and boy children," "girls and boys ready to be married," and "fully adult women and men," constructs similarities among them and differences between them, and assigns them to different roles and responsibilities. Personality characteristics, feelings, motivations, and ambitions flow from these different life experiences so that the members of these different groups become different kinds of people. The process of gendering and its outcome are legitimated by religion, law, science, and the society's entire set of values.

In order to understand gender as a social institution, it is important to distinguish human action from animal behavior. Animals feed themselves and their young until their young can feed themselves. Humans have to produce not only food but shelter and clothing. They also, if the group is going to continue as a social group, have to teach the children how their particular group does these tasks. In the process, humans reproduce gender, family, kinship, and a division of labor—social institutions that do not exist among animals. Primate social groups have been referred to as families, and their mating patterns as monogamy, adultery, and harems. Primate behavior has been used to prove the universality of sex differences—as built into our evolutionary inheritance (Haraway 1978). But animals' sex differences are not at all the same as humans' gender differences; animals' bonding is not kinship; animals' mating is not ordered by marriage; and animals' dominance hierarchies are not the equivalent of human stratification systems. Animals group on sex and age, relational categories that are physiologically, not socially, different. Humans create gender and age-group categories that are socially, and not necessarily physiologically, different.[4]

For animals, physiological maturity means being able to impregnate or conceive; its markers are coming into heat (estrus) and sexual attraction. For humans, puberty means being available for marriage; it is marked by rites that demonstrate this marital eligibility. Although the onset of physiological puberty is signaled by secondary sex characteristics (menstruation, breast development, sperm ejaculation, pubic and underarm hair), the onset of social adulthood is ritualized by the coming-out party or desert walkabout or bar mitzvah or graduation from college or first successful hunt or dreaming or inheritance of property. Humans have rituals that mark the passage from childhood into puberty and puberty into full adult status, as well as for marriage, childbirth, and death; animals do not (van Gennep 1960). To the extent that infants and the dead are differentiated by whether they are male or female, there are different birth rituals for girls and boys and different funeral rituals for men and women (Biersack 1984, 132–33). Rituals of puberty, marriage, and becoming a parent are gendered, creating a "woman," a "man," a "bride," a "groom," a "mother," a "father." Animals have no equivalents for these statuses.

Among animals, siblings mate and so do parents and children; humans have incest taboos and rules that encourage or forbid mating between members of different kin groups (Lévi-Strauss 1956, [1949] 1969). Any animal of the same species may feed another's young (or may not, depending on the species). Humans designate responsibility for particular children by kinship; humans frequently limit responsibility for children to the members of their kinship group or make them into members of their kinship group with adoption rituals.

Animals have dominance hierarchies based on size or on successful threat gestures and signals. These hierarchies are usually sexed, and in some species,

moving to the top of the hierarchy physically changes the sex (Austad 1986). Humans have stratification patterns based on control of surplus food, ownership of property, legitimate demands on others' work and sexual services, enforced determinations of who marries whom, and approved use of violence. If a woman replaces a man at the top of a stratification hierarchy, her social status may be that of a man, but her sex does not change.

Mating, feeding, and nurturant behavior in animals is determined by instinct and imitative learning and ordered by physiological sex and age (Lancaster 1974). In humans, these behaviors are taught and symbolically reinforced and ordered by socially constructed gender and age grades. Social gender and age statuses sometimes ignore or override physiological sex and age completely. Male and female animals (unless they physiologically change) are not interchangeable; infant animals cannot take the place of adult animals. Human females can become husbands and fathers, and human males can become wives and mothers, without sex-change surgery (Blackwood 1984). Human infants can reign as kings or queens.

Western society's values legitimate gendering by claiming that it all comes from physiology—female and male procreative differences. But gender and sex are not equivalent, and gender as a social construction does not flow automatically from genitalia and reproductive organs, the main physiological differences of females and males. In the construction of ascribed social statuses, physiological differences such as sex, stage of development, color of skin, and size are crude markers. They are not the source of the social statuses of gender, age grade, and race. *Social statuses* are carefully constructed through prescribed processes of teaching, learning, emulation, and enforcement. Whatever genes, hormones, and biological evolution contribute to human social institutions is materially as well as qualitatively transformed by social practices. Every social institution has a material base, but culture and social practices transform that base into something with qualitatively different patterns and constraints. The economy is much more than producing food and goods and distributing them to eaters and users; family and kinship are not the equivalent of having sex and procreating; morals and religions cannot be equated with the fears and ecstasies of the brain; language goes far beyond the sounds produced by tongue and larynx. No one eats "money" or "credit"; the concepts of "god" and "angels" are the subjects of theological disquisitions; not only words but objects, such as their flag, "speak" to the citizens of a country.

Similarly, gender cannot be equated with biological and physiological differences between human females and males. The building blocks of gender are *socially constructed statuses*. Western societies have only two genders, "man" and "woman." Some societies have three genders—men, women, and *berdaches* or *hijras* or *xaniths*. Berdaches, hijras, and xaniths are biological males who behave, dress, work, and are treated in most respects as social women; they are therefore not men, nor are they female women; they are, in our language, "male women."[5] There are African and American Indian societies that have a gender status called *manly hearted women*—biological females who work, marry, and parent as men; their social status is "female men" (Amadiume 1987; Blackwood 1984). They do not have to behave or dress as men to have the social responsibilities and prerogatives of husbands and fathers; what makes them men is enough wealth to buy a wife.

Modern Western societies' *transsexuals* and *transvestites* are the nearest equivalent of these crossover genders, but they are not institutionalized as third genders (Bolin 1987). Transsexuals are biological males and females who have sex-change operations to alter their genitalia. They do so in order to bring their physical anatomy into congruence with the way they want to live and with their own sense of gender identity. They do not become a third gender; they change genders. Transvestites are males who live as women and females who live as men but do not intend to have sex-change surgery. Their dress, appearance, and mannerisms fall within the range of what is expected from members of the opposite gender, so that they "pass." They also change genders, sometimes temporarily, some for most of their lives. Transvestite women have fought in wars as men soldiers as recently as the nineteenth century; some married women, and others went back to being women and married men once the war was over.[6] Some were discovered when their wounds were treated; others not until they died. In order to work as a jazz musician, a man's occupation, Billy Tipton, a woman, lived most of her life as a man. She died recently at seventy-four, leaving a wife and three adopted sons for whom she was husband and father, and musicians with whom she had played and traveled, for whom she was "one of the boys" (*New York Times* 1989).[7] There have been many other such occurrences of women passing as men to do more prestigious or lucrative men's work (Matthaci 1982, 192–93).[8]

Genders, therefore, are not attached to a biological substratum. Gender boundaries are breachable, and individual and socially organized shifts from one gender to another call attention to "cultural, social, or aesthetic dissonances" (Garber 1992, 16). These odd or deviant or third genders show us what we ordinarily take for granted—that people have to learn to be women and men. Men who cross-dress for performances or for pleasure often learn from women's magazines how to "do femininity" convincingly (Garber 1992, 41–51). Because transvestism is direct evidence of how gender is constructed, Marjorie Garber claims it has "extraordinary power . . . to disrupt, expose, and challenge, putting in question the very notion of the 'original' and of stable identity" (1992, 16).

GENDER BENDING

It is difficult to see how gender is constructed because we take it for granted that it's all biology, or hormones, or human nature. The differences between women and men seem to be self-evident, and we think they would occur no matter what society did. But in actuality, human females and males are physiologically more similar in appearance than are the two sexes of many species of animals and are more alike than different in traits and behavior (Epstein 1988). Without the deliberate use of gendered clothing, hairstyles, jewelry, and cosmetics, women and men would look far more alike.[9] Even societies that do not cover women's breasts have gender-identifying clothing, scarification, jewelry, and hairstyles.

The ease with which many transvestite women pass as men and transvestite men as women is corroborated by the common gender misidentification in Westernized societies of people in jeans, T-shirts, and sneakers. Men with long hair may be addressed as "miss," and women with short hair are often taken for men unless they offset the potential ambiguity with deliberate gender markers (Devor 1987, 1989). Jan Morris, in *Conundrum*, an autobiographical account of events just before and just after a sex-change operation, described how easy it was to shift back and forth from being a man to being a woman when testing how it would feel to change gender status. During this time, Morris still had a penis and wore more or less unisex clothing; the context alone made the man and the woman:

Sometimes the arena of my ambivalence was uncomfortably small. At the Travellers' Club, for example, I was obviously known as a man of sorts—women were only allowed on the premises at all during a few hours of the day, and even then were hidden away as far as possible in lesser rooms or alcoves. But I had another club, only a few hundred yards away, where I was known only as a woman, and often I went directly from one to the other, imperceptibly changing roles on the way—"Cheerio, sir," the porter would say at one club, and "Hello, madam," the porter would greet me at the other. (1975, 132)

Gender shifts are actually a common phenomenon in public roles as well. Queen Elizabeth II of England bore children, but when she went to Saudi Arabia on a state visit, she was considered an honorary man so that she could confer and dine with the men who were heads of a state that forbids unrelated men and women to have face-to-unveiled-face contact. In contemporary Egypt, lower-class women who run restaurants or shops dress in men's clothing and engage in unfeminine aggressive behavior, and middle-class educated women of professional or managerial status can take positions of authority (Rugh 1986, 131). In these situations, there is an important status change: These women are treated by the others in the situation as if they are men. From their own point of view, they are still women. From the social perspective, however, they are men.[10]

In many cultures, gender bending is prevalent in theater or dance—the Japanese kabuki are men actors who play both women and men; in Shakespeare's theater company, there were no actresses—Juliet and Lady Macbeth were played by boys. Shakespeare's comedies are full of witty comments on gender shifts. Women characters frequently masquerade as young men, and other women characters fall in love with them; the boys playing these masquerading women meanwhile, are acting out pining for the love of men characters.[11] In *As You Like It*, when Rosalind justifies her protective cross-dressing, Shakespeare also comments on manliness:

Were it not better,
Because that I am more than common tall,
That I did suit me all points like a man:
A gallant curtle-axe upon my thigh,

A boar-spear in my hand, and in my heart
Lie there what hidden women's fear there will,
We'll have a swashing and martial outside,
As many other mannish cowards have
That do outface it with their semblances.

(I, i, 115–22)

Shakespeare's audience could appreciate the double subtext: Rosalind, a woman character, was a boy dressed in girl's clothing who then dressed as a boy; like bravery, masculinity and femininity can be put on and taken off with changes of costume and role (Howard 1988, 435).[12]

M Butterfly is a modern play of gender ambiguities, which David Hwang (1989) based on a real person. Shi Peipu, a male Chinese opera singer who sang women's roles, was a spy as a man and the lover as a woman of a Frenchman, Gallimard, a diplomat (Bernstein 1986). The relationship lasted twenty years, and Shi Peipu even pretended to be the mother of a child by Gallimard. "She" also pretended to be too shy to undress completely. As "Butterfly," Shi Peipu portrayed a fantasy Oriental woman who made the lover a "real man" (Kondo 1990b). In Gallimard's words, the fantasy was "of slender women in chong sams and kimonos who die for the love of unworthy foreign devils. Who are born and raised to be perfect women. Who take whatever punishment we give them, and bounce back, strengthened by love, unconditionally" (Hwang 1989, 91). When the fantasy woman betrayed him by turning out to be the more powerful "real man," Gallimard assumed the role of Butterfly and, dressed in a geisha's robes, killed himself: "because 'man' and 'woman' are oppositionally defined terms, reversals . . . are possible" (Kondo 1990b, 18).[13]

But despite the ease with which gender boundaries can be traversed in work, in social relationships, and in cultural productions, gender statuses remain. Transvestites and transsexuals do not challenge the social construction of gender. Their goal is to be feminine women and masculine men (Kando 1973). Those who do not want to change their anatomy but do want to change their gender behavior fare less well in establishing their social identity. The women Holly Devor called "gender blenders" wore their hair short, dressed in unisex pants, shirts, and comfortable shoes, and did not wear jewelry or makeup. They described their everyday dress as women's clothing: One said, "I wore jeans all the time, but I didn't wear men's clothes"

(Devor 1989, 100). Their gender identity was women, but because they refused to "do femininity," they were constantly taken for men (1987, 1989, 107–42). Devor said of them: "The most common area of complaint was with public washrooms. They repeatedly spoke of the humiliation of being challenged or ejected from women's washrooms. Similarly, they found public change rooms to be dangerous territory and the buying of undergarments to be a difficult feat to accomplish" (1987, 29). In an ultimate ironic twist, some of these women said "they would feel like transvestites if they were to wear dresses, and two women said that they had been called transvestites when they had done so" (1987, 31). They resolved the ambiguity of their gender status by identifying as women in private and passing as men in public to avoid harassment on the street, to get men's jobs, and, if they were lesbians, to make it easier to display affection publicly with their lovers (Devor 1989, 107–42). Sometimes they even used men's bathrooms. When they had gender-neutral names, like Leslie, they could avoid the bureaucratic hassles that arose when they had to present their passports or other proof of identity, but because most had names associated with women, their appearance and their cards of identity were not conventionally congruent, and their gender status was in constant jeopardy.[14] When they could, they found it easier to pass as men than to try to change the stereotyped notions of what women should look like.

Paradoxically, then, bending gender rules and passing between genders do not erode but rather preserve gender boundaries. In societies with only two genders, the gender dichotomy is not disturbed by transvestites, because others feel that a transvestite is only transitorily ambiguous—is "really a man or woman underneath." After sex-change surgery, transsexuals end up in a conventional gender status—a "man" or a "woman" with the appropriate genitals (Eichler 1989). When women dress as men for business reasons, they are indicating that in that situation, they want to be treated the way men are treated; when they dress as women, they want to be treated as women:

> By their male dress, female entrepreneurs signal their desire to suspend the expectations of accepted feminine conduct without losing respect and reputation. By wearing what is "unattractive" they signify that they are not intending to display their physical charms while engaging in public activity. Their loud, aggressive banter contrasts with the modest demeanor that

attracts men. . . . Overt signalling of a suspension of the rules preserves normal conduct from eroding expectations. (Rugh 1986, 131)

FOR INDIVIDUALS, GENDER MEANS SAMENESS

Although the possible combinations of genitalia, body shapes, clothing, mannerisms, sexuality, and roles could produce infinite varieties in human beings, the social institution of gender depends on the production and maintenance of a limited number of gender statuses and of making the members of these statuses similar to each other. Individuals are born sexed but not gendered, and they have to be taught to be masculine or feminine.[15] As Simone de Beauvoir said: "One is not born, but rather becomes, a woman . . .; it is civilization as a whole that produces this creature . . . which is described as feminine" (1952, 267).

Children learn to walk, talk, and gesture the way their social group says girls and boys should. Ray Birdwhistell, in his analysis of body motion as human communication, calls these learned gender displays *tertiary sex characteristics* and argues that they are needed to distinguish genders because humans are a weakly dimorphic species—their only sex markers are genitalia (1970, 39–46). Clothing, paradoxically, often hides the sex but displays the gender.

In early childhood, humans develop gendered personality structures and sexual orientations through their interactions with parents of the same and opposite gender. As adolescents, they conduct their sexual behavior according to gendered scripts. Schools, parents, peers, and the mass media guide young people into gendered work and family roles. As adults, they take on a gendered social status in their society's stratification system. Gender is thus both ascribed and achieved (West and Zimmerman 1987). . . .

People go along with the imposition of gender norms because the weight of morality as well as immediate social pressure enforces them. Consider how many instructions for properly gendered behavior are packed into this mother's admonition to her daughter: "This is how to hem a dress when you see the hem coming down and so to prevent yourself from looking like the slut I know you are so bent on becoming" (Kincaid 1978).

Gender norms are inscribed in the way people move, gesture, and even eat. In one African society, men were supposed to eat with their "whole mouth, wholeheartedly, and not, like women, just with the lips, that is halfheartedly, with reservation and restraint" (Bourdieu [1980] 1990, 70). Men and women in this society learned to walk in ways that proclaimed their different positions in the society:

> The manly man . . . stands up straight into the face of the person he approaches, or wishes to welcome. Ever on the alert, because ever threatened, he misses nothing of what happens around him. . . . Conversely, a well brought-up woman . . . is expected to walk with a slight stoop, avoiding every misplaced movement of her body, her head or her arms, looking down, keeping her eyes on the spot where she will next put her foot, especially if she happens to have to walk past the men's assembly. (70)

Many cultures go beyond clothing, gestures, and demeanor in gendering children. They inscribe gender directly into bodies. In traditional Chinese society, mothers bound their daughters' feet into three-inch stumps to enhance their sexual attractiveness. Jewish fathers circumcise their infant sons to show their covenant with God. Women in African societies remove the clitoris of prepubescent girls, scrape their labia, and make the lips grow together to preserve their chastity and ensure their marriageability. In Western societies, women augment their breast size with silicone and reconstruct their faces with cosmetic surgery to conform to cultural ideals of feminine beauty. Hanna Papanek (1979) notes that these practices reinforce the sense of superiority or inferiority in the adults who carry them out as well as in the children on whom they are done: The genitals of Jewish fathers and sons are physical and psychological evidence of their common dominant religious and familial status; the genitals of African mothers and daughters are physical and psychological evidence of their joint subordination.[16]

Sandra Bem (1981, 1983) argues that because gender is a powerful "schema" that orders the cognitive world, one must wage a constant, active battle for a child not to fall into typical gendered attitudes and behavior. In 1972, *Ms.* magazine published Lois Gould's fantasy of how to raise a child free of gender-typing. The experiment calls for hiding the child's anatomy from all eyes except the parents' and treating the child as neither a girl nor a boy. The child, called X, gets to do all the things boys *and* girls do. The experiment is so successful that all the children in X's class at school want to look and behave like X. At the end of the story,

the creators of the experiment are asked what will happen when X grows up. The scientists' answer is that by then it will be quite clear what X is, implying that its hormones will kick in and it will be revealed as a female or male. That ambiguous, and somewhat contradictory, ending lets Gould off the hook; neither she nor we have any idea what someone brought up totally androgynously would be like sexually or socially as an adult. The hormonal input will not create gender or sexuality but will only establish secondary sex characteristics; breasts, beards, and menstruation alone do not produce social manhood or womanhood. Indeed, it is at puberty, when sex characteristics become evident, that most societies put pubescent children through their most important rites of passage, the rituals that officially mark them as fully gendered—that is, ready to marry and become adults.

Most parents create a gendered world for their newborn by naming, birth announcements, and dress. Children's relationships with same-gendered and different-gendered caretakers structure their self-identifications and personalities. Through cognitive development, children extract and apply to their own actions the appropriate behavior for those who belong in their own gender, as well as race, religion, ethnic group, and social class, rejecting what is not appropriate. If their social categories are highly valued, they value themselves highly; if their social categories are low status, they lose self-esteem (Chodorow 1974). Many feminist parents who want to raise androgynous children soon lose their children to the pull of gendered norms (Gordon 1990, 87–90). My son attended a carefully nonsexist elementary school, which didn't even have girls' and boys' bathrooms. When he was seven or eight years old, I attended a class play about "squares" and "circles" and their need for each other and noticed that all the girl squares and circles wore makeup, but none of the boy squares and circles did. I asked the teacher about it after the play, and she said, "Bobby said he was not going to wear makeup, and he is a powerful child, so none of the boys would either." In a long discussion about conformity, my son confronted me with the question of who the conformists were, the boys who followed their leader or the girls who listened to the woman teacher. In actuality, they both were, because they both followed same-gender leaders and acted in gender-appropriate ways. (Actors may wear makeup, but real boys don't.)

For human beings there is no essential femaleness or maleness, femininity or masculinity, womanhood or manhood, but once gender is ascribed, the social order constructs and holds individuals to strongly gendered norms and expectations. Individuals may vary on many of the components of gender and may shift genders temporarily or permanently, but they must fit into the limited number of gender statuses their society recognizes. In the process, they recreate their society's version of women and men: "If we do gender appropriately, we simultaneously sustain, reproduce, and render legitimate the institutional arrangements. . . . If we fail to do gender appropriately, we as individuals—not the institutional arrangements—may be called to account (for our character, motives, and predispositions)" (West and Zimmerman 1987, 146).

> The gendered practices of everyday life reproduce a society's view of how women and men should act (Bourdieu [1980] 1990). Gendered social arrangements are justified by religion and cultural productions and backed by law, but the most powerful means of sustaining the moral hegemony of the dominant gender ideology is that the process is made invisible; any possible alternatives are virtually unthinkable. (Foucault 1972; Gramsci 1971)[17]

FOR SOCIETY, GENDER MEANS DIFFERENCE

The pervasiveness of gender as a way of structuring social life demands that gender statuses be clearly differentiated. Varied talents, sexual preferences, identities, personalities, interests, and ways of interacting fragment the individual's bodily and social experiences. Nonetheless, these are organized in Western cultures into two and only two socially and legally recognized gender statuses, "man" and "woman."[18] In the social construction of gender, it does not matter what men and women actually do; it does not even matter if they do exactly the same thing. The social institution of gender insists only that what they do is *perceived* as different.

If men and women are doing the same tasks, they are usually spatially segregated to maintain gender separation, and often the tasks are given different job titles as well, such as executive secretary and administrative assistant (Reskin 1988). If the differences between women and men begin to blur, society's "sameness taboo" goes into action (G. Rubin 1975, 178). At a rock- and-roll dance at West Point in 1976, the year women were admitted to the prestigious

military academy for the first time, the school's administrators "were reportedly perturbed by the sight of mirror-image couples dancing in short hair and dress gray trousers," and a rule was established that women cadets could dance at these events only if they wore skirts (Barkalow and Raab 1990, 53).[19] Women recruits in the U.S. Marine Corps are required to wear makeup—at a minimum, lipstick and eye shadow—and they have to take classes in makeup, hair care, poise, and etiquette. This feminization is part of a deliberate policy of making them clearly distinguishable from men Marines. Christine Williams quotes a twenty-five-year-old woman drill instructor as saying: "A lot of the recruits who come here don't wear makeup; they're tomboyish or athletic. A lot of them have the preconceived idea that going into the military means they can still be a tomboy. They don't realize that you are a *Woman* Marine" (1989, 76–77).[20]

If gender differences were genetic, physiological, or hormonal, gender bending and gender ambiguity would occur only in hermaphrodites, who are born with chromosomes and genitalia that are not clearly female or male. Since gender differences are socially constructed, all men and all women can enact the behavior of the other, because they know the other's social script: "'Man' and 'woman' are at once empty and overflowing categories. Empty because they have no ultimate, transcendental meaning. Overflowing because even when they appear to be fixed, they still contain within them alternative, denied, or suppressed definitions" (Scott 1988, 49). Nonetheless, though individuals may be able to shift gender statuses, the gender boundaries have to hold, or the whole gendered social order will come crashing down.

Paradoxically, it is the social importance of gender statuses and their external markers—clothing, mannerisms, and spatial segregation—that makes gender bending or gender crossing possible—or even necessary. The social viability of differentiated gender statuses produces the need or desire to shift statuses. Without gender differentiation, transvestism and transsexuality would be meaningless. You couldn't dress in the opposite gender's clothing if all clothing were unisex. There would be no need to reconstruct genitalia to match identity if interests and lifestyles were not gendered. There would be no need for women to pass as men to do certain kinds of work if jobs were not typed as "women's work" and "men's work." Women would not have to dress as men in public life in order to give orders or aggressively bargain with customers.

Gender boundaries are preserved when transsexuals create congruous autobiographies of always having felt like what they are now. The transvestite's story also "recuperates social and sexual norms" (Garber 1992, 69). In the transvestite's normalized narrative, he or she "is 'compelled' by social and economic forces to disguise himself or herself in order to get a job, escape repression, or gain artistic or political 'freedom'" (Garber 1992, 70). The "true identity," when revealed, causes amazement over how easily and successfully the person passed as a member of the opposite gender, not a suspicion that gender itself is something of a put-on.

GENDER RANKING

Most societies rank genders according to prestige and power and construct them to be unequal, so that moving from one to another also means moving up or down the social scale. Among some North American Indian cultures, the hierarchy was male men, male women, female men, female women. Women produced significant durable goods (basketry, textiles, pottery, decorated leather goods), which could be traded. Women also controlled what they produced and any profit or wealth they earned. Since women's occupational realm could lead to prosperity and prestige, it was fair game for young men—but only if they became women in gender status. Similarly, women in other societies who amassed a great deal of wealth were allowed to become men—"manly hearts." According to Harriet Whitehead (1982):

Both reactions reveal an unwillingness or inability to distinguish the sources of prestige—wealth, skill, personal efficacy (among other things)—from masculinity. Rather there is the innuendo that if a person performing female tasks can attain excellence, prosperity, or social power, it must be because that person is, at some level, a man. . . . A woman who could succeed at doing the things men did was honored as a man would be. . . . What seems to have been more disturbing to the culture—which means, for all intents and purposes, to the men—was the possibility that women, within their own department, might be onto a good thing. It was into this unsettling breach that the berdache institution was hurled. In their social aspect, women were complimented by the berdache's imitation. In their anatomic aspect, they were subtly insulted by his vaunted superiority. (108)

In American society, men-to-women transsexuals tend to earn less after surgery if they change occupations; women-to-men transsexuals tend to increase their income (Bolin 1988, 153–60; Brody 1979). Men who go into women's fields, like nursing, have less prestige than women who go into men's fields, like physics. Janice Raymond, a radical feminist, feels that transsexual men-to-women have advantages over female women because they were not socialized to be subordinate or oppressed throughout life. She says:

We know that we are women who are born with female chromosomes and anatomy, and that whether or not we were socialized to be so-called normal women, patriarchy has treated and will treat us like women. Transsexuals have not had this same history. No man can have the history of being born and located in this culture as a woman. He can have the history of *wishing* to be a woman and of *acting* like a woman, but this gender experience is that of a transsexual, not of a woman. Surgery may confer the artifacts of outward and inward female organs but it cannot confer the history of being born a woman in this society. (1979, 114)

Because women who become men rise in the world and men who become women fall, Elaine Showalter (1987) was very critical of the movie *Tootsie*, in which Dustin Hoffman plays an actor who passes as a woman in order to be able to get work. "Dorothy" becomes a feminist "woman of the year" for standing up for women's rights not to be demeaned or sexually harassed. Showalter feels that the message of the movie is double-edged: "Dorothy's 'feminist' speeches . . . are less a response to the oppression of women than an instinctive situational male reaction to being treated like a woman. The implication is that women must be taught by men how to win their rights. . . . It says that feminist ideas are much less threatening when they come from a man" (123). Like Raymond, Showalter feels that being or having been a man gives a transsexual man-to-woman or a man cross-dressed as a woman a social advantage over those whose gender status was always "woman."[21] The implication here is that there is an experiential superiority that doesn't disappear with the gender shift.

For one transsexual man-to-woman, however, the experience of living as a woman changed his/her whole personality. As James, Morris had been a soldier, foreign correspondent, and mountain climber; as Jan, Morris is a successful travel writer. But socially, James was far superior to Jan, and so Jan developed the "learned helplessness" that is supposed to characterize women in Western society:

> We are told that the social gap between the sexes is narrowing, but I can only report that having, in the second half of the twentieth century, experienced life in both roles, there seems to me no aspect of existence, no moment of the day, no contact, no arrangement, no response, which is not different for men and for women. The very tone of voice in which I was now addressed, the very posture of the person next in the queue, the very feel in the air when I entered a room or sat at a restaurant table, constantly emphasized my change of status.
>
> And if other's responses shifted, so did my own. The more I was treated as woman, the more woman I became. I adapted willy-nilly. If I was assumed to be incompetent at reversing cars, or opening bottles, oddly incompetent I found myself becoming. If a case was thought too heavy for me, inexplicably I found it so myself. . . . Women treated me with a frankness which, while it was one of the happiest discoveries of my metamorphosis, did imply membership of a camp, a faction, or at least a school of thought; so I found myself gravitating always towards the female, whether in sharing a railway compartment or supporting a political cause. Men treated me more and more as junior, . . . and so, addressed every day of my life as an inferior, involuntarily, month by month I accepted the condition. I discovered that even now men prefer women to be less informed, less able, less talkative, and certainly less self-centered than they are themselves; so I generally obliged them. (1975, 165–66)[22]

COMPONENTS OF GENDER

By now, it should be clear that gender is not a unitary essence but has many components as a social institution and as an individual status.[23]

As a social institution, gender is composed of:

Gender statuses, the socially recognized genders in a society and the norms and expectations for their enactment behaviorally, gesturally, linguistically, emotionally, and physically. How gender statuses are evaluated depends on historical development in any particular society.

Gendered division of labor, the assignment of productive and domestic work to members of different gender statuses. The work assigned to those of different gender statuses strengthens the society's evaluation of those statuses—the higher the status, the more prestigious and valued the work and the greater its rewards.

Gendered kinship, the family rights and responsibilities for each gender status. Kinship statuses reflect and reinforce the prestige and power differences of the different genders.

Gendered sexual scripts, the normative patterns of sexual desire and sexual behavior, as prescribed for the different gender statuses. Members of the dominant gender have more sexual prerogatives; members of a subordinate gender may be sexually exploited.

Gendered personalities, the combinations of traits patterned by gender norms of how members of different gender statuses are supposed to feel and behave. Social expectations of others in face-to-face interaction constantly bolster these norms.

Gendered social control, the formal and informal approval and reward of conforming behavior and the stigmatization, social isolation, punishment, and medical treatment of nonconforming behavior.

Gender ideology, the justification of gender statuses, particularly, their differential evaluation. The dominant ideology tends to suppress criticism by making these evaluations seem natural.

Gender imagery, the cultural representations of gender and embodiment of gender in symbolic language and artistic productions that reproduce and legitimate gender statuses. Culture is one of the main supports of the dominant gender ideology.

For an individual, gender is composed of:

Sex category, to which the infant is assigned at birth based on appearance of genitalia. With prenatal testing and sex-typing, categorization is prenatal. Sex category may be changed later through surgery or reinspection of ambiguous genitalia.

Gender identity, the individual's sense of gendered self as a worker and family member.

Gendered marital and procreative status, fulfillment or nonfulfillment of allowed or disallowed mating, impregnation, childbearing, kinship roles.

Gendered sexual orientation, socially and individually patterned sexual desires, feelings, practices, and identification.

Gendered personality, internalized patterns of socially normative emotions as organized by family structure and parenting.

Gendered processes, the social practices of learning, being taught, picking up cues, enacting behavior already learned to be gender appropriate (or inappropriate, if rebelling, testing), developing a gender identity, "doing gender" as a member of a gender status in relationships with gendered others, acting deferent or dominant.

Gender beliefs, incorporation of or resistance to gender ideology.

Gender display, presentation of self as a certain kind of gendered person through dress, cosmetics, adornments, and permanent and reversible body markers.

For an individual, all the social components are supposed to be consistent and congruent with perceived physiology. The actual combination of genes and genitalia, prenatal, adolescent, and adult hormonal input, and procreative capacity may or may not be congruous with each other and with sex-category assignment, gender identity, gendered sexual orientation and procreative status, gender display, personality, and work and family roles. At any one time, an individual's identity is a combination of the major ascribed statuses of gender, race, ethnicity, religion, and social class, and the individual's achieved statuses, such as education level, occupation or profession, marital status, parenthood, prestige, authority, and wealth. The ascribed statuses substantially limit or create opportunities for individual achievements and also diminish or enhance the luster of those achievements.

GENDER AS PROCESS, STRATIFICATION, AND STRUCTURE

As a social institution, gender is a process of creating distinguishable social statuses for the assignment of rights and responsibilities. As part of a stratification system that ranks these statuses unequally, gender is a major building block in the social structures built on these unequal statuses.

As a *process,* gender creates the social differences that define "woman" and "man." In social interaction throughout their lives, individuals learn what is expected, see what is expected, act and react in expected ways, and thus simultaneously construct and maintain the gender order: "The very injunction to be a given gender takes place through discursive routes: to be a good mother, to be a heterosexually desirable object, to be a fit worker, in sum, to signify a multiplicity of guarantees in response to a variety of different demands all at once" (Butler 1990, 145). Members of a social group neither make up gender as they go along nor exactly replicate in rote fashion what was done before. In almost every encounter, human beings produce gender, behaving in the ways they learned were appropriate for their gender status, or resisting or rebelling against these norms. Resistance and rebellion have altered gender norms, but so far they have rarely eroded the statuses.

Gendered patterns of interaction acquire additional layers of gendered sexuality, parenting, and work behaviors in childhood, adolescence, and adulthood. Gendered norms and expectations are enforced through informal sanctions of gender-inappropriate behavior by peers and by formal punishment or threat of punishment by those in authority should behavior deviate too far from socially imposed standards for women and men.

Everyday gendered interactions build gender into the family, the work process, and other organizations and institutions, which in turn reinforce gender expectations for individuals.[24] Because gender is a process, there is room not only for modification and variation by individuals and small groups but also for institutionalized change (Scott 1988, 7).

As part of a *stratification* system, gender ranks men above women of the same race and class. Women and men could be different but equal. In practice, the process of creating difference depends to a great extent on differential evaluation. As Nancy Jay (1981) says: "That which is defined, separated out, isolated from all else is A and pure. Not-A is necessarily impure, a random catchall, to which nothing is external except A and the principle of order that separates it from Not-A" (45). From the individual's point of view, whichever gender is A, the other is Not-A; gender boundaries tell the individual who is like him or her, and all the rest are unlike. From society's point of view, however, one gender is usually the touchstone, the normal, the dominant, and the other is different, deviant, and subordinate. In Western society, "man" is A, "wo-man" is Not-A. (Consider what a society would be like where woman was A and man Not-A.)

The further dichotomization by race and class constructs the gradations of a heterogeneous society's stratification scheme. Thus, in the United States, white is A, African American is Not-A; middle class is A, working class is Not-A, and "African-American women occupy a position whereby the inferior half of a series of these dichotomies converge" (Collins 1990, 70). The dominant categories are the hegemonic ideals, taken so for granted as the way things should be that white is not ordinarily thought of as a race, middle class as a class, or men as a gender. The characteristics of these categories define the Other as that which lacks the valuable qualities the dominants exhibit.

In a gender-stratified society, what men do is usually valued more highly than what women do because men do it, even when their activities are very similar or the same. In different regions of southern India, for example, harvesting rice is men's work, shared work, or women's work: "Wherever a task is done by women it is considered easy, and where it is done by [men] it is considered difficult" (Mencher 1988, 104). A gathering and hunting society's survival usually depends on the nuts, grubs, and small animals brought in by the women's foraging trips, but when the men's hunt is successful, it is the occasion for a celebration. Conversely, because they are the superior group, white men do not have to do the "dirty work," such as housework; the most inferior group does it, usually poor women of color (Palmer 1989).

Freudian psychoanalytic theory claims that boys must reject their mothers and deny the feminine in themselves in order to become men: "For boys the major goal is the achievement of personal masculine identification with their father and sense of secure masculine self, achieved through superego formation and disparagement of women" (Chodorow 1978, 165). Masculinity may be the outcome of boys' intrapsychic struggles to separate their identity from that of their mothers, but the proofs of masculinity are culturally shaped and usually ritualistic and symbolic (Gilmore 1990).

The Marxist feminist explanation for gender inequality is that by demeaning women's abilities and keeping them from learning valuable technological skills, bosses preserve them as a cheap and exploitable reserve army of labor. Unionized men who could be easily replaced by women collude in this process because it allows them to monopolize the better paid, more interesting, and more autonomous jobs: "Two

factors emerge as helping men maintain their separation from women and their control of technological occupations. One is the active gendering of jobs and people. The second is the continual creation of subdivisions in the work processes, and levels in work hierarchies, into which men can move in order to keep their distance from women" (Cockburn 1985, 13).

Societies vary in the extent of the inequality in social status of their women and men members, but where there is inequality, the status "woman" (and its attendant behavior and role allocations) is usually held in lesser esteem than the status "man." Since gender is also intertwined with a society's other constructed statuses of differential evaluation—race, religion, occupation, class, country of origin, and so on—men and women members of the favored groups command more power, more prestige, and more property than the members of the disfavored groups. Within many social groups, however, men are advantaged over women. The more economic resources, such as education and job opportunities, are available to a group, the more they tend to be monopolized by men. In poorer groups that have few resources (such as working-class African Americans in the United States), women and men are more nearly equal, and the women may even outstrip the men in education and occupational status (Almquist 1987).

As a *structure*, gender divides work in the home and in economic production, legitimates those in authority, and organizes sexuality and emotional life (Connell 1987, 91–142). As primary parents, women significantly influence children's psychological development and emotional attachments, in the process reproducing gender. Emergent sexuality is shaped by heterosexual, homosexual, bisexual, and sadomasochistic patterns that are gendered—different for girls and boys, and for women and men—so that sexual statuses reflect gender statuses.

When gender is a major component of structured inequality, the devalued genders have less power, prestige, and economic rewards than the valued genders. In countries that discourage gender discrimination, many major roles are still gendered; women still do most of the domestic labor and child-rearing, even while doing full-time paid work; women and men are segregated on the job and each does work considered "appropriate"; women's work is usually paid less than men's work. Men dominate the positions of authority and leadership in government, the military, and the law; cultural productions, religions, and sports reflect men's interests.

In societies that create the greatest gender difference, such as Saudi Arabia, women are kept out of sight behind walls or veils, have no civil rights, and often create a cultural and emotional world of their own (Bernard 1981). But even in societies with less rigid gender boundaries, women and men spend much of their time with people of their own gender because of the way work and family are organized. This spatial separation of women and men reinforces gendered differentness, identity, and ways of thinking and behaving (Coser 1986).

Gender inequality—the devaluation of "women" and the social domination of "men"—has social functions and a social history. It is not the result of sex, procreation, physiology, anatomy, hormones, or genetic predispositions. It is produced and maintained by identifiable social processes and built into the general social structure and individual identities deliberately and purposefully. The social order as we know it in Western societies is organized around racial, ethnic, class, and gender inequality. I contend, therefore, that the continuing purpose of gender as a modern social institution is to construct women as a group to be the subordinates of men as a group. The life of everyone placed in the status "woman" is "night to his day—that has forever been the fantasy. Black to his white. Shut out of his system's space, she is the repressed that ensures the system's functioning" (Cixous and Clément [1975] 1986, 67).

THE PARADOX OF HUMAN NATURE

To say that sex, sexuality, and gender are all socially constructed is not to minimize their social power. These categorical imperatives govern our lives in the most profound and pervasive ways, through the social experiences and social practices of what Dorothy Smith calls the "everyday/everynight world" (1990, 31–57). The paradox of human nature is that it is *always* a manifestation of cultural meanings, social relationships, and power politics; "not biology, but culture, becomes destiny" (Butler 1990, 8). Gendered people emerge not from physiology or sexual orientation but from the exigencies of the social order, mostly from the need for a reliable division of the work of food production and the social (not physical) reproduction of new members. The moral imperatives of religion and cultural representations guard the boundary lines among genders and ensure that what is demanded, what is permitted, and what is tabooed for the people in each gender are well known and followed by most (Davies 1982). Political power, control of scarce resources, and, if necessary, violence uphold the gendered social order in the face of resistance and rebellion. Most people, however, voluntarily go along with their society's prescriptions for those of their gender status, because the norms and expectations get built into their sense of worth and identity as a certain kind of human being, and because they believe their society's way is the natural way. These beliefs emerge from the imagery that pervades the way we think, the way we see and hear and speak, the way we fantasize, and the way we feel.

There is no core or bedrock human nature below these endlessly looping processes of the social production of sex and gender, self and other, identity and psyche, each of which is a "complex cultural construction" (Butler 1990, 36). *For humans, the social is the natural.* Therefore, "in its feminist senses, gender cannot mean simply the cultural appropriation of biological sexual difference. Sexual difference is itself a fundamental—and scientifically contested—construction. Both 'sex' and 'gender' are woven of multiple, asymmetrical strands of difference, charged with multifaceted dramatic narratives of domination and struggle" (Haraway 1990, 140).

NOTES

1. Gender is, in Erving Goffman's words, an aspect of *Felicity's Condition:* "any arrangement which leads us to judge an individual's . . . acts not to be a manifestation of strangeness. Behind Felicity's Condition is our sense of what it is to be sane" (1983, 27). Also see Bem 1993; Frye 1983, 17–40; Goffman 1977.

2. In cases of ambiguity in countries with modern medicine, surgery is usually performed to make the genitalia more clearly male or female.

3. See J. Butler 1990 for an analysis of how doing gender *is* gender identity.

4. Douglas 1973; MacCormack 1980; Ortner 1974; Ortner and Whitehead 1981; Yanagisako and Collier 1987. On the social construction of childhood, see Ariès 1962; Zelizer 1985.

5. On the hijras of India, see Nanda 1990; on the xaniths of Oman, Wikan 1982, 168–86; on the American Indian berdaches, W. L. Williams 1986. Other societies that have similar institutionalized third-gender men are the Koniag of Alaska, the Tanala of Madagascar, the Mesakin of Nuba, and the Chukchee of Siberia (Wikan 1982, 170).

6. Durova 1989; Freeman and Bond 1992, Wheelwright 1989.

7. Gender segregation of work in popular music still has not changed very much, according to Groce and Cooper 1990, despite considerable androgyny in some very popular figures. See Garber 1992 on the androgyny. She discusses Tipton on pp. 67–70.
8. In the nineteenth century, not only did these women get men's wages, but they also "had male privileges and could do all manner of things other women could not: open a bank account, write checks, own property, go anywhere unaccompanied, vote in elections" (Faderman 1981, 44).
9. When unisex clothing and men wearing long hair came into vogue in the United States in the mid-1960s, beards and mustaches for men also came into style again as gender identifications.
10. For other accounts of women being treated as men in Islamic countries, as well as accounts of women and men cross-dressing in these countries, see Garber 1992, 304–52.
11. Dollimore 1986; Garber 1992, 32–40; Greenblatt 1987, 66–93; Howard 1988. For Renaissance accounts of sexual relations with women and men of ambiguous sex, see Laqueur 1990, 134–39. For modern accounts of women passing as men that other women find sexually attractive, see Devor 1989, 136–37; Wheelwright 1989, 53–59.
12. Females who passed as men soldiers had to "do masculinity," not just dress in a uniform (Wheelwright 1989, 50–78). On the triple entendres and gender resonances of Rosalind-type characters, see Garber 1992, 71–77.
13. Also see Garber 1992, 234–66.
14. Bolin describes how many documents have to be changed by transsexuals to provide a legitimizing "paper trail" (1988, 145–47). Note that only members of the same social group know which names are women's and which men's in their culture, but many documents list "sex."
15. For an account of how a potential man-to-woman transsexual learned to be feminine, see Garfinkel 1967, 116–85, 285–88. For a gloss on this account that points out how, throughout his encounters with Agnes, Garfinkel failed to see how he himself was constructing his own masculinity, see Rogers 1992.
16. Paige and Paige (1981, 147–49) argue that circumcision ceremonies indicate a father's loyalty to his lineage elders—"visible public evidence that the head of a family unit of their lineage is willing to trust others with his and his

family's most valuable political asset, his son's penis" (147). On female circumcision, see El Dareer 1982; Lightfoot-Klein 1989; van der Kwaak 1992; Walker 1992. There is a form of female circumcision that removes only the prepuce of the clitoris and is similar to male circumcision, but most forms of female circumcision are far more extensive, mutilating, and spiritually and psychologically shocking than the usual form of male circumcision. However, among the Australian aborigines, boys' penises are slit and kept open, so that they urinate and bleed the way women do (Bettelheim 1962, 165–206).
17. The concepts of moral hegemony, the effects of everyday activities (praxis) on thought and personality, and the necessity of consciousness of these processes before political change can occur are all based on Marx's analysis of class relations.
18. Other societies recognize more than two categories, but usually no more than three or four (Jacobs and Roberts 1989).
19. Carol Barkalow's book has a photograph of eleven first-year West Pointers in a math class, who are dressed in regulation pants, shirts, and sweaters, with short haircuts. The caption challenges the reader to locate the only woman in the room.
20. The taboo on males and females looking alike reflects the U.S. military's homophobia (Berube and D'Emilio 1984). If you can't tell those with a penis from those with a vagina, how are you going to determine whether their sexual interest is heterosexual or homosexual unless you watch them having sexual relations?
21. Garber feels that *Tootsie* is not about feminism but about transvestism and its possibilities for disturbing the gender order (1992, 5–9).
22. See Bolin 1988, 149–50, for transsexual men-to-women's discovery of the dangers of rape and sexual harassment. Devor's "gender blenders" went in the opposite direction. Because they found that it was an advantage to be taken for men, they did not deliberately cross-dress, but they did not feminize themselves either (1989, 126–40).
23. See West and Zimmerman 1987 for a similar set of gender components.
24. On the "logic of practice," or how the experience of gender is embedded in the norms of everyday interaction and the structure of formal organizations, see Acker 1990; Bourdieu [1980] 1990; Connell 1987; Smith 1987.

REFERENCES

Acker, Joan. 1990. Hierarchies, jobs, and bodies: A theory of gendered organizations. *Gender & Society* 4: 139–58.
Almquist, Elizabeth M. 1987. Labor market gendered inequality in minority groups. *Gender & Society* 1: 400–14.
Amadiume, Ifi. 1987. *Male daughters, female husbands: Gender and sex in an African society.* London: Zed Books.
Aries, Philippe. 1962. *Centuries of childhood: A social history of family life,* translated by Robert Baldick. New York: Vintage.
Austad, Steven N. 1986. Changing sex nature's way. *International Wildlife,* May–June, 29.
Barkalow, Carol, with Andrea Raab. 1990. *In the men's house.* New York: Poseidon Press.
Bem, Sandra Lipsitz. 1981. Gender schema theory: A cognitive account of sex typing. *Psychological Review* 88: 354–64.
———. 1983. Gender schema theory and its implications for child development: Raising gender-aschematic children in a gender-schematic society. *Signs* 8: 598–616.

———. 1993. *The lense of gender: Transforming the debate on sexual inequality.* New Haven: Yale University Press.

Bernard, Jessie. 1981. *The female world.* New York: Free Press.

Bernstein, Richard. 1986. France jails 2 in odd case of espionage. *New York Times,* 11 May.

Berube, Allan, and John D'Emilio. 1984. The military and lesbians during the McCarthy years. *Signs* 9: 759–75.

Bettelheim, Bruno. 1962. *Symbolic wounds: Puberty rites and the envious male.* London: Thames and Hudson.

Biersack, Aletta. 1984. Paiela "women-men": The reflexive foundations of gender ideology. *American Ethnologist* 11: 118–38.

Birdwhistell, Ray L. 1970. *Kinesics and context: Essays on body motion communications.* Philadelphia: University of Pennsylvania Press.

Blackwood, Evelyn. 1984. Sexuality and gender in certain Native American tribes: The case of cross-gender females. *Signs* 10: 27–42.

Bolin, Anne. 1987. Transsexualism and the limits of traditional analysis. *American Behavioral Scientist* 31: 41–65.

———. 1988. *In search of Eve: Transsexual rites of passage.* South Hadley, Mass.: Bergin and Garvey.

Bourdieu, Pierre. [1980] 1990. *The logic of practice.* Stanford, Calif.: Stanford University Press.

Brody, Jane E. 1979. Benefits of transsexual surgery disputed as leading hospital halts the procedure. *New York Times,* 2 October.

Butler, Judith. 1990. *Gender trouble: Feminism and the subversion of identity.* New York and London: Routledge.

Chodorow, Nancy. 1974. Family structure and feminine personality. In Rosaldo and Lamphere.

———. 1978. *The reproduction of mothering.* Berkeley: University of California Press.

Cixous, Hélène, and Catherine Clément. [1975] 1986. *The newly born woman,* translated by Betsy Wing. Minneapolis: University of Minnesota Press.

Cockburn, Cynthia. 1985. *Machinery of dominance: Women, men and technical know-how.* London: Pluto Press.

Collins, Patricia Hill. 1990. *Black feminist thought: Knowledge, consciousness, and the politics of empowerment.* Boston: Unwin Hyman.

Connell, R. [Robert] W. 1987. *Gender and power: Society, the person, and sexual politics.* Stanford, Calif.: Stanford University Press.

Coser, Rose Laub. 1986. Cognitive structure and the use of social space. *Sociological Forum* 1: 1–26.

Davies, Christie. 1982. Sexual taboos and social boundaries. *American Journal of Sociology* 87: 1032–63.

de Beauvoir, Simone. 1953. *The second sex,* translated by H. M. Parshley. New York: Knopf.

Devor, Holly. 1987. Gender blending females: Women and sometimes men. *American Behavioral Scientist* 31: 12–40.

———. 1989. *Gender blending: Confronting the limits of duality.* Bloomington: Indiana University Press.

Dollimore, Jonathan. 1986. Subjectivity, sexuality, and transgression: The Jacobean connection. *Renaissance Drama,* n.s. 17: 53–81.

Douglas, Mary. 1973. *Natural symbols.* New York: Vintage.

Durova, Nadezhda. 1989. *The calvary maiden: Journals of a Russian officer in the Napoleonic wars,* translated by Mary Fleming Zirin. Bloomington: Indiana University Press.

Eichler, Margrit. 1989. Sex change operations: The last bulwark of the double standard. In *Feminist frontiers,* edited by Laurel Richardson and Verta Taylor. New York: Random House.

El Dareer, Asma. 1982. *Woman, why do you weep? Circumcision and its consequences.* London: Zed Books.

Epstein, Cynthia Fuchs. 1988. *Deceptive distinctions: Sex, gender and the social order.* New Haven: Yale University Press.

Faderman, Lillian. 1981. *Surpassing the love of men: Romantic friendship and love between women from the Renaissance to the present.* New York: William Morrow.

Foucault, Michel. 1972. *The archeology of knowledge and the discourse on language,* translated by A. M. Sheridan Smith. New York: Pantheon.

Freeman, Lucy, and Alma Halbert Bond. 1992. *America's first woman warrior: The courage of Deborah Sampson.* New York: Paragon.

Frye, Marilyn. 1983. *The politics of reality: Essays in feminist theory.* Trumansburg, N.Y.: Crossing Press.

Garber, Marjorie. 1992. *Vested interests: Cross-dressing and cultural anxiety.* New York and London: Routledge.

Garfinkel, Harold. 1967. *Studies in ethnomethodology.* Engelwood Cliffs, N.J.: Prentice-Hall.

Gilmore, David D. 1977. The arrangement between the sexes. *Theory and Society* 4: 301–33.

———. 1990. *Manhood in the making: Cultural concepts of masculinity.* New Haven: Yale University Press.

Goffman, Erving. 1977. The arrangement between the sexes. *Theory and Society* 4: 301–33.

———. Felicity's condition. *American Journal of Sociology* 89: 1–53.

Gordon, Tuula. 1990. *Feminist mothers.* New York: New York University Press.

Gramsci, Antonio. 1971. *Selections from the prison notebooks,* translated and edited by Quintin Hoare and Geoffrey Nowell Smith. New York: International Publishers.

Greenblatt, Stephen. 1987. *Shakespearean negotiations: The circulation of social energy in Renaissance England.* Berkeley: University of California Press.

Groce, Stephen B., and Margaret Cooper. 1990. Just me and the boys? Women in local-level rock and roll. *Gender & Society* 4: 220–29.

Haraway, Donna. 1978. Animal sociology and a natural economy of the body politic. Part I: A political physiology of dominance. *Signs* 4: 21–36.

———. 1990. Investment strategies for the evolving portfolio of primate females. In Jacobus, Keller, and Shuttleworth.

Howard, Jean E. 1988. Crossdressing, the theater, and gender struggle in early modern England. *Shakespeare Quarterly* 39: 418–41.

Hwang, David Henry. 1989. *M Butterfly.* New York: New American Library.

Jacobs, Sue-Ellen, and Christine Roberts. 1989. Sex, sexuality, gender, and gender variance. In *Gender and anthropology,* edited by Sandra Morgen. Washington, D.C.: American Anthropological Association.

Jay, Nancy. 1981. Gender and dichotomy. *Feminist Studies* 7: 38–56.

Kando, Thomas. 1973. *Sex change: The achievement of gender identity among feminized transsexuals.* Springfield, Ill.: Charles C Thomas.

Kincaid, Jamaica. 1978. Girl. *The New Yorker,* 26 June.

Kondo, Dorinne K. 1990a. *Crafting selves: Power, gender, and discourses of identity in a Japanese workplace.* Chicago: University of Chicago Press.

———. 1990b. *M. Butterfly:* Orientalism, gender, and a critique of essentialist identity. *Cultural Critique,* no. 16 (Fall): 5–29.

Lancaster, Jane Beckman. 1974. *Primate behavior and the emergence of human culture.* New York: Holt, Rinehart and Winston.

Laqueur, Thomas. 1990. *Making sex: Body and gender from the Greeks to Freud.* Cambridge, Mass.: Harvard University Press.

Lévi-Strauss, Claude. 1956. The family. In *Man, culture, and society,* edited by Harry L. Shapiro, New York: Oxford.

———. [1949] 1969. *The elementary structures of kinship,* translated by J. H. Bell and J. R. von Sturmer. Boston: Beacon Press.

Lightfoot-Klein, Hanny. 1989. *Prisoners of ritual: An odyssey into female circumcision in Africa.* New York: Harrington Park Press.

MacCormack, Carol P. 1980. Nature, culture and gender: A critique. In *Nature, culture and gender,* edited by Carol P. MacCormack and Marilyn Strathern. Cambridge, England: Cambridge University Press.

Matthaei, Julie A. 1982. *An economic history of women's work in America.* New York: Schocken.

Mencher, Joan. 1988. Women's work and poverty: Women's contribution to household maintenance in South India. In Dwyer and Bruce.

Morris, Jan. 1975. *Conundrum.* New York: Signet.

Nanda, Serena. 1990. *Neither man nor woman: The hijiras of India.* Belmont, Calif.: Wadsworth.

New York Times. 1989. Musician's death at 74 reveals he was a woman. 2 February.

Ortner, Sherry B. 1974. Is female to male as nature is to culture? In Rosaldo and Lamphere.

Ortner, Sherry B., and Harriet Whitehead. 1981. Introduction: Accounting for sexual meanings. In Ortner and Whitehead.

Paige, Karen Ericksen, and Jeffrey M. Paige. 1981. *The politics of reproductive ritual.* Berkeley: University of California Press.

Palmer, Phyllis. 1989. *Domesticity and dirt: Housewives and domestic servants in the United States, 1920–1945.* Philadelphia: Temple University Press.

Papanek, Hanna. 1979. *Family status production:* The "work" and "non-work" of women. *Signs* 4: 775–81.

Raymond, Janice G. 1979. *The transsexual empire: The making of the she-male.* Boston: Beacon Press.

Reskin, Barbara F. 1988. Bringing the men back in: Sex differentiation and the devaluation of women's work. *Gender & Society* 2: 58–81.

Rogers, Mary F. 1992. They were all passing: Agnes, Garfinkel, and company. *Gender & Society* 6: 169–91.

Rosaldo, Michelle Zimbalist, and Louise Lamphere (eds.). 1974. *Woman, culture, and society.* Stanford, Calif.: Stanford University Press.

Rubin, Gayle. 1975. The traffic in women: Notes on the political economy of sex. In *Toward an anthropology of women,* edited by Rayna R[app] Reiter. New York: Monthly Review Press.

Rugh, Andrea B. 1986. *Reveal and conceal: Dress in contemporary Egypt.* Syracuse, N.Y.: Syracuse University Press.

Scott, Joan Wallach. 1988. *Gender and the politics of history.* New York: Columbia University Press.

Showalter, Elaine. 1987. Critical cross-dressing: Male feminists and the woman of the year. In *Men in feminism,* edited by Alice Jardine and Paul Smith. New York: Methuen.

Smith, Dorothy E. 1987. *The everyday world as problematic: A feminist sociology.* Toronto: University of Toronto Press.

———. 1990. *The conceptual practices of power: A feminist sociology of knowledge.* Toronto: University of Toronto Press.

van der Kwaak, Anke. 1992. Female circumcision and gender identity: A questionable alliance? *Social Science and Medicine* 35: 777–87.

van Gennep, Arnold. 1960. *The rites of passage,* translated by Monika B. Vizedom and Gabrielle L. Caffee. Chicago: University of Chicago Press.

Walker, Molly K. 1992. Maternal reactions to fetal sex. *Health Care for Women International* 13: 293–302.

West, Candace, and Don Zimmerman. 1987. Doing gender. *Gender & Society* 1: 125–51.

Wheelright, Julie. 1989. *Amazons and military maids: Women who cross-dressed in pursuit of life, liberty and happiness.* London: Pandora Press.

Whitehead, Harriet. 1982. The bow and the burden strap: A new look at institutionalized homosexuality in Native North America. In *Sexual meanings: The cultural construction of gender and sexuality,* edited by Sherry B. Ornter and Harriet Whitehead. New York: Cambridge University Press.

Wikan, Unni. 1982. *Behind the veil in Arabia: Women in Oman.* Baltimore, Md.: Johns Hopkins University Press.

Williams, Christine L. 1989. *Gender differences at work: Women and men in nontraditional occupations.* Berkeley: University of California Press.

Williams, Walter L. 1986. *The spirit and the flesh: Sexual diversity in American Indian culture.* Boston: Beacon Press.

Yanagisako, Sylvia Junko, and Jane Fishburne Collier. 1987. Toward a unified analysis of gender and kinship. In *Gender and kinship: Essays toward a unified analysis,* edited by Jane Fishburne Collier and Sylvia Junko Yanagisako. Berkeley: University of California Press.

Zelizer, Viviana A. 1985. *Pricing the priceless child: The changing social value of children.* New York: Basic Books.

READING 7   *Suzanne Kessler*

The Medical Construction of Gender
First published in 1998

The birth of intersexed infants, babies born with genitals that are neither clearly male nor clearly female, has been documented throughout recorded time.[1] In the late twentieth century, medical technology has become sufficiently advanced to allow scientists to determine chromosomal and hormonal gender, which is typically taken to be the real, natural, biological gender, usually referred to as "sex."[2] Nevertheless, physicians who handle cases of intersexed infants consider several factors beside biological ones in determining, assigning, and announcing the gender of a particular infant. Indeed, biological factors are often preempted in physicians' deliberations by such cultural factors as the "correct" length of the penis and capacity of the vagina.

In the literature on intersexuality, issues such as announcing a baby's gender at the time of delivery, postdelivery discussions with the parents, and consultations with patients in adolescence are considered only peripherally to the central medical issues—etiology, diagnosis, and surgical procedures.[3] Yet members of medical teams have standard practices for managing intersexuality, which rely ultimately on cultural understandings of gender. The process and guidelines by which decisions about gender (re)construction are made reveal the model for the social construction of gender generally. Moreover, in the face of apparently incontrovertible evidence—infants born with some combination of "female" and "male" reproductive and sexual features—physicians hold an incorrigible belief that female and male are the only "natural" options. This paradox highlights and calls into question the idea that female and male are biological givens compelling a culture of two genders.

Ideally, to undertake an extensive study of intersexed infant case management, I would like to have had direct access to particular events, for example the deliveries of intersexed infants and the initial discussions among physicians, between physicians and parents, between parents, and among parents and family and friends of intersexed infants. The rarity with which intersexuality occurs, however, made this unfeasible.[4] Alternatively, physicians who have had considerable experience dealing with this condition were interviewed. I do not assume that their "talk" about how they manage such cases mirrors their "talk" in the situation, but their words do reveal that they have certain assumptions about gender and that they impose those assumptions via their medical decisions on the patients they treat.

Interviews were conducted with six medical experts (three women and three men) in the field of pediatric intersexuality: one clinical geneticist, three endocrinologists (two of them pediatric specialists), one psycho-endocrinologist, and one urologist. All of them have had extensive clinical experience with various intersexed syndromes, and some are internationally known researchers in the field of intersexuality. They were selected on the basis of their prominence in the field and their representing four different medical centers in New York City. Although they know one another, they do not collaborate on research and are not part of the same management team. All were interviewed in the spring of 1985 in their offices. The interviews lasted between forty-five minutes and one hour. Unless further referenced, all quotations in this [reading] are from these interviews.[5]

THE THEORY OF INTERSEXUALITY MANAGEMENT

The sophistication of today's medical technology has led to an extensive compilation of various intersex categories based on the various causes of malformed genitals. The "true hermaphrodite" condition, where both ovarian and testicular tissue are present either in the same gonad or in opposite gonads, accounts for fewer than 5 percent of all cases of ambiguous genitals:[6] More commonly, the infant has either ovaries or testes, but the genitals are ambiguous. If the infant has two ovaries, the condition is referred to as female pseudohermaphroditism. If the infant has two testes, the condition is referred to as male pseudohermaphroditism. There are numerous causes of both forms of pseudohermaphroditism, and although there are life-threatening aspects to some of these conditions, having ambiguous genitals per se is not harmful to the infant's health.[7]Although most cases of ambiguous genitals do not represent true hermaphroditism, in keeping with the contemporary literature I will refer to all such cases as intersexed.

Current attitudes toward the intersex condition have been primarily influenced by three factors. First are the developments in surgery and endocrinology. Diagnoses of specific intersex conditions can be made with greater precision. Female genitals can be constructed that look much like "natural" ones, and some small penises can be enlarged with the exogenous application of hormones, although surgical skills are not sufficiently advanced to construct a "normal"-looking and -functioning penis out of other tissue.[8] Second, in the contemporary United States, the influence of the feminist movement has called into question the valuation of women according to strictly reproductive functions, and the presence or absence of functional gonads is no longer the only or the definitive criterion for gender assignment. Third, psychological theorists focus on "gender identity" (one's sense of oneself as belonging to the female or male category) as distinct from "gender role" (cultural expectations of one's behavior as "appropriate" for a female or male).[9] The relevance of this new gender identity theory for rethinking cases of ambiguous genitals is that gender

must be assigned as early as possible if gender identity is to develop successfully. As a result of these three factors, intersexuality is considered a treatable condition of the genitals, one that needs to be resolved expeditiously.

According to all of the specialists interviewed, management of intersexed cases is based upon the theory of gender proposed first by John Money, J. G. Hampson, and J. L. Hempson in 1955 and developed in 1972 by Money and Anke A. Ehrhardt. The theory argues that gender identity is changeable until approximately eighteen months of age.[10] "To use the Pygmalion allegory, one may begin with the same clay and fashion a god or a goddess."[11] The theory rests on satisfying several conditions: The experts must ensure that the parents have no doubt about whether their child is male or female; the genitals must be made to match the assigned gender as soon as possible; gender-appropriate hormones must be administered at puberty; and intersexed children must be kept informed about their situation with age-appropriate explanations. If these conditions are met, the theory proposes, the intersexed child will develop a gender identity in accordance with the gender assignment (regardless of the chromosomal gender) and will not question her or his assignment and request reassignment at a later age.

Supportive evidence for Money and Ehrhardt's theory is based on only a handful of repeatedly cited cases, but it has been accepted because of the prestige of the theoreticians and its resonance with contemporary ideas about gender, children, psychology, and medicine. Gender and children are malleable; psychology and medicine are the tools used to transform them. This theory is so strongly endorsed that it has taken on the character of gospel. "I think we [physicians] have been raised in the Money theory," one endocrinologist said. Another claimed, "We always approach the problem in a similar way and it's been dictated, to a large extent, by the work of John Money and Anke Ehrhardt because they are the only people who have published, at least in medical literature, any data, any guidelines." It is provocative that this physician immediately followed this assertion with: "And I don't know how effective it really is." Contradictory data are rarely cited in reviews of the literature, were not mentioned by any of the physicians interviewed, and have not reduced these physicians' belief in the theory's validity.[12]

The doctors interviewed concur with the argument that gender must be assigned immediately, decisively, and irreversibly, and that professional opinions be presented in a clear and unambiguous way. The psycho-endocrinologist said that when doctors make a statement about the infant, they should "stick to it." The urologist said, "If you make a statement that later has to be disclaimed or discredited, you've weakened your credibility." A gender assignment made decisively, unambiguously, and irrevocably contributes, I believe, to the general impression that the infant's true, natural "sex" has been discovered, and that something that was there all along has been found. It also serves to maintain the credibility of the medical profession, reassure the parents, and reflexively substantiate Money and Ehrhardt's theory.

Also according to this theory, if corrective surgery is necessary, it should take place as soon as possible. If the infant is assigned the male gender, the initial stage of penis repair is usually undertaken in the first year, and further surgery is completed before the child enters school. If the infant is assigned the female gender, vulva repair (including clitoral reduction) is usually begun by three months of age. Money suggests that if reduction of phallic tissue were delayed beyond the neonatal period, the infant would have traumatic memories of having been castrated.[13] Vaginoplasty, in those females having an adequate internal structure (e.g., the vaginal canal is near its expected location), is done between the ages of one and four years. Girls who require more complicated surgical procedures might not be surgically corrected until preadolescence.[14] The complete vaginal canal is typically constructed only when the body is fully grown, following pubertal feminization with estrogen, although some specialists have claimed surgical success with vaginal construction in the early childhood years.[15] Although physicians speculate about the possible trauma of an early-childhood "castration" memory, there is no corresponding concern that vaginal reconstructive surgery delayed beyond the neonatal period is traumatic.

Even though gender identity theory places the critical age limit for gender reassignment between eighteen months and two years, the physicians acknowledge that diagnosis, gender assignment, and genital reconstruction cannot be delayed for as long as two years, since a clear gender assignment and correctly formed genitals will determine the kind of interactions parents will have with their child.[16] The geneticist argued that when parents "change a diaper and see genitalia that don't mean much in terms of gender assignment, I think it prolongs the negative response to the baby. . . .

If you have clitoral enlargement that is so extraordinary that the parents can't distinguish between male and female, it is sometimes helpful to reduce that somewhat so that the parent views the child as female." Another physician concurred: Parents "need to go home and do their job as child rearers with it very clear whether it's a boy or a girl."

DIAGNOSIS

A premature gender announcement by an obstetrician, prior to a close examination of an infant's genitals, can be problematic. Money and his colleagues claim that the primary complications in case management of intersexed infants can be traced to mishandling by medical personnel untrained in sexology.[17] According to one of the pediatric endocrinologists interviewed, obstetricians improperly educated about intersexed conditions "don't examine the babies closely enough at birth and say things just by looking, before separating legs and looking at everything, and jump to conclusions, because 99 percent of the time it's correct. . . . People get upset, physicians I mean. And they say things that are inappropriate." For example, he said that an inexperienced obstetrician might blurt out, "I think you have a boy, or no, maybe you have a girl." Other inappropriate remarks a doctor might make in postdelivery consultation with the parents include, "You have a little boy, but he'll never function as a little boy, so you better raise him as a little girl." As a result, said the pediatric endocrinologist, "the family comes away with the idea that they have a little boy, and that's what they wanted, and that's what they're going to get." In such cases, parents sometimes insist that the child be raised male despite the physicians' instructions to the contrary. "People have in mind certain things they've heard, that this is a boy, and they're not likely to forget that, or they're not likely to let it go easily." The urologist agreed that the first gender attribution is critical: "Once it's been announced, you've got a big problem on your hands." "One of the worst things is to allow them [the parents] to go ahead and give a name and tell everyone, and it turns out the child has to be raised in the opposite sex."[18]

Physicians feel that the mismanagement of such cases requires careful remedying. The psychoendocrinologist asserted, "When I'm involved, I spend hours with the parents to explain to them what has happened and how a mistake like that could be made, *or not really a mistake but a different decision*" [my emphasis]. One pediatric endocrinologist said, "I try to dissuade them from previous misconceptions and say, 'Well, I know what they meant, but the way they said it confused you. This is, I think, a better way to think about it.'" These statements reveal physicians' efforts not only to protect parents from concluding that their child is neither male nor female or both, but also to protect other physicians' decision-making processes. Case management involves perpetuating the notion that good medical decisions are based on interpretations of the infant's real "sex" rather than on cultural understandings of gender.

"Mismanagements" are less likely to occur in communities with major medical centers where specialists are prepared to deal with intersexuality and a medical team (perhaps drawing physicians from more than one teaching hospital) can be quickly assembled. The team typically consists of the original referring doctor (obstetrician or pediatrician), a pediatric endocrinologist, a pediatric surgeon (urologist or gynecologist), and a geneticist. In addition, a psychologist, psychiatrist, or psychoendocrinologist might play a role. If an infant is born with ambiguous genitals in a small community hospital without the relevant specialists on staff, the baby is likely to be transferred to a hospital where diagnosis and treatment are available. Intersexed infants born in poor rural areas where there is less medical intervention might never be referred for genital reconstruction. Many of these children, like those born in earlier historical periods, will grow up and live through adulthood with the genital ambiguity—somehow managing.

The diagnosis of intersexed conditions includes assessing the chromosomal sex and the syndrome that produced the genital ambiguity and may include medical procedures such as cytologic screening; chromosomal analysis; assessing serum electrolytes; hormone, gonadotropin, and steroids evaluation; digital examination; and radiographic genitography.[19] In any intersexed condition, if the infant is determined to be a genetic female (having an XX chromosome makeup), then the treatment—genital surgery to reduce the phallus size—can proceed relatively quickly, satisfying what the doctors believe are psychological and cultural demands. For example, 21-hydroxylase deficiency, a form of female pseudohermaphroditism and one of the most common conditions, can be determined by a blood test within the first few days.

If, on the other hand, the infant is determined to have at least one Y chromosome, then surgery may be considerably delayed. A decision must be made

whether to test the ability of the phallic tissue to respond to human chorionic gonadotropin (HCG), a treatment intended to enlarge the microphallus enough to be a penis. The endocrinologist explained, "You do HCG testing and you find out if the male can make testosterone. . . . You can get those results back probably within three weeks. . . . You're sure the male is making testosterone—but can he respond to it? It can take three months of waiting to see whether the phallus responds."

If the Y-chromosome infant cannot make testosterone or cannot respond to the testosterone it makes, the phallus will not develop, and the Y-chromosome infant will not be considered to be a male after all. Should the infant's phallus respond to the local application of testosterone or a brief course of intramuscular injections of low-potency androgen, the gender assignment problem is resolved, but possibly at some later cost, since the penis will not grow again at puberty when the rest of the body develops.[20] Money's case-management philosophy assumes that while it may be difficult for an adult male to have a much smaller than average penis, it is very detrimental to the morale of the young boy to have a micropenis.[21] In the former case, the male's manliness might be at stake, but in the latter case, his essential maleness might be. Although the psychological consequences of these experiences have not been empirically documented, Money and his colleagues suggest that it is wise to avoid the problems of both the micropenis in childhood and the still-undersized penis postpuberty by reassigning many of these infants to the female gender.[22] This approach suggests that for Money and his colleagues, chromosomes are less relevant in determining gender than penis size, and, by implication, that "male" is defined not by the genetic condition of having one Y and one X chromosome or by the production of sperm but by the aesthetic condition of having an "appropriately" sized penis.

The tests and procedures required for diagnosis (and consequently for gender assignment) can take several months.[23] Although physicians are anxious not to make premature gender assignments, their language suggests that it is difficult for them to take a completely neutral position and to think and speak only of *phallic tissue* that belongs to an infant whose gender has not yet been determined or decided. Comments such as "seeing whether the male can respond to testosterone" imply at least a tentative male gender assignment of an XY infant. The psychoendocrinologist's explanations to parents of their infant's treatment program also illustrate this implicit male gender assignment. "Clearly this baby has an underdeveloped phallus. But if the phallus responds to this treatment, we are fairly confident that surgical techniques and hormonal techniques will help this child to look like a boy. But we want to make absolutely sure and use some hormone treatments and see whether the tissue reacts." The mere fact that this doctor refers to the genitals as an "underdeveloped" phallus rather than an overdeveloped clitoris suggests that the infant has been judged to be, at least provisionally, a male. In the case of the undersized phallus, what is ambiguous is not whether this is a penis but whether it is "good enough" to remain one. If, at the end of the treatment period, the phallic tissue has not responded, what had been a potential penis (referred to in the medical literature as a "clitoropenis") is now considered an enlarged clitoris (or "penoclitoris"), and reconstructive surgery is planned as for the genetic female.

The time-consuming nature of intersex diagnosis and the assumption, based on the gender identity theory, that gender be assigned as soon as possible thus present physicians with difficult dilemmas. Medical personnel are committed to discovering the etiology of the condition in order to determine the best course of treatment, which takes time. Yet they feel an urgent need to provide an immediate assignment and genitals that look and function appropriately. An immediate assignment that will need to be retracted is more problematic than a delayed assignment, since reassignment carries with it an additional set of social complications. The endocrinologist interviewed commented: "We've come very far in that we can diagnose, eventually, many of the conditions. But we haven't come far enough. . . . We can't do it early enough. . . . Very frequently a decision is made before all this information is available, simply because it takes so long to make the correct diagnosis. And you cannot let a child go indefinitely, not in this society you can't. . . . There's pressure on parents [for a decision], and the parents transmit that pressure onto physicians."

A pediatric endocrinologist agreed: "At times you may need to operate before a diagnosis can be made. . . . In one case parents were told to wait on the announcement while the infant was treated to see if the phallus would grow when treated with androgens. After the first month passed and there was some growth, the parents said they had given the child a boy's name. They could only wait a month."

Deliberating out loud on the judiciousness of making parents wait for assignment decisions, the endocrinologist asked rhetorically, "Why do we do all these tests if in the end we're going to make the decision simply on the basis of the appearance of the genitalia?" This question suggests that the principles underlying physicians' decisions are cultural rather than biological, based on parental reaction and the medical team's perception of the infant's societal adjustment prospects given the way the child's genitals look or could be made to look. Moreover, as long as the decision rests largely on the criterion of genital appearance, and male is defined as having a "good-sized" penis, more infants will be assigned to the female gender than the male.

THE WAITING PERIOD: DEALING WITH AMBIGUITY

During the period of ambiguity between birth and assignment, physicians not only must evaluate the infant's prospects of becoming a good male but also must manage the parents' uncertainty about a genderless child. Physicians advise that parents postpone announcing the gender of the infant until a gender has been explicitly assigned. They believe that parents should not feel compelled to disclose the baby's "sex" to other people. The clinical geneticist interviewed said that physicians "basically encourage them [parents] to treat it [the infant] as neuter." One of the pediatric endocrinologists reported that in France parents confronted with this dilemma sometimes give the infant a neuter name such as Claude. The psychoendocrinologist concurred: "If you have a truly borderline situation, and you want to make it dependent on the hormone treatment . . . then the parents are . . . told, 'Try not to make a decision. Refer to the baby as "baby." Don't think in terms of boy or girl.'" Yet, when asked whether this is a reasonable request to make of parents in our society, the physician answered: "I don't think so. I think parents can't do it."[24]

New York State requires that a birth certificate be filled out within forty-eight hours of delivery, but the certificate need not be filed with the state for thirty days. The geneticist tells parents to insert "child of" instead of a name. In one case, parents filled out two birth registration forms, one for each gender, and they refused to sign either until a final gender assignment had been made.[25] One of the pediatric endocrinologists claimed, "I heard a story, I don't know if it's true or not. There were parents of a hermaphroditic infant who told everyone they had twins, one of each gender.

When the gender was determined, they said the other had died."

The geneticist explained that when directly asked by parents what to tell others about the gender of the infant, she says, "Why don't you just tell them that the baby is having problems and as soon as the problems are resolved we'll get back to you." A pediatric endocrinologist echoes this suggestion in advising parents to say, "Until the problem is solved, [we] would really prefer not to discuss any of the details." According to the urologist, "If [the gender] isn't announced, people may mutter about it and may grumble about it, but they haven't got anything to get their teeth into and make trouble over for the child, or the parents, or whatever." In short, parents are asked to sidestep the infant's gender rather than admit that the gender is unknown, thereby collaborating in a web of white lies, ellipses, and mystifications.[26]

Even as physicians teach parents how to deal with those who may not find the infant's condition comprehensible or acceptable, they also must make the condition comprehensible and acceptable to the parents, normalizing the intersexed condition for them. In doing so, they help the parents consider the infant's condition in the most positive way. There are four key aspects to this "normalizing" process.

First, physicians teach parents usual fetal development and explain that all fetuses have the potential to be male or female. One of the endocrinologists explains, "In the absence of maleness, you have femaleness. . . . It's really the basic design. The other [intersex] is really a variation on a theme." This explanation presents the intersex condition as a natural phase of fetal development. Another endocrinologist "like[s] to show picture[s] to them and explain that at a certain point in development males and females look alike and then diverge for such and such reason." The professional literature suggests that doctors use diagrams that illustrate "nature's principle of using the same anlagen to produce the external genital parts of the male and female."[27]

Second, physicians stress the normalcy of other aspects of the infant. For example, the geneticist tells parents, "The baby is healthy, but there was a problem in the way the baby was developing." The endocrinologist says the infant has "a mild defect, [which] just like anything could be considered a birth defect, a mole, or a hemangioma." This language not only eases the blow to the parents but also redirects their attention. Terms like "hermaphrodite" or "abnormal" are not used. The urologist said that he advised parents "about the generalization of sticking to the good things and not confusing people with something that is unnecessary."

Third, physicians (at least initially) imply that it is not the gender of the child that is ambiguous but the genitals. They talk about "undeveloped," "maldeveloped," or "unfinished" organs. From a number of the physicians interviewed came the following explanations:

> At a point in time the development proceeded in a different way, and sometimes the development isn't complete and we may have some trouble . . . in determining what the *actual* sex is. And so we have to do a blood test to help us. [my emphasis]
>
> The baby may be a female, which you would know after the buccal smear, but you can't prove it yet. If so, then it's a normal female with a different appearance. This can be surgically corrected.
>
> The gender of your child isn't apparent to us at the moment.
>
> While this looks like a small penis, it's actually a large clitoris. And what we're going to do is put it back in its proper position and reduce the size of the tip of it enough so it doesn't look funny, so it looks right.

Money and his colleagues report a case in which parents were advised to tell their friends that the reason their infant's gender was reannounced from male to female is that "the baby was . . . 'closed up down there.' [. . .] When the closed skin was divided, the female organs were revealed, and the baby discovered to be, *in fact*, a girl" [my emphasis]. It was mistakenly assumed to be a male at first because "there was an excess of skin on the clitoris."[28]

The message in these examples is that the trouble lies in the doctor's ability to determine the gender, not in the baby's gender per se. The real gender will presumably be determined/proven by testing, and the "bad" genitals (which are confusing the situation for everyone) will be "repaired." The emphasis is not on the doctors' creating gender but in their completing the genitals. Physicians say that they "reconstruct" the genitals rather than "construct" them. The surgeons reconstitute from remaining parts what should have been there all along. The fact that gender in an infant is "reannounced" rather than "reassigned" suggests that the first announcement was a mistake because the announcer was confused by the genitals. The gender always was what it is now seen to be.[29]

Finally, physicians tell parents that social factors are more important in gender development than biological ones, even though they are searching for biological causes. In essence, the physicians teach the parents Money and Ehrhardt's theory of gender development.[30] In doing so, they shift the emphasis from the discovery of biological factors that are a sign of the "real" gender to providing the appropriate social conditions to produce the "real" gender. What remains unsaid is the apparent contradiction in the assumption that a "real" or "natural" gender can be or needs to be produced artificially. The physician/parent discussions make it clear to family members that gender is not a biological given [even though, of course, the physicians' own procedures for diagnosis assume that it is] and that gender is fluid: The psychoendocrinologist paraphrased an explanation to parents thus: "It will depend, ultimately, on how everybody treats your child and how your child is looking as a person. . . . I can with confidence tell them that generally gender [identity] clearly agrees with the assignment." A pediatric endocrinologist explained: "I try to impress upon them that there's an enormous amount of clinical data to support the fact that if you sex-reverse an infant . . . the majority of the time the alternative gender identity is commensurate with the socialization, the way that they're raised, and how people view them, and that seems to be the most critical."

The implication of these comments is that gender identity (of all children, not just those born with ambiguous genitals) is determined primarily by social factors, that the parents and community always construct the child's gender. In the case of intersexed infants, the physicians merely provide the right genitals to go along with the socialization. Of course at so-called normal births, when the infant's genitals are unambiguous, the parents are not told that the child's gender is ultimately up to socialization. In those cases, doctors do treat gender as a biological given.

SOCIAL FACTORS IN DECISION MAKING

Most of the physicians interviewed claimed that personal convictions of doctors ought to play no role in the decision-making process. The psychoendocrinologist explained:

> I think the most critical factors [are] what is the possibility that this child will grow up with genitals which look like that of the assigned gender and which will

ultimately function according to gender. . . . That's why it's so important that it's a well-established team, because [personal convictions] can't really enter into it. It has to be what is surgically and endocrinologically possible for that baby to be able to make it. . . . It's really much more within medical criteria. I don't think many social factors enter into it.

While this doctor eschews the importance of social factors in gender assignment, she argues forcefully that social factors are extremely important in the development of gender identity. Indeed, she implies that social factors primarily enter the picture once the infant leaves the hospital.

In fact, doctors make decisions about gender on the basis of shared cultural values that are unstated, perhaps even unconscious, and therefore considered objective rather than subjective. Money states the fundamental rule for gender assignment: "Never assign a baby to be reared, and to surgical and hormonal therapy, as a boy, unless the phallic structure, hypospadiac or otherwise, is neonatally of at least the same caliber as that of same-aged males with small–average penises."[31] Elsewhere, he and his colleagues provide specific measurements for what qualifies as a micropenis: "A penis is, by convention, designated as a micropenis when at birth its dimensions are three or more standard deviations below the mean. . . . When it is correspondingly reduced in diameter with corpora that are vestigial, . . . it unquestionably qualifies as a micropenis."[32] A pediatric endocrinologist claimed that although "the [size of the] phallus is not the deciding factor, . . . if the phallus is less than two centimeters long at birth and won't respond to androgen treatments, then it's made into a female." There is no clearer statement of the formula for gender assignment than the one given by one well-published pediatric surgeon: "The decision to raise the child with male pseudohermaphroditism as a male or female is dictated entirely by the size of the phallus."[33]

These guidelines are clear, but they focus on only one physical feature, one that is distinctly imbued with cultural meaning. This becomes especially apparent in the case of an XX infant with normal female reproductive gonads and a "perfect" penis. Would the size and shape of the penis, in this case, be the deciding factor in assigning the infant as a "male," or would the "perfect" penis be surgically destroyed and female genitals created? Money notes that this dilemma would be complicated by the anticipated reaction of the parents to seeing "their apparent son lose his penis."[34] Other researchers concur that parents are likely to want to raise a child with a normal-shaped penis (regardless of size) as "male," particularly if the scrotal area looks normal and if the parents have had no experience with intersexuality.[35] Elsewhere, Money argues in favor of not neonatally amputating the penis of XX infants since fetal masculinization of brain structures would predispose them "almost invariably [to] develop behaviorally as tomboys, even when reared as girls."[36] This reasoning implies first that tomboyish behavior in girls is bad and should be avoided and second that it is preferable to remove the internal female organs, implant prosthetic testes, and regulate the "boy's hormones for his entire life than to overlook or disregard the perfection of the penis."[37]

The ultimate proof to the physicians that they intervened appropriately and gave the intersexed infant the correct gender assignment is that the reconstructed genitals look normal and function normally in adulthood. The vulva, labia, and clitoris should appear ordinary to the woman and her partner(s), and the vagina should be able to receive a normal-sized penis. Similarly, the man and his partner(s) should feel that his penis (even if somewhat smaller than the norm) looks and functions in an unremarkable way. Although there are no published data on how much emphasis the intersexed person, him- or herself, places upon genital appearance and functioning, physicians are absolutely clear about what they believe is important. The clinical geneticist said, "If you have . . . a seventeen-year-old young lady who has gotten hormone therapy and has breast development and pubic hair and no vaginal opening, I can't even entertain the notion that this young lady wouldn't want to have corrective surgery." The urologist summarized his criteria: "Happiness is the biggest factor. Anatomy is part of happiness." Money states, "The primary deficit [of not having sufficient penis]—and destroyer of morale—lies in being unable to satisfy the partner."[38] Another team of clinicians reveals its phallocentrism and argues that the most serious mistake in gender assignment is to create "an individual unable to engage in genital [heterosexual] sex."[39]

The equation of gender with genitals could have emerged only in an age when medical science can create genitals that appear to be normal and to function adequately, and an emphasis on the good phallus above all else could have emerged only in a culture that has rigid aesthetic and performance criteria for what constitutes maleness. The formulation "Good penis equals male; absence of good penis equals female" is treated in the literature and by the physicians interviewed as an objective criterion, operative in all cases. There is a striking lack of attention to the size and shape requirements of the female genitals, other than that the clitoris not be too big and that the vagina be able to receive a penis.[40]

In the late nineteenth century, when women's reproductive function was culturally designated as their essential characteristic, the presence or absence of ovaries (whether or not they were fertile) was held to be the ultimate criterion of gender assignment for hermaphrodites. As recently as 1955, there was some concern that if people with the same chromosomes or gonads paired off, even if they had different genitals, that "might bring the physician in conflict with the law for abetting the pursuit of (technically) illegal sex practices."[41] The urologist interviewed recalled a case from that period of a male child reassigned to "female" at the age of four or five because ovaries had been discovered. Nevertheless, doctors today, schooled in the etiology and treatment of the various intersex syndromes, view decisions based primarily on chromosomes or gonads as wrong, although, they complain, the conviction that the presence of chromosomes or gonads is the ultimate criterion "still dictates the decisions of the uneducated and uninformed."[42] Presumably the educated and informed now know that decisions based primarily on phallic size, shape, and sexual capacity are right.

While the prospect of constructing good genitals is the primary consideration in physicians' gender assignments, another extramedical factor was repeatedly cited by the six physicians interviewed—the specialty of the attending physician. Although intersexed infants are generally treated by teams of specialists, only the person who coordinates the team is actually responsible for the case. This person, acknowledged by the other physicians as having chief responsibility, acts as spokesperson to the parents. Although all of the physicians claimed that these medical teams work smoothly, with few differences of opinion, several of them mentioned decision-making orientations that are grounded in particular medical specializations. One endocrinologist stated, "The easiest route to take, where there is ever any question, . . . is to raise the child as female. . . . In this country, that is usual if the infant falls into the hands of a pediatric endocrinologist. . . . If the decision is made by the urologists, who are mostly males, . . . they're always opting, because they do the surgery, they're always feeling they can correct anything." Another endocrinologist concurred: "[Most urologists] don't think in terms of dynamic processes. They're interested in fixing pipes and lengthening pipes, and not dealing with hormonal, and certainly not psychological issues. . . . 'What can I do with what I've got?'" Urologists were defended by the clinical geneticist: "Surgeons here, now I can't speak for elsewhere, they don't get into a situation where the child is a year old and they can't make anything."

Whether or not urologists "like to make boys," as one endocrinologist claimed, the following example from a urologist who was interviewed explicitly links a cultural interpretation of masculinity to the medical treatment plan. The case involved an adolescent who had been assigned the female gender at birth but was developing some male pubertal signs and wanted to be a boy. "He was ill-equipped," said the urologist, "yet we made a very respectable male out of him. He now owns a huge construction business—those big cranes that put stuff up on the building."

POSTINFANCY CASE MANAGEMENT

After the infant's gender has been assigned, parents generally latch onto the assignment as the solution to the problem—and it is. The physician as detective has collected the evidence, as lawyer has presented the case, and as judge has rendered a verdict. Although most of the interviewees claimed that parents are equal participants in the whole process, they gave no instances of parental participation prior to the gender assignment.[43] After the physicians assign the infant's gender, the parents are encouraged to establish the credibility of that gender publicly by, for example, giving a detailed medical explanation to a leader in their community, such as a physician or pastor, who will explain the situation to curious casual acquaintances. Money argues that "medical terminology has a special layman's magic in such a context, it is final and authoritative and closes the issue."[44] He also recommends that eventually the mother "settle [the] argument once and for all among her women friends by allowing some of them to see the baby's reconstructed genitalia." Apparently, the powerful influence of normal-looking genitals helps overcome a history of ambiguous gender.

Some of the same issues that arise in assigning gender recur some years later when, at adolescence, the

child may be referred to a physician for counseling.[45] The physician then tells the adolescent many of the same things his or her parents had been told years before, with the same language. Terms like "abnormal," "disorder," "disease," and "hermaphroditism" are avoided; the condition is normalized and the child's gender is treated as unproblematic. One clinician explains to his patients that sex organs are different in appearance for each person, not just those who are intersexed. Furthermore, he tells the girls "that while most women menstruate, not all do . . . that conception is only one of a number of ways to become a parent; [and] that today some individuals are choosing not to become parents."[46] The clinical geneticist tells a typical female patient: "You are female. Female is not determined by your genes. Lots of other things determine being a woman. And you are a woman but you won't be able to have babies."

A case reported by one of the pediatric endocrinologists involving an adolescent female with androgen insensitivity provides an intriguing insight into the postinfancy gender-management process. She was told at the age of fourteen "that her ovaries weren't normal and had been removed. That's why she needed pills to look normal. . . . I wanted to convince her of her femininity. Then I told her she could marry and have normal sexual relations. . . . [Her] uterus won't develop but [she] could adopt children." The urologist interviewed was asked to comment on this handling of the counseling. "It sounds like a very good solution to it. He's stating the truth, and if you don't state the truth . . . then you're in trouble later." This is a strange version of "the truth," however, since the adolescent was chromosomally XY and was born with normal testes that produced normal quantities of androgen. There *were* no ovaries or uterus. Another pediatric endocrinologist, in commenting on the management of this case, hedged the issue by saying that he would have used a generic term like "the gonads." A third endocrinologist said she would say that the uterus had never formed.

Technically, these physicians are lying when, for example, they explain to an adolescent XY female with an intersexed history that her "ovaries . . . had to be removed because they were unhealthy or were producing 'the wrong balance of hormones.'"[47] We can presume that these lies are told in the service of what physicians consider a greater good—keeping individual/concrete genders as clear and uncontaminated as the notions of female and male are in the abstract. One clinician suggests that with some female patients it eventually may be possible to talk to them "about their gonads having some structures and features that are testicular-like."[48] This call for honesty may be based, at least partly, on the possibility of the child's discovering his or her chromosomal sex inadvertently from a buccal smear taken in a high school biology class. Today's litigious climate may be another encouragement.

In sum, the adolescent is typically told that certain internal organs did not form because of an endocrinological defect, not because those organs could never have developed in someone with her or his sex chromosomes. The topic of chromosomes is skirted.

There are no published studies on how these adolescents experience their condition and their treatment by doctors. An endocrinologist interviewed mentioned that her adolescent patients rarely ask specifically what is wrong with them, suggesting that they are accomplices in this evasion. In spite of the "truth" having been evaded, the clinician's impression is that "their gender identities and general senses of well-being and self-esteem appear not to have suffered."[49]

LESSONS FROM INTERSEX MANAGEMENT

Physicians conduct careful examinations of the intersexed infant's genitals and perform intricate laboratory procedures. They are interpreters of the body, trained and committed to uncovering the "actual" gender obscured by ambiguous genitals. Yet they also have considerable leeway in assigning gender, and their decisions are influenced by cultural as well as medical factors. What is the relationship between the physician as discoverer and the physician as determiner of gender? Where is the relative emphasis placed in discussions with parents and adolescents and in the consciousness of the physicians? It is misleading to characterize the doctors whose words are provided here as presenting themselves publicly to the parents as discoverers of the infant's real gender but privately acknowledging that the infant has no real gender other than the one being determined or constructed by the medical professionals. They are not hypocritical. It is also misleading to claim that the physicians' focus shifts from discovery to determination over the course of treatment: first the doctors regard the infant's gender as an unknown but discoverable reality; then the doctors relinquish their attempts to find the real gender and treat the infant's gender as something they

must construct. They are not medically incompetent or deficient. Instead, I am arguing that the peculiar balance of discovery and determination throughout treatment permits physicians to handle very problematic cases of gender in the most unproblematic of ways.

This balance relies fundamentally on a particular conception of "natural."[50] Although the "deformity" of intersexed genitals would be immutable were it not for medical interference, physicians do not consider it natural. Instead, they think of, and speak of, the surgical/hormonal alteration of such "deformities" as natural because such intervention returns the body to what it ought to have been if events had taken their typical course. The nonnormative is converted into the normative, and the normative state is considered natural.[51] The genital ambiguity is remedied to conform to a "natural," that is, culturally indisputable gender dichotomy. Sherry Ortner's claim that the culture/nature distinction is itself a construction—a product of culture—is relevant here. Language and imagery help create and maintain a specific view of what is natural about the two genders and, I would argue, about the very idea of gender—that it consists of two exclusive types: female and male.[52] The belief that gender consists of two exclusive types is maintained and perpetuated by the medical community in the face of incontrovertible physical evidence that this is not mandated by biology.

The lay conception of human anatomy and physiology assumes a concordance among clearly dimorphic gender markers—chromosomes, genitals, gonads, hormones—but physicians understand that concordance and dimorphism do not always exist. Their understanding of biology's complexity, however, does not inform their understanding of gender's complexity. In order for intersexuality to be managed differently than it currently is, physicians would have to take seriously Money's assertion that it is a misrepresentation of epistemology to consider any cell in the body authentically male or female.[53] If authenticity for gender resides not in a discoverable nature but in someone's proclamation, then the power to proclaim something else is available. If physicians recognized that implicit in their management of gender is the notion that finally, and always, people construct gender, as well as the social systems that are grounded in gender-based concepts, the possibilities for real societal transformations would be unlimited. Unfortunately, neither in their representations to the families of the intersexed nor among themselves do the physicians interviewed for this study draw such far-reaching implications from their work. Their "understanding" that particular genders are medically (re)constructed in these cases does not lead them to see that gender *is always* constructed. Accepting genital ambiguity as a natural option would require that physicians also acknowledge that genital ambiguity is "corrected" not because it is threatening to the infant's life but because it is threatening to the infant's culture.

Rather than admit to their role in perpetuating gender, physicians "psychologize" the issue by talking about the parents' anxiety and humiliation in being confronted with an anomalous infant. They talk as though they have no choice but to respond to the parents' pressure for a resolution of psychological discomfort and as though they have no choice but to use medical technology in the service of a two-gender culture. Neither the psychology nor the technology is doubted, since both shield physicians from responsibility. Indeed, for the most part, neither physicians nor parents emerge from the experience of intersex case management with a greater understanding of the social construction of gender. Society's accountability, like their own, is masked by the assumption that gender is a given. Thus, the medical management of intersexuality, instead of illustrating nature's failure to ordain gender in these isolated, "unfortunate" instances, illustrates physicians' and Western society's failure of imagination—the failure to imagine that each of their management decisions is a moment when a specific instance of biological "sex" is transformed into a culturally constructed gender.

NOTES

1. For historical reviews of the intersexed person in ancient Greece and Rome, see Leslie Fiedler, *Freaks: Myths and Images of the Second Self* and Vern Bullough, *Sexual Variance in Society and History*. For the Middle Ages and Renaissance, see Michel Foucault, *History of Sexuality*. For the eighteenth and nineteenth centuries, see Michel Foucault, *Herculine Barbin* and Alice Domurat Dreger, *Hermaphrodites and the Medical Invention of Sex*. For the early twentieth century, see Havelock Ellis, *Studies in the Psychology of Sex*.

2. Traditionally, the term "gender" has designated psychological, social, and cultural aspects of maleness and femaleness, and the term "sex" has specified the biological and presumably more objective components. Twenty years ago, Wendy McKenna and I introduced the argument that "gender" should be used exclusively to refer to anything related to the categories "female" and "male," replacing the term "sex," which would be restricted to reproductive and "lovemaking" activities (Kessler and McKenna). Our reasoning was (and still is) that this would emphasize the socially constructed, overlapping nature of all category distinctions, even the biological ones. We wrote about gender chromosomes and gender hormones even though, at the time, doing so seemed awkward. I continue this practice here, but I follow the convention of referring to people with mixed biological gender cues as "intersexed" or "intersexuals" rather than as "intergendered" or "intergenderals." The latter is more consistent with my position, but I want to reflect both medical and vernacular usage without using quotation marks each time.

3. See, for example: M. Bolkenius, R. Daum, and E. Heinrich, "Paediatric Surgical Principles in the Management of Children with Intersex"; Kenneth I. Glassberg, "Gender Assignment in Newborn Male Pseudohermaphrodites"; and Peter A. Lee et al., "Micropenis. I. Criteria, Etiologies and Classification."

4. It is difficult to get accurate statistics on the frequency of intersexuality. Chromosomal abnormalities (like XOXX or XXXY) are registered, but those conditions do not always imply ambiguous genitals, and most cases of ambiguous genitals do not involve chromosomal abnormalities. None of the physicians interviewed would venture a guess on frequency rates, but all claimed that intersexuality is rare. One physician suggested that the average obstetrician may see only two cases in twenty years. Another estimated that a specialist may see only one a year or possibly as many as five a year. A reporter who interviewed physicians at Johns Hopkins Medical Center wrote that they treat, at most, ten new patients a year (Melissa Hendricks, "Is It a Boy or a Girl?"). The numbers are considerably greater if one adopts a broader definition of intersexuality to include all "sex chromosome" deviations and any genitals that do not look, according to the culturally informed view of the moment, "normal" enough. A urologist at a Mt. Sinai School of Medicine symposium on Pediatric Plastic and Reconstructive Surgery (New York City, 16 May 1996) claimed that one of every three hundred male births involves some kind of genital abnormality. A meticulous analysis of the medical literature from 1955 to 1997 led Anne Fausto-Sterling and her students to conclude that the frequency of intersexuality may be as high as 2 percent of live births, and that between 0.1 and 0.2 percent of newborns undergo some sort of genital surgery (Melanie Blackless et al., "How Sexually Dimorphic Are We?"). The Intersex Society of North America (ISNA) estimates that about five intersex surgeries are performed in the United States each day.

5. Although the interviews in this chapter were conducted more than ten years ago, interviews with physicians conducted in the mid-to late 1990s and interviews conducted with parents of intersexed children during that same time

period . . . indicate that little has changed in the medical management of intersexuality. This lack of change is also evident in current medical management literature. See, for example, F. M. E. Slijper et al., "Neonates with Abnormal Genital Development Assigned the Female Sex: Parent Counseling," and M. Rohatgi, "Intersex Disorders: An Approach to Surgical Management."

6. Mariano Castro-Magana, Moris Angulo, and Platon J. Collipp, "Management of the Child with Ambiguous Genitalia."

7. For example, infants whose intersexuality is caused by congenital adrenal hyperplasia can develop severe electrolyte disturbances unless the condition is controlled by cortisone treatments. Intersexed infants whose condition is caused by androgen insensitivity are in danger of eventual malignant degeneration of the testes unless these are removed. For a complete catalog of clinical syndromes related to the intersexed condition, see Arye Lev-Ran, "Sex Reversal as Related to Clinical Syndromes in Human Beings."

8. Much of the surgical experimentation in this area has been accomplished by urologists who are trying to create penises for female-to-male transsexuals. Although there have been some advancements in recent years in the ability to create a "reasonable-looking" penis from tissue taken elsewhere on the body, the complicated requirements of the organ (requiring both urinary and sexual functioning) have posed surgical problems. It may be, however, that the concerns of the urologists are not identical to the concerns of the patients. While data are not yet available from the intersexed, we know that female-to-male transsexuals place greater emphasis on the "public" requirements of the penis (for example, being able to look normal while standing at the urinal or wearing a bathing suit) than on its functional requirements (for example, being able to achieve an erection) (Kessler and McKenna, 128–132). As surgical techniques improve, female-to-male transsexuals (and intersexed males) might increase their demands for organs that look and function better.

9. Historically, psychology has tended to blur the distinction between the two by equating a person's acceptance of her or his genitals with gender role and ignoring gender identity. For example, Freudian theory posited that if one had a penis and accepted its reality, then masculine gender role behavior would naturally follow (Sigmund Freud, "Some Psychical Consequences of the Anatomical Distinctions Between the Sexes").

10. Almost all of the published literature on intersexed infant case management has been written or co-written by one researcher, John Money, professor of medical psychology and professor of pediatrics, emeritus, at Johns Hopkins University and Hospital, where he is director of the Psychohormonal Research Unit. Even the publications that are produced independently of Money reference him and reiterate his management philosophy. Although only one of the physicians interviewed has published with Money, they all essentially concur with his views and give the impression of a consensus that is rarely encountered in science. The one physician who raised some questions about Money's philosophy and the gender theory on which it is based has extensive experience with intersexuality in a nonindustrialized culture where the infant is matured differently with no apparent harm to gender development. Even though psychologists fiercely argue issues of gender identity and gender role development, doctors who treat intersexed infants seem untouched by these debates. There are still, in the late 1990s, few renegade voices from within the medical establishment. Why Money has been so single-handedly influential in promoting his ideas about gender is a question worthy of a separate substantial analysis. His management philosophy is conveyed in the following sources: John Money, J. G. Hampson, and J. L. Hampson, "Hermaphroditism: Recommendations Concerning Assignment of Sex, Change of Sex, and Psychologic Management"; John Money, *Sex Errors of the Body: Dilemmas, Education, Counseling;* John Money, Reynolds Potter, and Clarice S. Stoll, "Sex Reannouncement in Hereditary Sex Deformity: Psychology and Sociology of Habilitation"; Money and Ehrhardt; John Money, "Psychologic Consideration of Sex Assignment in Intersexuality"; John Money, "Psychological Counseling: Hermaphroditism"; John Money, Tom Mazur, Charles Abrams, and Bernard F. Norman, "Micropenis, Family Mental Health, and Neonatal Management: A Report on Fourteen Patients Reared as Girls"; and John Money, "Birth Defect of the Sex Organs: Telling the Parents and the Patient."

11. Money and Ehrhardt, 152.

12. One exception is the case followed by Milton Diamond in "Sexual Identity, Monozygotic Twins Reared in Discordant Sex Roles and a BBC Follow-up" and, with Keith Sigmundson, in "Sex Reassignment at Birth: Long-term Review and Clinical Applications."

13. Money, "Psychologic Consideration of Sex Assignment in Intersexuality."

14. Castro-Magana, Angulo, and Collipp.

15. Victor Braren et al., "True Hermaphroditism: A Rational Approach to Diagnosis and Treatment."

16. Studies of nonintersexed newborns have shown that, from the moment of birth, parents respond to their infant based on her or his gender. Jeffrey Rubin, F. J. Provenzano, and Z. Luria, "The Eye of the Beholder: Parents' Views on Sex of Newborns."

17. Money, Mazur, Abrams, and Norman.

18. There is evidence from other kinds of sources that once a gender attribution is made, all further information buttresses that attribution, and only the most contradictory new information will cause the original gender attribution to be questioned. Kessler and McKenna.

19. Castro-Magana, Angulo, and Collipp.

20. Money, "Psychologic Consideration of Sex Assignment in Intersexuality."

21. Technically, the term "micropenis" should be reserved for an exceptionally small but well-formed structure, a small, malformed "penis" should be referred to as a "microphallus" (Peter A. Lee et al.).

22. Money, Mazur, Abrams, and Norman, 26. A different view is argued by another leading gender-identity theorist: "When a little boy (with an imperfect penis) knows he is a male, he creates a penis that functions symbolically the same as those of boys with normal penises" (Robert J. Stoller, Sex and Gender).

23. W. Ch. Hecker, "Operative Correction of Intersexual Genitals in Children."

24. This way of presenting advice fails to understand that parents are part of a larger system. A pediatric endocrinologist told biologist Anne Fausto-Sterling that parents, especially young ones, are not independent actors. They rely on the advice of grandparents and older siblings, who, according to the physician, are more hysterical and push for an early gender assignment before all the medical data are analyzed (private communication, summer 1996).

25. Elizabeth Bing and Esselyn Rudikoff, "Divergent Ways of Parental Coping with Hermaphrodite Children."

26. These evasions must have many ramifications in everyday social interactions between parents, family, and friends. How people "fill in" the uncertainty such that interactions remain relatively normal is an interesting question that warrants further study. One of the pediatric endocrinologists interviewed acknowledged that the published literature discusses intersex management only from the physicians' point of view. He asks, "How [do parents] experience what they're told, and what [do] they remember . . . and carry with them?" One published exception to this neglect of the parents' perspective is a case study comparing two different coping strategies. The first couple, although initially distressed, handled the traumatic event by regarding the abnormality as an act of God. The second couple, more educated and less religious, put their faith in medical science and expressed a need to fully understand the biochemistry of the defect. Bing and Rudikoff.

27. Tom Mazur, "Ambiguous Genitalia: Detection and Counseling," and Money "Psychologic Consideration of Sex Assignment in Intersexuality," 218.

28. Money, Potter, and Stoll, 211.

29. The term "reassignment" is more commonly used to describe the gender changes of those who are cognizant of their earlier gender, e.g., transsexuals—people whose gender itself was a mistake.

30. Although Money and Ehrhardt's socialization theory is uncontested by the physicians who treat intersexuality and is presented to parents as a matter of fact, there is actually much debate among psychologists about the effect of prenatal hormones on brain structure and ultimately on gender-role behavior and even on gender

identity. The physicians interviewed agreed that the animal evidence for prenatal brain organization is compelling but that there is no evidence in humans that prenatal hormones have an inviolate or unilateral effect. If there is any effect of prenatal exposure to androgen, they believe it can easily be overcome and modified by psychosocial factors. It is this latter position, not the controversy in the field, that is communicated to the parents. For an argument favoring prenatally organized gender differences in the brain, see Milton Diamond, "Human Sexual Development: Biological Foundations for Social Development"; for a critique of that position, see Ruth Bleier, Science and Gender. A Critique of Biology and Its Theories on Women.

31. Money, "Psychological Counseling: Hermaphroditism," 610.

32. Money, Mazur, Abrams, and Norman, 18.

33. P. Donahoe, "Clinical Management of Intersex Abnormalities."

34. John Money, "Hermaphroditism and Pseudohermaphroditism."

35. Mojtaba Beheshti, Brian E. Hardy, Bernard M. Churchill, and Denis Daneman, "Gender Assignment in Male Pseudohermaphrodite Children." Of course, if the penis looked normal and the empty scrotum was overlooked, it might not be discovered until puberty that the male child was XX with a female internal structure.

36. Money, "Psychologic Consideration of Sex Assignment in Intersexuality," 216.

37. Weighing the probability of achieving a "perfect" penis against the probable trauma such procedures may entail is another social factor in decision making. According to an endocrinologist interviewed, if it seems that an XY infant with an inadequate penis would require as many as ten genital operations over a six-year period in order to have an adequate penis, the infant would be assigned the female gender. In this case, the endocrinologist's practical and compassionate concerns would override purely genital criteria.

38. Money, "Psychologic Consideration of Sex Assignment in Intersexuality," 217.

39. Castro-Magana, Angulo, and Collipp, 180.

40. It is unclear how much of this bias is the result of a general cultural devaluation of the female and how much is the result of physicians' belief in their ability to construct anatomically correct and functional female genitals.

41. John F. Oliven, Sexual Hygiene and Pathology: A Manual for the Physician.

42. Money, "Psychologic Consideration of Sex Assignment in Intersexuality," 215. Remnants of this anachronistic view can still be found, however, when doctors justify the removal of contradictory gonads on the grounds that they are typically sterile or at risk for malignancy (J. Dewhurst and D. B. Grant, "Intersex Problems"). Presumably, if the gonads were functional and healthy, their removal would provide an ethical dilemma for at least some medical professionals.

43. Although one set of authors argued that the views of the parents on the most appropriate gender for their child must be taken into account (Dewhurst and Grant, 1192), the physicians interviewed here denied direct knowledge of this kind of participation. They claimed that they personally had encountered few, if any, cases of parents who insisted on their child being assigned a particular gender. Yet each had heard about cases where a family's ethnicity or religious background biased them toward males. None of the physicians recalled whether this preference for male offspring meant the parents wanted a male regardless of the "inadequacy" of the penis, or whether it meant that the parents would have greater difficulty with a less-than-perfect male than with a "normal" female.

44. Money, "Psychological Counseling: Hermaphroditism," 613.

45. As with the literature on infancy, most of the published material on adolescents is on surgical and hormonal management rather than on social management. See, for example, Joel J. Roslyn, Eric W. Fonkalsrud, and Barbara Lippe, "Intersex Disorders in Adolescents and Adults."

46. Mazur, 421.

47. Dewhurst and Grant, 1193.

48. Mazur, 422.

49. Ibid.

50. For an extended discussion of different ways of conceptualizing what is natural, see Richard W. Smith, "What Kind of Sex Is Natural?"

51. This supports sociologist Harold Garfinkel's argument that we treat routine events as our *due* as social members and that we treat gender, like all normal forms, as a moral imperative. It is no wonder, then, that physicians conceptualize what they are doing as natural and unquestionably "right." Harold Garfinkel, *Studies in Ethnomethodology.*

52. Sherry B. Ortner, "Is Female to Male as Nature Is to Culture?"

53. Money, "Psychological Counseling: Hermaphroditism," 618.

REFERENCES

Beheshti, Mojtaba, Brian E. Hardy, Bernard M. Churchill, and Denis Daneman. "Gender Assignment in Male Pseudohermaphrodite Children." *Urology* 22, no. 6 (December 1983): 604–607.

Bing, Elizabeth, and Esselyn Rudikoff. "Divergent Ways of Parental Coping with Hermaphrodite Children." *Medical Aspects of Human Sexuality* (December 1970): 73–88.

Blackless, Melanie, Anthony Charuvastra, Amanda Derryck, Anne Fausto-Sterling, Karl Lauzanne, and Ellen Lee. "How Sexually Dimorphic Are We?" Unpublished manuscript, 1997.

Bleier, Ruth. *Science and Gender: A Critique of Biology and Its Theories on Women.* New York: Pergamon Press, 1984.

Bolkenius, M., R. Daum, and E. Heinrich. "Paediatric Surgical Principles in the Management of Children with Intersex." *Progress in Pediatric Surgery* 17 (1984): 33–38.

Braren, Victor, John J. Warner, Ian M. Burr, Alfred Slonim, James A. O'Neill Jr., and Robert K. Rhamy. "True Hermaphroditism: A Rational Approach to Diagnosis and Treatment." *Urology* 15 (June 1980): 569–574.

Bullough, Vern. *Sexual Variance in Society and History.* New York: John Wiley and Sons, 1976.

Castro-Magana, Mariano, Moris Angulo, and Platon J. Collipp. "Management of the Child with Ambiguous Genitalia." *Medical Aspects of Human Sexuality* 18, no. 4 (April 1984): 172–188.

Dewhurst, J., and D. B. Grant. "Intersex Problems." *Archives of Disease in Childhood* 59 (July–December 1984): 1191–1194.

Diamond, Milton. "Human Sexual Development: Biological Foundations for Social Development." In *Human Sexuality in Four Perspectives,* ed. Frank A. Beach, 22–61. Baltimore: The Johns Hopkins University Press, 1976.

———. "Sexual Identity, Monozygotic Twins Reared in Discordant Sex Roles and a BBC Follow-Up." *Archives of Sexual Behavior* 11, no. 2 (1982): 181–186.

———, and Keith Sigmundson. "Sex Reassignment of Birth: Long-term Review and Clinical Applications." *Archives of Pediatric and Adolescent Medicine* 151 (May 1997): 298–304.

Donahoe, P. "Clinical Management of Intersex Abnormalities." *Current Problems in Surgery* 28 (1991): 519–579.

Dreger, Alice Domurat. *Hermaphrodites and the Medical Invention of Sex.* Cambridge: Harvard University Press, 1998.

Ellis, Havelock. *Studies in the Psychology of Sex.* New York: Random House, 1942.

Fiedler, Leslie. *Freaks: Myths and Images of the Second Self.* New York: Simon and Schuster, 1978.

Foucault, Michael. *Herculine Barbin.* New York: Pantheon Books, 1978.

———. *History of Sexuality.* New York: Pantheon Books, 1980.

Freud, Sigmund. "Some Psychical Consequences of the Anatomical Distinctions Between the Sexes" (1925). In *The Complete Psychological Works,* trans. and ed. J. Strachy, vol. 18. New York: Norton, 1976.

Garfinkel, Harold. *Studies in Ethnomethodology.* Englewood Cliffs, N.J.: Prentice-Hall, 1967.

Glassberg, Kenneth I. "Gender Assignment in Newborn Male Pseudohermaphodites." *Urologic Clinics of North America* 7 (June 1980): 409–421.

Hecker, W. Ch. "Operative Correction of Intersexual Genitals in Children." *Progress in Pediatric Surgery* 17 (1984): 21–31.

Hendricks, Melissa. "Is It a Boy or a Girl?" *Johns Hopkins Magazine* 45, no. 5 (November 1993): 10–16.

Kessler, Suzanne J., and Wendy McKenna. *Gender: An Ethnomethodological Approach.* New York: Wiley-Interscience, 1978; Chicago: University of Chicago Press, 1985.

Lee, Peter A., Thomas Mazur, Robert Danish, James Amrhein, Robert M. Blizzard, John Money, and Claude J. Migeon. "Micropenis: I. Criteria, Etiologies and Classification." *The Johns Hopkins Medical Journal* 146 (1980): 156–163.

Lev-Ran, Arye. "Sex Reversal as Related to Clinical Syndromes in Human Beings." In *Handbook of Sexology II: Genetics, Hormones and Behavior,* ed. John Money and H. Musaph, 157–173. New York: Elsevier, 1978.

Mazur, Tom. "Ambiguous Genitalia: Detection and Counseling." *Pediatric Nursing* 9 (November/December 1983): 417–431.

Money, John. "Birth Defect of the Sex Organs: Telling the Parents and the Patient." *British Journal of Sexual Medicine* 10 (March 1983): 14.

———. "Hermaphroditism and Pseudohermaphroditism." In *Gynecologic Endocrinology,* ed. Jay J. Gold, 449–464. New York: Hoeber, 1968.

———. "Psychologic Consideration of Sex Assignment in Intersexuality." *Clinics in Plastic Surgery* 1 (April 1974): 215–222.

———. "Psychological Counseling: Hermaphroditism." In *Endocrine and Genetic Diseases of Childhood and Adolescence,* ed. L. I. Gardner, 609–618. Philadelphia: W. B. Saunders, 1975.

———. *Sex Errors of the Body: Dilemmas, Education, Counseling.* Baltimore: The Johns Hopkins University Press, 1968. Reprint, 1994.

———, and Anke A. Ehrhardt. *Man & Woman, Boy & Girl.* Baltimore: The Johns Hopkins University Press, 1972.

———, J. G. Hampson, and J. L. Hampson. "Hermaphroditism: Recommendations Concerning Assignment of Sex, Change of Sex, and Psychologic Management." *Bulletin of The Johns Hopkins Hospital* 97 (1955): 284–300.

———, Tom Mazur, Charles Abrams, and Bernard F. Norman. "Micropenis, Family Mental Health, and Neonatal Management: A Report on Fourteen Patients Reared as Girls." *Journal of Preventive Psychiatry* 1, no. 1 (1981): 17–27.

———, Reynolds Potter, and Clarice S. Stoll. "Sex Reannouncement in Hereditary Sex Deformity: Psychology and Sociology of Habilitation." *Social Science and Medicine* 3 (1969): 207–216.

Oliven, John F. *Sexual Hygiene and Pathology: A Manual for the Physician.* Philadelphia: J. B. Lippincott, 1955.

Ortner, Sherry B. "Is Female to Male as Nature Is to Culture?" In *Woman, Culture, and Society,* ed. Michelle Zimbalist Rosaldo and Louise Lamphere, 67–87. Stanford, Calif.: Stanford University Press, 1974.

Rohatgi, M. "Intersex Disorders: An Approach to Surgical Management." *Indian Journal of Pediatrics* 59 (1992): 523–530.

Roslyn, Joel J., Eric W. Fonkalsrud, and Barbara Lippe. "Intersex Disorders in Adolescents and Adults." *The American Journal of Surgery* 146 (July 1983): 138–144.

Rubin, Jeffrey, F. J. Provenzano, and Z. Luria. "The Eye of the Beholder: Parents' Views on Sex of Newborns." *American Journal of Orthopsychiatry* 44, no. 4 (1974): 512–519.

Slijper, F. M. E., S. L. S. Drop, J. C. Molenaar, and R. J. Scholtmeijer. "Neonates with Abnormal Genital Development Assigned the Female Sex: Parent Counseling." *Journal of Sex Education and Therapy* 20, no. 1 (1994): 9–17.

Smith, Richard W. "What Kind of Sex Is Natural?" In *The Frontiers of Sex Research,* ed. Vern Bullough, 103–111. Buffalo: Prometheus, 1979.

Stoller, Robert J. *Sex and Gender,* vol. 1. New York: J. Aronson, 1968.

READING *8* **Susan Stryker**

Transgender Feminism:
Queering the Woman Question[1]
First published in 2007

Many years ago, I paid a visit to my son's kindergarten room for parent-teacher night. Among the treats in store for us parents that evening was a chance to look at the *My Favorite Things* book that each child had prepared over the first few weeks of classes. Each page

was blank except for a pre-printed line that said "My favorite color is (blank)," or "My favorite food is (blank)," or "My favorite story is (blank)"; students were supposed to fill in the blanks with their favorite things and draw an accompanying picture. My son had filled the blanks and empty spaces of his book with many such things as "green," "pizza" and "*Good-night Moon*," but I was unprepared for his response to "My favorite animal is (blank)." His favorite animal was "yeast." I looked up at the teacher, who had been watching me in anticipation of this moment. "Yeast?" I said, and she, barely suppressing her glee, said, "Yeah. And when I asked why yeast was his favorite animal, he said, 'It just makes the category animal seem more interesting.'"

At the risk of suggesting that the category "woman" is somehow not interesting *enough* without a transgender supplement, which is certainly not my intent, I have to confess that there is a sense in which "woman," as a category of human personhood, is indeed, for me, *more* interesting when we include transgender phenomena within its rubric. The work required to encompass transgender within the bounds of womanhood takes women's studies, and queer feminist theorizing, in important and necessary directions. It takes us directly into the basic questions of the sex/gender distinction, and of the concept of a sex/gender system, that lie at the heart of Anglophone feminism. Once there, transgender phenomena ask us to follow basic feminist insights to their logical conclusion (biology is not destiny, and one is not born a woman, right?) And yet, transgender phenomena simultaneously threaten to refigure the basic conceptual and representational framework within which the category "woman" has been conventionally understood, deployed, embraced, and resisted.

Perhaps "gender," transgender tells us, is not related to "sex" in quite the same way that an apple is related to the reflection of a red fruit in the mirror; it is not a mimetic relationship. Perhaps "sex" is a category that, like citizenship, can be attained by the non-native residents of a particular location by following certain procedures. Perhaps gender has a more complex genealogy, at the level of individual psychobiography as well as collective sociohistorical process, than can be grasped or accounted for by the currently dominant binary sex/gender model of Eurocentric modernity. And perhaps what is to be learned by grappling with transgender concerns is relevant to a great many people, including nontransgendered women and men. Perhaps transgender discourses help us think in terms of embodied specificities, as *women's* studies has traditionally tried to do, while also giving us a way to think about gender as a system with multiple nodes and positions, as *gender* studies increasingly requires us to

do. Perhaps transgender studies, which emerged in the academy at the intersection of feminism and queer theory over the course of the last decade or so, can be thought of as one productive way to "queer the woman question."[2]

If we define "transgender phenomena" broadly as anything that disrupts or denaturalizes normative gender, and which calls our attention to the processes through which normativity is produced and atypicality achieves visibility, "transgender" becomes an incredibly useful analytical concept. What might "transgender feminism"—a feminism that focuses on marginalized gender expressions as well as normative ones—look like?

As an historian of the United States, my training encourages me to approach currently salient questions by looking at the past through new eyes. Questions that matter now, historians are taught to think, are always framed by enabling conditions that precede them. Thus, when I want to know what transgender feminism might be, I try to learn what it has already been. When I learned, for example, that the first publication of the post-WWII transgender movement, a short-lived early-1950s magazine called *Transvestia*, was produced by a group calling itself The Society for Equality in Dress,[3] I not only saw that a group of male transvestites in Southern California had embraced the rhetoric of first-wave feminism and applied the concept of gender equality to the marginalized topic of cross-dressing; I also came to think differently about Amelia Bloomer and the antebellum clothing reform movement. To the extent that breaking out of the conventional constrictions of womanhood is both a feminist and a transgender practice, what we might conceivably call transgender feminism arguably has been around since the first half of the nineteenth century.

Looking back, it is increasingly obvious that transgender phenomena are not limited to individuals who have "transgendered" personal identities. Rather, they are signposts that point to many different kinds of bodies and subjects, and they can help us see how gender can function as part of a more extensive apparatus of social domination and control. Gender as a form of social control is not limited to the control of bodies defined as "women's bodies," or the control of female reproductive capacities. Because genders are categories through which we recognize the personhood of others (as well as ourselves), because they are categories without which we have great difficulty in recognizing personhood at all, gender also functions as a mechanism of control when some loss of gender status is threatened, or when claims of membership in a gender are denied. Why is it considered a heterosexist put-down to call some lesbians mannish? Why, if a working-class woman does certain kinds of physically demanding labor, or if a middle-class woman surpasses a certain level of professional accomplishment, is their feminine respectability called into question? Stripping away gender, and misattributing gender, are practices of social domination, regulation, and control that threaten social abjection; they operate by attaching transgender stigma to various unruly bodies and subject positions, not just to "transgendered" ones.[4]

There is also, however, a lost history of feminist activism by self-identified transgender people waiting to be recovered. My own historical research into twentieth-century transgender communities and identities teaches me that activists on transgender issues were involved in multi-issue political movements in the 1960s and 1970s, including radical feminism. The ascendancy of cultural feminism and lesbian separatism by the mid-1970s—both of which cast transgender practices, particularly transsexuality, as reactionary patriarchal anachronisms—largely erased knowledge of this early transgender activism from feminist consciousness. Janice Raymond, in her outrageously transphobic book *The Transsexual Empire,* went so far as to suggest that "the problem of transsexualism would best be served by morally mandating it out of existence."[5] Even in this period, however, when identity politics effectively disconnected transgender feminism from the broader women's movement and before the queer cultural politics of the 1990s revitalized and expanded the transgender movement, it is possible to find startling historical episodes that compel us to reexamine what we think we know about the feminist history of the recent past. The Radical Queens drag collective in Philadelphia, for example, had a "sister house" relationship with a lesbian separatist commune during the early 1970s, and participated in mainstream feminist activism through involvement with the local chapter of N.O.W. In the later 1970s in Washington, D.C., secretive clubs for married heterosexual male cross-dressers began holding consciousness-raising sessions; they argued that to identify as feminine meant they were politically obligated to come out as feminists, speak out as transvestites, and work publicly for passage of the Equal Rights Amendment.[6]

In addition to offering a revisionist history of feminist activism, transgender issues also engage many of the foundational questions in the social sciences and life sciences as they pertain to feminist inquiry. The biological body, which is typically assumed to be a single organically unified natural object characterized by one and only one of two available sex statuses, is demonstrably no such thing. The so-called "sex of the body" is an interpretive fiction that narrates a complex amalgamation of gland secretions and reproductive organs, chromosomes and genes, morphological characteristics and physiognomic features. There are far more than two viable aggregations of sexed bodily being. At what cost, for what purposes, and through what means do we collapse this diversity of embodiment into the social categories "woman" and "man"? How does the psychical subject who forms in this material context become aware of itself, of its embodied situation, of its position in language, family, or society? How does it learn to answer to one or the other of the two personal pronouns "he" or "she," and to recognize "it" as a disavowed option that forecloses personhood? How do these processes vary from individual to individual, from place to place, and from time to time? These are questions of importance to feminism, usually relegated to the domains of biology and psychology, that transgender phenomena can help us think through. Transgender feminism gives us another axis, along with critical race studies or disability studies, to learn more about the ways in which bodily difference becomes the basis for socially constructed hierarchies, and helps us see in new ways how we are all inextricably situated, through the inescapable necessity of our own bodies, in terms of race, sex, gender, or ability.

When we look cross-culturally and trans-historically at societies, as anthropologists and sociologists tend to do, we readily see patterns of variations in the social organization of biological reproduction, labor, economic exchange, and kinship; we see a variety of culturally specific configurations of embodiment, identity, desire, social status, and social role. Which of these patterns do we call "gender," and which do we call "transgender"? The question makes sense only in reference to an unstated norm that allows us to distinguish between the two. To examine "transgender" cross-culturally and trans-historically is to articulate the masked assumptions that produce gender normativity in any given (time-bound and geographically constrained) context. To examine "transgender" is thus to risk decentering the privileged standpoint of white Eurocentric modernity. It is to denaturize and dereify the terms through which we ground our own genders, in order to confront the possibility of radically different ways of being in the world. This, too, is a feminist project.[7]

A third set of concerns that make transgender feminism interesting for women's studies is the extent to which "transgender," for more than a decade now, has served as a laboratory and proving ground for the various postmodern and poststructuralist critical theories that have transformed humanities scholarship in general over the past half century, and which have played a role in structuring the generational debates about "second wave" and "third wave" feminism. This is a debate in which I take an explicitly partisan position, largely in response to the utterly inexcusable level of overt transphobia in second-wave feminisim.

An unfortunate consequence of the second-wave feminist turn to an untheorized female body as the ultimate ground for feminist practice (which has to be understood historically in the context of reactionary political pressures that fragmented all sorts of movements posing radical threats to the established order and required them to find new, often ontological, bases for political resistance) was that it steered feminist analysis in directions that ill equipped it to engage theoretically with the emerging material conditions of social life within advanced capitalism that collectively have come to be called, more or less usefully, "postmodernity." The overarching tendency of second-wave feminism to couch its political analyses within moral narratives that link "woman" with "natural," "natural" with "good," "good" with "true," and "true" with "right" has been predicated on an increasingly non-utilitarian modernist epistemology. Within the representational framework of Eurocentric modernity, which posits gender as the superstructural sign of the material referent of sex, transgender practices have been morally condemned as unnatural, bad, false, and wrong, in that they fundamentally misalign the proper relationship between sex and gender. The people who engage in such misrepresentations can be understood only as duped or duplicitous, fools or enemies to be pitied or scorned. The failure of second-wave feminism to do justice to transgender issues in the 1970s; 1980s, and afterward is rooted in its more fundamental theoretical failure to recognize the conceptual limits of modernist epistemology.[8]

Transgender theorizing in third-wave feminism begins from a different—postmodern—epistemological standpoint which imagines new ways for sexed bodies to signify gender. Within the feminist third wave, and within humanities scholarship in general, transgender phenomena have come to constitute important evidence in recent arguments about essentialism and social construction, performativity and citationality, hybridity and fluidity, anti-foundationalist ontologies and non-referential epistemologies, the proliferation of perversities, the collapse of difference, the triumph of technology, the advent of posthumanism, and the end of the world as we know it. While it is easy to parody the specialized and sometimes alienating jargon of these debates, the issues at stake are quite large, involving as they do the actual as well as theoretical dismantling of power relations that sustain various privileges associated with normativity and injustices directed at minorities. Because these debates are irreducibly political, because they constitute an ideological landscape upon which material struggles are waged within the academy for research funds and promotions, for tenure and teaching loads, transgender phenomena have come to occupy a curiously strategic location in the working lives of humanities professionals, whether they like it or not. This brings me at last to the crux of my remarks.

For all the reasons I have suggested, transgender phenomena are *interesting* for feminism, women's studies, gender studies, sexuality studies, and so forth. But *interesting*, by itself, is not enough, when hard decisions about budgets and staffing have to be made in academic departments, priorities and commitments actualized through classroom allocations and affirmative action hiring goals. *Interesting* also has to be *important*, and transgender is rarely considered important. All too often transgender is thought to name only a largely irrelevant class of phenomena that occupy the marginal fringe of the hegemonic gender categories man and woman, or else it is seen as one of the later, minor accretions to the gay and lesbian movement, along with bisexual and intersexed. At best, transgender is considered a portent of a future that seems to await us, for good or ill. But it remains a canary in the cultural coal mine, not an analytical workhorse for pulling down the patriarchy and other associated social ills. As long as transgender is conceived as the fraction of a fraction of a fraction of a movement, as long as it is thought to represent only some inconsequential outliers in a bigger and more important set of data, there is very little reason to support transgender concerns at the institutional level. Transgender will always lose by the numbers. The transgender community is tiny. In (so-called) liberal democracies that measures political strength by the number of votes or the number of dollars, transgender doesn't count for much, or add up to a lot. But there is another way to think about the importance of transgender concerns at this moment in our history.

One measure of an issue's potential is not how many people directly identify with it, but rather, how many other issues it can be linked with in a productive fashion. How, in other words, can an issue be *articulated,* in the double sense of "articulation," meaning both "to bring into language," and "the act of flexibly conjoining."[9] Articulating a transgender politics is part of the specialized work that I do as an activist transgender intellectual. How many issues can I link together through my experience of the category transgender?

To the extent I am perceived as a woman (which is most of the time), I experience the same misogyny as other women, and to the extent that I am perceived as a man (which happens every now and then), I experience the homophobia directed at gay men—both forms of oppression, in my experience, being rooted in a cultural devaluation of the feminine. My transgender status, to the extent that it is apparent to others, manifests itself through the appearance of my bodily surface and my shape, in much the same way that race is constructed, in part, through visuality and skin, and in much the same way that the beauty system operates by privileging certain modes of appearance. My transsexual body is different from most other bodies, and while this difference does not impair me, it has been medicalized, and I am sometimes disabled by the social oppression that takes aim at the specific form of my difference. Because I am formally classified as a person with a psychopathology known as Gender Identity Disorder, I am subject to the social stigma attached to mental illness, and I am more vulnerable to unwanted medical-psychiatric interventions. Because changing personal identification documents is an expensive and drawn out affair, I have spent part of my life as an undocumented worker. Because identification documents such as drivers licenses and passports are coded with multiple levels of information, including previous names and "A.K.A.'s," my privacy, and perhaps my personal safety, are at risk every time

I drive too fast or cross a border. When I travel I always have to ask myself—will some aspect of my appearance, some bit of data buried in the magnetic strip on some piece of plastic with my picture on it, create suspicion and result in my detention? In this era of terror and security, we are all surveiled, we are all profiled, but some of us have more to fear from the state than others. Staying home, however, does not make me safer. If I risk arrest by engaging in non-violent demonstrations, or violent political protest, the incarceration complex would not readily accommodate my needs; even though I am a post-operative male-to-female transsexual, I could wind up in a men's prison where I would be at extreme risk of rape and sexual assault. Because I am transgendered, I am more likely to experience discrimination in housing, employment, and access to health care, more likely to experience violence. These are not abstract issues: I have lost jobs, and not been offered jobs, because I am transgendered. I have had doctors walk out of exam rooms in disgust; I have had more trouble finding and retaining housing because I am transgendered; I have had my home burglarized and my property vandalized, and I have been assaulted, because I am transgendered.

Let me recapitulate what I can personally articulate through transgender: misogyny, homophobia, racism, looksism, disability, medical colonization, coercive psychiatrization, undocumented labor, border control, state surveillance, population profiling, the prison-industrial complex, employment discrimination, housing discrimination, lack of health care, denial of access to social services, and violent hate crimes. These issues are my issues, not because I think it's chic to be politically progressive. These issues are my issues, not because I feel guilty about being white, highly educated, or a citizen of the United States. These issues are my issues because my bodily being lives in the space where these issues intersect. I articulate these issues when my mouth speaks the words that my mind puts together from what my body knows. It is by winning the struggles over these issues that my body as it is lived for me survives—or by losing them, that it will die. If these issues are your issues as well, then transgender needs to be part of your intellectual and political agenda. It is one of your issues.

I conclude now with some thoughts on yet another aspect of transgender articulation, the one mentioned in my title, which is how transgender issues articulate, or join together, feminist and queer projects. "Trans-" is troublesome for both LGBT communities and feminism, but the kind of knowledge that emerges from this linkage is precisely the kind of knowledge that we desperately need in the larger social arena.

Trans is not a "sexual identity," and therefore fits awkwardly in the LGBT rubric. That is, "transgender" does not describe a sexual orientation (like homosexual, bisexual, heterosexual, or asexual), nor are transgender people typically attracted to other transgender people in the same way that lesbians are attracted to other lesbians, or gay men to other gay men. Transgender status is more like race or class, in that it cuts across the categories of sexual identity.[10] Neither is transgender (at least currently, in Eurocentric modernity) an identity term like "woman" or "man" that names a gender category within a social system. It is a way of being a man or a woman, or a way of marking resistance to those terms. Transgender analyses of gender oppression and hierarchy, unlike more normative feminist analyses, are not primarily concerned with the differential operations of power upon particular identity categories that create inequalities within gender systems, but rather on how the system itself produces a multitude of possible positions that it then works to center or to marginalize.

Transgender practices and identities are a form of gender trouble, in that they call attention to contradictions in how we tend to think about gender, sex, and sexuality. But the transgender knowledges that emerge from these troubling contradictions, I want to argue, can yoke together queer and feminist projects in a way that helps break the impasse of identity politics that has so crippled progressive movements in the United States. Since the early 1970s, progressive politics have fragmented along identity lines practically to the point of absurdity. While it undoubtedly has been vital over the past few decades of movement history to enunciate the particularities of all our manifold forms of bodily being in the world, it is equally important that we now find new ways of articulating our commonalities without falling into the equally dead-end logic of totalizing philosophies and programs.

Transgender studies offers us one critical methodology for thinking through the diverse particularities of our embodied lives, as well for thinking through the commonalities we share through our mutual enmeshment in more global systems. Reactionary political movements have been very effective in telling stories about shared values—family, religion, tradition. We who work at the intersection of queer and feminist movements, we who have a different vision of our collective future, need to become equally adept in telling stories

that link us in ways that advance the cause of justice, and that hold forth the promise of happy endings for all our strivings. Bringing transgender issues into women's studies, and into feminist movement building, is one concrete way to be engaged in that important work.

While it is politically necessary to include transgender issues in feminist theorizing and organizing, it is not intellectually responsible, nor ethically defensible, to teach transgender studies in academic women's studies without being engaged in peer-to-peer conversations with various sorts of trans- and genderqueer people. Something crucial is lost when academically-based feminists fail to support transgender inclusion in the academic workplace. Genderqueer youth who have come of age after the "queer '90s" are now passing through the higher education system, and they increasingly fail to recognize the applicability of prevailing modes of feminist discourse for their own lives and experiences. How we each live our bodies in the world is a vital source of knowledge for us all, and to teach trans studies without being in dialog with trans people is akin to teaching race studies only from a position of whiteness, or gender studies only from a position of masculinity. Why is transgender not a category targeted for affirmative action in hiring, and valued the same way that racial diversity is valued? It is past time for feminists who have imagined that transgender issues have not been part of their own concerns to take a long, hard look in the mirror. What in their own constructions of self, their own experiences of gender, prevents their recognition of transgender people as being somehow like themselves—as people engaged in parallel, intersecting, and overlapping struggles, who are not fundamentally Other?

Transgender phenomena now present queer figures on the horizon of feminist visibility. Their calls for attention are too often received, however, as an uncomfortable solicitation from an alien and unthinkable monstrosity best left somewhere outside the village gates. But justice, when we first feel its claims upon us, typically points us toward a future we can scarcely imagine. At the historical moment when racial slavery in the United States at long last became morally indefensible, and the nation plunged into civil war, what did the future of the nation look like? When greenhouse gas emissions finally become equally morally indefensible, what shape will a post-oil world take? Transgender issues make similar claims of justice upon us all, and promise equally unthinkable transformations. Recognizing the legitimacy of these claims will change the world, and feminism along with it, in ways we can now hardly fathom. It's about time.

NOTES

1. This essay was first delivered as a keynote address at Third Wave Feminism, an international conference at the Institute for Feminist Theory and Research, University of Exeter, UK, July 25, 2002; and in revised form at the Presidential Session plenary on "Transgender Theory" at the National Women's Studies Association Annual Meeting, Oakland, California, June 17, 2006. Many of the ideas I present here have been worked out in greater detail in Stryker 1994, 1998, 2004, and 2006; see also Zalewski. For another account of the relationship between recent feminist scholarship and transgender issues, see Heyes.

2. Meyerowitz 2002, p. 179.

3. My thoughts on the role of transgender phenomena for understanding United States history in general are significantly indebted to Joanne Meyerowitz; see Meyerowitz 2006.

4. Raymond, 178. See also Hausman, 9–14, for an overview of cultural feminist critiques of transsexuality, and Billings

and Urban for a particularly cogent exposition and application of this approach.

5. Tommi Avicolli Mecca interview, November 19, 1998, in author's possession; see also Silverman and Stryker 2005, and Members of the Gay and Lesbian Historical Society 1998, for transgender involvement in progressive grassroots political activism in the San Francisco Bay Area in the 1960s.

6. See Blackwood and Wieringa, and Morgan and Towle, on cross-cultural studies of transgender phenomena.

7. For a post-structuralist, anti-foundationalist critique of second-wave feminism, see Butler.

8. The concept of "articulation" is taken from Laclau and Mouffe 2001.

9. See Gamson on the trouble transgender presents to identity movements.

10. On monstrosity and justice, see Sullivan 2006.

REFERENCES

Billings, Dwight B. and Thomas Urban. "The Sociomedical Construction of Transsexualism: An Interpretation and Critique." *Social Problems* 29 (1981), 266–282.

Blackwood, Evelyn and Saskia Wieringa, eds. *Female Desires: Same Sex Relations and Transgender Practices Across Cultures.* New York: Columbia University Press, 1999.

Butler, Judith. "Contingent Foundations: Feminism and the Question of 'Postmodernism.'" In Judith Butler and Joan Scott, eds., *Feminists Theorize the Political.* New York: Routledge, 1992. Pp. 3–21.

Gamson, Joshua. "Must Identity Movements Self-Destruct? A Queer Dilemma." *Social Problems* (1995) Vol. 42, no. 3, 390–406.

Heyes, Cressida. "Feminist Solidarity After Queer Theory: The Case of Transgender." *Signs* (2003) Vol. 28, no. 4, 1093–1120.

Laclau, Ernesto and Chantal Mouffe. *Hegemony and Socialist Strategy: Towards a Radical Democratic Politics.* London: Verso. 2001. Second Edition.

Mecca, Tommi Avicolli. Interview by Susan Stryker, November 19, 1998. Transcript in author's possession.

Members of the Gay and Lesbian Historical Society. "MTF Transgender Activism in San Francisco's Tenderloin: Commentary and Interview with Elliot Blackstone." *GLQ: A Journal of Lesbian and Gay Studies* 4:2 (1998), 349–372.

Meyerowitz, Joanne. *How Sex Changed: A History of Transsexuality in the United States.* Cambridge: Harvard University Press. 2002.

Meyerowitz, Joanne. "A New History of Gender." Paper delivered at Trans/Forming Knowledge: The Implications of Transgender Studies for Women's, Gender, and Sexuality Studies. University of Chicago, February 17,

2006. Podcast at http://humanities.uchicago.edu/orgs/cgs/Trans%20Conference%20Audio%20Files/Session%202_Intro_Meyerowitz.mp3. Accessed on June 27, 2006.

Morgan, Lynn M. and Evan B. Towle, "Romancing the Transgender Native: Rethinking the Use of the 'Third Gender' Concept." *GLQ: A Journal of Lesbian and Gay Studies* Vol. 8, no. 4, 469–497.

Raymond, Janice. *The Transsexual Empire: The Making of the She-Male.* New York: Teachers College Press. Reissued with new introduction, 1994; orig. pub. Boston: Beacon Press. 1979.

Silverman, Victor and Susan Stryker. *Screaming Queens: The Riot at Compton's Cafeteria.* Documentary film. (USA 2005).

Stryker, Susan. "(De)Subjugated Knowledges: An Introduction to Transgender Studies." In Susan Stryker and Stephen Whittle, eds., *The Transgender Studies Reader.* New York: Routledge. 2006. Pp. 1–18.

———. "My Words to Victor Frankenstein Above the Village of Chamounix: Performing Transgender Rage." *GLQ: A Journal of Lesbian and Gay Studies* 1:3 (1994), 237–254.

———. "Introduction: The Transgender Issue." *GLQ: A Journal of Lesbian and Gay Studies* 4:2 (1998), 145–158.

———. "Transgender Studies: Queer Theory's Evil Twin." *GLQ: A Journal of Lesbian and Gay Studies* 10:2 (Spring, 2004), 212–215.

Sullivan, Nikki. "Transmogrification: (Un)Becoming Others." In Susan Stryker and Stephen Whittle, eds., *The Transgender Studies Reader.* New York: Routledge. 2006. Pp. 552–564.

Zalewski, Marysia. "A Conversation with Susan Stryker." *International Feminist Journal of Politics* 5:1 (April 2003), 118–125.

Maxine Baca Zinn
Bonnie Thornton Dill

Theorizing Difference from Multiracial Feminism
First published in 1996

Women of color have long challenged the hegemony of feminisms constructed primarily around the lives of white middle-class women. Since the late 1960s, U.S. women of color have taken issue with unitary theories of gender. Our critiques grew out of the widespread concern about the exclusion of women of color from feminist scholarship and the misinterpretation of our experiences,[1] and ultimately "out of the very discourses, denying, permitting, and producing difference."[2] Speaking simultaneously from "within and against" *both* women's liberation *and* antiracist movements, we have insisted on the need to challenge systems of domination,[3] not merely as gendered subjects but as women whose lives are affected by our location in multiple hierarchies.

Recently, and largely in response to these challenges, work that links gender to other forms of domination is increasing. In this article, we examine this connection further as well as the ways in which difference and diversity infuse contemporary feminist studies. Our analysis draws on a conceptual framework that we refer to as "multiracial feminism."[4] This perspective is an attempt to go beyond a mere recognition of diversity and difference among women to examine structures of domination, specifically the importance of race in understanding the social construction of gender. Despite the varied concerns and multiple intellectual stances which characterize the feminisms of women of color, they share an emphasis on race as a primary force situating genders differently. It is the centrality of race, of institutionalized racism, and of struggles against racial oppression that link the various feminist perspectives within this framework. Together, they demonstrate that racial meanings offer new theoretical directions for feminist thought.

TENSIONS IN CONTEMPORARY DIFFERENCE FEMINISM

Objections to the false universalism embedded in the concept "woman" emerged within other discourses as well as those of women of color.[5] Lesbian feminists and postmodern feminists put forth their own versions of what Susan Bordo has called "gender skepticism."[6]

Many thinkers within mainstream feminism have responded to these critiques with efforts to contextualize gender. The search for women's "universal" or "essential" characteristics is being abandoned. By examining gender in the context of other social divisions and perspectives, difference has gradually become important—even problematizing the universal categories of "women" and "men." Sandra Harding expresses the shift best in her claim that "there are no gender relations *per se*, but only gender relations as constructed by and between classes, races, and cultures."[7]

Many feminists now contend that difference occupies center stage as *the* project of women studies today.[8] According to one scholar, "difference has replaced equality as the central concern of feminist theory."[9] Many have welcomed the change, hailing it as a major revitalizing force in U.S. feminist theory.[10] But if *some* priorities within mainstream feminist thought have been refocused by attention to difference, there remains an "uneasy alliance"[11] between women of color and other feminists.

If difference has helped revitalize academic feminisms, it has also "upset the apple cart" and introduced new conflicts into feminist studies.[12] For example, in a recent and widely discussed essay, Jane Rowland Martin argues that the current preoccupation with difference is leading feminism into dangerous traps. She fears that in giving privileged status to a predetermined set of analytic categories (race, ethnicity, and class), "we affirm the existence of nothing but difference." She asks, "How do we know that for us, difference does not turn on being fat, or religious, or in an abusive relationship?"[13]

We, too, see pitfalls in some strands of the difference project. However, our perspectives take their bearings from social relations. Race and class differences are crucial, we argue, not as individual characteristics (such as being fat) but insofar as they are primary organizing principles of a society which locates and positions groups within that society's opportunity structures.

Despite the much-heralded diversity trend within feminist studies, difference is often reduced to mere pluralism: a "live and let live" approach where principles of relativism generate a long list of diversities which begin with gender, class, and race and continue through a range of social structural as well as personal characteristics.[14] Another disturbing pattern, which bell hooks refers to as "the commodification of difference," is the representation of diversity as a form of exotica, "a spice, seasoning that livens up the dull dish that is mainstream white culture."[15] The major limitation of these approaches is the failure to attend to the power relations that accompany difference. Moreover, these approaches ignore the inequalities that cause some characteristics to be seen as "normal" while others are seen as "different" and thus, deviant.

Maria C. Lugones expresses irritation at those feminists who see only the *problem* of difference without recognizing *difference*.[16] Increasingly, we find that difference *is* recognized. But this in no way means that difference occupies a "privileged" theoretical status. Instead of using difference to rethink the category of women, difference is often a euphemism for women who differ from the traditional norm. Even in purporting to accept difference, feminist pluralism often creates a social reality that reverts to universalizing women:

> So much feminist scholarship assumes that when we cut through all of the diversity among women created by differences of racial classification, ethnicity, social class, and sexual orientation, a "universal truth" concerning women and gender lies buried underneath. But if we can face the scary possibility that no such certainty exists and that persisting in such a search will always distort or omit someone's experiences, with

what do we replace this old way of thinking? Gender differences and gender politics begin to look very different if there is no essential woman at the core.[17]

WHAT IS MULTIRACIAL FEMINISM?

A new set of feminist theories have emerged from the challenges put forth by women of color. Multiracial feminism is an evolving body of theory and practice informed by wide-ranging intellectual traditions. This framework does not offer a singular or unified feminism but a body of knowledge situating women and men in multiple systems of domination. U.S. multiracial feminism encompasses several emergent perspectives developed primarily by women of color: African Americans, Latinas, Asian Americans, and Native Americans, women whose analyses are shaped by their unique perspectives as "outsiders within"—marginal intellectuals whose social locations provide them with a particular perspective on self and society.[18] Although U.S. women of color represent many races and ethnic backgrounds—with different histories and cultures—our feminisms cohere in their treatment of race as a basic social division, a structure of power, a focus of political struggle, and hence a fundamental force in shaping women's and men's lives.

This evolving intellectual and political perspective uses several controversial terms. While we adopt the label "multiracial," other terms have been used to describe this broad framework. For example, Chela Sandoval refers to "U.S. Third World feminisms,"[19] while other scholars refer to "indigenous feminisms." In their theory text-reader, Alison M. Jagger and Paula M. Rothenberg adopt the label "multicultural feminism."[20]

We use "multiracial" rather than "multicultural" as a way of underscoring race as a power system that interacts with other structured inequalities to shape genders. Within the U.S. context, race, and the system of meanings and ideologies which accompany it, is a fundamental organizing principle of social relationships.[21] Race affects all women and men, although in different ways. Even cultural and group differences among women are produced through interaction within a racially stratified social order. Therefore, although we do not discount the importance of culture, we caution that cultural analytic frameworks that ignore race tend to view women's differences as the product of group-specific values and practices that often result in the marginalization of cultural groups which are then perceived as exotic expressions of a normative center. Our focus on race stresses the social construction of differently situated social groups and their varying degrees of advantage and power. Additionally, this emphasis on race takes on increasing political importance in an era where discourse about race is governed by color-evasive language[22] and a preference for individual rather than group remedies for social inequalities. Our analyses insist upon the primary and pervasive nature of race in contemporary U.S. society while at the same time acknowledging how race both shapes and is shaped by a variety of other social relations.

In the social sciences, multiracial feminism grew out of socialist feminist thinking. Theories about how political economic forces shape women's lives were influential as we began to uncover the social causes of racial ethnic women's subordination. But socialist feminism's concept of capitalist patriarchy, with its focus on women's unpaid (reproductive) labor in the home failed to address racial differences in the organization of reproductive labor. As feminists of color have argued, "reproductive labor has divided along racial as well as gender lines, and the specific characteristics have varied regionally and changed over time as capitalism has reorganized."[23] Despite the limitations of socialist feminism, this body of literature has been especially useful in pursuing questions about the interconnections among systems of domination.[24]

Race and ethnic studies was the other major social scientific source of multiracial feminism. It provided a basis for comparative analyses of groups that are socially and legally subordinated and remain culturally distinct within U.S. society. This includes the systematic discrimination of socially constructed racial groups and their distinctive cultural arrangements. Historically, the categories of African American, Latino, Asian American, and Native American were constructed as both racially and culturally distinct. Each group has a distinctive culture, shares a common heritage, and has developed a common identity within a larger society that subordinates them.[25]

We recognize, of course, certain problems inherent in an uncritical use of the multiracial label. First, the perspective can be hampered by a biracial model in which only African Americans and whites are seen as racial categories and all other groups are viewed through the prism of cultural differences. Latinos and Asians have always occupied distinctive places within the racial hierarchy, and current shifts in the composition of the U.S. population are racializing these groups anew.[26]

A second problem lies in treating multiracial feminism as a single analytical framework, and its principle [sic] architects, women of color, as an undifferentiated category. The concepts "multiracial feminism," "racial ethnic women," and "women of color" "homogenize quite different experiences and can falsely universalize experiences across race, ethnicity, sexual orientation, and age."[27] The feminisms created by women of color exhibit a plurality of intellectual and political positions. We speak in many voices, with inconsistencies that are born of our different social locations. Multiracial feminism embodies this plurality and richness. Our intent is not to falsely universalize women of color. Nor do we wish to promote a new racial essentialism in place of the old gender essentialism. Instead, we use these concepts to examine the structures and experiences produced by intersecting forms of race and gender.

It is also essential to acknowledge that race is a shifting and contested category whose meanings construct definitions of all aspects of social life.[28] In the United States it helped define citizenship by excluding everyone who was not a white, male property owner. It defined labor as slave or free, coolie or contract, and family as available only to those men whose marriages were recognized or whose wives could immigrate with them. Additionally, racial meanings are contested both within groups and between them.[29]

Although definitions of race are at once historically and geographically specific, they are also transnational, encompassing diasporic groups and crossing traditional geographic boundaries. Thus, while U.S. multiracial feminism calls attention to the fundamental importance of race, it must also locate the meaning of race within specific national traditions.

THE DISTINGUISHING FEATURES OF MULTIRACIAL FEMINISM

By attending to these problems, multiracial feminism offers a set of analytic premises for thinking about and theorizing gender. The following themes distinguish this branch of feminist inquiry.

First, multiracial feminism asserts that gender is constructed by a range of interlocking inequalities, what Patricia Hill Collins calls a "matrix of domination."[30] The idea of a matrix is that several fundamental systems work with and through each other. People experience race, class, gender, and sexuality differently depending upon their social location in the structures of race, class, gender, and sexuality. For example, people of the same race will experience race differently depending upon their location in the class structure as working class, professional managerial class, or unemployed; in the gender structure as female or male; and in structures of sexuality as heterosexual, homosexual, or bisexual.

Multiracial feminism also examines the simultaneity of systems in shaping women's experience and identity. Race, class, gender, and sexuality are not reducible to individual attributes to be measured and assessed for their separate contribution in explaining given social outcomes, an approach that Elizabeth Spelman calls "popbead metaphysics," where a woman's identity consists of the sum of parts neatly divisible from one another.[31] The matrix of domination seeks to account for the multiple ways that women experience themselves as gendered, raced, classed, and sexualized.

Second, multiracial feminism emphasizes the intersectional nature of hierarchies at all levels of social life. Class, race, gender, and sexuality are components of both social structure and social interaction. Women and men are differently embedded in locations created by these cross-cutting hierarchies. As a result, women and men throughout the social order experience different forms of privilege and subordination, depending on their race, class, gender, and sexuality. In other words, intersecting forms of domination produce *both* oppression *and* opportunity. At the same time that structures of race, class, and gender create disadvantages for women of color, they provide unacknowledged benefits for those who are at the top of these hierarchies—whites, members of the upper classes, and males. Therefore, multiracial feminism applies not only to racial ethnic women but also to women and men of all races, classes, and genders.

Third, multiracial feminism highlights the relational nature of dominance and subordination. Power is the cornerstone of women's differences.[32] This means that women's differences are *connected* in systematic ways.[33] Race is a vital element in the pattern of relations among minority and white women. As Linda Gordon argues, the very meanings of being a white woman in the United States have been affected by the existence of subordinated women of color: "They intersect in conflict and in occasional cooperation, but always in mutual influence."[34]

Fourth, multiracial feminism explores the interplay of social structure and women's agency. Within the constraints of race, class, and gender oppression, women create viable lives for themselves, their families, and their communities. Women of color have resisted and often undermined the forces of power that control them. From acts of quiet dignity and steadfast determination to involvement in revolt and rebellion, women struggle to shape their own lives. Racial oppression has been a common focus of the "dynamic of oppositional agency" of women of color. As Chandra Talpade Mohanty points out, it is the nature and organization of women's opposition which mediates and differentiates the impact of structures of domination.[35]

Fifth, multiracial feminism encompasses wide-ranging methodological approaches, and like other branches of feminist thought, relies on varied theoretical tools as well. Ruth Frankenberg and Lata Mani identify three guiding principles of inclusive feminist inquiry: "building complex analyses, avoiding erasure, specifying location."[36] In the last decade, the opening up of academic feminism has focused attention on social location in the production of knowledge. Most basically, research by and about marginalized women has destabilized what used to be considered as universal categories of gender. Marginalized locations are well suited for grasping social relations that remained obscure from more privileged vantage points. Lived experience, in other words, creates alternative ways of understanding the social world and the experience of different groups of women within it. Racially informed standpoint epistemologies have provided new topics, fresh questions, and new understandings of women and men. Women of color have, as Norma Alarcón argues, asserted ourselves as subjects, using our voices to challenge dominant conceptions of truth.[37]

Sixth, multiracial feminism brings together understandings drawn from the lived experiences of diverse and continuously changing groups of women. Among Asian Americans, Native Americans, Latinas, and Blacks are many different national cultural and ethnic groups. Each one is engaged in the process of testing, refining, and reshaping these broader categories in its own image. Such internal differences heighten awareness of and sensitivity to both commonalities and differences, serving as a constant reminder of the importance of comparative study and maintaining a creative tension between diversity and universalization.

DIFFERENCE AND TRANSFORMATION

Efforts to make women's studies less partial and less distorted have produced important changes in academic feminism. Inclusive thinking has provided a way to build multiplicity and difference into our analyses. This has led to the discovery that race matters for everyone. White women, too, must be reconceptualized as a category that is multiply defined by race, class, and other differences. As Ruth Frankenberg demonstrates in a study of whiteness among contemporary women, all kinds of social relations, even those that appear neutral, are, in fact, racialized. Frankenberg further complicates the very notion of a unified white identity by introducing issues of Jewish identity.[38] Therefore, the lives of women of color cannot be seen as a *variation* on a more general model of white American womanhood. The model of womanhood that feminist social science once held as "universal" is also a product of race and class.

When we analyze the power relations constituting all social arrangements and shaping women's lives in distinctive ways, we can begin to grapple with core feminist issues about how genders are socially constructed and constructed differently. Women's difference is built into our study of gender. Yet this perspective is quite far removed from the atheoretical pluralism implied in much contemporary thinking about gender.

Multiracial feminism, in our view, focuses not just on differences but also on the way in which differences and domination intersect and are historically and socially constituted. It challenges feminist scholars to go beyond the mere recognition and inclusion of difference to reshape the basic concepts and theories of our disciplines. By attending to women's social location based on race, class, and gender, multiracial feminism seeks to clarify the structural sources of diversity. Ultimately, multiracial feminism forces us to see privilege and subordination as interrelated and to pose such questions as: How do the existences and experiences of all people— women and men, different racial-ethnic groups, and different classes—shape the experiences of each other? How are those relationships defined and enforced through social institutions that are the primary sites for negotiating power within society? How do these differences contribute to the construction of both individual and group identity? Once we acknowledge that all women are affected by the racial order of society, then it becomes clear that the insights of multiracial feminism provide an analytical framework, not solely for understanding the experiences of women of color but for understanding *all* women, and men, as well.

NOTES

1. Maxine Baca Zinn, Lynn Weber Cannon, Elizabeth Higginbotham, and Bonnie Thornton Dill, "The Costs of Exclusionary Practices in Women's Studies," *Signs* 11 (winter 1986): 290–303.

2. Chela Sandoval, "U.S. Third World Feminism: The Theory and Method of Oppositional Consciousness in the Postmodern World," *Genders* (spring 1991): 1–24.

3. Ruth Frankenberg and Lata Mani, "Cross Currents, Crosstalk: Race, 'Postcoloniality,' and the Politics of Location," *Cultural Studies* 7 (May 1993): 292–310.

4. We use the term "multiracial feminism" to convey the multiplicity of racial groups and feminist perspectives.

5. A growing body of work on difference in feminist thought now exists. Although we cannot cite all the current work, the following are representative: Michèle Barrett, "The Concept of Difference," *Feminist Review* 26 (July 1987): 29–42; Christina Crosby, "Dealing with Difference," in *Feminists Theorize the Political*, ed. Judith Butler and Joan W. Scott (New York: Routledge, 1992), 130–43; Elizabeth Fox-Genovese, "Difference, Diversity, and Divisions in an Agenda for the Women's Movement," in *Color, Class, and Country: Experiences of Gender,* ed. Gay Young and Bette J. Dickerson (London: Zed Books, 1994), 232–48; Nancy A. Hewitt, "Compounding Differences," *Feminist Studies* 18 (summer 1992): 313–26; Maria C. Lugones, "On the Logic of Feminist Pluralism," in *Feminist Ethics*, ed. Claudia

Card (Lawrence: University of Kansas Press, 1991), 35–44; Rita S. Gallin and Anne Ferguson, "The Plurality of Feminism: Rethinking 'Difference,'" in *The Woman and International Development Annual* (Boulder: Westview Press, 1993), 3: 1–16; and Linda Gordon, "On Difference," *Genders* 10 (spring 1991): 91–111.

6. Susan Bordo, "Feminism, Postmodernism, and Gender Skepticism," in *Feminism/Postmodernism*, ed. Linda J. Nicholson (London: Routledge, 1990), 133–56.

7. Sandra G. Harding, *Whose Science? Whose Knowledge? Thinking from Women's Lives* (Ithaca: Cornell University Press, 1991), 179.

8. Crosby, 131.

9. Fox-Genovese, 232.

10. Faye Ginsberg and Anna Lowenhaupt Tsing, Introduction to *Uncertain Terms, Negotiating Gender in American Culture,* ed. Faye Ginsberg and Anna Lowenhaupt Tsing (Boston: Beacon Press, 1990), 3.

11. Sandoval, 2.

12. Sandra Morgan, "Making Connections: Socialist-Feminist Challenges to Marxist Scholarship," in *Women and a New Academy: Gender and Cultural Contexts*, ed. Jean F. O'Barr (Madison: University of Wisconsin Press, 1989), 149.

13. Jane Rowland Martin, "Methodological Essentialism, False Difference, and Other Dangerous Traps," *Signs* 19 (spring 1994): 647.

14. Barrett, 32.

15. bell hooks, *Black Looks: Race and Representation* (Boston: South End Press, 1992), 21.

16. Lugones, 35–44.

17. Patricia Hill Collins, Foreword to *Women of Color in U.S. Society,* ed. Maxine Baca Zinn and Bonnie Thornton Dill (Philadelphia: Temple University Press, 1994), xv.

18. Patricia Hill Collins, "Learning from the Outsider Within: The Sociological Significance of Black Feminist Thought," *Social Problems* 33 (December 1986): 514–32.

19. Sandoval, 1.

20. Alison M. Jagger and Paula S. Rothenberg, *Feminist Frameworks: Alternative Theoretical Accounts of the Relations Between Women and Men,* 3d ed. (New York: McGraw-Hill, 1993).

21. Michael Omi and Howard Winant, *Racial Formation in the United States: From the 1960s to the 1980s,* 2d ed. (New York: Routledge, 1994).

22. Ruth Frankenberg, *The Social Construction of Whiteness: White Women, Race Matters* (Minneapolis: University of Minnesota Press, 1993).

23. Evelyn Nakano Glenn, "From Servitude to Service Work: Historical Continuities in the Racial Division of Paid Reproductive Labor," *Signs* 18 (autumn 1992): 3. See also Bonnie Thornton Dill, "Our Mothers' Grief: Racial-Ethnic Women and the Maintenance of Families," *Journal of Family History* 13, no. 4 (1988): 415–31.

24. Morgan, 146.

25. Maxine Baca Zinn and Bonnie Thornton Dill, "Difference and Domination," in *Women of Color in U.S. Society,* 11–22.

26. See Omi and Winant, 53–76, for a discussion of racial formation.

27. Margaret L. Andersen and Patricia Hill Collins, *Race, Class, and Gender: An Anthology* (Belmont, Calif.: Wadsworth, 1992), xvi.

28. Omi and Winant.

29. Nazli Kibria, "Migration and Vietnamese American Women: Remaking Ethnicity," in *Women of Color in U.S. Society,* 247–61.

30. Patricia Hill Collins, *Black Feminist Thought: Knowledge, Consciousness, and the Politics of Empowerment* (Boston: Unwin Hyman, 1990).

31. Elizabeth Spelman, *Inessential Women: Problems of Exclusion in Feminist Thought* (Boston: Beacon Press, 1988), 136.

32. Several discussions of difference make this point. See Baca Zinn and Dill, 10; Gordon, 106; and Lynn Weber, in the "Symposium on West and Fenstermaker's 'Doing Difference,'" *Gender & Society* 9 (August 1995): 515–19.

33. Glenn, 10.

34. Gordon, 106.

35. Chandra Talpade Mohanty, "Cartographies of Struggle: Third World Women and the Politics of Feminism," in *Third World Women and the Politics of Feminism,* ed. Chandra Talpade Mohanty, Ann Russo, and Lourdes Torres (Bloomington: Indiana University Press, 1991), 13.

36. Frankenberg and Mani, 306.

37. Norma Alarcón, "The Theoretical Subject(s) of *This Bridge Called My Back* and Anglo-American Feminism," in *Making Face, Making Soul, Haciendo Caras: Creative and Critical Perspectives by Women of Color,* ed. Gloria Anzaldúa (San Francisco: Aunt Lute, 1990), 356.

38. Frankenberg. See also Evelyn Torton Beck, "The Politics of Jewish Invisibility," *NWSA Journal* (fall 1988): 93–102.

READING *10*   **Denise A. Segura**
Patricia Zavella

Gender in the Borderlands
First published in 2011

A border is a dividing line, a narrow strip along a steep edge. A borderland is a vague and undetermined place created by the emotional residue of an unnatural boundary. It is in a constant state of transition. The prohibited and forbidden are its inhabitants (Anzaldúa 1987, 3).

Borderlands theory offers new ways of exploring relationships of power and domination, resistance and agency among women and men hitherto cast as marginalized "others." Research utilizing borderlands theory has been increasing rapidly. One of the most influential thinkers about borderlands, the Chicana feminist lesbian poet and theorist Gloria Anzaldúa, argues that border-lands have multiple meanings (1987). Literally, the bor-derlands include the geopolitical space around the U.S.-Mexico border, where there is a great deal of move-ment of people, products and ideas. Borderlands also refer to how individuals cope with social inequalities based on racial, gender, class and/or sexual differences, as well as spiritual transformation and psychic processes of exclusion and identification—of feeling "in between" cultures, languages, or places. Borderlands are spaces where the "the prohibited and forbidden" marginalized voice their identities and resistance. All of these social, political, spiritual and emotional transitions transcend geopolitical space or national borders. In an often-cited statement, Anzaldúa writes, "The U.S.-Mexico border *es una herida abierta* (an open wound) where the Third World grates against the first and bleeds. And before a scab forms it hemorrhages again, the lifeblood of two worlds merging to form a third country—a border cul-ture. Borders are set up to define the places that are safe and unsafe, to distinguish us from them" (1987, 5).

We argue that there are two major approaches to borderlands studies relevant to feminist research. Within the social sciences, borderlands studies focus on transnational social formations, on how migrants engage in economic, political or socio-cultural activi-ties that transcend national borders and "deterritorial-ize," or span international boundaries. Increasingly ethnographers who use this approach conduct field research in multiple sites—"sending" and "receiving" communities—so as to concretize how sustained deter-ritorialized processes unfold. A second approach to borderlands within cultural studies "emphasize the ways in which identity formation is linked to multiple sites, both real and imagined, such that new hybrid-ized and creolized identity forms emerge. According to this perspective, identities shift and are negotiated in responses to forces from above and below and there-fore are never fixed or bounded" (Levitt 2001, 237–8). Both approaches provide insight on the multifaceted changes that women negotiate daily in the border-lands, how they adapt to structural transformations, contest or create representations of their identities in light of their marginality, and give voice to their com-plex human agency or what we refer to as "subjective transnationalism." Drawing on the work on transna-tionalism, feminist studies, and Chicana/o Studies,[1] we argue that women are constructing their identities in spaces "located in the interstices between the domi-nant national and cultural systems of both the United

States and Mexico" (Gutiérrez 1999, 488) as they live, work and play in communities on both sides of the border. Women in the borderlands construct a new dia-sporic subjectivity that may be oppositional and trans-formative as they reflect on their experiences of migration, settlement, work, or social reproduction that are affected by globalization and structural vio-lence. Subjective transnationalism reflects the experi-ence of feeling "at home" in more than one geographic location where identity construction is deterritorial-ized as part of a borderlands mixture of shifting race-ethnic boundaries and gendered transitions in a global economy. Conversely, subjective transnationalism includes feelings that one is neither from "here" nor from "there," not at home anywhere.

As a process subjective transnationalism occurs wherever "the Third World grates against the first" and transcends any one geographic space. Global and intra-national migrations provide a potent setting for new social forms as women's market activities increase accompanied by their negotiations for an enhanced social space in households, local communities and the state. These negotiation processes often contest patriar-chal ways of being as women increasingly engage in productive as well as reproductive labor. Even if this labor is viewed by more privileged "first world" inhab-itants as "low value and semi-skilled," women's par-ticipation in the peripheral sectors of the economy can facilitate a critique of the exploitative processes that characterize global economic transactions as vividly demonstrated by the rise of labor activism, the increase in the numbers of women utilizing social services, the growing participation of women's involvement in their children's schooling, and the development of economic strategies associated with the rise of female-headed households. While households headed by women are typically characterized by economic marginality, women increasingly demonstrate a preference for reli-ance on the fruits of their own labor when a partner-ship (either male or female) lowers the quality of their lives, creating a heightened subjectivity about their constraints and options. Borderlands approaches explore these negotiations which contextualize wom-en's lives across and within national borders.

U.S.-MEXICO INTEGRATION

The social, economic and cultural nexus between the United States and Mexico has inspired significant bor-derlands theorizing. The integration of the U.S. and

Mexican economies, which pre-date the passage of the North American Free Trade Agreement (NAFTA) in 1994 but accelerated once the two countries became formally allied, reflects the long-standing, complex relations between both societies. Historically, production has been binational with Mexico serving as the reserve army of labor for U.S. agriculture, manufacturing and service sectors (Palerm and Urquiola 1993). Over time, however, this relationship has changed. Increasingly social reproduction is taking place in the United States as more women migrate and form families here, whereas production relocates south as U.S. jobs are "outsourced." These changing economic relations frame the context for the emergence of borderlands politics facilitated by dual nationality, in social formations (such as binational families), and through transculturation—cultural expressions and identities that transcend the border (Paredes 1993).

At the macro level, the increasing interdependence of world economies, communications systems, and popular cultures are reshaping local and global political and economic dynamics. Remittances sent to Latin America by U.S.-based Latinas and Latinos now constitute one of the largest sources of capital to the area. Under NAFTA and other trade agreements, economic, social, environmental, and agricultural policies carried out by the United States now affect Mexico much more directly than in the past. At the same time, Mexico's economic and political strategies, particularly those related to migration, have consequences in the United States. For example, recent transformations in biomedical-environmental policies that have resulted in greater availability of more affordable AIDS treatments and additional regulation of genetically modified agricultural and medicinal products affect those on either side of the U.S.-Mexico border. The binational dialogue from these transformations is becoming more challenging in the post-9/11 era where calls for greater border controls and regulation of international migration are restructuring relations of scientific and cultural exchange between the United States and Mexico.

A key feature of contemporary U.S.-Mexico economic interdependence is women's growing mobility. More and more women migrate within Mexico and from Mexico to the United States. This development mirrors global migrations happening in other parts of the world, e.g., Filipina domestic workers to the Middle East, Hong Kong, Malaysia and Singapore (Guevarra 2010; Parreñas 2001, 2005). Global migrations exact particular regional effects in both countries,

including women's incorporation into the labor market and the feminization of specific occupations. With these changes come a number of contradictions, such as limited occupational mobility for women despite their higher educational attainment. This development, coupled with the growth of households headed by women, enlarges their numbers among the working poor. These global, regional, and local changes have far-reaching consequences for women's work experiences, their family lives, their social identities, and their cultural expressions.

Sociologist Shawn Kanaiaupuni (2000, 1316) argues that "migration as a response to macro level conditions is shaped by the relative opportunity structures for men and women in places of origin and destination." She suggests that migration from Mexico has been predominantly male because of three factors: patriarchal social norms, the presence of children, and occupational segregation. Patriarchal norms deem men to be breadwinners, so if the local employment structure does not provide adequate wages, the conditions favor male migration. The interplay between marital status, the presence of children, and the local opportunity structure is gendered. The presence of children influences men to migrate if they do not earn enough income to support their families in Mexico whereas this is not that direct among women. In general, the presence of children often makes geographical mobility difficult, and the cost of raising a family is lower in Mexico than in the United States; both factors discourage women from migrating. "Hence married women with children are more likely to remain in the sending communities while male family members migrate" (1318). More important predictors of women's migration include level of education, prior marital status, and the strength of their social networks in the United States. Women who are no longer in a conjugal relationships are more likely to migrate even if they had children and particularly if they have strong social ties in the United States. Women with higher levels of education also tend to migrate given the low returns on their human capital investments in Mexico vis-à-vis men (Reyes 1997).

In addition to these economic and social considerations in Mexico, U.S. immigration policies have strongly influenced gendered migration patterns, beginning with the Bracero Program (1942–1964), which constructed social networks for sharing knowledge about resources for migration but did not provide opportunities for women to work in the United States.

The 1965 Immigration law emphasized family reunification, which usually meant that wives and children of male migrants could legally join them. The Immigration Reform and Control Act of 1986 (IRCA), which offered amnesty to migrants who document their residency and employment, presented disadvantages to women who largely worked in the informal sector, and favored men, who were more likely to have formal employment and were thus able to document their status.

Despite such formidable barriers, migration by women (both documented and undocumented) has grown steadily. Between 1910–1939—an era that included both the Mexican Revolution and the Great Depression, which were characterized by significant Mexican repatriations—women constituted 5 percent of migrants from Mexico; that figure increased to 7 percent in the period between 1940–1964 (the era of the Bracero Program), and climbed to 20 percent after 1965, following the implementation of the 1965 Immigration Reform Act (Durand 1992, 121). During these same periods, the percentage of women who migrated within Mexico—one indicator of possible future transnational migration—increased from 15 percent, to 16 percent, to 27 percent, respectively (121). Thus, women were part of larger demographic changes in the migrant stream and in the political-economic forces, which pushed Mexicans to leave their home regions, attracted to jobs elsewhere (Durand 1992; Cardenas and Flores 1986).

More recently, migration to the United States has included even higher proportions of women. Since 1970, at least 6.8 million Mexican migrants have entered the United States with or without documents: "The percentage of women among documented migrants fluctuated around 46 percent before IRCA (1980–1986), during the post IRCA transition period (1987–1992), and after IRCA (1993 onward)" (Massey, Durand, and Malone 2002, 134). Other sources estimate that 57 percent of authorized Mexican migrants were women (Cerrutti & Massey 2001). Alongside the growth of documented female migration was an increase in the propensity for undocumented women to migrate. Prior to IRCA, undocumented women comprised about one quarter of all migrants. During the transition and post-IRCA periods, that figure rose to one third (Massey, Durand and Malone 2002, 134). At the same time, more indigenous Mexicans, including women, joined the migrant stream (Fox and Rivera-Salgado 2004; Gil-García 2010). These demographic changes point to the feminization of migration from Mexico. Other work concurs that global migration is increasingly feminized (UNFPA 2006; Castles and Miller 1998).

Clearly, we need to understand better the nature of this shift in the gender composition of transnational migrants and what it means for women's work and family experiences as well as women's identities and cultural expressions in the United States and in Mexico. Once women enter the migrant stream, they find themselves in the borderlands between the United States and Mexico with important political implications.

THE POLITICS OF TRANSNATIONAL MIGRATION

In the political realm, migration from Latin America has been a flashpoint in the United States, particularly visible in California where 40 percent of all Mexicans reside (Fry 2002). Anti-immigrant proponents often assume that all Latinas/os—whether citizens or authorized permanent residents—are migrants and therefore "illegal" (De Genova 2002). A series of propositions have been passed or proposed that aim to control the effects of a growing Latina/o presence: Proposition 63, "English as the Official Language of California," passed in 1986, was intended to preserve and enhance the role of English as the state's common language and includes a provision to allow anyone living or doing business in the state to sue state or local governments for actions that diminish this principle; Proposition 187, "Save Our State," passed in 1994, aimed to prevent "illegal aliens" from using health care, public education and other social services, but it was nullified by the courts as unconstitutional; Proposition 209, the anti-affirmative action "California Civil Rights Initiative," passed in 1996, amended the state constitution to prohibit public institutions from considering race, ethnicity, or sex in all programs and employment; Proposition 227, the anti-bilingual education "English for the Children" initiative, passed in 1998, requires a one-year transition to English language instruction for all school-children; Proposition 54, the so-called "Racial Privacy Initiative," defeated on 7 October 2003, would have disallowed the collecting of official statistics by race, ethnicity, or national origin. (The defeat was seen as a major victory for those who value monitoring discrimination against racial groups and their institutional under-representation.) These propositions mobilized citizens who felt they were defending the state, as well as activists who opposed racist exclusionary legislation.

At the national level, Congress passed legislation that affirmed some of the restrictionist sentiments in California's Proposition 187. The "Illegal Immigration Reform and Immigrant Responsibility Act," passed in 1996, restricted access to healthcare, except for emergency care, for undocumented migrants and further entrenched the border as a militarized zone with increased border patrols and technology. In addition, labor policy became integrally linked to migration issues and patterns of investment. This relationship was evident in the 2004 U.S. electoral season, during which various candidates promoted or opposed support for "offshore" investment in Latin America by U.S. corporations, for a guest worker program, or for making driver's licenses available for undocumented immigrants (Vieth and Chen 2004). More recently, SB1070 (the "Support Law Enforcement and Safe Neighborhoods Act") passed by the Arizona state legislature and signed into law by Governor Jan Brewer in June 2010, authorized local police to check the resident status of anyone suspected of being in the United States illegally. A temporary injunction has put key portions of this law "on hold" and bolsters the argument advanced by the Obama administration that a state cannot preempt federal authority on the matter of immigration. SB1070 and similar proposals being considered across the country reflect "hysterical nativism" and will likely intensify racial profiling by law enforcement agencies (*The Economist*, April 2, 2010). Such laws are particularly worrisome to Latinas and Latinos, 57 percent of whom worry that they, or someone they know will be deported (Lopez and Minushkin 2008). Analyzing these political mobilizations and narrow definitions of citizenship comprise borderlands projects that critique nativist ideologies and practices that are simultaneously raced, gendered, and classed.

For politically underrepresented and racially subordinated groups like Mexicans, cultural expressions—literature or film, popular music, visual arts such as murals or folk art, performance arts like dance or theater—provide essential social spaces and a sense of belonging within their local communities and in the larger, dominant society (Aparicio 2004; Iglesias and Fregoso 1998). In particular, popular culture provides important sites for contesting nativism and exploring issues such as bilingualism, immigration, and racism. In the context of globalization, migration, and marginalization as experienced by many migrants and citizens, cultural expressions are often key sites for expressing language, rituals, and cultural memories, and for affirming their identities.

All of these developments have an impact in the United States, leading to significant social, economic, and cultural transformations, including the growth in the Chicana/o and Latina/o populations. The 2000 census recorded 37.4 million Latinas/os in the U.S. Mexicans constituted 67 percent of the Latinas/os, who made up 13.7 percent of the total population. According to those numbers, Latinas/os had become the largest racial-ethnic minority group in the U.S. (U.S. Census Bureau 2003).[2] The increase in the numbers of Chicanas/os and Latinas/os in the United States is most pronounced in California where they comprise one-third of the most populous state in the nation and in Texas, which is 31 percent Latina/o (Texas State Data Center 1998).

In tandem with increased migration to the United States, policies have shifted in Mexico toward what Jorge Durand (2004) calls "shared responsibility." Vicente Fox, while a Presidential candidate, made several highly publicized trips to campaign in the United States. After he was elected President, Fox created the short-lived Presidential Office for Mexicans Abroad and promulgated a discourse about migrants being "heroes to the nation," a discourse that, while controversial, signaled a change in how Mexicans regard those who leave.[3] Mexico extended dual nationality to Mexicans who become American citizens as well as to their children (Levitt and de la Dehesa 2003). The Mexican congress passed legislation to enable citizens living abroad to vote in Mexican elections, thus joining 60 other nations that allow migrants to vote in their former countries' elections (Thompson 2005). The Mexican government also increased funding to hometown associations that channel U.S.-based resources in economic development projects in Mexico and often matches what they contribute through a program called "Three for One." Some of the federations of hometown associations, especially those formed by indigenous migrants, are active in the United States and Mexico and provide a source of identity and political activity (Fox and Rivera-Salgado 2004). Feminists are major contributors to the debates about politics, ethnic groups, classes and party affiliations in Mexico (Biron 1996).

One important consequence of increased migration to the United States is growing attention to Mexican women's fertility. Latinas overall have relatively higher fertility than Whites, African Americans, or Asians and Pacific Islanders (Johnson, Hill, and Heim 2001). In part, this reflects the larger number of Latinas in their childbearing years. Specifically, 51 percent of all Latinas are between 14–44 years old compared to 42 percent of white women (U.S. Census Bureau 2000). Furthermore, foreign-born Latinas have higher fertility rates than U.S.-born Latinas, a disparity that the demographer Hans Johnson and his colleagues (2001) attribute partially to IRCA, which provided amnesty for predominantly young men who then brought over their spouses and began families. Family reunification created a baby boom, which is predicted to be of short duration. Indeed, fertility rates for foreign-born Latinas declined between 1990 and 1997. What is critical for the quality of life of Latinas/os in the United States is that women's reproduction is seen as a threat to the racial purity and well-being of the nation (Chavez 2004; Inda 2002).

Surprisingly little attention has been paid to the *decline* in the fertility of the largest Latina/o group, namely Mexican women (Chavez 2004). In the early 1970's, the size of Mexican American families averaged 4.4 persons, as opposed to 3.5 persons for non-Latinas/os (Chavez 2004, 176). In order to examine whether Mexican women's fertility continued to decline, Leo Chavez undertook a survey in 1992–93 of 803 Latinas and 422 white women that revealed that the fertility rate for U.S.-born Mexicans was 1.81 and for White women was 1.27. Because reproduction is 2.0, these rates represent zero population growth for both groups. Fertility has also been declining in Mexico for several decades. In 1970, the lifetime number of children per woman was 7.5; that figure declined to 4.4 by 1980, and to 3.4 by 1990, and 2.4 by 2000 (Hirsch 1998, 540–1; Chavez 2004, 175). Jennifer Hirsch (2003) attributes this decline to changing beliefs about marriage, delays in bearing children, the spacing of births, and increased contraceptive use—processes found in the United States as well. Moreover, U.S.-born, second-and third-generation women of Mexican origin have lower fertility rates than either migrants or U.S. white women. Despite these shifts in fertility, Mexican women's reproduction is often represented as "out of control" and as largely responsible for Mexicans' low socio-economic status (Chavez 2004).

Changes in the political, economic and social environments in both countries alongside the changing character of fertility, employment, and migration have led to polarized debates about the appropriate constitution of national communities as well as the role of migrants in both nations (Chavez 2001, 2004). Mexican women are at the center of such immigration debates. Their reproductive bodies are represented as hostile and foreign, threatening the social safety net and thus the well-being of the nation. Such representations constitute a form of social violence (Chavez 1997, 2004; Inda 2002). Negative representations of Mexican migrants, women in particular, mask the state-sanctioned structural violence that pushes subjects into the migrant stream as well as the social violence that migrants negotiate in everyday life (Flores and Valdez Curiel 2009). Further, women's economic contributions, creative adaptation strategies, cultural expressions, and everyday contestations remain largely unrecognized in scholarship and in the media.

Mexican women have become key contributors to the "new" economy, which is characterized by flexible accumulation, borderless organizations of work and the expansion of low-wage jobs, all of which are consequences of structural violence. Disruptions in family life, brought on by migration and participation in the labor market, present challenges for women who have come to the United States in search of better lives and who cope with social violence in migrant communities and even within families. These changes have contributed to the development of new social identities and cultural formations that span national borders. Mexican women thus are situated within intersections of political, economic, and social transformations that the discourses on immigration, globalization, and Latin American and Chicano studies have approached in different ways.

PARALLEL CONVERSATIONS

Along with the feminization of migrant streams, the increased incorporation of women into the labor force has been approached using different analytical frameworks in Mexico and in the United States. Current research on women workers in Mexico demonstrates that the labor market is becoming feminized, particularly in the agricultural sector, as more women are recruited for seasonal jobs such as weeding, planting, and occasionally even harvesting (Flores 1995; González Montes and Salles 1995). Growing sources of women's employment include industrial homework in electronics (expanding as firms outsource production), manufacturing textiles or other products, and street vending. Women's employment in these sectors is changing household dynamics as women age or support families on their own. Sex work remains highly stigmatized even as women attempt to gain more control over the conditions of such work (Lamas 1996; Castañeda, Ortiz, Allen, García and Hernández-Avila 1996).

The Border Industrialization Program (BIP), initiated in the 1960s, attracted more women to the U.S.-Mexico border, one of the largest crossing points in the world, and exploited gendered dynamics. The BIP accelerated the development of maquiladoras (factories that produce for export), which targeted women as workers for "women's work" that required "nimble fingers" and docility, as well as participation in gendered social activities such as beauty pageants (Salzinger 2003; Cravey 1998). Since the factories at first predominantly employed women, they stimulated men's migration to the United States (Fernández-Kelly 1983). After restructuring in the 1980s, the factories employed more men as well (De la O Martínez 1995; Broughton 2008). The BIP stimulated urbanization in border "twin cities"—Juarez and El Paso, San Diego and Tijuana, for example—which grew tremendously. The BIP furthered the integration of the United States and Mexican economies and the fluidity of the border, generating frequent crossings for visiting, shopping, entertainment, and the like. In the late 1980s, the Reagan administration launched a War Against Drugs to counter the national security threat presented by the flow of drugs, particularly cocaine, heroin and marijuana, across the U.S.-Mexico border through personal possession or as cargo. Increasing attention to narco-trafficking stimulated violence within the border region, which continues to plague both countries.

The border is a region where power structures of capitalism, patriarchy, and racialization intersect, generating structural violence that is most visible in the deaths of migrants who cross the border and in the rise of *colonias*, communities characterized by underdeveloped or substandard housing, which can be found on either side of the border (Téllez 2008; Fregoso 2003). Structural violence is also apparent in the increase of female-headed households that live in conditions of poverty despite employment and in exploitative working conditions on either side of the border (Cravey 1998; Coronado 2006). Chant (1991, 1994, 2007) finds that households and labor markets are linked and that women are more likely to enter the labor market after becoming heads of households and when there is increased labor demand.

Excellent case studies of women working in the maquiladoras indicate that profound changes are occurring as women face the challenges of physically taxing, gendered work and polluted work sites where women are subject to sexual harassment and surveillance (Fernandez-Kelly 1983; De la O Martinez 1995; Salzinger 2003; Muñoz 2008). Similar to processes occurring in the United States, women's incorporation into the labor force in Mexico draws on and often reinforces traditional ideological notions that women's place should be within the home despite her contributions to household income (Fowler-Salamini and Vaughan 1994; González de la Rocha 1984). Furthermore, Mexican families are adapting varied forms, ranging from extended households to single families, to cope with women's labor market participation (González Montes and Tuñon 1997). Like women workers elsewhere, Mexican women living in poverty construct complicated survival strategies through the use of social exchange among social networks and fictive kin, including what anthropologist Carlos Vélez-Ibáñez (1983) calls "rituals of marginality" whereby they confront the conditions of poverty through organized resistance at work sites or within their communities.

Within labor markets and work sites segregated by race and gender in the United States, Chicanas and Latinas are also concentrated in "women's jobs," with migrants at the bottom of the occupational structure in the secondary labor market (Catzanarite 2000; Zavella 2002; Muñoz 2008; Mauricio Gaston Institute 1994). These jobs are often nonunion, pay minimum wages, have few benefits, are seasonal and/or subject to displacement (e.g. in agriculture or garments), and often require relatively low training or educational levels although the work itself may be quite difficult (Ruiz 1998; Ibarra 2000, 2002; Ehrenreich and Hochschild 2002). Those working in the informal sector (e.g. domestic workers, day care providers) are subject to irregular work hours, little oversight over the conditions of work, and little recourse if their employers do not pay or underpay. Even workers who are located in unionized sectors (e.g. food processing) find that unions are often unresponsive to their particular needs, and union democracy struggles have been waged over translating contracts and union meetings into Spanish, and electing representatives who understand the needs of the workers (Flores 1997; Lamphere and Zavella 1997).

Despite the passage of equal employment opportunity laws and increases in educational attainment by Mexican women born in the United States, patterns of occupational segregation continue. Analysts suggest that this is due to a combination of structural changes and vulnerabilities in human capital. Chicanas/os and Latinas/os often reside in regions where economic restructuring has dismantled industries such as steel or auto manufacturing which provided well-paying, stable jobs and shifted to other manufacturing sectors (garments, electronics) that hire predominantly migrant women at low wages (Ortiz 1996; Bonacich and Appelbaum 2000; Zentgraf 2005). Indeed, some argue that migrant labor, particularly that of women, is a central feature of a flexible, global economy (Sassen 1998, 2002; Morales and Bonilla 1993). Like electronics, garments and food processing industries have undergone outsourcing to the Third World, and to the extent that they remain in the United States, these industries increasingly rely on migrant labor forces, especially women. When downsizing occurs, those who have recently moved into jobs or up the job ladder (particularly women) are vulnerable to lay offs, long-term unemployment, and stress. These structural processes are fueled by increased immigration and by employers who prefer migrants, who often do not speak English, have few skills that are marketable here (although they may be well-trained in their home country), or are undocumented.

There is a clear relationship between occupational segregation in low-wage jobs and poverty. Mexicans have disproportionately high rates of poverty, and contrary to expectations of upward mobility through successive generations born in the United States, Mexican poverty rates remain disproportionately high even by the third generation (Telles and Ortiz 2008). Generally, Mexicans make up the working poor, where at least one member of the household has a low-wage job (Moore and Pinderhughes 1993; Pastor 2009). Mexicans in the Southwest for the most part experience structural forces which produce poverty differently than forces that affect other racial groups, notably African Americans in the Midwest and on the East Coast, where deindustrialization, white flight, inner-city residential segregation, employer perceptions of Blacks vs. migrants, and declining infrastructures create formidable barriers to job creation. Particularly in the Southwest, Mexicans living in poverty are likely to be located in suburban or rural areas. Like other racial-ethnic minorities, Mexicans have experienced a feminization of poverty: Mexican women consistently have higher poverty rates than men within each generation, and the percentage of women heading households has increased (Telles and Ortiz 2008; U.S. Bureau of the Census 2007).

Mexican and Latina women in the United States (whether migrants or not) often rely on their own resources and nurture intense social networks that help them get through the vicissitudes of poverty and social isolation (Vélez-Ibáñez and Greenberg 1992; Edin and Lein 1997; Menjivar 2000). Grassroots, community-based organizations are another venue through which women struggle to change the daily conditions of their lives and increasingly Mexican women are organizing *encuentros* that bring together activists from both sides of the border (Pardo 1990, 1998a, 1998b; Carrillo 1998; Coronado 2006; Pena 2007). Regarding family life, there are important differences between migrant Mexican women and second and third generation women of Mexican heritage who work in secondary labor market jobs, particularly in how they perceive themselves as working mothers (Segura 1994; Hirsch 2003). Some women migrate independently while others rely on direct sponsorship or are accompanied by men. Furthermore, women "consolidate settlement" after immigration differently than men: through community-wide social networks that originate in women's wage work, through women's relatively stable jobs, and through the utilization of private and public institutional forms of assistance, including credit (Hondagneu-Sotelo 1994, Deeb-Sosa and Bickham Mendez 2008). There is growing evidence that some transnational migrants retain close ties with families, extended kin, social networks, or communities in Mexico through the construction of binational households or families (Hondagneu-Sotelo and Avila 1997; Gil-García 2010). When speaking of poor Mexican women workers, then, one must often refer to processes occurring on both sides of the border, which are integral to women's daily life experiences.

BORDERLANDS PROJECTS

Despite the magnitude of the economic and social transformations in the borderlands, too little research has included migrant women's voices and built theory from their experiences. Indeed, much of the research on men's experiences has failed to include gender analysis that integrates ideologies of masculinity and femininity alongside of structural variations that generate unequal outcomes for men and women. Borderlands theory makes gender and gender oppression central in studies of migration, Chicana/o-Latina/o studies, Latin American studies, and globalization. Key investigations include how family/work intersections operate, new family forms, and the role of social networks, resistance and empowerment, and different modes of women's cultural expressions. A borderlands analysis contextualizes the many layers of violence that originate in structural dislocation and permeate family life as well as work sites and interpersonal relations. When women become the center of analysis, questions change and previously-held assumptions become subjects of inquiry. For example, how are decisions made within households regarding who migrates and who remains behind? Under which circumstances do women migrate alone, with children, or other family members? In view of global interpenetration, how are new identities and social formations being reconstructed on either side of the borders by migrant women? How are these reconfigured identities and social formations being represented in cultural expressions and imaginaries in the United States, Mexico or the Global South? Borderlands theory provides a site to bring together new research that inspires paradigm shifts. Scholarship framed within a borderlands perspective explores the range of women's experiences from reconstructions of "tradition" to contestations of racist, patriarchal and/or heteronormative structures in work sites, families, popular culture, and the state.

This work constitutes emerging feminist borderlands projects (Segura and Zavella 2008). Feminist borderlands projects interrogate the multiple meanings of borders and borderlands across four key dimensions: structural, discursive, interactional, and agentic (2008, 539). Structural dimensions of a feminist borderlands project critique the effects of globalizing economies, neoliberal state practices, and growing regional interdependence on women's life chances. Discursive elements of borderlands projects offer critiques of ideologies and practices that reinforce racializations and heteronormativity and resistance to unequal power relations. Interactional dimensions of borderlands projects interrogate the active accomplishments of unequal relations of race, class, gender and sexualities. Women's agency to negotiate and claim space within the local and global "matrices of domination" include, for example, activist mothering or transborder organizing projects. How women maneuver within structures of power that are often brutal, whether contesting personal or political abuse as well as discourses of state or social violence are critical borderlands projects.

The dialectic between borderlands theory and borderlands projects are dynamic and often incorporate interdisciplinary approaches to reveal the poetics and performance of women's agency, crafting a tapestry of voice and resistance to nativist politics and silencing discourse as well as traditional gendered expectations. By exploring multiple sites of gendered control and contestation, borderlands research reveals the complex representations, experiences and identities that women construct within the context of globalization and transnational migration. Within these structural and socially violent discourses, women continually challenge confining notions of citizenship and create community within and across national borders.

NOTES

1. The terms, "Chicanas and Chicanos" refer to people of Mexican descent in the United States who have a politicized consciousness. "Latina and Latino" is a broader term that typically refers to people of Latin American heritage, which also includes Mexicans. Latino is often used interchangeably with the term, "Hispanic." The terms, "Chicana" and "Latina" refer to women only whereas "Chicano" and "Latino" in many traditional texts have been used to refer to men or to both men and women. Increasingly, the terms, "Chicana/o" and "Latina/o" are being used to subvert the masculinist bias in the generic "Chicano" or "Latino" labels.

2. According to the 2000 Census, African Americans constitute 13 percent of the population. Latinas/os are undoubtedly undercounted by the census, which often misses migrants and the undocumented.

3. The discourse of transnational migrants as "heroes of the nation" extends to a number of countries including the Philippines (Guevarra 2010) and Indonesia (Silvey 2004), among others.

REFERENCES

Anzaldúa, Gloria. 1987. *Borderlands, La Frontera: The New Mestiza*. San Francisco: Spinsters/Aunt Lute Books.

Aparicio, Frances R. 2004. "U.S. Latino Expressive Cultures." In *The Columbia History of Latinos in the United States Since 1960*, edited by David G. Gutiérrez, 355–90. New York: Columbia University Press.

Biron, Rebecca E. 1996. "Feminist Periodicals and Political Crisis in Mexico: *Fem, Debate Feminista*, and *La Correa Feminista* in the 1990s." *Feminist Studies* 22, no. 1: 151–69.

Bonacich, Edna and Richard P. Applebaum. 2000. *Behind the Label: Inequality in the Los Angeles Apparel Industry*. Berkeley: University of California Press.

Broughton, Chad. 2008. "Migration as Engendered Practice: Mexican Men, Masculinity, and Northward Migration." *Gender & Society* 22, no. 5: 568–89.

Cardenas, Gilberto and Estevan T. Flores. 1986. *The Migration and Settlement of Undocumented Women.* Austin: University of Texas, Center for Mexican American Studies.

Carrillo, Teresa. 1998. "Cross-Border Talk: Transnational Perspectives on Labor, Race, and Sexuality." In *Talking Visions: Multicultural Feminism in a Transnational Age,* edited by Ella Habiba Shohat, 391–411. Cambridge: MIT Press.

Castles, Stephen and Mark J. Miller. 1998. *The Age of Migration: International Population Movements in the Modern World.* New York and London: The Guilford Press.

Castañeda, Xóchitl, Victor Ortiz, Betania Allen, Cecilia García, and Mauricio Hernández-Avila. 1996. "Sex Masks: The Double Life of Female Commercial Sex Workers in Mexico City." *Culture Medicine and Psychiatry* 20:229–247.

Catanzarite, Lisa and Lindsey Trimble. 2007. "The Latino Workforce at Mid-Decade." CSRC Research Report. Los Angeles, CA: UCLA Chicano Studies Research Center.

Cerrutti, Marcela and Douglas S. Massey. 2001. "On the Auspices of Female Migration from Mexico to the United States." *Demography* 38, no. 2: 187–200.

Chant, Sylvia H. 1991. *Women and Survival in Mexican Cities, Perspectives on gender, labour markets and low-income households.* Manchester, U. K.: Manchester University Press.

———. 1994. "Women, Work and Household Survival Strategies in Mexico, 1982–1992: Past Trends, Current Tendencies and Future Research." *Bulletin of Latin American Research* 13, no. 2: 203–33.

———. 2007. "Single-Parent Families: Choice or Constraint? The Formation of Female-Headed Households in Mexican Shanty Towns." In *Women and Migration in the U.S.-Mexico Borderlands: A Reader,* edited by Denise A. Segura and Patricia Zavella, 360–367. Durham and London: Duke University Press.

Chavez, Leo R. 1997. "Immigration Reform and Nativism: The Nationalist Response to the Transnationalist Challenge." In *Immigrants Out! In The New Nativism and the Anti-Immigrant Impulse in the United States,* edited by Juan Perea, 61–77. New York: New York University Press.

———. 2001. *Covering Immigration: Popular Images and the Politics of the Nation.* Berkeley: University of California Press.

———. 2004. "A Glass Half Empty: Latina Reproduction and Public Discourse." *Human Organization* 64, no. 2: 173–88.

Coronado, Irasema. 2006. "Styles, strategies, and issues of women leaders at the border." In *Women and change at the U.S.-Mexico border: mobility, labor, and activism,* edited by D. J. Mattingly and E.R. Hansen. Tucson: The University of Arizona Press.

Cravey, Altha J. 1998. *Women and Work in Mexico's Maquiladoras.* Lanham, Md.: Rowman and Littlefield.

Deeb-Sosa, Natalia and Jennifer Bickham Mendez. 2008. "Enforcing Borders in the Nuevo South: Gender and Migration in Williamsburg, Virgina, and the Research Triangle, North Carolina. *Gender & Society* 22, no. 5: 613–38.

De Genova, Nicholas P. 2002. "Migrant "Illegality" and Deportability in Everyday Life." *Annual Review of Anthropology* 31, no. 4: 19–47.

De la O Martínez, María Eugenia. 1995. "Maquiladora, Mujer y Cambios Productivos: Estudio de Caso en la Industria Maquiladora de Ciudad Juárez." In *Mujeres, Migración y Maquila en la Frontera,* edited by Soledad González Montes, Olivia Ruiz, Laura Velasco and Ofelia Woo, 241–70. Mexico City: El Colegio de la Frontera Norte, El Colegio de México.

Durand, Jorge. 1992. *Mas Alla de la Linea: Patrones migratorios entre México y Estados Unidos.* Ph.D diss., Departamento de Antropología, Colegio de Michoacán, Zamora.

The Economist. 2010. "Hysterical nativism: A conservative border state is at risk of becoming a police state." http://www.economist.com/node/15954262/print, April 22, 2010, (accessed on 29 June 2010).

Edin, Kathryn and Laura Lein. 1997. *Making Ends Meet: How Single Mothers Survive Welfare and Low-Wage Work.* New York: Russell Sage Foundation.

Ehrenreich, Barbara and Arlie Russell Hochschild (eds). 2002. *Global Woman: Nannies, Maids and Sex Workers in the New Economy.* New York: Metropolitan.

Fernández-Kelly, María Patricia. 1983. *For we are sold, I and my people: women and industry in Mexico's frontier.* Albany: State University of New York Press.

Flores, William V. 1997. "*Mujeres en Huelga:* Cultural Citizenship and Gender Empowerment in a Cannery Strike." In *Latino Cultural Citizenship: Claiming Identity, Space, and Rights,* edited by William V. Flores and Rina Benmayor, 210–254. Boston: Beacon Press.

Flores, Sara Maria, ed. 1995. *Jornaleras, Temporeras y Bóias-Frias: El rostro femenino del mercado de trabajo rural en América Latina.* United Nations Research Institute for Social Development. Caracas: Nueva Sociedad.

Flores, Yvette and Enriqueta Valdez Curiel. 2009. "Conflict Resolution and Intimate Partner Violence among Mexicans on both sides of the border." In *Mexicans in California: Tranformations and Challenges,* edited by Ramón Gutiérrez and Patricia Zavella, 183–205. Urbana and Chicago: University of Illinois Press.

Fowler-Salamini, Heather, and Mary Kay Vaughan, eds. 1994. *Women of the Mexican Countryside, 1850–1990: Creating Spaces, Shaping Transitions.* Tucson: University of Arizona Press.

Fox, Jonathan, and Gaspar Rivera-Salgado, eds. 2004. *Indigenous Mexican Migrants in the United States.* La Jolla: Center for U.S.-Mexican Studies and Center for Comparative Immigration Studies.

Fregoso, Rosa Linda. 2003. *meXicana Encounters: The Making of Social Identities on the Borderlands.* Berkeley: University of California Press.

Fry, Richard. 2002. *Latinos in Higher Education: Many Enroll, Too Few Graduate*. Washington, D.C.: PEW Hispanic Center.

———. 1997. *Chicana Feminist Thought: The Basic Historical Writings*. New York: Routledge.

Gil-García, Óscar. 2010. "Representations of Race, Class and Gender in Transnational Guatemalan Forced Migrant Communities." Ph.D diss., Department of Sociology, University of California, Santa Barbara.

González de la Rocha, Mercedes. 1984. *Urban Households and Domestic Cycles in Guadalajara, Mexico*. Ph.D. diss., Faculty of Social and Economic Studies, University of Manchester.

González Montes, Soledad, and Vania Salles, eds. 1995. *Relaciones de género y transformaciones agrarias: Estudios sobre el campo*. México City: El Colegio de México, Programa Interdisciplinario de Estudios de la Mujer.

González Montes, Soledad, and Julia Tuñón. 1997. *Familias y mujeres en México: Del modelo a la diversidad*. México City: El Colegio de México, Programa Interdisciplinario de Estudios de la Mujer.

Guevarra, Anna Romina. 2010. *Marketing Dreams, Manufacturing Heroes: The Transnational Labor Brokering of Filipino Workers*. New Brunswick, New Jersey and London: Rutgers University Press.

Gutiérrez, Elena Rebeca. 1999. "The Racial Politics of Reproduction: The Social Construction of Mexican-Origin Women's Fertility." Ph.D. diss., Department of Sociology, University of Michigan, Ann Arbor.

Hirsch, Jennifer S. 2003. *A Courtship After Marriage: Sexuality and Love in Mexican Transnational Families*. Berkeley: University of California Press.

Hondagneu-Sotelo, Pierrette. 1994. *Gendered Transitions: Mexican experiences of immigration* Berkeley: University of California Press.

Hondagneu-Sotelo, Pierrette and Ernestine Avila. 1997. "'I'm Here, but I'm There': The Meanings of Latina Transnational Motherhood." *Gender & Society* 11, no. 5: 548–71.

Ibarra, Maria de la Luz. 2000. "Mexican Immigrant Women and the New Domestic Labor." *Human Organization* 59, no. 4: 452–64.

———. 2002. "Emotional Proletarians in a Global Economy: Mexican Immigrant Women and Elder Care Work." *Urban Anthropology* 31, nos. 3-4: 317–51.

Iglesias-Prieto, Norma, and Rosa Linda Fregoso, eds. 1998. *Miradas de mujer: encuentro de cineastas y videoastas mexicanas y chicanas*. Tijuana, Mexico: El Colegio de la Frontera Norte.

Inda, Jonathan Xavier. 2002. "Biopower, Reproduction, and the Migrant Woman's Body." In *Decolonial Voices: Chicana and Chicano Cultural Studies in the 21st Century*, edited by Arturo J. Aldama and Naomi H. Quiñonez, 98–112. Bloomington: Indiana University Press.

Johnson, Hans P., Laura Hill, and Mary Heim. 2001. "New Trends in Newborns: Fertility Rates and Patterns in California." *California Counts: Population Trends and Profiles* 3, no. 1: 1–11.

Kanaiaupuni, Shawn Malia. 2000. "Reframing the Migration Question: An Analysis of Men, Women, and Gender in Mexico." *Social Forces* 78, no. 4: 1311–47.

Lamas, Marta. 1996. "Trabajadoras sexuales: Del estigma a la consciencia política." *Estudios Sociológicos* 14, no. 40: 33–52.

Lamphere, Louise and Patricia Zavella. 1997. "Women's Resistance in the Sunbelt: Anglos and Hispanas Respond to Managerial Control." In *Women and Work: Exploring Race, Ethnicity, and Class*, edited by Elizabeth Higginbotham and Mary Romero, 76–100. Thousand Oaks, Calif.: Sage Publications.

Levitt, Peggy. 2001. *The Transnational Villagers*. Berkeley: University of California Press.

Levitt, Peggy, and Rafael de la Dehesa. 2003. "Transnational Migration and the Redefinition of the State: Variations and Explanations." *Ethnic and Racial Studies* 26, no. 4: 587–611.

Lopez, Mark Hugo, and Susan Minushkin. 2008. "2008 National Survey of Latinos: Hispanics See Their Situation in U.S. Deteriorating; Opposed Key Immigration Enforcement Measures." Washington D.C.: Pew Hispanic Center.

Massey, Douglas S., Jorge Durand, and Nolan J. Malone. 2002. *Beyond Smoke and Mirrors: Mexican Immigration in an Era of Economic Integration*. New York: Russell Sage Foundation.

Mauricio Gastón Institute for Latino Community Development and Public Policy. 1994. "Barriers to Employment and Work-Place Advancement of Latinos: Report to The Glass Ceiling Commission, U.S. Department of Labor." Unpublished report, University of Massachusetts, Boston.

Menjívar, Cecilia. 2000. *Fragmented Ties: Salvadoran Immigrant Networks in America*. Berkeley: University of California Press.

Moore, Joan, and Raquel Pinderhughes, eds. 1993. *In the Barrios: Latinos and the Underclass Debate*. New York: Russell Sage Foundation.

Morales, Rebecca, and Frank Bonilla, eds. 1993. *Latinos in a Changing U.S. Economy: Comparative Perspectives on Growing Inequality*. Newbury Park, Calif.: Sage Publications.

Muñoz, Carolina Bank. 2008. *Transnational Tortillas: Race, Gender, and Shop-Floor Politics in Mexico and the United States*. Ithaca and London: Cornell University Press.

Ortiz, Vilma. 1996. "The Mexican Origin Population: Permanent Working Class or Emerging Middle Class?" In *Ethnic Los Angeles*, edited by Roger Waldinger and Mehdi Bozorgmehr, 247–278. New York: Russell Sage Foundation.

Palerm, Juan Vicente, and José Ignacio Urquiola. 1993. "A Binational System of Agricultural Production: The Case of the Mexican Bajío and California." In *Mexico and the United States: Neighbors in Crisis*, edited by Daniel G. Aldrich, Jr. and Lorenzo Meyer, 311–37. San Bernardino, Calif.: The Borgo Press.

Pardo, Mary S. 1990. "Mexican American Women Grassroots Community Activists: Mothers of East Los Angeles." *Frontiers, A Journal of Women's Studies* 11, no. 1: 1–7.

————. 1998a. "Creating Community: Mexican American Women in Eastside Los Angeles." In *Community Activism and Feminist Politics: Organizing Across Race, Class, and Gender,* edited by Nancy A. Naples, 275–300. New York: Routledge.

————. 1998b. *Mexican American Women Activists: Identity and Resistance in Two Los Angeles Communities.* Philadelphia: Temple University Press.

Paredes, Américo. 1993. "The Folklore of Groups of Mexican Origin in the United States." In *Folklore and Culture on the Texas-Mexico Border,* edited by Richard Bauman, 3–18. Austin: University of Texas at Austin, Center for Mexican American Studies.

Parreñas, Rhacel. 2001. *Servants of Globalization: Women, Migration, and Domestic Work.* Palo Alto, Calif.: Stanford University Press.

————. 2005. *Children of Global Migration: Transnational Families and Gendered Woes.* Palo Alto, Calif.: Stanford University Press.

Pastor, Manuel Jr. 2009. "Poverty, Work, and Public Policy: Latino Futures in California's New Economy." In *Mexicans in California: Transformations and Challenges,* edited by Ramón A. Gutiérrez and Patricia Zavella, 15–35. Urbana and Chicago: University of Illinois Press.

Peña, Milagros. 2007. *Latina Activists across borders: Women grassroots organizing in Mexico and Texas.* Durham, NC and London: Duke University Press.

Reyes, Belinda I. 1997. "Dynamics of Immigration: Return Migration to Western Mexico." San Francisco: Public Policy Institute of California.

Ruiz, Vicki L. 1998. *From Out of the Shadows: Mexican Women in Twentieth-Century America.* New York: Oxford University Press.

Salzinger, Leslie. 2003. *Genders in Production: Making Workers in Mexico's Global Factories.* Berkeley: University of California Press.

Sassen, Saskia. 1998. *Globalization and Its Discontents: Essays on the New Mobility of People and Money.* New York: New Press.

————. 2002. "Global Cities and Survival Circuits." In *Global Woman: Nannies, Maids and Sex Workers in the New Economy* edited by Barbara Ehrenreich and Arlie Russell Hochschild. New York: Metropolitan.

Segura, Denise A. 1994. "Working at Motherhood: Chicana and Mexican Immigrant Mothers and Employment." In *Mothering: Ideology, Experience, and Agency,* edited by Evelyn Nakano Glenn, Grace Chang and Linda Rennie Forcey, 211–236. New York: Routledge.

Segura, Denise A. and Patricia Zavella. 2008. "Introduction: Gendered Borderlands." *Gender & Society* 22 (special issue on Gendered Borderlands), no. 5: 537–544.

Silvey, Rachel. 2004. "Transnational Domestication: State Power and Indonesian Migrant Women in Saudi Arabia." *Political Geography* 23: 245–64.

Telles, Edward E. and Vilma Ortiz. 2008. *Generations of Exclusion: Mexican Americans, Assimilation, and Race.* New York: Russell Sage Foundation.

Téllez, Michelle. 2008. "Community of Struggle: Gender, Violence, and Resistance on the U.S./Mexico Border." *Gender & Society* 22, no. 5: 545–67.

Texas State Data Center. 1998. "Projections of the Population of Texas and Counties in Texas by Age, Sex and Race/Ethnicity, for 2000–2030." (http://txsdc.tamu.edu), Accessed on 4 March, 2005.

Thompson, Ginger. 2005. "Mexico's Migrants Profit From Dollars Sent Home." *New York Times,* 23 February, Al, 8.

UNFPA (United Nations Population Fund). 2006. "State of the World Population 2006: A Passage to Hope, Women and International Migration." New York: United Nations Population Fund.

U.S. Bureau of the Census. 2000. *Summary File 1. Table 3, Female Population by Age, Race, and Hispanic or Latino Origin for the United States: 2000.* Washington, D.C.: U.S. Government Printing Office.

————. 2003. *The Hispanic Population in the United States: March 2002,* Series P20, No. 545. Washington, D.C.: U.S. Government Printing Office.

————. 2007. *Age and sex of all people, family members and unrelated individuals iterated by income-to-poverty ratio and race: 2007.* Washington, D.C.: Retrieved from http://pubdb3 .census.gov/macro/032008/pov/new01_100_09. htm.

Vélez-Ibáñez, Carlos G. 1983. *Rituals of Marginality: Politics, Process, and Culture Change in Central Urban Mexico, 1969–74.* Berkeley: University of California Press.

Vélez-Ibáñez, Carlos G., and James B. Greenberg. 1992. "Formation and Transformation of Funds of Knowledge Among U.S.-Mexican Households." *Anthropology and Education Quarterly* 23, no. 4: 313–34;

Vieth, Warren, and Edward Chen. 2004. "Bush Supports Shift of Jobs Overseas." *Los Angeles Times,* 10 February, A14.

Zavella, Patricia. 2002. "Engendering Transnationalism in Food Processing: Peripheral Vision on Both Sides of the U.S.-Mexico Border." In *Transnationalism and Latino Communities: Politics, Processes and Cultures,* edited by Carlos G. Vélez-Ibáñez and Anna Sampaio, with Manolo González-Estay, 397–424. Lanham, MD: Rowman and Littlefield.

Zentgraf, Kristine M. 2005. "Why Women Migrate: Salvadoran and Guatemalan Women in Los Angeles." In *Latino Los Angeles: Transformations, Communities, and Activism,* edited by Enrique C. Ochoa and Gilda L. Ochoa, 63–82. Tucson: University of Arizona Press.

Masculinities and Globalization
First published in 1999

The current wave of research and debate on masculinity stems from the impact of the women's liberation movement on men, but it has taken time for this impact to produce a new intellectual agenda. Most discussions of men's gender in the 1970s and early 1980s centered on an established concept, the male sex role, and an established problem: how men and boys were socialized into this role. There was not much new empirical research. What there was tended to use the more abstracted methods of social psychology (e.g., paper-and-pencil masculinity/femininity scales) to measure generalized attitudes and expectations in ill-defined populations. The largest body of empirical research was the continuing stream of quantitative studies of sex differences—which continued to be disappointingly slight (Carrigan, Connell, and Lee 1985).

The concept of a unitary male sex role, however, came under increasing criticism for its multiple oversimplifications and its incapacity to handle issues about power (Kimmel 1987; Connell 1987). New conceptual frameworks were proposed that linked feminist work on institutionalized patriarchy, gay theoretical work on homophobia, and psychoanalytic ideas about the person (Carrigan, Connell, and Lee 1985; Hearn 1987). Increasing attention was given to certain studies that located issues about masculinity in a fully described local context, whether a British printing shop (Cockburn 1983) or a Papuan mountain community (Herdt 1981). By the late 1980s, a genre of empirical research based on these ideas was developing, most clearly in sociology but also in anthropology, history, organization studies, and cultural studies. This has borne fruit in the 1990s in what is now widely recognized as a new generation of social research on masculinity and men in gender relations (Connell 1995; *Widersprueche* 1995; Segal 1997).

Although the recent research has been diverse in subject matter and social location, its characteristic focus is the construction of masculinity in a particular milieu or moment—a clergyman's family (Tosh 1991), a professional sports career (Messner 1992), a small group of gay men (Connell 1992), a bodybuilding gym (Klein 1993), a group of colonial schools (Morrell 1994), an urban police force (McElhinny 1994), drinking groups in bars (Tomsen 1997), a corporate office on the verge of a decision (Messerschmidt 1997). Accordingly, we might think of this as the "ethnographic moment" in masculinity research, in which the specific and the local are in focus. (This is not to deny that this work *deploys* broader structural concepts simply to note the characteristic focus of the empirical work and its analysis.)

The ethnographic moment brought a much-needed gust of realism to debates on men and masculinity, a corrective to the simplifications of role theory. It also provided a corrective to the trend in popular culture where vague discussions of men's sex roles were giving way to the mystical generalities of the mythopoetic movement and the extreme simplifications of religious revivalism.

Although the rich detail of the historical and field studies defies easy summary, certain conclusions emerge from this body of research as a whole. In short form, they are the following.

Plural Masculinities A theme of theoretical work in the 1980s, the multiplicity of masculinities has now been very fully documented by descriptive research. Different cultures and different periods of history construct gender differently. Striking differences exist, for instance, in the relationship of homosexual practice to dominant forms of masculinity (Herdt 1984). In multicultural societies, there are varying definitions and enactments of masculinity, for instance, between Anglo and Latino communities in the United States (Hondagneu-Sotelo and Messner 1994). Equally important, more than one kind of masculinity can be found within a given cultural setting or institution. This is particularly well documented in school studies (Foley 1990) but can also be observed in workplaces (Messerschmidt 1997) and the military (Barrett 1996).

Hierarchy and Hegemony   These plural masculinities exist in definite social relations, often relations of hierarchy and exclusion. This was recognized early, in gay theorists' discussions of homophobia; it has become clear that the implications are far-reaching. There is generally a hegemonic form of masculinity, the most honored or desired in a particular context. For Western popular culture, this is extensively documented in research on media representations of masculinity (McKay and Huber 1992). The hegemonic form need not be the most common form of masculinity. Many men live in a state of some tension with, or distance from, hegemonic masculinity; others (such as sporting heroes) are taken as exemplars of hegemonic masculinity and are required to live up to it strenuously (Connell 1990a). The dominance of hegemonic masculinity over other forms may be quiet and implicit, but it may also be vehement and violent, as in the important case of homophobic violence.

Collective Masculinities   Masculinities, as patterns of gender practice, are sustained and enacted not only by individuals but also by groups and institutions. This fact was visible in Cockburn's (1983) pioneering research on informal workplace culture, and it has been confirmed over and over: in workplaces (Donaldson 1991), in organized sport (Whitson 1990; Messner 1992), in schools (Connell 1996), and so on. This point must be taken with the previous two: institutions may construct multiple masculinities and define relationships between them. Barrett's (1996) illuminating study of hegemonic masculinity in the U.S. Navy shows how this takes different forms in the different subbranches of the one military organization.

Bodies as Arenas   Men's bodies do not determine the patterns of masculinity, but they are still of great importance in masculinity. Men's bodies are addressed, defined and disciplined (as in sport; see Theberge 1991), and given outlets and pleasures by the gender order of society. But men's bodies are not blank slates.

The enactment of masculinity reaches certain limits, for instance, in the destruction of the industrial worker's body (Donaldson 1991). Masculine conduct with a female body is felt to be anomalous or transgressive, like feminine conduct with a male body; research on gender crossing (Bolin 1988) shows the work that must be done to sustain an anomalous gender.

Active Construction   Masculinities do not exist prior to social interaction, but come into existence as people act. They are actively produced, using the resources and strategies available in a given milieu. Thus the exemplary masculinities of sports professionals are not a product of passive disciplining, but as Messner (1992) shows, result from a sustained, active engagement with the demands of the institutional setting, even to the point of serious bodily damage from "playing hurt" and accumulated stress. With boys learning masculinities, much of what was previously taken as socialization appears, in close-focus studies of schools (Walker 1988; Thorne 1993), as the outcome of intricate and intense maneuvering in peer groups, classes, and adult-child relationships.

Contradiction   Masculinities are not homogeneous, simple states of being. Close-focus research on masculinities commonly identifies contradictory desires and conduct; for instance, in Klein's (1993) study of bodybuilders, the contradiction between the heterosexual definition of hegemonic masculinity and the homosexual practice by which some of the bodybuilders finance the making of an exemplary body. Psychoanalysis provides the classic evidence of conflicts within personality, and recent psychoanalytic writing (Chodorow 1994; Lewes 1988) has laid some emphasis on the conflicts and emotional compromises within both hegemonic and subordinated forms of masculinity. Life-history research influenced by existential psychoanalysis (Connell 1995) has similarly traced contradictory projects and commitments within particular forms of masculinity.

Dynamics   Masculinities created in specific historical circumstances are liable to reconstruction, and any pattern of hegemony is subject to contestation, in which a dominant masculinity may be displaced. Heward (1988) shows the changing gender regime of a boys' school responding to the changed strategies of the families in its clientele. Roper (1991) shows the displacement of a production-oriented masculinity among engineering managers by new financially oriented generic managers. Since the 1970s, the reconstruction of masculinities has been pursued as a conscious politics. Schwalbe's (1996) close examination of one mythopoetic group shows the complexity of the practice and the limits of the reconstruction.

If we compare this picture of masculinity with earlier understandings of the male sex role, it is clear that the ethnographic moment in research has already had important intellectual fruits.

Nevertheless, it has always been recognized that some issues go beyond the local. For instance, mythopoetic movements such as the highly visible Promise Keepers are part of a spectrum of masculinity politics; Messner (1997) shows for the United States that this spectrum involves at least eight conflicting agendas for the remaking of masculinity. Historical studies such as Phillips (1987) on New Zealand and Kimmel (1996) on the United States have traced the changing public constructions of masculinity for whole countries over long periods; ultimately, such historical reconstructions are essential for understanding the meaning of ethnographic details.

I consider that this logic must now be taken a step further, and in taking this step, we will move toward a new agenda for the whole field. What happens in localities is affected by the history of whole countries, but what happens in countries is affected by the history of the world. Locally situated lives are now (indeed, have long been) powerfully influenced by geopolitical struggles, global markets, multinational corporations, labor migration, transnational media. It is time for this fundamental fact to be built into our analysis of men and masculinities.

To understand local masculinities, we must think in global terms. But how? That is the problem pursued in this article. I will offer a framework for thinking about masculinities as a feature of world society and for thinking about men's gender practices in terms of the global structure and dynamics of gender. This is by no means to reject the ethnographic moment in masculinity research. It is, rather, to think how we can use its findings more adequately.

THE WORLD GENDER ORDER

Masculinities do not first exist and then come into contact with femininities; they are produced together, in the process that constitutes a gender order. Accordingly, to understand the masculinities on a world scale, we must first have a concept of the globalization of gender.

This is one of the most difficult points in current gender analysis because the very conception is counterintuitive. We are so accustomed to thinking of gender as the attribute of an individual, even as an unusually intimate attribute, that it requires a considerable wrench to think of gender on the vast scale of global society. Most relevant discussions, such as the literature on women and development, fudge the issue. They treat the entities that extend internationally (markets, corporations, intergovernmental programs, etc.) as ungendered in principle—but affecting unequally gendered recipients of aid in practice, because of bad policies. Such conceptions reproduce the familiar liberal-feminist view of the state as in principle gender-neutral, though empirically dominated by men.

But if we recognize that very large scale institutions such as the state are themselves gendered, in quite precise and specifiable ways (Connell 1990b), and if we recognize that international relations, international trade, and global markets are inherently an arena of gender formation and gender politics (Enloe 1990), then we can recognize the existence of a world gender order. The term can be defined as the structure of relationships that interconnect the gender regimes of institutions, and the gender orders of local society, on a world scale. That is, however, only a definition. The substantive questions remain: what is the shape of that structure, how tightly are its elements linked, how has it arisen historically, what is its trajectory into the future?

Current business and media talk about globalization pictures a homogenizing process sweeping across the world, driven by new technologies, producing vast unfettered global markets in which all participate on equal terms. This is a misleading image. As Hirst and Thompson (1996) show, the global economy is highly unequal and the current degree of homogenization is often overestimated. Multinational corporations based in the three major economic powers (the United States, European Union, and Japan) are the major economic actors worldwide.

The structure bears the marks of its history. Modern global society was historically produced as Wallerstein (1974) argued, by the economic and political expansion of European states from the fifteenth century on and by the creation of colonial empires. It is in this process that we find the roots of the modern world gender order. Imperialism was, from the start, a gendered process. Its first phase, colonial conquest and settlement, was carried out by gender-segregated forces, and it resulted in massive disruption of indigenous gender orders. In its second phase, the stabilization of colonial societies, new gender divisions of labor were produced in plantation economies and colonial cities, while gender ideologies were linked with racial hierarchies and the cultural defense of empire. The third phase, marked by political decolonization, economic neocolonialism, and the current growth of world markets and structures of financial control, has seen gender divisions of labor remade on a massive scale in the "global factory" (Fuentes and Ehrenreich 1983), as well as the spread of gendered violence alongside Western military technology.

The result of this history is a partially integrated, highly unequal and turbulent world society, in which gender relations are partly but unevenly linked on a global scale. The unevenness becomes clear when different substructures of gender (Connell 1987; Walby 1990) are examined separately.

The Division of Labor   A characteristic feature of colonial and neocolonial economies was the restructuring of local production systems to produce a male wage worker–female domestic worker couple (Mies 1986). This need not produce a "housewife" in the Western suburban sense, for instance, where the wage work involved migration to plantations or mines (Moodie 1994). But it has generally produced the identification of masculinity with the public realm and the money economy and of femininity with domesticity, which is a core feature of the modern European gender system (Holter 1997).

Power Relations   The colonial and postcolonial world has tended to break down purdah systems of patriarchy in the name of modernization, if not of women's emancipation (Kandiyoti 1994). At the same time, the creation of a westernized public realm has seen the growth of large-scale organizations in the form of the state and corporations, which in the great majority of cases are culturally masculinized and controlled by men. In *comprador* capitalism, however, the power of local elites depends on their relations with the metropolitan powers, so the hegemonic masculinities of neocolonial societies are uneasily poised between local and global cultures.

Emotional Relations   Both religious and cultural missionary activity has corroded indigenous homosexual and cross-gender practice, such as the native American

berdache and the Chinese "passion of the cut sleeve" (Hinsch 1990). Recently developed Western models of romantic heterosexual love as the basis for marriage and of gay identity as the main alternative have now circulated globally—though as Altman (1996) observes, they do not simply displace indigenous models, but interact with them in extremely complex ways.

Symbolization   Mass media, especially electronic media, in most parts of the world follow North American and European models and relay a great deal of metropolitan content; gender imagery is an important part of what is circulated. A striking example is the reproduction of a North American imagery of femininity by Xuxa, the blonde television superstar in Brazil (Simpson 1993). In counterpoint, exotic gender imagery has been used in the marketing strategies of newly industrializing countries (e.g., airline advertising from Southeast Asia)—a tactic based on the longstanding combination of the exotic and the erotic in the colonial imagination (Jolly 1997).

Clearly, the world gender order is not simply an extension of a traditional European-American gender order. That gender order was changed by colonialism, and elements from other cultures now circulate globally. Yet in no sense do they mix on equal terms, to produce a United Colours of Benetton gender order. The culture and institutions of the North Atlantic countries are hegemonic within the emergent world system. This is crucial for understanding the kinds of masculinities produced within it.

THE REPOSITIONING OF MEN AND THE RECONSTITUTION OF MASCULINITIES

The positioning of men and the constitution of masculinities may be analyzed at any of the levels at which gender practice is configured: in relation to the body, in personal life, and in collective social practice. At each level, we need to consider how the processes of globalization influence configurations of gender.

Men's bodies are positioned in the gender order, and enter the gender process, through body-reflexive practices in which bodies are both objects and agents (Connell 1995)—including sexuality, violence, and labor. The conditions of such practice include where one is and who is available for interaction. So it is a fact of considerable importance for gender relations that the global social order distributes and redistributes bodies, through migration, and through political controls over movement and interaction.

The creation of empire was the original "elite migration," though in certain cases mass migration followed. Through settler colonialism, something close to the gender order of Western Europe was reassembled in North America and in Australia. Labor migration within the colonial systems was a means by which gender practices were spread, but also a means by which they were reconstructed, since labor migration was itself a gendered process—as we have seen in relation to the gender division of labor. Migration from the colonized world to the metropole became (except for Japan) a mass process in the decades after World War II. There is also migration within the periphery, such as the creation of a very large immigrant labor force, mostly from other Muslim countries, in the oil-producing Gulf states.

These relocations of bodies create the possibility of hybridization in gender imagery, sexuality, and other forms of practice. The movement is not always toward synthesis, however, as the race/ethnic hierarchies of colonialism have been recreated in new contexts, including the politics of the metropole. Ethnic and racial conflict has been growing in importance in recent years, and as Klein (1997) and Tillner (1997) argue, this is a fruitful context for the production of masculinities oriented toward domination and violence. Even without the context of violence, there can be an intimate interweaving of the formation of masculinity with the formation of ethnic identity, as seen in the study by Poynting, Noble, and Tabar (1997) of Lebanese youths in the Anglo-dominant culture of Australia.

At the level of personal life as well as in relation to bodies, the making of masculinities is shaped by global forces. In some cases, the link is indirect, such as the working-class Australian men caught in a situation of structural unemployment (Connell 1995), which arises from Australia's changing position in the global economy. In other cases, the link is obvious, such as the executives of multinational corporations and the financial sector servicing international trade. The requirements of a career in international business set up strong pressures on domestic life: almost all multinational executives are men, and the assumption in business magazines and advertising directed toward them is that they will have dependent wives running their homes and bringing up their children.

At the level of collective practice, masculinities are reconstituted by the remaking of gender meanings and the reshaping of the institutional contexts of practice. Let us consider each in turn.

The growth of global mass media, especially electronic media, is an obvious "vector" for the globalization of gender. Popular entertainment circulates stereotyped gender images, deliberately made attractive for marketing purposes. The example of Xuxa in Brazil has already been mentioned. International news media are also controlled or strongly influenced from the metropole and circulate Western definitions of authoritative masculinity, criminality, desirable femininity, and so on. But there are limits to the power of global mass communications. Some local centers of mass entertainment differ from the Hollywood model, such as the Indian popular film industry centered in Bombay. Further, media research emphasizes that audiences are highly selective in their reception of media messages, and we must allow for popular recognition of the fantasy in mass entertainment. Just as economic globalization can be exaggerated, the creation of a global culture is a more turbulent and uneven process than is often assumed (Featherstone 1995).

More important, I would argue, is a process that began long before electronic media existed, the export of institutions. Gendered institutions not only circulate definitions of masculinity (and femininity), as sex role theory notes. The functioning of gendered institutions, creating specific conditions for social practice, calls into existence specific patterns of practice. Thus, certain patterns of collective violence are embedded in the organization and culture of a Western-style army, which are different from the patterns of precolonial violence. Certain patterns of calculative egocentrism are embedded in the working of a stock market; certain patterns of rule following and domination are embedded in a bureaucracy.

Now, the colonial and postcolonial world saw the installation in the periphery, on a very large scale, of a range of institutions on the North Atlantic model: armies, states, bureaucracies, corporations, capital markets, labor markets, schools, law courts, transport systems. These are gendered institutions and their functioning has directly reconstituted masculinities in the periphery. This has not necessarily meant photocopies of European masculinities. Rather, pressures for change are set up that are inherent in the institutional form.

To the extent that particular institutions become dominant in world society, the patterns of masculinity embedded in them may become global standards. Masculine dress is an interesting indicator: almost every political leader in the world now wears the uniform of the Western business executive. The more common pattern, however, is not the complete displacement of local patterns but the articulation of the local gender order with the gender regime of global model institutions. Case studies such as Hollway's (1994) account of bureaucracy in Tanzania illustrate the point; there, domestic patriarchy articulated with masculine authority in the state in ways that subverted the government's formal commitment to equal opportunity for women.

We should not expect the overall structure of gender relations on a world scale simply to mirror patterns known on the smaller scale. In the most vital of respects, there is continuity. The world gender order is unquestionably patriarchal, in the sense that it privileges men over women. There is a patriarchal dividend for men arising from unequal wages, unequal labor force participation, and a highly unequal structure of ownership, as well as cultural and sexual privileging. This has been extensively documented by feminist work on women's situation globally (e.g., Taylor 1985), though its implications for masculinity have mostly been ignored. The conditions thus exist for the production of a hegemonic masculinity on a world scale, that is to say, a dominant form of masculinity that embodies, organizes, and legitimates men's domination in the gender order as a whole.

The conditions of globalization, which involve the interaction of many local gender orders, certainly multiply the forms of masculinity in the global gender order. At the same time, the specific shape of globalization, concentrating economic and cultural power on an unprecedented scale, provides new resources for dominance by particular groups of men. This dominance may become institutionalized in a pattern of masculinity that becomes, to some degree, standardized across localities. I will call such patterns *globalizing masculinities,* and it is among them, rather than narrowly within the metropole, that we are likely to find candidates for hegemony in the world gender order.

GLOBALIZING MASCULINITIES

In this section, I will offer a sketch of major forms of globalizing masculinity in the three historical phases identified above in the discussion of globalization.

Masculinities of Conquest and Settlement

The creation of the imperial social order involved peculiar conditions for the gender practices of men. Colonial conquest itself was mainly carried out by segregated groups of men—soldiers, sailors, traders, administrators, and a good many who were all these by turn (such as the Rum Corps in early New South Wales, Australia). They were drawn from the more segregated occupations and milieu in the metropole, and it is likely that the men drawn into colonization tended to be the more rootless. Certainly the process of conquest could produce frontier masculinities that combined the occupational culture of these groups with an unusual level of violence and egocentric individualism. The vehement contemporary debate about the genocidal violence of the Spanish conquistadors—who in fifty years completely exterminated the population of Hispaniola—points to this pattern (Bitterli 1989).

The political history of empire is full of evidence of the tenuous control over the frontier exercised by the state—the Spanish monarchs unable to rein in the conquistadors, the governors in Sydney unable to hold back the squatters and in Capetown unable to hold back the Boers, gold rushes breaking boundaries everywhere, even an independent republic set up by escaped slaves in Brazil. The point probably applies to other forms of social control too, such as customary controls on men's sexuality. Extensive sexual exploitation of indigenous women was a common feature of conquest. In certain circumstances, frontier masculinities might be reproduced as a local cultural tradition long after the frontier had passed, such as the gauchos of southern South America and the cowboys of the western United States.

In other circumstances, however, the frontier of conquest and exploitation was replaced by a frontier of settlement. Sex ratios in the colonizing population changed, as women arrived and locally born generations succeeded. A shift back toward the family patterns of the metropole was likely. As Cain and Hopkins (1993) have shown for the British empire, the ruling group in the colonial world as a whole was an extension of the dominant class in the metropole, the landed gentry, and tended to reproduce its social customs and ideology. The creation of a settler masculinity might be the goal of state policy, as it seems to have been in late-nineteenth-century New Zealand, as part of a general process of pacification and the creation of an agricultural social order (Phillips 1987). Or it might be undertaken through institutions created by settler groups, such as the elite schools in Natal studied by Morrell (1994).

The impact of colonialism on the construction of masculinity among the colonized is much less documented, but there is every reason to think it was severe. Conquest and settlement disrupted all the structures of indigenous society, whether or not this was intended by the colonizing powers (Bitterli 1989). Indigenous gender orders were no exception. Their disruption could result from the pulverization of indigenous communities (as in the seizure of land in eastern North America and southeastern Australia), through gendered labor migration (as in gold mining with Black labor in South Africa; see Moodie 1994), to ideological attacks on local gender arrangements (as in the missionary assault on the *berdache* tradition in North America; see Williams 1986). The varied course of resistance to colonization is also likely to have affected the making of masculinities. This is clear in the region of Natal in South Africa, where sustained resistance to colonization by the Zulu kingdom was a key to the mobilization of ethnic-national masculine identities in the twentieth century (Morrell 1996).

Masculinities of Empire

The imperial social order created a hierarchy of masculinities, as it created a hierarchy of communities and races. The colonizers distinguished "more manly" from "less manly" groups among their subjects. In British India, for instance, Bengali men were supposed effeminate while Pathans and Sikhs were regarded as strong and warlike. Similar distinctions were made in South Africa between Hottentots and Zulus, in North America between Iroquois, Sioux, and Cheyenne on one side, and southern and southwestern tribes on the other.

At the same time, the emerging imagery of gender difference in European culture provided general symbols of superiority and inferiority. Within the imperial "poetics of war" (MacDonald 1994), the conqueror was virile, while the colonized were dirty, sexualized, and effeminate or childlike. In many colonial situations, indigenous men were called "boys" by the colonizers (e.g., in Zimbabwe; see Shire 1994). Sinha's (1995) interesting study of the language of political controversy in India in the 1880s and 1890s shows how the images of "manly Englishman" and "effeminate Bengali" were deployed to uphold colonial privilege

and contain movements for change. In the late nineteenth century, racial barriers in colonial societies were hardening rather than weakening, and gender ideology tended to fuse with racism in forms that the twentieth century has never untangled.

The power relations of empire meant that indigenous gender orders were generally under pressure from the colonizers, rather than the other way around. But the colonizers too might change. The barriers of late colonial racism were not only to prevent pollution from below but also to forestall "going native," a well-recognized possibility—the starting point, for instance, of Kipling's famous novel *Kim* ([1901] 1987). The pressures, opportunities, and profits of empire might also work changes in gender arrangements among the colonizers, for instance, the division of labor in households with a large supply of indigenous workers as domestic servants (Bulbeck 1992). Empire might also affect the gender order of the metropole itself by changing gender ideologies, divisions of labor, and the nature of the metropolitan state. For instance, empire figured prominently as a source of masculine imagery in Britain, in the Boy Scouts, and in the cult of Lawrence of Arabia (Dawson 1991). Here we see examples of an important principle: the interplay of gender dynamics between different parts of the world order.

The world of empire created two very different settings for the modernization of masculinities. In the periphery, the forcible restructuring of economics and workforces tended to individualize, on one hand, and rationalize, on the other. A widespread result was masculinities in which the rational calculation of self-interest was the key to action, emphasizing the European gender contrast of rational man/irrational woman. The specific form might be local—for instance, the Japanese "salaryman," a type first recognized in the 1910s, was specific to the Japanese context of large, stable industrial conglomerates (Kinmonth 1981). But the result generally was masculinities defined around economic action, with both workers and entrepreneurs increasingly adapted to emerging market economies.

In the metropole, the accumulation of wealth made possible a specialization of leadership in the dominant classes, and struggles for hegemony in which masculinities organized around domination or violence were split from masculinities organized around expertise. The class compromises that allowed the development of the welfare state in Europe and North America were paralleled by gender compromises—gender reform movements (most notably the women's suffrage movement) contesting the legal privileges of men and forcing concessions from the state. In this context, agendas of reform in masculinity emerged: the temperance movement, compassionate marriage, homosexual rights movements, leading eventually to the pursuit of androgyny in "men's liberation" in the 1970s (Kimmel and Mosmiller 1992). Not all reconstructions of masculinity, however, emphasized tolerance or moved toward androgyny. The vehement masculinity politics of fascism, for instance, emphasized dominance and difference and glorified violence, a pattern still found in contemporary racist movements (Tillner 1997).

Masculinities of Postcolonialism and Neoliberalism

The process of decolonization disrupted the gender hierarchies of the colonial order and, where armed struggle was involved, might have involved a deliberate cultivation of masculine hardness and violence (as in South Africa; see Xaba 1997). Some activists and theorists of liberation struggles celebrated this, as a necessary response to colonial violence and emasculation; women in liberation struggles were perhaps less impressed. However one evaluates the process, one of the consequences of decolonization was another round of disruptions of community-based gender orders and another step in the reorientation of masculinities toward national and international contexts.

Nearly half a century after the main wave of decolonization, the old hierarchies persist in new shapes. With the collapse of Soviet communism, the decline of postcolonial socialism, and the ascendancy of the new right in Europe and North America, world politics is more and more organized around the needs of transnational capital and the creation of global markets.

The neoliberal agenda has little to say, explicitly, about gender: it speaks a gender-neutral language of "markets," "individuals," and "choice." But the world in which neoliberalism is ascendant is still a gendered world, and neoliberalism has an implicit gender politics. The "individual" of neoliberal theory has in general the attributes and interests of a male entrepreneur, the attack on the welfare state generally weakens the position of women, while the increasingly unregulated power of transnational corporations places strategic power in the hands of particular groups of men. It is not surprising, then, that the installation of capitalism in Eastern Europe and the former Soviet Union has been accompanied by a reassertion of dominating masculinities and, in some situations, a sharp worsening in the social position of women.

We might propose, then, that the hegemonic form of masculinity in the current world gender order is the masculinity associated with those who control its dominant institutions: the business executives who operate in global markets, and the political executives who interact (and in many contexts, merge) with them. I will call this *transnational business masculinity*. This is not readily available for ethnographic study, but we can get some clues to its character from its reflections in management literature, business journalism, and corporate self-promotion, and from studies of local business elites (e.g., Donaldson 1997).

As a first approximation, I would suggest this is a masculinity marked by increasing egocentrism, very conditional loyalties (even to the corporation), and a declining sense of responsibility for others (except for purposes of image making). Gee, Hull and Lankshear (1996), studying recent management textbooks, note the peculiar construction of the executive in "fast capitalism" as a person with no permanent commitments, except (in effect) to the idea of accumulation itself. Transnational business masculinity is characterized by a limited technical rationality (management theory), which is increasingly separate from science.

Transnational business masculinity differs from traditional bourgeois masculinity by its increasingly libertarian sexuality, with a growing tendency to commodify relations with women. Hotels catering to businessmen in most parts of the world now routinely offer pornographic videos, and in some parts of the world, there is a well-developed prostitution industry catering for international businessmen. Transnational business masculinity does not require bodily force, since the patriarchal dividend on which it rests is accumulated by impersonal, institutional means. But corporations increasingly use the exemplary bodies of elite sportsmen as a marketing tool (note the phenomenal growth of corporate "sponsorship" of sport in the last generation) and indirectly as a means of legitimation for the whole gender order.

MASCULINITY POLITICS ON A WORLD SCALE

Recognizing global society as an arena of masculinity formation allows us to pose new questions about masculinity politics. What social dynamics in the global arena give rise to masculinity politics, and what shape does global masculinity politics take?

The gradual creation of a world gender order has meant many local instabilities of gender. Gender instability is a familiar theme of poststructuralist theory, but this school of thought takes as a universal condition a situation that is historically specific. Instabilities range from the disruption of men's local cultural dominance as women move into the public realm and higher education, through the disruption of sexual identities that produced "queer" politics in the metropole, to the shifts in the urban intelligentsia that produced "the new sensitive man" and other images of gender change.

One response to such instabilities, on the part of groups whose power is challenged but still dominant, is to reaffirm *local* gender orthodoxies and hierarchies. A masculine fundamentalism is, accordingly, a common response in gender politics at present. A soft version, searching for an essential masculinity among myths and symbols, is offered by the mythopoetic men's movement in the United States and by the religious revivalists of the Promise Keepers (Messner 1997). A much harder version is found, in that country, in the right-wing militia movement brought to world attention by the Oklahoma City bombing (Gibson 1994), and in contemporary Afghanistan, if we can trust Western media reports, in the militant misogyny of the Taliban. It is no coincidence that in the two latter cases, hardline masculine fundamentalism goes together with a marked anti-internationalism. The world system—rightly enough—is seen as the source of pollution and disruption.

Not that the emerging global order is a hotbed of gender progressivism. Indeed, the neoliberal agenda for the reform of national and international economics involves closing down historic possibilities for gender reform. I have noted how it subverts the gender compromise represented by the metropolitan welfare state. It has also undermined the progressive-liberal agendas of sex role reform represented by affirmative action programs, antidiscrimination provisions, child care services, and the like. Right-wing parties and governments have been persistently cutting such programs, in the name of either individual liberties or global competitiveness. Through these means, the patriarchal dividend to men is defended or restored, without an *explicit* masculinity politics in the form of a mobilization of men.

Within the arenas of international relations, the international state, multinational corporations, and global markets, there is nevertheless a deployment of masculinities and a reasonably clear hegemony. The transnational business masculinity described above has had only one major competitor for hegemony in recent decades, the rigid, control-oriented masculinity of the military, and the military-style bureaucratic dictatorships of Stalinism. With the collapse of Stalinism and the end of the cold war, Big Brother (Orwell's famous parody of this form of masculinity) is a fading threat, and the more flexible, calculative, egocentric masculinity of the fast capitalist entrepreneur holds the world stage.

We must, however, recall two important conclusions of the ethnographic moment in masculinity research: that different forms of masculinity exist together and that hegemony is constantly subject to challenge. These are possibilities in the global arena too. Transnational business masculinity is not completely homogeneous; variations of it are embedded in different parts of the world system, which may not be completely compatible. We may distinguish a Confucian variant, based in East Asia, with a stronger commitment to hierarchy and social consensus, from a secularized Christian variant, based in North America, with more hedonism and individualism and greater tolerance for social conflict. In certain arenas, there is already conflict between the business and political leaderships embodying these forms of masculinity: initially over human rights versus Asian values, and more recently over the extent of trade and investment liberalization.

If these are contenders for hegemony, there is also the possibility of opposition to hegemony. The global circulation of "gay" identity (Altman 1996) is an important indication that nonhegemonic masculinities may operate in global arenas, and may even find a certain political articulation, in this case around human rights and AIDS prevention.

REFERENCES

Altman, Dennis. 1996. Rupture or continuity? The internationalisation of gay identities. *Social Text* 48 (3): 77–94.

Barrett, Frank J. 1996. The organizational construction of hegemonic masculinity: The case of the U.S. Navy. *Gender Work and Organization* 3 (3): 129–42.

BauSteineMaenner, ed. 1996. *Kritische Maennerforschung* [Critical research on men]. Berlin: Argument.

Bitterli, Urs. 1989. *Cultures in conflict: Encounters between European and non-European cultures, 1492–1800.* Stanford, CA: Stanford University Press.

Bolin, Anne. 1988. *In search of Eve: Transexual rites of passage.* Westport, CT: Bergin & Garvey.

Bulbeck, Chilla. 1992. *Australian women in Papua New Guinea: Colonial passages 1920–1960.* Cambridge, U.K.: Cambridge University Press.

Cain, P. J., and A. G. Hopkins. 1993. *British imperialism: Innovation and expansion, 1688–1914.* New York: Longman.

Carrigan, Tim, Bob Connell, and John Lee. 1985. Toward a new sociology of masculinity. *Theory and Society* 14 (5): 551–604.

Chodorow, Nancy. 1994. *Femininities, masculinities, sexualities: Freud and beyond.* Lexington: University Press of Kentucky.

Cockburn, Cynthia. 1983. *Brothers: Male dominance and technological change.* London: Pluto.

Cohen, Jon. 1991. NOMAS: Challenging male supremacy. *Changing Men* (Winter/Spring): 45–46.

Connell, R. W. 1987. *Gender and power.* Cambridge, MA: Polity.

———. 1990a. An iron man: The body and some contradictions of hegemonic masculinity. In *Sport, men and the gender order: Critical feminist perspectives,* edited by Michael A. Messner and Donald F. Sabo, 83–95. Champaign, IL: Human Kinetics Books.

———. 1990b. The state, gender and sexual politics: Theory and appraisal. *Theory and Society* 19: 507–44.

———. 1992. A very straight gay: Masculinity, homosexual experience and the dynamics of gender. *American Sociological Review* 57 (6): 735–51.

———. 1995. *Masculinities.* Cambridge, MA: Polity.

———. 1996. Teaching the boys: New research on masculinity, and gender strategies for schools. *Teachers College Record* 98 (2): 206–35.

Cornwall, Andrea, and Nancy Lindisfarne, eds. 1994. *Dislocating masculinity: Comparative ethnographies.* London: Routledge.

Dawson, Graham. 1991. The blond Bedouin: Lawrence of Arabia, imperial adventure and the imagining of English-British masculinity. In *Manful assertions: Masculinities in Britain since 1800,* edited by Michael Roper and John Tosh, 113–44. London: Routledge.

Donaldson, Mike. 1991. *Time of our lives: Labour and love in the working class.* Sydney: Allen & Unwin.

———. 1997. Growing up very rich: The masculinity of the hegemonic. Paper presented at the conference Masculinities: Renegotiating Genders, June, University of Wollongong, Australia.

Enloe, Cynthia. 1990. *Bananas, beaches and bases: Making feminist sense of international politics.* Berkeley: University of California Press.

Featherstone, Mike. 1995. *Undoing culture: Globalization, postmodernism and identity.* London: Sage.

Foley, Douglas E. 1990. *Learning capitalist culture: Deep in the heart of Tejas.* Philadelphia: University of Pennsylvania Press.

Fuentes, Annette, and Barbara Ehrenreich. 1983. *Women in the global factory.* Boston: South End.

Gee, James Paul, Glynda Hall, and Colin Lankshear. 1996. *The new work order: Behind the language of the new capitalism.* Sydney: Allen & Unwin.

Gender Equality Ombudsman. 1997. *The father's quota.* Information sheet on parental leave entitlements, Oslo.

Gibson, J. William. 1994. *Warrior dreams: Paramilitary culture in post-Vietnam America.* New York: Hill & Wang.

Hagemann-White, Carol, and Maria S. Rerrich, eds. 1988. *FrauenMaennerBilder* [Women, imaging, men]. Bielefeld: AJZ-Verlag.

Hearn, Jeff. 1987. *The gender of oppression: Men, masculinity and the critique of Marxism.* Brighton, U.K.: Wheatsheaf.

Herdt, Gilbert H. 1981. *Guardians of the flutes: Idioms of masculinity.* New York: McGraw-Hill.

———, ed. 1984. *Ritualized homosexuality in Melanesia.* Berkeley: University of California Press.

Heward, Christine. 1988. *Making a man of him: Parents and their sons' education at an English public school 1929–1950.* London: Routledge.

Hinsch, Bret. 1990. *Passions of the cut sleeve: The male homosexual tradition in China.* Berkeley: University of California Press.

Hirst, Paul, and Grahame Thompson. 1996. *Globalization in question: The international economy and the possibilities of governance.* Cambridge, MA: Polity.

Hollstein, Walter. 1992. *Machen Sie Platz, mein Herr! Teilen statt Herrschen* [Sharing instead of dominating]. Hamburg: Rowohlt.

Hollway, Wendy. 1994. Separation, integration and difference: Contradictions in a gender regime. In *Power/gender: Social relations in theory and practice,* edited by H. Lorraine Radtke and Henderikus Stam, 247–69. London: Sage.

Holter, Oystein Gullvag. 1997. Gender, patriarchy and capitalism: A social forms analysis. Ph.D. diss., University of Oslo, Faculty of Social Science.

Hondagneu-Sotelo, Pierrette, and Michael A. Messner. 1994. Gender displays and men's power: The "new man" and the Mexican immigrant man. In *Theorizing masculinities,* edited by Harry Brod and Michael Kaufman, 200–218. Thousand Oaks, CA: Sage.

Ito Kimio. 1993. *Otokorashisa-no-yukue* [Directions for masculinities]. Tokyo: Shinyo-sha.

Jolly, Margaret. 1997. From point Venus to Bali Ha'i: Eroticism and exoticism in representations of the Pacific. In *Sites of desire, economies of pleasure: Sexualities in Asia and the Pacific,* edited by Lenore Manderson and Margaret Jolly, 99–122. Chicago: University of Chicago Press.

Kandiyoti, Deniz. 1994. The paradoxes of masculinity: Some thoughts on segregated societies. In *Dislocating masculinity: Comparative ethnographies,* edited by Andrea Cornwall and Nancy Lindisfame, 197–213. London: Routledge.

Kaufman, Michael. 1997. Working with men and boys to challenge sexism and end men's violence. Paper presented at UNESCO expert group meeting on Male Roles and

Masculinities in the Perspective of a Culture of Peace, September, Oslo.

Kimmel, Michael S. 1987. Rethinking "masculinity": New directions in research. In *Changing men: New directions in research on men and masculinity*, edited by Michael S. Kimmel, 9–24. Newbury Park, CA: Sage.

———. 1996. *Manhood in America: A cultural history*. New York: Free Press.

Kimmel, Michael S., and Thomas P. Mosmiller, eds. 1992. *Against the tide: Pro-feminist men in the United States, 1776–1990, a documentary history*. Boston: Beacon.

Kindler, Heinz. 1993. *Maske(r)ade: Jungen-und Maenner-arbeit fuer die Pratis* [Work with youth and men]. Neuling: Schwaebisch Gmuend und Tuebingen.

Kinmonth, Earl H. 1981. *The self-made man in Meiji Japanese thought: From Samurai to salary man*. Berkeley: University of California Press.

Kipling, Rudyard. [1901] 1987. *Kim*. London: Penguin.

Klein, Alan M. 1993. *Little big men: Bodybuilding subculture and gender construction*. Albany: State University of New York Press.

Klein, Uta. 1997. Our best boys: The making of masculinity in Israeli society. Paper presented at UNESCO expert group meeting on Male Roles and Masculinities in the Perspectives of a Culture of Peace, September, Oslo.

Lewes, Kenneth. 1988. *The psychoanalytic theory of male homosexuality*. New York: Simon & Schuster.

MacDonald, Robert H. 1994. *The language of empire: Myths and metaphors of popular imperialism, 1880–1918*. Manchester, U.K.: Manchester University Press.

McElhinny, Bonnie. 1994. An economy of affect: Objectivity, masculinity and the gendering of police work. In *Dislocating masculinity: Comparative ethnographies*, edited by Andrea Cornwall and Nancy Lindisfarne, 159–71. London: Routledge.

McKay, Jim, and Debbie Huber. 1992. Anchoring media images of technology and sport. *Women's Studies International Forum* 15 (2): 205–18.

Messerschmidt, James W. 1997. *Crime as structured action: Gender, race, class, and crime in the making*. Thousand Oaks, CA: Sage.

Messner, Michael A. 1992. *Power at play: Sports and the problem of masculinity*. Boston: Beacon.

———. 1997. *The politics of masculinities: Men in movements*. Thousand Oaks, CA: Sage.

Metz-Goeckel, Sigrid, and Ursula Mueller. 1986. *Der Mann: Die Brigitte-Studie* [The male]. Beltz: Weinheim & Basel.

Mies, Maria. 1986. *Patriarchy and accumulation on a world scale: Women in the international division of labour*. London: Zed.

Moodie, T. Dunbar. 1994. *Going for gold: Men, mines, and migration*. Johannesburg: Witwatersand University Press.

Morrell, Robert. 1994. Boys, gangs, and the making of masculinity in the White secondary schools of Natal, 1880–1930. *Masculinities* 2 (2): 56–82.

———, ed. 1996. *Political economy and identities in KwaZulu-Natal: Historical and social perspectives*. Durban, Natal: Indicator Press.

Nakamura, Akira. 1994. *Watashi-no Danseigaku* [My men's studies]. Tokyo: Kindaibugei-sha.

Oftung, Knut, ed. 1994. *Menns bilder og bilder av menn* [Images of men]. Oslo: Likestillingsradet.

Phillips, Jock. 1987. *A man's country? The image of the Pakeha male—a history*. Auckland: Penguin.

Poynting, S., G. Noble, and P. Tabar. 1997. "Intersections" of masculinity and ethnicity: A study of male Lebanese immigrant youth in Western Sydney. Paper presented at the conference Masculinities: Renegotiating Genders, June, University of Wollongong, Australia.

Roper, Michael. 1991. Yesterday's model: Product fetishism and the British company man, 1945–85. In *Manful assertions: Masculinities in Britain since 1800*, edited by Michael Roper and John Tosh, 190–211. London: Routledge.

Schwalbe, Michael. 1996. *Unlocking the iron cage: The men's movement, gender, politics, and the American culture*. New York: Oxford University Press.

Segal, Lynne. 1997. *Slow motion: Changing masculinities, changing men*. 2d ed. London: Virago.

Seidler, Victor J. 1991. *Achilles heel reader: Men, sexual politics and socialism*. London: Routledge.

Shire, Chenjerai. 1994. Men don't go to the moon: Language, space and masculinities in Zimbabwe. In *Dislocating masculinity: Comparative ethnographies*, edited by Andrea Cornwall and Nancy Lindisfarne, 147–58. London: Routledge.

Simpson, Amelia. 1993. *Xuxa: The mega-marketing of a gender, race and modernity*. Philadelphia: Temple University Press.

Sinha, Mrinalini. 1995. *Colonial masculinity: The manly Englishman and the effeminate Bengali in the late nineteenth century*. Manchester, U.K.: Manchester University Press.

Taylor, Debbie. 1985. Women: An analysis. In *Women: A world report*, 1–98. London: Methuen.

Theberge, Nancy. 1991. Reflections on the body in the sociology of sport. *Quest* 43:123–34.

Thorne, Barrie. 1993. *Gender play: Girls and boys in school*. New Brunswick, NJ: Rutgers University Press.

Tillner, Georg. 1997. Masculinity and xenophobia. Paper presented at UNESCO meeting on Male Roles and Masculinities in the Perspective of a Culture of Peace, September, Oslo.

Tomsen, Stephen. 1997. A top night: Social protest, masculinity and the culture of drinking violence. *British Journal of Criminology* 37 (1): 90–103.

Tosh, John. 1991. Domesticity and manliness in the Victorian middle class: The family of Edward White Benson. In *Manful assertions: Masculinities in Britain since 1800*, edited by Michael Roper and John Tosh, 44–73. London: Routledge.

United Nations Educational, Scientific and Cultural Organization (UNESCO). 1997. *Male roles and masculinities in the perspective of a culture of peace: Report of expert group meeting, Oslo, 24–28 September 1997*. Paris: Women and a Culture of Peace Programme, Culture of Peace Unit, UNESCO.

Walby, Sylvia. 1990. *Theorizing patriarchy*. Oxford, U.K.: Blackwell.

Walker, James C. 1988. *Louts and legends: Male youth culture in an inner-city school*. Sydney: Allen & Unwin.

Wallerstein, Immanuel. 1974. *The modern world-system: Capitalist agriculture and the origins of the European world-economy in the sixteenth century*. New York: Academic Press.

Whitson, David. 1990. Sport in the social construction of masculinity. In *Sport, men, and the gender order: Critical feminist perspectives*, edited by Michael A. Messner and Donald F. Sabo, 19–29. Champaign, IL: Human Kinetics Books.

Widersprueche. 1995. Special Issue: *Maennlichkeiten*. Vol. 56/57.

Williams, Walter L. 1986. *The spirit and the flesh: Sexual diversity in American Indian culture*. Boston: Beacon.

Xaba, Thokozani. 1997. Masculinity in a transitional society: The rise and fall of the "young lions." Paper presented at the conference Masculinities in Southern Africa, June, University of Natal-Durban, Durban.

PART TWO

GENDER, CULTURE, AND SOCIALIZATION

Everyone is born into a culture—a set of shared ideas about the nature of reality, standards of right and wrong, and concepts for making sense of social interactions. These ideas are put into practice in behaviors and material objects. As totally dependent infants, we are socialized—taught the rules, roles, and relationships of the social world we will inherit. In the process of growing up, we learn to think, act, and feel as we are "supposed to." As adults, we are embedded in our culture's assumptions and images of gender.

One of the earliest and most deeply seated ideas to which we are socialized is that of gender identity—the idea that "I am a boy" or "I am a girl." Because the culture promotes strong ideas about what boys and girls are like, most of us learn to think of ourselves in terms of our gender identity (our "boyness" or "girlness") and adopt behaviors that are sex-assigned in our culture. Thus, for example, a girl who plays quietly with dolls is viewed as behaving in a feminine or "ladylike" manner, and a boy who plays with trucks is seen as appropriately masculine, as "all boy." Children who do not display these gender-stereotypical behaviors may face disapproval or punishment from adults and teasing or shunning by other children. Children who do not feel that their gender is right—that their bodies do not match their sense of their own gender identity—have a very difficult time in our society. Consciously or unconsciously, adults and peers categorize children as boys or girls, respond to and regard them differently, and encourage them to adopt behaviors and attitudes on the basis of their sex. We raise, in effect, two different kinds of children: girls and boys.

Parents are strong socializing influences, and they provide the first and most deeply experienced socialization. Despite claims to the contrary, American parents treat girls and boys differently. Boys and girls have different toys, names, and room decor, and adults play with them in different ways. The stores in which parents shop for children's toys or clothing have separate aisles for boys' and girls' items, which can easily be identified by the dominant color (waves of pink packaging are a clue that the aisle contains girls' items). Even if parents monitor their actions in the hope of preventing sexism from affecting their child, other socializing influences—schools, mass media, and other children—bear down on children.

One of the primary socializing influences is language. When we learn to talk, we also learn the thought patterns and communication styles of our culture. Those patterns and styles reinforce differentiation by sex and perpetuate sex stereotyping, although the kind of stereotyping may vary from language to language. All languages teach their culture's ideas about men and women. In the English language, for example, the generic man is supposed to include males and females, as well as people of all races and ethnicities; but in linguistic practice, it does not, as Richardson shows in Section 3. People other than white and male are linguistically tagged in writing and in speech. For example, occupational categories are sex- or race-tagged if the person's sex or race does not fit cultural stereotypes about who will be in those occupations. Consider: doctor/woman doctor/black woman doctor or nurse/male nurse/Asian male nurse. Linguistic tags convey normative expectations about who should occupy particular positions in society and about the normality or legitimacy of white men's claim to powerful positions. When a child asks, "Were there any cave women?" for example, we realize the picture conveyed by the term "cavemen."

As societies have become more complex, the mass media increasingly have become centralized agents that transmit dominant cultural beliefs. Movements toward cultural heterogeneity are thwarted through the homogenizing effects of television, in particular. TV presents gender stereotypes in their purest and simplest forms. Whether the program is about African-American families, doctors at work, wealthy white teenagers in New York City, talking animals, or bachelors searching for the perfect wife, the stereotyping messages about gender and race are endlessly repetitive. Children in the United States spend more time watching TV than they spend in school or interacting with parents or peers. Moreover, they believe that what they see on TV is an accurate representation of how the world is and should be organized. White middle-class male dominance and sexualized, passive femininity are the repetitive themes.

The socialization effected by the family, language, and the mass media is continued in the educational system. Schools are formally charged with teaching the young. While teaching reading, writing, and arithmetic, however, schools also teach conventional views of gender. They do so through patterns of staffing (male principals and custodians, female teachers and food servers), curriculum, the sex segregation of sports and activities (whether formal or informal), and different expectations for boys and girls. Children themselves reinforce these messages through sex-segregated play and the teasing of children who do not conform.

Socialization—whether through the home, the school, language, or the mass media—creates and sustains gender differences. Boys are taught that they will inherit the privileges and prestige of manhood and that they must be tough, aggressive, and interested in cars, fighting, and sports. Girls, in contrast, learn that they are less socially valuable than boys and that they should be quiet, pretty, and interested in babies, fashion, and boys. Subcultures that promote values and beliefs different from the mainstream do exist, and individuals do not necessarily internalize every message from the dominant culture. In fact, many children and adults challenge the culture of gender difference directly, and many others live their lives in ways that do not conform to the stereotypes and expectations for their gender. Nevertheless, traditional cultural views of gender are ubiquitous and powerful.

Through influential social institutions, children learn and consume a culture. Our culture is one that views men and masculinity as superior to women and femininity. It is a system that assigns different behaviors and attitudes to males and females and that further distinguishes between people of different racial and ethnic groups. As adults, we continue to be shaped by the books and magazines we read, the movies and TV shows we see, the music we enjoy, and the people with whom we spend time. The ways that gender is portrayed or represented in the culture—in mass media, schools, and public discussions—provide us with our only conceptual tools for thinking about men and women. It becomes nearly impossible to think about gender without being shaped by the images that surround us.

The readings in this part of Feminist Frontiers illustrate and explain different aspects of cultural constructions of gender and the socialization process. These systems of meaning shape how we understand ourselves and our social institutions. The readings document both the prevalence of conventional understandings in the culture and the presence of alternative messages. As you read, consider what kinds of influences conventional representations of gender have and what sources exist for challenging these images.

Representation, Language, and Culture

Our gender culture includes the language we use and the images that surround us in advertising, mass media, and daily life. We are confronted by images of gender in all areas of our lives. In our language, mass media, and daily lives, we encounter particular definitions of what it means to be a woman or a man. Often we take these images for granted, and the ways that women and men are represented seem natural or inevitable. Yet language and media representations of gender shape the way we view ourselves and our relationships to each other and to the world around us. This section explores the images of women and men expressed in language and mass media, as well as their relationship to culture and daily life more broadly.

Laurel Richardson's "Gender Stereotyping in the English Language" demonstrates the major ways in which sexism pervades the structure and standard usage of modern American English. Her analysis reveals different expectations of women and men embedded in the language and shows how we internalize and reinforce gender differences, as we read, write, and speak English or hear it spoken. The reading raises questions about the relationships between language and social life, including connections between linguistic change and other forms of social change. What are some examples of sexist or nonsexist language? If you speak or have studied another language, compare its gender structure to that of English. Do you think using nonsexist language affects people's

attitudes toward women? How? An interesting question for classroom debate is whether the word "guy" or the phrase "you guys" is gender neutral. In "Sexing the Internet," danah boyd analyzes the use of sex as a marker of identity online. In the early days of the Internet, theorists imagined that the online world would allow users to define themselves flexibly, free of the categories and stereotypes that define us offline. Contrary to this utopian vision, boyd shows, users must enter their sex, and usually other identifiers such as age, location, and occupation, in order to create accounts on social networking and other Web sites. By doing so, they create online personas that rely on "coarse categorizations," meaning that when we meet people online, we rely on the stereotypes their limited information connotes. In this way, profiles affect interaction. The pressures of online advertising, which requires a demographic description of a site's traffic and targets advertisements based on individual users' profiles, makes it unlikely that major sites will abandon the use of sex as a category.

How is your online identity shaped by sex and by gender? In what ways do you observe gender affecting your online interactions? Think of examples of targeted advertising by gender. Examine your Facebook advertisements, if you have a Facebook page; how are they targeted to your gender, and how do they change if you change your gender on your Facebook profile? Even in the short time since boyd wrote her article and since this book was published, the online world has changed. What changes do you notice regarding sex and gender online? If you see these issues as problematic, can you think of solutions?

Josée Johnston and Judith Taylor's "Feminist Consumerism and Fat Activists" moves to the arena of advertising and daily life. Taylor contrasts how the Dove Campaign for Real Beauty talked about broader views of what kinds of bodies can be seen as beautiful with the much more radical redefinitions of feminine beauty advocated by a fat activist group. Although the Dove campaign challenged the view that only extremely thin women are beautiful, it nevertheless presented beauty as central to women's identities. In contrast, the fat activist group not only celebrated fat women's bodies but attempted to resist the idea that women are defined by their appearance. Yet while the Dove campaign reached a broad audience, the grassroots and radical nature of the fat activist group meant that it reached only a relatively small audience. What effect, if any, do you think the Dove campaign had on definitions of beauty and weight? Can you think of other advertising campaigns that challenged definitions of beauty or that presented alternative views of women or men more generally? How much power do you think advertising has to change gender? What limits its power? In contrast, what kinds of changes can grassroots campaigns like the one Taylor describes make?

Debra Gimlin describes one of the consequences of cultural messages of beauty on women: the high rates of cosmetic surgery. In "Cosmetic Surgery: Paying for Your Beauty," she discusses the phenomenal rise in the United States of elective cosmetic surgeries such as liposuction, breast augmentation (and reduction), blepharoplasty (eyelid surgery), facelift, and chemical peel. Ninety percent of patients undergoing such procedures are women. Criticism of such surgeries focus not only on the risks and costs but also on the increasing pressure for women to take advantage of medical advances to fight aging, imperfection, and ethnic deviations from an Anglo ideal of beauty.

Yet Gimlin, in interviewing women who had undergone plastic surgery, challenges the notion that women are simply dupes of the culture. She finds that women set realistic and limited goals—not the attainment of perfect beauty—when they seek plastic surgery, and that the surgery often makes them feel better about their bodies and themselves. Gimlin offers a complex view of cosmetic surgery. Do you think cosmetic surgery is a reasonable choice for women? How important are cultural ideals in making women dislike parts of their bodies? Can you imagine seeking cosmetic surgery for yourself?

In the next selection, Ingrid Banks, author of a book called *Hair Matters*, argues in "Hair Still Matters" that hair continues to carry complex meanings for African-American women. From Venus Williams and her controversial beaded braids to Yaya DaCosta Johnson, a contestant on "America's Next Top Model" who was considered "Afrocentric" because she did not straighten her hair, African-American women's hairstyles make statements about race, gender, sexuality, and culture. Banks listens to the voices of African-American women talking about how hair is perceived by others and how they feel about their own hair. She also connects the issue of hair to global issues of beauty and women's bodies. Can you think of examples from popular culture in which long hair signals beauty and femininity for African-American women? What are the standards for beautiful hair for other racial or ethnic groups? Do other ethnic groups also attempt to conform to white standards of beauty? Are there similar pressures for men? What do different hairstyles signal about the people who choose to wear them? Do you judge women's femininity and sexuality based on hairstyle?

Language and mass media are central to the construction of our understanding of women's and men's positions in society. We are exposed to these images continually. Because the language we have acquired and the images we use are so deeply rooted, it is very difficult for us to break free of them, to see and describe the world and our experiences in nonsexist ways. Yet women and other subordinate groups attempt to construct alternative systems of meaning and to draw strength from cultures of resistance. The power to define has a major influence on our conceptions of others and ourselves.

Gender Stereotyping in the English Language
First published in 1981

Everyone in our society, regardless of class, ethnicity, sex, age, or race, is exposed to the same language, the language of the dominant culture. Analysis of verbal language can tell us a great deal about a people's fears, prejudices, anxieties, and interests. A rich vocabulary on a particular subject indicates societal interests or obsessions (e.g., the extensive vocabulary about cars in America). And different words for the same subject (such as *freedom fighter* and *terrorist, passed away* and *croaked, make love* and *ball*) show that there is a range of attitudes and feelings in the society toward that subject.

It should not be surprising, then, to find differential attitudes and feelings about men and women rooted in the English language. Although English has not been completely analyzed, six general propositions concerning these attitudes and feelings about males and females can be made.

First, in terms of grammatical and semantic structure, women do not have a fully autonomous, independent existence; they are part of man. The language is not divided into male and female with distinct conjugations and declensions, as many other languages are. Rather, *women* are included under the generic *man*. Grammar books specify that the pronoun *he* can be used generically to mean *he or she*. Further, *man*, when used as an indefinite pronoun, grammatically refers to both men and women. So, for example, when we read *man* in the following phrases we are to interpret it as applying to both men and women: "man the oars," "one small step for man, one giant step for mankind," "man, that's tough," "man overboard," "man the tool-maker," "alienated man," "garbageman." Our rules of etiquette complete the grammatical presumption of inclusivity. When two persons are pronounced "man and wife," Miss Susan Jones changes her entire name to Mrs. Robert Gordon (Vanderbilt, 1972). In each of these correct usages, women are a part of man; they do not exist autonomously. The exclusion of women is well expressed in Mary Daly's ear-jarring slogan "the sisterhood of man" (1973:7–21).

However, there is some question as to whether the theory that *man* means everybody is carried out in practice (see Bendix, 1979; Martyna, 1980). For example, an eight-year-old interrupts her reading of "The Story of the Cavemen" to ask how we got here without cavewomen. A ten-year-old thinks it is dumb to have a woman post*man*. A beginning anthropology student believes (incorrectly) that all shamans ("witch doctors") are males because her textbook and professor use the referential pronoun *he*.

But beginning language learners are not the only ones who visualize males when they see the word *man*. Research has consistently demonstrated that when the generic *man* is used, people visualize men, not women (Schneider & Hacker, 1973; DeStefano, 1976; Martyna, 1978; Hamilton & Henley, 1982). DeStefano, for example, reports that college students choose silhouettes of males for sentences with the word *man* or *men* in them. Similarly, the presumably generic *he* elicits images of men rather than women. The finding is so persistent that linguists doubt whether there actually is a semantic generic in English (MacKay, 1983).

Man, then, suggests not humanity but rather male images. Moreover, over one's lifetime, an educated American will be exposed to the prescriptive *he* more than a million times (MacKay, 1983). One consequence is the exclusion of women in the visualization, imagination, and thought of males and females. Most likely this linguistic practice perpetuates in men their feelings of dominance over and responsibility for women, feelings that interfere with the development of equality in relationships.

Second, in actual practice, our pronoun usage perpetuates different personality attributes and career aspirations for men and women. Nurses, secretaries, and elementary school teachers are almost invariably referred to as *she;* doctors, engineers, electricians, and presidents as *he.* In one classroom, students referred to an unidentified child as *he* but shifted to *she* when discussing the child's parent. In a faculty discussion of the problems of acquiring new staff, all architects, engineers, security officers, faculty, and computer programmers were referred to as *he;* secretaries and file clerks were referred to as *she.* Martyna (1978) has noted that speakers consistently use *he* when the referent has a high-status occupation (e.g., doctor, lawyer, judge) but shift to *she* when the occupations have lower status (e.g., nurse, secretary).

Even our choice of sex ascription to nonhuman objects subtly reinforces different personalities for males and females. It seems as though the small (e.g., kittens), the graceful (e.g., poetry), the unpredictable (e.g., the fates), the nurturant (e.g., the church, the school), and that which is owned and/or controlled by men (e.g., boats, cars, governments, nations) represent the feminine, whereas that which is a controlling forceful power in and of itself (e.g., God, Satan, tiger) primarily represents the masculine. Even athletic teams are not immune. In one college, the men's teams are called the Bearcats and the women's teams the Bearkittens.

Some of you may wonder whether it matters that the female is linguistically included in the male. The inclusion of women under the pseudogeneric *man* and the prescriptive *he,* however, is not a trivial issue. Language has tremendous power to shape attitudes and influence behavior. Indeed, MacKay (1983) argues that the prescriptive *he* "has all the characteristics of a highly effective propaganda technique": frequent repetition, early age of acquisition (before age six), covertness (*he* is not thought of as propaganda), use by high-prestige sources (including university texts and professors), and indirectness (presented as though it were a matter of common knowledge). As a result, the prescriptive affects females' sense of life options and feelings of well-being. For example, Adamsky (1981) found that women's sense of power and importance was enhanced when the prescriptive *he* was replaced by *she.*

Awareness of the impact of the generic *man* and prescriptive *he* has generated considerable activity to change the language. One change, approved by the Modern Language Association, is to replace the prescriptive *he* with the plural *they*—as was accepted practice before the eighteenth century. Another is the use of *he or she.* Although it sounds awkward at first, the *he or she* designation is increasingly being used in the media and among people who have recognized the power of the pronoun to perpetuate sex stereotyping. When a professor, for example, talks about "the lawyer" as "he or she," a speech pattern that counteracts sex stereotyping is modeled. This drive to neutralize the impact of pronouns is evidenced further in the renaming of occupations: a policeman is now a police officer, a postman is a mail carrier, a stewardess is a flight attendant.

Third, linguistic practice defines females as immature, incompetent, and incapable and males as mature, complete, and competent. Because the words *man* and *woman* tend to connote sexual and human maturity, common speech, organizational titles, public addresses, and bathroom doors frequently designate the women in question as *ladies.* Simply contrast the different connotations of *lady* and *woman* in the following common phrases:

> *Luck, be a lady (woman) tonight.*
> *Barbara's a little lady (woman).*
> *Ladies' (Women's) Air Corps.*

In the first two examples, the use of *lady* desexualizes the contextual meaning of *woman.* So trivializing is the use of *lady* in the last phrase that the second is wholly anomalous. The male equivalent, *lord,* is never used, and its synonym, *gentleman,* is used infrequently. When *gentleman* is used, the assumption seems to be that certain culturally condoned aspects of masculinity (e.g., aggressivity, activity, and strength) should be set aside in the interests of maturity and order, as in the following phrases:

> *A gentlemen's (men's) agreement.*
> *A duel between gentlemen (men).*
> *He's a real gentleman (man).*

Rather than feeling constrained to set aside the stereotypes associated with *man,* males frequently find the opposite process occurring. The contextual connotation of *man* places a strain on males to be continuously sexually and socially potent, as the following examples reveal:

> *I was not a man (gentleman) with her tonight.*
> *This is a man's (gentleman's) job.*
> *Be a man (gentleman).*

Whether males, therefore, feel competent or anxious, valuable or worthless in particular contexts is influenced by the demands placed on them by the expectations of the language.

Not only are men infrequently labeled *gentlemen*, but they are infrequently labeled *boys*. The term *boy* is reserved for young males, bellhops, and car attendants, and as a putdown to those males judged inferior. *Boy* connotes immaturity and powerlessness. Only occasionally do males "have a night out with the boys." They do not talk "boy talk" at the office. Rarely does our language legitimize carefreeness in males. Rather, they are expected, linguistically, to adopt the responsibilities of manhood.

On the other hand, women of all ages may be called *girls*. Grown females "play bridge with the girls" and indulge in "girl talk." They are encouraged to remain childlike, and the implication is that they are basically immature and without power. Men can become men, linguistically, putting aside the immaturity of childhood; indeed, for them to retain the openness and playfulness of boyhood is linguistically difficult.

Further, the presumed incompetence and immaturity of women are evidenced by the linguistic company they keep. Women are categorized with children ("women and children first"), the infirm ("the blind, the lame, the women"), and the incompetent ("women, convicts, and idiots"). The use of these categorical designations is not accidental happenstance; "rather these selectional groupings are powerful forces behind the actual expressions of language and are based on distinctions which are not regarded as trivial by the speakers of the language" (Key, 1975:82). A total language analysis of categorical groupings is not available, yet it seems likely that women tend to be included in groupings that designate incompleteness, ineptitude, and immaturity. On the other hand, it is difficult for us to conceive of the word *man* in any categorical grouping other than one that extends beyond humanity, such as "Man, apes, and angels" or "Man and Superman." That is, men do exist as an independent category capable of autonomy; women are grouped with the stigmatized, the immature, and the foolish. Moreover, when men are in human groupings, they are invariably first on the list ("men and women," "he and she," "man and wife"). This order is not accidental but was prescribed in the sixteenth century to honor the worthier party.

Fourth, in practice women are defined in terms of their sexual desirability (to men); men are defined in terms of their sexual prowess (over women). Most slang words in reference to women refer to their sexual desirability to men (e.g., *dog, fox, broad, ass, chick*). Slang about men refers to their sexual prowess over women (e.g., *dude, stud, hunk*). The fewer examples given for men is not an oversight. An analysis of sexual slang, for example, listed more than a thousand words and phrases that derogate women sexually but found "nowhere near this multitude for describing men" (Kramarae, 1975:72). Farmer and Henley (cited in Schulz, 1975) list five hundred synonyms for *prostitute*, for example, and only sixty-five for *whoremonger*. Stanley (1977) reports two hundred twenty terms for a sexually promiscuous woman and only twenty-two for a sexually promiscuous man. Shuster (1973) reports that the passive verb form is used in reference to women's sexual experiences (e.g., *to be laid, to be had, to be taken*), whereas the active tense is used in reference to the male's sexual experience (e.g., *lay, take, have*). Being sexually attractive to males is culturally condoned for women and being sexually powerful is approved for males. In this regard, the slang of the street is certainly not countercultural; rather, it perpetuates and reinforces different expectations in females and males as sexual objects and performers.

Further, we find sexual connotations associated with neutral words applied to women. A few examples should suffice. A male academician questioned the title of a new course, asserting it was "too suggestive." The title? "The Position of Women in the Social Order." A male tramp is simply a hobo, but a female tramp is a slut. And consider the difference in connotation of the following expressions:

> *It's easy.*
> *He's easy.*
> *She's easy.*

In the first, we assume something is "easy to do"; in the second, we might assume a professor is an "easy grader" or a man is "easygoing." But when we read "she's easy," the connotation is "she's an easy lay."

In the world of slang, men are defined by their sexual prowess. In the world of slang and proper speech, women are defined as sexual objects. The rule in practice seems to be: If in doubt, assume that *any* reference to a women has a sexual connotation. For both genders, the constant bombardment of prescribed sexuality is bound to have real consequences.

Fifth, women are defined in terms of their relations to men; men are defined in terms of their relations to the world at large. A good example is seen in the words *master* and *mistress*. Originally these words had the same meaning—"a person who holds power over servants." With the demise of the feudal system, however, these words took on different meanings. The masculine variant metaphorically refers to power over something, as in "He is the master of his trade"; the feminine variant metaphorically (although probably not in actuality) refers to power over a man sexually, as in "She is Tom's mistress." Men are defined in terms of their power in the occupational world, women in terms of their sexual power over men.

The existence of two contractions for Mistress (*Miss* and *Mrs.*) and but one for Mister (*Mr.*) underscores the cultural concern and linguistic practice: women are defined in relation to men. Even a divorced woman is defined in terms of her no-longer-existing relation to a man (she is still *Mrs. Man's Name*). But apparently the divorced state is not relevant enough to the man or to the society to require a label. A divorced woman is a *divorcée*, but what do you call a divorced man? The recent preference of many women to be called *Ms.* is an attempt to provide for women an equivalency title that is not dependent on marital status.

Sixth, a historical pattern can be seen in the meanings that come to be attached to words that originally were neutral: those that apply to women acquire obscene and/or debased connotations, but no such pattern of derogation holds for neutral words referring to men. The processes of *pejoration* (the acquiring of an obscene or debased connotation) and *amelioration* (the reacquiring of a neutral or positive connotation) in the English language in regard to terms for males and females have been studied extensively by Muriel Schulz (1975).

Leveling is the least derogative form of pejoration. Through leveling, titles that originally referred to an elite class of persons come to include a wider class of persons. Such democratic leveling is more common for female designates than for males. For example, contrast the following: *lord–lady; baronet–dame; governor–governess*.

Most frequently what happens to words designating women as they become pejorated, however, is that they come to denote or connote sexual wantonness. *Sir* and *mister,* for example, remain titles of courtesy, but at some time *madam, miss,* and *mistress* have come to designate, respectively, a brothelkeeper, a prostitute, and

an unmarried sexual partner of a male (Schulz, 1975:66).

Names for domestic helpers, if they are females, are frequently derogated. *Hussy,* for example, originally meant "housewife." *Laundress, needlewoman, spinster* ("tender of the spinning wheel"), and *nurse* all referred to domestic occupations within the home, and all at some point became slang expressions for prostitute or mistress.

Even kinship terms referring to women become denigrated. During the seventeenth century, *mother* was used to mean "a bawd"; more recently *mother* (*mothuh f—*) has become a common derogatory epithet (Cameron, 1974). Probably at some point in history every kinship term for females has been derogated (Schulz, 1975:66).

Terms of endearment for women also seem to follow a downward path. Such pet names as Tart, Dolly, Kitty, Polly, Mopsy, Biddy, and Jill all eventually became sexually derogatory (Schulz, 1975:67). *Whore* comes from the same Latin root as *care* and once meant "a lover of either sex."

Indeed, even the most neutral categorical designations—*girl, female, woman, lady*—at some point in their history have been used to connote sexual immorality. *Girl* originally meant "a child of either sex"; through the process of semantic degeneration it eventually meant "a prostitute." Although *girl* has lost this meaning, *girlie* still retains sexual connotations. *Woman* connoted "a mistress" in the early nineteenth century; *female* was a degrading epithet in the latter part of the nineteenth century; and when *lady* was introduced as a euphemism, it too became deprecatory. "Even so neutral a term as *person,* when it was used as substitute for *woman,* suffered [vulgarization]" (Mencken, 1963:350, quoted in Schulz, 1975:71).

Whether one looks at elite titles, occupational roles, kinship relationships, endearments, or age-sex categorical designations, the pattern is clear. Terms referring to females are pejorated—"become negative in the middle instances and abusive in the extremes" (Schulz, 1975:69). Such semantic derogation, however, is not evidenced for male referents. *Lord, baronet, father, brother, nephew, footman, bowman, boy, lad, fellow, gentleman, man, male,* and so on "have failed to undergo the derogation found in the history of their corresponding feminine designations" (Schulz, 1975:67). Interestingly, the male word, rather than undergoing derogation, frequently is replaced by a female referent when the speaker wants to debase a male. A weak man, for example, is referred to as a *sissy* (diminutive of *sister*), and an army recruit during basic training is called a *pussy*. And when one is swearing at a male, he is referred to as a *bastard* or a *son of a bitch*—both appellations that impugn the dignity of a man's mother.

In summary, these verbal practices are consistent with the gender stereotypes that we encounter in everyday life. Women are thought to be a part of man, nonautonomous, dependent, relegated to roles that require few skills, characteristically incompetent and immature, sexual objects, best defined in terms of their relations to men. Males are visible, autonomous and independent, responsible for the protection and containment of women, expected to occupy positions on the basis of their high achievement or physical power, assumed to be sexually potent, and defined primarily by their relations to the world of work. The use of the language perpetuates the stereotypes for both genders and limits the options available for self-definition.

REFERENCES

Adamsky, C. 1981. "Changes in pronominal usage in a classroom situation." *Psychology of Women Quarterly* 5:773–79.

Bendix, J. 1979. "Linguistic models as political symbols: Gender and the generic 'he' in English." In J. Orasanu, M. Slater, and L. L. Adler, eds., *Language, Sex and Gender: Does la différence Make a Difference?* pp. 23–42. New York: New Academy of Science Annuals.

Cameron, P. 1974. "Frequency and kinds of words in various social settings, or What the hell's going on?" In M. Truzzi, ed., *Sociology for Pleasure*, pp. 31–37. Englewood Cliffs, N.J.: Prentice-Hall.

Daly, M. 1973. *Beyond God the Father.* Boston: Beacon Press.

DeStefano, J. S. 1976. Personal communication. Columbus: Ohio State University.

Hamilton, N., & Henley, N. 1982. "Detrimental consequences of the generic masculine usage." Paper presented to the Western Psychological Association meetings, Sacramento.

Key, M. R. 1975. *Male/Female Language.* Metuchen, N.J.: Scarecrow Press.

Kramarae, Cheris. 1975. "Woman's speech: Separate but unequal?" In Barrie Thorne and Nancy Henley, eds., *Language and Sex: Difference and Dominance*, pp. 43–56. Rowley, Mass.: Newbury House.

MacKay, D. G. 1983. "Prescriptive grammar and the pronoun problem." In B. Thorne, C. Kramarae, and N. Henley, eds., *Language, Gender, and Society*, pp. 38–53. Rowley, Mass.: Newbury House.

Martyna, W. 1978. "What does 'he' mean? Use of the generic masculine." *Journal of Communication* 28:131–38.

Martyna, W. 1980. "Beyond the 'he/man' approach: The case for nonsexist language." *Signs* 5:482–93.

Mencken, H. L. 1963. *The American Language.* 4th ed. with supplements. Abr. and ed. R. I. McDavis. New York: Knopf.

Schneider, J., & Hacker, S. 1973. "Sex role imagery in the use of the generic 'man' in introductory texts: A case in the sociology of sociology." *American Sociologist* 8.12–18.

Schulz, M. R. 1975. "The semantic derogation of women." In B. Thorne and N. Henley, eds., *Language and Sex: Difference and Dominance*, pp. 64–75. Rowley, Mass.: Newbury House.

Shuster, Janet. 1973. "Grammatical forms marked for male and female in English." Unpublished paper. Chicago: University of Chicago.

Stanley, J. P. 1977. "Paradigmatic woman: The prostitute." In D. L. Shores, ed., *Papers in Language Variation.* Birmingham: University of Alabama Press.

Vanderbilt, A. 1972. *Amy Vanderbilt's Etiquette.* Garden City, N.Y.: Doubleday.

Sexing the Internet: Reflections on the Role of Identification in Online Communities

First published in 2001

INTRODUCTION

On June 14 2001, the *New York Times* technology section carried a review of instant messaging software options (Biersdorfer 2001). Writing about his attempts to create user IDs across five different instant messengers, the reviewer, J.D. Biersdorfer, noted that, 'Moving on to register for Yahoo Messenger, I found myself asked to fill in fields marked gender and occupation before I could advance to the software downloading area. I tried to blow by but was hit with a stern error message: "Gender is a required value. Occupation is a required value." (I am sure there is a paper on contemporary American socialization or a post-postmodernism riff in there somewhere.)' This is that paper.

I came of age in America at a time when identity politics dominated most academic discourse, and carried over into popular culture and politics. At that same time, the PC was moving home, and the Internet, in its embryonic forms, gained acceptance beyond research environments. Without even realizing it, i learned to perform my identity simultaneously in digital, as well as physical, environments. As a precocious teenager, the multiple personalities of my online identity proved a terrific staging ground for learning about myself, and the world around me. While attending graduate school, i have been able to reexamine those experiences through an analytical lens, and to contextualize them more broadly. As a participant in online communities . . ., i have been witness to, and agent in, remarkable shifts in online social norms. In what follows, i draw on my experiences and interactions with others, as well as a few targeted conversations, in order to understand the impact of current practices on the online community.

In this [selection], i examine how demographic profiles can and do affect online social interactions. [I] begin with a review of the utopian ideals of online communities and the ways those ideals have been popularized. The remainder of the [selection] is concerned with the experience of getting and being online. [I] discuss how , in order to gain access to most online communities, one has to construct one's identities through a series of pre-selected and prescribed options, specifically age, sex and location. Here i am interested in the ways such identities are being manipulated. [I] conclude with a discussion of how sex as a marker of identity reproduces societal norms, both online and offline. It is my contention that the reliance on sex as a marker of identity online has encouraged a certain kind of re-embodiment of users (as sexed beings), with an attendant sexualizing of cyberspace. I suggest that the use of gender instead allows greater flexibility for users seeking to create new and fluid identities online.

THE IDEAL

In their 1996 novel *Nearly Roadkill,* Caitlin Sullivan and Kate Bornstein create a fictional society in which online communities thrive and social interaction is the primary use of networked technology (Sullivan 1996). Recognizing the economic possibilities of targeted advertising in these online worlds, the government and advertising industry work together to require that everyone register their identity through a list of markers including race, age, income, and sex. Initially, almost everyone in this fictional society accepts these markings. A few disgruntled members of the community decide that this practice needed to be questioned. Through their vocal rebellion, they gather massive support and the online community stages a successful 24-hour voluntary boycott of the Internet, resulting in systematic change. Although *Nearly Roadkill* was written in the mid-1990s, before the mass popularization of the Internet, its vision of a commercialized online world has certainly been realized. . . . It remains to be seen whether we will also realize a mass social resistance to these commercial practices.

In the late 1980s and early 1990s, many academics also imagined that virtual environments would offer a utopian world where sex, race, class, gender, age, and sexual orientation ceased to be relevant. While early systems appeared to offer these options, as the masses joined the Internet bandwagon, they brought many social norms with them. Although much of the early Internet, with its roots in research, was free, the growing population of users suggested commercial possibilities to many entrepreneurs. Working out how to make money on and offline been a complicated problem, but the first step has always been to have a better sense of who all these users are. As a result, commercialization of online environments has resulted in mandated profiling of individuals users.[1] These profiling practices have a wide variety of effects on the social environment, ranging from reemphasizing the male/female dichotomy to altering the social norms of introduction.

In order to profit from the tremendous expansion while still offering free access to consumers organizers of online communities, including large portal sites such as Microsoft and Yahoo! [and Facebook], sought advertising.[2] In order to directly target consumers, advertisers require that these sites collect and make available demographic information about users. To comply, most commercial sites require users to identify themselves through a collection of demographic labels, usually including sex, age, and zip code (which can predict race and socio-economic class with reasonable accuracy). In some sites, these labels are made part of the user's profile, and thus play a significant identifying role during social interactions online. For example, while Yahoo! does not publicly reveal one's email address, one's sex is automatically placed in parentheses next to one's membership; to change this, one must go click through six layers of personal information and then agree to Yahoo!'s terms of service.

Supporters of labeling suggest that this practice is beneficial, as it replicates the information available in physical interactions, allowing for appropriate behaviors and pronoun usage. Detractors claim that these coarsely drawn category labels are quite different from the more subtle cues present in real life and that they hinder the development of rich mediated communities by magnifying preexisting stereotypes, encouraging deception, and automatically sexualizing virtual spaces. Meanwhile, advertisers and those attempting to profit from online traffic continue to require collection of personalized information about individual users (and potential consumers), in ways simply not possible in offline spaces.

THE UTOPIA-IZATION OF ONLINE SPACES

As digital pioneers, Donna Haraway, Sandy Stone and Sherry Turkle imagined the possibility of life online as a way to transcend physical identity and marked bodies. Cyberspace became a site, or series of sites, in which identity might be deliberately and consciously performed (a la Judith Butler). This reading of cyberspace was seductive, and spread from the academy across a range of communities generating considerable discussion in academic, radical feminist, and queer circles. These ideas were played out in some . . . early virtual worlds, such as LambdaMOO, where you could identify yourself as belonging to a wide variety of races and genders, beyond those that exist in the physical world.

Although early digital writing suggested that this was the perfect frontier to escape the inequalities of the physical world, researchers quickly discovered that the physical problems did not disappear in a virtual world. Indeed, O'Brien argues that individuals tend to reproduce, if not hypergender, their real world identities (O'Brien 1999). More significantly, even when people attempt to escape their physical identities, their deception is often quite apparent to other people within the space (Donath 1998; Berman 2000).

While academics continue to hope that the cyberutopia will be realized, the ongoing commercialization of online communities only magnifies existing identity markers by continuing to legitimate, even demand, their use. Although the desired utopia is impractical, i believe that it's possible to improve on what is currently available and find ways to move beyond a rigid set of social classifications to something more fluid and flexible.

GETTING ONLINE IN THE REAL WORLD— IT'S ALL ABOUT AGE, SEX AND LOCATION (A/S/L)

. . . [I] was forced to join Yahoo! in order to manage the myriad of mailing list subscriptions that are an intimate part of my digital life. Although i had previously considered signing up with Yahoo! for instant messaging purposes, i had avoided doing so for fear of the initial, but required, questionnaire, challenging me with impossible questions. First, i must choose one of a series of pre-selected secret questions, in case i forget my password and need to ask the friendly customer service people; i can't answer any of them. I don't have an all-time favorite sports team; i don't remember my father's middle name, the name of my first school or my high school's mascot; i have never chosen a favorite pastime; i don't have a pet at this moment and i certainly don't know where i met my spouse. I answer one of them randomly, deciding to hope that i just remember my password. The next step, birth date, is . . . less challenging, as i am quite able to pull down the appropriate month and fill in the two blanks indicating day and year. Next, under language and content, i leave the default 'English-United States' and move on to zip code. I re-enter my college zip code even though i haven't lived there in over a year, but figure it is as good as any zip code. Moving on to the gender scrollbar, i choose the first of two options— male. Right below zip code and gender is the occupation scrollbar, allowing me to choose from a series of occupations with 'executive/managerial' and 'professional (doctor, lawyer, etc.)' being my first two choices. Next comes industry with another scrollbar of problematic options. I continue my systematic approach of selecting the first option, and become a male 'executive/managerial' in the 'banking/finance/real estate' industry. After removing the check from the 'contact me occasionally' toggle button and ignoring the optional interests, i proceed to submit the form.

It should go without saying that i don't identify as a man, nor as an executive in the financial sector. However, my decision to adopt those markers, and thus thwart a certain kind of profiling, is more than just a whim. It reflects my discomfort and inability to adequately place myself within the recognized boundaries. Additionally, by opting for the first markers, i chose to identify with the assumed 'norm,' in the hopes of being able to blend with greater ease. Needless to say, my difficulty in filling out these forms continues,

as i attempt to join a wide variety of digital spaces, from Salon.com to Excite to DisneyBlast, where i am required to define myself by a few 'simple' categories.

While Yahoo!'s sign-up process may seem particularly complicated, even the usual troika of age, sex and location is deceptively loaded. It appears so simple, so 'natural', a shorthand for who we are, or who we might be. Yet when scrutinized a little more closely, it immediately becomes more complicated. Online age, for instance, has legal implications. Since the passage of United States' Child Online Privacy Protection Act (COPPA) on April 21, 2000, American companies operating in cyberspace are required to ask a user's age and deny access to children under the age of 13 who do not have parental permission. In order to subvert these requirements, or perhaps to get around the letter of the law, some companies have designed scrollbar options that only present ages that are over 13, suggesting that those under 13 should just lie to acquire access.

Other categories, which are not required by law, are used for market research, and thus, reflect current marketing practices and assumptions. The 'gender' question is usually presented as either 'male/female' or 'Mr./Ms.'—an interesting collapsing of honorifics and sex. The significant slippage here, however, is between gender and sex—between the body and the performance of identities. The question might be framed as one of gender, but the answer is all about sex. The request for zip code seems innocuous enough, but it encodes a worldview with America at its center—not all countries have zip codes—and a view of users that requires they have permanent and fixed addresses. Zip codes are an attractive marker for marketers because they can convey an accurate estimate of a user's racial and socio-economic background.

In order to acquire a 'Passport,' which is the key to MSN's Hotmail, chatrooms and community webboards, Microsoft requires that you select your sex and your zip code. Their explanation is simple: 'This is one of the requirements for our banners advertisements, demographic purpose. I suggest that you give the appropriate gender.'[3] It is interesting to reflect on the ways in which MSN attempts to normalize the practice, by evoking 'passport,' requiring that users prove their identity in order to gain citizenship and the freedom to travel. One might also ponder, as i did, what an appropriate gender might be in these circumstances, and how would i know i had chosen the right one?

Talk City/Live World, whose partners and clients include a who's who list of mega-corporations including Cox Interactive, Mattel and About.com, 'pioneered the use of interactive online environments for promotion and brand extension.'[4] They suggest that accurate advertising demographics will make the experience better for the users.

> We will use the personal information in order to be able to determine the demographics of our users. This will allow us to provide a better experience for our users. The aggregate information, which does not contain any personal identifiable information, will be used for marketing and advertising purposes on our site . . . This information will allow us to better target any offerings we might have, appropriate content and ads to the specific user. (http://www.talkcity.com/csa/privacy.htmpl)

This stereotypical explanation suggests that consumers get something out of their 'act' of participation. By disclosing their identity, consumers will get better service, and more meaningful content. Here demographics create consumers; old vectors of social inequity become new marketing opportunities. For digital enterprises, accurate definition of user populations appears to have no obvious downsides: advertisers are happy, and consumers/users get a better experience. However, in these simple acts of definition, online business helps reinscribe existing social and cultural distinctions.

HAVING BODIES, CRAFTING SELVES

As there is a limited amount of information available in online environments, one would think that any additional information would help provide lacking context and enrich the barren virtual landscape. As O'Brien suggests,

> (Re)embodying the self in a disembodied realm is an exercise in textual production. Because physical cues are not available, online conversants must signal everything that they want others to know about them through a text-based medium. (O'Brien 1999: 87)

But in the online world, if we represent people solely as their demographics (age, sex, location, race), we have constructed coarse categorization schemes that force people to mentally over generalize. The result is an image that is even less accurate and more problematic than those developed during first impressions.

Consider, for example, the profile '23/white/female.' What image is drawn in the reader's mind? Does it resemble Britney Spears or someone you know? How long and what color is her hair? How heavy or tall is she? Is she attractive? Friendly? An introvert or an extrovert? What are her political views? What social communities does she participate in?

Drawing on a lifetime of social interactions, most people are able to develop a mental image using only vague descriptors, but that mental image rarely corresponds to the actual image of the person behind the given markers. That is, when presented with limited coarse information, people don't typically create an abstract mental construct existing solely of 23/white/female and devoid of other markers. Instead, they automatically conjure up an exemplar of a person who meets that description—but who also has other characteristics that have been unconsciously interpolated, although there is no particular reason to associate these characteristics with the given individual.

Providing coarse identifiers often generates inaccurate mental images that users must then overcome. In order to develop an accurate one, the reader is required to deconstruct this false initial impression, or view the differences from hir* imagined norms in a caricatured fashion. Although this is possible, it is difficult for people to adjust their initial categorizations; in fact, they are more likely to reinterpret the events than adjust their initial classification (Aronson 1995). While people usually have to overcome initial opinions in physical interaction, these are drawn from a greater context and understanding of the individual, based on what other information they visually convey in addition to sex/race/age.

The problem of coarse categorization is not just a concern for the reader, but also for the performer. When an individual embodies an identity, s/he has to be aware of how others are reading hir and react accordingly. In the physical world, this means knowing the social repercussions of wearing a trench coat to an American high school, or a party dress to a business office. For the online performer, knowing that the reader has been given the coarse category data, and has likely conjured an incorrect stereotype, s/he must go out of hir way to present further information to confirm, or combat, that stereotype. Instead of aiding in the development of a rich social environment, limited classification schemes offer new challenges for constructing complex and meaningful identities.[5]

*Hir is a gender-neutral pronoun.

In chatrooms, the usual formulation of age/sex/location still has a lot of currency. A/S/L acts as a social ritual—'formalized, socially prescribed symbolic behavior'—where the result is both a fulfillment of acceptable social behavior as well as informative (Winthrop 1991). The A/S/L ritual is invoked when there are a great number of newcomers, as a way to welcome people and offer them an opportunity for introduction and identification. The response is simple, 23/F/Boston or 34/F/Portland. This can create opportunities for conversation, most frequently based on location. Responses like 'Oh! I visited Boston once' or 'Is it still raining in Portland?' are quite common. While A/S/L identifications rarely lead to deep conversations, they have become an easy way of developing the necessary introductory rapport.

These acts of social checks and the resultant reactions do give participants in online spaces a sense of the social space at hand. Yet, the presentation of self . . . as a precise constellation of demographic information does not always meet all the social needs of an environment. Indeed, the A/S/L formulation can remove the spontaneous or crafted ways that we present ourselves to others. It should not be surprising then that sometimes the most interesting conversations stem from dissent or unwillingness to answer this social check, effectively questioning the social norms. This, in itself, also succeeds at allowing for an introduction where the rebel is telling a lot about hirself by refusing to answer or by questioning the purpose. Additionally, while the question suggests the type of answer—number, male/female, and simple phrase for location—this is not computationally mandated in the way birth date, M/F, zip code are in profiles. As a result, answers like 'old/?/bumblefuck USA' are perfectly reasonable and result in giving a personalized introduction, possibly with more depth than the statistical information.

However, there is more going on (t)here than just introductions and conversations. Age, sex and location are more than just a convenient shorthand, they are very specific markers that point to particular bodies in time and space. 23/F/Boston suggests not just a presence online, but also a very real person offline. With an obvious nod to personal ads, it is this slippage between online and offline identities, that a reliance on A/S/L allows, even in some ways encourages. Thus contextualized, the sexualization of online spaces seems almost inevitable.

Consider the environment that presents no information other than just the title of the online space, for instance 'rec.motorcyles', or CNN's 'Talkback Live' chat room. The initial image of individuals in that space—one of interest in the topic—is imprecise but fairly accurate. The reader can then use the language of the participants to develop a more detailed mental image, building from direct impressions instead of potentially inaccurate or meaningless labels. In a space focused on a nonsexual topic, such as gardening, the sex of participants should be irrelevant to the content. Appropriate markers would indicate skills, knowledge, and experience in the topic. But by presenting sex as the relevant marker, the implicit message is that sex is the most or the only significant characteristic.

Additionally, the social rules that govern a space are difficult to discern, as determining a digital space's history is impossible unless you have experienced it. Even in a physical space, it is challenging to read the subliminal signals that others project, or to determine what the norms are regarding sexual interactions. In a virtual space, these cues are even more obfuscated. Although inappropriate sexual innuendos would be quickly socially punished offline, they are all too pervasive online, with little social repercussions.

The most obvious way in which users attempt to desexualize the spaces is through using deception, or misidentification. Due to the lack of context in these spaces, human connection becomes difficult. Also, while mandated profiles only increase the sexual nature of these spaces, even the A/S/L social checks provide sexual context. Rather than ignoring this issue, thereby encouraging inappropriate behavior or deception, a better initial step would be to figure out how to develop social accountability in online environments.

An interesting consequence of the quasi-voluntary way identity is established online is that it provides opportunities for intentional deception. By offering explicit options for categorization, online profiling is bound to introduce a certain level of inaccuracy, either due to an individual being uncomfortable with the choices or feeling the need to misrepresent hirself in order to participate in a community. Some systems, such as those who do not allow users to choose options under 13, actively encourage dishonesty. Still others present the information in a way where dishonesty is likely to lean in one direction, by ordering the options in a specific fashion. While discussing how users react to these profiles, i found that many people share the same method of filling out the forms: choose the first choice available that will still let you join the site. This makes me wonder what the statistics are for self-reported 13-17 year old males. The users i spoke with seemed much more likely to record an accurate zip code, but quite a few preferred to indicate one that they felt could not exist, such as '12345.'

If deception is quite common, what is the social cost of doing so? While getting a gender specific advertisement might be annoying, there is no other systematic penalty for offering inaccurate information. The primary cost of deception lies within the social realm, potentially affecting the user and/or the community (Donath, 1999). Although deception is an advantageous coping mechanism, it may not aid in making a social space effective, as initial encounters are fraudulent and do not help people get to know one another. O'Brien writes,

> . . . even if it is possible for me to conceive and author characters that defy categorization along conventional lines, others cannot engage in meaningful interaction with me ('meaningful' being defined as mutually comprehensible and generative) unless they too know something about the 'script' through which I am representing myself and/or characterizing the situation. (O'Brien 1999: 85)

In order to stop deception, corporations want users to construct universal profiles. Microsoft's .NET initiative, initialized through their Passport system, suggests that it will make things easier for users, by consolidating their information and passwords. This is particularly important since there has been tremendous concern for how multiple identities may act as fronts for criminals, voyeurs, sexual deviants and stalkers. As a result, we are learning to distrust things that historically seemed very transparent. But by focusing on the dangers of online interaction and the problem of multiple identities, we fail to consider other ways in which we, as individuals, manipulate our own identities.

In the physical world, it is common for people to actualize different identities for different purposes, without any of these identities being 'inaccurate.' It is not uncommon for individuals to have multiple email addresses or phone numbers as a way of controlling access to them. Most people are not interested in consolidating all of their physical or virtual identities into one. Online, people sign up for multiple accounts and offline, one's party persona is different than one's work persona.

This does not mean that users don't intentionally lie on their Passport applications. For example, it has been shown that women regularly portray themselves as men in order to avoid being hassled as they access information (Bruckman 1993). Again, this does not mean that this is their universal persona, only one that they evoke for a purpose. Universal accounts with public profiles do not solve the problems of deception, only magnify it by forcing users to either have multiple accounts or lie more pervasively. Universal accounts also fail to address the underlying issues of power inequities and pervasive gender inequalities that have been re-established online.

MOVING BEYOND 'SEX'

The problem with sex as a principle marker online is that it adheres to a body—it is hard to think about sex without thinking about the biological ways that [it] is expressed. Even queer companies privilege the male/female body in cyberspace. For example, UK's Queer-Company offers potential users the usual male/female options, as well as MtF and FtM. While they are to be commended for attempting to address these issues, and while adding additional transsexual markers validates the existence of transgender individuals, they still fail to acknowledge that not everyone in the population fits comfortably into either two, or four, potential categories and that not everyone wants to have a sexed body online.

The use of 'sex' as a significant marker online has a negative, though little discussed, impact on the genderqueer community. Here, i am using genderqueer as an umbrella term for all those who don't simply fit into male/female, including those who identify as transgender, transsexual, intersexed, bois, grrls, drag artists and a wide variety of other identities. These people cannot comfortably be categorized as either female or male, either due to biological or psychological perceptions of self. Requiring a sex-specific identification reinforces the notion that there is a wide divide between two segments of the population, making invisible those who appear to fall in between. Genderqueer communities have gained a great deal by having the opportunity to present themselves online, as they perceive themselves, not just as society perceives them. And their ongoing online identity politics are instructive . . . as we think about the ways that 'gender' as a marker might have more flexibility than sex.

[These] concerns . . . do not mean that identifying elements should not be a factor of interaction, just that individuals should have the opportunity to perform the ways in which they present themselves, in the same way as they choose clothing and other markers to perform identity in the physical space. By limiting how, and with what language people are able to express their identity, profiling does a disservice to its users.

Although the practice of profiling affects users both personally and socially, the primary push for acquiring profiles is economic. For this reason, in order to eliminate forced profiling, it will require arguments that affect both the social element as well as the economic position of most companies.

Meanwhile, forced profiling continues to increase. Microsoft's Hailstorm[6] is being hailed by the media, although practically unnoticed by the public, as a way to make life quite a bit easier; to do so, Microsoft will handle, regulate and store everyone's private data. Although privacy should be a tremendous concern, when the apparent benefit of sharing your information overshadows any perceived problems, people are more than willing to share their data, as has been shown through grocery store savings cards. [Similarly, Facebook's collection and use of personal information has led to concern about online privacy.]

Since the majority of the population will happily convey their private data, and the majority of companies think that it is useful for gathering advertisements, eliminating forced profiling seems like an impossible goal. Those who recognize that the public doesn't necessarily want to walk around with this information, such as Yahoo!, allow users to turn off public perusal of this information, although the information is still gathered and still affects Yahoo!-user interaction, such as advertisement presentations. While this eliminates many of the perception concerns, it still enforces the binary assumptions and affects the privacy that users are able to maintain when online.

Although the ideal would be to allow users to construct their own representations, without encouragement or structure imposed by corporate interests, i know that this is not feasible. For that reason, i feel as though educating users to be aware of how their profiles affect their social interaction is the most obvious first step. Additionally, i feel that it's necessary to help construct social environments that offer better ways to assist users in constructing and maintaining their identities, and i am pursuing this in my own research. This work is far from complete, and the details are beyond the scope of this paper, but the salient features of our ideal space allow for localized self-identification, visual presentation of historical and current behavior characteristics, and visual mechanisms by which users can develop appropriate mental models of the people that surround them. If constructed appropriately, and these spaces actually improve social interaction, gradually the commercial environments will incorporate these mechanisms in order to remain competitive.

ACKNOWLEDGEMENTS

I would like to thank the MIT Media Lab, its sponsors, and particularly the Sociable Media Group for their support. In addition, this work would not have happened without Kate Bornstein's troublemaking ideas, Genevieve Bell's linguistic and conceptual magic, and the encouragement (and editing skills) of Judith Donath, Henry Jenkins, Ronen Barzel and Becky Hurwitz.

NOTES

1. Following the massive Internet boom, the vast majority of online environments are corporately controlled, relying on advertising revenues, or in rare cases, consumer subscriptions. Thus, for the purpose of this paper, we will only address such communities.
2. Microsoft network includes Chat, Communities, Hotmail, Instant Messenger; Yahoo! includes Chat, YahooMail, Messenger, eGroups/yahoogroups and GeoCities.
3. From MSN Hotmail Support <support_x@css.one .microsoft.com> on May 14, 2001.
4. Talk City/LiveWorld is a marketing research company that collects and manages the data gathered by providing free-to-users chats, bulletin boards and other web services. Its clients represent a who's who of megacorporations including media giants (such as Cox Interactive, ABC, NBC, CBS, CNBC, HBO, Disney, WB, Microsoft's WebTV, Sony Music), retail companies (such as Mattel, The Gap, Kodak, Johnson & Johnson), Internet sites (such as About.com, Alta Vista, Amazon.com, Ebay), as well as a wide variety of other corporations (such as American Heart Association, American Express, Charles Schwab, Intel, 3Com, HP). http://www.tcmg.com/about/background/index.html
5. When individuals construct virtual avatars to represent themselves, they also have to choose from a limited series of possibilities, similar to the demographic questions. For

example, newcomers to My Virtual Model.com must choose their race through a series of colors and possible slants of the eyes (www.mvm.com). As these models are to be used to help people shop, the avatars balance between possible variations in body type and acceptable norms for image.

6. .NET includes Hailstorm and Passport. Based on the Passport identification system, Hailstorm allows for universal collection and maintenance of all a user's activities, data, and information. http://www.microsoft.com/net/hailstorm.asp

REFERENCES

Aronson, Elliot (1995) *The Social Animal* (7th edition). New York: WH Freeman.

Berman, Joshua and Bruckman, Amy (2000) 'The Turing Game: A Participatory Exploration of Online Environments,' presented at the Conference on Cultural Diversity in/and Cyberspace, University of Maryland, College Park, MD, May 5.

Biersdorfer, JD (2001) 'State of the Art: Messengers That Carry Big Bundles', *New York Times*, June 14, 2001.

Bruckman, Amy (1993) 'Gender Swapping on the Internet,' *Proceedings of the Internet Society—INET'93*. San Francisco, CA, August.

Donath, Judith (1998) 'Identity and deception in the virtual community,' in Marc Smith, Peter Kollock (eds) *Communities in Cyberspace*. London: Routledge.

O'Brien, Jodi (1999) 'Writing in the body: Gender (re)production in online interaction,' in Marc Smith, Peter Kollock (eds) *Communities in Cyberspace*. London: Routledge.

Sullivan, Caitlin and Bornstein, Kate (1996) *Nearly Roadkill*. New York: High Risk Books.

Winthrop, Robert (1991) *Dictionary of Concepts in Cultural Anthropology*. Westport, CT: Greenwood Press.

READING *14* Josée Johnston
Judith Taylor

Feminist Consumerism and Fat Activists: A Comparative Study of Grassroots Activism and the Dove Real Beauty Campaign

First published in 2008

Corporations have a long history of incorporating emancipatory ideals into marketing campaigns, often with limited transformative outcomes (Frank 1997; Heath and Potter 2004). Virginia Slims, for instance, promotes an image of feminist independence in the "You've come a long way, baby" marketing campaign, and yet it sells women a highly addictive, cancer-causing product. While "feminist tobacco" contains obvious contradictions, today's transnational corporations employ a panoply of socially responsible wares ranging from fair-trade coffee to biodegradable yoga mats and organic frozen dinners (Johnston 2001). Because in some instances such corporate strategies appear both well intentioned and well received, we move beyond cynical dismissal to empirically investigate and analyze corporate discourse to identify its transformative possibilities and contradictions. In this article, we question whether transformative visions are exclusively linked with grassroots models for social change—models at the heart of feminist consciousness-raising.[1] Our primary goal is to compare the discursive contributions of

Dove's "Campaign for Real Beauty"—a corporate project that claims to oppose restrictive feminine beauty standards and promote a more democratic vision of beauty—with those made by a Toronto-based grassroots fat-activist organization that also targets feminine beauty ideals: Pretty, Porky, and Pissed Off (PPPO).[2] We use a comparative approach to evaluate how each case challenges feminine beauty ideology while also considering the scale of its activism. Our analysis of the PPPO case relies on interviews with PPPO members, archival documentation of their events provided by activists, and media profiles and reviews of their shows. The Dove case draws primarily on the company's Web site, multimedia advertisements, trade magazines and journals, and participant observation at Dove Real Beauty events. We also collected and analyzed mainstream news coverage of PPPO activities and the Dove campaign. This research enabled us to understand and compare these parallel but very different campaigns and pay particular attention to questions of scale and their different cultural contexts, ideologies, tactics, intended audiences, and goals.

At the same political moment when scholars bemoaned the constant assertion that feminism is dead (see Hawkesworth 2004; Staggenborg and Taylor 2005), Dove launched its Campaign for Real Beauty in 2004 using feminist critiques and concerns about beauty ideals to revitalize the Dove brand. Billboard, television, and magazine ads depicted women who were wrinkled, freckled, pregnant, had stretch marks, or might be seen as fat (at least compared with the average media representation of women).[3] The campaign has generated commercial success (e.g., sales of firming lotion, the campaign's flagship product, far exceeded forecasts), media sensation (see, e.g., *People* 2005), and endorsements from celebrities (e.g., Oprah Winfrey), gender scholars (e.g., Susie Orbach), and professional associations (e.g., American Women in Radio and Television). The campaign, which started in the United Kingdom and quickly spread to North America, is now a major feature of Dove's global marketing.

While Dove uses a multimillion dollar, multimedia marketing campaign, PPPO employed radically different tactics to challenge hegemonic beauty standards. Frustrated with ill-fitting clothing options for plus-size women, a group of artists and activists from women's studies and queer activist communities formed PPPO in 1996. Their first event was a street protest in a trendy shopping district in which members handed out candy

and questioned passersby about their attitudes toward fat. Members moved from street protest to creating cabaret shows with which they could more fully explore and enact their burgeoning politics. Pretty, Porky, and Pissed Off went on to become one of Toronto's most popular queer cabaret acts, using song and dance to challenge misogynist attitudes about fat women and sexuality.

Despite the belief that the beauty industry articulates and reproduces gendered beauty norms, PPPO's grassroots activism and Dove's corporate campaign appear to be countervailing forces pulling beauty ideology in opposite directions (Black 2004; Jeffreys 2005). The tendency is to summarily dismiss Dove's efforts to broaden beauty ideals, yet . . . , our hope is to better understand the nuances, possibilities, and contradictions of Dove's seemingly transformative aspirations, particularly when juxtaposed with the beauty critiques of grassroots activists. The Dove Real Beauty Campaign promotes itself as a progressive force for women, aligns itself with certain feminist ideals and scholars, engages in "grassroots" partnering to raise millions of dollars for eating disorder organizations and Girl Scouts programs to build self-esteem, has engaged with prominent gender scholars, and has been widely praised in the popular media. To make sense of its impact, our comparison of the Dove campaign with grassroots feminist activism aims to document Dove's campaign discourse as an example of corporate appropriation of social movement ideals, thereby contributing to the important, but sparse, critical scholarship on this topic (Frank 1997; Messner 2002; Heath and Potter 2004).[4] We examine the transformative potential of the corporate versus the grassroots, and speak to theoretical debates, suggesting the need for closer integration between political economic analysis and feminist scholarship of beauty ideology, cultural politics, and grassroots activisms.[5] Thus, our comparative project combines political-economic scholarship with feminist understandings of social change, shedding light on prospects for counterhegemonic action against oppressive feminine beauty standards.

We use the term "feminist consumerism," a phenomenon with the potential to partially disrupt gender norms, to emphasize the Dove campaign's evolution alongside a broader culture-ideology of consumerism, understood as a way of life dedicated to the possession and use of consumer goods (Kellner 1983, 74) and rooted in the capitalist need to sell an ever-expanding roster of commodities in a globalized economy

(Gottdiener 2000, 281; Sklair 2001).[6] In contrast, PPPO provides a counter-hegemonic critique of beauty and its relationship to capitalist consumerism, but we caution against a reification and romanticization of the scale of grassroots social activism and suggest that the limitations of both actors help explain the continued salience of beauty ideology in women's lives.

IDEOLOGICAL CONTEXT: FEMININE BEAUTY AND FEMINIST PRAXIS

Ideology is a useful tool for feminists interested in understanding how ideas enable and preclude possibilities for transformative change. Recent theorizing sees ideology as organized around a set of ideas, normative claims, and value structures that have an emotional component influencing their usage and appeal (see Fegan 1996; Ferree and Merrill 2000; Thompson 2001). Building on neo-Gramscian theories of hegemony, we argue that ideologies express degrees of hegemony depending on their ability to reinforce and naturalize power hierarchies and material inequality. Eileen Fegan, for instance, employs the example of motherhood to demonstrate how ideology is internalized by women in their intimate lives—providing meaning and personal satisfaction—while it [also] reproduces and legitimates gender inequality through its discursive operations in the legal system (1996, 183). For our case studies, ideology is essential to appreciating how subjects internalize and resist feminine beauty ideals in the larger context of corporate consumer culture, and this allows a substantive comparison of counterhegemonic potential.

Feminist scholarship and activism since the 1970s have critiqued oppressive beauty standards that repress women's freedom, inhibit personal power and self-acceptance, and promote a destructive relationship with the body.[7] Drawing on these critiques, in 1991 Naomi Wolf published *The Beauty Myth*, a feminist analysis of beauty standards that became one of the best-selling feminist books of all time and that suggested that women's gains from the second wave of the feminist movement were stymied by the existence of a beauty myth that disabled women from achieving full equality with men. While Wolf's work was a timely piece of public scholarship, exposing countless women to the idea of a hegemonic beauty regimen, more recent feminist scholarship on beauty draws from poststructuralism's emphasis on agency, focusing on the meaning embedded in beauty rituals. Scholars have observed women's collusion with, and participation

in, the social construction of beauty, suggesting that women's body work, whether through exercise, cosmetics, or plastic surgery, can function as a meaningful source of empowerment (Davis 1995; Frost 2001).

. . . Similarly, . . . feminist scholars . . . problematize the aesthetic ideals surrounding thin and fat bodies. Corpulence studies, for instance, draws on queer theory to question whether beauty standards surrounding body weight are straightforwardly oppressive, and it deconstructs dualisms of thin/successful versus fat/oppressed. Corpulence studies has developed significant insights into food, gender, sexuality, and the body, specifically in relationship to fat bodies reviled as asexual, out of control, or morally repugnant (Braziel 2001; Hartley 2001; LeBesco 2001). Significantly, this scholarship has identified agency in fat bodies previously assumed to be monolithically oppressed, depressed, and psychologically traumatized. Jana Evans Braziel and Kathleen LeBesco (2001) and Marilyn Wann (1999) suggest that not every fat girl wants to be thin and that fatness is experienced in a variety of ways betwixt stereotypes of the asexual obese woman and the fat femme (Braziel 2001; Mazer 2001). Corpulence studies identifies agency, everyday forms of resistance, and the varied ways gender is constructed in bodies that defy idealized feminine beauty.

Problematizing the existence of a singular, oppressive beauty standard has been a useful corrective to monochromatic understandings of gender inequality and oppression. However, the emphasis on feminine beauty and the body as a site of individual meaning and empowering play is prone to a naive [assumption] that women act completely voluntarily, thus minimizing corporate domination and the "normalizing power of cultural images" (Bordo 1993, 21, 275; see also Jeffreys 2005, 5). Even scholars who emphasize the agency present in beauty practices have produced evidence suggesting that internalized hatred of fat bodies persists despite willful individual resistance, and this is documented within the fat-acceptance movement (Gimlin 2002, 136). The persistence of domination in the realm of beauty ideals raises serious questions for our two cases of beauty rebellion, as well as for the cultural turn in beauty analysis. Can resistance to beauty ideals rely on therapeutic, individually focused strategies, or must activists also target the institutions and material structures that support hegemonic beauty standards?[8] How can individual transgression and resistance be reincorporated into corporate structures—say, in a jar of woman-affirming firming cream?[9]

[An analysis] of ideology . . . can clarify how hege-monic beauty standards dominate and oppress, while simultaneously recognizing the agency present in beauty practices.[10] Using ideology, feminist analyses of beauty standards can move away from a voluntaristic and idealistic approach that either suggests that women can readily eschew internalized beauty ideals and embrace their nonconforming bodies or sanctions gender conformity through fashion, makeup, and plastic surgery. . . . The concept of ideology particu-larly draws our attention to the role of corporations as key actors in the production and reproduction of beauty ideology. This industry perpetuates and insti-tutionalizes gender inequality by placing an inordi-nate emphasis on the personal appearance of women, (re)producing largely unattainable aesthetic standards (Hartley 2001, 64), and perpetuating misogynist and harmful cultural practices (e.g., labiaplasty and breast augmentation) (Jeffreys 2005). . . . Particularly relevant here is how the corporate and grassroots cases frame beauty ideology in relation to the capitalist ideology of consumerism. Consumerism puts forward a world-view in which consumption is "at the center of mean-ingful existence" (Sklair 2001, 5) and shopping is the ideal form of participation in struggles for social change. . . .

The ability of corporations to accommodate and capitalize on social dissent and alienation suggests the need to be skeptical of consumer-based strategies for social change. However, to understand women's rela-tionships with beauty ideology and the beauty indus-try, we need first to connect feminine beauty ideology to feminist social action. . . . A key insight of feminist politics and social change projects is that political inequalities and oppression are personalized and inter-nalized at the level of individual subjects. Because of this, addressing internalized feelings of inferiority is politically significant and can profoundly challenge the gender order (see Taylor 1996). Feminist scholars draw-ing on Michel Foucault have emphasized how "a soci-ety's imposition of discipline upon bodies depends on those bodies learning *to regulate themselves*," making the hatred of fat, nonconforming bodies a deeply internal-ized phenomenon (Hartley 2001, 62; emphasis added). In terms of beauty ideology, this suggests that a neces-sary (albeit insufficient) criterion for transformative social change is transformative individual change. These counterhegemonic strategies challenge the ideo-logical salience of consumerism and feminine beauty at the level of feelings, thoughts, and the lifeworld.

Feminist politics has been a central site for connect-ing personal and political battles, yet today the popu-lar consensus is that the women's movement is dead and that counterhegemonic feminist ideologies have lost their critical edge (see Hawkesworth 2004; Staggenborg and Taylor 2005).[11] Indeed, Dove's public campaign for a woman's right to feel beautiful might suggest that feminist ideals have become socially mainstream rather than socially marginalized. This begs the question of how to differentiate between the gender ideals used by Dove to promote women's self-esteem through brand-building and those promoted by grassroots fat activists like those in PPPO. Not all gender ideals are equally feminist, or equally commit-ted to women's equality and empowerment in the face of institutionalized gender inequality; nor do they equally challenge the naturalization of women's sub-ordinate status as it intersects with inequalities of class, race, and ethnicity. To explore the counterhegemonic challenge to beauty ideologies and their relationship to feminist activism, we turn to our case studies.

THE CASES: FAT ACTIVISTS AND A CORPORATE CAMPAIGN FOR REAL BEAUTY

Pretty, Porky, and Pissed Off (PPPO)

Pretty, Porky, and Pissed Off emerged the way many primary movement groups (Rosenthal and Schwartz 1989) do: based on friendship and characterized by informality. The idea arose from a 1996 conversation between Allyson Mitchell and Ruby Rowan, both of whom were artists and women's studies students. While attending a conference on subcultures, they lamented the absence of attention to lesbian feminists active in the queer arts scene—women writing, play-ing in bands, making films and art that expressed femi-nist politics in varied and nuanced ways. The conversation turned to mundane matters; not being able to find cool pants that fit. Mitchell recalled of this conversation, "It was so familiar and so yuck, and so a known story for fat girls. Ruby was really pivotal in saying 'Let's do something about it instead of bitching about it. We should start a fat girl group.'"[12]

Mitchell, Rowan, and many of their friends who had already explored body issues in their artistic work hoped the idea of a more formal group would reso-nate. However, friends needed to be out as fat, com-fortable enough to perform the role of fat activist, and able to both confront strangers' phobias and endure curious or contemptuous stares. They planned an action for the following weekend in a trendy shopping district, in which Mitchell, Rowan, and ten friends dressed in campy polyester dresses and feather boas, danced to electronic music, and passed out "fat facts," such as the average size of North American women. As shoppers passed by, the activists gave them stickers or flyers, and asked, "Do you think I'm fat?"

Participants found the event successful because they reached a large number of people and the event received significant media attention. Besides feeling that they had effectively communicated with the public, they gained an understanding of who they were and what they could do for and with one another. Characterizing participants as a "dyke network" of artists, performers, feminists, friends, and exes, Mitchell says the event solidified their identities as fat activists: "It was consciousness-raising among ourselves for us all to be there. It was borrowing from that feminist power in numbers, feeding off each other's affirmations and then trying to bleed that out to the crowd."

The group continued general interventions, like putting stickers and fliers in public spaces, but subsequent activism also focused on performance pieces within the queer arts community. Pretty, Porky, and Pissed Off officially came together as a troupe of three (gradually expanding to eight) at a benefit show for Pussy Palace, a women's bathhouse in Toronto facing legal challenges after a police raid. While two troupe members sang a rewritten version of the reggae song "Wide Load," the third passed out peanut butter and jelly sandwiches to onlookers. Later performances evolved along with the group's political consciousness and everyday lived experiences. Planning meetings, for instance, were as much concerned with processing feelings and experiences of fat phobia as they were with choreography; some pieces evolved organically out of these discussions and reflected the group's growing camaraderie. For example, one PPPO member was one day rendered speechless when told, "Move it, fatty," by a man getting off a streetcar. This experience was catalyst for a piece called "Move It Fatty," in which the girl-gang comes to the rescue, throwing the significance of female friendship into sharp relief. In addition to building solidarity and community, PPPO also experimented with importing a feminist politic and a therapeutic effect into spaces in which queer camp predominated, and it introduced increasingly complex political analyses of fat and

consumerism. In one show titled "Big Judy," each member introduced her performance by talking about the personal politics and experiences that led her to become a fat activist, while another show titled "Chubway" attempted to reckon with the political economy of fat by critiquing the food industry and its promotion of unhealthy diets. Thus, PPPO brought a complex feminist analysis into a queer arts space in which neither hegemonic beauty standards nor corporate capitalism were previously much critiqued.

In addition to cabaret-style shows, PPPO members held fundraisers for fat activism causes, such as Nomy Lamm's Phat Camp camp for kids, which focuses on positive body image rather than weight loss. These included clothing swaps in working-class neighborhoods, where women paid five dollars for a bag of clothing that fit them. For PPPO activists, this kind of work exemplified their politics: it was not simply that they wanted corporations to produce larger sizes; they also wanted to create opportunities to resist consumerism, while recognizing the gender and class implications of fat bodies.

The PPPO activists primarily performed in countercultural arts spaces, but they also performed in more mainstream venues and traveled outside Toronto, with mixed results. Some women did not understand the camp genre and complained that the show lampooned fat women. Arts-oriented audiences critiqued the group for not memorizing their lines or for having simplistic choreography, missing the fact that performance for PPPO was a vehicle for political and cultural expression. Wearing tennis shoes with bottle caps nailed to the bottom enabled tap dancing, and black body suits were used to critique, rather than compete within, an ultra-thin and competitive women's dance world. Another site of contention was the media: eager to communicate a message of health and bodily acceptance to large-bodied women and girls, PPPO activists regularly granted interviews, although members found it challenging to be cast opposite public health officials and represented as the voices denying the health risks of obesity.

At a meeting in 2003 to discuss a show that would require travel, arts grants, and significant time and resources, the group realized they did not want to take their activism to this new level, and PPPO disbanded. Expanding PPPO's reach would have required members to give up other activist, artistic, and employment commitments. Members celebrated the decision, however, proud of their accomplishments and committed to carrying on their fat activism. Members of PPPO hoped another group would pick up where it left off, and in 2005, one did: the Fat Femme Mafia, a fat activist performance group that performs and organizes fat events in the Toronto area, explicitly drew inspiration from PPPO's trailblazing work.[13] Thus far, Fat Femme Mafia is not the community PPPO once was, having only two members, but its intention to work within the public schools suggests a less insular approach to social change than that taken by its predecessors.

The Dove Campaign: Real Women, Real Beauty, Real Feminism?

Just as PPPO's grassroots activism was winding down, Dove, a subsidiary of Unilever, and the largest skin care brand in the world, launched the "Real Women" Campaign in Britain. The campaign hinged on selecting real women—rather than professional models—for television and print advertisements featuring its new line of firming products. The women appeared to be in their twenties and thirties, were multiracial, and posed together smiling and frolicking, all while wearing white cotton bras and underwear. Conventionally attractive, they radiated happiness and friendship. The success of this effort led to a significantly more complex and multitiered, multinational "Campaign for Real Beauty" launched in September 2004. The campaign was orchestrated by some of the most powerful advertising, research, and public relations firms in the world, including Ogilvy and Mather, the Downing Street Group, and others, in conjunction with creative teams within Unilever and Dove. Additionally, along with networking with university researchers and non-profit agencies, Dove commissioned a large-scale, multinational survey of women's conceptions and practices, hiring scholars like Nancy Etcoff, Susie Orbach, and Naomi Wolf to contribute to "The Real Truth about Beauty: A Global Report" (Etcoff et al. 2004). While some marketing gurus advised against such unusual strategies, others found such corporate sponsored research and engagement with ideas a good way to garner media attention and revitalize a fifty-year-old brand.

Dove's fluid, multipronged marketing approach made use of diverse organizational fields, including billboards, television, interactive Web sites, and tic-ins with the mass media, for example, *The Oprah Winfrey Show.* Initially, Dove focused on provocative, conversational billboards with images of women in which the public

was asked to adjudicate women's attractiveness (e.g., "fat or fabulous?"). This format provided a space to debate feminine beauty ideals and was a win-win situation for Dove: it could promote its products as beauty solutions and at the same time express concern with narrow beauty ideals. Dove soon moved toward a more explicitly normative position critiquing conventional beauty ideals. The Dove Real Beauty Campaign Web site launched with the following text floating over the Dove insignia: "For too long, beauty has been defined by narrow, stifling stereotypes. You've told us it's time to change all that. Doves agrees. We believe real beauty comes in many shapes, sizes, and ages. That is why Dove is launching the Campaign for Real Beauty" (Dove 2005b). Thus, while responding to real women with cellulite and wrinkles (rather than unattainable air-brushed features), Dove diagnoses the problem as one caused by unrealistic media and advertising images, communicating its intention to make women feel more beautiful.

On the Dove Web site, women can post their pictures, donate to one of Dove's campaigns, read Dove-commissioned research on beauty, or participate in Web conversations in multiple nations and languages. Seamlessly connecting Dove's politics to its products, the Web site also includes sections like "Let's Dare to Love Our Hair," which is followed by a list of Dove shampoos, conditioners, and styling aids. In another section, a list of Dove antiperspirants and lotions is prefaced by "Let's Make Peace with Our Bodies." This pairing is explicit, and corporate spokespersons speak plainly and consistently about their dual goals: to make women feel more beautiful and to sell more Dove beauty products (see *People* 2005). On the latter score, Dove attributes the success of its new product lines, such as the Dove Firming Range (exceeding expectations by 120 percent), to the Campaign for Real Beauty. Advertising trade magazines and business schools alike have applauded Dove for its marked financial success.

The Dove campaign also forged alliances, using what it termed grassroots partnering: for instance, the Dove Self-Esteem Fund was formed to educate and inspire girls on a wider definition of beauty in partnership with the American Girl Scouts. By 2005, Dove claimed to have already reached over 138,000 eight- to fourteen-year-old girls with programs like "Uniquely ME!" and "Body Talk." The campaign also expanded into the arts with an international photography exhibition, Beyond Compare, featuring the work of sixty female photographers from twenty-two countries. The exhibition featured images of women of various races and nationalities, including those portraying obesity, aging, dwarfism, eating disorders, lesbians, and female body builders. Dove asked photographers to donate pictures they took depicting real beauty as they saw it, and in exchange, Dove made a contribution to the National Eating Disorders Information Centre, a Toronto-based nonprofit agency whose Web site now features a prominent Dove hotlink.

...BEAUTY IDEOLOGIES, FEMINIST CONSUMERISM, AND GRASSROOTS ACTIVISM

Beauty Ideology: Dove Makes Peace While PPPO Wages War

Both the Dove Real Beauty Campaign and PPPO claim to challenge hegemonic beauty codes that articulate a virtually unachievable conception of physical beauty. Even defenders of beauty norms as socially and biologically inevitable, like evolutionary psychologist Nancy Etcoff, acknowledge that the top models exemplifying contemporary Western beauty are "genetic freaks" (1999, 12). Given the extent to which these images of models affect women's self-perceptions, it may come as little surprise that Dove's own multinational beauty survey, for instance, found that only two percent of women describe themselves as beautiful (Etcoff et al. 2004, 11). In response, Dove has committed itself to changing this statistic through its provocative billboard campaign, which partially disrupts the ideology of feminine beauty by publicly portraying women not conventionally seen as beautiful and hence not normally depicted on billboards advertising beauty products. By doing so, the campaign drew both criticism and compliments from men. *Chicago Sun-Times* columnist Richard Roeper criticized the campaign for depicting average women and suggested that if he wanted to see "plump gals baring too much skin," he would have simply gone to Taste of Chicago (*People* 2005, 17). Yet *Slate* advertising columnist Seth Stevenson said that the Dove models on giant billboards challenged his gendered beauty ideals in a positive way: "When I first saw one of these smiley, husky gals on the side of a building, my brain hiccupped. . . . Here I was, staring at a 'big-boned' woman in her underwear, but this wasn't an Adam Sandler movie,

and I wasn't supposed to laugh at her. It felt almost revolutionary" (Stevenson 2005).

While the Dove campaign challenges the key element of narrow beauty ideals within beauty ideology, theorists remind us that ideology is a complex creature; women are not simply tricked into seeking beauty. Beauty ideals . . . are internalized, rationalized, and socially legitimized: . . . the ideology of beauty suggests that every woman can, and should, feel beautiful, presenting beauty as a democratic gender good, akin to life, liberty, and the pursuit of happiness. Yet beauty codes make clear that most women do not measure up aesthetically. Women are penalized for not being beautiful and at the same time are stigmatized, even pathologized, for not feeling beautiful, for having low self-esteem, for engaging in behaviors like dieting and excessive exercising, or for having eating disorders.

The Dove campaign, while it contests narrow beauty codes, works within a hegemonic ideology of gendered beauty by refusing to challenge the idea that beauty is an essential part of a woman's identity, personhood, and social success and by legitimizing the notion that every woman should feel beautiful. For example, a television advertisement promoting Dove's Self-Esteem Fund for young girls features girls confessing their physical anxieties (e.g., they hate their freckles, feel fat, or want to be blonde), followed by a voice-over that issues the following commands projected over their faces: "Let's tell her she's wrong. Let's tell her to be real. And brave. And true. And she'll be beautiful. Beautiful. Beautiful. [Dove logo appears on screen.] Let's make peace with beauty" (Dove Real Beauty Campaign 2005a). In another advertisement, hundreds of women are seen converging at a city center in identical blonde wigs. They simultaneously tear off their wigs, thereby symbolically repudiating notions of attractive hair and embracing their locks. Reminiscent of Eve Ensler's *Vagina Monologues,* the accompanying video on Dove's Web site features women talking about learning to love their hair. Three women are featured: one is blonde, white, and attractive, with a slightly protruding stomach; the second has the appearance of a supermodel, being extremely thin and white, with lustrous long brown hair; and the third is an attractive, petite, light-skinned minority woman with blonde-frosted curly hair.

At the end of both commercials, and within the Dove campaign more generally, the social imperative for women to be and feel beautiful is not up for negotiation. Even though the social understanding of beauty is contested, the importance of beauty as a paramount value for women is reproduced and legitimized by the campaign's explicit and unceasing focus on beauty. Women's acceptance of their bodies as beautiful is demanded, rather than recognized as an inherently complex, fraught, and contradictory endeavor—particularly in the context of the mass media, the beauty industry, the weight-loss industry, and the industrial food complex—or in relation to what women accomplish apart from looking pretty.[14] . . .

Additionally, such gendered beauty depictions are significant because they allow the campaign to associate youth, slenderness, and conventional beauty (like beautiful hair) with the Dove brand, while simultaneously opening the door to a handful of deviations (like the slightly protruding stomach) that help to construct brand loyalty. This is part of a gender-specific marketing strategy that cultivates brand loyalty using models and imagery that women can identify with, while conveying an appearance of corporate philanthropy (Corbett 2006). The occasional image of an aging wrinkled face or a protruding stomach fits within consumer capitalism's need to continually incorporate deviant images (Bordo 1993, 25; Frank 1997; Frank and Weiland 1997). Thus, Dove channels women's dissent to rebuild its brand, while also deflecting attention away from the conventional depictions of feminine beauty relied upon in Dove marketing. By acknowledging that most women do not possess conventional beauty, the Dove campaign also allows them to participate in a critique of narrow beauty norms while encouraging women to "make peace with beauty" by channeling negative energy into self-acceptance, self-worth, and self-care via Dove products. In this sense, Dove's attempt to democratize beauty is deeply disingenuous. It . . . denies the hierarchical nature of beauty standards, and . . . obscures the [fact that] . . . thin, white, privileged women [find] it easier to achieve hegemonic beauty ideals.

One of the more insidious aspects of Dove's appropriation of feminist themes of empowerment and self-care is its reformulation of feminism as achieved principally through grooming and shopping. This association is ironic because many women have shied away from feminism precisely because they do not want to burn their bras or discontinue shaving, wearing makeup, and using deodorant. The radical feminism that might require them to be critical of gendered grooming and beauty ideology is absent in feminist consumerism, a corporate strategy that employs feminist themes of empowerment to market products to women and that shares consumerism's focus on individual consumption as a primary source of identity, affirmation, and social change. This reformulation enables women to wear an identity associated with self-respect, independence, personal strength, and collective identity and community without doing any of the hard consciousness-raising work usually required to produce collective (rather than simply individual) transformation.[15]

In addition, psychological and philosophical research on perceptions of beauty suggest that the male gaze is a strong determinant of the extent to which beauty ideals are prioritized; both straight women and gay men experience the comparative pressure of narrow beauty ideals more profoundly (Bordo 1993, 102; Etcoff 1999, 61). The . . . presence of the male gaze is an assumption running through the Dove campaign. One of the inspirational articles featured on the Dove Real Beauty Web site is a faux-blog titled "A Day without Makeup." When the fictitious blogger is challenged by the prospect of meeting her friends for drinks after work, after a moment of self-doubt, she thinks of her husband: "I remember my husband's look at lunch, and hear his words again: 'You look pretty.'" By replaying and internalizing these words, she is able to face the situation with confidence: "I stand a little straighter and toss my hair back. I look at my friends, smiling and laughing, all gorgeous in their own way. . . . Just like me" (Dove Real Beauty Campaign 2007). The male gaze assuages the woman's doubts; she gains an inner confidence that acknowledges and legitimizes her physical appearance as an important prelude to her social confidence in the public sphere.

Like the Dove campaign, the PPPO critique did not reject the idea of physical feminine beauty altogether. Yet a closer examination of PPPO's approach to beauty reveals important differences between the two campaigns, namely, PPPO's more complex and ambivalent relationship to the idealization of women's physical beauty, an interest in exploring the pain caused by beauty ideals, and a refusal to prioritize looking or feeling beautiful as cornerstones of gendered identity. Rather than take on the lofty concept of beauty, the activists in PPPO appropriated a more accessible moniker, "pretty," and immediately and alliteratively knocked the gender ideal of "pretty" off its social pedestal by linking it to "porky" and "pissed off." In so doing, PPPO members embraced their nonconforming fat bodies and waged war with hegemonic beauty standards—actions far removed from Dove's reformist peacemaking.

Unlike Dove's demand that women feel beautiful and love their curves, PPPO activists did not straightforwardly celebrate fat as fabulous.[16] Instead, PPPO activism involved open discussion of the terrors, contradictions, and pain involved with living in a fat body: as one PPPO activist, speaking on a local radio program, commented, "I am a fat activist with an eating disorder."[17] PPPO performances presented large bodies as sexually attractive and confident, but fat was not uncritically or automatically linked to beauty. Instead, the whole complex politics of judging women based on their physical appearance—and the kinds of gendered obsessions this creates—were themselves challenged through PPPO's activist performances. In "Big Judy," for instance, PPPO activists explored how obsession with their nonconforming bodies caused physical discomfort, emotional suffering, and enduring pain.[18] . . .

PPPO activism contained a reconstructive program for self-worth and esteem that played with nonconventional fashion and beauty imagery. Like Dove, PPPO targeted women's feelings of inadequacy in relation to beauty, but unlike Dove's equation of feeling beautiful with being beautiful, PPPO recognized that not everyone would perceive their dancing, performing, nonconforming bodies as attractive. While the Dove campaign implicitly relied on images of attractive women, PPPO activist-performances explicitly constructed dissonant images of beauty (e.g., dressing in body-hugging black leotards and dancing with iced cakes); these images engaged the obesophobia (e.g., the performance, "Move It Fatty") underlying harmful body practices such as eating disorders and other contortions (Bordo 1993, 141). In addition, PPPO's radical disruption of hegemonic beauty ideology worked to destabilize the heteronormative gaze. Strongly linked to a lesbian arts community, PPPO activists did not prioritize the approval of men socially or performatively, and this may have allowed a more radical rejection of beauty as feminine aspiration. Whether a radical rejection of both beauty ideology and the male gaze is a likely strategy for a corporate campaign is an important question for feminist praxis, one to which we now turn.

Feminist Praxis: Consciousness, Community, and Consumerism

. . . The critical differences between Dove's and PPPO's contributions to feminist praxis . . . [center] on the contrast between feminist consumerism and feminist community building and consciousness-raising.

The goal of facilitating women's emotional transformation and creating therapeutic spaces for women to process their feelings about hegemonic beauty standards is central to both campaigns; however, the emotion cultures and emotion work of each are constitutively distinct. In its performances and discourse, PPPO modeled therapeutic consciousness-raising: members narrated painful stories, while song and dance segments were built around accessible stories of rejection, social exclusion, self-loathing, and reclaiming painful epithets (e.g., "fatty," "porky"). Actors modeled an emotional trajectory of pain and isolation giving way to anger and eventually ending in either a bold assertion of self-worth or a collective assertion of burlesque sensuality.

Conversely, in the Dove campaign, both pain and anger are avoided, suggesting a more limited model of consciousness-raising, a greater focus on building positive associations that can be converted to brand loyalty, and an explicit connection between self-love and self-care through commodity consumption. Women featured on the Dove Web site and the advertisements convey that they have been unhappy with different aspects of their bodies and appearances, but any emotional pain such self reflection caused is sanitized and appears easy to overcome. Consciousness-raising in the Dove campaign is presented as a happy awakening by casting off limited notions of attractiveness and working with what one has to accentuate inner and outer beauty. For Dove, social acceptance and beauty should not be uncoupled; rather, beauty should be reconceived and made accessible—a process that occurs through self-care via Dove beauty products. Because the central importance of feminine beauty is not questioned by the Dove campaign, its architects need not include anger as an emotional stage. Anger would be required only if women were rejecting, rather than coming to terms with, this basic social tenet. Dove's emotional register erases shame, fear, and anger, making personal pride and social change appear painless, simple achievements—as simple as shopping itself.

Furthermore, Dove and PPPO had very different ideas concerning deviance and challenging gendered beauty norms. On a basic level, PPPO did not prescribe changes in women's appearance but instead advocated female solidarity to alleviate the psychological toll of nonconformity. In stark contrast, Dove uses a smattering of deviant images to suggest a feeling of solidarity with real women, followed by product promotion framed as a way to express self-care. While both Dove and PPPO ask women to embrace their nonconforming bodies, Dove advocates feminist consumerism as a primary form of social critique. Most significantly, this critique obscures the contradictory desires underlying the Dove campaign: to condemn beauty standards while promoting conformity to these same standards—like, for example, promoting firming and antiaging creams. While Dove legitimizes conformity, PPPO asserts the coolness of feminine deviance in their performances, such as their mock *West Side Story* featuring a protagonist rejected from the gang for not being fat enough.[19] Perhaps because PPPO emerged from a queer feminist friendship and activist network, deviance was already a central mode of operation and criterion for membership. Conversely, the Dove campaign enables more people to feel successful in achieving (heterosexual) mainstream social acceptance. Even the "uniform" of the two groups conveys this different approach to deviance: while the Dove campaign dresses models in white cotton bras and underwear, signifying cleanliness and purity, PPPO activists wore fat drag, donning black leotards and feather boas.

Dove's and PPPO's approaches to diversity and inequality reflect the differing goals of feminist consumerism versus grassroots community building. Consumer culture allows for, and encourages, individual difference but does not emphasize structural hierarchies or collective strategies for social change. In Dove's approach, multicultural diversity is embraced through visual images of women of different races, but the structural inequalities facing citizens (e.g., injustice, racism, inequality) and the disparate, racialized effects of beauty standards are not openly discussed. Interracial harmony is performed but is never part of the written text, or, to state it another way, is seen but not heard. The Dove Web site similarly represents the problem of hegemonic beauty standards as global and as universally experienced. Dove's message, "Women of the World—Unite!" reflects a simplistic understanding of how women across different national contexts may share a common interest in beauty, while it disregards the significant barriers dividing women along lines of class, citizenship, race, ethnicity, religion, and language. In this way, feminist consumerism is a politically problematic strategy that resists naming structural inequality, classism, or institutionalized racism and presents "an undifferentiated pastiche of differences, a grab bag in which no items are assigned any more importance or centrality than others" (Bordo 1993, 258).

In contrast to Dove's consumerist recognition of diversity without inequality, PPPO employed what it conceived of as a third-wave feminist approach to fat activism and community building that explicitly recognized multiple axes of inequality. As a group, PPPO spent considerable time discussing intersectionality and providing community opportunities to address social inequality but was less concerned with representing racial difference through its performances. While PPPO was somewhat ethnically diverse, the group's commitment to antiracism did not make its way into its activism. The issue of class featured more prominently in PPPO's actions, such as in fundraisers for low-income children to attend fat-positive camps and clothing swaps in low-income neighborhoods. . . .

In sum, while each case displays a concern with feminine beauty ideology, the two represent very different approaches to feminist praxis—a difference we would characterize as a disjuncture between feminist consumerism and a grassroots feminist focus on community building and consciousness-raising. As with consumerism more generally (Sklair 2001, 5), feminist consumerism prioritizes commodity purchases above more ambitious goals such as decentering the role of beauty in women's lives, processing negative emotions, or challenging men's relationship with feminine beauty. As such, feminist consumerism tends to obscure and minimize both structural and institutionalized gender inequalities that are difficult to resolve and that might cause negative emotional associations with brands. Thus, from a marketing perspective, feminist consumerism makes business sense, operating as it does within a larger pattern of consumer culture that markets dissent to build brand loyalty and increase sales.[20]

The fact that the Dove campaign reached a wide audience cannot be denied, yet we question whether corporate channels enable counterhegemonic critique, particularly given the campaign's complicity with beauty ideology outlined above. In contrast, PPPO's ability to incorporate negative emotions and build spaces for deviant behavior allowed it to construct a counterhegemonic feminist project of community building and consciousness-raising. This grassroots activism included a radical intersectional critique focused on women's personal relationships with food and fat but also critiqued corporate capitalism and its role in promoting unhealthy eating habits and destructive body image. Although the scale on which these activities occurred was clearly limited when compared to Dove's multinational campaign, PPPO provided more room to process the negative emotions generated by gender inequality and beauty ideology and raised awareness and solidarity among fat activists at the local scale.

CONCLUSION

Our objective has been to assess how the Dove Campaign for Real Beauty and the grassroots group Pretty, Porky, and Pissed Off did and did not challenge beauty ideology and how their relative successes either circumscribe or enable possibilities for feminist transformation. We conclude that while the Dove Campaign for Real Beauty provides a critique that partially disrupts the narrowness of Western contemporary beauty codes, at the same time it systematically reproduces and legitimizes the hegemony of beauty ideology in women's personal lives in the service of expanding sales and corporate growth. Dove's approach, which we term feminist consumerism, encourages women to channel dissent and practice self-care by engaging with corporate marketing campaigns and purchasing beauty products. Although broadly accessible, Dove's critique of beauty ideology is diluted by its contradictory imperative to promote self-acceptance and at the same time increase sales by promoting women's consumption of products that encourage conformity to feminine beauty ideology. The Dove campaign does not decenter the role of beauty in women's lives but rather suggests that beauty and self-acceptance can be accessed through the purchase of Dove beauty products. Dove's profit imperative helps explain the campaign's reproduction of hegemonic beauty ideologies and its place within a larger hegemonic culture-ideology of consumerism. A more radical critique might negatively affect sales by alienating women who are emotionally invested in beauty ideology and/or promote a kind of self-acceptance not contingent on beautification and commodification. Because the Dove campaign was framed in a market context that prioritizes profits and corporate growth, the critique of hegemonic beauty standards could not incorporate a critique of consumerism as an avenue to self-acceptance or meaningfully address the class and racial inequalities linked with beauty ideals in late capitalist societies.

In the case of grassroots fat activists PPPO, we identified a more substantive counterhegemonic attack on beauty standards that mocked these norms and offered a radical, intersectional critique identifying the role of political-economic variables underlying women's unhealthy relationships to food, beauty, and the body. While offering a therapeutic venue for processing pain caused by the failure to conform to ideological beauty codes, the PPPO case suggests that countercultural activism is not necessarily solipsistic navel-gazing; its performances challenged the capitalist ideology of consumerism, offered a critique of hegemonic standards by attacking market institutions like corporations, and occurred within the more democratic context of civil society organizing, public sphere interventions, and the local spaces of queer theater. These are significant achievements, but what should not be forgotten are the limits of the local: these grassroots actors were unable to connect with the scores of women and girls reached through the Dove campaign. While narrow in its reach, the impact of PPPO's counterhegemonic critique of the beauty industry appears deep in terms of community building and identity construction for the women involved. Corporate entities were not transformed in such a grassroots project, but a critical consciousness was fostered and developed. This is no small accomplishment. . . .

The limitations of both the corporate and grassroots actors help explain the continued salience of beauty ideology in contemporary women's lives. While both corporations and grassroots feminists challenge hegemonic notions of feminine beauty, the scale and market location of the Dove case allow it to have considerably greater influence through the mass market. Meanwhile, beauty ideology works to reproduce and legitimate gender inequality that generates billions of dollars in profit for the diet, cosmetic, and plastic surgery industries. This conclusion has implications for feminist praxis and method. Our case comparison speaks to the pressing need for collective action that can raise critical consciousness about beauty ideology among women and girls over a long time frame; our cases suggest that such a critique will not emerge from a corporate market context but is nonetheless required at a scale that transcends grassroots resistance projects. . . .

NOTES

1. While national organizations and feminist campaigns define feminism in the national public consciousness, collective identities are arguably forged at the local level (Reger 2002). Movement scholars have long understood the centrality of grassroots organizing to feminist (and other) social change initiatives, even though the political is often narrowly defined as a national-level occurrence targeting the state (Bookman and Morgen 1988; Naples 1998).

2. Dove is a beauty products company owned by international Dutch corporation Unilever.

3. The Dove models range in dress sizes from 6 to 12. While larger than the average fashion model (size 4), they are still smaller than the average American woman, who is a size 14.

4. This objective also responds to Avery Gordon's decade-old assertion that corporate discourse is an important yet neglected element of cultural studies scholarship (1995).

5. In part, this echoes Nancy Fraser's call for closer attention to how feminist struggles involve elements of symbolic recognition and material redistribution (Fraser and Naples 2004, 1113).

6. Analyses of Nike's campaigns surrounding women and sports have inspired concepts similar to ours, and these are useful in explaining how corporations appropriate feminist ideas in marketing campaigns. Such analyses use terms such as "corporate feminism" (Messner 2002) and "celebrity feminism" (Cole and Hribar 1995). We are indebted to anonymous reviewers at *Signs* for flagging these parallel analyses. We use the term "feminist consumerism" to emphasize its origins in consumerism's focus on commodity purchase and acquisition as a primary means to assert an identity, achieve a common good, express ethical (feminist) principles, and seek personal pleasure and social approval. Feminist consumerism is an effective marketing tool because it is part of a hegemonic common sense of consumerism that allows Dove to credibly present itself as the vanguard of a consumer movement facilitating women's agitation and channeling resistance into commodity purchases. This involves a degree of agency, but as Messner notes, it is a "reproductive agency" that channels "women's actions and bodies within the power relations of the current gender order" (2002, 87).

7. See Dworkia 1974; Chernin 1981; Banner 1983; Brownmiller 1984; Bartky 1990; Bovey 1994.

8. While LeBesco uses queer theory to deconstruct the discourse of fatness as revolting, her suggestion that rat bodies are necessarily in revolt obscures the link between discursive constructions and material institutions. Using Judith Butler as her reference point, LeBesco suggests that "we just might be able to talk our way out of anything,

even seemingly entrenched fat oppression, because speaking builds subjects" (2001 , 77).

9. These questions are posed to the progressive Left and feminists by critics who question the assumption that countetcultural actions and nonconformist play necessarily subvert capitalist institutions and material structures (Frank 1997; Heath and Potter 2005, 21; Jeffreys 2005).

10. Following McLellan's writings on ideology, we suggest that a theoretically sophisticated conception of ideology would retain, first, a self-reflexive "hermeneutic subtlety" rejecting the Archimedean standpoint toward ideology (versus science); and, second, an interest in ideology's role in domination and social control (1995, 83).

11. Pronouncements on the death of feminism are themselves ideological, naturalizing the end of an era of feminist activism and suggesting that women's concerns have been addressed and are not worth fighting for (see Hawkesworth 2004).

12. Unpublished interview with Allyson Mitchell and Mariko Tamaki conducted by Judith Taylor and Josée Johnston at Mitchell's studio in the Gladstone Hotel, Toronto, June 17, 2005.

13. In an interview, Fat Femme Mafia activist Liz Brockest said, "My dream is to be half as fundamental to fat folks as PPPO was and still is" (in Foad 2006, 25).

14. A long-standing marketing strategy is to superficially acknowledge women's problematic and conflicted relationship with food (e.g., emphasizing themes of obsession, danger, and loss of control) while denying or minimizing the darker realities of these relationships. Susan Bordo's deconstruction of advertisements suggests that even ads that destabilize gender expectations can work to reify inequitable gender norms (1993, 105-10, 131–34).

15. Cogent analyses of Nike's advertisements in the mid-1990s indicate a strikingly similar and successful precedent for selling feminism to women who need only wear Nike clothing to be "empowered," thereby channeling dissent into individual consumption rather than collective organizing around the concept of "women" (Cole and Hribar 1995; Messner 2002, 88).

16. Celebrating fat as fabulous is a theme of many fat acceptance organizations and activists (see, e.g., Wann 1999).

17. Interview with PPPO activist Allyson Mitchell, January 3, 2005, "Big City, Small World," CBC Radio, produced by Garvia Bailey.

18. Interview, Mitchell and Tamaki, 2005.

19. Fat deviance is cool, yet unhealthy eating encouraged by the contemporary industrial-food system is also acknowledged. Performances mounted by PPPO demonstrated a complex attraction/repulsion to food (e.g., performers

sit on cakes and then eat the mashed remnants off their own bodies).

20. Dove is not the only corporation to use the marketing strategy of feminist consumerism. Nike also uses this strategy in various girl-power campaigns; the most recent features disaggregated women's body parts that reappropriates derogatory labels (e.g., "thunder thighs") to sell athletic wear featured on well-toned (but not anorexic) body parts.

REFERENCES

Banner, Lois W. 1983. *American Beauty*. New York: Knopf.

Bartky, Sandra Lee. 1990. *Femininity and Domination: Studies in the Phenomenology of Oppression*. New York: Routledge.

Black, Paula. 2004. *The Beauty Industry: Gender, Culture, Pleasure*. New York: Routledge.

Bookman, Ann, and Sandra Morgen, eds. 1988. *Women and the Politics of Empowerment*. Philadelphia: Temple University Press.

Bordo, Susan. 1993. *Unbearable Weight: Feminism, Western Culture, and the Body*. Berkeley: University of California Press.

Bovey, Shelley. 1994. *The Forbidden Body: Why Being Fat Is Not a Sin*. London: Pandora.

Braziel, Jana Evans. 2001. "Sex and Fat Chics: Deterritorializing the Fat Female Body." In Braziel and LeBesco 2001, 231–56.

Braziel, Jana Evans, and Kathleen LeBesco, eds. 2001. *Bodies Out of Bounds. Fatness and Transgression*. Berkeley: University of California Press.

Brownmiller, Susan. 1984. *Femininity*. New York: Linden.

Chernin, Kim. 1981. *The Obsession: Reflections on the Tyranny of Slenderness*. New York: Harper & Row.

Cole, Cheryl L., and Amy Hribar. 1995. "Celebrity Feminism: Nike Style—Post-Fordism, Transcendence, and Consumer Power." *Sociology of Sport Journal* 12(4): 347–69.

Corbett, Rachel. 2006. "Dove's Larger Models Spur Sales and Attention." *Women's ENews*, January 29. http://womensenews.org/article.cfm/dyn/aid/2617/context/cover/.

Davis, Kathy. 1995. *Reshaping the Female Body: The Dilemma of Cosmetic Surgery*. New York: Routledge.

Dove Real Beauty Campaign. 2005a. "The NEW Dove Self-Esteem Fund TV Ad." Unilever Canada, Inc. http://www.campaignforrealbeauty.ca/flat2.asp?url=flat2.asp&id=1607.

———. 2005b. "Why the Campaign for Real Beauty?" Unilever Canada, Inc. http://www.campaignforrealbeauty.ca/supports.asp?id=1560&length=short&section=campaign.

———. 2007. "Expert Advice: Inspiration from and for Real Women." Unilever, Inc. http://www.dove.us/real_beauty/article.asp?id=256.

Dworkin, Andrea. 1974. *Woman Hating*. New York: Dutton.

Etcoff, Nancy. 1999. *Survival of the Prettiest: The Science of Beauty*. New York: Random House.

Etcoff, Nancy, Susie Orbach, Jennifer Scott, and Heidi D'Agostino. 2004. "The Real Truth about Beauty: A Global Report." Unilever Canada, Inc. http://www.campaignforrealbeauty.ca/uploadedFiles/dove_white_paper_final.pdf.

Fegan, Eileen. 1996. "'Ideology' after 'Discourse': A Reconceptualization for Feminist Analyses of Law." *Journal of Law and Society* 23(2):173–97.

Ferree, Myra Marx, and David A. Merrill. 2000. "Hot Movements, Cold Cognition: Thinking about Social Movements in Gendered Frames." *Contemporary Sociology* 29(3): 454–62.

Foad, Lisa. 2006. "A Big Fat Revolution." *XTRA!* February 16, 25.

Frank, Thomas. 1997. *The Conquest of Cool: Business Culture, Counterculture, and the Rise of Hip Consumerism*. Chicago: University of Chicago Press.

Frank, Thomas, and Matt Weiland, eds. 1997. *Commodify Your Dissent: Salvos from the Baffler*. New York: Norton.

Fraser, Nancy, and Nancy A. Naples. 2004. "To Interpret the World and to Change It: An Interview with Nancy Fraser." *Signs: Journal of Women in Culture and Society* 29(4):1103–24.

Frost, Liz. 2001 *Young Women and the Body: A Feminist Sociology*. Houndmills: Palgrave.

Gimlin, Debra L. 2002. *Body Work: Beauty and Self-Image in American Culture*. Berkeley: University of California Press.

Gordon, Avery. 1995. "The Work of Corporate Culture." *Social Text* 44(3):3–30.

Gottdiener, Mark, ed. 2000. *New Forms of Consumption: Consumers, Culture, and Commodification*. Lanham, MD: Rowman & Littlefield.

Hartley, Cecilia. 2001. "Letting Ourselves Go: Making Room for the Fat Body in Feminist Scholarship." In Braziel and LeBesco 2001, 60–73.

Hawkesworth, Mary. 2004. "The Semiotics of Premature Burial: Feminism in a Postfeminist Age." *Signs* 29(4):961–85.

Heath, Joseph, and Andrew Potter. 2004. *The Rebel Sell: Why the Culture Can't Be Jammed*. Toronto: HarperCollins.

——— 2005 "Feminism for Sale." *This Magazine*, May/June, 20–27.

Jeffreys, Sheila. 2005. *Beauty and Misogyny: Harmful Cultural Practices in the West*. New York: Routledge.

Johnston, Josée. 2001. "Consuming Global Justice: Fair Trade Shopping and the Search for Alternative Development Strategies." In *Protest and Globalisation: Prospects for Transnational Solidarity*, ed. J. Goodman, 38–56. Sydney: Pluto.

Kellner, Douglas. 1983. "Critical Theory, Commodities and Consumer Society." *Theory, Culture and Society* 1(3): 66–83.

LeBesco, Kathleeen. 2001. "Queering Fat Bodies/Politics." In Braziel and LeBesco 2001, 74–90.

Mazer, Sharon. 2001. "'She's so fat . . .': Facing the Fat Lady at Coney Island's Sideshows by the Seashore." In Braziel and LeBesco 2001, 257–76.

McLellan, David. 1995. *Ideology.* 2nd ed. Buckingham: Open University Press.

Messner, Michael. 2002. *Taking the Field: Women, Men, and Sports.* Minneapolis: University of Minnesota Press.

Naples, Nancy A., ed. 1998. *Community Activism and Feminist Politics: Organizing across Race, Class, and Gender.* New York: Routledge.

People, 2005. "Fat or Flab?" August 15, 116–17.

Reger, Jo. 2002. "Organizational Dynamics and Construction of Multiple Feminist Identities in the National Organization for Women." *Gender and Society* 16(5): 710–27.

Rosenthal, Naomi, and Michael Schwartz. 1989. "Spontaneity and Democracy in Social Movements." In *Organizing for Social Change: Social Movement Organizations in Europe and the United States,* ed. Bert Klandermans, 33–59. Greenwich, CT: JAI.

Sklair, Leslie. 2001. *The Transnational Capitalist Class.* Malden, MA: Blackwell.

Staggenborg, Suzanne, and Verta Taylor. 2005. "Whatever Happened to the Women's Movement?" *Mobilization* 10(1):37–52.

Stevenson, Seth. 2005. "When Tush Comes to Dove: Real Women; Real Curves; Really Smart Ad Campaign." *Slate,* August 1. http://www.slate.com/id/ 2123659/.

Taylor, Verta. 1996. *Rock-a-by Baby: Feminism, Self-Help, and Postpartum Depression,* New York: Routledge.

Thompson, Denise. 2001. *Radical Feminism Today.* London: Sage.

Wann, Marilyn. 1999. *Fat! So? Because You Don't Have to Apologize for Your Size!* Berkeley, CA: Ten Speed.

Wolf, Naomi. 1991. *The Beauty Myth.* Toronto: Random House.

READING *15* **Debra L. Gimlin**

Cosmetic Surgery: Paying for Your Beauty

First published in 2002

After several unsuccessful attempts to schedule an appointment, I finally managed to meet with Jennifer, a twenty-nine-year-old grade school teacher who volunteered to talk with me about her cosmetic surgery. On a typically cold November afternoon, I spoke with Jennifer in her apartment on the south shore of Long Island. Jennifer is 5 feet 6 inches tall and has long, straight blonde hair and expressive light blue eyes. That day she was dressed in an oversized gray pullover and black sweatpants. While we talked, she peeled and sliced the crudites that would be her contribution to the potluck engagement party that she was attending later that evening.

During our conversation, I noticed that by far the most prominent feature in her small studio apartment was the enormous black and chrome stair-climbing machine set slightly off from the center of the living room/bedroom. I learned that Jennifer spends forty minutes each day on this machine and works out with weights at a nearby gym three to four times a week. She eats no meat, very little oil or fat, and no sweets, and she drinks very little alcohol. Despite her rigorous body work routine, Jennifer's legs have remained a disappointment to her. Rather than lean and muscular, they look, by her account, thick and shapeless—particularly around her lower thighs and knees. Jennifer says that her decision to have liposuction was motivated primarily by her inability to reshape her legs through diet and exercise. During the procedure, the fatty deposits were removed from the insides of Jennifer's knees, making her legs appear slimmer and more toned.

Jennifer acknowledged her own significant ambivalence about taking surgical steps to alter her body. If possible, she would have preferred to shape her legs through aerobics, weight training, and dieting, rather than through liposuction, which Jennifer described as a final and desperate option. By her account, plastic surgery was the only way to alter physical attributes that she referred to as "genetic flaws," features that she could change through no other available means. Expressing some shame, as she says, "for taking the easy way out," Jennifer's guilt is not so great that she regrets having surgery. Indeed, she plans to have a second liposuction in the near future, this time to remove the fatty tissue from her upper and inner thighs.

Cosmetic surgery stands, for many theorists and social critics, as the ultimate invasion of the human body for the sake of physical beauty. It epitomizes the astounding lengths to which contemporary women will go to obtain bodies that meet current ideals of attractiveness. As such, plastic surgery is perceived by many to be qualitatively different from aerobics, hair styling, or even dieting. In this view, cosmetic surgery is not about controlling one's own body but is instead an activity so extreme, so invasive that it can only be interpreted as subjugation. Even more than women who may participate in other types of body-shaping activities, those who undergo cosmetic surgery appear to many observers—both casual and academic—to be so obsessed with physical appearance that they are willing to risk their very existence to become more attractive.

Not surprisingly, cosmetic surgery has been attacked by the scores of feminist writers who criticize body work generally.[1] While these attacks may be well deserved, the cosmetic surgery industry is expanding rapidly nevertheless. Board-certified plastic surgeons performed more than 2.2 million procedures in 1999, a 44 percent increase since 1996 and striking 153 percent increase since 1992. Liposuction, the most common cosmetic procedure in the United States, was performed 230,865 times (up 57 percent since 1996 and 264 percent since 1992), at a cost of approximately $2,000 per patient. Breast augmentation, with its price tag of nearly $3,000, was the second most common procedure, at 167,318 (a 51 percent increase since 1996). Blepharoplasty (eyelid surgery), the third most common, was performed on 142,033 patients at a cost of just under $3,000, followed by face-lift (72,793) at over $5,000, and chemical peel (51,519), at nearly $1,300.[2] Ninety percent of these operations are performed on women, as are virtually all breast augmentations and reductions, 87 percent of liposuctions, 91 percent of face-lifts, and 85 percent of blepharoplastics. In 1999, American women had 167,318 breast augmentations,

120,160 blepharoplasties, 201,083 liposuction procedures, and 66,096 face-lifts.[3]

Although strategies for surgically altering the body's appearance have been available for centuries, the practice has only recently become a mass phenomenon. Until recently, patients were most often men disabled by war or industrial accidents. Now the recipients are overwhelmingly women who are dissatisfied with their looks.[4] Today, aesthetic operations make up 45 percent of all plastic surgery.[5]

Cosmetic surgery is one of the fastest-growing specialities in American medicine.[6] Although the total number of physicians in the United States has little more than doubled in the last quarter of a century, the number of plastic surgeons has increased fourfold. At the end of World War II, there were only about 100 plastic surgeons in the country; in 1965, there were 1,133. By 1990, that number had tripled to 3,850. Moreover, these figures may underrepresent the total number of individuals performing aesthetic procedures today. Because it is not necessary to be a licensed plastic surgeon to perform cosmetic surgery, procedures such as face-lifts, eyelid corrections, and chemical peels may be performed by other specialists, such as dermatologists.[7]

Criticisms of surgical alternation of the female body multiply nearly as rapidly as the procedures themselves. One of the main critiques of cosmetic surgery derives from the dangers involved. Cosmetic surgery is undeniably painful and risky, and each operation involves specific potential complications. For instance, pain, numbness, bruising, discoloration, and depigmentation frequently follow a liposuction, often lingering up to six months after the operation. Face-lifts can damage nerves, leaving the patient's face permanently numb. More serious complications include fat embolisms, blood clots, fluid depletion, and even death. Health experts estimate that the chance of serious side effects from breast augmentation are between 30 percent and 50 percent. The least dramatic and most common of these include decreased sensitivity in the nipples, painful swelling or congestion of the breasts, and hardening of the breasts that makes it difficult to lie down comfortably or to raise the arms without shifting the implants.[8] More serious is the problem of encapsulation, in which the body reacts to foreign materials by forming a capsule of fibrous tissue around the implants. This covering can sometimes be broken down manually by the surgeon, but, even when successful, the procedure is extremely painful.

When it is unsuccessful, the implants must be removed; in some cases, the surgeon must chisel the hardened substance from the patient's chest wall.

Clearly, the recipient of cosmetic surgery may emerge from the operation in worse shape than when she went in. Unsuccessful breast augmentations are often disfiguring, leaving the patient with unsightly scars and deformation. An overly tight face-lift produces a "zombie" look, in which the countenance seems devoid of expression. Following liposuction, the skin can develop a corrugated, uneven texture.

Finally, some criticisms of plastic surgery focus on the implications of such procedures for contemporary conceptualizations of the body and identity. Cosmetic surgery has expanded alongside specific technological developments, including advances in medical equipment like magnifying lenses, air drills for severing bone and leveling skin, and improved suturing materials, all of which enable surgical interventions to be performed with better results and less trauma for the patient.[9] According to some critics, these developments, and the increasing flexibility in body altering that they permit, are linked to cultural discourses likening the body to what Susan Bordo has called "cultural plastic." The body is now understood as having a potential for limitless change, "undetermined by history, social location or even individual biography."[10] Not only has the body come to stand as a primary symbol of identity, but it is a symbol with an unlimited capacity for alteration and modification. The body is not a dysfunctional object requiring medical intervention but a commodity, not unlike "a car, a refrigerator, a house, which can be continuously upgraded and modified in accordance with new interests and greater resources."[11] The body is a symbol of selfhood, but its relation to its inhabitant is shaped primarily by the individual's capacity for material consumption.

Of the various forms of body work, plastic surgery is surely the hardest to justify. The physical dangers are real. The symbolic damage done to all women by the apparent surrender of some to unattainable ideals of beauty is significant. Yet the criticisms also leave out a good deal. Most important, the criticisms operate either at the grand level of cultural discourse or the highly grounded level of physiological effect. As a result, they overlook the experience of the women who have plastic surgery. In this [reading], after first discussing the role of the doctor as a gatekeeper to plastic surgery, I focus on that experience.

First—and most important to those who undergo it—plastic surgery often works. This fact stands in contrast to a rhetoric that concentrates on the unattainable character of contemporary beauty ideals, portraying plastic surgery as a Sisyphean task. Critics of plastic surgery imply that those who undergo it will complete one operation only to discover some new flaw. Yet this is not the case. Somewhat to my surprise, many of the women I interviewed expressed enormous satisfaction with their procedures. While some did, indeed, intend to return for additional operations, others seemed content to have fixed a particular "flaw." I do not mean to argue that all contemporary ideals of beauty are, in fact, attainable. They are not. Neither do I mean to argue that women in contemporary America can escape the nagging self-doubts caused by those unattainable ideals. They cannot. But the ambitions of those women who undergo plastic surgery often stop far short of attaining ideal beauty. And given these limited ambitions—and within the cultural space marked out for the expression of female beauty—plastic surgery frequently achieves the exact goals intended by those who undergo it.

Second, criticisms of plastic surgery directed at gender issues often understate the extent to which this activity involves gender at an intersection with age, race, ethnicity, and even class. Many women surely undertake plastic surgery, most notably in the case of breast enlargement, to enhance distinctively female attributes. Others, however—Jewish and Italian women who have rhinoplasty, Chinese and Japanese women who have their eyes reshaped—do so in a distinctively ethnic context. And many others have plastic surgery in an attempt to reproduce the bodies of their youth. If plastic surgery speaks to the depredations of gender domination, we should recognize that it also speaks to the depredations of Anglo-Saxon ideals of beauty and the idealization of youth.

Third, the criticisms of plastic surgery ignore the complicated process by which the women who undergo surgical procedures integrate them into their identities. If not in feminist theory, then in popular culture, there lies an implicit notion that the benefits of plastic surgery are somehow inauthentic and, therefore, undeserved. Although the critics of plastic surgery insist that appearance should not be the measure of a woman's worth, the women who have plastic surgery are nonetheless participants in a culture in which appearance is taken as an expression of an inner state. To be able to purchase a new nose or wider eyes or thinner thighs seems, then, to sever the relationship between inner states and their outer expression. Where the women in aerobics classes are working hard to detach their identities from their bodies, the women who undergo plastic surgery must work even harder to reattach their identities to their new appearances. On the one hand, they are using plastic surgery to tell a story about themselves: I am the woman with svelte thighs or a button nose. On the other hand, they must also tell a story about plastic surgery in order to counter the charges of its inauthenticity. They must somehow show, to themselves even more than to others, that the new appearance is both deserved and a better indicator of the self than the old appearance—an appearance necessarily repositioned as "accidental." The result, then, is that the woman who has plastic surgery finds herself in a double bind. She is unhappy with her appearance, and so she takes the only steps she can to improve it. No matter how successful her efforts are—or how pleased she is with their outcome—the woman must ultimately defend her decision to purchase appearance and identity.

RESEARCH AND METHODS

The research for this [reading] involved fieldwork in a Long Island plastic surgery clinic and interviews with the surgeon and twenty of his female patients. Finding a location to study cosmetic surgery proved difficult because many women hesitate to admit that they have undergone such procedures and physicians are bound by doctor-patient confidentiality. Having organized my research around interviews and fieldwork in identifiable physical locations, I knew that I wanted to talk with a single surgeon's female patients, rather than a "snowball" sample of surgery clients, whom I could have located easily through advertisements in local newspapers, gyms, universities, or hairstyling salons. As a result, I needed to find a cosmetic surgeon who would permit me access to patients. My search for this doctor took nearly six months, during which time I contacted over twenty clinics and interviewed seven physicians.

I eventually chose to focus on the clinic of Dr. John Norris, a local surgeon specializing in aesthetic procedures. My discussions with the six other physicians proved to be a rich source of data about the cosmetic surgery industry and cosmetic surgeons themselves. I learned, for example, that cosmetic surgeons are frequently critical of their female clientele, seeing them as obsessed and impossible to please. Moreover, often believing that the physical imperfections that their clients observe are insignificant, surgeons sometimes suspect their patients of trying to solve emotional problems by altering their bodies.

I met John Norris at the gym where I studied aerobics. As a member of the gym, I spent a considerable amount of time there each week, both in research and on my own body work. John and his wife, Monica, were gym regulars who, like me, tended to exercise in the mornings, and I saw them several times each week. Even though I had met him previously, I contacted John formally, as I did the other cosmetic surgeons in the area. I explained my project to his receptionist and made an appointment to speak with him. After our second meeting, I asked John to allow me to interview twenty of his female clients. He agreed and asked his receptionist to contact women who might be willing to talk with me. After obtaining his patients' approval, John provided me with their names and telephone numbers. This procedure surely biased my sample in favor of successful cases. In addition to interviewing patients (one of whom I was able to interview both before and after she had surgery), I conducted several interviews with John. I also attended informational sessions at another local clinic to learn more about many of these procedures.

John conducts his enormously successful practice in two offices, one on Long Island and the other in Manhattan. I spoke with him at some length about his interest in aesthetic plastic surgery. He explained that although he had originally aspired to be a sculptor, he soon decided that a career in art would not provide an adequate income. As his interest in science developed, John opted instead for a medical career and for what he now refers to as the "excitement of sculpting human appearance." Believing that his work helps his patients to feel more satisfied with the way they look, more desirable, and more confident in their professional and private lives, John says that he derives enormous satisfaction from his career.

John is interested not only in "sculpting" the appearances of others; he is himself heavily involved in the culture of body work. In particular, John has participated in bodybuilding since he was fifteen years old and, at age fifty-one, still participates regularly in bodybuilding competitions. Moreover, John has personally undergone plastic surgery to remove the "love handles" that he says will develop at his waistline unless he maintains a body composition of no more than 3 percent body fat. As his medical career has progressed, John's training and competition have both fueled and been fueled by his interest in using surgery to rework the aesthetics of the body. While he began his career doing reconstructive and burn-correcting surgery in addition to cosmetic procedures, he now focuses almost exclusively on aesthetic plastic surgery, which he finds equally rewarding and more enjoyable.

Similar to the staff of Pamela's Hair Salon [discussed in another part of *Body Work: Beauty and Self-image in American Culture* (Berkeley: University of California Press, 2002), from which this reading is taken], John is a "true believer" in beauty ideology. Like the stylists, John not only dispenses the means of altering appearance but also is deeply involved in reworking his own appearance. Nevertheless, he is differentiated from them by his higher social status. Like Pamela's staff, John is able both to assess his clients' appearance "flaws" and to suggest particular techniques for correcting them. But, unlike Pamela's staff—and primarily because of his status as a medical professional—John's patients nearly always accept his advice. Simply put, John is different from Pamela's stylists because he not only dispenses "beauty" to his patients but also shapes the choices they make about their appearances.

Moreover, John regularly denies surgical candidates access to the body work he provides. He is selective in choosing his clientele, screening patients to ensure that they are suitable for the operations they request. Listening to the client's description of her physical imperfections, John determines whether or not her complaint is reasonable—whether or not her nose is really inappropriate for her face, her breasts are really too small, her ankles are really too thick, and so on. In making such judgments, John (like the beauticians at Pamela's) blurs the line between technique and aesthetics, effectively broadening his area of expertise. While understanding his activity as a process of determining the "appropriateness" of surgical candidates, he actually selects patients based in large part on his personal taste and sense of aesthetics. As a purveyor of body work, John positions himself not only as a surgeon but also as an expert in contemporary standards for female beauty.

In deciding whether patients are suitable candidates for the procedures they request, John judges not only the aesthetics of their appearance but also their psychological health. By his own account, John attempts to determine whether patients are trying to deal with personal crises (such as divorce) through plastic surgery. John says that when he talks with potential patients about their motivations for having cosmetic surgery, many express sadness or fear regarding a significant personal relationship, even to the point of breaking down in tears in his office. This reaction, he claims, suggests that patients should seek the services of "some other type" of professional presumably, a psychologist or marital counselor—rather than those of a cosmetic surgeon.

John has come to categorize patients in four conceptual types, distinguished primarily by their motivations for having surgery. The first of the groups includes individuals who are "self-motivated and realistic." These patients pursue surgery as a means of bringing their appearances in line with their inner self. Claiming that their bodies fail to represent them as the people they truly are, individuals in this group explain their desire for cosmetic surgery with statements such as "I don't feel like an old person. I don't want to look like one," or "I exercise and diet. I want to look like I do." These candidates, according to John, are adequately prepared for cosmetic surgery, with expectations that will likely be met by the procedures they undergo.

The second type of patient seeks out plastic surgery to please someone else. In John's description, this patient—usually a woman—is going through a painful breakup and, hoping that changing her appearance will reignite her partner's interest, turns to plastic surgery as a "last-ditch effort" to save her relationship. Breast augmentation—which, John notes with some amusement, is the surgical procedure most likely to precede divorce—is a common request among members of this category. John typically refuses to perform such procedures on patients who hope to use plastic surgery to solve some personal problem.

The third group in John's typology involves children, usually brought to the office by their parents. According to John, these patients' parents frequently say things such as "She has her father's nose," which the parents, rather than the children themselves, judge as unattractive and requiring change. John makes it a practice to ask the adolescents what they think about the particular body part. According to him, they tend to be relatively satisfied with the "nose" or other problematic feature, finding it far less objectionable than the parents do. John advises parents not to "fix what isn't broken," to give the child a few years to "grow into" the feature and then broach the topic of surgery again if they feel it necessary.

The last group includes individuals John refers to as "flighty," who want surgery for any number of "bizarre" reasons. As an example, John described one woman who wanted to have rhinoplasty because a favorite movie star had undergone the procedure. In another case, a potential patient requested breast augmentation in order to look more like a celebrity her boyfriend admired. In such cases, John refuses to operate because he considers these individuals to be psychologically unstable and impossible to satisfy.

All told, John claims that he rejects two or three requests per week. His ability and willingness to deny service suggest another comparison between the plastic surgeon and the hairstylist: John is less dependent on his clientele than are the beauticians at Pamela's, who have little choice concerning whose hair they style or how they style it. At the same time, John's decisions to reject patients are linked to his medical and legal responsibility for the surgeries that he performs. Indeed, his motivations for denying surgical procedures suggest a wariness about trying to satisfy the desires of individuals whose expectations are unreasonable and who might hold him legally responsible for their inevitable dissatisfaction. In this sense, John is even more vulnerable to his clients than are the stylists at Pamela's. While a beautician might lose a client who dislikes her haircut, John could potentially lose much more to a patient who claims that he is responsible for some physical deformity, particularly if that patient decides to sue.

The patients I interviewed ranged in age from twenty-four to fifty. The procedures they underwent included breast augmentations, nose jobs, face-lifts, eye-reshaping procedures, tummy tucks, and liposuctions. All of the women were Asian-American or European American; three were of Semitic ancestry; and all but one (a full-time mother) held salaried jobs or were students at the time of the interviews. They were employed as opticians, medical technicians, receptionists, insurance agents, teachers, office administrators, hairstylists, and secretaries.

THE STORY OF A FACE-LIFT: ANN MARIE

Ann Marie, a slender, soft-spoken fifty-year-old medical technician with upswept blonde hair, was one of the first patients I interviewed. Married to her current and only husband for nearly thirty years, Ann Marie carries herself with a careful gentility. Dressed in snug-fitting woolen pants, low-heeled brown pumps and a fuzzy light mauve sweater, Ann Marie invites me into her small, tidy home and asks if I would like coffee. Anxious to begin my first interview, I refuse. Ann Marie brings her own drink back from the kitchen in a tiny, flower-painted china cup and saucer and begins telling me about her experiences with plastic surgery.

Ann Marie is not at all shy about discussing her face-lift. She actually seems eager to tell me the reasons for her decision. Her appearance began to change in her late thirties and forties when she developed "puffiness underneath the eyes" and "drooping upper eyelids." Most unattractive, by Ann Marie's account, "the skin of my throat started getting creepy." In her words, "You get to an age" when "you look in the mirror and see lines that were not there before." Because her physical appearance had begun to reflect the aging process, she explains, "All of a sudden, the need [for cosmetic surgery] was there."

While Ann Marie describes her need for a face-lift as "sudden," she had planned to have the procedure long before. She recalls that "about ten years ago," she spoke with several close friends about having a face-lift at some point in the future. She explains, "We talked about it a long time ago. I guess I have never accepted the axiom of growing old gracefully. I have always sworn I would never picture myself as a chubby old lady." Ann Marie and her friends "talked and decided that when the time was just right, we would definitely do it." Ann Marie is the only member of the group who actually went through with surgery.

Despite her resolve, Ann Marie did not enter into cosmetic surgery lightly. Instead, for several years she "thought about it from time to time. There was a lot to be considered." Among the issues she contemplated were the physical dangers involved in the operation, the risk of looking worse after the surgery than before, and the importance of choosing a well-qualified doctor with an excellent reputation. She explains, "You are putting your face in the hands of a surgeon; there is the possibility of absolute disaster, very possibly permanently. You have to choose the surgeon very carefully."

Ann Marie chose John Norris to perform the face-lift. Largely because he had performed an emergency procedure for her just over one year earlier, Ann Marie claims that she felt completely comfortable with him. "John was recommended to me by my dermatologist. I had an infection on my face; it was quite serious. The dermatologist told me I had to go to a plastic surgeon, and John was the only one he would recommend." Because of the dermatologist's recommendation and her satisfaction with John's earlier work, Ann Marie returned to him for the face-lift. She visited his office in Long Island for a consultation and, not long after her appointment, decided to go ahead with the procedure.

During their first meeting, Ann Marie had what she refers to as two "surprises": one was the price of the operation and the other the news that she would have to stop smoking. According to Ann Marie, John explained that "you will not heal as well if you continue to smoke. Because it impedes circulation, smoking decreases your ability to heal properly." She says, "The most difficult part was to stop smoking. I was puffing away a pack and a half a day for over twenty years." John told Ann Marie that she would not be able to smoke for three months before the surgery. She says, "I thought, What? I will never be able to do this. But I did, I stopped cold. That was the real sacrifice for me."

While giving up cigarettes may have been the greatest sacrifice for Ann Marie, there were clearly many others. For a full year, Ann Marie had to work "one day job, one night job, occasionally a third job" to afford the surgery. She had to "bank" four weeks of overtime at her primary job so she could take time off to recover from the procedure. She also postponed repairs on her home. She explains, "There were things my house needed, but my feeling was, I needed a face-lift more than my house did."

By providing me with a long and detailed account of her need for a face-lift and the sacrifices she was willing to make to have the procedure, Ann Marie hints at an awareness that her behavior is somehow subject to criticism, that it might be construed by others as superficial or shallow. With a hint of defensiveness, Ann Marie explains that she "needed" the face-lift—despite its financial costs and physical risks—not merely because she is concerned with her appearance, but because of pressures in "the workfield." She says, "Despite the fact that we have laws against age discrimination, employers do find ways of getting around it. I know women my age who do not get jobs or are relieved of jobs because of age. . . . [The face-lift] will ensure my work ability." Ann Marie, by her account, decided to have cosmetic surgery not due to narcissism but to concern for her professional well-being. Justifying her behavior as a career decision, she implies that she is sensitive to the social disapproval of

plastic surgery, that she knows that the behavior requires some justification.

Even though Ann Marie believes that looking younger will help her professionally, she also admits that she has "not seen anything that has really changed in that area." Instead, the procedure has affected her primarily "on a personal basis, a social basis." Explaining these effects in more detail, she says, "I meet people I haven't seen for two or three years who will say, 'There is something different about you, but I don't know what it is.' I met a sister of a very good friend of mine in June, which is five months after my surgery. She looked at me and said, 'I don't know you.' I said, 'Of course you do. I've known you nearly all of my life.' She realized who I was and was astounded at my appearance."

This incident, along with several similar ones, has, by Ann Marie's account, improved her self-image. By attributing these experiences—and the resulting improvement in her self-perception—to her face-lift, Ann Marie justifies her decision to have cosmetic surgery. In contemporary Western culture, "feeling good" about oneself is understood to be worth considerable effort because it makes us better workers, spouses, and citizens. Among children, self-esteem is credited with the ability to improve grades and to discourage sex and illegal drug use. Ann Marie explains her choice to have plastic surgery as "a matter of personal esteem. If you feel you look better, you feel better about yourself." By granting cosmetic surgery the power to provide self-esteem, Ann Marie—like many of the other women I spoke with—effectively legitimizes an otherwise illegitimate activity.

At the same time, Ann Marie's defensiveness suggests that she is somewhat self-conscious about her choice. She describes her decision to have a face-lift as "not purely vanity," and then adds, "If it is vanity, so what? That does not make me a bad person. I don't want to look bad. I don't want to look my age. I want to look younger. I want smoother skin." By her account, Ann Marie is not "bad" or vain; in fact, she is actually a good person, as evidenced by the other forms of body work in which she participates. She explains, "My weight is only a variance of six pounds heavier from what it was thirty years ago. I keep in shape in addition to the surgery. I jog, I exercise, I diet." Ann Marie has maintained her physical appearance of youth in every way possible—failing only to control the appearance of her facial skin, which she could not keep from "getting creepy." In her account, Ann Marie deserved the surgery—an act tinged with deception—because she has proved her moral character through other (physically demanding and highly symbolic) forms of work on her body. Ann Marie is entitled to an appearance that reflects those efforts, even if that appearance is obtainable only through cosmetic surgery.

"A DEEP, DARK SECRET": HAVING LIPOSUCTION

John arranged for me to speak with a twenty-seven-year-old woman named Bonnie who was planning to have cosmetic surgery. In sharp contrast to the other women I interviewed, Bonnie was hesitant to speak with me about the procedure, because, as she later said, she considered it to be "a deep, dark secret" that she had discussed with no one but her husband of five months. Bonnie worked out at the same gym that both John and I attended. Because she and I were previously acquainted, John suggested that Bonnie speak with me about the procedure she was considering, and she agreed. Over the next six months, Bonnie and I met several times to discuss cosmetic surgery; during that period, she decided to have liposuction, underwent the procedure, and recovered from it.

Having recently completed a master's degree at a New England university, Bonnie moved to the east end of Long Island to take a position as a chemist in a pharmaceutical firm. She explained to me that over the years she had spoken casually to various women about cosmetic surgery and had "fantasized about" having liposuction herself, though she had never considered it seriously. Prior to having the operation, Bonnie told me why she was reluctant to have cosmetic surgery:

> It's always seemed to me to be one step too far. I have dieted and exercised my whole life, and sometimes I've gone over the edge and done some things that probably weren't very healthy, but I could always stop myself before I became totally obsessed. I guess I have always thought that I would never get so obsessed that I would allow my body to be cut into just so I could look better. At least that's what I had always hoped. I couldn't imagine myself as one of "them," as one of those weak women who would go that far.

Despite her stated objections to cosmetic surgery and her characterization of its patients as "weak," Bonnie

underwent liposuction on the outside of her upper thighs. Bonnie described this area of her body as "flabby, no matter what I do. I exercise five or six times a week; I cycle with my husband. I do all the weight lifting that is supposed to tone up the muscles in those areas. Nothing works!" Nevertheless, Bonnie never seriously investigated the procedure until she finished graduate school and began full-time employment. She explained, "This is the first time I've ever made enough money to think about doing something like this. The liposuction will cost $2,000, which is less than it usually costs because I won't have to have general anesthesia, but it's still a lot of money."

Referring to her new job and home, Bonnie noted that she would never have considered having cosmetic surgery while she was living near her family and friends. "I wouldn't want any of my friends or my family to know about it, only my husband. My family would all be like, 'You don't need to have that done. You're crazy. You are thin enough already.' That doesn't keep me from thinking these lumps on my thighs are really ugly. They are the only thing I see when I look in the mirror."

Bonnie's hesitance to discuss liposuction with her friends stems from her perception of cosmetic surgery as part of a process of "giving in to pressure, giving in to these ideals about how women should look, when none of us real women are ever going to look like that." Bonnie believes that her friends would react to her interest in plastic surgery by making her "feel so ashamed, like I am not strong enough to accept myself like I am."

Unlike most of John's patients, Bonnie articulates her ambivalence about plastic surgery primarily in political rather than personal terms. Her description of her friends' imagined objections is one of many examples of her concern with the political meaning of her actions. In another, Bonnie explains that her own political view of cosmetic surgery is the main source of her conflict over having the procedure. She says, "I am not worried about problems with the operation itself. I know that Dr. Norris has a great reputation. I've talked to other people at the gym who have used him, and they were all really happy. He does so much of this stuff, I'm sure he's really good at it." Bonnie's concerns focus instead on the social and cultural significance of her action. "If I am proud to be a woman, then I should be proud to look like a woman, with a woman's butt and a woman's thighs." Reacting to her own accusations, she notes, "I am proud to be a woman, but I really hate it when I get a glimpse of my backside and I just look big. I feel terrible knowing that it is those areas of my body which are understood to be most 'female' that I dislike the most." Expressing her interest in cosmetic surgery as her only viable option for reducing her dissatisfaction with her appearance, she adds,

> I don't really know how to get around it, though, because I really do not like those parts of my figure. Plastic surgery seems like a pretty good way, and really, a pretty easy way, to deal with that dissatisfaction, to put those negative feelings behind me . . . to move on with the rest of my life. . . . I'd love to get dressed for work in the morning and have only the work in front of me, rather than, you know, what's literally behind me, be the thing that concerns me the most.

Bonnie is explicitly aware that the body and the self are linked. When she says that she dislikes the "female" parts of her figure, one can easily imagine replacing the term "figure" with the term "self." Indeed, it is Bonnie's ambivalence about her female identity that is most troubling to her; eradicating the physical signs of femininity—and the flaws inherent in those attributes—may enable her to construct a self that she believes to be less imperfect, more culturally acceptable, and that will allow her to focus more attention on other activities and concerns, including her career, the sports she enjoys, and her new marriage. At the same time, her decision to undergo liposuction comes at a considerable cost; Bonnie says explicitly that, if possible, she would prefer to change her perceptions rather than her body. The "pressure" she feels, however, limits her ability to rework her self-image, leaving her to choose between plastic surgery and a negative self-concept, two options that are unsatisfying. Bonnie's decision to undergo liposuction suggests that, in the end, the costs associated with plastic surgery are somehow less significant than those attached to her appearance flaws.

Obviously, Ann Marie and Bonnie present two quite disparate facets of the concerns women face as they consider having cosmetic surgery. While Ann Marie struggled to meet the financial and physical requirements of her face-lift, Bonnie agonized over the political dimension of her decision to have liposuction. So distinct are these preoccupations, in fact, that they can be conceptualized as opposite ends of a continuum, along which the perspectives of the other eighteen women I interviewed can be placed. For most of these women, the political implications of cosmetic surgery, though not entirely insignificant, were far less important than they were for Bonnie. The other women I interviewed were more often concerned with the health risks and financial costs of cosmetic surgery and with how they would look after their procedures.

While Ann Marie's and Bonnie's preoperative anxieties took different forms, both constructed elaborate justifications for plastic surgery. Like the other women I interviewed, Bonnie responds to the negative identity implications of plastic surgery by explaining that she has done all that is humanly possible to alter an imperfect body but that no act short of plastic surgery will allow her to live peacefully with herself. Invariably, the women's accounts involve bodies that were flawed in some way for which the individual claimed not to be responsible. Each woman's body was imperfect not because she had erred in her body work but because of aging, genetics, or some other physical condition that she could not control. Their flawed bodies are inaccurate indicators of character, and so they effectively lie about who the women really are. Accounts like these permit women to engage in cosmetic procedures with less guilt. Plastic surgery becomes for them not an act of deception but an attempt to align body with self.

"THE BODY I WAS MEANT TO HAVE": WHY WOMEN HAVE COSMETIC SURGERY

Whereas some writers have dealt with cosmetic surgery as if it were an attempt to attain idealized female beauty in order to gain the approval of men,[12] the women I interviewed claim that their goal in undergoing plastic surgery is neither to become beautiful nor to be beautiful specifically for husbands, boyfriends, or other significant individuals. Rather, they alter their bodies for their own satisfaction, in effect utilizing such procedures to create what they consider a normal appearance, one that reflects a normal self. While I do not accept their accounts without some skepticism, I believe that women who have plastic surgery are not necessarily doing so in order to become beautiful or to please particular individuals. Instead they are responding to highly restrictive notions of normality and the "normal" self, notions that neither apply to the population at large (in fact, quite the reverse) nor leave space for ethnic variation. Plastic surgery "works" for women who have these procedures, but it works only within the context of a culture of appearance that is less about beauty than it is about control based on the physical representations of gender, age, and ethnicity.

My respondents claim that prior to having surgery, some particular physical feature stood in the way of their looking "normal." This feature distinguished them from others and prohibited them from experiencing "a happy, regular life," as Marcy, a twenty-five-year-old student, put it. Marcy decided at twenty-one to have the bony arch in the middle of her nose removed and its tip shortened. Before the procedure, Marcy had never been involved in a romantic relationship, a fact that she attributed to her "hook" nose and unattractive appearance. Marcy says, "I have always felt terrible about how pronounced it was. No matter how I wore my hair, it was in the middle of my face, and everybody noticed it. It's not like I could just wear my bangs long."

Marcy decided to have rhinoplasty near a date that was particularly symbolic for her. "I was having my nose done just before Valentine's Day. I thought to myself, maybe if I have my nose done for Valentine's Day, by next Valentine's Day, I'll have a Valentine!" Although she did not find a Valentine for the following year—she explained that dating "didn't happen until a few years later"—Marcy claimed that over time, the surgery allowed her to experience pleasure that she would otherwise have missed.

Because Marcy uses cosmetic surgery to make herself more appealing to others, her experience seemingly supports the criticisms of authors like Naomi Wolf. However, Marcy stresses that she does not expect plastic surgery to make her beautiful. Neither does she believe that winning male affection requires her to be beautiful. Quite the contrary, Marcy clearly imagines that a merely normal appearance is sufficient to garner the male attention she desires.

The women describe several ways in which their physical features have kept them from living ordinary lives. For example, Barbara, a twenty-nine-year-old bookkeeper, says that her breasts—which were, by her account, too small to fill out attractive clothing—made her appear "dumpy" and ill-proportioned. Her "flaw" contributed to a negative self-image, which in turn served to limit the education and career goals Barbara set for herself, the friendships she fostered, and the romantic and sexual relationships she pursued. Barbara decided to have her breasts augmented (from a 36A to a 36D) to become, in her words, "more attractive to myself and others." While her larger breasts have in fact made Barbara feel more attractive, she, like other patients I interviewed, nevertheless laments women's inability to be self-confident despite their physical shortcomings. She says, "For women, the appearance is the important thing. That's too bad that we can't worry about not being judged. [Small breasts] made a big difference in how I felt myself being perceived and how I felt about myself as a person."

Because physical attractiveness shapes the way women are "judged," appearance must be protected as women age. Like Ann Marie, several of the patients I interviewed underwent cosmetic procedures aimed at reducing the natural signs of aging. These women claim that aging had changed an acceptable appearance into an unacceptable one that reflected negatively on their identity. For instance, Sue, a forty-four-year-old optician, decided to have the loose skin around her eyes tightened. She discusses her motivations for having the operation: "My eyes had always been all right, nice eyes. I guess I had always liked my face pretty well, but with age, the skin around them started getting puffy. They just didn't look nice anymore. I looked tired, tired and old. That's why I had them fixed." While Sue had, according to her own account, once been satisfied with her appearance, she grew to dislike her face as the signs of aging became apparent. She used cosmetic surgery to regain the face she liked "pretty well."

Several women told me that they chose to have cosmetic surgery not to make themselves beautiful or outstanding in any particular way but simply to regain normal physical characteristics they had lost through aging.[13] Like Sue and Ann Marie, Tina, a forty-eight-year-old receptionist, used cosmetic surgery to combat the physical changes associated with growing older. Tina underwent liposuction to reduce what she referred to as "secretarial spread," the widening of her hips and buttocks that she believed had come with her twenty-five-year career in office management. She explains, "When I was younger, I had nice hips, curvy but narrow enough, and my rear was well-shaped. After a lifetime of sitting, growing older and flabbier, it had gotten really huge." Tina hoped to restore her appearance to its more youthful form. Believing that her only means of doing so was cosmetic surgery, Tina opted to have liposuction rather than surrender to the aging process that had so drastically altered her body.

Youth—or at least a youthful appearance—is not the only characteristic women attempt to construct or regain through aesthetic procedures. Indeed, three of the patients I interviewed—all under the age of thirty—had cosmetic surgery to reduce the physical markers of ethnicity. These women underwent procedures intended to make their physical features more Anglo-Saxon. Marcy, a Jewish woman, notes that her rhinoplasty removed physical features "more frequently associated with Jewish people." Jodie, a twenty-eight-year-old student who also had her nose reshaped, says, "I had this Italian bump on my nose. It required a little shaving. Now, it looks better." By a "better" nose, Jodie implies a more Anglo-Saxon, less Italian, and therefore less ethnic nose. And Kim, a twenty-two-year-old Taiwanese American student, underwent a procedure to make her eyes appear more oval in shape. She said, "[Taiwanese people] regard girls with wide, bright eyes as beautiful. My eyes used to look a little bit as if I was staring at somebody. The look is not soft; it is a very stiff look." While none of these women consciously attempted to detach themselves from ethnicity, they nevertheless chose to ignore the fact that their efforts to appear "normal" explicitly diminished the physical markers of that ethnicity. Seemingly indifferent to this loss, they accept the notion that normalized (i.e., Anglo-Saxon) features are more attractive than ethnic ones.

All the women claimed that plastic surgery was, for them, a logical, carefully thought-out response to distressing circumstances that could not be otherwise remedied. They now perceive themselves to be more socially acceptable, more normal, and, in several cases, more outgoing. As Bonnie explains, "I got exactly what I wanted from this. My body isn't extraordinarily different, but now, I feel like, well, I have a cute bottom. I have a cuter figure. I don't feel like the one with the big butt anymore. And for me, that lets me put my body issues away pretty much."

At the same time, displaying some remnants of her original ambivalence about cosmetic surgery, Bonnie notes, "I wish that I could have said, 'To hell with it, I am going to love my body the way it is' . . . but I had tried to do that for fifteen years, and it didn't work." She adds, "Now, I know I'll never look like Cindy Crawford, but I can walk around and feel like everything is good enough."

Women who undergo plastic surgery report various other benefits. For instance, some say that they can now wear clothes that they could not have worn prior to their operations; others attest to having greater self-confidence or to being more extroverted. Jennifer explains, "When I walk out that door in the morning, my head might be a little bit higher when I'm wearing a certain outfit. Like, before I had [liposuction] done, it used to be, I feel good, but I hope no one will notice that my legs aren't too nice."

These women now wear bathing suits, dresses with low-cut necklines, and feminine and revealing lingerie. Wearing these clothes, and believing themselves to be attractive in them, shapes the women's perceptions of themselves and increases their self-confidence. Tara, a twenty-seven-year-old student, told me that before she had breast augmentation surgery, she avoided wearing bathing suits in public and rarely shopped for bras. She says, "[Breast augmentation] has given me more self-confidence than I ever had. I fit in when I'm with my girlfriends now. Before, I never went to the beach with anybody around. After I had [plastic surgery], I couldn't wait to buy a bra. I could never buy one before because I was so pathetically small." Having plastic surgery made Tara appear more "normal." She is now able to participate in activities from which she previously felt excluded.

Barbara, who also had breast augmentation surgery, recounted a similar experience. She says, "I used to wear super-padded bras when I dressed up, but they just never did it for me. I didn't look like the other women. But now, like tonight, I am going to a party, and I know I'll be able to fill out the dress." She added, "[Breast augmentation] has made me feel very confident. I think that's the difference."

Sandra, a forty-three-year-old office manager who had liposuction to reduce her "thick thighs" and "saddlebag" hips, explains that she underwent the procedure not only to appear youthful and wear feminine clothing, but also to approximate a cultural ideal involving social class. "I used to put on nice clothes and still look like a bag lady, you know, unsophisticated. Now I feel like I can wear good clothes and look like they are appropriate for me. Now, my body fits the clothes." Sandra likens appearance to a tableau of social class, both in the context of the clothing one chooses and the extent to which one's body appears to be "appropriate" for that clothing (and the social standing that it implies). Simply put, before Sandra's surgery, her "flabby" body had less class than her clothing. Her body undermined her efforts to use appearance to stake out a particular social location. In effect, it not only made her clothing an ineffective class identifier but also invalidated her claims to a particular status. Plastic surgery, however, has allowed Sandra to display social class through clothing. Cosmetic surgery legitimizes Sandra's claims to social status.

Other women I interviewed also claimed that cosmetic surgery helped them feel more self confident. For example, Kim says, "I guess I feel better when I am out with friends, like maybe people will think I am attractive. I feel attractive and I guess, I act more attractive." Thus, the women imagine that they are now perceived more favorably and so behave in a manner that they believe is appropriate for "attractive" women. At the same time, the women recognize that they may simply be imagining others' perceptions of them and that their behaviors may have changed independently of any alteration in the way they are viewed. Kim says, "Maybe nobody even notices, but I feel like I look better. I guess just thinking I look better changes the way I act a little "

Nearly all of the women told me that their romantic partners believed the cosmetic procedures were unnecessary. Before her breast augmentation procedure, Tara's boyfriend voiced significant apprehension. "He was very, very frightened about it. He kept on telling me, 'I love you just the way you are,' that type of thing." And Barbara's fiance blamed himself for her dissatisfaction with her breasts. She recalls, "My fiance thought he was doing something wrong that would make me feel like this about myself." In many cases, the women's partners attempted to convince them not to undergo the surgery. Jennifer says her boyfriend "tried to talk me out of it, but finally he decided, 'If it's going to make you happy, go ahead and do it.'" Some of John's patients report that their partners have had mixed reactions to the results of the procedures. Barbara says that even though she has always considered her husband a "breast man, because his eyes would pop out if he saw a big-breasted woman," he nevertheless told her that she was "perfect" with small breasts. She adds, laughing, "He still says he liked me better before, but I'll tell you, I can't keep him off of me. I keep saying I'm taking them back for a refund."

The frequency with which I heard such assertions points to the considerable importance women attach to having "freely" chosen to have cosmetic surgery, independent of coercion by their lovers or the desire to please someone other than themselves. These assertions make sense in light of the women's accounts of their surgery. Plastic surgery cannot be both something women "deserve" and something that they are forced or manipulated into doing. In their accounts, plastic surgery is positioned as a final option for correcting a tormenting problem. This conception of plastic surgery is clearly inconsistent with an image of acts forced on them by others—particularly others who might actually benefit more from the procedures than do the women themselves.

PLASTIC SURGERY AND INAUTHENTICITY: THE HIGH PRICE OF BODY WORK

In turning "abnormal" bodies into "normal" ones, plastic surgery succeeds: the woman who participates in plastic surgery comes to possess the foundation (i.e., a normal body) of a normative self. However, plastic surgery fails as a method for constructing a positive self-concept because of the negative social and political meanings attached to it. Women participate in cosmetic surgery in a world that limits their choices and in which the flawed body is taken as a sign of a flawed character. Despite the negative connotations of plastic surgery, women opt to engage in such procedures because the alternative is more detrimental to self-image. However, most of the women I interviewed carry with them the burden of their decisions; the process of dealing with that burden exacts from them a considerable price.

Some of the costs of cosmetic surgery—including the danger of physical damage and the high financial price—are obvious to those who have undergone these procedures and perhaps even to those who have not. Most of these women had plastic surgery only after serious consideration (often accompanied by research into the medical technology involved in the operations). Likewise, few could easily afford the surgery they underwent; nearly all of them had to sacrifice some other large purchase or to weather financial hardship. Some have accrued considerable debt, while others had to request financial help from relatives. Only a very few of the women had health insurance that covered part of the cost.

Other costs associated with cosmetic surgery, while less concrete, are no less substantial. Specifically, after surgery, women must attempt to deal with the taint of inauthenticity these procedures imply. Although the body appears more normal, the character becomes suspect, with the self, by implication, becoming deviant. The unacceptable act of cosmetic surgery displaces the normative body as an indicator of character. Although the women I interviewed do not formulate the complexities and contradictions involved in their activities in the way I have here, their accounts show that they struggle with a self-concept that continues to be deviant despite their now-normal appearance. Indeed, the accounts themselves—which attempt to deny inauthenticity by positioning cosmetic surgery as somehow owed to the women who partake of it— show that plastic surgery fails to align body and self.

These accounts suggest a singular conclusion with regard to the success of plastic surgery for establishing the normative identity. Women like Ann Marie and Bonnie—like participants in the aerobics classes [discussed in another part of *Body Work*]—invoke their rigorous body work regimens as evidence of moral rectitude and as the basis for their entitlement to cosmetic surgery. But although cosmetic surgery patients and aerobics participants seem to rely on the same symbols of identity, for women who undergo cosmetic surgery, those symbols fail to mitigate the body's negative implications for self. Had these women accepted their body work as an adequate indicator of identity, they would not have needed to turn to plastic surgery to correct their bodies' failings. Moreover, still needing to establish the "deceptive" act of plastic surgery as irrelevant to self (and to position the surgically altered, normative body as the true indicator of selfhood), these women revert to accounts that have already proved unsuccessful. Indeed, the negative implications for self inherent in cosmetic surgery require women to resort to accounts that they know—consciously or not—fail to support the normative identity. In so doing, these women attest to the failure of cosmetic surgery to position the transformed body as symbolic of self. Simply put, if plastic surgery were a successful method for constructing identity, these women would argue that the surgically altered body—rather than body work that has proved unsuccessful at shaping the body or establishing the self—serves to symbolize identity.

CONCLUSION

My research points to three general conclusions. The first bears on the reasons women have plastic surgery and suggests a modification of the criticisms of such procedures. The second bears on the ways in which women create accounts of plastic surgery, which are ignored by the criticisms of plastic surgery to date. The third returns more sympathetically to those criticisms.

None of the women I spoke to embarked casually on plastic surgery. The costs associated with these procedures—measured in dollars and the risk of physical damage—are well known. Although physicians may serve as gatekeepers by preventing some women from undergoing surgery, they rarely recruit patients directly. When surgeons actively market their practices—as did John Norris—they tend to do so indirectly, through advertisements in local magazines and shopping malls. And the women I interviewed did not report that they underwent surgery at the urging of a husband, parent, lover, or friend. Rather, the decision to seek surgery seems to have been theirs alone, at least in the immediate circumstances. To be sure, these decisions were shaped by broader cultural considerations— by notions of what constitutes beauty, by distinctively ethnic notions of beauty, and, most important, by the assumption that a woman's worth is measured by her appearance. Yet to portray the women I talked to as cultural dupes, as passively submitting to the demands of beauty, is to misrepresent them badly. A more appropriate image, I would suggest, is to present them as savvy cultural negotiators, attempting to make out as best they can within a culture that limits their options. Those who undergo plastic surgery may (ultimately) be misguided, but they are not foolish. They know what they are doing. Their goals are realistic, and they in fact achieve most of what they set out to accomplish with plastic surgery. Although their actions surely do, in the long run, contribute to the reproduction of a beauty culture that carries heavy costs for them and for all women, in the short run they have succeeded in their own limited purposes.

Second, plastic surgery requires a defense. Much like the women I studied in the aerobics classes, those who underwent plastic surgery are working hard to justify themselves. But the accounts of the women who have plastic surgery are very different from those of the women who attend the aerobics classes. The aerobics women use hard physical work as an indicator of character that allows them to sever their conception of the self from the body. In contrast, the women who have had plastic surgery work hard to reattach the self to the body. First, they must convince themselves that they deserve the surgery, whether by the hard work they put in at the gym or the effort they invest in saving the money for the procedure. In so doing, they make the surgery psychologically and ideologically their own. Second, they must convince themselves that their revised appearance is authentically connected to the self.[14] To do this, they invoke essentialist notions of the self and corresponding notions of the body as accidental, somehow inessential or a degeneration from a younger body that better represented who they truly are.

I do not mean these observations as a defense of plastic surgery so much as an effort to understand that surgery and its implications. Indeed, if we are to distinguish plastic surgery from other forms of body work, we can do so on precisely the grounds I have just suggested. I am not convinced that reducing facial wrinkles is somehow less "real" than dyeing hair from gray to brown or even that eye surgery or rhinoplasty is somehow less authentic than a decision to have straight rather than curly hair. However, what characterizes the efforts of women in aerobics, hair salons, and, . . . in NAAFA [National Association to Advance Fat Acceptance], is that they attempt, in somewhat different ways and with varying degrees of success, to neutralize appearance as a measure of character. Far more than the other women I studied, the women who undergo plastic surgery help to reproduce some of the worst aspects of the beauty culture, not so much through the act of the surgery itself as through their ideological efforts to restore appearance as an indicator of character.

My own criticisms of plastic surgery are tempered by observations of [other] women described in [my book] *Body Work*. Although I have characterized plastic surgery as a research "site," parallel to an aerobics class or a group of women in a hair salon or the members of NAAFA, this parallel is in certain respects misleading. In the hair salon, in the aerobics class, and especially in NAAFA, I found women working together to find common solutions to a shared problem. But women who underwent plastic surgery were not a group in the same sense. For the most part, they did not know each other. They did not speak to each other. And although they may have had common problems with a common solution, they did not develop this solution cooperatively. In the other settings I studied, the local production of an alternative culture was very much in evidence. In the plastic surgery group, however, there were the aesthetic judgments of the plastic surgeon, the ignored opposition of friends and family, but no culture of its own. The women in the aerobics class, in the hair salon, and especially in NAAFA, all challenged a beauty culture, however haltingly, however partially. In contrast, the women who undergo plastic surgery are simply making do within a culture that they believe judges and rewards them for their looks.

NOTES

1. Ann Dally, *Women Under the Knife: A History of Surgery* (London: Hutchinson Radius, 1991); Eugenia Kaw, "Opening Faces: The Politics of Cosmetic Surgery and Asian-American Women," in *Many Mirrors: Body Image and Social Relations*, ed. N. Sank (New Brunswick, N.J.: Rutgers University Press, 1994), 241–65.

2. American Society of Plastic and Reconstructive Surgeons, *1999 Plastic Surgery Procedural Statistics* (Arlington Heights, Ill.: American Society of Plastic and Reconstructive Surgeons, www.plasticsurgery.org, March 2000); American Society of Plastic and Reconstructive Surgeons, *1999 Average Surgeon's Fees* (Arlington Heights, Ill.: American Society of Plastic and Reconstructive Surgeons, www.plasticsurgery.org, March 2000). Generally, surgeons' fees do not include anesthesia, operating-room facilities, or other related expenses.

3. American Society of Plastic and Reconstructive Surgeons, *1999 Gender Distribution. Cosmetic Procedures* (Arlington Heights, Ill.: American Society of Plastic and Reconstructive Surgeons, www.plasticsurgery.org, March 2000).

4. American Society of Plastic and Reconstructive Surgeons, *1999 Plastic Surgery Procedural Statistics* (Arlington Heights, Ill.: www.plasticsurgery.org, March 2000).

5. Joachim Gabka and Ekkehard Vaubel, *Plastic Surgery Past and Present: Origin and History of Modern Lines of Incision* (Basel: Karger, 1983), 29.

6. Susan Faludi, *Backlash: The Undeclared War on Women* (New York: Crown, 1991), 217.

7. Kathy Davis, *Reshaping the Female Body: The Dilemma of Cosmetic Surgery* (New York: Routledge, 1995), 21.

8. Robert M. Goldwyn, ed., *Long-Term Results in Plastic and Reconstructive Surgery*, 2d ed. (Boston: Little, Brown, 1980).

9. Barbara Meredith, *A Change for the Better* (London: Grafton Books, 1988).

10. Susan Bordo, "'Material Girl': The Effacements of Postmodern Culture," *Michigan Quarterly Review* 29 (1990): 657.

11. Joan Finkelstein, *The Fashioned Self* (Philadelphia: Temple University Press, 1991), 87.

12. Naomi Wolf, *The Beauty Myth: How Images of Beauty Are Used against Women* (New York: William Morrow, 1991).

13. See Davis, *Reshaping the Female Body*, for similar findings.

14. Concern about authenticity may well be class-specific; however, because my sample is based on references from a plastic surgeon, it is likely to include those patients who are least troubled by what they have done.

Hair Still Matters

First published in 2004

Williams' beaded braids, though popular with her fans and part of her identity the past few years, have long been a matter of annoyance to some opponents even when they don't come undone. . . . To bead or not to bead, that is the question now facing Williams. For the moment, she plans only to braid them a little tighter. "I shouldn't have to change," she said. "I like my hair."

—Associated Press, 1999

INTRODUCTION

I've always liked tennis, as both a player and fan. But who knew back in 1999 when Venus Williams was beginning to light a fire to the women's professional circuit that my interest in tennis and my scholarly research on black women and hair would collide? Though troubled by the racial, gendered, and cultural meanings of Williams being penalized for wearing beads in her hair during the Australian Open, I knew that once again I had some phat fodder for continuing to argue that hair STILL matters for black women.[1] The expectation to conform to white standards is nothing new in a society that privileges whiteness, and the expectation is becoming magnified for blacks in predominantly white spaces like professional tennis. In fact, in the late 1990s, descriptions of Venus Williams and basketball sensation Allen Iverson often included allusions to their hairstyles, braided and in rows, respectively. The coded racial language of sportscasters' coverage of Williams's tennis matches or Iverson's basketball games is indicative of the fascination and discomfort that white mainstream U.S. society continues to feel regarding African Americans in general, and particular black hairstyles and what they signify, whether real or imagined. Like the Afro, Williams's

beaded braids and Iverson's cornrows are exotic to some and threatening to others because they display a black aesthetic that is linked to an authentic or radical blackness in the imagination of many whites. Still, the gendered component of Williams's sanctioning during her 1999 match is equally as important as the racial one. For example, Williams's choice of hairstyle was rooted outside of mainstream constructions of femininity. By wearing beaded braids, Williams's expression of racialized gender sent the message to a predominantly white professional women's tennis circuit that mainstream constructions of womanhood are insufficient in understanding black women's relationship to beauty culture. In fact, Williams's hairstyle sent a bold statement that the very notion of what constitutes femininity must not only be contested, but our understanding of womanhood must be expanded. Feminist scholars have done well in unmasking the gender politics of femininity and sexuality that are embedded in how the female body has been, for example, treated in popular media and science (Jaggar and Bordo 1989; Bordo 1993). The female body in general, as a site where both empowerment and repression are played out, must be central to feminist projects in the twenty-first century. From a woman's right to choose what happens to her body with regard to abortion to female circumcision to the covering of women's bodies among Muslims, feminists, locally and globally, must continue to illuminate the contexts under which women's bodies are politicized, as well as depoliticized.

SITUATING HAIR IN ACADEMIA AND POPULAR CULTURE

To be sure, this is not fetish or trendy scholarship. Hair has been of interest to social theorists spanning the twentieth century from Freud to Robin D. G. Kelley.

Psychoanalysts were waxing theoretical poetic about the sexual symbolism of hair during the earlier period (Freud 1922). In reaction to psychoanalytic readings of hair symbolism, social meanings of hair emerged. More specifically in the latter part of the century, scholars focusing on blacks and hair emphasize the importance of hair among blacks in relationship to Africa (Morrow 1973), enslavement (Patterson 1982), constructions of race (Mercer 1990), skin color, self-esteem, ritual, aesthetics, and adornment (Mercer 1990), appropriate grooming practices (Tyler 1990), images of beauty, politics, and identity (Grier and Cobbs 1968; Mercer 1990), and the intersection of race and gender (Craig 1997; Kelley 1997).

The scholarship on blacks and hair highlighting the difference that gender makes in understanding hairstyling practices among African Americans provides a similar gender intervention to that within general hair theorizing scholarship (Eilberg-Schwartz and Doniger 1995).

Several works have been written that engage beauty culture and black women (Giddings 1984; Hill Collins 1990; Caraway 1991; Rooks 1996; Craig 2002). In particular, discussions by black women moved the debate about hair among people of African descent to one that also focuses on experience (Okazawa-Rey et al. 1986; Benton Rushing 1988; hooks 1988; Walker 1988; Hill Collins 1990; Caldwell 1991; Norsworthy 1991; Cleage 1993; Wade Gayles 1993; Davis 1994; Jones 1994; Gibson 1995; DuCille 1996; Rooks 1996). In these works the authors discuss personal experiences involving hair that intersect with race, gender, motherhood, freedom, law, appropriation, and identity. In one of the most important texts focusing on black women and hair, *Hair Raising: Beauty, Culture, and African American Women,* Noliwe Rooks (1996) examines black hair care advertisements at the turn of the century in her investigation of how dominant or mainstream ideologies of race and beauty forced African American women to produce and sell beauty products for an African American female market. Rooks makes a strong case for understanding why gendered investigations of hair meanings in black communities are central for understanding how black women negotiate mainstream beauty culture. More recently, provocative texts that examine the history of black hair in the U.S. (Byrd and Tharps, 2001) and personal reflections on hair (Harris and Johnson, 2001) have contributed greatly to scholarship on black women and hair.

Similar to early anthropological writings that do not take into consideration the difference culture and gender make in understandings about hair, early feminist discussions about the relationship between femininity and hair focus on hair as an indelible marker of femininity. For example, Susan Brownmiller (1984) conflates the meanings of hair by reducing the interpretation of "good" hair and "bad" hair to mean the same thing for black women as it does for white women. Brownmiller collapses these terms despite racial and cultural difference. Her analysis demonstrates why these types of comparisons are problematic and how they disclaim the cultural significance of hair for black women by treating the issue as if it were *merely* a women's issue, and not an issue that traverses lines of race and culture.

Black hair is certainly not simply an academic matter. In fact, the debates that scholars engage [in] are clearly indicative of real-world tensions, as the literature on blacks and hair demonstrates. Within the context of black popular culture, hair has always been "pop." Spike Lee films such as *School Daze* and *Jungle Fever,* as well as the prime-time TV shows *Any Day Now, Girlfriends, Moesha, The Parkers,* and *The Practice,* have engaged the politically charged issue of black women's hair. For example, in Spike Lee's *School Daze,* a scene unfolds in the film that illustrates the intraracial tensions embedded in constructions of "good" hair and "bad" hair. In one episode of Lifetime Television Network's drama *Any Day Now,* a story line involving the different cultural meanings that black and white women ascribe to hair grooming practices illustrates difference race makes in understanding how women relate to beauty culture.

Rap artists such as Lauryn Hill and her former Fugees crew, The Lost Boyz, and The Roots have laced particular songs with explicit references to nappy hair.[2] Preceding the attention given to black hair on prime time and in popular music in the late twentieth century and early twenty first century was the emergence of the Afro almost three decades ago. Though today the Afro has less political meaning, in the late 1960s it was associated with a movement and a black woman. The movement was black power and the black woman was (and still is, even without her late 1960s, early 1970s Afro) Angela Davis. During an interview for *Hair Matters,* Taylor, a 48-year-old accountant, reminisced about her desire to wear an "Angela Davis Afro" during the early 1970s. Similar [to] yet different from Davis's recognition that law enforcement officers used her image (i.e., Afro) as a reason to detain and harass black women, Taylor explained that it was her Afro and *assumed* gender that led to her being detained during the early 1970s:

> When Afros came out, I wanted to wear an Afro. So I did everything and I finally got me a great big huge Angela Davis Afro. Whenever I would wear my Afro I'd get pulled over by the police because I drove a very sleek car and they always thought from the back of the head that I had to be male a lot of times because we [Black women and Black men] all wore the same hairstyle.

Taylor's understanding of why she was detained by police officers was based on both her Afro and mistaken gender-identity. Whereas Taylor presented an image of the Afro-wearing militant as male, which was supported by the general perception of the black militant at the time, Davis describes how race and gender merged to stigmatize and repress black women, a point that would surface almost twenty years later when black women's hair was at the center of legal battles.

In the late 1980s black female employees went to court to challenge a policy by Hyatt Hotels and American Airlines against the wearing of braids.[3] These companies couched their policy in terms that related to "appropriate" grooming practices, which they argued braids violated. In November 1996, another hair controversy hit a suburban middle school in Chicago. *The Atlanta Journal/Atlanta Constitution* ran a story that highlighted a ban on hairstyles, along with certain clothes and jewelry that school officials defined as "gang related paraphernalia." Hairstyles such as cornrows, dreadlocks, braids, and ponytails for boys would lead to suspension; hairstyles with zigzag parts for girls were disallowed. With a similar argument as the one used against Hyatt Hotels and American Airlines, critics argued that the school's policy appeared to restrict African Americans. To add, the weekly ABC news show *20/20* aired a segment that examined the tensions that many black professional women face when hair is at issue. Oprah Winfrey dedicated an entire show to the "black hair question." As the *Los Angeles Times* reported in an article that examined the rise in natural hairstyles among black women (and men), the *20/20* episode illustrated how "one woman was terminated because management saw her hair-

style as 'extreme,' and another woman was written up because her braids were deemed 'too ethnic'" (George 1998, E4).

MY RESEARCH ON BLACK WOMEN AND HAIR

My research is a departure from previous research and discussions as it serves as the first empirical study that examines why hair matters to black women and girls. Prior to my research, an empirically based book that centers on black women's views was absent in the literature and to this end, the study fills a void in the literature. Given that I identified a gap in research on this topic, how did I go about collecting data? By the fall of 1998, I completed forty-three individual interviews and five focus group interviews with African-American women and girls. The interviewees consisted of girls and women ranging from ages 12 to 76, from various walks of life. Individuals were recruited and interviewed in the San Francisco Bay Area, Los Angeles, Santa Barbara, and Atlanta. During a focus group interviewee, Wixie, a 45-year-old physician explained to me, "There's always a question of race, money, and sex. But I think for black women, it's race, money, sex, and hair. It transcends a cosmetic [or esthetic] issue because it is at the base historically, culturally, and socially." Indeed, the argument here presents hair as a cultural tool that shapes black women's ideas about race, gender, class, sexuality and images of beauty and power. In addition, my research illustrates that hair matters for black women are never merely arrested within esthetics. Indeed, it serves cultural theorists well in paying close attention to why hair matters to black women. In stating that hair matters, I argue that identity matters.

HAIR AND FEMININITY

On January 3, 1999, hair, in relationship to black women, made prime time again on the ABC weekly one-hour drama *The Practice*. The show focuses on a group of attorneys in a Boston law firm. In this particular episode, Lucy, the white female receptionist in her early twenties, asks the black female attorney, Rebecca, if she's a lesbian. Rebecca, somewhat puzzled, replies no, but wonders why anyone would assume she is a lesbian. Lucy replies, "With that rump and no guy in your life, and that crop-cut butchy-do hair [I just assumed you were a lesbian]." Rebecca commences to wonder if the reason she doesn't get asked out is because she "looks butch." Though Rebecca's femininity is marked through her shapely posterior, which is loaded with racialized images of Black women's bodies, her hair becomes the ultimate marker of both her womanhood and sexuality. Ideas about the relationship between hair, femininity, and sexuality, as well as images of beauty and male perceptions of femininity, surfaced as the women and girls addressed the question of whether hair is associated with femininity in any way.

Several of the women explained how long hair is associated with femininity and how their beliefs have been nurtured through the mainstream media or other external forces. For example, Pearl, a 45-year-old college counselor, explained that she felt most sexy with long hair:

PEARL: Oh I have [associated hair with femininity]. I think the sexiest hairstyle was for me, and this could come from advertisements, television, anywhere, was when my hair was longer and it was piled on top of my head and I would always have little ringlets on the side. And that could also be from my southern background and that's how southern women wore their hair a long time ago. It could stem from my mom. I'm not exactly sure where those images come from but I would look in the mirror and I would see how I look and say, "God, that is sexy, that looks gorgeous."

Pearl also associated her perception of long hair with her southern roots and mother, but still questioned how she learned what is feminine or sexy. Aria, a 30-year-old undergraduate student, also explained the relationship between long hair, femininity, and constructions of beauty but unlike Pearl, Aria perceived this relationship through gender and racial readings of hair:

ARIA: Oh please, yes. If I said no I'd be lying because for years we have been inundated with magazine pictures of white women and their beautiful bodies and their long flowing locks. We have seen commercials, they're [white women] in the magazine ads. You see them in school flippin' their hair all through the classroom. I mean I sit in class and I see these women changing their hairstyles in a fifty-minute class at least four

different times, you know. It's like come on. We have romance novels that accentuate the long, silken tresses so there's so many different mediums that portray [long] hair as beautiful, as feminine, as silky. And then if you have a lack of hair, then your femininity sometimes is questioned.

Aria pointed to the white women on TV, in magazines, and in romance novels with long, flowing hair as representative of femininity in U.S. society. Therefore, femininity is not merely associated with long hair as described by Pearl but with white women. Aria made a connection to the historical construction of womanhood, also known as the "cult of the lady" or the "cult of true womanhood" that represented ninetieth century U.S. Victorian society (Giddings 1984). Similar to Aria's construction of femininity that does not include black women, this was also the case with the cult of true womanhood. Given that the cult was based on a socioeconomic class hierarchy,[4] as well as racist and sexist ideologies, there was no place for black women regardless of class status in the definition of "true" womanhood.

Aria ends by stating that if a woman lacks hair, her femininity is questioned. This idea was common among the women. They associated their understanding of what short hair means in relationship to sexuality and masculinity. Dianne, a 50-year-old retired material handler, explained that an understanding of what it means to be male and female is embedded in readings of hair length. She also presented a different way of approaching the image of long flowing hair among black women:

DIANNE: Oh yeah. Right or wrong, you'll say stuff like that's a feminine cut, that's not a feminine cut, or whatever. I think to the extent that you have this long flowing hair that's perceived as very feminine. And the shorter you go, the less feminine it seems to be. So I definitely think that there's some association with that. And the whole interesting thing with the long hair [is] that [it] has some tie back to mainstream culture because not a lot of people in our community have this flowing long hair, but that's defined as being feminine. So when [women] go really short, [people say] that looks too mannish or something. My sister got her hair cut really short one time and she was like, "oh now people are going to think that I look like a boy or something."

In Dianne's explanation of the relationship between femininity and hair, she presented a scale in which long hair (feminine) and short hair (masculine) exists at the extremes. "Mannish" is associated with "looking like a boy" and long, flowing hair becomes a powerful feminine trait. However, Dianne questioned placing the image of long flowing hair among black people outside of black communities when she stated that based on her observations, there is not a critical mass of black folk who have long flowing hair. The more telling issue is how black people in general, and black women in particular, understand these meanings and how ideas that link long hair to femininity are actually acted out. In fact Indigo, a 28-year-old independent filmmaker and teacher, explained how her decision to grow dreadlocks has allowed her to fulfill the dream of having long hair.

INDIGO: I think certainly. I've just begun to take a look at the issue of dreadlocks because I look at myself and all my life I wanted to have long hair and now I get to have it with dreadlocks. The longer I let it grow I can have this long, flowing hair. Of course it won't look like Cheryl Tiegs's hair or, you know, Farah Fawcett's, but it will be my own hair.

Although similar to Aria's observation that white women's hair is the standard of long, flowing hair, Indigo sees length as outweighing texture. She demonstrated her perception of femininity through hair, and although she recognizes the problem in reinforcing the belief that long hair characterizes femininity, she challenged mainstream standards of beauty through the length of her dreadlocks. Although she doesn't have the stuff, in terms of texture and color, as do Tiegs and Fawcett, she does possess the feminine trait, long hair. Thus, Indigo's reading of hair permits black women to sit at the table of femininity, despite historical constructions of what constitutes womanhood and, therefore, beauty. But the desire to have long hair relates to perceptions of what is considered feminine and it is associated with white women. That is, even with long dreadlocks, the model of long hair, and therefore femininity, is white women like Cheryl Tiegs and Farah Fawcett.

Indigo also explained how shaving her head and having short hair shaped her understanding about hair and femininity. Like other women, she discussed the relationship between sexuality or perceived sexuality with hair, particularly in relationship to lesbianism.

INDIGO: For women, you know, it is a very important part of your appearance. Your face, your hair. I mean you can still be feminine and have no hair on your head. But you know, we have these judgments that only certain women can pull that off. I mean actually be bald, and still be considered feminine. I know when I shaved off [my hair or the] many times I've had my hair short, I was trying to compensate with earrings and all this kind of stuff. Trying not to wear as many pants because I felt like I was going to be, you know, categorized as a dyke, or you know, just deemed unattractive.

Cheryl, Jean, Kaliph, and Barbara[5] made similar comments in linking hair to sexuality, as well as being masculine:

CHERYL: Yeah, I think it is, unfortunately. I cut my hair [short] [and] the day I did it I went out to a club with my girl [in the nonromantic sense]. It wasn't that crowded, so we were kinda hangin' out together and I think we went on the dance floor. We weren't even really dancing together but we were, you know, dancing without partners and somebody came up to me and asked me if like we were together as like a lesbian couple. And she [my friend] wears dreads. And I was like, it's the hair, isn't it?

JEAN: Oh yeah, definitely. So you know, especially in this town [San Francisco Bay Area, California] people see a haircut and they say, oh, dyke.

KALIPH: Yes, definitely yes because, and now I'm thinking in terms of length and lack of length. I hear one of the concerns among my friends who wear their hair short and natural, that there is sometimes a misperception around sexuality like, oh you must be a lesbian if you wear your hair like that. And by definition if you're a lesbian that somehow there's a lack of femininity, you know, you're trying to be a man. You're trying to be male, masculine. So I think there is something about hair, particularly length of hair, that speaks to being feminine and being a woman.

BARBARA: In my view, no. But some men will see a woman with short hair, real short hair, and will think negatively. [Like] a butch cut. I've heard that.

Words such as "butch" and "dyke" describe how ideas about sexuality can be read through hair. Sexual identities are often placed on individuals based on hair, which is why Cheryl concluded that it was her short haircut and her friend's dreadlocks that made others think they were a lesbian couple on the dance floor. Kaliph even shared that she has black female friends with close-cropped and natural hair that are concerned with being perceived as lesbian. Kaliph explained that hair length is related not only to sexuality but also to female attractiveness. For example, when Indigo compensated for the lack of hair on her head, she did so by accentuating what she understood as feminine. It was Indigo's concern with being labeled a lesbian and therefore unfeminine that guided her practice of wearing big earrings and more skirts and dresses. In fact, as if in a dialogue with Indigo, Mrs. Franklin, a 70-year-old retired instructor's assistant, supported this reading of hair and femininity:

MRS. FRANKLIN: Yes, I do [think hair is associated with femininity]. Because I like to see women with hair. Most women when they have their hair short, [they] got to get up in the morning [and start] puttin' on make-up, puttin' on earrings and all this kind of stuff so people won't take a second look and say, "Is that a man or a lady?"

Even though Mrs. Franklin appeared to be making a presumption that women with short hair have to highlight their femininity, her thoughts resonate in Indigo's personal account of her insecurities about how her womanhood, in relationship to sexuality, would be read. What Mrs. Franklin and Indigo demonstrate is that black women understand that femininity cannot be reduced to one thing. Although hair is important in black women's understanding of what constitutes femininity, it is not the only marker. However, their comments also contradict their understanding of a more complicated reading of femininity because if a black woman has long hair, it is not necessary for her to "play up" her femininity by adorning her body in ways that are defined as "feminine." Even if hair is only one of many markers of femininity, or lack thereof, it is definitely one of the most powerful.

Habiba is a 50-year-old writer and teacher. In her reading of the relationship between hair and femininity, she also discussed long hair but used the example of (black) men wearing dreads as indicative of femininity. Femininity is still read through long hair, but Habiba challenged the belief that only women possess feminine characteristics when they have long hair. She also *explicitly* stated that hair is associated with femininity *and* sexuality:

HABIBA: [Hair is associated with femininity] and sexuality. People often times have their hands in each other's hair, pubic [for example]. So [hair] is very, very sensual. Very, very feminine. And I think men growing the long hair, men with dreads, are also activating that. What is it? They're activating the feminine side. Yes, yes, yes. For men to have the long hair and the dreads. Oh, that's incredible.

Habiba also provided a different view of the sexual nature of hair. Her reading of the relationship between hair and sexuality involves sensuality. Although her discussion supports how long hair is associated with femininity, Habiba's perception of what it means to be masculine is not questioned when she sees black men with long hair. Unlike the explanations of what it means for a woman to wear particular short hairdos[6] that are perceived as male "do's" Habiba questioned static notions of gender identities for women and men even as she supported the idea that long hair is associated with femininity. However it is Semple's critique of gender readings of hair (she is a 22-year-old undergraduate student), like that posed by Habiba's, that view long hair as feminine, that present a challenge to how gender is socially constructed. Unlike other women, Semple discussed this matter within the context of black males and how their hairstyling practices relate to how they are perceived:

SEMPLE: Is hair associated with femininity? I mean, I can see where we've maybe been socialized to think certain hairstyles [are feminine]. [The artist formally known as] Prince is always thought of as being out the box because he wants to wear a perm and a short cut. Michael Jackson got a little bob cut and people wanted to feminize that whole image. But at the same time, a brother can grow locks down his back and still be seen as extremely masculine. I mean brothers are wearing braids now and people are still [associating certain hair-styles with femininity]. I mean there's an element of "gang society" who walks around with permed hair and curls in their hair.

Unlike Habiba, Semple sees long dreadlocks worn by black men as indicative of masculinity, not femininity. Styles or lengths that are perceived as feminine do not necessarily question the masculinity or sexuality of black men. Semple's discussion of femininity as being read through the hairstyling practices of black men provided a different lens from which to view how black women understand gender through their ideas about hair. Although Semple discussed the hairstyling practices of Michael Jackson and The Artist as influencing their feminization, it is in her discussion of gang culture and the hairstyling practices among younger black males, particularly those in urban areas, that undoubtedly influence and have been influenced by hip-hop culture and rap music, that she contested feminine constructions of hair. Although I am in no way suggesting that rap artist Snoop Dog is a gangster, his hairstyling practices sheds light on Semple's critique. When Snoop appeared on the MTV Music Awards show in New York City a few years ago his hair was freshly straightened with lots of "Shirley Temple" curls. A year or two later, he was on the same awards show with straightened hair that touched his shoulders. Despite Snoop's hairstyling practices that imitate popular hairstyling practices by (Black) women, his "manhood" is not called into question. Like other younger black males who are straightening their hair, wearing braids and cornrows, as well as barrettes and rubber bands [in] their hair, Snoop is still seen as masculine. In a recent DJ Quik music video "Youz a Gangsta," Snoop appears with individual braids with beads dangling elegantly at the end of each braid. DJ Quik's hairstyle changes from cornrows to a straightened style by the end of the video. In another recent video, "Thug Mentality," rap artist Krayzie Bone appears with beautiful cornrows, and one of his posse members stands by his side with the same type of braided and beaded style as Snoop in DJ Quik's video. The video represents the life of a thug, with car chases and gambling rounding out the message of the video. Despite their hairdos, in both of these videos, the masculinity and sexuality of the main characters are never questioned because they are gangstas and thugs. This was true in the 1970s as well within the urban pimp culture scene. No one challenged Ron

O'Neal's masculinity in the blaxploitation film *Super Fly*. If anything, he was hyper-masculinized and seen as the perfect example of a "brother's brother." That is, a man's man. He had women, money, sharp clothes, a nice apartment, and a fancy car. And he had straightened ("fly") hair.

What Semple's observation suggests is that gender identity is not static, but given the comments by other women who addressed the relationship between hair and femininity, a nonstatic or even a cross-reading of gender does not occur when women's hairstyling practices resemble those that are considered masculine. Whereas all black men are not labeled as feminine or gay when they sport hairdos that are perceived as feminine, when black women wear their hair close-cropped, for example, they are constructed as being unfeminine, unattractive, masculine, and lesbian. As Indigo and Mrs. Franklin's comments demonstrate above, women have to play up their femininity in other ways.

CONCLUSION: FEMININITY, HAIR, AND GLOBALIZATION

Hair still matters, and though differences arise in different cultural and political contexts, for women, hair is never *simply* arrested within the aesthetic. Though global-studies scholars are raising important questions concerning globalization and its relationship to not merely Western societies, but the entire planet, hair went global a while back. "Through the seventies, stock imported from Europe was the only hair product sold to what the industry calls the 'Caucasian Trade.' Now that the European market is drying up, Asian hair goes to all races, in most cases, unless specially ordered. When you buy human hair in lengths for weaving and braiding, in wigs, and as male-replacement product, what you buy nine times out often is Asian hair" (Jones, 1994, p. 282). The average woman from Asia growing her hair for profit lives in poverty. It is an eerie feeling to realize that though these women will most likely remain living in a cycle of poverty, their hair exists within a global context.

Hair has gone global culturally as well. During the post–September 11 era, hair matters continue to make news, though within a different global and cultural context than what went down with Venus Williams in Australia in 1999. Consider the eyes of the Western/Christian world not merely on the Taliban restrictions placed on Afghani women, but also on the wider

Islamic faith's teachings concerning the presentation of the female body. The hijab (veil) that covers the hair continues to be a source of great debate within and outside feminist circles. With the downfall of the Taliban government, some Afghani women proudly shed the all-encompassing burka (full body veil). However, many women continue to follow Afghan culture by continuing to wear the burka. As feminists, we would be remiss if we discounted the views of Islamic women outside and inside of Afghanistan who continue to don the hijab. Certainly, the issue of covering women's bodies among Muslims cannot be disengaged from patriarchy and the state, but as my research on U.S. black women conveys, women must be given a platform to speak, to theorize, about *their* existence from *their* various standpoints. Indeed, hair still matters, and it matters for women of color in profound ways as exemplified by what we can learn by recent events in the global culture.

ACKNOWLEDGMENT

I am indebted to Hung Cam Thai for his insightful comments and unwavering support. He is one of the finest *feminists* that I know.

NOTES

1. Ingrid Banks, *Hair Matters: Beauty, Power, and Black Women's Consciousness* (New York: New York University Press, 2000).
2. See Lauryn Hill's "Doo Wop (That Thing)," the Fugees' "Nappy Hair," and The Lost Boyz album "Love, Peace, and Nappiness."
3. See Paulette Caldwell's (1991) discussion of these cases.
4. For example, poor and working-class women, regardless of race, were not viewed as "true women." Those women who had to work outside of the home for economic necessity were excluded from the definition of a lady.
5. Cheryl is a 22-year-old graduate student, Jean is a 37-year-old architect, Kaliph is a 28-year-old graduate student, and Barbara is a 49-year-old Administrative Assistant II.
6. Not all short hairdos worn by women are viewed as unfeminine; what is meant here is particularly those hairdos that resemble traditional men's hairdos (e.g., short, cropped, buzz cuts).

REFERENCES

Banks, Ingrid. 2000. *Hair Matters: Beauty, Power and Black Women's Consciousness.* New York: University Press.

Benton Rushing, Andrea. 1988. "Hair-Raising." *Feminist Studies* 14(2) (Summer): 325–335.

Bordo, Susan. 1993. *Unbearable Weight: Feminism, Western Culture, and the Body.* Berkeley: University of California Press.

Brownmiller, Susan. 1984. *Femininity.* New York: London Press/Simon & Schuster.

Byrd, Ayana D., and Lori L. Tharps. 2001. *Hair Story: Untangling the Roots of Black Hair in America.* New York: St. Martin's Press.

Caldwell, Paulette M. 1991. "A Hair Piece: Perspectives on the Intersection of Race and Gender." *Duke Law Review*: 365–397.

Caraway, Nancie. 1991. *Segregated Sisterhood: Racism and the Politics of American Feminism.* Knoxville: University of Tennessee Press.

Cleage, Pearl. 1993. "Hairpeace: Requirement for Afro-American Women Writers to Discuss Hair." *African-American Review* 27(1) (Spring): 37.

Craig, Maxine. 2002. *Ain't I a Beauty Queen? Black Women, Beauty, and the Politics of Race.* New York: Oxford University Press.

———. 1997. "The Decline and the Fall of the Conk; or, How to Read a Process." *Fashion Theory: The Journal of Dress, Body and Culture* 1(4) (December): 399–419.

Davis, Angela Y. 1994. "Afro Images: Politics, Fashion, and Nostalgia." *Critical Inquiry* 21(1) (Autumn): 37.

DuCille, Ann. 1996 *Skin Trade.* Cambridge: Harvard University Press.

Eilberg-Schwartz, Howard, and Wendy Doniger, eds. 1995. *Off with Her Head! The Denial of Woman's Identity in Myth, Religion, and Culture.* Berkeley: University of California Press.

Freud, Sigmund. 1922. "Medusa's Hair." In *Collected Papers*, 105–106. London: Hogarth Press and the Institute of Psychoanalysis.

George, Lynell. 1998. "The Natural Look." *The Los Angeles Times*, August 6, E1.

Gibson, Aliona. 1995. *Nappy: Growing Up Black and Female in America.* New York: Harlem River Press.

Giddings, Paula. 1984. *When and Where I Enter: The Impact of Black Women on Race and Sex in America*. New York: Bantam Books.

Grier, William H., and Price M. Cobbs. 1968. *Black Rage*. New York: Basic Books.

Harris, Juliette, and Pamela Johnson. 2001. *Tenderheaded: A Comb-Bending Collection of Hair Stories*. New York: Pocket Books.

Hill Collins, Patricia. 1990. *Black Feminist Thought: Knowledge, Consciousness, and the Politics of Empowerment*. London: HarperCollins.

hooks, bell. 1988. "Straightening Our Hair." *Z Magazine* (Summer): 14–18.

Jagger, Alison, and Susan Bordo. 1989. *Gender/Body/Knowledge: Feminist Reconstructions of Knowing*. Newark, NJ: Rutgers University Press.

Jones, Lisa. 1994. *Bulletproof Diva: Tales of Race, Sex, and Hair*. New York: Doubleday.

Kelley, Robin D. G. 1997. "Nap Time: Historicizing the Afro." *Fashion Theory: The Journal of Dress, Body and Culture* 1(4) (December): 339–351.

Mercer, Kobena. 1990. "Black Hair/Style Politics." In *Out There: Marginalization and Contemporary Cultures*, Russell Ferguson et al., eds., 247–264. New York: The New Museum of Contemporary Art and MIT Press.

Morrow, Willie. 1973. *400 Years Without a Comb*. San Diego: Black Publishers of San Diego.

Norsworthy, Kym. 1991. "Hair Discovery." *Real News*, 2(1): 3, 8.

Okazawa-Rey, Margo, et al. 1986. "Black Women and the Politics of Skin Color and Hair." *Women's Studies Quarterly* 14 (1 and 2) (Spring/Summer): 13–14.

Patterson, Orlando. 1982. *Slavery and Social Death: A Comparative Study*. Cambridge: Harvard University Press.

Rooks, Noliwe. 1996. *Hair Raising: Beauty, Culture, and African American Women*. New Brunswick, NJ: Rutgers University Press.

Tyler, Bruce M. 1990. "Black Hairstyles: Cultural and Sociopolitical Implications." *The Western Journal of Black Studies* 14(4): 235–250.

Wade-Gayles, Gloria. 1993. "The Making of a Permanent Afro." In *Pushed Back to Strength: A Black Woman's Journey Home*, 133–158. Boston: Beacon Press.

Walker, Alice. 1988. "Oppressed Hair Puts a Ceiling on the Brain." In *Living by the Word*, 69–74. Orlando: Harcourt Brace Jovanovich.

SECTION 4
Socialization

We are born into cultures that have definite ideas about men and women and their appropriate attitudes, values, and behaviors, although those ideas may differ dramatically across time and place. The dominant U.S. culture defines certain traits as masculine or feminine and values behaviors, occupations, and attitudes deemed the characteristics of men more highly than those associated with women. It assumes that what men do is right and normal. Women are judged in accordance with how well they conform to the male standard. This way of thinking is known as *androcentrism*. As children, we learn to see ourselves and others as girls or boys and to judge our own and others' behaviors according to standards of gender-appropriate behavior, which is why a boy wearing a skirt or liking the color pink can be so disconcerting. If we don't know a person's gender, we barely know how to interact, which is why people whose gender cannot be easily discerned or is easily mistaken or is not consistent with the physical body have such a hard time.

The articles in this section analyze the complex process of gender socialization from various perspectives. Learning about our culture begins in the family. We learn about gender not only from what our parents say but from what they do. When mothers have primary responsibility for raising children, both girls and boys learn that nurturing is more a responsibility of women than of men. Gender socialization continues in schools, peer groups, and religious institutions, and can be ongoing throughout life, as we learn the expectations of our college contexts, our workplaces, and the families we form as adults.

One important way we are socialized into gender and sexuality is through the media. From a very young age, children encounter lessons about what it means to be a woman or a man in our society. In "Hetero-Romantic Love and Heterosexiness in Children's G-Rated Films," Martin and Kazyak analyze the messages about heterosexuality that bombard young viewers. In contrast to the way that other scholars have characterized heteronormativity as ordinary and taken for granted, the authors argue that children's films portray heterosexual romance as exceptional, magical, powerful, and transformative. When heterosexuality is portrayed outside of romantic relationships, the films sexualize (and racialize) women's bodies through the eyes of male characters. Both kinds of representations shore up heteronormativity. While Martin and Kazyak make no claims about what children actually take away from viewing such films, what lessons do you think they learn? Do you think girls and boys are affected differently? How do you think children from different class and ethnic backgrounds might react differently to the films discussed in the article? Did you watch these kinds of films? If so, how do you think they might have had an impact on your thinking about love and romance?

"Pretty Baby" tells the story of a young boy who loves the color pink. Despite the societal association of pink with girls, he chooses pink whenever possible and combines interest in activities that are traditionally coded feminine as well as those socially approved for boys. What does this story tell us about the ways that boys and girls are expected to behave in U.S.

society? What do people assume about a boy who loves pink? Why does a boy wearing pink carry so much more weight than a girl wearing blue? What does the ending of the story tell us about the reactions his mother must often encounter?

As we have all experienced, schools play an important role in gender socialization as well. By the time children are in school, they not only have been socialized into their gender but also are able to negotiate how and in which situations gender will be socially salient. Barrie Thorne, in her classic article "Girls and Boys Together . . . but Mostly Apart: Gender Arrangements in Elementary Schools," argues for a more complex idea of gender as socially constructed and context specific. In her observations of social relations among children in elementary school, she finds that boys and girls are segregated and seen as different in the classroom and on the playground due both to teachers' actions and to the ways children socialize each other. Did your own experiences in elementary school conform to the patterns Thorne describes? Do you think anything has changed since Thorne first published this research in 1986?

Because gender intersects with race, ethnicity, and class, our socialization experiences differ in complex ways. What a woman of color, for example, needs to teach her sons and daughters to enable them to survive in a white-male-dominated society is different from what a white mother needs to teach her children. These kinds of ethnic and racial differences, in turn, are compounded by differences in class status. Yen Le Espiritu, in "We Don't Sleep Around Like White Girls Do," explores the ways that gendered sex norms in Filipina-American families serve as a strategy of resistance to oppression for the community as a whole and at the same time limit the autonomy of Filipina women. By emphasizing the sexual looseness of white girls, Filipina girls and their parents assert their moral superiority and counter the stereotypes of Filipinas as either prostitutes or submissive mail-order brides. Rather than consider dominant white conceptions of racial and ethnic "others," Espiritu looks at Filipina constructions of whiteness. What generational differences are there between the Filipina girls Espiritu studies and their parents? What is the Filipina-American notion of white society? Do you think it is accurate?

Socialization, as you can see, is not a simple process; rather, it is shaped in profound ways by class, race, ethnicity, and sexuality. Why is gender socialization such a powerful force? How much agency do you think people have in accepting or resisting the forces of socialization?

17 **Karin A. Martin**
Emily Kazyak

Hetero-Romantic Love and Heterosexiness in Children's G-Rated Films

First published in 2009

The role that Disney plays in shaping individual identities and controlling fields of social meaning through which children negotiate the world is far too complex to be simply set aside as a form of reactionary politics. If educators and other cultural workers are to include the culture of children as an important site of contestation and struggle, then it becomes imperative to analyze how Disney's animated films powerfully influence the way America's cultural landscape is imagined.

—*Giroux (1996, 96)*

Multiple ethnographic studies suggest that by elementary school, children understand the normativity of heterosexuality. That is, by elementary school, children have a heteronormative understanding of the world (Best 1983; Renold 2002, 2005; Thorne 1993). Yet we know little about what children bring with them to the peer cultures these ethnographers describe and how these understandings develop before elementary school. Martin (2009) finds that mothers' conversations with young children normalize heterosexuality, but children's social worlds are larger than the mother-child dyad. Research on adolescence suggests that alongside parents and peers, the media are important in shaping cultural understandings of sexuality (Kim et al. 2007; Ward 1995, 2003). This article provides a beginning step toward understanding the role of the media in the development of children's heteronormativity. We ask, *How are heteronormativity and heterosexuality constructed in children's top-selling G-rated movies between 1990 and 2005?* Before answering this question, we sketch our understanding of heteronormativity and explain why we chose this genre of media, why we analyze the content of these films, and the limits of such analysis. We then review the existing literature on children's movies and finally turn to our study, which finds heterosexuality in children's movies is not entirely as theorists of heteronormativity describe. That is, heterosexuality within the context of romantic relationships in G-rated movies is not ordinary or mundane but, rather, is powerful, exceptional, and magical. Outside of romantic relationships, heterosexual desire is much less serious.

HETERONORMATIVITY

Heteronormativity includes the multiple, often mundane ways through which heterosexuality overwhelmingly structures and "pervasively and insidiously" orders "everyday existence" (Jackson 2006, 108; Kitzinger 2005). Heteronormativity structures social life so that heterosexuality is always assumed, expected, ordinary, and privileged. Its pervasiveness makes it difficult for people to imagine other ways of life. In part, the assumption and expectation of heterosexuality is linked to its status as natural and biologically necessary for procreation (Lancaster 2003). Anything else is relegated to the nonnormative, unusual, and unexpected and is, thus, in need of explanation. Specifically, within heteronormativity, homosexuality becomes the "other" against which heterosexuality defines itself (Johnson 2005; Rubin 1984).

But not just any kind of heterosexuality is privileged. Heteronormativity regulates those within its boundaries as it marginalizes those outside of it. According to Jackson (2006), heteronormativity works to define more than normative sexuality, insofar as it also defines normative ways of life in general. Heteronormativity holds people accountable to reproductive procreative sexuality and traditional gendered domestic arrangements of sexual relationships, and it is linked to particular patterns of consumerism and consumption (Ingraham 1999). In other words, while heteronormativity regulates people's sexualities, bodies, and sexual relationships (for both those nonheterosexuals on the "outside" and heterosexuals on the "inside"), it regulates nonsexual aspects of life as well.

Heteronormativity also privileges a particular type of heterosexual. Among those aspects desired in heterosexuals, Rubin (1984) includes being married, monogamous, and procreative. We might also include that heterosexuality is most sanctioned when it is intraracial and that other inequalities, like race and class, intersect and help construct what Rubin calls "the inner charmed circle" in a multitude of complicated ways (e.g., Whose married sex is most sanctioned? Whose reproductive sex is most normal?). Heteronormativity also rests on gender asymmetry, as heterosexuality depends on a particular type of normatively gendered women and men (Jackson 2006). In this article, we examine how children's movies construct heterosexuality to better understand what information is available in media that might contribute to children's heteronormative social worlds.

CHILDREN, MEDIA, AND MOVIES

The media are an important avenue of children's sexual socialization because young children are immersed in media-rich worlds. Thirty percent of children under three years old and 43 percent of four- to six-year-olds have a television in their bedrooms, and one-quarter of children under six years old have a VCR/DVD player in their bedrooms (Rideout, Vandewater, and Wartella 2003). Since the deregulation of television in the 1980s, there has been more and more content produced on television for children. Children's programming produced for television, however, must still meet educational regulations. Films produced with young children as a significant intended portion of the audience are under no such obligations. However, to attract young children (and their parents) to films, filmmakers must

get their movies a G-rating. Film producers are interested in doing this because the marketing advantages that accompany a successful children's film are enormous (Thomas 2007). The Motion Picture Association of America rates a film G for "General Audience" if the film "contains nothing in theme, language, nudity, sex, violence or other matters that, in the view of the Rating Board, would offend parents whose younger children view the motion picture. . . . No nudity, sex scenes or drug use are present in the motion picture" (Motion Picture Association of America 2009). Thus, a G-rating signals that these films expect young children in their audience.

We examine the top-selling G-rated movies to challenge the idea that these movies are without (much) sexual content and the notion that young children are therefore not exposed to matters relating to sexuality. As theorists of heteronormativity suggest, heterosexuality is pervasive, and we want to examine how it makes its way into films that are by definition devoid of sexuality. If heteronormativity structures social life well beyond the sexual arena, then it is likely at work even in films that announce themselves as free of sexuality.

We look at movies themselves rather than children's reception of them because of the difficulty of research with young children generally, especially around issues of sexuality (Martin, Luke, and Verduzco-Baker 2007) and around media (Thomas 2007). Parents, human subjects review boards, and schools all serve as barriers to research with children on these topics. Given that we know little about how heteronormativity is constructed for children, examining the content of these films seems a logical first step before asking what children take from them. Although we will not be able to say whether or which accounts of heteronormativity children take away with them after watching these movies, current research about children's relationships to such movies indicates that children are engaged with these media and the stories they tell. Enormous numbers of children watch Disney and other G-rated children's movies. In a 2006 survey of more than 600 American mothers of three- to six-year-olds, only 1 percent reported that their child had not seen any of the films we analyze here; half had seen 13 or more (Martin, Luke, and Verduzco-Baker 2007).

Many children also watch these movies repeatedly (Mares 1998). The advent of videos made it possible for children to watch and rewatch movies at home. In fact, preschool children enjoy watching videos/DVDs repeatedly, and this has implications for the way they comprehend their messages. Crawley et al. (1999) discovered that children comprehended more from repeated viewing. Repeated viewing may also mean that jokes or innuendo intended for adults in these films may become more visible and curious, if not more intelligible, to young children. Further work by Schmitt, Anderson, and Collins (1999) also suggests that young children's attention is most focused and content best understood when watching media that includes animation, child characters, nonhuman characters, animals, frequent movement, and purposeful action (as opposed to live action; adults, especially adult men; and characters who only converse without much action). These are prominent features of most of the G-rated films we analyze here, suggesting that they are certainly vehicles for children's attention and comprehension.

We also know young children are engaged by many such films as the plots and toys marketed from them are used in many creative ways in children's fantasy and play. Not only do movies make social worlds visible on screen, but the mass marketing surrounding these movies invites young people to inhabit those worlds (Giroux 1996). These media not only offer what is normal but also actively ensure that children understand it and compel them to consume it (Schor 2004). Researchers have demonstrated the depth of children's engagement with such media and how they adapt it for their own uses. For example, Hadley and Nenga (2004) find that Taiwanese kindergartners used everything from *Snow White* to *Digimon* to demonstrate and challenge their Confucian values at school. Gotz et al. (2005) similarly find that eight-year-old children across the United States, Israel, Germany, and South Korea make use of the media in constructing the "fantasylands" they imagine and play in. Thus, while we must look at particular groups of children's reception of particular media to see what they do with it (Tobin 2000), there is evidence that children certainly incorporate such media into their learning and play.

Finally, with respect to heterosexuality specifically, there is some evidence that suggests even young children learn from media accounts. Kelley, Buckingham, and Davies (1999) find that six- to eleven-year-old children incorporate what they learn about sexuality on television into their talk and identity work in their peer groups. Martin (2009) finds mothers of children ages

three to six years old suggest that children, especially girls, know about heterosexual falling in love, weddings, and marriage from "movies," "princesses," and "Disney." Again, our research cannot address what children take away from their repeated viewings of such movies, but given that the extant research suggests they take something, we analyze what is there for the taking.

Some scholarship has begun to look at what kinds of narratives, accounts, and images are available in children's movies, and especially in Disney movies. Most useful for our purposes is the research on gender (Thompson and Zerbinos 1995; Witt 2000) and on gender and race stereotypes in young children's media (Giroux 1996; Hurley 2005; Mo and Shen 2000; Pewewardy 1996; Witt 2000). Most of this research indicates that there are fewer portrayals of women and of nonwhites and that those portrayals often rely on stereotypes. Analyses of the stereotypes and discourses of race and gender sometimes embed some discussion of sexuality within them. A smattering of research on race examines how some racial/ethnic groups are portrayed as exoticized and more sexualized than white women (Lacroix 2004). Research that examines gender construction in the media sometimes links heterosexuality and romantic love to femininity and discusses the importance of finding a man/prince for the heroines (Junn 1997; Thompson and Zerbinos 1995). But heterosexuality is a given in such analyses. The existing research does not fully analyze how heterosexuality is constructed in these films.

In a different vein, media scholars have offered queer readings of some children's and especially Disney films (Byrne and McQuillan 1999; Griffin 2000). Employing a poststructuralist lens that privileges the radically indeterminate meaning of texts, Byrne and McQuillan (1999) highlight how certain characters and story lines in Disney movies can be read as queer. They discuss the many queer or ambiguous characters populating these films, such as Quasimodo and the gargoyles in *The Hunchback of Notre Dame*. They describe the character Mulan as a "transvestite bonanza," representing "Disney's most sustained creation of lesbian chic" (1999, 143). Moreover, they highlight the queerness of certain story lines in Disney movies. For instance, they argue that homosocial desire and bonds between men structure many of the films, and they explicate the queerness of the portrayal of monstrous desire, a desire that threatens the family unit, in *Beauty and the Beast*. These readings do not argue that particular characters or plots are gay or lesbian per se; rather, they emphasize their queer potential. Similarly, Griffin (2000) aims to queer Disney by analyzing how gay and lesbian viewers might understand these films with gay sensibilities. He highlights how Disney characters who do not fit into their societies echo the feeling of many gays and lesbians. He also argues that many characters (especially villains) lend themselves to queer readings because of how they overperform their gender roles. Villainesses often look like drag queens, such as Ursula in *The Little Mermaid*, a character modeled after the transvestite star Divine. These analyses rest on the desire to destabilize the meanings of characters and story lines in movies to open them up and discover their queer potential. This scholarship, however, presumes a sophisticated and knowledgeable reader of culture. It does not consider children as the audience or address whether such readings are possible for young children. It overlooks, for example, that while there are transvestite characters like Mulan, the Mulan toys marketed to children were feminine, long-haired, non-sword-wielding ones (Nguyen 1998), perhaps making such readings less sustainable for children even if they are possible. Again, we will need research on what children take away from such media to address these issues.

OUR RESEARCH

In this article, we do not aim to do a queer reading of these films as such readings have already been done. Instead, we analyze *how* heterosexuality is constructed in children's G-rated films. We ask not how characters might be read as queer but what accounts these films offer of heterosexuality and how such accounts serve heteronormativity. Unpacking the construction of heterosexuality in these films is a first step toward understanding what social-sexual information is available to the children who watch them.

SAMPLE AND METHOD

The data for this study come from all the G-rated movies released (or rereleased) between 1990 and 2005 that grossed more than $100 million in the United States (see Table 1).[1] Using this sample of widely viewed films overcomes the limitations of previous analyses of children's, and especially Disney, movies, which often

focus on a few particular examples. Here we have tried to examine all the most viewed films within this genre and time period. The films in our sample were extremely successful and widely viewed, as evidenced by their sales numbers in theaters. Home videos/DVDs sales and rentals of these films are also very high (Arnold 2005), including direct-to-video/DVD sequels of many of these films, for example, *Lion King 1.5, Ariel's Beginning,* and *Beauty and the Beast's Enchanted Christmas*. While the audience for these films is broader than children, children are certainly centrally intended as part of the audience. G is the rating given to films that contain nothing that "would offend parents whose younger children view the motion picture" according to the Motion Picture Association of America (2009). Sixteen (80 percent) of these films are animated, and 17 are produced by Disney, a major producer of children's consumption and socialization (Giroux 1997).

After collecting this sample, the first author screened all the films and then trained three research assistants to extract any story lines, images, scenes, songs, or dialogue that depicted anything about sexuality, including depictions of bodies, kissing, jokes, romance, weddings, dating, love, where babies come from, and pregnancy. The research assistants then wrote descriptions of the scenes in which they found material related to sexuality. They described the visuals of the scenes in as vivid detail as possible and transcribed the dialogue verbatim. Two research assistants watched each film and extracted the relevant material. The first author reconciled the minimal differences between what each research assistant included by rescreening the films herself and adding or correcting material.

This text describing the material in each film was then inductively coded using the qualitative software program QSR-Nvivo. The themes that emerged from this open-coding were then developed in a series of initial and then integrative memos. The movies were re-viewed again by both authors as needed to further explicate the categories of understanding that emerged from first round coding. The memos were then developed into the results below (Emerson, Fretz, and Shaw 1995).

RESULTS AND DISCUSSION

We describe two ways that heterosexuality is constructed in these films. The primary account of heterosexuality in these films is one of hetero-romantic love and its exceptional, magical, transformative power. Secondarily, there are some depictions of heterosexuality outside of this model. Outside of hetero-romantic love, heterosexuality is constructed as men gazing desirously at women's bodies. This construction rests on gendered and racialized bodies and is portrayed as less serious and less powerful than hetero-romantic love.

Magical, Exceptional, Transformative Hetero-Romantic Love

Hetero-romantic love is the account of heterosexuality that is most developed in these films. Only two films have barely detectable or no hetero-romantic references (see Table 1). In eight of these films hetero-

romance is a major plot line, and in another seven films it is a secondary story line. Those films not made by Disney have much less hetero-romantic content than those made by Disney.

Films where we coded hetero-romantic love as a major plot line are those in which the hetero-romantic story line is central to the overall narrative of the film. In *The Little Mermaid*, for instance, the entire narrative revolves around the romance between Ariel, a mermaid, and Eric, a human. The same is true of movies like *Beauty and the Beast, Aladdin,* and *Santa Clause 2.* There would be no movie without the hetero-romantic story line for these films. In others, the hetero-romantic story line is secondary. For example, in *Chicken Run* the romance develops between Ginger and Rocky as they

TABLE 1   SAMPLE: $100 MILLION G-RATED MOVIES, 1990-2005

| Movie | Year | Produced By | HETERO-ROMANTIC STORY LINE | | | HETEROSEXUALITY | |
			Any Reference	Major Plot	Minor Plot	Sexiness	Ogling of Women's Bodies
Chicken Little	2005	Disney	x		x	x	
The Polar Express	2004	Castle Rock					
Finding Nemo	2003	Disney/Pixar	x				
The Santa Clause 2	2002	Disney	x	x			
Monsters, Inc.	2001	Disney/Pixar	x		x		x
The Princess Diaries	2001	Disney	x	x		x	x
Chicken Run	2000	DreamWorks	x		x		x
Tarzan	1999	Disney	x		x		
Toy Story 2	1999	Disney/Pixar	x			x	x
A Bug's Life	1998	Disney/Pixar	x		x		x
Mulan	1998	Disney	x		x		x
The Rugrats Movie	1998	Nickelodeon					
101 Dalmatians	1996	Disney	x		x		
The Hunchback of Notre Dame	1996	Disney	x	x		x	x
Toy Story	1995	Disney/Pixar	x			x	
Pocahontas	1995/2005	Disney	x	x			
The Lion King	1994/2002	Disney	x	x			
Aladdin	1994	Disney	x	x		x	x
Beauty and the Beast	1991/2002	Disney	x	x		x	x
The Little Mermaid	1989/1997	Disney	x	x		x	x

help organize the chicken revolt—the heart of the movie—although the movie ends with them coupled, enjoying their freedom in a pasture. While removing the hetero-romantic story line would still leave other stories in place in such films, the romance nonetheless exists. In other movies, like *Toy Story*, references are made to hetero-romance but are not developed into a story line. For instance, this film suggests romantic interest between Woody and Little Bo Peep, but their romance is not woven throughout the film.

While our focus is on the construction of heterosexuality, we recognize that other stories exist in these films. For instance, there are stories about parent-child relationships (e.g., Chicken Little wants his father to be proud of him; Nemo struggles against his overprotective father). Stories about workers, working conditions, and collective revolt also appear, for instance, in *Monsters, Inc.* (whose characters, working for the city's power company that relies on scaring children to generate electricity, successfully stop an evil corporate plan to kidnap children and eventually change their policy to making children laugh) and *Chicken Run* (whose main character, Ginger, successfully organizes all of her fellow chickens to escape their farm after learning of the farmers' plan to begin turning them into chicken pies). Though certainly there is much analysis that could be done around such stories, we do not do so here. Rather, we turn our attention to the hetero-romantic story lines and the work they do in constructing heterosexuality.

Theorists of heteronormativity suggest that the power of heteronormativity is that heterosexuality is assumed, mundane, ordinary, and expected. In contrast, we find that in these films, while it is certainly assumed, heterosexuality is very often not ordinary or mundane. Rather, romantic heterosexual relationships are portrayed as a special, distinct, exceptional form of relationship, different from all others. Characters frequently defy parents, their culture, or their very selves to embrace a hetero-romantic love that is transformative, powerful, and (literally) magical. At the same time, these accounts are sometimes held in tension with or constructed by understandings of the naturalness of heterosexuality. Below, we describe how the films construct these relationships as distinct, set apart, and different from others. We also describe how they are constructed as powerful, transformative, and magical.

These films repeatedly mark relationships between cross-gender lead characters as special and magical by utilizing imagery of love and romance. Characters in love are surrounded by music, flowers, candles, magic, fire, ballrooms, fancy dresses, dim lights, dancing, and elaborate dinners. Fireflies, butterflies, sunsets, wind, and the beauty and power of nature often provide the setting for—and a link to the naturalness of—hetero-romantic love. For example, in *Beauty and the Beast*, the main characters fall in love frolicking in the snow; Aladdin and Jasmine fall in love as they fly through a starlit sky in *Aladdin*; Ariel falls in love as she discovers the beauty of earth in *The Little Mermaid*; Santa and his eventual bride ride in a sleigh on a sparkling snowy night with snow lightly falling over only their heads in *Santa Clause 2*; and *Pocahontas* is full of allusion to water, wind, and trees as a backdrop to the characters falling in love. The characters often say little in these scenes. Instead, the scenes are overlaid with music and song that tells the viewer more abstractly what the characters are feeling. These scenes depicting hetero-romantic love are also paced more slowly with longer shots and with slower and soaring music.

These films also construct the specialness of hetero-romantic love by holding in tension the assertion that hetero-romantic relationships are simultaneously magical and natural. In fact, their naturalness and their connection to "chemistry" and the body further produce their exceptionalness. According to Johnson (2005), love and heterosexuality become interwoven as people articulate the idea that being in love is overpowering and that chemistry or a spark forms the basis for romantic love. These formulations include ideas about reproductive instincts and biology, and they work to naturalize heterosexuality. We see similar constructions at work in these G-rated movies where the natural becomes the magical. These films show that, in the words of Mrs. Pots from *Beauty and the Beast*, if "there's a spark there," then all that needs to be done is to "let nature take its course." However, this adage is usually not spoken. Rather, the portrayal of romantic love as occurring through chemistry or a spark is depicted by two characters gazing into each other's eyes and sometimes stroking each other's faces. The viewer usually sees the two characters up close and in profile as serious and soaring music plays as this romantic chemistry is not explained with words but must be felt and understood via the gazing eye contact between the characters. Disney further marks the falling in love and the triumphs of hetero-romantic love by wrapping the characters in magical swirls of sparks, leaves, or fireworks as they stare into each other's eyes.

The music accompanying such scenes is momentous and triumphant.

We asked whether all sorts of relationships might be magical, special, and exceptional in similar ways, as it is possible that many types of relationships have these qualities in these imaginative fantasies where anything is possible. However, we found that romantic heterosexual relationships in G-rated movies are set apart from other types of relationships. This serves to further define them as special and exceptional. All other love relationships are portrayed without the imagery described above. The pacing of friendship scenes is also faster and choppier, and the music is quicker and bouncy. Nor do friendships and familial relationships start with a "spark."

Parent-child relationships are portrayed as restrictive, tedious, and protective. The child is usually escaping these relationships for the exciting adolescent or adult world. Friendships are also set aside as different from romantic love. There are many close friendships and buddies in these stories, and none are portrayed with the imagery of romantic love. Cross-gender friends are often literally smaller and a different species or object in the animated films, thus making them off limits for romance. For example, Mulan's friend is Mushoo, a small, red dragon; Pocahontas is friends with many small animals (a raccoon; a hummingbird); Ariel is looked after by Sebastian (a crab) and Flounder (a fish); and Belle is befriended by a range of small household items (teapot, candlestick, broom). Same–sex friendships or buddies are unusual for girls and women unless the friends are maternal (e.g., Willow in *Pocahontas,* Mrs. Pots in *Beauty and the Beast*). The lead male characters, however, often have comical buddies (e.g., Timon in *The Lion King,* Abu in *Aladdin,* the gargoyles in *The Hunchback of Notre Dame,* Mike in *Monsters, Inc.*). These friendships are often portrayed as funny, silly, gross, and fun but certainly not as serious, special, powerful, important, or natural. For example, in *The Lion King,* Timon (a meerkat), Pumba (a boar), and Simba (a lion) all live a carefree life together in the jungle as the best of friends, but Simba quickly deserts them for Nala, a female lion, once he is an adolescent. Throughout the film, Timon and Pumba provide comic relief from the serious business of the lions falling in (heterosexual) love and saving the kingdom. Thus, the construction of friendships and family relationships reveal that hetero-romantic relationships in contrast are serious, important, and natural.

Furthermore, while friendships provide comic relief and friends and family are portrayed as providing comfort or advice to lead characters, these relationships are not portrayed as transformative, powerful, or magical. Hetero-romantic love is exceptional in these films because it is constructed as incredibly powerful and transformative. Throughout many of these films with a primary plot about hetero-romantic love, such love is depicted as rebellious, magical, defiant, and with a power to transform the world. This is quite different from our understanding of heterosexuality as normative, ordinary, and expected. The hetero-romantic relationships in these films are extraordinary. Falling in heterosexual love can break a spell (*Beauty and the Beast*) or cause one to give up her identity (*The Little Mermaid*). It can save Santa Claus and Christmas (*Santa Clause 2*). It can lead children (e.g., Ariel, Jasmine, Pocahontas, Belle) to disobey their parents and defy the social rules of their culture (e.g., Jasmine, Pocahontas). It can stop a war that is imminent (*Pocahontas*) or change an age-old law (*Aladdin*).

Hetero-romantic love is constructed as being in a realm of freedom and choice, a realm where chemistry can flourish and love can be sparked and discovered. Thus, romantic love is so exceptional it is positioned "outside of the control of any social or political force" (Johnson 2005, 37). This construction appears in G-rated movies and intertwines race and heteronormativity as characters who are nonwhite critique arranged marriages as backward and old-fashioned and celebrate a woman's ability to choose her own husband. For example, in *Aladdin,* Jasmine protests the law that dictates that she must marry a prince and says, "The law is wrong. . . . I hate being forced into this . . . if I do marry, I want it to be for love." Later, Aladdin agrees with her that being forced to be married by her father is "awful." Pocahontas faces a similar dilemma, as her father insists that she marry Kocoum. When she disagrees and asks him, "Why can't I choose?" he says, "You are the daughter of the chief . . . it is your time to take your place among our people." While arranged marriages are portrayed as something outdated, these characters "choose" whom they will love, thus simultaneously securing hetero-romantic love's naturalness and extraordinariness and its position beyond the prescriptions of any social-political context. In fact, their love changes these prescriptions in both of these examples. Jasmine and Aladdin's love overturns the age-old law that the princess must marry a prince when she is of age, and Pocahontas's love for John Smith ends the war between her tribe and colonizers. This transformative power of hetero-romantic love is echoed throughout these films.

Finally, we observe that hetero-romantic love is not sexually embodied in these films except through kissing. The power of hetero-romantic love is often delivered through a heterosexual kiss. A lot of heterosexual kissing happens in G-rated films. *Princess Diaries,* with its live-action teenage characters, contains the most explicit kissing, as the main character daydreams that a boy kisses her passionately, open-mouthed as she falls back against the lockers smiling and giggling. Most animated kisses are with closed mouths (or the viewer cannot fully see the mouths) and of shorter duration, but they are often even more powerful. Throughout these films, but especially in the animated ones, a heterosexual kiss signifies heterosexual love and in doing so is powerful. Ariel of *The Little Mermaid* must secure a kiss from the prince to retain her voice and her legs. In *The Lion King,* when Nala and Simba kiss (lick and nuzzle) as they are reunited, they not only realize their love, but Simba realizes he must return to his rightful place as king and save his family and the entire kingdom. We often see these powerful kisses first very close-up and in profile and then moving outward to show the wider world that the powerful kisses are transforming. For example, once the Beast is transformed back into a man by Belle's declaration of love, they kiss, and the entire kingdom appears to turn from winter to springtime, flowers bloom, and others who had been damaged by the same spell as the Beast are restored to their personhood.

In one case, the kiss of love initially leads to making the world worse. When Pocahontas kisses John Smith, others see them, and this leads to the death of the man Pocahontas's father wanted her to marry. Eventually, however, their love is what brings peace between the Native Americans and European colonizers. Even this negative transformation brought on by a kiss is different from kisses outside of hetero-romantic love. Take, for example, the only same-gender kiss in these films. In *The Lion King,* Pumba and Timon are eating dinner and sucking on opposite ends of a worm (reminiscent of the classic *Lady and the Tramp* spaghetti vignette). When they reach the middle, their lips touch with a smooch, and they both look toward the camera aghast, seemingly both at the deed (the "kiss") and having been "caught" by the camera. This kiss is treated as humorous and not as serious or powerful as the kisses of hetero-romantic love. Even heterosexual kisses outside of love relationships are not serious, powerful, or transformative. For example, Jasmine kisses the evil Jafar in *Aladdin,* but she does so to trick him. It works as a trick and distraction, but it is not powerful or transformative. Only hetero-romantic kissing is powerful in that it signifies love and in doing so can change the world.

Heterosexiness and the Heterosexual Gaze: Heterosexuality Outside of Love

Thus far, we have described how heterosexuality is constructed through depictions of hetero-romantic love relationships in these films. There is also heterosexuality depicted outside of romantic relationships, though this heterosexuality is quite different and more ordinary. As such, it is depicted not as earnest or transformative but as frivolous, entertaining, and crude. This nonromantic heterosexuality is constructed through the different portrayals of women's and men's bodies, the heterosexiness of the feminine characters, and the heterosexual gaze of the masculine ones.

Heteronormativity requires particular kinds of bodies and interactions between those bodies. Thus, as heterosexuality is constructed in these films, gendered bodies are portrayed quite differently, and we see much more of some bodies than others. Women throughout the animated features in our sample are drawn with cleavage, bare stomachs, and bare legs. Women of color are more likely to be drawn as young women with breasts and hips and white women as delicate girls (Lacroix 2004). Men are occasionally depicted without their shirts, such as in *Tarzan;* or without much of a shirt, as in *Aladdin;* and in one scene in *Mulan,* it is implied that men have been swimming naked. However, having part of the body exposed is more common among the lead women characters and among the women who make up the background of the scenes.

Women's nudity is also often marked as significant through comment or reaction. Women are often "almost caught" naked by men. For example, Mia of the *Princess Diaries* has her dressing area torn down by jealous girls, almost revealing her naked to a group of male photographers. Mulan bathes in a lake when she thinks she is alone, but when male soldiers come to swim, Mushoo refers to her breasts, saying, "There are a couple of things they're bound to notice," and she sneaks away. Similarly, Quasimodo accidentally stumbles into Esmeralda's dressing area, and she quickly covers up with a robe and hunches over so as not to expose herself. She ties up her robe as Quasimodo apologizes again and again and hides his eyes. However, as he exits, he glances back toward her with a smile signifying for the viewer his love for her. A glimpse of her body has made her even more lovable and desirable.

Men's bodies are treated quite differently in these films. Male bodies, to the extent they are commented on at all, are the site of jokes. Men's crotches, genitals, and backsides are funny. For example, in *Hunchback of Notre Dame*, a cork from a bottle of champagne flies between a man's legs and knocks him over and the man yells in pain; later in that movie, during a fight, someone says, "That's hitting a little below the belt," and the woman says, "No this is!" and aims to strike him in the groin but is deflected by a sword. A boy in *Princess Diaries* is doubled over in pain as a baseball hits him in the groin. This scene is played as funny and the result of another character extracting her vengeance. *The Rugrats Movie* is full of jokes and images of boys' bare bottoms and penises. There are also references in other films to "a limp noodle" (*Mulan*) and "a shrinky winky" (*101 Dalmatians*). Mushoo in *Mulan* also jokes about male nudity, saying, "I hate biting naked butts." Women's genitals are never mentioned or invoked in any way. Their bodies are not the sites of jokes. Rather, women's bodies become important in the construction of heteronormative sexuality through their "sexiness" at which men gaze.

Much of the sexuality that these gendered bodies engage in has little to do with heterosexual sex narrowly defined as intercourse or even behaviors that might lead to it, but rather with cultural signs of a gendered sexuality for women. These signs are found in subplots, musical numbers, humorous scenes, and scenes depicting women's bodies, rather than in the main story lines of hetero-romantic true love. Such scenes contain sexual innuendo based in gesture, movement, tone of voice, and expression. Importantly, in all cases, sexiness is depicted as something women possess and use for getting men's attention. Sexiness is more often an attribute of female characters of color (e.g., Esmeralda, Jasmine, Ursula) (Hurley 2005) and is implicitly heterosexual given that the films construct the intended spectator of this sexiness as male (Mulvey 1975).

The best example of the representation of sexiness appears in *The Hunchback of Notre Dame*. Esmeralda, the Gypsy female lead, is drawn with dark hair, big green eyes, a curvy body, cleavage, and a small waist. She is also drawn with darker skin than other lead Disney characters like Belle (*Beauty and the Beast*) and Ariel (*Little Mermaid*). Darker skin and hair and "exotic" features are part of the representation of heterosexual sexiness for women. Moreover, Esmeralda spends much time in this film swaying her hips and dancing "sexily" while men admire her. An early scene in the film resembles a striptease, although all the character's clothes do not come off. The scene begins with the song, "Come one, come all! Hurry, hurry, here's your chance. See the mystery and romance . . . See the finest girl in France . . . Make an entrance to entrance . . . Dance la Esmeralda . . . Dance!" Esmeralda begins to dance. She is dressed seductively, and her dancing is provocative. We then see the men who are watching her. Frollo says, "Look at that disgusting display" to which Captain replies, "YES SIR!" and opens his eyes wider. She perches in front of Frollo and then tosses her scarf around his neck, pulls him in as if she is going to kiss him, puts her lips on his nose, and then pushes his hat over his face. She dances back to the stage where she does a split in front of Quasimodo and gives him a wink. She then steals a large spear from a security guard, stabs it into the stage and begins to swing and twist around the pole. The men in the crowd are all wide-eyed, screaming and cheering, and then they all toss money on stage for her performance.

Not all scenes with the signification of sexiness are so elaborated. When the candlestick and duster are turned back into people in *Beauty and the Beast*, the now-voluptuous maid prances bare-shouldered in front of the chef who stares. Throughout *Aladdin*, especially in fast-paced musical scenes, sexy women prance, preen, bat their eyelashes, shake their hips, and reveal their cleavage. When Genie sings to Aladdin, he produces three women with bare stomachs and bikini-like outfits who dance around him, touch him, bat their eyes at him, and kiss him. He stares at them sometimes unsure, but wide-eyed and smiling. When Prince Ali comes to ask Princess Jasmine for her hand in marriage, his parade to the castle is adorned with writhing, dancing women with bare stomachs and cleavage. Later, Jasmine sees Prince Ali as a fraud and tricks him with similarly sexy moves. Heterosexiness in *Aladdin* is delivered through the bodies of women of color who are exoticized.

There are a few examples of white women depicted as "sexy," although these are more delimited and do not involve the main white women/girl characters.

In *Princess Diaries,* a group of teenage friends are shown doing many of the same things as the animated women in *Aladdin.* They dance, shake their hips, make faces with curled and puckered lips and squinting eyes, play with their hair, and slap their hips. In *Beauty and the Beast,* a man is hit on the head for talking to a large-breasted woman with cleavage and much lipstick who moves and speaks in a sexy, flirtatious manner. *Toy Story 2* has a group of singing, dancing, nearly all-white Barbies who are ogled by the masculine toys. These scenes make it clear that women move and adorn their bodies and contort their faces for men.

While the women are being sexy, the (usually white) men are performing a different role as these films construct heterosexuality. As evident from some of the examples above, there is much explicit heterosexual gazing at or ogling of women's bodies in these films. Sometimes such gazing establishes that a woman is worth the pursuit of men and the fight for her that will develop the plot of the film, as in *Beauty and the Beast.* In an early scene in this film, when Belle walks out of a bookshop, three men who had been peering through the window turn around as if to pretend that they had not been staring. The man in the middle is then held up by the other two so that he can stare at Belle's backside as she walks away. All three men stare and then start to sing of her beauty. In other films, sexualized gazing is not so tightly attached to beauty but to the performance of heterosexual masculinity. In one instance in *Chicken Run,* the chickens are "exercising," and Rocky (a chicken) stares at Ginger's (a chicken) backside. She catches him, and he smiles, slyly. When the main characters refrain from overt ogling and sexual commentary, the "sidekicks" provide humor through this practice. For example, in *Toy Story 2,* Rex, Potato Head, Slinky Dog, and Piggy Bank drive through aisles of a toy store and stop at a "beach party" where there are many Barbies in bathing suits, laughing and dancing. As the male characters approach, a jackpot sound ("ching") is heard, and all four male characters' jaws drop open. Then "Tour Guide Barbie" acrobatically lands in their car and says she will help them. They all stare at her with open eyes and mouths. Mr. Potato Head recites again and again, "I'm a married spud, I'm a married spud, I'm a married spud," and Piggy Bank says, "Make room for single fellas" as he jumps over Potato Head to sit next to Barbie. They remain mesmerized by Barbie as she gives them a tour of the store.

The objectifying gaze at women's bodies is often translated into objectifying, sexist language. Girl/ women characters are called doll face, chicks, cuties, baby doll, angel face, sweet cheeks, bodacious, succulent little garden snail, tender oozing blossom, temptress snake, and tramp; and the boys/men say things like "I'll give you a tune up any time" and "give her some slack and reel her in." The desiring gazes, the commentary, and the depictions of them (large eyes, staring, open mouths, sound effects, and anxiousness) are constructed as competitive and conquering or frivolous, in stark contrast to the exceptional, magical, powerful hetero-romantic love described above. These depictions of heterosexual interactions have the effect of normalizing men's objectification of women's bodies and the heterosexual desire it signifies.

CONCLUSION

Despite the assumption that children's media are free of sexual content, our analyses suggest that these media depict a rich and pervasive heterosexual landscape. We have illustrated two main ways that G-rated films construct heterosexuality. First, heterosexuality is constructed through depictions of hetero-romantic love as exceptional, powerful, transformative, and magical. Second, heterosexuality is also constructed through depictions of interactions between gendered bodies in which the sexiness of feminine characters is subjected to the gaze of masculine characters. These accounts of heterosexuality extend our understandings of heteronormativity.

First, the finding that heterosexuality is constructed through heterosexiness points to the ways that heteronormativity intersects with gender, race, and class in its constructions. While heterosexuality is normalized and expected, it takes different forms for different sorts of bodies, and this is especially true for heterosexuality outside of romantic relationships. Second, the finding that hetero-romantic love is depicted as exceptional, powerful, and transformative runs counter to current theoretical understandings of heteronormativity's scaffolding being the ordinary, expected, everydayness of heterosexuality. These films show heterosexuality to be just the opposite. Heterosexuality achieves a taken-for-granted status in these films not because it is ordinary, but because hetero-romance is depicted as powerful. This finding in no way negates previous understandings of heteronormativity but rather extends another theoretical tenet—that is, that heterosexuality and its normativity are pervasive. Heterosexual exceptionalism extends the pervasiveness of heterosexuality and may serve as a means of inviting investment in it. Furthermore, heterosexuality is glorified here in mass culture but is also ordinary and assumed in everyday life. Thus, its encompassing pervasiveness lends it its power. Both ordinary and exceptional constructions of heterosexuality work to normalize its status because it becomes difficult to imagine anything other than this form of social relationship or anyone outside of these bonds.

Finally, we want to again emphasize that we cannot know what understandings and interpretations children might take away from these films or how they make sense of them alongside all the other social and cultural information they acquire. Others have shown

that queer readings of such films are possible for adults (Griffin 2000). Children may have their own queer readings of such films. Without future work with children directly, we cannot know. However, these films are widely viewed by many very young children who are engaged with media rich worlds. It is likely that these accounts of heterosexuality make it into their understanding of the world in some way, albeit likely with layers of misunderstanding, reinterpretation, and integration with other information. Regardless, these films provide powerful portraits of a multifaceted and pervasive heterosexuality that likely facilitates the reproduction of heteronormativity.

NOTE

1. http://www.washingtonpost.com/wp-srv/style/daily/movies/100million/article.htm.

REFERENCES

Arnold, Thomas K. 2005. Kids' DVDs are in a growth spurt. *USA Today*, http://www.usatoday.com/life/movies/news/2005-04-04-kids-dvds_x.htm.

Best, Raphaela. 1983. *We've All Got Scars: What Boys and Girls Learn in Elementary School*. Bloomington, IN: Indiana University Press.

Byrne, Eleanor, and Martin McQuillan. 1999. *Deconstructing Disney*. London: Pluto Press.

Crawley, Alisha M., D. R. Anderson, A. Wilder, M. Williams, and A. Santomero. 1999. Effects of repeated exposures to a single episode of the television program *Blue's Clues* on the viewing behaviors and comprehension of preschool children. *Journal of Educational Psychology* 91:630–37.

Emerson, Robert, Rachel Fretz, and Linda Shaw. 1995. *Writing ethnographic fieldnotes*. Chicago: University of Chicago Press.

Giroux, Henry A. 1996. Animating youth: The Disneyfication of children's culture. In *Fugitive cultures: Race, violence, and youth*. New York: Routledge.

———. 1997. Are Disney movies good for your kids? In *Kinderculture: The corporate construction of childhood*, edited by Shirley R. Steinberg and Joe L. Kincheloe. Boulder, CO: Westview.

Gotz, Maya, Dafna Lemish, Amy Aidman, and Hyesung Moon. 2005. *Media and the make believe worlds of children: When Harry Potter meets Pokemon in Disneyland*. Mahwah, NJ: Lawrence Erlbaum.

Griffin, Sean. 2000. *Tinker Belles and evil queens: The Walt Disney Company from the inside out*. New York: New York University Press.

Hadley, Kathryn Gold, and Sandi Kawecka Nenga. 2004. From Snow White to Digimon: Using popular media to confront Confucian Values in Taiwanese peer cultures. *Childhood* 11 (4): 515–36.

Hurley, Dorothy L. 2005. Seeing white: Children of color and the Disney fairy tale princess. *Journal of Negro Education* 74:221–32.

Ingraham, Chrys. 1999. *White weddings: Romancing heterosexuality in popular culture*. New York: Routledge.

Jackson, Stevi. 2006. Gender, sexuality and heterosexuality: The complexity (and limits) of heteronormativity. *Feminist Theory* 7:105–21.

Johnson, Paul. 2005. *Love, heterosexuality, and society*. London: Routledge.

Junn, Ellen N. 1997. Media portrayals of love, marriage & sexuality for child audiences. Paper presented at the Biennial Meeting, Society for Research in Child Development, Washington, DC.

Kelley, P., D. Buckingham, and H. Davies. 1999. Talking dirty: Sexual knowledge and television. *Childhood* 6:221–42.

Kim, J. L., C. L. Sorsoll, K. Collins, and B. A. Zylbergold. 2007. From sex to sexuality: Exposing the heterosexual script on primetime network television. *Journal of Sex Research* 44:145.

Kitzinger, Celia. 2005. Heteronormativity in action: Reproducing the heterosexual nuclear family in after-hours medical calls. *Social Problems* 52:477–98.

Lacroix, Celeste. 2004. Images of animated others: The orientalization of Disney's cartoon heroines from *The Little Mermaid* to *The Hunchback of Notre Dame*. *Popular Communication* 2:213–29.

Lancaster, Roger. 2003. *The trouble with nature.* Berkeley: University of California Press.

Mares, M. L. 1998. Children's use of VCRs. *Annals of the American Academy of Political and Social Science* 557:120–31.

Martin, Karin A. 2009. Normalizing heterosexuality: Mothers' assumptions, talk, and strategies with young children. *American Sociological Review* 74: 190–207.

Martin, Karin A., Katherine Luke, and Lynn Verduzco-Baker. 2007. The sexual socialization of young children: Setting the agenda for research. In *Advances in group processes,* vol. 6, *Social psychology of gender,* edited by Shelly Correll. Oxford, UK: Elsevier Science.

Mo, W., and W. Shen. 2000. A mean wink at authenticity: Chinese images in Disney's Mulan. *New Advocate* 13:129–42.

Motion Picture Association of America, "Film Ratings," Motion Picture Association of America, http://www.mpaa.org/FilmRatings.asp

Mulvey, Laura. 1975. Visual pleasure and narrative cinema. *Screen* 16:6–18.

Nguyen, Mimi. 1998. A feminist fantasia, almost. *San Jose Mercury News,* July 5.

Pewewardy, Cornel. 1996. The Pocahontas paradox: A cautionary tale for educators. *Journal of Navajo Education* 14:20–25.

Renold, Emma. 2002. Presumed innocence: (Hetero)Sexual, heterosexist and homophobic harassment among primary school girls and boys. *Childhood* 9:415–34.

———. 2005. *Girls, boys, and junior sexualities: Exploring children's gender and sexual relations in the primary school.* London: Routledge Falmer.

Rideout, V., E. A. Vandewater, and E. A. Wartella, 2003. *Zero to six: Electronic media in the lives of infants, toddlers, and preschoolers.* Washington, DC: Henry J. Kaiser Family Foundation.

Rubin, Gayle. 1984. Thinking sex: Notes for a radical theory of the politics of sexuality. In *Pleasure and danger,* edited by Carol Vance. Boston: Routledge.

Schmitt, K. L., D. R. Anderson, and P. A. Collins 1999. Form and content: Looking at visual features of television. *Developmental Psychology* 35:1156–67.

Schor, Juliet B. 2004. *Born to buy: The commercialized child and the new consumer culture.* New York: Scribner.

Thomas, Susan Gregory. 2007. *Buy, buy, baby: How consumer culture manipulates parents.* New York: Houghton Mifflin.

Thompson, T. L., and E. Zerbinos. 1995. Gender roles in animated cartoons: Has the picture changed in 20 years? *Sex Roles: A Journal of Research* 32:651–73.

Thorne, Barrie. 1993. *Gender play: Girls and boys in school.* New Brunswick, NJ: Rutgers University Press.

Tobin, Joseph. 2000. *"Good guys don't wear hats": Children's talk about the media.* Williston, VT: Teachers College Press.

Ward, L. Monique. 1995. Talking about sex: Common themes about sexuality in the prime-time television programs children and adolescents view most. *Journal of Youth and Adolescence* 24:595–615.

———. 2003. Understanding the role of entertainment media in the sexual socialization of American youth: A review of empirical research. *Developmental Review* 23:347–88.

Witt, Susan D. 2000. The influence of television on children's gender role socialization. *Childhood Education* 76:322–24.

Pretty Baby

First published in 2005

Was that you, sitting behind us at *The Nutcracker on Ice?* Remember? Your kid was tangled up in her own scarf and then weeping over a box of spilled raisins before she peed "one tiny, tiny drop" into her tights? But still you could hear our Ben's sharp intake of breath when the skaters all glided out in pairs. You heard his whispery loud "That's so beautiful!" about their powdered white wigs and spingly-spangly outfits, real pretend snow fluttering around them as they twirled their romantic figure eights. Oh, those fancy parents of the *Nutcracker* children! Those mothers skating around in fitted pink-satin waistcoats and full pink-satin skirts, those fathers just barely distinct in their own cotton candy waistcoats, although they weren't wearing skirts, of course—I mean, it wasn't *Nutcracker on Castro Street*, for God's sake. No, the fathers were sporting the super-manly pink-satin *knickers*. And Ben loved them.

Later, when we were zipping up our jackets in the lobby—after the scuffling soldier mice and the various Freudian dream sequences of hunky toys that may or may not come to life and look like a person's dad, after the "Dance of the Sugar Plum Fairy" and Ben's baby sister falling asleep in my lap like a thirty-pound sack of sausages—Ben identified "that pink part" as the very best segment of the entire evening.

I was not surprised. Ben is five, and pink has always been his favorite color. Just to be clear, we're not talking *pale* pink—which he will tolerate but has no special affinity for (it ranks seventh on his list, behind even *teal*)—but bright pink, or what he sometimes calls "darky pink." When, for instance, I wore my reversible down jacket with the black side out, he thought I was insane. "If I had all that nice darky pink in my coat, I would definitely show it." (He had a point, I reversed it.) His own jacket is silver, but his snow boots are

flamingo pink, as is the fraying plastic lei from a midwinter luau. His favorite flowers are pink roses. And his most special outfit—the one he wears only for such extraordinary occasions as a birthday party or the weekly show-and-tell at his preschool—involves a floral-printed t-shirt with fuchsia velour sleeves, and the pants that I myself made (with much saying of the F-word and sewing of my actual hand to the fabric) from the magenta-striped terry cloth that Ben picked out from Jo-Ann Fabrics.

Right about now you're probably sending enthusiastic "You go, boy!" vibes in Ben's direction—and you should be. For one thing, he looks absolutely fabulous. And for another, maybe pink is the new navy blue. After all, P. Diddy swaggers in sweatpants the color of a seashell, and Demi Moore ogles her young hottie in his taffy-hued suit. Briefcase-carrying hominids seem to have worn sherbety-pink shirts beneath their ties since the Dawn of Business Attire. And yet the color rules are different for little boys. Is that because we imagine a grown man's gender is already hardened and set, like the steely abdomen of masculinity itself, the threat of pink bouncing off it like so many girly punches? While evidently for budding young manhood—the preschool type—pink must be shunned like gender-bending kryptonite. Like it's some queer wolf in powdery-pale clothing. Pink might *seem* to be a swishy little color— but it's got the strength of entire armies. Why, merely gazing too long at a carnation could prevent your son's very testicles from descending! And forget the actual *wearing* of the color—that could send his Y chromosomes leaping for their lives onto the nearest testosterone-leaking Arnold Schwarzenegger look-alike.

I know this must be true, because I write an online parenting column, and whenever I post a picture of Ben in this or that pink outfit—or with the rolling pink

Hello Kitty suitcase he wanted (and got) for his fourth birthday—the message boards fill with enraged, apocalyptic postings about our family's imminent nellification. "Why is your son wearing pink?" is what people want to know—although they don't tend to ask quite so politely. (And you'd be surprised at how unsatisfactory they find the perfectly logical answer "Because pink is his favorite color.") From the shrillness of their indignation, you'd think we were taking Ben back-to-school shopping at Frederick's of Hollywood instead of Old Navy, which is where we actually go (when we're not at the Salvation Army).

And all I'll say is, *you* try convincing a young child to choose from the racks of boy clothes. Do we really expect boys to thrill to one of those midget salesmen outfits—the tomato-red polo shirts and pleated khaki slacks—or over an oatmeal-colored sweater vest and army-green camouflage sweatpants? Are we genuinely shocked that the girls' section—with its plush bubblegum everything, its rhinestones and puppies and velvet detailing—calls out to some boys like a pastel siren song? Of course not. But even when nobody says it outright, we know what the critics are thinking: Let your son wear pink, and you might as well enroll him in Camp Fire Island. Because pink isn't just nouveau Hollywood-hip and retro neo-preppy golf sweaters. It's still totally Elton John and Village People. It still means taking out a lease in Gayville—with an option to buy.

Yes, nobody likes to come right out and say it (actually, plenty do), but that's what all of this is about. Everyone wants to be sure that, a dozen years from now, our sons will have the right kind of prom date— the *vagina* kind of prom date. Which they surely won't, unless we police their color choices a little more rigorously. But here's where I get confused—simple pinheaded bigotry aside. If "pink" and "gay" go together like Froot Loops and Toucan Sam, is pink imagined to be the *effect* of gayness? Or its cause? Because if it's the former—if pink is the mere expression of some extant *essential* gayness—well then, what's the point of worrying about it? It's a fait accompli, so pour me a glass of champagne, pop in a Barbra Streisand movie, and let's celebrate. But if it's taken instead to be the cause, then how, exactly *does* pink make a boy gay? Does he grow up to be a pink-wearing adult, at which point other men—woops!—mistake him for a Victoria's Secret model and hit on him by accident and, well, one thing leads to another, when in Rome, etc.? Or do the color waves actually alter his brain chemistry such that his ideal wife spontaneously becomes Tom Selleck?

For one thing: I doubt it. And for another: Great— even if it's not Tom Selleck. I'll be delighted. (Wouldn't you much rather, for instance, that your son be *shacked up with* the Queer Eye Fab Five than waiting shlubbily for them to come and fix him?)

Or is the worry just that pink will keep Ben from achieving his proper patriarchal birthright? *Oh masculinity! So natural and true! As teetering and precarious as an ice-fishing house built from fairy wings!* Will Ben's preschool class photo be uncovered one day and threaten his entry into the World Wrestling Federation? Will those pink-threaded boyhood outfits prevent him from registering a firearm or sucking bear out of somebody's ass crack at a fraternity hazing? Will he be clinically incapable of slouching in front of the Super Bowl like an overgrown, chili-fed larva? Or do we just worry that he won't know how to camouflage himself properly as an *imbecile stone* when a lover tries to enter together with him into the world of human feelings? I mean, men are great and everything—my own dearly beloved is a man, for example—but the last time I checked, gender roles didn't seem to be working so well for everyone. Why would we take such good care of something that seems to make so many people—gay and straight, men and women—so unhappy? And why on earth would we start so young?

Or younger. Because even when Ben was a mere wisp of a newborn, boyness seemed to cast its peculiar blue shadow over him. Our best friends had had a baby before us, and Ben wore her hand-me-down onesies and rompers, all of them decorated variously with whimsical fruits and zoo animals. Nothing was frilly or girly or even pink, but because these were not typical boy-baby clothes—insofar as they were without the obligatory decals of footballs and bulldozers and naked women—Ben was often mistaken for a girl. Which was fine with us—I mean, it wasn't like we needed him to hop up and carve our Thanksgiving turkey or anything. He was only fifteen seconds old, after all. But people would gush over him—"Oh what a pretty baby! Oh she's gorgeous!"—and we would beam and nod until the moment they asked "her" name, when we would have to confess, "Well, actually, it's Ben." And then his admirer would fall into fits of apology. "Oh my God! I'm so sorry! I don't know how I missed it! I mean, now that I really look—he's so handsome. So *manly*." Even though little Ben would just be dozing neutrally in the front pack, with his rosebud lips and male pattern baldness. It wasn't like he was cruising for a fiancé. "Oh that's okay," we always said. "We don't care!"

And we didn't. Or at least not about that. Because we do care—so much that it's like an ache at the bottom of my throat—about other things. Like Ben's happiness. His wholeness. We want him to be himself, to do the things he likes—however contradictory these things may be. Like the time he was two, and he toddled into the living room with a beaded pink-and-orange evening bag slung elegantly over his shoulder—then turned it over and dumped out a heap of Matchbox cars, *vroomed* them around like a maniac. Or the summer he wore the t-shirt our artist friend Meg made him: a little pink scoop-neck with the word "boy" silk-screened in black. He loves glittery purple eye shadow (which he applies only to the groove between his nose and mouth) and his iridescent strawberry-kiwi Bonne Bell Lipsmacker—and also running around, yelling, with a plastic baseball bat stuck out from between his legs. He loves his stuffed Snow Bear so tenderly that his eyes glisten while he cuddles her—but play the associations game with him, and the prompt "boring" will cause him to spit out the words "baby doll" like so much chewed-up tobacco.

Ben wants to decorate his birthday cake with rose petals and also gummy worms. He covets (and wears) bejeweled hair accessories although his hair is cut short, and he loves stringing glass beads and setting up elaborate tracks for his trains. His very best friend is a girl, but his second- and third-best friends are both boys. He likes to arrange the pansies and bleeding hearts in his grandmother's flower press. Dinosaurs scare him. He's a fearless climber. He recently told me that he thinks he's a fan of the Red Sox, "but," he admitted, "only because of the word "socks"—not because of how they play that game." He's happy and funny and smart. And he's very kind.

Which may be why, at *The Nutcracker*, after we'd gathered up all our mittens and scarves and Ben was twirling merrily toward the exit in blue racing-stripe sweatpants and a pink shirt with a heart on its sleeve, *you* leaned over your sleeping daughter and whispered to me, "Your son is lovely." And my eyes filled with tears—I could only smile and nod—because it's true. He is. And it was lovely of you to notice.

READING *19* **Barrie Thorne**

Girls and Boys Together ... but Mostly Apart: Gender Arrangements in Elementary Schools
First published in 1986

Throughout the years of elementary school, children's friendships and casual encounters are strongly separated by sex. Sex segregation among children, which starts in preschool and is well established by middle childhood, has been amply documented in studies of children's groups and friendships (e.g., Eder & Hallinan, 1978; Schofield, 1981) and is immediately visible in elementary school settings. When children choose seats in classrooms or the cafeteria, or get into line, they frequently arrange themselves in same-sex clusters. At lunchtime, they talk matter-of-factly about "girls' tables" and "boys' tables." Playgrounds have gendered turfs, with some areas and activities, such as large playing fields and basketball courts, controlled mainly by boys, and others smaller enclaves like jungle-gym areas and concrete spaces for hopscotch or jump rope—more often controlled by girls. Sex segregation is so common in elementary schools that it is meaningful to speak of separate girls' and boys' worlds.

Studies of gender and children's social relations have mostly followed this "two worlds" model, separately describing and comparing the subcultures of girls and boys (e.g., Lever, 1976; Maltz & Borker, 1983). In brief summary: Boys tend to interact in larger, more age-heterogeneous groups (Lever, 1976; Waldrop & Halverson, 1975; Eder & Hallinan, 1978). They engage in more rough and tumble play and physical fighting (Maccoby & Jacklin, 1974). Organized sports are both a central activity and a major metaphor in boys' subcultures; they use the language of "teams" even when not engaged in sports, and they often construct interaction in the form of contests. The shifting hierarchies of boys' groups (Savin-Williams, 1976) are evident in their more frequent use of direct commands, insults, and challenges (Goodwin, 1980).

Fewer studies have been done of girls' groups (Foot, Chapman, & Smith, 1980; McRobbie & Garber, 1975), and—perhaps because categories for description and analysis have come more from male than female experience—researchers have had difficulty seeing and analyzing girls' social relations. Recent work has begun to correct this skew. In middle childhood, girls' worlds are less public than those of boys; girls more often interact in private places and in smaller groups or friendship pairs (Eder & Hallinan, 1978; Waldrop & Halverson, 1975). Their play is more cooperative and turn-taking (Lever, 1976). Girls have more intense and exclusive friendships, which take shape around keeping and telling secrets, shifting alliances, and indirect ways of expressing disagreement (Goodwin, 1980; Lever, 1976; Maltz & Borker, 1983). Instead of direct commands, girls more often use directives which merge speaker and hearer, e.g., "let's" or "we gotta" (Goodwin, 1980).

Although much can be learned by comparing the social organization and subcultures of boys' and of girls' groups, the separate-worlds approach has eclipsed full, contextual understanding of gender and social relations among children. The separate-worlds model essentially involves a search for group sex differences and shares the limitations of individual sex difference research. Differences tend to be exaggerated and similarities ignored, with little theoretical attention to the integration of similarity and difference (Unger, 1979). Statistical findings of difference are often portrayed as dichotomous, neglecting the considerable individual variation that exists; for example, not all boys fight, and some have intense and exclusive friendships. The sex difference approach tends to abstract gender from its social context, to assume that males and females are qualitatively and permanently

different (with differences perhaps unfolding through separate developmental lines). These assumptions mask the possibility that gender arrangements and patterns of similarity and difference may vary by situation, race, social class, region, or subculture.

Sex segregation is far from total, and is a more complex and dynamic process than the portrayal of separate worlds reveals. Erving Goffman (1977) has observed that sex segregation has a "with–then apart" structure; the sexes segregate periodically, with separate spaces, rituals, [and] groups, but they also come together and are, in crucial ways, part of the same world. This is certainly true in the social environment of elementary schools. Although girls and boys do interact as boundaried collectivities—an image suggested by the separate-worlds approach—there are other occasions when they work or play in relaxed and integrated ways. Gender is less central to the organization and meaning of some situations than others. In short, sex segregation is not static, but is a variable and complicated process.

To gain an understanding of gender which can encompass both the "with" and the "apart" of sex segregation, analysis should start not with the individual, nor with a search for sex differences, but with social relationships. Gender should be conceptualized as a system of relationships rather than as an immutable and dichotomous given. Taking this approach, I have organized my research on gender and children's social relations around questions like the following: How and when does gender enter into group formation? In a given situation, how is gender made more or less salient or infused with particular meanings? By what rituals, processes, and forms of social organization and conflict do "with–then apart" rhythms get enacted? How are these processes affected by the organization of institutions (e.g., different types of schools, neighborhoods, or summer camps), varied settings (e.g., the constraints and possibilities governing interaction on playgrounds vs. classrooms), and particular encounters?

METHODS AND SOURCES OF DATA

This study is based on two periods of participant observation. In 1976–1977 I observed for eight months in a largely working-class elementary school in California, a school with 8 percent Black and 12 percent Chicana/o students. In 1980 I did fieldwork for three months in a Michigan elementary school of similar size (around 400 students), social class, and racial composition.

I observed in several classrooms—a kindergarten, a second grade, and a combined fourth-fifth grade—and in school hallways, cafeterias, and playgrounds. I set out to follow the round of the school day as children experience it, recording their interactions with one another, and with adults, in varied settings.

Participant observation involves gaining access to everyday, "naturalistic" settings and taking systematic notes over an extended period of time. Rather than starting with preset categories for recording, or with fixed hypotheses for testing, participant observers record detail in ways which maximize opportunities for discovery. Through continuous interaction between observation and analysis, "grounded theory" is developed (Glaser & Strauss, 1967).

The distinctive logic and discipline of this mode of inquiry emerges from: (1) theoretical sampling—being relatively systematic in the choice of where and whom to observe in order to maximize knowledge relevant to categories and analysis which are being developed; and (2) comparing all relevant data on a given point in order to modify emerging propositions to take account of discrepant cases (Katz, 1983). Participant observation is a flexible, open-ended and inductive method, designed to understand behavior within, rather than stripped from, social context. It provides richly detailed information anchored in everyday meanings and experience.

DAILY PROCESSES OF SEX SEGREGATION

Sex segregation should be understood not as a given, but as the result of deliberate activity. The outcome is dramatically visible when there are separate girls' and boys' tables in school lunchrooms or sex-separated groups on playgrounds. But in the same lunchroom one can also find tables where girls and boys eat and talk together, and in some playground activities the sexes mix. By what processes do girls and boys separate into gender-defined and relatively boundaried collectivities? And in what contexts, and through what processes, do boys and girls interact in less gender-divided ways?

In the school settings I observed, much segregation happened with no mention of gender. Gender was implicit in the contours of friendship, shared interest, and perceived risk which came into play when children chose companions—in their prior planning, invitations, seeking of access, saving of places, denials of entry, and allowing or protesting of "cuts" by those

who violated the rules for lining up. Sometimes children formed mixed-sex groups for play, eating, talking, working on a classroom project, or moving through space. When adults or children explicitly invoked gender—and this was nearly always in ways which separated girls and boys—boundaries were heightened and mixed-sex interaction became an explicit arena of risk.

In the schools I studied, the physical space and curricula were not formally divided by sex, as they have been in the history of elementary schooling (a history evident in separate entrances to old school buildings, where the words "Boys" and "Girls" are permanently etched in concrete). Nevertheless, gender was a visible marker in the adult-organized school day. In both schools, when the public address system sounded, the principal inevitably opened with: "Boys and girls ... ," and in addressing clusters of children, teachers and aides regularly used gender terms ("Heads down, girls"; "The girls are ready and the boys aren't"). These forms of address made gender visible and salient, conveying an assumption that the sexes are separate social groups.

Teachers and aides sometimes drew upon gender as a basis for sorting children and organizing activities. Gender is an embodied and visual social category which roughly divides the population in half, and the separation of girls and boys permeates the history and lore of schools and playgrounds. In both schools—although through awareness of Title IX, many teachers had changed this practice—one could see separate girls' and boys' lines moving, like caterpillars, through the school halls. In the fourth–fifth-grade classroom the teacher frequently pitted girls against boys for spelling and math contests. On the playground in the Michigan school, aides regarded the space close to the building as girls' territory, and the playing fields "out there" as boys' territory. They sometimes shooed children of the other sex away from those spaces, especially boys who ventured near the girls' area and seemed to have teasing in mind.

In organizing their activities, both within and apart from the surveillance of adults, children also explicitly invoked gender. During my fieldwork in the Michigan school, I kept daily records of who sat where in the lunchroom. The amount of sex segregation varied: it was least at the first-grade tables and almost total among sixth-graders. There was also variation from classroom to classroom within a given age and from day to day. Actions like the following heightened the gender divide: In the lunchroom, when the two second-grade tables were filling, a high-status boy walked by the inside table, which had a scattering of both boys and girls, and said loudly, "Oooo, too many girls," as he headed for a seat at the far table. The boys at the inside table picked up their trays and moved, and no other boys sat at the inside table, which the pronouncement had effectively made taboo. In the end, that day (which was not the case every day), girls and boys ate at separate tables.

Eating and walking are not sex-typed activities, yet in forming groups in lunchrooms and hallways children often separated by sex. Sex segregation assumed added dimensions on the playground, where spaces, equipment, and activities were infused with gender meanings. My inventories of activities and groupings on the playground showed similar patterns in both schools: boys controlled the large fixed spaces designated for team sports (baseball diamonds, grassy fields used for football or soccer); girls more often played closer to the building, doing tricks on the monkey bars (which, for sixth-graders, became an area for sitting and talking) and using cement areas for jump rope, hopscotch, and group games like four-square. (Lever, 1976, provides a good analysis of sex-divided play.) Girls and boys most often played together in kickball, and in group (rather than team) games like four-square, dodgeball, and handball. When children used gender to exclude others from play, they often drew upon beliefs connecting boys to some activities and girls to others: A first-grade boy avidly watched an all-female game of jump rope. When the girls began to shift positions, he recognized a means of access to the play and he offered, "I'll swing it." A girl responded, "No way, you don't know how to do it, to swing it. You gotta be a girl." He left without protest. Although children sometimes ignored pronouncements about what each sex could or could not do, I never heard them directly challenge such claims.

When children had explicitly defined an activity or a group as gendered, those who crossed the boundary—especially boys who moved into female-marked space—risked being teased. ("Look! Mike's in the girls' line!"; "That's a girl over there," a girl said loudly, pointing to a boy sitting at an otherwise all-female table in the lunchroom.) Children, and occasionally adults, used teasing—especially the tease of "liking" someone of the other sex, or of "being" that sex by virtue of being in their midst—to police gender boundaries. Much of the teasing drew upon heterosexual romantic

definitions, making cross-sex interaction risky and increasing social distance between boys and girls.

RELATIONSHIPS BETWEEN THE SEXES

Because I have emphasized the "apart" and ignored the occasions of "with," this analysis of sex segregation falsely implies that there is little contact between girls and boys in daily school life. In fact, relationships between girls and boys—which should be studied as fully as, and in connection with, same-sex relationships—are of several kinds:

1. "Borderwork," or forms of cross-sex interaction which are based upon and reaffirm boundaries and asymmetries between girls' and boys' groups.
2. Interactions which are infused with heterosexual meanings.
3. Occasions where individuals cross gender boundaries to participate in the world of the other sex.
4. Situations where gender is muted in salience, with girls and boys interacting in more relaxed ways.

Borderwork

In elementary school settings, boys' and girls' groups are sometimes spatially set apart. Same-sex groups sometimes claim fixed territories such as the basketball court, the bars, or specific lunchroom tables. However, in the crowded, multifocused, and adult-controlled environment of the school, groups form and disperse at a rapid rate and can never stay totally apart. Contact between girls and boys sometimes lessens sex segregation, but gender-defined groups also come together in ways which emphasize their boundaries.

"Borderwork" refers to interaction across, yet based upon and even strengthening, gender boundaries. I have drawn this notion from Fredrik Barth's (1969) analysis of social relations which are maintained across ethnic boundaries without diminishing dichotomized ethnic status.[1] His focus is on more macro, ecological arrangements; mine is on face-to-face behavior. But the insight is similar: groups may interact in ways which strengthen their borders, and the maintenance of ethnic (or gender) groups can best be understood by examining the boundary that defines the groups, "not the cultural stuff that it encloses" (Barth, 1969:15). In elementary schools there are several types of borderwork: contests or games where gender-defined teams compete; cross-sex rituals of chasing and pollution; and group invasions. These interactions are asymmetrical, challenging the separate-but-parallel model of "two worlds."

Contests   Boys and girls are sometimes pitted against each other in classroom competitions and playground games. The fourth–fifth-grade classroom had a boys' side and a girls' side, an arrangement that reemerged each time the teacher asked children to choose their own desks. Although there was some within-sex shuffling, the result was always a spatial moiety system— boys on the left, girls on the right—with the exception of one girl (the "tomboy" whom I'll describe later), who twice chose a desk with the boys and once with the girls. Drawing upon and reinforcing the children's self-segregation, the teacher often pitted the boys against the girls in spelling and math competitions, events marked by cross-sex antagonism and within-sex solidarity. The teacher introduced a math game; she would write addition and subtraction problems on the board, and a member of each team would race to be the first to write the correct answer. She wrote two scorekeeping columns on the board: "Beastly Boys" ... "Gossipy Girls." The boys yelled out, as several girls laughed, "Noisy girls! Gruesome girls!" The girls sat in a row on top of their desks; sometimes they moved collectively, pushing their hips or whispering "Pass it on." The boys stood along the wall, some reclining against desks. When members of either group came back victorious from the front of the room, they would do the "giving five" hand-slapping ritual with their team members.

On the playground a team of girls occasionally played a team of boys, usually in kickball or team two-square. Sometimes these games proceeded matter-of-factly, but if gender became the explicit basis of team solidarity, the interaction changed, becoming more antagonistic and unstable. Two fifth-grade girls played against two fifth-grade boys in a team game of two-square. The game proceeded at an even pace until an argument ensued about whether the ball was out or on the line. Karen, who had hit the ball, became annoyed, flashed her middle finger at the other team, and called to a passing girl to join their side. The boys then called out to other boys, and cheered as several arrived to play. "We got five and you got three!" Jack yelled. The game continued, with the girls yelling, "Bratty boys! Sissy boys!" and the boys making noises—"Weee haw," "Ha-ha-ha"—as they played.

Chasing   Cross-sex chasing dramatically affirms boundaries between girls and boys. The basic elements of chase and elude, capture and rescue (Sutton-Smith, 1971) are found in various kinds of tag with formal rules and in informal episodes of chasing which punctuate life on playgrounds. These episodes begin with a provocation (taunts like "You can't get me!" or "Slobber monster!"; bodily pokes or the grabbing of possessions). A provocation may be ignored or responded to by chasing. Chaser and chased may then alternate roles. In an ethnographic study of chase sequences on a school playground, Christine Finnan (1982) observes that chases vary in number of chasers to chased (e.g., one chasing one or five chasing two); form of provocation (a taunt or a poke); outcome (an episode may end when the chased outdistances the chaser, or with a brief touch, being wrestled to the ground, or the recapturing of a hat or a ball); and use of space (there may or may not be safety zones).

Like Finnan (1982) and Sluckin (1981), who studied a playground in England, I found that chasing has a gendered structure. Boys frequently chase one another, an activity which often ends in wrestling and mock fights. When girls chase girls, they are usually less physically aggressive; they less often, for example, wrestle one another to the ground.

Cross-sex chasing is set apart by special names— "girls chase the boys"; "boys chase the girls"; "the chase"; "chasers"; "chase and kiss"; "kiss chase"; "kissers and chasers"; "kiss or kill"—and by children's animated talk about the activity. The names vary by region and school, but contain both gender and sexual meanings (this form of play is mentioned, but only briefly analyzed, in Finnan, 1982; Sluckin, 1981; Parrott, 1972; and Borman, 1979).

In "boys chase the girls" and "girls chase the boys" (the names most frequently used in both the California and Michigan schools) boys and girls become, by definition, separate teams. Gender terms override individual identities, especially for the other team ("Help, a girl's chasin' me!"; "C'mon, Sarah, let's get that boy"; "Tony, help save me from the girls"). Individuals may also grab someone of their sex and turn them over to the opposing team: Ryan grabbed Billy from behind, wrestling him to the ground. "Hey, girls, get 'im," Ryan called.

Boys more often mix episodes of cross-sex with same-sex chasing. Girls more often have safety zones, places like the girls' restroom or an area by the school wall, where they retreat to rest and talk (sometimes in animated postmortems) before new episodes of cross-sex chasing begin.

Early in the fall in the Michigan school, where chasing was especially prevalent, I watched a second-grade boy teach a kindergarten girl how to chase. He slowly ran backwards, beckoning her to pursue him, as he called, "Help, a girl's after me." In the early grades chasing mixes with fantasy play, e.g., a first-grade boy who played "sea monster," his arms out-flung and his voice growling, as he chased a group of girls. By third grade, stylized gestures—exaggerated stalking motions, screams (which only girls do), and karate kicks—accompany scenes of chasing.

Names like "chase and kiss" mark the sexual meanings of cross-sex chasing, a theme I return to later. The threat of kissing—most often girls threatening to kiss boys—is a ritualized form of provocation. Cross-sex chasing among sixth-graders involves elaborate patterns of touch and touch avoidance, which adults see as sexual. The principal told the sixth-graders in the Michigan school that they were not to play "pom-pom," a complicated chasing game, because it entailed "inappropriate touch."

Rituals of Pollution Cross-sex chasing is sometimes entwined with rituals of pollution, as in "cooties," where specific individuals or groups are treated as contaminating or carrying "germs." Children have rituals for transferring cooties (usually touching someone else and shouting, "You've got cooties!"), for immunization (e.g., writing "CV" for "cootie vaccination" on their arms), and for eliminating cooties (e.g., saying "no gives" or using "cootie catchers" made of folded paper) (described in Knapp & Knapp, 1976). While girls may give cooties to girls, boys do not generally give cooties to one another (Samuelson, 1980).

In cross-sex play, either girls or boys may be defined as having cooties, which they transfer through chasing and touching. Girls give cooties to boys more often than vice versa. In Michigan, one version of cooties is called "girl stain"; the fourth-graders whom Karkau (1973) describes used the phrase "girl touch." "Cootie queens" or "cootie girls" (there are no "kings" or "boys") are female pariahs, the ultimate school untouchables, seen as contaminating not only by virtue of gender, but also through some added stigma such as being overweight or poor.[2] That girls are seen as more polluting than boys is a significant asymmetry, which echoes cross-cultural patterns, although in other cultures female pollution is generally connected to menstruation and not applied to prepubertal girls.

Invasions Playground invasions are another asymmetric form of borderwork. On a few occasions I saw girls invade and disrupt an all-male game, most memorably a group of tall sixth-grade girls who ran onto the playing field and grabbed a football which was in play. The boys were surprised and frustrated, and, unusual for boys this old, finally tattled to the aide. But in the majority of cases, boys disrupt girls' activities rather than vice versa. Boys grab the ball from girls playing four-square, stick feet into a jump-rope and stop an ongoing game, and dash through the area of the bars where girls are taking turns performing, sending the rings flying. Sometimes boys ask to join a girls' game and then, after a short period of seemingly earnest play, disrupt the game. Two second-grade boys begged to "twirl" the jump rope for a group of second-grade girls who had been jumping for some time. The girls agreed, and the boys began to twirl. Soon, without announcement, the boys changed from "seashells, cockle bells" to "hot peppers" (spinning the rope very fast), and tangled the jumper in the rope. The boys ran away laughing.

Boys disrupt girls' play so often that girls have developed almost ritualized responses: they guard their ongoing play, chase boys away, and tattle to the aides. In a playground cycle which enhances sex segregation, aides who try to spot potential trouble before it occurs sometimes shoo boys away from areas where girls are playing. Aides do not anticipate trouble from girls who seek to join groups of boys, with the exception of girls intent on provoking a chase sequence. And indeed, if they seek access to a boys' game, girls usually play with boys in earnest rather than breaking up the game.

A close look at the organization of borderwork—or boundaried interactions between the sexes—shows that the worlds of boys and girls may be separate, but they are not parallel, nor are they equal. The worlds of girls and boys articulate in several asymmetric ways:

1. On the playground, boys control as much as ten times more space than girls, when one adds up the area of large playing fields and compares it with the much smaller areas where girls predominate. Girls, who play closer to the building, are more often watched over and protected by the adult aides.

2. Boys invade all-female games and scenes of play much more than girls invade boys'. This, and boys' greater control of space, correspond with other findings about the organization of gender, and inequality, in our society: compared with men and boys, women and girls take up less space, and their space and talk are more often violated and interrupted (Greif, 1982; Henley, 1977; West & Zimmerman, 1983).

3. Although individual boys are occasionally treated as contaminating (e.g., a third-grade boy who both boys and girls said was "stinky" and "smelled like pee"), girls are more often defined as polluting. This pattern ties to themes that I discuss later: it is more taboo for a boy to play with (as opposed to invade) girls, and girls are more sexually defined than boys.

A look at the boundaries between the separated worlds of girls and boys illuminates within-sex hierarchies of status and control. For example, in the sex-divided seating in the fourth–fifth-grade classroom, several boys recurringly sat near "female space": their desks were at the gender divide in the classroom, and they were more likely than other boys to sit at a predominantly female table in the lunchroom. These boys—two nonbilingual Chicanos and an overweight "loner" boy who was afraid of sports—were at the bottom of the male hierarchy. Gender is sometimes used as a metaphor for male hierarchies; the inferior status of boys at the bottom is conveyed by calling them "girls." Seven boys and one girl were playing basketball. Two younger boys came over and asked to play. While the girl silently stood, fully accepted in the company of players, one of the older boys disparagingly said to the younger boys, "You girls can't play."[3]

In contrast, the girls who more often travel in the boys' world, sitting with groups of boys in the lunchroom or playing basketball, soccer, and baseball with them, are not stigmatized. Some have fairly high status with other girls. The worlds of girls and boys are asymmetrically arranged, and spatial patterns map out interacting forms of inequality.

Heterosexual Meanings

The organization and meanings of gender (the social categories "woman/man," "girl/boy") and of sexuality vary cross-culturally (Ortner & Whitehead, 1981)—and, in our society, across the life course. Harriet Whitehead (1981) observed that in our (Western) gender system, and that of many traditional North American Indian cultures, one's choice of a sexual object, occupation, and dress and demeanor are closely associated with gender. However, the "center of gravity" differs in the two gender systems. For Indians, occupational pursuits provide the primary imagery of gender; dress and demeanor are secondary, and sexuality is least important. In our system, at least for adults, the order is reversed: heterosexuality is central to our definitions of "man" and "woman" ("masculinity/femininity") and the relationships that obtain between them, whereas occupation and dress/demeanor are secondary.

Whereas erotic orientation and gender are closely linked in our definitions of adults, we define children as relatively asexual. Activities and dress/demeanor are more important than sexuality in the cultural meanings of "girl" and "boy." Children are less heterosexually defined than adults, and we have nonsexual imagery for relations between girls and boys. However, both children and adults sometimes use heterosexual language—"crushes," "like," "goin' with," "girlfriends," and "boyfriends"—to define cross-sex relationships. This language increases through the years of elementary school; the shift to adolescence consolidates a gender system organized around the institution of heterosexuality.

In everyday life in the schools, heterosexual and romantic meanings infuse some ritualized forms of interaction between groups of boys and girls (e.g., "chase and kiss") and help maintain sex segregation. "Jimmy likes Beth" or "Beth likes Jimmy" is a major form of teasing, which a child risks in choosing to sit by or walk with someone of the other sex. The structure of teasing and children's sparse vocabulary for relationships between girls and boys are evident in the following conversation, which I had with a group of third-grade girls in the lunchroom. Susan asked me what I was doing, and I said I was observing the things children do and play. Nicole volunteered, "I like running, boys chase all the girls. See Tim over there? Judy chases him all around the school. She likes him." Judy, sitting across the table, quickly responded, "I hate him. I like him for a friend." "Tim loves Judy," Nicole said in a loud, singsong voice.

In the younger grades, the culture and lore of girls contain more heterosexual romantic themes than those of boys. In Michigan, the first-grade girls often jumped rope to a rhyme which began: "Down in the valley where the green grass grows, there sat Cindy [name of jumper], as sweet as a rose. She sat, she sat, she sat so sweet. Along came Jason and kissed her on the cheek. First comes love, then comes marriage, then along comes Cindy with a baby carriage." Before a girl took her turn at jumping, the chanters asked her, "Who do you want to be your boyfriend?" The jumper always proffered a name, which was accepted matter-of-factly. In chasing, a girl's kiss carried greater threat than a boy's kiss; "girl touch," when defined as contaminating, had sexual connotations. In short, starting at an early age, girls are more sexually defined than boys.

Through the years of elementary school, and increasing with age, the idiom of heterosexuality helps maintain the gender divide. Cross-sex interactions, especially when children initiate them, are fraught with the risk of being teased about "liking" someone of the other sex. I learned of several close cross-sex friendships, formed and maintained in neighborhoods and church, which went underground during the school day.

By the fifth grade a few children began to affirm, rather than avoid, the charge of having a girlfriend or a boyfriend; they introduced the heterosexual courtship rituals of adolescence. In the lunchroom in the Michigan school, as the tables were forming, a high-status fifth-grade boy called out from his seat at the table: "I want Trish to sit by me." Trish came over, and almost like a king and queen, they sat at the gender divide—a row of girls down the table on her side, a row of boys on his. In this situation, which inverted earlier forms, it was not a loss but a gain in status to publicly choose a companion of the other sex. By affirming his choice, the boy became unteasable (note the familiar asymmetry of heterosexual courtship rituals: the male initiates). This incident signals a temporal shift in arrangements of sex and gender.

Traveling in the World of the Other Sex

Contests, invasions, chasing, and heterosexually defined encounters are based upon and reaffirm boundaries between girls and boys. In another type of cross-sex interaction, individuals (or sometimes pairs) cross gender boundaries, seeking acceptance in a group of the other sex. Nearly all the cases I saw of this were tomboys—girls who played organized sports and frequently sat with boys in the cafeteria or classroom. If these girls were skilled at activities central in the boys' world, especially games like soccer, baseball,

and basketball, they were pretty much accepted as participants.

Being a tomboy is a matter of degree. Some girls seek access to boys' groups but are excluded; other girls limit their "crossing" to specific sports. Only a few—such as the tomboy I mentioned earlier, who chose a seat with the boys in the sex-divided fourth-fifth grade—participate fully in the boys' world. That particular girl was skilled at the various organized sports which boys played in different seasons of the year. She was also adept at physical fighting and at using the forms of arguing, insult, teasing, naming, and sports-talk of the boys' subculture. She was the only Black child in her classroom, in a school with only 8 percent Black students; overall that token status, along with unusual athletic and verbal skills, may have contributed to her ability to move back and forth across the gender divide. Her unique position in the children's world was widely recognized in the school. Several times, the teacher said to me, "She thinks she's a boy."

I observed only one boy in the upper grades (a fourth-grader) who regularly played with all-female groups, as opposed to "playing at" girls' games and seeking to disrupt them. He frequently played jump rope and took turns with girls doing tricks on the bars, using the small gestures—for example, a helpful push on the heel of a girl who needed momentum to turn her body around the bar—which mark skillful and earnest participation. Although I never saw him play in other than an earnest spirit, the girls often chased him away from their games, and both girls and boys teased him. The fact that girls seek and have more access to boys' worlds than vice versa, and the fact that girls who travel with the other sex are less stigmatized for it, are obvious asymmetries, tied to the asymmetries previously discussed.

Relaxed Cross-Sex Interactions

Relationships between boys and girls are not always marked by strong boundaries, heterosexual definitions, or interacting on the terms and turfs of the other sex. On some occasions girls and boys interact in relatively comfortable ways. Gender is not strongly salient nor explicitly invoked, and girls and boys are not organized into boundaried collectivities. These "with" occasions have been neglected by those studying gender and children's relationships, who have emphasized either the model of separate worlds (with little attention to their articulation) or heterosexual forms of contact.

Occasions when boys and girls interact without strain, when gender wanes rather than waxes in importance, frequently have one or more of the following characteristics:

1. The situations are organized around an absorbing task, such as a group art project or creating a radio show, which encourages cooperation and lessens attention to gender. This pattern accords with other studies finding that cooperative activities reduce group antagonism (e.g., Sherif & Sherif, 1953, who studied divisions between boys in a summer camp; and Aronson et al., 1978, who used cooperative activities to lessen racial divisions in a classroom).
2. Gender is less prominent when children are not responsible for the formation of the group. Mixed-sex play is less frequent in games like football, which require the choosing of teams, and more frequent in games like handball or dodgeball, which individuals can join simply by getting into a line or a circle. When adults organize mixed-sex encounters—which they frequently do in the classroom and in physical education periods on the playground—they legitimize cross-sex contact. This removes the risk of being teased for choosing to be with the other sex.
3. There is more extensive and relaxed cross-sex interaction when principles of grouping other than gender are explicitly invoked—for example, counting off to form teams for spelling or kickball, dividing lines by hot lunch or cold lunch, or organizing a work group on the basis of interests or reading ability.
4. Girls and boys may interact more readily in less public and crowded settings. Neighborhood play, depending on demography, is more often sex- and age-integrated than play at school, partly because with fewer numbers, one may have to resort to an array of social categories to find play partners or to constitute a game. And in less crowded environments there are fewer potential witnesses to "make something of it" if girls and boys play together.

Relaxed interactions between girls and boys often depend on adults to set up and legitimize the contact.[4] Perhaps because of this contingency—and the other, distancing patterns which permeate relations between girls and boys—the easeful moments of interaction

rarely build to close friendship. Schofield (1981) makes a similar observation about gender and racial barriers to friendship in a junior high school.

IMPLICATIONS FOR DEVELOPMENT

I have located social relations within an essentially spatial framework, emphasizing the organization of children's play, work, and other activities within specific settings and in one type of institution, the school. In contrast, frameworks of child development rely upon temporal metaphors, using images of growth and transformation over time. Taken alone, both spatial and temporal frameworks have shortcomings; fitted together, they may be mutually correcting.

Those interested in gender and development have relied upon conceptualizations of "sex-role socialization" and "sex differences." Sexuality and gender, I have argued, are more situated and fluid than these individualist and intrinsic models imply. Sex and gender are differently organized and defined across situations, even within the same institution. This situational variation (e.g., in the extent to which an encounter heightens or lessens gender boundaries, or is infused with sexual meanings) shapes and constrains individual behavior. Features which a developmental perspective might attribute to individuals and understand as relatively internal attributes unfolding over time may, in fact, be highly dependent on context. For example, children's avoidance of cross-sex friendship may be attributed to individual gender development in middle childhood. But attention to varied situations may show that this avoidance is contingent on group size, activity, adult behavior, collective meanings, and the risk of being teased.

A focus on social organization and situation draws attention to children's experiences in the present. This helps correct a model like "sex-role socialization," which casts the present under the shadow of the future, or presumed "endpoints" (Speier, 1976). A situated analysis of arrangements of sex and gender among those of different ages may point to crucial disjunctions in the life course. In the fourth and fifth grades, culturally defined heterosexual rituals ("goin' with") begin to suppress the presence and visibility of other types of interaction between girls and boys, such as nonsexualized and comfortable interaction and traveling in the world of the other sex. As "boyfriend/girlfriend" definitions spread, the fifth-grade tomboy I described had to work to sustain "buddy" relationships with boys.

Adult women who were tomboys often speak of early adolescence as a painful time when they were pushed away from participation in boys' activities. Other adult women speak of the loss of intense, even erotic ties with other girls when they entered puberty and the rituals of dating, that is, when they became absorbed into the situation of heterosexuality (Rich, 1980). When Lever (1976) describes best-friend relationships among fifth-grade girls as preparation for dating, she imposes heterosexual ideologies onto a present which should be understood on its own terms.

As heterosexual encounters assume more importance, they may alter relations in same-sex groups. For example, Schofield (1981) reports that for sixth- and seventh-grade children in a middle school, the popularity of girls with other girls was affected by their popularity with boys, while boys' status with other boys did not depend on their relations with girls. This is an asymmetry familiar from the adult world; men's relationships with one another are defined through varied activities (occupations, sports), while relationships among women—and their public status—are more influenced by their connections to individual men.

A full understanding of gender and social relations should encompass cross-sex as well as within-sex interactions. "Borderwork" helps maintain separate, gender-linked subcultures, which, as those interested in development have begun to suggest, may result in different milieux for learning. Daniel Maltz and Ruth Borker (1983), for example, argue that because of different interactions within girls' and boys' groups, the sexes learn different rules for creating and interpreting friendly conversation, rules which carry into adulthood and help account for miscommunication between men and women. Carol Gilligan (1982) fits research on the different worlds of girls and boys into a theory of sex differences in moral development. Girls develop a style of reasoning, she argues, which is more personal and relational; boys develop a style which is more positional, based on separateness. Eleanor Maccoby (1982), also following the insight that because of sex segregation, girls and boys grow up in different environments, suggests implications for gender-differentiated prosocial and antisocial behavior.

This separate-worlds approach, as I have illustrated, also has limitations. The occasions when the sexes are together should also be studied, and understood as contexts for experience and learning. For example, asymmetries in cross-sex relationships convey a series of messages: that boys are more entitled to space and to the nonreciprocal right of interrupting or invading the activities of the other sex; that girls are more in need of adult protection, lower in status, more defined by sexuality, and may even be polluting. Different types of cross-sex interaction—relaxed, boundaried, sexualized, or taking place on the terms of the other sex—provide different contexts for development.

By mapping the array of relationships between and within the sexes, one adds complexity to the overly static and dichotomous imagery of separate worlds. Individual experiences vary, with implications for development. Some children prefer same-sex groupings; some are more likely to cross the gender boundary and participate in the world of the other sex; some children (e.g., girls and boys who frequently play "chase and kiss") invoke heterosexual meanings, while others avoid them.

Finally, after charting the terrain of relationships, one can trace their development over time. For example, age variation in the content and form of borderwork, or of cross- and same-sex touch, may be related to differing cognitive, social, emotional, or physical capacities, as well as to age-associated cultural forms. I earlier mentioned temporal shifts in the organization of cross-sex chasing, from mixing with fantasy play in the early grades to more elaborately ritualized and sexualized forms by the sixth grade. There also appear to be temporal changes in same- and cross-sex touch. In kindergarten, girls and boys touch one another more freely than in fourth grade, when children avoid relaxed cross-sex touch and instead use pokes, pushes, and other forms of mock violence, even when the touch clearly expresses affection. This touch taboo is obviously related to the risk of seeming to *like* someone of the other sex. In fourth grade, same-sex touch begins to signal sexual meanings among boys as well as between boys and girls. Younger boys touch one another freely in cuddling (arm around shoulder) as well as mock-violence ways. By fourth grade, when homophobic taunts like "fag" become more common among boys, cuddling touch begins to disappear for boys, but less for girls.

Overall, I am calling for more complexity in our conceptualizations of gender and of children's social relationships. Our challenge is to retain the temporal sweep, looking at individual and group lives as they unfold over time, while also attending to social structure and context and to the full variety of experiences in the present.

ACKNOWLEDGMENTS

I would like to thank Jane Atkinson, Nancy Chodorow, Arlene Daniels, Peter Lyman, Zick Rubin, Malcolm Spector, Avril Thorne, and Margery Wolf for comments on an earlier version of this paper. Conversations with Zella Luria enriched this work.

NOTES

1. I am grateful to Frederick Erickson for suggesting the relevance of Barth's analysis.
2. Sue Samuelson (1980) reports that in a racially mixed playground in Fresno, California, Mexican-American but not Anglo children gave cooties. Racial as well as sexual inequality may be expressed through these forms.
3. This incident was recorded by Margaret Blume, who, for an undergraduate research project in 1982, observed in the California school where I earlier did fieldwork. Her observations and insights enhanced my own, and I would like to thank her for letting me cite this excerpt.
4. Note that in daily school life depending on the individual and the situation, teachers and aides sometimes lessened and at other times heightened sex segregation.

REFERENCES

Aronson, E., et al. 1978. *The Jigsaw Classroom*. Beverly Hills, Calif.: Sage.

Barth, F., ed. 1969. *Ethnic Groups and Boundaries*. Boston: Little, Brown.

Borman, K. M. 1979. "Children's interactions in playgrounds." *Theory into Practice* 18: 251–57.

Eder, D., & Hallinan, M. T. 1978. "Sex differences in children's friendships." *American Sociological Review* 43: 237–50.

Finnan, C. R. 1982. "The ethnography of children's spontaneous play." In G. Spindler, ed., *Doing the Ethnography of Schooling*, pp. 358–80. New York: Holt, Rinehart & Winston.

Foot, H. C., Chapman, A. J., & Smith, J. R. 1980. "Introduction." *Friendship and Social Relations in Children*, pp. 1–14. New York: Wiley.

Gilligan, C. 1982. *In a Different Voice: Psychological Theory and Women's Development*. Cambridge: Harvard University Press.

Glaser, B. G., & Strauss, A. L. 1967. *The Discovery of Grounded Theory*. Chicago: Aldine.

Goffman, E. 1977. "The arrangement between the sexes." *Theory and Society* 4: 301–36.

Goodwin, M. H. 1980. "Directive-response speech sequences in girls' and boys' task activities." In S. McConnell-Ginet, R. Borker, & N. Furman, eds., *Women and Language in Literature and Society*, pp. 157–73. New York: Praeger.

Greif, E. B. 1982. "Sex differences in parent–child conversations." *Women's Studies International Quarterly* 3: 253–58.

Henley, N. 1977. *Body Politics: Power, Sex, and Nonverbal Communication*. Englewood Cliffs, N.J.: Prentice-Hall.

Karkau, K. 1973. *Sexism in the Fourth Grade*. Pittsburgh: KNOW, Inc. (pamphlet).

Katz, J. 1983. "A theory of qualitative methodology: The social system of analytic fieldwork." In R. M. Emerson, ed., *Contemporary Field Research*, pp. 127–48. Boston: Little, Brown.

Knapp, M., & Knapp, H. 1976. *One Potato, Two Potato: The Secret Education of American Children*. New York: W. W. Norton.

Lever, J. 1976. "Sex differences in the games children play." *Social Problems* 23: 478–87.

Maccoby, E. 1982. "Social groupings in childhood: Their relationship to prosocial and antisocial behavior in boys and girls." Paper presented at conference on The Development of Prosocial and Antisocial Behavior, Voss, Norway.

Maccoby, E., & Jacklin, C. 1974. *The Psychology of Sex Differences*. Stanford, Calif.: Stanford University Press.

Maltz, D. N., & Borker, R. A. 1983. "A cultural approach to male–female miscommunication." In J. J. Gumperz, ed., *Language and Social Identity*, pp. 195–216. New York: Cambridge University Press.

McRobbie, A., & Garber, J. 1975. "Girls and subcultures." In S. Hall & T. Jefferson, eds., *Resistance Through Rituals*, pp. 209–23. London: Hutchinson.

Ortner, S. B., & Whitehead, H. 1981. *Sexual Meanings*. New York: Cambridge University Press.

Parrott, S. 1972. "Games children play: Ethnography of a second-grade recess." In J. P. Spradley & D. W. McCurdy, eds., *The Cultural Experience*, pp. 206–19. Chicago: Science Research Associates.

Rich, A. 1980. "Compulsory heterosexuality and lesbian existence." *Signs* 5: 631–60.

Samuelson, S. 1980. "The cooties complex." *Western Folklore* 39: 198–210.

Savin-Williams, R. C. 1976. "An ethological study of dominance formation and maintenance in a group of human adolescents." *Child Development* 47: 972–79.

Schofield, J. W. 1981. "Complementary and conflicting identities: Images and interaction in an interracial school." In S. R. Asher & J. M. Gottman, eds., *The Development of Children's Friendships,* pp. 53–90. New York: Cambridge University Press.

Sherif, M., & Sherif, C. 1953. *Groups in Harmony and Tension.* New York: Harper.

Sluckin, A. 1981. *Growing Up in the Playground.* London: Routledge & Kegan Paul.

Speier, M. 1976. "The adult ideological viewpoint in studies of childhood." In A. Skolnick, ed., *Rethinking Childhood,* pp. 168–86. Boston: Little, Brown.

Sutton-Smith, B. 1971. "A syntax for play and games." In R. E. Herron and B. Sutton-Smith, eds., *Child's Play,* pp. 298–307. New York: Wiley.

Unger, R. K. 1979. "Toward a redefinition of sex and gender." *American Psychologist* 34: 1085–94.

Waldrop, M. F., & Halverson, C. F. 1975. "Intensive and extensive peer behavior: Longitudinal and cross-sectional analysis." *Child Development* 46: 19–26.

West, C., & Zimmerman, D. H. 1983. "Small insults: A study of interruptions in cross-sex conversations between unacquainted persons." In B. Thorne, C. Kramarae, & N. Henley, eds., *Language, Gender, and Society.* Rowley, Mass.: Newbury House.

Whitehead, H. 1981. "The bow and the burden strap: A new look at institutionalized homosexuality in Native America." In S. B. Ortner & H. Whitehead, eds., *Sexual Meanings,* pp. 80–115. New York: Cambridge University Press.

R E A D I N G *20*   *Yen Le Espiritu*

"We Don't Sleep Around Like White Girls Do": Family, Culture, and Gender in Filipina American Lives

First published in 2001

I want my daughters to be Filipino especially on sex. I always emphasize to them that they should not participate in sex if they are not married. We are also Catholic. We are raised so that we don't engage in going out with men while we are not married. And I don't like it to happen to my daughters as if they have no values. I don't like them to grow up that way, like the American girls.

—*Filipina Immigrant Mother*

I found that a lot of the Asian American friends of mine, we don't date like white girls date. We don't sleep around like white girls do. Everyone is really

mellow at dating because your parents were constraining and restrictive.

—*Second-Generation Filipina daughter*

Focusing on the relationship between Filipino immigrant parents and their daughters, this article argues that gender is a key to immigrant identity and a vehicle for racialized immigrants to assert cultural superiority over the dominant group. In immigrant communities, culture takes on a special significance: not only does it form a lifeline to the home country and a basis for group identity in a new country, it is also a base from which immigrants stake their political and sociocultural claims on their new country (Eastmond 1993, 40). For Filipino immigrants, who come from a homeland that was once a U.S. colony, cultural reconstruction has been especially critical in the assertion of their presence in the United States—a way to counter the cultural Americanization of the Philippines, to resist the assimilative and alienating demands of U.S. society, and to reaffirm to themselves their self-worth in the face of colonial, racial, class, and gendered subordination. Before World War II, Filipinos were barred from becoming U.S. citizens, owning property, and marrying whites. They also encountered discriminatory housing policies, unfair labor practices, violent physical encounters, and racist as well as anti-immigrant discourse.[1] While blatant legal discrimination against Filipino Americans is largely a matter of the past, Filipinos continue to encounter many barriers that prevent full participation in the economic, social, and political institutions of the United States (Azores-Gunter 1986–87; Cabezas, Shinagawa, and Kawaguchi 1986–87; Okamura and Agbayani 1997). Moreover, the economic mobility and cultural assimilation that enables white ethnics to become "unhyphenated whites" is seldom extended to Filipino Americans (Espiritu 1994). Like other Asians, the Filipino is "always seen as an immigrant, as the 'foreigner-within,' even when born in the United States" (Lowe 1996, 5). Finally, although Filipinos have been in the United States since the middle of the 1700s and Americans have been in the Philippines since at least the late 1800s, U.S. Filipinos—as racialized nationals, immigrants, and citizens—are "still practically an invisible and silent minority" (San Juan 1991, 117). Drawing from my research on Filipino American families in San Diego, California, I explore in this article the ways racialized immigrants claim through gender the power denied them by racism.

My epigraphs, quotations of a Filipina immigrant mother and a second-generation Filipina daughter, suggest that the virtuous Filipina daughter is partially constructed on the conceptualization of white women as sexually immoral. This juxtaposition underscores the fact that femininity is a relational category, one that is co-constructed with other racial and cultural categories. These narratives also reveal that women's sexuality and their enforced "morality" are fundamental to the structuring of social inequalities. Historically, the sexuality of racialized women has been systematically demonized and disparaged by dominant or oppressor

groups to justify and bolster nationalist movements, colonialism, and/or racism. But as these narratives indicate, racialized groups also criticize the morality of white women as a strategy of resistance—a means of asserting a morally superior public face to the dominant society.

By exploring how Filipino immigrants characterize white families and white women, I hope to contribute to a neglected area of research: how the "margins" imagine and construct the "mainstream" in order to assert superiority over it. But this strategy is not without costs. The elevation of Filipina chastity (particularly that of young women) has the effect of reinforcing masculinist and patriarchal power in the name of a greater ideal of national/ethnic self-respect. Because the control of women is one of the principal means of asserting moral superiority, young women in immigrant families face numerous restrictions on their autonomy, mobility, and personal decision making. Although this article addresses the experiences and attitudes of both parents and children, here I am more concerned with understanding the actions of immigrant parents than with the reactions of their second-generation daughters.

STUDYING FILIPINOS IN SAN DIEGO

San Diego, California has long been a favored area of settlement for Filipinos and is today the third-largest U.S. destination for Filipino immigrants (Rumbaut 1991, 220).[2] As the site of the largest U.S. naval base and the Navy's primary West Coast training facility, San Diego has been a primary area of settlement for Filipino navy personnel and their families since the early 1900s. As in other Filipino communities along the Pacific Coast, the San Diego community grew dramatically in the twenty-five years following passage of the 1965 Immigration Act. New immigration contributed greatly to the tripling of San Diego county's Filipino American population from 1970 to 1980 and its doubling from 1980 to 1990. In 1990, nearly 96,000 Filipinos resided in the county. Although they made up only 4 percent of the county's general population, they constituted close to 50 percent of the Asian American population (Espiritu 1995). Many post-1965 Filipino immigrants have come to San Diego as professionals—most conspicuously as health care workers. A 1992 analysis of the socioeconomic characteristics of recent Filipino immigrants in San Diego indicated that they were predominantly middle-class, college-educated, and English-speaking professionals who were more likely to own than rent their homes (Rumbaut 1994). At the same time, about two-thirds of the Filipinos surveyed indicated that they had experienced racial and ethnic discrimination (Espiritu and Wolf, forthcoming).

The information on which this article is based comes mostly from in-depth interviews that I conducted with almost one hundred Filipinos in San Diego.[3] Using the "snowball" sampling technique, I started by interviewing Filipino Americans whom I knew and then asking them to refer me to others who might be willing to be interviewed. In other words, I chose participants not randomly but rather through a network of Filipino American contacts whom the first group of respondents trusted. To capture the diversity within the Filipino American community, I sought and selected respondents of different backgrounds and with diverse viewpoints. The sample is about equally divided between first-generation immigrants (those who came to the United States as adults) and Filipinas/os who were born and/or raised in the United States. It is more difficult to pinpoint the class status of the people I interviewed. To be sure, they included poor working-class immigrants who barely eked out a living, as well as educated professionals who thrived in middle- and upper-class suburban neighborhoods. However, the class status of most was much more ambiguous. I met Filipinos/as who toiled as assembly workers but who, through the pooling of income and finances, owned homes in middle-class communities. I also discovered that class status was transnational, determined as much by one's economic position in the Philippines as by that in the United States. For example, I encountered individuals who struggled economically in the United States but owned sizable properties in the Philippines. And I interviewed immigrants who continued to view themselves as "upper class" even while living in dire conditions in the United States. These examples suggest that the upper/middle/working-class typology, while useful, does not capture the complexity of immigrant lives. Reflecting the prominence of the U.S. Navy in San Diego, more than half of my respondents were affiliated with or had relatives affiliated with the U.S. Navy.

My tape-recorded interviews, conducted in English, ranged from three to ten hours each and took place in offices, coffee shops, and homes. My questions were open-ended and covered three general areas: family and immigration history, ethnic identity and practices,

and community development among San Diego's Filipinos. The interviewing process varied widely: some respondents needed to be prompted with specific questions, while others spoke at great length on their own. Some chose to cover the span of their lives; others focused on specific events that were particularly important to them. The initial impetus for this article on the relationship between immigrant parents and their daughters came from my observation that the dynamics of gender emerged more clearly in the interviews with women than in those with men. Because gender has been a marked category for women, the mothers and daughters I interviewed rarely told their life stories without reference to the dynamics of gender (see Personal Narratives Group 1989, 4–5). Even without prompting, young Filipinas almost always recounted stories of restrictive gender roles and gender expectations, particularly of parental control over their whereabouts and sexuality.

I believe that my own personal and social characteristics influenced the actual process of data collection, the quality of the materials that I gathered, and my analysis of them. As a Vietnam-born woman who immigrated to the United States at the age of twelve, I came to the research project not as an "objective" outsider but as a fellow Asian immigrant who shared some of the life experiences of my respondents. During the fieldwork process, I did not remain detached but actively shared with my informants my own experiences of being an Asian immigrant woman: of being perceived as an outsider in U.S. society, of speaking English as a second language, of being a woman of color in a racialized patriarchal society, and of negotiating intergenerational tensions within my own family. I do not claim that these shared struggles grant me "insider status" into the Filipino American community; the differences in our histories, cultures, languages, and, at times, class backgrounds, remain important. But I do claim that these shared experiences enable me to bring to the work a comparative perspective that is implicit, intuitive, and informed by my own identities and positionalities—and with it a commitment to approach these subjects with both sensitivity and rigor. In a cogent call for scholars of color to expand on the premise of studying "our own" by studying other "others," Ruby Tapia argues that such implicitly comparative projects are important because they permit us to "highlight the different and *differentiating* functional forces of racialization" (1997, 2). It is with this deep interest in discovering—and forging—

commonalities out of our specific and disparate experiences that I began this study on Filipino Americans in San Diego.

"AMERICAN" AND WHITENESS: "TO ME, AMERICAN MEANS WHITE"

In U.S. racial discourse and practices, unless otherwise specified, "Americans" means "whites" (Lipsitz 1998, 1). In the case of Asian Americans, U.S. exclusion acts, naturalization laws, and national culture have simultaneously marked Asians as the inassimilable aliens and whites as the quintessential Americans (Lowe 1996). Excluded from the collective memory of who constitutes a "real" American, Asians in the United States, even as citizens, remain "foreigners-within"—"non-Americans." In a study of third- and later-generation Chinese and Japanese Americans, Mia Tuan (1998) concludes that, despite being longtime Americans, Asians—as racialized ethnics—are often assumed to be foreign unless proven otherwise. In the case of Filipinos who emigrated from a former U.S. colony, their formation as racialized minorities does not begin in the United States but rather in a "homeland" already affected by U.S. economic, social, and cultural influences (Lowe 1996, 8).

Cognizant of this racialized history, my Filipino respondents seldom identify themselves as American. As will be evident in the discussion below, they equate "American" with "white" and often use these two terms interchangeably. For example, a Filipina who is married to a white American refers to her husband as "American" but to her African American and Filipino American brothers-in-law as "black" and "Filipino," respectively. Others speak about "American ways," "American culture," or "American lifestyle" when they really mean white American ways, culture, and lifestyle. A Filipino man who has lived in the United States for thirty years explains why he still does not identify himself as American: "I don't see myself just as an American because I cannot hide the fact that my skin is brown. To me, American means white." A second-generation Filipina recounted the following story when asked whether she defined herself as American:

I went to an all-white school. I knew I was different. I wasn't American. See, you are not taught that you're American because you are not white. When I was in the tenth grade, our English teacher asked us what our

nationality was, and she goes how many of you are Mexican, how many of you are Filipino, and how many of you are Samoan and things like that. And when she asked how many of you are American, just the white people raised their hands.

Other Asian Americans also conflate *American* and *white*. In an ethnographic study of Asian American high school students, Stacey Lee reports that Korean immigrant parents often instructed their children to socialize only with Koreans and "Americans." When asked to define the term *American,* the Korean students responded in unison with "White! Korean parents like white" (Lee 1996, 24). Tuan (1998) found the same practice among later-generation Chinese and Japanese Americans: the majority use the term *American* to refer to whites.

CONSTRUCTING THE DOMINANT GROUP: THE MORAL FLAWS OF WHITE AMERICANS

Given the centrality of moral themes in popular discussions on racial differences, Michele Lamont (1997) has suggested that morality is a crucial site to study the cultural mechanisms of reproduction of racial inequality. While much has been written on how whites have represented the (im)morality of people of color (Collins 1991; Marchetti 1993; Hamamoto 1994), there has been less critical attention to how people of color have represented whites.[4] Shifting attention from the otherness of the subordinate group (as dictated by the "mainstream") to the otherness of the dominant group (as constructed by the "margins"), this section focuses on the alternative frames of meaning that racially subordinate groups mobilize to (re)define their status in relation to the dominant group. I argue that female morality—defined as women's dedication to their families and sexual restraint—is one of the few sites where economically and politically dominated groups can construct the dominant group as other and themselves as superior. Because womanhood is idealized as the repository of tradition, the norms that regulate women's behaviors become a means of determining and defining group status and boundaries. As a consequence, the burdens and complexities of cultural representation fall most heavily on immigrant women and their daughters. Below, I show that Filipino immigrants claim moral distinctiveness for their community by representing "Americans" as morally flawed, themselves as family-oriented model minorities, and their wives and daughters as paragons of morality.

FAMILY-ORIENTED MODEL MINORITIES: "WHITE WOMEN WILL LEAVE YOU"

In his work on Italian immigrant parents and children in the 1930s, Robert Anthony Orsi (1985) reports that the parents invented a virtuous Italy (based on memories of their childhood) that they then used to castigate the morality of the United States and their U.S.-born or -raised children. In a similar way, many of my respondents constructed their "ethnic" culture as principled and "American" culture as deviant. Most often, this morality narrative revolves around family life and family relations. When asked what set Filipinos apart from other Americans, my respondents—of all ages and class backgrounds—repeatedly contrasted close-knit Filipino families to what they perceived to be the more impersonal quality of U.S. family relations.[5] In the following narratives, "Americans" are characterized as lacking in strong family ties and collective identity, less willing to do the work of family and cultural maintenance, and less willing to abide by patriarchal norms in husband/wife relations:

> American society lacks caring. The American way of life is more individual rather than collective. The American way is to say I want to have my own way. (Filipina immigrant, fifty-four years old)
>
> Our [Filipino] culture is different. We are more close-knit. We tend to help one another. Americans, ya know, they are all right, but they don't help each other that much. As a matter of fact, if the parents are old, they take them to a convalescent home and let them rot there. We would never do that in our culture. We would nurse them; we would help them until the very end. (Filipino immigrant, sixty years old)
>
> Our [Filipino] culture is very communal. You know that your family will always be there, that you don't have to work when you turn eighteen, you don't have to pay rent when you are eighteen, which is the American way of thinking. You also know that if things don't work out in the outside world, you can always come home and mommy and daddy will always take you and your children in. (Second-generation Filipina, thirty-three years old)
>
> Asian parents take care of their children. Americans have a different attitude. They leave their children to

their own resources. They get baby sitters to take care of their children or leave them in day care. That's why when they get old, their children don't even care about them. (Filipina immigrant, forty-six years old)

Implicit in negative depictions of U.S. families as uncaring, selfish, and distant is the allegation that white women are not as dedicated to their families as Filipina women are to theirs. Several Filipino men who married white women recalled being warned by their parents and relatives that "white women will leave you." As one man related, "My mother said to me, 'Well, you know, don't marry a white person because they would take everything that you own and leave you.'" For some Filipino men, perceived differences in attitudes about women's roles between Filipina and non-Filipina women influenced their marital choice. A Filipino American navy man explained why he went back to the Philippines to look for a wife:

> My goal was to marry a Filipina. I requested to be stationed in the Philippines to get married to a Filipina. I'd seen the women here and basically they are spoiled. They have a tendency of not going along together with their husband. They behave differently. They chase the male, instead of the male, the normal way of the traditional way is for the male to go after the female. They have sex without marrying. They want to do their own things. So my idea was to go back home and marry somebody who has never been here. I tell my son the same thing: if he does what I did and finds himself a good lady there, he will be in good hands.

Another man who had dated mostly white women in high school recounted that when it came time for him to marry, he "looked for the kind of women" he met while stationed in the Philippines: "I hate to sound chauvinistic about marriages, but Filipinas have a way of making you feel like you are a king. They also have that tenderness, that elegance. And we share the same values about family, education, religion, and raising children."

The claims of family closeness are not unique to Filipino immigrants. For example, when asked what makes their group distinctive, Italian Americans (di Leonardo 1984), Vietnamese Americans (Kibria 1993), South Asian Americans (Hickey 1996), and African Americans (Lamont 1997) all point proudly to the close-knit character of their family life. Although it is difficult to know whether these claims are actual perceptions or favored self-legitimating answers, it is nevertheless important to note the gender implications of these claims. That is, while both men and women identify the family system as a tremendous source of cultural pride, it is women—through their unpaid housework and kin work—who shoulder the primary responsibility for maintaining family closeness. As the organizers of family rituals, transmitters of homeland folklores, and socializers of young children, women have been crucial for the maintenance of family ties and cultural traditions. In a study of kinship, class, and gender among California Italian Americans, di Leonardo argues that women's kin work, "the work of knitting households together into 'close, extended families,'" maintains the family networks that give ethnicity meaning (1984, 229).

Because the moral status of the community rests on women's labor, women, as wives and daughters, are expected to dedicate themselves to the family. Writing on the constructed image of ethnic family and gender, di Leonardo argues that "a large part of stressing ethnic identity amounts to burdening women with increased responsibilities for preparing special foods, planning rituals, and enforcing 'ethnic' socialization of children" (1984, 222). A twenty-three-year-old Filipina spoke about the reproductive work that her mother performed and expected her to learn:

> In my family, I was the only girl, so my mom expected a lot from me. She wanted me to help her to take care of the household. I felt like there was a lot of pressure on me. It's very important to my mom to have the house in order: to wash the dishes, to keep the kitchen in order, vacuuming, and dusting and things like that. She wants me to be a perfect housewife. It's difficult. I have been married now for about four months and my mother asks me every now and then what have I cooked for my husband. My mom is also very strict about families getting together on holidays, and I would always help her to organize that. Each holiday, I would try to decorate the house for her, to make it more special.

The burden of unpaid reproductive and kin work is particularly stressful for women who work outside the home. In the following narrative, a Filipina wife and mother described the pulls of family and work that she experienced when she went back to school to pursue a doctoral degree in nursing:

> The Filipinos, we are very collective, very connected. Going through the doctoral program, sometimes I think it is better just to forget about my relatives and just concentrate on school. All that connectedness, it steals parts of myself because all of my energies are devoted to my family. And that is the reason why I think Americans are successful. The majority of the American people they can do what they want. They don't feel guilty because they only have a few people to relate to. For us Filipinos, it's like roots under the tree, you have all these connections. The Americans are more like the trunk. I am still trying to go up to the trunk of the tree but it is too hard. I want to be more independent, more like the Americans. I want to be good to my family but what about me? And all the things that I am doing. It's hard. It's always a struggle.

It is important to note that this Filipina interprets her exclusion and added responsibilities as only racial when they are also gendered. For example, when she says, "the American people they can do what they want," she ignores the differences in the lives of white men and white women—the fact that most white women experience similar competing pulls of family, education, and work.

RACIALIZED SEXUALITY AND (IM)MORALITY: "IN AMERICA, . . . SEX IS NOTHING"

Sexuality, as a core aspect of social identity, is fundamental to the structuring of gender inequality (Millett 1970). Sexuality is also a salient marker of otherness and has figured prominently in racist and imperialist ideologies (Gilman 1985; Stoler 1991). Historically, the sexuality of subordinate groups—particularly that of racialized women—has been systematically stereotyped by the dominant groups.[6] At stake in these stereotypes is the construction of women of color as morally lacking in the areas of sexual restraint and traditional morality. Asian women—both in Asia and in the United States—have been racialized as sexually immoral, and the "Orient"—and its women—has long served as a site of European male-power fantasies, replete with lurid images of sexual license, gynecological aberrations, and general perversion (Gilman 1985, 89). In colonial Asia in the nineteenth and early twentieth centuries, for example, female sexuality was a site for colonial rulers to assert their moral superiority and thus their supposed natural and legitimate right to rule. The colonial rhetoric of moral superiority was based on the construction of colonized Asian women as subjects of sexual desire and fulfillment and European colonial women as the paragons of virtue and the bearers of a redefined colonial morality (Stoler 1991). The discourse of morality has also been used to mark the "unassimilability" of Asians in the United States. At the turn of the twentieth century, the public perception of Chinese women as disease-ridden, drug-addicted prostitutes served to underline the depravity of "Orientals" and played a decisive role in the eventual passage of exclusion laws against all Asians (Mazumdar 1989, 3–4). The stereotypical view that all Asian women were prostitutes, first formed in the 1850s, persisted. Contemporary American popular culture continues to endow Asian women with an excess of "womanhood," sexualizing them but also impugning their sexuality (Espiritu 1997, 93).

Filipinas—both in the Philippines and in the United States—have been marked as desirable but dangerous "prostitutes" and/or submissive "mail-order brides" (Halualani 1995; Egan 1996). These stereotypes emerged out of the colonial process, especially the extensive U.S. military presence in the Philippines. Until the early 1990s, the Philippines, at times unwillingly, housed some of the United States's largest overseas airforce and naval bases (Espiritu 1995, 14). Many Filipino nationalists have charged that "the prostitution problem" in the Philippines stemmed from U.S. and Philippine government policies that promoted a sex industry—brothels, bars, and massage parlors— for servicemen stationed or on leave in the Philippines. During the Vietnam War, the Philippines was known as the "rest and recreation" center of Asia, hosting approximately ten thousand U.S. servicemen daily (Coronel and Rosca 1993; Warren 1993). In this context, *all* Filipinas were racialized as sexual commodities, usable and expendable. A U.S.-born Filipina recounted the sexual harassment she faced while visiting Subic Bay Naval Station in Olongapo City:

One day, I went to the base dispensary. . . . I was dressed nicely, and as I walked by the fire station, I heard catcalls and snide remarks being made by some of the firemen. . . . I was fuming inside. The next thing I heard was, "How much do you charge?" I kept on

walking. "Hey, are you deaf or something? How much do you charge? You have a good body." That was an incident that I will never forget. (Quoted in Espiritu 1995, 77)

The sexualized racialization of Filipina women is also captured in Marianne Vilanueva's short story "Opportunity" (1991). As the protagonist, a "mail-order bride" from the Philippines, enters a hotel lobby to meet her American fiancé, the bellboys snicker and whisper *puta* (whore): a reminder that U.S. economic and cultural colonization in the Philippines always forms a backdrop to any relations between Filipinos and Americans (Wong 1993, 53).

Cognizant of the pervasive hypersexualization of Filipina women, my respondents, especially women who grew up near military bases, were quick to denounce prostitution, to condemn sex laborers, and to declare (unasked) that they themselves did not frequent "that part of town." As one Filipina immigrant said,

Growing up [in the Philippines], I could never date an American because my dad's concept of a friendship with an American is with a G.I. The only reason why my dad wouldn't let us date an American is that people will think that the only way you met was because of the base. I have never seen the inside of any of the bases because we were just forbidden to go there.

Many of my respondents also distanced themselves culturally from the Filipinas who serviced U.S. soldiers by branding them "more Americanized" and "more Westernized." In other words, these women were sexually promiscuous because they had assumed the sexual mores of white women. This characterization allows my respondents to symbolically disown the Filipina "bad girl" and, in so doing, to uphold the narrative of Filipina sexual virtuosity and white female sexual promiscuity. In the following narrative, a mother who came to the United States in her thirties contrasted the controlled sexuality of women in the Philippines with the perceived promiscuity of white women in the United States:

In the Philippines, we always have chaperons when we go out. When we go to dances, we have our uncle, our grandfather, and auntie all behind us to make sure that we behave in the dance hall. Nobody goes necking outside. You don't even let a man put his hand on your shoulders. When you were brought up in a conservative country, it is hard to come here and see that it is all freedom of speech and freedom of action. Sex was never mentioned in our generation. I was thirty already when I learned about sex. But to the young generation in America, sex is nothing.

Similarly, another immigrant woman criticized the way young American women are raised: "Americans are so liberated. They allow their children, their girls, to go out even when they are still so young." In contrast, she stated that, in "the Filipino way, it is very important, the value of the woman, that she is a virgin when she gets married."

The ideal "Filipina," then, is partially constructed on the community's conceptualization of white women. She is everything that they are not: she is sexually modest and dedicated to her family; they are sexually promiscuous and uncaring. Within the context of the dominant culture's pervasive hypersexualization of Filipinas, the construction of the "ideal" Filipina—as family-oriented and chaste—can be read as an effort to reclaim the morality of the community. This effort erases the Filipina "bad girl," ignores competing sexual practices in the Filipino communities, and uncritically embraces the myth of "Oriental femininity." Cast as the embodiment of perfect womanhood and exotic femininity, Filipinas (and other Asian women) in recent years have been idealized in U.S. popular culture as more truly "feminine" (i.e., devoted, dependent, domestic) and therefore more desirable than their more modern, emancipated sisters (Espiritu 1997, 113). Capitalizing on this image of the "superfemme," mail-order bride agencies market Filipina women as "'exotic, subservient wife imports' for sale and as alternatives for men sick of independent 'liberal' Western women" (Halualani 1995, 49; see also Ordonez 1997, 122).

Embodying the moral integrity of the idealized ethnic community, immigrant women, particularly young daughters, are expected to comply with male-defined criteria of what constitute "ideal" feminine virtues. While the sexual behavior of adult women is confined to a monogamous, heterosexual context, that of young women is denied completely (see Dasgupta and DasGupta 1996, 229–31). In the next section, I detail the ways Filipino immigrant parents, under the rubric of "cultural preservation," police their daughters' behaviors in order to safeguard their sexual innocence and virginity. These attempts at policing generate hierarchies and tensions within immigrant families— between parents and children and between brothers and sisters.

THE CONSTRUCTION(S) OF THE "IDEAL" FILIPINA: "BOYS ARE BOYS AND GIRLS ARE DIFFERENT"

As the designated "keepers of the culture" (Billson 1995), immigrant women and their behavior come under intensive scrutiny both from men and women of their own groups and from U.S.-born Americans (Gabbacia 1994, xi). In a study of the Italian Harlem community from 1880 to 1950, Orsi reports that "all the community's fears for the reputation and integrity of the domus came to focus on the behavior of young women" (1985, 135). Because women's moral and sexual loyalties were deemed central to the maintenance of group status, changes in female behavior, especially that of growing daughters, were interpreted as signs of moral decay and ethnic suicide and were carefully monitored and sanctioned (Gabbacia 1994, 113).

Although details vary, young women of various groups and across space and time—for example, second-generation Chinese women in San Francisco in the 1920s (Yung 1995), U.S.-born Italian women in East Harlem in the 1930s (Orsi 1985), young Mexican women in the Southwest during the interwar years (Ruiz 1992), and daughters of Caribbean and Asian Indian immigrants on the East Coast in the 1990s (Dasgupta and DasGupta 1996; Waters 1996)—have identified strict parental control on their activities and movements as the primary source of intergenerational conflict. Recent studies of immigrant families also identify gender as a significant determinant of parent-child conflict, with daughters more likely than sons to be involved in such conflicts and instances of parental derogation (Rumbaut and Ima 1988; Woldemikael 1989; Matute-Bianchi 1991; Gibson 1995).

Although immigrant families have always been preoccupied with passing on their native culture, language, and traditions to both male and female children, it is daughters who have the primary burden of protecting and preserving the family. Because sons do not have to conform to the image of an "ideal" ethnic subject as daughters do, they often receive special day-to-day privileges denied to daughters (Haddad and Smith 1996, 22–24; Waters 1996, 75–76). This is not to say that immigrant parents do not place undue expectations on their sons; rather, these expectations do not pivot around the sons' sexuality or dating choices.[7] In contrast, parental control over the movement and action of daughters begins the moment they are perceived as young adults and sexually vulnerable. It regularly consists of monitoring their whereabouts and forbidding dating (Wolf 1997). For example, the immigrant parents I interviewed seldom allowed their daughters to date, to stay out late, to spend the night at a friend's house, or to take an out-of-town trip.

Many of the second-generation women I spoke to complained bitterly about these parental restrictions. They particularly resented what they saw as gender inequity in their families: the fact that their parents placed far more restrictions on their activities and movements than on their brothers'. Some decried the fact that even their younger brothers had more freedom than they did. "It was really hard growing up because my parents would let my younger brothers do what they wanted but I didn't get to do what I wanted even though I was the oldest. I had a curfew and my brothers didn't. I had to ask if I could go places and they didn't. My parents never even asked my brothers when they were coming home." As indicated in the following excerpt, many Filipino males are cognizant of this double standard in their families:

I have that Filipino mentality that boys are boys and girls are different. Girls are supposed to be protected, to be clean. In the early years, my daughters have to have chaperons and curfews. And they know that they have to be virgins until they get married. The girls always say that is not fair. What is the difference between their brothers and them? And my answer

My sister would always say to me, "It's not fair, just because you are a guy, you can go wherever you want." I think my parents do treat me and my sister differently. Like in high school, maybe 10:30 at night, which is pretty late on a school night, and I say I have to go pick up some notes at my friend's house, my parents wouldn't say anything. But if my sister were to do that, there would be no way. Even now when my sister is in college already, if she wants to leave at midnight to go to a friend's house, they would tell her that she shouldn't do it.

When questioned about this double standard, parents generally responded by explaining that "girls are different":

I have that Filipino mentality that boys are boys and girls are different. Girls are supposed to be protected, to be clean. In the early years, my daughters have to have chaperons and curfews. And they know that they have to be virgins until they get married. The girls always say that is not fair. What is the difference between their brothers and them? And my answer

always is, "In the Philippines, you know, we don't do that. The girls stay home. The boys go out." It was the way that I was raised. I still want to have part of that culture instilled in my children. And I want them to have that to pass on to their children.

Even among self-described Western-educated and "tolerant" parents, many continue to ascribe to "the Filipino way" when it comes to raising daughters. As one college-educated father explains,

Because of my Western education, I don't raise my children the way my parents raised me. I tended to be a little more tolerant. But at times, especially in certain issues like dating, I find myself more towards the Filipino way in the sense that I have only one daughter so I tended to be a little bit stricter. So the double standard kind of operates: it's alright for the boys to explore the field but I tended to be overly protective of my daughter. My wife feels the same way because the boys will not lose anything, but the daughter will lose something, her virginity, and it can be also a question of losing face, that kind of thing.

Although many parents discourage or forbid dating for daughters, they still fully expect these young women to fulfill their traditional roles as women: to marry and have children. A young Filipina recounted the mixed messages she received from her parents:

This is the way it is supposed to work: Okay, you go to school. You go to college. You graduate. You find a job. *Then* you find your husband, and you have children. That's the whole time line. *But* my question is, if you are not allowed to date, how are you supposed to find your husband? They say "no" to the whole dating scene because that is secondary to your education, secondary to your family. They do push marriage, but at a later date. So basically my parents are telling me that I should get married and I should have children but that I should not date.

In a study of second-generation Filipino Americans in northern California, Diane Wolf (1997) reports the same pattern of parental pressures: Parents expect daughters to remain virgins until marriage, to have a career, *and* to combine their work lives with marriage and children.

The restrictions on girls' movement sometimes spill over to the realm of academics. Dasgupta and

DasGupta (1996, 230) recount that in the Indian American community, while young men were expected to attend faraway competitive colleges, many of their female peers were encouraged by their parents to go to the local colleges so that they could live at or close to home. Similarly, Wolf (1997, 467) reports that some Filipino parents pursued contradictory tactics with their children, particularly their daughters, by pushing them to achieve academic excellence in high school but then "pulling the emergency brake" when they contemplated college by expecting them to stay at home, even if it meant going to a less competitive college, or not going at all. In the following account, a young Filipina relates that her parents' desire to "protect" her surpassed their concerns for her academic preparation:

> My brother [was] given a lot more opportunity educationally. He was given the opportunity to go to Miller High School that has a renowned college preparatory program but [for] which you have to be bussed out of our area [8] I've come from a college prep program in junior high and I was asked to apply for the program at Miller. But my parents said "No, absolutely not." This was even during the time, too, when Southside [the neighborhood high school] had one of the lowest test scores in the state of California. So it was like, "You know, mom, I'll get a better chance at Miller." "No, no, you're going to Southside. There is no ifs, ands, or buts. Miller is too far. What if something happens to you?" But two years later, when my brother got ready to go on to high school, he was allowed to go to Miller. My sister and I were like, "Obviously, whose education do you value more? If you're telling us that education is important, why do we see a double standard?"

The above narratives suggest that the process of parenting is gendered in that immigrant parents tend to restrict the autonomy, mobility, and personal decision making of their daughters more than that of their sons. I argue that these parental restrictions are attempts to construct a model of Filipina womanhood that is chaste, modest, nurturing, and family-oriented. Women are seen as responsible for holding the cultural line, maintaining racial boundaries, and marking cultural difference. This is not to say that parent-daughter conflicts exist in all Filipino immigrant families. Certainly, Filipino parents do not respond in a uniform way to the challenges of being racial-ethnic minorities, and I met parents who have had to change some of

their ideas and practices in response to their inability to control their children's movements and choices:

> I have three girls and one boy. I used to think that I wouldn't allow my daughters to go dating and things like that, but there is no way I could do that. I can't stop it. It's the way of life here in America. Sometimes you kind of question yourself, if you are doing what is right. It is hard to accept but you got to accept it. That's the way they are here. (Professional Filipino immigrant father)

> My children are born and raised here, so they do pretty much what they want. They think they know everything. I can only do so much as a parent. . . . When I try to teach my kids things, they tell me that I sound like an old record. They even talk back to me sometimes. . . . The first time my daughter brought her boyfriend to the house, she was eighteen years old. I almost passed away, knocked out. Lord, tell me what to do? (Working-class Filipino immigrant mother)

These narratives call attention to the shifts in the generational power caused by the migration process and to the possible gap between what parents say they want for their children and their ability to control the young. However, the interview data do suggest that intergenerational conflicts are socially recognized occurrences in Filipino communities. Even when respondents themselves had not experienced intergenerational tensions, they could always recall a cousin, a girlfriend, or a friend's daughter who had.

SANCTIONS AND REACTIONS: "THAT IS NOT WHAT A DECENT FILIPINO GIRL SHOULD DO"

I do not wish to suggest that immigrant communities are the only ones in which parents regulate their daughters' mobility and sexuality. Feminist scholars have long documented the construction, containment, and exploitation of women's sexuality in various societies (Maglin and Perry 1996). We also know that the cultural anxiety over unbounded female sexuality is most apparent with regard to adolescent girls (Tolman and Higgins 1996, 206). The difference is in the ways immigrant and nonimmigrant families sanction girls' sexuality. To control sexually assertive girls nonimmigrant parents rely on the gender-based good girl/bad girl dichotomy in which "good girls" are passive, threatened sexual objects while "bad girls" are active, desiring sexual agents (Tolman and Higgins 1996). As Dasgupta and DasGupta write, "the two most pervasive images of women across cultures are the goddess and whore, the good and bad women" (1996, 236). This good girl/bad girl cultural story conflates femininity with sexuality, increases women's vulnerability to sexual coercion, and justifies women's containment in the domestic sphere.

Immigrant families, though, have an additional strategy: they can discipline their daughters as racial/national subjects as well as gendered ones. That is, as self-appointed guardians of "authentic" cultural memory, immigrant parents can attempt to regulate their daughters' independent choices by linking them to cultural ignorance or betrayal. As both parents and children recounted, young women who disobeyed parental strictures were often branded "non-ethnic," "untraditional," "radical," "selfish," and "not caring about the family." Female sexual choices were also linked to moral degeneracy, defined in relation to a narrative of a hegemonic white norm. Parents were quick to warn their daughters about "bad" Filipinas who had become pregnant outside marriage.[9] As in the case of "bar girls" in the Philippines, Filipina Americans who veered from acceptable behaviors were deemed "Americanized"—as women who have adopted the sexual mores and practices of white women. As one Filipino immigrant father described "Americanized" Filipinas: "They are spoiled because they have seen the American way. They go out at night. Late at night. They go out on dates. Smoking. They have sex without marrying."

From the perspective of the second-generation daughters, these charges are stinging. The young women I interviewed were visibly pained—with many breaking down and crying—when they recounted their parents' charges. This deep pain, stemming in part from their desire to be validated as Filipina, existed even among the more "rebellious" daughters. One twenty-four-year-old daughter explained:

> My mom is very traditional. She wants to follow the Filipino customs, just really adhere to them, like what is proper for a girl, what she can and can't do, and what other people are going to think of her if she doesn't follow that way. When I pushed these restrictions, when I rebelled and stayed out later than allowed, my mom would always say, "That is not what a decent Filipino girl should do. You should come home at a decent hour. What are people going to think of you?" And that would get me really upset, you know, because I think that my character is very much the way it should be for a Filipina. I wear my hair long, I wear decent makeup. I dress properly, conservative. I am family oriented. It hurts me that she doesn't see that I am decent, that I am proper and that I am not going to bring shame to the family or anything like that.

This narrative suggests that even when parents are unable to control the behaviors of their children, their (dis)approval remains powerful in shaping the emotional lives of their daughters (see Wolf 1997). Although better-off parents can and do exert greater controls over their children's behaviors than do poorer parents (Wolf 1992; Kibria 1993), I would argue that all immigrant parents—regardless of class background—possess this emotional hold on their children. Therein lies the source of their power: As immigrant parents, they have the authority to determine if their daughters are "authentic" members of their racial-ethnic community. Largely unacquainted with the "home" country, U.S.-born children depend on their parents' tutelage to craft and affirm their ethnic self and thus are particularly vulnerable to charges of cultural ignorance and/or betrayal (Espiritu 1994).

Despite these emotional pains, many young Filipinas I interviewed contest and negotiate parental restrictions in their daily lives. Faced with parental restrictions on their mobility, young Filipinas struggle to gain some control over their own social lives, particularly over dating. In many cases, daughters simply misinform their parents of their whereabouts or date without their parents' knowledge. They also rebel by vowing to create more egalitarian relationships with their own husbands and children. A thirty-year-old Filipina who is married to a white American explained why she chose to marry outside her culture:

> In high school, I dated mostly Mexican and Filipino. It never occurred to me to date a white or black guy. I was not attracted to them. But as I kept growing up and my father and I were having all these conflicts, I knew that if I married a Mexican or a Filipino, [he] would be exactly like my father. And so I tried to date anyone that would not remind me of my dad. A lot of my Filipina friends that I grew up with had similar experiences. So I knew that it wasn't only me. I was

determined to marry a white person because he would treat me as an individual.[10]

Another Filipina who was labeled "radical" by her parents indicated that she would be more open-minded in raising her own children: "I see myself as very traditional in upbringing but I don't see myself as constricting on my children one day and I wouldn't put the gender roles on them. I wouldn't lock them into any particular way of behaving." It is important to note that even as these Filipinas desired new gender norms and practices for their own families, the majority hoped that their children would remain connected to Filipino culture.

My respondents also reported more serious reactions to parental restrictions, recalling incidents of someone they knew who had run away, joined a gang, or attempted suicide. A Filipina high-school counselor relates that most of the Filipinas she worked with "are really scared because a lot of them know friends that are pregnant and they all pretty much know girls who have attempted suicide." A 1995 random survey of San Diego public high schools conducted by the federal Centers for Disease Control and Prevention (CDC) found that, in comparison with other ethnic groups, female Filipino students had the highest rates of seriously considering suicide (45.6 percent) as well as the highest rates of actually attempting suicide (23 percent) in the year preceding the survey. In comparison, 33.4 percent of Latinas, 26.2 percent of white women, and 25.3 percent of black women surveyed said they had suicidal thoughts (Lau 1995).

CONCLUSION

Mainstream American society defines white middle-class culture as the norm and whiteness as the unmarked marker of others' difference (Frankenberg 1993). In this article, I have shown that many Filipino immigrants use the largely gendered discourse of morality as one strategy to decenter whiteness and to locate themselves above the dominant group, demonizing it in the process. Like other immigrant groups, Filipinos praise the United States as a land of significant economic opportunity but simultaneously denounce it as a country inhabited by corrupted and individualistic people of questionable morals. In particular, they criticize American family life, American individualism, and American women (see Gabbacia 1994, 113). Enforced by distorting powers of memory and nostalgia, this rhetoric of moral superiority often leads to patriarchal calls for a cultural "authenticity" that locates family honor and national integrity in the group's female members. Because the policing of women's bodies is one of the main means of asserting moral superiority, young women face numerous restrictions on their autonomy, mobility, and personal decision making. This practice of cultural (re)construction reveals how deeply the conduct of private life can be tied to larger social structures.

The construction of white Americans as the "other" and American culture as deviant serves a dual purpose: It allows immigrant communities both to reinforce patriarchy through the sanctioning of women's (mis)behavior and to present an unblemished, if not morally superior, public face to the dominant society. Strong in family values, heterosexual morality, and a hierarchical family structure, this public face erases the Filipina "bad girl" and ignores competing (im)moral practices in the Filipino communities. Through the oppression of Filipina women and the denunciation of white women's morality, the immigrant community attempts to exert its moral superiority over the dominant Western culture and to reaffirm to itself its self-worth in the face of economic, social, political, and legal subordination. In other words, the immigrant community uses restrictions on women's lives as one form of resistance to racism. This form of cultural resistance, however, severely restricts the lives of women, particularly those of the second generation, and it casts the family as a potential site of intense conflict and oppressive demands in immigrant lives.

ACKNOWLEDGMENTS

I gratefully acknowledge the many useful suggestions and comments of George Lipsitz, Vince Rafael, Lisa Lowe, Joane Nagel, Diane Wolf, Karen Pyke, and two anonymous reviewers for *Signs*. I also would like to thank all those Filipinos/as who participated in this study for their time, help, and insights into immigrant lives.

NOTES

1. Cordova 1983; Sharma 1984; Scharlin and Villanueva 1992; Jung 1999.

2. Filipino settlement in San Diego dates back to 1903, when a group of young Filipino *pensionados* enrolled at the State Normal School (now San Diego State University).

3. My understanding of Filipino American lives is also based on the many conversations I have had with my Filipino American students at the University of California, San Diego, and with Filipino American friends in the San Diego area and elsewhere.

4. A few studies have documented the ways racialized communities have represented white Americans. For example, in his anthropological work on Chicano joking, José Limón (1982) reports that young Mexican Americans elevate themselves over whites through the telling of "Stupid-American" jokes in which an Anglo American is consistently duped by a Mexican character. In her interviews with African American working-class men, Michele Lamont (1997) finds that these men tend to perceive Euro Americans as immoral, sneaky, and not to be trusted. Although these studies provide an interesting and compelling window into racialized communities' views of white Americans, they do not analyze how the rhetoric of moral superiority often depends on gender categories.

5. Indeed people around the world often believe that Americans have no real family ties. For example, on a visit to my family in Vietnam, my cousin asked me earnestly if it was true that American children put their elderly parents in nursing homes instead of caring for them at home. She was horrified at this practice and proclaimed that, because they care for their elders, Vietnamese families are morally superior to American families.

6. Writing on the objectification of black women, Patricia Hill Collins (1991) argues that popular representations of black females—mammy, welfare queen, and Jezebel—all pivot around their sexuality, either desexualizing or hypersexualizing them. Along the same line, Native American women have been portrayed as sexually excessive (Green 1975), Chicana women as "exotic and erotic" (Mirande 1980), and Puerto Rican and Cuban women as "tropical bombshells, . . . sexy, sexed and interested" (Tafolla 1985, 39).

7. The relationship between immigrant parents and their sons deserves an article of its own. According to Gabbacia, "Immigrant parents fought with sons, too, but over different issues: parents' complaints about rebellious sons focused more on criminal activity than on male sexuality or independent courtship" (1994, 70). Moreover, because of their mobility, young men have more means to escape—at least temporarily—the pressures of the family than young women. In his study of Italian American families, Orsi reports that young men rebelled by sleeping in cars or joining the army, but young women did not have such opportunities (1985, 143).

8. The names of the two high schools in this excerpt are fictitious.

9. According to a 1992 health assessment report of Filipinos in San Francisco, Filipino teens have the highest pregnancy rates among all Asian groups and, in 1991, the highest rate of increase in the number of births as compared with all other racial or ethnic groups (Tiongson 1997, 257).

10. The few available studies on Filipino American intermarriage indicate a high rate relative to other Asian groups. In 1980, Filipino men in California recorded the highest intermarriage rate among all Asian groups, and Filipina women had the second-highest rate, after Japanese American women (Agbayani-Siewert and Revilla 1995, 156).

REFERENCES

Agbayani-Siewert, Pauline, and Linda Revilla. 1995. "Filipino Americans." In *Asian Americans: Contemporary Trends and Issues,* ed. Pyong Gap Min, 134–68. Thousand Oaks, Calif.: Sage.

Azores-Gunter, Tania Fortunata M. 1986–87. "Educational Attainment and Upward Mobility: Prospects for Filipino Americans." *Amerasia Journal* 13(1):39–52.

Billson, Janet Mancini. 1995. *Keepers of the Culture: The Power of Tradition in Women's Lives.* New York: Lexington.

Cabezas, Amado, Larry H. Shinagawa, and Gary Kawaguchi. 1986–87. "New Inquiries into the Socioeconomic Status of Pilipino Americans in California." *Amerasia Journal* 13(1):1–21.

Collins, Patricia Hill. 1991. *Black Feminist Thought: Knowledge, Consciousness, and the Politics of Empowerment.* New York: Routledge.

Cordova, Fred. 1983. *Filipinos: Forgotten Asian Americans, a Pictorial Essay, 1763–1963.* Dubuque, Iowa: Kendall/ Hunt.

Coronel, Sheila, and Ninotchka Rosca. 1993. "For the Boys: Filipinas Expose Years of Sexual Slavery by the U.S. and Japan." *Ms.,* November/December, 10–15.

Dasgupta, Shamita Das, and Sayantani DasGupta. 1996. "Public Face, Private Space: Asian Indian Women and Sexuality." In *"Bad Girls/Good Girls": Women, Sex, and Power in the Nineties,* ed. Nan Bauer Maglin and Donna Perry, 226–43. New Brunswick, N.J.: Rutgers University Press.

di Leonardo, Micaela. 1984. *The Varieties of Ethnic Experience: Kinship, Class, and Gender Among California Italian-Americans.* Ithaca, N.Y.: Cornell University Press.

Eastmond, Marita. 1993. "Reconstructing Life: Chilean Refugee Women and the Dilemmas of Exile." In *Migrant Women: Crossing Boundaries and Changing Identities,* ed. Gina Buijs, 35–53. Oxford: Berg.

Egan, Timothy. 1996. "Mail-Order Marriage, Immigrant Dreams and Death." *New York Times,* May 26, 12.

Espiritu, Yen Le. 1994. "The Intersection of Race, Ethnicity, and Class: The Multiple Identities of Second Generation Filipinos." *Identities* 1(2–3):249–73.

———. 1995. *Filipino American Lives.* Philadelphia: Temple University Press.

———. 1997. *Asian American Women and Men: Labor, Laws, and Love.* Thousand Oaks, Calif.: Sage.

Espiritu, Yen Le, and Diane L. Wolf. Forthcoming. "The Paradox of Assimilation: Children of Filipino Immigrants in San Diego." In *Ethnicities: Children of Immigrants in America,* ed. Ruben Rumbaut and Alejandro Portes. Berkeley: University of California Press; New York: Russell Sage Foundation.

Frankenberg, Ruth. 1993. *White Women, Race Matters: The Social Construction of Whiteness.* Minneapolis: University of Minnesota Press.

Gabbacia, Donna. 1994. *From the Other Side: Women, Gender, and Immigrant Life in the U.S., 1820–1990.* Bloomington: Indiana University Press.

Gibson, Margaret A. 1995. "Additive Acculturation as a Strategy for School Improvement." In *California's Immigrant Children: Theory, Research, and Implications for Educational Policy,* ed. Ruben Rumbaut and Wayne A. Cornelius, 77–105. La Jolla: Center for U.S.-Mexican Studies, University of California, San Diego.

Gilman, Sander L. 1985. *Difference and Pathology: Stereotypes of Sexuality, Race, and Madness.* Ithaca, N.Y.: Cornell University Press.

Green, Rayna. 1975. "The Pocahontas Perplex: The Image of Indian Women in American Culture." *Massachusetts Review* 16(4):698–714.

Haddad, Yvonne Y., and Jane I. Smith. 1996. "Islamic Values Among American Muslims." In *Family and Gender Among American Muslims: Issues Facing Middle Eastern Immigrants and Their Descendants,* ed. Barbara C. Aswad and Barbara Bilge, 19–40. Philadelphia: Temple University Press.

Halualani, Rona Tamiko. 1995. "The Intersecting Hegemonic Discourses of an Asian Mail-Order Bride Catalog: Pilipina 'Oriental Butterfly' Dolls for Sale." *Women's Studies in Communication* 18(1):45–64.

Hamamoto, Darrell Y. 1994. *Monitored Peril: Asian Americans and the Politics of Representation.* Minneapolis: University of Minnesota Press.

Hickey, M. Gail. 1996. "'Go to College, Get a Job, and Don't Leave the House Without Your Brother': Oral Histories with Immigrant Women and Their Daughters." *Oral History Review* 23(2):63–92.

Jung, Moon-Kie. 1999. "No Whites: No Asians: Race, Marxism and Hawaii's Pre-emergent Working Class." *Social Science History* 23(3):357–93.

Kibria, Nazli. 1993. *Family Tightrope: The Changing Lives of Vietnamese Immigrant Community.* Princeton, N.J.: Princeton University Press.

Lamont, Michele. 1997. "Colliding Moralities Between Black and White Workers." In *From Sociology to Cultural Studies: New Perspectives,* ed. Elisabeth Long, 263–85. New York: Blackwell.

Lau, Angela. 1995. "Filipino Girls Think Suicide at Number One Rate." *San Diego Union-Tribune,* February 11, A-1.

Lee, Stacey J. 1996. *Unraveling the "Model Minority" Stereotype: Listening to Asian American Youth.* New York: Teachers College Press.

Limón, José E. 1982. "History, Chicano Joking, and the Varieties of Higher Education: Tradition and Performance as Critical Symbolic Action." *Journal of the Folklore Institute* 19(2/3):141–66.

Lipsitz, George. 1998. *The Possessive Investment in Whiteness: How White People Profit from Identity Politics.* Philadelphia: Temple University Press.

Lowe, Lisa. 1996. *Immigrant Acts: On Asian American Cultural Politics.* Durham, N.C.: Duke University Press.

Maglin, Nan Bauer, and Donna Perry. 1996. "Introduction." In *"Bad Girls/Good Girls": Women, Sex, and Power in the Nineties,* ed. Nan Bauer Maglin and Donna Perry, xiii–xxvi. New Brunswick, N.J.: Rutgers University Press.

Marchetti, Gina. 1993. *Romance and the "Yellow Peril": Race, Sex, and Discursive Strategies in Hollywood Fiction.* Berkeley: University of California Press.

Matute-Bianchi, Maria Eugenia. 1991. "Situational Ethnicity and Patterns of School Performance among Immigrant and Nonimmigrant Mexican-Descent Students." In *Minority Status and Schooling: A Comparative Study of Immigrant and Involuntary Minorities,* ed. Margaret A. Gibson and John U. Ogbu, 205–47. New York: Garland.

Mazumdar, Suchetta. 1989. "General Introduction: A Woman-Centered Perspective on Asian American History." In *Making Waves: An Anthology by and About Asian American Women,* ed. Asian Women United of California, 1–22. Boston: Beacon.

Millett, Kate. 1970. *Sexual Politics.* Garden City, N.Y.: Doubleday.

Mirande, Alfredo. 1980. "The Chicano Family: A Reanalysis of Conflicting Views." In *Rethinking Marriage, Child Rearing, and Family Organization,* ed. Arlene S. Skolnick and Jerome H. Skolnick, 479–93. Berkeley: University of California Press.

Okamura, Jonathan, and Amefil Agbayani. 1997. "*Pamantasan:* Filipino American Higher Education." In *Filipino Americans: Transformation and Identity,* ed. Maria P. Root, 183–97. Thousand Oaks, Calif.: Sage.

Ordonez, Raquel Z. 1997. "Mail-Order Brides: An Emerging Community." In *Filipino Americans: Transformation and Identity,* ed. Maria P. Root, 121–42. Thousand Oaks, Calif.: Sage.

Orsi, Robert Anthony. 1985. *The Madonna of 115th Street: Faith and Community in Italian Harlem, 1880–1950*. New Haven, Conn.: Yale University Press.

Personal Narratives Group. 1989. "Origins." In *Interpreting Women's Lives: Feminist Theory and Personal Narratives*, ed. Personal Narratives Group, 3–15. Bloomington: Indiana University Press.

Ruiz, Vicki L. 1992. "The Flapper and the Chaperone: Historical Memory among Mexican-American Women." In *Seeking Common Ground: Multidisciplinary Studies*, ed. Donna Gabbacia. Westport, Conn.: Greenwood.

Rumbaut, Ruben. 1991. "Passages to America: Perspectives on the New Immigration." In *America at Century's End*, ed. Alan Wolfe, 208–44. Berkeley: University of California Press.

———. 1994. "The Crucible Within: Ethnic Identity, Self-Esteem, and Segmented Assimilation Among Children of Immigrants." *International Migration Review* 28(4):748–94.

Rumbaut, Ruben, and Kenji Ima. 1988. *The Adaptation of Southeast Asian Refugee Youth: A Comparative Study*. Washington, D.C.: U.S. Office of Refugee Resettlement.

San Juan, E., Jr. 1991. "Mapping the Boundaries: The Filipino Writer in the U.S." *Journal of Ethnic Studies* 19(1):117–31.

Scharlin, Craig, and Lilia V. Villanueva. 1992. *Philip Vera Cruz: A Personal History of Filipino Immigrants and the Farmworkers Movement*. Los Angeles: University of California, Los Angeles Labor Center, Institute of Labor Relations, and Asian American Studies Center.

Sharma, Miriam. 1984. "Labor Migration and Class Formation among the Filipinos in Hawaii, 1906–46." In *Labor Immigration Under Capitalism: Asian Workers in the United States Before World War II*; ed. Lucie Cheng and Edna Bonacich, 579–611. Berkeley: University of California Press.

Stoler, Ann Laura. 1991. "Carnal Knowledge and Imperial Power: Gender, Race, and Morality in Colonial Asia." In *Gender at the Crossroads of Knowledge: Feminist Anthropology in the Postmodern Era*, ed. Micaela di Leonardo, 51–104. Berkeley: University of California Press.

Tafolla, Carmen. 1985. *To Split a Human: Mitos, Machos y la Mujer Chicana*. San Antonio, Tex.: Mexican American Cultural Center.

Tapia, Ruby. 1997. "Studying Other 'Others.'" Paper presented at the Association of Pacific Americans in Higher Education, San Diego, Calif., May 24.

Tiongson, Antonio T., Jr. 1997. "Throwing the Baby out with the Bath Water." In *Filipino Americans: Transformation and Identity*, ed. Maria P. Root, 257–71. Thousand Oaks, Calif.: Sage.

Tolman, Deborah L., and Tracy E. Higgins. 1996. "How Being a Good Girl Can Be Bad for Girls." In *"Bad Girls/Good Girls": Women, Sex, and Power in the Nineties*, ed. Nan Bauer Maglin and Donna Perry, 205–25. New Brunswick, N.J.: Rutgers University Press.

Tuan, Mia. 1998. *Forever Foreigners or Honorary Whites? The Asian Ethnic Experience Today*. New Brunswick, N.J.: Rutgers University Press.

Villanueva, M. 1991. *Ginseng and Other Tales from Manila*. Corvallis, Oreg.: Calyx.

Warren, Jenifer. 1993. "Suit Asks Navy to Aid Children Left in Philippines." *Los Angeles Times*, March 5, A3.

Waters, Mary C. 1996. "The Intersection of Gender, Race, and Ethnicity in Identity Development of Caribbean American Teens." In *Urban Girls: Resisting Stereotypes, Creating. Identities*, ed. Bonnie J. Ross Leadbeater and Niobe Way, 65–81. New York: New York University Press.

Woldemikael, T. M. 1989. *Becoming Black American: Haitians and American Institutions in Evanston, Illinois*. New York: AMS Press.

Wolf, Diane L. 1992. *Factory Daughters: Gender; Household Dynamics, and Rural Industrialization in Java*. Berkeley: University of California Press.

———. 1997. "Family Secrets: Transnational Struggles Among Children of Filipino Immigrants." *Sociological Perspectives* 40(3):457–82.

Wong, Sau-ling. 1993. *Reading Asian American Literature: From Necessity to Extravagance*. Princeton, N.J.: Princeton University Press.

Yung, Judy. 1995. *Unbound Feet: A Social History of Chinese Women in San Francisco*. Berkeley: University of California Press.

PART THREE

SOCIAL ORGANIZATION OF GENDER

The processes of gender socialization that begin in early childhood prepare us for participation in society as adult women and men. Socialization alone, however, cannot account for the differences in power and prestige between men and women in almost all societies. Gender encompasses more than the socialized differences between individual women and men. As Judith Lorber points out in Section 2, gender also affects the way that social institutions—from family to medicine to politics—are structured. Key to feminist analyses is an understanding of the role of a society's institutions in perpetuating gender inequality.

Like other forms of social inequality, gender inequality includes the unequal distribution of three different kinds of valued commodities. First, inequality entails differential access to power, defined as the ability to carry out one's will despite opposition. Second, inequality includes differential access to the sources of prestige, defined as the ability to command respect, honor, and deference. Third, differential access to wealth, or economic and material resources, is central to inequality. Those who have access to any one of these resources—power, prestige, or wealth—occupy a position from which they are likely to gain access to the others and thereby reinforce their status over those who have less. In the case of gender-stratified social systems, men's greater access to power, prestige, and wealth enhances their opportunities in relationship to women of their social group.

Of course, not all men have equal access to power, prestige, or wealth. Men of subordinated racial or ethnic groups, working-class and poor men, disabled men, transsexual and transgendered men, and many gay or old men are also excluded from socially sanctioned sources of power, prestige, and wealth. Women, too, vary in their degree of access

to power, prestige, and wealth; white or upper-class women receive benefits from their class and race. As we have seen, gender is one system of domination that interacts with other systems based on race, class, ethnicity, sexuality, nationality, and ability. The task of feminist scholars is to trace the intersections of gender and other systems of domination, examining the varied ways that gender inequality is expressed and reinforced in social institutions.

Institutions construct systems of inequality in a variety of ways. Economic and legal systems; political, educational, medical, religious, and familial institutions; mass media; and the institutions of science and technology—all reinforce the ideology of women's inferiority and preserve men's greater access to power, prestige, and wealth. How? The structures of institutions are gendered in that they privilege men and those traits labeled masculine, and penalize women and the traits labeled feminine. Such institutions engage in practices that discriminate against women, exclude or devalue women's perspectives, and perpetuate the idea that differences between women and men and the dominance of men are natural. In addition, the control of these institutions usually rests in the hands of men, and as social scientists understand, dominant groups tend to behave in ways that enhance their own power.

Some institutions operate in quite subtle ways. For example, a complex social system throughout much of the world—what feminist poet and scholar Adrienne Rich called "compulsory heterosexuality"—exerts strong pressures on women to enter into heterosexual marriages. In the United States, families train daughters to be wives and mothers; high school events encourage opposite-sex dates; college fraternities and sororities promote heterosexual coupling; widespread violence against women encourages them, ironically, to seek male protection; and men's higher incomes mean that heterosexual marriage tends to improve a woman's standard of living.

A woman's failure to marry constitutes a violation of social prescriptions and often leaves her economically disadvantaged and socially suspect. On the other hand, despite women's increasing participation in the paid labor force, in heterosexual marriage the burden of care work—raising children and attending to the home—still usually falls disproportionately on women, a dynamic that helps maintain the inequality between men and women in the work world.

It is important to reiterate that gender stratification is not the only form of inequality affecting women's and men's lives and the structure of social institutions. Institutions that disadvantage racial or ethnic groups, sexual minorities, older people, people with disabilities, the poor, or particular religious or class-based groups also discriminate against both women and men who belong to those groups. Understanding women's oppression as a function of the social organization of gender necessitates understanding the intersectionality of systems of domination.

The following articles examine how particular institutions express, construct, and maintain gender inequality. They analyze the ways that women's subordination is maintained in work, families, sexuality, treatment of and attitudes about bodies, and violence against women. The articles do not simply document women's inequality, however. They also describe the ways that women and men in various groups resist oppression and attempt to exercise control over their choices and their lives. To what extent are women and men able to resist the structures of gender, and to what extent are they controlled by gendered institutions?

SECTION 5

Work

Work for pay influences many aspects of our lives: our economic prosperity, our social status, our residence, our relationships with family members and friends, our health, and our access to health care. Our work experiences influence how we come to view others, ourselves, and the social world around us. Reciprocally, how we are situated in society often influences the kind of work we do and our compensation for that work.

A division of labor based on sex—some tasks defined as "men's work" and others as "women's work"—does not necessarily mean that one kind of work is considered more important than the other. But in contemporary industrialized societies, as well as earlier economic forms, social divisions of labor based on gender, race, ethnicity, age, and other factors reflect and perpetuate power differences among groups. As we have already seen in Section 1, "Diversity and Difference," and Section 2, "Theoretical Perspectives," gender is profoundly shaped by class, race, and ethnicity in ways that are especially critical in the realm of work.

This section begins with Christine Bose and Rachel Whaley's exploration of the continued concentration of women in predominantly female and men in predominantly male occupations. The most common occupations for women include secretary, cashier, and nurse, while truck drivers and carpenters are almost always men. In "Sex Segregation in the U.S. Labor Force," Bose and Whaley discuss the different ways of measuring sex segregation; the nature of sex segregation in white-collar, pink-collar, clerical, and blue-collar jobs; and the various explanations for the persistence of sex segregation into the twenty-first century. They also argue that sex segregation matters: It is a cause of inequities

in earnings (see Nancy Whittier's table on earnings) and leads to tokenism and lack of occupational mobility. Thinking about the people you know, how many are in non-sex-segregated jobs? Are the jobs that you and your friends hold and hope to move into in the future gendered? What factors hinder people from finding work outside the traditional gender-appropriate occupations? How important is outright discrimination compared to people's socialization? What do you think can be done to end sex segregation in the labor force?

The next article in this section looks at a form of gendered and embodied labor that can be found in Korean nail salons across the country. Class, race, and ethnicity are central to Miliann Kang's story, not just in terms of the characteristics of the labor force but also with regard to the style of "body labor" expected by clients. In her rich ethnographic study, Kang differentiates white upper- and middle-class women's interest in pampering from black working-class women's preference for technical skill from the expectation of efficiency at a reasonable price on the part of the clients of a mixed-race, midlevel salon. What do the different interests of manicurists' clients tell us about racialized gender? What other jobs involve "body labor"? What does Kang see as positive about the interactions among women that she documents?

Sex segregation and racial-ethnic patterns of employment are also at the heart of Pierrette Hondagneu-Sotelo's "Maid in L.A.," a study of Latina domestic workers in Los Angeles. Talking with immigrant women, mostly from Latin America, who work as live-in and live-out nannies and housekeepers and as housecleaners, Hondagneu-Sotelo learns why they choose particular kinds of jobs at different times. New immigrants without the support of family and friends must often take jobs as live-ins, the least desirable position because of the lack of privacy, social isolation, long hours, incessant demands, and low pay. We hear how these Latina women feel about the houses they must clean, the children they care for, and the food (or lack thereof) their employers provide. We understand why, as soon as they can, women choose to work on a live-out basis, in their own homes and communities, and why some choose housecleaning as the most autonomous job.

Hondagneu-Sotelo puts these women's experiences into the context of immigration, transnational motherhood, and racial stereotyping. Like Kang's manicurists, Hondagneu-Sotelo's domestic workers are part of a global economy that is shaped by gender, class, and race/ethnicity. In what ways are the domestics similar to manicurists in New York? In what ways are they different? What determines whether domestic workers see their jobs as good jobs? Think about the relationship between their lives and the lives of the women who employ them. What do the experiences of Latina domestics tell us about why a living wage is a women's issue?

In the last article in this section, we turn to another kind of care work with the same kind of racialized and gendered nature as domestic work. As families become less able to care for elders and the disabled in the home, a population of poorly paid people, mostly black, Latina, and immigrant women, have taken up the slack. Jennifer Klein and Eileen Boris, in a piece originally published online, explain how, in the United States, what was once the private work of women has become a fast-growing occupation. Beginning in the New Deal in the 1930s, the government hired unemployed poor women to help care for old people in their homes, relieving some of the burden on overcrowded hospitals. Such home care has always been excluded, in the United States, from the protections accorded other kinds of work, such as minimum wage and overtime laws, old-age insurance, unemployment benefits, and the right to collective bargaining. Increasingly, work as a "home health attendant" has come to substitute for welfare benefits as the government cuts back social services. As with immigrant domestic workers, home care workers end up leaving their own families to care for the members of others. Despite all the odds against them, however, home care workers are increasingly organizing to win union recognition and an improvement in their pay and conditions of work.

How does the system of home care in the United States illustrate the intersectionality of gender, race, and class? What historical and contemporary developments in the United States contribute to a situation in which poor women care for the elderly and disabled in someone else's home? Who cares for the elderly in your family? What kinds of policies might improve the situation for everyone?

As these articles demonstrate, women's race, ethnicity, nationality, age, and social class affect both the structural opportunities available to them in the labor force and their interpretations of these experiences. What experiences, if any, do you think women in the labor force share by virtue of their gender?

READING *21* **Christine E. Bose**
Rachel Bridges Whaley[1]

Sex Segregation in the U.S. Labor Force

First published in 2001

Sex segregation in the workplace is manifested in many ways—in the extent to which women and men are concentrated in different industries, establishments, occupations, and jobs, and in the extent to which any particular job is dominated by workers of one sex. An occupation is usually considered female or male dominated if it is at least 75 percent female or male. For example, 7 of the 10 most common occupations for women are dominated by female workers including secretary (98 percent), cashier (78 percent), and registered nurse (93 percent) (Women's Bureau 1999) (see Table 1). Similarly, the majority of the most common occupations for men are male dominated, such as truck

driver (94 percent) and carpenter (98 percent) (U.S. Census Bureau 1998a) (see Table 2). The only occupation among the top 10 (largest numbers) for both men and women is miscellaneous salaried manager, which is 70 percent male (Women's Bureau 1999). Such occupational "integration" is rare and its positive effects are frequently diluted because the particular jobs offered by employers or firms are sex segregated.

Occupational segregation may entail the physical separation of workers of different social groups (sex and racial or ethnic groups). For example, between 1920 and 1940 in North Carolina's tobacco industry, workers were

TABLE 1   TEN MOST COMMON OCCUPATIONS FOR WOMEN, 1998

Women's Common Occupations[1]	Percent Women
Secretaries	98
Cashiers	78
Managers and administrators, n.e.c.[1]	30
Sales supervisors and proprietors	40
Registered nurses	93
Nursing aides, orderlies, and attendants	89
Elementary school teachers	84
Bookkeepers, accounting clerks	93
Waiters and waitresses	78
Sales workers, other commodities[2]	68
Average labor-force occupation	46

[1]Not elsewhere classified or miscellaneous.
[2]Includes foods, drugs, health, and other commodities.

TABLE 2   TEN MOST COMMON OCCUPATIONS FOR MEN, 1998

Men's Common Occupations	Percent Women
Managers and administrators, n.e.c.	30
Truck drivers	5
Sales supervisors and proprietors	40
Construction laborers	16
Freight, stock, and material handlers	24
Janitors and cleaners	35
Fabricators and assemblers	33
Carpenters	1
Cooks	41
Sales representatives, commodities, wholesale	26

Source: U.S. Census, Statistical Abstract accessed on 4/10/00 at http://www.census.gov/prod/99pubs/99statab/sec13.pdf
Note: Occupational categories drawn from this source are slightly less detailed than those for women's occupations.

physically separated and segregated into sex-typed and race-typed tasks. Black women tobacco workers were located in one building or on one floor, designed for "dirty" prefabrication work such as stripping the leaves, and white women were in another building or on another floor, inspecting and packing the product. Meanwhile black men hauled materials between locales and white men acted as supervisors and inspectors (Jones 1984). A more recent example can be found in the baking industry. Female bakers are located in retail establishments (e.g., supermarkets) while men make up the majority of wholesale bakers (Steiger and Reskin 1990).

The sex segregation of any occupation can change over time, even while the segregation of the entire labor force remains fairly stable. Occupations are more likely to shift from male to female domination than the reverse. Public-school teaching made this transition in the late nineteenth century; clerical workers, telephone operators, waiters and waitresses, and bank tellers were resegregated by the middle of the twentieth century from male to female jobs. More recently, residential real estate sales and pharmacy work have become female dominated. Women have made significant inroads into other male-dominated jobs such as bartending and insurance adjustment, which now appear to be sex integrated but may be merely in transit to becoming female dominated. According to Barbara Reskin and Patricia Roos (1990), the fundamental reason that a job is resegregated from male to female domination is a shortage of male workers. That shortage occasionally happens when an occupation is rapidly expanding, using up the supply of suitable men. In most cases, however, men are leaving a job that has become less attractive because the work process has been downgraded in terms of skills or the job rewards are less. Consequently, the decrease in prestige and pay of an occupation occurs before women enter it. As a result, women's integration into apparently prestigious male-dominated jobs can be a hollow victory.

MEASURING SEX SEGREGATION

One way to understand the extent to which men and women do different work is to examine the proportion of workers of the same sex in each occupation, as was done above. To this end, it is seen that most men and women work in occupations where workers of the same sex predominate. Indeed, only a fraction of women work in occupations that are dominated by men (Kraut and Luna 1992).

Another method is to examine the extent to which male and female workers are clustered in a small number of occupations. Reskin and Irene Padavic (1994) report that 33 percent of women workers are employed in the top 10 occupations sex-typed female compared to about 25 percent of men being clustered in the top 10 occupations sex-typed male.

The most common way to measure sex segregation is to calculate an index of sex segregation, also called an *index of dissimilarity,* which ranges from 0 to 100. Its value is interpreted as the percentage of workers of one sex that would have to change occupations so that men and women have the same distribution in each occupation. An index of 0 implies perfect integration while an index of 100 suggests that the sexes are completely segregated from each other. In 1990 the index was 53, which means 53 percent of women workers (or approximately 28 million individuals) would need to be redistributed into other occupations if all occupations were to have the same percentage of women and men that are in the entire labor force (Reskin and Padavic 1994).

Researchers have calculated the occupational sex segregation index, using the preferred detailed Census job categories, for different historical periods. It is generally agreed that the index stayed fairly high and steady, between 65 and 69, from 1900 through 1960 (Gross 1968) and perhaps as late as 1970 (Jacobs 1989). If one focuses on nonagricultural jobs, there was only a six-point decline in sex segregation in the 60 years between 1910 and 1970, dropping from 74 to 68. Through the 1970s, however, it dropped another 8 points to 60 in 1980 (Jacobs 1989). In the 1980s, the segregation index continued to drop but at a much slower rate (Reskin and Roos 1990).

In 1940 a comparable index of occupational *race* segregation, calculated separately for blacks and whites of each sex, was rather high at 65 among women and 44 among men. These rates actually increased through 1960 but declined thereafter with the advent of affirmative-action legislation. By 1980, the greater racial segregation among working women had declined to match that of men, reaching 26 to men's 30 by 1990 (King 1992; Reskin 1994). During this same 50-year time span, occupational sex segregation rates among both blacks and whites remained almost twice as high as race segregation among men (Reskin and Padavic 1994). Indeed, Joyce Jacobsen (1994) has concluded that the slowed decline in occupational sex segregation, combined with high rates of firm-level segregation, make it unlikely that sex segregation rates will become as low as race segregation rates by the 2000 census.

SEX SEGREGATION IN SPECIFIC CATEGORIES OF OCCUPATIONS

White-Collar Occupations

As a group, white-collar occupations typically command high salaries, prestige, and autonomy. Yet further inspection reveals considerable variation in their earnings as well as considerable sex segregation. There is a hierarchy of occupations within the classification white-collar. Imagine a pyramid. Executives, physicians, lawyers, and college professors are at the top of the pyramid, while nurses, librarians, and elementary school and secondary-school teachers form part of the middle third. The bottom third includes clerical workers, sales workers, and some service workers. More women are in white-collar occupations today than ever before but where?

In 1900 only 9 percent of women workers were employed in professional occupations and only 1 percent in managerial occupations. Ninety years later 17 percent of working women are in a professional specialty and 11 percent are in executive, administrative, and managerial occupations (U.S. Census Bureau 1990). In fact, women are 49 percent of all workers in executive, administrative, and managerial occupations and 53 percent in professional specialties, respectively (U.S. Census Bureau 1998a). Does this mean occupational sex segregation is no longer a problem? Unfortunately the answer is no.

Industry, firm, and job segregation channels women into the lower-paid, less autonomous, and less prestigious positions that often lack opportunities for upward advancement. For example, although women are about 50 percent of financial managers, they tend to be segregated in small bank branches rather than in loan and investment departments at headquarters (Silver 1981, cited in Reskin and Phipps 1988). Women are 63 percent of personnel and labor relations managers, a service-focused occupation with median annual earnings of $50,080, but only 35 percent of managers in marketing, advertising, and public relations who earn an average $57,100 a year (U.S. Census Bureau 1998a; U.S. Bureau of Labor Statistics 1997).

Women are currently about 27 percent of all lawyers, a remarkable increase from the 1900 figure of .8 percent. Yet, in a recent study of 200 male and female lawyers, Patricia MacCorquodale and Gary Jensen found that "Not a single respondent, male or female, would choose an equally qualified female attorney over a male attorney when considering who would command more respect in court" (1993, 590). Stereotypes and prejudices influence which firms hire women lawyers, the cases they are given, and whether they make partner. Research suggests that the path to partnership is considerably more demanding for women, who must present themselves as "super lawyers" to dissuade the sexist doubts of current partners (Kay and Hagan 1998, 741).

The barriers that women face when they attempt to move into higher-status positions, with greater responsibility, decision-making power, and authority, are widespread in male-dominated occupations. The phenomenon is so common that it has been termed the *glass-ceiling effect*, a phrase that helps people visualize the very real barrier to upward mobility on the job for women workers. The glass ceiling is created by a variety of organizational barriers and discrimination. . . .

Although the gender balance in the broad categories of executive, administrative, and managerial occupations and professional specialties appears to be about 50–50 and thousands of women are managers, doctors, and college professors, occupational segregation continues to limit women's options. In fact, 70 percent of women professionals, but only 27 percent of men professionals, are employed as teachers, librarians, and counselors or in health assessment and treating occupations such as nurse or dietitian (U.S. Census Bureau 1990).

Pink-Collar Occupations

There is a cluster of white-collar occupations that are more commonly labeled pink-collar occupations because they are female dominated. For example, women are approximately 93 percent of registered nurses, 98 percent of preschool and kindergarten teachers, 84 percent of elementary-school teachers, and 81 percent of librarians (U.S. Census Bureau 1998a; Women's Bureau 1999). These professional jobs are occasionally labeled semiprofessions because they lack some of the characteristics that identify an occupation as professional. Semiprofessions tend to be less prestigious, have less autonomy, and command lower salaries than full professions. Nursing and teaching at the elementary-school level are among the top 10 occupations for women, but women earn an average of only $38,168 as registered nurses and $35,204 as elementary-school teachers. Semiprofessionals are usually located in a bureaucratic setting where persons other than fellow professional workers set most administrative rules and professional norms.

In contrast to the relatively large proportion of women who have attempted to enter traditionally male-dominated occupations (e.g., manager, doctor, or lawyer), men are much less likely to enter the traditionally female-dominated domain of pink-collar occupations. Currently, 8 percent of registered nurses, 16 percent of elementary-school teachers, and 20 percent of librarians are men (U.S. Census Bureau 1998a; Women's Bureau 1999). Contrary to the lower wages that women command when they enter male-dominated occupations, men who enter female-dominated occupations often receive higher wages than women in similar positions. Yet the wage gap is almost negligible in nursing and elementary-school teaching, where women earn 95 percent and 90 percent of what men earn. It is important that both women and men who work in female-dominated occupations earn relatively less than women and men who work in male-dominated occupations; "women's work" is generally devalued and underpaid (England and Herbert 1993). Men in female-dominated occupations often find themselves on the fast track or on a "glass escalator"; upward mobility is encouraged and supported for them, for example, in occupations such as bank teller or airline flight attendant.

Clerical Occupations

The history of clerical work represents an example of the feminization of an occupation. At the beginning of the twentieth century, women were only 4 percent of clerical workers. Clerical work was a small, male-dominated occupation with relatively high prestige; it incorporated a diversity of tasks ranging from correspondence to bookkeeping. As the economy grew to be dominated by business and as paperwork proliferated, the need for clerical workers increased drastically. Employers drew on the ready supply of educated, working-class women who were eager to leave domestic service and factory work and enter these "cleaner" jobs. Companies intentionally divided up and restructured clerical work, creating female-dominated typists, whose jobs were mechanized by the previously invented typewriter, and filers, both having less autonomy than the accounting, bookkeeping, and cashier work initially reserved for men (Davies 1982).

Today women are 99 percent of secretaries, 94 percent of typists, and 97 percent of receptionists (U.S. Census Bureau 1998a), while being only 31 percent of shipping clerks, 41 percent of purchasing managers, and 57 percent of accountants and auditors. Secretarial work now employs more women than any other occupation. Compared to other prevalent women's occupations, the median weekly salary for secretaries ($430) is ranked fifth, well behind the higher earnings of the top-ranked registered nurses ($734) (Women's Bureau 1999). Secretarial work and other clerical positions tend to have short promotion ladders and typically do not lead to professional or managerial positions (Nakano Glenn and Feldberg 1989). Over the last century, clerical work has become tedious, requires lower skills, and is highly supervised. Clerical workers are often overeducated and find the work does not allow them to utilize all their skills (Nakano Glenn and Feldberg 1989).

Blue-Collar Occupations

Approximately 39 percent of men and 11 percent of women work in blue-collar occupations, which are counted by the Census under the headings of precision production, craft, and repair occupations and as machine operators, fabricators, and laborers (U.S. Census Bureau 1990). Like most occupational categories, blue-collar work includes a diverse array of occupations ranging from skilled through semiskilled to unskilled. Four blue-collar jobs—truck driver, carpenter, construction laborer, and automobile mechanic—were among the 10 leading occupations for men in 1990. All four are almost completely male dominated ranging from 99 percent (automobile mechanic) to 89 percent male (truck driver). Except for skilled occupations (e.g., electrician, carpenter, and plumber) and supervisory positions, blue-collar work offers little room for autonomy or creativity, requires hard physical labor, and is often dangerous.

Blue-collar work appeals to women although they find it hard to gain access to such positions. Historically, work in the manufacturing sector, particularly in unionized mills and plants, offered several advantages over the service jobs traditionally open to women. A study of women in the steel industry in the 1970s found that they preferred the higher wages, job security, health-care benefits, opportunity for shift work, and slower pace of blue-collar work over the harsh reality of working in sales or waitressing (Fonow 1993). In fact these tangible benefits outweighed the negative experiences in blue-collar work.

EXPLANATIONS OF SEX SEGREGATION

The history of work in the United States and elsewhere reveals a pattern of sex typing, defining some jobs as appropriate for men and others as women's work. But the origins of sex segregation in work are usually attributed to emerging industrialization. Sex segregation was created, in part, by gendered social expectations for women and men. For example, the ideas surrounding men as breadwinners and the "family wage" functioned to keep married women out of the labor force; and when single, divorced, or widowed women worked, these notions kept their wages lower than men's. The assumption was that all women had fathers and then husbands to care for them. Since men were considered the typical employees, part-time work, which women needed to be compatible with children's school hours, was virtually nonexistent except in the form of factory outwork or taking in laundry. Legal barriers constrained women's opportunities as well. Protective legislation limited women's options by defining how many hours, when (day versus night), and in which occupations they could work. In a reciprocal fashion, such segregation reinforced gendered power relations by limiting women's access to good jobs and by increasing their dependency on men. Through these processes, jobs became gendered. In other words, certain job titles as well as work tasks and skills became defined as male as distinct from female. This process is almost unnoticeable except when a job is newly created (and fought over by men and women) or its stereotype changes. A clear example of the latter case is the redefinition of clerical work as women's work by 1940 when, previously, it had been dominated by men.

Present-day researchers explain sex segregation in a variety of ways ranging from theories about individuals' behaviors to those emphasizing labor-market processes and social structure. The earliest sociological explanation focused on individual socialization, suggesting that the gender-stereotypical lessons people learn in childhood about masculine men and feminine women determine the academic fields they study and the occupations they choose. This view, however, is only partially supported. The jobs available to members of different social groups, such as women, blacks, or Hispanics, play a much greater role in determining our occupational status than any gender (or race) lessons we were taught as children. Workers are constrained by the opportunities available to them, by structural forces external to individuals.

One of the most important economic perspectives that, like socialization theory, focuses on individuals is human capital theory. Human capital is considered to be those characteristics or skills that make a worker more productive and attractive to an employer. To explain why women are predominantly employed in female-dominated occupations, human-capital theorists make many assumptions. First, they assume that all workers choose educational fields and occupations primarily with an eye toward maximizing lifetime earnings. They further assume that women consider work to be secondary to family and are only employed for short periods of time. Following from these assumptions, human-capital theorists expect women to select educational fields that require little investment in training and occupations that require skills that will not depreciate during occasional absences from the labor force. The assumption is that the resulting female-dominated occupations will be low skilled, have short career ladders, be amenable to intermittent employment, and pay more at entry than male-dominated jobs, where pay increases depend on on-the-job training. These assumptions are based on a 1950s understanding of women's roles.

Thus it is not surprising that researchers have shown that the human-capital perspective does not explain occupational sex segregation. It cannot explain why women enter low-skilled, female-dominated jobs when there are low-skilled, male-dominated jobs available. Worse still, most female-dominated occupations do not make it any easier to combine work and family than male-dominated occupations.

Counter to human-capital or socialization theorists, structural theorists argue that features of work can create behaviors, rather than individual behavior shaping occupational characteristics. For example, working in female-dominated occupations that are monotonous, have poor benefits and low wages, and lack autonomy can lead to high turnover rates. Researchers found that the same negative occupational characteristics lead to turnover among male workers, too (Reskin and Hartmann 1986). In other words, jobs can influence the attitudes, ambitions, and job preferences of workers, who are malleable and responsive to changing job situations.

The notion that institutional forces largely determine people's life chances is central to the various social-structural perspectives on occupational sex segregation. Social-control theory points to the social pressures that women and men encounter before and during employment. Both men and women are often discouraged from seeking employment in sex-atypical positions. Steel mill jobs were offered to women only after a federal court ordered steel companies to end discrimination against them. Even then the mills and male workers did not embrace the idea of women workers with open arms. In fact, women applicants reported feeling strongly discouraged by management, who questioned their interest and ability to deal with the negative aspects of the work (Fonow 1993). Men who attempt to enter traditionally female occupations are similarly discouraged by questions concerning their sexual orientation, manhood, and reasons for wanting to work with children or patients (Williams 1992).

In spite of such stereotyping, working people are not merely at the mercy of social institutions. They are also active participants in shaping sex segregation. Both sex typing and race typing of jobs can develop out of workers' struggles over new or existing occupations (Baron 1991; Milkman 1987). When the occupations of typist (originally called typewriter) or computer programmer were created, workers contended over which sex should fill them. When the existing occupation of typesetter changed from using hot-metal type to electronic composition in the 1970s, women actively entered jobs that men chose to leave (Roos 1990). Such resegregation in jobs from male to female is partially, but not entirely, responsible for the gradual decline in sex segregation during the 1980s (Jacobs 1989).

Other processes, such as hiring procedures, help explain why women find employment in female-dominated occupations. When employers depend upon referrals from current employees for new employees, they tend to receive applications from workers of the same sex and race as those currently employed. The reason is that workers' informal networks of friends and family tend to include people of their own sex or racial group. Thus if an employer asks white men for referrals, names of other white men are proposed. Informal networks have been found to be very helpful for applicants; the sharing of information about job openings and promotion opportunities is critical to gaining access to higher-status and better-paying positions. This benefit, however, appears to be an advantage only for men. When women rely upon informal networks to learn about job openings, more often than not they end up in female-dominated occupations (Drentea 1998). When employers use open-recruitment methods, which they have to do if they are subject to affirmative-action laws, they are more likely to receive applications from workers who differ in sex, race, and ethnicity.

Open recruitment does not guarantee women access to sex-atypical jobs, however. Other organizational barriers make it difficult for women to break away from female-dominated occupations. For example, apprenticeship programs for various blue-collar jobs may have age limits, so that women who try to enter programs after having children are deemed too old, or they may require unnecessary previous experience including high school shop class. Seniority systems that are not plantwide and thus not transferable across departments may discourage women in clerical positions from taking more traditionally male jobs. The use of secretarial and typing pools in large offices hurts women's opportunities to be noticed and considered for promotion. Recent evidence suggests that sex segregation has a feedback effect. That is, employers tend to promote or hire women into management-level positions only if other women currently hold positions at the same level (Cohen, Broschak, and Haveman 1998). In other words, promotion or advancement in management for women occurs more often in female-dominated ladders. Until employers take the "risk" and hire women for positions not currently held by women, current practices will perpetuate sex segregation.

While many organizational or geographic barriers to sex-atypical occupations are grounded in administrative policies that have little to do with an employer's prejudices, discriminatory actions by employers and other male workers play an important role in the perpetuation of segregation. Recall the situation of women lawyers discussed above. Current law firm partners, who make decisions about granting new partnerships, have prejudices that can make it difficult for women to obtain partner status (Kay and Hagan 1998). Although discrimination against workers on the basis of sex and race is illegal, it persists nonetheless, as evidenced by the number of legitimate complaints of discrimination heard by the Equal Employment Opportunity Commission and other institutions.

CONSEQUENCES OF SEX SEGREGATION

Why does it matter that men and women are physically separated at work? What are the implications of sex-typed occupations? Sex segregation in the workplace matters for the same reason that the U.S. Supreme Court outlawed school segregation in 1964; among socially unequal groups, separate is not equal. The separation of men and women, as well as members of different racial or ethnic groups, into different jobs makes it easier to treat them differently and helps maintain stereotypes about men's and women's work-related characteristics (skills, aspirations, experience). It makes possible the devaluation of women's skills and abilities.

The remainder of this [reading] briefly highlights some of the major consequences of occupational sex segregation, including the wage gap, tokenism, and hindered mobility. Other consequences include women's lower Social Security and retirement benefits as a result of earning less during employment and having worked in less profitable industries that may not provide pensions (Hogan, Perrucci, and Wilmoth 2000). Sexual harassment appears to be a major consequence of sex segregation. When women are a numerical minority in an office or section of a plant, they are very likely to experience various forms of sexual harassment ranging from hostile environment to sexual coercion. . . .

The wage gap is a major consequence of occupational sex segregation. Among full-time, year-round workers age 25 years and over, women earn an average of 74 cents for every men's dollar (U.S. Bureau of Labor Statistics, 1999). The current wage gap represents a historical narrowing of earnings inequality; between 1930 and 1980 it fluctuated between 55 and 64 percent (Reskin and Padavic 1994, 103). However, only two-fifths of women's wage improvement in the last 20 years is due to an increase in their real wages; the remaining three-fifths is due to the fall in men's real wages.

Occupational sex segregation helps explain the wage gap in several ways. First, women and men work in different occupations. The occupations in which men predominate pay higher wages. Second, even when one compares women and men in the same occupational grouping, one finds that sex segregation in industries, establishments, departments, and jobs results in lower wages for women workers. Women engineers earn $800 less per week than men engineers (Andersen 1997, 105). The median weekly income for female machine operators is $228, yet for male machine operators it is $415 (Andersen 1997, 105). Although the occupations of engineer and machine operator are male dominated, sales occupations appear well integrated; 50 percent of sales workers are women (U.S. Census Bureau 1998a); however, retail or wholesale, men and women sell different items. In large department stores, for example, men sell large appliances on commission, while women work in noncommission departments such as sportswear. Consequently, the median weekly earning for men in this "integrated" occupational category is $603 while women earn $352

(U.S. Census Bureau 1998b). The broad categorization of sales occupations only appears integrated. Upon closer examination, the segregation of women into the retail industry and into positions such as cashier reveal the extent to which sales occupations are really not integrated. Third, female-dominated jobs often have a shorter career ladder and fewer possibilities for upward job mobility. As a result, women's jobs not only have a glass ceiling but also a "sticky floor" (Berheide 1992).

Researchers have debated the extent to which sex segregation actually explains the wage gap. Other explanations point to human-capital characteristics, job characteristics, and organizational and regional differences. Donald Tomaskovic-Devey (1995) compared the ability of sex composition to explain the wage gap in both jobs and occupations. He found that the number of women employees in jobs explains 46 percent of the earnings differential for women and men while sex composition in occupations explains 33 percent. Similarly, the segregation of men and women into different occupations and industries when they begin their careers explains 42 percent of the earnings gap while gender differences in human capital and occupational aspirations account for only 14 and 10 percent of the gap, respectively (Marini and Fan 1997). . . .

Women and men who enter nontraditional occupations may encounter varieties of "boundary heightening" by majority-group members; this situation also occurs when people of color enter predominantly white organizations (Kanter 1977). When one class of worker makes up only 15 percent of a work group or organization, majority-group members are likely to act in ways that strengthen or make more visible the differences between their own group and the minority group. Much of this activity involves discriminatory treatment that may have direct impact on a token person's work environment, physical and mental well-being, and opportunity for advancement. In the case of female tokens, employee events may take on a decidedly masculine theme involving football or cars to which female co-workers may not even be invited. Thus women may be effectively excluded from the informal networks that prove so important in obtaining better jobs. Dress codes also set women apart in a very visible manner. In addition to boundary-heightening actions, majority-group workers may attempt to discourage women workers altogether. When women first entered steel work, male workers attempted to sabotage their work. Women fire fighters report concerns as to whether co-workers will back them up in dangerous situations. Finally, when women are members of a token group in the workplace they are often "oversupervised" and scrutinized.

The discriminatory treatment of women in male-dominated occupations does not mirror the experience of men in female-dominated occupations. Although female nurses and librarians often interact with male nurses and librarians in stereotypical ways (e.g., asking a male nurse to help change a tire), male tokens receive more rewards as a result of their numerical minority than disadvantages (Williams 1992). For example, rather than being labeled a "bitch" or an "Iron Maiden" for working hard and overachieving, a man in a sex-atypical position will be encouraged to move ahead and will often be placed on the fast track. The glass escalator experienced by many token male employees reveals the extent to which the token's experience is dependent upon gender. Female and male tokens are not treated similarly by co-workers, potential mentors, and bosses.

In sum, the consequences of occupational segregation are substantial. Occupations can provide income, autonomy, security, social status, and upward mobility. Occupational segregation, however, serves as a major institutional factor shaping and limiting women's (and men's) employment options, ultimately, reinforcing a gendered distribution of power and social status.

CONCLUSION

Throughout much of the twentieth century, rates of occupational sex segregation were consistent and high,

only declining since 1970 from 68 to 53. In white-collar, pink-collar, clerical, and blue-collar occupations, the jobs at the top of the hierarchy tend to be male dominated; when women are allowed into those specialties, it is usually because the jobs have changed in some way to be less attractive to men. Although occupational segregation per se is not illegal, discriminatory hiring and promotion practices are prohibited in firms covered by affirmative-action legislation. Unfortunately, many states are overturning affirmative-action laws and policies. This trend is likely to slow any progress made toward the inclusion of more women and minorities in highly skewed male occupations. The best-supported explanations for the persistence of occupational sex segregation are those that focus on institutional and socially constructed antecedents rather than individual characteristics or gender differences. Perhaps surprisingly, the rapid, large increase in women's recorded employment over the last few decades has done proportionally little to reduce occupational sex stereotyping and the overall sex segregation of workers. Attitudes about the desirability of women's work may have changed, but the social organization of the specific jobs women hold has not always done so. Some occupations have become more sex integrated or have switched from male to female dominated. Yet other factors have counterbalanced this trend, including the decline of sex-integrated occupations in agriculture or the growth of new and existing sex-segregated occupations in the service sector. The consequence is continuing high rates of sex segregation that foster gender inequities.

NOTE

1. The co-authors have equally contributed to this chapter and their order is alphabetical.

REFERENCES

Andersen, Margaret L. (1997). *Thinking About Women: Sociological Perspectives on Sex and Gender*. Boston: Allyn and Bacon.

Baron, Ava. (1991). *Work Engendered: Toward a New History of American Labor*. Ithaca, NY: Cornell University Press.

Berheide, Catherine White. (1992). "Women still 'stuck' in low level jobs." *Women in Public Services: A Bulletin for the Center for Women in Government* 3 (Fall). Albany: Center for Women in Government, State University of New York.

Cohen, Lisa E., Joseph P. Broschak, and Heather A. Haveman. (1998). "And then there were more? The effect of organizational sex composition on the hiring and promotion of managers." *American Sociological Review*, 63:711–727.

Davies, Margery W. (1982). *Women's Place Is at the Typewriter: Office Work and Office Workers 1870–1930*. Philadelphia: Temple University Press.

Drentea, Patricia. (1998). "Consequences of women's formal and informal job search methods for employment in female-dominated jobs." *Gender & Society*, 12:321–338.

England, Paula and Melissa S. Herbert. (1993). "The pay of men in 'female' occupations: Is comparable worth only for women?" Pp. 28–48 in *Doing "Women's Work": Men in Nontraditional Occupations*. Christine L. Williams (ed.). Newbury Park, CA: Sage.

Fonow, Mary Margaret. (1993). "Occupation/steelworker: Sex/female." Pp. 217–222 in *Feminist Frontiers III.* Laurel Richardson and Verta Taylor (eds.). New York: McGraw-Hill.

Gross, Edward. (1968). "*Plus ça change:* The sexual segregation of occupations over time." *Social Problems,* 16:198–208.

Hogan, Richard, Carolyn C. Perrucci, and Janet M. Wilmoth. (2000). "Gender inequality in employment and retirement income effects of marriage, industrial sector, and self-employment." Pp. 27–54 in *Advances in Gender Research, Vol. 4, Social Change for Women and Children.* Vasilikie Demos and Marcia Texler Segal (eds.). Stamford, CT: JAI.

Jacobs, Jerry (1989). "Long-term trends in occupational segregation by sex." *American Journal of Sociology,* 95:160–173.

Jacobsen, Joyce P. (1994). "Trends in work force sex segregation: 1960–1990." *Social Science Quarterly,* 75(1):204–211.

Jones, Beverly W. (1984). "Race, sex, and class; black female tobacco workers in Durham, North Carolina, 1920–1940, and the development of female consciousness." Pp. 228–233 in *Feminist Frontiers IV.* Laurel Richardson, Verta Taylor, and Nancy Whittier (eds.). New York: McGraw-Hill.

Kanter, Rosabeth Moss. (1977). *Men and Women of the Corporation.* New York: Basic.

Kay, Fiona M. and John Hagan (1998). "Raising the bar: The gender stratification of law-firm capital." *American Sociological Review,* 63:728–743.

King, Mary C. (1992). "Occupational segregation by race and sex, 1940–88." *Monthly Labor Review,* 115:30–36.

Kraut, Karen and Molly Luna. (1992). *Work and Wages: Facts on Women and People of Color in the Workforce.* Washington, DC: National Committee on Pay Equity.

MacCorquodale, Patricia and Gary Jensen. (1993). "Women in the law: Partners or tokens?" *Gender & Society,* 7:582–593.

Marini, Margaret Mooney and Pi-Ling Fan. (1997). "The gender gap in earnings at career entry." *American Sociological Review,* 62:588–604.

Milkman, Ruth. (1987). *Gender at Work: The Dynamics of Job Segregation by Sex During World War II.* Urbana: University of Illinois Press.

Nakano Glenn, Evelyn and Roslyn L. Feldberg. (1989). "Clerical work: The female occupation." Pp. 287–311 in *Women: A Feminist Perspective.* Jo Freeman (ed.). Mountain View, CA: Mayfield.

Reskin, Barbara F. (1994). "Segregating workers: Occupational differences by sex, race, and ethnicity." Paper presented at the annual meeting of the Population Association of America in San Francisco.

Reskin, Barbara F. and Heidi I. Hartmann. (1986). *Women's Work, Men's Work: Sex Segregation on the Job.* Washington, DC: National Academy Press.

Reskin, Barbara F. and Irene Padavic. (1994). *Women and Men at Work.* Thousand Oaks, CA: Pine Forge.

Reskin, Barbara F. and Patricia A. Roos (eds.). (1990). *Job Queues, Gender Queues: Explaining Women's Inroads into Male Occupations.* Philadelphia: Temple University Press.

Reskin, Barbara F. and Polly A. Phipps. (1988). "Women in male-dominated professional and managerial occupations." Pp. 190–205 in *Women Working: Theories and Facts in Perspective,* Second Edition. Ann Helton Stromberg and Shirley Harkess (eds.). Mountain View, CA: Mayfield.

Roos, Patricia A. (1990). "Hot metal to electronic composition: Gender, technology, and social change." Pp. 275–298 in *Job Queues, Gender Queues: Explaining Women's Inroads into Male Occupations.* Barbara F. Reskin and Patricia A. Roos (eds.). Philadelphia: Temple University Press.

Silver, Catherine Bodare. (1981). "Public bureaucracy and private enterprise in the U.S.A. and France: Contexts for the attainment of executive positions by women." In *Access to Power: Cross-National Studies of Women and Elites.* Cynthia Fuchs Epstein and Rose Laub Coser (eds.). London: George Allen and Unwin.

Steiger, Thomas and Barbara F. Reskin. (1990). "Baking and baking off: Deskilling and the changing sex makeup of bakers." Pp. 257–274 in *Job Queues, Gender Queues: Explaining Women's Inroads into Male Occupations.* Barbara F. Reskin and Patricia A. Roos (eds.). Philadelphia: Temple University Press.

Tomaskovic-Devey, Donald. (1995). "Sex composition and gendered earnings inequality: A comparison of job and occupational models." Pp. 23–56 in *Gender Inequality at Work.* Jerry A. Jacobs (ed.). Thousand Oaks, CA: Sage.

U.S. Bureau of Labor Statistics. (1997). "Table 1. Table A-1. National employment and wage data from the occupational employment statistics survey by occupation, 1997." [Web Page]. Accessed 3 August 1999. Available at http://stats.bls.gov;80/news.release/ocwage.t01.htm.

———. (1999). "D-20 median weekly earnings of full-time wage and salary workers by selected characteristics." [Web Page]. Accessed 13 August 1999. Available at http://www.bls.gov/cpseeq.htm.

U.S. Census Bureau. (1990). "Table 20. Occupation of employed persons: 1990." P. 20 in *Census of the Population. Social and Economic Characteristics. United States.* Washington, DC: Bureau of the Census.

———. (1998a). *The Official Statistics™.* "No. 672. Employed civilians, by occupations, sex, race, and Hispanic origin: 1983 and 1997." *Statistical Abstract of the United States.* [Web Page]. Accessed 7 August 1999. Available at http://www.census.gov/prod/3/98pubs/98statab/cc98stab.htm.

———. (1998b). *The Official Statistics™.* "No. 696. Full-time wage and salary workers—number and earnings: 1985 to 1997." *Statistical Abstract of the United States.* [Web Page]. Accessed 7 August 1999. Available at http://www.census.gov/prod/3/98pubs/98statab/cc98stab.htm.

Williams, Christine L. (1992). "The glass escalator: Hidden advantages for men in the 'female' professions." Pp. 193–207 in *Men's Lives,* Third Edition. Michael S. Kimmel and Michael A. Messner (eds.). Boston: Allyn and Bacon.

Women's Bureau, Department of Labor. (1999) "20 leading occupations of employed women: 1998 annual averages." [Web Page]. Accessed 7 August 1999. Available at http://www.dol.gov/dol/wb/public/wb_pubs/20lead98.htm.

Median Annual Earnings of Full-Time, Year-Round Workers by Education, Race, and Hispanic Origin, 2009

	WOMEN			
Education	All Races	White	Black	Hispanic	Asian
Overall	37,264	37,918	32,829	28,627	44,823
Less than 9th grade	18,480	18,124	*	17,727	20,247
9-12th grade, non-grad.	21,226	20,933	22,298	20,038	*
High school graduate	29,150	29,907	26,843	25,768	27,266
Some college	34,087	34,962	31,724	31,566	35,022
Associate's degree	37,267	38,353	31,936	31,974	38,089
Bachelor's degree	46,832	46,648	46,224	44,085	51,089
Master's degree	61,068	60,906	55,875	55,187	72,415
Professional degree	83,905	85,964	*	*	*
Doctoral degree	76,581	76,486	*	*	*

	MEN			
Education	All Races	White	Black	Hispanic	Asian
Overall	49,904	50,600	40,030	32,348	52,408
Less than 9th grade	23,945	23,992	22,732	23,476	*
9-12th grade, non-grad.	28,023	29,073	26,524	25,086	23,737
High school graduate	39,478	40,546	32,325	31,668	32,291
Some college	47,097	49,086	40,138	41,274	42,129
Associate's degree	50,303	50,974	41,797	42,348	46,074
Bachelor's degree	62,444	65,467	51,504	55,867	60,044
Master's degree	79,342	80,101	61,101	72,180	89,472
Professional degree	123,243	123,186	*	*	150,125
Doctoral degree	100,740	100,912	*	*	98,530

Note: The category Hispanic includes Hispanics of any race. All other racial categories refer to people who reported only that category. Figures are for workers over age 25.
*No data were available for these categories due to small sample size.
Source: U.S. Census Bureau, Current Population Survey, 2010 Annual Social and Economic Supplement. Table PINC-03. "Educational Attainment—People 25 Years Old and Over, by Total Money Earnings in 2009, Work Experience in 2009, Age, Race, Hispanic Origin and Sex." http://www.census.gov/hhes/www/cpstables/032010/perinc/new03_000.htm

The Managed Hand: The Commercialization of Bodies and Emotions in Korean Immigrant–Owned Nail Salons

First published in 2003

The title of [Arlie] Hochschild's (1983) groundbreaking study of emotional labor, *The Managed Heart*, provides a rich metaphor for the control and commercialization of human feeling in service interactions. The title of this article, "The Managed Hand," plays on Hochschild's to capture the commercialization of both human feelings and bodies and to introduce the concept of body labor, the provision of body-related services and the management of feelings that accompanies it. By focusing on the case study of Korean immigrant manicurists and their relations with racially and socioeconomically diverse female customers in New York City nail salons, I broaden the study of emotional labor to illuminate its neglected embodied dimensions and to examine the intersections of gender, race, and class in its performance.

The past decade has witnessed a turn toward "Bringing Bodies Back In" (Frank 1990) to theory and research in sociology and feminist scholarship. What can be gained by "bringing the body back in" to the study of emotional labor and, more broadly, of gendered work? What are the dimensions of body labor, and what factors explain the variation in the quality and quantity of its performance? An embodied perspective on gendered work highlights the feminization of the body-related service sector and the proliferation of intricate practices of enhancing the appearance of the female body. A race, gender, and class perspective highlights the increasing role of working-class immigrant women in filling body-related service jobs and the racialized meanings that shape the processes of emotional management among service workers.

This study compares nail salons in three racially and socioeconomically diverse settings, employing participant observation and in-depth interviews ($N = 62$) in the tradition of feminist ethnography and the extended case method. After providing a brief overview of the case study of Korean-owned nail salons in New York City, the data presentation maps out the physical and emotional dimensions of body labor in three different nail salons and explains patterns of variation according to the race and class of the clientele and neighborhood.

In addition to contributing original empirical research on Korean immigrant women's work in the new and expanding niches of body service work, this article broadens the scholarship on emotional labor by addressing its performance by racial-ethnic and immigrant women in the global service economy. It demonstrates how the gendered processes of physical and emotional labor in nail salon work are steeped with race and class meanings that reinforce broader structures of inequality and ideologies of difference between women.

THEORETICAL FRAMEWORK

Emotional Labor in Body Service Work: Race, Gender, and Class Intersections

Work on the body requires not only physical labor but extensive emotional management, or what Hochschild's (1983) seminal work describes as emotional labor. The concept of body labor makes two important contributions to the study of emotional labor: (1) It explores the embodied dimensions of emotional labor and (2) it investigates the intersections of race, gender, and class in shaping its performance. By bringing together an embodied analysis of emotional labor with an integrative race, gender, and class perspective, I show how this case study of nail salon work retheorizes emotional labor to have greater applicability to gendered occupations dominated by racialized immigrant women.

Building on Hochschild's (1983) work, studies of emotional labor have illuminated the increasing prevalence of emotional management in specific occupations and industries, the gendered composition of the emotional labor force, wage discrimination, burnout, and other occupational health issues (Hall 1993; Leidner 1999; Lively 2000; Wharton 1999). Steinberg and Figart (1999) provide a comprehensive overview of the field that examines both qualitative case studies of the contours of emotional labor in specific work sites and quantitative investigations of its prevalence and its impact on job satisfaction and compensation. Despite the many dimensions of emotional labor that have been addressed by feminist scholars, the body-related contours of emotional labor as it is manifested in low-wage service work dominated by racial-ethnic women, particularly in the beauty industry, have yet to be examined in depth.

While the study of beauty and the beauty industry presents a rich opportunity to explore the emotional work involved in servicing female bodies, this literature has focused attention almost exclusively on the experiences of middle-class white women consumers and their physical and psychological exploitation by the male-dominated beauty industry (Banner 1983; Bordo 1993; Chapkis 1986; Wolf 1991), neglecting the substandard working conditions, unequal power relations, and complex emotional lives of the women who provide these services. Several excellent ethnographies of beauty salons (Gimlan 1996; Kerner Furman 1997) have explored the dimensions of class and age in beauty shop culture, but they have not addressed the experiences of women of color as either customers or body service workers. Studies of the bodies of women of color, while illuminating cultural representations of racialized bodies as inferior and exotic (hooks 1990) and studying the politics of body alteration, particularly regarding hair (Banks 2000; Rooks 1996), have also neglected the actual interactions between consumers and providers of body-related services and the hierarchies that govern these exchanges.

In addition to neglecting emotional work in body service jobs, the literature on emotional labor has framed the processes of interactive service work primarily through a gender lens and paid less attention to the crosscutting influences of gender, race and class. Russell Hochschild's original case study of flight attendants and subsequent applications to other female-dominated occupations have emphasized the gendered employment experiences of native-born white women as paralegals (Pierce 1995), nannies and au pairs (Macdonald 1996), fast food and insurance sales workers (Leidner 1993), and police officers (Schmitt and Yancey Martin 1999). My research expands this work not only in its empirical focus on immigrant women of color doing gendered, emotional labor but through the theoretical framework of race, gender, and class as "interactive systems" and "interlocking categories of experience" (Anderson and Hill Collins 2001, xii). This framework critiques additive models that append race and class to the experiences of white middle-class women and instead highlights the simultaneity and reciprocity of race, gender, and class in patterns of social relations and in the lives of individuals (Baca Zinn 1989; Hill Collins 1991; hooks 1981; Hurtado 1989; Nakano Glenn 1992; Ngan-Ling Chow 1994). Thus, I demonstrate that different expectations or "feeling rules" (Hochschild 1983, x) shape the performance of emotional labor by women according to the racial and class context.

Drawing from Hochschild's (1983) definition of emotional labor, I incorporate this intersectional analysis to define important parallels and distinctions between the concepts of body labor and emotional labor. First, Hochschild's definition of emotional labor focuses on a particular form that "requires one to induce or suppress feeling in order to sustain the outward countenance that produces the proper state of mind in others—in this case, the sense of being cared for in a convivial and safe place" (1983, 7). While Hochschild develops this definition in reference to the specific case of flight attendants and the feeling rules that govern their work, this kind of caring, attentive service has become a widely generalized definition, rather than being regarded as one particular form of emotional labor performed by mostly white, middle-class women largely for the benefit of white, middle- and upper-class men. Korean-owned nail salons thus serve as a contrasting site to explore other forms of emotional labor that emerge in work sites that are differently gendered, differently racialized, and differently classed. The patterns of emotional labor described in this study can illuminate similar sites in which emotional labor involves women serving women (as opposed to mainly women serving men), and is not necessarily governed by the social feeling rules of white, middle-class America.

Furthermore, while Hochschild and other scholars of emotional labor have examined certain embodied aspects of emotional labor concerned with gendered bodily display, ranging from control of weight to smiles, this study highlights emotional management regarding bodily contact in service interactions. The dynamics of extended physical contact between women of different racial and class positions complicate and intensify the gendered performance of emotional labor. Body labor not only demands that the service worker present and comport her body in an appropriate fashion but also that she induces customers' positive feelings about their own bodies. This is a highly complicated enterprise in a culture that sets unattainable standards for female beauty and pathologizes intimate, nurturing physical contact between women, while it normalizes unequal relations in the exchange of body services.

By investigating the understudied area of body-related service occupations through an intersectional race, gender, and class analysis, this study of body labor reformulates the concept of emotional labor to dramatize how the feeling rules governing its exchange are shaped by interlocking oppressions that operate at the macro level (Hill Collins 1991) and then emerge as different styles of emotional service at the micro level.

BACKGROUND FOR THE STUDY

In this section, I provide context for my study by describing nail salons as a niche for Korean immigrant women's work and discussing the dynamics of race and ethnicity in its development. As one of the few arenas in which immigrant and native-born women encounter each other in regular, sustained, physical contact, Korean immigrant women–owned nail salons in New York City illuminate the complex performance and production of race, gender, and class as they are constructed in feminized work sites in the global service economy. Since the early 1980s, Korean women in New York City have pioneered this new ethnic niche with more than 2,000 Korean-owned nail salons throughout the metropolitan area, or approximately 70 percent of the total, as estimated by the Korean American Nail Association of New York. Each salon employs an average of five workers, suggesting an occupational niche of roughly 10,000 women. While the New York State licensing bureau does not keep track of nail salon licenses by ethnic group, their figures reveal an overall 41-percent growth in the nail industry (from 7,562 licensed nail technicians in 1996 to 10,684 in 2000) in New York City, Westchester County, and Nassau County. These numbers undercount a sizable number of women who do not possess licenses or legal working status.

While concentrating on Korean immigrant women, this study examines both race and ethnicity as salient categories of analysis. I designate the salon owners and workers according to ethnicity, but I recognize shared racial positions that push not only Korean but also other Asian immigrant women into this niche. For example, in New York, there is a significant presence of Chinese- and Vietnamese- as well as Korean-owned nail salons, and on the West Coast, the niche is almost solely dominated by Vietnamese women (www.nails-mag.com). Common factors such as limited English-language ability, unrecognized professional credentials from their countries of origin, undocumented immigration status, and coethnic resources in the form of labor, start-up capital, and social networks explain why Asian immigrant women of various ethnic groups cluster in the nail salon industry. Similarities across Asian ethnic groups include not only the human capital of the women themselves but also the conditions of the labor market and the U.S. racial hierarchy that they encounter. Through their shared race, gender, and class locations, Asian women have been coveted as productive and docile workers, whose "nimble fingers" (Ong 1987) make them desirable and exploitable in an increasingly feminized, impoverished, and unprotected labor force (Cheng and Bonacich 1984; Hu-DeHart 1999). Racialized perceptions of Asian women as skilled in detailed handiwork and massage further contribute to customers' preference for their manicuring services, as evidenced by the fact that many customers racially identify the salons as owned by Asians or "Orientals," as opposed to by specific ethnic group.

In sum, because it would be methodologically unsound to generalize findings based on a limited sample of Korean women to include all Asian immigrant women in the nail industry, this study maintains ethnicity as the significant category for describing the workers and owners but frames differences between the customers and variation in service interactions according to race. Thus, I discuss the different dimensions of Korean-immigrant women's performance of body labor through the integrative lens of race, gender, and class rather than a more specific focus on Korean ethnicity.

RESEARCH DESIGN AND METHOD

This study situates itself within feminist methodology and epistemology by beginning from the standpoint of women to investigate the "relations of ruling" in contemporary capitalist society (Smith 1987). At the same time, it does not privilege gender as the only or the most important framework for defining and investigating differences and aims instead for an understanding of race, gender, and class as crosscutting forces. By examining contrasting patterns of body labor between women of different racial and class backgrounds, this study reconstructs theories of emotional labor by addressing its embodied dimensions and the simultaneous influence of gender, race, and class on its performance. In doing so, it follows the extended case method of making critical interventions in existing theory by explaining anomalies between similar phenomena, rather than seeking generalizations toward the discovery of new theory, as in the contrasting approach of grounded theory. According to Burawoy (1991, 281), the primary architect of the extended case method, "The importance of the single case lies in what it tells us about society as a whole rather than about the population of similar cases." Thus, my study examines cases of specific nail salons, not to formulate generalizations about all similar nail salons but instead to explain how social forces influence variation in the service interactions at these sites.

The data collection for this project involved 14 months of fieldwork in New York City nail salons. The research design included in-depth interviews ($N = 62$) and participant observation at three sites: (1) "Uptown Nails," located in a predominantly white, middle- and upper-class commercial area; (2) "Downtown Nails," located in a predominantly Black (African American and Caribbean) working- and lower-middle-class commercial neighborhood; and (3) "Crosstown Nails," located in a racially mixed lower-middle and middle-class residential and commercial area. I spent at least 50 hours at each salon over the course of several months. In the case of Crosstown Nails, which was located near my home, visits were shorter (2 to 3 hours) and more frequent (several times a week). The other two salons required long commutes, so I usually visited once a week for 6 to 7 hours.

In addition to hundreds of unstructured conversational interviews conducted as a participant-observer, the research included in-depth structured interviews with 10 Korean nail salon owners, 10 Korean nail salon workers, 15 Black customers, and 15 white customers. The customers interviewed at each salon are as follows. Uptown Nails included a lawyer, professor, pharmacist, flight attendant, secretary, personal trainer, accessories importer, homemaker (formerly a computer programmer), fashion designer, and real estate broker. Customers interviewed at Downtown Nails included a package clerk, student/waitress, student/mother, grocery cashier, ambulatory service driver, county government administrative assistant, laboratory technician, nanny, therapist, and elementary school principal. At Crosstown Nails, I interviewed 10 customers (five white, five Black). The white customers included a bartender, high school teacher, hairdresser, homemaker, and retired insurance bookkeeper. The Black customers included a clinical researcher, theater technician/musician, management consultant, homemaker, and student.

In-depth interviews averaged 45 minutes for customers and two hours for owners and workers. Customers were interviewed in English at the salon while they were having their manicures, and when necessary, a follow-up meeting or telephone interview was arranged. Owners and workers were interviewed in both Korean and English, depending on their preference and level of fluency. Bilingual research assistants helped with translation, transcription, and follow-up interviews. I tape-recorded interviews in which consent was given, but in cases in which respondents refused, I took extensive handwritten notes that I typed immediately afterward. Both customers and service providers are referred to by pseudonyms that approximate the names they use in the salons. This convention captures the naturalistic setting where even coworkers commonly refer to each other by the "American name" that they employ at work. I have added a surname to citations and descriptions of owners and workers to differentiate customers from service providers.

Finally, I conducted key respondent interviews with two officials of the Korean Nail Salon Association of New York, two Korean ethnic press journalists, one New York State licensing official, and a representative of a Korean-operated nail school. I interviewed two Vietnamese nail salon owners and one Chinese and one Russian manicurist to provide preliminary comparisons to other ethnically owned nail salons. To provide comparisons to other Korean-owned small businesses, I engaged in limited participant observation in a Korean-owned grocery store and interviewed the owner and manager.

FINDINGS

The Contours of Body Labor

Body labor involves the exchange of body-related services for a wage and the performance of physical and emotional labor in this exchange. My study's findings illustrate three dimensions of body labor: (1) the physical labor of attending to the bodily appearance and pleasure of customers, (2) the emotional labor of managing feelings to display certain feeling states and to create and respond to customers' feelings regarding the servicing of their bodies, and (3) variation in the performance of body labor as explained through the intersection of gender with race and class. These dimensions vary across the different research sites and emerge as three distinct patterns of body labor provision: (1) high-service body labor involving physical pampering and emotional attentiveness serving mostly middle- and upper-class white female customers, (2) expressive body labor involving artistry in technical skills and communication of respect and fairness when serving mostly working- and lower-middle-class African American and Caribbean female customers, and (3) routinized body labor involving efficient, competent physical labor and courteous but minimal emotional labor when serving mostly lower-middle and middle-class racially mixed female customers. The data presentation admittedly flattens some of the variation within each site to clarify distinctions between them, but this typology highlights the dominant physical and emotional style of service at each salon.

Uptown Nails: High-Service Body Labor

A seasoned Korean manicurist who has worked at Uptown Nails for nearly 10 years, Esther Lee is in high demand for her relaxing and invigorating hand massages. She energetically kneads, strokes, and pushes pressure points, finishing off the massage by holding each of the customer's hands between her own and alternately rubbing, slapping, and gently pounding them with the flare that has wooed many a customer into a regular nail salon habit. Margie, a white single woman in her mid-30s who works for an accounting firm, smiles appreciatively and squeezes Esther's hand: "I swear, I couldn't stay in my job without this!" Esther reciprocates a warm, somewhat shy smile.

Uptown Nails boasts leafy green plants, glossy framed pictures of white fashion models showing off well-manicured hands, recent fashion magazine subscriptions stacked neatly on a coffee table, and classical CDs on the stereo system. The salon has been in operation for 13 years, and three of the six employees have worked there for more than 10 years. The customers sit quietly sipping their cappuccinos, updating their appointment books, or at times politely conversing with each other about the weather or the color of the nail polish they are wearing. Located in a prosperous business district of Manhattan, an Uptown Nails manicuring experience involves not only the filing and polishing of nails but attention to the customer's physical and emotional comfort. From the gentle removal of undernail dirt, to the careful trimming of cuticles and buffing of calluses, to the massaging of hands and feet, Korean manicurists literally rub up against their customers, who are mostly white middle- and upper-class women. The owner, one of the earliest pioneers in the nail salon industry, currently operates six very profitable salons in prime Manhattan locations and visits this salon only once a week to take care of paperwork. The owner, manager, and employees are all middle-aged Korean women with fluent English-language ability, reflecting the greater expectations for communications with customers. The physical dimensions of body labor in Uptown Nails, including hot cotton towels, bowls of warm soaking solution, sanitized utensils, and calming background music, all indicate considerable attention to creating a pleasurable sensory experience for the customer. Particular attention is given to avoiding nicks and cuts and sterilizing and apologizing profusely when they occur.

In addition to this extensive physical pampering, Uptown Nails prioritizes the emotional needs of customers regarding the servicing of their bodies. The mostly white middle-class customers at this salon place great importance on emotional attentiveness as a crucial component of the service interaction. Kathy, a personal trainer, elaborated,

> Having them done is a pleasure, a luxury. Doing them myself is tedious, having them done is a treat. It's the whole idea of going and having something nice done for myself. If I do them myself, it's just routine upkeep of my body—like washing your hair or keeping your clothes clean. . . . Of course it makes it more enjoyable if they are friendly and can talk to you. If they can't remember my name that's okay, but I think they should recognize me.

The proper performance of body labor thus transforms a hygienic process, otherwise equated with washing hair or clothes, into a richly rewarding physical and emotional experience. The satisfaction Kathy experiences from the manicure derives not only from the appearance of the nails but the feeling of being special that accompanies attentive body servicing. To generate this feeling, customers expect the manicurist to display a caring demeanor and engage in pleasant one-on-one conversation with them.

Service providers recognize customers' high expectations with regard to both the physical and emotional dimensions of body labor, and they respond accordingly. Judy Cha, a 34-year-old who immigrated in 1993, describes the emotional and physical stressors that accompany high-service body labor, particularly giving massages to earn tips and engaging in conversation.

> Three years ago we didn't give a lot of massages but now customers ask more and more. It makes me weak and really tired. . . . I guess because I don't have the right training to do it in a way that doesn't tire my body. Some manicurists give massage all the time to get tips, but sometimes I don't even ask them if I'm tired. Owners keep asking you to ask them, but on days I'm not feeling well, I don't ask. . . . One of my biggest fears working in the salon is, what if I don't understand what the customer is saying? They don't really talk in detail, just say, "how is the weather." But in order to have a deeper relationship, I need to get past that and to improve my English. It makes it very stressful.

Thus, manicurists work hard to conform to the high service expectations of middle-class white women, but while the performance of caring, attentive emotional labor is noticeably higher than that afforded in the other research sites, it often does not meet customers' expectations. In particular, many Uptown Nails customers disapprove of the use of Korean language by the manicurists as a violation of proper attentiveness in beauty service transactions and suspect that they are being talked about (Kang 1997).

Cathy Hong, a 32-year-old manicurist who immigrated in 1999, sums up the assumptions many of the Uptown Nails customers have regarding access to a regular manicure delivered with high-service body labor: "These women get their nails done regularly because it has become a habit to them, they take it for granted. Just as we wash our face daily, American women get their nails done."

Downtown Nails: Expressive Body Labor

Entering another borough, the scene inside Downtown Nails differs as radically as the neighborhoods in which these two salons are located. Squeezed between a Caribbean bakery and a discount clothing store, a worn-out signboard displays the single word "NAILS" and a painting of a graceful, well-manicured hand holding a long-stemmed rose and pointing to a staircase leading to the second-story entrance. Upon being buzzed in through the locked door, the customer is greeted with a display of hundreds of brightly colored airbrushed nail tips lining an entire wall. The noise level in the salon is high, as various electronic nail-sculpting tools create a constant buzz to match the flow of the lively conversations among the mostly Black customers. On a weekend afternoon, Downtown Nails is filled to capacity, and the wait for a preferred "nail artist" can be more than an hour. Mostly Caribbean and African American women, the customers engage in animated conversations while sharing coco buns and currant rolls from the downstairs bakery. The banter ranges from vivid accounts of a recent mugging near the salon to news about the pay freeze in the nearby hospital where many of the women work as nurses or technicians.

A far cry from the spa-like pampering experience of Uptown Nails, a nail job at Downtown Nails is closer to a stint on a factory assembly line: highly mechanized and potentially toxic. Absent are the elaborate sanitizing machines and solutions, let alone the soft pampering touches. Despite these appearances, body labor at Downtown Nails involves a complex mix of physical and emotional labor that accommodates customers' desires to express a unique sense of self through their nail designs and their expectations that service providers demonstrate both individual respect and appreciation to the community.

The manicurists, or nail artists, provide less of the traditional, attentive style of emotional labor but focus their emotional management on communicating a sense of respect and fairness. These women tend to be more recent immigrants from more working-class backgrounds with less English-language fluency and are more likely to be working without legal immigration status or licenses. The owners, Mr. and Mrs. Lee, are a married couple, both formerly school teachers, who immigrated in 1981 to pursue better educational opportunities for their children. Two years after their arrival, they opened a salon in this location because the rent was affordable, the customer base was strong, and they reside in a nearby neighborhood. The customers at Downtown Nails span a broad range in socioeconomic status but most are working to lower-middle class.

The importance of the physical appearance of the nails themselves as opposed to the pampering experience of receiving these services is dramatized by customers' concern with the design of the nails versus the massage and other services that customers at Uptown Nails regard as integral and Downtown Nails customers view as extraneous. Jamilla, a 26-year-old African American part-time student and waitress, proudly displays her inch-and-a-half-long nails, each one adorned with the skyline of New York City in bold black, framed by an orange and yellow sunset. A regular patron of Downtown Nails for six years, she explains why she is willing to spend "$50–$60 every two weeks" for elaborate hand-painted designs:

> Because I don't like looking like anyone else. My nails say "me." They're the first thing people notice about me. I have big hands for a female. I never had those long, thin ladylike fingers. My father used to say my hands were bigger than his. I want long nails because they make my hands look more feminine.

Indicating a preference for nails that reflect very different norms of femininity than the demure, pastel tones prevalent at Uptown Nails, Jamilla elaborates further on her nail aesthetics. "It all depends on my mood. Like this design makes me feel like I'm on top of the city, like it can't bring me down [laughing]. . . . No one's gonna mess with you when you got nails like these." Jamilla's pride in having originally designed nails that no one else can reproduce suggests the importance of her nails as an expression of her individuality that also communicate a sense of self-efficacy and protection, as indicated in her comments that no one would "mess" with a woman with nails like hers. To meet the expectations of customers such as Jamilla, body labor at Downtown Nails calls for development of expertise in sculpting and painting original nail designs rather than in the soothing, pampering services offered at Uptown Nails. Thus, the physical demands of body labor are not less but simply of a different type.

Similarly, the emotional dimensions of body labor at Downtown Nails are not different in degree so much as kind. The customer's race and class location intersect to produce much lower expectations among working-class Black customers for emotional attentiveness than the white middle-class women at Uptown Nails. While it is clearly less attentive, Serena, an African American grocery store cashier, assesses the emotional labor at Downtown Nails positively.

> It's very good, I'm satisfied with it. They really just do the nails, no massages. That's fine with me. I just go in with my Walkman and listen to some good music and maybe just have a little basic conversation.

Customers at Downtown Nails rarely are on a first-name basis with the service providers, and their preference for a particular manicurist is based much more on her technical skills than her emotional attentiveness. Serena elaborated,

> There are a few people I like and I go to whoever's open, but I'll stay away from certain people. I know they're not good cause I hear other people complain—I see someone come back and say that their nail cracked the next day, or I see someone get nicked with a filer. . . . No, it's not because they're rude or anything, it's because I know they don't do a good job. . . . Just like some people just can't do hair, some people just can't do nails.
>
> [Regarding relations with her current manicurist] I feel comfortable with her, but it's more that she does an excellent job. If a wrap cracks or looks funny or I lose a nail, I'm not going back to her no matter how nice she is.

While many working-class Black customers like Serena give little importance to a caring, attentive emotional display, they demand another style of emotional labor.

Emotional labor at Downtown Nails calls less for sensitivity to pampering of individual customers and more for demonstration of values of respect and fairness that recognize the complex dynamics of Korean businesses operating in Black neighborhoods. This includes efforts such as sponsoring a Christmas party to thank customers for their patronage, participating in community events, displaying Afro-centric designs, and playing R&B and rap music. Mrs. Lee, the co-owner of the salon, allows regulars to run an informal tab when they are short of money and keeps a change jar that customers dip into for bus fare, telephone calls, or other incidentals. It is not uncommon for customers to drop by even when they are not getting their nails done to use the bathroom or leave shopping bags behind the front desk while they complete errands. These efforts at "giving back to the community" entail a distinct form of emotional labor that conforms not to white middle-class women's feeling rules of privilege and pampering but to Black working-class women's concerns about being treated with respect and fairness.

Jamilla described the importance of a sense of fairness and respect to Black customers and how this demands a particular form of emotional labor from Korean manicurists.

> It's kind of a Catch-22. Some customers feel like they're getting disrespected if you don't refer back to them or if you're having a side conversation. Then the Koreans get upset and think African Americans have an attitude, which then makes them talk more about us. You see, in the African American community, you can't outright say anything you want to say because we always have our guard up. We get it all the time, from the cops or whoever. I've seen it in the Hispanic community too—this thing about honor and respect. "Don't disrespect me just because I'm Black or Hispanic. What I say does count."

Thus, while the caring, pampering style of service is virtually absent at Downtown Nails, another form of emotional labor is necessary to negotiate and avoid conflicts with customers that can quickly become racialized into heated confrontations (Lee 2002). Serena described a scene at another salon that illustrates how the failure to perform appropriately respectful emotional labor can quickly erupt into shouting matches that take on racialized and anti-immigrant overtones: "I've seen some customers really go off on them, 'You're not in your country, speak English.'" Her comments underscore how the race and class of the neighborhood complicate the processes of emotional management inside the salons.

Although disagreements between Downtown Nails' customers and workers do arise, at times resulting in heated exchanges, the relations in the salon are congenial overall, as the expressive style of emotional labor enables customers and service providers to voice and, for the most part, "work out" their differences. Mrs. Lee explained that she prefers serving Black customers for this reason and actually moved back to working in a low-income Black neighborhood after working for a period in Long Island.

> Working in the white neighborhood didn't match my personality. I don't deal well with picky customers. . . . In the Black neighborhood, it's more relaxed. They don't leave tips but they don't expect so much service either. . . . [In Long Island] they want you to go slow and spend time with them. Here I just concentrate on doing a good job and working quickly.

Service providers invest less energy in displaying and creating convivial feeling states, which in some cases allows for a genuine affinity with Black customers and less of a sense of burnout from the effort involved in the manufacture of falsely convivial feelings.

Expressive body labor thus prioritizes both the meanings of the nails as a form of self-expression to working-class Black customers and the expression of symbolic but tangible efforts to respond to the feeling rules of respect and fairness governing Korean immigrant service providers in predominantly Black working-class neighborhoods.

Crosstown Nails: Routinized Body Labor

Located on the second floor above a fashionable boutique, Crosstown Nails is clean but sparse and utilitarian. In many ways, this salon is representative of the most prevalent style of service offered in Korean-owned nail salons: fast, cheap, basic manicures and pedicures with no frills. The McDonald's of the nail salon industry, Crosstown Nails offers a manicure that is standardized and predictable in both its physical and emotional aspects.

This salon often has customers waiting, but even when it is busy, the line moves quickly as each customer is whisked in and out of the manicuring seat with crisp efficiency. The customer chooses her nail color, presents it to the manicurist who asks her to specify the desired shape of the nail, and then soaks her nails briefly in a softening solution. Depending on her preference, her nails are either trimmed or pushed back. The manicurist offers to give a massage, but it is perfunctory and lasts usually not more than a minute. After carefully layering on two coats of polish and a quick-drying topcoat, the customer moves to a heated hand dryer where she converses with other customers or more often "zones out."

Many customers come from the neighboring hospital during lunch hour or after work. Situated on the edge of a fashionable, high-rent, racially diverse residential district and a lower-income but also racially mixed neighborhood, Crosstown Nails captures the broad range of customer interactions that many Korean service providers negotiate in a given day. In large, high-immigrant-receiving cities such as New York, service interactions often involve multiracial rather than binary interactions between Korean and Blacks or Koreans and whites.

Susan Lee, age 39, founded Crosstown Nails in 1989 and is the sole owner. Divorced with one son, age 10, she emigrated in 1982 from Seoul with her husband, a graduate student. She graduated college with a degree in tourism and worked as a travel agent in Korea. In New York City, she first worked in a retail store in Manhattan, then began to work in a nail salon in Brooklyn to support her husband while he studied. After their marriage ended, she brought her mother from Korea in 1988 and with her help opened a convenience store, which failed shortly thereafter. She then opened Crosstown Nails a year later, and the business has thrived.

The secret of Crosstown Nail's success is its ability to appeal to customers who lack excess disposable income and normally would not indulge in a professional manicure but are attracted by the convenience and price. Julia, a white bartender, commented,

> I'm kind of a ragamuffin, so it kind of surprises me that I get them done as often as I do, which is still much less than most people in the city. It's just so easy to do here, and cheap.

Julia's description of herself as a "ragamuffin" suggests that she does not adhere to strict codes of femininity in her dress or other beauty routines, as indicated by her casual peasant skirt and no makeup. Nonetheless, easy and cheap access draws her into purchasing regular manicures.

Many customers at Crosstown Nails seek manicures not as a pampering experience or as creative expression but as a utilitarian measure to enhance their self-presentation at work. Merna, an Afro-Caribbean clinical researcher, explained,

> I only get them done about every two months. I don't want to get attached to it. For some women it's such a ritual, it becomes a job—maintaining the tips and stuff.

> I'm presenting my hands all day long so it's worth it to me to spend some time and money to make sure they look good.

Merna regards manicured nails as a professional asset more than a core aspect of a gendered self. Thus, the style of her nails and the meaning she gives to them is more similar to the white middle-class customers at Crosstown Nails than to the Black working-class customers at Downtown Nails.

In general, middle-class Black customers like Merna mostly exhibited similar nail aesthetics to those of middle-class white women, suggesting the greater importance of class over race in influencing nail styles and expectations of body labor, particularly in routinized settings such as Crosstown Nails.

DISCUSSION

The concept of emotional labor addresses how service providers present and manipulate their feelings to communicate a sense of caring and attentiveness to customers, or in Hochschild's (1983, 6) words, where "the emotional style of offering service is part of the service itself." This study of interactions in Korean-owned nail salons enriches the literature on emotional labor by expanding it to include embodied dimensions, or body labor. The embodied aspects of emotional labor not only heighten the intensity of commercialized feeling exchanges but they also point out variation in these exchanges beyond the white middle-class settings explored by most researchers. Nail salon services, and body labor more generally, are gendered work processes, but they are enacted in different forms according to the influences of race and class.

In what ways is nail salon work gendered? In what ways are these gendered work processes remolded by race and class? Understanding the influence of race and class on the gendered performance of body labor in Korean-owned nail salons illuminates how gendered work processes reflect and reproduce racial and class inequalities at the level of social structures. Nail salon work is gendered in four major dimensions: (1) It involves mostly female actors, as both service providers and customers; (2) it focuses on the construction of beauty according to feminine norms; (3) it is situated in feminized, semiprivate spaces; and (4) it involves the gendered performance of emotional labor.

In describing each of these dimensions, I do not emphasize how socialized gender roles are acted out in these establishments, but rather how gender operates as a social institution that lays the groundwork for the very existence of these businesses and frames the interactions that occur within them. Thus, I conceptualize these small businesses according to the model of gendered institutions (Marx Ferree and Hall 1996) and examine how they are constructed from the ground up through gendered ideologies, relations, and practices that sustain systematic gender inequality at the micro level of sex differences, at the meso level of group conflict, and [at] the macro levels of power, social control, and the division of labor. At the same time, I argue that as gendered institutions, they cannot be separated from forces of racial and class inequality.

If, as Paul Gilroy (1993, 85) asserted, "gender is the modality in which race is lived," then race, and I argue class as well, are lived in these nail salons and other body-service sites as differences in gendered styles of body labor. Interactions in Korean female immigrant–owned nail salons illustrate how the gendered practices of body labor become the locus of expressing and negotiating race and class hierarchies between white, Black, and Asian women. High-service body labor, as performed at Uptown Nails, is similar to the style of caring, attentive emotional labor practiced by Hochschild's flight attendants and conforms to the feeling rules of white middle-class women. Expressive body labor focuses on the physical appearance and artistry of the nails and the communication of respect and fairness in serving mostly working- and lower-middle-class African American and Caribbean women customers at Downtown Nails. Routinized body labor stresses efficiency, predictability, affordability, and competency in physical labor and a courteous but no-frills style of emotional labor geared toward mostly lower-middle- and middle-class racially mixed female customers at Crosstown Nails.

These patterns of body labor conform to the racial and class positions of the customers and the associated feeling rules that define their service expectations. At Uptown Nails, race, gender, and class intersect to produce an emotionally and physically pampering form of body labor that conforms to the expectations of white, professional women for caring and attentive service. These women have high expectations regarding massages, cleanliness, sensitive touch, and friendly conversation while Black, working-class women at Downtown Nails expect minimal pampering and focus on the appearance, originality, and durability of

the nails themselves. At Crosstown Nails, class prevails over race as both Black and white women of middling socioeconomic status view the nails instrumentally as a no-nonsense professional asset rather than conforming to traditional notions of pampered femininity. Thus, they trade off the physical pleasure and emotional attentiveness of high-service treatment for the convenience and price of routinized body labor.

Black middle-class women at Crosstown Nails share this instrumental view of nails and a preference for a routinized, hassle-free manicure. The style of nails and the meaning given to them by Black middle-class women radically differ from the working-class Black women at Downtown Nails, who value nail art as a form of self-expression and demand emotional labor that communicates respect and fairness. This contrast between the Black middle-class and working-class women customers at Crosstown and Downtown Nails again suggests the greater salience of class over race in determining the type of body labor.

What structural factors explain the differences in the provision of body labor in these three sites? These body labor types, while enacted at the micro level, reflect the social conditions of the neighborhoods in which the salons are located and the clientele they serve. Because of the reliance on tips in white middle-class neighborhoods, service providers have greater incentive to cater to the emotional needs of customers such as those at Uptown Nails to increase their earnings. In the Black working-class neighborhoods where tipping is not a widespread practice, nail salon workers guarantee their economic livelihood by establishing a base of regular customers who seek them out for their technical and artistic abilities more than their emotional or physical attentiveness. In routinized body labor settings serving lower-middle-class women of mixed races, service providers maximize their earnings by generating a high turnover of customers who receive satisfactory but not special emotional and physical treatment.

These patterns of body labor service reflect and reproduce racial and class inequalities between women. Korean service providers learn to respond to white middle- and upper-class customers' emotional pampering and physical pleasure, thereby reinforcing the invisible sense of privilege claimed by these customers. The expressive practices of creating artful nails and troubleshooting potential problems with Black working-class customers, while helping to smooth relations, can also serve to emphasize racial meanings in these interactions and enforce a sense of difference. The routinized style of body labor reflects the generic social position of women whose bodies are neither privileged nor pathologized but simply treated with routine efficiency.

CONCLUSIONS

Exchanges of manicuring services set up complex emotional and embodied interactions between diverse women. In introducing and exploring the dimensions of body labor, this article challenges the scholarship on emotional labor to take more seriously the growth in body-related service jobs and to address the differences in these service interactions not simply in terms of gendered processes but through the lens of race, gender, and class intersections. Thus, not only does the concept of body labor add embodied dimensions to emotional labor, but it also makes it more applicable to low-wage service work performed by immigrant women of color.

This study situates the practice of body labor in Korean-owned nail salons within the restructuring of the global economy and the transplantation of the practices of enhancing bodily appearance from private households into new forms of public urban space. A manicure is no longer something a woman gives herself, her daughter, or a girlfriend in the quiet of her own bathroom, but it is something that she increasingly purchases in a nail salon. In purchasing these services, she not only expands the boundaries of the service economy to include formerly private regimens of personal hygiene, but she also encounters the "other," often an immigrant woman of different racial and class background through physical contact that can generate highly charged feelings on both sides. These feelings manifest and are worked out differently in distinct styles of body labor that emerge through the intersection of gendered work processes with customers' racial and class positions and their associated service expectations.

Although so far I have drawn parallels between this process of exchanging body services for a wage with the commercialization of feelings in emotional labor, another parallel can be drawn to the encroachment of the capitalist system into the area of social reproduction. Nakano Glenn (1992) and others have illuminated how the performance of household work such as cleaning, cooking, and caring for children and the

elderly has become increasingly part of the capitalist market, and these low-paying, unprotected jobs (nanny, elderly caregiver, nurses, aide) are most often filled by immigrant women of color. This study has illustrated how similar to these dynamics of commodifying reproductive labor and farming it out at low wages to less privileged women, body services and the emotional labor accompanying it (what I have conceptualized as body labor) have become increasingly commercialized and designated as racialized immigrant women's work.

While this article has concentrated on my case study of nail salons, the concept of body labor can be applied to many other occupations, especially female-dominated service professions in which service providers and customers are of different race and class origins, including hairdressers, masseuses, nannies, nurses, doctors, personal trainers, and prostitutes.

Finally, in mapping out the racial, gendered, and classed complexity of body labor, this article highlights a kernel of social change that lies in negotiating service interactions between women of different classes, racial and ethnic backgrounds, and immigrant statuses. While these interactions often mimic structures of power and privilege, they also create opportunities to contest these structures. The Korean salon owner of Downtown Nails learns to respect and show appreciation for Black working-class patrons. Korean manicurists at Uptown Nails assert their knowledge and expertise over their white middle-class customers. Routinized service at Crosstown Nails equalizes treatment of women across race and class.

From the customer's side, a weekly trip to the local nail salon can become a lesson in relating to a woman of a radically different social position, whom she would rarely encounter in her own milieu. As these emotional and embodied interactions reflect larger systems of status and power, by rewriting the unspoken feeling rules of these interactions, women can take small but important steps in the creation of more equal relations with other women. Nakano Glenn (2002, 16–17) wrote that "contesting race and gender hierarchies may involve challenging everyday assumptions and practices, take forms that do not involve direct confrontation, and occur in locations not considered political." Exchanges involving body labor in Korean-owned nail salons are one such location where these everyday assumptions and practices can be recognized and possibly renegotiated.

ACKNOWLEDGMENTS

I would like to thank Catherine Berheide, C. N. Le, Jennifer Lee, Sara Lee, Susan Walzer and Chris Bose, Minjeong Kim, and the *Gender & Society* anonymous reviewers for valuable comments and suggestions. My dissertation committee at New York University, Craig Calhoun, Jeff Goodwin, and Ruth Horowitz, and readers, Troy Duster and Kathleen Gerson, guided the theory and research design. Thanks to Liann Kang, Wi Jo Kang, Nora Choi-Lee, Jung-hwa Hwang, Eunja Lee, and especially Jiwon Lee for research assistance. Research was supported in part by New York University, the Social Science Research Council's Committee on International Migration, Skidmore College, and Grinnell College. By recognizing this study with the Cheryl Allyn Miller award, Sociologists for Women in Society provided encouragement and intellectual community. I am grateful to Myra Marx Ferree, Mitchell Duneier, and members of the Feminist Seminar and Race and Ethnicity Seminar for inviting me to present and for responding to an earlier version of this article at the University of Wisconsin–Madison, 2001.

REFERENCES

Anderson, Margaret, and Patricia Hill Collins. 2001. *Race, class, and gender: An anthology.* Belmont, CA: Wadsworth.

Baca Zinn, Maxine. 1989. Family, race, and poverty in the eighties. *Signs: Journal of Women in Culture and Society* 14:856–74.

Banks, Ingrid. 2000. *Hair matters: Beauty, power, and Black women's consciousness.* New York: New York University Press.

Banner, Lois. 1983. *American beauty.* New York: Alfred A. Knopf.

Bordo, Susan. 1993. *Unbearable weight: Feminism, Western culture and the body.* Berkeley: University of California Press.

Burawoy, Michael. 1991. *Ethnography unbound.* Berkeley: University of California Press.

Chapkis, Wendy. 1986. *Beauty secrets.* Boston: South End.

Cheng, Lucie, and Edna Bonacich. 1984. *Labor immigration under capitalism: Asian workers in the United States before World War 2.* Berkeley: University of California Press.

Frank, Arthur W. 1990. Bringing bodies back in: A decade review. *Theory, Culture, and Society* 7:131–62.

Gilroy, Paul. 1993. *The Black Atlantic: Modernity and double consciousness.* Cambridge, MA: Harvard University Press.

Gimlan, Debra. 1996. Pamela's place: Power and negotiation in the hair salon. *Gender & Society* 10:505–26.

Hall, Elaine J. 1993. Waitering/waitressing: Engendering the work of table servers. *Gender & Society* 7:329–46.

Hill Collins, Patricia. 1991. *Black feminist thought: Knowledge, consciousness, and the politics of empowerment.* New York: Routledge.

Hochschild, Arlie. 1983. *The managed heart: The commercialization of human feeling.* Berkeley: University of California Press.

hooks, bell. 1981. *Ain't I a woman: Black women and feminism.* Boston: South End.

———. 1990. *Black looks: Race and representation.* Boston: South End.

Hu-DeHart, Evelyn. 1999. *Across the Pacific: Asian Americans and globalization.* Philadelphia: Temple University Press.

Hurtado, Aida. 1989. Relating to privilege: Seduction and rejection in the subordination of white women and women of color. *Signs: Journal of Women in Culture and Society* 14:833–55.

Kang, Miliann. 1997. Manicuring race, gender, and class: Service interactions in New York City Korean nail salons. *Race, Gender, and Class* 4:143–64.

Kerner Furman, Frida. 1997. *Facing the mirror: Older women and the beauty shop culture.* New York: Routledge.

Lee, Jee-Young Jennifer. 2002. *Civility in the city: Blacks, Jews, and Koreans in urban America.* Cambridge, MA: Harvard University Press.

Leidner, Robin. 1993. *Fast food, fast talk: Service work and the routinization of everyday life.* Berkeley: University of California Press.

———. 1999. Emotional labor in service work. *Annals of the American Academy of Political and Social Science* 561:81–95.

Lively, Kathryn. 2000. Reciprocal emotion management: Working together to maintain stratification in private law firms. *Work and Occupations* 27:32–63.

Macdonald, Cameron. 1996. Shadow mothers: Nannies, au pairs, and invisible work. In *Working in the service society,* edited by Cameron Lynne Macdonald and Carmen Sirianni. Philadelphia: Temple University Press.

Marx Ferree, Myra, and Elaine J. Hall. 1996. Rethinking stratification from a feminist perspective: Gender, race, and class in mainstream textbooks. *American Sociological Review* 61:929–50.

Nakano Glenn, Evelyn. 1992. From servitude to service work: Historical continuities in the racial division of paid reproductive labor. *Signs: Journal of Women in Culture and Society* 18:1–43.

———. 2002. *Unequal freedom: How race and gender shaped American citizenship and labor.* Cambridge, MA: Harvard University Press.

Ngan-Ling Chow, Esther. 1994. Asian American women at work. In *Women of color in U.S. society,* edited by Maxine Baca Zinn and Bonnie Dill Thornton. Philadelphia: Temple University Press.

Ong, Aihwa. 1987. *Spirits of resistance and capitalist discipline: Factory women in Malaysia.* Albany: State University of New York Press.

Pierce, Jennifer L. 1995. *Gender trials: Emotional lives in contemporary law firms.* Berkeley: University of California Press.

Rooks, Noliwe. 1996. *Hair rising: Beauty, culture, and African American women.* New Brunswick. NJ: Rutgers University Press.

Schmitt, Frederika E., and Patricia Yancey Martin. 1999. Unobtrusive mobilization by an institutionalized rape crisis center. "All we do comes from victims." *Gender & Society* 13:364–84.

Smith, Dorothy. 1987. *The everyday world as problematic: A feminist sociology.* Boston: Northeastern University Press.

Steinberg, Ronnie, and Deborah Figart. 1999. Emotional labor since *The Managed Heart. Annals of the American Academy of Political and Social Science* 561:8–26.

Wharton, Amy. 1999. The psychological consequences of emotional labor. *Annals of the American Academy of Political and Social Science* 561:158–77.

Wolf, Naomi. 1991. *The beauty myth: How images of beauty are used against women.* New York: William Morrow

READING *24* **Pierrette Hondagneu-Sotelo**

Maid in L.A.

First published in 2001

The title of this [reading] was inspired by Mary Romero's 1992 book, *Maid in the U.S.A.*, but I am also taking the pun to heart: most Latina immigrant women who do paid domestic work in Los Angeles had no prior experience working as domestics in their countries of origin. Of the 153 Latina domestic workers that I surveyed at bus stops, in ESL classes, and in parks, fewer than 10 percent reported having worked in other people's homes, or taking in laundry for pay, in their countries of origin. This finding is perhaps not surprising, as we know from immigration research that the poorest of the poor rarely migrate to the United States; they simply cannot afford to do so.

Some of the Latina immigrant women who come to Los Angeles grew up in impoverished squatter settlements, others in comfortable homes with servants. In their countries of origin, these women were housewives raising their own children, or college students, factory workers, store clerks, and secretaries; still others came from rural families of very modest means. Regardless of their diverse backgrounds, their transformation into housecleaners and nanny/housekeepers occurs in Los Angeles. I emphasize this point because images in popular culture and the media more or less identify Latinas with domestic workers—or, more precisely, as "cleaning gals" and "baby-sitters," euphemisms that mask American discomfort with these arrangements. Yet they take on these roles only in

the United States, at various points in their own migration and settlement trajectories, in the context of private households, informal social networks, and the larger culture's racialized nativism.

Who are these women who come to the United States in search of jobs, and what are those jobs like? Domestic work is organized in different ways, and in this [reading] I describe live-in, live-out, and house-cleaning jobs and profile some of the Latina immigrants who do them and how they feel about their work. The [reading] concludes with a discussion of why it is that Latina immigrants are the primary recruits to domestic work, and I examine what they and their employers have to say about race relations and domestic work.

LIVE-IN NANNY/HOUSEKEEPER JOBS

For Maribel Centeno, newly arrived from Guatemala City in 1989 at age twenty-two and without supportive family and friends with whom to stay, taking a live-in job made a lot of sense. She knew that she wouldn't have to spend money on room and board, and that she could soon begin saving to pay off her debts. Getting a live-in job through an agency was easy. The *señora*, in her rudimentary Spanish, only asked where she was from, and if she had a husband and children. Chuckling, Maribel recalled her initial misunderstanding when the *señora*, using her index finger, had drawn an imaginary "2" and "3" in the palm of her hand. "I thought to myself, well, she must have two or three bedrooms, so I said, fine. 'No,' she said. 'Really, really big.' She started counting, 'One, two, three, four . . . two-three rooms.' It was twenty-three rooms! I thought, huy! On a piece of paper, she wrote '$80 a week,' and she said, 'You, child, and entire house.' So I thought, well, I have to do what I have to do, and I happily said, 'Yes.'"

"I arrived on Monday at dawn," she recalled, "and I went to the job on Wednesday evening." When the *señora* and the child spoke to her, Maribel remembered "just laughing and feeling useless. I couldn't understand anything." On that first evening, the *señora* put on classical music, which Maribel quickly identified. "I said, 'Beethoven.' She said, 'Yeah,' and began asking me in English, 'You like it?' I said 'Yes,' or perhaps I said, 'Si,' and she began playing other cassettes, CDs. They had Richard Clayderman and I recognized it, and when I said that, she stopped in her tracks, her jaw fell open, and she just stared at me. She must have been thinking, 'No schooling, no preparation, no English, how does she know this music?'" But the *señora*, perhaps because of the language difficulty, or perhaps because she felt upstaged by her live-in's knowledge of classical music, never did ask. Maribel desperately wanted the *señora* to respect her, to recognize that she was smart, educated, and cultivated in the arts. In spite of her best status-signaling efforts, "They treated me," she said, "the same as any other girl from the countryside." She never got the verbal recognition that she desired from the *señora*.

Maribel summed up her experiences with her first live-in job this way: "The pay was bad. The treatment was, how shall I say? It was cordial, a little, uh, not racist, but with very little consideration, very little respect." She liked caring for the little seven-year-old boy, but keeping after the cleaning of the twenty-three-room house, filled with marble floors and glass tables, proved physically impossible. She eventually quit not because of the polishing and scrubbing, but because being ignored devastated her socially.

Compared to many other Latina immigrants' first live-in jobs, Maribel Centeno's was relatively good. She was not on call during all her waking hours and throughout the night, the parents were engaged with the child, and she was not required to sleep in a child's bedroom or on a cot tucked away in the laundry room. But having a private room filled with amenities did not mean she had privacy or the ability to do simple things one might take for granted. "I had my own room, with my own television, VCR, my private bath, and closet, and a kind of sitting room—but everything in miniature, Thumbelina style," she said. "I had privacy in that respect. But I couldn't do many things. If I wanted to walk around in a T-shirt, or just feel like I was home, I couldn't do that. If I was hungry in the evening, I wouldn't come out to grab a banana because I'd have to walk through the family room, and then everybody's watching and having to smell the banana. I could never feel at home, never. Never, never, never! There's always something invisible that tells you this is not your house, you just work here."

It is the rare California home that offers separate maid's quarters, but that doesn't stop families from hiring live-ins; nor does it stop newly arrived Latina migrant workers from taking jobs they urgently need. When live-ins cannot even retreat to their own rooms, work seeps into their sleep and their dreams. There is no time off from the job, and they say they feel confined, trapped, imprisoned.

"I lose a lot of sleep," said Margarita Gutiérrez, a twenty-four-year-old Mexicana who worked as a live-in nanny/housekeeper. At her job in a modest-sized condominium in Pasadena, she slept in a corner of a three-year-old child's bedroom. Consequently, she found herself on call day and night with the child, who sometimes went several days without seeing her mother because of the latter's schedule at an insurance company. Margarita was obliged to be on her job twenty-four hours a day; and like other live-in nanny/housekeepers I interviewed, she claimed that she could scarcely find time to shower or brush her teeth. "I go to bed fine," she reported, "and then I wake up at two or three in the morning with the girl asking for water, or food." After the child went back to sleep, Margarita would lie awake, thinking about how to leave her job but finding it hard to even walk out into the kitchen. Live-in employees like Margarita literally have no space and no time they can claim as their own.

Working in a larger home or staying in plush, private quarters is no guarantee of privacy or refuge from the job. Forty-four-year-old Elvia Lucero worked as a live-in at a sprawling, canyon-side residence, where she was in charge of looking after twins, two five-year-old girls. On numerous occasions when I visited her there, I saw that she occupied her own bedroom, a beautifully decorated one outfitted with delicate antiques, plush white carpet, and a stenciled border of pink roses painstakingly painted on the wall by the employer. It looked serene and inviting, but it was only three steps away from the twins' room. Every night one of the twins crawled into bed with Elvia. Elvia disliked this, but said she couldn't break the girl of the habit. And the parents' room lay tucked away at the opposite end of the large (more than 3,000 square feet), L-shaped house.

Regardless of the size of the home and the splendor of the accommodations, the boundaries that we might normally take for granted disappear in live-in jobs. They have, as Evelyn Nakano Glenn has noted, "no clear line between work and non-work time," and the line between job space and private space is similarly blurred.[1] Live-in nanny/housekeepers are at once socially isolated and surrounded by other people's territory; during the hours they remain on the employers' premises, their space, like their time, belongs to another. The sensation of being among others while remaining invisible, unknown and apart, of never being able to leave the margins, makes many live-in employees sad, lonely, and depressed. Melancholy sets in and doesn't necessarily lift on the weekends.

Rules and regulations may extend around the clock. Some employers restrict the ability of their live-in employees to receive telephone calls, entertain friends, attend evening ESL classes, or see boyfriends during the workweek. Other employers do not impose these sorts of restrictions, but because their homes are located on remote hillsides, in suburban enclaves, or in gated communities, their live-in nanny/housekeepers are effectively kept away from anything resembling social life or public culture. A Spanish-language radio station, or maybe a *telenovela*, may serve as their only link to the outside world.

Food—the way some employers hoard it, waste it, deny it, or just simply do not even have any of it in their kitchens—is a frequent topic of discussion among Latina live-in nanny/housekeepers. These women are talking not about counting calories but about the social meaning of food on the job. Almost no one works with a written contract, but anyone taking a live-in job that includes "room and board" would assume that adequate meals will be included. But what constitutes an adequate meal? Everyone has a different idea, and using the subject like a secret handshake, Latina domestic workers often greet one another by talking about the problems of managing food and meals on the job. Inevitably, food enters their conversations.

No one feels the indignities of food more deeply than do live-in employees, who may not leave the job for up to six days at a time. For them, the workplace necessarily becomes the place of daily sustenance. In some of the homes where they work, the employers are out all day. When these adults return home, they may only snack, keeping on hand little besides hot dogs, packets of macaroni and cheese, cereal, and peanut butter for the children. Such foods are considered neither nutritious nor appetizing by Latina immigrants, many of whom are accustomed to sitting down to meals prepared with fresh vegetables, rice, beans, and meat. In some employers' homes, the cupboards are literally bare. Gladys Villedas recalled that at one of her live-in jobs, the *señora* had graciously said, " 'Go ahead, help yourself to anything in the kitchen.' But at times," she recalled, "there was nothing, nothing in the refrigerator! There was nothing to eat!" Even in lavish kitchens outfitted with Subzero refrigerators and imported cabinetry, food may be scarce. A celebrity photographer of luxury homes that appear in posh magazines described to a reporter what he sees when he opens the doors of some of Beverly Hills' refrigerators: "Rows of cans of Diet Coke, and maybe a few remains of pizza."[2]

Further down the class ladder, some employers go to great lengths to economize on food bills. Margarita Gutiérrez claimed that at her live-in job, the husband did the weekly grocery shopping, but he bought things in small quantities—say, two potatoes that would be served in half portions, or a quarter of a watermelon to last a household of five all week. He rationed out the bottled water and warned her that milk would make her fat. Lately, she said, he was taking both her and the children to an upscale grocery market where they gave free samples of gourmet cheeses, breads, and dips, urging them all to fill up on the freebies. "I never thought," exclaimed Margarita, formerly a secretary in Mexico City, "that I would come to this country to experience hunger!"

Many women who work as live-ins are keenly aware of how food and meals underline the boundaries between them and the families for whom they work. "I never ate with them," recalled Maribel Centeno of her first live-in job. "First of all, she never said, 'Come and join us,' and secondly, I just avoided being around when they were about to eat." Why did she avoid mealtime? "I didn't feel I was part of that family. I knew they liked me, but only because of the good work I did, and because of the affection I showered on the boy; but apart from that, I was just like the gardener, like the pool man, just one more of their staff." Sitting down to share a meal symbolizes membership in a family, and Latina employees, for the most part, know they are not just like one of the family.

Food scarcity is not endemic to all of the households where these women work. In some homes, ample quantities of fresh fruits, cheeses, and chicken stock the kitchens. Some employer families readily share all of their food, but in other households, certain higher-quality, expensive food items may remain off-limits to the live-in employees, who are instructed to eat hot dogs with the children. One Latina live-in nanny/housekeeper told me that in her employers' substantial pantry, little "DO NOT TOUCH" signs signaled which food items were not available to her; and another said that her employer was always defrosting freezer-burned leftovers for her to eat, some of it dating back nearly a decade.

Other women felt subtle pressure to remain unobtrusive, humble, and self-effacing, so they held back from eating even when they were hungry. They talked a lot about how these unspoken rules apply to fruit. "Look, if they [the employers] buy fruit, they buy three bananas, two apples, two pears. So if I eat one, who took it? It's me," one woman said, "they'll know it's me." Another nanny/housekeeper recalled: "They would bring home fruit, but without them having to say it, you just knew these were not intended for you. You understand this right away, you get it." Or as another put it, *"Las Americanos* have their apples counted out, one for each day of the week." Even fruits growing in the garden are sometimes contested. In Southern California's agriculture-friendly climate, many a residential home boasts fruit trees that hang heavy with oranges, plums, and peaches, and when the Latina women who work in these homes pick the fruit, they sometimes get in trouble.[3] Eventually, many of the women solve the food problem by buying and bringing in their own food; early on Monday mornings, you see them walking with their plastic grocery bags, carting, say, a sack of apples, some chicken, and maybe some prepared food in plastic containers.

The issue of food captures the essence of how Latina live-in domestic workers feel about their jobs. It symbolizes the extent to which the families they work for draw the boundaries of exclusion or inclusion, and it marks the degree to which those families recognize the live-in nanny/housekeepers as human beings who have basic human needs. When they first take their jobs, most live-in nanny/housekeepers do not anticipate spending any of their meager wages on food to eat while on the job, but in the end, most do—and sometimes the food they buy is eaten by members of the family for whom they work.

Although there is a wide range of pay, many Latina domestic workers in live-in jobs earn less than minimum wage for marathon hours: 93 percent of the live-in workers I surveyed in the mid-1990s were earning less than $5 an hour (79 percent of them below minimum wage, which was then $4.25), and they reported working an average of sixty-four hours a week.[4] Some of the most astoundingly low rates were paid for live-in jobs in the households of other working-class Latino immigrants, which provide some women their first job when they arrive in Los Angeles. Carmen Vasquez, for example, had spent several years working as a live-in for two Mexican families, earning only $50 a week. By comparison, her current salary of $170 a week, which she was earning as a live-in nanny/housekeeper in the hillside home of an attorney and a teacher, seemed a princely sum.

Many people assume that the rich pay more than do families of modest means, but working as a live-in in an exclusive, wealthy neighborhood, or in a twenty-three-room house, provides no guarantee of a high salary. Early one Monday morning in the fall of 1995, I was standing with a group of live-in nanny/housekeepers on a corner across the street from the Beverly Hills Hotel. As they were waiting to be picked up by their employers, a large Mercedes sedan with two women (a daughter and mother or mother-in-law?) approached, rolled down the windows, and asked if anyone was interested in a $150-a-week live-in job. A few women jotted down the phone number, and no one was shocked by the offer. Gore Vidal once commented that no one is allowed to fail within a two-mile radius of the Beverly Hills Hotel, but it turns out that plenty of women in that vicinity are failing in the salary department. In some of the most affluent Westside areas of Los Angeles—in Malibu, Pacific Palisades, and Bel Air—there are live-in nanny/housekeepers earning $150 a week. And in 1999, the *Los Angeles Times* Sunday classified ads still listed live-in nanny/housekeeper jobs with pay as low as $100 and $125.[5] Salaries for live-in jobs, however, do go considerably higher. The best-paid live-in employee whom I interviewed was Patricia Paredes, a Mexicana who spoke impeccable English and who had legal status, substantial experience, and references. She told me that she currently earned $450 a week at her live-in job. She had been promised a raise to $550, after a room remodel was finished, when she would assume weekend house-cleaning in that same home. With such a relatively high weekly salary she felt compelled to stay in a live-in job during the week, away from her husband and three young daughters who remained on the east side of Los Angeles. The salary level required that sacrifice.

But once they experience it, most women are repelled by live-in jobs. The lack of privacy, the mandated separation from family and friends, the round-the-clock hours, the food issues, the low pay, and especially the constant loneliness prompt most Latina immigrants to seek other job arrangements. Some young, single women who learn to speak English fluently try to move up the ranks into higher-paying live-in jobs. As soon as they can, however, the majority attempt to leave live-in work altogether. Most live-in nanny/housekeepers have been in the United States for five years or less; among the live-in nanny/housekeepers I interviewed, only two (Carmen Vasquez and the relatively high-earning Patricia Paredes) had been in the United States for longer than that. Like African American women earlier in the century, who tired of what the historian Elizabeth Clark-Lewis has called "the soul-destroying hollowness of live-in domestic work,"[6] most Latina immigrants try to find other options.

Until the early 1900s, live-in jobs were the most common form of paid domestic work in the United States, but through the first half of the twentieth century they were gradually supplanted by domestic "day work."[7] Live-in work never completely disappeared, however, and in the last decades of the twentieth century, it revived with vigor, given new life by the needs of American families with working parents and young children—and, as we have seen, by the needs of newly arrived Latina immigrants, many of them unmarried and unattached to families. When these women try to move up from live-in domestic work, they see few job alternatives. Often, the best they can do is switch to another form of paid domestic work, either as a live-out nanny/housekeeper or as a weekly housecleaner. When they do such day work, they are better able to circumscribe their work hours, and they earn more money in less time.[8]

LIVE-OUT NANNY/HOUSEKEEPERS

When I first met twenty-four-year-old Ronalda Saavedra, she was peeling a hard-boiled egg for a dog in the kitchen of a very large home where I was interviewing the employer. At this particular domestic job, the fifth she had held since migrating from El Salvador in 1991, she arrived daily around one in the afternoon and left after the children went to bed. On a typical day, she assisted the housekeeper, a middle-aged woman, with cleaning, laundry, and errands, and at three o'clock she drove off in her own car to pick up the children—a nine-year-old boy, whom she claimed was always angry, and his hyperactive six-year-old brother.

Once the children were put to bed, Ronalda Saavedra drove home to a cozy apartment that she shared with her brother in the San Fernando Valley. When I visited her, I saw that it was a tiny place, about half the size of the kitchen where we had first met; but it was pleasantly outfitted with new bleached oak furniture, and the morning sunshine that streamed in through a large window gave it a cheerful, almost spacious feel. Ronalda kept a well-stocked refrigerator, and during our interview she served me *pan dulce*, coffee, and honeydew melon.

Like many other women, Ronalda had begun her work stint in the United States with a live-in job, but she vastly preferred living out. She slept through the night in peace, attended ESL classes in the morning, ate what she wanted when she wanted it, and talked daily on the phone with her fiancé. All this was possible because live-out jobs are firmly circumscribed. Even when women find it difficult to say no to their employers when they are asked, at the last minute, to stay and work another hour or two, they know they will eventually retreat to their own places. So while the workday tasks and rhythms are similar to those of live-ins, the job demands on live-outs stop when they exit the houses where they work and return to their own homes, usually small and sometimes crowded apartments located in one of Los Angeles' many Latino neighborhoods. For such women with husbands or with children of their own, live-out jobs allow them to actually live with their family members and see them daily.

Live-out nanny/housekeepers also earn more money than live-ins. Most of them work eight or nine hours a day, and of those I surveyed, 60 percent worked five days a week or fewer. Their mean hourly wages were $5.90—not an exorbitant wage by any means, but above the legal minimum, unlike the wages of their peers in live-in jobs. Ronalda earned $350 for her forty-hour workweek, making her hourly wage $8.75. On top of this, her employer gave her an additional $50 to cover gasoline expenses, as Ronalda spent a portion of each afternoon driving on errands, such as going to the dry cleaners, and ferrying the children home from school and then to and from soccer practices, music lessons, and so on. In the suburban landscape of Los Angeles, employers pay an extra premium for nanny/housekeepers who can provide this shuttling service. Only Latina nanny/housekeepers with experience, strong references, English skills, and an impressive array of certificates and licenses enjoy earnings that reach Ronalda's level.

Today, most Americans who hire a domestic worker to come into their homes on a daily basis do so in order to meet their needs for *both* housecleaning and child care. Most Latina nanny/housekeepers work in households where they are solely responsible for these tasks, and they work hard to fit in the cleaning and laundry (most of them don't cook) while the children are napping or at school. Some of them feel, as one woman said, that they need to be "octopuses," with busy arms extended simultaneously in all directions. A big part of their job requires taking care of the children; and various issues with the children present nanny/housekeepers with their greatest frustrations. Paradoxically, they also experience some of their deepest job satisfaction with these children with whom they spend so much time.

After what may be years of watching, feeding, playing with, and reprimanding the same child from birth to elementary school, day in and day out, some nanny/housekeepers grow very fond of their charges and look back nostalgically, remembering, say, when a child took her first steps or first learned nursery rhymes in Spanish. Ronalda, an articulate, highly animated woman who told stories using a lot of gestures and facial expressions, talked a great deal about the children she had cared for in her various jobs. She imitated the voices of children she had taken care of, describing longingly little girls who were, she said, "*muy* nice" or "*tan* sweet," and recalled the imaginary games they would play. Like many other nanny/housekeepers, she wept freely when she remembered some of the intimate and amusing moments she had spent with children she no longer saw. She also described other children who, she said, were dour, disrespectful, and disobedient.

Many live-out nanny/housekeepers made care work—the work of keeping the children clean, happy, well nourished, and above all safe—a priority over housecleaning duties. This sometimes created conflicts with their employers, who despite saying that their children should come first still expected a spotless house. "The truth is," explained Teresa Portillo, who looked after a child only on the weekends, "when you are taking care of children, you can't neglect anything, absolutely nothing! Because the moment you do, they do whatever little *travesura*, and they scrape their knees, cut themselves or whatever." Nanny/housekeepers fear they will be sent to jail if anything happens to the children.

Feeding the children is a big part of the job. Unlike their live-in peers, when live-out nanny/housekeepers talk about food, they're usually concerned with what the children eat or don't eat. Some of them derive tremendous pleasure and satisfaction from bringing the children special treats prepared at their own homes—maybe homemade flan or *pan con crema*, or simply a mango. Some nanny/housekeepers are also in charge, to their dismay, of feeding and cleaning the children's menagerie of pets. Many feel disgusted when they have to bathe and give eyedrops to old, sick dogs, or clean the cages of iguanas, snakes, lizards, and various rodents. But these tasks are trivial in comparison to the difficulties they encounter with hard-to-manage children. Mostly, though, they complain about permissive, neglectful parents.

Not all nanny/housekeepers bond tightly with their employers' children, but most are critical of what they perceive as their employers' careless parenting—or, more accurately, mothering, for their female employers typically receive the blame. They see mothers who may spend, they say, only a few minutes a day with their babies and toddlers, or who return home from work after the children are asleep. Soraya Sanchez said she could understand mothers who work "out of necessity," but all other mothers, she believed, hired nanny/housekeepers because they just didn't like being with their own kids. "*La Americana* is very selfish, she only thinks about herself," she said. "They prefer not to be with their children, as they find it's much easier to pay someone to do that." Her critique was shared by many nanny/housekeepers; and those with children of their own, even if they didn't live with them, saw their own mothering as far superior. "I love my kids, they don't. It's just like, excuse the word, 'shitting kids'" said Patricia Paredes. "What they prefer is to go to the salon, get their nails done, you know, go shopping, things like that. Even if they're home all day, they don't want to spend time with the kids because they're paying somebody to do that for them." For many Latina nanny/housekeepers, seething class resentments find expression in the rhetoric of comparative mothering.

When Latina immigrant women enter the homes of middle-class and upper-middle-class Americans, they encounter ways of raising children very different from those with which they are familiar. As Julia Wrigley's research has shown, the child-rearing values of many Latina and Caribbean nannies differ from those of their employers, but most are eager to do what middle-class parents want—to adopt "time out" discipline measures instead of swatting, or to impose limits on television viewing and Nintendo.[9] Some of them not only adapt but come to genuinely admire and appreciate such methods of child rearing. Yet they, too, criticize the parenting styles they witness close up in the homes where they work.

Some nanny/housekeepers encounter belligerent young children, who yell at them, call them names, and throw violent temper tantrums; and when they do, they blame the parents. They are aghast when parents, after witnessing a child scratch or bite or spit at them, simply shrug their shoulders and ignore such behavior. Parents' reactions to these incidents were a litmus test of sorts. Gladys Villedas, for example, told me that at her job, a five-year-old "grabbed my hair and pulled it really hard. Ay! It hurt so much I started crying! It really hurt my feelings because never in my own country, when I was raising my children, had this happened to me. Why should this happen to me here?" When she complained to her employer, she said the employer had simply consulted a child-rearing manual and explained that it was "a stage." Not all nanny/housekeepers encounter physically abusive children, but when they do, they prefer parents who allow them the authority to impose discipline, or who back them up by firmly instructing their children that it is not okay to kick or slap the nanny. Nanny/housekeepers spoke glowingly about these sorts of employers.

When nanny/housekeepers see parent-child interactions in the homes where they work, they are often put off and puzzled by what they observe. In these moments, the huge cultural gulf between Latina nanny/housekeepers and their employers seems even wider than they had initially imagined. In the home where Maribel Centeno was working as a live-out nanny/housekeeper, she spent the first few hours of her shift doing laundry and housecleaning, but when a thirteen-year-old boy, of whom she was actually very fond, arrived home from school, her real work began. It was his pranks, which were neither malicious nor directed at her, and parental tolerance of these, that drove her crazy. These adolescent pranks usually involved items like water balloons, firecrackers, and baking soda made to look like cocaine. Recently the boy had tacked up on his parents' bedroom door a condom filled with a small amount of milk and a little sign that read, "Mom and Dad, this could have been my life." Maribel thought this was inappropriate behavior; but more bewildering and disturbing than the boy's prank was his mother's reaction—laughter. Another nanny/housekeeper had reacted with similar astonishment when, after a toddler tore apart a loaf of French bread and threw the pieces, balled like cotton, onto the floor, the father came forward not to reprimand but to record the incident with a camcorder. The regularity with which their employers waste food astounds them, and drug use also raises their eyebrows. Some nanny/housekeepers are instructed to give Ritalin and Prozac to children as young as five or six, and others tell of parents and teens locked in their separate bedrooms, each smoking marijuana.

Nanny/housekeepers blame permissive and neglectful parents, who they feel don't spend enough time with their own children, for the children's unruly behavior and for teen drug use. "The parents, they say 'yes' to everything the child asks," complained one woman. "Naturally," she added, "the children are going to act spoiled." Another nanny/housekeeper analyzed the situation this way: "They [the parents] feel guilty because they don't spend that much time with the kids, and they want to replace that missed time, that love, with toys."

Other nanny/housekeepers prided themselves on taming and teaching the children to act properly. "I really had to battle with these children just to get them to pay attention to me! When I started with them, they had no limits, they didn't pick up their toys, and they couldn't control their tempers. The eldest—oof! He used to kick and hit me, and in public! I was mortified," recalled Ronalda Saavedra. Another woman remarked of children she had looked after, "These kids listened to me. After all, they spent most of the time with me, and not with them [the parents]. They would arrive at night, maybe spend a few moments with the kids, or maybe the kids were already asleep." Flvia Areola highlighted the injustice of rearing children whom one will never see again. Discussing her previous job, she said, "I was the one who taught that boy to talk, to walk, to read, to sit! Everything! She [the child's mother] almost never picked him up! She only picked him up when he was happy." Another nanny/housekeeper concluded, "These parents don't really know their own children. Just playing with them, or taking them to the park, well, that's not raising children. I'm the one who is with them every day."

Nanny/housekeepers must also maneuver around jealous parents, who may come to feel that their children's affections have been displaced. "The kids fall in love with you and they [the parents] wonder why. Some parents are jealous of what the kids feel toward you," said Ronalda Saavedra, "I'm not going to be lying, 'I'm your mommy,' but in a way, children go to the person who takes care of them, you know? That's just the way it is." For many nanny/housekeepers, it is these ties of affection that make it possible for them to do their job by making it rewarding. Some of them say they can't properly care for the children without feeling a special fondness for them; others say it just happens naturally. "I fall in love with all of these children. How can I not? That's just the way I am," one nanny/housekeeper told me. "I'm with them all day, and when I go home, my husband complains that that's all I talk about, what they did, the funny things they said." The nanny/housekeepers, as much as they felt burdened by disobedient children, sometimes felt that these children were also a gift of sorts, one that parents—again, the mothers—did not fully appreciate. "The babies are so beautiful!" gushed Soraya Sanchez. "How is it that a mother can lose those best years, when their kids are babies. I mean, I remember going down for a nap with these little babies, how we'd cuddle. How is it that a person who has the option of enjoying that would prefer to give that experience to a stranger?" Precisely because of such feelings, many Latina immigrants who have children try to find a job that is compatible with their own family lives. Housecleaning is one of those jobs.

HOUSECLEANERS

Like many working mothers, every weekday morning Marisela Ramírez awoke to dress and feed her preschooler, Tomás, and drive him to school (actually, a Head Start program) before she herself ventured out to work, navigating the dizzying array of Los Angeles freeways. Each day she set off in a different direction headed for a different workplace. On Mondays she maneuvered her way to Pasadena, where she cleaned the stately home of an elderly couple; on Tuesdays she alternated between cleaning a home in the Hollywood Hills and a more modest-sized duplex in Glendale; and Wednesdays took her to a split-level condominium in Burbank. You had to keep alert, she said, to remember where to go on which days and how to get there!

By nine o'clock she was usually on the job, and because she zoomed through her work she was able to finish, unless the house was extremely dirty, by one or two in the afternoon. After work, there were still plenty of daylight hours left for Marisela to take Tomás to the park, or at least to take him outside and let him ride down the sidewalk on his kid-sized motorized vehicle before she started dinner. Working as a housecleaner allowed Marisela to be the kind of wife and mother she wanted to be. Her job was something she did, she said, "because I have to"; but unlike her peers who work in live-in jobs, she enjoyed a fairly regular family life of her own, one that included cooking and eating family meals, playing with her son, bathing him, putting him to bed, and then watching *telenovelas* in the evenings with her husband and her sister. On the weekends, family socializing took center stage, with *carne asadas* in the park; informal gatherings with her large Mexican family, which extended throughout Los Angeles; and music from her husband, who worked as a gardener but played guitar in a weekend *ranchera* band.

Some might see Marisela Ramírez as just another low-wage worker doing dirty work, but by her own account—and gauging by her progress from her starting point—she had made remarkable occupational strides. Marisela had begun working as a live-in nanny/housekeeper in Los Angeles when she was only fifteen years old. Ten years later, the move from live-in work to housecleaning had brought her higher hourly wages, a shorter workweek, control over the pace of work, and flexibility in arranging when she worked. Cleaning different houses was also, she said, less boring than working as a nanny/housekeeper, which entailed passing every single day "in just one house, all week long with the same routine, over and over."

For a while she had tried factory work, packaging costume jewelry in a factory warehouse located in the San Fernando Valley, but Marisela saw housecleaning as preferable on just about every count. "In the factory, one has to work very, very fast!" she exclaimed. "And you can't talk to anybody, you can't stop, and you can't rest until it's break time. When you're working in a house, you can take a break at the moment you wish, finish the house when you want, and leave at the hour you decide. And it's better pay. It's harder work, yes," she conceded, "but it's better pay."

"How much were you earning at the factory?" I asked.

"Five dollars an hour; and working in houses now, I make about $11, or even more. Look, in a typical house, I enter at about 9 A.M., and I leave at 1 P.M., and they pay me $60. It's much better [than factory work]." Her income varied, but she could usually count on weekly earnings of about $300. By pooling these together with her husband's and sister's earnings, she was able to rent a one-bedroom bungalow roofed in red tile, with a lawn and a backyard for Tomás's sandbox and plastic swimming pool. In Mexico, Marisela had only studied as far as fifth grade, but she wanted the best for Tomás. Everyone doted on him, and by age four he was already reading simple words.

Of the housecleaners I surveyed, the majority earned, like Marisela, between $50 and $60 per housecleaning, which usually took about six hours. This suggests an average hourly wage of about $9.50, but I suspect the actual figure is higher.[10] Women like Marisela, who drive their own cars and speak some English, are likely to earn more than the women I surveyed, many of whom ride the buses to work. Marisela was typical of the housecleaners whom I surveyed in having been in the United States for a number of years. Unlike nanny/housekeepers, most of the housecleaners who were mothers themselves had all their children with them in the United States. Housecleaning, as Mary Romero has noted, is a job that is quite compatible with having a family life of one's own.

Breaking into housecleaning is tough, often requiring informal tutelage from friends and relatives. Contrary to the image that all women "naturally" know how to do domestic work, many Latina domestic workers discover that their own housekeeping experiences do not automatically transfer to the homes where they work. As she looked back on her early days in the job, Marisela said, "I didn't know how to clean or anything. My sister taught me." Erlinda Castro, a middle-aged women who had already run her own household and raised five children in Guatemala, had also initially worked in live-in jobs when she first came to Los Angeles. Yet despite this substantial domestic experience, she recalled how mystified she was when she began housecleaning. "Learning how to use the chemicals and the liquids" in the different households was confusing, and, as friends and employers instructed her on what to do, she began writing down in a little notebook the names of the products and what they cleaned. Some women learn the job by informally

apprenticing with one another, accompanying a friend or perhaps an aunt on her housecleaning jobs.

Establishing a thriving route of *casas* requires more than learning which cleaning products to use or how to clean quickly and efficiently. It also involves acquiring multiple jobs, which housecleaners typically gain by asking their employers if they have friends, neighbors, or acquaintances who need someone to clean their houses; and because some attrition is inevitable, they must constantly be on the lookout for more *casas*. Not everyone who wants to can fill up her entire week.

To make ends meet when they don't have enough houses to clean, Latina housecleaners in Los Angeles find other ways to earn income. They might prepare food—say, tamales and *crema*—which they sell door-to-door or on the street; or they might sell small amounts of clothing that they buy wholesale in the garment district, or products from Avon, Mary Kay cosmetics, and Princess House kitchenware. They take odd jobs, such as handing out flyers advertising dental clinics or working at a swap meet; or perhaps they find something more stable, such as evening janitorial work in office buildings. Some housecleaners work swing shift in garment factories, while others work three days a week as a nanny/housekeeper and try to fill the remaining days with housecleaning jobs. Some women supplement their husband's income by cleaning only one or two houses a week, but more often they patch together a number of jobs in addition to housecleaning.

Housecleaning represents, as Romero has written, the "modernization" of paid domestic work. Women who clean different houses on different days sell their labor services, she argues, in much the same way that a vendor sells a product to various customers.[11] The housecleaners themselves see their job as far preferable to that of a live-in or live-out nanny/housekeeper. They typically work alone, during times when their employers are out of the home; and because they are paid "by the job" instead of by the hour, they don't have to remain on the job until 6 or 7 P.M., an advantage much appreciated by women who have families of their own. Moreover, because they work for different employers on different days, they are not solely dependent for their livelihood on one boss whom they see every single day. Consequently, their relationships with their employers are less likely to become highly charged and conflictual; and if problems do arise, they can leave one job without jeopardizing their entire weekly earnings. Since child care is not one of their tasks, their responsibilities are more straightforward and there are fewer points of contention with employers. Housecleaning is altogether less risky.

Housecleaners also see working independently and informally as more desirable than working for a commercial cleaning company. "The companies pay $5 an hour," said Erlinda Castro, whose neighbor worked for one, "and the women have to work their eight hours, doing up to ten, twenty houses a day! One does the vacuuming, the other does the bathroom and the kitchen, and like that. It's tremendously hard work, and at $5 an hour? Thank God, I don't have to do that." Two of the women I interviewed, one now a live-out nanny/housekeeper and the other a private housecleaner, had previously worked for cleaning services, and both of them complained bitterly about their speeded-up work pace, low pay, and tyrannical bosses.

Private housecleaners take enormous pride in their work. When they finish their job, they can see the shiny results, and they are proud of their job autonomy, their hours, their pay, and, most important, what they are able to do with their pay for themselves and for their families. Yet housecleaning brings its own special problems. Intensive cleaning eventually brings physical pain, and sometimes injury. "Even my bones are tired," said fifty-three-year-old Lupe Vélez; and even a relatively young woman like Celestina Vigil at age thirty-three was already reporting back problems that she attributed to her work. While most of them have only fleeting contact with their employers, and many said they work for "good people," just about everyone has suffered, they said, "inconsiderate persons" who exhort them to work faster, humiliate them, fail to give raises, add extra cleaning tasks without paying extra, or unjustly accuse them of stealing or of ruining a rug or upholstery. And the plain old hard work and stigma of cleaning always remain, as suggested by the answer I got when I asked a housecleaner what she liked least about her job. "The least?" she said, with a wry smile. "Well, that you have to clean."

DOMESTIC JOB TRAJECTORIES AND TRANSNATIONAL MOTHERHOOD

As we have seen, private paid domestic work is organized into suboccupations, each with different pay scales, tasks, and hours.[12] Although they share many similarities, each job arrangement has its own different

TABLE 1   TYPE OF DOMESTIC WORK, LENGTH OF RESIDENCE IN THE UNITED STATES, AND MEAN HOURLY WAGES

	Live-ins (percent) (n = 30)	Live-outs (percent) (n = 64)	Housecleaners (percent) (n = 59)
Five years or less in United States	60	31	17
More than five years in United States	40	69	83
Mean hourly wage	$3.80	$5.90	$9.50

problems and rewards. In this section I discuss the movement between the three suboccupations and some of the family characteristics of the women who fill these jobs.

Some researchers have called live-in domestic work "the bridging occupation," because in various periods and places, it allowed rural migrant women to acculturate to the city and learn new ways of living.[13] Unlike Irish immigrant women or the black women who went from the South to the North to work as domestics in the early twentieth century, and unlike many private domestics in Europe and Latin America in the past, most Latina immigrants doing paid domestic work in the United States are *not* new to the city. Yet for many of them in Los Angeles today, especially those who are single and have very limited options for places to work and live, live-in jobs do serve as an initial occupational step. As Table 1 shows, new arrivals and women who have lived in the United States five years or less concentrate in live-in jobs (60 percent). In contrast, the majority of housecleaners (83 percent) and live-out nanny/housekeepers (69 percent) have lived in the United States for more than five years. Some begin their live-in jobs literally within forty-eight hours after arriving in Los Angeles, while some housecleaners have lived in the United States for twenty years or more. For newly arrived immigrant women without papers, a live-in job in a private home may feel safer, as private homes in middle- and upper-middle-class neighborhoods are rarely, if ever, threatened by Immigration and Naturalization Service raids.[14]

As the years pass, the women who took live-in jobs learn some English, gain knowledge of other job possibilities, and learn to use their social networks to their occupational advantage. Most of them eventually move out of live-in work. Some return to their countries of origin, and others look to sales, factory work, or janitorial work. But given the low pay of those jobs—in 1999, garment workers in Los Angeles were earning $5.00 an hour, and nonunion janitors with six years of experience were earning $6.30 an hour—many of them transition into some form of domestic day work.[15]As they abandon their live-in positions for live-out nanny/housekeeper and housecleaner jobs, their wages increase. For these women, the initial misery suffered in their live-in jobs makes other domestic work look if not good then at least tolerable—and certainly better than where they started.

For Latina immigrants in Los Angeles today, live-in domestic work does serve as an occupational bridge of sorts, but it often leads only to other types of domestic jobs. These individual trajectories match historical transformations in the occupation. Much as live-in jobs were once the dominant form of paid domestic work, and then gave way to arrangements in which domestics continued to work daily for one employer but lived with their own families, and finally to modernized "job work" or periodic housecleaning, so many Latina immigrants today traverse these three different types of jobs. Some roughly follow the historical order, moving from live-in to live-out nanny/housekeeper jobs, and then to housecleaning, but their modest occupational mobility does not always follow such a linear course.

As Mexican and Central American immigrant women move into live-out and housecleaning jobs, their family lives change. With better pay and fewer hours of work, they become able to live with their own family members. Among those I surveyed, about 45 percent of the women doing day work were married, but only 13 percent of the live-ins were married. Most women who have husbands and children with them in Los Angeles do not wish to take live-in jobs; moreover, their application for a live-in job is likely to be rejected if they reveal that they have a husband, a boyfriend, or children living in Los Angeles. As one job seeker in an employment agency waiting room put it, "You can't have a family, you can't have anyone [if you want a live-in job]." Live-out nanny/housekeepers often face this family restriction too, as employers are wary of hiring someone who may not report for work when her own children come down with the flu.

Their subminimum wages and long hours make it impossible for many live-in workers to bring their children to Los Angeles; other live-ins are young women who do not have children of their own. Once they do have children who are either born in or have immigrated to Los Angeles, most women try to leave live-in work to be with them. Not all the women can do so, and sometimes their finances or jobs force them to send the children "back home" to be reared by grandmothers. Clearly, performing domestic work for pay, especially in a live-in job, is often incompatible with caring for one's own family and home.[16]

The substantial proportion of Latina domestic workers in Los Angeles whose children stay in their countries of origin are in the same position as many Caribbean women working in domestic jobs on the East Coast, and as the Filipinas who predominate in domestic jobs in many cities around the globe. This is what I label "transnational motherhood" . . . ; in a 1997 article Ernestine Avila and I coined this term as we examined how Latina immigrant domestic workers are transforming their own meanings of motherhood to accommodate these spatial and temporal separations.[17] As Table 2 suggests, these arrangements are most common among women with live-in jobs, but live-in domestic workers and single mothers are not the only ones who rely on them.[18]

TABLE 2   TYPE OF DOMESTIC WORK, MARITAL STATUS, AND LOCATION OF CHILDREN

	Live-ins (percent) (n = 30)	Live-outs (percent) (n = 64)	Housecleaners (percent) (n = 59)
Single (included the widowed, divorced, or separated)	87	55	54
Married	13	45	46
	DOMESTIC WORKERS WITH CHILDREN		
	(n = 16)	(n = 53)	(n = 45)
All children in United States	18	58	76
At least one child "back home"	82	42	24

These transnational arrangements are not altogether new. The United States has a long history of incorporating people of color through coercive systems of labor that do not recognize family rights, including the right to care for one's own family members. As others have pointed out, slavery and contract labor systems were organized to maximize economic productivity, and offered few supports to sustain family life.[19] Today, international labor migration and the job characteristics of paid domestic work, especially live-in work, virtually impose transnational motherhood on many Mexican and Central American women who have children of their own.

At the other end of the spectrum are the housecleaners, who earn higher wages than live-ins (averaging $9.50 an hour vs. $3.80) and who work fewer hours per week than live-ins (twenty-three vs. sixty-four). The majority of them (76 percent) have all their children in the United States, and they are the least likely to experience transnational spatial and temporal separations from their children. Greater financial resources and more favorable job terms enhance housecleaners' abilities to bring their children to the United States. As we have seen, weekly housecleaning is dominated by relatively well-established women with more years of experience in the United States, who speak some English, who have a car, and who have job references. Because their own position is more secure, they are also more likely to have their children here. And because they tend to work fewer hours per week, have greater flexibility in scheduling, and earn higher wages than the live-ins, they can live with and care for their children.

With respect to their ability to care for their own children, live-out nanny/housekeepers fall between live-ins and weekly cleaners—predictably, since they are also in an intermediate position in their earnings, rigidity of schedule, and working hours. Live-out domestic workers, according to the survey, earn $5.90 an hour and work an average workweek of thirty-five hours, and 42 percent of those who are mothers reported having at least one of their children in their country of origin.

THE DOMINANCE OF CENTRAL AMERICAN AND MEXICAN IMMIGRANT WOMEN

Paid domestic work has long been a racialized and gendered occupation, but why today are Central American women hugely over-represented in these jobs in Los Angeles in comparison with Mexicans (whose immigrant population is of course many times larger)? In the survey I conducted of 153 Westside Latina domestic workers, 75 percent of the respondents were from Central America; of those, most were from El Salvador and Guatemala. And in census counts, Salvadoran and Guatemalan women are, respectively, twelve times and thirteen times more likely than the general population to be engaged in private domestic work in Los Angeles.[20] Numerous studies paint a similar picture in other major U.S. cities, such as Washington, D.C., Houston, and San Francisco; one naturally wonders why this should be so.[21]

In Los Angeles, the heavy concentration of Central American women in paid domestic work is partially explained by the location of L.A.'s primary Central American immigrant neighborhood, the Pico-Union/ Westlake area, just west of the small, high-rise downtown. As UCLA sociologist David Lopez and his colleagues explain, "A large proportion of Central Americans tend to reside closer to the middle-class neighborhoods of the Westside and the San Fernando Valley . . . while Mexicans are concentrated in the more isolated areas east and south of Downtown Los Angeles.[22] It is certainly quicker to drive or take a bus to the Westside from the Pico Union area than it is from East L.A. But there is more to this story than spatial location and L.A. transportation systems: distinct migration patterns have also influenced these occupational concentrations.

Mexican migration to the United States goes back over a hundred years, initially driven by labor recruitment programs designed to bring in men to work in agriculture. Since the late 1960s, it has shifted from a primarily male population of temporary or sojourner workers to one that includes women and entire families; these newcomers have settled in rural areas, cities, and suburbs throughout the United States, but disproportionately in California. Many Mexican women who migrated in the 1970s and 1980s were accompanied by their families and were aided by rich social networks; the latter helped prevent the urgency that leads new immigrants to take live-in jobs. Even those unmarried Mexican women who did migrate on their own, despite being opposed and sometimes stigmatized by their family and community, were often assisted by friends and more sympathetic family members. By the 1990s, more unmarried Mexican women were going north, encouraged in part by help from female friends and kin. When Mexican women arrive in the United

States, many of them enjoy access to well-developed, established communities whose members have long been employed in various industries, particularly agriculture, construction, hotels, food-processing plants, and garment factories. Compared to their Central American peers, Mexican women are more likely to have financial support from a husband; because fewer Mexican immigrant women must work outside their home, they have lower rates of overall participation in the labor force than do Central American women.[23] Their social networks also give Mexican women greater variety in their employment options; paid domestic work is only one of their alternatives.

Salvadoran and Guatemalan women migrating to the United States have done so under different circumstances than Mexican women. For Central Americans coming to *el norte*, there was no long-standing labor program recruiting men who could then bring, or encourage the migration of, their wives and daughters. In fact, as Terry Repak's study shows, some of the early pioneers of Salvadoran migration to Washington, D.C., were women, themselves informally recruited by individual members of the diplomatic corps precisely because they were desired as private domestics.[24] More significantly, Salvadoran and Guatemalan women and men left their countries in haste, often leaving their children behind, as they fled the civil wars, political violence, and economic upheaval of the 1980s. Theirs are immigrant communities that subsisted without legal status for nearly two decades, grew rapidly, and remain very poor. Even Guatemalan and Salvadoran women who arrived in the United States in the late 1980s and early 1990s could not count on finding communities of well-established compatriots who could quickly and efficiently situate them in jobs in restaurants, hotels, factories, or other industries. In fact, as some of the most compelling ethnographies of Salvadorans in San Francisco and on Long Island have shown, Central Americans' relatively shallow U.S. roots have left their social networks extremely impoverished and sometimes fractured.[25] For Central American women arriving on their own, without husbands and children in tow, desperate and lacking information about jobs—and at a crucial historical moment when American families were seeking to resolve their own child care and housekeeping problems—live-in jobs were both attractive and available.

Family structures and marriage patterns may have also contributed to the preponderance of Central American women in paid domestic work. El Salvador has traditionally had one of the lowest marriage rates in the hemisphere, especially among the urban poor, where common-law marriages and legacies of internal and intra–Central America labor migration—mostly for work on coffee plantations—have encouraged the formation of female-headed households.[26] Thus Salvadoran women have been more likely to migrate on their own and accept live-in jobs.[27] Their large numbers in this lowest rung of domestic work would then explain their eventual disproportionate concentration in all types of private paid domestic work, following the pattern discussed above.

The experience of Central American women might also be compared to that of Asian immigrant women, who have been entering the United States at increasing rates. The latter are an extremely heterogeneous group, but on average—and this is particularly true of Chinese, Indian, and Filipina women—they arrive with much higher levels of education, better English language skills, and more professional credentials than do their Latina peers. They are also more likely to have legal status; and members of some groups, especially Korean immigrant women, enjoy access to jobs in family businesses and ethnic enclaves.[28] At the same time, the generally poorer and less-educated women from Vietnam, Laos, and Cambodia have been able to withstand periods of underemployment and unemployment because they are officially sanctioned political refugees and therefore enjoy access to welfare and resettlement assistance from the federal government. While some individual Asian immigrant women are working in paid domestic work, they have not developed social networks that channel them into this niche.

It is particularly striking that Filipina immigrants predominate in this occupation elsewhere around the globe, but not in the United States. Worldwide, about two-thirds of Filipina migrants in countries as different as Italy, Canada, Hong Kong, Taiwan, Singapore, Saudi Arabia, and Jordan, do paid domestic work; but in the United States, their high levels of education and fluent English enable most of them to enter higher status occupations that require more skills than does domestic work. In 1990, 71 percent of the Filipinas in the United States were working in managerial, professional, technical/sales, and administrative support jobs, and only 17 percent were employed in service jobs.[29] They are disproportionately concentrated in the health professions, the result of formal recruitment programs designed to fill U.S. nursing shortages.[30] Experience in the health professions leads many

Filipinas to take jobs in elder care; and though some work as nanny/housekeepers in Los Angeles, many of them as live-ins, in my numerous discussions with employers, Latina employees, attorneys, and owners and employees of domestic employment agencies, no one ever mentioned Filipina housecleaners.

Nevertheless, Filipina immigrants are doing paid domestic work in the United States. Interviews conducted by Rhacel Parreñas with twenty-six Filipina domestic workers in Los Angeles reveal that many of these women have college diplomas and are working in homes because they are older and face age discrimination; they tend to earn more as care providers for the elderly ($425 per week) and more as nanny/housekeepers ($350 per week) than do Latina immigrants in these same jobs.[31] When it comes to caring for their children, some employers prefer Filipina nanny/housekeepers because they speak English well (English is the official language of schools and universities in the Philippines), and because they tend to be highly educated. Paradoxically, these qualities may predispose some employers to *not* choose Filipinas as domestic employees. At three domestic employment agencies, the owners told me that they rarely placed Filipina job applicants, because they were deemed "uppity," demanding, and likely to lie about their references. Racial preferences, as the next section suggests, shape the formation of Latina domestic workers and their employment in Los Angeles.

NARRATIVES OF RACIAL PREFERENCES

In a race-conscious society, everyone has racial preferences and prejudices, and Latina domestic workers and the women who employ them are no exception. When choosing someone to work in their homes, many employers prefer Latinas, because as "others" in language, race-ethnicity, and social class, they are outside white, English-speaking, middle-class social circles and are thus seen as unlikely to reveal family secrets and intimacies. If they do tell someone about the family fight they witnessed, that someone is likely to be another Latina nanny or a member of their own family—in either case, no one who matters to the employers. This fear of exposure sometimes prevents employers from choosing white, English-speaking job candidates. "She was non-Hispanic, and I wasn't sure if I could trust her," said one woman of a prospective employee. Another employer had been advised not to hire a white woman as a nanny/housekeeper because

an immigrant would be less likely to recognize her philanthropic family's name and to engage in bribery or kidnapping. Other women told me that they did not want a European au pair or midwestern (white) teenager taking care of their children because they would probably be young, irresponsible teens, more interested in cavorting with boyfriends, cruising the beach, and stargazing in Hollywood than in doing their job. Employers may also prefer to hire Latina nannies, as research conducted by Julia Wrigley suggests, because they view them as more submissive than whites.[32]

While some of the older employers I interviewed had hired African American housecleaners and domestics in the past, none were now doing so. Of the relatively few black women working in paid domestic work in contemporary Los Angeles, most are immigrants from Belize and Brazil, and some employers remain adamantly opposed to hiring black women to work in their homes. One domestic employment agency owner told me that some clients had requested that he never send black women to interview for a job. And at an informal luncheon, arranged by one of the employer interviewees, one of them cleared her throat and then offered, with some awkward hesitation, "Uhm, ah, I would never hire a black woman. I'd be too scared to, and I'd be especially scared if her boyfriend came around." The women, all of them relatively upper-class white matrons, had nodded in silent agreement. The old stereotype of the bossy black maid is apparently alive and well, now joined by newer terrifying images associated with young black men; but since African-American women are not pursuing domestic work jobs in Los Angeles, most employers need never confront their own racial fears directly. It is, after all, Latina immigrant women who are queuing up for domestic jobs in private homes.

When I talked with them, most employers expressed genuine appreciation for the effort, dedication, and work that these women put into their homes and children. They viewed Latina domestic workers as responsible, trustworthy, and reliable employees who have "a really strong work ethic." And while plenty of employers spoke at length about Latina women as ideally suited to caring for children, relying on images of Latinas as exceptionally warm, patient, and loving mothers, there was no similar racialized image of cleanliness. No one said, for instance, "She cleans like a Mexican." Such a phrase may sound offensive, but the absence of any such generalization is striking when nearly everyone hired to do cleaning in Los Angeles is Mexican or Central American.

Indeed, some of the employers I interviewed did make this kind of statement—to associate their own northern European heritage with superior cleaning and hygiene. A few of them offered remarks such as "People associate very clean homes with Dutch people," or "My mother's German and she cleans, you know, like Germans clean." These women did not necessarily claim that they were excellent cleaners, only that they belonged to racial-ethnic groups associated with cleanliness. None of them described their domestic employees as "dirty," but the adjective has been commonly featured in racial epithets directed at Mexicans in the Southwest and at domestic workers just about everywhere. The historian Phyllis Palmer, who has written compellingly about dirt, domesticity, and racialized divisions among women, notes that while dirt and housework connote inferior morality, white middle-class women transcend these connotations by employing women different from themselves to do the work. "Dirtiness," Palmer notes, "appears always in a constellation of the suspect qualities that, along with sexuality, immorality, laziness, and ignorance, justify social rankings of race, class and gender. The 'slut,' initially a shorthand for 'slattern' or kitchen maid, captures all of these personifications in a way unimaginable in a male persona."[33]

Employers are not the only ones who hold strong racial-ethnic preferences and prejudices. Latina domestic workers at the bus stops, at the agencies, and in the public parks readily agreed on who were their worst employers: Armenians, Iranians, Asians, Latinos, blacks, and Jews, especially Israeli Jews. "I'll never work again for *un chino!*" or *"Los armenios* [Armenians] are the worst," they tell each other. These statements were echoed in the individual interviews, as well as by the preferences job candidates register at employment agencies, and they seem to mirror what Latino men who work as day laborers think about their similarly racialized employers in Los Angeles.[34] Anyone marked as "nonwhite," it seems, is at risk of being denounced as a cheap, abusive, and oppressive employer, one to be avoided at all costs.

There are a number of factors at work here. Many of the employers in these racial-ethnic groups are immigrants themselves, albeit entrepreneurial and professional immigrants with substantially more resources than the Latinas they hire to care for their homes and children. Many had belonged to elites in their countries of origin, accustomed to having servants in their homes who would be expected to perform all sorts of

jobs on demand. Some of them bring these expectations with them when they come to the United States. When Latina domestic workers are expected to massage the *señora's* feet with oil, or scrub the kitchen floor on their hands and knees, they take offence. Others are wholly unprepared to iron Hindu saris, or to follow kosher food preparation and serving practices in the homes of Orthodox Jews. At the same time, the immigrant and ethnic employers may have been accustomed in their countries of origin to paying slave wages, and the tenuous financial situations of some makes them unable to pay minimum wage. Some newly arrived women who find their first job working as a live-in for other working-class Latino immigrant families may receive as little as $25 or $50 a week in exchange for their round-the-clock services.

Latina immigrants also operate under racist assumptions, many of which they learn in the United States. They quickly pick up the country's racial hierarchies and racist stereotypes. "Jews are cheap," "Mexican Americans and blacks are lazy," or *"Los chinos* are too bossy," they say. The regional racial hierarchy also fixes Jews, Armenians, and Iranians in low positions. *"Los Americanos,"* the term they typically use to refer to employers marked only "white," are almost never singled out by ethnicity and are rarely criticized or negatively labeled as a group.

Conversely, Latina domestic workers single out the race of particular employers who happen to be both "bad employers" and "racialized" as nonwhite. One Mexican housecleaner who maintained that Latino employers were among the most exploitative was Lupe Vélez. When I probed why she felt this way, she cited as evidence her experiences with one employer, a man from Monterrey, Mexico. A large, verbally abusive man, he had called her a pig, he went out of his way to deny her food when he sat down to eat with his family, and he had unfairly accused her of scratching and ruining a stove top. These deeply felt, painful experiences were recounted tearfully.

Yet as we talked longer, I discovered that in Los Angeles, Lupe had worked in three different Latino homes; she spoke of a Mexican American teacher who had treated her well and paid her fairly. Mutual fondness, respect, and closeness had grown between the two, who had unsuccessfully conspired at matchmaking between their young adult children. How could she maintain that Latinos were the "worst" employers when in fact a Mexican American had been among her best employers? In recalling her bad experience with the Mexican man, Lupe Vélez singled out his racial-ethnic identity. As she recalled that painful experience, his being Mexican and consistently acting abusively toward her became the most salient features about him. She applied "Latino," a racial marker, to this man, labeled an abusive, bad employer, but not to the teacher whom she had favored.

I suspect that when Latina domestic workers denounce Jewish employers, a similar process is at work. In those cases, they may only identify as Jewish those employers who are abusive and who are, as Orthodox Jews or recently emigrated Israeli Jews, unambiguously marked as Jewish. They might not recognize the other Jews for whom they work. Or perhaps Latina domestic workers' disdain for Jewish employers is testimony to the force of contemporary anti-Semitism. It is no small irony that a major provider of legal services for Latina domestic workers in Los Angeles is a Jewish nonprofit organization.[35]

Some Latina domestic workers related counternarratives, criticizing their peers for relying on racial stereotypes and hasty racial judgments. One Salvadoran housecleaner cited her Moroccan employer as one of the most gracious because she always served her a hot lunch, sitting down to chat with her; another related her appreciation of an African American bachelor, an ex-basketball player, who kept a messy house but paid her very generously; still another felt warmly toward her Korean employer who did not pay well, but who passed many choice housecleaning jobs on to her. Yet the voices of these women were drowned out by the louder, frequently blanket condemnations that other Latina domestic workers offered about their racially marked minority and immigrant employers. Amid the public clamor of racialized nativism that propelled California ballot initiatives against health and education services for undocumented immigrants and their children, against affirmative action, and against bilingual education (Propositions 187, 209, and 227 respectively), Latina immigrant domestic workers learn their own version of regional racism.

In this [reading], I conveyed briefly some of the life textures and the daily trials and triumphs experienced by Latina immigrants who work as housecleaners, live-out nanny/housekeepers, and live-in nanny/housekeepers. The Mexican, Salvadoran, and Guatemalan women who occupy these jobs come from diverse class, regional, and cultural locations, and they bring different expectations to their jobs. Once in the United States, however, they share a set of similar experiences part because of the way that their domestic work is structured.

NOTES

1. Glenn 1986: 141.
2. Lacher 1997: 1.
3. One nanny/housekeeper told me that a *señora* had admonished her for picking a bag of fruit, and wanted to charge her for it; another claimed that her employer had said she would rather watch the fruit fall off the branches and rot than see her eat it.
4. Many Latina domestic workers do not know the amount of their hourly wages; and because the lines between their work and nonwork tend to blur, live-in nanny/housekeepers have particular difficulty calculating them. In the survey questionnaire I asked live-in nanny/housekeepers how many days a week they worked, what time they began their job, and what time they ended, and I asked them to estimate how many hours off they had during an average workday (39 percent said they had no time off, but 32 percent said they had a break of between one and three hours). Forty-seven percent of the women said they began their workday at 7 a.m. or earlier, with 62 percent ending their workday at 7 p.m. or later. With the majority of them (71 percent) working five days a week, their average workweek was sixty-four hours. This estimate may at first glance appear inflated; but consider a prototypical live-in nanny/housekeeper who works, say, five days a

week, from 7 a.m. until 9 p.m., with one and a half hours off during the children's nap time (when she might take a break to lie down or watch television). Her on-duty work hours would total sixty-four and a half hours per week. The weekly pay of live-in nanny/housekeepers surveyed ranged from $130 to $400, averaging $242. Dividing this figure by sixty-four yields an hourly wage of $3.80. None of the live-in nanny/housekeepers were charged for room and board—and . . . this practice is regulated by law—but 86 percent said they brought food with them to their jobs. The majority reported being paid in cash.
5. See, e.g., Employment Classified Section 2, *Los Angeles Times*, June 6, 1999, G9.
6. Clark-Lewis 1994: 123. "After an average of seven years," she notes in her analysis of African American women who had migrated from the South to Washington, D.C., in the early twentieth century, "all of the migrant women grew to dread their live-in situation. They saw their occupation as harming all aspects of their life" (124). Nearly all of these women transitioned into day work in private homes. This pattern is being repeated by Latina immigrants in Los Angeles today, and it reflects local labor market opportunities and constraints. In Houston, Texas, where many Mayan Guatemalan immigrant women today work as

live-ins, research by Jacqueline Maria Hagan (1998) points to the tremendous obstacles they face in leaving live-in work. In Houston, housecleaning is dominated by better-established immigrant women, by Chicanas and, more recently, by the commercial cleaning companies—so it is hard for the Maya to secure those jobs. Moreover, Hagan finds that over time, the Mayan women who take live-in jobs see their own social networks contract, further reducing their internal job mobility.

7. Several factors explain the shift to day work, including urbanization, interurban transportation systems, and smaller private residences. Historians have also credited the job preferences of African American domestic workers, who rejected the constraints of live-in work and chose to live with their own families and communities, with helping to promote this shift in the urban North after 1900 (Katzman 1981; Clark-Lewis 1994: 129–35). In many urban regions of the United States, the shift to day work accelerated during World War I, so that live-out arrangements eventually became more prevalent (Katzman 1981; Palmer 1989). Elsewhere, and for different groups of domestic workers, these transitions happened later in the twentieth century. Evelyn Nakano Glenn (1986: 143) notes that Japanese immigrant and Japanese American women employed in domestic work in the San Francisco Bay Area moved out of live-in jobs and into modernized day work in the years after World War II.

8. Katzman 1981; Glenn 1986.

9. Wrigley 1995.

10. Keep in mind that the survey questionnaire was administered at three different types of sites: bus stops, ESL evening classes, and parks where nannies congregate with the children in their charge. Housecleaners who drive and have their own cars, and who speak some English, typically earn more money and are able to clean more houses per week. Because my survey is biased toward Latina domestic workers who ride the buses and attend ESL classes, those housecleaners earning higher wages are not taken into account.

11. Romero 1992.

12. In addition to the jobs of live-in nanny/housekeepers, live-out nanny/housekeepers, and weekly or biweekly housecleaners, an increasingly important and growing segment of the domestic workforce is engaged in elder care. That, too, is organized in different ways; and though the occupation lies beyond the parameters of this study (much of it is formally organized and contracted for by the state or medical organizations), some Latina immigrants are privately contracted for jobs as elders' companions and caretakers, as *damas de compañía*.

13. Smith 1973; McBride 1976.

14. The only news report of INS raids involving nannies working in private homes in Los Angeles that came to my attention as I did this research involved a nanny working for a top-ranking Latino INS agent, Jorge Guzman. In 1996 armed plainclothes INS agents illegally raided Guzman's home, and allegedly fondled and made sexual advances toward the domestic worker. Guzman claimed that the raid was part of a ten-year program of internal anti-Latino harassment directed at him. After he filed suit, the U.S. Justice Department agreed to pay him $400,000 to settle (McDonnell 1999).

15. Personal communication, Cynthia Cranford, March 1999; Cleeland 1999.

16. Rollins 1985; Glenn 1986; Romero 1992. See Romero 1997 for a study focusing on the perspective of domestic workers' children. Although the majority of respondents in that study were children of day workers, and none appear to have been children of transnational mothers, they still recall that their mothers' occupation had significant costs for them.

17. Hondagneu-Sotelo and Avila 1997.

18. Central American women seem more likely than Mexican women to leave their children in their country of origin, even if their husbands are living with them in the United States, perhaps because of the multiple dangers and costs associated with undocumented travel from Central America to the United States. The civil wars of the 1980s, continuing violence and economic uncertainty, greater difficulties and costs associated with crossing multiple national borders, and stronger cultural legacies of socially sanctioned consensual unions may also contribute to this pattern for Central Americans.

19. Glenn 1986; Dill 1988.

20. The figures on Salvadoran and Guatemalan women are taken from an analysis of the 1990 census data by the sociologists David E. Lopez, Eric Popkin, and Edward Telles (1996); they also found that Mexican immigrants were only 2.3 times as likely as those in the general population to be engaged in paid domestic work.

21. See Salzinger 1991; Hagan 1994, 1998; Repak 1995.

22. Lopez, Popkin, and Telles 1996: 298.

23. According to 1990 PUMS Census data, about 70 percent of Central American women between the ages of 24 and 60 in Los Angeles County are in the labor force, while only 56 percent of their Mexican peers are. Among this same group, 71 percent of Mexican immigrant women but only 56 percent of their Central American peers are married and living with a spouse. To put it even more starkly, 28 percent of Mexican immigrant women and 43 percent of Central American women report living with family members or adults other than their spouses.

24. Repak 1995.

25. Mahler 1995; Menjívar 2000.

26. Some studies estimate that as many as 50 percent of poor households in San Salvador were formed by "free unions" rather than marriage by law. This pattern is related not just to internal and intra-Central American labor migration but also to urban poverty, as there is no need to secure inheritance rights when there is no property to share (Nieves 1979; Repak 1995).

27. Countries with traditions of consensual marriages afford women more migration opportunities (Donato 1992).

28. A survey conducted in Los Angeles and Orange County in 1986 revealed that 45 percent of Korean immigrants were self-employed; many were business owners in the Korean ethnic economy (Min 1996: 48).

29. Mar and Kim 1994.

30. Between 1966 and 1985 nearly 25,000 Filipina nurses came to work in the United States, and another 10,000 came between 1989 and 1991. Filipinas who were formally recruited through government programs then informally recruited their friends and former nursing school classmates (Ong and Azores 1994).

31. Parreñas 2001.

32. Wrigley 1995.

33. Palmer 1989: 140.

34. Personal communication with UCLA professor Abel Valenzuela, fall 1998.

35. Bet Tzedek Legal Services.

REFERENCES

Clark-Lewis, Elizabeth. 1994. *Living In, Living Out: African American Domestics in Washington, D.C. 1910–1940.* Washington, D.C.: Smithsonian Institution Press.

Cleeland, Nancy. 1999. "Garment Jobs: Hard, Bleak, and Vanishing." *Los Angeles Times,* March 11, A1, A14–16.

Dill, Bonnie Thornton. 1988. "'Making Your Job Good Yourself': Domestic Service and the Construction of Personal Dignity." In *Women and the Politics of Empowerment,* edited by Ann Bookman and Sandra Morgen, 33–52. Philadelphia: Temple University Press.

Donato, Katharine. 1992. "Understanding U.S. Immigration: Why Some Countries Send Women and Others Send Men." In *Seeking Common Ground: Multidisciplinary Studies of Immigrant Women in the United States,* edited by Donna Gabaccia, 159–84. Westport, Conn.: Praeger.

Glenn, Evelyn Nakano. 1986. *Issei, Nisei, Warbride.* Philadelphia: Temple University Press.

Hagan, Jacqueline Maria. 1994. *Deciding to Be Legal: A Maya Community in Houston.* Philadelphia: Temple University Press.

———. 1998. "Social Networks, Gender, and Immigrant Incorporation." *American Sociological Review* 63: 55–67.

Hondagneu-Sotelo, Pierrette, and Ernestine Avila. 1997. "'I'm Here, But I'm There': The Meanings of Latina Transnational Motherhood." *Gender and Society* 11: 548–71.

Katzman, David M. 1981. *Seven Days a Week: Women and Domestic Service in Industrializing America.* Urbana: University of Illinois Press.

Lacher, Irene. 1997. "An Interior Mind." *Los Angeles Times,* March 16, E1, E3.

Lopez, David E., Eric Popkin, and Edward Telles. 1996. "Central Americans: At the Bottom, Struggling to Get Ahead." In *Ethnic Los Angeles,* edited by Roger Waldinger and Mehdi Bozorgmehr, 279–304. New York: Russell Sage Foundation.

Mahler, Sarah J. 1995. *American Dreaming: Immigrant Life on the Margins.* Princeton: Princeton University Press.

Mar, D., and M. Kim. 1994. "Historical Trends." In *The State of Asian Pacific America: Economic Diversity, Issues, and Policies,* edited by Paul Ong, 13–30. Los Angeles: LEAP Asian Pacific American Public Policy Institute and UCLA Asian American Studies Center.

McBride, Theresa. 1976. *The Domestic Revolution: The Modernization of Household Service in England and France, 1820–1920.* New York: Holmes and Meier.

McDonnell, Patrick J. 1999. "U.S. to Pay $400,000 to INS Agent in Bias Suit." *Los Angeles Times,* January 21, B1, B5.

Menjívar, Cecilia. 2000. *Fragmented Ties: Salvadoran Immigrant Networks in America.* Berkeley: University of California Press.

Min, Pyong Gap. 1996. *Caught in the Middle: Korean Communities in New York and Los Angeles.* Berkeley: University of California Press.

Nieves, Isabel, 1979. "Household Arrangements and Multiple Jobs in San Salvador." *Signs* 5: 139–50.

Ong, Paul, and Tania Azores. 1994. "Health Professionals on the Front Line." In *The State of Asian Pacific America: Economic Diversity, Issues, and Policies,* edited by Paul Ong, 139–63. Los Angeles: LEAP Asian Pacific American Public Policy Institute and UCLA Asian American Studies Center.

Palmer, Phyllis. 1989. *Domesticity and Dirt: Housewives and Domestic Servants in the United States, 1920–1945.* Philadelphia: Temple University Press.

Parrenas, Rhacel Salazar. 2001. *Servants of Globalization: Women, Migration, and Domestic Work.* Stanford, Calif.: Stanford University Press.

Repak, Terry A. 1995. *Waiting on Washington: Central American Workers in the Nation's Capital.* Philadelphia: Temple University Press.

Rollins, Judith. 1985. *Between Women: Domestics and Their Employers.* Philadelphia: Temple University Press.

Romero, Mary. 1992. *Maid in the U.S.A.* New York: Routledge.

Romero, Mary. 1997. "Who Takes Care of the Maid's Children? Exploring the Costs of Domestic Service." In *Feminism and Families,* edited by Hilde L. Nelson, 63–91. New York: Routledge.

Salzinger, Leslie. 1991. "A Maid by Any Other Name: The Transformation of 'Dirty Work' by Central American Immigrants." In *Ethnography Unbound: Power and Resistance in the Modern Metropolis,* by Michael Burawoy et al., 139–60. Berkeley: University of California Press.

Smith, Margo L. 1973. "Domestic Service as a Channel of Upward Mobility for the Lower-Class Woman: The Lima Case." In *Female and Male in Latin America: Essays,* edited by Ann Pescatello, 192–207. Pittsburgh: University of Pittsburgh Press.

Wrigley, Julia. 1995. *Other People's Children.* New York: Basic Books.

Jennifer Klein
Eileen Boris

Organizing Home Care

First published in 2009

After fracturing her hip in 1981, Ethel Hunter, an 80-year-old stroke survivor, just "needed somebody to take care of [her]" so she could remain in her Forest Hills, New York apartment. She gained that aid through the minimum wage labor of Haitian immigrant Maryse Williams, who was paid by the city to "help her bathe and dress, cook the broiled chicken that she likes, clean her house and take her outside in a wheelchair." Williams was one of what was then 28,000 New York City home attendants providing personal care and undertaking household chores for frail elderly and non-elderly disabled persons who qualified for Medicaid. Such "domestic workers," as the press and public officials called attendants like Williams, allowed people to avoid institutionalization by substituting for absent family members. Their "humane and vital service" also saved the government the cost of "more expensive nursing homes"—but only because of minimum wages and lack of benefits that kept workers poor despite state promotion of such jobs as an alternative to welfare dependency.[1] From the early 1990s until 2005, home care and health care jobs accounted for the most employment growth in New York City.[2]

Personal attendants and home health aides like Maryse Williams are America's front-line caregivers. Predominantly Latina, Black, and immigrant women, they labor without health insurance, paid sick leave and vacations, or worker compensation.[3] Because of their location in client homes and the dense network of state contracts to private agencies, both the public nature of the job and the employment status of the worker are obscured. With workers employed by a municipal or proprietary agency, private charity, public hospital, or family, home care has existed in a clouded netherworld between public and private, employment and family labor, health care and household service.

As the population in the U.S. ages and family members are less available to care for elders, we have come to rely on this vast "invisible" workforce to provide long-term care. But the U.S. has never implemented a social insurance or dedicated program for long-term care at home. Instead, it has relied primarily on means-tested social services available only to the poorest people. This financing of care through the welfare system has fundamentally shaped the entire labor market for care, whether "public" or "private." State policies have made it difficult for even middle-class people to go out and hire someone to look after their loved ones because it has turned home care into a low-paid job.

Home care emerged as a modernized form of domestic work when state policies transformed intimate labor, performed by wives and mothers, into a social service authorized by state bureaucracies and financed by taxpayer funds. State policy both mirrored and facilitated the restructuring of domestic labor from an informal agreement between mistress and maid to a formal labor market in which a third party—a nonprofit, proprietary, or government agency—functioned as the employer, standing between worker and client. This "modernization" was never complete; a gray market expanded to offer attendants to those ineligible for state services. This largely affected the vast middle class, which otherwise has to spend down its assets to qualify for publicly funded care. By the late twentieth century, home aide was one of the fastest growing occupations in America; yet the occupation had no clear-cut employer, common workplace, or recognition under the nation's primary labor law, the Fair Labor Standards Act (FLSA).[4]

Home care, as a distinct occupation, emerged in the Great Depression both as work relief for New York's unemployed Black women who had previously worked as domestic servants, and as an alternative to fiscally strained public hospitals.[5] The New Deal employed what at the time were called visiting home-makers directly through the Works Progress Administration (WPA) to help poor families and individuals with medical emergencies, chronic illness, and health problems surrounding old age, while curtailing the costs of institutionalization. The WPA also initiated programs to move such people out of hospitals and give them the necessary assistance to become "independent" at home.

While New Dealers developed home care as a form of relief for both providers and receivers, they ignored it as an occupation. When the Democratic Congress passed old-age insurance, unemployment benefits, collective bargaining, minimum wages, and other labor standards, it excluded nurse companions, home-makers, and in-home workers from coverage.[6] Even when Congress amended the FLSA in 1974 to include domestic workers, it specifically exempted home care workers from coverage. The Supreme Court reaffirmed this exclusion in 2007.

After World War II, New York City's Department of Welfare offered the most successful model of a public program for home health care services. It directly employed home aids, still called homemakers, worked closely with private social welfare agencies, secured federal funding, and extended the service from child to elder care. Home care further grew as both an expansion of the hospital and as an attempt to alleviate the number of charity and chronic cases overburdening hospitals. The Great Society, the domestic programs initiated by President Lyndon B. Johnson in the 1960s, enhanced home care through new services for the aged and poor, especially Medicare and Medicaid. Specifically, War on Poverty training programs sought to channel poor women into these jobs. Recruited from families on public assistance, homemakers cared for others from the same social class.

From 1945 until the 1970s, these workers belonged to a booming municipal public sector, despite their actual workplaces being private homes. New York defined them as public employees able to receive benefits with limited Civil Service protections. Unlike a typical domestic, city homemakers officially worked a forty-hour week and received health insurance, sick leave, and paid vacation. In the early 1960s, the City employed 263 full-time workers, covered by a collective bargaining contract with the American Federation of State, County, and Municipal Workers (AFSCME).

In the late 1960s, however, New York State started to change course as it sought to counter militant public sector unionism, the welfare rights movement, and growing public welfare spending. After 1969, it began to privatize the home aide workforce, reclassifying workers as independent contractors. A new part-time and casualized employment structure emerged. Renamed home health attendants, their numbers soared to over 12,000 by the mid 1970s.

The contractor strategy resulted in marked deterioration of both the conditions of labor and the care received. Repeated investigations found egregious problems for both workers and clients. As a consequence of not being covered for over-time, some home attendants ended up making less than minimum wage. Audits found "inordinate delays and errors in payment," with workers waiting weeks or even months for wages. Attendants often called the mayor's office to complain of utility shut-off notices. Elderly and disabled clients reportedly drew upon "their own Supplemental Security Income checks" to help attendants. The Division of Home Attendant Service and its vendor agencies also seemed to exploit the caring part of home health care.[7] For example, there were weeks in which housekeepers received no paychecks at all, yet they continued working, since they could not abandon their clients. Despite these known problems, policymakers continued to insist that welfare recipients be pushed into these jobs to end their "dependency" on the state.

Workers began to organize and fight back in the late 1970s, especially as they came to recognize that they were largely serving clients of the Division of Home Attendant Service. During August 1977, a grassroots organizing effort emerged in the South Bronx amongst disgruntled home care aides who had not been paid for weeks. With guidance from a grass-roots neighborhood organization, La Raza Unida, a core group of Afro-Caribbean, African-American, and Puerto Rican women organized a union. Although employed through the Morrisania Community Corporation, a vendor agency, they went to the city government to demand redress. After waging an eight-day strike, with help from the Teamsters the women won union recognition. The City, however, had no intention of bargaining and instead terminated its contract with Morrisania and reassigned the women to other agencies. While not an individual success, this was just the beginning of a new social struggle.

Other unions started paying attention. The civil rights movement had begun to emphasize the status of domestic workers, pushing New York State to pass collective bargaining legislation for household workers. In response, New York's flagship local of the Service Employees International Union (SEIU), 32B-32J, launched an organizing campaign among household workers "to organize and to free you good people from slavery."[8] When SEIU sought to win bargaining rights for household workers as public employees, the city outmaneuvered them by shifting all clients to agency vendors. Thus, the union had to organize each agency, whatever the size, one at a time. The initial response was tremendous, but this strategy soon succumbed to the hassle of having to define bargaining units piecemeal, and to an ever-shifting labor force while state budgets constrained agencies from negotiating real wage increases.

New York's hospital workers' movement, Local 1199, however, knew how to turn workplace drives into political campaigns. In 1987, it launched (with AFSCME) the Campaign for Justice for Home Care Workers, joining forces with non-profit vendor agencies to press for greater appropriations from Albany. It mobilized significant community pressure, as well as support from clergy, including Cardinal John O'Connor, and political leaders, such as Jesse Jackson. In 1988, after unprecedented negotiations between Governor Mario Cuomo's office and the unions, the state allocated more funds to home health care and agreed to a major wage increase, health insurance, guaranteed days off, and prescription drug coverage.

This political deal was not enough to resolve the ambiguities of employment that hampered long-term rights and job security. Workers still lacked the protection of the nation's basic employment law. The intimacy of the work and its location in private homes continued to obscure care work as labor in multiple ways: through ideological and discursive dismissal of such labor as real or worthy work; through the service ethos of some care workers that leads them to work beyond their paid hours; and through legal classification that refuses to recognize the home as a workplace and the care worker as a worker. Home care workers and their disabled and senior clients and allies have both had to challenge pervasive stereotypes and representations. Home care workers are characterized as self-sacrificing workers,

while their clients are stigmatized as helplessly dependent on others, as well as on the state. . . .

Before the current recession, New York's home care aides made less than those in California, where unions more successfully gained higher wages through bargaining with the state. Many still had to rely on the strategies of the poor—turning to welfare or Medicaid, living with relatives, and taking on extra jobs. One of these retired workers, Jamaican immigrant Evelyn Coke, became the plaintiff in a high-profile lawsuit initiated by SEIU to challenge their exclusion from FLSA. Coke spent twenty years cooking for, cleaning up after, and bathing clients on Long Island, sometimes working twenty-four-hour shifts but rarely paid for overtime.[9]

Coke v. Long Island Care at Home exposed the limits of the search for care on the cheap. In its brief to the Supreme Court, New York City rationalized the exemption on the basis of expense. In contrast, civil, women's, and immigrant rights groups stressed the need to correct prior discrimination against household workers and revalue domestic labor. In foregrounding the concerns of receivers of domestic and personal services, Associate Justice Stephen Breyer erased the presence of providers. The Court unanimously ruled against Coke in 2007.[10] However, it left open the door for Congressional action or administrative rule changes. Long-term care could be added to social insurance, so that it becomes a right of citizenship.

Yet as our historical research has found, it takes personal and social transformation to tackle the more fundamental challenge: revaluing the labor of care. Trade unionism or other forms of collective organization, as with Domestic Workers United in New York, enables home-based caregivers to find others doing the same labor, recognize it as real work, form cultures of solidarity across race and ethnic lines, and become active political agents who put in the forefront the most urgent needs of our society. Such care worker unionism pleads for larger social benefits, advocating better care and better jobs. It not only seeks to make the home a place of dignity and respect for all those who labor there, but to recognize our fundamental human connection.

NOTES

1. Robin Herman, "Demand for Home-Care Workers Is Rising in City," *New York Times* 2 October 1981.
2. Patrick McGeehan, "For New York, Big Job Growth in Home Care," *New York Times* 25 May 2007.

3. Rhonda J.V. Montgomery, Lyn Holley, Jerome Deichert, and Karl Kosloski, "A Profile of Home Care Workers from the 2000 Census: How It Changes What We Know," *The Gerontologist* 45: 5 (2005), 593–600.

4. See "Demand Still Rising Fast for Direct Care Workers" on the Direct Care Alliance, Inc. blog (accessed 27 December 2009).

5. This narrative appears in another from in our book, *Caring for America: Home Health Workers Under the Shadow of the Welfare State*, forthcoming from Oxford University Press.

6. Mary Poole, *The Segregated Origins of Social Security: African Americans and the Welfare State* (Chapel Hill: University of North Carolina Press, 2006).

7. "Report on the Quality of Care and Operating Practices of the Home Attendant Program: Summary of Significant Observations," Oct. 25, 1978, unpublished manuscript, New York State Library; Metropolitan Regional Audit Office, "Audit of Home Attendant Services, New York City, Department of Social Services, #76-835-S-029-58,"

Aug. 1977, McMillan Library, NYC, 8, 14–18; Joan Shepard, "Payroll Foulup Angers Home Health Attendants," *New York Daily News*, 16 December 1977; Peter Khiss, "Program to Aid Elderly Sick Poor Marked by Fraud, State Audit Says," New York Times, 15 December 1977; Richard Severo, "Troubled Program for the Disabled," New York Times, 27 December 1977.

8. "Union Steps up Drive to Organize Household Workers," 32B-32J Newsletter, 46 (May 1978), 1.

9. Steven Greenhouse, "Justices to Hear Care on Wages of Home Aides," *New York Times* 25 March 2007.

10. *Long Island Care at Home, Ltd. v. Evelyn Coke,* 127 S.Ct. 2339 (2007).

SECTION 6

Families

Families are a fundamental social unit. In families we develop a sense of ourselves as individuals and as members of a primary group. We internalize messages about our position in the community, the nation, and the world. We are taught systems of belief, usually consistent with the society in which we live, about appropriate roles for particular kinds of people. For example, we learn to think differently about men and women, elders and children, and people of various races, classes, and social statuses. We also learn how we are expected to treat the people we encounter in the world around us.

It is within families that members of a society first develop ideas and feelings about themselves as gendered individuals. When we are children, the socialization we receive contains strong messages about the appropriate attitudes and behaviors for males and females. When we are adults, families are where we spend much of our time, divide up the work of meeting our physical and emotional needs, and care for others, such as children or aging family members. Families usually organize these interpersonal roles according to what they consider appropriate for men or women. Yet families come in many forms, even within one society. The normative family structure of a married mother and father, in which the man is employed outside the home while the woman cares for their children, no longer represents the majority of families. Instead, a family may be a single parent with children, a couple with no children, lesbian or gay parents and their children, or a group of people who share a household. As a result, individuals' experiences with families vary widely.

Feminist scholars examine the family as a major source of the reproduction of inequality in a society. Researchers investigate how the organization of family life supports women's oppression in society through its ideologies, economics, distribution of domestic tasks, and intimate relations. Reciprocally, researchers examine the impact of demographic, technological, economic, and political structures on women's and men's power and positions in their families.

At the same time, feminist scholars examine families as a source of women's strength and resistance. Alternative family forms are one way to restructure family lives; in addition, families may provide a source of resistance to other forms of oppression, such as racism or poverty. Feminist family studies emphasize the ways that race, ethnicity, sexuality, and class influence our family experiences.

The first selection, Carolyn Herbst Lewis's "Waking Sleeping Beauty: The Premarital Pelvic Exam and Heterosexuality During the Cold War," looks back in time to the 1950s, showing how the family is more than an intimate institution. Doctors in the 1950s saw families as the building block of a strong nation, one able to resist the Communist threat, and offered their expertise in teaching brides-to-be how to have appropriate sex on their wedding nights as the key to marital harmony, happy families, and national security. Through the premarital pelvic exam, they sought to ensure that what they assumed would be a woman's first experience with sexual intercourse would be pleasurable and appropriately gendered. What assumptions did doctors make about how couples should have sex? How did they connect sexual inter-course to the fight against Communism? In what ways are families and sexuality politicized today?

In "What If Marriage Is Bad for Us?" Laurie Essig and Lynn Owens look at marriage from a different angle in order to debunk many ideas about the bene-fits of marriage. They suggest that, contrary to popu-lar wisdom and public policy, marriage does not make people more economically secure (instead, the better-off are more likely to marry), does not improve health (married and never-married people are equally healthy and happy, while divorce makes health worse), and isn't "traditional" in its current form (marriages in the past were based on economic dependency rather than romantic love, were embedded in extended fam-ily networks, and were shorter because people died younger). While many assume that increasing mar-riage in poor communities will improve people's lives, Essig and Owens suggest that, "we should consider that those avoiding marriage might know exactly what they are doing." The debates over gay marriage, in their view, are based on an inaccurate view of mar-riage. As they write, "it's not the gay part we object to; it's the marriage part."

What might the consequences of legalizing same-sex marriage be for the institution of marriage as Essig and Owens describe it? How do the debates over this issue reflect the assumptions they identify? Can you find examples from news coverage to illustrate these assumptions at work? Overall, do you agree with Essig and Owens? As you read the rest of this section, look for evidence to support or dispute their claims that marriage is "bad for us," and that the people who ben-efit most from marriage are those who need it the most, in other words, those who are already advantaged.

In the next selection, "Moral Dilemmas, Moral Strategies, and the Transformation of Gender: Lessons from Two Generations of Work and Family Change," Kathleen Gerson addresses the relationship between work and family. For young heterosexual women and men, dividing up the responsibilities of earning income and caring for children and home is a major challenge. Gerson argues that the idea that women and men have different moral responsibilities—with women responsible for caring for others and men responsible

for supporting others through their work—is at the core of this dilemma. Although this ideology remains powerful, Gerson shows that contemporary reality is far different. Large numbers of women work for pay, and men's incomes have declined to the point that many of them could no longer play the breadwinner role in any case. Yet change in the work of caring for others has been slower, with women still expected to do the bulk of child care.

When Gerson interviewed women and men com-ing of age around the turn of the millennium, she found that they sought to achieve relationships in which they could be both autonomous and connected, and in which they would share work and child care. Overall, neither young men nor young women expected to find fulfillment solely through either work or family. But both women and men had fallback positions in case their ideals did not work out: women felt strongly that they wanted to be economically self-supporting, and men expected to be the primary breadwinners despite desiring connections with wives and children.

What are your own expectations about work and family? What kinds of jobs and family support systems would you need in order to fulfill these expectations? To what extent have you been able to fulfill these expectations, if you have already formed your own independent household? As you reflect on the choices and situations faced by your own parents, how do your experiences compare to theirs, and to those of the people Gerson interviewed? What changes have occurred in family and paid labor over the past gen-eration, and what has remained unchanged? What do you see as the main obstacles to further change in work and family lives?

In "For Better or Worse: Gender Allures in the Vietnamese Global Marriage Market," Hung Cam Thai shows how ideas of gender shape marriage strategies in quite different ways for Vietnamese male migrants to the United States and for women living in Vietnam. Women in Vietnam, he argues, are expected to "marry up" to men who are more highly educated, better employed, and older. But women who pursue higher education may lose their opportunity to marry up—in effect, "pricing themselves out" of the marriage market because by the time they finish their education they are not only too highly educated but too old to marry up. Reluctant to marry down in Vietnam and sacrifice their status and independence, they look for spouses who have immigrated to the United States, hoping to find a more egalitarian gender system there. Vietnamese male migrants to the United States, in contrast, often find themselves in low-status and low-paying jobs, despite their education or higher class status in Vietnam. For them, a wife from Vietnam provides the hope of a traditional marriage in which they can gain the respect that they have lost in the workplace. As Thai shows, these women and men bring very different hopes to their marriages, both shaped by complicated intersections of gender, nationality, class, and culture. What do you think will happen to couples like these?

How do their expectations compare to those of other cultures and communities with which you are familiar?

For most women, these articles suggest, family relationships are a complicated mixture of accommodation and resistance to gender oppression. Nevertheless, expectations and experiences within families differ for women and men of different races, ethnicities, classes, and sexual identities. In what ways do women, in these readings and in your own observation, accept or challenge traditional definitions of their family roles? How do they make choices about the relationship of paid employment to mothering? How do they gain power and fulfillment through family relationships, and how do these relationships constrict them? How are the answers to these questions different for men?

Waking Sleeping Beauty: The Premarital Pelvic Exam and Heterosexuality During the Cold War

First published in 2005

In 1966 physician William F. Sheeley wrote an editorial for the *Journal of the American Medical Association* urging his colleagues to take a more active interest in the sex lives of their patients. "That basic unit without which few societies can survive—the family—depends upon discipline and control of sexual behavior," he cautioned. "Without such control, the family soon breaks down, and soon thereafter the whole society comes crashing down—like the mighty Roman Empire, which is no more."[1]

Although it would be easy to dismiss Sheeley's editorial as overly dramatic, in fact, his statements echo the fears and anxieties expressed by numerous physicians writing in American medical journals throughout the 1950s and 1960s. In essence, these physicians engaged in a three-part dialogue over female heterosexual health, marital stability, and community security. At the intersection of these three conversations was the premarital consultation and physicians' efforts at sexual instruction as a means of ensuring both the psychosexual adjustment of their patients and the stability of their patients' marriages. The healthy female orgasm was the key to it all.

In the 1950s and 1960s, physicians devoted a great deal of attention to marking the accepted parameters of "normal" female heterosexual behavior, particularly the distinction between vaginal and clitoral orgasms. Their efforts were, in part, a response to the 1953 publication of Alfred Kinsey's *Sexual Behavior in the Human Female*. While Kinsey dismissed the vaginal orgasm and instead pointed to the clitoris as the site of female sexual pleasure, physicians, with little dissent, maintained their commitment to the vaginal orgasm well into the mid-1960s, when the conversation on female heterosexual health began to wane in medical journals.[2]

At the same time that physicians honed their definition of female heterosexual health, they also stressed the importance of a healthy sex life to the marital relationship. Physicians asserted that just as a vaginal orgasm was integral to a woman's psychosexual health, the performance of healthy heterosexual gender and sexual roles—as evidenced by a satisfying sexual relationship—was crucial to the establishment and maintenance of a stable marriage.[3] Physicians ultimately extended their concern for marital stability out into the larger community, arguing that marriages and the families they created were the foundations of a morally secure citizenry. Moral security translated into political stability and military strength. Writing during the turbulence and uncertainty of the Cold War, physicians worried that "unhealthy," "maladjusted," and even extramarital sexual behavior was just as threatening to American society as were the Soviets and their nuclear bombs. Some physicians even went so far as to assert that changing trends in American sexual behavior were "part and parcel of the Communist program to change American sexual mores, [resulting] in a breakdown of the family and collapse of society as a whole, clearing the way for an easy Communist takeover."[4]

Citing rising rates of venereal disease and divorce, as well as the increasing sexual permissiveness of the nation's youth, physicians throughout these decades likened what they saw as "sexual chaos" to a contagion threatening the very health and safety of the nation—a contagion that could only be checked by containing sexual behavior within heterosexual marriage.[5] Physicians did not stop there; containment was only the first step. As Sheeley illustrated, physicians believed that the family units created by heterosexual marriages formed the building blocks of the national community. Physicians therefore sought to reinforce American society against moral and political subversion by strengthening individual marriages.[6] They insisted that the most effective means of doing so was to ensure that couples were practicing the "right kind" of sex.

In articles, letters, and editorials in the professional medical journals, as well as in conference presentations and books, physicians promoted a model of heterosexuality that underscored the era's prescribed gender roles, including their race- and class-based assumptions.[7] Using a specific definition of sexual health, physicians did not assume that heterosexual performance indicated a patient was sexually "normal." In fact, sexual "deviancy" was not their only concern. Instead, physicians maintained distinctions between "good" and "bad" heterosexual identity and performance. In their estimation, sexual preference and conduct were inseparable from gender identification and performance. Consequently, physicians claimed a passive and receptive vaginal orgasm as the hallmark of a well-adjusted and normal femininity. A woman's ability to achieve vaginal orgasm during intercourse with her husband was both symptom and cure, as it verified her appropriate gender and sexual role performance—a passive and feminine wife yielding to her active and masculine husband.[8] Vaginal intercourse that culminated in a vaginal orgasm was, therefore, the definition of the "right kind" of sex.

Yet despite the assumption that this was the normal and healthy exercise of heterosexuality, it was not presumed to be instinctive. For example, physicians and psychiatrists cited the rising divorce rate as a sign of widespread sexual maladjustment caused by ignorance and fear, particularly on the part of women. Young brides approached their wedding nights ill-prepared for initiation into marital heterosexuality; consequently, as physician Nadina Kavinoky maintained, the trauma of even a small amount of bleeding and pain often led to unhappy marriages and divorce.[9]

Proper instruction and preparation before the marriage promised a quick antidote to the nation's sexual difficulties. This article considers how physicians proposed to communicate their definition of healthy marital heterosexuality to their patients through the use of a premarital pelvic examination. The pelvic exam, as part of a state-mandated premarital consultation

intended to monitor the spread of venereal disease, enabled physicians to monitor a woman's response to penetration and thereby estimate her ability to experience vaginal orgasm. Physicians asserted that, by ensuring that young women knew what to expect on their wedding nights, and, even more importantly, how to have the right kind of orgasm, they had a special role to play in contributing to marital stability. These stable marriages, in turn, would serve as the foundation for a morally secure nation.[10] In short, physicians believed that the fully functioning American family—including healthy sexual performance—was part of the national arsenal used to combat the chaos and immorality encouraged by the looming Soviet threat. Thus, the premarital pelvic exam stood at the intersection of physicians' assertions regarding heterosexual health, marital stability, and community security. In the ideological battle against communism, the premarital pelvic exam afforded the ideal opportunity for them to practice a unique form of preventive medicine.

THE FATHERLY PHYSICIAN AS SEXUAL INSTRUCTOR

While American medicine was already a prestigious profession in the mid-twentieth century, the standardization of various specialties, including obstetrics and gynecology as distinct from general family practice, was still underway.[11] This drive towards specialization and standardization encouraged the emergence of medical journals such as *General Practice, Fertility and Sterility,* and *Obstetrics and Gynecology* in the early 1950s. Like the *Journal of the American Medical Association (JAMA),* they quickly became more than a forum for informing physicians of advances in medical science. They also served as a means of reinforcing hegemony among physicians both as a larger group and within various specialties. This growth of professional identity was aided by the heightened prestige attached to Cold War science and the role of modern medicine in preventing the spread of infectious disease and improving the quality of life for the nation's citizens.[12]

In this context, physicians came to believe that they—even more than ministers or parents—were the best guides for a young couple seeking a mutually satisfying marital relationship. Their medical and anatomical expertise as well as their role as "father-confessor" to their patients made them knowledgeable and authoritative advisors.[13] As physician Jed Pearson explained, "The physician wishing to do premarital counseling is admirably equipped because of his broad medical and cultural education. In addition he needs only the attributes of personal warmth, sympathetic understanding, and an objectivity in approach to each patient's problems in order to succeed."[14] Although general practitioners and obstetrician-gynecologists emphasized how particularly well-suited their fields were to addressing matters related to female heterosexual health, they also claimed responsibility for ensuring the sexual well-being of the entire family unit on a long-term basis.

This emphasis on treating the family as well as the individual reflected physicians' concern with the family as the site of psychosexual development. Psychoanalytic theories of sexuality had become increasingly influential in the United States throughout the 1930s and 1940s. European psychiatrists seeking refuge in the United States brought with them a commitment to Freudian methods and theories. At the same time, the nature of psychiatric treatment shifted from rural state institutions for the "disturbed" to urban psychoanalysts treating a middle-class clientele with the time and money to attend to their mental and emotional well-being. Thus, psychiatrists became increasingly concerned not simply with curing the insane, but tending to the maladjusted as well. In this context, sexual behavior became an indicator of psychological health.[15] The rejection of more than one million men from military service due to mental and neurological disorders, coupled with those dismissed for being homosexuals, suggested to many in positions of power that the mental and sexual health problems of individuals were adversely affecting the nation. This was well demonstrated in 1950 Congressional hearings on the "homosexual problem," which linked medical discourse on homosexuality with issues of national security.[16] Because homosexuality was classified as a psychiatric disorder, the medical profession was the logical place to look for a solution to the problem.

General practitioners and psychiatrists agreed that prevention was just as important as treatment. Because the family played a pivotal role in Freudian theories of psychosexual development, the medical profession turned to the home as the main bastion against homosexuality and other psychosexual disturbances, such as frigidity. With the focus on the family, general practitioners became the primary source of medical intervention. Obstetrician-gynecologists were a close second. If they were successful, then the healthy families they produced would nurture healthy individuals. These families would serve as the building blocks of a healthy community and, by extension, a healthy nation.

THE RIGHT KIND OF SEX

The key to understanding how and why physicians constructed their role as sexual counselor lies in their belief that psychosexual development, while a natural and predetermined process, was not innate. Various factors could disrupt an individual's advancement to normal, mature, adult heterosexuality—a mother who was too doting, a father who was too distant, and, for women, a wedding night that was less than tender. An individual's psychosexual maladjustment held the potential for long-term impact on society, for psychosexually maladjusted parents—especially mothers—could not help but raise psychosexually maladjusted children.[17] Consequently, physicians placed great importance on a woman's transition into marital heterosexuality. In some sense, the wedding night was considered the last chance to overcome any previously induced sexual trauma and to set women on the path to psychosexual wellness. Surely, this was all much too important to be left to chance.

Greatly influenced by Freudian theories of psychosexual development, physicians characterized healthy female heterosexuality by such factors as passive acceptance of male sexual direction, a soft and submissive femininity, and a self-sacrificial drive to motherhood. The vagina formed the epicenter of this heterosexuality, as it served both as the site of the successful performance of heterosexual intercourse and as the only healthy outlet for female orgasm. Unlike male orgasm, which was considered necessary for male sexual health as well as for reproduction, female orgasm was a *goal*, but certainly not a *necessity*. As obstetrician Eugene Hamilton reminded readers of *Missouri Medicine*, "The male orgasm is a biologic necessity for the preservation of the species. For the female it is a luxury."[18] As evidence that the female orgasm was superfluous, physicians offered the explanation that "the normal woman is not so easily aroused [as the male] and may only on occasion achieve a climax."[19] Female sexual responsiveness, they asserted, was a latent energy that must be awakened by the more active energy of their partners, presumably their husbands. As psychoanalyst Helen Deutsch concluded, "The awakening of the vagina to full sexual functioning is entirely dependent upon the man's activity; and [the] absence of spontaneous vaginal activity constitutes the physiologic background of feminine passivity."[20] An active, or sexually aggressive, woman might arouse male anxieties of castration and thereby interfere with male heterosexual performance and psychosexual adjustment. Thus, female sexual passivity, as demonstrated through a woman's vaginal orgasm, was important not only to experiencing a satisfying and healthy sex life, but also to ensuring that a woman as well as her husband would be able to maintain the roles and identities "normal" for their sex.

The emphasis placed on vaginal orgasm reflected the discourse surrounding the nature of female sexuality that engaged the medical profession in the mid-twentieth century, particularly the debate over the valid definition of frigidity and the superiority of the vagina over the clitoris as the locus of female heterosexual pleasure. Neither physicians nor psychiatrists denied the existence of or possibility for clitoral orgasm; rather, they insisted that the clitoris was the primary organ of sexual pleasure during childhood, but in puberty, and particularly with the approach of marriage, a healthy, mature woman transferred her focus to the vagina.[21] This transfer was not so much physical as it was psychological; thus, the woman who failed to transfer suffered from a psychological neurosis that manifested itself in the inability to have a vaginal orgasm. In other words, she was frigid. Although a clitoral orgasm would still be physically possible, the mature woman would willingly and consciously defer to the vagina, maintaining a role of passive reception of the penis and restricting her sexual pleasure to that induced by penetration. The definition of frigidity used by physicians and psychiatrists in the mid-twentieth century did not simply correlate to the absence of sexual desire or sensation. Certainly, that was one form of frigidity, but physicians and psychiatrists primarily stressed the importance and pervasiveness of frigidity as *inappropriate*, not absent, sexual outlet. This frigidity would manifest itself in the failure to achieve a vaginal orgasm—or, worse yet, a consistent reliance on the clitoris for pleasure.[22]

Linked to this inappropriate sexual outlet was inappropriate gender role behavior. In addition to her improper sexual performance, a frigid woman would display improper gender identifications as well. If these women married in an attempt to create a normal life for themselves or to mask their psychosexual immaturity, "the marital union may be characterized by refusal to assume any serious obligation of wifehood or motherhood." Two of the era's most widely cited medical theorists of female sexuality, Edmund Bergler and William Kroger, warned that symptoms included interest in such activities as playing cards, participating in sports, traveling alone, and "perhaps even [the] aggressive pursuit of a career." At the same time, wives who became so obsessively involved in their homemaker duties that they stifled or neglected their husbands might also be frigid.[23]

Conversely, the psychosexually well-adjusted woman would recognize her husband's role as the head of the household and eagerly embrace her duties in the home. This included submitting to his sexual direction. Her ability to experience exclusively vaginal orgasm served as evidence of the extent to which a woman had adjusted to her role as wife and mother. Likewise, a truly healthy heterosexuality was indicated by appropriate psychosexual gender identity and corresponding heterosexual and social role performance. In the 1950s and 1960s, physicians writing in medical journals often cited a subconscious rejection of femininity and the maternal role as the main factor in female sexual disorder.[24] Women who failed to conform to expected standards of femininity were considered to be cases of latent frigidity or undiagnosed sexual dysfunction.

The definition of "healthy" sexuality and its accompanying gender ideology were further marked by assumptions of race and class. Throughout the medical journals, patients, like their physicians, were presumed to be white, heterosexual, and middle class. In fact, from 1950 to 1969 homosexuals, the working class, and women of color appeared in *JAMA* and the *New England Journal of Medicine* only in discussions of abnormal cases, pathologic behaviors, and especially in regard to lesbians, as the causes of neurosis in men. Chastity and modesty were often linked to the patient's (white) race, as physicians believed that "[e]mbarrassment at having the vulva exposed, looked at, or touched is a normal reaction, more deeply instilled in some racial groups than others."[25] As a result, physicians expected that their white patients would be in greater need of sensitivity and reassurance during the pelvic exam than their patients of color would be. Physicians also asserted that class and cultural backgrounds would determine a couple's "ability to fulfill their masculine or feminine destiny as parents" as well as "the pattern of the couple's relationship."[26] Intermarriage between different socioeconomic backgrounds produced further complications because, as one physician explained in 1966, "It is difficult for the middle class people to understand the behavior of the lower class male, and even more difficult for the female to understand comparable behavior." Although "lower class" men generally had more sexual experience, according to the physicians, middle-class men were more sophisticated and more sensitive to the needs of their partners. While the lower-class man was "unconcerned" with his partner's pleasure, the middle-class man "considers himself a failure if his wife doesn't have an orgasm."[27]

These assumptions are extremely important when we consider that physicians repeatedly stressed the need for a well-adjusted heterosexuality as the basis for a healthy femininity and maternal role. The implication of the race and class biases of the physicians was that only white and middle-class women could fully adjust to their own "psychosexual destinies" and, by extension, ensure that they would be able to guide the next generation to healthy adulthood. Perhaps fortunately, physicians did not attempt to "cure" the sexual problems of those who were neither white nor middle-class. Instead, they focused their attention on the psychosexual development of their patients—white, middle-class, and heterosexual women. For these women, unhealthy sexual behavior, such as frigidity, homosexuality, or nymphomania, indicated a maladjusted psychosexual identity or a rejection of femininity that needed remedying before a woman damaged herself, her children, and her community.[28]

Because the vaginal orgasm was the epicenter of healthy heterosexuality, the bride became the focus of the physician's premarital consultation, and the pelvic exam became the most important part of the office visit. Physicians worried that if a woman was too anxious, she might resist penetration and thereby undermine the successful performance of heterosexuality in her marriage. They imagined that the patient who was fearful of the pelvic exam would most likely be fearful of penetration in general.[29] Rather than approaching the exam as a means of observing how well patients had adjusted to intercourse after marriage, physicians in the 1950s and 1960s proposed using the pelvic exam as a means of instructing unmarried women in how to prepare for marital intercourse. In particular, physicians hoped to pre-empt any emotional or physical trauma that might be inflicted by a less-than-tender wedding night, which, of course, was presumed to be the patient's initial sexual intercourse. Consequently, physicians repeatedly advised their colleagues to per-

form a thorough, yet gentle, premarital pelvic exam that would quell any unspoken fears their patient might have of penetration.[30]

In their concern for the psychosexual development of their female patients, physicians expected women to lack both sexual knowledge and experience. While physicians recognized that information about marriage and sexuality was readily available to the public, they dismissed many of the sources as inadequate or misleading. Much of this information, they insisted, left young women confused, anxious, and ill-prepared. They asserted that physicians should employ their medical knowledge and moral authority to set the record straight about healthy and normal heterosexual performance. For example, at the same time that editor Helen Gurley Brown was advising women to explore the joys of premarital sexuality, one *JAMA* editor reminded her colleagues that, "As every nice girl in Western culture knows, it is the male who is the [sexual] aggressor, while the passive female submits with either good or bad grace."[31] In particular, physicians sought to combat any anxieties regarding painful penetration or sexual incompatibility induced by misinformed gossip with girlfriends by educating women in just "how adequately [their] own sex organs are prepared to receive the erect penis."[32] The premarital pelvic exam offered the perfect opportunity for them to do so.

THE PREMARITAL PELVIC EXAM

By the end of the Second World War, widespread state premarital exam legislation had been in effect for only a decade at best. Although Oregon, Texas, and Wisconsin had laws as early as 1913 requiring a signed certificate verifying that a physical examination had confirmed that a man was free of venereal disease before a marriage ceremony could be performed, no state presumed to require a comparable declaration from a woman. Indeed, Wisconsin legislators had repeatedly killed bills proposing physical inspections for VD for brides because they "objected to having their young daughters 'pawed over'" by physicians.[33] But in the 1930s this sentiment had begun to change. The increasing professionalization of American medicine brought new respect and authority to physicians, interfering with legislators' ability to object to their examinations on grounds of decency and morality. At the same time, physicians began to organize as a force lobbying for public health policy.[34] While some physicians, legislators, and public health officials continued to protest that mandatory exams were a gross invasion of their patients' privacy, lawmakers' desire to eradicate VD and preserve the health of the population proved more persuasive.[35] In 1935, the Connecticut legislature passed the first state law mandating premarital physical examinations for both men and women prior to the issuance of a marriage license. Within four years, seventeen additional states enacted similar legislation.[36]

Generally speaking, state laws simply required blood tests and venereal disease screenings for brides and grooms. However, within fifteen years of the initial Connecticut legislation, physicians also advocated the use of the premarital consultation to discuss matters of sexual adjustment with their patients.[37] Although control of VD remained the original intent of the laws, physicians acknowledged that "the clear objective [of the premarital consultation was] to foster and preserve a sound family unit, a happy marriage, and healthy children." By 1964, the number of states with such laws had doubled to thirty-seven. "Thus," wrote the editors of *JAMA*, "the legal machinery is set up to bring young people to the physician before marriage, at a time when ignorance and fear about sex can be evaluated most easily and, hopefully, overcome."[38]

Recognizing that restrictions on time and expenses meant that premarital counseling was usually limited to a single visit with the bride alone, physicians focused their attention on the pelvic exam. The model premarital pelvic exam was outlined in a 1954 article in *JAMA* by obstetrician-gynecologist Nadina Kavinoky. Following inspection of the female genitalia, Kavinoky suggested that the physician should approach the topic of sexual adjustment. Because "a fearful virgin must first be taught to cooperate and relax," the physician should instruct the patient in relaxing and contracting the vaginal sphincter and pubococcygeus muscles. This exercise, Kavinoky promised, would enable "even the fearful virgin" to learn "how to cooperate and develop a more spontaneous rhythm." Once the patient was comfortable with these exercises, then the physician should proceed with the second step in the premarital pelvic examination: the insertion of a well-lubricated instrument into the patient's vagina so that "the virgin [could] realize that there is a normal opening in the hymen that leads into a deep vaginal canal." After the initial penetration, the physician should instruct the patient to "bear down" and insert the tube further into the vaginal canal. "The rate at which [the patient] introduces the tube and her

facial expression reveal her anxiety," Kavinoky explained matter-of-factly, but "the return of color to her face and her relief, as she discovers no bleeding and no pain, convinces the physician of the therapeutic value of this simple procedure."[39]

Kavinoky's method of introducing the young woman to penetration became the accepted method for the premarital exam for the next two decades.[40] The exercises she implemented reflected the influence of psychoanalytic theories of psychosexual development, particularly the emphasis on penetration and the vagina's welcoming reception of the penis. In addition, Kavinoky was clearly relying on the work of gynecologist Arnold Kegel, who developed the series of vaginal and pubococcygeal contractions that became known as "Kegel exercises."

Like most physicians and psychiatrists of the time, Kegel pointed to involuntary muscular contractions during orgasm as the true indicator of mature female sexuality. While Kegel recognized that many women who experienced solely clitoral orgasms considered their sex lives to be satisfactory, he dismissed the clitoral orgasm as a crutch. Once women were able to transfer their focus to the vagina, Kegel reported in a 1953 letter to the editors of the *JAMA*, they appeared to "forget the clitoris" entirely.[41] But Kegel warned that even a woman who was otherwise sexually well-adjusted could be traumatized by a "rough first experience."[42] Like the other physicians writing in American medical journals at this time, Kegel failed to see the premarital consultation as an opportunity to advise grooms on how best to approach the act of initial penetration. Instead, physicians seemed to suggest that warning the bride to be patient and not resistant would be enough to get the couple through their first attempts at intercourse. Kegel's letter reflects a common suggestion that so long as the vagina was not resistant to penetration, marital heterosexuality would work itself out. After all, a woman's orgasm was more emotional than it was physical, and motherhood, not orgasm, was the ultimate fulfillment of her psychosexual destiny.

Perhaps this insistence on a compliant vagina and an emotional orgasm explains why virtually none of the material on the premarital consultation, including Kegel's letter to the editor and Kavinoky's article, made any mention of female arousal. Even Kavinoky's educational exercise in heterosexual performance remained just as clinical as the standard pelvic exam. Although the exercise was intended to prepare women for intercourse, it was not meant to replicate the sex act exactly. Consequently, physicians who used or advocated the use of Kavinoky's model premarital pelvic exam created a tricky situation. On the one hand, they wanted to demonstrate to their patients that penetration was nothing to fear and to convey the message that penetration should lead to orgasm. On the other hand, they did not want to arouse their patients. This fine line that physicians walked was illustrated by physician Janet Towne, whose article on premarital counseling offered a perplexing scenario.[43]

Towne described a patient having difficulty performing Kegel exercises. Her proposed solution was to induce muscular contraction by penetrating the vagina—in effect attempting to trick the vagina into an instinctive contraction. But, Towne warned, if the patient displayed an "erotic" response to the doctor's penetration, then the exam must end immediately. In short, while doctors wanted to tell their female patients how to respond sexually, they did not actually want to make them do it in their offices. This is certainly understandable. After all, it had been several decades since physicians had last advocated stimulating their patients to orgasm as a course of treatment for various nervous disorders. But, whereas the physicians administering "therapeutic massage" were able to argue that their activities were not sexual because penetration had not occurred, physicians administering exams such as Towne's or Kavinoky's could not claim the same.[44] Penetration had, in fact, taken place. Instead, physicians identified their procedure as non-sexual on the basis of their definitions of what heterosexual intercourse looked like, specifically penetration by a penis.

For example, Towne made a telling assumption: she only warned that attempting to induce a "vaginal response" was dangerous if the physician was male. Towne did not imagine a situation in which a woman might respond erotically to penetration by another woman. This reflects the physicians' assumption that lesbians, as psychosexually maladjusted women, would rely on clitoral stimulation rather than vaginal penetration in their lovemaking.[45] At the same time, Towne's assumption reinforced the assertion that the medical instrument should not be viewed as a mere substitute for the penis. Without a penis, it could not really be sex.

But there is something else at work here. In Towne's illustration, sexual response and sexual arousal are two separate and independent things. Most impor-

tantly, sexual arousal was not necessary to evoke "erotic" response. This helps to explain why Towne, like Kegel and Kavinoky, believed it was possible for physicians to train their patients in vaginal response without arousing them. In essence, the woman's sexual needs or desires were peripheral to her passive reception of the penis, as demonstrated by her embrace of the medical instrument without any need for sexual stimulation. Therefore, despite their purported concern for ensuring that women had satisfying sexual experiences in marriage, physicians actually endorsed a vision of "normal" heterosexual performance that perpetuated the emphasis on male sexual needs—a compliant vagina—rather than encouraging women to pursue physical sexual pleasure.

In fact, the physicians' goal was to create sexual partners who were compliant rather than eager. Physicians advised their female patients that pleasure would come later, once they had "gotten used to" penetration; women should be neither too fearful nor too eager. In the midst of all this discussion of fearful virgins, the idea that a woman might be too eager to begin heterosexual intercourse might seem a bit counterintuitive. Yet physicians repeatedly insisted that couples must not bring unrealistic expectations to the marriage bed. Wilfred Hulse warned that "[o]wing to the increased emphasis on female orgasm, the young bride and her spouse may occasionally become depressed and discouraged if she does not experience orgasm from the very beginning of married life."[46] In order to reassure the husband that it was no masculine failing on his part and the wife that it was no reflection on her femininity, physicians were urged to advise couples that it often took time and patience before a young bride could experience a fully satisfying sexual life. Like Kegel, these physicians believed that vaginal orgasm, while the only natural expression of female sexuality, was not necessarily instinctive. In some sense, they imagined themselves as coaches—not only overseeing their athletes' performance training, but also counseling them in reasonable goals and expectations. Gynecologist Patricia Lawrence cautioned that marital sexuality "is a learned technique requiring experience and practice," and "for the bride, responsiveness must often be cultivated."[47] Another gynecologist, Charles Flowers, advised that a woman should not expect to orgasm on her wedding night. Instead, "the bride should understand that coitus is a beautiful and tender expression of affection in which she achieves the giving of herself and body." Flowers continued, "She may be reminded of the first party or dance that she attended. The newness of the occasion, her excitement in wearing her first evening dress and high heeled shoes compensated for the lack of agility in herself and her dancing partner."[48] But why, after all their talk about the importance of the wedding night for setting the stage for healthy sexual and marital adjustment, would physicians counsel brides not to expect to orgasm on their wedding nights?

WAKING SLEEPING BEAUTY

Physicians stressed the need to coax women into orgasm because their vision of normal heterosexuality relied upon a confluence of gender performance, heterosexual development, and psychological health. This vision was best depicted in psychoanalyst Marie Bonaparte's 1953 volume *Female Sexuality*. The volume's cover professed that while "The Kinsey Report Gives the Facts—This Book Explains the *WHY* and *WHEREFORE*" of female sexuality. Bonaparte likened healthy female heterosexual development to the fairytale Sleeping Beauty. She asserted that "the little girl who is destined to be truly feminine must generally have abandoned clitoridal [sic] masturbation before she succeeds in obtaining end-pleasure [vaginal orgasm]." Bonaparte continued, "[L]ike the Sleeping Beauty, pierced in the hand—the hand of guilty masturbation . . . the preformed libidinal organization of the little girl will sink into slumber until such time as the husband's advent through the briars of the hymeneal forest awakes her from sleep. Such would be the ideal development of our little girls."[49]

In the traditional story of Sleeping Beauty, an evil witch puts a curse on a beautiful young princess. Despite all the efforts of her parents and their subjects to circumvent the conditions of the curse, on her sixteenth birthday the princess pricks her hand on a spinning wheel and she and the kingdom fall into a deep slumber. One hundred years later, a brave prince penetrates the forest that has grown around the castle. Finding Sleeping Beauty, he takes the liberty of kissing her motionless lips. Much to his joy, his kiss breaks the spell and she awakens and gratefully marries him.

In the fairytale maintained by Bonaparte and the physicians, Sleeping Beauty—personifying the ideal sexuality of all women—is asleep and will only be roused by the passions of the bridegroom. Unlike the woman in the fairytale who woke after just one kiss,

the real-life Sleeping Beauty will awaken slowly, by the gentle persistence of her prince. But this version of the story has a second hero, as only the efforts of the physician will ensure that the prince succeeds, particularly in his navigation of the "hymeneal forest" that stands between him and his bride. Indeed, while the prince in the fairytale simply had to hack his way through a century's worth of briar growth, the real-life groom faced the physical and psychological barrier of the hymen.

Physicians agreed that the hymen was "the most misunderstood structure of feminine anatomy."[50] They cautioned that women coming in for their first pelvic exam might fear that inspection of the hymen would expose "past indiscretions or evidence of masturbation" or, conversely, that the exam would rupture the hymen, removing all evidence of virginity.[51] A ruptured or softened hymen, they assumed, indicated that counseling was not needed. Gynecologist Eleanor Easley explained, "If the hymen is well dilated already . . . I don't want to waste time on unnecessary or inappropriate advice."[52]

But physicians expected that most women would approach their first pelvic exam as well as their wedding night with their hymens intact. They also expected these women to be afraid that rupturing the hymen would be painful. Physician Martin Goldberg warned that "there is often considerable fear that sex will be terribly painful, that the hymen will be resistant, or that somehow the vagina is not 'big enough'." He continued, "Conversely, some young husbands may fear hurting their wives and may be concerned about rupturing the hymen or making first entry. Or they, too, may fear that their genitals are not large enough to perform the sex act successfully."[53] Physicians noted that this anxiety on the part of the bridegroom as well as the bride could easily be overcome by premarital dilation of the hymen. As Easley noted, "men are happy for the doctor to take over part of the job of preparing the hymen for intercourse." But, she explained, "some gynecologists . . . believe that unless the difficulties are insurmountable, dilation is the husband's job, and that it teaches him fundamental lessons in consideration for his wife."[54]

Easley's suggestion that the hymen should be left intact so that the husband can learn "fundamental lessons" in how to approach his wife on their wedding night was not one that was lauded by other physicians. Indeed, most physicians believed that hymeneal dilation was too sensitive of a job for a "bungling" bridegroom.[55] Physician Irving J. Sands cautioned readers of the *New York State Journal of Medicine* that "The act of defloration in the female may set up a chain of reactions either for a happy and satisfying sexual marital life or for a frustrating and disappointing one."[56] Guiding a fearful bride into a healthy sexuality rooted in her openness to penetration was more important than a husband's right to conquest. Thus, physicians' focus was entirely on the bride's fear of penetration and removing any physical or psychological obstacles that might exist.[57]

In addition to verbally reassuring the patient about the elasticity of her vagina, physicians also advocated performing exercises to dilate the hymen prior to marriage. The patient could be instructed in digitally stretching her vaginal opening in a warm bath. Other women were given a dilator to use, for, as one physician explains, "This will accomplish not only dilation of the hymen but also get the patient used to something being inserted into the vagina."[58] In the case of the patient who objected to self-dilation on the grounds that it too closely resembled masturbation, one physician advised that "The remark that she is now a grown woman about to enter marriage and that she should take an adult attitude about such things suffices to reassure her."[59] Most physicians, however, accepted the idea that many women found manipulating their own genitals to be "distasteful" and instead expected patients to prefer that the physician use a set of dilators to gradually increase vaginal elasticity for them.[60] Many authors noted that consent (often written) was required from the patient's fiancé, and, in some cases, her parents, in order to perform this dilation.[61] They repeatedly emphasized that the decision to pursue this course of treatment was one that must be considered carefully *by the couple.* Even though physicians preferred dilation to take place within a situation they controlled so as to best avoid physical or emotional trauma, they assumed that a woman's body belonged not merely to their patient, but also to her future husband and even her family. Their authority as physicians only extended so far as the husband-to-be was willing to grant it. If a groom refused to agree to medical dilation, the physician could not perform it, no matter how despicable he found the groom's attitude to be.[62]

Like Kavinoky's exercise, the methods of dilation of the hymen recommended by physicians clearly served several functions. At the most basic level, premarital dilation ensured that the vagina was able to be penetrated and that no physical impediments to intercourse remained. This included rupturing or stretching the hymen so that penetration would not be painful or traumatic. There was also a psychological or emotional dimension to dilation. If the woman was frightened, then the various exercises would allow her to experience "first hand" the elasticity of her vagina without any pressure to perform sexually. There was also a psychological or emotional effect for the absent groom, as premarital dilation removed any fears he might have had about injuring his bride. The result of this premarital preparation via both hymeneal dilation and Kavinoky's exercises was a woman who came to her marriage bed with an open mind and a compliant vagina. If all went as physicians hoped, marital consummation would be painless. The groom had no reason to fear causing pain or bleeding, and yet he could still feel secure in the fact that he was the first man to have intercourse with his wife. Likewise, the bride had no reason to fear penetration, but she could still offer herself to her husband with a clear conscience. Even if she did not orgasm, the couple would surely be on the path to a healthy sexual relationship. Although the physician might never hear a word of thanks from either of them, he could feel confident that he had played a key role in effecting this fairytale ending.

CONCLUSION

"The family," physician Verna Stevens-Young explained, "is in essence the unit around which our communities are built."[63] Psychosexually well-adjusted individuals engaging in normal heterosexual intercourse promised to create stable marriages and secure families. And, according to the logic driving physicians in the decades of the Cold War, these strong families would produce strong communities, which would come together to form a strong nation capable of leading the free world. Marriages thus became imbued with great social and political, as well as personal, significance in the 1950s and 1960s. Conforming to the accepted model of heterosexual performance—both within the bedroom and outside of it—indicated not only a couple's sexual health, but also their adherence to the "American" way of life. Those who did not (because they could not or would not) were suspect.

In the premarital consultation, physicians intended to guide their patients into these satisfying and healthy marital relationships. Although their focus was on the heterosexual behavior of newly married couples, their motives clearly extended further, into the moral security of the community. With most states mandating premarital medical examinations as a prerequisite to obtaining a marriage license, physicians believed that they had both the opportunity and the expertise to discuss matters of sexual adjustment with their female patients, and thereby strengthen the moral fiber of American society.[64] If, as physician H. T. McGuire claimed in 1952, "the family unit is the keystone of the arch of our democracy," then satisfying marital sexuality was the foundation of the family unit. Making sure that women were not fearful of penetration was the physician's role in ensuring its success.[65]

In the decades before the resurgent feminist movement insisted that the personal is political, American physicians made the same point by linking healthy heterosexual vaginal orgasm, which they considered the prerequisite for marital stability, to the shoring up of the national security state. Sexuality therefore became part of the domestic policies of the Cold War not only in the exclusion and persecution of those individuals labeled as deviants, but also in the disciplining and control of the sexual behavior of those individuals considered to be normal. The line between the personal and the political did, in fact, blur as sexuality was used as a weapon of both national defense and political subterfuge. In matters of the state, as well as in matters of the heart, sex and politics make frequent, if somewhat strange, bedfellows.

ACKNOWLEDGMENTS

I would like to thank Leila Rupp, Jane Sherron De Hart, Katherine Jellison, Sandra Dawson, April Haynes, Elizabeth Stordeur Pryor, David Schuster, Matt Sutton, Warren Wood, A. J. Lewis, and the anonymous readers for the *Journal of Women's History* for their helpful comments.

NOTES

1. William F. Sheeley, M.D., "Sex and the Practicing Physician," *Journal of the American Medical Association,* hereafter *JAMA,* 195 (January 1966): 133.

2. Alfred C. Kinsey, Wardell B. Pomeroy, Clyde E. Martin, and Paul H. Gebhard, *Sexual Behavior in the Human Female* (Philadelphia: W. B. Saunders Company, 1953). Although Jane Gerhard has situated Kinsey as a link between the conservative definitions of heterosexual health that appeared in the early twentieth century and the sexually liberating ideology of second-wave feminism, Kinsey's research had little impact on the discussion of heterosexual health in the professional journals during the 1950s and early 1960s. Most mention of Kinsey was to dismiss his research and reaffirm the profession's commitment to the vaginal orgasm. Jane Gerhard, *Desiring Revolution: Second-Wave Feminism and the Rewriting of American Sexual Thought 1920–1982* (New York: Columbia University Press, 2001), chap. 2.

3. Sex as a cornerstone of stable marriage became well accepted among psychologists and marriage experts in the early twentieth century. Perhaps the best known proponent is Th. H. Van de Velde, M.D., *Ideal Marriage: Its Physiological and Technique* (New York: Random House, 1930).

4. Collin E. Cooper, M.D., Letter to the Editor, *JAMA* 209 (August 1969): 941. Cooper's letter was one of nine written to the editors of *JAMA* condemning their recent advocacy of secular sex education programs in the nation's schools. Other authors suggested that sex education was Communist inspired, based on a Swedish model of immorality, and anti-Christian. Editorial, "Sex Education in the Schools," *JAMA* 2008 (May 1969): 1016. Physicians were not the only authorities linking sexual behavior and citizenship. During the height of the Cold War, sexual "deviance" was suspect at best and treasonous at worst. See John D'Emilio, "The Homosexual Menace: The Politics of Sexuality in Cold War America," in *Passion and Powers: Sexuality in History,* eds. Kathy Peiss and Christina Simmons (Philadelphia: Temple University Press, 1989), 226–40; David Caute, *The Great Fear: The Anti-Communist Purge Under Truman and Eisenhower* (New York: Simon & Schuster, 1978); Margot Canaday, "Building a Straight State: Sexuality and Social Citizenship Under the 1944 G.I. Bill," *Journal of American History* 90 (December 2003): 935–57; Robert J. Corber, *In the Name of National Security: Hitchcock, Homophobia, and the Political Construction of Gender in Postwar America* (Durham, NC: Duke University Press, 1993); David Campbell, *Writing Security: United States Foreign Policy and the Politics of Identity* (Minneapolis: University of Minnesota Press, 1992), 150–60; and Robert D. Dean, *Imperial Brotherhood: Gender and the Making of Cold War Foreign Policy* (Amherst: University of Massachusetts Press, 2001).

5. In 1958, the editors of the *New England Journal of Medicine,* hereafter *NEJM,* attributed the decline in the nation's morals (as evidenced by increasing pre- and extra-marital sexual activity among women) to three factors: the culture of leisure and self-indulgence that characterized American society at mid-century, the sexual emancipation of women, and Cold War uncertainty about the future. Editorial, "Syphilis on the March," *NEJM* 259 (September 1958): 496. See also Nicholas J. Fiumara, M.D., M.Ph., Bernard Appel, M.D., William Hill, M.D., and Herbert Mescon, M.D.,

"Venereal Disease Today," *NEJM* 260 (September 1959): 863–68.

6. Sheeley, "Sex and the Practicing Physician," 133; Editorial, "Stock of the Puritans," *NEJM* 270 (January 1964): 104–5; Irving J. Sands, M.D., "Marriage Counseling as a Medical Responsibility," *New York State Journal of Medicine* 54 (July 1954): 2050–56; Jed W. Pearson, Jr., M.D., "The Physician's Role in Premarriage Counseling," *American Journal of Obstetrics and Gynecology,* hereafter *AJOG,* 71 (February 1956): 363–67; Raymond W. Waggoner, M.D., Sc.D., "Marriage Counseling as a Responsibility of the Physician," *Journal of the Arkansas Medical Society,* hereafter *JAMS,* 64 (November 1967): 211–14; O. Sturgeon English, M.D., "The Role of the General Practitioner in Counselling [*sic*] Before and After Marriage," *Delaware State Medical Journal* 24 (November 1952): 312–19; Robert H. Fagan, M.D., "The Role of the Obstetrician-Gynecologist in Marital Maladjustment," *AJOG* 89 (June 1964): 328–34; and Herman I. Kantor, M.D., "The Premarital Consultation," *The Mississippi Doctor* 64 (February 1968): 79–81.

7. Elaine Tyler May, *Homeward Bound: American Families in the Cold War Era* (New York: Basic Books, 1988); Stephanie Coontz, *The Way We Never Were: American Families and the Nostalgia Trap* (New York: Basic Books, 1992); Joanne Meyerowitz, ed., *Not June Cleaver: Women and Gender in Postwar America 1945–1960* (Philadelphia: Temple University Press, 1994); and Jessica Weiss, *To Have and to Hold: Marriage, the Baby Boom, and Social Change* (Chicago: University of Chicago Press, 2000).

8. Sheeley, "Sex and the Practicing Physician," 133; "Medical News: Submissive Women Arise and Marriages Fall," *JAMA* 184 (April 1963): 47; Charles E. Flowers, Jr., M.D., "Premarital Examination and Counseling," *Obstetrics & Gynecology,* hereafter *OG,* 20 (July 1962): 143–47; Sands, "Marriage Counseling as a Medical Responsibility," 2050–56; Janet E. Towne, M.D., "Premarital Counseling," *The Medical Clinics of North America* 45 (January 1961): 53–62; Pearson, "The Physician's Role," 363–67; Waggoner, "Marriage Counseling as a Responsibility of the Physician," 211–14; English, "The Role of the General Practitioner," 312–19; and Eugene G. Hamilton, M.D., "Frigidity in the Female," *Missouri Medicine* 58 (October 1961): 1040–51.

9. Nadina R. Kavinoky, M.D., "Premarital Medical Examination," *JAMA* 156 (October 1954): 692. See also Congress on Medical Education, "Obstacles to Population Control," *JAMA* 197 (April 1966): 643–54; Max Levin, M.D., "The Physician and the Sexual Revolution," *NEJM* 273 (December 1965): 1366–69; Wilfred C. Hulse, M.D., "The Management of Sexual Conflict in General Practice," *JAMA* 150 (November 1952): 846–49; Seymour L. Halleck, M.D., "Sex and Mental Health on Campus," *JAMA* 200 (May 1967): 684–90; Robert L. Tolle, M.D., "Sex and Marriage," *Southern Medical Journal* 60 (June 1967): 615–18; Lena Levine, M.D., "The Young Man and Woman Marry: Diagnosis and Treatment of Pre-Marital and Marital Ills," *Journal of the*

American Medical Woman's Association, hereafter JAMWA, 18 (March 1963): 227–31; Martin Goldberg, M.D., "Counseling Sexually Incompatible Marriage Partners," *Postgraduate Medicine,* hereafter *PM,* 42 (July 1967): 62–68; Eleanor B. Easley, "The Premarital Examination." *North Carolina Medical Journal* 15 (March 1954): 105–10; John Parks, "Premarital Gynecologic Examination," *PM* 30 (November 1961): 476–78; and Patricia Ann Lawrence, M.D., "The Responsibility of the Gynecologist in Premarital Counseling," *AJOG* 96 (September 1966): 80–86.

10. Ibid. See also Sheeley, "Sex and the Practicing Physician," 133; Flowers, "Premarital Examination and Counseling," 143–47; Sands, "Marriage Counseling as a Medical Responsibility," 2050–56; Towne, "Premarital Counseling," 53–62; Pearson, "The Physician's Role," 363–67; Waggoner, "Marriage Counseling as a Responsibility of the Physician," 211–44; Editorial, "Sex and Medicine," *JAMA* 197 (July 1966): 643–54; J. P. Greenhill, M.D., Letter to the Editor, *JAMA* 159 (September 1955): 398; S. Leon Israel, M.D., "Teaching the Art of Caring for Women," *JAMA* 191 (February 1965): 393–96; S. Leon Israel, M.D., "The Role of the Physician in Family Life Education," *Michigan Medicine* 66 (May 1967): 567–71; Mary S. Calderone, "Sexual Problems in Medical Practice," *JAMWA* 23 (February 1968): 140–46; Lena Levine, M.D., "Preventive Measures for Marital Adjustment," *JAMA* 61 (August 1964): 72–74; John H. Holzaepfel, M.D., "Premarital Examinations and Conception Control," *Western Journal of Surgery Obstetrics & Gynecology* (November–December 1957): 379–81; English, "The Role of the General Practitioner," 312–19; J. Allan Offen, M.D., "The Role of the Gynecologist in Family and Marriage Counseling," *OG* 13 (March 1959): 302–10; Jed W. Pearson, Jr., M.D., "Premarital Counseling," *Medical Annals of the District of Columbia* 36 (January 1967): 1–2, 76; Sylvester W. Trythall, M.D., "The Premarital Law: History and a Survey of Its Effectiveness in Michigan," *JAMA* 187 (March 1964): 900–903; James R. Rappaport, M.D., "Sex in Marriage Counseling," *Maryland State Medical Journal* (September 1966): 35–40; Robert H. Fagan, M.D., "Premarital and Marital Counseling and the Family Doctor," *Medical Times,* hereafter *MT,* 93 (June 1965): 671–74; C. A. Johnson, M.D., "The Pre-Marital Lecture," *South Dakota Journal of Medicine and Pharmacy* (February 1959): 91–92, 106; Frederick J. Hofmeister and Robert P. Reik, "The Complete Office Examination," *PM* (February 1960): 235–40; Robert Chez, M.D., "Obtaining the Sexual History in the Female Patient," *General Practice,* hereafter *GP,* 30 (October 1964): 120–24; and Paul Popenoe, Sc.D., "Marriage Counseling," *GP* 6 (October 1952): 53–60.

11. Paul Starr, *The Social Transformation of American Medicine: The Rise of a Sovereign Profession and the Making of a Vast Industry* (New York: Basic Books, 1982); John Duffy, *From Humors to Medical Science: A History of American Medicine* (Chicago: University of Illinois Press. 1993); Stuart W. Leslie, *The Cold War and American Science: The Military-*

Industrial-Academic Complex at MIT and Stanford (New York: Columbia University Press, 1993); and Rosemary Stevens, *American Medicine and the Public Interest: A History of Specialization* (Berkeley: University of California Press, 1971, 1998). Although obstetrician-gynecologists and general practitioners were struggling to distinguish their practices from one another, the material I am discussing in this article reveals a striking agreement on methods and ideology. Therefore, when I use the term "physicians" in this article, I am referring to both unless otherwise stated.

12. Starr, *The Social Transformation of American Medicine,* 333–51.

13. Luigi Mastroianni, M.D., discussion of Fagan, "The Role of the Obstetrician-Gynecologist," 334. See also Kavinoky, "Premarital Medical Examination," 692; Congress on Medical Education, "Obstacles to Population Control," 643–54; Sheeley, "Sex and the Practicing Physician," 133; Levin, "Preventive Measures," 1366–69; Hulse, "The Management of Sexual Conflict in General Practice," 846–49; Tolle, "Sex and Marriage," 615–18; Levine, "The Young Man and Woman Marry," 227–31; Flowers, "Premarital Examination and Counseling," 143–47; Sands, "Marriage Counseling as a Medical Responsibility," 2050–56; Towne, "Premarital Counseling," 53–62; Pearson, "The Physician's Role," 363–67; Waggoner, "Marriage Counseling as a Responsibility of the Physician," 211–14; Goldberg, "Counseling Sexually Incompatible Marriage Partners," 62–68; Easley, "The Premarital Examination," 105–10; Parks, "Premarital Gynecologic Examination," 476–78; Lawrence, "The Responsibility of the Gynecologist in Premarital Counseling," 80–86; "Sex and Medicine," 643–54; Greenhill, Letter to the Editor, 398; Israel, "Teaching the Art of Caring for Women," 393–96; Israel, "The Role of the Physician," 567–71; Calderone, "Sexual Problems in Medical Practice," 140–46; Levine, "Preventive Measures," 72–74; Holzaepfel, "Premarital Examinations and Conception Control," 379–81; English, "The Role of the General Practitioner," 312–19; Offen, "The Role of the Gynecologist in Family and Marriage Counseling," 302–10; Pearson, "Premarital Counseling," 1–2, 76; Trythall, "The Premarital Law," 900–903; Rappaport, "Sex in Marriage Counseling," 35–40; Fagan, "The Role of the Obstetrician-Gynecologist," 328–34; Fagan, "Premarital and Marital Counseling," 671–74; Johnson, "The PreMarital Lecture," 91–92, 106; Hofmeister and Reik, "The Complete Office Examination," 235–40; Chez, "Obtaining the Sexual History in the Female Patient," 120–24; and Popenoe, "Marriage Counseling," 53–60.

14. Pearson, "The Physician's Role," 693.

15. On shifts in psychiatric practices, see Starr, *The Social Transformation of American Medicine;* Juliet Mitchell, *Psychoanalysis and Feminism: A Radical Reassessment of Freudian Psychoanalysis* (1974; reprint, New York: Basic Books, 1974, 2000); and Joseph Schwartz, *Cassandra's Daughter: A History of Psychoanalysis* (New York: Penguin Books, 1999).

The correlation between sexual behavior and mental health became increasingly racialized in the postwar period—especially for unwed mothers. See Rickie Solinger, *Wake Up Little Susie: Single Pregnancy and Race Before Roe v. Wade* (New York: Routledge, 2000); and Regina G. Kunzel, "White Neurosis, Black Pathology: Constructing Out-of-Wedlock Pregnancy in the Wartime and Postwar United States," in Meyerowitz, *Not June Cleaver,* 304–31. On the medicalization of sexual behavior and identity, see Jennifer Terry, *An American Obsession: Science, Medicine, and Homosexuality in Modern Society* (Chicago: University of Chicago Press, 1999); Joanne Meyerowitz, *How Sex Changed: A History of Transsexuality in the United States* (Cambridge, MA: Harvard University Press, 2002); and Carol Groneman, *Nymphomania: A History* (New York: W.W. Norton & Company, 2000).

16. See Terry, *An American Obsession,* chap. 11; and Allen Bérubé, *Coming Out Under Fire: The History of Gay Men and Women in World War Two* (New York: The Free Press, 1990).

17. Philip Wylie, *Generation of Vipers* (New York: Rinehart & Co., 1942); Edward A. Strecker, M.D., *Their Mothers' Sons: The Psychiatrist Examines an American Problem* (New York: J.B. Lippincott and Co., 1946); Strecker and Vincent T. Lathbury, M.D., *Their Mothers' Daughters* (New York: J.B. Lippincott and Co., 1956); and Ferdinand Lundberg and Marynia F. Farnham, M.D., *Modern Woman: The Lost Sex* (New York: Harper & Brothers, Publishers, 1947).

18. Hamilton, "Frigidity in the Female," 1043. See also Flowers, "Premarital Examination and Counseling," 146.

19. Towne, "Premarital Counseling," 58.

20. Helene Deutsch, *The Psychology of Women, Volume II—Motherhood* (New York: Grune & Stratton, 1945).

21. G. Lombard Kelly, M.D., "Query: Vaginal Orgasm," *JAMA* 146 (July 1951): 978–79; Hamilton, "Frigidity in the Female," 1040; William S. Kroger, M.D., and S. Charles Freed, M.D., "Psychosomatic Aspects of Frigidity," *JAMA* 143 (June 1950): 526–32; Edmund Bergler, M.D., "The Problem of Frigidity," *Psychiatric Quarterly* 18 (July 1944): 374–90; and William S. Kroger, M.D., and S. Charles Freed, M.D., Letter to the Editor, *JAMA* 144 (October 1950): 570–71.

22. According to Edmund Bergler and William Kroger, Freud called this transfer a "push of passivity" that occurred around the onset of puberty. Failure to transfer resulted in the "penalty" of frigidity. Edmund Bergler and William S. Kroger, *Kinsey's Myth of Female Sexuality* (New York: Grune & Stratton, 1954), 69–70.

23. Kroger and Freed, "Psychosomatic Aspects," 526–32.

24. Beverley T. Mead, M.D., "Sexual Problems," *MT* 90 (October 1962): 1033–37; Kroger and Freed, "Psychosomatic Aspects"; Goldberg, "Counseling Sexually Incompatible Marriage Partners," 62–68; and Hamilton, "Frigidity in the Female," 1040–51.

25. Kavinoky, "Premarital Medical Examination," 692. As if to prove this point, the only photographic representations of

female genitalia that I have found in my research were of African American women. See Hofmeister and Reik, "The Complete Office Examination," 235–40. Emily Martin provides an excellent discussion of the racialization of women's healthcare in *The Woman in the Body: A Cultural Analysis of Reproduction* (Boston: Beacon Press, 1992).

26. Kavinoky, "Premarital Medical Examination," 694.

27. Rappaport, "Sex in Marriage Counseling," 36.

28. See, for example, Lawrence, "The Responsibility of the Gynecologist in Premarital Counseling," 84; and Hamilton, "Frigidity in the Female," 1040–51.

29. Lena Levine suggested that observing a patient's reaction to penetration during the pelvic exam would "serve as a guide to the physician as to the kind of information and explanations required" of sexual behavior. Levine, "The Young Man and Woman Marry," 228. Similar opinions are implied by Blanche Lockard, M.D., "A Program for Pre-Marital Counseling," *Mississippi Doctor* 37 (June 1959): 9–11; Kavinoky, "Premarital Medical Examination," 692–93; Paul Scholten, M.D., "The Premarital Examination," *JAMA* 168 (November 1958): 1173; and Towne, "Premarital Counseling," 56. Health educator Terri Kapsalis has argued that "the pelvic exam is in effect the staging of sex and gender, particularly the staging of femininity and female sexuality" in *Public Privates: Performing Gynecology from Both Ends of the Speculum* (Durham, NC: Duke University Press, 1997), 14. Barbara Ehrenreich and Deirdre English have discussed physicians' belief that the pelvic exam simulated heterosexual intercourse and therefore could be used to evaluate a woman's sexual adjustment in *For Her Own Good:150 Years of the Experts' Advice to Women* (New York: Anchor Books, 1978), 274–80.

30. The importance of a gentle pelvic exam was best described by Louis G. Fournier, M.D., in "Practical Considerations for the General Practitioner in His Role as a Gynecologist," *New York State Journal of Medicine* (November 1952): 2765–70: "You cannot roughly barge into a vagina, causing 'embarrassment, discomfort, and pain, and expect to outline adequately the contents of that particular pelvis." Unlike today, physicians writing in these journals expected this to be a woman's first visit to the gynecologist, unless she had some sort of medical condition that would have necessitated an earlier visit. So in addition to assuaging fears about sexual intercourse, physicians also had to keep in mind that this was probably the patient's first experience with the speculum.

31. Ethel M. Albert, PhD, "Modern Women—Freedom or Bondage," *JAMA* 183 (March 1963), 38.

32. Kavinoky, "Premarital Medical Examination," 693.

33. Carl N. Neupert, M.D., to Lee D. Cady, M.D., 28 October 1937, Lee D. Cady Papers, Western Historical Manuscript Collection, University of Missouri, Columbia MO, hereafter Cady Papers.

34. For further reading on physicians as public health advocates, see Allan M. Brandt, *No Magic Bullet: A Social History of Venereal Disease in the United States Since 1880* (New York: Oxford University Press, 1985); Leslie J. Reagan, *When Abortion Was a Crime: Women, Medicine and Law in the United States, 1867–1973* (Berkeley: University of California Press, 1997); Starr, *Social Transformation*; and Stevens, *American Medicine and the Public Interest*.

35. Physician Lee D. Cady, who led the medical profession's campaign for premarital syphilis testing in Missouri, repeatedly emphasized the privacy violation inherent in a mandated physical exam. See, for example, Cady's 1939 radio address, "Missouri's Pre-marital Examination Laws," f. 22, Cady Papers.

36. Trythall, "The Premarital Law," 900; and Phillip K. Condit, M.D., M.P.H., and A. Frank Brewer, M.D., "Premarital Examination Laws—Are They Worthwhile?" *American Journal of Public Health* 43 (July 1953): 880–87.

37. Robert Latou Dickinson advocated the use of the premarital consultation to discuss matters of sexual adjustment with their patients as early as 1928; however, widespread support of this idea did not appear in the medical journals for nearly twenty-five years. Wendy Kline has discussed Dickinson's position in *Building a Better Race: Gender, Sexuality, and Eugenics from the Turn of the Century to the Baby Boom* (Berkeley: University of California Press, 2001), chap. 5. See also Ethel M. Nash, M.A., Lucie Jessner, M.D., and D. Wilfred Abse, M.D., *Marriage Counseling in Medical Practice* (Chapel Hill: University of North Carolina Press, 1964), 223; and R. L. Dickinson, "Premarital Consultation," *JAMA* 117 (November 1941): 1687–92.

38. Editorial, "Premarital Laws," *JAMA* 187 (March 1964): 948. Physicians repeatedly described the laws necessitating a premarital physical or venereal exam as an "opportunity" to provide premarital counseling about sex. See, for example, Condit and Brewer, "Premarital Examination Laws," 880–87; Levine, "The Young Man and Woman Marry," 227–31; English, "The Role of the General Practitioner," 312–19; and Waggoner, "Marriage Counseling as a Responsibility of the Physician," 211–14.

39. Kavinoky, "Premarital Medical Examination," 692–95.

40. Articles that specifically cited Kavinoky as a model include Towne, "Premarital Counseling," 53–62; Pearson, "The Physician's Role," 363–67; Scholten, "The Premarital Examination," 117–77; and Ethel M. Nash, M.A., and Lois M. Louden, M.A., "The Premarital Medical Examination and the Carolina Population Center: What Patients Desire," *JAMA* 210 (December 1969): 2365–69. See also Clark E. Vincent, *Human Sexuality in Medical Education and, Practice* (Springfield, IL: Charles C Thomas Publisher, 1968), 21. The editors of the 1964 volume *Marriage Counseling in Medical Practice*, listed Kavinoky's article as an important step "in the evolution of the premarital examination." Nash, Jessner, and Abse, *Marriage Counseling in Medical Practice*, 223. Although they do not cite Kavinoky, Abraham Stone, M.D., and Lena Levine, M.D., emphasize the importance of the initial pelvic exam in establishing

the pattern for women's response to penetration in general. See Stone and Levine, *The Premarital Consultation: A Manual for Physicians* (New York: Grune & Stratton, 1956).

41. Arnold H. Kegel, M.D., Letter to the Editor, *JAMA* 153 (December 1953): 1303–4.

42. Ibid.

43. Towne, "Premarital Counseling," 57.

44. Rachel Maines, *The Technology of Orgasm* (Baltimore: Johns Hopkins University Press, 1999).

45. The medical community's discussion of frigidity makes clear that physicians and psychiatrists associated clitoral stimulation with latent or active lesbianism and vaginal orgasm with "normal" heterosexual response. Kroger and Freed, "Psychosomatic Aspects," 526–32; Bergler, "The Problem of Frigidity," 374–90; Deutsch, *The Psychology of Women* and Marie Bonaparte, *Female Sexuality* (New York: International Universities Press, Inc., 1953).

46. Hulse, "The Management of Sexual Conflict in General Practice," 848.

47. Lawrence, "The Responsibility of the Gynecologist in Premarital Counseling," 83.

48. Flowers, "Premarital Examination and Counseling," 146.

49. Bonaparte, *Female Sexuality*, 56. One physician not only cited Bonaparte in his bibliography, but also used the language of "sleeping beauty" to describe the normal sexual awakening for women. See Hamilton, "Frigidity in the Female," 1044.

50. Parks, "Premarital Gynecologic Examination," 477. One article described the pelvic exam as a planned invasion: "The hymen can be easily and almost painlessly infiltrated with 2% Xylocaine, beginning at 6 o'clock and proceeding around the entire periphery of the hymeneal ring." Flowers, "Premarital Examination and Counseling," 144. Flowers's article was reprinted in Nash, Jessner, and Abse, *Marriage Counseling in Medical Practice.*

51. Kavinoky, "Premarital Medical Examination," 692–95.

52. Easley, "The Premarital Examination," 107. The only physician who suggested that premarital sexual activity did not indicate sexual satisfaction was Lawrence, "The Responsibility of the Gynecologist in Premarital Counseling," 81. Likewise, because the pregnant bride was already on the path to fulfilling her psychosexual destiny, most physicians assumed that she had fully adjusted to heterosexuality, even if she had done so beyond the parameters of a legal and moral marriage.

53. Goldberg, "Counseling Sexually Incompatible Marriage Partners," 64.

54. Easley, "The Premarital Examination," 108.

55. Questions and Answers: Frigidity," *JAMA* 173 (June 1960): 971.

56. Sands, "Marriage Counseling as a Medical Responsibility," 2052.

57. Several physicians used the term "snug," including Fagan, "Premarital and Marital Counseling," 671, and "The Role of the Obstetrician-Gynecologist," 330; and Lawrence, "The Responsibility of the Gynecologist," 81.

58. Lockard, "A Program for Pre-Marital Counseling," 10.

59. Holzaepfel, "Premarital Examinations and Conception Control," 380.

60. Kavinoky, "Premarital Medical Examination," 693. The term "super-virgin" was used by Kavinoky to indicate a woman with a malformed hymen or vaginal canal that made the vaginal opening less than 1 cm. She emphasized that the physician should use this term when consulting with the couple regarding the appropriate course of treatment, because "The word 'small' has too many inaccurate implications." Similarly, John Parks advised that "Great care must be taken to avoid giving the patient a feeling that she is small, infantile, or genitally inferior." Parks, "Premarital Gynecologic Examination," 478.

61. Flowers, "Premarital Examination and Counseling," 144; Fagan, "Premarital and Marital Counseling," 672; Easley, "The Premarital Examination," 108; Lockard, "A Program for Pre-Marital Counseling," 10; and Pearson, "Premarital Counseling," 2. Parks suggested that the decision to dilate would be made solely by the fiancé, "Premarital Gynecologic Examination," 477; Towne indicates that the permission of the patient's family may also be necessary even before the pelvic exam can be administered ("Premarital Counseling," 55).

62. There is no indication of how many fiancés actually refused to grant permission for dilation. As physician Charles E. Flowers, Jr., noted, "It is indeed a rare and poorly adjusted groom who must reassure himself at the expense of his wife's dyspareunia." "Premarital Examination and Counseling," 144.

63. Verna Stevens-Young, M.D., discussion of English, "The Role of the General Practitioner," 317.

64. The ideological struggles of the Cold War were often cloaked in the language of sexual morality and gender performance. Consider, for example, the infamous Kitchen Debate between Soviet Premier Nikita Khrushchev and American Vice President Richard Nixon, or the gendered language of George Kennan's Long Telegram. See May, *Homeward Bound*, chap. 1; and Frank Costigliola, "'Unceasing Pressure for Penetration': Gender, Pathology, and Emotion in George Kennan's Formation of the Cold War," in *Journal of American History* (March 1997): 1309–39.

65. H. T. McGuire, M.D., discussion of English, "The Role of the General Practitioner," 317.

Laurie Essig
Lynn Owens

What if Marriage Is Bad for Us?

First published in 2009

Sometimes a belief becomes so strong that suggesting it might be wrong is nearly impossible. One such belief is that marriage is good for us. Last April, when Vermont finally recognized same-sex marriage, many of our fellow Vermonters rushed to celebrate. Neither one of us did. They were puzzled by our lack of enthusiasm. "You have to support gay marriage," a straight colleague angrily shouted at one of us. But why do we have to celebrate any marriage? Unlike conservatives who attack gay marriage, it's not the gay part we object to; it's the marriage part. What does it even mean? Over the past 15 years, Americans have been fighting about that, and therefore about what it means to be a citizen and an adult.

In 1996, as Congress turned "welfare" into "workfare," it proclaimed that "marriage is the foundation of a successful society." A few years ago, President George W. Bush created the Healthy Marriage Initiative to promote marriage as a solution to poverty and for the well-being of children. Currently the government spends about $150-million annually to promote marriage among our country's poorest citizens. In *The Audacity of Hope,* President Obama claims that supporting marriage among low-income couples should be "something everyone can agree upon." As one of his earliest acts as president, with two wars and an economic meltdown on his hands, Obama took time to approve taking $5-million out of antipoverty funds to promote marriage for young people.

The belief that marriage is good for us also explains why gay and lesbian activists have been fighting so hard for same-sex marriage. According to Freedom to Marry, the national organization behind much of the gay-marriage movement, marriage is "the most powerful expression we have for the affirmation of love and commitment, a source of social

recognition . . . that hold(s) two people together through life's ups and downs." Marriage is also the source of more than a thousand federal rights and responsibilities, not to mention cheaper gym memberships, social approval, and all those gifts that arrive on your wedding day.

Where there are policy disputes, you can expect social scientists to weigh in with their supposedly objective data. One noteworthy example is Mark Regnerus's recent op-ed essay in *The Washington Post,* urging young people to get married. Regnerus argues that "today, as ever, marriage wisely entered into remains good for the economy and the community, good for one's personal well-being, good for wealth creation, and, yes, good for the environment, too."

Marriage promises to save the poor, empower gays and lesbians, and socialize the young. In support of those promises, the romantics wax about love and happiness, the pragmatics tout rights and security, and the experts crunch the numbers. But as critical sociologists, we find ourselves agreeing most strongly with Marx— Groucho—who quipped, "Marriage is a wonderful institution, but who wants to live in an institution?"

Institutions serve two purposes, practical and ideological. We will do well to keep both in mind in evaluating the benefits that marriage supposedly offers.

Marriage Makes You Rich Advocates claim that marriage increases wealth. That makes sense; if the key to a successful marriage is hard work, you should at least get paid for it. It's true that married people are wealthier than unmarried people, but it's not marriage that makes you rich. Marriage is not randomly distributed across the population. People who get married (and stay married) tend to be wealthier and whiter than people who do not. For instance, 95 percent of white women will marry at some point in their lifetime, while only 43 percent of black women will.

To say marriage creates wealth is to confuse correlation with causation. If there is more wealth in Manhattan than in Brooklyn, that does not mean that moving to Manhattan will make you wealthier. In fact, moving—and marrying—may make you poorer, given the high start-up costs. A move requires first and last months' rent, a moving van, and lots of bubble wrap. A marriage often demands a wedding, and with the average cost of weddings at $30,000, getting married is going to cost you.

Nor will moving into marriage necessarily increase your earnings or earning potential. If you're poor and have little education, saying "I do" won't get you off welfare or make minimum wage any less a dead end. If you already have means, marriage might help. Be careful, though, because even when marriage does produce wealth, divorce often destroys it. If you are getting married for the economic benefits, better make sure it's forever.

Marriage Is Traditional   As Frank Sinatra once crooned: "Love and marriage / go together like a horse and carriage / . . . It's an institute you can't disparage / Ask the local gentry and they will say it's elementary." But there is nothing elementary about the form of marriage as we practice it today. Despite the claims of sociologists, politicians, and marriage advocates on all sides, marriage has changed over time and exists differently in different cultures.

Marriage as we imagine it today developed during the late 1800s, when it became "for love" and "companionate." Until that point, one married for material and social reasons, not romance. Women required marriage for survival; men did not. That left men free to behave as they wished: Prostitutes and buggery were part of many a married man's sexual repertoire. But then the Victorians (with their sexual prudishness) and first-wave feminists (with their sense that what's good for the goose is good for the gander) insisted that antiprostitution and antisodomy laws be enacted, and that married men confine their sexual impulses to the conjugal bed. The result was enforced lifelong sexual monogamy for both parties, at least in theory.

That might have seemed reasonable in 1900, when the average marriage lasted about 11 years, a consequence of high death rates. But these days, when a marriage can drag on for half a century, it can be a lot of work. Laura Kipnis calls marriage a "domestic gulag," a

forced-labor camp where the inmates have to spend all their time outside of work working on their marriage.

And if the dyadic couple locked in lifelong monogamy was a radical new form, so was the family structure it spawned. The nuclear family is primarily a mutant product of the nuclear age. Before World War II, most Americans lived among extended family. The definition of family was not the couple and their offspring, but brothers, sisters, aunts, uncles, and grandparents as well. With the creation of suburbs for the middle classes, large numbers of white Americans began participating in the radical family formation of two married parents plus children in a detached house separated from extended family.

Although the nuclear family is idealized as "natural" and "normal" by our culture (*Leave It to Beaver*) and our government ("family values"), it has always been both a shockingly new way of living and a minority lifestyle. Even at its height, in the early 1970s, only about 40 percent of American families lived that way. Today that number is about 23 percent, including stepfamilies. The nuclear family is not only revolutionary; it is a revolution that has failed for most of us.

Marriage Makes You Healthy   According to the Centers for Disease Control and Prevention, married people have better health than those who are not married. A closer look at the data, however, reveals that married and never-married Americans are similar; it's the divorced who seem to suffer. The lesson might be to never divorce, but an even more obvious lesson to be drawn from the research might be to never marry.

Naomi Gerstel and Natalia Sarkisian's research shows that married couples are more isolated than their single counterparts. That is not a function just of their having children. Even empty-nesters and couples without children tend to have weak friendship networks. Marriage results in fewer rather than more social ties because it promises complete fulfillment through the claims of romance. We are instructed by movies, pop songs, state policy, and sociology to get married because "love is all you need." But actually we humans need more. We need both a sense of connection to larger networks—to community, to place—and a sense of purpose that is beyond our primary sexual relationships.

For those reasons, marriage has been self-destructing as a social form. The marriage rate in the United States is at an all-time low. In 1960 about two-thirds of adult Americans were married. Today only slightly more than half of Americans live in wedded bliss. Actually, even the bliss is declining, with fewer married Americans describing their unions as "very happy."

Maybe it's the decline in happiness that has caused an increasing number of Americans to say "I don't," despite Hollywood's presenting us with happy ending after happy ending and a government bent on distributing civil rights on the basis of marital status. Apparently no amount of propaganda or coercion can force humans to participate in a family form so out of sync with what we actually need.

With all that marriage supporters promise—wealth, health, stability, happiness, sustainability—our country finds itself confronted with a paradox: Those who would appear to gain the most from marriage are the same ones who prove most resistant to its charms. Study after study has found that it is the poor in the United States who are least likely to wed. The people who get married are the same ones who already benefit most from all our social institutions: the "haves." They benefit even more when they convince everyone that the benefits are evenly distributed.

Too often we are presented with the false choice between a lifelong, loving marriage and a lonely, unmarried life. But those are far from the only options. We should consider the way people actually live: serial monogamy, polyamory, even polygamy.

Instead of "blaming the victims" for failing to adopt the formative lifestyles of the white and middle class, we should consider that those avoiding marriage might know exactly what they are doing. Marriage is not necessarily good for all of us, and it might even be bad for most of us. When there is broad, seemingly unanimous support for an institution, and when the institution is propped up by such disparate ideas as love, civil rights, and wealth creation, we should wonder why so many different players seem to agree so strongly. Perhaps it's because they are supporting not just marriage but also the status quo.

We can dress up marriage in as many beautiful white wedding gowns as we like, but the fundamental fact remains: Marriage is a structure of rights and privileges for those who least need them and a culture of prestige for those who already have the highest levels of racial, economic, and educational capital.

So when you hear activists and advocates—gay, Christian, and otherwise—pushing to increase not only marriage rights but also marriage rates, remember these grouchy words of Marx: "Politics is the art of looking for trouble, finding it everywhere, diagnosing it incorrectly, and applying the wrong remedies." Marriage is trouble. Americans haven't failed at marriage. Marriage has failed us.

28   **Kathleen Gerson**

Moral Dilemmas, Moral Strategies, and the Transformation of Gender: Lessons from Two Generations of Work and Family Change[1]

First published in 2002

Choosing between self-interest and caring for others is one of the most fundamental dilemmas facing all of us. To reconcile this dilemma, modern societies in general—and American society in particular—have tried to divide women and men into different moral categories. Since the rise of industrialism, the social organization of moral responsibility has expected women to seek personal development by caring for others and men to care for others by sharing the rewards of independent achievement.

Although labeled "traditional," this gendered division of moral labor represents a social form and cultural mandate that rose to prominence in the mid-twentieth century but reached an impasse as the postindustrial era opened new avenues for work and family life. (Among the voluminous works on this subject, see Kimmel 1996; Ryan 1981; Welter 1966.) At the outset of the twenty-first century, women and men face rising conflicts over how to resolve the basic tensions between family and work, public and private, autonomy and commitment. They are searching for new strategies for reconciling an "independent self" with commitment to others.

While the long-term trajectory of change remains unclear, new social conditions have severely undermined the link between gender and moral obligation. The young women and men who have come of age amid this changing social landscape face risks and dangers, but they also inherit an unprecedented opportunity to forge new, more egalitarian ways to balance self-development with commitment to others. To enable them to do so, however, we must reshape work

and family institutions in ways that overcome beliefs and practices that presume gender differences in moral responsibility.

Drawing on insights from my research on how contemporary young women and men negotiate the conflicts between family and work, I explore how new social conditions are compelling them to reconsider traditional strategies for reconciling self-development with caring for others. Social change has undermined earlier resolutions to these dilemmas but does not offer clear avenues for creating new ones. My research on the "children of the gender revolution" suggests that young women and men cannot rely on inflexible gender categories to resolve the conflict between autonomy and care, but they are encountering social and cultural obstacles to creating gender-neutral strategies for apportioning moral labor. . . .

STUDYING GENDER CHANGE: FINDINGS FROM A NEW GENERATION

During the last several decades, I have studied two pivotal generations. My earlier research examined how the women and men who came of age in the 1970s and 1980s helped forge changes in gender, work, and family life as they reacted to new structural and cultural conditions (Gerson 1985, 1993). My current research focuses on how the generation who grew up in these changing households and are now entering adulthood are responding to a world where nontraditional family forms predominate and gender inequality has been seriously questioned. In significant ways, the older group can be viewed as the "parents of the gender revolution" and the generation now coming of age as the "children of the revolution" (Gerson 2001). They have watched their parents cope with the erosion of the breadwinner-homemaker ethos, and they must now devise their own strategies in the face of continuing work and family change.

To discover how new generations are experiencing and responding to these vast social changes, I conducted in-depth, life history interviews with 120 young women and men between the ages of 18 and 32. They were randomly selected from a range of economic and social contexts, including inner-city, outer-city, and suburban neighborhoods throughout the New York metropolitan area. They are evenly divided between women and men, with an average age of 24, and are economically and racially diverse, with 54 percent non-Hispanic whites, 21 percent African Americans, 18 percent Hispanics, and 8 percent Asians.

Most lived in families that underwent changes that cannot be captured in the static categories of household types. That said, a large majority lived in some form of nontraditional arrangement before reaching 18. About 40 percent lived in a single-parent home at some point in their childhood, and 7 percent saw their parents break up after they left home.[2] About one-third grew up in homes where both parents held full-time jobs of relatively equal importance, at least at some point during their childhood.[3] The remaining 27 percent described growing up in homes that were generally traditional in the sense that mothers worked intermittently, secondarily, or not at all, although most of these households underwent some form of change as mothers went to work or marriages faced crises. As a whole, the group experienced the full range of changes now emerging in family, work, and gender arrangements.

The interviews reveal how growing up amid a shifting gender and family order has prompted a new generation to rethink the age-old conflict between self-interest and responsibility to others. Taking lessons from their parents and their parents' generation, but facing new quandaries of their own, these young women and men are crafting moral strategies that challenge traditional views of gender. Their emerging views on how to balance autonomy and commitment, to define care, and to develop a personal identity amid ambiguous social shifts are presented below. While these views suggest a blurring of gender boundaries, they also underscore how persisting obstacles are

creating a gap between young women's and men's emerging egalitarian aspirations and their far more limited opportunities for achieving them. The next section thus considers how pervasive barriers to both gender equality and work-family integration are creating a new gender divide between women who seek personal independence and men who worry about losing traditional privileges.

NEW DILEMMAS, AMBIGUOUS STRATEGIES

How does this generation view its moral choices? As adult partnerships have become more fluid and voluntary, they are grappling with how to form relationships that balance commitment with autonomy and self-sufficiency. As their mothers have become essential and often sole breadwinners for their households, they are searching for new ways to define care that do not force them to choose between spending time with their children and earning an income. And in the face of rising work-family conflicts, they are looking for definitions of personal identity that do not pit their own development against creating committed ties to others. As young women and men wrestle with these dilemmas, they are questioning a division of moral responsibility that poses a conflict between personal development and caring for others.

Seeking Autonomy, Establishing Commitment

The decline of permanent marriage has raised new and perplexing questions about how to weigh the need and desire for self-sufficiency against the hope of creating an enduring partnership. In wrestling with this quandary, young women and men draw on lessons learned in their families and personal relationships. Yet, they also recognize that past experiences and encounters can provide, at best, a partial and uncertain blueprint for the future.

Few of the women and men who were interviewed reacted in a rigidly moralistic way to their parents' choices. Among those whose parents chose to divorce (or never marry), about 45 percent viewed the breakup as a prelude to growing difficulty, but the other 55 percent supported the separation and felt relief in its aftermath. Danisha, a 21-year-old African American, concluded that conflict would have emerged had her parents stayed together:

I have personally met a lot of miserable children whose parents stayed together. For me, it would have been worse—because eventually, a lot of the civility they had toward each other would have broken down into hostility. They got out while it was good.

And at 26, Erica, who grew up in a white middle-class suburb, supported her parents' decision to separate and received more support from each of them in its aftermath:

I knew my parents were going to get divorced, because I could tell they weren't getting along. They were acting out roles rather than being involved. They were really drifting apart, so it was something perfectly natural to me. In the new situation, I spent more valuable time with my parents as individuals. So time with my father and mother was more meaningful to me and more productive.

Among those whose parents stayed together, almost 60 percent were pleased with and, indeed, inspired by, their parents' lifelong commitment, but about 40 percent concluded that a breakup would have been better than the persistently unhappy, conflict-ridden relationship they watched unfold. Amy, a 24-year-old Asian American, explains:

I always felt my parents would have divorced if they didn't have kids and didn't feel it was so morally wrong. They didn't really stick together because they were in love. I know all couples go through fights and stuff, but growing up, it seemed like they fought a lot, and each of them has made passing comments—like "Oh, I would have divorced your mom by now" or "I would have left your dad a thousand times." [So] I wouldn't have broken down or been emotionally stressed if my parents divorced. I didn't want to hear the shouting, and I didn't want to see my mom cry anymore. And I was also afraid of my dad, because he would never lay a hand on my mom, but he's scary. He could be violent.

Whether their parents stayed together or parted, most concluded that neither steadfast commitment nor choosing to leave has moral meaning in the abstract. The value of enduring commitment depends on the quality of the relationship it embodies.

When considering their own aspirations, almost everyone hopes to establish a committed, lasting rela-

tionship with one partner. Yet, they also hold high standards for what a relationship should provide and anticipate risks in sustaining such a commitment. Across the divides of gender, race, and class, most agree that a satisfying and worthwhile relationship should offer a balance between autonomy and sharing, sacrifice and support. At 26, Michael, an African American who was raised by his mother in a working-class suburb, is convinced that only economic independence can provide a proper base for commitment with his girlfriend:

I don't want the fifties type of marriage, where I come home with a briefcase and she's cooking. She doesn't have to cook. I just want her to have a career of her own. I want things to be comfortable. And somewhere down the line, if I lose my job or things start going crazy in the marriage, I want to be able to set my goals, and she can do what she wants, because we both have this economic base and the attitude to do it. That's what marriage is about.

Amy imagines a partnership that is equal and fluid, capable of adapting to circumstances without relinquishing equity:

I want a fifty-fifty relationship, where we both have the potential of doing everything. Both of us working, and in dealing with kids, it would be a matter of who has more flexibility with regard to their career. And if neither does, then one of us will have to sacrifice for one period, and the other for another.

Most acknowledge, however, that finding a lasting and satisfying relationship represents an ideal that is hard to reach. If it proves unattainable, they agree that being alone is better than remaining in an unhappy or destructive union. Building a full life thus means developing the self in multiple ways. At 29, Maria, who grew up in a close-knit Hispanic household where both parents worked, is careful to build her life in many directions:

I want to be with somebody, to have this person to share your life with—that you're there for as much as they're there for you. But I can't settle. If I don't find it, then I cannot live in sorrow. It's not the only thing that's ultimately important. If I didn't have my family, if I didn't have a career, if I didn't have friends, or if I didn't have the things that I enjoy doing, I would be equally unhappy. This is just one thing. Maybe it takes a little bit more of the pie than some other things—but it's still just a slice of the pie.

Across the range of personal family experiences, most also agree that children suffer more from an unhappy home than from separated parents.[4] Miranda, whose parents parted when her father returned to Mexico in her teens, looks back from the vantage point of 27 and concludes,

> For people to stay together in spite of themselves, just for the child, they're damaging the child. It's almost like a false assumption that you can do something for the sake of the child while you're being drained. Because the life is getting sucked out of you. How can you give life when it's sucked out of you?

Women and men both wonder if it is possible to establish relationships that strike a good balance between self-affirmation and commitment, providing and receiving support. Having observed their parents and others struggle with varying degrees of success against the strictures of traditional gender categories, they are hopeful but guarded about the possibilities for resolving the tension between autonomy and commitment in their own lives.[5] At 20, Chris, a Native American whose parents shared work and caretaking, is thus beginning to wonder:

> I thought you could just have a relationship, that love and being happy was always needed in life, and I've learned that you've got to be able to draw that line. It's a difficult thing, and you've got to know how to do it. And that would be my fear. Where am I cutting into my job too much? Where am I cutting into the relationship too much? And how do I divide it, and can it actually be done at all? Can you blend these two parts of your world?

Care as Time, Care as Money

If the rise of fluid adult partnerships has heightened the strains between commitment and autonomy, then the rise of employed mothers and the decline of sole male breadwinners have made the meaning of care ambiguous. Now that most children—whether living in single-parent or two-parent households—depend on the earnings of their mothers, parents face conflicts

in balancing the need to provide economic support with the need to devote time and attention.

Rigid notions of gendered caring do not fit well with most family experiences, and the majority express support for parents who transgressed traditional gender categories. Among those who grew up in two-earner households, four out of five support such an arrangement, most with enthusiasm. Across race, class, and gender groups, they believe that two incomes provided the family with increased economic resources, more flexibility against the buffeting of economic winds, and greater financial security. For Serena, a 26-year-old African American, her parents' two jobs allowed her to avoid the privations of her friends and peers:

> Both my parents worked and a lot of parents in this neighborhood, one stayed home or some were on welfare. So a lot of my peers thought we were, like, upper class because both parents had cars and we went to private schools. When I was in my late teens and actually realized where I fit into the picture, it made me really appreciate my parents.

And Jason, also 26 and white, finds inspiration in his upwardly mobile parents' example as hard workers who made things better for their children in the process:

> I would say [both parents' working] made things better for the family because their being so dedicated to providing, to working, they helped that ethic of having to work and not wasting time. So it's instilled in me and my sister the ethic to work.

Of course, this means they see a mother's employment as largely beneficial. Whether in a two-parent or single-parent home, women and men agree that an independent base enhanced a mother's sense of self, contributed to greater parental equality, and provided an uplifting model. Rachel, 24 and from a white, working-class background, explains,

> I don't think that I missed out on anything. I think it served as a more realistic model. I've heard all that stuff about how children need a parent at home, but I don't think that having her stay home with me, particularly considering her temper, would have been anything other than counterproductive. The reality is that I'm going to have to work, and a lot of women in

her generation chose not to work and did or didn't have the option. She had a choice, and she did what she wanted, and I think that's really great.

Kevin, 25 and from a middle-class, white family, agrees:

For quite a while, my mom was the main breadwinner. She was the one who was the driving force in earning money. My mother's persona was really hard working, and that's something I've strived to be with and to emulate. I didn't think it was wrong in any way. I actually feel it's a very positive thing. Whatever my relationships, I always want and appreciate people who work, and I'm talking about female involvement. It's part of who I am, and it makes me very optimistic knowing that hard work can get you somewhere.

They also deemed highly involved fathers, whether in two-earner or single-parent households, as worthy examples. Daniel, now 23, describes his Irish father's atypical working hours and parental involvement:

My father was always around. He's a fire fighter, so he had a lot of free time. When he was home, he was usually coaching me and my brother or cooking dinner or taking us wherever we wanted to go. He was the only cook up until me and my brother started doing it. So I want to make sure that, if I get married and have kids, I'm there for my kids.

In contrast, those who grew up in a largely traditional household expressed more ambivalence. Although half felt fortunate to have had a mother devoted primarily to their care, the other half would have preferred for their mothers to pursue a more independent life. At 21, Justin, who grew up in a white, largely middle-class suburb, looks back on his mother's domestic focus with a strong conviction that it took its toll on the whole household:

She was very involved [and] always around. And I appreciated it, but I felt guilty that maybe I was taking too much. It's just that she wasn't happy. And she didn't give us any responsibilities at all. I guess that made her feel good to have someone rely on her. She felt needed more. And in the long run, obviously that's not something good.

And at 30, Sarah, also white and middle-class, agreed, pointing out that a mother's "sacrifice" may evoke mixed feelings:

I wish my mom had worked so that she would have been happier. Her identity was very much as a mother, and that was a sort of a void and pain. Because that's all she was, and that was not enough. She would say that it was, but that's not what I saw. She just seemed really unhappy a lot of time. She was just overinvolved with us, and if we did something separate from her, that was a major problem. I wouldn't mind her being supermom if that was really okay with her. But I got the message that she was giving up all of this other stuff to do it, and we should feel bad about it.

Breadwinning fathers may also elicit mixed reactions. Their economic contributions are appreciated but not necessarily deemed sufficient. A good father, most concluded, takes time and offers emotional support as well. At 29, Nick, who grew up in a white working-class neighborhood and remembers feeling frustrated by his own father's distance, is seeking joint custody of his own young daughter:

I have seen a lot of guys who have kids and have never changed a diaper, have never done anything for this child. Don't call yourself daddy. Even when she was saying, "Oh, she might not be yours," it didn't matter to me. This child is counting on me.

In this context, care becomes a slippery concept. Across family circumstances, these young adults judge an ideal parent—whether mother or father—to be one who supports her or his children both economically and emotionally. At 21, Antonio, who grew up in a three-generational Hispanic household and whose father died of alcoholism, has concluded that fathers should give their children the time and emotional support typically expected of a mother:

[An ideal father] is a strong, balanced man. He's a daddy but he has the understanding of a mommy. He can care for you and protect you and guide you. . . . That's what I want to do with my kids. I want to make sure that I have time. I don't want to leave them in front of a TV set all day, because what they're learning is not coming from me. So I want to be there or, if not, I want to be in a position where I can take you with me.

If fathers should resemble traditional conceptions of mothers, then mothers should resemble fathers when it comes to work outside the home. Gabriel, a white 25-year-old who was raised by his father after his parents divorced when he was in grade school, explains,

> In terms of splitting parental stuff, it should be even. Kids need a mother and a father. And I'm really not high on the woman giving up her job. I have never wanted to have a wife who didn't make a salary. But not for the sake of leeching off of her, but so that she was independent.

And Miranda agrees that mothering means providing money as well as care:

> My mother has completely and entirely dedicated herself to me in the true sense; she has always been very selfless and very involved and fully responsible for me financially. I wouldn't feel comfortable if I didn't think I could make that kind of commitment.

If such an ideal proves beyond reach, as many expect it will be, women and men agree that families should apportion moral labor however best fits their circumstances—whether or not this means conforming to classic notions of gender difference. Mothers can and often do demonstrate care through paid work and fathers through involvement. Now 26 and raising a child on her own, Crystal, an African American, rejects a natural basis for mothering:

> I don't really believe in the mother instinct. I don't believe that's natural. Some people really connect with their children, and some people just don't. I think it should be whoever is really going to be able to be there for that child.

In the end, the material and emotional support a child receives matters more than the type of household arrangement in which it is provided. Michelle, a 24-year-old of Asian descent who watched her parents struggle in an unhappy marriage and then separate after she and her brother left home, focuses on emotional support rather than family composition:

> As long as the child feels supported and loved, that's the most important thing. Whether it's a two-parent home, a single-parent home, the mother is working, or

anything, it's just really important for the child to have a good, strong foundation.

Identity Through Love, Identity Through Work

In a world where partnerships are fragile and domesticity is devalued, young women and men are confronting basic questions about identity and self-interest. Do they base their personal well-being and sense of self on public pursuits or private attachments? What balance can or should be struck between them?

In pondering their parents' lives, most could find no simple way to define or measure self-interest. While a minority uphold traditional gendered identities, most do not find such resolutions viable. Women are especially likely to conclude that it is perilous to look to the home as the sole source of satisfaction or survival. Reflecting on the many examples of mothers and other women who languished at home, who were bereft when marriages broke up, or who found esteem in the world of paid work, 9 out of 10 express the hope that their lives will include strong ties to the workplace and public pursuits. Sarah, now a psychologist with a long-term lesbian partner who works "constantly," has high hopes but also nagging worries:

> I have a lot of conflicts now—work versus home and all of that stuff. But I would feel successful if I had a life with a lot of balance and that I'd made time for people who were important to me and made a real commitment to the people that I care about. And also, to work— I would be dedicated to work. And work and home would be connected. It would all be integrated, and it would be an outgrowth of my general way of being.

On the other side of the gender divide, many men have also become skeptical of work-centered definitions of masculine identity. As traditional jobs have given way to unpredictable shifts in work prospects, they are generally guarded about the prospect of achieving stable work careers. Having observed fathers and friends who found work either dissatisfying or too demanding, two-thirds of the men concluded that, while important, work alone could not provide their lives with meaning. These young men hope to balance paid work and personal attachments without having to sacrifice the self for a job or paycheck. Traditional views persist, but they increasingly compete with perspectives that define identity in more fluid ways. Widely shared by those who grew up in different types of families, these outlooks also transcend class and race differences. They cast doubt on some postfeminist assertions that a "new traditionalism" predominates among young women and men (Crittenden 1999). When asked how he would like to divide care-taking and breadwinning, Kevin considers the possibilities:

> Whoever can do it and whoever's capable of doing it, but it should be divided evenly. If there's something I can't do, just that I don't have the talent to do it, I would hope the other person would be able to. And the same goes the other way. My parents were like that. It was a matter of who was able to do what. There were hundreds of times when my dad made our lunches. And my sister claims that his were better than my mom's.

Yet, beyond the apparent similarities, a gender divide emerges. With one-third of men—but far fewer women—preferring traditional arrangements over all others, women are more likely to uphold flexible views of gender for themselves and their partners. More important, women and men both distinguish between their ideals and their chances of achieving them. If most hope to integrate family and work—and to find partners with whom to share the rewards and burdens of both—far fewer believe they can achieve this lofty aspiration. It is difficult to imagine integrating private with public obligations when most workplaces continue to make it difficult to balance family and job. And it is risky to build a life dependent on another adult when relationships are unpredictable. In this context, both women and men acknowledge that their actual options may fall substantially short of their ideals. For women, finding the right job and the right partner may seem too much to expect. Maria laments,

> Sometimes I ask myself if it's unrealistic to want everything. I think a lot of people would settle for something that is not what they wished, and, to me, that feels worse. It's a Catch 22, because you could wait so long, you never get anything, or you could settle for something and then be cut off from something else.

And men agree, although they are more likely to focus on the constraints of the workplace, as Peter, 27 and white, implies: "I want as even a split as possible. But with my hours, I don't think it could be very even."

AN EMERGING GENDER DIVIDE: AUTONOMY AND NEOTRADITIONALISM AS FALLBACK POSITIONS

The ideal of a balanced self continues to collide with an intransigent social world. New generations must thus develop contingent strategies for less than ideal circumstances. If egalitarian aspirations cannot be reached, what options remain? Here, women and men tend to diverge. Indeed, even as they are developing similar ideals, they are preparing for different outcomes. If an egalitarian commitment proves unworkable, most men would prefer a form of "modified traditionalism" in which they remain the primary if not sole family breadwinner and look to a partner to provide the lion's share of domestic care. Women, in contrast, tend to look toward autonomy as preferable to any form of traditionalism that would leave them and their children economically dependent on someone else.

As young women and men consider the difficulties of building balanced, integrated lives, they move from ideals to consider the fallback positions that would help them avert worst-case scenarios. Here, as we see below, the gender gap widens. Women, in hoping to avoid economic and social dependence, look toward autonomy, while men, in hoping to retain some traditional privileges, look toward modified forms of traditional arrangements. Yet, both groups hope to resolve these conflicts as they construct their lives over time.

Women and Autonomy

Among the women, 9 out of 10 hope to share family and work in a committed, mutually supportive, and egalitarian way. Yet, most are skeptical that they can find a partner or a work situation that will allow them to achieve this ideal. Integrating caretaking with committed work remains an uphill struggle, and it seems risky to count on a partner to sustain a shared vision in the long run. Even a modified version of traditionalism appears fraught with danger, for it creates economic vulnerability and constricted options in the event that a relationship sours or a partner decides to leave. Four out of five women thus prefer autonomy to a traditional marriage, concluding that going it alone is better than being trapped in an unhappy relationship or being abandoned by an unreliable partner. Danisha explains,

Let's say that my marriage doesn't work. I won't ever go into marriage believing that, but just in case, I want to establish myself, because I don't ever want to end up, like, "What am I gonna do?" I want to be able to do what I have to do and still be okay. You can't take a cavalier attitude that things will just work out. Things will work out if you put some effort into making it work out.

Autonomy for women means, at its core, economic self-sufficiency. A life that is firmly rooted in the world of paid work provides the best safeguard against being stuck in a destructive relationship or being left without the means to support a family. Healthy relationships, they reason, are based on a form of economic individualism in which they do not place their economic fate in the hands of another. Rachel declares,

I'm not afraid of being alone, but I am afraid of being with somebody who's a jerk. I can spend the rest of my life alone, and as long as I have my sisters and my friends, I'm okay. I want to get married and have children, but I'm not willing to just do it. It has to be under the right circumstances with the right person.

Men and Neotraditionalism

Young men express more ambivalence about the choice between autonomy and traditionalism. If a committed, egalitarian ideal proves out of reach, about 40 percent would opt for independence, preferring to stress the autonomous self so long associated with manhood and now increasingly affirmed by women as well. But 6 out of 10 men would prefer a modified traditionalism in which two earners need not mean complete equality. This split among men reflects the mix of options they confront. Work remains central to constructing a masculine identity, but it is difficult to find work that offers either economic security or good opportunities for family involvement. Without these supports, men are torn between avoiding family commitments and trying to retain some core advantages provided by traditional arrangements.

From men's perspective, opting for the autonomy conferred by remaining unmarried, unattached, or childless relieves them of the economic burden of earning a family wage in an uncertain economy, but it also risks cutting them off from close, committed, and lasting intimate connections. A neotraditional arrangement, in contrast, offers the chance to create a family built around shared breadwinning but less than equal caretaking. In this scenario, men may envision a dual earner arrangement but still expect their partner to place family first and weave work around it. Josh, a white 27-year-old who was raised by his father after his mother was diagnosed with severe mental illness, asserts,

All things being equal, it should be shared. It may sound sexist, but if somebody's gonna be the breadwinner, it's going to be me. First of all, I make a better salary. If she made a much better salary, then I would stay home, but I always feel the need to work, even if it's in the evenings or something. And I just think the child really needs the mother more than the father at a young age.

Modified traditionalism provides a way for men to cope with economic uncertainties and women's shifting status without surrendering some valued privileges. It collides, however, with women's growing desire for equality and rising need for economic self-sufficiency.

Resolving Moral Dilemmas over Time

In the absence of institutional supports, postponing ultimate decisions becomes a key strategy for resolving the conflicts between commitment and self-development. For women as much as men, the general refrain is, "You can't take care of others if you don't take care of yourself." Michael wants to be certain his girlfriend has created a base for herself at the workplace before they marry, hoping to increase the chances the marriage will succeed and to create a safety net if it fails:

There are a lot of problems when two people are not compatible socially, economically. When Kim gets these goals under her belt, and I have my goals established, it'll be a great marriage. You have to nurture the kind of marriage you want. You have to draw it out before you can go into it.

For Jennifer, 19 and white, autonomy also comes first. Commitment may follow, but only when she knows there is an escape route if the relationship deteriorates:

I will have to have a job and some kind of stability before considering marriage. Too many of my mother's friends went for that—let him provide everything—and they're stuck in a relationship they're not happy with because they can't provide for themselves or the children they now have. The man is not providing for them the way they need, or he's just not a good person. Most of them have husbands who make a lot more money, or they don't even work at all, and they're very unhappy, but they can't leave. So it's either welfare or putting up with somebody else's crap.

Establishing an independent base becomes an essential step on the road to other goals, and autonomy becomes a prerequisite for commitment. This developmental view rejects the idea that individualism and commitment are in conflict by defining the search for independence as a necessary part of the process of becoming able to care for others. To do that, women as well as men tend to look to work, and its promise of autonomy, to complete the self. For those with children as well as those who are childless, lifelong commitments can be established when "you feel good enough about yourself to create a good relationship." Shauna, a 30-year-old African American who was raised by her mother and stepfather, explains,

If you're not happy with yourself, then you can't be happy with someone else. I'm not looking for someone to fill a void. I think that's what a lot of people do when they look for relationships, and that's not what it's about. It's about sharing yourself with the other person, and when you're content and happy with who you are, then you can give more of yourself to someone else, and that's the type of person that I want to be with.

These strategies are deeply felt and intensely private responses to social and personal conflicts that seem intractable. More fundamental solutions await the creation of systematic supports for balancing work and family and for providing women and men with equal opportunities at the workplace and in the home. Without these supports, new generations must cope as best they can, remaining both flexible and guarded. Andrew, a white 27-year-old, has concluded that rigid positions are not helpful in an unpredictable world:

I would like to have an equal relationship, but I don't have a set definition for what that would be like. I would be fine if both of us were working and we were doing the same thing, but it would depend on what she wants, too. If she thought, "Well, at this point in my life, I don't want to work," or if I felt that way, then it would be fine for one person to do more work in some respects. But I would like it to be equal—just from what I was exposed to and what attracts me.

Anita, a 26-year-old Hispanic, agrees:

I don't want to be on my own for the rest of my life, but right now it's fine, so I can figure out who I am. I don't want to look back later and say I totally ignored my needs. I'm realizing that things are so impermanent, and my expectations can only get me so far.

CONCLUSION: TOWARD A NEW MORAL ORDER?

Deeply rooted social and cultural changes have created new moral dilemmas while undermining a traditional gendered division of moral labor. The widespread and interconnected nature of these changes suggests that a fundamental, irreversible realignment is under way. Less clear is whether it will produce a more gender-equal moral order or will, instead, create new forms of inequality. The long-term implications are necessarily cloudy, but this ambiguity has created some new opportunities along with new risks.

While large-scale social forces are propelling change in a general direction, the specific forms it takes will depend on how women and men respond, individually and collectively, to the dilemmas they face. Those who have come of age during this period are adopting a growing diversity of moral orientations that defies dichotomous gender categories. Their experiences point to a growing desire for a social order in which women and men alike are afforded the opportunity to integrate the essential life tasks of achieving autonomy and caring for others.

Yet, persistent inequalities continue to pose dilemmas, especially for those who aspire to integrate home and work in a balanced, egalitarian way. To understand these processes, we need to focus on the social conditions that create such dilemmas and can transform, and potentially dissolve, the link between gender and moral responsibility. Of course, eradicating this link might only mean that women are allowed to adopt the moral strategies once reserved for men. We also need to discover how to enable everyone, regardless of gender, class, or family situation, to balance care of others with care of self.

The possibilities have never been greater for creating humanistic, rather than gendered, conceptions of moral obligation. New moral dilemmas have prompted women and men to develop innovative strategies, but the long-term resolution of these dilemmas depends on reorganizing our social institutions to foster gender equality and a better balance between family and work. Freud once commented that a healthy person is able "to love and to work." Achieving this vision depends on creating a healthy society, where all citizens are able to combine love and work in the ways they deem best.

NOTES

1. My deep thanks go to Sociologists for Women in Society for honoring me with the 1998 Feminist Lectureship and to the sociology departments and Women's Studies Programs at the University of Georgia and the University of North Texas for their generous support and warm hospitality.

2. Of this group, more than 27 percent lived largely with a single parent, including 7 percent whose parents shared joint custody and 5 percent who lived with single, custodial fathers. The rest saw one or both of their parents remarry and form a new, two-parent household.

3. A larger proportion of households were dual-earning, but they varied in the degree of equality between parents' jobs and did not necessarily include both biological parents.

4. Amato and Booth (1997) confirmed this viewpoint. Respondents also argue that both parents should sustain strong ties to their children whether or not they remain together.

5. Cancian (1987) provided an in-depth analysis of innovative attempts among couples to create interdependent relationships, in which both women and men are responsible for love.

REFERENCES

Amato, Paul, and Alan Booth. 1997. *A generation at risk: Growing up in an era of family upheaval.* Cambridge, MA: Harvard University Press.

Cancian, Francesca M. 1987. *Love in America: Gender and self-development.* Cambridge, UK, and New York: Cambridge University Press.

Crittenden, Danielle. 1999. *What our mothers didn't tell us: Why happiness eludes the modern woman.* New York: Simon & Schuster.

Gerson, Kathleen. 1985. *Hard choices: How women decide about work, career, and motherhood.* Berkeley and Los Angeles: University of California Press.

———. 1993. *No man's land: Men's changing commitments to family and work.* New York: Basic Books.

———. 2001. Children of the gender revolution: Some theoretical questions and findings from the field. In *Restructuring work and the life course,* edited by Victor W. Marshall, Walter R. Heinz, Helga Krueger, and Anil Verma. Toronto, Canada: University of Toronto Press.

Kimmel, Michael. 1996. *Manhood in America: A cultural history.* New York: Free Press.

———. 2000. *The gendered society.* New York: Oxford University Press.

Ryan, Mary. 1981. *Cradle of the middle class.* New York and Cambridge, UK: Cambridge University Press.

Welter, Barbara. 1966. The Cult of True Womanhood: 1820–1860. *American Quarterly* 18(2):151–174.

For Better or Worse: Gender Allures in the Vietnamese Global Marriage Market

First published in 2003

Men and women like Minh and Thanh have dreams, but their dreams clash. He wants the best of tradition and she wants the best of modernity. He believes the respect he has been searching for did not arrive with him when he migrated to the United States almost 20 years ago, but instead was left back safely in Vietnam. She feels that the marital respect she needs is waiting for her in the United States and that she will get it when she joins him through marriage migration. Minh, 37, represents one of the more than two million *Viet Kieus*, or Vietnamese people living overseas, who make up an aging diaspora that largely began in the mid-1970s, after the postwar years. He is also one of over a million *Viet Kieus* who returned to visit family and friends during the year 2000, a dramatic increase from the 160,000 who did so in 1993 (Nhat 1999). Thanh, 32, will soon join Minh as one of over 200,000 women *and* men worldwide who come to the United States each year through marriage migration, the number one mechanism for contemporary *legal* migration to the United States. In general, females have dominated in U.S.-bound migration since the 1930s (Houstoun, Kramer, and Barrett 1984) and, historically, women more often than men have migrated as spouses (Thornton 1992). Women currently make up more than 65 percent of all marriage migrants. While male marriage migrants make up about a quarter of all men who enter the United States each year, female marriage migrants make up over 40 percent of all women who enter (USINS 1999a; USINS 1999b).

During 14 months of fieldwork done in phases in Vietnam and in the United States from 1997 to 2001, I got to know couples like Minh and Thanh. In addition to understanding their distinct national and local cul-tures, I paid particular attention to some of their most private matrimonial thoughts—thoughts that they have not yet disclosed to each other. For they are in a migration waiting period, a period in which the women are waiting to be united with their husbands through migration. In this distinct and emergent global marriage market, the immigrant Vietnamese men typically go to Vietnam to marry through arrangement and subsequently return to their places of residence in the Vietnamese diaspora (most are from the United States, Canada, France, and Australia) to initiate paperwork to sponsor their wives. During this waiting period, I came to know them by first entering the lives of the brides in Vietnam and later the U.S.-based grooms.

The marriage of Minh and Thanh characterizes a distinct and growing global stream over the past 40 years of immigrant or immigrant-origin men returning to their home countries for marriage partners through processes of family-forming migration (Lievans 1999), thus significantly transforming gender and race relations in the communities of both origin and destination. Same-ethnic individuals constitute an estimated two-thirds of all marriage migration couples, and among international marriage migrants of U.S. non-citizen permanent residents, who are presumably immigrants, almost 90 percent of them are women (Thornton 1992; USINS 1999a; USINS 1999b). Like many international marriages between same-ethnic individuals, especially in Asia, the marriage of Minh and Thanh was arranged. While there are varying flexible meanings of marriage arrangements and class compositions, I focus on marriages of the two "unmarriageables"—highly educated women in Vietnam and overseas Vietnamese men who do low-wage work.

These couples make up roughly 55 percent (n = 38) of the 69 marriages I studied.

GLOBALIZATION AND MARRIAGE SQUEEZES ACROSS THE VIETNAMESE DIASPORA

Before I began this study, I was fully aware that Vietnamese people worldwide are pressed unusually, if not uniquely, by what demographer Daniel Goodkind (1997) calls the "double marriage squeeze," which has resulted from a high male mortality rate during the Vietnam War and the larger number of men than women who emigrated during the last quarter of the twentieth century. A shortage of one sex or the other in the age group in which marriage generally occurs is often termed a marriage squeeze (Guttentag and Secord 1983). The Vietnamese double marriage squeeze specifically refers to the low ratio of males to females in Vietnam and the unusually high ratio of males to females in the Vietnamese diaspora, especially in Australia and in the United States. For example, by 1999, among people between the ages of 30 to 34 years in Vietnam, statistically speaking, there were approximately 92 men for every 100 women. At the other end of the diaspora in 2000, among Vietnamese Americans between 25 to 29 years, there were 129 men for every 100 women; for the age group of 30 to 34, there were about 135 men for every 100 women. While these numbers are important, they tell only part of the story about the recent dramatic rise in Vietnamese transpacific marriages. The link between demographic numbers, intensified transnational and global processes in Vietnam and worldwide, new contours of kinship, and the intersection of gender and class in marriage markets throughout the Vietnamese diaspora provides a much more in-depth look at social processes involved in the emergence of a Vietnamese transpacific marriage market.

The most striking aspect about marriages of the two unmarriageables like Minh and Thanh is that they have globalized and reversed the marriage gradient, an old and almost universal pattern that women "marry up" and men "marry down," which is to say women marry older men who earn more money and have more education and, conversely, men marry younger women who earn less money and have less education (Fitzgerald 1999). But depending on the measure one uses in the marriages I studied, it is difficult to tell who is "from below." In demographic mar-

riage market language (Guttentag and Secord 1983), women worldwide often find that the pool of marriageable men declines as they move up the educational ladder. Thanh is part of this emerging group of highly educated women in Vietnam who have delayed or avoided marriage with local men. These women have found the pool of marriageable men in Vietnam, who are employed and successful relative to them, to be too small. More importantly, Thanh's status as a highly educated woman made her unmarriageable to many men still influenced by the Asian and Confucian ideologies of hierarchical relations in terms of gender, age, and class. Like highly educated African-American women, women like Thanh in Vietnam are a "surplus" relative to their educated male counterparts. Minh, on the other hand, belongs to a group of surplus men, accumulated in part by the scattering of post-war Vietnamese migration, who are unable to find marriage partners partly because of their current low-wage work status. Some of these men, though certainly not all, experienced tremendous downward mobility as they migrated overseas.

Men like Minh who work in the low-wage labor market made up 80 percent of the men in my study. These men generally work for hourly wages, though some work in ethnic enterprises where salaries are negotiated "under the table." For the most part, they work long hours for low pay. In contrast, women like Thanh represent almost 70 percent of the brides. These women come from college-educated backgrounds, with about 40 percent having advanced degrees and working as doctors, lawyers, computer programmers, and the like. The remaining 60 percent are teachers, service sector workers in foreign companies, etc. To be sure, not all college-educated women in my study married low-wage working men, and not all low-wage working men married college-educated women. Men like Minh and women like Thanh are unmarriageable along both gender and class lines. Statistically, because of the double marriage squeeze, there is simply a surplus of women relative to men in Vietnam and a surplus of *Viet Kieu* men relative to *Viet Kieu* women overseas. But their unmarriageability does not end there. If the demography of the double marriage squeeze is a structural condition propelling these transpacific marriages, the cultural belief in the marriage gradient is perhaps a more powerful force driving these marriages. Vietnamese women and men worldwide have not dared to break the marriage-gradient norm in their local marriage market. They believe, as other unmarriageables do, that by globalizing the gradient, they have somehow solved the potential problem of breaking the marriage-gradient norm. That is, if a man is from a first-world country, he has the "up," while a woman from third-world Vietnam has the "down." And though it is no surprise that the economic divide between the "first-world" and "third-world" would inherently penetrate deeply into the private lives of Vietnamese transpacific couples, it is not always clear *who* has the third-world life in marriages of the two unmarriageables.

Globalization seems like a perfect solution to the dual problem facing the Vietnamese diaspora of "too few women here" and "too few men there," yet there is an untold story about the unanticipated collision of gender ideologies and strategies many of these couples will face.

Couples like Minh and Thanh—the unmarriageables—will bump into a clash of dreams as the women join their husbands overseas. Looking far across the Pacific, both were enamored, not necessarily by the economic, but powerfully by the gender allures of the other side: on one end of the Vietnamese diaspora, for educated women like Thanh, a man living overseas in a modern country will respect women more than men still held back by ancient traditions in Vietnam; on the other end of the diaspora, for low-wage working men like Minh, it is precisely these ancient traditions that he desired and perceived [that] are still maintained by women in Vietnam, the sort of traditions that he believes have been eroded by America's modernity.

Both have turned to the old and new, relying foremost on the tradition of marriage arrangements vis-à-vis family members to introduce them to each other. Yet, it is the new globalizing culture of Vietnam that offered them that opportunity. In 1986, after having no contact with the outside world for over a decade, the Vietnamese government adopted a new economic policy known as *doi moi*. It did not end state ownership, but encouraged private enterprise, free markets, and global engagement. Particularly in the 1990s, Saigon was reemerging as a major international city, first within the Asian landscape and soon to the rest of the world. At the time, Vietnam was in the news and was projected to be one of Asia's next "tigers" (Pierre 2000). Recognizing an enticing labor and consumer market of 80 million people, foreign companies were eager to move their factories there and make their products known. Globalization rapidly opened impersonal markets of capital, goods, and labor, and in conjunction with these markets, it also opened a rather personal market of emotions and marriages. Like global corporations and factories that recently moved to Vietnam because of its large supply of labor, one of the reasons *Viet Kieu* men go there for brides is because they have a much larger selection of marriage partners. However, unlike locals who eagerly work at foreign factories mainly for the monetary rewards, Vietnamese transpacific brides don't always share the same reasons for choosing to marry *Viet Kieu* men.

THE HIGHLY EDUCATED BRIDE'S STORY

Twenty years ago, Thanh's father was a math teacher at Le Buon Phong, a prestigious high school in Saigon. After the war, Thanh's uncle, her mother's younger brother, and his family were among the few thousands of Vietnamese who were airlifted out of Vietnam on April 30, 1975, when Saigon surrendered to North Vietnamese military troops. They eventually settled in Houston, one of the larger Vietnamese enclaves in the United States, and started a successful restaurant business specializing in *pho*, the popular Vietnamese beef noodle soup. Remittances—money sent back—from Thanh's uncle helped her parents open a small candy factory in the late 1980s which now has over 40 employees. Like the "new class of everywhere" in the global economy, her parents are now members of a class that represents a small but very visible percentage of families in Vietnam who enjoy access to overseas resources, such as Thanh's uncle and the remittances he sends home. They are part of a *Viet Kieu economy*, of which remittance plays an important role, that has grown from roughly $35 million in 1993 to an estimated $2 billion in 2000 (Pierre 2000). The remittance upward mobility is of course associated with Thanh's educational and social mobility. It has helped Thanh, her parents' only child, earn not only a good high school education, but also continue to study law and take lessons at international English schools in Saigon.

After graduating from Le Buon Phong High School, Thanh and a small group of her female friends did not choose early marriage, a path that most of their peers took soon after high school. Although Thanh and her friends did want to marry one day, they all wanted to further their schooling. Of her seven close female friends from high school, only one did not go to college. That friend opted for early marriage. The rest, including Thanh, quietly took various professional routes. Most went into fields traditionally reserved for women, including education and nursing. Two went on for higher education. Thanh obtained a law degree, and the other friend went on to become a prestigious physician at Vinh Bien, a private hospital catering to Saigon's middle class. Four of the seven, now in their early 30s, remain single. The pathways of Thanh and her four friends who chose singlehood illustrate a quiet gender revolution among highly educated women in Vietnam. These women have opted for singlehood in a culture where marriage is not only presumed, but often coerced. And if marriage is not achieved by a certain age, women and men are often dismissively referred to as simply "e," a derogatory term referring to commodities that are unmarketable. In contrast, women (often young and beautiful) and men (often educated and financially secure) who fare well on the marriage market are considered "dat," or scarce goods. As Thanh explained to me:

> I am already "e" in Vietnam. You know, at 32 here, it's hard to find a decent husband. I knew that when I decided to get a good education here that many men would be intimidated by me. But it was important to me to get an education, and I know that for women, marriage is more important. In Asian cultures, but maybe in Vietnam especially, the men do not want their wives to be better than them. I think for me it's harder, too, because my parents are successful here so on the outside [to the outsider] we are very successful.

In truth, Thanh is not completely "e" for there have been several men who, sometimes with their families, have come to propose marriage to her. In contemporary Vietnam, arranging marriage remains common practice, though more so in villages than in urban areas. For women in Vietnam, especially those who have passed the social marriageability age, individual and family success often come with being unmarriageable. Thanh had several proposals for marriage arrangements when she was in her mid-20s before she got her law degree, all from men who wanted to marry down socially and economically. Now, at age 32 and highly educated, she believes that marrying up is no longer an option as there are few available men in that category. Marrying down is not an appealing choice either, although she has many suitors in that category. Speaking in the marriage gradient mode, Thanh explains:

> When I look up, there are few men "up there" who I could see as suitable husbands. But those men, the few men I know who have more education and who are more successful than I am, usually want to marry young, beautiful women. To them, I am now too old. The backward thing about life is that the men below are very unappealing. And of course there are many of them! There are many, many non-quality men I could choose from, but that's what they are—non-quality.

Thanh's marriage procrastination was partially anchored in her confused class and gender status, for her educational and remittance upward mobility puts her one up locally, but one down globally. On the one hand, if by tradition, a man is to be above her, he must be the one to provide economically, but given that she married a low-wage worker, she may end up being the one to seek economic security through her own means. On the other hand, by traditional Vietnamese culture, Thanh knows her high educational status would not necessarily help her escape the gender subordination in marital life in Vietnam for few men she knows respect women in the every-day contours of marriage. On our third and final interview, Thanh and I walked along the Saigon River early one evening. As the city's buildings rose arrogantly in the background through the din of countless motorcycles, cycles, and taxis, she explained to me, with a sense of disconsolation:

> In Vietnam, it is hard being single, female, and old. People will criticize and laugh at you. People always ask me, "Where are your husband and children? And when I think about that, I realize that I have two choices. I can marry a man in Vietnam who is much less educated and less successful than me who I will have to support and who will likely abuse me emotionally or physically or dominate me in every possible way. Or I can marry a *Viet Kieu* man. *At least Viet Kieu men live in modern countries where they respect women.*

Ultimately, Thanh's priority, as an educated woman, in the selection of a marriage partner is for someone to respect her and for a marriage in which a man does not control her like most men in Vietnam she observes do. As Thanh explained to me:

> When I find a nice man "below" me who I could marry, he wouldn't want to marry me because he's afraid that I'll take control of the house or that if anything goes wrong in the marriage, I could turn to my family for

help. Most men in Vietnam want to control their wives, they want their wives to be subordinate even when she is more successful and educated. That leaves me with very few choices in Vietnam, you see, because I for sure don't want a man to take control of me.

THE LOW-WAGE WORKING GROOM'S STORY

Through complicated logics of transnationality, Thanh found a suitable spouse across the Pacific. But if Thanh's desire for respect was prompted by her educational and remittance upward mobility, her husband's need for respect was prompted by his migratory downward mobility. Minh, whose hands, facial expressions, and graying hair make him seem older than his 37 years, was the only member of his family to leave Vietnam during "wave II" of the boat refugee exodus that took place after the war (Zhou and Bankston 1998). As the eldest son, he holds a position of distinction and responsibility of six siblings in a family of educators. Both of his parents were teachers of philosophy at Le Buon Phong, where they have known Thanh's parents for many years. Today, three of Minh's sisters are teachers and his two brothers are successful merchants in Saigon.

In 1985, at the age of 21, Minh, then a man of intellectual ambition and curiosity, had just completed his third year of engineering school when his parents asked him if he wanted to go to America. They didn't know anyone overseas at the time, but they knew of several people, among the many hundreds of thousands of refugees, who had fled and safely reached a Western country. Of those who successfully made the trip, over 90 percent eventually settled in France, Australia, Canada, or the United States (Merli 1997). Minh's parents also knew that as many as half of the refugees on any particular boat trip did not succeed. They died along the way due to starvation, pirate attacks, and often, in the case of women and children, rape and murder en route to a refugee camp. Many were also caught by the Vietnamese government and severely punished with long prison sentences. Nevertheless, his parents were confident that he would make it and have a better life abroad. After all, they spent their entire life savings to put him on one of the safest and most reputable boats run by private individuals, to leave the Mekong Delta for Western lands of opportunity via refugee camps in Southeast Asia. Like the

Underground Railroad established for slave escapes during the American civil war, details about these refugee boats were kept secret. But unlike the railroads, the boats were made accessible only to wealthy or well-connected families. Many who were not wealthy, such as Minh's family, managed to pool their resources so that one person could go, usually a son. They saw this as an investment made with a hope of high returns, as in the case of Minh's family.

Today, Minh considers himself one of the lucky ones. After surviving two years—a lifetime to Minh—in a refugee camp in Malaysia, he was selected in 1987 for entry to the United States. Many people he met at the camp ended up in less desirable places, like Finland, Belgium, or Hungary. As with current migration from Vietnam, the United States was then considered the top destination choice, followed by Canada, France, and Australia. Minh arrived in rural Wyoming under the sponsorship of a local Catholic church. Like many of the churches scattered across the United States who sponsored Indochinese refugees from the late 1970s to the mid-1990s (Zhou and Bankston 1998), his church sponsored only one individual. He spent the first five years of his life in America as the only person of color in a rural town in Wyoming, the name of which he doesn't even want to remember. Like many Vietnamese refugees of the past three decades, Minh decided to migrate a second time. He wanted to go to Little Saigon, the most highly concentrated Vietnamese enclave outside of Vietnam, located in a seemingly quiet Los Angeles suburb, though today plagued by urban problems reported regularly by the media (Leonard and Tran 2000a; 2000b; *Los Angeles Times* 1995; Marosi and Tran 2000; Paddock and Dizon 1991; Terry 1999). But he had little money and no connections in or around Los Angeles. Then one day, in one of the Vietnamese-produced newspapers in the United States that flourished following the influx of refugees, Minh read about a Chinese restaurant called the Panda Garden that needed dishwashers. Unfortunately, it was not in Los Angeles but in a small town called Quincy, ninety miles from Seattle. Minh heard that Seattle also had many Vietnamese people and he thought a move there would bring him closer to other refugees.

Eleven years later, at age 37, Minh still lives in Quincy and works at the Panda Garden. He is now a deep fryer and an assistant cook, which is several steps up from the dishwashing position he was first given. Although to him, an assistant cook carries less stigma than a dishwasher, it is far from the engineering career he envisaged in his pre-migration years. Though known as one of the best and most authentic ethnic restaurants in town, the Panda mainly serves a "white American" clientele who, according to the owners, probably wouldn't know the differences between authentic Chinese food and Sara Lee frozen dinners. Quincy is similar to many suburban towns in Middle America—not quite rural, but far from urban. People who live here drive to Seattle to shop and eat if they have money, but stay in town if they want to see a movie. Minh knows five other Vietnamese people in the town, all men, and three of them work with him at the restaurant. He shares a modest three-bedroom apartment with the barest of furnishings with these co-workers.

Similar to many *Viet Kieu* people, Minh is a good example of a giver caught in the irony of a remittance-ship. Receivers of remittances enjoy first-world consumption, while their givers often only enjoy it when they go to Vietnam: on returning to a first-world setting, some givers, like Minh, regress to a third-world consumption pattern. Like Thanh's family, Minh's family enjoys remittances, albeit much smaller ones than Thanh's family enjoys from her uncle. He earns approximately $1,400 a month in Quincy and sends $500 of that back to his family. That amount is much higher than the average of $160 the grooms in my study send to their wives and/or families on a monthly basis. At $900, his remaining budget would be considered way below the poverty level anywhere in the United States. But his family has more than enough constant capital from his remittances to keep connected in the small, though conspicuous, circles of families who have overseas kin networks.

And while Minh's family enjoy their new consumption patterns, Minh finds himself lacking the luxury they afford—most importantly the luxury of having the kind of respect he was used to before migration, particularly the kind of respect he once had in intimate markets. Minh remembered vividly that in his early 20s, he had been considered a good catch among his peers. He was heading for an engineering career and was from a well-respected family. Recounting stories of masculinity from his early adulthood, Minh told me that young men he knew had not one, but several, girlfriends at a time, and that it was accepted and celebrated. After all, life after the war was particularly difficult for many families he knew. But he was relatively fortunate, for his parents were well-respected teachers with a small, but steady, income and, there-fore, could afford to spend small amounts of money on leisure activities and materials that bought them some status in their pre-remittance circles. As he told me in one conversation when we were talking, with beers and cigarettes in our hands, rather loudly in the hot and sizzling kitchen where he worked:

> Life here now is not like life in Vietnam back then. My younger brothers and sisters used to respect me a lot because I was going to college and I was about to get my degree. Many young women I met at the time liked me, too, because I came from a good family and I had status [*dia di*]. But now, because I don't have a good job here, people don't pay attention to me. That's the way my life has been since I came to the United States. And I don't know if I'm lucky or unlucky, but I think it's hard for a [Vietnamese] man to find a wife here if he doesn't make good money. If you have money, everyone will pay attention [to you], but if you don't, you have to live by yourself.

For the most part, that's what Minh has done in the 16 years since he arrived in the United States. In his social world, Minh believes money can, and often does, buy love, and that if you don't have much of it, you live "by yourself." His yearly income puts him just above the poverty level for a single man, but when I did a budget analysis of his expenditures, I discovered that after remittances, his available funds place him well below the poverty level. The long hours that often accompany low-wage work have also made it particularly difficult for him to meet and court marriage partners. If Minh worked long hours for a law firm or a large business corporation, he would not only get financial rewards, but also the status and prestige which men often use as a trade-off in marriage markets. If he were a blue collar white man in Quincy, he could go to church functions, bowling alleys, or bars to meet and court women in the local marriage market. For Minh—a single immigrant man—who does low-wage work in a low-status job with long hours in Middle America, the prospect of marriage has been, and remains, low. Like highly educated women such as Thanh, men like Minh are on the market for more than just intimacy. They are on it for respect, a sense of respect for marital life which they perceive they cannot find in their local marriage market. For men in general, but especially for working-class men, as sociologist Lillian Rubin (1994) argues in a compelling study, a sense of self is deeply connected to the ability to provide economically for the family. For low-wage workers like Minh, the ability to provide, or lack thereof, is sharply linked to earning respect in marital life. As Minh movingly explained to me:

> I don't know if other men told you this, but I think the main reason why a lot of *Viet Kieu* men go back to Vietnam for a wife is because the women here [*Viet Kieu*] do not respect their husbands if the husbands can not make a lot of money. I think that's why there are a lot of *Viet Kieu* women who marry white men, because the white men have better jobs than us. Many *Viet Kieu* women, even though they are not attractive and would not be worth much if there were a lot of them, would not even look at men like me because we can't buy them the fancy house or the nice cars. *I need my wife to respect me as her husband. If your wife doesn't respect you, who will?*

AND SO THEY MEET

Although Minh was headed for upward mobility in 1985 before he migrated to the United States, and would have become an engineer one day if he had remained in Vietnam, he is now an assistant cook and has spent the bulk of his adult working life in the confines of a small Chinese restaurant in Middle America. He hasn't read a book in recent memory. In fact, he didn't have much to share about what he does, except work, or what he owns, except a used Toyota Tercel he recently bought. Meanwhile, Thanh is a relatively successful lawyer in urban Saigon, where Chanel perfume from Paris and American designer Ann Taylor's shirts are essential components of her daily life. Thanh speaks very good English, the language we used when she and I met in Vietnam; Minh and I spoke Vietnamese when I interviewed him in Quincy, Washington. Thanh is currently attending an international adult English school to obtain her English proficiency degree and her current reading list includes Fitzgerald's *The Great Gatsby*. She often prides herself on the fact that she is not as thin as the average woman in Vietnam, nor does she conform to the stereotypical image of Vietnamese women with long, straight black hair. Instead, Thanh has a perm with red highlights and she spends a large part of her leisure time taking aerobics classes at the Saigonese Women's Union, an emerging activity among Saigon's middle class. Pointing to her access to and practice of modernity, she often joked, "Some people in Vietnam think that I'm a *Viet Kieu* woman."

Minh and Thanh, thus, live in noticeably different social worlds. They were united by a network of kin and acquaintanceship that was spatially separated, yet held together by the histories, memories, and connections of the prewar years. This network of kin helped arrange the marriage of the two and started when Minh's siblings expressed concerns that their eldest brother appeared lonely and "needed" a wife, though they never asked him. After all, he was the eldest brother and the only sibling not yet married and still childless. The average age of marriage for his three younger sisters was 21 and for his two brothers, 24. His next brother's eldest child is now attending her first year at Le Buon Phong High School, a sign to Minh that he's getting old. Minh was often embarrassed when asked, "Why didn't you bring your lady friend back to visit us, too?" What his family did not understand on his first few visits back was that long hours of work, as well as the scarcity of Vietnamese women (relative to men) in the United States in general and Quincy in particular, were reasons why the "lady friend generally was too busy to make the trip home *this time*."

If Minh's choice to return to Vietnam to find a wife was propelled by siblings and then followed by his individual discretion, Thanh's entrance into the transpacific marriage market was the complete opposite. Both faced structural and demographic limitations in their local marriage markets, but in different and reversed ways. On the one hand, Minh knew very *few* Vietnamese-American women, and those he knew usually earned the same amount of, or more, money than he did, which made him a *less* attractive marriage candidate in the United States. Research has shown that in the low-wage labor market among Asian Americans, especially in California, women tend to get jobs more easily, work longer hours, and earn more money than men (Espiritu 1999). In contrast, Thanh knew *many* single men in Saigon, but those she knew were far below her in educational status and made much *less* money than she did working as a part-time lawyer and for her father's factory, all of which made her a *less* attractive marriage candidate in Vietnam. By Vietnamese standards—and for some, by any global standard—women like Thanh come from solidly middle-class backgrounds, through acquired or inherited wealth, educational mobility, or remittances. Thanh's education, combined with the income she and her family generate, have been real trade-offs on the transpacific marriage market. As Thanh explained to me:

Any *Viet Kieu* man can come here to find a wife. And he can surely find a beautiful woman if he wants because there are many beautiful young women willing to marry anyone to go overseas. I think there is something different when you talk about *Viet Kieu* men coming back here to marry. They look for a real marriage. And a marriage that will last forever. And so it's important to them to check everything about the woman they will marry and her background. These men [*Viet Kieu* men] want a woman who is educated and who comes from an educated family, because that means she comes from a good family. And if her family has money, he knows she just doesn't want to marry him to go overseas because she already has a comfortable life in Vietnam.

Fearful that they may be seen as sex-workers, local women in Vietnam who want a transpacific spouse rarely allow themselves to be courted by foreign men in public spaces as is the case for women in Taiwan, Thailand, Singapore, Malaysia, Hong Kong, and other Asian countries I've visited and learned about. According to most women and men I talked to in Vietnam, *Viet Kieu* men often come back and visit local bars and dance clubs in search of "one-night stands" either with prostitutes or non-prostitutes, but they would never marry women they meet in those public spaces. If women are fearful of the possibility of being sexually exploited, *Viet Kieu* men are wary of being used as a "bridge" to cross the Pacific (Ong 1999). These reasons, as well as the availability of transnational networks, have propelled women in Vietnam and Vietnamese men who live overseas to rely on the old practice of marriage arrangements by family and kin members, rather than engaging in individual courtship, what we call "free love" practices of choosing a marriage partner. As in the case of arranged marriages among other ethnic groups, marriage candidates in the Vietnamese diaspora believe that family members make the best judgements in their interests when looking for a spouse. Here, Thanh explained the logics of marriage arrangements that may seem illogical to a foreigner:

It's very easy to trick people now. Both men and women can trick each other. Women will pretend to love so they can go abroad and men will pretend to love so they can get a one-night relationship. And so that is why people will choose a family member who could investigate both sides for them. Most of the cases I know are similar to mine. Usually a *Viet Kieu* man says he wants a wife,

and then he will call a family here who will search for him. His family member will try to contact friends, neighbors, whoever he can in search of a suitable wife who happens to also be waiting for an overseas man to court her. There's always a lot of women willing to marry a *Viet Kieu* man, even though she may never have thought about it until someone asks them. If you have a family member to choose for you, as my uncle helped me get to know my husband, you will end up with a real marriage. Otherwise, it can be risky for both people if they meet each other on their own.

The marriage arrangement between Minh and Thanh was initiated by Minh's parents, who have known Thanh's family for over two decades. Even though Thanh's father taught at Le Buon Phong two decades ago, and was a friend and colleague of Minh's parents, the current consumption gap between the two families has created a social distance over the years. When Minh's siblings convinced him to search for a wife in Vietnam, he was hesitant at first, but later followed their advice when his parents promised that they would invest time and care in finding the most suitable spouse. According to Minh, however, they were surprised to discover that arranging a marriage for a *Viet Kieu* was more complicated than they had anticipated:

I thought that it would be easy for them to find someone. I thought all they had to do was mention a few things to their friends, and within days, they could describe a few possible people to me. But my parents told me that they were afraid that women just wanted to use our family to go abroad. We had many people get involved, many people wanted to be matchmakers for the family and added so much anxiety and fear about people's intentions. But the first choice for them was to find a woman from a wealthy family so that they were sure she wasn't just interested in money because if she has money, she would already be comfortable in Vietnam. And it would have been best if she had family in the United States already, because we would know that they already have overseas people who help them out so they would not expect to become dependent on us. In Vietnamese, you know, there is this saying, "When you choose a spouse, you are choosing his/her whole family."

Thanh's family was finally contacted by Minh's parents, a traditional way of arranging marriages in which a groom's parents represent him to propose, often with rituals and a ceremonial language that date back for centuries. Like most brides in my study, Thanh relied on an overseas relative—in this case, Thanh's uncle, Tuan—for advice on Minh's economic and social situation in the United States. The family discovered that Minh was a low-wage worker, but a full-time worker nonetheless. Virtually all of the locals I met in Vietnam viewed overseas men as a two-tiered group: the "successful" who succeeded in owning ethnic enterprises or through obtaining an education, and the "indolent" without full-time jobs who were perceived as being welfare-dependent or as participants in underground economies, such as gambling. Some saw the latter group as men who took up valuable "spots" that others from Vietnam could have filled. "If I had gotten a chance to go," I heard many men say, "I would be so rich by now." Most people, however, did not have an explanation for a man like Minh, who is neither lazy nor extremely successful. Thanh's uncle, Tuan, seemed to know more men in Houston who were not only unemployed, but also alcoholics and gamblers. Her parents were worried that their daughter was unmarriageable as there was certainly no shortage of young and younger women in Vietnam for local men *her* age to marry. In addition, Thanh was already convinced that she was "*e*." All three were concerned that Thanh was facing a life of permanent singlehood for she was getting old by Vietnamese standards. In the back and front of these pre-arrangement thoughts, all three parties—Thanh's uncle, her parents, and herself—saw the option of marrying Minh, a *Viet kieu* man, [as] more desirable than marrying a local man in Vietnam. For Thanh's parents, Minh's status as a full-time worker *and* someone who sent remittances back home to his family translated into a potentially suitable husband. For her uncle, most *Viet Kieu* single men he knew were part of an underclass of which Minh was not a part. For Thanh, Minh's geographical advantage translated into something socially priceless: a man living in a modern country will respect women.

CLASH OF DREAMS

Women like Thanh want a respectful marriage based on principles of gender equality. By these principles, women expect to work for a wage, share in making social and economic decisions for their future households, and have their husbands share in the household

division of labor. Above all, they did *not* want to live in multi-generational households serving as the dutiful daughter-in-law and housewife, the two often inseparable and presumed roles historically delegated to women in Vietnam. Many express that reluctance, for they know numerous *Viet Kieu* men who live with their parents or plan to do so in the future when their parents are old. The women's concern about having to live in multi-generational households is anchored in the fact that in Vietnamese culture, and more generally in Asia, elderly parents prefer to, and often do, live with their sons, usually the eldest one. Much less is known about the fact that it is their daughters-in-law, the wives of their sons, who do the fundamental daily caring work.

For Thanh, living with one's in-laws is the most symbolic act of feminine submission. For Minh, a wife's insistence on a nuclear household represents a desire for an equal marriage—and is one of the gendered anxieties of modernity:

> Vietnamese women, they care for their husbands and they are more traditional. I think non-VN women and *Viet Kieu* women, are too modern. just want to be equal with their husbands and I don't think that it is the way husband and wife should be. [What do you mean?] I mean that husband and wife should not be equal. The wife should listen to husband most of the time. That is how they will have a happy life together. If the woman try to be equal they will have problems. . . . I know many Vietnamese men here who abandon their parents because their wives refuse to live with their parents. If my parents were in America, I would definitely plan for them to live with me when they are old. But because they are in Vietnam, they are living with one of my brothers.

Instead of seeking peasant village women or uneducated ones like white Europeans and Americans who search for wives through commercialized systems of mail-order brides, men like Minh seek marriage arrangement with educated women as part of a careful gender strategy for a perceived future marital stability. Minh outlines his strategy:

> For me, I want to marry an educated woman because she comes from a good, educated family. It's very hard to find a poor woman or an uneducated woman who comes from an uneducated family, because if they are uneducated [the family] they don't know how to teach

their daughters about morals and values. I know many men, *Viet Kieu* and foreign men, who go to Vietnam to marry beautiful young women, but they don't ask why do those women marry them? Those women only want to use their beauty to go overseas and they will leave their husbands when they get the chance. They can use their beauty to find other men. I would never marry a beautiful girl from a poor, uneducated family. You see, the educated women, they know it's important marry and stay married forever. As they say in Vietnam, "tram nam han phuc," [a hundred years of happiness]. Educated women must protect their family's reputation in Vietnam by having a happy marriage, not end in divorce.

UNIMAGINABLE FUTURES

At first glance, Minh and Thanh seem as if they are from different social worlds, two worlds accidentally assembled by a complex Vietnamese history. But once closely acquainted with them, we learn that they are very much alike. First is the class of their past—both sets of their parents were educated and middle class. Second, they are both lonely human faces of globalization who lack the emotional and intimate details that adults of their social worlds enjoy. Most importantly, it seems, because of the gendered meanings embedded in their opposite trails of class mobility, they both long for marital respect, the kind of respect they perceive is scarce in their local marriage market. From Minh's side of the gender scene, he experienced downward mobility quickly and immensely as a result of migration and is eager to get back the respect he has lost. Thanh, a woman who has, in part, priced herself out of the local marriage market by acquiring a higher education, paid for by a remittance upward mobility, wants a man who respects her as an equal and as a woman who embraces modernity. He wants to regain what he sees as something men like him have lost, while she has, in part, challenged the local marriage norm and, in effect, the "control-norm" in the gender world of Vietnam.

The global forces and global histories that have mobilized their marriage—and their clashed dreams—

will assuredly usher in marital conflicts. These conflicts will lead to several possibilities as women quietly migrate to join their husbands overseas. In a happy global story, Minh will join in the feminist revolution and leave behind the tradition he never had as he moves forward with his new marriage. I believe some, but few, men will join women in this revolution. In a tragic global story, these couples may end in divorce or worse, women like Thanh will be abused by their husbands. Many women like Thanh have thought about this possibility and have told me that their connection to transnational networks will ensure that they avoid abusive marriages. The most likely possibility for married couples like Minh and Thanh is that men will get what they want in the market of respect and women will consent to subordination in the name of family and kinship. Thanh will enjoy some aspects of modernity she cannot acquire in Vietnam, but she will be burdened by tradition she doesn't expect to see in the United States. For she will be going from a patriarchal frying pan to a patriarchal fire, but with one big difference. In the United States she has more support for her desire for gender equity where more women dare to quit a marriage if they don't get it. But she has the powerful burden of tradition in Vietnam to hold her back from choosing this option.

In Vietnam, marriage is an important matter not only because it unites two people, but also because it has significant implications for extended networks of kin (Tran 1991). In a culture where divorce is stigmatized and where saving face is a sacred activity especially among the educated and middle class, if Thanh daringly divorces her husband, she will cause her family and kin a loss of reputation in Vietnam and overseas, a risk she told me she is unlikely to take. If she stays in the marriage, she will give up her need for the respect and equality she thinks are waiting for her in the United States. And she will likely serve as the traditional wife Minh needs in order for him to gain back the respect he left back in Vietnam almost 20 years ago. Simply put, Vietnamese politics of kinship promise that couples like Minh and Thanh will remain married—for better or worse.

ACKNOWLEDGMENTS

This is a revised version of another paper previously published under the title "Clashing Dreams: Highly-Educated Vietnamese Brides and Their Low-Wage Overseas Husbands," in *Global Woman* (New York: Metropolitan Books, 2003), edited by Arlie Russell Hochschild and Barbara Ehrenreich. Versions of this paper were also presented at the 2002 annual meetings of American Sociological Association in Chicago, and at the 2003 annual meetings of the West and the Pacific Regional Association for Asian American Studies in Pomona, California. I would like to very much thank Arlie Russell Hochschild, Barbara Ehrenreich, Verta Taylor, and Leila Rupp for comments on previous drafts. Thanks to Ingrid Banks for conversations and feedback. And to Barrie Thorne for guidance at every step of the way.

REFERENCES

Espiritu, Yen Le. 1999. "Gender and Labor in Asian Immigrant Families." *American Behavioral Scientist* 42: 628–647.

Fitzgerald, Tina Katherine. 1999. *Who Marries Whom? Attitudes in Marital Partner Selection.* Ph.D. Dissertation: University of Colorado.

Goodkind, Daniel. 1997. "The Vietnamese Double Marriage Squeeze." *The Center for Migration Studies of New York* 31: 108–128.

Guttentag, Marcia, and Paul F. Secord. 1983. *Too Many Women? The Sex Ratio Question.* Beverly Hills: Sage Publications.

Houstoun, Marion F., Roger G. Kramer, and Joan Mackin Barrett. 1984. "Female Predominance in Immigration to the United States since 1930s: A First Look." *International Migration Review* 18: 908–963.

Leonard, Jack, and Mai Tran. 2000a. "Agents Target Little Saigon Crime Groups." *Los Angeles Times*, October 7, p. A1.

Leonard, Jack, and Mai Tran. 2000b. "Probes Take Aim at Organized Crime in Little Saigon; Crackdown: Numerous Agencies Target Gambling, Drug Sales, Counterfeit Labels and Credit Card Scams." *Los Angeles Times*, October 7, p. B7.

Lievans, John. 1999. "Family Forming Migration from Turkey and Morocco to Belgium." *International Migration Review* 33: 717–744.

Los Angeles Times. 1995. "Cooler Days in Little Saigon." *Los Angeles Times*, August 8, p. B8.

Marosi, Richard, and Mai Tran. 2000. "Little Saigon Raids Dismantle Crime Ring, Authorities Say; Probe: Asian Syndicate Supplied Most Illegal Gambling Machines in Orange County, Police Say. Fifteen Are Arrested." *Los Angeles Times*, September 29, p. B3

Merli, Giovanna M. 1997. "Estimation of International Migration for Vietnam, 1979–1989." Unpublished paper, Department of Sociology and Center for Studies in Demography and Ecology. Seattle: University of Washington.

Nhat, Hong. 1999. "Hankering for '*Viet Kieu*' Money." *Vietnam Economic News* 9, no. 50 (December), p. 12.

Ong, Aihwa. 1999. *Flexible Citizenship: The Cultural Logics of Transnationality.* Durham, N.C.: Duke University Press.

Paddock, Richard C., and Lily Dizon. 1991. "3 Vietnamese Brothers in Shoot-out Led Troubled Lives." *Los Angeles Times*, p. A3.

Pierre, Andrew J. 2000. "Vietnam's Contradictions." *Foreign Affairs* 79.

Rubin, Lillian. 1994. *Families on the Fault Line: America's Working Class Speaks About the Family, the Economy, Race and Ethnicity.* New York: HarperCollins.

Terry, Don. 1999. "Passions of Vietnam War Are Revived in Little Saigon; Shop's Ho Chi Minh Poster Sets off Violence." *New York Times*, February 11, p. A20.

Thornton, Michael C. 1992. "The Quiet Immigration: Foreign Spouses of U.S. Citizens, 1945–1985." Pp. 64–76 in *Racially Mixed People in America*, edited by Maria P. Root. Newbury Park, CA: Sage Publications.

Tran, Dinh Huou. 1991. "Traditional Families in Vietnam and the Influence of Confucianism." Pp. 27–53 in *Sociological Studies on the Vietnamese Family*, edited by Rita Lijestrom and Tuong Lai. Hanoi: Social Sciences Publishing House.

USINS. 1999a. "International Matchmaking Organizations: A Report to Congress by the Immigration & Naturalization Service." *A Report to Congress.*

USINS. 1999b. *Statistical Yearbook of the Immigration and Naturalization Service, 1997.* Washington, D.C.: U.S. Government Printing Office.

Zhou, Min, and Carl L. Bankston. 1998. *Growing Up American: How Vietnamese Children Adapt to Life in the United States.* New York: Russell Sage Foundation.

SECTION 7

Sexualities

The processes of socialization encourage women and men to develop different views of and approaches to sexuality and intimate relationships. Women learn strong interpersonal and emotional skills in preparation for roles as wives and mothers and for employment in professions associated with care work, such as teaching and nursing. At the same time, women's and men's different positions in social institutions mean that we enter our intimate and sexual relationships with different amounts and kinds of resources, power, networks, and expectations. In addition, we are surrounded by a culture that portrays women and men as having intrinsically different sexual needs, desires, and obligations. And as we have already seen, such differences between women and men are shaped as well by class, race, ethnicity, sexuality, nationality, ability, and age. The readings in this section discuss how even such a seemingly personal matter as sexuality is *socially constructed* in various ways in different contexts.

We begin with Deborah Tolman's "Doing Desire: Adolescent Girls' Struggles for/with Sexuality," an examination of how adolescent girls understand their sexuality. Adolescents have been the subject of considerable recent public debate over sexuality, with many politicians suggesting that teenage sexual activity should be discouraged. Yet adolescence is the life stage during which we begin to develop our sexual selves and form a sense of our intimate connections to others. Tolman examines how diverse adolescent girls construct desire, tracing the complex mix of pleasure and desire with danger and fear, highlighting

differences of sexual identity. As a result of the cultural repression of women's sexuality, Tolman argues, adolescent girls are "denied full access to the power of their own desire." How do the girls Tolman discusses come to understand their sexual selves in this context? What are the "possibilities of empowerment"? Do you see your own experiences or the experiences of female friends reflected in Tolman's findings?

In the next selection, "Shopping for love," Sophia deMasi considers the reasons why online dating has become so common and acceptable in U.S. society. While more and more people are turning to the Internet to meet potential partners, deMasi argues that online dating shuts down alternatives to a traditional heterosexual dating and marriage scenario, and so in that sense is not as alternative as it might seem. Why does she think online dating has become so popular? Do you know people who use the Internet to find sexual or romantic partners? What do you see as the advantages and disadvantages of online dating?

As college students across the country do not need to be told, "hooking up" has largely replaced dating, at least for those who are not in a committed relationship. As the authors of "Is Hooking Up Bad for Young Women?" point out, there is a great deal of disagreement among both scholars and popular culture commentators about the relative merits of hooking up. Elizabeth Armstrong, Laura Hamilton, and Paula England, on the basis of both interviews and a large-scale quantitative study of the hookup, dating, and relationship experiences of college students on campuses across the country, argue that both hooking up and relationships have their advantages and disadvantages for women. They debunk some of the myths about hooking up: that college students have much more sex than earlier generations, that hooking up has replaced relationships, and that the way college students interact sexually is entirely new. They also compare the positive and negative aspects of both hookups and relationships, concluding that the fundamental problem is the continuing sexual double standard.

What are the benefits and drawbacks of hooking up versus forming a relationship that they identify? Do you agree with their analysis? Why or why not? Do you agree that the double standard remains alive and well in young people's worlds? What could be done to improve sexual and intimate relationships on campus?

Zooming in on another aspect of campus life (and beyond), "Straight Girls Kissing" takes a look at the widespread practice at parties and bars of presumably heterosexual women kissing and making out with each other. Rupp and Taylor argue that more is going on here than grabbing the attention of men, which is what most commentators assume. The hookup culture, although determinedly heterosexual, provides a space for some young women to experiment with or act on same-sex desire. The concept of "heteroflexibility" allows them options, while the same freedoms are not accorded to women who identify as or are deemed lesbian.

Why do you think the practice of girls kissing girls has become so prominent in the party scene? Why is it considered sexy to witness women kissing, but not two men doing the same thing? Do you think sexual identities are becoming more fluid on campus?

In the final article in this section, "Doing Gender, Doing Heteronormativity," Kristen Schilt and Laurel Westbrook explore the different ways that nontransgender (known as "cisgender") women and men respond to transgender people in both public settings and intimate encounters. On the basis of two different studies, one of transitions in the workplace and the other on media reports on violence against transgender people, they detail the gender differences in the ways people respond, as well as differences between interactions in the workplace and in sexual encounters. Men tend to welcome transmen (females who transition to male) into masculine circles at work, while cisgender women are more nervous, since the transition opens up the possibility of intimate heterosexual relationships. Media reports make clear that, in intimate relations, men are more likely to react violently to transwomen (males who transition to female).

How do Schilt and Westbrook explain the gender differences in responses to transgender people? What do such reactions tell us about gender, sexuality, and the relation between them? What do these reactions, in conjunction with the phenomenon of "straight girls kissing," tell us about the institution of heterosexuality in U.S. society?

Like family life, sexuality and intimate relationships are both a source of support and strength for women and a location of inequality. What do these readings suggest about how diverse women find sexuality to be a means of fulfillment and an expression of self-definition? In contrast, how do the readings show sexuality to be a means of social control? How is sexuality shaped differently for people in different social groups?

Doing Desire: Adolescent Girls' Struggles for/with Sexuality

First published in 1994

In order to perpetuate itself, every oppression must corrupt or distort those various sources of power within the culture of the oppressed that can provide energy for change. For women, this has meant suppression of the erotic as a considered source of power and information within our lives. (Lorde 1984, 53)

Recent research suggests that adolescence is the crucial moment in the development of psychological disempowerment for many women (e.g., Brown and Gilligan 1992; Gilligan 1990). As they enter adolescence, many girls may lose an ability to speak about what they know, see, feel, and experience evident in childhood as they come under cultural pressure to be "nice girls" and ultimately "good women" in adolescence. When their bodies take on women's contours, girls begin to be seen as sexual, and sexuality becomes an aspect of adolescent girls' lives; yet "nice" girls and "good" women are not supposed to be sexual outside of heterosexual, monogamous marriage (Tolman 1991). Many girls experience a "crisis of connection," a relational dilemma of how to be oneself and stay in relationships with others who may not want to know the truth of girls' experiences (Gilligan 1989). In studies of adolescent girls' development, many girls have demonstrated the ironic tendency to silence their own thoughts and feelings for the sake of relationships, when what they think and feel threatens to be disruptive (Brown and Gilligan 1992). At adolescence, the energy needed for resistance to crushing conventions of femininity often begins to get siphoned off for the purpose of maintaining cultural standards that stand between women and their empowerment. Focusing

explicitly on embodied desire, Tolman and Debold (1993) observed similar patterns in the process of girls learning to look at, rather than experience, themselves, to know themselves from the perspective of men, thereby losing touch with their own bodily feelings and desires. It is at this moment in their development that many women will start to experience and develop ways of responding to their own sexual feelings. Given these realities, what are adolescent girls' experiences of sexual desire? How do girls enter their sexual lives and learn to negotiate or respond to their sexuality?

Despite the real gains that feminism and the sexual revolution achieved in securing women's reproductive rights and increasing women's sexual liberation (Rubin 1990), the tactics of silencing and denigrating women's sexual desire are deeply entrenched in this patriarchal society (Brown 1991). The Madonna/whore dichotomy is alternately virulent and subtle in the cultures of adolescents (Lees 1986; Tolman 1992). Sex education curricula name male adolescent sexual desire; girls are taught to recognize and to keep a lid on the sexual desire of boys but not taught to acknowledge or even to recognize their own sexual feelings (Fine 1988; Tolman 1991). The few feminist empirical studies of girls' sexuality suggest that sexual desire is a complicated, important experience for adolescent girls about which little is known. In an ethnographic study, Fine noticed that adolescent girls' sexuality was acknowledged by adults in school, but in terms that denied the sexual subjectivity of girls; this "missing discourse of desire" was, however, not always absent from the ways girls themselves spoke about their sexual experiences (Fine 1988). Rather than being "educated," girls' bodies are suppressed under surveillance and silenced in the schools (see also Lesko 1988). Although Fine ably conveys the existence of girls' discourse of desire, she does not articulate that discourse. Thompson collected 400 girls' narratives about sexuality, romance, contraception, and pregnancy (Thompson 1984, 1990) in which girls' desire seems frequently absent or not relevant to the terms of their sexual relationships. The minority of girls who spoke of sexual pleasure voiced more sexual agency than girls whose experiences were devoid of pleasure. Within the context of girls' psychological development, Fine's and Thompson's work underscores the need to understand what girls' experiences of their sexual desire are like.

A psychological analysis of this experience for girls can contribute an understanding of both the possibilities and limits for sexual freedom for women in the current social climate. By identifying how the culture has become anchored in the interior of women's lives—an interior that is birthed through living in the exterior of material conditions and relationships—this approach can keep distinct women's psychological responses to sexual oppression and also the sources of that oppression. This distinction is necessary for avoiding the trap of blaming women for the ways our minds and bodies have become constrained.

METHODOLOGICAL DISCUSSION

Sample and Data Collection

To examine this subject, I interviewed thirty girls who were juniors in an urban and a suburban public high school ($n = 28$) or members of a gay and lesbian youth group ($n = 2$). They were 16.5 years old on average and randomly selected. The girls in the larger study are a heterogeneous group, representing different races and ethnic backgrounds (Black, including Haitian and African American; Latina, including Puerto Rican and Colombian; Euro-American, including Eastern and Western European), religions (Catholic, Jewish, and Protestant), and sexual experiences. With the exception of one Puerto Rican girl, all of the girls from the suburban school were Euro-American; the racial/ethnic diversity in the sample is represented by the urban school. Interviews with school personnel confirmed that the student population of the urban school was almost exclusively poor or working class and the students in the suburban school were middle and upper-middle class. This information is important in that my focus is on how girls' social environments shape their

understanding of their sexuality. The fact that girls who live in the urban area experience the visibility of and discourse about violence, danger and the consequences of unprotected sex, and that the suburban girls live in a community that offers a veneer of safety and stability, informs their experiences of sexuality. Awareness of these features of the social contexts in which these girls are developing is essential for listening to and understanding their narratives about sexual experiences.

The data were collected in one-on-one, semistructured clinical interviews (Brown and Gilligan 1992). This method of interviewing consists of following a structured interview protocol that does not direct specific probes but elicits narratives. The interviewer listens carefully to a girl, taking in her voice, and responding with questions that will enable the girl to clarify her story and know she is being heard. In these interviews, I asked girls direct questions about desire to elicit descriptions and narratives. Most of the young women wove their concerns about danger into the narratives they told.

Analytic Strategy

To analyze these narratives, I used the Listening Guide—an interpretive methodology that joins hermeneutics and feminist standpoint epistemology (Brown et al. 1991). It is a voice-centered, relational method by which a researcher becomes a listener, taking in the voice of a girl, developing an interpretation of her experience. Through multiple readings of the same text, this method makes audible the "polyphonic and complex" nature of voice and experience (Brown and Gilligan 1992, 15). Both speaker and listener are recognized as individuals who bring thoughts and feelings to the text, acknowledging the necessary subjectivity of both participants. Self-consciously embedded in a standpoint acknowledging that patriarchal culture silences and obscures women's experiences, the method is explicitly psychological and feminist in providing the listener with an organized way to respond to the coded or indirect language of girls and women, especially regarding topics such as sexuality that girls and women are not supposed to speak of. This method leaves a trail of evidence for the listener's interpretation, and thus leaves room for other interpretations by other listeners consistent with the epistemological stance that there is multiple meaning in such stories. I present a way to understand the stories these young women chose to tell me, our story as I have heard and understood it. Therefore, in the interpretations that follow I include my responses, those of an adult woman, to these girls' words, providing information about girls' experiences of sexual desire much like counter-transference informs psychotherapy.

Adolescent Girls' Experiences of Sexual Desire

The first layer of the complexity of girls' experiences of their sexual desire was revealed initially in determining whether or not they felt sexual feelings. A majority of these girls (two-thirds) said unequivocally that they experienced sexual desire; in them I heard a clear and powerful way of speaking about the experience of feeling desire that was explicitly relational and also embodied. Only three of the girls said they did not experience sexual feelings, describing silent bodies and an absence of or intense confusion about romantic or sexual relationships. The remaining girls evidenced confusion or spoke in confusing ways about their own sexual feelings. Such confusion can be understood as a psychic solution to sexual feelings that arise in a culture that denigrates, suppresses, and heightens the dangers of girls' sexuality and in which contradictory messages about women's sexuality abound.

For the girls who said they experienced sexual desire, I turned my attention to how they said they responded to their sexual feelings. What characterized their responses was a sense of struggle; the question of "doing desire"—that is, what to do when they felt sexual desire—was not straightforward for any of them. While speaking of the power of their embodied feelings, the girls in this sample described the difficulties that their sexual feelings posed, being aware of both the potential for pleasure and the threat of danger that their desire holds for them. The struggle took different shapes for different girls, with some notable patterns emerging. Among the urban girls, the focus was on how to stay safe from bodily harm, in and out of the context of relational or social consequences, whereas among the suburban girls the most pronounced issue was how to maintain a sense of themselves as "good" and "normal" girls (Tolman 1992). In this article, I will offer portraits of three girls. By focusing on three girls in depth, I can balance an approach to "variance" with the kind of case study presentation that enables me to illustrate both similarities and differences in how girls in the larger sample spoke about their sexual

feelings. These three girls represent different sexual preferences—one heterosexual, one bisexual, and one lesbian.[1] I have chosen to forefront the difference of sexual preference because it has been for some women a source of empowerment and a route to community; it has also been a source of divisiveness among feminists. Through this approach, I can illustrate *both* the similarities and differences in their experiences of sexual desire, which are nested in their individual experiences as well as their social contexts. Although there are many other demarcations that differentiate these girls—social class, race, religion, sexual experience—and this is not the most pervasive difference in this sample,[2] sexual preference calls attention to the kinds of relationships in which girls are experiencing or exploring their sexual desire and which take meaning from gender arrangements and from both the presence and absence of institutionalization (Fine 1988; Friend 1993). Because any woman whose sexuality is not directly circumscribed by heterosexual, monogamous marriage is rendered deviant in our society, all adolescent girls bear suspicion regarding their sexuality, which sexual preference highlights. In addition, questions of identity are heightened at adolescence.

Rochelle Doing Desire   Rochelle is a tall, larger, African-American girl who is heterosexual. Her small, sweet voice and shy smile are a startling contrast to her large body, clothed in white spandex the day of our interview. She lives in an urban area where violence is embedded in the fabric of everyday life. She speaks about her sexual experience with a detailed knowledge of how her sexuality is shaped, silenced, denigrated, and possible in relationships with young men. As a sophomore, she thought she "had to get a boyfriend" and became "eager" for a sexual relationship. As she describes her first experience of sexual intercourse, she describes a traditional framing of male–female relationships:

> I felt as though I had to conform to everything he said that, you know, things that a girl and a guy were supposed to do, so like, when the sex came, like, I did it without thinking, like, I wish I would have waited . . . we started kissing and all that stuff and it just happened. And when I got, went home, I was like, I was shocked, I was like, why did I do that? I wish I wouldn't a did it.
> *Did you want to do it?*
> Not really. Not really. I just did it because, maybe because he wanted it, and I was always like tryin' to

please him and like, he was real mean, mean to me, now that I think about it. I was like kind of stupid, cause like I did everything for him and he just treated me like I was nothing and I just thought I had just to stay with him because I needed a boyfriend so bad to make my life complete but like now it's different.

Rochelle's own sexual desire is absent in her story of defloration—in fact, she seems to be missing altogether. In a virtual caricature of dominant cultural conventions of femininity, Rochelle connects her disappearance at the moment of sex—"it just happened"—to her attempts to fulfill the cultural guidelines for how to "make [her] life complete." She has sex because "he wanted it," a response that holds no place for whether or not she feels desire. In reflecting on this arrangement, Rochelle now feels she was "stupid . . . to do everything for him" and in her current relationship, things are "different." As she explains: "I don't take as much as I did with the first guy, cause like, if he's doin' stuff that I don't like, I tell him, I'll go, I don't like this and I think you shouldn't do it and we compromise, you know. I don't think I can just let him treat me bad and stuff."

During the interview, I begin to notice that desire is not a main plot line in Rochelle's stories about her sexual experiences, especially in her intimate relationships. When I ask her about her experiences of sexual pleasure and sexual desire, she voices contradictions. On one hand, as the interview unfolds, she is more and more clear that she does not enjoy sex: "I don't like sex" quickly becomes "I hate sex . . . I don't really have pleasure." On the other hand, she explains that

> there are certain times when I really really really enjoy it, but then, that's like, not a majority of the times, it's only sometimes, once in a while . . . if I was to have sex once a month, then I would enjoy it . . . if I like go a long period of time without havin' it then, it's really good to me, cause it's like, I haven't had something for a long time and I miss it. It's like, say I don't eat cake a lot, but say, like every two months, I had some cake, then it would be real good to me, so that's like the same thing.

Rochelle conveys a careful knowledge of her body's hunger, her need for tension as an aspect of her sexual pleasure, but her voiced dislike of sex suggests that she does not feel she has much say over when and how she engages in sexual activity.

In describing her experiences with sexuality, I am overwhelmed at how frequently Rochelle says that she "was scared." She is keenly aware of the many consequences that feeling and responding to her sexual desire could have. She is scared of being talked about and getting an undeserved reputation: "I was always scared that if I did that (had sexual intercourse) I would be portrayed as, you know, something bad." Even having sex within the confines of a relationship, which has been described by some girls as a safe haven for their sexuality (Rubin 1990; Tolman 1992), makes her vulnerable; she "could've had a bad reputation, but luckily he wasn't like that"; he did not choose to tell other boys (who then tell girls) about their sexual activity. Thinking she had a sexually transmitted disease was scary. Because she had been faithful to her boyfriend, having such a disease would mean having to know that her boyfriend cheated on her and would also make her vulnerable to false accusations of promiscuity from him. Her concern about the kind of woman she may be taken for is embedded in her fear of using contraception: "When you get birth control pills, people automatically think you're having sex every night and that's not true." Being thought of as sexually insatiable or out of control is a fear that many girls voice (Tolman 1992); this may be intensified for African-American girls, who are creating a sexual identity in a dominant cultural context that stereotypes Black women as alternately asexual and hypersexual (Spillers 1984).

Rochelle's history provides other sources of fear. After her boyfriend "flattened [her] face," when she realized she no longer wanted to be with him and broke off the relationship, she learned that her own desire may lead to male violence. Rochelle confided to me that she has had an abortion, suffering such intense sadness, guilt, and anxiety in the wake of it that, were she to become pregnant again, she would have the baby. For Rochelle, the risk of getting pregnant puts her education at risk, because she will have to sacrifice going to college. This goal is tied to security for her; she wants to "have something of my own before I get a husband, you know, so if he ever tries leavin' me, I have my own money." Given this wall of fears, I am not surprised when Rochelle describes a time when simply feeling desire made her "so scared that I started to cry." Feeling her constant and pervasive fear, I began to find it hard to imagine how she can feel any other feelings, including sexual ones.

I was thus caught off guard when I asked Rochelle directly if she has felt desire and she told me that she does experience sexual desire; however, she explained "most of the time, I'm by myself when I do." She launched, in breathless tones, into a story about an experience of her own sexual desire just the previous night:

> Last night, I had this crank call…. At first I thought it was my boyfriend, cause he likes to play around, you know. But I was sitting there talking, you know, and thinking of him and then I found out it's not him, it was so crazy weird, so I hang the phone up and he called back, he called back and called back. And then I couldn't sleep, I just had this feeling that, I wanted to have sex so so bad. It was like three o'clock in the morning. And I didn't sleep the rest of the night. And like, I called my boyfriend and I was tellin' him, and he was like, what do you want me to do, Rochelle, I'm sleeping! [Laughs.] I was like, okay, okay, well I'll talk to you later, bye. And then, like, I don't know, I just wanted to, and like, I kept tossin' and turnin'. And I'm trying to think who it was, who was callin' me, cause like, it's always the same guy who always crank calls me, he says he knows me. It's kinda scary. . . . I can't sleep, I'm like, I just think about it, like, oh I wanna have sex so bad, you know, it's like a fever, drugs, something like that. Like last night, I don't know, I think if I woulda had the car and stuff, I probably woulda left the house. And went over to his house, you know. But I couldn't, cause I was baby-sitting.

When I told her that it sounds a little frightening but it sounds like there's something exciting about it, she smiled and leaned forward, exclaiming, "Yeah! It's like sorta arousing." I was struck by the intensity of her sexual feelings and also by the fact that she is alone and essentially assured of remaining alone due to the late hour and her responsibilities. By being alone, not subject to observation or physical, social, emotional, or material vulnerability, Rochelle experienced the turbulent feelings that are awakened by this call in her body. Rochelle's desire has not been obliterated by her fear; desire and fear both reverberate through her psyche. But she is not completely alone in this experience of desire, for her feelings occur in response to another person, whom she at first suspects is her boyfriend speaking from a safe distance, conveying the relational contours of her sexual desire. Her wish to bring her desire into her relationship, voiced in her response of calling her boyfriend, is in conflict with her fear of what might happen if she did pursue her wish—

getting pregnant and having a baby, a consequence that Rochelle is desperate to avoid.

I am struck by her awareness of both the pleasure and danger in this experience and how she works the contradiction without dissociating from her own strong feelings. There is a brilliance and also a sadness in the logic her body and psyche have played out in the face of her experiences with sexuality and relationships. The psychological solution to the dilemma that desire means for her, of feeling sexual desire only when she cannot respond as she says she would like to, arises from her focus on these conflicts as personal experiences, which she suffers and solves privately. By identifying and solving the dilemma in this way, Rochelle is diminished, as is the possibility of her developing a critique of these conflicts as not just personal problems but as social inequities that emerge in her personal relationships and on her body. Without this perspective, Rochelle is less likely to become empowered through her own desire to identify that the ways in which she must curtail herself and be curtailed by others are socially constructed, suspect, and in need of change.

Megan Doing Desire Megan, a small, freckled, perky Euro-American, is dressed in baggy sweats, comfortable, unassuming, and counterpointed by her lively engagement in our interview.[3] She identifies herself as "being bisexual" and belongs to a gay youth group; she lives in a city in which wealth and housing projects coexist. Megan speaks of knowing she is feeling sexual desire for boys because she has "kind of just this feeling, you know? Just this feeling inside my body." She explains: "My vagina starts to kinda like act up and it kinda like quivers and stuff, and like I'll get like tingles and and, you can just feel your hormones (laughing) doing something weird, and you just, you get happy and you just get, you know, restimulated kind of and it's just, and Oh! Oh!" and "Your nerves feel good." Megan speaks about her sexual desire in two distinct ways, one for boys and one for girls. In our interview, she speaks most frequently about her sexual feelings in relation to boys. The power of her own desire and her doubt about her ability to control herself frighten her: "It scares me when I'm involved in a sexual situation and I just wanna go further and further and cause it just, and it scares me that, well, I have control, but if I even just let myself not have control, you know? … I'd have sex and I can't do that." Megan knows that girls who lose control over their desire like that can be called "sluts" and ostracized.

When asked to speak about an experience of sexual desire, Megan chooses to describe the safety of a heterosexual, monogamous relationship. She tells me how she feels when a boyfriend was "feeling me up"; not only is she aware of and articulate about his bodily reactions and her own, she narrates the relational synergy between her own desire and his:

I just wanted to go on, you know? Like I could feel his penis, you know, 'cause we'd kinda lied down you know, and, you just really get so into it and intense and, you just wanna, well you just kinda keep wanting to go on or something, but it just feels good. . . . His penis being on my leg made, you know, it hit a nerve or something, it did something because it just made me start to get more horny or whatever, you know, it just made me want to do more things and stuff. I don't know how, I can't, it's hard for me to describe exactly how I felt, you know like, (intake of breath) . . . when he gets more excited then he starts to do more things and you can kind of feel his pleasure and then you start to get more excited.

With this young man, Megan knows her feelings of sexual desire to be "intense," to have a momentum of their own, and to be pleasurable. Using the concrete information of his erection, she describes the relational contours of her own embodied sexual desire, a desire that she is clear is her own and located in her body but that also arises in response to his excitement.

Although able to speak clearly in describing a specific experience she has had with her desire, I hear confusion seep into her voice when she notices that her feelings contradict or challenge societal messages about girls and sexuality:

It's so confusing, 'cause you have to like say no, you have to be the one to say no, but why should you be the one to, cause I mean maybe you're enjoying it and you shouldn't have to say no or anything. But if you don't, maybe the guy'll just keep going and going, and you can't do that, because then you would be a slut. There's so [much] like, you know, stuff that you have to deal with and I don't know, just I keep losing my thought.

Although she knows the logic offered by society—that she must "say no" to keep him from "going and going," which will make her "a slut"—Megan identifies what is missing from that logic, that "maybe you're"—she, the girl—"the one who is enjoying it."

The fact that she may be experiencing sexual desire makes the scripted response—to silence his body—dizzying. Because she does feel her own desire and can identify the potential of her own pleasure, Megan asks the next logical question, the question that can lead to outrage, critique, and empowerment: "Why should you have to be the one to [say no]?" But Megan also gives voice to why sustaining the question is difficult; she knows that if she does not conform, if she does not "say no"—both to him and to herself—then she may be called a slut, which could lead to denigration and isolation. Megan is caught in the contradiction between the reality of her sexual feelings in her body and the absence of her sexual feelings in the cultural script for adolescent girls' sexuality. Her confusion is an understandable response to this untenable and unfair choice: a connection with herself, her body, and sexual pleasure or a connection with the social world.

Megan is an avid reader of the dominant culture. Not only has she observed the ways that messages about girls' sexuality leave out or condemn her embodied feelings for boys, she is also keenly aware of the pervasiveness of cultural norms and images that demand heterosexuality:

Every teen magazine you look at is like, guy this, how to get a date, guys, guys, guys, guys, guys. So you're constantly faced with I have to have a boyfriend, I have to have a boyfriend, you know, even if you don't have a boyfriend, just [have] a fling, you know, you just want to kiss a guy or something. I've had that mentality for so long.

In this description of compulsory heterosexuality (Rich 1983), Megan captures the pressure she feels to have a boyfriend and how she experiences the insistence of this demand, which is ironically in conflict with the mandate to say no when with a boy. She is aware of how her psyche has been shaped into a "mentality" requiring any sexual or relational interests to be heterosexual, which does not corroborate how she feels. Compulsory heterosexuality comes between Megan and her feelings, making her vulnerable to a dissociation of her "feelings" under this pressure.

Although she calls herself bisexual, Megan does not describe her sexual feelings for girls very much in this interview. In fact, she becomes so confused that at one point she says she is not sure if her feelings for girls are sexual:

I mean, I'll see a girl I really really like, you know, because I think she's so beautiful, and I might, I don't know. I'm so confused. . . . But there's, you know, that same mentality as me liking a guy if he's really cute, I'm like, oh my God, you know, he's so cute. If I see a woman that I like, a girl, it's just like wow, she's so pretty, you know. See I can picture like hugging a girl; I just can't picture the sex, or anything, so, there's something being blocked.

Megan links her confusion with her awareness of the absence of images of lesbian sexuality in the spoken or imagistic lexicon of the culture, counterpointing the pervasiveness of heterosexual imagery all around her. Megan suggests that another reason that she might feel "confused" about her feelings for girls is a lack of sexual experience. Megan knows she is feeling sexual desire when she can identify feelings in her own body—when her "vagina acts up"—and these feelings occur for her in the context of a sexual relationship, when she can feel the other person's desire. Because she has never been in a situation with a girl that would allow this embodied sexual response, she posits a connection between her lack of sexual experience with girls and her confusion.

Yet she has been in a situation where she was "close to" a girl and narrates how she does not let her body speak:

There was this one girl that I had kinda liked from school, and it was like really weird 'cause she's really popular and everything. And we were sitting next to each other during the movie and, kind of her leg was on my leg and I was like, wow, you know, and that was, I think that's like the first time that I've ever felt like sexual pleasure for a girl. But it's so impossible, I think I just like block it out, I mean, it could never happen. . . . I just can't know what I'm feeling. . . . I probably first mentally just say no, don't feel it, you know, maybe. But I never start to feel, I don't know. It's so confusing. 'Cause finally it's all right for me to like a girl, you know? Before it was like, you know, the two times that I really, that it was just really obvious that I liked them a lot, I had to keep saying no no no no no, you know, I just would not let myself. I just hated myself for it, and this year now that I'm talking about it, now I can start to think about it.

Megan both narrates and interprets her dissociation from her embodied sexual feelings and describes the disciplinary stance of her mind over her body in how she "mentally" silences her body by saying "no," preempting her embodied response. Without her body's feelings, her embodied knowledge, Megan feels confused. If she runs interference with her own sexual feelings by silencing her body, making it impossible for her to feel her desire for girls, then she can avoid the problems she knows will inevitably arise if she feels sexual feelings she "can't know"—compulsory heterosexuality and homophobia combine to render this knowledge problematic for her. Fearing rejection, Megan keeps herself from feelings that could lead to disappointment, embarrassment, or frustration, leaving her safe in some ways, yet also psychologically vulnerable.

Echoing dominant cultural constructions of sexual desire, Megan links her desire for girls with feelings of fear: "I've had crushes on some girls . . . you can picture yourself kissing a guy but then if you like a girl a lot and then you picture yourself kissing her, it's just like, I can't, you know, oh my God, no (laughs), you know it's like scary . . . it's society . . . you never would think of, you know, it's natural to kiss a girl." Megan's fear about her desire for girls is different from the fears associated with her desire for boys; whereas being too sexual with boys brings the stigma of being called a "slut," Megan fears "society" and being thought of as "unnatural" when it comes to her feelings for girls. Given what she knows about the heterosexual culture in which she is immersed—the pressure she feels to be interested in "guys" and also given what she knows about homophobia—there is an inherent logic in Megan's confused response to her feelings for girls.

Melissa Doing Desire   Melissa, dressed in a flowing gypsy skirt, white skin pale against the lively colors she wears, is clear about her sexual desire for girls, referring to herself as "lesbian"; she is also a member of a gay/lesbian youth group. In speaking of her desire, Melissa names not only powerful feelings of "being excited" and "wanting," but also more contained feelings; she has "like little crushes on like millions of people and I mean, it's enough for me." Living in a world defined as heterosexual, Melissa finds that "little crushes" have to suffice, given a lack of opportunity for sexual exploration or relationship: "I don't know very many people my age that are even bisexual or lesbians . . . so I pretty much stick to that, like, being hugely infatuated with straight people. Which can get a little touchy at times . . . realistically, I can't like get too ambitious, because that would just not be realistic."

At the forefront of how Melissa describes her desire is her awareness that her sexual feelings make her vulnerable to harm. Whereas the heterosexual girls in this study link their vulnerability to the outcomes of responding to their desire—pregnancy, disease, or getting a bad reputation—Melissa is aware that even the existence of her sexual desire for girls can lead to anger or violence if others know of it: "Well I'm really lucky that like nothing bad has happened or no one's gotten mad at me so far, that, by telling people about them, hasn't gotten me into more trouble than it has, I mean, little things but not like, anything really awful. I think about that and I think it, sometimes, I mean, it could be more dangerous." In response to this threat of violence, Melissa attempts to restrain her own desire: "Whenever I start, I feel like I can't help looking at someone for more than a few seconds, and I keep, and I feel like I have to make myself not stare at them or something." Another strategy is to express her desire covertly by being physically affectionate with other girls, a behavior that is common and acceptable; by keeping her sexuality secret, she can "hang all over [girls] and stuff and they wouldn't even think that I meant anything by it." I am not surprised that Melissa associates feeling sexual desire with frustration; she explains that she "find(s) it safer to just think about the person than what I wanna do, because if I think about that too much and I can't do it, then that'll just frustrate me," leading her to try to intervene in her feelings by "just think[ing] about the person" rather than about the more sexual things she "want(s) to do." In this way, Melissa may jeopardize her ability to know her sexual desire and, in focusing on containing what society has named improper feelings, minimize or exorcise her empowerment to expose that construction as problematic and unjust.

My questions about girls' sexual desire connect deeply with Melissa's own questions about herself; she is in her first intimate relationship, and this interview proves an opportunity to explore and clarify painful twinges of doubt that she had begun to have about it. This relationship began on the initiative of the other girl, with whom she had been very close, rather than out of any sexual feelings on Melissa's part. In fact, Melissa was surprised when her friend had expressed a sexual interest, because she had not "been thinking that" about this close friend. After a history of having to hold back her sexual desire, of feeling

"frustrated" and being "hugely infatuated with straight people," rather than having the chance to explore her sexuality, Melissa's response to this potential relationship was that she "should take advantage of this situation." As the interview progresses, Melissa begins to question whether she is sexually attracted to this girl or "it's just sort of like I just wanted something like this for so long that I'm just taking advantage of the situation."

When I ask Melissa questions about the role of her body in her experience of sexual desire, her confusion at first intensifies:

Is that [your body] part of what feels like it might be missing?
   (eight-second pause) It's not, well, sometimes, I mean I don't know how, what I feel all the time. It's hard like, because I mean I'm so confused about this. And it's hard like when it's actually happening to be like, OK, now how do I feel right now? How do I feel right now? How am I gonna feel about this? . . . I don't know, 'cause I don't know what to expect, and I haven't been with anyone else so I don't know what's supposed to happen. So, I mean I'm pretty confused.

The way she speaks about monitoring her body suggests that she is searching for bodily feelings, making me wonder what, if anything, she felt. I discern what she does not say directly: that her body was silent in these sexual experiences. Her hunger for a relationship is palpable: "I really wanted someone really badly, I think, I was getting really sick of being by myself. . . . I would be like God, I really need someone." The desperation in her voice, and the sexual frustration she describes, suggest that her "want" and "need" are distinctly sexual as well as relational.

One reason that Melissa seems to be confused is that she felt a strong desire to be "mothered," her own mother having died last year. In trying to distinguish her different desires in this interview, Melissa began to distinguish erotic feelings from another kind of wanting she also experienced: she said that "it's more of like but I kind of feel like it's really more of like a maternal thing, that I really want her to take care of me and I just wanna touch someone and I just really like the feeling of just how I mean I like, when I'm with her and touching her and stuff. A lot, but it's not necessarily a sexual thing at this point." In contrast to her feelings for her girlfriend, Melissa describes feeling sexually attracted to another girl. In so doing, Melissa clarifies what is missing in these first sexual adventures, enabling her to know what had bothered her about her relationship with her girlfriend:

> I don't really think I'm getting that much pleasure, from her, it's just, I mean it's almost like I'm getting experience, and I'm sort of having fun, it's not even that exciting, and that's why I think I don't really like her . . . because my friend asked me this the other day, well, I mean does it get, I mean when you're with her does it get really, I don't remember the word she used, but just really, like what was the word she used? But I guess she meant just like, exciting [laughing]. But it doesn't, to me. It's weird, because I can't really say that, I mean I can't think of like a time when I was really excited and it was like really, sexual pleasure, for me, because I don't think it's really like that. I mean not that I think that this isn't good because, I don't know, I mean, I like it, but I mean I think I have to, sort of realize that I'm not that much attracted to her, personally.

Wanting both a relationship and sexual pleasure, a chance to explore closeness and her sexual curiosity, and discovering that this relationship leaves out her sexual desire, Melissa laments her silent body: "I sort of expect or hope or whatever that there would be some kind of more excited feeling just from feeling sexually stimulated or whatever. I would hope that there would be more of a feeling than I've gotten so far." Knowing consciously what she "knows" about the absence of her sexual feelings in this relationship has left her with a relational conflict of large proportions for her: "I'm not that attracted to her and I don't know if I should tell her that. Or if I should just kind of pretend I am and try to . . . anyway." I ask her how she would go about doing that—pretending that she is. She replies, "I don't think I could pretend it for too long." Not being able to "pretend" to have feelings that she knows she wants as part of an intimate relationship, Melissa faces a dilemma of desire that may leave her feeling isolated and lonely or even fraudulent.

ADOLESCENT GIRLS' SEXUAL DESIRE AND THE POSSIBILITIES OF EMPOWERMENT

All of the girls in this study who said they felt sexual desire expressed conflict when describing their responses to their sexual feelings—conflict between their embodied sexual feelings and their perceptions of how those feelings are, in one way or another, anathema or problematic within the social and relational contexts of their lives. Their experiences of sexual desire are strong and pleasurable, yet they speak very often not of the power of desire but of how their desire may get them into trouble. These girls are beginning to voice the internalized oppression of their women's bodies; they knew and spoke about, in explicit or more indirect ways, the pressure they felt to silence their desire, to dissociate from those bodies in which they inescapably live. Larger societal forces of social control in the form of compulsory heterosexuality (Rich 1983), the policing of girls' bodies through school codes (Lesko 1988), and media images play a clear part in forcing this silence and dissociation. Specific relational dynamics, such as concern about a reputation that can easily be besmirched by other girls and by boys, fear of male violence in intimate relationships, and fear of violent repercussion of violating norms of heterosexuality are also audible in these girls' voices.

To be able to know their sexual feelings, to listen when their bodies speak about themselves and about their relationships, might enable these and other girls to identify and know more clearly the sources of oppression that press on their full personhood and their capacity for knowledge, joy, and connection. Living in the margins of a heterosexual society, the bisexual and lesbian girls voice an awareness of these forces as formative of the experiences of their bodies and relationships; the heterosexual girls are less clear and less critical about the ways that dominant constructions of their sexuality impinge on their embodied and relational worlds. Even when they are aware that societal ambivalence and fears are being played out on their minds and bodies, they do not speak of a need for collective action, or even the possibility of engaging in such activities. More often, they speak of the danger of speaking about desire at all. By dousing desire with fear and confusion, or simple, "uncomplicated" denial, silence, and dissociation, the girls in this study make individual psychological moves whereby they distance or disconnect themselves from discomfort and danger. Although disciplining their bodies and curbing their desire are a very logical and understandable way to stay physically, socially, and emotionally safe, they also heighten the chance that girls and women may lose track of the fact that an inequitable social system, and not a necessary situation, renders women's sexual desire a source of danger rather than one of pleasure and power in their lives. In "not knowing" desire, girls and women are at risk for not knowing that there is nothing wrong with having sexual feelings and responding to them in ways that bring joy and agency.

Virtually every girl in the larger study told me that no woman had ever talked to her about sexual desire and pleasure "like this"—in depth, listening to her speak about her own experiences, responding when she asked questions about how to masturbate, how to have cunnilingus, what sex is like after marriage. In the words of Rubin: "The ethos of privacy and silence about our personal sexual experience makes it easy to rationalize the refusal to speak [to adolescents]" (1990, 83; Segal 1993). Thompson (1990) found that daughters of women who had talked with them about pleasure and desire told narratives about first intercourse that were informed by pleasure and agency. The recurrent strategy the girls in my study describe of keeping their desire under wraps as a way to protect themselves also keeps girls out of authentic relationships with other girls and women. It is within these relationships that the empowerment of women can develop and be nurtured through shared experiences of both oppression and power, in which collectively articulated critiques are carved out and voiced. Such knowledge of how a patriarchal society systematically keeps girls and women from their own desire can instigate demand and agency for social change. By not talking about sexual desire with each other or with women, a source for empowerment is lost. There is a symbiotic interplay between desire and empowerment: to be empowered to desire one needs a critical perspective, and that critical perspective will be extended and sustained through knowing and experiencing the possibilities of desire and healthy embodied living. Each of these girls illustrates the phenomenon observed in the larger study—the difficulty for girls in having or sustaining a critical perspective on the culture's silencing of their sexual desire. They are denied full access to the power of their own desire and to structural supports for that access.

Common threads of fear and joy, pleasure and danger, weave through the narratives about sexual desire in this study, exemplified by the three portraits. Girls have the right to be informed that gaining pleasure and a strong sense of self and power through their bodies does not make them bad or unworthy. The experiences of these and other adolescent girls illustrate why girls deserve to be educated about their sexual desire. Thompson concludes that "to take pos-

session of sexuality in the wake of the anti-erotic sexist socialization that remains the majority experience, most teenage girls need an erotic education" (1990, 406). Girls need to be educated about the duality of their sexuality, to have safe contexts in which they can explore both danger and desire (Fine 1988), and to consider why their desire is so dangerous and how they can become active participants in their own redemption. Girls can be empowered to know and act on their own desire, a different educational direction than the simplistic strategies for avoiding boys' desire that they are offered. The "just say no" curriculum obscures the larger social inequities being played out on girls' bodies in heterosexual relationships and is not relevant for girls who feel sexual feelings for girls. Even adults who are willing or able to acknowledge that girls experience sexual feelings worry that knowing about their own sexual desire will place girls in danger (Segal 1993). But keeping girls in the dark about their power to choose based on their own feelings fails to keep them any safer from these dangers. Girls who trust their minds and bodies may experience a stronger sense of self, entitlement, and empowerment that could enhance their ability to make safe decisions. One approach to educating girls is for women to speak to them about the vicissitudes of sexual desire—which means that women must let themselves speak and know their own sexual feelings, as well as the pleasures and dangers associated with women's sexuality and the solutions that we have wrought to the dilemma of desire: how to balance the realities of pleasure and danger in women's sexuality.

Asking these girls to speak about sexual desire, and listening and responding to their answers and also to their questions, proved to be an effective way to interrupt the standard "dire consequences" discourse adults usually employ when speaking at all to girls about their sexuality. Knowing and speaking about the ways in which their sexuality continues to be unfairly constrained may interrupt the appearance of social equity that many adolescent girls (especially white, middle-class young women) naively and trustingly believe, thus leading them to reject feminism as unnecessary and mean-spirited and not relevant to their lives. As we know from the consciousness-raising activities that characterized the initial years of second-wave feminism, listening to the words of other girls and women can make it possible for girls to know and voice their experiences, their justified confusion and fears, their curiosities. Through such relationships, we help ourselves and each other to live in our different female bodies with an awareness of danger, but also with a desire to feel the power of the erotic, to fine-tune our bodies and our psyches to what Audre Lorde has called the "yes within ourselves" (Lorde 1984, 54).

NOTES

1. The bisexual girl and the lesbian girl were members of a gay/lesbian youth group and identify themselves using these categories. As is typical for members of privileged groups for whom membership is a given, the girls who feel sexual desire for boys and not for girls (about which they were asked explicitly) do not use the term "heterosexual" to describe themselves. Although I am aware of the debate surrounding the use of these categories and labels to delimit women's (and men's) experience, because my interpretive practice is informed by the ways society makes meaning of girls' sexuality, the categories that float in the culture as ways of describing the girls are relevant to my analysis. In addition, the bisexual and lesbian girls in this study are deeply aware of compulsory heterosexuality and its impact on their lives.

2. Of the thirty girls in this sample, twenty-seven speak of a desire for boys and not for girls. This pattern was ascertained by who appeared in their desire narratives and also by their response to direct questions about sexual feelings for girls, designed explicitly to interrupt the hegemony of heterosexuality. Two of the thirty girls described sexual desire for both boys and girls and one girl described sexual desire for girls and not for boys.

3. Parts of this analysis appear in Tolman (1994).

REFERENCES

Brown, L. 1991. Telling a girl's life: Self authorization as a form of resistance. In *Women, Girls and Psychotherapy: Reframing Resistance*, ed. C. Gilligan, A. Rogers, and D. Tolman. New York: Haworth.

Brown, L., E. Debold, M. Tappan, and C. Gilligan. 1991. Reading narratives of conflict for self and moral voice: A relational method. In *Handbook of Moral Behavior and Development: Theory, Research, and Application*, ed. W. Kurtines and J. Gewirtz. Hillsdale, NJ: Lawrence Erlbaum.

Brown, L., and C. Gilligan. 1992. *Meeting at the Crossroads: Women's Psychology and Girls' Development*. Cambridge, MA: Harvard University Press.

Fine, Michelle. 1988. Sexuality, schooling and adolescent females: The missing discourse of desire. *Harvard Educational Review* 58:29–53.

Friend, Richard. 1993. Choices, not closets. In *Beyond Silenced Voices*, ed. M. Fine and L. Weis. New York: State University of New York Press.

Gilligan, Carol. 1989. Teaching Shakespeare's sister. In *Making Connections: The Relational World of Adolescent Girls at Emma Willard School*, ed. C. Gilligan, N. Lyons, and T. Hamner. Cambridge, MA: Harvard University Press.

———. 1990. Joining the resistance: Psychology, politics, girls and women. *Michigan Quarterly Review* 29:501–36.

Lees, Susan. 1986. *Losing Out: Sexuality and Adolescent Girls*. London: Hutchinson.

Lesko, Nancy. 1988. The curriculum of the body: Lessons from a Catholic high school. In *Becoming Feminine: The Politics of Popular Culture*, ed. L. Roman. Philadelphia: Falmer.

Lorde, Audre. 1984. The uses of the erotic as power. In *Sister Outsider: Essays and Speeches*. Freedom, CA: Crossing Press.

Rich, Adrienne. 1983. Compulsory heterosexuality and lesbian existence. In *Powers of Desire: The Politics of Sexuality*, ed. A. Snitow, C. Stansell, and S. Thompson. New York: Monthly Review Press.

Rubin, Lillian. 1990. *Erotic Wars: What Happened to the Sexual Revolution?* New York: HarperCollins.

Segal, Lynne. 1993. Introduction. In *Sex Exposed: Sexuality and the Pornography Debate*, ed. L. Segal and M. McIntosh. New Brunswick, NJ: Rutgers University Press.

Spillers, Hortense. 1984. Interstices: A small drama of words. In *Pleasure and Danger: Exploring Female Sexuality*, ed. C. Vance. Boston: Routledge and Kegan Paul.

Thompson, Sharon. 1984. Search for tomorrow: On feminism and the reconstruction of teen romance. In *Pleasure and Danger: Exploring Female Sexuality*, ed. C. Vance. Boston: Routledge and Kegan Paul.

———. 1990. Putting a big thing in a little hole: Teenage girls' accounts of sexual initiation. *Journal of Sex Research* 27:341–61.

Tolman, Deborah L. 1991. Adolescent girls, women and sexuality: Discerning dilemmas of desire. *Women, Girls, and Psychotherapy: Reframing Resistance*, ed. C. Gilligan, A. Rogers, and D. Tolman. New York: Haworth.

———. 1992. Voicing the body: A psychological study of adolescent girls' sexual desire. Unpublished dissertation, Harvard University.

———. 1994. Daring to desire: Culture and the bodies of adolescent girls. In *Sexual Cultures: Adolescents, Communities and the Construction of Identity*, ed. J. Irvine. Philadelphia: Temple University Press.

Tolman, Deborah, and Elizabeth Debold. 1993. Conflicts of body and image: Female adolescents, desire, and the no-body. In *Feminist Treatment and Therapy of Eating Disorders*, ed. M. Katzman, P. Failon, and S. Wooley. New York: Guilford.

Shopping for Love: Online Dating and the Making of a Cyber Culture of Romance[1]

First published in 2006

Ten years ago, a reader of any mainstream national publication or local weekly could not have helped but notice the ubiquitous personal advertisements that saturated their back pages. Today, these same personal advertisements have migrated to the virtual pages of the World Wide Web. A casual glance at the content of online personal advertisements suggests that their writers solicit readers for a variety of reasons, including friendship, a long-term relationship, and casual sex; however, dating dominates the virtual landscape. The vast majority of online personal ads are written by people who want to date as a prelude to a satisfying long-term relationship (Brym and Lenton 2001). With an estimated 2,500 dating websites in operation entertaining approximately 40 million visitors each month (Sullivan 2002), internet dating is now a popular and vital part of the process by which people seek and find intimate partners.

Until recently, the use of personal advertisements to locate intimate partners was understood as a deviant activity resorted to only by "losers" left out of the marriage market, or "perverts" seeking illicit sexual encounters. In addition, the stigma attached to users of personal ads made many reluctant to reveal the activity to others (Darden and Koski 1988; Rajecki and Rasmussen 1992). Those days are gone. Now it is quite common for people to publicly reveal their experiences with online dating. It is not at all unusual to hear coworkers, friends, and acquaintances shamelessly boast about a successful date or to confess to a dating fiasco that began with an online personal advertisement. In offices, classrooms, and living rooms across the country, online daters boldly relate the latest update to their online profile and how many "hits" it got.

Another sign of the astonishing popularity of online dating is its visibility in popular culture. Currently available are over thirty self-help books that instruct users of dating websites in the finer points of creating an effective online profile. Book titles like *E Dating Secrets: How to Surf for your Perfect Love Match on the Internet, Everything you Need to Know about Romance and the Internet, 50+ and Looking for Love Online,* and *Worldwide Search: The Savvy Christian's Guide to Online Dating* indicate that online dating now has mass appeal across sexual orientation, race, age and religious groups. The popular press has also put internet dating in the spotlight by publishing the revelations of ordinary people who found their companions through online personals (Foston 2003; Wilkinson 2005). Self-help books and the public testimony of online daters help put to rest the belief that online dating is something resorted to only by desperate people.

The tremendous expansion of online personals, along with the public pronouncements of the people who use them, suggests that technologically mediated dating is now a socially acceptable method for finding intimate partners. Stigma and shame are no longer associated with people who seek to connect with others through personal advertisements. How has the formerly "deviant" activity of using print personal ads to seek and find partners given way to the apparently routine practice of seeking and finding companions through online personal advertisements? Moreover, what consequences might this change in medium have on the process of finding romantic and/or sexual partners?

Recent technological innovations and demographic changes are part of the reason why online dating has become such a common practice in the first decade of the twenty-first century. More significant, however, are the deliberate marketing strategies used to increase the appeal of online dating. Together, these factors work to expand possibilities for finding partners and establishing intimate relationships. But, paradoxically, online dating also limits the possibilities for creating relationships, particularly those that exist outside the narrow confines of relationship ideals historically identified with heterosexual intimacy. To attract a larger number of participants, dating websites rely primarily on a particular construction of intimate relationships that emphasizes love, romance, and monogamy; they rarely mention sex for pleasure and the desire for physical intimacy. Moreover, embedded in the structure of online dating websites are existing gender and sexual identity categories that preclude explorations of novel identity constructions. Consequently, online dating ensures homogeneity in the types of relationships that are sought and found online.

"ANYONE CAN DO IT": THE NORMALIZATION OF INTERNET DATING

It is impossible to understand how online dating has become mainstream without mentioning the rise of internet technology. Access to the internet rose steadily throughout the 1990s. In 1995, only 9 percent of adults in the United States were online. This figure increased to 56 percent by 1999 and to 67 percent by 2003 (Harris Poll 2003). Along with increased access to the internet, its ease of use has increased as low-cost, high-speed connections have become available to more people. Also significant is the demographics of internet users. Initially, the use of internet technology was limited to the young, affluent, and highly educated. Though these groups are still slightly more likely than older, poorer, and less educated groups to use internet technology, a . . . Harris Poll (2003) reveals that the internet population is beginning to look more like the general US population in terms of education, income, and age. As internet use expands to include more people, it provides the mass audience needed for internet dating.

When internet technology was first made available to the general public in the mid-1990s, it was enthusiastically hailed as an innovation that would funda-

mentally alter the way individuals accomplish the routine tasks of life. Today, the internet is used to do practically everything from reading the newspaper, paying bills, buying a home, searching for a job, taking educational courses, and purchasing consumer items. Finding a partner through the internet represents just one more of the many activities that the technology enables.

In addition to technological innovation, demographic changes have contributed to the growth of internet dating. According to social historian Barbara Dafoe Whitehead (2003), in the last three decades there has been a tremendous increase in the pool of people seeking mates. Thirty years ago, the dating pool was limited to young people who had never married. Today, it includes never-married men and women across a much wider age range, because both men and women marry at much later ages. In addition, the high divorce rate has created a large number of people who are looking for second and even third relation-ships. As well, older people who are living longer are also seeking companionship. Finally, the rise in the legitimacy of gay and lesbian relationships has propelled these individuals into the open market for relationships. Gays and lesbians are now able to seek partners through more conventional channels than they did thirty years ago, when they suffered greater public condemnation of their relationships. A large audience of actual and potential online daters has been created by these cultural changes.

While technological and demographic changes are part of the explanation for the rise of internet dating, they are not sufficient to explain why it has become such an enormously popular and commonplace activity. Equally significant is the purposeful effort by marketeers to construct online dating as a legitimate way for ordinary people to meet partners. In order to increase revenues through paid customer subscriptions, marketeers of online dating sites have deployed strategies to increase their mass appeal (Sullivan 2002). One approach has been to promote online dating websites as places where romantic relationships are easily acquired by all participants, a strategy evident in print advertisements and on network and cable television.

Typically, advertisements for online dating services promise quickly to transform unhappy, lonely, single people into blissful, content couples, if they just take the initiative to join and post a personal profile. For example, the advertising copy of a recent television ad campaign by Match.com, an online dating site that claims to have the largest number of personal profiles, asks potential members: "Will you ever find the person who will change your life?" This rhetorical question is, of course, followed by an emphatic "Yes!" By using the free guide from Match.com entitled "How to find the right person in 90 days," the ad implies that finding a partner online is so easy that *anyone* can do it. Advertisements such as these present online dating as an efficient and utterly conventional activity. Moreover, they help convince the public that internet dating is a viable way to meet a partner.

The legitimacy and appeal of online dating is further enhanced by the prominent suggestion that it is fundamentally about realizing the relationship goals of romance, love, and monogamous coupling. Regardless of whether online dating services are intended for heterosexual, gay, or lesbian users, they are typically constructed as places where conventionally established ideals of intimacy can be attained. For example, a visitor to the home page of EHarmony, a popular website for heterosexuals, is told that it is the website to use "when you are ready to find the love of your life." Similarly, Match.com proclaims itself to be "the world's number 1 place for love." Almost identical declarations are made on dating websites intended exclusively for lesbians and gays. Visitors to Planet Out will immediately notice the advertising copy that reads: "Find your Mr. or Ms. Right now!" Just underneath the bold headline is a link to the personal ads that reads: "Find Love." Although the home page of Gay-FriendFinder, an online dating site for gay men, carefully alludes to the possibility of a purely sexual relationship, it too makes love and romance a central part of its purpose. Its banner exclaims: "Find sexy single men for dating, romance, and *more*" [italics mine]. For additional emphasis, the headlines plastered across the home pages of heterosexual and gay and lesbian dating websites are routinely accompanied by visual graphics that conspicuously display stereotypical images of love and romance. Pictures that accompany print banners typically show two people holding hands, locked in a warm embrace, or gazing into each other's eyes over a candlelit dinner.

The inclusion of gays and lesbians within the rubric of love, romance, and monogamy is ironic precisely because gays and lesbians have historically been seen as incapable of achieving the relationship ideals typically linked to heterosexuality. Indeed, the idea that gays and lesbians are so far outside the

boundaries of intimate convention that they cannot sustain intimate relationships based on love and monogamous commitment is an argument made by gay marriage opponents today. Of course, gay and lesbian patterns of intimacy do not . . . preclude love, romance, and monogamy, but these options are not always the fundamental criteria around which lesbians and gays construct their relationships. A variety of historically unique types of intimate relationship characterize gay and lesbian subcultures: serial monogamy among lesbians, gay male subcultures based on sex, lesbian "Boston marriages" where physical intimacy is apparently absent, and butch-femme relationships that play on a heightened awareness of gender. Dating websites ignore these complex relationships in favor of assimilating gay and lesbian intimacy into a framework modeled on heterosexual standards of intimacy.

Indeed, most dating websites follow a similarly generic formula that includes the relentless depiction of words and images associated with heterosexual romance and a calculated muting of the sexual possibilities that might inspire or follow online encounters. Certainly, many online services exist primarily to link people who desire to meet others only for sexual activity, but websites whose business is limited to dating intentionally desexualize their content. The specific rules many dating sites have for creating profiles illustrate this point. For instance, Match.com expressly prohibits "overt solicitation for sex or descriptions of sexual activity, anatomy, etc." Similarly, YahooPersonals .com warns prospective ad writers not to "post detailed descriptions of physical characteristics or the types of sexual activities that interest you [*sic* them]" and forbids any video greetings that contain nudity or sexual language. Many dating sites also preempt the potential for any relationship that might develop outside the boundaries of monogamous coupling by forbidding the "solicitation of multiple or additional partners." In addition, some online dating sites seek to ensure that subscribers who deviate from the normative standards of heterosexual coupling are excluded from participation. People who are married, partnered, incarcerated, or under age 18 are generally not permitted to post profiles.

Also significant is the absence of questions about sex on the lengthy questionnaires that prospective members of dating websites must fill out before they make their profiles available to other members. Most dating websites require the completion of a comprehensive questionnaire that covers minute details regarding the social, recreational, and relational interests of the applicant and those attributes sought in a partner. The questionnaires typically include inquiries about the kinds of sports activities members enjoy, the type of pets they have or would like to have (or not), the foods they eat, their sense of humor, their political views, and even their astrological sign. Questionnaires on dating sites exclusively targeted at gays and lesbians generally contain additional questions about identity disclosure (that is, how "out" the person is, questions about a person's membership in established lesbian and gay subcultures, for example "butch-femme," "lipstick lesbian," "leather," etc.). Each of these categories is usually covered in extensive detail. For example, the question on the Match.com questionnaire that asks "What kind of sport and exercise do you enjoy?" lists twenty-two activities ranging from aerobics to yoga. But curiously absent from the questionnaires are any questions about the type of erotic and sexual practices users enjoy and/or are seeking.

It would seem that people interested in finding someone to connect with, on an intimate level, might want to know something about the sexual desires, interests, and experiences of their prospective partner. Yet questionnaires on both heterosexual and gay and lesbian dating sites are entirely devoid of questions about prospective partners' definition of sex, the kind of sex members expect to have, the sexual experiences they have had, where they like to have sex, how often they like to have sex, or whether they even want to have sex. A few dating sites that serve gay men do ask whether the prospective member is specifically looking for sex, but remarkably the questionnaires on these sites also fail to ask any detailed questions about sexual practice preferences. The exclusion of explicit questions about sex on gay male questionnaires is particularly surprising in light of the fact that gay men have established subcultures of intimacy that are based entirely on sex. The omission of inquiries about sexual desires and interests serves to normalize the practice of online dating by cleansing it of the taint of sexual perversion.

Almost without exception, internet dating sites are marketed to mass audiences as user-friendly venues where heterosexual, lesbian, and gay participants can secure the relationship goals historically associated with idealized heterosexuality: namely, a long-term, monogamous, and preferably connubial relationship

between two people. This vision is reinforced by the "success" stories regularly found on the homepages of dating websites. Couples who have realized a committed and exclusive relationship, or become engaged or married as a result of "meeting" through a particular online dating service, are counted among the website's success stories. To reinforce this point, online dating websites routinely publish the sometimes lengthy testimonials—along with photos of course—of members who have secured their relationship through the site. Typical are narratives that make reference to the esteemed status of couplehood or that invoke the idealized concepts of "romance" and "soul-mate":

> Gay FriendFinder helped me find my soul mate. I work hard and don't really have time or energy to go out to bars and clubs to meet people. I tried Gay FriendFinder mostly out of curiosity and met Jeff— he's too good to be true! Thank you, thank you, thank you (BizGal28).
>
> I just wanted to tell you that I have found that special someone and also wanted to say thanks. If it hadn't been for your site [curiouslove.com], I would probably be single and very miserable. Just wanted to say that your site is very awesome . . .
>
> As Ryan walked me to my car we kissed again. And he invited me to spend the following day wandering in San Francisco. I had really planned to spend the day getting a bunch of errands done, but his talk of sipping tea at the Japanese Tea Garden and a romantic picnic in Golden Gate Park was too much to pass up. We decided to meet the next morning. For the first time in years I've found a man that I can have a real relationship with (Julie; perfectmatch.com).

On heterosexual dating websites, testimonial narratives are often supplemented by statistics on how many marriages have been produced through the site. An illustration of this common practice can be seen on EHarmony's home page. Here, a selection of smiling, apparently happy, hand-holding couples is continuously flashed on the background of the page along with the prominent display of the date of their first meeting and the date of their subsequent engagement or marriage. With the exception of marriage, the definition of "success" in online dating does not appear to vary by sexual orientation. A successful online dater is one who has secured the ideal type of pairing historically linked to heterosexuality—a monogamously committed coupling of two people who are thereafter forever linked through romance and love.

The visual images and advertising copy displayed by online dating services make it clear to potential subscribers that these are not venues in which to find casual sexual encounters, non-monogamous relationships, or experiment with new gender or sexual identities. They are places where one can safely seek and find intimate relationships that embody the ideals of love and romance. Consistent reinforcement of the idea that romance, love, and long-term monogamous coupling can be realized through online dating eases the public's fear that sexual deviants are lurking behind the online profiles. Moreover, it induces confidence in the belief that placing or responding to an advertisement online is not a stigmatized activity undertaken by sexual deviants and losers, but an activity that anyone can easily and safely engage in.

Technological and demographic changes, along with deliberate marketing strategies that link internet dating with conventional relationship goals, have helped make the process of seeking and finding partners through online personal advertisements attractive to a mass audience. Today, people who, in the past, may have hesitated to meet someone in a virtual space eagerly participate in placing and reading online personal profiles. Indeed, Whitehead suggests that internet dating is "likely to be as influential in shaping the patterns of mating in the early twenty-first century as the internal combustion engine was in shaping patterns of youthful dating in the early twentieth century" (2003: 175). . . .

In theory, online dating should . . . expand opportunities to create new forms of relationships, courtship patterns, and identity expressions. In the online environment, relationships can take place entirely in virtual space. Contact between a reader and the originator of an online profile may begin in a public chatroom and then proceed to private emails and perhaps Instant Messages, but need never be realized in a face-to-face encounter. In this sense, online dating provides the potential to go beyond existing categories of gender, sexuality, and even race, because relationships that take place entirely online are not mediated by voices, bodies, smells, or—in the case where pictures are unavailable—faces. New forms of sexual relationships may also be defined because online sexual partnerships can and do develop without physical sexual contact. As well, traditional patterns of courtship where men have historically been the initiators may also give way to greater freedom for women to initiate

romantic and sexual encounters and exercise control over the process and content of their interactions. But the realization of these possibilities is incomplete, largely because online dating websites construct intimate relationships along the constricted confines of romance, love and monogamy, and rely on existing categories of sexuality and gender to make the sale.

CONSUMING LOVE: THE COMMERCIALIZATION OF INTIMACY

Online dating transforms the search for intimate partners into a consumer activity. The process can be likened to a retail shopping experience that provides patrons with expansive options in partner selection. Each dating website resembles a store that stocks an enormous variety of "products." Shoppers who visit an online dating website browse among the many items available and, like their counterparts in the mall, specify the size, color, and overall quality of the one they are seeking. If buyers don't like what is offered, they can easily move on to the next store until they find exactly what they are interested in. Moreover, if the product does not perform as promised, shoppers may return to the store for a replacement model. Similar to consumer protection agencies that police conventional retail shops, websites like Truedater.com allow online daters to "turn in" writers of advertisements who are less than candid about their appearance, or marital, or financial status. Indeed, online dating transforms people into rational consumers who scrutinize the marketplace for the "best available deal" on intimate relationships.

A consumer market model may provide the greatest number of choices for people who are looking for a date, but it simultaneously reproduces the boundaries of existing gender and sexual identity categories and, therefore, may actually limit the relationship choices people have. Like their more conventional retail counterparts; online dating websites categorize the products they sell in a way that makes them easy to find. As such, they structure the options shoppers may select along the lines of established identity categories that consumers easily recognize. When shoppers search for partners online, they make their initial selection on the basis of gender, sexual orientation, race, and age. Already embedded in the software are the categories "man," "woman," "gay," "straight," "white" and "black." Online daters decide on the prescribed criteria for the "product" they want and then the computerized sorting mechanism returns only profiles of those people who represent the specific categories selected. The online format does not permit people to consider or define alternatives to the categories already given.

Gender, sexual orientation, race, and age are invisible in virtual space; therefore, online dating contains the potential to create relationships that are modeled outside the boundaries of these established identities. Online dating websites could, for example, allow users to define searches around specific personal character traits, shared interests, or life goals. To be sure, these criteria are often used in the secondary aspects of a partner search, but the primary step in the selection process involves choosing candidates by gender, sexual orientation, age, and race. The paradox here is that the very efficiencies of online dating that expand the possibilities of finding partners also confine the parameters of the search and, therefore, limit the prospects of expanding conventional constructions of intimate relationships.

The potential for online dating to transcend established identity categories is further constrained by the fact that, as mentioned earlier, online dating sites are increasingly targeted toward particular sexual orientation, racial/ethnic, social class, religious, and age groups. Inarguably, the separation of dating websites by specific identity categories makes it easier to find someone who meets one's desires. After all, gay people don't ordinarily yearn to date heterosexuals. But the construction of online dating sites by narrowly-bounded definitions of gender and sexuality compels the users of online websites to express their allegiance to a set of fixed identities prior to engaging in the activity of searching for an intimate partner. Online dating websites do not encourage users to explore the space in between categories, nor do they promote the possibility of creating new ones beyond existing constructs.

Because online dating websites compel users to identify with established gender and sexual categories, they may also encourage writers of personal profiles to rearticulate rather than transform the boundaries of gender. Though social scientists have yet to produce a systematic study that explores gender expression in online advertisements, a casual overview of online profiles suggests that writers typically adhere to established social meanings around masculinity and femininity. For instance, the online profiles of heterosexual and lesbian females routinely make references to a desire for love and romance. In contrast, both gay and straight male profiles tend to describe the physical attributes of the partner(s) they are interested in. If online personal profiles solidify rather than expand conventionally understood meanings of gender, they too are unlikely to offer possibilities for creating relationships outside of conventionally established frameworks.

Online dating represents a spectacular change in the process of finding partners, and provides more efficient ways for people to meet their relationship needs, but it has yet to transform prevailing ideas about intimate relationships. Just as internet users shop the net for retail items, they can search the global marketplace for intimacy. Indeed, finding relationships in virtual space now has mass appeal. But online dating websites sustain their mass appeal through the insistent and ever-present reliance on a particular relationship model that embodies the characteristics historically tied to heterosexual couplings. Online dating websites construct ideal relationships within the boundaries of convention. The trilogy of romance, love, and monogamy dominates the online dating scene, while alternative models of intimacy and the sexual possibilities of intimate relationships are de-emphasized. Moreover, online dating websites provide few opportunities to contest socially imposed boundaries around sexuality and gender because these recognized identity categories are embedded in the very structure of the websites themselves. As a result, internet dating strengthens rather than expands the boundaries of the categories through which people imagine their intimate relationships and, therefore, limits ideas about alternative forms they might take.

NOTE

1. The writer thanks Susan Bass and Anne Colvin for helpful comments on earlier versions of this essay.

REFERENCES

Brym, R. and R. Lenton 2001. *Love Online: A Report on Digital Dating in Canada*. Available online at http://www.nelson .com/nelson/harcourt/sociology/newsociety3e/loveonline .pdf (accessed March 15 2006).

Darden, D. and P. Koski 1988 "Using the Personal Ads: A Deviant Activity", *Deviant Behavior* 9: 383–400.

Foston, N. 2003 "I met my husband online!", *Ebony*, April.

Harris Poll 2003. *Those With internet Access Continue to Grow But at a Slower Rate*, February 5th. Available online at http://www.harrisinteractive.com/harris_poll/index.asp?PID = 356 (accessed March 15 2006).

Rajecki, D. W. and J. L. Rasmussen 1992 "Personal ads as deviant and unsatisfactory: Support for evolutionary hypothesis", *Behavioral and Brain Sciences* 15: 107.

Sullivan, B. 2002 *Online Dating: Everyone's doing it: A dot-com business that actually makes a profit*, September 19. Available online at http://msnbc.msn.com/id/3078729 (accessed March 15 2006).

Whitehead, B. Dafoe 2003. *Why There are No Good Men Left*. New York: Broadway Books.

Wilkinson, D. 2005 "Online: A Search for Act II", *New York Times*, April 12th p.12.

R E A D I N G *32* **Elizabeth A. Armstrong**
Laura Hamilton
Paula England

Is Hooking Up Bad for Young Women?

First published in 2010

"Girls can't be guys in matters of the heart, even though they think they can," says Laura Sessions Stepp, author of *Unhooked: How Young Women Pursue Sex, Delay Love, and Lose at Both*, published in 2007. In her view, "hooking up"—casual sexual activity ranging from kissing to intercourse — places women at risk of "low self-esteem, depression, alcoholism, and eating disorders." Stepp is only one of half a dozen journalists currently engaged in the business of detailing the dangers of casual sex.

On the other side, pop culture feminists such as Jessica Valenti, author of *The Purity Myth: How America's Obsession with Virginity is Hurting Young Women* (2010), argue that the problem isn't casual sex, but a "moral panic" over casual sex. And still a third set of writers like Ariel Levy, author of *Female Chauvinist Pigs: Women and the Rise of Raunch Culture* (2005), questions whether it's empowering for young women to show up at parties dressed to imitate porn stars or to strip in "Girls Gone Wild" fashion. Levy's concern isn't necessarily moral, but rather that these young women seem less focused on their own sexual pleasure and more worried about being seen as "hot" by men.

Following on the heels of the mass media obsession, sociologists and psychologists have begun to investigate adolescent and young adult hookups more systematically. In this essay, we draw on systematic data and studies of youth sexual practices over time to counter claims that hooking up represents a sudden and alarming change in youth sexual culture. The research shows that there is some truth to popular claims that hookups are bad for women. However, it also demonstrates that women's hookup experiences are quite varied and far from uniformly negative and that monogamous, long-term relationships are not an ideal alternative. Scholarship suggests that pop culture feminists have correctly zeroed in on sexual double standards as a key source of gender inequality in sexuality.

THE RISE OF LIMITED LIABILITY HEDONISM

Before examining the consequences of hooking up for girls and young women, we need to look more carefully at the facts. *Unhooked* author Stepp describes girls "stripping in the student center in front of dozens of boys they didn't know." She asserts that "young people have virtually abandoned dating" and that "relationships have been replaced by the casual sexual encounters known as hookups." Her sensationalist tone suggests that young people are having more sex at earlier ages in more casual contexts than their Baby Boomer parents.

This characterization is simply not true. Young people today are not having more sex at younger ages than their parents. The sexual practices of American youth changed in the twentieth century, but the big change came with the Baby Boom cohort who came of age more than 40 years ago. The National Health and Social Life Survey—the gold standard of American sexual practice surveys—found that those born after 1942 were more sexually active at younger ages than those born from 1933–42. However, the trend toward greater sexual activity among young people appears to halt or reverse among the youngest cohort in the NHSLS, those born from 1963–72. Examining the National Survey of Family Growth, Lawrence B. Finer, Director of Domestic Research for the Guttmacher Institute, found that the percent of women who have had premarital sex by age 20 (65–76 percent) is roughly the same for all cohorts born after 1948. He also found that the women in the youngest cohort in this survey—those born from 1979–1984—were less likely to have premarital sex by age 20 than those born before them. The Centers for Disease Control, reporting on the results of the National Youth Risk Behavior Survey, report that rates of sexual intercourse among 9th–12th graders decreased from 1991–2007, as did numbers of partners. Reports of condom use increased. So what are young people doing to cause such angst among Boomers?

The pervasiveness of *casual* sexual activity among today's youth may be at the heart of Boomers' concerns. England surveyed more than 14,000 students from 19 universities and colleges about their hookup, dating, and relationship experiences. Seventy-two percent of both men and women participating in the survey reported at least one hookup by their senior year in college. What the Boomer panic may gloss over, however, is the fact that college students don't, on average, hook up that much. By senior year, roughly 40 percent of those who ever hooked up had engaged in three or fewer hookups, 40 percent between four and nine hookups, and only 20 percent in ten or more hookups. About 80 percent of students hook up, on average, less than once per semester over the course of college.

In addition, the sexual activity in hookups is often relatively light. Only about one third engaged in intercourse in their most recent hookup. Another third had engaged in oral sex or manual stimulation of the genitals. The other third of hookups only involved kissing and non-genital touching. A full 20 percent of survey respondents in their fourth year of college had never had vaginal intercourse. In addition, hookups between total strangers are relatively uncommon, while hooking up with the same person multiple times is common. Ongoing sexual relationships without commitment are labeled as "repeat," "regular," or "continuing" hookups, and sometimes as "friends with benefits." Often there is friendship or socializing both before and after the hookup.

Hooking up hasn't replaced committed relationships. Students often participate in both at different times during college. By their senior year, 69 percent of heterosexual students had been in a college relationship of at least six months. Hookups sometimes became committed relationships and vice versa; generally the distinction revolved around the agreed upon level of exclusivity and the willingness to refer to each other as "girlfriend/boyfriend."

And, finally, hooking up isn't radically new. As suggested above, the big change in adolescent and young adult sexual behavior occurred with the Baby Boomers. This makes sense, as the forces giving rise to casual sexual activity among the young—the availability of birth control pill, the women's and sexual liberation movements, and the decline of *in loco parentis* on college campuses—took hold in the 1960s. But changes in youth sexual culture did not stop with the major behavioral changes wrought by the Sexual Revolution.

Contemporary hookup culture among adolescents and young adults may rework aspects of the Sexual Revolution to get some of its pleasures while reducing its physical and emotional risks. Young people today—particularly young whites from affluent families—are expected to delay the commitments of adulthood while they invest in careers. They get the message that sex is okay, as long as it doesn't jeopardize their futures;

STDs and early pregnancies are to be avoided. This generates a sort of limited liability hedonism. For instance, friendship is prioritized a bit more than romance, and oral sex appeals because of its relative safety. Hookups may be the most explicit example of a calculating approach to sexual exploration. They make it possible to be sexually active while avoiding behaviors with the highest physical and emotional risks (e g., intercourse, intense relationships). Media panic over hooking up may be at least in part a result of adult confusion about youth sexual culture—that is, not understanding that oral sex and sexual experimentation with friends are actually some young people's ways of balancing fun and risk.

Even though hooking up in college isn't the rampant hedonistic free-for-all portrayed by the media, it does involve the movement of sexual activity outside of relationships. When *Contexts* addressed youth sex in 2002, Barbara Risman and Pepper Schwartz speculated that the slowdown in youth sexual activity in the 1990s might be a result of "girls' increasing control over the conditions of sexual intercourse," marked by the restriction of sex to relationships. They expressed optimism about gender equality in sexuality on the grounds that girls are more empowered in relationship sex than casual sex. It appears now that these scholars were overly optimistic about the progress of the gender revolution in sex. Not only is casual sex common, it seems that romantic relationships themselves are riddled with gender inequality.

HOOKUP PROBLEMS, RELATIONSHIP PLEASURES

Hookups are problematic for girls and young women for several related reasons. As many observers of American youth sexual culture have found, a sexual double standard continues to be pervasive. As one woman Hamilton interviewed explained, "Guys can have sex with all the girls and it makes them more of a man, but if a girl does then all of a sudden she's a 'ho' and she's not as quality of a person." Sexual labeling among adolescents and young adults may only loosely relate to actual sexual behavior; for example, one woman complained in her interview that she was a virgin the first time she was called a "slut." The lack of clear rules about what is "slutty" and what is not contribute to women's fears of stigma.

On college campuses, this sexual double standard often finds its most vociferous expression in the Greek scene. Fraternities are often the only venues where large groups of underage students can readily access alcohol. Consequently, one of the easiest places to find hookup partners is in a male-dominated party context. As a variety of scholars have observed, fraternity men often use their control of the situation to undermine women's ability to freely consent to sex (e.g., by pushing women to drink too heavily, barring their exit from private rooms, or refusing them rides home). Women report varying degrees of sexual disrespect in the fraternity culture, and the dynamics of this scene predictably produce some amount of sexual assault.

The most commonly encountered disadvantage of hookups, though, is that sex in relationships is far better for women. England's survey revealed that women orgasm more often and report higher levels of sexual satisfaction in relationship sex than in hookup sex. This is in part because sex in relationships is more likely to include sexual activities conducive to women's orgasm. In hookups, men are much more likely to receive fellatio than women are to receive cunnilingus. In relationships, oral sex is more likely to be reciprocal. In interviews conducted by England's research team, men report more concern with the sexual pleasure of girlfriends than hookup partners, while women seem equally invested in pleasing hookup partners and boyfriends.

The continuing salience of the sexual double standard mars women's hookup experiences. In contrast, relationships provide a context in which sex is viewed as acceptable for women, protecting them from stigma and establishing sexual reciprocity as a basic expectation. In addition, relationships offer love and companionship.

RELATIONSHIP PROBLEMS, HOOKUP PLEASURES

Relationships are good for sex but, unfortunately, they have a dark side as well. Relationships are "greedy," getting in the way of other things that young women want to be doing as adolescents and young adults, and they are often characterized by gender inequality—sometimes even violence.

Talking to young people, two of us (Hamilton and Armstrong) found that committed relationships detracted from what women saw as main tasks of college. The women we interviewed complained, for example, that relationships made it difficult to meet people. As a woman who had just ended a relationship explained:

I'm happy that I'm able to go out and meet new people . . . I feel like I'm doing what a college student should be doing. I don't need to be tied down to my high school boyfriend for two years when this is the time to be meeting people.

Women also complained that committed relationships competed with schoolwork. One woman remarked, "[My boyfriend] doesn't understand why I can't pick up and go see him all the time. But I have school . . . I just want to be a college kid." Another told one of us (Hamilton) that her major was not compatible with the demands of a boyfriend. She said, "I wouldn't mind having a boyfriend again, but it's a lot of work. Right now with [my major] and everything . . . I wouldn't have time even to see him." Women feared that they would be devoured by relationships and sometimes struggled to keep their self-development projects going when they did get involved.

Subjects told us that relationships were not only time-consuming, but also marked by power inequalities and abuse. Women reported that boyfriends tried to control their social lives, the time they spent with friends, and even what they wore. One woman described her boyfriend, saying. "He is a very controlling person. . . . He's like, 'What are you wearing tonight?' . . . It's like a joke but serious at the same time." Women also became jealous. Coping with jealousy was painful and emotionally absorbing. One woman noted that she would "do anything to make this relationship work." She elaborated, "I was so nervous being with Dan because I knew he had cheated on his [prior] girlfriend . . . [but] I'm getting over it. When I go [to visit him] now . . . I let him go to the bar, whatever. I stayed in his apartment because there was nothing else to do." Other women changed the way they dressed, their friends, and where they went in the hope of keeping boyfriends.

When women attempted to end relationships, they often reported that men's efforts to control them escalated. In the course of interviewing 46 respondents, two of us (Hamilton and Armstrong) heard ten accounts of men using abuse to keep women in relationships. One woman spent months dealing with a boyfriend who accused her of cheating on him. When she tried to break up, he cut his wrist in her apartment. Another woman tried to end a relationship, but was forced to flee the state when her car windows were broken and her safety was threatened. And a third woman reported that her ex-boyfriend stalked her for months—even showing up at her workplace, showering her with flowers and gifts, and blocking her entry into her workplace until the police arrived. For most women, the costs of bad hookups tended to be less than costs of bad relationships. Bad hookups were isolated events, while bad relationships wreaked havoc with whole lives. Abusive relationships led to lost semesters, wrecked friendships, damaged property, aborted pregnancies, depression, and time-consuming involvement with police and courts.

The abuse that women reported to us is not unusual. Intimate partner violence among adolescents and young adults is common. In a survey of 15,000 adolescents conducted in 2007, the Centers for Disease Control found that 10 percent of students had been "hit, slapped, or physically hurt on purpose by their boyfriend or girlfriend" in the last 12 months.

If relationships threaten academic achievement, get in the way of friendship, and can involve jealousy, manipulation, stalking, and abuse, it is no wonder that young women sometimes opt for casual sex. Being open to hooking up means being able to go out and fit into the social scene, get attention from young men, and learn about sexuality. Women we interviewed gushed about parties they attended and attention they received from boys. As one noted, "Everyone was so excited. It was a big fun party." They reported turning on their "make out radar," explaining that "it's fun to know that a guy's attracted to you and is willing to kiss you." Women reported enjoying hookups, and few reported regretting their last hookup. Over half the time women participating in England's survey reported no relational interest before or after their hookup, although more women than men showed interest in a relationship both before and after hookups. The gender gap in relationship interest is slightly larger after the hookup, with 48 percent of women and 36 percent of men reporting interest in a relationship.

TOWARD GENDER EQUALITY IN SEX

Like others, Stepp, the author of *Unhooked,* suggests that restricting sex to relationships is the way to challenge gender inequality in youth sex. Certainly, sex in relationships is better for women than hookup sex. However, research suggests two reasons why Stepp's strategy won't work: first, relationships are also plagued by inequality. Second, valorizing relationships as the ideal context for women's sexual activity reinforces the notion that women shouldn't want sex outside of relationships and stigmatizes women who do. A better approach would challenge gender inequality in both relationships and hookups. It is critical to attack the tenacious sexual double standard that leads men to disrespect their hookup partners. Ironically, this could improve relationships because women would be less likely to tolerate "greedy" or abusive

relationships if they were treated better in hookups. Fostering relationships among young adults should go hand-in-hand with efforts to decrease intimate partner violence and to build egalitarian relationships that allow more space for other aspects of life—such as school, work, and friendship.

REFERENCES

Kathleen A. Bogle. *Hooking Up: Sex, Dating, and Relationships on Campus* (New York University Press, 2008).

Paula England, Emily Fitzgibbons Shafer, and Alison C. K. Fogarty. "Hooking Up and Forming Romantic Relationships on Today's College Campuses." In M. Kimmel and A. Aronson (eds.), *The Gendered Society Reader*, 3rd edition (Oxford University Press, 2008).

Norval Glenn and Elizabeth Marquardt. *Hooking Up, Hanging Out, and Hoping for Mr. Right: College Women on Mating and Dating Today* (Institute for American Values, 2001).

Laura Hamilton and Elizabeth A. Armstrong. "Double Binds and Flawed Options: Gendered Sexuality in Early Adulthood," *Gender & Sexuality* (2009), 23: 589–616.

Derek A. Kreager and Jeremy Staff. "The Sexual Double Standard and Adolescent Peer Acceptance," *Social Psychology Quarterly* (2009), 72: 143–164.

Wendy D. Manning, Peggy C. Giordano, and Monica A. Longmore. "Hooking Up: The Relationship Contexts of 'Nonrelationship' Sex," *Journal of Adolescent Research* (2006), 21: 459–483.

READING *33* Leila J. Rupp
Verta Taylor

Straight Girls Kissing

First published in 2010

The phenomenon of presumably straight girls kissing and making out with other girls at college parties and at bars is everywhere in contemporary popular culture, from Katy Perry's hit song, "I Kissed a Girl," to a Tyra Banks online poll on attitudes toward girls who kiss girls in bars, to AskMen.com's "Top 10: Chick Kissing Scenes." Why *do* girls who aren't lesbians kiss girls? Some think it's just another example of "girls gone wild," seeking to attract the boys who watch. Others, such as psychologist Lisa Diamond, point to women's "sexual fluidity," suggesting that the behavior could be part of how women shape their sexual identities, even using a heterosexual social

scene as a way to transition to a bisexual or lesbian identity.

These speculations touch on a number of issues in the sociology of sexuality. The fact that young women on college campuses are engaging in new kinds of sexual behaviors brings home the fundamental concept of the social construction of sexuality—that whom we desire, what kinds of sexual acts we engage in, and how we identify sexually is profoundly shaped by the societies in which we live. Furthermore, boys enjoying the sight of girls making out recalls the feminist notion of the "male gaze," calling attention to the power embodied in men as viewers and women as the viewed. The sexual fluidity that is potentially embodied in women's intimate inter-actions in public reminds us that sexuality is gendered and that sexual desire, sexual behavior, and sexual iden-tity do not always match. That is, men do not, at least in contemporary American culture, experience the same kind of fluidity. Although they may identify as straight and have sex with other men, they certainly don't make out at parties for the pleasure of women.

The hookup culture on college campuses, as depicted in another [reading], facilitates casual sexual interactions (ranging from kissing and making out to oral sex and intercourse) between students who meet at parties or bars. Our campus is no exception. The University of California, Santa Barbara, has a long-standing reputation as a party school (much to the administration's relief, it's declining in those rankings). In a student population of twenty thousand, more than half of the students are female and slightly under half are students of color, primarily Chicano/Latino and Asian American. About a third are first-generation col-lege students. Out of over two thousand female UC Santa Barbara students who responded to sociologist Paula England's online College and Social Life Survey on hooking-up practices on campus, just under one percent identified as homosexual, three percent as bisexual, and nearly two percent as "not sure."

National data on same-sex sexuality shows that far fewer people identify as lesbian or gay than are sexu-ally attracted to the same sex or have engaged in same-sex sexual behavior. Sociologist Edward Laumann and his colleagues, in the National Health and Social Life Survey, found that less than two percent of women identified as lesbian or bisexual, but over eight percent had experienced same-sex desire or engaged in lesbian sex. The opposite is true for men, who are more likely to have had sex with a man than to report finding men attractive. Across time and cultures (and, as sociologist Jane Ward has pointed out, even in the present among white straight-identified men), sex with other men, as long as a man plays the insertive role in a sexual encounter, can bolster, rather than undermine, hetero-sexuality. Does the same work for women?

The reigning assumption about girls kissing girls in the party scene is that they do it to attract the attention of men. But the concept of sexual fluidity and the lack of fit among desire, behavior, and identity suggest that there may be more going on than meets the male gaze. A series of formal and informal interviews with diverse female college students at our university, conducted by undergraduates as part of a class assignment,

supports the sociological scholarship on the complex-ity of women's sexuality.

THE COLLEGE PARTY SCENE

What is most distinctive about UC Santa Barbara is the adjacent community of Isla Vista, a densely populated area made up of two-thirds students and one-third pri-marily poor and working-class Mexican American families. House parties, fraternity and sorority parties, dance parties (often with, as one woman student put it, "some sort of slutty theme to them"), and random par-ties open to anyone who stops by flourish on the week-ends. Women students describe Isla Vista as "unrealistic to the rest of the world . . . It's a little wild," "very pro-miscuous, a lot of experimenting and going crazy," and "like a sovereign nation . . . a space where people feel really comfortable to let down their guards and to kind of let loose." Alcohol flows freely, drugs are available, women sport skimpy clothing, and students engage in a lot of hooking up. One sorority member described parties as featuring "a lot of, you know, sexual dance. And some people, you know, like pretty much are fucking on the dance floor even though they're really not. I feel like they just take it above and beyond." Another student thinks "women have a little bit more freedom here." But despite the unreality of life in Isla Vista, there's no reason to think life here is fundamen-tally different than on other large campuses.

At Isla Vista parties, the practice of presumably het-erosexual women kissing and making out with other women is widespread. As one student reported, "It's just normal for most people now, friends make out with each other." The student newspaper sex colum-nist began her column in October 2008, "I kissed a girl and liked it," recommending "if you're a girl who hasn't quite warmed up to a little experimentation with one of your own, then I suggest you grab a gal and get to it." She posed the "burning question on every male spectator's mind . . . Is it real or is it for show?" As it turns out, students offered three different explanations of why students do this: to get attention from men, to experiment with same-sex activity, and out of same-sex desire.

GETTING ATTENTION

Girls kissing other girls can be a turn-on for men in our culture, as the girls who engage in it well know. A stu-dent told us, "It's usually for display for guys who are usually surrounding them and like cheering them on. And it seems to be done in order to like, you know, for the guys, not like for their own pleasure or desire, but to like, I don't know, entertain the guys." Alcohol is usually involved: "It's usually brought on by, I don't know, like shots or drinking, or people kind of saying something to like cheer it on or whatever. And it's usually done in order to turn guys on or to seek male attention in some way." One student who admits to giving her friend what she calls "love pecks" and engaging in some "booby grabbing" says "I think it's mainly for attention definitely. It's usually girls that are super drunk that are trying to get attention from guys or are just really just having fun like when my roommate and I did it at our date party . . . It is alcohol and for show. Not experimentation at all." Another student, who has had her friends kiss her, insists that "they do that for attention . . . kind of like a circle forms around them . . . egging them on or taking pictures." One woman admitted that she puckered up for the attention, but when asked if it had anything to do with experimentation, added "maybe with some people. I think for me it was a little bit, yeah."

EXPERIMENTATION

Other women agree that experimentation is part of the story. One student who identifies as straight says "I have kissed girls on multiple occasions." One night she and a friend were "hammered, walking down the street, and we're getting really friendly and just started making out and taking pictures," which they then posted on Facebook. "And then the last time, this is a little bit more personal, but was when I actually had a threesome. Which was at a party and obviously didn't happen during the party." She mentions "bisexual tendencies" as an explanation, in addition to getting attention: "I would actually call it maybe more like experimentation." Another student, who calls herself straight but "bi-curious," says girls do it for attention, but also, "It's a good time for them, something they may not have the courage to express themselves otherwise, if they're in a room alone, it makes them more comfortable with it because other people are receiving pleasure from them." She told us about being drunk at a theme party ("Alice in Fuck-land"): "And me and 'Maria' just started going at it in the kitchen. And this dude, he whispers in my ear, 'Everyone's watching. People can see you.' But me and 'Maria' just like to kiss. I don't think it was like really a spectacle thing, like we

weren't teasing anybody. We just like to make out. So we might be an exception to the rule," she giggled.

In another interview, a student described a friend as liking "boys and girls when she's drunk . . . But when she's sober she's starting to like girls." And another student who called herself "technically" bisexual explained that she hates that term because in Isla Vista "it basically means that you make out with girls at parties." Before her first relationship with a woman, she never thought about bisexuality: "The closest I ever came to thinking that was, hey, I'd probably make out with a girl if I was drinking." These stories make clear that experimentation in the heterosexual context of the hookup culture and college party scene provides a safe space for some women to explore non-heterosexual possibilities.

SAME-SEX DESIRE

Some women go beyond just liking to make out and admit to same-sex desire as the motivating factor. One student who defined her sexuality as liking sex with men but feeling "attracted more towards girls than guys" described her coming out process as realizing, "I really like girls and I really like kissing girls." Said another student, "I've always considered myself straight, but since I've been living here I've had several sexual experiences with women. So I guess I would consider myself, like, bisexual at this point." She at first identified as "one of those girls" who makes out at parties, but then admitted that she also had sexual experiences with women in private. At this point she shifted her identification to bisexual: "I may have fallen into that trap of like kissing a girl to impress a guy, but I can't really recollect doing that on purpose. It was more of just my own desire to be with, like to try that with a woman." Another bisexual woman who sometimes makes out with one of her girlfriends in public thinks other women might "only do it in a public setting because they're afraid of that side of their sexuality, because they were told to be heterosexual you know . . . So if they make out, it's only for the show of it, even though they may like it they can't admit that they do."

The ability to kiss and make out with girls in public without having to declare a lesbian or bisexual identity makes it possible for women with same-sex desires to be part of the regular college party scene, and the act of making out in public has the potential to lead to more extensive sexual activity in private. One student described falling in love with her best friend in middle school, but being "too chicken shit to make the first move" because "I never know if they are queer or not." Her first sexual relationship with a bisexual woman included the woman's boyfriend as well. In this way, the fact that some women have their first same-sex sexual encounter in a threesome with a man is an extension of the safe heterosexual space for exploring same-sex desire.

HETEROFLEXIBILITY

Obviously, in at least some cases, more is going on here than drunken women making out for the pleasure of men. Sexual fluidity is certainly relevant; in Lisa Diamond's ten-year study of young women who originally identified as lesbian or bisexual, she found a great deal of movement in sexual desire, intimate relationships, and sexual identities. The women moved in all directions, from lesbian to bisexual and heterosexual, bisexual to lesbian and heterosexual, and, notably, from all identities to "unlabeled." From a psychological perspective, Diamond argues for the importance of both biology and culture in shaping women as sexually fluid, with a greater capacity for attractions to both female and male partners than men. Certainly the women who identify as heterosexual but into kissing other women fit her notion of sexual fluidity. Said one straight-identified student, "It's not like they're way different from anyone else. They're just making out."

Mostly, though, students didn't think that making out had any impact on one's identity as heterosexual: "And yeah, I imagine a lot of the girls that you know just casually make out with their girlfriends would consider themselves straight. I consider myself straight." Said another, "I would still think they're straight girls. Unless I saw some, like level of like emotional and like attraction there." A bisexual student, though, thought "they're definitely bi-curious at the least . . . I think that a woman who actually does it for enjoyment and like knows that she likes that and that she desires it again, I would say would be more leaning towards bisexual."

EVERYBODY BUT LESBIANS

So, although girls who kiss girls are not "different from anyone else," if they have an emotional reaction or *really* enjoy it or want to do it again, then they've apparently crossed the line of heterosexuality. Diamond found that lesbians in her study who had been exclusively attracted to and involved with other women were the only group that didn't report changes in their sexual identities. Sociologist Arlene Stein, in her study of lesbian feminist communities in the 1980s, also painted a picture of boundary struggles around the identity "lesbian." Women who developed relationships with men but continued to identify as lesbians were called "ex-lesbians" or "fakers" by those who considered themselves "real lesbians." And while straight college students today can make out with women and call themselves "bi-curious" without challenge to their heterosexual identity, the same kind of flexibility does not extend to lesbians. A straight, bi-curious woman explained that she didn't think "the lesbian community would accept me right off because I like guys too much, you know." And she didn't think she had "enough sexual experience with the women to be considered bisexual." Another student, who described herself as "a free flowing spirit" and has had multiple relationships with straight-identified women, rejected the label "lesbian" because "I like girls" but "guys are still totally attractive to me." She stated that "to be a lesbian meant . . . you'd have to commit yourself to it one hundred percent. Like you'd have to be in it sexually, you'd have to be in it emotionally. And I think if you were you wouldn't have that attraction for men . . . if you were a lesbian."

In contrast to "heteroflexibility," a term much in use by young women, students hold a much more rigid, if unarticulated, notion of lesbian identity. "It's just like it's okay because we're both drunk and we're friends. It's not like we identify as lesbian in any way. . . ." One woman who has kissed her roommate is sure that she can tell the difference between straight women and lesbians: "I haven't ever seen like an actual like lesbian couple enjoying themselves." Another commented, "I mean, it's one thing if you are, if you do identify as gay and that you're expressing something." A bisexual woman is less sure, at first stating that eighty percent of the making out at parties is for men, then hesitating because "that totally excludes the queer community and my own viewing of like women who absolutely love other women, and they show that openly so, I think that it could be either context." At that point she changed the percentage to fifty percent: "Cause I guess I never know if a woman is like preferably into women or if it's more of a social game." A bisexual woman described kissing her girlfriend at a party "and some guy came up and poured beer on us and said something like 'stop kissing her you bitch,'" suggesting that any sign that women are kissing for their own pleasure puts them over the line. She went on to add that "we've gotten plenty of guys staring at us though, when we kiss or whatever, [and] they think that we're doing it for them, or we want them to join or whatever. It gets pretty old."

So there is a lot of leeway for women's same-sex behavior with a straight identity. But it is different than for straight men, who experience their same-sex interactions in a more private space, away from the gaze of women. Straight women can be "barsexual" or "bi-curious" or "mostly straight," but too much physical attraction or emotional investment crosses over the line of heterosexuality. What this suggests is that heterosexual women's options for physical intimacy are expanding, although such activity has little salience for identity, partner choice, or political allegiances. But the line between lesbian and non-lesbian, whether bisexual or straight, remains firmly intact.

REFERENCES

Lisa M. Diamond. *Sexual Fluidity: Understanding Women's Love and Desire*. (Harvard University Press, 2009).

Laura Hamilton. "Trading on Heterosexuality: College Women's Gender Strategies and Homophobia." *Gender & Society* (2007), 21:145–72.

Arlene Stein. *Sex and Sensibility: Stories of a Lesbian Generation* (University of California Press, 1997).

Elisabeth Morgan Thompson and Elizabeth M. Morgan. "'Mostly Straight' Young Women. Variations in Sexual Behavior and Identity Development." *Developmental Psychology* (2008), 44/1 15–21.

Jane Ward. "Dude-Sex: White Masculinities and 'Authentic' Heterosexuality Among Dudes Who Have Sex With Dudes." *Sexualities* (2008), 11:414–434.

READING *34* **Kristen Schilt**
Laurel Westbrook

Doing Gender, Doing Heteronormativity: "Gender Normals," Transgender People, and the Social Maintenance of Heterosexuality

First published in 2009

In "Feminism, Marxism, Method and the State," Catherine MacKinnon (1982, 533) argued that "sexuality is the linchpin of gender inequality." This argument

AUTHORS' NOTE: We are extremely grateful to Beth Schneider, Jane Ward, Dana Britton, and the anonymous reviewers at Gender & Society for the detailed and thoughtful feedback that they provided on earlier versions of this article. In addition, we wish to thank Wendy Brown, Karl Bryant, Richard Juang, Dawne Moon, Charis Thompson, Barrie Thorne, Aliya Saperstein, and Mel Stanfill for comments on previous versions of this work. Portions of this research have been supported by funding from the Regents of the University of California.

echoed earlier conceptualizations of heterosexuality as a compulsory, institutionalized system that supports gender inequality (Rich 1980). Despite these important insights, however, theorizing heterosexuality did not become central to feminist sociology (Ingraham 1994). Rather, it was queer theory that picked up the theoretical mantle, turning the gaze onto how the "heterosexual matrix" (Butler 1989) maintains inequality between men and women (see Seidman 1995). Shifting the object of analysis from the margins (women, homosexuals) to the center (men, heterosexuals) allowed for the theorization of heteronormativity—the suite of cultural, legal, and institutional practices that maintain normative assumptions that there are two and only two genders, that gender reflects biological sex, and that only sexual attraction between these "opposite" genders is natural or acceptable (Kitzinger 2005). Heterosexuality plays a central role in "maintaining the gender hierarchy that subordinates women to men" (Cameron and Kulick 2003, 45). Yet the relationship between heterosexuality and gender oppression remains undertheorized in social science research.

In this article, we bring attention to the everyday workings of heteronormativity by examining potential challenges to this "sex/gender/sexuality system" (Seidman 1995): people who live their lives in a social gender that is not the gender they were assigned at birth. People who make these social transitions—often termed "transgender" people—disrupt cultural expectations that gender identity is an immutable derivation of biology (Garfinkel 1967; Kessler and McKenna 1978). In social situations, transgender people—as all people—have "cultural genitalia" that derive from their gender presentation (Kessler and McKenna 1978). Yet in sexual and sexualized situations—interactional contexts that allow for the performance of both gender and heterosexuality—male-bodied women and female-bodied men present a challenge to heteronormativity. As we demonstrate, analyzing these situations can illuminate the relationship between the maintenance of gender and the maintenance of (hetero)sexuality.

Taking methodological insights from queer theory, we consider how cisgender men and women[1]–whom Garfinkel (1967) terms "gender normals"—react to transgender people. This focus inverts the typical model of using transgender people (the margins) to illuminate the workings of everybody else (the center) (see Garfinkel 1967; Kessler and McKenna 1978; West and Zimmerman 1987). We draw on two cases studies: an ethnographic study of transmen who socially transition from female to male (FtM) in the workplace and a textual analysis of media narratives about the killings predominantly of transwomen who socially transition from male to female (MtF). Attention to how gender normals react to the discovery of what they perceive as a mismatch between gender identity and biological sex in these public and private relationships reveals the interactional precariousness of the seemingly natural heterosexual gender system. We argue that these responses demonstrate that the processes of "doing gender" (West and Zimmerman 1987) are

difficult to separate from the maintenance of heteronormativity. Our case studies show that doing gender in a way that does not reflect biological sex can be perceived as a threat to heterosexuality. Cisgender men and women attempt to repair these potential ruptures through the deployment of normatively gendered tactics that reify gender and sexual difference. These tactics simultaneously negate the authenticity of transmen and transwomen's gender and sexual identities and reaffirm the heteronormative assumption that only "opposite sex" attraction between two differently sexed and gendered bodies is normal, natural, and desirable.

LITERATURE REVIEW

The persistence of gender inequality is well documented within sociology. Behind this reproduction of inequality are cultural schemas about the naturalness of a binary gender system in which there are two, and only two, genders that derive from biology (chromosomes and genitalia) (West and Zimmerman 1987). These schemas constitute and are constituted by our current gender order—the patterns of power relations between men and women that shape norms for femininity and masculinity by defining what is gender-appropriate in arenas such as romantic partner selection, occupational choice, and parental roles. The gender order is hierarchical, which means there is consistently a higher value on masculinity than on femininity (Connell 1987; Schippers 2007).

Ethnomethodological theories of gender (see Garfinkel 1967; Kessler and McKenna 1978; West and Zimmerman 1987) argue that an empirical focus on social interactions makes the mechanisms that maintain this gender system visible, as "social interactions can reflect and reiterate the gender inequality characteristic of society more generally" (Fenstermaker, West, and Zimmerman 2002, 28). This theoretical body of work examines what has come to be termed "doing gender" (West and Zimmerman 1987)—the interactional process of crafting gender identities that are then presumed to reflect and naturally derive from biology. As masculinity and femininity are not fixed properties of male and female bodies, the meanings and expectations for being men and women differ both historically and across interactional settings. Normative expectations for men and women maintain gender inequality, as strictures of masculinity push men to "do dominance" and strictures of femininity push women to "do submission" (West and Zimmerman 1987). Taken together, these expectations about natural gender differences translate into an unreflexive production of doing inequality that reproduces the hierarchical gender system more broadly (Fenstermaker, West, and Zimmerman 2002).

Fully illuminating the mechanisms that uphold gender inequality, however, requires a more thorough analysis of the interplay between gender and sexuality—what some feminists have termed the connection between patriarchy and compulsory heterosexuality (Rich 1980)—than is offered in these theories. Heterosexuality—like masculinity and femininity—is taken for granted as a natural occurrence derived from biological sex. Heterosexual expectations are embedded in social institutions, "guarantee [ing] that some people will have more class status, power, and privilege than others" (Ingraham 1994, 212). The hierarchical gender system that privileges masculinity also privileges heterosexuality. Its maintenance rests on the cultural devaluation of femininity and homosexuality. Showing the effects of this socialization, violent crimes against gay men—individuals who are culturally stereotyped as feminine (Hennen 2008)—typically are propagated by men (Franklin 2000). The gender system must be conceived of as *heterosexist*, as power is allocated via positioning in gender and sexual hierarchies. As such, understanding the persistence of gender inequality necessitates an understanding of the relationality between heterosexuality and gender.

Heterosexuality requires a binary sex system, as it is predicated on the seemingly natural attraction between two types of bodies defined as opposites. The taken-for-granted expectation that heterosexuality and gender identity follow from genitalia produces heteronormativity—even though in most social interactions genitals are not actually visible. People do not expect a mismatch between "biological" credentials and gender presentations but rather assume that gendered appearances reflect a biologically sexed reality (West and Zimmerman 1987). This assumption is not always warranted. Transgender people—people who live with a social gender identity that differs from the gender they were assigned at birth—can successfully do masculinity or femininity without having the genitalia that are presumed to follow from their outward appearance.

In many social interactions, transgender people's private bodies matter little, as—if they "pass" in their desired social gender—their appearance is taken to be proof of their biological sex. Sexual encounters, however, can disrupt the taken-for-granted assumptions that people who look like women have vaginas and people who look like men have penises. In these situations gender normals, particularly men, can have strong, even violent reactions. A question arises: Is the reaction related to (trans)gender or (hetero)sexuality? Framed as a (trans)gender issue, this violence operates as a disciplinary force on bodies that transgress the seemingly natural gender binary. Yet (hetero)sexuality is also an important factor as "the heterosexual framework that centers upon the model of penis-vagina penetration undoubtedly informs the genital division of male and female" (Bettcher 2007, 56). Transgender people have their claim to their gender category of choice challenged in these situations on the basis of genitalia, which in turn calls the heterosexuality of cisgender people they have been sexual with into question. How people respond to breaches to naturalized attitudes about gender and sexuality can illuminate the processes and mechanisms behind the everyday unfolding of not just doing gender but also doing heteronormativity.

METHODS

The first case study examined reactions to open workplace transitions—situations in which transgender people announce their intention to undergo a gender transition and remain in the same job. Between 2003 and 2007, Schilt conducted in-depth interviews with 54 transmen in Southern California and Central Texas. Generating a random sample of transmen is not possible, as there is not an even dispersal of transmen by state or transgender-specific neighborhoods from which to sample. Respondents were recruited from transgender activist groups, listservs, support groups, and personal contacts. After the interview, each respondent was asked if he felt comfortable recommending any coworkers for an interview about their experience of the workplace transition. Fourteen coworkers (10 women and four men) of eight transmen in professional and blue-collar jobs were interviewed.

There were few demographic differences between transmen from the two regions. Thirty-five of these men had openly transitioned at one point in their lives, 19 in California and 16 in Texas. The majority were white (86 percent), with relatively equal numbers of queer, bisexual, and gay men and heterosexual men. The average age of California respondents was higher than that of the Texas respondents (35 vs. 25).

California transmen also had a wider range of years of transition—from the mid-1980s to the mid-2000s—while all of the transmen interviewed in Texas openly transitioned in the early to mid-2000s. In both states, most transmen transitioned in professional occupations or in service industry/retail occupations (72 percent), with a minority transitioning in blue-collar occupations and "women's professions."

In the second case study, Westbrook systematically collected all the available nonfiction texts produced by the mainstream news media in the United States between 1990 and 2005 about the murders of people described as doing gender so as to possibly be seen as a gender other than the one they were assigned at birth. Texts included those identifying a murder victim as wearing clothing, jewelry, and/or makeup associated with a gender other than the one they were labeled at birth; naming a murder victim as *transsexual, transgender,* a *cross-dresser,* or a *transvestite;* and/or describing the victim of fatal violence as *a man in a dress, a man posing as a woman, passed as a man, a woman posing as a man, female impersonator,* or *a woman who is really a man.* For this article, we will refer to this group of people using the term "transgender."

In total, Westbrook collected and analyzed 7,183 individual news stories about 232 homicides. Most texts came from searches of the databases Lexis Nexis and Access World News and included print newspaper articles and news magazine articles produced for a general audience. To gather these texts, Westbrook compiled a list of names of people identified as transgender murder victims by transgender activists and then searched for articles about these victims. She then assembled a list of names and terms used to describe victims in these news stories, such as "posed as a woman," and performed a new search using those terms. This process was repeated a number of times. The extensiveness of the search makes these texts a census of all available stories, not just a sample, and all cases identified by transgender activists were written about at least once in the mainstream press. . . .

There are some potential limitations to this comparative model. The first lies in the populations we compare. While transmen and transwomen are lumped together as "transgender" in many situations, their experiences do not mirror one another. Still, we find these comparisons to be fruitful for our analyses for several reasons. First, while the selection of transmen in the first case study was purposive, the focus on transwomen in the second case study was not. The lack

of any documented incidents involving heterosexual cisgender women killing transmen suggests that the tactics used to police gender and sexual transgressions are themselves gendered—a point we develop in our analysis. Second, this comparison reveals how responses to transmen and transwomen vary across public and private sexualized/sexual relationships. This comparison illuminates how criteria for membership in gender categories differ in sexual, as compared to non-sexual, situations.

DOING GENDER AND HETERONORMATIVITY IN PUBLIC RELATIONSHIPS

Open workplace transitions—situations in which a transgender employee informs her employers that she intends to begin living and working as a man—present an interesting empirical setting for examining how gender and heteronormativity "work" in public relationships. Reactions to this announcement could play out in multiple ways. Transmen could be fired for making a stigmatized identity public, thus neutralizing this potential challenge to the binary gender order. They could experience no change to their workplace experiences. Or they could be repatriated as men by being expected to follow the men's dress and behavioral codes and being moved into new jobs or positions that employers see as better suited to masculine abilities and interests.

The experiences of transmen in both Texas and California are largely consistent: They are incorporated into men's jobs and men's workplace cultures. These incorporations are not seamless, however. When transmen's (hetero)sexuality is raised at work, heterosexual men often encourage an open display of shared sexual desire for women—emphasizing their new sameness with transmen. Heterosexual women, in contrast, police the boundaries of who can be counted as a man—negating their new "oppositeness" with transmen. In sexualized situations, transmen's masculinity is simultaneously reinforced—as men frame them as heterosexual men—and challenged—as women position them as homosexual women.

Reaffirming "Natural" Gender Difference

Employers and coworkers find new ways to do gender "naturally" by incorporating transmen into the workplace as one of the guys. On an organizational level, some employers rehire transmen as men, institutionally sanctioning their transition into a man's career track. Preston received a directive from his boss that he should adopt the men's dress code at his blue-collar job, which meant the removal of a single earring he had worn unproblematically for years as a woman in the same workplace. John's employer in his service industry job required that he retain the women's uniform until he started testosterone—at which point he could legitimately don a men's uniform. Employers also issue top-down dictates that give transmen access to men's restrooms and lockers and ask coworkers to change names and pronouns with their transgender colleague. These employer responses show how gender boundaries can shift—former women can be accepted as men—without a change in structural gender relations or organizational policies.

When transmen receive top-down support for their workplace transitions, men and women coworkers often show their adherence to these dictates by enlisting transmen into masculine "gender rituals" (Goffman 1977). For the first few weeks of Jake's transition, heterosexual men colleagues began signaling in an obvious way that they were treating him like a guy:

A lot of my male colleagues started kind of like slapping me on the back [laughs]. But I think it was with more force than they probably slapped each other on the back. . . . And it was not that I had gained access to "male privilege" but they were trying to affirm to me that they saw me as a male. . . . That was the way they were going to be supportive of me as a guy, or something of the sort [laughs].

The awkwardness of these backslaps illustrates his colleagues' own hyper-awareness of trying to do gender with someone who is becoming a man. Jake felt normalized by this incorporation and made frequent references to himself as a *trans*man to disrupt his colleagues' attempts to naturalize his transition.

Women also engage transmen in heterosocial gender rituals, such as doing heavy lifting around the office. The change is so rapid that many transmen are, at first, not sure how to make sense of these new expectations. Kelly, who transitioned in a semiprofessional job, notes,

Before [transition] no one asked me to do anything really and then [after], this one teacher, she's like, "Can you hang this up? Can you move this for me?" . . . Like

if anything needed to be done in this room, it was me. Like she was just, "Male? Okay you do it." That took some adjusting. I thought she was picking on me.

Ken describes a similar experience in his semiprofessional workplace. While his coworkers were slow to adopt masculine pronouns with him, his women coworkers did enlist him in carrying heavy items to the basement and unloading boxes. This enlistment into heterosocial gender rituals suggests that while open transitions might make gender trouble for coworkers who struggle with how they should treat their transgender colleague, this disruption does not make them reconsider the naturalness of the gender binary. Treating transmen as men gives them their "rightful" place in the dichotomy—and allows schemas about men and women's natural differences to go unchanged.

Interviews with coworkers illuminate how they grapple with this potential breach to their ideas about gender. Heterosexual men emphasized that if they were not discussing the transition in an interview, it would not cross their minds. They position this transition from female to male as "natural" for a masculine woman. One man in a blue-collar job says,

I chuckle to myself every now and then, how just natural it seems. [It] took a while for the pronouns to catch on but now it just comes out naturally. It just seems like a natural fit. It just seems like my inclination or my intuition at the beginning was correct; it just seemed, like, natural that she should go through with something like this because she was gonna be more comfortable as a man than as a woman.

Another man says he was unsurprised about the transition because his colleague "was an unattractive woman." As many transmen move from being masculine (e.g., gender nonconforming) women to gender-conforming men, their decisions to transition can be seen as a natural fit for someone who was viewed as doing femininity unsuccessfully. Many transmen also move from being gender nonconforming women who are assumed to be lesbians to gender-conforming men who are assumed to be heterosexual—a move that coworkers can justify as confirmation of the naturalness and desirability of a heteronormative gender system.

Women coworkers express more hesitation about seeing transmen as men. Several women discuss their concern about what they perceive as mismatch between their colleague's gender presentation—male—and his biological sex—female. One woman who works with a transman in a female-dominated job says,

It's a hard thing for me [to say I see him as a man]. . . . On some levels yes, but in other ways, no. If I think about it, I start thinking about his body. I feel that his body would be different than any man that I would know. . . . When I think a lot about it, I definitely think about his body and what's happened to it. I wouldn't think of him as I would another male friend.

Another woman in a blue collar job makes a similar comment, saying,

I can't say yes [I see him as a man] but I can't really say no. The appearance has changed. You know . . . he always looked like a guy . . . dressed like a guy . . . and what's changed is that his hair is cut short. But I can't really say I accept him as a guy.

These comments demonstrate the power of gender attributions as, on one hand, these women see their colleagues as men because they look like men. However, when they think too much about their bodies—what they see as an authentic and unchangeable sexed reality—they are hesitant to include them in the category of man.

Yet, showing the power of institutionally supported public relationships, many coworkers will validate transmen's new social identities as men regardless of their personal acceptance of this identity—in effect "passing" as supportive colleagues. While sociologists have positioned transgender people as gender over-achievers who attempt to be 120 percent male or female (see Garfinkel 1967), coworkers' adherence to these gender rituals suggests that in these public interactions, gender normals may have more anxiety about how gender *should* be done than the person who is transitioning. Whether or not this adherence reflects authentic support for transmen *as men*, it maintains the idea of natural gender differences that create "opposite" personality types with different abilities and interests.

Gendered Responses to Heterosexuality

The incorporation of transmen as one of the guys at work is not seamless. Where this incorporation comes apart highlights the connection between doing gender and maintaining heteronormativity. While the workplace often is framed as nonsexual, interactions can become sexualized, as in sex talk and sexual banter; and/or sexual, in ways both consensual and nonconsensual (Williams, Giuffre, and Dellinger 1999). Heterosexual women's perception of a mismatch between their colleague's biological sex and gender identity comes to the forefront in (hetero) sexualized interactions. Women can accept transmen as men when doing masculine roles at work—heavy lifting, killing spiders—but not in sexualized relationships with female-bodied people. Illustrating this, Preston remembers telling a woman coworker that he had a new girlfriend. He was shocked when she yelled across the room, "How do you have sex if you don't have a dick?" Her comment shows that in his coworker's mind, Preston does not have the essential signifier of manhood and therefore cannot *really* have penis-vagina intercourse—the hallmark of heterosexuality.

In sexualized situations, women frame transmen as deceptive—tricking women into seemingly heterosexual relationships without the necessary biological marker of manhood. At a volunteer organization Peter participated in for many years, before and after his transition, he developed a flirtatious relationship with a woman volunteer. He says, "We were flirting a bit and someone noticed. She pulled me aside and said, 'Does she know about you? I am concerned she doesn't know about you. What is going on between you two? This is totally inappropriate.'" Having known his co-volunteers for several years, he was surprised to realize they saw him as suspicious and threatening. Chris encountered a similar experience in his first job as a man. Hired as a man, he planned not to come out as transgender at work. However, his transition became public knowledge when a high school colleague recognized him. While she originally agreed not to tell anyone, she changed her mind. He says, "So basically for the first time in my life—I was nineteen—I had girls *like* like me, you know. And I think what happened was [this former classmate] was thinking, 'Oh that's sick, I better warn them.'" While his coworkers continued to treat him as a man in nonsexual interactions, a woman he had set up a date with cancelled. He had no further romantic interest shown to him by women at that job. His experience shows how women's acceptance of transmen's gender can be negated in sexualized interactions. In these situations, women regender transmen as biological females passing as men in an attempt to trick women into homosexuality.

Conversely, rather than policing transmen's heterosexuality, heterosexual men encourage it by engaging them in sex talk about women. Kelly notes,

I definitely notice that the guys . . . they will say stuff to me that I know they wouldn't have said before [when I was working as a female]. . . . One guy, recently we were talking and he was talking about his girlfriend and he's like, "I go home and work it [have sex] for exercise."

He adds that this same coworker went out of his way to avoid him before his transition. The coworker later told Kelly that he was uncomfortable with gays and lesbians. This disclosure reflects heteronormativity, as becoming a presumably heterosexual man can be viewed more positively than being a lesbian. While some transmen personally identify as gay or queer men, heteronormativity ensures that their coworkers imagine they are transitioning to become heterosexual men. These responses show that when an open transition has employer support, heterosexual men are willing in many cases to relate to transmen they see as heterosexual on the basis of shared sexual desire for women. Illustrating this, one coworker describes taking his transman colleague to Hooters because they both enjoy looking at "scantily clad women."

As heteronormativity requires men to ignore other men's bodies, heterosexual men do masculinity, and simultaneously uphold their heterosexuality, by ignoring the bodily details of transmen's transitions. Cisgender men are hesitant to admit any interest in genital surgery. Those who did ask questions about genital surgery in their interview qualified that this interest was purely "scientific," rather than prurient. Ignoring genitalia gives transmen a "sameness" with heterosexual men at work. This sameness allows cisgender men to enlist transmen into discussions of heterosexuality that never go beyond the theoretical. Heterosexual women, in contrast, now have an "oppositeness" with transmen, making them and other women at work part of a potential dating pool. This transition moves transmen's heterosexuality closer to practice than theory—a move that accounts for the reactive, policing steps to thwart transmen's heterosexuality by placing emphasis on genitalia. Perhaps drawing on their own surprise at learning that someone who looks like a man might not have a penis, they want to alert other women who could be "tricked" into homosexuality.

These experiences illustrate that while both cisgender men and women treat transmen as socially male in nonsexualized public interactions, there are gender differences in responses to sexualized public interactions. In these situations, men gender transmen as heterosexually male on the basis of gender presentation, while women gender them as homosexually female on the basis of biological sex. When gender category and heterosexual authenticity are policed through reference to genitalia, the choice of targets is gendered. Further illustrating this, heterosexual cisgender men often engage in policing and harassing behaviors toward transwomen's public workplace transitions (Schilt 2009; Schilt and Connell 2007). This difference suggests that cisgender people react more strongly toward transgender people who become the "opposite gender" but are presumed to still be the "same sex," as they—and their entire gender—now run the risk of unwittingly engaging in homosexuality. Yet the public context of these relationships still mediates the methods used to enforce heteronormativity. As the next section shows, in private, sexual relationships, men show more extreme reactions.

DOING GENDER AND HETERONORMATIVITY IN PRIVATE RELATIONSHIPS

Examining media accounts of killings of transgender people provides important insight into the beliefs that maintain gender inequality and heteronormativity. Journalists frame a minority of the murders of transpeople in the United States between 1990 and 2005 as caused by reasons wholly, or mostly, unrelated to their membership in the group "transgender." These sorts of cases—the result of personal conflict, random violence, or membership in categories such as "woman" or "person of color"—account for about 33 percent of transgender homicides in which reporters provide a cause for the violence. Journalists attribute the other 67 percent to reasons more closely related to being transgender. Articles describe homophobia or transphobia as the primary cause of violence in only 6 percent of the total cases, while in the majority of cases, 56 percent, journalists depict violence as resulting from private, sexual interactions in which the perpetrator feels "tricked" into homosexuality by "gender deceivers." An additional 5 percent depict the murder as resulting from cisgender men defending themselves from unwanted sexual advances.

As with reactions to public, sexualized relationships, the response patterns in these private, sexual interactions are gendered. Almost ninety-five percent of reported cases involve a cisgender man murdering a transwoman, while no articles describe a cisgender woman killing a transman.[2] The gendered pattern of violence represented in mainstream news stories echoes, although significantly exceeds, that for all reported homicides in the United States, as 65.3 percent involve a male offender and male victim and 2.4 percent of cases are females killing females (Bureau of Justice Statistics 2007). While reports of homicides, whether they be from the Bureau of Justice Statistics or transgender activists and the mainstream news, are unlikely to include every murder in the United States, the extremity of the gender gap in identified fatal violence against transgender people demonstrates that, while doing masculinity and doing violence are socially linked, the combined threat to both gender and sexuality posed by transgender bodies in private, sexual relationships can result in hypergendered responses by cisgender men.

Gender and Heterosexuality in Private

Most of the transgender homicides covered in the mainstream news media occur in what can be understood as private relationships, such as those between lovers, family members, friends, acquaintances, and strangers met on the street or in bars; or outside the realm of socially authorized public relationships, such as people engaged in illegal activities like prostitution and drug dealing. Of the 136 cases in which journalists identify the relationship between the perpetrator and victim, only one is said to be a relationship between coworkers, and it occurs far outside the realm of legally sanctioned working relationships—an MtF prostitute portrayed as killing her transsexual madam in an argument over money (Grace 2003). Similarly, although many of these murders occurred in public spaces, such as in parks and on the street, they rarely took place within the more regulated spaces of retail stores or other places of business.

Almost two-thirds of the reported fatal violence in these private interactions transpired within sexual relationships of short duration, such as the victim and perpetrator engaging in a physical sexual encounter for the first time, or the perpetrator or victim propositioning the other for a sexual relationship (either with or without the exchange of money). Many articles describe the perpetrators and victims as strangers or very recent acquaintances. In these narratives, cisgender men approach or are approached by a woman for sex and the pair immediately go to a place where they can engage in such an encounter. Upon becoming sexual, the cisgender man discovers the transwoman's penis and reacts with physical violence. Articles explain the resulting violence as caused by the perpetrators feeling deceived by the transwomen about their "true gender" and "tricked" into a homosexual encounter.

News articles described the murder of Chrissey Johnson (nee Marvin Johnson) in such a way:

Man charged in death of transvestite

A Baltimore man has been arrested for killing a 29-year-old man whom he had brought home believing the victim was a woman. The police said that Allen E. Horton, 22, went into a rage Saturday night when he discovered Marvin Johnson, who was dressed as a woman, was really a man, a police spokesman said yesterday. (*Washington Times* 1993)

News coverage frames fatal sexual encounters between cisgender men and transwomen sex workers similarly, as this description of the murder of Jesse Santiago (nee Jesus) shows:

Man Kills Transvestite, Then Himself, Police Say

A bizarre case of mistaken sexual identity ended in the fatal screwdriver stabbing of a transvestite Bronx prostitute and the suicide of his killer early yesterday, police said. It began late Friday night when 47-year-old Augustin Rosado propositioned what he believed was a female prostitute in the University Heights section. The two headed to Rosado's fourth-floor furnished room in a transient hotel on Cresten Avenue, police said. Once inside, Rosado discovered the prostitute was a male transvestite and flew into a rage, stabbing the unidentified 30-year-old man repeatedly with a screwdriver and hitting him with a metal pipe, police said . . . . A detective working on the case said it is nearly impossible to tell on sight which prostitutes plying their trade in the area are men and which are women. "Some of these transvestites look sexier than some women," he said. "I could see how someone could be surprised." (Jamieson 1992)

The "deception" in these frames is a dual one; articles portray victims as lying both about their gender and about their sexual orientation. Showing how the sexual context of the relationship matters, reporters never use the deception frame for cases in which there has been no sexual interaction between the transgender person and a cisgender person. This lack of the deception frame in these nonsexual situations highlights the salience of genitalia as the key determiner of gender and sexual identity in sexual situations.

Gender "Deception" and the Precariousness of (Male) Heterosexuality

Accusations of false doings of gender in sexual interactions dominate the news coverage of the murder of transwomen by cisgender men through phrases such as "secret," "lied," "tricked," "misled," "avoid detection," "posed as a woman," "true gender," "really a woman," "true identity," "double life," "fooled," "deceit," "pretended," "masquerade," and "gender secret." One typical news story opened,

> Gregory Johnson's friends and a cousin think they know why someone shot the 17-year-old boy and his 18-year-old friend, and then left their bodies to burn beyond recognition inside a blazing SUV. Rage. Johnson, they say, was a sweet and funny young man who liked to dress as a woman, fooling his dates. They suspect one of them became enraged upon learning the truth and killed Johnson and his female friend. (Horne and Spalding 2003)

Journalists, and the people they quote, say that transwomen victims mis-portrayed their gender through the clothing they wore, the names they used, and often the timbre of their voices. To utilize gender deception as the explanation for violence requires an underlying conception of a true gender that the victim intentionally did not display to the perpetrator. Indeed, the phrase "true gender" is often used in these articles, and the idea of a truth of gender is constructed using other terms; for example, reporters often say that victims had a "gender secret" and were "actually" or "really" another gender. "True gender" in these stories functions both as a synonym for "sex" as well as a reference to the ways that journalists and perpetrators feel that the victims *should* have been doing gender. Although these victims presented as women socially, in the minds of the journalists and perpetrators, they

were *really* men for the purposes of sexual interactions because they had penises. Descriptions of the murder of MtF Gwen Araujo, who had not had genital surgery, illustrate this point, as journalists regularly defined her "true gender" as male.

Passion Blamed for Teen's Slaying: Client's discovery of victim's true gender led to chaos, attorney for one murder suspect says

A defense attorney for one of three men charged with killing a transgender teen described his client Thursday as a quiet, even-tempered man caught up by ungovernable passions the night he discovered he had unwittingly had sex with a man. "What followed was absolute pandemonium and chaos," said attorney Michael Thorman, who described the killing as "classic manslaughter," not murder. . . . The four men met Araujo, whom they knew as "Lida," in the summer of 2002. Merel and Magidson, according to Nabors, had sex with Araujo, but became suspicious about the teen's gender after comparing notes. On Oct. 3, 2002, the men confronted Araujo at Merel's house in Newark, a San Francisco suburb, and demanded: "Are you a woman or a man?" Another woman at the house found out the truth by grabbing Araujo's genitals. Uproar ensued. The 17-year-old Araujo was punched, choked, hit with a skillet, kneed in the face, tied up and strangled. Araujo was buried in a remote area near Lake Tahoe; about two weeks later Nabors led police to the victim's body. (Associated Press 2004)

In sexual interactions such as this one, "true gender" is often determined by touching the genitals, showing that truth here is determined by bodily, rather than social, criteria. In sexual relationships, biological sex and social gender are expected to "match." As a result, women with penises are seen as sexual deceivers.

We can see the importance of the shape of genitals, rather than transgender status, in determining "true gender" by comparing journalists' explanations of murders of transwomen who have and have not had genital surgery. Between 1990 and 2005, the mainstream news reported on the murder of six transwomen who had had genital surgery. None of them were said to have been killed because they "deceived" their sexual partner about their "true gender." Journalists do not use the deception frame to explain the murder of postoperative transwomen, as they possess the "correct" biological credentials to do gender as women in sexual interactions. In contrast, journalists portray transwomen who have not had genital surgery as being truly men and, as such, engaging in a double deception—about both their gender and sexual orientation—if they have sex with heterosexual men. Shawn Wilson assumed that Robert Gibson must be a homosexual after discovering Gibson's male genitalia during a sexual encounter:

Man to stand trial in stabbing death of female impersonator

A 21-year-old man was ordered yesterday to stand trial on a murder charge in the stabbing death of an El Cajon hairdresser who moonlighted as a female impersonator. Shawn Keith Wilson told police after his arrest that he allowed 32-year-old Robert Howard Gibson to perform a sex act on him, then "tripped out" when he realized that Gibson was a man. Gibson was stabbed 25 times late on the night of July 30. . . . Shortly after Wilson's arrest, [Wilson's friend, Laree] Stemen told detectives that Wilson had told her that a homosexual "tried to rape him." (Wolf 1998)

Transwomen who desire men are assumed to be gay men because they have penises and want to engage in sex with other people with penises. Without the biological credentials to prove their desire as heterosexual, they are presumed to be homosexual.

In many of these murder cases, journalists and perpetrators portray transwomen as deceptive gay men, seeking to trick innocent heterosexual men into homosexuality. This "trick" carries a heavy social weight through what we term the "one-act rule of homosexuality." Similar to the idea that anyone with one drop of black blood is black (Davis 1991), both straight and gay people often believe that engaging in sexual encounters with people of the same sex demonstrates an innate, previously hidden, homosexuality, no matter what sexual identity one may personally avow (Ward 2006). In interviews and court testimony, the accused killers of Gwen Araujo articulate a belief that for a man to have sex with a person who has male-shaped genitals makes him homosexual, even if he were unaware of those genitals at the time. Mainstream news stories describe one of the convicted killers as starting to cry and repeating "I can't be gay" over and over again when the group of men "discovered" that Gwen Araujo had testicles. The punishment for

attempting to "trick" someone into homosexuality is death—the only way to literally destroy the evidence of the violation of the one-act rule. Because the "true gender" for sexual encounters is determined by genital shape, self-identity is not sufficient for deciding either gender or sexuality. Thus, heterosexual men are constantly at risk of losing their claim to heterosexual status—just as transwomen are at risk for losing their claim to their chosen gender identity—because both gender and sexuality are produced in interaction. Individuals alone cannot determine their gender or sexuality and must, instead, prove them through fulfilling the appropriate criteria, including having the "right" genitals and never desiring someone with the "wrong" genitals.

The belief that gender deception in a sexual relationship would result in fatal violence is so culturally resonant that, even in cases where there is evidence that the perpetrator knew the victim was transgender prior to the sexual act, many people involved in the case, including journalists and police officers, still use the deception frame.[3] In one such case, that of the murder of Chanelle Pickett (nee Roman Pickett) by William Palmer in 1995, Palmer claimed that he only discovered that Pickett had male genitals once they were engaged in sex. Countering this, a few news articles include quotes from friends of Pickett's who said that Palmer was a regular at transgender hangouts and intentionally pursued transwomen who had not had genital surgeries. Despite these claims, journalists usually explain the murder as resulting from the discovery of Pickett's gender. During the trial, both framings of the violence were told, and the jury found the deception narrative more convincing, convicting Palmer of only assault and battery and sentencing him to two years in jail. Following the logics of heteronormativity and gender inequality, people often ignore counterevidence in these cases and accept the violence as justified.

In mainstream news media portrayals, when faced with the discovery of the transgender status of a sexual partner, men and women respond differently. We cannot account for this gap by only attending to questions of gender. Instead, we must look to the intersections of gender and sexuality. When heterosexual cisgender men and women discover that their sexual partner is transgender, this new information could challenge their claims to heterosexuality, as well as to their gender category of choice. As we saw with the cases of cisgender men, their masculinity is challenged as they feel "raped" and feminized through their connection to homosexuality. To repair this breach, they respond with violence—a masculine-coded act. Because of the interconnectedness of gender and sexuality, cisgender men reclaim their heterosexuality by emphasizing their masculinity. News articles described how when Jose Merel feared that his sexual contact with Gwen Araujo would mark him as gay, his friend Nicole Brown attempted to sooth[e] him through references to his masculinity, saying, "This is not your fault. You were a football player." By highlighting his participation in a masculine sport, she tries to cleanse him of homosexual stigma.

But while cisgender men can repair the sexuality breach by emphasizing masculinity through violence, cisgender women cannot use the same tactic. To do violence and, thus, do masculinity would further destabilize women's claims to both femininity and heterosexuality. Given that masculine behavior in women is associated with lesbianism, cisgender women who wish to emphasize heterosexuality must respond differently—either ending the relationship or accepting their partner in one way or another. This gender difference can be seen clearly in portrayals of the life of Brandon Teena. Before he was killed by two men enraged by his sexual encounters with the local women, he had several heterosexually identified cisgender women partners "discover" his "true gender," but not one responded with fatal violence. Thus, men, not women, can use violence to repair the breach in gender and the challenge to their sexuality caused by the discovery of transgender status in private, casual sexual relationships. The extremity of men's responses shows the depth of the threat of trans-gender bodies to heteronormativity within sexual situations and the need to neutralize that threat through hypergendered reactions.

CONCLUSION

This [reading] examines how responses by gender normals to transmen and transwomen demonstrate the ways gender and (hetero)sexuality are interrelated. The sex/gender/sexuality system rests on the belief that there are two, and only two, opposite sexes, determined by biology and signaled primarily by the shape of genitals. The idea of sexual difference naturalizes sexual interactions between "opposite" bodies; within

this logic it seems obvious, to paraphrase a slang phrase, to "insert tab A into slot B." Sex between two tabs or two slots, in contrast, is unnatural. Similarly, this sex/gender/sexuality system rests on the belief that gendered behavior, (hetero)sexual identity, and social roles flow naturally from biological sex, creating attraction between two opposite personalities. This belief maintains gender inequality, as "opposites"—bodies, genders, sexes—cannot be expected to fulfill the same social roles and, so, cannot receive the same resources.

The case studies in this [reading] improve our understandings of the workings of a heteronormative gender system predicated on people being clearly categorized as one of two sexes. Much of the literature on violence against transpeople points to gender norm transgression as the cause of violence and assumes that all transgender people are at risk for the same type of violence across social situations. Our two studies complicate this explanation. In public interactions not coded as sexual, self-identity and gender presentation can be sufficient to place someone in his or her gender category of choice—particularly in situations where this new identity is supported by people in authority positions. This adherence reflects the accountability to situational norms in public interactions (Goffman 1966). Highlighting the importance of these public norms, when open workplace transitions do not receive top-down support, cisgender men and women are more likely to express resistance to their transgender colleague (Schilt 2009)—even when they have worked unproblematically for many years with their transgender colleague prior to his or her transition. This resistance is heightened when public interactions become sexualized. In these situations, responses that police heterosexuality are, in themselves, gendered: cisgender women regulate transmen's sexualized behaviors through talk and gossip, whereas cisgender men police transwomen through aggressive verbal harassment (Schilt 2009; Schilt and Connell 2007).

Examining gender normals' reactions to private, sexual interactions with transmen and transwomen presents something of a paradox, however. The majority of cases in the textual analysis present cisgender men murdering transwomen after learning that their sexual partner is transgender. Yet although surely interactions occur in which cisgender women "discover" that the transmen with whom they have been sexually intimate were assigned female at birth, there were no reported cases of cisgender women reacting violently to such a discovery. The gender gap in use of violence to repair the breach in gender and (hetero)sexuality occurs because violence can be used to claim masculine, but not feminine, hetero-sexuality. Although the one-act rule of homosexuality may well apply equally to men and women, a woman cannot undo the violation by responding with violence.

The extremity of the violence cisgender men use to punish transwomen in private, sexual situations high-lights gender inequality in the forms of the cultural devaluation of femininity, homosexuality, and, partic-ularly, males choosing to take on characteristics coded as feminine. The violent reactions from men illustrate the real-life outcomes of gender socialization that requires men to demonstrate their own masculinity and hetero-sexuality through the devaluation and ridi-cule of male homosexuality and any presentations—by men or by women—of femininity (Hennen 2008; Pascoe 2007). Similarly, the intense harassment of transwomen by cisgender men in the workplace derives from the valuation of masculinity over femi-ninity. Whereas transmen may face less censure because they are adopting the socially respected traits of masculinity, transwomen are understood as com-mitting the double sin of both abandoning masculinity and choosing femininity.

These gender differences further suggest the importance of the context of interactions (nonsexual/sexualized/sexual; public/private). Sexual and non-sexual situations require different degrees of "oppo-siteness." Heterosexual interactions entail both opposite genitals as well as opposite gendered behav-ior. By contrast, nonsexual heterosocial interactions only require opposite gendered behavior, so self-identity can be accepted without biological creden-tials. As genitals are not visible in nonsexual situations, and are not needed to engage in any of the expected behaviors of the interaction, they are not required to establish membership in a gender cate-gory for nonsexual relationships. By contrast, genitals are a central part of the social interaction of a sexual encounter, and so are used both to determine the gen-ders of the people involved as well as the sexual ori-entation of the encounter. Thus, the criteria for gender membership are different in social versus (hetero)sexual circumstances; only in sexual situations is there a requirement that gender (self-presentation) equals sex (genitals). Accepting transgender people's

self-identity in nonsexual situations does not threaten cisgender people's claims to heterosexual status. Men can be *homosocial* with other men, including those who lack the biological credentials for maleness, without being *homosexual*. In sexualized circum-stances, however, heterosexuality is threatened by the one-act rule of homosexuality. Cisgender men stand to lose not just their sexual identity but also their standing as "real" men.

Illustrating the connection between gender and sexuality, gender normals react most strongly to trans-gender people who become, via gender transitions, part of the "opposite gender." The content of these reactions, however, is mediated by the context of the relationship (public/private) and the degree of sexual-ization of the interaction. In the public context of the workplace, cisgender men and women can incorporate transmen as men into interactions coded as gendered—lifting boxes, backslapping. When interactions become sexualized, however, men emphasize their sameness with transmen while women reject their new opposite-ness. These patterns suggest that when a transgender person is not a potential sexual partner, biological cre-dentials (the "right" genitalia) are not required to claim membership in a gender category. By contrast, when the transgender person is in theory part of a potential pool of sexual partners, the criteria for gender mem-bership becomes much more strict—cultural genitals are no longer enough and biological genitals are a necessity.

Examining the reactions of cisgender people to transgender people helps to illuminate the mecha-nisms that uphold the heteronormative sex/gender/sexuality system and illustrates the lengths to which gender normals will go to maintain a gender/sexual order that occurs "naturally." However, it would be a mistake to assume cisgender sexual desire for trans-gender bodies "must be paid for in blood," as Halberstam (2005) has argued. Some cisgender people—men, women, gay, straight, bisexual, pansexual—seek sex-ual and romantic partnerships with people they know to be transgender. Under a heternormative system, this open desire for transgender bodies typically is framed as pathological or fetishistic (Serano 2009). Future research should examine the purposeful sexual and romantic relationships between cisgender and trans-gender people outside of this pathological frame, as these relationships have the potential to create (hetero)sexual trouble within a heteronormative gender system.

NOTES

1. *Cis* is the Latin prefix for "on the same side." It compliments *trans,* the prefix for "across" or "over." "Cisgender" replaces the terms "nontransgender" or "bio man/bio woman" to refer to individuals who have a match between the gender they were assigned at birth, their bodies, and their personal identity.

2. Of the reported murders in which both the gender of the victim and perpetrator were known, 94.9 percent (149 of 157 cases) were instances of cisgender men killing transwomen. The remaining cases included three in which a cisgender woman killed a transwoman (1.91 percent), two in which a transwoman killed another transwoman (1.27

percent), and three in which one or more cisgender men killed a transman (1.91 percent).

3. Perpetrators may claim deception, even when none occurred, to try to reduce both legal and social castigation. As desire for opposite gender transgender bodies is culturally understood as *homosexual* desire, following the belief that genitalia determine gender in sexual interactions, perpetrators may claim they were deceived to try to cleanse themselves of the stigma from the one-act rule of homosexuality. They may also make such a claim to attempt to reduce criminal charges from homicide to manslaughter.

REFERENCES

Associated Press. 2004. Passion blamed for teen's slaying: client's discovery of victim's true gender led to chaos, attorney for one murder suspect says. *Los Angeles Times,* 16 April.

Bettcher, Talia. 2007. Evil deceivers and make believers: On transphobic violence and the politics of illusion. *Hypatia* 22:45–62.

Bureau of Justice Statistics. 2007. Homicide trends in the U.S.: Trends by gender. http://www.ojp.usdoj.gov/bjs/homicide/gender.htm (accessed 7 March, 2009).

Butler, Judith. 1989. *Gender trouble: Feminism and the subversion of identity.* New York: Routledge.

Cameron, Deborah, and Don Kulick. 2003. *Language and sexuality.* Cambridge: Cambridge University Press.

Connell, R. W. 1987. *Gender & power.* Berkeley: University of California Press.

Davis, Floyd James. 1991. *Who is Black? One nation's definition.* University Park: Pennsylvania State University Press.

Fenstermaker, Sarah, Candace West, and Don Zimmerman. 2002. Gender inequality: New conceptual terrain. In *Doing gender, doing difference,* edited by Sarah Fenstermaker and Candace West, 25–40. New York: Routledge.

Franklin, Karen. 2000. Antigay behaviors among young adults: Prevalence, patterns and motivators in a noncriminal population. *Journal of Interpersonal Violence* 15:339–62.

Garfinkel, Harold. 1967. *Studies in ethnomethodology.* Englewood Cliffs, NJ: Prentice Hall.

Goffman, Erving. 1966. *Behavior in public places. On the social organization of groups.* New York: Free Press.

———. 1977. The arrangement between the sexes. *Theory & Society* 4 (3): 301–31.

Grace, Melissa. 2003. Nabbed in tricky transsexual slay. *Daily News* (New York), 21 May.

Halberstam, Judith. 2005. *In a queer time and place: Transgender bodies, sub-cultural lives.* New York: New York University Press.

Hennen, Peter. 2008. *Faeries, bears, and leathermen: Men in community queering the masculine.* Chicago: University of Chicago Press.

Horne, Terry, and Tom Spalding. 2003. Dating habits may have led to teen's death. *Indianapolis Star,* 26 July.

Ingraham, Chrys. 1994. The heterosexual imaginary: Feminist sociology and theories of gender. *Sociological Theory* 12:203–19.

Jamieson, Wendell. 1992. Man kills transvestite, then himself, police say. *Newsday* (Melville, NY), 9 February.

Kessler, Suzanne, and Wendy McKenna. 1978. *Gender: An ethnomethodological approach.* Chicago: University of Chicago Press.

Kitzinger, Celia. 2005. Heteronormativity in action: Reproducing the heterosexual nuclear family in after-hours medical calls. *Social Problems* 52 (4): 477–98.

MacKinnon, Catherine. 1982. Feminism, Marxism, method and the state: An agenda for theory. *Signs: Journal of Women in Culture and Society* 7 (13): 515–44.

Pascoe, C. J. 2007. *Dude, you're a fag: Masculinity and sexuality in high school.* Berkeley: University of California Press.

Rich, Adrienne. 1980. Compulsory heterosexuality and lesbian existence. *Signs: Journal of Women in Culture and Society* 5 (4): 631–60.

Schilt, Kristen. 2009. (Trans)gender at work: The persistence of gender inequality. Manuscript.

Schilt, Kristen, and Catherine Connell. 2007. Do workplace gender transitions make gender trouble? *Gender, Work and Organization* 14 (6): 596–618.

Schippers, Mimi. 2007. Recovering the feminine other: Masculinity, femininity, and gender hegemony. *Theory & Society* 36 (1): 85–102.

Seidman, Steven. 1995. Deconstructing queer theory or the under-theorization of the social and the ethical. In *Social postmodernism: Beyond identity politics,* edited by Linda Nicholson and Steven Seidman. Cambridge: Cambridge University Press.

Serano, Julia. 2009. Why feminists should be concerned with the impending revisions of the DSM. http://www.feministing.com/archives/015254.html (accessed 6 May, 2009).

Ward, Jane. 2006. Straight dude seeks same: Mapping the relationship between sexual identities, Practices, and cultures. In *Sex matters: The sexuality and society reader*, 2nd ed., edited by Mindy Stombler. Needham Heights, Massachusetts: Allyn & Bacon.

Washington Times. 1993. Man charged in death of transvestite. 4 January.

West, Candace, and Don Zimmerman. 1987. Doing gender. *Gender & Society* 1 (2): 125–51.

Williams, Christine, Patti Giuffre, and Kirsten Dellinger. 1999. Sexuality in the workplace. *Annual Review of Sociology* 25:73–93.

Wolf, Leslie. 1998. Man to stand trial in stabbing death of female impersonator. *San Diego Union-Tribune*, 21 October.

SECTION 8

Bodies

It might seem that women's bodies and physical health are biological rather than social matters. However, factors such as access to health care, working conditions, and nutrition are all socially determined and have a big impact on our physical selves. In addition, cultural ideologies about women's bodies affect how we perceive our own bodies, as well as how social institutions regulate women's bodies and health. As with the other aspects of women's lives that we have explored so far, class, race, ethnicity, nationality, sexuality, and ability intersect with gender in shaping the social and cultural forces that affect women's health and physical well-being.

Women's bodies are contested terrain, the subject of struggle over political rights, reproductive rights, health care, and medical research. The ability to control reproduction, to live and work in conditions not injurious to health, and to receive safe, effective, and affordable medical care are central to all women's welfare. In recent decades, feminists have devoted considerable energy to changing public health policy on women's behalf and to increasing research funding for women's health issues.

In the 1970s, a women's health movement developed in the United States as an outgrowth of the feminist and consumer health movements. Women's health advocates criticized and challenged the medical establishment's tendency to view women as abnormal and inherently diseased simply because the female reproductive cycle deviates from that of the male. Today, women across the world are asserting the right to control their own bodies by exposing and resisting the medical abuse of women in forms ranging from forced sterilization and sex selection favoring male children to pharmaceutical experimentation. Women are also increasing their control over their own health care by enhancing access to information and specialized training that allows them more accurately to assess their health care needs and make informed decisions about medical treatment. These movements focused on improving women's health care have recently worked alongside other movements, such as those organizing against AIDS or providing support for women with postpartum depression or working for improved nutrition and preventive health care for the poor in the United States as well as in Third World countries.

This section explores different aspects of the social construction of women's bodies and the experiences of diverse women with body issues. Suzanne Kessler's article in Section 2 ("The Medical Construction of Gender") showed that the medical system actively constructs sex categories. In "The Bare Bones of Sex: Part 1—Sex and Gender," biologist Anne Fausto-Sterling uses the case of bone density and bone health to show how aspects of bodies that are generally considered purely biological are in fact affected in profound ways by cultural factors. Her analysis once again raises questions about the relationship of sex and gender, nature and nurture. Fausto-Sterling proposes a life course systems approach to thinking about bodies and culture. She argues that a consideration of biological and social factors at different stages of life, from the womb to old age, not only helps us to think in a more complex way about sex and gender but also has important consequences for public health policy. What are the factors that make women's bones different from men's? What are some of the examples that Fausto-Sterling gives for how bones are affected by the way we live? What other conditions that we think of as physical might be shaped by culture?

Social contexts shape and create health problems as well. Becky Wangsgaard Thompson also explores the ways that social contexts shape and create health problems. In "'A Way Outa No Way': Eating Problems Among African-American, Latina, and White Women," she argues that compulsive eating, compulsive dieting, anorexia, and bulimia are all coping strategies that women employ in response to sexual abuse, poverty, heterosexism, racism, and "class injuries." Eating problems thus are not just about conforming to a norm of physical appearance but are also a "serious response to injustices." Thompson's article illustrates how examining women's multiple oppressions—race, class, and sex, as well as gender—can alter feminist analyses. What differences does she see between the different groups she examines? What kinds of social change would be necessary to eliminate eating problems?

In "Loose Lips Sink Ships," Simone Weil Davis looks at a different kind of bodily "problem" beginning to gain attention in the United States: droopy labia. She compares women's dissatisfaction with their genitals, leading them to embrace cosmetic surgery, to the motivations behind genital cutting in some African societies. At the same time that she argues against genital surgery of any kind, she challenges us to forego the assumption that U.S. women "choose" such surgeries while African women are helpless victims forced to undergo them. What are the forces that lead women in different contexts to alter their bodies? How does Davis's analysis compare to Debra Gimlin's article in Section 3 about other forms of cosmetic surgery? What do you think about the practice of labiaplasty? About other kinds of genital surgery?

In "Google Babies," France Winddance Twine analyzes the growing practice of gestational surrogacy, in which women carry fetuses whose genetic material comes from egg or sperm donors or from the intended parents. Twine shows how advertisements for surrogates downplay the physical and emotional

work of surrogacy, emphasizing instead financial benefits and altruism. Surrogates can carry babies of different racial or ethnic makeup from themselves, and Twine shows how white surrogates refuse to carry black babies, while women in India, where many surrogates carry babies for American or European parents, frequently carry white babies. White parents may even prefer surrogates from different racial or ethnic groups in order to decrease the likelihood of custody battles. Twine writes, "Surrogacy is an industry that is embedded in racial and class hierarchies," because of the economic and racial differences between surrogates and intended parents. It is also an industry that is regulated very differently in different locations, producing "reproductive tourism" in which parents from countries or states in which it is illegal to hire surrogates travel elsewhere. The title of this article, "Google Babies," highlights the way that people rely on the Internet to find both surrogates and donated eggs or sperm. Twine argues that we need to understand the issue in terms of the historical use of the bodies of women of color for the benefit of whites under slavery, and that we need to consider global economic and racial inequality in efforts to regulate and understand surrogacy.

Twine suggests that access to reproductive technology is also connected to other kinds of reproductive rights such as access to birth control, abortion, and prenatal care. How are these issues connected? How are they shaped by race and by class? Do you agree with Twine about the dynamics of gestational surrogacy? Do you think her argument can be applied to other kinds of reproductive technology, such as IVF (in vitro fertilization) or egg or sperm donation? Do you think surrogacy is a legitimate form of labor for women? Should the practice be regulated or banned, as it is in many countries? Who would benefit and who would suffer as a result?

Karen McCormack, in "Stratified Reproduction and Poor Women's Resistance," uses interviews with women on welfare to explore the ways that their conceptions of what it means to be a good mother both resist dominant notions of welfare mothers as bad mothers and at the same time exacerbate the difficulties of raising children in poverty. The interviews took place at a critical moment, when the 1996 "welfare reform," criticized elsewhere in this volume, made it even more difficult for women in need of public assistance to care for their children. How did these women define the characteristics of a good mother? How did their situations make it difficult to meet those demands? How do they resist stereotypes of the bad welfare mother, and what does McCormack see as the limitations of this resistance? What might be a more fruitful way to think about mothering?

Andrea Smith, in the last article in this section, "Beyond Pro-Choice Versus Pro-Life," questions the approaches of both sides of the abortion debate from the perspective of women of color, poor women, and women with disabilities. Beginning with the complicated responses of Native American women to the

question of whether they were "pro-choice" or "pro-life," Smith challenges the reliance of both groups on criminalization or choice as an approach to issues of reproductive rights. Arguing that neither side attends to the issues of marginalized women, she advocates a more complex response to the barriers to reproductive justice for women both in the United States and abroad. What kinds of approaches might make a difference? How might feminists go about fighting for what Smith calls "reproductive justice"? Do you agree with analysis of both sides of the debate over abortion?

Together, these articles show the diverse ways in which bodies are socially constructed. What might a feminist agenda for the body include?

The Bare Bones of Sex: Part 1—Sex and Gender

First published in 2005

Here are some curious facts about bones. They can tell us about the kinds of physical labor an individual has performed over a lifetime and about sustained physical trauma. They get thinner or thicker (on average in a population) in different historical periods and in response to different colonial regimes (Molleson 1994; Larsen 1998). They can indicate class, race, and sex (or is it gender—wait and see). We can measure their mineral density and whether on average someone is likely to fracture a limb but not whether a particular individual with a particular density will do so. A bone may break more easily even when its mineral density remains constant (Peacock et al. 2002).[1]

Culture shapes bones. For example, urban ultraorthodox Jewish adolescents have lowered physical activity, less exposure to sunlight, and drink less milk than their more secular counterparts. They also have greatly decreased mineral density in the vertebrae of their lower backs, that is, the lumbar vertebrae (Taha et al. 2001). Chinese women who work daily in the fields have increased bone mineral content and density. The degree of increase correlates with the amount of time spent in physical activity (Hu et al. 1994); weightlessness in space flight leads to bone loss (Skerry 2000); gymnastics training in young women ages seventeen to twenty-seven correlates with increased bone density despite bone resorption caused by total lack of menstruation (Robinson et al. 1995). Consider also some recent demographic trends: in Europe during the past thirty years, the number of vertebral fractures has increased three- to fourfold for women and more than fourfold for men (Mosekilde 2000); in some groups the relative proportions of different parts of the skeleton have changed in recent generations.[2]

What are we to make of reports that African Americans have greater peak bone densities than Caucasian

Americans (Aloia et al. 1996; Gilsanz et al. 1998),[3] although this difference may not hold when one compares Africans to British Caucasians (Dibba et al. 1999), or that white women and white men break their hips more often than black women and black men (Kellie and Brody 1990)?[4] How do we interpret reports that Caucasian men have a lifetime fracture risk of 13–25 percent compared with Caucasian women's lifetime risk of 50 percent even though once peak bone mass is attained men and women lose bone at the same rate (Seeman 1997, 1998; NIH Consensus Statement Online 2000)?

Such curious facts raise perplexing questions. Why have bones become more breakable in certain populations? What does it mean to say that a lifestyle behavior such as exercise, diet, drinking, or smoking is a risk factor for osteoporosis? Why do we screen large numbers of women for bone density even though this information does not tell us whether an individual woman will break a bone?[5] Why was a major public policy statement on women's health unable to offer a coherent account of sex (or is it gender?) differences in bone health over the life cycle (Wizemann and Pardue 2001)? Why, if bone fragility is so often considered to be a sex-related trait, do so few studies examine the relationships among childbirth, lactation, and bone development (Sowers 1996; Glock, Shanahan, and McGowan 2000)?

Such curious facts and perplexing questions challenge both feminist and biomedical theory. If "facts" about biology and "facts" about culture are all in a muddle, perhaps the nature/nurture dualism, a mainstay of feminist theory, is not working as it should. Perhaps, too, parsing medical problems into biological (or genetic or hormonal) components in opposition to cultural or lifestyle factors has outlived its usefulness for biomedical theory. I propose that already well-developed dynamic systems theories can provide a better understanding of how social categories act on bone production. Such a framework, especially if it borrows from a second analytic trend called "life course analysis of chronic disease epidemiology" (Kuh and Ben-Shlomo 1997; Ben-Shlomo and Kuh 2002; Kuh and Hardy 2002), can improve our approaches to public health policy, prediction of individual health conditions, and the treatment of individuals with unhealthy bones.[6] To see why we should follow new roads, I consider gender, examining where we—feminist theorists and medical scientists—have recently been. . . .

SEX AND GENDER (AGAIN)

For centuries, scholars, physicians, and lay people in the United States and Western Europe used biological models to explain the different social, legal, and political statuses of men and women and people of different hues.[7] When the feminist second wave burst onto the political arena in the early 1970s, we made the theoretical claim that sex differs from gender and that social institutions produce observed social differences between men and women (Rubin 1975). Feminists assigned biological (especially reproductive) differences to the word *sex* and gave to *gender* all other differences.

"Sex," however, has become the Achilles' heel of 1970s feminism. We relegated it to the domain of biology and medicine, and biologists and medical scientists have spent the past thirty years expanding it into arenas we firmly believed to belong to our ally gender. Hormones, we learn (once more), cause naturally more assertive men to reach the top in the workplace (Dabbs and Dabbs 2001). Rape is a behavior that can be changed only with the greatest difficulty because it is wired somehow into men's brains (Thornhill and Palmer 2001). The relative size of eggs and sperm dictate that men are naturally polygamous and women naturally monogamous. And more. (See Zuk 2002; Travis 2003 for a critique of these claims.) Feminist scholars have two choices in response to this spreading oil spill of sex. Either we can contest each claim, one at a time, doing what Susan Oyama calls "hauling the theoretical body back and forth across the sex/gender border" (2000a, 190), or, as I choose to do here, we can reconsider the 1970s theoretical account of sex and gender.

In thinking about both gender and race, feminists must accept the body as simultaneously composed of genes, hormones, cells, and organs—all of which influence health and behavior—and of culture and history (Verbrugge 1997). As a biologist, I focus on what it might mean to claim that our bodies physically imbibe culture. How does experience shape the very bones that support us?[8] Can we find a way to talk about the body without ceding it to those who would fix it as a naturally determined object existing outside of politics, culture, and social change? This is a project already well under way, not only in feminist theoretical circles but in epidemiology, medical sociology, and anthropology as well.

EMBODIMENT MERGES BIOLOGY AND CULTURE

During the 1990s, feminist reconsideration of the sex/gender problem moved into full swing.[9] Early in the decade Judith Butler argued compellingly for the importance of reclaiming the term *sex* for feminist inquiry but did not delve into the nuts and bolts of how sex and gender materialize in the body. Philosopher Elizabeth Grosz (1994) claimed that sex is neither fixed nor given. In drawing on philosophers such as Maurice Merleau-Ponty (1962) and Alfred North Whitehead ([1929] 1978), Grosz differentiates herself from Butler, holding that materiality is "primordial, not merely the effect of power" (Alcoff 2000, 858). Primordial materiality, however, does not mean that purely biological accounts of human development—no matter how intricate their stories of cellular function—can explain the emergence of lived and differently gendered realities. . . .[10]

Efforts to reincorporate the body into social theory also come from the field of disability studies. Here too an emphasis on the social construction of disability has been enormously productive. Yet several authors have broached the limitations of an exclusively constructivist approach. At least two different types of critique parallel and foreshadow possible feminist approaches to a reconsideration of the body. The first demands that we recognize the material constraints on the disabled body in its variable forms and that we integrate that recognition into theory (Williams and Busby 2000). The second, more radical move is to suggest that "the disabled body changes the process of representation itself" (Siebers 2001, 738). This latter approach offers a rich resource for feminist theories of representation and another possible entry point into the analysis of materiality in actual, lived-in bodies (see also Schriempf 2001).

SEX AND GENDER IN THE WORLD OF BIOLOGY AND MEDICINE

In contrast to these new feminist explorations of the body, in the field of medicine a more limited view of sex differences prevails. Consider a recent report on sex differences issued by the National Institute of Medicine and, more broadly, the professional movement called "gender-based medicine" promoted by the Society for Women's Health Research (SWHR). The SWHR describes itself as "the nation's only not-for-profit organization whose sole mission is to improve the health of women through research. . . . The Society . . . encourages the study of sex differences that may affect the prevention, diagnosis and treatment of disease and promotes the inclusion of women in medical research studies" (Schachter 2001, 29).[11] The society lobbies Congress, sponsors research conferences, and publishes a peer-reviewed academic journal, the *Journal of Women's Health and Gender-Based Medicine*.

A traditional biomedical model of health and disease provides the intellectual framework for the research conferences (Krieger and Zierler 1995). Although much of the research publicized through such conferences seems strictly to deal with *sex* in the 1970s feminist meaning of the word, sex sometimes strays into arenas that traditional feminists claim for gender. Consider a presentation that was said to provide evidence that prenatal testosterone exposure affects which toys little girls and boys prefer to play with (Berenbaum 2001). Working within a 1970s definition of the sex/gender dualism, the author of this study logically extends the term *sex* into the realm of human behavior.

For those familiar with contemporary feminist theory, it might seem that the large number of biological psychologists who follow similar research programs and the biomedical researchers interested in tracking down all of the medically interesting differences between men and women live in a time warp. But members of the feminist medical establishment, that is, those researchers and physicians for whom the activities and programs of the SWHR make eminent sense, see themselves perched on the forward edge of a nascent movement to bring gender equity to the health care system. These feminists work outside of an intellectual milieu that would permit the more revolutionary task proposed by Grosz and Wilson, among others, that of contesting not only "the domination of the body by biological terms but

also [contesting] the terms of biology itself" (Grosz 1994, 20). . . .

Helen Keane and Marsha Rosengarten (2002) have explored the body as a dynamic process out of which gender emerges. . . . I have chosen bone development—an area often accepted as an irrefutable site of sex difference—to examine Keane and Rosengarten's formulation. First, to what extent can we understand bone formation as an effect of culture rather than a passive unfolding of biology? Second, can we use dynamic (developmental) systems to ask better research questions and to formulate better public-health responses to bone disease?

WHY BONES?

Bones are eloquent. Archaeologists read old bone texts to find out how prehistoric peoples lived and worked. A hyperflexed and damaged big toe, a bony growth on the femur, the knee, or the vertebrae, for example, tell bioarchaeologist Theya Molleson that women in a Near Eastern agricultural community routinely ground grain on all fours, grasping a stone grinder with their hands and pushing back and forth on a saddle-shaped stone. The bones of these neolithic people bear evidence of a gendered division of labor, culture, and biology intertwined (Molleson 1994).[12]

. . . Osteoporosis is a condition that reveals all of the problems of defining sex apart from gender. A close reading of the osteoporosis literature further reveals the difficulties of adding the variable of race to the mix (a point I will develop in a forthcoming paper [Fausto-Sterling in preparation]) while also exemplifying the claim that disease states are socially produced, both by rhetoric and measurement (e.g., Petersen 1998 and by the manner in which cultural practice shapes the very bones in our bodies (Krieger and Zierler 1995).

OF BONES AND (WO)MEN

The accuracy of the claim that osteoporosis occurs four times more frequently in women than in men (Glock, Shanahan, and McGowan 2000) depends on how we define osteoporosis, in which human populations (and historical periods) we gather statistics, and what portions of the life cycle we compare. The NIH (2000) defines osteoporosis as a skeletal disorder in which weakened bones increase the risk of fracture. When osteoporosis first wandered onto the medical radar screen, the only signal that a person suffered from it was a bone fracture. Post hoc, a doctor could examine a person with a fracture either [by] using a biopsy to look at the structural competence of the bone or by assessing bone density.

If one looks at lifetime risks for fracture, contemporary Caucasian men range from 13 to 25 percent (Bilezikian, Kurkland, and Rosen 1999) while Caucasian women (who also live longer) have a 50 percent risk. But not all fractures result from osteoporosis. One study looked at fracture incidence in men and women at different ages and found that between the ages of five and forty-five men break more limbs than women.[13] The breaks, however, result from significant work- and sports-related trauma suffered by healthy bones. After the age of fifty, women break their bones more often than men, although after seventy years of age men do their best to catch up (Melton 1988).

The most commonly used medical standard for a diagnosis of osteoporosis no longer depends on broken bones. With the advent of machines called densitometers used to measure bone mineral density (of which more in a moment), the World Health Organization (WHO) developed a new "operational" definition: a woman has osteoporosis if her bone mineral density measures 2.5 times the standard deviation below a peak reference standard for young (white) women. The densitometer manufacturer usually provides the reference data to a screening facility (Seeman 1998), and thus rarely, if ever, do assessments of osteoporosis reflect what Margaret Lock calls "local biologies" (Lock 1998, 39).[14] With the WHO definition, the prevalence of osteoporosis for white women is 18 percent, although there is not necessarily associated pathology, since now, by definition, one can "get" or "have" osteoporosis without ever having a broken bone. The WHO definition is controversial, since bone mineral density (BMD, or grams/cm^2) accounts for approximately 70 percent of bone strength, while the other 30 percent derives from the internal structure of bone and overall bone size. And while women with lower bone density are 2.5 times more likely to experience a hip fracture than women with high bone densities, high risks of hip fracture emerge even in women with high bone densities when five or more other risk factors are present (Cummings et al. 1995).[15] Furthermore, it is hard to know how to apply the criterion, based on a baseline of young white women, to men, children, and members of other ethnic groups. To make matters

worse, there is a lack of standardization between instruments and sites at which measurements are taken.[16] Thus it comes as no surprise that "controversy exists among experts regarding the continued use of this [WHO] diagnostic criterion" (NIH Consensus Statement Online 2000, 3).

There is a complicated mixture at play. First, osteoporosis—whether defined as fractures or bone density—is on the rise, even when the increased age of a population is taken into account (Mosekilde 2000). At the same time, it is hard to assess the danger of osteoporosis, in part due to drug company–sponsored "public awareness" campaigns. For example, in preparation for the sales campaign for its new drug, Fosamax, Merck Pharmaceuticals gave a large osteoporosis education grant to the National Osteoporosis Foundation to educate older women about the dangers of osteoporosis (Tanouye 1995).[17] Merck also directly addressed consumers with television ads contrasting frail, pain-wracked older women with lively, attractive seniors, implying the urgent need for older women to use Fosamax (Fugh-Berman, Pearson, Allina, Zones, Worcester, and Whatley 2002).

Mass marketing a new drug, however, requires more than a public awareness campaign. There must also be an easy, relatively inexpensive method of diagnosis. Here the slippage between the new technological measure—bone density—and the old definition of actual fractures and direct assessment of bone structure looms large. Merck promoted affordable bone density testing even before it put Fosamax on the market. The company bought an equipment manufacturing company and ramped up its production of bone density machines while at the same time helping consumers find screening locations by giving a grant to the National Osteoporosis Foundation to push a toll-free number that consumers (presumably alarmed by the Merck TV ads) could call to find a bone density screener in a locale near them (Tanouye 1995; Fugh-Berman, Pearson, Allina, Zones, Worcester, and Whatley 2002).

The availability of a simple technological measure for osteoporosis also made scientific research easier and cheaper. The majority of the thousands upon thousands of research papers on osteoporosis published in the ten years from 1995 to 2005 use BMD as a proxy for osteoporosis. This is true despite a critical scientific literature that insists that the more expensive volumetric measure (grams/cm^3) more accurately measures bone strength and that knowledge of internal bone structure (bone histomorphometry) provides essential information for understanding the actual risk of fracture (Meunier 1988).[18] The explosion of knowledge about osteoporosis codifies a new disorder, still called osteoporosis but sporting a newly simplified account of bone health and disease.[19] . . .

Weaving together these threads—increasing lifetime risk, new disease definitions, and easier measurement—produces an epistemological transformation in our scientific accounts of bones and why they break. The transformation is driven by a combination of cultural forces (why are fracture rates increasing?) and new technologies generated by drug companies interested in creating new markets, disseminated with the help of market forces drummed up by the self-same drug companies, and aided by consumer health movements, including feminist health organizations such as the Society for Women's Research, which argue that gender-based differences in disease have been too long neglected.

Analyzing bone development within the framework of sex versus gender (nature vs. nurture) makes it difficult to understand bone health in men as well as women. Those trying to decide on a proper standard to measure fracture risk in men (should they use a separate male baseline or the only one available, which is for young, white women?) struggle with this problem of gender standardization (Melton et al. 1998). There are differences between men and women, although osteoporosis in men is vastly understudied. In a bibliography of 2,449 citations of papers from 1995 to 1999 (Glock, Shanahan, and McGowan 2000), only 47 (2 percent) addressed osteoporosis in men. But making sense of patterns of bone health for either or both sexes requires a dynamic systems approach. A basic starting place is to ask the development question.

For instance, we find no difference in bone mineral density in (Caucasian) boys and girls under age sixteen but a higher bone mineral density in males than in females thereafter (Zanchetta et al. 1995). This difference (combined with others that develop during middle adulthood) becomes important later in life, since men and women appear to lose bone at the same rate once they have reached a peak bone mass; those starting the loss phase of the life cycle with more bone in place will be less likely to develop highly breakable bones. Researchers offer different explanations for this divergence. Some note that boys continue to grow for an average of two years longer

than girls (Seeman 1997). The extra growth period strengthens their bones by adding overall size. Others point additionally to hormones, diet, physical activity, and body weight as contributing to the emerging sex (or is it gender?) difference at puberty (Rizzoli and Bonjour 1999).

So differences in bone mineral density between boys and girls emerge during and after puberty, while for both men and women peak bone mass and strength is reached at twenty-five to thirty years of age (Seeman 1999). Vertebral height is the same in men and women, but vertebral width is greater in men. The volume of the inner latticework does not differ in men and women, but the outer layer of bone (periosteum) is thicker in men. Both width and outer thickness strengthen the bone. In general, sex/gender bone differences at peak are in size rather than density (Bilezikian, Kurkland, and Rosen 1999).

This life-cycle analysis reveals three major differences in the pattern of bone growth and loss in men compared with that in women. First, at peak, men have 20 to 30 percent more bone mass and strength than women. Second, following peak, men but not women compensate for bone loss with new increases in vertebral width that continue to strengthen the vertebrae. Over time both men and women lose 70 to 80 percent of bone strength (Mosekilde 2000), but the pattern of loss differs. In men the decline is gradual, barring secondary causes.[20] In women it is gradual until perimenopause, accelerates for several years during and after the menopause, and then resumes a gradual decline.[21] Lis Moskilde (2000) points out that the rush to link menopause to osteoporosis has led to the neglect of two of the three major differences in the pattern of bone growth between men and women. Yet these two factors are specifically linked to physical activity, and thus amenable to change earlier in life.

Indeed, many studies on children and adolescents address the contribution sociocultural components of bone development make to male-female differences that emerge just after puberty. But the overwhelming focus on menopause as the period of the life cycle in which women enter the danger zone steers us away from examining how earlier sociocultural events shape our bones (see Lock 1998). Once menopause enters the picture, the idea that hormones are at the heart of the problem overwhelms other modes of thought.[22] Nor is it clear how hormones affect bone development and loss. In childhood, growth hormone is essential for long bone growth, the gonadal steroids are important for the cessation of bone growth at puberty, and probably both estrogen and testosterone are important for bone health maintenance (Damien, Price, and Lanyon 1998). The details at the cellular level have yet to be understood (Gasperino 1995).[23] . . .

THINKING SYSTEMATICALLY ABOUT BONE

There are better ways to think about gender and the bare bones of sex. One cannot easily separate bone biology from the experiences of individuals growing, living, and dying in particular cultures and historical periods and under different regimens of social gender.[24] But how can we integrate the varied information presented in this essay in a manner that helps us ask better research and public policy questions and that, in posing better questions, allows us to find better answers? By *better*, I mean several things: in terms of the science I want to take more of the "curious facts" about bone into account when responding to public health problems. I favor emphasizing lifelong healthful habits that might prevent or lessen the severity of bone problems in late life, but I would also like us to have a better idea of how to help people whose bones are already thin. What dietary changes, what regimens of exercise and sun exposure, what body mass index work best with which medications? How do the medications we choose work? What unintended effects do they have? Finally, *better* includes an ability to predict outcomes for individuals, based on their particular life histories and genetic makeups, rather than merely making probability statements about large and diverse categories of people.

How can we get there from here? Below, I outline in fairly general form the possibilities of dynamic systems and developmental systems approaches. Such formulations allow us to work with the idea that we are always 100 percent nature and 100 percent nurture. I further point to important theoretical and empirical work currently under way by social scientists who study chronic diseases using a life-course approach. Before turning to the specifics of bone development, let me offer a general introduction to these complementary modes of thought.

. . . Ludwig von Bertalanffy is usually cited as the originator of "general systems theory," a program for studying complex systems such as organisms as whole

entities rather than the traditional approach of reducing the whole to its component parts (Bertalanffy 1969), but the idea of studying developmental outcomes as a result of the combined action of genes and environment began in the early twentieth century before a clear theoretical statement was achieved in the 1940s.[25]

Systems theorists also write about the brain and behavior. D. O. Hebb (1949) linked psychology and physiology by thinking about how functional cellular groups develop in the brain, thus developing a form of systems theory called connectionism. As Esther Thelen and Linda Smith put it, "the connection weights between layers—the response of the network to a particular input—thus depend on the statistical regularities in the network's *history* of experiences" (Thelen and Smith 1998, 580). Thus an organism's current and future behaviors are shaped by past experiences via a direct effect on the strength of connections between cells in the brain.[26]

The varied systems approaches to understanding development share certain features in common. All understand that cells, nervous systems, and whole organisms develop through a process of self-organization rather than according to a preformed set of instructions.[27] The varying relationships among system components lead to change, and new patterns are dynamically stable because the characteristics of the system confer stability. But if the system is sufficiently perturbed, instability ensues and significant fluctuations occur until a new pattern, again dynamically stable, emerges. Bone densities, for example, are often dynamically stable in midlife but destabilize during old age; most medical interventions aim to restabilize the dynamic system that maintains bone density. But we really do not understand how the transition from a stable to an unstable system of bone maintenance occurs.

To address the bare bones of sex, I highlight, in figure 1, seven systems that contribute to bone strength throughout the life cycle.[28] I also describe some of the known interrelationships between them.[29] Each of the seven—physical activity, diet, drugs, bone formation in fetal development, hormones, bone cell metabolism, and biomechanical effects on bone formation—can be analyzed as a complex system in its own right. Bone strength emerges from the interrelated actions of each (and all) of these systems as they act throughout the life cycle. As a first step toward envisioning bone from a systems viewpoint we can construct a

FIGURE I: A LIFE HISTORY–SYSTEMS OVERVIEW OF BONE DEVELOPMENT. (1) PHYSICAL ACTIVITY HAS DIRECT EFFECTS ON BONE CELL RECEPTORS AND INDIRECT EFFECTS BY BUILDING STRONGER MUSCLES, WHICH EXERT PHYSICAL STRAIN ON BONES, THUS STIMULATING BONE SYNTHESIS. (2) PHYSICAL ACTIVITY THAT TAKES PLACE OUTDOORS INVOLVES EXPOSURE TO SUNLIGHT, THUS STIMULATING VITAMIN D SYNTHESIS, PART OF THE HORMONAL SYSTEM REGU-LATING CALCIUM METABOLISM. (3) BIOMECHANICAL STRAIN AFFECTS BONE CELL METABOLISM BY ACTIVATING GENES CONCERNED WITH BONE CELL DIVISION AND BONE (RE)MODELING. (4) HORMONES AFFECT BONE CELL METABOLISM BY ACTIVATING GENES CONCERNED WITH BONE CELL DIVISION, CELL DEATH, BONE (RE)MODELING, AND NEW HORMONE SYNTHESIS.

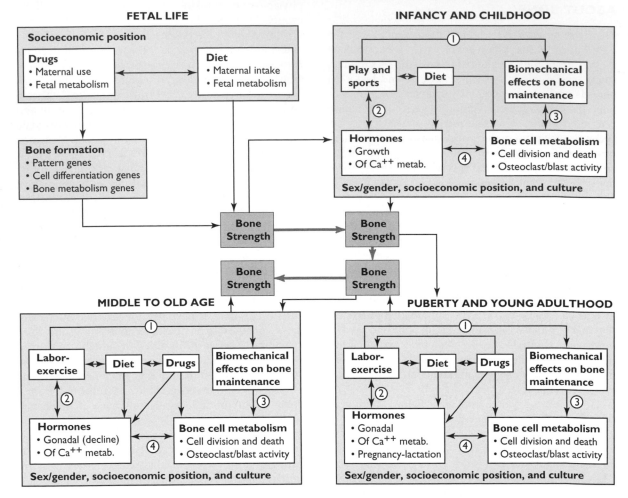

theoretical diagram of their interactions. The diagram in systems approaches can be thought of as a theoretical model, to be tested in part or whole and modified as needed.[30] As ways to describe each component system using numerical proxies become available, the pictorial model can provide the framework for a mathematical model. Figure 1 represents one possible diagram of a life-course systems account of bone development.

This feminist systems account embeds the proposed subsystems within the dimensions of gender, socioeconomic position, and culture.[31] Consider the diet system. Generally, of course, diet is shaped by culture and subculture, including race and ethnicity (Bryant, Cadogan, and Weaver 1999). But gender further influences diet. For example, one study reports that 27 percent of U.S. teenage girls (compared with 10 percent of adolescent boys) who think they weigh the correct amount are nevertheless trying to lose weight (Walsh and Devlin 1998). It may also be true that there are sex/gender differences in basal metabolism rates that influence food intake.

Figure 1 also indicates the cumulative effects of diet on bone formation. Key events may be clustered at certain points in the life cycle.[32] For example, adolescent girls in the United States often diet more and exercise less than during earlier childhood. Diseases such as anorexia nervosa, which have devastating effects on bone development, may also emerge during adolescence. As Yoav Ben-Shlomo and Diana Kuh (2002) point out, such clustering of adverse events is common and may be thought of in terms of "chains of risk" (or benefit). In a life-course approach, prior events set the limits on later ones. If girls and women enter into adulthood with weakened bones, therefore, they can rebuild them, but their peak density may be less than if they had built stronger bones in adolescence.[33] Alternatively, achieving a safe peak bone density might require more sustained and intense work for a person of one history compared with a person of a different history.

Sex/gender, race, class, and culture also differentiate individuals by forms of play in childhood and beyond (Boot et al. 1997), by choices of formal exercise programs, and, in adulthood, by forms of labor, physical and otherwise. In analyzing the system of physical activity one again applies life-course principles by considering that what happens at any one point builds on what has gone before. Important events with regard to bone development may be clustered and interrelated. For both the diet and physical activity systems, it should be possible to design mathematical models based on some measure of bone strength that would incorporate the effects of each of these social systems on bone development throughout the life cycle; once we have plausible models of each system, we can ask questions about their interactions.

The remaining four systems are often considered within the realm of biology, as if biology were separate from culture, although recent work from some medical epidemiologists challenges this distinction

(Ellison 1996; Hertzman 1999; Lamont et al. 2000). The system of biomechanical effects on bone synthesis, for example, requires further investigation of all of its inputs (physical strain, activation of genes that stimulate bone cell development or death, etc. [Harada and Rodan 2003]), but these must then be studied in relationship to the gender-differentiated physical activity system. The different body shapes of adult men and women (related to hormones at puberty among other things) may also affect bone biomechanics, and we need, too, to know more about how growth and development affect the number of bone mechanoreceptors—molecules that translate mechanical stress in biochemical activity (Boman et al. 1998; Pavalko et al. 2003).

The impact of hormones on bone development and maintenance requires research attention of a sort currently lacking in the bone literature. We need to know both about the molecular biology of hormones and bone cell hormone receptors and about life-course effects on hormone systems (Ellison 1996; Worthman 2002). Finally, genes involved in bone cell metabolism, pattern formation, hormone metabolism, drug processing, and many other processes contribute importantly to the development of bone strength (Zelzer and Olsen 2003). Understanding how they function within both the local and global (body and sociocultural) networks contributing to bone development requires a systems-level analysis not yet found in the literature.

CONCLUSION

This article is a call to arms. The sex-gender or nature-nurture accounts of difference fail to appreciate the degree to which culture is a partner in producing body systems commonly referred to as biology—something apart from the social. I introduce an alternative—a life-course systems approach to the analysis of sex/gender. Figure 1 is a research proposal for multiple programs of investigation in several disciplines. We need to ask old questions in new ways so that we can think systematically about the interweaving of bodies and culture. We will not lay bare the bones of sex, but we will come to understand, instead, that our skeletons are part of a life process. If process rather than stasis becomes our intellectual goal, we will improve medical practice and have a more satisfying account of gender and sex as, to paraphrase the phenomenologists, being-in-the-world.

ACKNOWLEDGMENTS

Thanks to the members of the Pembroke Seminar on Theories of Embodiment for a wonderful year of thinking about the process of body making and for their thoughtful response to an earlier draft of this essay. Credit for the title goes to Greg Downey. Thanks also to anonymous reviewers from *Signs* for making me sharpen some of the arguments.

NOTES

1. Munro Peacock et al. write: "The pathogenesis of a fragility fracture almost always involves trauma and is not necessarily associated with reduced bone mass. Thus, fragility fracture should neither be used synonymously nor interchangeably as a phenotype for osteoporosis" (2002, 303).

2. For example, sitting height reflects trunk length (vertebral height) vs. standing height, which reflects the length of the leg bones. These can change independently of one another. Thus height increases can result from changes in long bone length, vertebral height, or both. See Meredith 1978; Tanner et al. 1982; Malina, Brown, and Zavaleta 1987; Balthazart, Tlemçani, and Ball 1996; Seeman 1997.

3. The use of racial terms such as *Caucasian* and others in this article is fraught. But for the duration of this article I will use the terms as they appear in the sources I cite, leaving an analysis of this problematic terminology to future publications, e.g., Fausto-Sterling 2004.

4. Since a number of studies show no sex difference in hip fracture incidence between African American men and women, the "well-known" gender difference in bone fragility may really only be about white women. As so often happens, the word *gender* excludes women of color (Farmer et al. 1984).

5. Peacock et al. write, "Key bone phenotypes involved in fracture risk relate not only to bone mass but also to bone structure, bone loss, and possibly bone turnover" (2002, 306).

6. I am grateful to Peter Taylor for insisting that I read the work in life-course analysis.

7. Stepan 1982; Russett, 1989; Hubbard 1990; Fausto-Sterling 1992.

8. I use the term *experience* rather than the term *environment* here to refer to functional activity. For more detail see Gottlieb, Whalen, and Lickliter 1998.

9. Butler 1990, 1993; Gatens 1996; Kirby 1997; Birke 1999.

10. The "rediscovery" of phenomenology and its application to gendered body image remains a fruitful arena of feminist body theory, e.g., Weiss 1999.

11. Since the society receives both foundation and pharmaceutical company funding, its claim to independence requires scrutiny. The Sex and Gene Expression conferences were funded by Aventis Pharmaceuticals as well as private foundations. Industry and mainstream medical care sponsorship does not unethically direct work, but it limits the permissible ontological and epistemological approaches to the study of women's health and sex differences.

12. Perhaps because the field of archaeology is still struggling to bring gender into the fold, its practitioners often insist on the centrality of the sex/gender distinction. Yet their own conclusions undermine this dualism, precisely because they use a biological product, bone, to draw conclusions about culture and behavior (Ehrenberg 1989; Gero and Conkey 1991; Wright 1996; Armelagos 1998).

13. This study (cited in Melton 1988) dates from 1979, and it seems likely that subsequent cultural changes have led to different patterns of breakage; fracture incidence is a moving target.

14. Local biologies reflect local differences in biology. For example, hot flashes are far less frequent in Japan than in the United States, possibly for reasons pertaining to diet. The normalization question here is: Is it best to compare a population to its own group or some group with similar environmental and genetic histories, or to some outgroup standard?

15. These factors include: a mother having broken her hip, especially before age eighty; height at age twenty-five (taller women are more likely to break hips); extreme thinness; sedentary lifestyle; poor vision; high pulse rate; the use of certain drugs; etc.

16. One researcher states: "I think what is also of note, is that the between-center differences are greater than between-sex differences within certain centers" (Lips 1997, 95).

17. Fosamax seems to be able to prevent further bone loss in people who are losing bone and to build back lost bone at least in the hip and spine. In discussing Merck's campaign, I do not argue that the drug is useless (in fact, I am taking it!), merely (!) that drug companies play an important role in the creation of new "disease" and profit as a result.

18. "An association between the change in areal bone density and the change in fracture rates has never been documented" (Seeman 1997, 517). According to the NIH Consensus Statement Online: "Currently there is no accurate measure of overall bone strength" (2000, 5). But BMD is

often used as a proxy. The National Women's Health Network cites the pitfalls of using BMD to predict future fractures (Fugh-Berman, Pearson, Allina, Zones, Worcester, Whatley, Massion, et al. 2002), but others cite a strong association between BMD and fracture rate (e.g., Melton et al. 1998; Siris et al. 2001). One overview of studies that attempted to predict osteoporosis-linked fractures with bone mineral density concluded: "Measurements of bone mineral density can predict fracture risk but cannot identify individuals who will have a fracture. We do not recommend a programme of screening menopausal women for osteoporosis by measuring bone density" (Marshall, Johnell, and Wedell 1996, 1254). See also Nelson et al. 2002.

19. For a history of the concept of osteoporosis, see Klinge 1998.

20. A secondary cause might be bone loss due to an eating disorder or a metabolic disease, or the prolonged use of a bone-leaching drug such as cortisone.

21. When I use the words *men* and *women* I refer to particular populations on which these studies were done. These are mostly Caucasian and Northern European or North American. Most of the studies have been done since the 1980s, but bone size, shape, and growth patterns would have differed at the beginning of the twentieth century compared with their appearance at the beginning of the twenty-first. I will not make these points every time I use these words.

22. So powerful is the focus on old age that the long NIH bibliography on menopause completely ignores the possible importance of pregnancy and lactation on bone development. These two processes are profoundly implicated in calcium metabolism, and if there is *no* effect on later bone strength it would be important to find out why. What physiological mechanisms protect the bone of pregnant and lactating women? This is an example of a biological question that lies fallow because of the focus on supposed estrogen deficiency in old age.

23. For a discussion of bone biology, see the full article from which this reading as excerpted.

24. I found one eloquent but wordless example on the Web in an article on causes of vitamin D deficiency. The short segment titled "Insufficient Exposure to Sunlight" was accompanied by a photograph of two women, standing in the blazing sun, covered from head to toe in burkas, clearly insufficiently exposed to sunlight but not for want of being outdoors in the sun.

25. Brief histories of these ideas as well as accounts of present-day embryology, genetics, and evolution based on systems theory may be found in Waddington 1957; Kauffman 1993; Webster and Goodwin 1996; Schlichting and Pigliucci 1998; van der Weele 1999; Oyama 2000a, 2000b.

26. The implications of these ideas for an integrative theory of the development of gender differences in behavior and psychological skills have not escaped me and are the subject of a work in progress. The explosion of knowledge about the plastic nature of brain development and an increasing understanding of neuroplasticity in adults suggest that far from being destiny, anatomy is dynamic history. A rich literature that joins mathematical models of nonlinear equations (Kelso 1995) has begun to join forces with experimental scientists who study animal behavior (Gottlieb 1997) and those who now use dynamic systems approaches to reconceptualize human behavioral development (Smith and Thelen 1993; Thelen and Smith 1994, 1998; Thelen 1995; Thelen et al. 2001).

27. Among biologists the idea that genes provide such instructions is giving way to a systems account of cell function. The metaphor of the genome (DNA) as a blueprint or set of direction for building cells and organisms is giving way to a new metaphor—genomes as parts list (Vukmirovic and Tilghmann 2000; Tyson, Csikasz-Nagy, and Novak 2002). If the genome lists only the component parts (codes for RNA and protein), the location of the assembly directions becomes uncertain: one needs to specify a cell or organism's past history and current conditions in order to predict a current developmental event accurately. Cell biologists have now turned in earnest to complexity and systems theory to help learn the rules by which organisms are assembled. (See entire December 2002 issue of *Bioessays* devoted to "Modeling Complex Biological Systems.") In another example, authors extend and twist the book metaphor. "Just as words must be assembled into sentences, paragraphs, chapters and books to make sense, vital cellular functions are performed by structured ensembles of proteins . . . not by freely diffusing and occasionally colliding proteins" (Sali et al. 2003, 216).

28. I use Peter Taylor's definition of systems as "units that have clearly defined boundaries, coherent internal dynamics, and simply mediated relations with their external context" (personal communication 2003).

29. This choice of systems emerges from the data presented earlier in this article. Since this is a model, others might argue for dividing the pie in a different way. To keep the diagram readable and the discussion manageable, I have not emphasized that the entire grouping of systems is embedded in a larger system I call "general health." There are many disease states that secondarily affect bone (e.g., kidney disease or endocrine disorders) by affecting calcium metabolism or preventing exercise. The relationships among the systems affecting bone strength would be shifted in dramatic ways worthy of study in their own right under such circumstances.

30. Choice of model has profound implications. For a discussion of a lifestyle model of disease that emphasizes individual choice vs. a "social production model," see Krieger and Zierler 1995. For an update on current theories of social epidemiology, see Krieger 2001.

31. To the extent that race is a legitimate category separate from class and culture, I will incorporate it into the bone systems story in pt. 2 of this work. For a model of social pathways in childhood that lead to adult health, see Kuh and Ben-Shlomo 1997.

32. Bonjour et al. 1997; Boot et al. 1997; Perry 1997; Wang et al. 2003.

33. For the effects of dietary calcium later in life, see Heaney 2000.

REFERENCES

Alcoff, Linda Martín. 2000. "Philosophy Matters: A Review of Recent Work on Feminist Philosophy." *Signs: Journal of Women in Culture and Society* 25(3):841–42.

Aloia, J. F., A. N. Vaswani, J. K. Yeh, and E. Flaster. 1996. "Risk for Osteoporosis in Black Women." *Calcified Tissue International* 59(6):415–23.

Armelagos, George J. 1998. "Introduction: Sex, Gender and Health Status in Prehistoric and Contemporary Populations." In *Sex and Gender in Paleopathological Perspective*, ed. Anne L. Grauer and Patricia Stuart-Macadam, 1–10. Cambridge: Cambridge University Press.

Balthazart, Jacques, Omar Tlemçani, and Gregory F. Ball. 1996. "Do Sex Differences in the Brain Explain Sex Differences in Hormonal Induction of Reproductive Behavior? What 25 Years of Research on the Japanese Quail Tells Us." *Hormones and Behavior* 30(4):627–61.

Ben-Shlomo, Yoav, and Diana Kuh. 2002. "A Life Course Approach to Chronic Disease Epidemiology: Conceptual Models, Empirical Challenges, and Interdisciplinary Perspectives." *International Journal of Epidemiology* 31(2):285–93.

Berenbaum, Sheri. 2001. "Prenatal Androgen Effects on Cognitive and Social Development." Paper presented at the Second Annual Conference on Sex and Gene Expression, March 8–11, Winston-Salem, North Carolina.

Bertalanffy, Ludwig von. 1969. *General System Theory: Foundations, Development, Applications.* New York: Braziller.

Bilezikian, John P., Etah S. Kurland, and Clifford S. Rosen. 1999. "Male Skeletal Health and Osteoporosis." *Trends in Endocrinology and Metabolism* 10(6):244–50.

Birke, Lynda. 1999. *Feminism and the Biological Body.* Edinburgh: Edinburgh University Press.

Boman, U. Wide, A. Möller, and K. Albertsson-Wikland. 1998. "Psychological Aspects of Turner Syndrome." *Journal of Psychosomatic Obstetrics and Gynaecology* 19(1):1–18.

Bonjour, Jean-Phillippe, Anne-Lise Carrie, Serge Ferrari, Helen Clavien, Daniel Slosman, and Gerald Theintz. 1997. "Calcium-Enriched Foods and Bone Mass Growth in Prepubertal Girls: A Randomized, Double-Blind, Placebo-Controlled Trial." *Journal of Clinical Investigation* 99(6): 1287–94.

Boot, Annemieke M., Maria A. J. de Ridder, Huibert A. P. Pols, Eric P. Krenning, and Sabine M. P. F. de Muinck Keizer-Schrama. 1997. "Bone Mineral Density in Children and Adolescents: Relation to Puberty, Calcium Intake, and Physical Activity." *Journal of Clinical Endocrinology and Metabolism* 82(1):57–62.

Bryant, Rebecca J., Jo Cadogan, and Connie M. Weaver. 1999. "The New Dietary Reference Intakes for Calcium: Implications for Osteoporosis." *Journal of the American College of Nutrition* 18(5):S406–S412.

Butler, Judith. 1990. *Gender Trouble: Feminism and the Subversion of Identity.* New York: Routledge.

———. 1993. *Bodies That Matter: On the Discursive Limits of "Sex."* New York: Routledge.

Cummings, Steven R., Michael C. Nevitt, Warren S. Browner, Katie Stone, Kathleen M. Fox, Kristine E. Ensrud, Jane Cauley, Dennis Black, and Thomas M. Vogt. 1995. "Risk Factors for Hip Fracture in White Women." *New England Journal of Medicine* 332(12):767–73.

Dabbs, James McBride, and Mary Godwin Dabbs. 2001. *Heroes, Rogues, and Lovers: Testosterone and Behavior,* New York: McGraw-Hill.

Damien, E., J. S. Price, and L. E. Lanyon. 1998. "The Estrogen Receptor's Involvement in Osteoblasts' Adaptive Response to Mechanical Strain." *Journal of Bone and Mineral Research* 13(8):1275–82.

Dibba, Bakary, Ann Prentice, Ann Laskey, Dot Stirling, and Tim Cole. 1999. "An Investigation of Ethnic Differences in Bone Mineral, Hip Axis Length, Calcium Metabolism and Bone Turnover Between West African and Caucasian Adults Living in the United Kingdom." *Annals of Human Biology* 26(3):229–42.

Ehrenberg, Margaret. 1989. *Women in Prehistory.* London: British Museum Press.

Ellison, Peter T. 1996. "Developmental Influences on Adult Ovarian Hormonal Function." *American Journal of Human Biology* 8(6):725–34.

Farmer, Mary E., Lon R. White, Jacob A. Brody, and Kent R. Bailey. 1984. "Race and Sex Differences in Hip Fracture Incidence." *American Journal of Public Health* 74(12): 1374–80.

Fausto-Sterling, Anne. 1992. *Myths of Gender: Biological Theories About Women and Men.* 2d ed. New York: Basic Books.

———. 2004. "Refashioning Race: DNA and the Politics of Health Care." *Differences: A Journal of Feminist Cultural Studies.* In Press.

———. In preparation. "The Bare Bones of Sex: Part II—Race."

Fugh-Berman, Adriane, C. K. Pearson, Amy Allina, Jane Zones, Nancy Worcester, and Mariamne Whatley. 2002. "Manufacturing Need, Manufacturing 'Knowledge.'" *Network News* (May/June):1, 4.

Fugh-Berman, Adriane, C. K. Pearson, Amy Allina, Jane Zones, Nancy Worcester, Mariamne Whatley, Charlea Massion, and

Ellen Michaud. 2002. "Hormone Therapy and Osteoporosis: To Prevent Fractures and Falls, There Are Better Options Than Hormones." *Network News* (July/August): 4–5.

Fujita, Y., K. Katsumata, A. Unno, T. Tawa, and A. Tokita. 1999. "Factors Affecting Peak Bone Density in Japanese Women." *Calcified Tissue International* 64(2):107–11.

Gasperino, James. 1995. "Androgenic Regulation of Bone Mass in Women." *Clinical Orthopaedics and Related Research* 311:278–86.

Gatens, Moira. 1996. *Imaginary Bodies: Ethics, Power, and Corporeality*. London: Routledge.

Gero, Joan M., and Margaret W. Conkey, eds. 1991. *Engendering Archeology: Women in Prehistory*. Oxford: Blackwell.

Gilsanz, Vicente, David L. Skaggs, Arzu Kovanlikaya, James Sayre, M. Luiza Loro, Francine Kaufman, and Stanley G. Korenman. 1998. "Differential Effect of Race on the Axial and Appendicular Skeletons of Children." *Journal of Clinical Endocrinology and Metabolism* 83(5):1420–27.

Glock, Martha, Kathleen A. Shanahan, Joan A. McGowan, and compilers, eds. 2000. "Osteoporosis [Bibliography Online]: 2,449 Citations from January 1995 Through December 1999." Available online at http://www.nlm.nih.gov/pubs/cbm/osteoporosis.html. Last accessed May 5, 2004.

Goodman, Alan H. 1997. "Bred in the Bone?" *Sciences* 37(2):20–25.

Gottlieb, Gilbert. 1997. *Synthesizing Nature-Nurture: Prenatal Roots of Instinctive Behavior*. Mahwah, N.J.: Erlbaum.

Gottlieb, Gilbert, Richard E. Whalen, and Robert Lickliter. 1998. "The Significance of Biology for Human Development: A Developmental Psychobiological Systems View." In *Handbook of Child Psychology*, ed. Richard M. Lerner, 233–73. New York: Wiley.

Grosz, Elizabeth. 1994. *Volatile Bodies: Toward a Corporeal Feminism*. Bloomington: Indiana University Press.

Harada, Shun-ichi, and Gideon A. Rodan. 2003. "Control of Osteoblast Function and Regulation of Bone Mass." *Nature* 423 (May 15):349–55.

Heaney, Robert P. 2000. "Calcium, Dairy Products, and Osteoporosis." *Journal of the American College of Nutrition* 19(2):S83–S99.

Hebb, D. O. 1949. *The Organization of Behavior: A Neuropsychological Theory*. New York: Wiley.

Hertzman, Clyde. 1999. "The Biological Embedding of Early Experience and Its Effects on Health in Adulthood." *Annals of the New York Academy of Science* 896:85–95.

Hu, J. F., X. H. Zhao, J. S. Chen, J. Fitzpatrick, B. Parpia, and T. C. Campbell. 1994. "Bone Density and Lifestyle Characteristics in Premenopausal and Postmenopausal Chinese Women." *Osteoporosis International* 4:288–97.

Hubbard, Ruth. 1990. *The Politics of Women's Biology*. New York: Routledge.

Kauffman, Stuart. 1993. *The Origins of Order: Self-Organization and Selection in Evolution*. New York: Oxford University Press.

Keane, Helen, and Marsha Rosengarten. 2002. "On the Biology of Sexed Subjects." *Australian Feminist Studies* 17(39):261–79.

Kellie, Shirley E., and Jacob A. Brody. 1990. "Sex-Specific and Race-Specific Hip Fracture Rates." *American Journal of Public Health* 80(3):326–28.

Kelso, J. A. Scott. 1995. *Dynamic Patterns: The Self-Organization of Brain and Behavior*. Cambridge, Mass.: MIT Press.

Kirby, Vicki. 1997. *Telling Flesh: The Substance of the Corporeal*. New York: Routledge.

Klinge, Ineke. 1998. "Gender and Bones: The Production of Osteoporosis, 1941–1996." Ph.D. dissertation, University of Utrecht.

Krieger, Nancy. 2001. "Theories for Social Epidemiology in the Twenty-First Century: An Ecosocial Perspective." *International Journal of Epidemiology* 30(4): 668–77.

Krieger, Nancy, and Sally Zierler. 1995. "Accounting for Health of Women." *Current Issues in Public Health* 1:251–56.

Kuh, Diana, and Yoav Ben-Shlomo, eds. 1997. *A Life Course Approach to Chronic Disease Epidemiology*. Oxford: Oxford University Press.

Kuh, Diana, and Rebecca Hardy, eds. 2002. *A Life Course Approach to Women's Health*. Oxford: Oxford University Press.

Lamont, Douglas, Louise Parker, Martin White, Nigel Unwin, Stuart M. A. Bennett, Melanie Cohen, David Richardson, Heather O. Dickinson, K. G. M. M. Alberti, and Alan W. Kraft. 2000. "Risk of Cardiovascular Disease Measured by Carotid Intima-Media Thickness at Age 49–51: A Lifecourse Study." *British Medical Journal* 320 (January 29): 273–78.

Larsen, Clark Spencer. 1998. "Gender, Health, and Activity in Foragers and Farmers in the American Southeast: Implications for Social Organization in the Georgia Bight." In *Sex and Gender in Paleopathological Perspective*, ed. Anne L. Grauer and Patricia Stuart-Macadam, 165–87. Cambridge: Cambridge University Press.

Lips, Paul. 1997. "Epidemiology and Predictors of Fractures Associated with Osteoporosis." *American Journal of Medicine* 103(2A): S3–S11.

Lock, Margaret. 1998. "Anomalous Ageing: Managing the Postmenopausal Body." *Body and Society* 4(1):35–61.

Malina, Robert M., Kathryn H. Brown, and Antonio N. Zavaleta. 1987. "Relative Lower Extremity Length in Mexican American and in American Black and White Youth." *American Journal of Physical Anthropology* 72:89–94.

Marshall, Deborah, Olof Johnell, and Hans Wedel. 1996. "Meta-Analysis of How Well Measures of Bone Mineral Density Predict Occurrence of Osteoporotic Fractures." *British Medical Journal* 312(7041):1254–59.

Melton, L. Joseph, III. 1988. "Epidemiology of Fractures." In *Osteoporosis: Etiology, Diagnosis, and Management*, ed. B. Lawrence Riggs and L. Joseph Melton, III, 133–54. New York: Raven.

Melton, L. Joseph, III, Elizabeth J. Atkinson, Michael K. O'Connor, W. Michael O'Fallon, and B. Lawrence Riggs.

1998. "Bone Density and Fracture Risk in Men." *Journal of Bone and Mineral Research* 13(12): 1915–23.

Meredith, Howard V. 1978. "Secular Change in Sitting Height and Lower Limb Height of Children, Youths, and Young Adults of Afro-Black, European, and Japanese Ancestry." *Growth* 42(1):37–41.

Merleau-Ponty, Maurice. 1962. *Phenomenology of Perception.* Trans. Colin Smith. New York: Humanities Press.

Meunier, Pierre J. 1988. "Assessment of Bone Turnover by Histormorphometry." In *Osteoporosis: Etiology, Diagnosis, and Management,* ed. B. Lawrence Riggs and L. Joseph Melton III, 317–32. New York: Raven.

Molleson, Theya. 1994. "The Eloquent Bones of Abu Hureyra." *Scientific American* 2:70–75.

Mosekilde, Lis. 2000. "Age-Related Changes in Bone Mass, Structure, and Strength—Effects of Loading." *Zeitschrift für Rheumatologie* 59 (Supplement 1): I/1–I/9.

Nelson, Heidi D., Mark Helfand, Steven H. Woolf, and Janet D. Allan. 2002. "Screening for Postmenopausal Osteoporosis: A Review of the Evidence for the U.S. Preventive Services Task Force." *Annals of Internal Medicine* 137(6):529–41.

NIH Consensus Statement Online. 2000. 17(1):1–36.

Oyama, Susan. 2000a. *Evolution's Eye: A System's View of the Biology-Culture Divide.* Durham, N.C.: Duke University Press.

———. 2000b. *The Ontogeny of Information: Developmental Systems and Evolution.* Durham, N.C.: Duke University Press.

Pavalko, Fred M., Suzanne M. Norvell, David B. Burr, Charles H. Turner, Randall L. Duncan, and Joseph P. Bidwell. 2003. "A Model for Mechanotransduction in Bone Cells: The Load-Bearing Mechanosomes." *Journal of Cellular Biochemistry* 88(1):104–12.

Peacock, Munro, Charles H. Turner, Michael J. Econs, and Tatiana Foroud. 2002. "Genetics of Osteoporosis." *Endocrine Reviews* 23(3):303–26.

Pead, Matthew J., Timothy M. Skerry, and Lance E. Lanyon. 1988. "Direct Transformation from Quiesence to Bone Formation in the Adult Periosteum Following a Single Brief Period of Bone Loading." *Journal of Bone and Mineral Research* 3(6):647–56.

Perry, Ivan J. 1997. "Fetal Growth and Development: The Role of Nutrition and Other Factors." In Kuh and Ben-Schlomo 1997, 145–68.

Petersen, Alan. 1998. "Sexing the Body: Representations of Sex Differences in *Gray's Anatomy*, 1858 to the Present." *Body and Society* 4(1):1–15.

Rizzoli, R., and J.-P. Bonjour. 1999. "Determinants of Peak Bone Mass and Mechanisms of Bone Loss." *Osteoporosis International* 9 (Supplement 2): S17–S23.

Robinson, T. L., C. Snow-Harter, D. R. Taaffe, D. Gillis, J. Shaw, and R. Marcus. 1995. "Gymnasts Exhibits Higher Bone Mass Than Runners Despite Similar Prevalence of Amenorrhea and Oligomenorrhea." *Journal of Bone and Mineral Research* 10(1):26–35.

Rubin, Gayle. 1975. "The Traffic in Women: Notes on the 'Political Economy' of Sex." In *Toward an Anthropology of Women,* ed. Rayna R. Reiter, 157–210. New York: Monthly Review Press.

Russett, Cynthia Eagle. 1989. *Sexual Science: The Victorian Construction of Womanhood.* Cambridge, Mass.: Harvard University Press.

Sali, Andrej, Robert Glaeser, Thomas Earnest, and Wolfgang Baumeister. 2003. "From Words to Literature in Structural Proteins." *Nature* 422(6928):216–55.

Schacter, Beth. 2001. "About the Society for Women's Health Research." Proceedings from the Second Annual Conference on Sex and Gene Expression, March 8–11, Winston-Salem, North Carolina.

Schlichting, Carl D., and Massimo Pigliucci. 1998. *Phenotypic Evolution: A Reaction Norm Perspective.* Sunderland, Mass.: Sinauer Associates.

Schriempf, Alexa. 2001. "(Re)fusing the Amputated Body: An Interactionist Bridge for Feminism and Disability." *Hypatia* 16(4): 53–79.

Seeman, E. 1997. "Perspective: From: Density to Structure: Growing Up and Growing Old on the Surfaces of Bone." *Journal of Bone and Mineral Research* 12(4):509–21.

———. 1998. "Editorial: Growth in Bone Mass and Size—Are Racial and Gender Differences in Bone Mineral Density More Apparent Than Real?" *Journal of Clinical Endocrinology and Metabolism* 83(5): 1414–19.

———. 1999. "The Structural Basis of Bone Fragility in Men." *Bone* 25 (1):143–47.

Siebers, Tobin. 2001. "Disability in Theory: From Social Constructionism to the New Realism of the Body." *American Literary History* 13(4): 737–54.

Siris, Ethel S., Paul D Miller, Elizabeth Barrett-Connor, Kenneth G. Faulkner, Lois E. Wehren, Thomas A. Abbott, Marc L. Berger, Arthur C. Santora, and Louis M. Sherwood. 2001. "Identification and Fracture Outcomes of Undiagnosed Low Bone Mineral Density in Postmenopausal Women: Results from the National Osteoporosis Risk Assessment." *Journal of the American Medical Association* 286(22):2815–22.

Skerry, Tim. 2000. "Biomechanical Influences on Skeletal Growth and Development." In *Development, Growth, and Evolution: Implications for the Study of the Hominid Skeleton,* ed. Paul O' Higgins and Martin J. Cohn, 29–39. London: Academic Press.

Skerry, Tim, and Lance E. Lanyon. 1995. "Interruption of Disuse by Short Duration Walking Exercise Does Not Prevent Bone Loss in the Sheep Calcaneus." *Bone* 16(2): 269–74.

Smith, Linda B., and Esther Thelen, eds. 1993. *A Dynamic Systems Approach to Development: Applications.* Cambridge, Mass.: MIT Press.

Sowers, Maryfran. 1996. "Pregnancy and Lactation as Risk Factors for Subsequent Bone Loss and Osteoporosis." *Journal of Bone and Mineral Research* 11(8):1052–60.

Stepan, Nancy. 1982. *The Idea of Race in Science: Great Britain, 1800–1960*. London: Macmillan.

Taha, Wael, Daisy Chin, Arnold Silverberg, Larisa Lashiker, Naila Khateeb, and Henry Anhalt. 2001. "Reduced Spinal Bone Mineral Density in Adolescents of an Ultra-Orthodox. Jewish Community in Brooklyn." *Pediatrics* 107 (5): e79–e85.

Tanner, J. M., T. Hayashi, M. A. Preece, and N. Cameron. 1982. "Increase in Length of Leg Relative to Trunk in Japanese Children and Adults from 1957 to 1977: Comparison with British and Japanese Children." *Annals of Human Biology* 9(5): 411–23.

Tanouye, Elyse. 1995. "Merck's Osteoporosis Warnings Pave the Way for Its New Drug." *Wall Street Journal*, June 28, B1, B4.

Thelen, Esther. 1995. "Motor Development: A New Synthesis." *American Psychologist* 50(2): 79–95.

Thelen, Esther, Gregor Schoner, Christian Scheier, and Linda B. Smith. 2001. "The Dynamics of Embodiment: A Field Theory of Infant Perseverative Reaching" *Behavioral and Brain Sciences* 24(1): 1–86.

Thelen, Esther, and Linda B. Smith. 1994. *A Dynamic Systems Approach to the Development of Cognition and Action*. Cambridge, Mass: MIT Press.

———. 1998. "Dynamic Systems Theories," In *Handbook of Child Psychology: Theoretical Models of Human Development*, ed. Richard M. Lerner, 563–634. New York: Wiley.

Thornhill, Randy, and Craig T. Palmer. 2001. *A Natural History of Rape*. Cambridge, Mass.: MIT Press.

Travis, Cheryl Brown, ed. 2003. *Evolution, Gender, and Rape*. Cambridge, Mass.: MIT Press.

Tyson, John J., Attila Csikasz-Nagy, and Bela Novak. 2002. "The Dynamics of Cell Cycle Regulation." *BioEssays:* 24(12):1095–1109.

Van der Weele, Cor. 1999. *Images of Development: Environmental Causes of Ontogeny*. Albany: State University of New York Press.

Verbrugge, Marth H. 1997. "Recreating the Body. Women's Physical Education and the Science of Sex Differences in America, 1900–1940." *Bulletin of the History of Medicine* 71(2):273–304.

Vukmirovic, Ognenka Gog, and Shirley M. Tilghmann. 2000. "Exploring Genome Space." *Nature* 405(6793): 820–22.

Waddington, C. H. 1957. *The Strategy of the Genes: A Discussion of Some Aspects of Theoretical Biology*. London: Allen & Unwin.

Walsh, Timothy B., and Michael J. Devlin. 1998. "Eating Disorders: Progress and Problems." *Science* 280(5638): 1387–90.

Wang, May-Choo, Patricia B. Crawford, Mark Hudes, Marta Van Loan, Kirstin Siemering, and Laura K. Bachrach. 2003. "Diet in Midpuberty and Sedentary Activity in Prepuberty Predict Peak Bone Mass." *American Journal of Clinical Nutrition* 77(2):495–503.

Webster, Gerry, and Brian Goodwin. 1996. *Form and Transformation: Generative and Relational Principles in Biology*. Cambridge: Cambridge University Press.

Weiss, Gail. 1999. *Body Images: Embodiments as Intercorporeality*. New York: Routledge.

Whitehead, Alfred North. (1929) 1978. *Process and Reality: An Essay in Cosmology*. New York: Macmillan.

Williams, Gareth, and Helen Busby. 2000. "The Politics of 'Disabled' Bodies." In *Health, Medicine and Society: Key Theories, Future Agendas*, ed. Simon J. Williams, Jonathan Gabe, and Michael Calnan, 169–85. London: Routledge.

Wizemann, Theresa M., and Mary-Lou Pardue, eds. 2001. *Exploring the Biological Contributions to Human Health: Does Sex Matter?* Washington, D.C.: National Academy Press.

Worthman, Carol M. 2002. "Endocrine Pathways in Differential Well-Being Across the Life Course." In Kuh and Hardy 2002, 197–216.

Wright, Rita P., ed. 1996. *Gender and Archeology*. Philadelphia: University of Pennsylvania Press.

Zanchetta, J. R., H. Plotkin, and M. L. Alvarez Filgueira. 1995. "Bone Mass in Children: Normative Values for the 2–20-Year-Old Population." *Bone* 16 (Supplement 4): S393–S399.

Zelzer, Elazar, and Bjorn R. Olsen. 2003. "The Genetic Basis for Skeletal Diseases." *Nature* 423(6937):343–48.

Zuk, Marlene. 2002. *Sexual Selections: What We Can and Can't Learn About Sex from Animals*. Berkeley: University of California Press.

"A Way Outa No Way": Eating Problems Among African-American, Latina, and White Women

First published in 1992

Bulimia, anorexia, binging, and extensive dieting are among the many health issues women have been confronting in the last twenty years. Until recently, however, there has been almost no research about eating problems among African-American, Latina, Asian-American, or Native American women, working-class women, or lesbians.[1] In fact, according to the normative epidemiological portrait, eating problems are largely a white, middle-, and upper-class heterosexual phenomenon. Further, while feminist research has documented how eating problems are fueled by sexism, there has been almost no attention to how other systems of oppression may also be implicated in the development of eating problems.

In this article, I reevaluate the portrayal of eating problems as issues of appearance based in the "culture of thinness." I propose that eating problems begin as ways women cope with various traumas, including sexual abuse, racism, classism, sexism, heterosexism, and poverty. Showing the interface between these traumas and the onset of eating problems explains why women may use eating to numb pain and cope with violations to their bodies. This theoretical shift also permits an understanding of the economic, political, social, educational, and cultural resources that women need to change in correcting their relationship to food and their bodies.

EXISTING RESEARCH ON EATING PROBLEMS

There are three theoretical models used to explain the epidemiology, etiology, and treatment of eating problems. The biomedical model offers important scientific research about possible physiological causes of eating problems and the physiological dangers of purging and starvation (Copeland 1985; Spack 1985). However, this model adopts medical treatment strategies that may disempower and traumatize women (Garner 1985; Orbach 1985). In addition, this model ignores many social, historical, and cultural factors that influence women's eating patterns. The psychological model identifies eating problems as "multidimensional disorders" that are influenced by biological, psychological, and cultural factors (Garfinkel and Garner 1982). While useful in its exploration of effective therapeutic treatments, this model, like the biomedical one, tends to neglect women of color, lesbians, and working-class women.

The third model, offered by feminists, asserts that eating problems are gendered. This model explains why the vast majority of people with eating problems are women, how gender socialization and sexism may relate to eating problems, and how masculine models of psychological development have shaped theoretical interpretations. Feminists offer the culture-of-thinness model as a key reason why eating problems predominate among women. According to this model, thinness is a culturally, socially, and economically enforced requirement for female beauty. This imperative makes women vulnerable to cycles of dieting, weight loss, and subsequent weight gain, which may lead to anorexia and bulimia (Chernin 1981; Orbach 1978, 1985; Smead 1984).

Feminists have rescued eating problems from the realm of individual psychopathology by showing how the difficulties are rooted in systematic and pervasive attempts to control women's body sizes and appetites.

However, researchers have yet to give significant attention to how race, class, and sexuality influence women's understanding of their bodies and appetites. The handful of epidemiological studies that include African-American women and Latinas casts doubt on the accuracy of the normative epidemiological portrait. The studies suggest that this portrait reflects which particular populations of women have been studied rather than actual prevalence (Andersen and Hay 1985; Gray, Ford, and Kelly 1987; Hsu 1987; Nevo 1985; Silber 1986)

More important, this research shows that bias in research has consequences for women of color. Tomas Silber (1986) asserts that many well-trained professionals have either misdiagnosed or delayed their diagnoses of eating problems among African-American and Latina women due to stereotypical thinking that these problems are restricted to white women. As a consequence, when African-American women or Latinas are diagnosed, their eating problems tend to be more severe due to extended processes of starvation prior to intervention. In her autobiographical account of her eating problems, Retha Powers (1989), an African-American woman, describes being told not to worry about her eating problems since "fat is more acceptable in the Black community" (p. 78). Stereotypical perceptions held by her peers and teachers of the "maternal Black woman" and the "persistent mammy-brickhouse Black woman image" (p. 134) made it difficult for Powers to find people who took her problems with food seriously.

Recent work by African-American women reveals that eating problems often relate to women's struggles against a "simultaneity of oppression" (Clarke 1982; Naylor 1985; White 1991). Byllye Avery (1990), the founder of the National Black Women's Health Project, links the origins of eating problems among African-American women to the daily stress of being undervalued and overburdened at home and at work. In Evelyn C. White's (1990) anthology, *The Black Woman's Health Book: Speaking for Ourselves*, Georgiana Arnold (1990) links her eating problems partly to racism and racial isolation during childhood.

Recent feminist research also identifies factors that are related to eating problems among lesbians (Brown 1987; Dworkin 1989; Iazzetto 1989; Schoenfielder and Wieser 1983). In her clinical work, Brown (1987) found that lesbians who have internalized a high degree of homophobia are more likely to accept negative attitudes about fat than are lesbians who have examined their internalized homophobia. Autobiographical accounts by lesbians have also indicated that secrecy about eating problems among lesbians partly reflects their fear of being associated with a stigmatized illness ("What's Important" 1988).

Attention to African-American women, Latinas, and lesbians paves the way for further research that explores the possible interface between facing multiple oppressions and the development of eating problems. In this way, this study is part of a larger feminist and sociological research agenda that seeks to understand how race, class, gender, nationality, and sexuality inform women's experiences and influence theory production.

METHODOLOGY

I conducted eighteen life history interviews and administered lengthy questionnaires to explore eating problems among African-American, Latina, and white women. I employed a snowball sample, a method in which potential respondents often first learn about the study from people who have already participated. This method was well suited for the study since it enabled women to get information about me and the interview process from people they already knew. Typically, I had much contact with the respondents prior to the interview. This was particularly important given the secrecy associated with this topic (Russell 1986; Silberstein, Striegel-Moore, and Rodin 1987), the necessity of women of color and lesbians to be discriminating about how their lives are studied, and the fact that I was conducting across-race research.

To create analytical notes and conceptual categories from the data, I adopted Glaser and Strauss's (1967) technique of theoretical sampling, which directs the researcher to collect, analyze, and test hypotheses during the sampling process (rather than imposing theoretical categories onto the data). After completing each interview transcription, I gave a copy to each woman who wanted one. After reading their interviews, some of the women clarified or made additions to the interview text.

Demographics of the Women in the Study

The eighteen women I interviewed included five African-American women, five Latinas, and eight white women. Of these women, twelve are lesbian and six are heterosexual. Five women are Jewish, eight are

Catholic, and five are Protestant. Three women grew up outside of the United States. The women represented a range of class backgrounds (both in terms of origin and current class status) and ranged in age from nineteen to forty-six years old (with a median age of 33.5 years).

The majority of the women reported having had a combination of eating problems (at least two of the following: bulimia, compulsive eating, anorexia, and/or extensive dieting). In addition, the particular types of eating problems often changed during a woman's life span. (For example, a woman might have been bulimic during adolescence and anorexic as an adult.) Among the women, 28 percent had been bulimic, 17 percent had been bulimic and anorexic, and 5 percent had been anorexic. All of the women who had been anorexic or bulimic also had a history of compulsive eating and extensive dieting. Of the women, 50 percent were compulsive eaters and dieters (39 percent) or compulsive eaters (11 percent) but had not been bulimic or anorexic.

Two-thirds of the women have had eating problems for more than half of their lives, a finding that contradicts the stereotype of eating problems as transitory. The weight fluctuation among the women varied from 16 to 160 pounds, with an average fluctuation of 74 pounds. This drastic weight change illustrates the degree to which the women adjusted to major changes in body size at least once during their lives as they lost, gained, and lost weight again. The average age of onset was eleven years old, meaning that most of the women developed eating problems prior to puberty. Almost all of the women (88 percent) consider themselves as still having a problem with eating, although the majority believe they are well on the way to recovery.

THE INTERFACE OF TRAUMA AND EATING PROBLEMS

One of the most striking findings in this study was the range of traumas the women associated with the origins of their eating problems, including racism, sexual abuse, poverty, sexism, emotional or physical abuse, heterosexism, class injuries, and acculturation.[2] The particular constellation of eating problems among the women did not vary with race, class, sexuality, or nationality. Women from various race and class backgrounds attributed the origins of their eating problems to sexual abuse, sexism, and emotional and/or physical abuse. Among some of the African-American and Latina women, eating problems were also associated

with poverty, racism, and class injuries. Heterosexism was a key factor in the onset of bulimia, compulsive eating, and extensive dieting among some of the lesbians. These oppressions are not the same nor are the injuries caused by them. And certainly, there are a variety of potentially harmful ways that women respond to oppression (such as using drugs, becoming a workaholic, or committing suicide). However, for all these women, eating was a way of coping with trauma.

Sexual Abuse

Sexual abuse was the most common trauma that the women related to the origins of their eating problems. Until recently, there has been virtually no research exploring the possible relationship between these two phenomena. Since the mid-1980s, however, researchers have begun identifying connections between the two, a task that is part of a larger feminist critique of traditional psychoanalytic symptomatology (DeSalvo 1989; Herman 1981; Masson 1984). Results of a number of incidence studies indicate that between one-third and two-thirds of women who have eating problems have been abused (Oppenheimer et al. 1985; Root and Fallon 1988). In addition, a growing number of therapists and researchers have offered interpretations of the meaning and impact of eating problems for survivors of sexual abuse (Bass and Davis 1988; Goldfarb 1987; Iazzetto 1989; Swink and Leveille 1986). Kearney-Cooke (1988) identifies dieting and binging as common ways in which women cope with frequent psychological consequences of sexual abuse (such as body image disturbances, distrust of people and one's own experiences, and confusion about one's feelings). Root and Fallon (1989) specify ways that victimized women cope with assaults by binging and purging: bulimia serves many functions, including anesthetizing the negative feelings associated with victimization. Iazzetto's innovative study (1989), based on in-depth interviews and art therapy sessions, examines how a woman's relationship to her body changes as a consequence of sexual abuse. Iazzetto discovered that the process of leaving the body (through progressive phases of numbing, dissociating, and denying) that often occurs during sexual abuse parallels the process of leaving the body made possible through binging.

Among the women I interviewed, 61 percent were survivors of sexual abuse (eleven of the eighteen women), most of whom made connections between sexual abuse and the beginning of their eating problems. Binging was the most common method of coping identified by the survivors. Binging helped women "numb out" or anesthetize their feelings. Eating sedated, alleviated anxiety, and combated loneliness. Food was something that they could trust and was accessible whenever they needed it. Antonia (a pseudonym) is an Italian-American woman who was first sexually abused by a male relative when she was four years old. Retrospectively, she knows that binging was a way she coped with the abuse. When the abuse began, and for many years subsequently, Antonia often woke up during the middle of the night with anxiety attacks or nightmares and would go straight to the kitchen cupboards to get food. Binging helped her block painful feelings because it put her back to sleep.

Like other women in the study who began binging when they were very young, Antonia was not always fully conscious as she binged. She described eating during the night as "sleep walking. It was mostly desperate—like I had to have it." Describing why she ate after waking up with nightmares, Antonia said, "What else do you do? If you don't have any coping mechanisms, you eat." She said that binging made her "disappear," which made her feel protected. Like Antonia, most of the women were sexually abused before puberty; four of them before they were five years old. Given their youth, food was the most accessible and socially acceptable drug available to them. Because all of the women endured the psychological consequences alone, it is logical that they coped with tactics they could do alone as well.

One reason Antonia binged (rather than dieted) to cope with sexual abuse is that she saw little reason to try to be the small size girls were supposed to be. Growing up as one of the Italian Americans in what she described as a "very WASP town," Antonia felt that everything from her weight and size to having dark hair on her upper lip were physical characteristics she was supposed to hide. From a young age she knew she "never embodied the essence of the good girl. I don't like her. I have never acted like her. I can't be her. I sort of gave up." For Antonia, her body was the physical entity that signified her outsider status. When the sexual abuse occurred, Antonia felt she had lost her body. In her mind, the body she lived in after the abuse was not really hers. By the time Antonia was eleven, her mother put her on diet pills. Antonia began to eat behind closed doors as she continued to cope with the psychological consequences of sexual abuse and feeling like a cultural outsider.

Extensive dieting and bulimia were also ways in which women responded to sexual abuse. Some women thought that the men had abused them because of their weight. They believed that if they were smaller, they might not have been abused. For example when Elsa, an Argentine woman, was sexually abused at the age of eleven, she thought her chubby size was the reason the man was abusing her. Elsa said, "I had this notion that these old perverts liked these plump girls. You heard adults say this too. Sex and flesh being associated." Looking back on her childhood, Elsa believes she made fat the enemy partly due to the shame and guilt she felt about the incest. Her belief that fat was the source of her problems was also supported by her socialization. Raised by strict German governesses in an upper-class family, Elsa was taught that a woman's weight was a primary criterion for judging her worth. Her mother "was socially conscious of walking into places with a fat daughter and maybe people staring at her." Her father often referred to Elsa's body as "shot to hell." When asked to describe how she felt about her body when growing up, Elsa described being completely alienated from her body. She explained,

> Remember in school when they talk about the difference between body and soul? I always felt like my soul was skinny. My soul was free. My soul sort of flew. I was tied down by this big bag of rocks that was my body. I had to drag it around. It did pretty much what it wanted and I had a lot of trouble controlling it. It kept me from doing all the things that I dreamed of.

As is true for many women who have been abused, the split that Elsa described between her body and soul was an attempt to protect herself from the pain she believed her body caused her. In her mind, her fat body was what had "bashed in her dreams." Dieting became her solution, but, as is true for many women in the study, this strategy soon led to cycles of binging and weight fluctuation.

Ruthie, a Puerto Rican woman who was sexually abused from twelve until sixteen years of age, described bulimia as a way she responded to sexual abuse. As a child, Ruthie liked her body. Like many Puerto Rican women of her mother's generation, Ruthie's mother did not want skinny children, interpreting that as a sign that they were sick or being fed improperly. Despite her mother's attempts to make her gain weight, Ruthie remained thin through puberty. When a male relative began sexually abusing her, Ruthie's sense of her body changed dramatically. Although she weighed only 100 pounds, she began to feel fat and thought her size was causing the abuse. She had seen a movie on television about Romans who made themselves throw up and so she began doing it, in hopes that she could look like the "little kid" she was before the abuse began. Her symbolic attempt to protect herself by purging stands in stark contrast to the psychoanalytic explanation of eating problems as an "abnormal" repudiation of sexuality. In fact, her actions and those of many other survivors indicate a girl's logical attempt to protect herself (including her sexuality) by being a size and shape that does not seem as vulnerable to sexual assault.

These women's experiences suggest many reasons why women develop eating problems as a consequence of sexual abuse. Most of the survivors "forgot" the sexual abuse after its onset and were unable to retrieve the abuse memories until many years later. With these gaps in memory, frequently they did not know why they felt ashamed, fearful, or depressed. When sexual abuse memories resurfaced in dreams, they often woke feeling upset but could not remember what they had dreamed. These free-floating, unexplained feelings left the women feeling out of control and confused. Binging or focusing on maintaining a new diet were ways women distracted or appeased themselves, in turn, helping them regain a sense of control. As they grew older, they became more conscious of the consequences of these actions. Becoming angry at themselves for binging or promising themselves they would not purge again was a way to direct feelings of shame and self-hate that often accompanied the trauma.

Integral to this occurrence was a transference process in which the women displaced onto their bodies painful feelings and memories that actually derived from or were directed toward the persons who caused the abuse. Dieting became a method of trying to change the parts of their bodies they hated, a strategy that at least initially brought success as they lost weight. Purging was a way women tried to reject the body size they thought was responsible for the abuse. Throwing up in order to lose the weight they thought was making them vulnerable to the abuse was a way to try to find the body they had lost when the abuse began.

Poverty

Like sexual abuse, poverty is another injury that may make women vulnerable to eating problems. One woman I interviewed attributed her eating problems directly to the stress caused by poverty. Yolanda is a Black Cape Verdean mother who began eating compulsively when she was twenty-seven years old. After leaving an abusive husband in her early twenties, Yolanda was forced to go on welfare. As a single mother with small children and few financial resources, she tried to support herself and her children on $539 a month. Yolanda began binging in the evenings after putting her children to bed. Eating was something she could do alone. It would calm her, help her deal with loneliness, and make her feel safe. Food was an accessible commodity that was cheap. She ate three boxes of macaroni and cheese when nothing else was available. As a single mother with little money, Yolanda felt as if her body was the only thing she had left. As she described it,

> I am here, [in my body] 'cause there is no where else for me to go. Where am I going to go? This is all I got . . . that probably contributes to putting on so much weight cause staying in your body, in your home, in yourself, you don't go out. You aren't around other people. . . . You hide and as long as you hide you don't have to face . . . nobody can see you eat. You are safe.

When she was eating, Yolanda felt a momentary reprieve from her worries. Binging not only became a logical solution because it was cheap and easy but also because she had grown up amid positive messages about eating. In her family, eating was a celebrated and joyful act. However, in adulthood, eating became a double-edged sword. While comforting her, binging also led to weight gain. During the three years Yolanda was on welfare, she gained seventy pounds.

Yolanda's story captures how poverty can be a precipitating factor in eating problems and highlights the value of understanding how class inequalities may shape women's eating problems. As a single mother, her financial constraints mirrored those of most female heads of households. The dual hazards of a race- and sex-stratified labor market further limited her options (Higginbotham 1986). In an article about Black women's health, Byllye Avery (1990) quotes a Black woman's explanation about why she eats compulsively. The woman told Avery,

> I work for General Electric making batteries, and, I know it's killing me. My old man is an alcoholic. My kid's got babies. Things are not well with me. And one

thing I know I can do when I come home is cook me a pot of food and sit down in front of the TV and eat it. And you can't take that away from me until you're ready to give me something in its place. (p. 7)

Like Yolanda, this woman identifies eating compulsively as a quick, accessible, and immediately satisfying way of coping with the daily stress caused by conditions she could not control. Connections between poverty and eating problems also show the limits of portraying eating problems as maladies of upper-class adolescent women.

The fact that many women use food to anesthetize themselves, rather than other drugs (even when they gained access to alcohol, marijuana, and other illegal drugs), is partly a function of gender socialization and the competing demands that women face. One of the physiological consequences of binge eating is a numbed state similar to that experienced by drinking. Troubles and tensions are covered over as a consequence of the body's defensive response to massive food intake. When food is eaten in that way, it effectively works like a drug with immediate and predictable effects. Yolanda said she binged late at night rather than getting drunk because she could still get up in the morning, get her children ready for school, and be clearheaded for the college classes she attended. By binging, she avoided the hangover or sickness that results from alcohol or illegal drugs. In this way, food was her drug of choice since it was possible for her to eat while she continued to care for her children, drive, cook, and study. Binging is also less expensive than drinking, a factor that is especially significant for poor women. Another woman I interviewed said that when her compulsive eating was at its height, she ate breakfast after rising in the morning, stopped for a snack on her way to work, ate lunch at three different cafeterias, and snacked at her desk throughout the afternoon. Yet even when her eating had become constant, she was still able to remain employed. While her patterns of eating no doubt slowed her productivity, being drunk may have slowed her to a dead stop.

Heterosexism

The life history interviews also uncovered new connections between heterosexism and eating problems. One of the most important recent feminist contributions has been identifying compulsory heterosexuality as an institution which truncates opportunities for heterosexual and lesbian women (Rich 1986). All of the women interviewed for this study, both lesbian and heterosexual, were taught that heterosexuality was compulsory, although the versions of this enforcement were shaped by race and class. Expectations about heterosexuality were partly taught through messages that girls learned about eating and their bodies. In some homes, boys were given more food than girls, especially as teenagers, based on the rationale that girls need to be thin to attract boys. As the girls approached puberty, many were told to stop being athletic, begin wearing dresses, and watch their weight. For the women who weighed more than was considered acceptable, threats about their need to diet were laced with admonitions that being fat would ensure becoming an "old maid."

While compulsory heterosexuality influenced all of the women's emerging sense of their bodies and eating patterns, the women who linked heterosexism directly to the beginning of their eating problems were those who knew they were lesbians when very young and actively resisted heterosexual norms. One working-class Jewish woman, Martha, began compulsively eating when she was eleven years old, the same year she started getting clues of her lesbian identity. In junior high school, as many of her female peers began dating boys, Martha began fantasizing about girls, which made her feel utterly alone. Confused and ashamed about her fantasies, Martha came home every day from school and binged. Binging was a way she drugged herself so that being alone was tolerable. Describing binging, she said, "It was the only thing I knew. I was looking for a comfort." Like many women, Martha binged because it softened painful feelings. Binging sedated her, lessened her anxiety, and induced sleep.

Martha's story also reveals ways that trauma can influence women's experience of their bodies. Like many other women, Martha had no sense of herself as connected to her body. When I asked Martha whether she saw herself as fat when she was growing up she said, "I didn't see myself as fat. I didn't see myself. I wasn't there. I get so sad about that because I missed so much." In the literature on eating problems, *body image* is the term that is typically used to describe a woman's experience of her body. This term connotes the act of imagining one's physical appearance. Typically, women with eating problems are assumed to have difficulties with their body image. However, the term *body image* does not adequately capture the complexity and range of bodily responses to trauma experienced by the women. Exposure to trauma did much more than distort the women's visual image of themselves. These traumas often jeopardized their capacity to consider themselves as having bodies at all.

Given the limited connotations of the term *body image*, I use the term *body consciousness* as a more useful way to understand the range of bodily responses to trauma.[3] By body consciousness I mean the ability to reside comfortably in one's body (to see oneself as embodied) and to consider one's body as connected to oneself. The disruptions to their body consciousness that the women described included leaving their bodies, making a split between their body and mind, experiencing being "in" their bodies as painful, feeling unable to control what went in and out of their bodies, hiding in one part of their bodies, or simply not seeing themselves as having bodies. Binging, dieting, or purging were common ways women responded to disruptions to their body consciousness.

Racism and Class Injuries

For some of the Latinas and African-American women, racism coupled with the stress resulting from class mobility related to the onset of their eating problems. Joselyn, an African-American woman, remembered her white grandmother telling her she would never be as pretty as her cousins because they were lighter skinned. Her grandmother often humiliated Joselyn in front of others, as she made fun of Joselyn's body while she was naked and told her she was fat. As a young child, Joselyn began to think that although she could not change her skin color, she could at least try to be thin. When Joselyn was young, her grandmother was the only family member who objected to Joselyn's weight. However, her father also began encouraging his wife and daughter to be thin as the family's class standing began to change. When the family was working class, serving big meals, having chubby children, and keeping plenty of food in the house was a sign the family was doing well. But, as the family became mobile, Joselyn's father began insisting that Joselyn be thin. She remembered, "When my father's business began to bloom and my father was interacting more with white businessmen and seeing how they did business, suddenly thin became important. If you were a truly well-to-do family, then your family was slim and elegant."

As Joselyn's grandmother used Joselyn's body as territory for enforcing her own racism and prejudice about size, Joselyn's father used her body as the territory through which he channeled the demands he faced in the white-dominated business world. However, as Joselyn was pressured to diet, her father still served her large portions and bought treats for her and the neighborhood children. These contradictory messages made her feel confused about her body. As was true for many women in this study, Joselyn was told she was fat beginning when she was very young even though she was not overweight. And, like most of the women, Joselyn was put on diet pills and diets before even reaching puberty, beginning the cycles of dieting, compulsive eating, and bulimia.

The confusion about body size expectations that Joselyn associated with changes in class paralleled one Puerto Rican woman's association between her eating problems and the stress of assimilation as her family's class standing moved from poverty to working class. When Vera was very young, she was so thin that her mother took her to a doctor who prescribed appetite stimulants. However, by the time Vera was eight years old, her mother began trying to shame Vera into dieting. Looking back on it, Vera attributed her mother's change of heart to competition among extended family members that centered on "being white, being successful, being middle class, . . . and it was always, 'Ay Bendito. She is so fat. What happened?'"

The fact that some of the African-American and Latina women associated the ambivalent messages about food and eating to their family's class mobility and/or the demands of assimilation while none of the eight white women expressed this (including those whose class was stable and changing) suggests that the added dimension of racism was connected to the imperative to be thin. In fact, the class expectations that their parents experienced exacerbated standards about weight that they inflicted on their daughters.

EATING PROBLEMS AS SURVIVAL STRATEGIES

Feminist Theoretical Shifts

My research permits a reevaluation of many assumptions about eating problems. First, this work challenges the theoretical reliance on the culture-of-thinness model. Although all of the women I interviewed were manipulated and hurt by this imperative at some point in their lives, it is not the primary source of their problems. Even in the instances in which a culture of thinness was a precipitating factor in anorexia, bulimia, or binging, this influence occurred in concert with other oppressions.

Attributing the etiology of eating problems primarily to a woman's striving to attain a certain beauty ideal is also problematic because it labels a common way that women cope with pain as essentially appearance-based disorders. One blatant example of sexism is the notion that women's foremost worry is about their appearance. By focusing on the emphasis on slenderness, the eating-problems literature falls into the same trap of assuming that the problems reflect women's "obsession" with appearance. Some women were raised in families and communities in which thinness was not considered a criterion for beauty. Yet, they still developed eating problems. Other women were taught that women should be thin, but their eating problems were not primarily in reaction to this imperative. Their eating strategies began as logical solutions to problems rather than problems themselves as they tried to cope with a variety of traumas.

Establishing links between eating problems and a range of oppressions invites a rethinking of both the groups of women who have been excluded from research and those whose lives have been the basis of theory formation. The construction of bulimia and anorexia as appearance-based disorders is rooted in a notion of femininity in which white middle- and upper-class women are portrayed as frivolous, obsessed with their bodies, and overly accepting of narrow gender roles. This portrayal fuels women's tremendous shame and guilt about eating problems—as signs of self-centered vanity. This construction of white middle- and upper-class women is intimately linked to the portrayal of working-class white women and women of color as their opposite: as somehow exempt from accepting the dominant standards of beauty or as one step away from being hungry and therefore not susceptible to eating problems. Identifying that women may binge to cope with poverty contrasts the notion that eating problems are class bound. Attending to the intricacies of race, class, sexuality, and gender pushes us to rethink the demeaning construction of middle-class femininity and establishes bulimia and anorexia as serious responses to injustices.

Understanding the link between eating problems and trauma also suggests much about treatment and prevention. Ultimately, their prevention depends not simply on individual healing but also on changing the social conditions that underlie their etiology. As Bernice Johnson Reagon sings in Sweet Honey in the Rock's song "Oughta Be a Woman," "A way outa no way is too much to ask/too much of a task for any one woman" (Reagon 1980).[4] Making it possible for women to have healthy relationships with their bodies and eating is a comprehensive task. Beginning steps in this direction include insuring that (1) girls can grow up without being sexually abused, (2) parents have adequate resources to raise their children, (3) children of color grow up free of racism, and (4) young lesbians have the chance to see their reflection in their teachers and community leaders. Ultimately, the prevention of eating problems depends on women's access to economic, cultural, racial, political, social, and sexual justice.

NOTES

1. I use the term *eating problems* as an umbrella term for one or more of the following: anorexia, bulimia, extensive dieting, or binging. I avoid using the term *eating disorder* because it categorizes the problems as individual pathologies, which deflects attention away from the social inequalities underlying them (Brown 1985). However, by using the term *problem* I do not wish to imply blame. In fact, throughout, I argue that the eating strategies that women develop begin as logical solutions to problems, not problems themselves.

2. By trauma I mean a violating experience that has long-term emotional, physical, and/or spiritual consequences that may have immediate or delayed effects. One reason the term *trauma* is useful conceptually is its association with the diagnostic label *post-traumatic stress disorder (PTSD)* (American Psychological Association 1987). PTSD is one of the few clinical diagnostic categories that recognize social problems (such as war or the Holocaust) as responsible for the symptoms identified (Trimble 1985). This concept adapts well to the feminist assertion that a woman's symptoms cannot be understood as solely individual, considered outside of her social context, or prevented without significant changes in social conditions.

3. One reason the term *consciousness* is applicable is its intellectual history as an entity that is shaped by social context and social structures (Delphy 1984; Marx 1964). This link aptly applies to how the women described their bodies because their perceptions of themselves as embodied (or not embodied) directly relate to their material conditions (living situations, financial resources, and access to social and political power).

4. Copyright © 1980. Used by permission of Songtalk Publishing.

REFERENCES

American Psychological Association. 1987. *Diagnostic and Statistical Manual of Mental Disorders.* 3rd ed. rev. Washington, DC: American Psychological Association.

Andersen, Arnold, and Andy Hay. 1985. Racial and socioeconomic influences in anorexia nervosa and bulimia. *International Journal of Eating Disorders* 4:479–87.

Arnold, Georgiana. 1990. Coming home: One Black woman's journey to health and fitness. In *The Black Women's Health Book: Speaking for Ourselves,* Evelyn C. White. Seattle, WA: Seal Press.

Avery, Byllye Y. 1990. Breathing life into ourselves: The evolution of the National Black Women's Health Project. In *The Black Women's Health Book: Speaking for Ourselves,* Evelyn C. White. Seattle, WA: Seal Press.

Bass, Ellen, and Laura Davis. 1988. *The Courage to Heal: A Guide for Women Survivors of Child Sexual Abuse.* New York: Harper & Row.

Brown, Laura S. 1985. Women, weight and power: Feminist theoretical and therapeutic issues. *Women and Therapy* 4:61–71.

———. 1987. Lesbians, weight and eating: New analyses and perspectives. In *Lesbian Psychologies,* the Boston Lesbian Psychologies Collective. Champaign: University of Illinois Press.

Chernin, Kim. 1981. *The Obsession: Reflections of the Tyranny of Slenderness.* New York: Harper & Row.

Clarke, Cheryl. 1982. *Narratives.* New Brunswick, NJ: Sister Books.

Copeland, Paul M. 1985. Neuroendocrine aspects of eating disorders. In *Theory and Treatment of Anorexia Nervosa and Bulimia: Biomedical, Sociocultural, and Psychological Perspectives,* Steven Wiley Emmett. New York: Brunner/Mazel.

Delphy, Christine. 1984. *Close to Home: A Materialist Analysis of Women's Oppression.* Amherst: University of Massachusetts Press.

DeSalvo, Louise. 1989. *Virginia Woolf: The Impact of Childhood Sexual Abuse on Her Life and Work.* Boston, MA: Beacon.

Dworkin, Sari H. 1989. Not in man's image: Lesbians and the cultural oppression of body image. In *Loving Boldly: Issues Facing Lesbians,* Ester D. Rothblum and Ellen Cole. New York: Harrington Park Press.

Garfinkel, Paul E., and David M. Garner. 1982. *Anorexia Nervosa: A Multidimensional Perspective.* New York: Brunner/Mazel.

Garner, David. 1985. Iatrogenesis in anorexia nervosa and bulimia nervosa. *International Journal of Eating Disorders* 4:701–26.

Glaser, Barney G., and Anselm L. Strauss. 1967. *The Discovery of Grounded Theory: Strategies for Qualitative Research.* New York: Aldine DeGruyter.

Goldfarb, Lori. 1987. Sexual abuse antecedent to anorexia nervosa, bulimia and compulsive overeating: Three case reports. *International Journal of Eating Disorders* 6:675–80.

Gray, James, Kathryn Ford, and Lily M. Kelly. 1987. The prevalence of bulimia in a Black college population. *International Journal of Eating Disorders* 6:733–40.

Herman, Judith. 1981. *Father-Daughter Incest.* Cambridge, MA: Harvard University Press.

Higginbotham, Elizabeth. 1986. We were never on a pedestal: Women of color continue to struggle with poverty, racism and sexism. In *For Crying Out Loud,* Rochelle Lefkowitz and Ann Withorn. Boston, MA: Pilgrim Press.

Hsu, George. 1987. Are eating disorders becoming more common in Blacks? *International Journal of Eating Disorders* 6:113–24.

Iazzetto, Demetria. 1989. When the body is not an easy place to be: Women's sexual abuse and eating problems. Ph.D. diss., Union for Experimenting Colleges and Universities, Cincinnati, Ohio.

Kearney-Cooke, Ann. 1988. Group treatment of sexual abuse among women with eating disorders. *Women and Therapy* 7:5–21.

Marx, Karl. 1964. *The Economic and Philosophic Manuscripts of 1844.* New York: International.

Masson, Jeffrey. 1984. *The Assault on the Truth: Freud's Suppression of the Seduction Theory.* New York: Farrar, Strauss & Giroux.

Naylor, Gloria. 1985. *Linden Hills.* New York: Ticknor & Fields.

Nevo, Shoshana. 1985. Bulimic symptoms: Prevalence and the ethnic differences among college women. *International Journal of Eating Disorders* 4:151–68.

Oppenheimer, R., K. Howells, R. L. Palmer, and D. A. Chaloner. 1985. Adverse sexual experience in childhood and clinical eating disorders: A preliminary description. *Journal of Psychiatric Research* 19:357–61.

Orbach, Susie. 1978. *Fat Is a Feminist Issue.* New York: Paddington.

———. 1985. Accepting the symptom: A feminist psychoanalytic treatment of anorexia nervosa. In *Handbook of Psychotherapy for Anorexia Nervosa and Bulimia,* David M. Garner and Paul E. Garfinkel. New York: Guilford.

Powers, Retha. 1989. Fat is a Black women's issue. *Essence,* Oct., 75, 78, 134, 136.

Reagon, Bernice Johnson. 1980. "Oughta be a woman." On Sweet Honey in the Rock's album *Good News.* Music by Bernice Johnson Reagon; lyrics by June Jordan. Washington, DC: Songtalk.

Rich, Adrienne. 1986. Compulsory heterosexuality and lesbian existence. In *Blood, Bread and Poetry.* New York: Norton.

Root, Maria P. P., and Patricia Fallon. 1988. The incidence of victimization experiences in a bulimic sample. *Journal of Interpersonal Violence* 3:161–73.

———. 1989. Treating the victimized bulimic: The functions of binge–purge behavior. *Journal of Interpersonal Violence* 4:90–100.

Russell, Diana E. 1986. *The secret trauma: Incest in the lives of girls and women.* New York: Basic Books.

Silber, Tomas. 1986. Anorexia nervosa in Blacks and Hispanics. *International Journal of Eating Disorders* 5:121–28.

Silberstein, Lisa, Ruth Striegel-Moore, and Judith Rodin. 1987. Feeling fat: A woman's shame. In *The role of shame in symptom formation,* edited by Helen Block Lewis. Hillsdale, NJ: Lawrence Erlbaum.

Smead, Valerie. 1984. Eating behaviors which may lead to and perpetuate anorexia nervosa, bulimarexia, and bulimia. *Women and Therapy* 3:37–49.

Spack, Norman. 1985. Medical complications of anorexia nervosa and bulimia. In *Theory and treatment of anorexia nervosa and bulimia: Biomedical sociocultural and psychological perspectives,* edited by Steven Wiley Emmett. New York: Brunner/Maze.

Swink, Kathy, and Antoinette E. Leveille. 1986. From victim to survivor: A new look at the issues and recovery process for adult incest survivors. *Women and Therapy* 5:119–43.

Trimble, Michael. 1985. Post-traumatic stress disorder: History of a concept. In *Trauma and its wake: The study and treatment of post-traumatic stress disorder,* edited by C. R. Figley. New York: Brunner/Mazel.

READING *37* **Simone Weil Davis**

Loose Lips Sink Ships

First published in 2002

[They are] two excrescences of muscular flesh which hang, and in some women, fall outside the neck of the womb; lengthen and shorten as does the comb of a turkey, principally when they desire coitus. . . .

—Ambroise Paré (1579), quoted in Lisa Jean Moore and Adele E. Clarke, "Clitoral Conventions and Transgressions: Graphic Representations in Anatomy Texts, c1900–1991," *Feminist Studies* 21 (summer 1995)

DESIGNER VAGINAS

Perhaps you noticed some of the articles in women's magazines that came out in 1998, *Cosmopolitan, Marie Claire,* and *Harper's Bazaar* each carried one, as did *Salon* on-line, articles with titles like "Labia Envy," "Designer Vaginas," and "The New Sex Surgeries." More recently, *Jane* magazine covered the topic, and Dan Savage's nationally syndicated advice column, "Savage Love," stumbled explosively upon it as well. These pieces all discussed labiaplasty, a relatively recent plastic surgery procedure that involves trimming away labial tissue

and sometimes injecting fat from another part of the body into labia that have been deemed excessively droopy. In contrast to the tightening operation known as "vaginal rejuvenation," labiaplasty is sheerly cosmetic in purpose and purports to have no impact on sensation (unless something were to go terribly awry).[1] Throughout coverage here and in Canada, the aptly named Doctors Alter, Stubbs, and Matlock shared much of the glory and the public relations. In the name of consumer choice, these articles provoke consumer anxiety. The *Los Angeles Times* quotes Dr. Matlock: "The woman is the designer . . . the doctor is just the instrument. . . . Honestly, if you look at *Playboy,* those women, on the outer vagina area, the vulva is very aesthetically appealing, the vulva is rounded. It's full, not flat. . . . Women are coming in saying, I want something different, I want to change things. They look at *Playboy,* the ideal woman per se, for the body and the shape and so on. You don't see women in there with excessively long labia minora."[2]

All the popular articles about the "new sex surgeries" that I've reviewed also include remarks from skeptical colleagues and from polled readers who feel okay about their labia. (In an unfortunate turn of phrase, one plastic surgeon describes Dr. Matlock as a bit too "cutting edge.") Despite this apparently balanced coverage, a brand-new worry is being planted, with the declaration in *Salon* that "many women had been troubled for years about the appearance of their labia minora," and with the use of words like "normal" and "abnormal" to describe nonpathological variations among genitalia. The November 1998 article in *Cosmopolitan* has an eye-catching blurb: "My labia were so long, they'd show through my clothes!" Having taken *that* in, the reader suddenly looks up at the accompanying photo with new eyes: the photograph is of a slim woman in fairly modest underwear; because of the picture's cropping, she is headless, but the posture is distinctive, awkward. She's somewhat hunched forward, her hands are both crotch-bound, and one finger slips beneath the edge of her panties. Having read the caption, you think, "My God, she's tucking in her labia!"[3]

Ellen Frankfort's 1972 book, the women's liberationist *Vaginal Politics,* begins with the following scene.[4] Carol from the Los Angeles Self-Help Clinic "slips out of her dungarees and underpants," hops onto a long table in an old church basement and inserts a speculum into her vagina. The 50 other women present file up and look with a flashlight, and learn, too, how to self-examine with a speculum and a dimestore mirror. This self-exploration of what has often been referred to as "the dark continent" or just "down there" seemed the perfect symbol for the early claim of women's liberation that "the personal is political." How could a woman call for sexual autonomy without self-awareness? To reverse the phrasing of one of Second Wave feminism's most famous byproducts, how could we know "our selves" without knowing "our bodies" first?[5] This image of women using a well-placed mirror to demystify and reclaim their own bodies is rooted dimly in my teen-years memory. I found it eerily resurrected when the *Salon* piece by Louisa Kamps came up on my computer screen. Kamps starts off like this: "'Ladies, get out your hand mirrors,' begins a curious press release I find at my desk one Monday morning. 'Yes, it is true . . . the newest trend in surgically enhanced body beautification: Female Genital Cosmetic Surgery.'" The hand mirror this time is used to alert the would-be vagina shopper to any deficiencies "down below" that she may have been blithely ignoring. From 1970s' consciousness-raising groups and Judy Chicago's dinner plates, through Annie Sprinkle's speculum parties of the 1980s, and on to Eve Ensler's collaborative *Vagina Monologues,*[6] we came at the end of the 1990s to Dr. Alter and Dr. Stubbs. What's the trajectory from Second Wave feminist "self-discovery and celebration"

to the current almost-craze for labiaplasty? And does the fact of this trajectory provide us with a warning?

THE CLEAN SLIT

The vagina. According to Freud, its first sighting is the first scandal. It is *the* secret, invariably broken, that, once seen, changes you forever, especially if "you" are a little boy in turn-of-the-century Vienna, stumbling in upon your mother *en déshabillé.* You discover, all at once, in a rude shock, that she lacks a penis. You tremble at the threat that her missing phallus implies to *your* little member: if it happened to her, it could happen to you (especially because you've got the gall to compete with your father for your mother's affections). For Freud, his followers, and even many of his feminist revisionists, the "scandal" of a woman's genitals is supposed to be due to what *isn't* there, not what *is.* This article is not about lack, however. It is about excess. And it is not (exactly) about what Jacques Lacan and Hélène Cixous celebrated as *jouissance.* It's about labia.

So the vagina betokens the horror of castration, we're told. Many have remarked that perhaps this scandal is more accurately defined as one of interiority. In a society that revolves around the visual, an orgasm that doesn't include ejaculation can seem maddeningly uncontrollable: you can't prove it (outside of a laboratory), and thus it can be faked.[7] Discussing hardcore cinematic pornography, Linda Williams claims that "[t]he woman's ability to fake the orgasm that the man can never fake . . . seems to be at the root of all the genre's attempts to solicit what it can never be sure of: the out-of-control confession of pleasure, a hard-core 'frenzy of the visible.'"[8]

In the Amero-European world of the late-eighteenth and the early-nineteenth centuries, an earlier notion of women's natural lustiness was transformed into the myth of feminine modesty.[9] This purported lady-like decorum has always been depicted as simultaneously innate for the female *and* a massively big job. For the same social world that generated the mythos of the delicate, proper lady has also continually spawned and recycled dirty jokes about "vagina dentata," fatal odors, and other horror-story imagery about female genitalia.[10] The off-color disgust has always been tied in a complex way to a vast, off-color desire, and these both have been concomitant with the prescription to stay dainty—no matter what—for at least three hundred years. The paradoxical welding of abhorrence and adoration is often "resolved" socially through a stereotyped decoupling of the two, although mythologies of the lurid and the pure female are in fact too interdependent ever to be truly unbraided. Women have been branded good or bad, refined or fallen, on the basis of their race, their profession, their station in life, and so forth, with the judgments conveniently supporting the political, economic, and racial status quo (about which, more later). That being said, the paradox is also one that women negotiate individually, and this has been so for a remarkably long time. . . .

Although "feminine modesty" used to be the answer to this subtextual concern about vaginas, now the shameful zone needs to be brought into line for display, rather than hidden. The vulva is becoming a pioneer territory for cosmetic enhancement—surgical practitioners need above all to capitalize both on that preexisting shame and on the ever-greater need to provide a cyborgian spectacle of porno-gloss. The relative mainstreaming of the sex industry (think of Demi Moore in *Striptease,* for example) and the blurring of the lines between hard-core and advertising imagery (think Calvin Klein) have led to a perpetually increasing sense of pressure among many women, the pressure to develop and present a seamlessly sexualized, "airbrushed" body.[11] Drs. Alter, Stubbs, and Matlock want that sought-after body to include a specific labial look, one desirable enough to be worth "buying."

Before people will spend money on something as expensive and uncomfortable as cosmetic surgery, they need to be motivated not only by desire but by concern or self-doubt. Bringing the authoritative language of medical science to the aestheticization of the vagina is one key way to trigger such anxiety. Advertisers have frequently invoked and generated medicalized norms to sell products. Roland Marchand describes perhaps the classic example of this phenomenon: after the liquid known as Listerine proved a lackluster general antiseptic, it was decided to dramatize its function as a mouthwash. Foul tasting as it was, consumer incentive would be needed. The term "halitosis" was "exhumed from an old medical dictionary" by an advertising firm and became the driving force behind a subsequent, energetic scare campaign about the medical, social, and romantic risks of bad breath.[12] Advertisers have always been both matter-of-fact and explicit about delineating and then steadily working to create a sense of deficiency where once there was indifference or even, God forbid, enjoyment, working to incite new arenas of insecurity, new personal anxieties, so that more things can be marketed and sold.

Cosmetic surgery has worked with the same principles throughout its more than 100-year history, as detailed in histories of the profession by Kathy Davis, Elizabeth Haiken, and Sander Gilman.[13] For instance, in a particularly unnerving chapter on "micromastia" (the "disease" of flat-chestedness) and the surgeries developed to "correct" it, Haiken quotes a 1958 article by plastic surgeon Milton T. Edgerton and psychiatrist A. R. McClary, on "the psychiatry of breast augmentation": "Literally thousands of women in this country alone, are seriously disturbed by feelings of inadequacy in regard to concepts of the body image. Partly as a result of exposure to advertising propaganda and questionable publicity, many physically normal women develop an almost paralyzing self-consciousness focused on the feeling that they do not have the correct size bosom."[14] The rationale laid out here, which explains *but also helps create* "inferiority complexes," can be applied across the full topography of the human form, as borne out by the increasing prevalence of liposuction, face-lifts, buttock and tummy tucks. The latest realm to be scoured for "abnormalities" is the vagina, formerly spared from the scrutiny of the market because it was considered both too reviled and too quakingly desired to be addressed commercially.

These days, in part because of the video dissemination and the main-streaming of pornography, women, regardless of gender preference, can see the vaginas of a lot of different other women. They may desire those vaginas, they may simultaneously identify with them, but if they are rich enough or have great credit, they can definitely have them built.[15] A 1997 article in the Canadian magazine *See* interviews a patient of Dr. Stubbs in Toronto. Deborah "has had her eyes done and had breast implants and some liposuction. She says that she started thinking about her labia when her first husband brought home porn magazines and she started comparing herself. 'I saw some other ones that were cuter than mine' and I thought, 'Hey, I want that one,' she laughs."[16] Of course, the images we relish or bemoan in pornography are almost always tweaked technically. As Deborah did her "catalog shopping," the women she was admiring were perhaps themselves surgically "enhanced," but additionally, they were posed, muted with makeup and lighting, and the resultant photographic images were then edited with an airbrush or the digital modifications of Photoshop.

This is especially true of pornography that presents itself as "upscale," whether soft or hard core. As Laura Kipnis helps us realize, there's a crucial link between

Hustler's targeting of a working-class market and its being the first of the big three glossy "wank mags" to show what it called "the pink."[17] *Hustler*'s aggressive celebration of vulgarity informed its initial rejection of soft-core decorum about genitals; thus, its representations of vaginas were matter-of-fact, and often enough contextualized with very explicit, poorly lit Polaroid shots sent in by readers. When the vagina finally came to the pages of *Penthouse*, by contrast, it was as flaw-free and glossy as the rest of the models' figures. In "The Pussy Shot: An Interview with Andrew Blake," sex writer Susie Bright discusses the classed aesthetics of this pornographer, whose trademarks are his lavish sets (straight out of *Architectural Digest*, Bright remarks) and high-end production values: in this posh setting, it comes as no surprise that the star's labia are small and her "pussy is perfectly composed, with every hair in place."[18]

The evolution of a new strict standard of "beauty," rigid enough to induce surgery, does not occur in a vacuum. Among other factors, economics are in play—not just in the eagerness of a few cosmetic surgeons to up their patient load but in a far more intricate web of drives and desires intersecting with technological shifts and cultural and financial power plays. I will only nod here to the complexity of this phenomenon. A first example: in *Venus Envy: A History of Cosmetic Surgery*, Haiken points out that research catalyzed by World War I and II led to technological innovations that furthered the cosmetic surgery industry. Wars, which maim and disfigure people, increase the demand for and respectability of plastic surgery, allowing surgeons the grim opportunity to improve their skills and their public relations. Additionally, war means the invention and/or increased availability of new materials, like silicone and polyurethane, both of which were used for breast augmentation in the wake of World War II.[19] Could this new material on hand have *led* (in part) to the 1950s' notorious obsession with large breasts?

Here is a more recent example of the subtle interplay of cultural and economic forces that can help shape changes in beauty standards: Perhaps Rudolph Giuliani's New York City should be thought of as undergoing an urban labiaplasty. In this zoned, regulated era, newly comfortable for tourists if not for New Yorkers, the sex industry has been radically curtailed. This change has meant, tellingly enough, that almost all the sex clubs "connected" enough to remain open after 1998 favor "clone" women—Caucasian bodies, tidy tan lines, big blonde hair, collagen lips, surgically removed ribs, liposucked bottoms, and implanted breasts. With time, their labia may also be ubiquitously trimmed. Many women with bodies that diverge from the approved stereotype—biker chicks, Latina and Black dancers, plump or small-breasted women, the pierced girl with the monster tattoo—women who used to be able to dance erotically for an income, have been "sheered away," forced into unemployment, prostitution, or departure. These days in New York, only the clones can dance, and it is clone bodies alone that New York City strip club patrons now ogle.[20] The ripple effects such a change works, no doubt, multiply, and the Bloomberg era will see them continue.

In part because of the prevalence of just such a mainstreamed *Penthouse* and *Playboy* aesthetic, labias in pornography are often literally tucked away (in the most low-tech variant of body modification).[21] If you review enough porn, however, especially lesbian porn or that which is unsqueamishly "déclassé" as in *Hustler*, you will see a wide variety in the female genitalia on display—wide enough to evoke the "snowflake uniqueness" analogy that is bandied around in popular coverage of the new cosmetic enhancement surgeries. And indeed the before-and-after shots available at some of the surgeons' web sites that I've found so far do reveal, unsurprisingly, that the single favored look for these "designer vaginas" is . . . the clean slit. Louisa Kamps of *Salon* magazine agrees: "What strikes me in the 'after' shots is the eerie similarity between the women . . . their genitalia are carbon copies of each other."

In a subtle but nontrivial way, this particular aesthetic and the surgery that manifests it cut back on women's experience of self-on-self contact, of tactility: Luce Irigaray celebrates the nonvisual, sensory experience women perpetually enjoy as their vaginal lips press and move against one another. She suggests that this physiological status makes women psychologically less invested in the myth of the monadic, self-reliant individual than are men. Irigaray's "two lips which are not one" would not touch each other much in a world of women "Altered."[22] What do the aesthetics of a streamlined vulva signify? The smooth groin of our favorite plastic android prototype, Barbie? A desire to approximate prepubescence? A fastidious minimization of marginal zones?[23]

Mary Russo writes of "the female grotesque" in terms that are relevant here: "The images of the grotesque body are precisely those which are abjected from the bodily canons of classical aesthetics. The classical body is transcendent and monumental, closed, static, self-contained, symmetrical, and sleek. . . . The grotesque body is open, protruding, secreting, multiple and changing. . . ."[24] Russo's contrasting of the grotesque with the classical is particularly resonant in this context, as plastic surgeons often invoke classical aesthetics and the metaphor of surgeon-as-sculptor; Stubbs even illustrates his site with photographs of classical statuary and presents his "before-and-after" shots in a "Surgical Art Gallery" captioned by Hippocrates: "'*Ars longa, vita brevis*'—Art is long and life is short.'"[25] Elizabeth Haiken discusses "the classical context in which [early plastic surgeons] wished to place themselves; the term *plastic surgery* derives from the Greek *plastikos*, to shape or mold."[26] The asymmetries, protrusions, and changeability of Russo's grotesque are what the labiaplasty is meant to "shape or mold" and *cut* away.

Bodies do change with the passage of time, of course. If the living body is to approximate sculpture, change itself must be managed, *fixed*. Reading the following quote from Dr. Alter's website, one is reminded of the Renaissance theory of the wandering womb, whereby female hysteria and misbehavior were deemed the results of a uterus that had dislodged and begun to storm about internally, wreaking havoc. A woman's "womb was like a hungry animal; when not amply fed by sexual intercourse or reproduction, it was likely to wander about her body, overpowering her speech and senses."[27] In Dr. Alter's prose, the older woman, "in dialogue with gravity,"[28] may find her previously pleasing vagina dangerously "on the move": "The aging female may dislike the descent of her pubic hair and labia and desire re-elevation to its previous location," Dr. Alter warns. So, it is woman's work to make sure her genitalia are snug, not wayward.

We are talking about vaginal aesthetics, and aesthetic judgments almost always evidence socially relevant metaphors at work on the material and visual planes. Ideas about feminine beauty are ever-changing: the classic example is a comparison of Rubens's fleshy beauties and the wraithlike super-model Kate Moss (who succeeded Twiggy). But, in a world where many women have never thought about judging the looks of their genitals, even if they care about their appearance more generally, we should ask what criteria make for a good-looking vagina, and who is assigned as arbiter. These (mutating) criteria should tell us something about the value system that generates them. To tease out some answers to these questions, this article goes on to put the labiaplasty phenomenon in a contextual frame with other vaginal modifications.

MODIFYING/CLASSIFYING

What representations of vulvas circulate in our society? And who, beyond Dr. Tight, is modifying the female genitalia, how and why? For one, among alternative youth (and the not-so-alternative, not-so-youthful, too) piercings are being sought to modify and decorate the labia, sometimes to extend them, and, ideally, to add to clitoral stimulation. What sensibilities mark these changes? Among body modifiers on the Web, conversation about body image, self-mutilation, and, contrarily, healing, is common, with an accepted understanding that many turn to piercing as a means of overcoming perceived past abuse. "'Most folks use BodMod to get back in touch with the parts of themselves that were hurt or misused by others.' 'BodMod has helped me undemonize pain. . . . I was able to handle [childbirth] better, knowing that I'd survived . . . two ten-gauge labial piercings. . . .'" Changing one's relationship to one's genitalia by becoming their "modifier" leads here to an aesthetic reassessment: "'You know, I never liked to look at my puss until I got my rings. I have well-developed inner labia that always show, and I was always envious of those women who seemed to have nice neat little pussies with everything tucked inside. My puss looked like an old whore's cunt to me! So one reason I *know* I wasn't mutilating myself when I got my privates pierced was how much I liked to look at myself after the work was done. You might actually say I'm *glad* my labia are the way they are now.'"[29]

"Glad" is what the cosmetic surgeons do *not* want you to be about prominent labia minora. If you look at the opening paragraph of Ensler's *Vagina Monologues*, you begin to wonder if the unruliness now coming under the governance of the cosmetic surgeon isn't at least as symbolic as it is aesthetic. This is Ensler, introducing her project (interviews with real women, transcribed, performed onstage, and then collected in a book):

> I was worried about vaginas. I was worried about what we think about vaginas, and even more worried that we don't think about them. . . . So I decided to talk to women about their vaginas, to do vagina interviews, which became vagina monologues. I talked with over two hundred women. I talked to old women, young women, married women, single women, lesbians, college professors, actors, corporate professionals, sex workers, African American women, Hispanic women, Asian American women, Native American women, Caucasian women, Jewish women. At first women were reluctant to talk. They were a little shy. But once they got going, you couldn't stop them.[30]

Just as Ensler's own catalog of interviewees seems to burgeon and proliferate, so too the women with whom she spoke were "unstoppable." With a similar metaphoric expansion, in the cosmetic surgeons' promotional material, not only are women's *labia* depicted as in danger of distention, but one woman customer also described her *"hang-up"* about her preoperative labia as "just growing and growing," until the doctor cut it short, that is. Loose lips sink ships.

I received a "free consultation" from one doctor who performs labiaplasties, and this doctor explained to me that the ideal look for labia minora was not only minimal and unextended but also symmetrical, "homogeneously pink," and "not wavy."[31] To the dangers and allures of what's hidden about the vagina, now is added the "too muchness" of labial tissue. In their heterogeneous dappling and their moist curves, labia mark the lack of tidy differentiation between inside and outside and that's just *too much*. One effect of this procedure is to reduce this sense of a "marginal" site between exterior and interior corporeality. Labia can be seen as "gateway" tissue, in other words, tissue that is somewhat indeterminate in texture and hue, yielding slowly from outer to inner and blurring the boundary between the fetishized gloss of the outer dermis and the wet, mushy darkness of the inside. This indeterminacy, actually a function of the labia's protective role, may be part of their association with excess.[32] In *Public Privates: Performing Gynecology from Both Ends of the Speculum,* Terry Kapsalis "reads" the images in a widely used medical text, *Danforth's Obstetrics and Gynecology*. She is struck by the lack of representations of healthy vaginas in *Danforth's* and argues that ultimately the work's visual logic pathologizes female genitalia per se. Using language parallel to that which I have used here, she writes: "Perhaps it is not a lack that is threatening, but an excess. The fact is that even if no pathology exists, there *is* something there—namely, a vulva with labia, a clitoris, and so on, a marginal site occupying both the inside and the outside, an abject space (according to Julia Kristeva) that threatens to devour the penis (vagina dentata)."[33]

In the medical realm, much effort is expended to overcome the mysterious liminality of the vagina. Since the eras of the ancient anatomists Galen and Hippocrates and especially since the rise of gynecology in the nineteenth century, vaginas have been diagrammed and cataloged in medical textbooks. Running parallel, a variant of pornography has always picked up and parodied the objectifying eroticism of scientific conquest.[34] In this realm, large labia have often been associated with

deviance—at least since the sixteenth century they have indicated to doctors the alleged presence of hypersexuality, onanism, and possible "tribadism" or lesbian tendencies. Jennifer Terry discusses a 1930s' study conducted in New York City, "under the auspices of the Committee for the Study of Sex Variants," in order "to identify, treat, and prevent homosexuality." A moderate-sized group of self- proclaimed lesbians were examined by a battery of experts, so that their "traits" could be characterized and profiled. These experts included gynecologists. The overseer of the project, one Dr. Dickinson, ultimately "identified ten characteristics which he argued set the sex variant [lesbian] apart from 'normal' women: (1) larger than average vulvas; (2) longer labia minora; (3) 'labia minora protrude between the labia majora and are wrinkled, thickened, or *brawny'*; (4) 'the prepuce is large or wrinkled or in folds'; (5) the clitoris is 'notably erectile' . . . , (6) 'eroticism is clearly in evidence on examination, as shown by dusky flush of the parts, with free flow of clear, glairy mucus, and with definite clitoris erection. . . .'" The study concludes that all "these findings can be the result of strong sex urge [presumably an innate or congenital condition], plus: (a) Vulvar and vulvovaginal self-friction; or (b) Homosexual digital or oral play; or (c) Heterosexual manual or coital techniques, singly or in any combination."[35] Terry rightly emphasizes the researchers' apparent fascination with the concept that homo/hypersexual desire (often conflated) could be strong enough that it could make the vulva a site of transformation. The prurience behind this possibility that perverted sex play could "rebuild" a vagina seems great enough that it is allowed to overshadow the theory of a congenital distinction between heterosexual and homosexual anatomy.

Many American and British clitoridectomies and female castrations (the removal of healthy ovaries) were performed in the nineteenth century and as recently as the 1970s, as a response to just such indicators.[36] Isaac Baker Brown began to perform clitoridectomies in Britain in 1858, in order to reduce "hysteria" and other nervous ailments, but particularly to combat "excessive" masturbation. He was, by the 1860s, soundly critiqued in his own country and indeed expelled from Britain's Obstetrical Society in 1867; but his procedure (and its milder variant, circumcision of the clitoral hood) became popular in the United States by the late 1860s and was performed in this country for decades. Although experimentation in the development phases of sexual surgeries generally was exacted on the bodies of poor and disenfranchised women (mostly African American), the lady of leisure became the expressed target for these operations. Upper-middle-class and upper-class women had disposable incomes and time on their hands (to masturbate . . . or to recover from genital surgery). Robert Battey developed the practice of removing healthy ovaries to address a whole slew of complaints, from kleptomania to epilepsy, and this procedure was surprisingly widespread, particularly between 1880 and 1910. One 1893 proponent of female castration claimed that "the moral sense of the patient is elevated. . . . She becomes tractable, orderly, industrious and cleanly." Although depleted misrule seems an unsurprising "benefit" of such operations, one would not expect *aesthetics* to spring up as a concern in this context, but Ben Barker-Benfield cites some clitoridectomy and castration patients who thought of the trend as a "fashionable fad" and found their scars "as pretty as the dimple on the cheek of sweet sixteen."[37]

In the 1970s and 1980s, James Burt, an Ohio gynecologist, gained notoriety—and eventually lost his license—performing what he called "the surgery of love" on more than 4,500 patients, apparently often without even garnering the pretense of informed consent, while they were anesthetized and "on the table" for another procedure. This procedure included a clitoral circumcision and a vaginal reconstruction that changed the angle of the vagina; he insisted before and after the malpractice suits that he had enhanced the sexual pleasure of 99 percent of the women upon whom he'd operated and that he was "correcting" the female anatomy, which he saw as God's mistake, by repositioning the genitalia. Women were left with loss of erotic sensation, enormous pain during intercourse, chronic bowel and urination problems requiring regular catheter use, and ongoing serious infections; the same set of medical sequelae have been reported among infibulated women.[38] In 1997, the Ohio Supreme Court ultimately awarded forty women compensation amounting to a total of $20 million. This award came after spectacular struggles in the courts over an eleven-year-period. The organization Patients-in-Arms, led by Carla Miller (who describes herself as "a victim of FGM" [female genital mutilation]), is devoted to helping women speak out about abuse and disfigurement at the hands of gynecologists. A review of the cases toward which Ms. Miller can direct one makes it excruciatingly clear both that this phenomenon is quite widespread and that it is made possible by the common and interlinked phenomenon of the "white wall of silence" that reduces the doctors' risk of being brought to task.[39]

In a related phenomenon that persists to this day, the erotic tissue of "intersexed" or ambiguously gendered babies and children is routinely, in fact just about ubiquitously, modified through surgery without the minor's consent, in what the medical profession calls a "psychosocial emergency." These modifications have been shown to leave behind serious psychological scarring; often enough, the surgeries profoundly compromise the sexual sensation of the people forced to undergo them. In a piece called "The Tyranny of the Aesthetic: Surgery's Most Intimate Violation," Martha Coventry explains that "girlhood is [almost always] the gender approximated through surgery in such circumstances." "It's easier to poke a hole than build a pole," as one surgeon remarks. Coventry quotes Suzanne Kessler, whose work represents an important contribution to the study of intersexed experience: "Genital ambiguity is corrected not because it is threatening to the infant's life, but because it is threatening to the infant's culture."[40]

The genitalia are cultural terrain that must conform to identificatory norms; this has been driven home by the historians of gynecological science. When mid-nineteenth-century physician Marion Sims developed the duck-billed speculum and an examination protocol that gave him a good view, he used the language of an imperial conquistador, beholding still uncharted territory: "I saw everything, as no man had seen before."[41] Much has been written, particularly by Irigaray, about the mythologization of female genitalia as "the dark continent," the "nothing to see," an Unknown supposedly waiting to be penetrated by pioneering masculine experts; Mary Ann Doane and Anne McClintock are among those who have etched out the linkage that such a metaphor immediately suggests between gender politics and racial imperialism.[42]

What if the "nothing," the furor about female absence, is in part a stand-in scandal for the *something* that is the vaginal bloom—just as the "vast wildernesses" of the Americas and Africa were an invader's myth that suppressed the inconvenient fact of inhabitation? It is exactly in the realms where gender and race intersect that we can see this being played out. Sander Gilman and Michele Wallace are among those who have discussed Saartjie (or Sara) Baartman, dubbed the Hottentot Venus. She and other African women were taken from their homes and put on show in the early nineteenth century; in this display, their labial "aprons" were rumored about and peeked at with as much eroticized condemnation as were their "steoptygic" buttocks, although the latter were more plainly in view.[43] When George Cuvier, Geoffrey St. Hilaire, and Henri de Blainville, eminent naturalists all, attempted to force a scientific examination of

Baartman, de Blainville reported that "she hid her apron carefully between her thighs—her movements were brusque and capricious like those of apes. . . . It was only with great sorrow that she let drop her handkerchief for a moment."[44] The outrage of invasion so evident here is aggravated by the dehumanization of Baartman that drove the tragic endeavor. In the same commentary, Cuvier describes elements of her appearance as being "like an orangutan," "like an animal," and "like a dog."[45] Eager to inspect her labia, particularly as they were seeking a classificatory wedge that would distinguish the Hottentot from the European on the level of species, the scientists spent three days trying to convince Baartman to submit to the physical, even offering her money, which she refused. Alas, her early death afforded them ready access to her private parts, however, and Cuvier made a plaster cast of her body and had her brain and genitals preserved in jars. Although the skeleton remains at Paris's Musée de l'Homme, her body is due to be returned to South Africa for burial . . . and her brain and genitals have disappeared.[46]

It is no coincidence that the aforementioned Marion Sims, early American gynecologist, developed his surgery techniques only by repeated, public operations on the bodies of African American slaves and poor, white "washerwomen."[47] Doing symbolic work, nonwhite women in the Euro-American context have endured the exposure of their bodies only to have them decried and desired, first as heathenish, then as "abnormal." Meanwhile, the nonprostitute white woman's vagina was hidden, protected—shamed, too, but out of the limelight.

OUR VULVAS, OUR SELVES

Perhaps this context needs to be kept in mind when we consider another role played contemporarily by images of female genitals: among activists opposed to the circumcision of African females, even among those who are extremely sensitive to the liabilities of cultural bias, the documenting photo has a special, and somewhat problematic, status. In "Desiring the 'Mutilated' African Woman," Wacuka Mungai points out that there is a heated and eerily prurient interest expressed over the Web in accessing documentary photos of girls and women who have undergone cliterodectomies, excisions, and infibulation.[48] Although photographs of excised and infibulated vaginas are available at "kinky" web sites alongside other images deemed

freakish or gory, I agree with Mungai that, even beyond the overtly pornographic, their status as emblems of an "Othered" barbarity is also tinged with unacknowledged eroticism. As Mungai explains, these photos are typically taken with something like consent, but under circumstances when a girl would be hard pressed to withhold permission—in exchange for treatment, a foreign, light-skinned doctor who doesn't speak your language asks that you let her photograph you. You are not likely to refuse her, even though there may be trauma in the taking, and even though the photos then circulate the globe, representing only the wounded status of the African female. Like the gynecological diagram, like Baartman's genitals so long on formaldehyde display in Paris, like the "monster shot" in porn flicks, these images are partial, headless . . . vaginas emphatically dissevered from whole people, made creatures of their own—treated perhaps as the essence of the woman, the cut vagina the truest thing about her, a dangerous metonymy. Mungai points out that, by the same token, in media coverage of the debates over female circumcision among immigrants, the portraits of "cut" women's faces that accompany articles decrying the practice often serve to bring about the same delimiting reduction.

One North American woman with whom I spoke who had elected to have a labiaplasty laughed uproariously with me at the nerve of a European television news program that had approached her to ask if she'd like to do a segment on their show about her operation. The very *thought* of her face being linked to her imagined, modified vagina was preposterous to her, and she would certainly never have consented to being part of the show. Our laughter should continue to ring until it has turned livid, as we think about the many African girls and women who experience just this representational conflation. . . .

CONFOUNDING THE BOUNDARIES

The U.S. Congress passed a measure criminalizing the circumcision of a minor female in 1996, and nine or ten states have passed anti-FGO acts since 1996 as well. In Illinois, Minnesota, Rhode Island, and Tennessee, this legislation felonizes operations performed on adults as well as on minors. But *which* operations? Anti-FGO laws that now exist in a number of U.S. states describe procedures that would definitely include those practiced by Drs. Alter and Matlock, but they use only language that addresses the "ritual" or custom and belief-based cutting of African immigrant bodies. Meanwhile, this legal language either elides or okays both the "corrective" cutting of the intersexed child and the surgery sought by the unsettled consumer who has been told by plastic surgeons that her labia are unappealing and aberrant. Thus American law marks out relations between the state and its citizen bodies that differ depending on birthplace, cultural context, and skin color.

In fact, however, it is a (prevalent) mistake to imagine a quantum distinction between Euro-American and African reshapings of women's bodies: far too often, they are measured with entirely different yardsticks, rather than on a continuum. Nahid Toubia, executive director of the advocacy group Rainbo, remarks that "[t]he thinking of an African woman who believes that 'FGM is the fashionable thing to do to become a real woman' is not so different from that of an American woman who has breast implants to appear more feminine."[49] In keeping with Toubia's remark, I propose here that a subtler and less culturally binaristic analysis of such phenomena will lead, not to political paralysis in the name of cultural relativism, but to deeper understanding of core issues like the nature of consent, of bodily aesthetics and social control, and of cross-cultural activist collaboration.[50]

Soraya Miré, Somali maker of the film *Fire Eyes*, remarks in Inga Muscio's (wo)manifesto, *Cunt: A Declaration of Independence:* "[Western women] come into conversations waving the American flag, forever projecting the idea that they are more intelligent than I am. I've learned that American women look at women like me to hide from their own pain. . . . In America, women pay *the money that is theirs and no one else's* to go to a doctor who cuts them up so they can create or sustain an image men want. Men are the mirror. Western women cut themselves up voluntarily."[51] Significantly, in Miré's construction, consent to genital surgery does *not* okay it so much as it marks the degrading depths of women's oppression. Although consent is at the heart of the issue of genital operations on children, a topic both urgent and not to be downplayed, we must also look at the social and cultural means whereby consent is manufactured, regardless of age, in the West as well as in African and other countries engaging in FGOs. In the North American popular imagination, the public address of advertising is not understood as infringing upon our power of consent. Indeed, the freedom to "pay the money that is [one's] own" is too often inscribed as the quintessential exemplar of life in a

democracy. Perhaps due to that presumption, beauty rituals hatched on Madison Avenue or in Beverly Hills do not bear the onus of "barbarism" here, despite the social compulsions, psychological drives, and magical thinking that impel them.

By the same token, American oversimplifications suppress the fact that African women's relations to female genital operations are complex and variable, as are the operations themselves, of course. The operations can be roughly grouped into four sorts: circumcision, the removal of the clitoral hood or "female prepuce"; clitoridectomy, "the partial or total removal of the clitoris"; excision, "the removal of the clitoris and all or part of the labia minora"; and infibulation, "the removal of all external genitalia followed by the stitching together of most of the vaginal opening."[52] As will be discussed, motivations for any of these practices are highly variable across time and between individuals as well as between cultures. Vicki Kirby points out the distortions that come with Western monolithizing: "What is 'other' for the West must thereby forfeit its own internal contradictions and diversities in this singular and homogenizing determination of alterity."[53]

Additionally, African vaginal aesthetics are not limited to such sheerings away of vulvular tissue. Although now it is predominantly the members of the royal family who still practice this technique (which is thus a sign of status), the Buganda people in Uganda have a tradition of stretching and massaging the labia and clitoris from childhood to extend them (for feminine beautification). As Londa Schiebinger describes, some say that the "Hottentot aprons," so fetishized by Europeans, were also the result of cosmetic manipulations, on the part of African women seeking beauty.[54]

If one considers all female circumcision practices in Africa to be analogous, as is too commonly the case in popular American analysis of the phenomenon, not only does one miss the dramatic differences between the different forms of FGO, but one also fails to understand the relevant differences between people who practice it as a part of their cultural life and those who experience it as a part of their religious life. Crucial issues of consent are blurred with such elisions. Western critics of African genital surgeries can also miss completely the role that it often plays in the symbolism of resistance and political struggle, both colonial and tribal.[55] In *Facing Mt. Kenya: The Tribal Life of the Kikuyu* (1953), Jomo Kenyatta remarks that "the overwhelming majority of [the local people] believe that it is the secret aim of those who attack this country's old customs to disintegrate their social order and thereby hasten their Europeanization."[56] An additional point: although female circumcision is not explicitly directed by any religious text, it is practiced as an expression of Muslim, Christian, and Jewish religious observance among various African populations. Overall, it should not be imagined as concomitant with Islam (which it regularly is, often in an anti-Arab conflation), or even as a primarily religious practice.

In most regions, female circumcision practices are determined more by cultural factors, and by ethnic, national, tribal, and postcolonial politics, than by religion. They are by no means solely or exotically "ritualistic" in a way that entirely distinguishes them from nonimmigrant American operations on vaginas. Female genital operations are understood, variously, as hygiene, as beautification, as a curb to female sexuality, as a clarification of the difference between the sexes, as an enhancement of male sexual pleasure, as conducive to fertility and/or monogamy, as disease prevention, and as a means of conforming with social norms and ensuring that one's daughter will be marriageable, that she will be able to take her place among her age set, and that the solidarity and social strength of older women's organizations will be able to flourish.[57]

SURGERY, SISTERLINESS, AND THE "RIGHT TO CHOOSE"

Among the key motivating factors raised by African women who favor female genital surgeries are beautification, transcendence of shame, and the desire to conform; these clearly matter to American women seeking cosmetic surgery on their labia, as well. Thus, the motivations that impel African-rooted FGOs and American labiaplasties should not be envisioned as radically distinct. Not only does such oversimplification lead to a dangerous reanimation of the un/civilized binary, but it also leaves the feminist with dull tools for analysis of either phenomenon. There are aesthetic parallels between the Western and the African procedures. The enthusiasm for the clean slit voiced so vigorously by the American plastic surgeon I consulted is echoed among a group of Egyptian mothers discussing female genital operations for their daughters in the 1990 documentary, *Hidden Faces*. Although several of the women laughingly nudge each other and say they wouldn't want the excisers to interfere much with "the front" (showing a clear zest

for clitoral pleasure), one woman voices an aesthetic principle about which she feels strongly. Energetically, she decries the ugliness of dangling labia, and explains to the filmmaker, with appropriate hand gestures, "Do you want her to be like a boy, with this floppy thing hanging down? Now, it should be straight. Shhh. Smooth as silk." This aesthetic judgment is in keeping not only with the views of labiaplasters in the United States but also with the vocabulary of Mauritanian midwives: one such woman, who has argued to her colleagues for a milder version of circumcision in place of vigorous excision, "use[s] two words to refer to female circumcision, 'tizian,' which means to make more beautiful, and 'gaaad,' which means to cut off and make even."[58]

The group of women chatting on a rooftop in *Hidden Faces* invokes another continuum between African and American women's approaches to feminine beauty rituals and vaginal modifications. Simplistic depictions of a global patriarchy, wherein men curb, cow, cut, and dominate "their" women, may drive home the ubiquity of female subjugation, but they leave out an important factor at the same time: although both labiaplasties and African female circumcision should be (and are here) investigated through a feminist lens, that feminism should be informed by an awareness of women's agency. A knee-jerk celebration of that agency misleads, but its disavowal in the name of victimhood leads to dangerous blind spots. Across many different cultural contexts, female genital operations are contemplated and undergone by girls and women in a social and psychological framework shaped *in part* by other women.

The plastic surgeon whose office I visited provided me with two referrals, patients who had had the procedure done by him. As part of what seemed a well-worn sales pitch, he referred often to "self-help groups," a network of supportive, independent women helping each other find the professional care they wanted and deserved, in the face of an unfeeling, disbelieving medical profession. I was interested by what seemed an invocation of rather feminist sensibilities and wondered about this swelling, grassroots support group he seemed to be conjuring up for me. And, indeed, the image of the surgery consumer as a liberated woman and an independent self-fashioner did provide a crucial spin for the doctor, throughout his consultation. The consumer-feminist in support of other women he condoned; by contrast, he expressed an avowed disapproval of the women who came to him solely to please a domineering partner. He brought up this posited bad, weak, man-centric woman three times as we spoke, and each time his face clouded, he frowned, and his brow furrowed: he said that it was only this type of woman who complained of pain after the procedure, for instance, just to get the attention of her partner, whereas for most women, he insisted, the pain was minimal. He seemed to use these diverging models of female behavior to answer in advance any reservations the prospective client might have about a cosmetic operation on the genitalia (such as, "Should I really do something so drastic to my body just to please men?"). By insisting on his antipathy toward women who kowtowed to the male perspective, and celebrating the fearless vision of the pioneer consumer of "cutting edge" surgery, the doctor tried, I suspect, to ward off potential surges of feminist resistance to the procedure.

In the same spirit, one website advertising the surgery fuels itself on a long-standing feminist call for a more responsive medical establishment by contrasting the surgeon being advertised with other doctors less sensitive to the needs of women. "Very few physicians are concerned with the appearance of the female external genitalia. A relative complacency exists that frustrates many women."[59] Rachel Bowlby has addressed the theoretical conflations between feminist freedom and the "freedom" to choose as a consumer.[60] The surgeon to whose sales pitch I listened and the creators of the web site noted here certainly understood that the feminist discourse of choice can be appropriated, funneled toward the managed choosing-under-duress of the consumer, becoming saturated along the way with commodity culture's directives.

One goal of this article is to raise the question of this ready appropriation. In *States of Injury: Power and Freedom in Late Modernity,* Wendy Brown examines some of the liabilities of the Left's reliance on the rhetoric of identity, injury, and redress, suggesting that it can result in a politics of state domination.[61] From Bakke on, we have certainly seen the language of affirmative action hauled into the arena of "reverse racism." Perhaps by the same token, the language of choice, as central to the feminist project in this country as we could imagine, sprang up in a culture where the glories of consumer "choice" had already been mythologized. Revisiting and perhaps refiguring the conceptual framework behind "choice" in the face of manufactured consent, then, is to enable, not critique feminism. The hand mirror that allowed feminists of the 1960s

and 1970s to get familiar with "our bodies, our selves" is positioned again so that we can see our vaginas. Only, it comes now with the injunction to look critically at what we see and to exert our selfhood through expenditure and remodeling of a body that is not "ourself" any longer but which is "ours," commodified and estranged, to rebuild.

Although the approach of the doctor I visited seemed agenda-driven and rather theatricalized, when I talked with the women to whom he referred me, I was struck by how very friendly and supportive they *did* seem. I had found the doctor likable but showy, like a much rehearsed salesman, but these women were engaged, candid, and genuinely warm. They were generous with their time (and with their permission to be cited anonymously in the present article), and they made it clear that they really did want to help other women with their "experience, strength, and hope." Perhaps these women were "incentivized" to speak well of the doctor (about whose care they raved): maybe they received discounted work in exchange for talking with prospective clients. Even with this possibility in mind they seemed sincerely ready to assume a common perspective, in fact an intimacy, between women discussing their bodies and body image. To overlook their candor, generosity, and *sisterliness* in order to critique the misogynist judgments that may have driven them to surgery would be to mischaracterize the phenomenon of gender display. We typically learn about and develop a gendered bodily performance, not in isolation, but as members of both real and imagined female "communities."[62] And in 2002, one senses the cultural shading that twentieth-century feminism has, ironically, brought to this community building: the rhetoric of choice making and of solidarity developed during the Second Wave ghosts through our conversations. It's a stereotypical joke that women *really* dress for each other—a deeper look at how this female-to-female hodgepodge of peer pressure and peer support really manifests itself is useful. And again, a look at the web of relations among women is helpful in understanding African female genital operations as well.

One on-line World Health Organization report discusses the impact of female circumcisions on girls' psychological health. Importantly, it mentions not only "experiences of suffering, devaluation and impotence" but also the "desirability of the ceremony for the child, with its social advantage of peer acceptance, personal pride and material gifts." Claire Robertson points out that among the functions of the circumcision ceremony in Central Kenya is the role female initiation plays in maintaining the social strength of organizations of older women.[63] The flip side of approving support, of course, is peer pressure. "When girls of my age were looking after the lambs, they would talk among themselves about their circumcision experiences and look at each other's genitals to see who had the smallest opening. If there was a girl in the group who was still uninfibulated, she would always feel ashamed since she had nothing to show the others."[64]

A reminiscent bodily shame lurks behind the support for labial modifications that my American patient contacts expressed. One (heterosexual) woman explained to me that although none of her boyfriends had ever remarked on her labia, "ever since I was fourteen, I felt like I had this abnormalcy; I felt uncomfortable changing in front of girl-friends." She went on to say that she felt she had to hide her vagina around other women and could never enjoy skinny-dipping because of her concerns about other women judging her appearance. Another labiaplasty patient reported a "120% shift" in her "mental attitude," and a "night-and-day" improvement in the looks of her genitalia, thanks to the surgery. "As sad as it is, it makes you feel inferior," she commented.[65] Her use of the second person (or the ethical dative, as it's known), so intimate in its extension of subjectivity, meant that her language included me. . . . I too felt sad, I too felt inferior. And for a fee, the kind doctor was there to correct me.

NEW RITES

It is probably obvious from this piece that, even in the age where both informational and medical technology have led to bodies being reshaped, extended, reconfigured, and reconceptualized like never before, I believe that erotic tissue is far better enjoyed than removed.[66] In approaching the politics of female genital operations, however, I would argue that it is imperative that both consent issues and vaginal modifications themselves be considered *on a continuum* that is not determined along hemispheric, national, or racial lines. Instead, we peer at female genital operations with a prurient, bifurcating tunnel vision and pretend a clean break between the "primitive barbarism" of "ritual" cutting of African women, who are far too often represented as undifferentiated victims, and the aesthetic or medical "fixings" of those Amero-European women who are presented as either mildly deformed people in

the wise hands of experts or consumer-designers of a cyborgian gender display.

In "Arrogant Perception, World-Traveling, and Multicultural Feminism: The Case of Female Genital Surgeries," Isabelle R. Gunning attempts to define and model a responsible approach to thinking about genital operations across cultures. She urges activists "to look at one's own culture anew and identify [. . .] practices that might prove 'culturally challenging' or negative to some other," and "to look in careful detail at the organic social environment of the 'other' which has produced the culturally challenging practice being explored."[67] I have tried, in this article, to meet her first criterion, and I hope that rendering American cosmetic surgery strange through a heedful look at this latest, not-yet-naturalized procedure can aid us in contextualizing and understanding genital surgeries born in other contexts as well.

Gunning examines some of the ramifications of legal "remedies" for African genital operations and concludes that criminalization of FGOs, whether on the grounds of violating human rights, women's rights, or children's rights, can seem to characterize African women and men as morally blighted, criminally bad parents, and blinded by a cultural tradition that would best be replaced with Western values. Stan Meuwese and Annemieke Wolthuis of Defense for Children International remark that a "legal approach to the phenomenon . . . especially the use of criminal law, shows very clearly the limitations of the juridical system to combat historically and socially deeply-rooted behavior." One Somali woman points out that "if Somali women change, it will be a change done by us, among us. When they order us to stop, tell us what we must do, it is offensive to the black person or Muslim person who believes in circumcision. To advise is good, but not to order."[68]

Gunning, Robertson, and writers at Rainbo's website are among those who advise that the socioeconomic dependency of women upon men is perhaps the key context for understanding and ultimately abandoning female genital surgeries.[69] They call for a two-pronged strategy: (1) work to improve women's socioeconomic autonomy, both globally and locally and (2) facilitate autonomous, community-generated cultural evolution rather than imposing punitive restrictions. These do seem fruitful emphases, as applicable in the American as in the African context. That they are realizable can be seen with the following story.

In 1997, Malik Stan Reaves reported in the *African News Service* about an alternative ritual that was replacing female circumcision in some rural sections of Kenya. I quote from his article:

A growing number of rural Kenyan families are turning to an alternative to the rite of female circumcision for their daughters. "Circumcision Through Words" grows out of collaborations between rural families and the Kenyan national women's group, Maendeleo ya Wanawake Organization (MYWO), which is committed to ending FGM in Kenya, . . . with the close cooperation of the Program for Appropriate Technology in Health (PATH), a nonprofit, nongovernmental, international organization which seeks to improve the health of women and children. . . .

"People think of the traditions as themselves," said Leah Muuya of MYWO. "They see themselves in their traditions. They see they are being themselves because they have been able to fulfill some of the initiations." . . . Circumcision Through Words brings the young candidates together for a week of seclusion during which they learn traditional teachings about their coming roles as women, parents, and adults in the community, as well as more modern messages about personal health, reproductive issues, hygiene, communications skills, self-esteem, and dealing with peer pressure. The week is capped by a community celebration of song, dancing, and feasting which affirms the girls and their new place in the community.[70]

Willow Gerber, of PATH, confirms that as of December 2001, the Circumcision Through Words program is still ongoing and has been, over the last several years, expanded to other districts by a consortium of donors.[71] Considering this impressive endeavor, which has seen more than 1,900 girls grow to womanhood uncut, one is reminded of the words of Claire Robertson: "Central Kenyan women have been making increasingly successful efforts to stop FGM . . . [they show] strengths that U.S. women might well emulate in seeking to better their own status.[72]

How *might* we emulate "Circumcision Through Words"? Newly formed rituals in this country, at least those formally recognized as such, usually emerge in either New Age or evangelical settings and can grate the sensibilities of people beyond those spheres. Initiation of our girls into womanhood is often enough left to the devices of Madison Avenue and magazines like *YM, Teen People,* and *CosmoGirl.* And yet, for all the

unconsciousness with which so many of us muddle through our life transitions in this country, nonetheless we too "feel that we have been ourselves" when we fulfill what we see as society's expectations for people at our stage of life. This is not an emotion to be belittled. (One Arabic term for the genital scar is *nafsi* , "my own self.")[73] Without the "years of research and discussion" that helped MYWO develop Circumcision Through Words, we would be hard pressed to generate new ways of bringing "our bodies, ourselves" into a symbolic relation with the social world that would prove both intelligible and affirmative. Just as analogies between genital cuttings are both important and exceedingly difficult to draw, so too is the conscious development of new, performative practices both worth emulating and only circuitously "applicable." Even in rural Kenya, the approach to "circumcision through words" varies dramatically from district to district."[74]

So I will not conclude this article with a glib, faux ritual for American women trained to hate the specificities of their bodies in the interest of capital accumulation. I will see, however, if I can leave you in a performative mode, offering a coda that I hope can "act" upon and through the reader as a textual "rite of antidote," speaking back to the cited language of abnormality, pathology, and sexual distrust with which this article began.

CODA

Dan Savage, syndicated sex advice columnist, responded to one reader concerned about the aesthetic effect of her long labia minora, by suggesting the work of Dr. Stubbs. He received many letters of protest, providing paeans to the appeal of prominent labia and/or suggesting that he advise self-admiration, not surgery. The enthusiastic adjectives these letter writers employed ("lavish," "luscious," "extravagant"), coupled with their emphasis on erotic pleasure, can remind us that perhaps "beauty" results from a harmony between form and function, and one key genital function is *pleasure.* I offer excerpts from some of these letters here.[75]

- . . . You might have told Jagger Lips to toss her unappreciative lovers out of bed and find a boyfriend who sees the beauty of her as she exists. . . .
- . . . I have long inner labia and most of the women I've seen naked have inner labia that extend past the

- outer labia. . . . If someone wants to see what vulvas really look like, they should put down *Penthouse* and start sleeping with lots of women.
- . . . many men, myself included, don't find a thing wrong with longer labia minora. My girlfriend has one [*sic*] and I find it quite the enjoyable thing to suck on. . . .
- Does female sexual pleasure mean anything to you? Not only do the labia minora engorge during sexual stimulation and have lots of nerve endings, they also increase friction. . . .
- I am writing to Jagger Lips to discourage her from chopping off her labia minora. I prefer long labia. I find that they lend themselves more readily to being tugged, stretched, nibbled, etc. . . .
- . . . I remember a gorgeous actor, Savannah, who sadly committed suicide in the mid-1990s, who had a beautiful snatch with extravagant labia spilling (an inch and a half, easy) from her soft and salty cornucopia of love. She was rad, I hope she's resting in peace, and I'd recommend your reader try and rustle up a video. . . .
- Our society tends not to be so pussy-positive, and most commercial pussy pictures are airbrushed on Planet Barbie, and shouldn't be considered reality. Labia (inner and outer) have lots of nerves and feel really good when they get stroked.
- . . . Please tell the woman with the lavish labia not to have them removed. . . . You were much too hasty to recommend clipping her butterfly wings! . . .

ACKNOWLEDGMENTS

Thanks to former students Jenn Sanders and Wacuka Mungai for their help in developing this article.

NOTES

1. Things certainly can happen. See Louisa Kamps, "Labia Envy," 16 March 1998, <http://www.salon.com/mwt/feature/1998/03/16feature.html> (9 Dec. 2001).
2. *Los Angeles Times*, 5 Mar. 1998. See, too, the following Internet resources on labiaplasty: Dr. Alter: "Female Cosmetic and Reconstructive Genital Surgery," <http://www.altermd.com/female/index.html> (9 Dec. 2001); Julia Scheeres, "Vaginal Cosmetic Surgery," 16 Apr. 2001, <http://thriveonline.oxygen.com/sex/sexpressions/vaginal-cosmetic-surgery.html> (9 Dec. 2001); Dr. Stubbs, <http://psurg.com>; Laser Rejuvenation Center of LA, <http://www.drmatlock.com>; Dan Savage, "Long in the Labia," 16 Dec. 1999, <http://www.thestranger.com/1999-12-16/savage.html> (13 Dec. 2001); iVillage.com Archive Message Board, "Cosmetic Surgery," 7 Jan. 2000, <http://boards.allhealth.com/messages/get/bhcosmeticsx2.html> (13 Dec. 2001); Patients' chatboard, <http://boards.allhealth.com/messages/get/bhcosmeticsx2.html>
3. See Kamps. Also, see Carrie Havranek, "The New Sex Surgeries," *Cosmopolitan*, November 1998, 146.
4. Ellen Frankfort, *Vaginal Politics* (New York: Quadrangle, 1972). See, too, Julia Scheeres, "Vulva Goldmine: How Cosmetic Surgeons Snatch Your Money," *Bitch* 11 (January 2000): 70–84.
5. Boston Women's Health Collective, *Our Bodies, Ourselves* (New York: Simon ; Schuster, 1973). Updated editions have continued to be released. See Boston Women's Health Collective, *Our Bodies, Ourselves for the New Century: A Book by and for Women* (New York: Simon ; Schuster, 1998).
6. See Amelia Jones, ed., *Sexual Politics: Judy Chicago's Dinner Party in Feminist Art History* (Berkeley: University of California Press, 1996); Shannon Bell, "Prostitute Performances: Sacred Carnival Theorists of the Female Body," from her *Reading, Writing, and Rewriting the Prostitute Body* (Bloomington: Indiana University Press, 1994), 137–84; and Eve Ensler, *The Vagina Monologues* (New York: Villard Press, 1998).
7. Although some women enjoy orgasmic ejaculation, it remains an exception to the rule.
8. Linda Williams's book is about pornographic films, especially those of the 1970s: *Hard Core: Power, Pleasure, and the "Frenzy of the Visible"* (Berkeley: University of California Press, 1989), 50.
9. See Michel Foucault, *The History of Sexuality,* vol. 1, *An Introduction* (New York: Random House, 1978).
10. See Gershon Legman, *Rationale of the Dirty Joke: An Analysis of Sexual Humor* (New York: Breaking Point Press, 1975), 547.
11. In a mode that both ridicules and familiarizes the body modifications of plastic surgery, tabloids regularly feature articles about the "work" being done on celebrities, with a special emphasis on implant disasters. See, for instance, "Hollywood's Plastic Surgery Nightmares: When Breast Implants Go Bad," *National Enquirer,* 4 May 1999, 28–33. Kathy Davis discusses popular coverage of celebrity

surgeries in *Reshaping the Female Body: The Dilemma of Cosmetic Surgery* (New York: Routledge, 1995), 18.

12. See the work of the late historian Roland Marchand, *Advertising the American Dream: Making Way for Modernity, 1920–1940* (Berkeley: University of California Press, 1985), 18–20.

13. Davis; Elizabeth Haiken, *Venus Envy: A History of Cosmetic Surgery* (Baltimore: Johns Hopkins University Press, 1997); Sander Gilman, *Making the Body Beautiful: A Cultural History of Aesthetic Surgery* (Princeton: Princeton University Press, 1999). Also, see Claudia Springer, *Electronic Eros: Bodies and Desire in the Postindustrial Age* (Austin: University of Texas Press, 1996).

14. Milton T. Edgerton and H.R. McClary, quoted in Haiken, 244.

15. On the thin line between identification and desire, between wanting to be like someone and wanting to bed down with them (so exploited in consumer culture), see Diana Fuss, "Fashion and the Homospectatorial Look," in *On Fashion*, ed. Shari Benstock and Suzanne Ferriss (New Brunswick, N.J.: Rutgers University Press, 1994), 211–32; and Judith Butler, *Gender Trouble: Feminism and the Subversion of Identity* (New York: Routledge, 1990), esp. 57–72.

16. Josey Vogels, "My Messy Bedroom," *See*, 10 July 1997, <http://www.greatwest.ca/SEE/Issues/1997/970710/josey.html> (13 Dec. 2001).

17. Laura Kipnis, *Bound and Gagged: Pornography and the Politics of Fantasy in America* (New York: Grove, 1996).

18. Susie Bright, "The Pussy Shot: An Interview with Andrew Blake," *Sexwise* (New York: Cleis Press, 1995), 82.

19. Haiken, 29–34, 136–45, 237, 246.

20. See Richard Goldstein, "Porn Free," *Village Voice*, 1 Sept. 1998, 28–34. My own research for a work-in-progress, "Choosing the Moves: Choreography in the Strip Club," also bears this out.

21. See Nedahl Stelio, "Do You Know What a Vagina Looks Like?" *Cosmopolitan*, August 2001, 126–28, on sex magazines' doctoring of vaginas and the increased prevalence of labiaplasty.

22. Luce Irigaray, *This Sex Which Is Not One*, trans. Catherine Porter (Ithaca: Cornell University Press, 1985), 209. Also see her *Speculum of the Other Woman* (Ithaca: Cornell University Press, 1986).

23. See Mary Douglas on a cross-cultural tendency to approach marginal zones, marginal people, and marginal periods with great apprehension, in *Purity and Danger: An Analysis of the Concepts of Pollution and Taboo* (1966; reprint, New York: Routledge, 1992).

24. Mary Russo, *The Female Grotesque: Risk, Excess, and Modernity* (New York: Routledge, 1994), 8.

25. See <http://www.psurg.com/gallery.html> (13 Dec. 2001).

26. Haiken, 5.

27. Natalie Zemon Davis, "Women on Top," in her *Society and Culture in Early Modern France* (Stanford: Stanford University Press, 1975), 124. See 124–31.

28. Denise Stoklos, remark made in Solo Performance Composition, her course offered by the Performance Studies Department, New York University, Spring 2000. "Our primary dialogue is with gravity," Stoklos says.

29. See Ambient, Inc., "Body Modification: Is It Self-Mutilation—Even if Someone Else Does It for You?" 2 Feb. 1998, <http://www.ambient.on.ca/bodmod/mutilate.htm> (13 Dec. 2001). Another web site dealing with body modification is <www.perforations.com> (13 Dec. 2001).

30. Ensler, 3–5.

31. This and all subsequent quotations from this plastic surgeon are from an office visit in a major American city—location to remain unspecified to ensure anonymity—in April 1999.

32. Elizabeth Grosz: "[W]omen's corporeality is inscribed as a mode of seepage." See her *Volatile Bodies: Toward a Corporeal Feminism* (Bloomington: Indiana University Press, 1994), 203.

33. Terri Kapsalis, *Public Privates: Performing Gynecology from Both Ends of the Speculum* (Durham: Duke University Press, 1997), 89. She references Julia Kristeva, *Powers of Horror: An Essay on Abjection* (New York: Columbia University Press, 1982). On the cultural and political implications of representations of genitalia in anatomical textbooks, see Lisa Jean Moore and Adele E. Clarke, "Clitoral Conventions and Transgressions: Graphic Representations in Anatomy Texts, c1900–1991," *Feminist Studies* 21 (summer 1995): 255–301; and Susan C. Lawrence and Kae Bendixen, "His and Hers: Male and Female Anatomy in Anatomical Texts for U.S. Medical Students, 1890–1989," *Social Science and Medicine* 35 (October 1992): 925–34. Also, see Katharine Young, "Perceptual Modalities: Gynecology," in her *Presence in the Flesh* (Cambridge: Harvard University Press, 1997), 46–79.

34. Thomas Laqueur, *Making Sex: Body and Gender from the Greeks to Freud* (Cambridge: Harvard University Press, 1990). And see Lynn Hunt, *The Invention of Pornography* (New York: Zone, 1993).

35. Jennifer Terry, "Lesbians under the Medical Gaze: Scientists Search for Remarkable Differences," *Journal of Sex Research* 27 (August 1990): 317–39, 332 (emphasis added), 333.

36. See Ben Barker-Benfield, "Sexual Surgery in Late-Nineteenth-Century America," *International Journal of Health Services* 5, no. 2 (1975): 279–98; Andrew Scull and Diane Favreau, "The Clitoridectomy Craze," *Social Research* 53 (summer 1986): 243; Barbara Ehrenreich and Deirdre English, *Complaints and Disorders: The Sexual Politics of Sickness* (New York: City University of New York Press, 1973); and Rachel P. Maines, *The Technology of Orgasm: "Hysteria," the Vibrator, and Women's Sexual Satisfaction* (Baltimore: Johns Hopkins University Press, 1999).

37. Barker-Benfield, 287, 298.

38. See Daniel Gordon, "Female Circumcision and Genital Operations in Egypt and the Sudan: A Dilemma for

Medical Anthropology," *Medical Anthropology Quarterly* 5 (March 1991): 7.

39. For more on this and similar cases, see Carla Miller's statement at <www.InMemoryoftheSufferingChild.com>. For coverage of the Burt case, see, for instance, Sandy Theis, "His Peers Waved Red Flags: Monitors' Concern Went Beyond Love Surgery," *Dayton Daily News*, 4 Aug. 1991, 1A; Rob Modic, "Painful Testimony: Woman Testifies of Trust for Gynecologist Burt," *Dayton Daily News*, 1 June 1991, 1A; Judith Adler Hennessee, "The Love Surgeon," *Mademoiselle*, August 1989, 206; Gerry Harness and Judy Kelman, "A Mother's True Story: 'My Gynecologist Butchered Me!'" *Redbook* , July 1989, 22. Also see <http://www.nocirc.org> (13 Dec. 2001); <http://www.SexuallyMutilatedChild.org/index.html> (13 Dec. 2001).

40. See Suzanne Kessler, *Gender: An Ethnomethodological Approach* (1978; reprint, Chicago: University of Chicago Press, 1985), quoted by Martha Coventry in "The Tyranny of the Aesthetic: Surgery's Most Intimate Violation," <http://www.fgm.org/coventryarticle.html> (20 Dec. 2001).

41. Deborah Kuhn McGregor, *From Midwives to Medicine: The Birth of American Gynecology* (New Brunswick, N. J.: Rutgers University Press, 1998), 49. She is quoting Sims's autobiography. See also Kapsalis, chap. 2.

42. Mary Ann Doane, "Dark Continents: Epistemologies of Racial and Sexual Difference in Psychoanalysis and the Cinema," in her *Femmes Fatales: Feminism, Film Theory, Psychoanalysis* (New York: Routledge, 1991), 209–48; and Anne McClintock, *Imperial Leather: Race Gender, and Sexuality in the Colonial Contest* (New York: Routledge, 1995), esp. 1–4, and 21–31.

43. See Zola Maseko, director, *The Life and Times of Sara Baartman, "The Hottentot Venus,"* videorecording, London: Dominant 7, Mail and Guardian Television, France 3, and SABC 2, 1998.

44. Henri de Blainville, quoted in Maseko.

45. See Londa Schiebinger, *Nature's Body: Gender in the Making of Modern Science* (Boston: Beacon, 1995), chap. 5.

46. Maseko.

47. McGregor, 46–51.

48. Wacuka Mungai, "Desiring the 'Mutilated' African Woman," paper, 1999. Mungai is a doctoral student at New York University and assistant program director at Rainbo, an organization devoted in large part to advocating for African women around the issue of female circumcision.

49. Nahid Toubia, *Female Genital Mutilation: A Call for Global Action*, 3d ed. (New York: Women, Ink, 1995), 35.

50. See Janice Boddy, "Body Politics: Continuing the Anticircumcision Crusade"; and Faye Ginsburg, "What Do Women Want? Feminist Anthropology Confronts Clitoridectomy," both in *Medical Anthropology Quarterly* 5 (March 1991): 15–19.

51. Inga Muscio, *Cunt: A Declaration of Independence* (Toronto: Seal Press, 1998), 134–35.

52. "Female Genital Mutilation: A Human Rights Information Pack" (London: Amnesty International, 1997).

53. Vicki Kirby, "On the Cutting Edge: Feminism and Clitoridectomy," *Australian Feminist Studies* 5 (summer 1987): 35–56.

54. In New York City, March 1999, Wacuka Mungai shared one anecdote with me about a Buganda woman who took one trip to a gynecologist in North America: the doctor was flabbergasted and wanted to rush in a crowd of residents to stare at her. Of course, this reaction was not welcomed by the patient and she shied away from the entire profession afterward, rather than risk a reoccurrence of the circus atmosphere the doctor had created. See also, Lauran Neergard, "Doctors See More Female Circumcision," 17 Sept. 1999, posted at <http://www.worldafricannet.com/news/news7861.html>. And see this web site, that catalogs body modifications across cultures: <http://www.cadewalk.com/mods/modify.htm>. Also, see Schiebinger.

55. See Claire Robertson, "Grassroots in Kenya: Women, Genital Mutilation, and Collective Action, 1920–1990," *Signs* 21 (spring 1996): 615–42, on some of the history of circumcision's changing meaning in Kenya over the course of the twentieth century. Mungai suggested that the *tribal* politics, in addition to the politics of colonial resistance, were perhaps more complex than Robertson's article describes. See also, Isabelle R. Gunning, "Arrogant Perception, World Traveling, and Multicultural Feminism: The Case of Female Genital Surgeries," *Columbia Human Rights Law Review* 23 (Summer 1992): 189–248.

56. Jomo Kenyatta, quoted in Gunning, 228.

57. See, for instance, Nadia Kamal Khalifa, "Reasons Behind Practicing Re-circumcision among Educated Sudanese Women," *Ahfad Journal* 11, no. 2 (1994): 16–32; Anke van der Kwaake, "Female Circumcision and Gender Identity: A Questionable Alliance?" *Social Science and Medicine* 35, no. 6 (1992): 777–87.

58. Claire Hunt and Kim Longinotto, with Safaa Fathay, *Hidden Faces,* videorecording (New York: Twentieth Century Vixen Production/Women Make Movies, 1990). And see Elizabeth Oram, introduction to Zainaba's "Lecture on Clitoridectomy to the Midwives of Touil, Mauritania" (1987), in *Opening the Gates: A Century of Arab Feminist Writing,* ed. Margot Badran and Miriam Cooke (Bloomington: Indiana University Press, 1990), 63–71.

59. See <http://www.altermd.com/female/index.html> (13 Dec. 2001).

60. See Rachel Bowlby, in *Shopping with Freud: Items on Consumerism, Feminism, and Psychoanalysis* (New York: Routledge, 1993), on theoretical conflations between feminist freedom and the "freedom" to choose as a consumer.

61. Wendy Brown, *States of Injury: Power and Freedom in Late Modernity* (Princeton: Princeton University Press, 1995).

62. Anonymous telephone interviews with two West Coast labiaplasty patients, August 1999. For an on-line example

of this, see the fascinating archived chat between women about cosmetic surgery at iVillage, "Cosmetic Surgery Archive Board," 7 Jan. 2001, <http://boards.allhealth.com/messages/get/bhcosmeticsx2.html> (13 Dec. 2001).

63. See Robertson.

64. Anab's story, from "Social and Cultural Implications of Infibulation in Somalia," by Amina Wasame, in *Female Circumcision: Strategies to Bring about Change* (Somali Women's Democratic Organization), quoted in Toubia, 41.

65. Anonymous telephone interview with author, August 1999.

66. An important caveat: As the transgendered community has made clear, for some individuals, erotic enjoyment is enhanced via the genital modification that comes along with reassigning gender, even if that surgery has resulted in a reduction in nerve endings or sensation.

67. Gunning, 213.

68. See Frances A. Althaus, "Female Circumcision: Rite of Passage or Violation of Rites?" *International Family Planning Perspectives* 23 (September 1997), <http://www.agi-usa.org/pubs/journals/2313097.html#21> (20 Dec. 2001).

69. Alan Worsley, "Infibulation and Female Circumcision," *Journal of Obstetrics and Gynecology of the British Empire* 45, no. 4 (1938): 687.

70. For more information, see the web site for the Gender Learning Network, a partnership between twenty-three women-run NGOs, including MYWO, "working to promote women's rights and status in Kenya," <http://arcc.or.ke/gln/glnl3sec.html> (13 Dec. 2001). And here are two relevant links to PATH's web site: (1) Anonymous, "Alternative rituals raise hope for eradication of Female Genital Mutilation," 20 Oct. 1997, <http://www.path.org/resources/press/19971020-FGM.html> (13 Dec. 2001), and (2) Anonymous, "Modern Rites of Passage," <http://www.path.org/resources/closerlooks/f_modern_rites_of_passage.htm> (13 Dec. 2001).

71. PATH's Michelle Folsom heads a ten-year office in Kenya, and oversees the organization's collaboration on this and other projects with MYWO, and their work receives the support of the Kenyan government. See "Program for Appropriate Technology in Health," *Promoting a Healthy Alternative to FGM: A Tool for Program Implementers* (Washington, D.C.: PATH, 2001). See also, Davan Maharaj, "Kenya to Ban Female Genital Excision," *Los Angeles Times*, 15 Dec. 2001.

72. Robertson, 615. See also, Carolyn Sargent, "Confronting Patriarchy: The Potential for Advocacy in Medical Anthropology," *Medical Anthropology Quarterly* 5 (March 1991): 24–25.

73. Alan Worsley, 687.

74. See "Modern Rites of Passage," <http://www.path.org/closerlooks/f_modern_rites_of_passage.html> (13 Dec. 2001).

75. All letters quoted in Dan Savage, "Savage Love," *Village Voice*, 18 Jan. 2000, 126.

READING *38*   **France Winddance Twine**

Google Babies: Race, Class, and Gestational Surrogacy

First published in 2011

Google Baby, a 2009 documentary produced by the Israeli Zippi Brand Frank, a former Fellow at Harvard University, premiered in the United States on HBO in the summer of 2010. This documentary follows Doron, a gay Israeli entrepreneur who provides fertility services, including womb rental, to gay men in Israel trying to form a family that includes children to whom they are genetically related. His customers use Google to shop on-line for genetic material that they wish to purchase. They use the Internet to identify women willing to sell their eggs. The viewers see Israeli men reviewing the egg donor profiles of U.S. white women and purchasing ova to be gestated in the wombs of Indian gestational surrogates, also referred to as gestational carriers, in the Akanksha Clinic in Anand, a city in the western state of Gujarat.

Outsourcing reproductive labor to commercial surrogates who carry pregnancies to term under pre-conception labor contracts has been neglected by economic sociologists, feminist sociologists, and political sociologists, yet it is one of the fastest growing sectors of the global fertility industry. Poor women, under-employed stay-at-home mothers, military wives, and others are increasingly turning to this form of service work to support their families. A quiet revolution has been taking place during the past three decades. The way that children enter families has changed radically among upper-middle-class families. In the 1980s infertility increasing became defined as a medical problem that could be solved with assisted reproductive technologies (ART) rather than through adoption. Asexual or "assisted conception" involving medical technologies such as in vitro fertilization and embryo transfers began to replace sexual reproduction for infertile couples. Third parties, referred to as surrogates, are hired to assist individuals and/or couples who wish to conceive a child with whom they share a genetic tie. This has resulted in a "surrogate baby boom."

Commercial surrogacy is a contractual arrangement in which a woman signs a pre-conception contract in which she agrees to become pregnant, carry to term (gestate) and give birth to a child, which she will relinquish at birth in exchange for payment. She may be the child's biological mother (also referred to as the genetic mother) or more likely she may be implanted with the embryo produced with the sperm and ovum of the intended parents (the contractual parents) who are hiring her. Unlike traditional surrogacy, in gestational surrogacy, the intended parent or couple can hire a woman who is classified as belonging to a different racial, ethnic and/or religious group because the surrogate does not share genetic ties with the child she carries to term. For example, a European same-sex couple can outsource this labor to a woman in California or India. Gestational surrogacy challenges the idea of "natural" reproduction and the meaning of parenthood.

Gestational surrogacy, in which women rent out their wombs, is a form of industrial pregnancy or contract labor that involves purchasing the "reproductive labor" of a third party in order to conceive and bring to term a baby. It includes in vitro fertilization, embryo transfers, and other forms of assisted reproduction. This form of labor involves the purchase of the bodily functions of a woman and the child that results from this labor in exchange for payment. Surrogacy is a gender-specific form of industrial labor. Surrogacy has been described by feminist opponents as "the industrialization of pregnancy" and as a "degradation" of women's reproductive labor. Despite the altruistic motives that may inspire some women to serve as gestational surrogates, this is a form of reproductive labor that involves physical risks, pain, possible death, as well as invasive medical procedures.

Imagine that you can hire someone to carry a pregnancy to term for around the cost of a mid-sized car. And you can be assured that the woman's medical condition is monitored during the entire pregnancy. You are relieved because she is receiving adequate nutrition and under continual medical supervision. Thus, there are no opportunities for your gestational surrogate to consume alcohol, use recreational drugs, or smoke. If you have donated the eggs and the sperm, then the child also has a genetic tie to you. In other words, it belongs to you "genetically" because the genetic material (ovum, sperm) belongs to you or a sibling.

Commercial surrogacy is severely restricted or banned in most industrialized nations. Australia, Canada, Denmark, France, Germany, Britain, Italy, the Netherlands, Norway, Spain, Sweden, and Switzerland all have national laws that prohibit or discourage the practice. The United Kingdom and Germany have imposed criminal sanctions as well. In some U.S. states, this practice is legal.

FROM TEST-TUBE BABIES TO GESTATIONAL SURROGATES

Aldous Huxley introduced the term "test-tube" babies in his 1932 novel *Brave New World,* in which he described a world where children were fertilized and incubated in artificial wombs. The term "test-tube" baby refers to the fact that the fertilization takes place outside of the womb. "In vitro," which literally means "in glass," refers to a biological process that ordinarily takes place within the body but occurs in a petri dish or a glass laboratory receptacle. On July 25, 1978, Louise Brown, the first "test-tube" baby, was born in Oldham, England. Her parents were from working-class backgrounds and had struggled to form a family for years.

Today, according to the Centers for Disease Control, one percent of U.S. live births involved some assisted reproductive technologies. Embryos can be produced by in vitro fertilization (IVF) using sperm and/or eggs from third parties (sellers or donors) and then transferred to a woman who is the gestational surrogate but may not be the intended parent. IVF has made it possible for lesbian couples and for gay male couples to have children biologically related to them. An embryo contains the full and unique genome of a potential human being, with all of his or her traits. Embryos are often frozen and stored for later use because the retrieval of eggs is an invasive and risky procedure. Consequently doctors prefer to use hormones to over-stimulate the ovaries to produce more eggs. Then multiple eggs (between 10 and 15) can be harvested in one procedure. Embryos withstand the cryopreservation process much better than do eggs.

BECOMING A GESTATIONAL SURROGATE

You would like to earn some fast cash. You are a full-time homemaker and the mother of one or two children. You are married. You would like to supplement your family's income to pay for a vacation, your children's education, a room addition, tutoring for a child who has special needs, or to pay off debt. You may be employed but would like to supplement your income to pay for unusual expenses. You have a child who has special medical needs and you want to convert your basement into a physical therapy gym for your child. You want to have a financial cushion because, although your spouse or domestic partner is employed, s/he earns a modest income that doesn't cover all of the household's needs. In other words, you are working class or middle class and financially challenged.

You can go on the Internet and find out which agencies are recruiting surrogates in your region. If you are fortunate and live in a highly competitive market such as southern California or parts of the Northeast, where there is a concentration of agencies who are in competition for surrogates, this will increases the potential fees. You can either register with an agency or you can place your own advertisement on Craigslist, indicating that you are available. Placing your own advertisement gives you more control over whom you sell your reproductive services to in this market.

Three recruitment advertisements by surrogacy agencies from the Northeast, one from California's Central Coast, and another from Los Angeles illustrate the wages available and the type of language used by these agencies to present gestational surrogacy as a safe and easy way to make fast cash.

MASSACHUSETTS
   Boston Craigslist: The Center for Surrogacy and Egg Donation, Inc.

   SUBJECT HEADING: SURROGATE MOTHER NEEDED—HELP A COUPLE HAVE A CHILD, EARN $35K PLUS (Boston and Surrounding Areas)

- Earn between $20,000 and $25,000 for a first-time surrogacy, and significantly more as an experienced surrogate.
- Enjoy the financial freedom of being able to pay off student loan, make a down payment on a home, or create a college fund for your own children.
- Retain 100% of your fee, as all expenses will be paid through our agency.

CALIFORNIA
   San Luis Obispo Craigslist: Circle Surrogacy
   SUBJECT HEADING: Looking for Surrogate Mothers $25,000
   Circle Surrogacy has been helping create families through egg donation and gestational surrogacy for over 15 years. Headed by one of Boston's finest attorneys we are looking forward to our 400th baby being born this next year. Surrogate mother must be:

- 21–38 years of age
- BMI no higher than 32
- Healthy (mentally, physically, emotionally)
- Healthy family history
- Has given birth on at least one occasion
- No use of illegal drugs, cigarettes, alcohol abuse or anti-depressant use
- Healthy, full term pregnancies

Los Angeles Craigslist
   SUBJECT HEADING: SURROGACY MOTHERS NEEDED NOW—NO WAIT (ENCINO, LOS ANGELES);
   We have immediate openings for gestational surrogate mothers at our Encino facility. Our surrogates carry an unrelated child to birth for an infertile couple by undergoing a simple, painless, medical procedure that transfers the surrogate pregnancy to you. We are a

full service infertility center, not a surrogate agency so we subtract NO agency fees from you and are able to match our surrogates directly with waiting couples in need of a surrogate. Our surrogates are paid a base compensation rate of $24,000 for a successful pregnancy and delivery in addition to having all direct medical expenses and personal pregnancy related expenses paid for. . . . You must be between the ages of 21 and 43, and must be drug, alcohol and tobacco free. Drug, alcohol and tobacco testing will be carried out.

What we see from these recruitment advertisements is that the discomfort, health risks and any potential medical dangers are not mentioned or addressed. There is also an emphasis on earning "fast cash."

INDEPENDENT ADVERTISEMENTS BY SURROGATES

Some surrogates place their own advertisements on the Internet. This gives them more control over the characteristics of the couple for whom they would carry a child. It allows surrogates to set limits because they can represent themselves without having to conform to the constraints of the agencies, which may have non-discrimination policies. For example, some prospective surrogates may hold strong religious beliefs and may not want to carry a child for same-sex couples or for individuals who are not Christians. Here are some examples of how surrogates represent themselves as "free agents."

- I am a non-religious 35 year-old happily married mother of three (7, 4, 17 months) who wants to help you realize your dream of being a parent. I have had 3 full-term pregnancies with no complications.

Within the gestational surrogacy market, a niche has emerged for surrogates willing to carry babies to term for same-sex couples. Agencies such as Surrogate Alternatives.com advertise to same-sex couples seeking a surrogate. Its website reaches out to same-sex couples with assurance and emphasizes the legal support they offer and the changes in attitudes. For example:

Years ago being gay meant living a life without children. Never being able to hold or love a child that is biologically your own. That has all changed!!! You are no longer restricted due to your sexuality and people aren't as closed minded about men raising children

without a mother in the dynamic. . . . This medical procedure allows for BOTH parents to fertilize the embryo and to transfer one embryo fertilized by one parent and the second fertilized by the other, thus if both embryos grow into the babies, the clients would know each has a biological child on the way.

Sometimes single gay men post their own ads for surrogates while working with an attorney who specializes in surrogacy. These men tend to be well-paid professionals who are seeking a surrogate because they do not have a sibling or close female friend who can serve as a surrogate for them. In other words, they do not have access to an altruistic surrogate within their familial or friendship network. Like heterosexual couples they use the sperm of the intended father and purchase ovum; they are splitting the function between the donor (genetic mother) and the carrier (gestational surrogate), which also minimizes legal problems since the gestational surrogate who gives birth to the child has no genetic tie to the child she carries. An example of an ad posted in the summer of 2010 on Craigslist represents the approach of single gay men:

ALL I NEED IS YOU . . . HOPEFUL DAD ISO[1] GESTATIONAL SURROGATE $22K (PHILADELPHIA, PA)
PHYSICIAN SEEKS GESTATIONAL SURROGATE
My name is Edward. . . . And I am looking for a Gestational Surrogate to help me become a father. I have many close friends and loving parents, but something is missing in my life—a family of my own. . . . I have found an Egg Donor, but still need a special woman to carry the child. Could that woman be you? . . . Please respond if you are wiling to join my team and be my Gestational Surrogate, and if you:

- are comfortable carrying a child for a single gay father
- are 21–40 years old
- have given birth
- have a healthy lifestyle with no smoking, drug use or alcohol abuse
- reside in a surrogacy-friendly state in the Northeast

Compensation: $22,000–27,000 depending on your experience and health insurance. Plus generous benefits . . . $5,000 twins supplement and more.

This ad also shows the market value of experience. Having previously carried a pregnancy to term and given birth as a gestational surrogate increases one's market value and the wages that one can command because it demonstrates that a woman is already familiar with the process and has delivered a desirable product. Depending upon the region, wealth, and desperation of the contracting person, this experience can translate into an additional $5,000–$10,000 in wages. Another factor however, is the number of available (and acceptable) surrogates in a region. In a competitive region where agencies and intended parents are competing for the most desirable surrogates, the price that a surrogate (as well as an egg donor) can command increases.

RACISM AMONG U.S. GESTATIONAL SURROGATES: A SAN FRANCISCO CASE

Commercial surrogacy contracts allow women from racial and ethnic minorities to carry and bear children for women from high income and racially dominant groups—thus extending a long history of poor women and women of color doing a form of service—work and nurturing labor—modern day "wet nurses."

In her research in the San Francisco Bay Area, Gillian Goslinga-Roy (2000) found that 'race' was a significant factor in how the white gestational surrogate she followed during the entire process maintained her bodily integrity. She uncovered the racist ideologies that structured this woman's experience of the surrogacy process. Some white surrogates will refuse to carry a child who is the product of black parents. According to Goslinga-Roy's analysis, the absolute rejection of blacks and refusal to serve as a gestational surrogate for a black couple enabled this white surrogate to maintain a feeling of bodily integrity. She notes that Julie explained that:

It feels foreign to me. Different. I could carry a Japanese baby or a Chinese baby because they are white to me. Society sees them as white. But a Black child is more difficult. I'm already surrounded by controversy: I married a man thirty-two years older than me. I work in a later-term, problem-pregnancy abortion facility, and I'm a surrogate. To give birth to a Black child would add one more controversial aspect to my life and I'm not ready to be on the front page of the *National Enquirer*.

In her analysis, Goslinga-Roy argues that "What struck me more, however, was how carrying someone else's (white) child provoked no gut reaction in her whatsoever. . . But the mere thought of carrying someone else's Black child immediately made her experience of surrogacy as a very intimate and at once very public violation of her bodily and moral boundaries. Whiteness, I had to conclude was the invisible glue that held her narrative of gestational surrogacy together" (116).

Innovations in reproductive technologies have allowed people to select surrogates who are classified as racially different from them to carry their fetus because there is no genetic tie, thus it is simply a form of labor. During the past decades there has been a dramatic change in the fertility industry with higher income people primarily of European, European-American, Canadian, and Japanese origins selecting surrogates from a racial, ethnic or national group presumed to be different from their own. Helena Ragone (2000) identified an emerging preference for gestational surrogates whom parents perceive as racially or ethnically different from themselves (2000). In the aftermath of the Calvert trial, in which a surrogate and the genetic parents fought over the right to the child, some argue that this is an attempt by intended parents to minimize their exposure to legal conflicts over infants born under surrogacy contracts.

In her analysis of the shifting and paradoxical meaning of the genetic tie, Dorothy Roberts (1995) argues that "The institution of slavery made the genetic tie to the slave mother critical to determining a child's social status, yet legally insignificant to the relationship between male slave owners and their mulatto children. Although today we generally assume that the genetic tie creates an enduring bond between parents and their children, the law often disregards it in the cases of surrogate mothers, sperm donors and unwed fathers" (210–211).

TOWARDS A MODEL OF REPRODUCTIVE JUSTICE

The economic benefits of motherhood are structured along racial, ethnic, caste, and class lines, with poor women renting their wombs out for service to higher income women (and often racially dominant or higher caste individuals and couples) in exchange for capital. They are selling their bodily labor to more economically privileged women. Surrogacy is an industry that is embedded in racial and class hierarchies. Amrita Pande (2009) has argued that "Commercial surrogacy is an unusual type of work that has characteristics of both sex work and care work and, thus becomes an exciting way to extend the literature on gender and work." I agree with Pande. However, her analysis is limited by its failure to adequately consider racial inequalities in the U.S. or caste hierarchies in India. Pande's analysis is not in dialogue with critical race theorists, thus it provides little insight into the racial and ethnic hierarchies in the U.S. market. Commercial surrogacy can best be understood as a form of *stratified reproduction* in which poor women and increasingly women from racial and ethnic backgrounds are renting their wombs or selling their uteruses to wealthier women and men. Surrogates lack the economic, social and cultural resources of the couple whom they serve.

In U.S. policy debates for and against surrogacy there has been insufficient analytical attention given to the role that economic privilege plays in access to ART and whether this form of inequality should be supported. With a few notable exceptions debates about the ethics of commercial surrogacy have been framed in ways that avoid obvious histories of the commodification of slave children and the contemporary commodification of white children (Markens 2007). In an analysis of the competing frames of surrogacy, Susan Markens concludes that "the analysis also shows how those advocates both for and against commercial surrogacy shared many fundamental assumptions about the nature of the family and were similarly blind to the significant disparities between racial/ethnic groups' real access to procreative rights" (81). Markens acknowledges that these frames reflect the priorities and racialized concerns of affluent white women.

Black feminists and critical race scholars have opposed commercial surrogacy and have expressed skepticism about the meaning of consumer choice and free markets in a nation's whose early economy was built on enslaved labor and slave-produced crops. For almost 300 years women of African ancestry worked as slave laborers and produced children who were commodities in a stratified system (Allen 1991, Roberts 1995, Sanders 1992). As the mothers of children who constituted a form of wealth for their owners (and sometimes their biological fathers), they did not possess what Dorothy Roberts calls "reproductive liberty." In other words, they did not have control over their reproductive labor. They could not choose when to have children or how many children to bear, and their children were commodities that did not belong to them.

Control over one's reproductive labor remains a privilege, rather than a right, in the United States. Access to abortion, contraception, IVF fertility treatments, and services related to women's reproductive functions . . . are all highly stratified along racial, ethnic, class, and religious lines. In the United States assisted reproductive technologies are not accessible to the poor, the working class, or to many members of racial and ethnic minorities. Access to fertility treatments are available primarily to the wealthy, the upper middle class, or those able and willing to borrow the money required.

Israel is distinct as the first and only country in the world that allows and funds surrogacy but regulates it in accordance with religious law at the state level (Kahn 2000, Teman 2010). The surrogacy market in Israel is an internal market, in that it is restricted to Israeli citizens. Israeli gestational surrogates are only allowed to work for Israeli citizens. The Israeli government does not support or encourage reproductive tourism for heterosexual couples or unmarried women, although, with prior approval, Israelis can purchase genetic material (such as sperm) from individuals in other countries. All surrogacy contracts must be pre-approved in advance by a screening committee. In Israel screening committees employ a set of strict criteria that are applied to all couples seeking state-funded support for in vitro fertilization (IVF) and surrogacy. Couples must be Israeli citizens or permanent residents, which prevents Israel from becoming a global commercial destination for surrogacy. Couples seeking surrogates are also religiously matched to a gestational surrogate, which means that no Muslims and few Christian Arabs have participated in or have access to gestational surrogates.

The U.S. federal government does not regulate commercial surrogacy, and the U.S. Department of Labor does not keep statistics on this category of workers. The federal government's failure to regulate this industry has left politics up to individual states. Consequently we have a patchwork of laws and competing and contradictory legislation in the United States. Some states, such as Arizona and the District of Columbia, ban all commercial surrogacy contracts, while others (Florida, Nevada, New York, New Hampshire, Virginia, Washington) ban payments but allow for services, while California has become the interstate and international destination of choice for couples wishing to purchase reproductive services and hire surrogates.

California remains the global destination of choice for reproductive tourists from countries where commercial surrogacy is banned. Individuals from other countries seeking to form a family by employing assisted reproductive technologies can use search engines such as Google to identify, evaluate, and hire a gestational carrier in California to carry their child for them. The Internet has transformed the experience of commercial pregnancy and family formation for same-sex and heterosexual couples.

"Google Babies," then, illustrate the complex ways that racial, class, and global inequalities are played out on the bodies of women who bear children for others. Gestational surrogacy can be understood only in the context of racism and the enduring legacies of slavery, white supremacy, historical commodification of black children, global and national racial and caste inqualities, and the persistence of white supremacist hierarchies in the fertility industry.

NOTE

1. ISO stands for International Organization for Standardization.

REFERENCES

Allen, Anita. 1991. "The Black Surrogate Mother", in *Harvard Blackletter Journal,* Vol. 8, pp. 17–31.

Goslinga-Roy, Gillian. 2000. "Body Boundaries, Fiction of the Female Self: an ethnography of power," *Feminist Studies,* Vol. 26, No. 1 (Spring 2000):113–140.

Kahn, Susan Martha. 2000. *Reproducing Jews: a cultural account of assisted conception in Israel.* Durham and London: Duke University Press.

Markens, Susan. 2007. *Surrogate Motherhood and the Politics of Reproduction.* Berkeley/Los Angeles: University of California Press.

Pande, Amrita. 2009. "It May Be Her Eggs, But It's My Blood: Surrogates and Everyday Forms of Kinship in India", *Qualitative Sociology,* Vol. 32(4): 379–397.

Ragonè, Helena. 2000. "Of Likeness and Difference: How Race Is Being Transfigured by Gestational Surrogacy," in *Ideologies and Technologies of Motherhood,* eds Helena Ragone and France Winddance Twine, 2000 (New York: Routledge), 65.

Roberts, Dorothy. 1995. "The Genetic Tie", *University of Chicago Law Review,* Vol. 62: 209–273

Sanders, Cheryl J. 1992. "Surrogate Motherhood and Reproductive Technologies: An African American Perspective", *Creighton Law Review,* Vol. 25: 1707–1723.

Teman, Ely. 2010. *Birthing the Mother: The Surrogate Body and the Pregnant Self.* Berkeley/Los Angeles/London: University of California Press.

Beyond Pro-Choice Versus Pro-Life: Women of Color and Reproductive Justice

First published in 2005

Once, while taking an informal survey of Native women in Chicago about their position on abortion—were they "pro-life" or "pro-choice"—I quickly found that their responses did not neatly match up with these media-mandated categories.

Example I:

ME: Are you pro-choice or pro-life?
RESPONDENT 1:   Oh I am definitely pro-life.
ME: So you think abortion should be illegal?
RESPONDENT 1:   No, definitely not. People should be able to have an abortion if they want.
ME: Do you think then that there should not be federal funding for abortion services?
RESPONDENT 1:   No, there should be funding available so that anyone can afford to have one.

Example 2:

ME: Would you say you are pro-choice or pro-life?
RESPONDENT 2:   Well, I would say that I am pro-choice, but the most important thing to me is promoting life in Native communities.

These responses make it difficult to categorize the Native women queried neatly into "pro-life" or "pro-choice" camps. Is Respondent #1 pro-life because she says she is pro-life? Or is she pro-choice because she supports the decriminalization of and public funding for abortion? I would argue that, rather than attempt to situate these respondents in pro-life or pro-choice camps, it is more useful to recognize the limitations of the pro-life/pro-choice dichotomy for understanding the politics around reproductive justice. Unlike pro-life versus pro-choice advocates who make their overall political goal either the criminalization or decriminalization of abortion, the reproductive frameworks these Native women are implicitly articulating are based on fighting for life and self-determination of their communities. The criminalization of abortion may or may not be a strategy for pursuing that goal.

In previous works, I have focused more specifically on Native women and reproductive justice (Smith 2001). Here, I am using these Native women's responses to questions about abortion to argue that the pro-life versus pro-choice paradigm is a model that marginalizes women of color, poor women, and women with disabilities. The pro-life versus pro-choice paradigm reifies and masks the structures of white supremacy and capitalism that undergird the reproductive choices that women make, and it also narrows the focus of our political goals to the question of criminalization of abortion. Ironically, I will contend, while the pro-choice and pro-life camps on the abortion debate are often articulated as polar opposites, both depend on similar operating assumptions that do nothing to support either life or real choice for women of color. In developing this analysis, I seek to build on previous scholarship that centers women of color as well as reflect on my fifteen years as an activist in the reproductive justice movement through such organizations as Illinois National Abortion and Reproductive Rights Action League (NARAL), the Chicago Abortion Fund, Women of All Red Nations, Incite! Women of Color Against Violence, and Committee on Women, Population and the Environment. I begin by examining the limitations of the pro-life position. I then explore the problems with the pro-choice position. The paper concludes with suggestions for moving beyond this binary stalemate between "pro-life" and "pro-choice."

PRO-LIFE POLITICS, CRIMINALIZATION OF ABORTION, AND THE PRISON INDUSTRIAL COMPLEX

The fetus is a life but sometimes that life must be ended.

—*Jeanette Bushnell, Seattle-based Native health activist (2004)*

The pro-life position maintains that the fetus is a life; hence abortion should be criminalized. Consequently, the pro-life camp situates its position around moral claims regarding the sanctity of life. In a published debate on pro-life versus pro-choice positions on the issue of abortion, Gray Crum (former vice-president of South Carolina Citizens for Life) argues that the pro-life position is "ethically pure" (Crum and McCormack 1992, 54). Because of the moral weight he grants to the protection of the life of the fetus, Crum contends that abortion must be criminalized. Any immoral actions that impact others should be a "serious crime under the law" (1992, 28). The pro-choice position counters this argument by asserting that the fetus is not a life, and hence policy must be directed toward protecting a woman's ability to control her own body. To quote sociologist Thelma McCormack's response to Crum: "Life truly begins in the . . . hospital room, not in the womb" (Crum and McCormack 1992, 121). Gloria Feldt, president of Planned Parenthood, similarly asserts that if the fetus is established as a life, the principles of *Roe v. Wade* must necessarily be discarded (Feldt 2004, 90).

Jeanette Bushnell's statement that *"The fetus is a life—but sometimes that life must be ended"* suggests, however, a critical intervention in the pro-life argument. That is, the major flaw in the pro-life position is NOT the claim that the fetus is a life, but the conclusion it draws from this assertion: that because the fetus is a life, abortion should be criminalized. In this regard, reproductive rights activists and scholars could benefit from the analysis of the anti-prison movement which questions criminalization as an appropriate response to social issues. As I shall demonstrate, assuming a

criminal justice regime fails to address social problems or to adjudicate reproductive issues and results in further marginalization of poor women and women of color. To make this connection, I must first provide a critical history of the failures of the prison system to deal effectively with social problems.

The anti-prison industrial complex movement has highlighted the complete failure of the prison system to address social concerns. In fact, not only do prisons not solve social problems, such as "crime," they are more likely to increase rather than decrease crime rates (Currie 1998; Donziger 1996; Walker 1998). Most people in prison are there for drug or poverty-related crimes. Prisons do not provide treatment for drug addiction, and it is often easier to access drugs in prison than on the outside. For people who are in prison because of poverty-related crimes, a prison record ensures that it will be much more difficult for them to secure employment once they are released. Consistently, study after study indicates that prisons do not have an impact on decreasing crime rates. . . . In fact, changes in crime rates often have more to do with fluctuations in employment rates than with increased police surveillance or increased incarceration rates (Box and Hale 1982; Jankovic 1977). In addition, as documented by prison activist groups such as the Prison Activist Resource Center, government monies are siphoned away from education and social services into prisons, thus destabilizing communities of color and increasing their vulnerability to incarceration (Prison Activist Resource Center 2004).

The failure of prisons is well known to policymakers. . . . Given that this failure is well known, it then becomes apparent that the purpose of prisons has never been to stop crime. Rather, as a variety of scholars and activists have argued, the purpose has been in large part to control the population of communities of color. . . . In 1994, for instance, one out of every three African American men between the ages of 20 and 29 was under some form of criminal justice supervision (Mauer 1999). Two-thirds of men of color in California between the ages of 18 and 30 have been arrested (Donziger 1996, 102–4). Six of every ten juveniles in federal custody are American Indian and two-thirds of women in prison are women of color (Prison Activist Resource Center 2004).

In a statement that also applies to the criminalization of abortion, Davis further argues that it is critical to disarticulate the equation between crime and punishment because the primary purpose is not to solve the problem of crime. . . . Prisons simply are not only ineffective institutions for addressing social concerns, they drain resources from institutions that could be more effective. They also mark certain peoples, particularly people of color, as inherently "criminal," undeserving of civil and political rights—thus increasing their vulnerability to poverty and further criminalization.

Davis's principle of disarticulation is critical in reassessing the pro-life position. That is, whether or not one perceives abortion to be a crime, it does not therefore follow that punishment in the form of imprisonment is a necessary response. Criminalization individualizes solutions to problems that are the result of larger economic, social, and political conditions. Consequently, it is inherently incapable of solving social problems or addressing crime. . . . Thus, even if we hold that a top social priority is to reduce the number of abortions, there is no evidence to suggest that involving the criminal justice system will accomplish that goal, given that it has not been effective in reducing crime rates or addressing social problems. In addition, increased criminalization disproportionately affects people of color—and in the case of abortion, women of color and poor women. An interrogation of the assumptions behind the pro-life movement suggests that what distinguishes the pro-life position is not so much a commitment to life (since criminalization promotes death rather than life, particularly in communities of color and poor communities), but rather a commitment to criminal justice interventions in reproductive justice issues. . . .

. . . The pro-life position implicitly supports the prison industrial complex by unquestioningly supporting a criminal justice approach that legitimizes rather than challenges the prison system. As Davis (2003) argues, it is not sufficient to challenge the criminal justice system; we must build alternatives to it. Just as the women of color anti-violence movement is currently developing strategies for ending violence (Smith 2005/in press), a consistent pro-life position would require activists to develop responses to abortion that do not rely on the prison industrial complex. Otherwise, these pro-life activists will continue to support policies that are brutally oppressive, particularly to communities of color and poor communities.

Interestingly, this critique of the prison system is prevalent even within conservative evangelical circles. For example, Charles Colson, a prominent Christian Right activist, founder of Prison Fellowship, and for-

mer attorney with the Nixon administration, served time in prison for his role in the Watergate break-in. Following his imprisonment, Colson began to work on prison reform, organizing the Prison Fellowship and its associated lobbying arm, Justice Fellowship. . . . In fact, Colson argues that 50 percent of people in prison today should be released immediately (Fager 1982, 23). To quote Colson:

> The whole system of punishment today is geared toward taking away people's dignity, putting them in an institution, and locking them up in a cage. Prisons are overcrowded, understaffed, dirty places. Eighty percent of American prisons are barbaric—not just brutal, but barbaric. . . . Prison as a punishment is a failure. Mandatory sentences and longer sentences are counterproductive . . . the tougher the laws, I'm convinced, the more lawless and violent we will become. As for public safety, it can hardly be said that prisons contribute to public safety. . . . Prisons obviously are not deterring criminal conduct. The evidence is overwhelming that the more people we put in prison, the more crime we have. All prisons do is warehouse human beings and at exorbitant cost. (Colson 1983, 15; Fager 1982, 23; Forbes 1982, 34)[1]

Yet, despite his sustained critique of the failure of the prison system, Colson never critiques the wisdom of criminalization as the appropriate response to abortion. In the name of promoting life, the pro-life movement supports one of the biggest institutions of violence and death in this society. But given that this critique of criminalization is not inaccessible to large sectors of the pro-life movement, there should be opportunities to make anti-criminalization interventions into pro-life discourse. Thus, the major flaw in the pro-life position is not so much its claim that the fetus is a life, but its assumption that because the fetus is a life, abortion should be criminalized. A commitment to criminalization of social issues necessarily contributes to the growth of the prison system because it reinforces the notion that prisons are appropriate institutions for addressing social problems rather than causes of the problems. Given the disproportionate impact of criminalization on communities of color, support for criminalization as public policy also implicitly supports racism.

In addition, I am suggesting that those committed to pro-choice positions will be more effective and politically consistent if they contest the pro-life position from an anti-prison perspective. For instance, increasingly, poor women and women of color are finding their pregnancies criminalized. As Dorothy Roberts (1997) and others have noted, women of color are more likely to be arrested and imprisoned for drug use because, as a result of greater rates of poverty in communities of color, they are more likely to be in contact with government agencies where their drug use can be detected. While white pregnant women are slightly *more* likely to engage in substance abuse than black women, public health facilities and private doctors are more likely to report black women than white women to criminal justice authorities (Maher 1990; Roberts 1997, 175). Meanwhile, pregnant women who would like treatment for their addiction can seldom get it because treatment centers do not meet the needs of pregnant women. One study found that two-thirds of drug treatment centers would not treat pregnant women (Roberts 1997, 189). Furthermore, the criminalization approach is more likely to drive pregnant women who are substance abusers from seeking prenatal or other forms of health care for fear of being reported to the authorities (Roberts 1997, 190). Roberts critiques communities of color for often supporting the criminalization of women of color who have addictions and for failing to understand this criminalization as another strategy of white supremacy that blames women for the effects of poverty and racism. Lisa Maher (1990) and Rickie Solinger (2001, 148) note that a simple choice perspective is not effective for addressing this problem because certain women become marked as women who make "bad choices" and hence deserve imprisonment.

Similarly, Elizabeth Cook-Lynn (1998) argues in "The Big Pipe Case" that at the same time Native peoples were rallying around Leonard Peltier, no one stood beside Marie Big Pipe when she was incarcerated on a felony charge of "assault with intent to commit serious bodily harm" because she breast-fed her child while under the influence of alcohol. She was denied services to treat her substance abuse problem and access to abortion services when she became pregnant. But not only did her community not support her, it supported her incarceration. Cook-Lynn argues that in doing so, the community supported the encroachment of U.S. federal jurisdiction on tribal lands for an issue that would normally be under tribal jurisdiction (1998, 110–25). Cook-Lynn recounts how this demonization of Native women was assisted by the publication of Michael Dorris's (1989) *The Broken Cord*, which

narrates his adoption of a Native child who suffered from fetal alcohol syndrome. While this book has been crucial in sensitizing many communities to the realities of fetal alcohol syndrome, it also portrays the mother of the child unsympathetically and advocates repressive legislative solutions targeted against women substance abusers. Thus, within Native communities, the growing demonization of Native women substance abusers has prompted tribes to collude with the federal government in whittling away their own sovereignty.

In the larger society, Barbara Harris started an organization called CRACK (Children Requiring a Caring Kommunity) in Anaheim, California, which gives women $200 to have sterilizations. Their mission is to "'save our welfare system' and the world from the exorbitant cost to the taxpayer for each 'drug addicted birth' by offering 'effective preventive measures to reduce the tragedy of numerous drug-affected pregnancies'" (Kigvamasud'Vashi 2001). Some of CRACK's initial billboards read, "Don't let a pregnancy ruin your drug habit" (Kigvamasud'Vashi 2001). The organization has since opened chapters in several cities around the country, and has changed its name to Positive Prevention to present a less inflammatory image. Nonetheless, its basic message is the same—that poor women who are substance abusers are the cause of social ills and that the conditions that give rise to poor women becoming substance abusers do not need to be addressed.

Unfortunately, as both Roberts (1997) and Cook-Lynn (1998) point out, even communities of color, including those who identify as both pro-life and pro-choice, have supported the criminalization of women of color who have addiction issues. The reason they support this strategy is because they focus on what they perceive to be the moral culpability of women of color for not protecting the life of their children. If we adopt an anti-prison perspective, however, it becomes clear that even on the terms of moral culpability (which I am not defending) it does not follow that the criminal justice approach is the appropriate way to address this social concern.[2] In fact, criminal justice responses to unwanted pregnancies and/or pregnant women who have addiction issues demonstrate an inherent contradiction in the pro-life position. Many pro-life organizations have been ardent opponents of population control programs and policies—advocating against the promotion of dangerous contraceptives or the promotion of sterilization in third-world countries. Yet, their position depends on the prison industrial complex that is an institution of population control for communities of color in the United States.

Meanwhile, many pro-choice organizations, such as Planned Parenthood, have supported financial incentives for poor and criminalized women to be sterilized or to take long-acting hormonal contraceptives (Saletan 2003).[3] As I will discuss later, part of this political inconsistency is inherent in the articulation of the pro-choice position. But another reason is that many in the pro-choice camp have also not questioned criminalization as the appropriate response for addressing reproductive health concerns. The pro-choice camp may differ from pro-life groups regarding which acts should be criminalized, but it does not necessarily question the criminalization regime itself.

THE PRO-CHOICE POSITION AND CAPITALISM

The pro-choice camp claims a position that offers more choices for women making decisions about their reproductive lives. A variety of scholars and activists have critiqued the choice paradigm because it rests on essentially individualist, consumerist notions of "free" choice that do not take into consideration all the social, economic, and political conditions that frame the so-called choices that women are forced to make (Patchesky 1990; Smith 1999; Solinger 2001). Solinger further contends that in the 1960s and 1970s, abortion rights advocates initially used the term "rights" rather than choice; rights are understood as those benefits owed to all those who are human regardless of access to special resources. By contrast, argues Solinger, the concept of choice is connected to possession of resources, thus creating a hierarchy among women based on who is capable of making legitimate choices (2001, 6). Consequently, since under a capitalist system, those with resources are granted more choices, it is not inconsistent to withdraw reproductive rights choices from poor women through legislation such as the Hyde Amendment (which restricts federal funding for abortion) or family caps for TANF (Temporary Assistance for Needy Families) recipients.[4] Solinger's argument can be demonstrated in the writings of Planned Parenthood. In 1960, Planned Parenthood commissioned a study which concluded that poor and working-class families lacked the rationality to do family planning, and that this lack of "rationality and early family planning as middle-class couples"

was "embodied in the particular personalities, world views, and ways of life" of the poor themselves (Rainwater 1960, 5, 167). As Solinger states:

> "Choice" also became a symbol of middle-class women's arrival as independent consumers. Middle-class women could afford to choose. They had earned the right to choose motherhood, if they liked. According to many Americans, however, when choice was associated with poor women, it became a symbol of illegitimacy. Poor women had not earned the right to choose. (2001, 199–200)

What Solinger's analysis suggests is that, ironically, while the pro-choice camp contends that the pro-life position diminishes the rights of women in favor of "fetal" rights; the pro-choice position actually does not ascribe inherent rights to women either. Rather, women are viewed as having reproductive choices if they can afford them or if they are deemed legitimate choice-makers.

William Saletan's (1998) history of the evolution of the pro-choice paradigm illustrates the extent to which this paradigm is a conservative one. Saletan contends that pro-choice strategists, generally affiliated with National Abortion and Reproductive Rights Action League (NARAL), intentionally rejected a rights-based framework in favor of one that focused on privacy from *big government*. That is, government should not intervene in the woman's right to decide if she wants to have children. This approach appealed to those with libertarian sensibilities who otherwise might have had no sympathy with feminist causes. The impact of this strategy was that it enabled the pro-choice side to keep *Roe v. Wade* intact—but only in the most narrow sense. This strategy undermined any attempt to achieve a broader pro-choice agenda because the strategy could be used against a broader agenda. For instance, the argument that government should not be involved in reproductive rights decisions could also be used by pro-life advocates against federal funding for abortions (Saletan 2003). Consequently, Saletan argues, "Liberals have not won the struggle for abortion rights. Conservatives have" (1998, 114).

Furthermore, this narrow approach has contributed to some pro-choice organizations, such as Planned Parenthood and NARAL, often developing strategies that marginalize women of color. Both supported the Freedom of Choice Act in the early 1990s that retained the Hyde Amendment (Saletan 2003). The Hyde Amendment, besides discriminating against poor women by denying federal funding for abortion services, discriminates against American Indian women who largely obtain healthcare through Indian Health Services, a federal agency. One of NARAL's petitions stated: "The Freedom of Choice Act (FOCA) will secure the original vision of *Roe v. Wade,* giving *all* women reproductive freedom and securing that right for future generations [emphasis mine]."[5] Apparently, poor women and indigenous women do not qualify as "women."[6]

Building on this analysis, I would argue that while there is certainly a sustained critique of the choice paradigm, particularly among women of color reproductive rights groups, the choice paradigm continues to govern much of the policies of mainstream groups in a manner that sustains the marginalization of women of color, poor women, and women with disabilities. One example is the extent to which pro-choice advocates narrow their advocacy around legislation that affects the one choice of whether or not to have an abortion without addressing all the conditions that gave rise to a woman having to make this decision in the first place. Consequently, politicians, such as former President Bill Clinton, will be heralded as "pro-choice" as long as they do not support legislative restrictions on abortion regardless of their stance on other issues that may equally impact the reproductive choices women make. Clinton's approval of federal welfare reform that places poor women in the position of possibly being forced to have an abortion because of cuts in social services, while often critiqued, is not viewed as an "anti-choice" position. On Planned Parenthood's and NARAL's websites (www.plannedparenthood.org; www.naral.org) there is generally no mention of welfare policies in these organizations' pro-choice legislation alerts.

A consequence of the choice paradigm is that its advocates frequently take positions that are oppressive to women from marginalized communities. For instance, this paradigm often makes it difficult to develop nuanced positions on the use of abortion when the fetus is determined to have abnormalities. Focusing solely on the woman's choice to have or not have the child does not address the larger context of a society that sees children with disabilities as having worthless lives and that provides inadequate resources to women who may otherwise want to have them. As Martha Saxton notes: "Our society profoundly limits the 'choice' to love and care for a baby with a disability" (1998, 375). If our response to disability is to simply facilitate the process by which women can abort

fetuses that may have disabilities, we never actually focus on changing economic policies that make raising children with disabilities difficult. Rashmi Luthra (1993) notes, by contrast, that reproductive advocates from other countries such as India, who do not operate from this same choice paradigm, are often able to develop more complicated political positions on issues such as this one.

Another example is the difficulty pro-choice groups have in maintaining a critical perspective on dangerous or potentially dangerous contraceptives, arguing that women should have the "choice" of contraceptives. Many scholars and activists have documented the dubious safety record of Norplant and Depo-Provera, two long-acting hormonal contraceptives (Krust and Assetoyer 1993; Masterson and Guthrie 1986; Roberts 1997; Smith 2001). In fact, lawsuits against Norplant have forced an end to its distribution (although Norplant that remains on the shelves can be sold to women). In 1978, the FDA denied approval for Depo-Provera on the grounds that: (1) dog studies confirmed an elevated rate of breast cancer; (2) there appeared to be an increased risk of birth defects in human fetuses exposed to the drug; and (3) there was no pressing need shown for use of the drug as a contraceptive (Masterson and Guthrie 1986). In 1987, the FDA changed its regulations and began to require cancer testing in rats and mice instead of dogs and monkeys; Depo-Provera did not cause cancer in these animals, but major concerns regarding its safety persist (Feminist Women's Health Centers 1997). Also problematic is the manner in which these contraceptives are frequently promoted in communities of color and often without informed consent (Krust and Assetoyer 1993; Masterson and Guthrie 1986; Smith 2001).[7] Yet none of the mainstream pro-choice organizations have ever seriously taken a position on the issue of informed consent as part of their agenda.[8] Indeed, Gloria Feldt, president of Planned Parenthood, equates opposition to Norplant and Depo-Provera as opposition to "choice" in her book *The War on Choice* (Feldt 2004, 34, 37). Planned Parenthood and NARAL opposed restrictions against sterilization abuse, despite the thousands of women of color who were being sterilized without their consent, because they saw such policies as interfering with a woman's "right to choose" (Nelson 2003, 144; Patchesky 1990, 8).

Particularly disturbing has been some of the support given by these organizations to the Center for Research on Population and Security, headed by

Stephen Mumford and Elton Kessel, which distributes globally a form of sterilization, Quinacrine. Quinacrine is a drug that is used to treat malaria. It is inserted into the uterus where it dissolves, causing the fallopian tubes to scar, rendering the woman irreversibly sterile. Family Health International conducted four *in vitro* studies and found Quinacrine to be mutagenic in three of them (Controversy over Sterilization Pellet 1994; Norsigian 1996). It, as well as the World Health Organization, recommended against further trials for female sterilization, and no regulatory body supports Quinacrine. However, the North Carolina–based Center for Research on Population and Security has circumvented these bodies through private funding from such organizations as the Turner Foundation and Leland Fykes organization (which incidentally funds pro-choice *and* anti-immigrant groups). The Center for Research on Population and Security has been distributing Quinacrine for free to researchers and government health agencies. There are field trials in eleven countries, with more than 70,000 women sterilized. In Vietnam, a hundred female rubber plant workers were given routine pelvic exams during which the doctor inserted the Quinacrine without their consent. Thus far, the side effects linked to Quinacrine include ectopic pregnancy, puncturing of the uterus during insertion, pelvic inflammatory disease, and severe abdominal pains. Other possible concerns include heart and liver damage and exacerbation of pre-existing viral conditions. In one of the trials in Vietnam, a large number of cases that had serious side effects were excluded from the data (Controversy over Sterilization Pellet 1994; Norsigian 1996).

Despite the threat to reproductive justice that this group represents, Feminist Majority Foundation featured the Center for Research on Population and Security at its 1996 Feminist Expo because, I was informed by the organizers, they promoted choice for women. Then in 1999, Planned Parenthood almost agreed to sponsor a Quinacrine trial in the United States until outside pressure forced it to change its position (Committee on Women, Population and the Environment 1999). A prevalent ideology within the mainstream pro-choice movement is that women should have the choice to use whatever contraception they want. This position does not consider: (1) that a choice among dangerous contraceptives is not much of a choice; (2) the millions of dollars pharmaceutical companies and the medical industry have to promote certain contraceptives, compared to the few resources women's advocacy groups have to provide alternative information on these same

contraceptives; and (3) the social, political, and economic conditions in which women may find themselves are such that using dangerous contraceptives may be the best of even worse options.

One reason that such groups have not taken a position on informed consent in the case of potentially dangerous contraceptives is due to their investment in population control. As Betsy Hartmann (1995) has argued, while contraceptives are often articulated as an issue of choice for white women in the first world, they are articulated as an instrument of population control for women of color and women in the third world (Hartmann 1995). The historical origins of Planned Parenthood are inextricably tied to the eugenics movement. Its founder, Margaret Sanger, increasingly collaborated with eugenics organizations during her career and framed the need for birth control in terms of the need to reduce the number of those in the "lower classes" (Roberts 1997, 73). In a study commissioned in 1960, Planned Parenthood concluded that poor people "have too many children" (Rainwater 1960, 2); yet something must be done to stop this trend in order to "disarm the population bomb" (Rainwater 1960, 178). Today, Planned Parenthood is particularly implicated in this movement as can be seen clearly by the groups it lists as allies on its website (www.plannedparenthood.org): Population Action International, the Population Institute, Zero Population Growth, and the Population Council. A central campaign of Planned Parenthood is to restore U.S. funding to the United Nations Population Fund. In addition it asserts its commitment to addressing *rapid population growth* on this same website. I will not repeat the problematic analysis, critiqued elsewhere, of this population paradigm that essentially blames third-world women for poverty, war, environmental damage, and social unrest, without looking at the root causes of all these phenomena (including population growth)—colonialism, corporate policies, militarism, and economic disparities between poor and rich countries (Bandarage 1997; Hartmann 1995; Silliman and King 1999).

As Hartmann (1995) documents, the United Nations Population Fund has long been involved in coercive contraceptive policies throughout the world. The Population Council produced Norplant and assisted in Norplant trials in Bangladesh and other countries without the informed consent of the trial participants (Hartmann 1995). In fact, trial administrators often refused to remove Norplant when requested (Cadbury 1995). All of these population organizations intersect to promote generally long-acting hormonal contraceptives of dubious safety around the world (Hartmann 1995). Of course, Planned Parenthood provides valuable family planning resources to women around the world as well, but it does so through a population framework that inevitably shifts the focus from family planning as a right in and of itself to family planning as an instrument of population control. While population control advocates, such as Planned Parenthood, are increasingly more sophisticated in their rhetoric and often talk about ensuring social, political, and economic opportunity, the *population* focus of this model still results in its advocates working to reduce population rather than to provide social, political, and economic opportunity.

Another unfortunate consequence of uncritically adopting the choice paradigm is the tendency of reproductive rights advocates to make simplistic analyses of who our political friends and enemies are in the area of reproductive rights. That is, all those who call themselves pro-choice are our political allies while all those who call themselves pro-life are our political enemies. An example of this rhetoric is Gloria Feldt's description of anyone who is pro-life as a "right-wing extremist" (Feldt 2004, 5). As I have argued elsewhere, this simplistic analysis of who is politically progressive versus conservative does not actually do justice to the complex political positions people inhabit (Smith 2002). As a result, we often engage uncritically in coalitions with groups that, as anti-violence activist Beth Richie states, "do not pay us back" (2000, 31). Meanwhile, we often lose opportunities to work with people with whom we may have sharp disagreements, but who may, with different political framings and organizing strategies, shift their positions.

To illustrate: Planned Parenthood is often championed as an organization that supports women's rights to choose with whom women of color should ally. Yet, as discussed previously, its roots are in the eugenics movement and today it is heavily invested in the population establishment. It continues to support population control policies in the third world, it almost supported the development of Quinacrine in the United States, and it opposed strengthening sterilization regulations that would protect women of color. Meanwhile, the North Baton Rouge Women's Help Center in Louisiana is a crisis pregnancy center that articulates its pro-life position from an anti-racist perspective. It argues that Planned Parenthood has advocated population control, particularly in communities of color. It critiques the Black Church Initiative for the Religious Coalition for Reproductive Choice for contending that charges of racism against Sanger are

scare tactics (Blunt 2003, 22). It also attempts to provide its services from a holistic perspective—it provides educational and vocational training, GED classes, literacy programs, primary health care and pregnancy services, and child placement services. Its position: "We cannot encourage women to have babies and then continue their dependency on the system. We can't leave them without the resources to care for their children and then say, 'Praise the Lord, we saved a baby'" (Blunt 2003, 23).

It would seem that while the two organizations support some positions that are beneficial to women of color, they both equally support positions that are detrimental to them. If we are truly committed to reproductive justice, why should we presume that we should necessarily work with Planned Parenthood and reject the Women's Help Center? Why would we not instead position ourselves independently from both of these approaches and work to shift their positions to a stance that is truly liberatory for all women?

BEYOND PRO-LIFE VERSUS PRO-CHOICE

To develop an independent position, it is necessary to reject the pro-life versus pro-choice model for understanding reproductive justice. Many reproductive advocates have attempted to expand the definitions of either pro-life or pro-choice depending on which side of this divide they may rest. Unfortunately, they are trying to expand concepts that are inherently designed to exclude the experiences of most women, especially poor women, women of color, indigenous women, and women with disabilities.

If we critically assess the assumptions behind both positions, it is clear that these camps are more similar than they are different. As I have argued, they both assume a criminal justice regime for adjudicating reproductive issues (although they may differ as to which women should be subjected to this regime). Neither position endows women with inherent rights to their body—the pro-life position pits fetal rights against women's rights whereas the pro-choice position argues that women should have freedom to make choices rather than possess inherent rights to their bodies regardless of their class standing. They both support positions that reinforce racial and gender hierarchies that marginalize women of color. The pro-life position supports a criminalization approach that depends on a racist political system that will necessarily impact poor women and women of color who are less likely to have alternative strategies for addressing unwanted pregnancies. Meanwhile, the pro-choice position often supports population control policies and the development of dangerous contraceptives that are generally targeted toward communities of color. And both positions do not question the capitalist system—they focus solely on the decision of whether or not a woman should have an abortion without addressing the economic, political, and social conditions that put women in this position in the first place.

Consequently, it is critical that reproductive advocates develop a framework that does not rest on the pro-choice versus pro-life framework. Such a strategy would enable us to fight for reproductive justice as a part of a larger social justice strategy. It would also free us to think more creatively about who we could work in coalition with while simultaneously allowing us to hold those who claim to be our allies more accountable for the positions they take. To be successful in this venture, however, it is not sufficient to simply articulate a women of color reproductive justice agenda—we must focus on developing a nationally coordinated women of color movement. While there are many women of color reproductive organizations, relatively few actually focus on bringing new women of color into the movement and training them to organize on their own behalf. And to the extent that these groups do exist, they are not generally coordinated as national mobilization efforts. Rather, national work is generally done on an advocacy level with heads of women of color organizations advocating for policy changes, but often working without a solid base to back their demands (Silliman et al. 2005/in press).

Consequently, women of color organizations are not always in a strong position to negotiate with power brokers and mainstream pro-choice organizations or to hold them accountable. As an example, many women of color groups mobilized to attend the 2004 March for Women's Lives in Washington, D.C., in order to expand the focus of the march from a narrow pro-choice abortion rights agenda to a broad-based reproductive rights agenda. While this broader agenda was reflected in the march, it became co-opted by the pro-choice paradigm in the media coverage of the event. My survey of the major newspaper coverage of the march indicates that virtually no newspaper described it as anything other than a pro-choice or abortion rights march.[9] To quote New Orleans health activist Barbara Major, "When you go to power without a base, your demand becomes a request" (2003). Base-building work, on which many women of color organizations are beginning to focus, is very slow work that may not show results for a long time. After all, the base-building of the Christian Right did not become publicly visible for 50 years (Diamond 1989). Perhaps one day, we will have a march for women's lives in which the main issues addressed and reported will include: (1) repealing the Hyde Amendment; (2) stopping the promotion of dangerous contraceptives; (3) decriminalizing women who are pregnant and who have addictions; and (4) ending welfare policies that punish women, in addition to other issues that speak to the intersections of gender, race, and class in reproductive rights policies.

At a meeting of the United Council of Tribes in Chicago, representatives from the Chicago Pro-Choice Alliance informed us that we should join the struggle to keep abortion legal or else we would lose our reproductive rights. A woman in the audience responded, "Who cares about reproductive rights; we don't have any rights, period." What her response suggests is that a reproductive justice agenda must make the dismantling of capitalism, white supremacy, and colonialism *central* to its agenda, and not just as principles added to organizations' promotional material designed to appeal to women of color, with no budget to support making these principles a reality. We must reject single-issue, pro-choice politics of the mainstream reproductive rights movement as an agenda that not only does not serve women of color, but actually promotes the structures of oppression which keep women of color from having real choices or healthy lives.

NOTES

1. This block quote is a compilation of Colson quotes from three different sources (Colson 1983, 15; Fager 1982, 23; Forbes 1982, 34).
2. As Roberts (1997) and Maher (1990) note, addiction is itself a result of social and political conditions, such as racism and poverty, which the U.S. government does not take steps to alleviate, and then blames women who are victimized by these conditions. Furthermore, the government provides no resources for pregnant women to end their addictions; it simply penalizes them for continuing a pregnancy. Thus assigning moral culpability primarily to pregnant women with addiction problems is a dubious prospect.

3. Additionally, several reproductive rights advocates at the historic *SisterSong* Conference on Women of Color and Reproductive Justice held in Atlanta, November 13–16, 2003, noted that some local Planned Parenthood agencies were currently offering financial incentives for women who are addicted to accept long-acting contraceptives or were distributing literature from CRACK. This policy was not uniform among Planned Parenthood chapters, however, and many Planned Parenthood chapters condemn this practice.

4. For further analysis of how welfare reform marks poor women and women of color as women who make "bad choices" and hence should have these choices restricted through marriage promotion, family caps (or cuts in payments if recipients have additional children), and incentives to use long-acting hormonal contraceptives, see Mink 1999.

5. The petition can be found on the Web at http://www.wanaral.org/s01takeaction/200307101.shtml

6. During this period, I served on the board of Illinois National Abortion and Reproductive Rights Action League (NARAL), which was constituted primarily of women of color. Illinois NARAL broke with National NARAL in opposing the Freedom of Choice Act (FOCA). Despite many heated discussions with NARAL president Kate Michelman, she refused to consider the perspective of women of color on this issue.

7. I was a co-organizer of a reproductive rights conference in Chicago in 1992. There, hotline workers from Chicago Planned Parenthood reported that they were told to tell women seeking contraception that Norplant had no side effects. In 2000, women from a class I was teaching at University of California, Santa Cruz, informed the class that when they asked Planned Parenthood workers what were the side effects of Depo-Provera, the workers said that they were not allowed to tell them the side effects because they were supposed to promote Depo-Provera. Similar problems in other Planned Parenthood offices were reported at the previously mentioned *SisterSong* conference. These problems around informed consent are not necessarily a national Planned Parenthood policy or uniform across all Planned Parenthood agencies.

8. In 1994 when NARAL changed its name from the National Association for the Repeal of Abortion Laws to the National Abortion and Reproductive Rights Action League, it held a strategy session for its state chapters which I attended. Michelman and her associates claimed that this name change was reflective of NARAL's interest in expanding its agenda to new communities, and informed consent around contraceptives would be included in this expanded agenda. I asked how much of NARAL's budget was going to be allocated to this new agenda. Their reply: none. They were going to release a report on these new issues, but they were going to work only on the issues NARAL had addressed traditionally.

9. Newspapers surveyed which focused solely on abortion rights include *The New York Times* (Toner 2004); *Connecticut Post* ("Abortion-Rights Marchers Crowd D.C." 2004); *New York Newsday* (Phelps 2004); *Syracuse Post Standard* (Gadoua 2004); *The Record* (Varoqua 2004); *The Baltimore Sun* (Gibson 2004); *The Commercial Appeal* (Wolfe 2004); *Richmond Times Dispatch* (Smith 2004); *Marin Independent Journal* ("Marchers Say Bush Policies Harm Women" 2004); *Salt Lake Tribune* (Stephenson 2004); *The Capital Times* (Segars 2004); *Dayton Daily News* (Dart 2004); *Milwaukee Journal Sentinel* (Madigan 2004); *Cleveland Plains Dealer* (Diemer 2004); *Minneapolis Star Tribune* (O'Rourke 2004); *Chicago Daily Herald* (Ryan 2004); *Chicago Sun-Times* (Sweeney 2004); *The Columbus Dispatch* (Riskind 2004); *San Francisco Chronicle* (Marinucci 2004); and *Dayton Daily News* (Wynn 2004). The coverage of "other" issues in a few papers was limited to "The concerns they voiced extended beyond the issues of abortion to health care access, AIDS prevention, birth control and civil rights" in *San Francisco Chronicle* (Marinucci 2004); "Another group flashed signs calling for the government to recognize same-sex marriage" in the *Houston Chronicle* (Black 2004); "Various trends and vendors on the Mall also promoted other political causes, including welfare, the Falun Gong movement in China, homosexual 'marriage,' the socialist movement, environmentalism, and striking Utah coal miners" in the *Atlanta Journal-Constitution* (Dart and Pickel 2004); "'This morning I was saying that I was mainly here for abortion,' said Gresh, reflecting on the march. 'But now, going through this, I realize that there are so many issues. Equal pay is a big issue. And globalization, and women's rights around the world'" in the *Pittsburgh Post-Gazette* (Belser 2004).

REFERENCES

"Abortion-Rights Marchers Crowd D.C." 2004. *Connecticut Post*, April 26.

Bandarage, Asoka. 1997. *Women, Population and Global Crisis*. London: Zed.

Belser, Ann. 2004. "Local Marchers Have Many Issues." *Pittsburgh Post-Gazette*, April 26, A4.

Black, Joe. 2004. "Marchers Rally for Abortion Rights." *Houston Chronicle*, April 26, A1.

Blunt, Sheryl. 2003. "Saving Black Babies." *Christianity Today* 47 (February):21–23.

Box, Steve, and Chris Hale. 1982. "Economic Crisis and the Rising Prisoner Population in England and Wales." *Crime and Social Justice* 17:20–35.

Bushnell, Jeanette. 2004. Interview with author, 21 May.

Cadbury, Deborah. 1995. *Human Laboratory*. Video, BBC.

Colson, Charles. 1983. "Why Charles Colson's Heart is Still in Prison." *Christianity Today* 27 (September 16):12–4.

Committee on Women, Population and the Environment. 1999. Internal correspondence.

Controversy over Sterilization Pellet. 1994. *Political Environments* 1 (Spring):9.

Cook-Lynn, Elizabeth. 1998. *Why I Can't Read Wallace Stegner and Other Essays.* Madison: University of Wisconsin Press.

Crum, Gary, and Thelma McCormack. 1992. *Abortion: Pro-Choice or Pro-Life?* Washington, DC: American University Press.

Currie, Elliott. 1998. *Crime and Punishment in America.* New York: Metropolitan Books.

Dart, Bob. 2004. "Abortion-Rights Backers March." *Dayton Daily News,* April 26, A1.

Dart, Bob, and Mary Lou Pickel. 2004. "Abortion Rights Supporters March." *Atlanta Journal-Constitution,* April 26, 1A.

Davis, Angela. 2003. *Are Prisons Obsolete?* New York: Seven Stories Press.

Diamond, Sara. 1989. *Spiritual Warfare.* Boston: South End Press.

Diemer, Tom. 2004. "Thousands Rally for Choice: 500,000 to 800,000 March in D.C. in Support of Abortion Rights." *Cleveland Plains Dealer,* April 26, A1.

Donziger, Steven. 1996. *The Real War on Crime.* New York: HarperCollins.

Dorris, Michael. 1989. *The Broken Cord.* New York: Harper & Row.

Fager, Charles. 1982. "No Holds Barred." *Eternity* 33 (April 1982):20–4.

Forbes, Cheryl. 1982. "What Hope for America's Prisons." *Christian Herald* 105 (April): 32–40.

Feldt, Gloria. 2004. *The War on Choice.* New York: Bantam Books.

Feminist Women's Health Centers. 1997. "Depo-Provera (The Shot)," http://www.fwhc.org/bcdepo.html.

Gadoua, Renee. 2004. "A Woman Should Decide." *Post-Standard,* April 26, B1.

Gibson, Gail. 2004. "Thousands Rally for Abortion Rights." *Baltimore Sun,* April 26, 1A.

Hartmann, Betsy. 1995. *Reproductive Rights and Wrongs: The Global Politics of Population Control.* Boston: South End Press.

Jankovic, Ivan. 1977. "Labour Market and Imprisonment." *Crime and Social Justice* 8:17–31.

Kigvamasud'Vashi, Theryn. 2001. "Fact Sheet on Positive Prevention/CRACK (Children Requiring a Caring Kommunity)." Seattle: Communities Against Rape and Abuse.

Krust, Lin, and Charon Assetoyer. 1993. "A Study of the Use of Depo-Provera and Norplant by the Indian Health Services." Lake Andes: South Dakota: Native American Women's Health Education Resource Center.

Luthra, Rashmi. 1993. "Toward a Reconceptualization of 'Choice': Challenges at the Margins." *Feminist Issues* 13 (Spring):41–54.

Madigan, Erin. 2004. "Hundreds of Thousands March for Abortion Rights." *Milwaukee Journal Sentinel,* April 26, 3A.

Maher, Lisa. 1990. "Criminalizing Pregnancy—The Downside of a Kinder, Gentler Nation?" *Social Justice* 17 (Fall): 111–35.

Major, Barbara. 2003. Keynote Address, National Women's Studies Association National Conference. New Orleans, June.

"Marchers Say Bush Policies Harm Women." 2004. *Marin Independent Journal,* April 26, Nation/World.

Marinucci, Carla. 2004. "Hundreds of Thousands in D.C. Pledge to Take Fight to Polls." *San Francisco Chronicle,* April 26, A1.

Masterson, Mike, and Patricia Guthrie. 1986. "Taking the Shot." *Arizona Republic,* n.p.

Mauer, Marc. 1999. *Race to Incarcerate.* New York: New Press/ W.W. Norton.

Mink, Gendolyn, ed. 1999. *Whose Welfare?* Ithaca: Cornell University Press.

Nelson, Jennifer. 2003. *Women of Color and the Reproductive Rights Movement.* New York: New York University Press.

Norsigian, Judy. 1996. "Quinacrine Update." *Political Environments* 3 (Spring):26–27.

O'Rourke, Lawrence. 2004. "Thousands Rally for Abortion Rights." *Star Tribune,* April 26, 1A.

Patchesky, Rosalind. 1990. *Abortion and Woman's Choice.* Boston: Northeastern University Press.

Phelps, Timothy. 2004. "Demonstration in D.C." *New York Newsday,* April 26, A05.

Prison Activist Resource Center. 2004. http://www.prisonactivist.org.

Rainwater, Lee. 1960. *And the Poor Get Children.* Chicago: Quadrangle Books.

Richie, Beth. 2000. "Plenary Presentation." In *The Color of Violence: Violence Against Women of Color,* ed. Incite! Women of Color Against Violence, 124. University of California, Santa Cruz: Incite! Women of Color Against Violence.

Riskind, Jonathan. 2004. "Supporters of Abortion Rights Seek Forefront." *The Columbus Dispatch,* April 25, 1A.

Roberts, Dorothy. 1997. *Killing the Black Body.* New York: Pantheon Books.

Ryan, Joseph. 2004. "Abortion Rights Supporters Jump in to Rejuvenate Cause." *Chicago Daily Herald,* April 26, 15.

Saletan, William. 2003. *Bearing Right.* Berkeley: University of California Press.

———. 1998. "Electoral Politics and Abortion." In *The Abortion Wars,* ed. Rickie Solinger, 111–23. Berkeley: University of California Press.

Saxton, Martha. 1998. "Disability Rights." In *The Abortion Wars,* ed. Rickie Solinger, 374–93. Berkeley: University of California Press.

Segars, Melissa. 2004. "Rally for Women's Rights." *The Capital Times,* April 26, 1A.

Silliman, Jael, Loretta Ross, Marlene Gerber Fried, and Elena Gutierrez. 2005/in press. *Undivided Rights.* Boston: South End Press.

Silliman, Jael, and Ynestra King, eds. 1999. *Dangerous Intersections: Feminist Perspectives on Population, Environment and Development.* Boston: South End Press.

Smith, Andrea. 2005/in press. "Domestic Violence, the State, and Social Change." In *Domestic Violence at the Margins: A Reader at the Intersections of Race, Class, and Gender,* ed. Natalie Sokoloff. New Brunswick: Rutgers University Press.

———. 2002. "Bible, Gender and Nationalism in American Indian and Christian Right Activism." Santa Cruz: University of California.

———. 2001. "'Better Dead Than Pregnant' The Colonization of Native Women's Health." In *Policing the National Body,* ed. Anannya Bhattacharjee and Jael Silliman, 123–46. Boston: South End Press.

Smith, Justine. 1999. "Native Sovereignty and Social Justice: Moving Toward an Inclusive Social Justice Framework." In *Dangerous Intersections: Feminist Perspectives on Population, Environment and Development,* ed. Jael Silliman and Ynestra King, 202–13. Boston: South End Press.

Smith, Tammie. 2004. "Marchers Call for 'A Choice' About Reproductive Rights." *Richmond Times Dispatch,* April 26, A1.

Solinger, Rickie. 2001. *Beggers and Choosers.* New York: Hill and Wang.

Stephenson, Kathy. 2004. "Utahns Take Part in D.C. and at Home." *Salt Lake Tribune,* April 26, A6.

Sweeney, Annie. 2004. "Chicagoans Head to D.C. for Pro-Choice March." *Chicago Sun-Times,* April 26, 18.

Toner, Robin. 2004. "Abortion Rights Marches Vow to Fight Another Bush Term." *The New York Times,* April 26, A1.

Varoqua, Eman. 2004. "N.J. Supporters Form Large Column for Rights." *The Record,* April 26, A01.

Walker, Samuel. 1998. *Sense and Nonsense About Crime.* Belmont: Wadsworth.

Wolfe, Elizabeth. 2004. "Rights March Packs Mall." *The Commercial Appeal,* April 26, A4.

Wynn, Kelli. 2004. "Hundreds Go to D.C. for March Today." *Dayton Daily News,* April 25, B1.

SECTION 9

Violence Against Women

Violence against women manifests itself in many forms. Verbal harassment, sexual imposition, sexual assault, rape, domestic battering, lesbian bashing, and child abuse all contribute to a social climate that encourages women to comply with men's desires or to restrict their activities in order to avoid assault. The threat of violence against women is pervasive across cultures. In addition to violence against women and girls, other forms of violence—against lesbians and gay men (or those presumed to be gay), boys, people of color, and transgendered people—serve to reinforce the subordination of those groups and, often, to reinforce the notion that transgressing acceptable boundaries of gender is risky and dangerous. Feminist analyses of violence against women focus on the extent to which violence serves as a means for the institutionalized control of women, children, and sexual minorities. The articles in this section analyze various forms of violence against women and contrast beliefs and actualities about various kinds of male violence. Often, sexist ideologies encourage us to accept violence against women as either harmless or deserved. Feminist analyses take the position that this violence constitutes a system through which men frighten, and therefore control and dominate, women.

Women and girls also commit violent acts. In "Violence Against Girls Provokes Girls' Violence: From Private Injury to Public Harm," Laurie Schaffner takes on the increasing rate of violent offenses committed by girls. Based on in-depth interviews with girls in the juvenile correctional system, Schaffner finds that these girls experienced sexual, physical, and emotional abuse

at disproportionately high rates. Without access to high-quality psychotherapeutic care or protection from additional violence, Schaffner argues, they respond to their experiences of violence by committing violence themselves, in what Schaffner calls a "coping strategy to survive within an increasingly violent culture." Schaffner's case studies show how one girl's battery of her girlfriend was shaped by experiences with homophobia, anger, and domestic violence, and how another girl's knife stabbing was a response to attempted rape and prior experiences of violence. Schaffner is clear that we cannot understand girls' violence as a result of either poverty and discrimination or of psychological pathology, but as an interaction between the two.

How did the girls Schaffner studied understand their experiences with violence? Why did they see them this way? What kinds of solutions does Schaffner's article suggest for reducing violent offenses committed by girls? Think about antirape or antiviolence materials distributed on your campus. What kinds of resources do they suggest? How would these resources work for the girls Schaffner studies?

In "My Strength Is Not for Hurting: Men's Anti-Rape Websites and Their Construction of Masculinity and Male Sexuality," N. Tatiana Masters examines efforts to prevent rape. Focusing on Web sites aimed at men, Masters examines representations of "good" and "bad" masculinity, of the rapist, and consensual sexual activity. She shows that these Web sites attempt to construct an alternative masculinity that does not rely on power and sexual conquest. While some sites emphasize androgyny, others focus on redefining macho masculinity, with slogans like "Real Men Don't Rape." In the end, Masters argues, these Web sites are helpful, but they can also reinforce definitions of masculinity and femininity that "may need to be softened as part of norm change." Similarly, by talking about the rapist as the "other," the Web sites may allow readers to rationalize their own behavior as not part of the problem even when it is.

What kinds of Web sites does Masters think are most effective, and why? Do you agree with her? Look at a rape prevention Web site or the rape prevention materials distributed on your campus. Do they address men, women, or both? Compare the way they discuss rape and gender with Masters's description. Masters analyzes the discourse of these Web sites, that is, looking at how they talk about rape and gender. What other ways might you analyze rape prevention? What kind of rape prevention programs exist on your campus or in your community?

Patricia Yancey Martin and Robert A. Hummer explore the forces that lead to rape in "Fraternities and Rape on Campus." Fraternity members' negative attitudes toward women, rigid ideas about masculinity, and pressures to demonstrate simultaneously their heterosexuality and their utter loyalty to the "brotherhood" create fraternity cultures in which men use women to prove their masculinity and worth. What are some other social contexts in which similar pressures for men to be hypermasculine exist? How does

this research relate to Masters's on rape prevention? Are the messages Masters finds in Web sites aimed at men relevant to the forces that promote rape in Martin and Hummer's view?

Violence against women is shaped by the intersections between race, class, and gender. In "Mapping the Margins: Intersectionality, Identity Politics, and Violence Against Women of Color," Kimberlé Crenshaw examines the relationship between gender and race in domestic violence. Domestic violence, she shows, is shaped by race in several ways. First, there are proscriptions within communities of color against publicizing or politicizing domestic violence, out of the fear of reinforcing stereotypes of black men as violent. Controversy over feminism (often seen as a white movement) and reluctance to report violence to an often-racist police force further contribute to the problem. At the same time, efforts to address domestic violence by feminists and policy makers often either ignore women of color or include them in a tokenistic way. Services to help women who are battered, such as shelters, are often inaccessible to women of color because of language barriers or the lack of incorporation of women of color into leadership positions in shelters. What does Crenshaw suggest would be necessary to address domestic violence more effectively in all communities? To what extent do the other readings in this section use an intersectional approach to violence, taking into account how it is shaped by race as well as gender?

Violence Against Girls Provokes Girls' Violence: From Private Injury to Public Harm

First published in 2007

Hidden in accounts of the rise in girls' arrests for violent offenses lies an alarming and undertheorized trend. A disproportionate number of girls come into the juvenile system with family histories of physical and sexual violence and emotional neglect. This link between childhood victimization and later juvenile offending has been confirmed by research in a variety of academic disciplines and by practitioners in social work, sociology, public health, and criminology (Belknap & Holsinger, 1998; Miller, 2001; Owen, Bloom, & Covington, 2003).

Some studies now estimate that more than 90% of girls in the juvenile legal system have histories of sexual, physical, or emotional abuse (Acoca & Dedel, 1998). Compared to sexual abuse reported by approximately 7% of teenage girls in general, this figure is staggering (Moore, Winquist Nord, & Peterson, 1989). In a 1995 national study, about 20% of women reported that at some time in their lives they had been forced by a man to have intercourse (Abma, Chandra, Mosher, Peterson, & Piccinino, 1997). One nationwide study conducted by the American Correctional Association (1990) of girls in juvenile correctional facilities found that 61% of girls had been physically abused and 54% had been sexually abused. In a nationwide study of

adult women in the criminal justice system, researchers found that almost 68% of incarcerated women reported being violently victimized as young girls (Acoca & Austin, 1996). So among the population of court-involved girls, we find a disproportionate representation of girls who are also victims of abuse.

According to a comparative longitudinal study, abused and neglected girls are nearly twice as likely to be arrested as juveniles (Widom, 2000). Researchers find that children exposed to multiple forms of family violence report more than twice the rate of youth violence as those from nonviolent families (Thornberry, 1994). At the Harvard School of Public Health, scholars studied the connection between delinquency and depression and found that 82% of girls suffering depression committed crimes against persons, compared to 42% of other girls in their study (Obeidallah & Earls, 1999). These data reveal that similar to young men, young women express depression and distress as aggression (Campbell, 1994; Lamb, 1999). Understanding this link between coercion, injury, emotions, and subsequent female delinquency becomes salient as the prevalence of abuse and its chronic and long-term effects are more widely known to health specialists and as arrest and detention rates for girls remain at unprecedented levels.

To apprehend the complete ramifications of the experiences of abuse, they must be contextualized. For example, poverty and socioeconomic class status influence girls' outcomes differentially because of a lack of opportunities and diminished decisional avenues available to less advantaged young women. Poor girls of color are more vulnerable to predation by local idle older men, less likely to be protected by the law, and

AUTHOR'S NOTE: This article draws from ideas developed in my book *Girls in Trouble With the Law* (Rutgers University Press, 2006). The research was supported in part by a Woodrow Wilson Fellowship for Children's Health, as well as the Great Cities Institute at the University of Illinois at Chicago, I would like to thank the young women who shared the stories of their lives for this project. The article is dedicated to the memory of Esther Madriz, *"Que descanse en paz."*

lack access to resources to heal from previous trauma (Levine, 2003; Rogers Park Young Women's Action Team, 2003; Veysey, 2003). For these reasons, it becomes relatively meaningless to think about abuse on its own, separated from its racial, gendered, and sexist content and meaning.

This point cannot be overemphasized: Violence against women animates women's violence. It is time we unmask the now rather flatly coined term *abuse* and reinvigorate it as the traumatic ground that provides explanatory links in girls' pasts, presents, and futures. The social consequences of the emotional injuries that girls in trouble with the law have sustained have been inadequately theorized, partially because these topics are so segregated by disciplinary boundaries. Important features of their trauma have not been afforded the primacy they deserve when working to understand the distinct experiences of court-involved girls, for it is precisely at the location of injury that the psychic and structural are inexorably intertwined. A sociology of emotion allows us to theorize how the social is imbibed, mapped onto the body, in psychological ways. The abuse and harm of young girls comes to be seen as a process, not an event. And although this harm may take place in the private sphere, as individual or personal events altering girls' very sense of self, it contributes to drastic public behaviors with social consequences. The injuries sustained, invisible to the (social scientist's) eye, cannot be understood as simply phenomenological events to be recorded or analyzed as variables. This harm must be articulated and theorized to be apprehended. These human experiences are not uniform, regardless of age, race, or gender, and especially not, as this article illuminates, for low-income girls of color in troubled urban communities. We hear in their accounts how court-involved young women worked through these processes of injury in their adolescence and find that some of that emotional work involved aggression.

A correlation can be drawn between young women's early experiences of harm and exploitation and later problems with juvenile authorities (Acoca, 1998; Thornberry, 1994; Widom, 2000). The research presented in this article introduces a sociological link that articulates a deep intersectionality among sexual and violent experiences as embedded locations where structural damages, such as sexism and racism, are heaped upon the emotional life of individuals. Listening to young women who are being adjudicated delinquent illuminates that it is impossible to comprehend girls' offenses without considering their prior victimization, but not in deterministically causal or quantitatively measurable ways. To theorize girls' offending, we must consider the distinct significance of the experiences of this harm for unprotected girls, often low-income minorities, who are then punished for coping mechanisms they deploy in response to their victimization.

Young women in the juvenile legal system report enduring prior trauma that was sustained, chronic, and acute. Whereas for boys, abuse goes against what they are taught to expect from their gender position of superiority, abuse of girls confirms their place in the gender hierarchy. A distinct process needs to be enacted for girls to heal and to achieve a sense of safety and psychological integrity. The social forces of gender influence how childhood abuse is processed emotionally and how recovery occurs. This article argues several related points. Sexual violence is fundamentally gendered and racialized, experienced differently by different girls. Abuse plays a special role in the lives of many girls who come to the attention of authorities. This role must be theorized because its meaning cannot be determined empirically. Girls' agentic aggression, contextualized, can then be seen for what it is: a coping strategy to survive within an increasingly violent culture. This theoretical process allows us to broaden the definition of community violence and capture more accurate accounts of sexual, gendered, and physical violence in girls' lives because the violence girls experience in so-called private is deeply interrelated to the community experience of public harm.

Two interrelated factors will be highlighted. First, in studies of girls who were being adjudicated delinquent from the 1990s to the present, reports indicate that they witnessed and were the victims of inordinately high rates of what is termed domestic and community violence. Second, there has been an alarming increase in girls' offenses for violent crime. Although quantitative data have not consistently yielded statistical significance linking these factors causally, interviews with young women reveal an undeniable connection between their having been harmed earlier in their lives and later court involvement, often for violent offending.

This article draws from a larger study of court-involved girls conducted between 1994 and 2004 (Schaffner, 2006). Interviews were gathered from girls who were being adjudicated delinquent in the juvenile legal system in 22 facilities across the United States. A total of 42 adults who worked with young women were interviewed as well. Interviews were life history in nature, included open-ended questions, and often lasted 2 hours. Of the 100 young women discussed in this article, 37% were African American, 35% Latina, 4% Asian, 3% Native American, and 8% biracial. Girls ranged in age from 13 to 18 years. Participant observation ethnography was also conducted in various agencies and other settings frequented by adolescent girls.

After a brief review of research regarding child abuse and violence in the lives of youth, including an outline of studies of the quantity of violence and the social consequences of the abuse, the article proceeds in the following manner. First, I highlight two different contexts where girls' violence led them to come into the juvenile legal system: lesbian battery and fighting back from sexual harassment. Second, I present a discussion of how witnessing violence is learning violence. I conclude with recommendations for future research.

LITERATURE REVIEW: REVISITING THE TERM *ABUSE*

Child abuse—its study, measurement, prevention, and treatment, and the punishment of offenders—has become a veritable cottage industry. Social work, law, public health, psychiatry, psychology, and criminology have developed definitions, course-work, even diplomas. Legal experts and government officials make their cases and win elections by focusing on attendant popular moral outrage. Meanwhile, young women across the United States are quietly dying from it. In the course of this research, I found it increasingly disturbing to hear from everyone—from Oprah Winfrey to both Presidents Bush—about prostitution, trafficking, and child abuse, while defenseless young women continue to be punished for defense mechanisms that they deploy in response to the onslaught against them.

The Amount of Harm

Family researchers and social service providers consider violence against children one of the most serious social problems of our times. According to a special report investigating violence among family members and intimate partners, more than 1,550,000 incidents of family violence were reported between 1996 and 2001 (Federal Bureau of Investigation, 2003). An estimated 906,000 children were determined to be victims of child abuse or neglect in 2003. More than 60% experienced neglect, almost 19% were physically abused, 10% were sexually abused, and 5% were emotionally maltreated (National Clearinghouse on Child Abuse and Neglect Information, 2005). Even though the rates of victimization in the national population declined between 1990 and 2003, the rate of 12.4 children per 1,000 is unacceptably high. In a national study, 33% of high school youth reported having been in at least one physical fight during the preceding year. Seventeen percent of students reported that they had carried a weapon. In 2003, one out of nine (12%) high school girls reported having been raped at some point in their lives (Centers for Disease Control and Prevention, 2004).

In one U.S. study, 8% of women reported their first intercourse to be nonvoluntary (Abma et al., 1997). Of all Americans who do report episodes of nonvoluntary sexual intercourse, women were more likely than men to report having had this experience, with just under one half of all nonvoluntary experiences among women occurring before age 14 (Moore et al., 1989). Numerous national reports indicate that sexual offenses against children are widespread (Finkelhor, 1994; Moore et al., 1989; Runtz & Briere, 1986; Stock, Bell, Boyer, & Connell, 1997). It is now generally known that girls are sexually abused and raped more often than boys (Finkelhor & Baron, 1986). Most abuse (90%) is committed by men and by persons known to the child (70%–90%) (Finkelhor, 1994). Indeed, one scholar frames sexual coercion of girls and women as so prevalent as to be a kind of a new norm (Schur, 1989). The victims of one in four persons incarcerated for sexual assault in the United States were the assaulters' own children or their stepchildren. Convicted violent sexual assault offenders revealed that more than 75% of their victims were younger than 18. Almost 85% of their victims were females (Greenfield, 1997). These data point to a crisis of violence in the everyday lives of U.S. youth.

As girls in general were disproportionately victims of abuse, so too were girls in trouble with the law. In a recent report of girls in the California juvenile correctional system, 92% reported experiencing sexual, physical, or emotional abuse; many reported combinations of multiple forms of abuse and experiencing abuse on multiple occasions (Acoca, 1998). Of the participants in my study, 53% had experienced physical injury, 53% sexual injury, and 71% reported that they had been neglected emotionally (Schaffner, 2006).

The Price of Harm

Abuse of girls takes its toll in many alarming ways: from psychological problems ranging from depression to suicide, to problems with the criminal justice system resulting in incarceration. Almost 68% of adult women in the U.S. criminal justice system reported having been beaten, abused, molested, or burned when they were young girls (Acoca & Austin, 1996). Survivors of sexual injury develop common psychological effects such as depression, anxiety, low self-esteem, loss of trust, and difficulty establishing intimacy (Herman, 1992; Powers & Jaklitsch, 1989). Researchers note a variety of problems: complex posttraumatic stress disorder, feelings of hopelessness, feelings of angry aggression, disassociative behaviors, self-mutilation, and suicide attempts are common for survivors of sexual abuse (Briere & Elliott, 1994; Herman, 1992; Holden, Geffner, & Jouriles, 1998). Substance dependency has been linked to sexual abuse (Briere & Elliott, 1994). Girls may also become pregnant as a result of the abuse, with some obtaining an abortion and others giving birth. Bulimia, anorexia, eating disorders, and self-loathing related to being overweight and underweight also manifest among adolescent girls as responses to abuse or emotional neglect (Acoca & Dedel, 1998).

Many girls being adjudicated delinquent are not formally diagnosed. For some, their emotional conditions are not recognized by parents or authorities as the results of sexual victimization (Powers & Jaklitsch, 1989). Adults sometimes characterize these kinds of female troubles as part of "teenage angst" or "raging hormones." Probation officers are known to consider girls in trouble as "liars" and "manipulators" (Gaarder, Rodriguez, & Zatz, 2004). Socioeconomic differences exist as well. Compared to privileged girls, poor girls are less likely to be seen by medical and mental health personnel. Girls from no-income and low-income families have less access than middle-class girls to the most highly skilled therapists and their careful guidance through psychopharmaceuticals (Duncan, Yeung, Brooks-Gunn, & Smith, 1998). Girls report feeling that nobody was listening or taking the time to notice and proactively help them (Apter, 1990; Bernardez, 1991).

Studies suggest a correlation between early injury and female trouble behavior such as psychological disturbances and juvenile delinquency (Goldman, 1987; Herman, 1992; Runtz & Briere, 1986). In one study of homeless youth, 75% of female adolescent prostitutes had been sexually abused (Deisher & Rogers, 1991). . . . Owen and Bloom's (1997) study of young women in the California Youth Authority found that 85% indicated some type of abuse in their lives. It is possible that for injured girls, subsequent decisions they made seemed to them to actually "solve" their sexual abuse problem or heal prior hurt and injury (Runtz & Briere, 1986; Schaffner, 1997).

The choices that harmed girls made in response to their injuries may have led them to the attention of juvenile authorities. Often living in a fast "culture of urgency" moment, their impetuous or numbed solutions may lead to involvement in aggressive and violent situations. Young women report that they often find themselves in situations where they need to protect themselves physically, or they get so angered at being injured that they fight back (Wolfe & Tucker, 1998). Others report feeling generally demoralized and debased, so they "jus' go off and do things." It is often at this point that girls come to the attention of the juvenile legal system. Thus, it is plausible that many young women involved in behaviors that draw attention from juvenile corrections may be fleeing, and otherwise responding to, childhood sexual and physical injury.

FINDINGS: GIRL FIGHTS IN DIFFERENT SETTINGS

Among commentators who notice the rise in girls' arrests for violent offenses, disagreement remains as to why. Is it the case that girls are actually more violent than ever before (Putallaz & Bierman, 2004)? Alternative explanations include that decreases in chivalry on the part of police officers and judges draw girls into the system at higher rates, that violent offenses by girls are so few that any increase in numbers creates huge gains in proportions, that mandatory arrests for intimate violence increase girls' chances for arrest at the scenes of domestic disputes, that police categorize girls' fights as more serious assaults, and that the media have jumped onto a bandwagon of sensationalizing an increase in rates of violence among girls (Artz, 1998; Chesney-Lind, 2004). Whatever the reasons, we do a grave disservice not to notice, contextualize, and analyze the system response to experiences of young women who are being adjudicated delinquent for violent offenses. The current judicial penalization of gender transgression is important because it profoundly affects young women's developmental courses and life trajectories. When young women are treated with disrespect and aggression, they learn to respond with it.

Context One: Cora Winfield Confronting Homophobia

During fieldwork in a juvenile detention facility, I met Cora Winfield, a 15-year-old raised in a White East Coast working-class family by a proud Irish father and U.S.-born mother.[1] In detention for aggravated assault, Cora explained to me that "I don't how else to say it. I get drunk and kick my girlfriend's ass just like my dad gets drunk and kicks my mom's." Her management of her adolescent knowledge of her homosexuality was complicated by the homophobia and misogyny in her family of origin. Expressing a disturbing self-hatred, Cora talked to me about how she wasn't going to "stay gay."

> I ain't gonna be gay my whole life, you know . . . I can't take it. I probably won't stay gay. Hidin,' pretendin,' gettin' hassled all the time at school or even just hangin' out—I can't take it. I'm always stressin' over where the next fight is gonna go down. I'm sick of being called "lezzie." I kick it fine with my homeys. They just treat me like another lil' dude anyways. I don't know . . .

Cora was lanky and long-legged, slim and tall. Her dirty blonde hair, bobbed straight and tucked behind her ears, fell forward onto her cheeks as she hung her head and talked. I found hers to be a particularly disturbing confession, given the high rate of suicide attempts among queer youth. In a 1989 report on teen suicide, the U.S. Department of Health and Human Services concluded that 30% of teen suicides were among lesbian and gay youth and that these were largely the result of antigay attitudes within the society. In other words, these deaths were preventable (Owens, 1998). When Cora said she was not going to be gay her whole life, I hoped she did not intend it as a statement of suicidal ideation.

There is no safe space in the dominant culture for girls to explore same-sex desire: Rarely are girls given open social permission to explore lesbian sexuality and identity as a normative option (Fontaine & Hammond, 1996; Weston, 1991; Zemsky, 1998). Sexual diversity manifests in various ways among troubled girls. Gen-

dered norms of beauty, especially for butch girls, as well as norms toward heterosexuality can impede psychological and emotional development of queer and questioning girls by tagging them with the label *deviant.* Confusingly, even though a hypersexualization of adolescence in the West since the 1960s included a sense of entitlement to explore sexualities (Rubin, 1990), for young women caught exploring same-sex desire, extreme forms of social exclusion and marginalization can result.

At the turn of the twenty-first century, a tension exists in the dominant Western culture between an increased sense of entitlement to sexual rights, a heightened homophobia and heteronormativity, and a hypersexualization of youth culture. What is historically new about attention to cases of homophobia and same-sex desire among children in trouble with the law is that for the first time in the history of modem sexuality, it is possible for youth to adopt identity categories such as lesbian, gay, transgender, bisexual, questioning, or queer (D'Emilio, 1983; Herdt, 1989). Thus, uneducated, confused, and unprepared families—and sociolegal and delinquency systems—have meager experience in raising gay children, processing their cases, and, most important, protecting their human and civil rights. . . .

Homophobia includes feelings of confusion, disgust, anger, hatred, or fear of people who are homosexual. In my research, descriptions of events surrounding homophobic feelings—which girls expressed toward each other and toward themselves—was a pattern that emerged from listening to the accounts of girls' troubles and their behaviors of anger- and aggression-related offending. In an ominous development for queer and questioning young women who struggle simultaneously with their sexuality, self-love, and a need to avoid juvenile corrections, homophobia was on the rise in schools, and gay bashing among youth was widespread in the United States (Brooke, 1998; D'Augelli & Dark, 1995; Kurwa, 1998; Sullivan, 1998). In a recent poll of thousands of the highest achieving American high school students, almost half admitted prejudice against gays and lesbians (Ness, 1998). Ten percent of girls reported "being called lesbian" in a national survey of sexual harassment in schools (American Association of University Women, 2001).

An achievement of a sexual identity is a complex developmental process during puberty and adolescence (Braverman & Strasburger, 1993). In contemporary Western culture, a society-wide and cross-cultural homophobia provokes a disproportionate number of lesbian and gay teens into inordinate emotional struggle. Those who work with gay and lesbian teen populations report that these youth describe feelings of self-hatred, withdrawal, and anger that seem to lead them to indulge in alcohol and other drugs as a way to hide from their problems or attempt to fit in with peers (Fleisher & Fillman, 1995).

Researchers find that this unique population drops out of school, runs away from home, lives without shelter, and self-medicates with street drugs and alcohol at high rates (D'Augelli, 1998; Fleisher & Fillman, 1995). Some queer teenagers—especially young women with butch demeanor, such as Cora Winfield—report that they suffer such vilification at home or in school that they are forced out onto the streets. Government agencies estimate that approximately 25% of gay and lesbian youth are forced to flee homophobia from their families and schools and that from a quarter to a third of the runaway, homeless, and street youth population are gay or lesbian (Los Angeles County Task Force on Runaway and Homeless Youth, 1988; U.S. Department of Health and Human Services, 1989).

Others note that teenagers living on the street are forced into survival sex, the sex trade, and the street economy in order to live (Pfeffer, 1997; Yates, Mackenzie, Pennbridge, & Swofford, 1991). In a study of U.S. adolescents living in the street economy, Yates and colleagues (1991) found that youth involved in prostitution were more than 5 times as likely to report homosexual or bisexual identities.

In the United States, runaway, homeless, and street youth then come to the attention of the state (juvenile authorities and emergency rooms) in disproportionate numbers (Kruks, 1991; Scholinski, 1997). In addition, the *Diagnostic and Statistical Manual* diagnoses of "Sexual Dysfunctions" and "Gender Identity Disorders" provide pathways to psychiatric wards and other juvenile "correctional" systems (American Psychiatric Association, 1994; Herdt, 1989; Hunter, 1990; Kennedy, 1991).

Data on the number of lesbian, bisexual, and questioning female youth in U.S. juvenile correctional facilities are difficult to obtain. Given the widespread stigma attached to coming out and identifying as gay, many young women do not openly identify as lesbian or queer even as they pursue sexual experiences and deep emotional relationships with other females. Despite the absence of systematic data, anecdotal information confirms the reality that homophobia in the lives of queer teenage girls can be a challenge that often includes traversing a juvenile corrections system.

Homophobia affects girls in juvenile corrections in different ways (Curtin, 2002; Dang, 1997; see also Owens, 1998). One young woman testified that when she was locked in detention, she was "never given a roommate because she was a lesbian" and that "special showering arrangements were made to prevent her from showering with other girls" (Dang, 1997, p. 17). One girl told her story of living in a group home: "I prepared myself to get in a fight the very first night when I went downstairs later that night for dinner." This young woman had been driven out of her house by her homophobic mother, but the girls in the group home finally accepted her (Foster Care Youth United, 1994). Findings from one Human Rights Commission report found that "many youth who enter the juvenile justice system for hate-related crimes have committed crimes *against* [italics added] LGBTQQ [lesbian, gay, bisexual, transgendered, queer, and questioning] people" (Dang, 1997, p. 17).

Battery between lesbian couples is another hidden problem among girls in trouble (Lobel, 1986; Scherzer, 1998). Three young women from my study (of the nine who talked about their lesbian relationships) revealed that they had beat up their girlfriends/lovers. For example, they said,

> I was involved with a hooker—she was bisexual. I was always buyin' her things but we fought a lot. I beat her up off crystal so I got an ADW off that. (Claudia Sereno, 16 years old, Los Angeles, possession and sale of marijuana)

> I beat my girl 'cause she ran away with Miguel. First we left him, but then he started buggin' her. Then we fought. I beat her bad. (Leslie Rollins, 15 years old, Marin County, CA, simple assault)

Lesbian, bisexual, and questioning girls may be victimized by violence perpetrated by males or females when they strike out in anger and fear towards each other (Pastor, McCormick, & Fine, 1996; Way, 1996). Thus, the effects of homophobia, both on queer girls who are victims of violence and on those girls who perpetrate violence, must be taken into account when theorizing girls' offending behaviors.

Cora Winfield learned her anger and physical fighting at home and spent a lot of time in public facilities because of it. She turned her discomfort with her own sexuality aggressively outward, resulting in her getting into emotional and legal trouble. Cora talked about her situation, her fears, and her father:

> My father is some bigwig in his company and he thinks he owns the whole damn world! He thinks he can push me and my mom around. If he had any idea about me and my girl he will kill me. And now he's gonna find out because they're gonna tell him I'm in here on a DV [domestic violence] charge. Like they're gonna tell him I beat up my girlfriend—not just some girl. Shit! I am so totally fucked! I hate this stupid life. I ain't never heard anyone had it so bad as me. I cannot always be like this. This is the worst! I super need me a cold one [beer] just to get through today . . .

One advantage Cora enjoyed at the time of our interview was luck—luck to be in a location where service providers could identify and locate community support for her. In the particular facility where she was detained, her well-trained gender-aware public defender put Cora in contact with a local queer youth center to assist Cora with her feelings and her case. Countless other teens around the world go through the agonies of adolescence—as well as "corrections"—feeling hopeless, angry, fearful, and sad, but with no such access to a supportive community.

Despite the sexualization of the adolescent female, mainstream American culture and law lag in the recognition of homosexuality and lesbian desire as legitimate experiences. These institutions and systems fail to acknowledge that being gay is about more than just sex, that homophobia has a devastating impact upon young people struggling to form their sense of self, and that elimination of prejudice is essential to fair treatment in the juvenile justice system (Owens, 1998). State response to gender transgressions such as "intimate violence" of gay and lesbian youth demands inclusion in any contemporary theory of girls' violence.

Context Two: Mylen Cruz's Fight Back Against "Sexual Harassment"

Mylen Cruz's story illustrates her attempt to manage misogyny and sexual harassment—an attempt that went terribly awry. Mylen grew up in Northern California, in a semihomeless situation with her mother and younger brother. She moved from home to home, in other people's houses, staying with relatives and her mother's boyfriends. Mylen Cruz was Filipina American, 16 years old, and in detention for attempted murder.

> Mommy was always totally stressing. I mean, it got me worried all the damn time. Was there food? Did Eddie [her little brother] need shoes? Where we gonna live next? I seen my mom get beat out on the corner—hell, *I* got beat out on the corner. . . . It was always some crazy shit goin' on. I din't get to have any kind of childhood, like, um, be a little girl and all—uh uh, no how.
>
> In the schools I went to, you hadda be bad if you were goin' to make it. Is jus' like that. I'm not no bad-ass but I ain't take shit offa nobody. Especially no boy gonna disrespect me like that! You got to come at me correct if you want some of this. He jus' all, "hey was-sup, girl" and all that.

Mylen talked about how Jackson, her assailant, had approached her. She required young men to approach her with respect and decency. According to Mylen, Jackson had basically just sidled up to her and started teasing her in a threatening way, putting his hands all over her body.

> I was in the office at my school and this boy come up to me to fuck with me. He was all, "I'ma get me some of this shit, man." He all started to touch my butt! He thought we gonna be kickin' it or some shit! We got into a violent fight. I did a violent act. I don't know. I was mad. I couldn't deal, I couldn't hold it. I'm not a killer but I would be able to do it. I hoped he wouldn't die but . . . I wasn't scared to come to Juvey.

She said that first she froze, and then she was overcome by her feelings:

> See I had this little knife in my bag that I always carry with me. So he's all touchin' me and tryin' to feel me up and um, and first I couldn't believe it. I was just like, you know, stuck there or something. Then, I just got it out my bag and started swingin' it at him. I went crazy!—I really did. I jus' felt it sooo mad and like felt all hot and I don't know . . . and I jus' . . . I don't know how, I just did it.

"He got stabbed," she said, oddly passive in her language. It was as if Mylen could not process her own actions, that *she* had stabbed him.

In her file, I read that her mother was often home-less with Mylen and her little brother. I asked her about her family.

> Mommy is there for me sometimes. She's always busy 'cause she has a lot of problems: the rent, money. We used to be close but her stress affects me. I never ran away, but we always got evicted. Out in the shelters, well, it's crazy. They's some crazy motherfuckers out there.

Mylen described a situation in which her family was staying with another family and her mother "had to serve him [the other family's father] coffee and take a lot of shit like she was the slave." Mylen said she hated school and knew she shouldn't have gone that day. "I knew I was gonna go off on somebody eventually." Mylen was very upset at this point in our conversation and started crying. She said she felt like so many things were wrong with her life, she couldn't figure out how to begin to fix it.

Mylen's situation—fighting off a possible rapist—was not framed as self-defense. She was actually being adjudicated in adult court for attempted homicide. Factors such as being subjected to cruelty during an unprotected childhood and witnessing her mother (her only caregiver) receive consistent maltreatment must be taken into account when adjudicating girls as perpetrators of violence.

DISCUSSION: WITNESSING VIOLENCE IS LEARNING VIOLENCE

In academic and public discourse, community violence is represented, in the main, by facts and accounts of guys in gangs with guns. Definitions of community violence need to be broadened to include what girls see, face, and deal with in everyday life at home, at school, and out on the streets (Garbarino, Dubrow, Kostelny, & Pardo, 1992; Holden et al., 1998; Osofsky, 1997; Zimring, 1998). Recognizing the gravity of wit-nessing violence and its long-term impact on the life course and development of healthy children will fuel the reinvigoration of state response to perpetration of gender and sexual violence and revive community, school, and family recognition of gender violence as dangerous and destructive.

Not until blood was spilled or police were called could the young women in my study "see" the community and family violence surrounding them.

Whereas 53% of the young women reported being physically or sexually injured directly, when asked if they had ever witnessed their parents or other combi-nations of family and household members in physical battle, 71% of the young women in this project answered in the affirmative. However, when asked if they had ever witnessed abuse or if they felt that there was violence in their homes, only a small portion framed abuse and fights as violence. A relationship between witnessing violence and subsequent offend-ing was certainly suggested by these findings, but it was as if young women did not see it, and if they did, it was not that bad, according to them.

Research in psychology reveals, however, that abuse and subsequent anger may result in aggressive behavior (Herman, 1992.)

At first, young women expressed no discord with the chaos and violence they reported witnessing. Upon follow-up questions that signaled to the girls that I thought it was crucial, they began to unfurl details of powerful events that had made up just four- or five-word phrases in their files (and lives): "gfa [grandfa-ther] raped her mo [mother] in her room one night"; "was kidnapped and forced to watch pornographic sex acts before being released"; or "was raped with a gun inserted into her vagina." Upon prompts from me such as "So, how do you feel about what happened that night?" or "What do you think that means to you now?" girls reported feeling frozen with fear, terrified at seeing their mothers and siblings being hurt and unable to do anything to stop it, and panicked when recalling harm. Of course, who can know how much of our discussion was prompted by my very questioning? Even so, that to become disturbed about violent mistreatment would need provocation was interesting in itself.

Some girls explored the idea that exposure to trauma was linked to their current troubles. A few insisted there was no connection whatsoever. Others seemed disassociated from the terror while recounting it. But many more appeared a little bored by telling their sto-ries over and over to yet another social worker, which I believe is how I was often perceived. For example, one young woman related an account of watching her mother get raped by some men who stopped to "help" them when they had a flat tire on a Colorado highway one night. Yet there was a way that she repeated the story in such a monotonous tone, as if, "Oh well, this is what happened." She knew it was an extraordinary experience, but I got the sense from her that it had become so normalized in a way, made into a notation in her file, that she did not seem to think it was of much importance or that out of the ordinary anymore. Children are now considered "invisible victims" of domestic and community violence (Osofsky, 1998.)

The girls' accounts in my research exemplify why definitions of community violence need to be broadened to include what youths (including girls) experience.

Court-involved girls revealed that they witnessed an inordinate amount of violence on a regular, routine basis. They talked about seeing brothers, friends, cousins, fathers, and boyfriends being kicked, beaten, punched, knifed, shot, and killed. In interviews, young women reported witnessing their mothers being devalued and hurt physically by fathers, stepfathers, and boyfriends. Well over half of the girls in my sample reported witnessing physical, sexual, or emotional abuse of others. Almost every girl had accounts to relate regarding this. Most recounted multiple events. Many intertwined tales of abuse and mistreatment among the regular stories of their daily lives:

My mom drinks 2 cups of vodka every day. My dad was arrested for beating on my mom. They have 6 kids, but only my brother is my real brother. I used to put my head under my pillow when I was little so I wouldn't hear my brother cry when he got hit. (Ilsa Davis, 14 years old, simple assault)

My best friend's brother hanged himself. I found him there. . . . I'm stressin' now because my friend Benito got killed in Bayview and they wouldn't let me go to the *funeraria.* See what happened is, um, *chiflaron y salio mucha gente. Luego lo malaron* [They whistled and a bunch of people came out of the house and then they killed Benito]. (Claudia Sereno, 16 years old, arrested for assault, relating various events strung together)

I got cut off Home Detention cause I didn't go to school. I need to stay at my boyfriend's [apartment] 'cause he lives nearby my school and I can just go from there. My mom's always goin' to jail.

  For what?

  For partyin'—I don't know what you call it. She freaked out because my cousin got shot so my brother shot the people who shot him and then *he* got shot. Me and my mom aren't getting along ever since my brother died. I probably want to go to NA for crank [Narcotics Anonymous for taking speed]—I been doin' like 6 lines a day to forget about my problems. (Cheyanne McDerby, 17 years old, probation violation)

My daddy gets in jail a lot for drinking. I run away from home because it is loud and noisy there—the music—it's hard to concentrate. I've run from placements and hospitals, too! My mom and her boyfriend hit each other and hit me too. They give me bloody lips. But I went to a hospital for cutting my arm. [File reads: "Body covered with scars from cutting herself."] (Sasha Rudnik, 15 years old, CA PC 245 assault with a deadly weapon)

I came to consider the young women in this population as unnoticed, mute witnesses of frontline violence in day-to-day urban life. Girls in my study reported living in worlds tainted daily by aggression and assault. Many adolescents experience power struggles with siblings and parents, but for these girls common household conflicts, such as not being able to use the telephone or go out with friends, or discussions over their chores, turned into physically violent disputes.

For some people in some situations, violence becomes normalized, even utilized, as an emotional strategy and a psychological response to troubles and frustrations (see Dougherty, 1998; Scheper-Hughes, 1992; Stein, Katz, Madriz, & Shick, 1997; van der Kolk & Greenberg, 1987). A certain routinization of violence in girls' everyday lives was embedded in their decision making. Girls interspersed accounts about throwing coffee cans, seeing their mothers get hit, and whacking folks on the head in the street all in one breath. They called it "goin'" off—meaning losing one's temper, letting frustrations build up, and then pouring it out in violent expressions, as if that were how things just were. The social logic to these expressions of anger was that, unfortunately, they were a normal and natural part of day-to-day interactions.

Data from my interviews and observations indicated that factors such as witnessing sexual and physical trauma were salient when interpreting girls' violent offenses. It is impossible to understand girls' troubles with juvenile authorities without contextualizing them within the violence they suffer, including listening to fighting and watching brutal assaults.

My dad was an abusive alcoholic and the divorce helped him straighten up. But since their divorce when I was 11, all went downhill from there for me. I grew up in a bad household, I seen my dad pound on my mom. I can't blame it on my mom and dad but ever since my mom and dad got their divorce I haven't got through it yet. I never thought it could happen to our family. Now I'm in here for jumping this girl and beatin' on her—I stole her chain, too. It's jus' all bad for me. (Doris Montoya, 14 years old, assault and battery)

I even had to call the police on my own dad. He used to fight with my mom, with my uncle, even our neighbors! Fights: my dad taught me, "If someone hits you then hit them back!" I don't know how many times he's been in jail for assault and battery! He taught me how to fight pretty good, well, not that good [laughs], I lost the fight I'm in here for. (Joanne Billingsly, 15 years old, assault and battery on school grounds)

In accounts from court-involved girls' everyday lives, some girls were able to relate aggression and anger, and their parents' marital discord, to their offending behaviors. Yet mainstream criminology fails to capture the ways girls growing up in homes where there was wife beating responded by being aggressive themselves (see, for example, Siegel, 2005). Studies cannot prove that witnessing or being victimized by brutality in childhood directly caused later offending behaviors, nor can they predict which witness will become an offender. Yet plausible links among factors such as exposure to violence, girls' anger, and subsequent offenses, especially girls' involvement in violent crimes, became easy to verify by hearing the voices of girls who were locked up for violent offenses.

CONCLUSION: FROM PRIVATE HARM TO PUBLIC INJURY

Children are born into families where they learn their culture and family history, values, and how to love and work. We know that young people gravitate to safe and loving places in which to grow up. As one group of feminist scholars found in their work with urban girls,

> "Homeplaces" can be broadly defined to include comforting, safe spaces in institutions such as schools or in social groups such as clubs, social movements, or gangs. Listening to young women's critiques of schooling, domestic spaces, gender relations, racial hierarchies, and social violence, we have learned that homeplaces, broadly defined, can also become con-

stricting places from which they often try to break free. (Pastor et al., 1996, p. 15)

Cora's and Mylen's experiences typify how families can simultaneously offer girls and young women love, care, nurturing, and encouragement—and also violence, incest, neglect, abuse, and homophobia.

When we dig deeper in court-involved girls' accounts, we see how their private anguish affects us as a public. In their families, friendships, neighborhoods, and schools, young women were provoked to astonishing levels of aggressive assaults. Their injuries were connected to their sexual misconduct as well. Young women who were sexually exploited and witnessed violence in their daily lives came to the attention of juvenile correctional systems with psychiatric diagnoses of "oppositional defiant conduct disorders" and probation conditions regarding "disorderly conduct." The explanatory power of listening to their narratives revealed neither a simple structural determinism from being poor or discriminated against nor facile psychosexual dysfunction or pathology. Instead, girls' involvement in juvenile corrections resulted from interplay between these forces and others, mediated by a less protective culture and more punitive social stance.

This study raises important questions for further research about the relationship between violence and female offending. For example, some gender scholars find that the anger that girls express through violence is framed as more a "relational" anger than boys' anger (Crick et al., 2001; Crick & Grotpeter, 1995). More thought needs to attend to exactly what happens to these analyses as we challenge essentialist or binary characterizations (see, for example, Butler, 2004). Much needed is comparative research into how masculinities are adopted into the socialization of court-involved girls' identities and the role of emotionality in the lives of boys in trouble with the law. Yet empirical data provided here yield glimpses of typologies and symbolic meanings of the emotion work beneath accounts of juvenile offending, lending insight into the connections among sexual and violent victimization and the state's interventions into gender transgressions.

NOTE

1. All names, descriptions, locations, details of cases, exact situations, charges, job titles, and any other identifying features have been altered to protect project participants' anonymity and confidentiality. This research was conducted with informed consent and under the guidelines of university human subjects review.

REFERENCES

Abma, J. C., Chandra, A., Mosher, W. D., Peterson, L., & Piccinino, L. (1997). *Fertility, family planning, and women's health: New data From the 1995 National Survey of Family Growth*. Hyattsville, MD: National Center for Health Statistics.

Acoca, L. (1998). Outside/inside: The violation of American girls at home, on the streets, and in the juvenile justice system, *Crime and Delinquency, 44,* 561–589.

Acoca, L., & Austin, J. (1996). *The crisis: Women in prison*. San Francisco: National Council on Crime and Delinquency, the Women Offender Sentencing Study and Alternative Sentencing Recommendations Project.

Acoca, L., & Dedel, K. (1998). *No place to hide: Understanding and meeting the needs of girls in the California Juvenile Justice System*. San Francisco: National Council on Crime and Delinquency.

American Association of University Women. (2001). *Hostile hallways: The AAUW survey of sexual harassment in America's schools*. Washington, DC: Author.

American Correctional Association. (1990). *The female offender: What does the future hold?* Washington, DC: St. Mary's Press.

American Psychiatric Association. (1994). *Diagnostic and statistical manual of mental disorders* (4th ed.). Washington, DC: Author.

Apter, T. (1990). *Altered loves: Mothers and daughters during adolescence*. New York: Fawcett Columbine.

Artz, S. (1998). *Sex, power, and the violent school girl*. New York: Teacher's College Press.

Belknap, J., & Holsinger, K. (1998). An overview of delinquent girls: How theory and practice have failed and the need for innovative changes. In R. Zaplin (Ed.), *Female offenders: Critical perspectives and effective interventions* (pp. 31–64). Gaithersburg, MD: Aspen.

Bernardez, T. (1991). Adolescent resistance and the maladies of women: Notes from the underground. In C. Gilligan, A. G. Rogers, & D. L. Tolman (Eds.), *Women, girls, and psychotherapy* (pp. 213–222). New York: Haworth.

Braverman, P., & Strasburger, V. (1993). Adolescent sexual activity. *Clinical Pediatrics, 32*(11), 658–668.

Briere, J. N., & Elliott, D. M. (1994). Immediate and long-term impacts of child sexual abuse. In *The future of children: Sexual abuse of children* (Vol. 4, No. 2, pp. 54–69). Los Altos, CA: David and Lucile Packard Foundation.

Brooke, J. (1998, October 14). Homophobia often found in schools, data shows. *New York Times*, p. A19.

Butler, J. (2004). *Undoing gender*. New York: Routledge.

Campbell, A. (1994). *Men, women, and aggression*. New York: Basic Books.

Centers for Disease Control and Prevention. (2004). *Youth risk behavior surveillance, United States, 2003*. Washington DC: U.S. Department of Health and Human Services.

Chesney-Lind, M. (2004). *Girls and violence: Is the gender gap closing?* (Applied Research Forum). Available from Violence Against Women Net, a project of the National Resource Center on Domestic Violence; http://www.vawnet.org

Crick, N., & Grotpeter, J. (1995). Relational aggression, gender, and social-psychological adjustment. *Child Development, 66,* 710–722.

Crick, N., Nelson, D., Morales, J., Cullerton-Sen, C., Casas, J., & Hickman, S. (2001). Relational victimization in childhood and adolescence: I hurt you through the grapevine. In J. Juvonen & S. Graham (Eds.), *Peer harassment in school: The plight of the vulnerable and victimized* (pp. 196–214). New York: Guilford.

Curtin, M. (2002). Lesbian and bisexual girls in the juvenile justice system. *Child and Adolescent Social Work Journal, 19,* 285–301.

Dang, Q. H. (1997). *Investigation into the needs of lesbian, gay, bisexual, transgender, queer, and questioning youth*. San Francisco: Human Rights Commission City and County of San Francisco.

D'Augelli, A. (1998). Developmental implications of victimization of lesbian, gay, and bisexual youths. In G. Herek (Ed.), *Stigma and sexual orientation* (pp. 187–210). Thousand Oaks, CA: Sage.

D'Augelli, A., & Dark, L. (1995). Lesbian, gay, and bisexual youths. In L. Eron, J. Gentry, & P. Schlegel (Eds.), *Reason to hope: A psychosocial perspective on violence and youth* (pp. 177–196). Washington, DC: American Psychological Association.

Deisher, R., & Rogers, W. (1991). The medical care of street youth. *Journal of Adolescent Health, 12,* 500–503.

D'Emilio, J. (1983). Capitalism and gay identity. In A. Snitow, C. Stansell, & S. Thompson (Eds.), *Powers of desire* (pp. 100–113), New York: Monthly Review Press.

Dougherty, J. (1998). Female offenders and childhood maltreatment: Understanding the connections. In R. Zaplin (Ed.), *Female offenders: Critical perspectives and effective interventions* (pp. 227–244). Gaithersburg, MD: Aspen.

Duncan, G. J., Yeung, W. J., Brooks-Gunn, J., & Smith, J. R. (1998). How much does childhood poverty affect the life chances of children? *American Sociological Review, 63,* 406–423.

Federal Bureau of Investigation. (2003). *Crime in the United States, 2001*. Washington, DC: U.S. Department of Justice.

Finkelhor, D. (1994). Current information on the scope and nature of child sexual abuse. In *The future of children: Sexual abuse of children* (Vol. 4, No. 2, pp. 31–53). Los Altos, CA: David and Lucile Packard Foundation.

Finkelhor, D., & Baron, L. (1986). Risk factors for child sexual abuse. *Journal of Interpersonal Violence, 1,* 43–71.

Fleisher, J., & Fillman, J. (1995, January/February). Lesbian and gay youth: Treatment issues. *The Counselor*, pp. 27–28.

Fontaine, J., & Hammond, N. (1996). Counseling issues with gay and lesbian adolescents. *Adolescence, 31,* 817–830.

Foster Care Youth United. (1994). *Interview with "Sandra," a lesbian in the system.* New York: Youth Communications, Inc.

Gaarder, E., Rodriguez, N., & Zatz, M. (2004). Criers, liars, and manipulators: Probation officers' views of girls. *Justice Quarterly, 21,* 547–578.

Garbarino, J., Dubrow, N., Kostelny, K., & Pardo, C. (1992). *Children in danger: Coping with consequences of community violence.* San Francisco: Jossey-Bass.

Goldman, M. (1987). Prostitution, economic exchange, and the unconscious. In J. Rabow, G. Platt, & M. Goldman (Eds.), *Advances in psychoanalytic sociology* (pp. 187–209). Malabar, FL: Krieger.

Greenfield, L. (1997). *Sex offenses and offenders: An analysis of data on rape and sexual assault.* Washington, DC: U.S. Department of Justice, Bureau of Justice Statistics.

Herdt, G. (Ed.). (1989). *Gay and lesbian youth.* New York: Harrington Park Press.

Herman, J. (1992). *Trauma and recovery.* New York: Basic Books.

Holden, G., Geffner, R., & Jouriles, E. (Eds.). (1998). *Children exposed to marital violence: Theory, research, and applied issues.* Washington, DC: American Psychological Association.

Hunter, J. (1990). Violence against lesbian and gay male youths. *Journal of Interpersonal Violence, 5,* 295–300.

Kennedy, M. (1991). Homeless and runaway youth mental health issues: No access to the system. *Journal of Adolescent Health, 12,* 576–579.

Kruks, G. (1991). Gay and lesbian homeless/street youth: Special issues and concerns. *Journal of Adolescent Health, 12,* 515–518.

Kurwa, N. (1998, May 19). Do schools condone harassment of gay students? *San Francisco Examiner,* p. D7.

Lamb, S. (Ed.). (1999). *New versions of victims: Feminists struggle with the concept.* New York: New York University Press.

Levine, K. (2003). *Prosecution, politics and pregnancy: Enforcing statutory rape in California.* Unpublished doctoral dissertation, University of California, Berkeley.

Lobel, K. (Ed.). (1986). *Naming the violence: Speaking out about lesbian battering.* Denver, CO: National Coalition Against Domestic Violence, Lesbian Task Force.

Los Angeles County Task Force on Runaway and Homeless Youth. (1988). *Report and recommendations of the task force.* Los Angeles: City and County of Los Angeles.

Miller, J. (2001). *One of the guys: Girls, gangs, and gender.* New York: Oxford University Press.

Moore, K. A., Winquist Nord, C., & Peterson, J. L. (1989). Nonvoluntary sexual activity among adolescents. *Family Planning Perspectives, 21,* 110–114.

National Clearinghouse on Child Abuse and Neglect Information. (2005). *Childhood maltreatment 2003.* Washington, DC: U.S. Department of Health and Human Services.

Ness, C. (1998, November 12). Gay bias rising among top students. *San Francisco Examiner,* p. A1.

Obeidallah, D., & Earls, F. (1999). *Adolescent girls: The role of depression in the development of delinquency.* Washington, DC: U.S. Department of Justice, National Institute of Justice.

Osofsky, J. (Ed.). (1997). *Children in a violent society.* New York: Guilford.

Osofsky, J. (1998). Children as invisible victims of domestic and community violence. In G. Holden, R. Geffner, & E. Jouriles (Eds.), *Children exposed to marital violence: Theory, research, and applied issues* (pp. 95–120). Washington, DC: American Psychological Association.

Owen, B., & Bloom, B. (1997). *Profiling the needs of young female offenders: Final report to the executive staff of the California Youth Authority.* Washington, DC: U.S. Department of Justice, National Institute of Justice.

Owen, B., Bloom, B., & Covington, S. (2003). *Gender-responsive strategies: Research, practice, and guiding principles for women offenders.* Washington, DC: U.S. Department of Justice, National Institute of Corrections.

Owens, R. (1998). *Queer kids: The challenges and promise for lesbian, gay, and bisexual youth.* New York: Haworth.

Pastor, J., McCormick, J., & Fine, M. (1996). Makin' homes: An urban girl thing. In B. R. Leadbeater & N. Way (Eds.), *Urban girls* (pp. 15–34), New York: New York University Press.

Pfeffer, R. (1997). *Surviving the streets: Girls living on their own.* New York: Garland.

Powers, J., & Jaklitsch, B. (1989). *Understanding survivors of abuse. Stories of homeless and runaway adolescents.* Lexington, MA: Lexington Books.

Putallaz, M., & Bierman, K. (Eds.) (2004). *Aggression, antisocial behavior, and violence among girls.* New York: Guilford.

Rogers Park Young Women's Action Team. (2003). *"Hey cutie, can I get your digits!" A report about the street harassment of girls in Rogers Park.* Chicago: Friends of Battered Women and Their Children.

Rubin, L. (1990). *Erotic wars: What happened to the sexual revolution?* New York: HarperPerennial.

Runtz, M., & Briere, J. (1986). Adolescent "acting out" and childhood history of sexual abuse. *Journal of Interpersonal Violence, 1,* 326–334.

Schaffner, L. (1997). Families on probation: Court-ordered parenting skills classes for parents of juvenile offenders. *Crime and Delinquency, 43,* 412–437.

Schaffner, L. (2006). *Girls in trouble with the law.* New Brunswick, NJ: Rutgers University Press.

Scheper-Hughes, N. (1992). *Death without weeping: The violence of everyday life in Brazil.* Berkeley: University of California Press.

Scherzer, T. (1998). Domestic violence in lesbian relationships: Findings of the Lesbian Relationships Research Project. In C. Ponticelli (Ed.). *Gateways to improving lesbian health and health care* (pp. 29–47). New York: Haworth.

Scholinski, D. (1997). *The last time I wore a dress.* New York: Riverhead Books.

Schur, E. (1989). *The Americanization of sex.* Philadelphia: Temple University Press.

Siegel, L. (2005). *Criminology: The core* (2nd ed.). Belmont, CA: Thomson Wadsworth.

Stein, N., Katz, S., Madriz, E., & Shick, S. (Eds.). (1997). Losing a generation: Probing the myths and lealities of youth and violence [Special issue]. *Social Justice, 24*(4).

Stock, J., Bell, M., Boyer, D., & Connell, F. (1997). Adolescent pregnancy and sexual risk-taking among sexually abused girls, *Family Planning Perspectives, 29,* 200–203.

Sullivan, K. (1998, July 26). Gay youths struggle in personal hell. *Sunday San Francisco Examiner and Chronicle,* pp. Dl, D4.

Thornberry, T. (1994). *Violent families and violent youths* (Fact Sheet No. 21). Washington, DC: Office of Juvenile Justice and Delinquency Prevention.

U.S. Department of Health and Human Services. (1989). *Report of the Secretary's Task Force on Youth Suicide: Vol. 3. Prevention and interventions in youth suicide.* Rockville, MD: Author.

van der Kolk, B., & Greenberg, M. (1987). The psychobiology of the trauma response: Hyperarousal, constriction, and addiction to traumatic re-exposure. In B. van der Kolk (Ed.), *Psychological trauma* (pp. 63–88). Washington, DC: American Psychiatric Press.

Veysey, B. (2003). *Adolescent girls with mental health disorders involved with the juvenile justice system.* Washington, DC: National Center for Mental Health and Juvenile Justice. Retrieved from www.ncmhjj.com

Way, N. (1996). Between experiences of betrayal and desire: Close friendships among urban adolescents. B. R.

Leadbeater & N. Way (Eds.), *Urban girls* (pp. 173–182). New York: New York University Press.

Weston, K. (1991). *Families we choose: Lesbians, gays, kinship.* New York: Columbia University Press.

Widom, C. S. (2000, January). Childhood victimization: Early adversity, later psychopathology. *National Institute of Juvenile Justice Journal,* pp. 3–9.

Wolfe, L. & Tucker, J. (1998). *Report of the Summit on Girls and Violence.* Washington, DC: Center for Women Policy Studies.

Yates, G., Mackenzie, R., Pennbridge, J., & Swofford, A. (1991). A risk profile comparison of homeless youth involved in prostitution and homeless youth not involved. *Journal of Adolescent Health, 12,* 545–548.

Zemsky, B. (1991). Coming out against all odds: Resistance in the life of a young lesbian. *Women and Therapy, 11,* 185–200.

Zimring, F. (1998). *American youth violence.* New York: Oxford University Press.

Laurie Schaffner is a sociologist at the University of Illinois at Chicago and a 2007–2008 Fullbright–Garcia Robles scholar at the Universidad de Guadalajara, Mexico. Her book *Girls in Trouble With the Law* (Rutgers University Press, 2006) won the 2007 award for Distinguished Contribution to Scholarship from the Section on Childhood and Youth of the American Sociological Association.

READING *41*   **N. Tatiana Masters**

"My Strength Is Not for Hurting":[1] Men's Anti-Rape Websites and Their Construction of Masculinity and Male Sexuality

First published in 2010

Sexual assault of women by male acquaintances is common in the USA. Research demonstrates that 20 percent of young women have been victims of rape in their lifetimes (Koss et al., 1987; Brener et al., 1999); acquaintance rape comprises the majority of these assaults (Koss et al., 1987). Some feminist scholars argue that in order to understand and prevent acquaintance sexual assault, it is critical to view it as a crime while simultaneously recognizing its continuity with heterosexual courtship norms in which men push for sex and women act as 'gatekeepers' (Gavey, 2005).

Acquaintance sexual assault prevention has focused on education aimed at changing these 'rape supportive' norms. Most programs have been carried out on college campuses (for reviews, see Anderson and Whiston, 2005; Brecklin and Forde, 2001; Rozee and Koss, 2001; Schewe, 2002; Sochting et al., 2004). While review articles mention the need to do acquaintance sexual assault prevention programming for men, its most common perpetrators, the majority of interventions are directed at women, its most common victims. Acquaintance sexual assault prevention that targets college men has demonstrated modest though real effectiveness (Fabiano et al., 2003; Heppner et al., 1995; Heppner et al., 1999). However, there is no literature to date that characterizes acquaintance sexual assault prevention programs offered to non-college populations of men, whose need for such programs surely matches that of university men.

A little studied type of anti-rape programming, the men's anti-rape website, reaches out to men specifically and addresses non-college groups. These sites focus on sexual assault and its prevention; they are an interesting example of the Internet as a source of information and opinion on sexuality-related topics (Gauntlett, 1999; Pequegnat et al., 2007). Anti-rape websites provide data on current social constructions of sexual assault and related topics in the USA. Different cultures frame sex, gender and sexual violence with different categories, and these categories construct individual subject positions and behavior and collective experience (Vance, 1991). The language used by these websites to frame categories such as men, rape, and consensual sex helps to construct gendered subject positions and collective experiences of sex and sexual coercion, and as such may be able to influence structures of sexual gender inequality that result in women being denied their right to sexual autonomy. A systematic description of the discourses promulgated by anti-rape websites is important to considering their potential utility as acquaintance sexual assault prevention interventions. This research note describes a sample of men's anti-rape websites and the social discourses on masculinity, rape, and consensual sex that they both produce and reflect.

METHOD

Data

I selected websites for this analysis through internet searches on terms such as 'men against rape' and 'men against sexual assault'. Once several sites had been identified, I followed each site's links to similar sites to create a 'snowball' sample. When this process led only to already sampled sites, the process ended. I screened sites to ensure that only those focused on (1) sexual assault, rather than violence against women in general, and (2) reaching men outside the university campus context, were included, identifying six websites. I used a discourse analytic framework to examine the sites' organizational mission statements and recommendations for action.

Analytic Framework and Process

Discourse analysis operates from a theoretical perspective that treats social realities such as masculinity, femininity and sexuality itself as being socially constructed through language and practices (Cameron and Kulick, 2003). This framework treats language as a topic in itself rather than a resource that provides clues about people's internal experiences (Edley, 2001). It focuses on what people do with language: they 'produce versions of events, objects, and people' (Horton-Salway, 2001: 153).

In analyzing this sample of anti-rape websites, I looked at them in terms of what they did to or for their audiences, the rhetorical strategies they employed, and the versions of events and people they produced. I also considered the social contexts around sexuality and gender that these website texts were part of. My analytical process involved identifying statements on, for example, masculinity by examining the texts for statements on men's characteristics or behavior. Comparison and examination of statements referring to what a man could, should, or might be or do provided insight into alternative masculinities, and statements that referred to the way men were or the things men did now represented current mainstream masculinity. The exemplars that follow illustrate the types of discursive moves identified in these websites.

FINDINGS

. . . Sites' language falls into two categories: Some speak ambitiously of their organizational missions in terms of 'ending', 'stopping', or 'eradicating' rape, while others more modestly discuss 'addressing', 'preventing', or 'reducing' rape. Likewise, one group of mission statements emphasizes men's participation in anti-rape efforts with language such as 'Since men are overwhelmingly the ones responsible, we have to be the ones who put an end to it', while the others link men's efforts with those of women by speaking of working 'as allies with women' to be 'part of the solution'.

Masculinity and Male Sexuality

It is analytically useful to keep gender and sexuality separate (Rubin, 1984) in many situations, with gender referring to a person's masculine or feminine social identity while sexuality refers to a person's sexual behaviors and erotic desires (Cameron and Kulick, 2003). However, male sexuality and masculinity are tightly woven together on anti-rape websites. These sites construct and advocate alternative masculinities to affect men's sexual behavior and make it less coercive; for example, forcing sex on a female partner (sexuality) is talked about as a possible consequence of mainstream masculinity (gender). Sexual behavior is also used to delineate the boundary between 'good', non-rapist masculinity and 'bad', rapist masculinity, treating gender as emerging from sexuality. Since masculinity and male sexuality are mutually productive and reinforcing categories on anti-rape websites, I adopt the sites' practice of referring to them in tandem in this analysis.[2]

A major activity of anti-rape websites is constructing alternative masculinities. Some sites openly situate themselves in a social con-structionist perspective to carry out this project:[3]

> We help young men first become more aware of the dominant stories of . . . traditional masculinity, which consists of social pressure on men to play typecast roles representing aggression, toughness, and various other characteristics typically associated with the desire to dominate. We have to offer them positive alternatives . . . Men Can Stop Rape defines counter-story as a personal story or a story in popular culture that represents a healthier, nonviolent masculinity . . . a man listening to a woman when she says she wants to stop, or a man asking how a woman feels when he isn't sure. (MCSR)

Other sites simply assume social construction and provide 'counter-stories' of masculinity and male sexuality.

Men's anti-rape websites, with a few interesting exceptions, use the rhetorical strategy of othering the rapist in their construction of masculinity. 'Othering' is a discursive process by which a group identity is delineated through defining and excluding other groups. Sites construct two main types of masculinities and styles of sexual behavior, which can be described as 'Real Men Don't Rape' and 'Androgyny Advocacy'.

Othering the Rapist, Claiming the Rapist

Most anti-rape websites, while stating that their goal is to have men take responsibility for preventing rape, cast this responsibility as preventing other men from committing sexual assault. This example presents the rapist as someone else:

> Most of us will probably never see a rape in progress. However, we will all see and hear attitudes and behaviors that degrade women and that promote rape. We all have a moral responsibility to those around us to both safeguard the rights of individuals and to make every attempt to limit the culture of male dominance that exists in America. (MASV)

Even 'attitudes and behaviors that . . . promote rape' are spoken of as things that a man is likely to see and have an opportunity to confront in others rather than in himself. Another site takes a playful tone but places similar stress on men's responsibility to guide other men's social and sexual behavior:

> Have you ever seen another guy act the fool and thought to yourself 'This Ass is making us all look bad'? Well, there's people out there making us all look bad, and we've got no choice but to rise up and respond to it. (SN)

Gender structures are reinforced by speaking of men as a unitary group using the words 'us all,' and the reader is encouraged to keep his gender looking good by excluding the rapist/fool/ass.

The othering strategy is understandable given these sites' need to engage men's interest in order to influence their beliefs and behavior. Men might be alienated by being addressed as potential rapists, while the notion that they can purify and reinforce masculinity through monitoring other men's behavior may be easier to accept. In spite of the potential strategic pitfalls involved, some of the same sites also use a strategy of inclusion that I call 'claiming the rapist,' as in this example:

> Do you use pressure to get sex? 'You would do it if you really loved me, you have to do it now that you led me on, just do it just do it just do it . . .' Sound familiar? If it does, you ARE the problem. Every time you do that and

get away with it, you make it easier for it to happen to your sister, or your Mother, or your girlfriend. (SN)

A similar tale is told here: 'Many men, perhaps even a majority, have done something that could qualify as a sexual assault, though most wouldn't identify their behavior as such' (MSR).

The claiming strategy is subtler than the othering strategy, but it too provides a desirable subject position for men. While few men would publicly identify themselves as potential rapists, some may harbor doubts about past behavior or perceived social norms for masculinity. The claiming strategy may reach such men by offering them participation in a narrative of confession and redemption. As we contrast the classically 'macho' and the androgynous masculinities being constructed by these websites, we will see both strategies at work.

Real Men Don't Rape

The 'My strength is not for hurting' campaign typifies the way some of these sites claim positive characteristics of traditional masculinity, such as strength, bravery, and power, in order to divide 'real men' from rapists. This campaign includes photographs of muscular, handsome men and attractive, traditionally feminine women of different races and ethnicities embracing or standing near one another, offering subject positions designed to engage a variety of viewers. Captions begin with the 'My strength is not for hurting' line and continue with phrases such as 'so when she said NO, I said OK'. This juxtaposition opposes 'my' strength, the strength of the real man which is 'not for hurting', to the strength of the rapist, used for assaulting women, and once again identifies the rapist as the other.

In the next example, publicly opposing date rape becomes a test of masculinity. The inclusion of profanity and the implied physical challenge construct the man opposing rape as a real man, and the man staying silent as a wimp:

There comes a time in a guy's life when he has to act like a man, not a wimp. So, Take a fucking stand. Tell people how you feel. Tell them that anyone who disrespects women, who abuses, who date rapes, who thinks he can get over is going to have to talk to you about it. (SN)

This excerpt from the same site others the rapist as 'not man enough' while claiming him as part of the masculine community with the words 'we' and 'ourselves':

When someone tells you something just happened or that it was an accident, what they're really saying is 'I'm not man enough to accept the responsibility for what I do'. If we can't control ourselves, is there anything in the world we can ever hope to do right? (SN)

The rapist who is claimed can be encouraged to practice non-coercive, non-violent sexual behavior with women as a defining part of masculinity. The same move occurs here when men are addressed 'as males' and their masculine power invoked: 'We as males have the power to address this important problem. It is our responsibility to challenge ourselves as well as those around us to take steps to end sexual violence' (MASV).

Androgyny Advocacy

The websites just described reinforce traditional masculinity but attempt to reclaim it as against sexual violence. Others construct a more androgynous type of masculinity by encouraging men to embrace the feminine. This site portrays rape as a result of dichotomous gender structures, and invites men to connect to 'feminine' emotions as a way to begin addressing the problem of rape:

We have learned to divide feelings into masculine and feminine . . . We pretend that men can only be aggressive and strong, logical and unemotional. In fact, we are also at times confused, nurturing, intuitive, and sad . . . Misogyny is the often-disguised yet widespread fear or hatred of women, including the attributes in ourselves which are traditionally labeled feminine. (MSR)

Another site suggests that a more androgynous masculinity could be more pleasurable to men while making them less liable to commit sexual assault:

Many of us grow up with unrealistic beliefs about sex: that we should instinctively know what to do; that we should be ready to achieve an erection instantly and maintain it for hours; and that it is unmasculine to have to talk about what gives us (or our partner) pleasure. These beliefs and others keep us from knowing our own sexuality and from enjoying our sexual relationships. (MASV)

The site Walk a Mile in Her Shoes provides a novel example of the androgynous masculinity constructed by some anti-rape websites. The site organizes men's marches against sexual assault; men seek sponsors who will pay them to march, and funds are donated to local rape crisis centers. The men march in women's high-heeled shoes, and much of the site's content is photographs of participants.

> There is an old saying: 'You can't really understand another person's experience until you've walked a mile in their shoes'. Walk a Mile in Her Shoes® asks men to literally walk one mile in women's high-heeled shoes. It's not easy walking in these shoes, but it's fun and it gets the community to talk about something that's really difficult to talk about: gender relations and sexual violence. (WMHS)

WMHS plays around the line between masculine and feminine clothing in order to evoke consideration of the gender line regarding sexuality.

Rape and Consensual Sex

In addition to constructing masculinities that rule out rape and male sexualities that redefine masculinity, these websites construct rape in ways that serve their goals of ending or reducing it. Sexual assault is constructed as a communication breakdown using the discursive strategy of othering discussed earlier, but it is rape that is othered by contrasting it with consensual sex. This construction makes rape a problem with a solution: Better communication between men and women, some sites claim, can prevent rape.

Most anti-rape websites talk about rape occurring as a result of bad sexual communication, as opposed to consensual 'healthy' sex, in which communication flows freely. The word 'communication' is used repeatedly on these sites, along with its linguistic cousins 'express,' 'listen,' 'ask,' 'state' and 'understand'. Men Ending Violence provides a typical example:

> Sexual violence often goes hand in hand with poor communication . . . By learning effective sexual communication—stating your desires clearly, listening to your partner, and asking when the situation is unclear—men make sex safer for themselves and others. (MEV)

The difference between rape and consensual sex is described as successful communication, as in this example:

> Without mutual agreement, sex becomes rape. Sex is healthy when it reflects the free and mutual sharing of

one another. When we discuss what makes us comfortable and uncomfortable and try new ways to express ourselves, we also greatly reduce the risk of sexual assault. (MASV and MSR)

Both examples make a discursive move that shifts the focus from individual men's accountability to generalized notions of risk and safety. Talk about men using sexual communication to make sex 'safer for themselves and others' creates a false equivalency between a woman's risk of being sexually assaulted by her date and a man's risk of committing an assault.

One exception to the communication breakdown construction of sexual assault is a site that describes rape as a 'choice men make to exert power and control over others' (MCSR). This statement moves sexual assault from misunderstanding to decision. Most of the websites analyzed speak of rape as inadvertent miscommunication, though these two sites, which share content, make a link between choice and communication:

> Expectations are hopes crystallized by silence. Acting on our expectations without sufficient information can cause serious misunderstandings and can lead to rape . . . we project our interest in sex onto our partner . . . we misinterpret any friendliness as invitation . . . Acting on our assumptions may seem more spontaneous but often leads us to be dishonest, manipulative, or to use physical force to get what we want. (MASV and MSR)

The preceding excerpts illustrate the use of communicative, consensual sex to construct rape as a problem caused by poor communication. Consensual sex also appears when sites emphasize their enthusiasm for it while deploring rape. This move bolsters the anti-rape man's masculinity by portraying him as highly sexed, as in this example:

> You guys got a problem with sex?—That would suck. Big fans of sex, actually. Sex isn't the problem. If everyone were running people over with their Volkswagens, it wouldn't be anti-Volkswagen to tell people it's time to stop driving on the sidewalks . . . Be close to your friends, girlfriends, listen to them, try to understand what they want . . . These are all tips for how to avoid being in a situation where you take the other person's choices away, but they're also good tips on how to be a responsible lover when the time is right. (SN)

Something subtler than masculinity reinforcement also seems to be going on in this excerpt. The Volkswagen metaphor communicates the elements of rape and consensual sex that overlap within a system of norms that assigns men to 'accelerator' and women to 'brakes'. The metaphor also points to men's responsibility regarding sexual assault by placing them in the 'driver's seat.'

DISCUSSION

Considering men's anti-rape websites has provided some insights into their constructions of masculinity, rape, and consensual sex, which in turn reflect and reproduce larger social discourses on gender and sexuality. These sites' possible implications for sexual assault prevention will be discussed next.

From a rape-prevention standpoint, the idea that socially constructed gender norms rather than biological sex differences shape men's sexually assaultive behavior seems like a useful one. The 'Real Men Don't Rape' masculinity constructed by some websites is less rape-supportive than stereotypical masculinities that construct men as unable to control their violent sexual urges. But when sites claim positive characteristics of traditional masculinity such as strength, bravery and power to divide the 'real men' from the rapists, they solidify distinctions between masculinity and femininity that may need to be softened as part of norm change. The 'androgyny advocacy' masculinity offered by several sites advocates this softening of the gender line at the risk of sacrificing the appeal the 'we're still real men, just not rapists' discourse could have to an audience of mainstream US men. The photos of men marching in high heels from the Walk a Mile in Her Shoes site demonstrate this point. The marchers have donned pumps but been careful to keep the rest of their attire masculine. Their baseball caps, athletic jerseys, and baggy gym shorts leave the viewer in no danger of mistaking this for a group of women: embracing the feminine only goes so far.

The principle rhetorical strategies—othering the rapist and claiming the rapist—used by men's anti-rape websites each have implications for sexual assault prevention. Othering the rapist serves to label sexually coercive behavior as non-normative and shameful. However, one in every five US women has been raped by the time she is in her mid-20s, and over 80 percent of these assaults are committed by acquaintances, which suggests it is most likely not some 'other' who is the rapist. Rather, sexual coercion may be a fairly common element of some US men's sexual repertoires. Depicting acquaintance sexual assault as a crime committed by others may lull sites' male audiences into believing their own practices do not require interrogation. The strategy of claiming the rapist acknowledges that sexual coercion may not be some other man's problem and exhorts men to monitor their own beliefs and behavior. Making men both part of the problem and part of the solution in this way could lead to more powerful anti-rape messages.

Another discourse produced by men's anti-rape websites is that of acquaintance sexual assault as a communication breakdown. Since communication is not solely the responsibility of one person, this construction allows responsibility for preventing rape to be covertly placed back on women even as these sites overtly claim it as men's. Language about reducing the 'risk of sexual assault' through discussion elides differences between being the victim of a sexual assault and being its perpetrator. Minority constructions of rape as being about power and control as well as about communication complicate the simplistic majority construction of rape. Their message is less straightforward but may be more fruitful for sexual assault prevention.

Discourses on sexuality are a resource that people draw upon as they construct their gender identities and socio-sexual practices (Cameron and Kulick, 2003), including masculinities and the sexually violent behavior associated with some of them. The internet provides a platform for norm-changing education and, perhaps, a place for experimentation with discourses of non-violent masculinity and male sexuality that can be enacted in sexual relationships with women in the real world.

NOTES

1. Statement appearing on several men's anti-rape websites.
2. Although I have chosen to refer to 'sexuality' in this analysis for the sake of simplicity, it is important to note that the male and female sexualities that are constructed by these sites are overwhelmingly heterosexual. Several websites mention male-on-male sexual assault; one (Men Against Sexual Violence) provides a list of steps to take and things to know for male rape victims. However, most men's anti-rape websites refer exclusively to male perpetrators and female victims. Same-sex rape, when it is mentioned, is surrounded by affirmations that it is not related to the victim's sexual orientation; this is the only acknowledgement of sexualities other than hetero that appears in these sites.
3. Websites were viewed during August 2007; analyses and quotations reflect their content during that period.

REFERENCES

Anderson, L.A. and Whiston, S.C. (2005) 'Sexual Assault Education Programs: A Meta-Analytic Examination of their Effectiveness', *Psychology of Women Quarterly* 29 (4): 374–88.

Brecklin, L.R. and Forde, D.R. (2001)'A Meta-Analysis of Rape Education Programs', *Violence and Victims* 16(3): 303–21.

Brener, N.D., McMahon, P.M., Warren, C.W. and Douglas, K.A. (1999) 'Forced Sexual Intercourse and Associated Health-Risk Behavior among Female College Students in the United States', *Journal of Consulting and Clinical Psychology* 67(2): 252–9.

Cameron, D. and Kulick, D. (2003) *Language and Sexuality.* Cambridge: Cambridge University Press.

Edley, N. (2001) 'Analysing Masculinity: Interpretive Repertoires, Ideological Dilemmas and Subject Positions', in M. Wetherell, S. Taylor, and S.J. Yates (eds) *Discourse as Data,* pp. 189–228. London: SAGE.

Fabiano, P.M., Perkins, H.W., Berkowitz, A., Linkenbach, J. and Stark, C. (2003) 'Engaging Men as Social Justice Allies in Ending Violence against Women: Evidence for a Social Norms Approach', *Journal of American College Health* 52(3): 105–12.

Gauntlett, David (1999) 'Digital Sexualities: A Guide to Internet Resources', *Sexuaties* 2(3): 327–32.

Gavey, Nicola (2005) *Just Sex? The Cultural Scaffolding of Rape.* New York: Routledge.

Heppner, M.J., Humphrey, C.F., Hillenbrand-Gunn, T.L. and DeBord, K.A. (1995) 'The Differential Effects of Rape Prevention Programming on Attitudes, Behavior, and Knowledge', *Journal of Counseling Psychology* 42(4): 508–18.

Heppner, M.J., Neville, H.A., Smith, K., Kivlighan, D.M., Jr. and Gershuny, B.S. (1999) 'Examining Immediate and Long-Term Efficacy of Rape Prevention Programming with Racially Diverse College Men', *Journal of Counseling Psychology* 46(1): 16–26.

Horton-Salway, M. (2001) 'The Construction of M.E.: The Discursive Action Model', in M. Wetherell, S. Taylor and S.J. Yates (eds) *Discourse as Data,* pp. 147–88. London: SAGE.

Koss, M.P., Gidycz, C.A. and Wisniewski, N. (1987) 'The Scope of Rape: Incidence and Prevalence of Sexual Aggression and Victimization in a National Sample of Higher Education Students', *Journal of Consulting and Clinical Psychology* 55(2): 162–70.

Pequegnat, W., Rosser, B.R.S., Bowen, A.M., Bull, S.S., DiClemente, R.J., Bockting, W.O., Elford, J., Fishbein, M., Gurak, L., Horvath, K., Konstan, J., Noar, S.M., Ross, M.W., Sherr, L., Spiegel, D. and Zimmerman, R. (2007) 'Conducting internet-based HIV/ STD prevention survey research: Considerations in design and evaluation', *AIDS and Behavior* 11(4): 505–21.

Rozee, P.D. and Koss, M.P. (2001) 'Rape: A Century of Resistance', *Psychology of Women Quarterly* 25(4): 295–311.

Rubin, Gayle S. (1984) 'Thinking Sex: Notes for a Radical Theory of the Politics of Sexuality', in R. Parker and P. Aggleton (eds) *Culture, Society and Sexuality: A Reader* (2007), pp. 150–87. New York: Routledge.

Schewe, P.A. (2002) 'Guidelines for Developing Rape Prevention and Risk Reduction Interventions', in P.A. Schewe (ed.) *Preventing Violence in Relationships,* pp. 163–96. Washington, DC: APA Press.

Sochting, L, Fairbrother, N. and Koch, W.J. (2004) 'Sexual Assault of Women: Prevention Efforts and Risk Factors', *Violence Against Women* 10(1): 73–93.

Vance, Carole S. (1991) 'Anthropology Rediscovers Sexuality', in R. Parker and P. Aggleton (eds) *Culture, Society and Sexuality: A Reader* (2007), pp. 41–57. New York: Routledge.

WEBSITES DISCUSSED

All websites were accessed in August 2007

(MASV) Men Against Sexual Violence. http://www.menagainstsexual violence.org/what.html

(MCSR) Men Can Stop Rape. http://www.mencanstoprape.org/info-url_nocat2701/info-url_nocat.htm

(MEV) Men Ending Violence. http://www.vahealth.org/civp/sexualviolence/menendingviolence/aboutus.html

(MSR) Men Stopping Rape. http://www.men-stopping-rape.org/

(SN) The Safety Net. http://www.thesafetynet.org/index.cfm?id=3

(WMHS) Walk a Mile in Her Shoes. http://www.walkamileinhershoes.org/aboutus.html

42   **Patricia Yancey Martin**
Robert A. Hummer

Fraternities and Rape on Campus

First published in 1989

Rapes are perpetrated on dates, at parties, in chance encounters, and in specially planned circumstances. That group structure and processes, rather than individual values or characteristics, are the impetus for many rape episodes was documented by Blanchard (1959) thirty years ago (also see Geis 1971), yet sociologists have failed to pursue this theme (for an exception, see Chancer 1987). A recent review of research (Muehlenhard and Linton 1987) on sexual violence, or rape, devotes only a few pages to the situational contexts of rape events, and these are conceptualized as potential risk factors for individuals rather than qualities of rape-prone social contexts.

Many rapes, far more than come to the public's attention, occur in fraternity houses on college and university campuses, yet little research has analyzed fraternities at American colleges and universities as rape-prone contexts (cf. Ehrhart and Sandler 1985). Most of the research on fraternities reports on samples of individual fraternity men. One group of studies compares the values, attitudes, perceptions, family socioeconomic status, psychological traits (aggressiveness, dependence), and so on, of fraternity and nonfraternity men (Bohrnstedt 1969; Fox, Hodge, and Ward 1987; Kanin 1967; Lemire 1979; Miller 1973). A second group attempts to identify the effects of fraternity membership over time on the values, attitudes, beliefs, or moral precepts of members (Hughes and Winston 1987; Marlowe and Auvenshine 1982; Miller 1973; Wilder, Hoyt, Doren, Hauck, and Zettle 1978; Wilder, Hoyt, Surbeck, Wilder, and Carney 1986). With minor exceptions, little research addresses the group and organizational context of fraternities or the social construction of fraternity life (for exceptions, see Letchworth 1969; Longino and Kart 1973; Smith 1964).

Gary Tash, writing as an alumnus and trial attorney in his fraternity's magazine, claims that over 90 percent of all gang rapes on college campuses involve fraternity men (1988, p. 2). Tash provides no evidence to substantiate this claim, but students of violence against women have been concerned with fraternity men's frequently reported involvement in rape episodes (Adams and Abarbanel 1988). Ehrhart and Sandler (1985) identify over fifty cases of gang rapes on campus perpetrated by fraternity men, and their analysis points to many of the conditions that we discuss here. Their analysis is unique in focusing on conditions in fraternities that make gang rapes of women by fraternity men both feasible and probable. They identify excessive alcohol use, isolation from external monitoring, treatment of women as prey, use of pornography, approval of violence, and excessive concern with competition as precipitating conditions to gang rape (also see Merton 1985; Roark 1987).

The study reported here confirmed and complemented these findings by focusing on both conditions and processes. We examined dynamics associated with the social construction of fraternity life, with a focus on processes that foster the use of coercion, including rape, in fraternity men's relations with women. Our examination of men's social fraternities on college and university campuses as groups and organizations led us to conclude that fraternities are a physical and sociocultural context that encourages the sexual coercion of women. We make no claims that all fraternities are "bad" or that all fraternity men are rapists. Our observations indicated, however, that rape is especially probable in fraternities because of the kinds of organizations they are, the kinds of members they have, the practices their members engage in, and a virtual absence of university or community oversight.

Analyses that lay blame for rapes by fraternity men on "peer pressure" are, we feel, overly simplistic (cf. Burkhart 1989; Walsh 1989). We suggest, rather, that fraternities create a sociocultural context in which the use of coercion in sexual relations with women is normative and in which the mechanisms to keep this pattern of behavior in check are minimal at best and absent at worst. We conclude that unless fraternities change in fundamental ways, little improvement can be expected.

METHODOLOGY

Our goal was to analyze the group and organizational practices and conditions that create in fraternities an abusive social context for women. We developed a conceptual framework from an initial case study of an alleged gang rape at Florida State University that involved four fraternity men and an eighteen-year-old coed. The group rape took place on the third floor of a fraternity house and ended with the "dumping" of the woman in the hallway of a neighboring fraternity house. According to newspaper accounts, the victim's blood-alcohol concentration, when she was discovered, was .349 percent, more than three times the legal limit for automobile driving and an almost lethal amount. One law enforcement officer reported that sexual intercourse occurred during the time the victim was unconscious: "She was in a life-threatening situation" (*Tallahassee Democrat* 1988b). When the victim was found, she was comatose and had suffered multiple scratches and abrasions. Crude words and a fraternity symbol had been written on her thighs (*Tampa Tribune* 1988). When law enforcement officials tried to investigate the case, fraternity members refused to cooperate. This led, eventually, to a five-year ban of the fraternity from campus by the university and by the fraternity's national organization.

In trying to understand how such an event could have occurred, and how a group of over 150 members (exact figures are unknown because the fraternity refused to provide a membership roster) could hold rank, deny knowledge of the event, and allegedly lie to a grand jury, we analyzed newspaper articles about the case and conducted open-ended interviews with a variety of respondents about the case and about fraternities, rapes, alcohol use, gender relations, and sexual activities on campus. Our data included over 100 newspaper articles on the initial gang rape case; open-ended interviews with Greek (social fraternity and

sorority) and non-Greek (independent) students (n = 20); university administrators (n = 8, five men, three women); and alumni advisers to Greek organizations (n = 6). Open-ended interviews were held also with judges, public and private defense attorneys, victim advocates, and state prosecutors regarding the processing of sexual assault cases. Data were analyzed using the grounded theory method (Glaser 1978; Martin and Turner 1986). In the following analysis, concepts generated from the data analysis are integrated with the literature on men's social fraternities, sexual coercion, and related issues.

FRATERNITIES AND THE SOCIAL CONSTRUCTION OF MEN AND MASCULINITY

Our research indicated that fraternities are vitally concerned—more than with anything else—with masculinity (cf. Kanin 1967). They work hard to create a macho image and context and try to avoid any suggestion of "wimpishness," effeminacy, and homosexuality. Valued members display, or are willing to go along with, a narrow conception of masculinity that stresses competition, athleticism, dominance, winning, conflict, wealth, material possessions, willingness to drink alcohol, and sexual prowess vis-à-vis women.

Valued Qualities of Members

When fraternity members talked about the kind of pledges they prefer, a litany of stereotypical and narrowly masculine attributes and behaviors was recited and feminine or woman-associated qualities and behaviors were expressly denounced (cf. Merton 1985). Fraternities seek men who are "athletic," "big guys," good in intramural competition, "who can talk college sports." Males "who are willing to drink alcohol," "who drink socially," or "who can hold their liquor" are sought. Alcohol and activities associated with the recreational use of alcohol are cornerstones of fraternity social life. Nondrinkers are viewed with skepticism and rarely selected for membership.[1]

Fraternities try to avoid "geeks," nerds, and men said to give the fraternity a "wimpy" or "gay" reputation. Art, music, and humanities majors, majors in traditional women's fields (nursing, home economics, social work, education), men with long hair, and those whose appearance or dress violate current norms are rejected. Clean-cut, handsome men who dress well (are clean, neat, conforming, fashionable) are preferred. One sorority woman commented that "the top-ranking fraternities have the best looking guys."

One fraternity man, a senior, said his fraternity recruited "some big guys, very athletic" over a two-year period to help overcome its image of wimpiness. His fraternity had won the interfraternity competition for highest grade-point average several years running but was looked down on as "wimpy, dancy, even gay." With their bigger, more athletic recruits, "our reputation improved; we're a much more recognized fraternity now." Thus a fraternity's reputation and status depend on members' possession of stereotypically masculine qualities. Good grades, campus leadership, and community service are "nice" but masculinity dominance—for example, in athletic events, physical size of members, athleticism of members—counts most.

Certain social skills are valued. Men are sought who "have good personalities," are friendly, and "have the ability to relate to girls" (cf. Longino and Kart 1973). One fraternity man, a junior, said: "We watch a guy [a potential pledge] talk to women . . . we want guys who can relate to girls." Assessing a pledge's ability to talk to women is, in part, a preoccupation with homosexuality and a conscious avoidance of men who seem to have effeminate manners or qualities. If a member is suspected of being gay, he is ostracized and informally drummed out of the fraternity. A fraternity with a reputation as wimpy or tolerant of gays is ridiculed and shunned by other fraternities. Militant heterosexuality is frequently used by men as a strategy to keep each other in line (Kimmel 1987).

Financial affluence or wealth, a male-associated value in American culture, is highly valued by fraternities. In accounting for why the fraternity involved in the gang rape that precipitated our research project had been recognized recently as "the best fraternity chapter in the United States," a university official said: "They were good-looking, a big fraternity, had lots of BMWs [expensive, German-made automobiles]." After the rape, newspaper stories described the fraternity members' affluence, noting the high number of members who owned expensive cars (*St. Petersburg Times* 1988).

The Status and Norms of Pledgeship

A pledge (sometimes called an associate member) is a new recruit who occupies a trial membership status for a specific period of time. The pledge period (typically ranging from ten to fifteen weeks) gives fraternity brothers an opportunity to assess and socialize new recruits. Pledges evaluate the fraternity also and decide if they want to become brothers. The socialization experience is structured partly through assignment of a Big Brother to each pledge. Big Brothers are expected to teach pledges how to become a brother and to support them as they progress through the trial membership period. Some pledges are repelled by the pledging experience, which can entail physical abuse; harsh discipline; and demands to be subordinate, follow orders, and engage in demeaning routines and activities, similar to those used by the military to "make men out of boys" during boot camp.

Characteristics of the pledge experience are rationalized by fraternity members as necessary to help pledges unite into a group, rely on each other, and join together against outsiders. The process is highly masculinist in execution as well as conception. A willingness to submit to authority, follow orders, and do as one is told is viewed as a sign of loyalty, togetherness, and unity. Fraternity pledges who find the pledge process offensive often drop out. Some do this by openly quitting, which can subject them to ridicule by brothers and other pledges, or they may deliberately fail to make the grades necessary for initiation or transfer schools and decline to reaffiliate with the fraternity on the new campus. One fraternity pledge who quit the fraternity he had pledged described an experience during pledgeship as follows:

> This one guy was always picking on me. No matter what I did, I was wrong. One night after dinner, he and two other guys called me and two other pledges into the chapter room. He said, "Here, X, hold this 25-pound bag of ice at arms' length 'til I tell you to stop." I did it even though my arms and hands were killing me. When I asked if I could stop, he grabbed me around the throat and lifted me off the floor. I thought he would choke me to death. He cussed me and called me all kinds of names. He took one of my fingers and twisted it until it nearly broke. . . . I stayed in the fraternity for a few more days, but then I decided to quit. I hated it. Those guys are sick. They like seeing you suffer.

Fraternities' emphasis on toughness, withstanding pain and humiliation, obedience to superiors, and using physical force to obtain compliance contributes to an interpersonal style that de-emphasizes caring and sensitivity but fosters intragroup trust and loyalty. If the least macho or most critical pledges drop out, those who remain may be more receptive to, and influenced by, masculinist values and practices that encourage the use of force in sexual relations with women and the covering up of such behavior (cf. Kanin 1967).

Norms and Dynamics of Brotherhood

Brother is the status occupied by fraternity men to indicate their relations to each other and their membership in a particular fraternity organization or group. Brother is a male-specific status; only males can become brothers, although women can become "Little Sisters," a form of pseudomembership. "Becoming a brother" is a rite of passage that follows the consistent and often lengthy display by pledges of appropriately masculine qualities and behaviors. Brothers have a quasifamilial relationship with each other, are normatively said to share bonds of closeness and support, and are sharply set off from nonmembers. Brotherhood is a loosely defined term used to represent the bonds that develop among fraternity members and the obligations and expectations incumbent upon them (cf. Marlowe and Auvenshine [1982] on fraternities' failure to encourage "moral development" in freshman pledges).

Some of our respondents talked about brotherhood in almost reverential terms, viewing it as the most valuable benefit of fraternity membership. One senior, a business-school major who had been affiliated with a fairly high-status fraternity throughout four years on campus, said:

> Brotherhood spurs friendship for life, which I consider its best aspect, although I didn't see it that way when I joined. Brotherhood bonds and unites. It instills values of caring about one another, caring about community, caring about ourselves. The values and bonds [of brotherhood] continually develop over the four years [in college] while normal friendships come and go.

Despite this idealization, most aspects of fraternity practice and conception are more mundane. Brotherhood often plays itself out as an overriding concern with masculinity and, by extension, femininity. As a consequence, fraternities comprise collectivities of highly masculinized men with attitudinal qualities and behavioral norms that predispose them to sexual coercion of women (cf. Kanin 1967; Merton 1985;

Rapaport and Burkhart 1984). The norms of masculinity are complemented by conceptions of women and femininity that are equally distorted and stereotyped and that may enhance the probability of women's exploitation (cf. Ehrhart and Sandler 1985; Sanday 1981, 1986).

Practices of Brotherhood

Practices associated with fraternity brotherhood that contribute to the sexual coercion of women include a preoccupation with loyalty, group protection and secrecy, use of alcohol as a weapon, involvement in violence and physical force, and an emphasis on competition and superiority.

Loyalty, Group Protection, and Secrecy   Loyalty is a fraternity preoccupation. Members are reminded constantly to be loyal to the fraternity and to their brothers. Among other ways, loyalty is played out in the practices of group protection and secrecy. The fraternity must be shielded from criticism. Members are admonished to avoid getting the fraternity in trouble and to bring all problems "to the chapter" (local branch of a national social fraternity) rather than to outsiders. Fraternities try to protect themselves from close scrutiny and criticism by the Interfraternity Council (a quasigoverning body composed of representatives from all social fraternities on campus), their fraternity's national office, university officials, law enforcement, the media, and the public. Protection of the fraternity often takes precedence over what is procedurally, ethically, or legally correct. Numerous examples were related to us of fraternity brothers' lying to outsiders to "protect the fraternity."

Group protection was observed in the alleged gang rape case with which we began our study. Except for one brother, a rapist who turned state's evidence, the entire remaining fraternity membership was accused by university and criminal justice officials of lying to protect the fraternity. Members consistently failed to cooperate even though the alleged crimes were felonies, involved only four men (two of whom were not even members of the local chapter), and the victim of the crime nearly died. According to a grand jury's findings, fraternity officers repeatedly broke appointments with law enforcement officials, refused to provide police with a list of members, and refused to cooperate with police and prosecutors investigating the case (*Florida Flambeau* 1988).

Secrecy is a priority value and practice in fraternities, partly because full-fledged membership is premised on it (for confirmation, see Ehrhart and Sandler 1985; Longino and Kart 1973; Roark 1987). Secrecy is also a boundary-maintaining mechanism, demarcating in-group from out-group, us from them. Secret rituals, handshakes, and mottoes are revealed to pledge brothers as they are initiated into full brotherhood. Since only brothers are supposed to know a fraternity's secrets, such knowledge affirms membership in the fraternity and separates a brother from others. Extending secrecy tactics from protection of private knowledge to protection of the fraternity from criticism is a predictable development. Our interviews indicated that individual members knew the difference between right and wrong, but fraternity norms that emphasize loyalty, group protection, and secrecy often overrode standards of ethical correctness.

Alcohol as Weapon   Alcohol use by fraternity men is normative. They use it on weekdays to relax after class and on weekends to "get drunk," "get crazy," and "get laid." The use of alcohol to obtain sex from women is pervasive—in other words, it is used as a weapon against sexual reluctance. According to several fraternity men whom we interviewed, alcohol is the major tool used to gain sexual mastery over women (cf. Adams and Abarbanel 1988; Ehrhart and Sandler 1985). One fraternity man, a twenty-one-year-old senior, described alcohol use to gain sex as follows: "There are girls that you know will fuck, then some you have to put some effort into it. . . . You have to buy them drinks or find out if she's drunk enough."

A similar strategy is used collectively. A fraternity man said that at parties with Little Sisters: "We provide them with 'hunch punch' and things get wild. We get them drunk and most of the guys end up with one." "'Hunch punch,'" he said, "is a girls' drink made up of overproof alcohol and powdered Kool-Aid, no water or anything, just ice. It's very strong. Two cups will do a number on a female." He had plans in the next academic term to surreptitiously give hunch punch to women in a "prim and proper" sorority because "having sex with prim and proper sorority girls is definitely a goal." These women are a challenge because they "won't openly consume alcohol and won't get openly drunk as hell." Their sororities have "standards committees" that forbid heavy drinking and easy sex.

In the gang rape case, our sources said that many fraternity men on campus believed the victim had a drinking problem and was thus an "easy make." According to newspaper accounts, she had been drinking alcohol on the evening she was raped; the lead assailant is alleged to have given her a bottle of wine after she arrived at his fraternity house. Portions of the rape occurred in a shower, and the victim was reportedly so drunk that her assailants had difficulty holding her in a standing position (*Tallahassee Democrat* 1988a). While raping her, her assailants repeatedly told her they were members of another fraternity under the apparent belief that she was too drunk to know the difference. Of course, if she was too drunk to know who they were, she was too drunk to consent to sex (cf. Allgeier 1986; Tash 1988).

One respondent told us that gang rapes are wrong and can get one expelled, but he seemed to see nothing wrong in sexual coercion one-on-one. He seemed unaware that the use of alcohol to obtain sex from a woman is grounds for a claim that a rape occurred (cf. Tash 1988). Few women on campus (who also may not know these grounds) report date rapes, however; so the odds of detection and punishment are slim for fraternity men who use alcohol for "seduction" purposes (cf. Byington and Keeter 1988; Merton 1985).

Violence and Physical Force   Fraternity men have a history of violence (Ehrhart and Sandler 1985; Roark 1987). Their record of hazing, fighting, property destruction, and rape has caused them problems with insurance companies (Bradford 1986; Pressley 1987). Two university officials told us that fraternities "are the third riskiest property to insure behind toxic waste dumps and amusement parks." Fraternities are increasingly defendants in legal actions brought by pledges subjected to hazing (Meyer 1986; Pressley 1987) and by women who were raped by one or more members. In a recent alleged gang rape incident at another Florida university, prosecutors failed to file charges but the victim filed a civil suit against the fraternity nevertheless (*Tallahassee Democrat* 1989).

Competition and Superiority   Interfraternity rivalry fosters in-group identification and out-group hostility. Fraternities stress pride of membership and superiority over other fraternities as major goals. Interfraternity rivalries take many forms, including competition for desirable pledges, size of pledge class, size of membership, size and appearance of fraternity house, superiority in intramural sports, highest grade-point averages, giving the best parties, gaining the best or most campus leadership roles, and, of great importance, attracting and displaying "good-looking women." Rivalry is particularly intense over members, intramural sports, and women (cf. Messner 1989).

FRATERNITIES' COMMODIFICATION OF WOMEN

In claiming that women are treated by fraternities as commodities, we mean that fraternities knowingly, and intentionally, *use* women for their benefit. Fraternities use women as bait for new members, as servers of brothers' needs, and as sexual prey.

Women as Bait

Fashionably attractive women help a fraternity attract new members. As one fraternity man, a junior, said, "They are good bait." Beautiful, sociable women are believed to impress the right kind of pledges and give the impression that the fraternity can deliver this type of woman to its members. Photographs of shapely, attractive coeds are printed in fraternity brochures and videotapes that are distributed and shown to potential pledges. The women pictured are often dressed in bikinis, at the beach, and are pictured hugging the brothers of the fraternity. One university official says such recruitment materials give the message: "Hey, they're here for you, you can have whatever you want," and, "we have the best-looking women. Join us and you can have them too." Another commented: "Something's wrong when males join an all-male organization as the best place to meet women. It's so illogical."

Fraternities compete in promising access to beautiful women. One fraternity man, a senior, commented that "the attraction of girls [i.e., a fraternity's success in attracting women] is a big status symbol for fraternities." One university official commented that the use of women as a recruiting tool is so well entrenched that fraternities that might be willing to forgo it say they cannot afford to unless other fraternities do so as well. One fraternity man said, "Look, if we don't have Little Sisters, the fraternities that do will get all the good pledges." Another said, "We won't have as good a rush [the period during which new members are assessed and selected] if we don't have these women around."

In displaying good-looking, attractive, skimpily dressed, nubile women to potential members, fraternities implicitly, and sometimes explicitly, promise sexual access to women. One fraternity man commented

that "part of what being in a fraternity is all about is the sex" and explained how his fraternity uses Little Sisters to recruit new members:

> We'll tell the sweetheart [the fraternity's term for Little Sister], "You're gorgeous; you can get him." We'll tell her to fake a scam and she'll go hang all over him during a rush party, kiss him, and he thinks he's done wonderful and wants to join. The girls think it's great too. It's flattering for them.

Women as Servers

The use of women as servers is exemplified in the Little Sister program. Little Sisters are undergraduate women who are rushed and selected in a manner parallel to the recruitment of fraternity men. They are affiliated with the fraternity in a formal but unofficial way and are able, indeed required, to wear the fraternity's Greek letters. Little Sisters are not full-fledged fraternity members, however; and fraternity national offices and most universities do not register or regulate them. Each fraternity has an officer called Little Sister Chairman who oversees their organization and activities. The Little Sisters elect officers among themselves, pay monthly dues to the fraternity, and have well-defined roles. Their dues are used to pay for the fraternity's social events, and Little Sisters are expected to attend and hostess fraternity parties and hang around the house to make it a "nice place to be." One fraternity man, a senior, described Little Sisters this way: "They are very social girls, willing to join in, be affiliated with the group, devoted to the fraternity." Another member, a sophomore, said: "Their sole purpose is social—attend parties, attract new members, and 'take care' of the guys."

Our observations and interviews suggested that women selected by fraternities as Little Sisters are physically attractive, possess good social skills, and are willing to devote time and energy to the fraternity and its members. One undergraduate woman gave the following job description for Little Sisters to a campus newspaper:

> It's not just making appearances at all the parties but entails many more responsibilities. You're going to be expected to go to all the intramural games to cheer the brothers on, support and encourage the pledges, and just be around to bring some extra life to the house. [As a Little Sister] you have to agree to take on a new responsibility other than studying to maintain your

grades and managing to keep your checkbook from bouncing. You have to make time to be a part of the fraternity and support the brothers in all they do. (*The Tomahawk* 1988)

The title of Little Sister reflects women's subordinate status; fraternity men in a parallel role are called Big Brothers. Big Brothers assist a sorority primarily with the physical work of sorority rushes, which, compared to fraternity rushes, are more formal, structured, and intensive. Sorority rushes take place in the daytime and fraternity rushes at night so fraternity men are free to help. According to one fraternity member, Little Sister status is a benefit to women because it gives them a social outlet and "the protection of the brothers." The gender-stereotypic conceptions and obligations of these Little Sister and Big Brother statuses indicate that fraternities and sororities promote a gender hierarchy on campus that fosters subordination and dependence in women, thus encouraging sexual exploitation and the belief that it is acceptable.

Women as Sexual Prey

Little Sisters are a sexual utility. Many Little Sisters do not belong to sororities and lack peer support for refraining from unwanted sexual relations. One fraternity man (whose fraternity has sixty-five members and eighty-five Little Sisters) told us they had recruited "wholesale" in the prior year to "get lots of new women." The structural access to women that the Little Sister program provides and the absence of normative supports for refusing fraternity members' sexual advances may make women in this program particularly susceptible to coerced sexual encounters with fraternity men.

Access to women for sexual gratification is a presumed benefit of fraternity membership, promised in recruitment materials and strategies and through brothers' conversations with new recruits. One fraternity man said: "We always tell the guys that you get sex all the time, there's always new girls. . . . After I became a Greek, I found out I could be with females at will." A university official told us that, based on his observations, "no one [i.e., fraternity men] on this campus wants to have 'relationships.' They just want to have fun [i.e., sex]." Fraternity men plan and execute strategies aimed at obtaining sexual gratification, and this occurs at both individual and collective levels.

Individual strategies include getting a woman drunk and spending a great deal of money on her. As for

collective strategies, most of our undergraduate interviewees agreed that fraternity parties often culminate in sex and that this outcome is planned. One fraternity man said fraternity parties often involve sex and nudity and can "turn into orgies." Orgies may be planned in advance, such as the Bowery Ball party held by one fraternity. A former fraternity member said of this party:

> The entire idea behind this is sex. Both men and women come to the party wearing little or nothing. There are pornographic pinups on the walls and usually porno movies playing on the TV. The music carries sexual overtones. . . . They just get schnockered [drunk] and, in most cases, they also get laid.

When asked about the women who come to such a party, he said: "Some Little Sisters just won't go. . . . The girls who do are looking for a good time, girls who don't know what it is, things like that."

Other respondents denied that fraternity parties are orgies but said that sex is always talked about among the brothers and they all know "who each other is doing it with." One member said that most of the time, guys have sex with their girlfriends "but with socials, girlfriends aren't allowed to come and it's their [members'] big chance [to have sex with other women]." The use of alcohol to help them get women into bed is a routine strategy at fraternity parties.

CONCLUSIONS

In general, our research indicated that the organization and membership of fraternities contribute heavily to coercive and often violent sex. Fraternity houses are occupied by same-sex (all men) and same-age (late teens, early twenties) peers whose maturity and judgment is often less than ideal. Yet fraternity houses are private dwellings that are mostly off-limits to, and away from scrutiny of, university and community representatives, with the result that fraternity house events seldom come to the attention of outsiders. Practices associated with the social construction of fraternity brotherhood emphasize a macho conception of men and masculinity, a narrow, stereotyped conception of women and femininity, and the treatment of women as commodities. Other practices contributing to coercive sexual relations and the coverup of rapes include excessive alcohol use, competitiveness, and normative support for deviance and secrecy (cf. Bogal-Allbritten and Allbritten 1985; Kanin 1967).

Some fraternity practices exacerbate others. Brotherhood norms require "sticking together" regardless of right or wrong; thus rape episodes are unlikely to be stopped or reported to outsiders, even when witnesses disapprove. The ability to use alcohol without scrutiny by authorities and alcohol's frequent association with violence, including sexual coercion, facilitates rape in fraternity houses. Fraternity norms that emphasize the value of maleness and masculinity over femaleness and femininity and that elevate the status of men and lower the status of women in members' eyes undermine perceptions and treatment of women as persons who deserve consideration and care (cf. Ehrhart and Sandler 1985; Merton 1985).

Androgynous men and men with a broad range of interests and attributes are lost to fraternities through their recruitment practices. Masculinity of a narrow and stereotypical type helps create attitudes, norms, and practices that predispose fraternity men to coerce women sexually, both individually and collectively (Allgeier 1986; Hood 1989; Sanday 1981, 1986). Male athletes on campus may be similarly disposed for the same reasons (Kirshenbaum 1989; Telander and Sullivan 1989).

Research into the social contexts in which rape crimes occur and the social constructions associated with these contexts illumine rape dynamics on campus. Blanchard (1959) found that group rapes almost always have a leader who pushes others into the crime. He also found that the leader's latent homosexuality, desire to show off to his peers, or fear of failing to prove himself a man are frequently an impetus. Fraternity norms and practices contribute to the approval and use of sexual coercion as an accepted tactic in relations with women. Alcohol-induced compliance is normative, whereas, presumably, use of a knife, gun, or threat of bodily harm would not be because the woman who "drinks too much" is viewed as "causing her own rape" (cf. Ehrhart and Sandler 1985).

Our research led us to conclude that fraternity norms and practices influence members to view the sexual coercion of women, which is a felony crime, as sport, a contest, or a game (cf. Sato 1988). This sport is played not between men and women but between men and men. Women are the pawns or prey in the interfraternity rivalry game; they prove that a fraternity is successful or prestigious. The use of women in this way encourages fraternity men to see women as objects and sexual coercion as sport. Today's societal norms support young women's right to engage in sex at their discretion, and coercion is unnecessary in a mutually desired encounter. However, nubile young women say they prefer to be "in a relationship" to have sex while young men say they prefer to "get laid" without a commitment (Muehlenhard and Linton 1987). These differences may reflect, in part, American puritanism and men's fears of sexual intimacy or perhaps intimacy of any kind. In a fraternity context, getting sex without giving emotionally demonstrates "cool" masculinity. More important, it poses no threat to the bonding and loyalty of the fraternity brotherhood (cf. Farr 1988). Drinking large quantities of alcohol before having sex suggests that "scoring" rather than intrinsic sexual pleasure is a primary concern of fraternity men.

Unless fraternities' composition, goals, structures, and practices change in fundamental ways, women on campus will continue to be sexual prey for fraternity men. As all-male enclaves dedicated to opposing faculty and administration and to cementing in-group ties, fraternity members eschew any hint of homosexuality. Their version of masculinity transforms women, and men with womanly characteristics, into the outgroup. "Womanly men" are ostracized; feminine women are used to demonstrate members' masculinity. Encouraging renewed emphasis on their founding values (Longino and Kart 1973), service orientation and activities (Lemire 1979), or members' moral development (Marlowe and Auvenshine 1982) will have little effect on fraternities' treatment of women. A case for or against fraternities cannot be made by studying individual members. The fraternity qua group and organization is at issue. Located on campus along with many vulnerable women, embedded in a sexist society, and caught up in masculinist goals, practices, and values, fraternities' violation of women—including forcible rape—should come as no surprise.

ACKNOWLEDGMENTS

We gratefully thank Meena Harris and Diane Mennella for assisting with data collection. The senior author thanks the graduate students in her fall 1988 graduate research methods seminar for help with developing the initial conceptual framework. Judith Lorber and two anonymous *Gender & Society* referees made numerous suggestions for improving our article and we thank them also.

NOTE

1. Recent bans by some universities on open-keg parties at fraternity houses have resulted in heavy drinking before coming to a party and an increase in drunkenness among those who attend. This may aggravate, rather than improve, the treatment of women by fraternity men at parties.

REFERENCES

Adams, Aileen, and Gail Abarbanel. 1988. *Sexual Assault on Campus: What Colleges Can Do.* Santa Monica, CA: Rape Treatment Center.

Allgeier, Elizabeth. 1986. "Coercive Versus Consensual Sexual Interactions." G. Stanley Hall Lecture to American Psychological Association Annual Meeting, Washington, DC, August.

Blanchard, W. H. 1959. "The Group Process in Gang Rape." *Journal of Social Psychology* 49: 259–66.

Bogal-Allbritten, Rosemarie B., and William L. Allbritten. 1985. "The Hidden Victims: Courtship Violence Among College Students." *Journal of College Student Personnel* 43: 201–4.

Bohrnstedt, George W. 1969. "Conservatism, Authoritarianism and Religiosity of Fraternity Pledges." *Journal of College Student Personnel* 27: 36–43.

Bradford, Michael. 1986. "Tight Market Dries Up Nightlife at University." *Business Insurance* (March 2): 2, 6.

Burkhart, Barry. 1989. Comments in Seminar on Acquaintance/Date Rape Prevention: A National Video Teleconference, February 2.

Byington, Diane B., and Karen W. Keeter. 1988. "Assessing Needs of Sexual Assault Victims on a University Campus." Pp. 23–31 in *Student Services: Responding to Issues and Challenges.* Chapel Hill: University of North Carolina Press.

Chancer, Lynn S. 1987. "New Bedford, Massachusetts, March 6, 1983–March 22, 1984: The 'Before and After' of a Group Rape." *Gender & Society* 1: 239–60.

Ehrhart, Julie K., and Bernice R. Sandler. 1985. *Campus Gang Rape: Party Games?* Washington, DC: Association of American Colleges.

Farr, K. A. 1988. "Dominance Bonding Through the Good Old Boys Sociability Network." *Sex Roles* 18: 259–77.

Florida Flambeau. 1988. "Pike Members Indicted in Rape." (May 19): 1, 5.

Fox, Elaine, Charles Hodge, and Walter Ward. 1987. "A Comparison of Attitudes Held by Black and White Fraternity Members." *Journal of Negro Education* 56: 521–34.

Geis, Gilbert. 1971. "Group Sexual Assaults." *Medical Aspects of Human Sexuality* 5: 101–13.

Glaser, Barney G. 1978. *Theoretical Sensitivity: Advances in the Methodology of Grounded Theory.* Mill Valley, CA: Sociology Press.

Hood, Jane. 1989. "Why Our Society Is Rape-Prone." *New York Times,* May 16.

Hughes, Michael J., and Roger B. Winston, Jr. 1987. "Effects of Fraternity Membership on Interpersonal Values." *Journal of College Student Personnel* 45: 405–11.

Kanin, Eugene J. 1967. "Reference Groups and Sex Conduct Norm Violations." *The Sociological Quarterly* 8: 495–504.

Kimmel, Michael, ed. 1987. *Changing Men: New Directions in Research on Men and Masculinity.* Newbury Park, CA: Sage.

Kirshenbaum, Jerry. 1989. "Special Report, An American Disgrace: A Violent and Unprecedented Lawlessness Has Arisen Among College Athletes in all Parts of the Country." *Sports Illustrated* (February 27): 16–19.

Lemire, David. 1979. "One Investigation of the Stereotypes Associated with Fraternities and Sororities." *Journal of College Student Personnel* 37: 54–57.

Letchworth, G. E. 1969. "Fraternities Now and in the Future." *Journal of College Student Personnel* 10: 118–22.

Longino, Charles F., Jr., and Cary S. Kart. 1973. "The College Fraternity: An Assessment of Theory and Research." *Journal of College Student Personnel* 31: 118–25.

Marlowe, Anne F., and Dwight C. Auvenshine. 1982. "Greek Membership: Its Impact on the Moral Development of College Freshmen." *Journal of College Student Personnel* 40: 53–57.

Martin, Patricia Yancey, and Barry A. Turner. 1986. "Grounded Theory and Organizational Research." *Journal of Applied Behavioral Science* 22: 141–57.

Merton, Andrew. 1985. "On Competition and Class: Return to Brotherhood." *Ms.* (September): 60–65, 121–22.

Messner, Michael. 1989. "Masculinities and Athletic Careers." *Gender & Society* 3: 71–88.

Meyer, T. J. 1986. "Fight Against Hazing Rituals Rages on Campuses." *Chronicle of Higher Education* (March 12): 34–36.

Miller, Leonard D. 1973. "Distinctive Characteristics of Fraternity Members." *Journal of College Student Personnel* 31: 126–28.

Muehlenhard, Charlene L., and Melaney A. Linton. 1987. "Date Rape and Sexual Aggression in Dating Situations: Incidence and Risk Factors." *Journal of Counseling Psychology* 34: 186–96.

Pressley, Sue Anne. 1987. "Fraternity Hell Night Still Endures." *Washington Post* (August 11): B1.

Rapaport, Karen, and Barry R. Burkhart. 1984. "Personality and Attitudinal Characteristics of Sexually Coercive College Males." *Journal of Abnormal Psychology* 93: 216–21.

Roark, Mary L. 1987. "Preventing Violence on College Campuses." *Journal of Counseling and Development* 65: 367–70.

Sanday, Peggy Reeves. 1981. "The Socio-Cultural Context of Rape: A Cross-Cultural Study." *Journal of Social Issues* 37: 5–27.

———. 1986. "Rape and the Silencing of the Feminine." Pp. 84–101 in *Rape*, ed. S. Tomaselli and R. Porter. Oxford: Basil Blackwell.

St. Petersburg Times. 1988. "A Greek Tragedy." (May 29): 1F, 6F.

Sato, Ikuya. 1988. "Play Theory of Delinquency: Toward a General Theory of 'Action.'" *Symbolic Interaction* 11: 191–212.

Smith, T. 1964. "Emergence and Maintenance of Fraternal Solidarity." *Pacific Sociological Review* 7: 29–37.

Tallahassee Democrat. 1988a. "FSU Fraternity Brothers Charged" (April 27): 1A, 12A.

———. 1988b. "FSU Interviewing Students about Alleged Rape" (April 24): 1D.

———. 1989. "Woman Sues Stetson in Alleged Rape" (March 19): 3B.

Tampa Tribune. 1988. "Fraternity Brothers Charged in Sexual Assault of FSU Coed" (April 27): 6B.

Tash, Gary B. 1988. "Date Rape." *The Emerald of Sigma Pi Fraternity* 75(4): 1–2.

Telander, Rick, and Robert Sullivan. 1989. "Special Report, You Reap What You Sow." *Sports Illustrated* (February 27): 20–34.

The Tomahawk. 1988. "A Look Back at Rush, a Mixture of Hard Work and Fun" (April/May): 3D.

Walsh, Claire. 1989. Comments in Seminar on Acquaintance/Date Rape Prevention: A National Video Teleconference, February 2.

Wilder, David H., Arlyne E. Hoyt, Dennis M. Doren, William E. Hauck, and Robert D. Zettle. 1978. "The Impact of Fraternity and Sorority Membership on Values and Attitudes." *Journal of College Student Personnel* 36: 445–49.

Wilder, David H., Arlyne E. Hoyt, Beth Shuster Surbeck, Janet C. Wilder, and Patricia Imperatrice Carney. 1986. "Greek Affiliation and Attitude Change in College Students." *Journal of College Student Personnel* 44: 510–19.

READING *43* *Kimberlé Crenshaw*

Mapping the Margins: Intersectionality, Identity Politics, and Violence Against Women of Color

First published in 1991

. . . My objective [is to explore] the race and gender dimensions of violence against women of color. . . . I consider how the experiences of women of color are frequently the product of intersecting patterns of racism and sexism. . . .

[Based on] a brief field study of battered women's shelters located in minority communities in Los Angeles,[1] [I found that in most cases], the physical assault that leads women to these shelters is merely the most immediate manifestation of the subordination they experience. Many women who seek protection are unemployed or under-employed, and a good number of them are poor. Shelters serving these women cannot afford to address only the violence inflicted by the batterer; they must also confront the other multilayered and routinized forms of domination that often converge in these women's lives, hindering their ability to create alternatives to the abusive relationships that brought them to shelters in the first place. Many women of color, for example, are burdened by poverty, child care responsibilities, and the lack of job skills.[2] These burdens, largely the consequence of gender and class oppression, are then compounded by the racially discriminatory employment and housing practices women of color often face, as well as by the disproportionately high unemployment among people of color that makes battered women of color less able to depend on the support of friends and relatives for temporary shelter.[3]

Where systems of race, gender, and class domination converge, as they do in the experiences of battered women of color, intervention strategies based solely on the experiences of women who do not share the same class or race backgrounds will be of limited help to women who because of race and class face different obstacles.[4] Such was the case in 1990 when Congress amended the marriage fraud provisions of the Immigration and Nationality Act to protect immigrant women who were battered or exposed to extreme cruelty by the United States citizens or permanent residents these women immigrated to the United States to marry. Under the marriage fraud provisions of the Act, a person who immigrated to the United States to marry a United States citizen or permanent resident had to remain "properly" married for two years before even applying for permanent resident status,[5] at which time applications for the immigrant's permanent status were required of both spouses. Predictably, under these circumstances, many immigrant women were reluctant to leave even the most abusive of partners for fear of being deported.[6] When faced with the choice between protection from their batterers and protection against deportation, many immigrant women chose the latter. Reports of the tragic consequences of this double subordination put pressure on Congress to include in the Immigration Act of 1990 a provision amending the marriage fraud rules to allow for an explicit waiver for hardship caused by domestic violence.[7] Yet many immigrant women, particularly immigrant women of color, have remained vulnerable to battering because they are unable to meet the conditions established for a waiver. The evidence required to support a waiver "can include but is not limited to, reports and affidavits from police, medical personnel, psychologists, school officials, and social service agencies."[8] For many immigrant women, limited access to these resources can make it difficult for them to obtain the evidence needed for a waiver. And cultural barriers

often further discourage immigrant women from reporting or escaping battering situations. Tina Shum, a family counselor at a social service agency, points out that "[t]his law sounds so easy to apply, but there are cultural complications in the Asian community that make even these requirements difficult. . . . Just to find the opportunity and courage to call us is an accomplishment for many."[9] The typical immigrant spouse, she suggests, may live "[i]n an extended family where several generations live together, there may be no privacy on the telephone, no opportunity to leave the house and no understanding of public phones."[10] As a consequence, many immigrant women are wholly dependent on their husbands as their link to the world outside their homes.

Immigrant women are also vulnerable to spousal violence because so many of them depend on their husbands for information regarding their legal status.[11] Many women who are now permanent residents continue to suffer abuse under threats of deportation by their husbands. Even if the threats are unfounded, women who have no independent access to information will still be intimidated by such threats. And even though the domestic violence waiver focuses on immigrant women whose husbands are United States citizens or permanent residents, there are countless women married to undocumented workers (or who are themselves undocumented) who suffer in silence for fear that the security of their entire families will be jeopardized should they seek help or otherwise call attention to themselves.

Language barriers present another structural problem that often limits opportunities of non-English-speaking women to take advantage of existing support services. Such barriers not only limit access to information about shelters, but also limit access to the security shelters provide. Some shelters turn non-English-speaking women away for lack of bilingual personnel and resources.[12]

These examples illustrate how patterns of subordination intersect in women's experience of domestic violence. . . .

A. THE POLITICIZATION OF DOMESTIC VIOLENCE

[T]he political interests of women of color are obscured and sometimes jeopardized by political strategies that ignore or suppress intersectional issues, [as] is illustrated by my [research]. I attempted to review

Los Angeles Police Department statistics reflecting the rate of domestic violence interventions by precinct because such statistics can provide a rough picture of arrests by racial group, given the degree of racial segregation in Los Angeles.[13] L.A.P.D., however, would not release the statistics. A representative explained that one reason the statistics were not released was that domestic violence activists both within and outside the Department feared that statistics reflecting the extent of domestic violence in minority communities might be selectively interpreted and publicized so as to undermine long-term efforts to force the Department to address domestic violence as a serious problem. I was told that activists were worried that the statistics might permit opponents to dismiss domestic violence as a minority problem and, therefore, not deserving of aggressive action.

The informant also claimed that representatives from various minority communities opposed the release of the statistics. They were concerned, apparently, that the data would unfairly represent Black and Brown communities as unusually violent, potentially reinforcing stereotypes that might be used in attempts to justify oppressive police tactics and other discriminatory practices. These misgivings are based on the familiar and not unfounded premise that certain minority groups—especially Black men—have already been stereotyped as uncontrollably violent. Some worry that attempts to make domestic violence an object of political action may only serve to confirm such stereotypes and undermine efforts to combat negative beliefs about the Black community.

This account sharply illustrates how women of color can be erased by the strategic silences of antiracism and feminism. The political priorities of both were defined in ways that suppressed information that could have facilitated attempts to confront the problem of domestic violence in communities of color.

I. Domestic Violence and Antiracist Politics

Within communities of color, efforts to stem the politicization of domestic violence are often grounded in attempts to maintain the integrity of the community. The articulation of this perspective takes different forms. Some critics allege that feminism has no place within communities of color, that the issues are internally divisive, and that they represent the migration of white women's concerns into a context in which they are not only irrelevant but also harmful. At its most

extreme, this rhetoric denies that gender violence is a problem in the community and characterizes any effort to politicize gender subordination as itself a community problem. This is the position taken by Shahrazad Ali in her controversial book, *The Blackman's Guide to Understanding the Blackwoman*.[14] In this stridently antifeminist tract, Ali draws a positive correlation between domestic violence and the liberation of African Americans. Ali blames the deteriorating conditions within the Black community on the insubordination of Black women and on the failure of Black men to control them.[15] Ali goes so far as to advise Black men to physically chastise Black women when they are "disrespectful."[16] While she cautions that Black men must use moderation in disciplining "their" women, she argues that Black men must sometimes resort to physical force to reestablish the authority over Black women that racism has disrupted.[17]

Ali's premise is that patriarchy is beneficial for the Black community, and that it must be strengthened through coercive means if necessary. Yet the violence that accompanies this will to control is devastating, not only for the Black women who are victimized, but also for the entire Black community. The recourse to violence to resolve conflicts establishes a dangerous pattern for children raised in such environments and contributes to many other pressing problems. It has been estimated that nearly forty percent of all homeless women and children have fled violence in the home,[18] and an estimated sixty-three percent of young men between the ages of eleven and twenty who are imprisoned for homicide have killed their mothers' batterers.[19] And yet, while gang violence, homicide, and other forms of Black-on-Black crime have increasingly been discussed within African-American politics, patriarchal ideas about gender and power preclude the recognition of domestic violence as yet another compelling incidence of Black-on-Black crime.

Efforts such as Ali's to justify violence against women in the name of Black liberation are indeed extreme. The more common problem is that the political or cultural interests of the community are interpreted in a way that precludes full public recognition of the problem of domestic violence. While it would be misleading to suggest that white Americans have come to terms with the degree of violence in their own homes, it is nonetheless the case that race adds yet another dimension to why the problem of domestic violence is suppressed within nonwhite communities.

People of color often must weigh their interests in avoiding issues that might reinforce distorted public perceptions against the need to acknowledge and address intracommunity problems. Yet the cost of suppression is seldom recognized in part because the failure to discuss the issue shapes perceptions of how serious the problem is in the first place.

The controversy over Alice Walker's novel *The Color Purple* can be understood as an intracommunity debate about the political costs of exposing gender violence within the Black community.[20] Some critics chastised Walker for portraying Black men as violent brutes.[21] One critic lambasted Walker's portrayal of Celie, the emotionally and physically abused protagonist who finally triumphs in the end. Walker, the critic contended, had created in Celie a Black woman whom she couldn't imagine existing in any Black community she knew or could conceive of.[22]

The claim that Celie was somehow an unauthentic character might be read as a consequence of silencing discussion of intracommunity violence. Celie may be unlike any Black woman we know because the real terror experienced daily by minority women is routinely concealed in a misguided (though perhaps understandable) attempt to forestall racial stereotyping. Of course, it is true that representations of Black violence—whether statistical or fictional—are often written into a larger script that consistently portrays Black and other minority communities as pathologically violent. The problem, however, is not so much the portrayal of violence itself as it is the absence of other narratives and images portraying a fuller range of Black experience. Suppression of some of these issues in the name of antiracism imposes real costs. Where information about violence in minority communities is not available, domestic violence is unlikely to be addressed as a serious issue.

The political imperatives of a narrowly focused antiracist strategy support other practices that isolate women of color. For example, activists who have attempted to provide support services to Asian- and African-American women report intense resistance from those communities.[23] At other times, cultural and social factors contribute to suppression. Nilda Rimonte, director of Everywoman's Shelter in Los Angeles, points out that in the Asian community, saving the honor of the family from shame is a priority.[24] Unfortunately, this priority tends to be interpreted as obliging women not to scream rather than obliging men not to hit.

Race and culture contribute to the suppression of domestic violence in other ways as well. Women of color are often reluctant to call the police, a hesitancy likely due to a general unwillingness among people of color to subject their private lives to the scrutiny and control of a police force that is frequently hostile. There is also a more generalized community ethic against public intervention, the product of a desire to create a private world free from the diverse assaults on the public lives of racially subordinated people. The home is not simply a man's castle in the patriarchal sense, but may also function as a safe haven from the indignities of life in a racist society. However, but for this "safe haven" in many cases, women of color victimized by violence might otherwise seek help.

There is also a general tendency within antiracist discourse to regard the problem of violence against women of color as just another manifestation of racism. In this sense, the relevance of gender domination within the community is reconfigured as a consequence of discrimination against men. Of course, it is probably true that racism contributes to the cycle of violence, given the stress that men of color experience in dominant society. It is therefore more than reasonable to explore the links between racism and domestic violence. But the chain of violence is more complex and extends beyond this single link. Racism is linked to patriarchy to the extent that racism denies men of color the power and privilege that dominant men enjoy. When violence is understood as an acting-out of being denied male power in other spheres, it seems counterproductive to embrace constructs that implicitly link the solution to domestic violence to the acquisition of greater male power. The more promising political imperative is to challenge the legitimacy of such power expectations by exposing their dysfunctional and debilitating effect on families and communities of color. Moreover, while understanding links between racism and domestic violence is an important component of any effective intervention strategy, it is also clear that women of color need not await the ultimate triumph over racism before they can expect to live violence-free lives.

2. Race and the Domestic Violence Lobby

Not only do race-based priorities function to obscure the problem of violence suffered by women of color; feminist concerns often suppress minority experiences as well. Strategies for increasing awareness of domestic violence within the white community tend to begin by citing the commonly shared assumption that battering is a minority problem. The strategy then focuses on demolishing this strawman, stressing that spousal abuse also occurs in the white community. Countless first-person stories begin with a statement like, "I was not supposed to be a battered wife." That battering occurs in families of all races and all classes seems to be an ever-present theme of anti-abuse campaigns. First-person anecdotes and studies, for example, consistently assert that battering cuts across racial, ethnic, economic, educational, and religious lines.[25] Such disclaimers seem relevant only in the presence of an initial, widely held belief that domestic violence occurs primarily in minority or poor families. Indeed some authorities explicitly renounce the "stereotypical myths" about battered women.[26] A few commentators have even transformed the message that battering is not exclusively a problem of the poor or minority communities into a claim that it equally affects all races and classes.[27] Yet these comments seem less concerned with exploring domestic abuse within "stereotyped" communities than with removing the stereotype as an obstacle to exposing battering within white middle- and upper-class communities.

Efforts to politicize the issue of violence against women challenge beliefs that violence occurs only in homes of "others." While it is unlikely that advocates and others who adopt this rhetorical strategy intend to exclude or ignore the needs of poor and colored women, the underlying premise of this seemingly universalistic appeal is to keep the sensibilities of dominant social groups focused on the experiences of those groups. Indeed, as subtly suggested by the opening comments of Senator David Boren (D-Okla.) in support of the Violence Against Women Act of 1991, the displacement of the "other" as the presumed victim of domestic violence works primarily as a political appeal to rally white elites. Boren said:

> Violent crimes against women are not limited to the streets of the inner cities, but also occur in homes in the urban and rural areas across the country.
>
> Violence against women affects not only those who are actually beaten and brutalized, but indirectly affects all women. Today, our wives, mothers, daughters, sisters, and colleagues are held captive by fear generated from these violent crimes—held captive not for what they do or who they are, but solely because of gender.[28]

Rather than focusing on and illuminating how violence is disregarded when the home is "othered," the strategy implicit in Senator Boren's remarks functions instead to politicize the problem only in the dominant community. This strategy permits white women victims to come into focus, but does little to disrupt the patterns of neglect that permitted the problem to continue as long as it was imagined to be a minority problem. The experience of violence of minority women is ignored, except to the extent it gains white support for domestic violence programs in the white community.

Senator Boren and his colleagues no doubt believe that they have provided legislation and resources that will address the problems of all women victimized by domestic violence. Yet despite their universalizing rhetoric of "all" women, they were able to empathize with female victims of domestic violence only by looking past the plight of "other" women and by recognizing the familiar faces of their own. The strength of the appeal to "protect our women" must be its race and class specificity. After all, it has always been someone's wife, mother, sister, or daughter that has been abused, even when the violence was stereotypically Black or Brown, and poor. The point here is not that the Violence Against Women Act is particularistic on its own terms, but that unless the senators and other policymakers ask why violence remained insignificant as long as it was understood as a minority problem, it is unlikely that women of color will share equally in the distribution of resources and concern. It is even more unlikely, however, that those in power will be forced to confront this issue. As long as attempts to politicize domestic violence focus on convincing whites that this is not a "minority" problem but their problem, any authentic and sensitive attention to the experiences of Black and other minority women probably will continue to be regarded as jeopardizing the movement.

While Senator Boren's statement reflects a self-consciously political presentation of domestic violence, an episode of the CBS news program *48 Hours*[29] shows how similar patterns of "othering" nonwhite women are apparent in journalistic accounts of domestic violence as well. The program presented seven women who were victims of abuse. Six were interviewed at some length along with their family members, friends, supporters, and even detractors. The viewer got to know something about each of these women. These victims were humanized. Yet the seventh woman, the only nonwhite one, never came into focus. She was literally unrecognizable throughout the segment, first introduced by photographs showing her face badly beaten and later shown with her face electronically altered in the videotape of a hearing at which she was forced to testify. Other images associated with this woman included shots of a bloodstained room and blood-soaked pillows. Her boyfriend was pictured handcuffed while the camera zoomed in for a close-up of his bloodied sneakers. Of all the presentations in the episode, hers was the most graphic and impersonal. The overall point of the segment "featuring" this woman was that battering might not escalate into homicide if battered women would only cooperate with prosecutors. In focusing on its own agenda and failing to explore why this woman refused to cooperate, the program diminished this woman, communicating, however subtly, that she was responsible for her own victimization.

Unlike the other women, all of whom, again, were white, this Black woman had no name, no family, no context. The viewer sees her only as victimized and uncooperative. She cries when shown pictures. She pleads not to be forced to view the bloodstained room and her disfigured face. The program does not help the viewer to understand her predicament. The possible reasons she did not want to testify—fear, love, or possibly both—are never suggested. Most unfortunately, she, unlike the other six, is given no epilogue. While the fates of the other women are revealed at the end of the episode, we discover nothing about the Black woman. She, like the "others" she represents, is simply left to herself and soon forgotten.

I offer this description to suggest that "other" women are silenced as much by being relegated to the margin of experience as by total exclusion. Tokenistic, objectifying, voyeuristic inclusion is at least as disempowering as complete exclusion. The effort to politicize violence against women will do little to address Black and other minority women if their images are retained simply to magnify the problem rather than to humanize their experiences. Similarly, the antiracist agenda will not be advanced significantly by forcibly suppressing the reality of battering in minority communities. As the *48 Hours* episode makes clear, the images and stereotypes we fear are readily available and are frequently deployed in ways that do not generate sensitive understanding of the nature of domestic violence in minority communities.

3. Race and Domestic Violence Support Services

Women working in the field of domestic violence have sometimes reproduced the subordination and marginalization of women of color by adopting policies, priorities, or strategies of empowerment that either elide or wholly disregard the particular intersectional needs of women of color. While gender, race, and class intersect to create the particular context in which women of color experience violence, certain choices made by "allies" can reproduce intersectional subordination within the very resistance strategies designed to respond to the problem.

This problem is starkly illustrated by the inaccessibility of domestic violence support services to many non-English-speaking women. In a letter written to the deputy commissioner of the New York State Department of Social Services, Diana Campos, Director of Human Services for Programas de Ocupaciones y Desarrollo Economico Real, Inc. (PODER), detailed the case of a Latina in crisis who was repeatedly denied accommodation at a shelter because she could not prove that she was English-proficient. The woman had fled her home with her teenaged son, believing her husband's threats to kill them both. She called the domestic violence hotline administered by PODER seeking shelter for herself and her son. Because most shelters would not accommodate the woman with her son, they were forced to live on the streets for two days. The hotline counselor was finally able to find an agency that would take both the mother and the son, but when the counselor told the intake coordinator at the shelter that the woman spoke limited English, the coordinator told her that they could not take anyone who was not English-proficient. When the women in crisis called back and was told of the shelter's "rule," she replied that she could understand English if spoken to her slowly. As Campos explains, Mildred, the hotline counselor, told Wendy, the intake coordinator

that the woman said that she could communicate a little in English. Wendy told Mildred that they could not provide services to this woman because they have house rules that the woman must agree to follow. Mildred asked her, "What if the woman agrees to follow your rules? Will you still not take her?" Wendy responded that all of the women at the shelter are required to attend [a] support group and they would not be able to have her in the group if she could not communicate. Mildred mentioned the severity of this woman's case. She told Wendy that the woman had been wandering the streets at night while her husband is home, and she had been mugged twice. She also reiterated the fact that this woman was in danger of being killed by either her husband or a mugger. Mildred expressed that the woman's safety was a priority at this point, and that once in a safe place, receiving counseling in a support group could be dealt with.[30]

The intake coordinator restated the shelter's policy of taking only English-speaking women, and stated further that the woman would have to call the shelter herself for screening. If the woman could communicate with them in English, she might be accepted. When the woman called the PODER hotline later that day, she was in such a state of fear that the hotline counselor who had been working with her had difficulty understanding her in Spanish.[31] Campos directly intervened at this point, calling the executive director of the shelter. A counselor called back from the shelter. As Campos reports,

Marie [the counselor] told me that they did not want to take the woman in the shelter because they felt that the woman would feel isolated. I explained that the son agreed to translate for his mother during the intake process. Furthermore, that we would assist them in locating a Spanish-speaking battered women's advocate to assist in counseling her. Marie stated that utilizing the son was not an acceptable means in communication for them, since it further victimized the victim. In addition, she stated that they had similar experiences with women who were non-English-speaking, and that the women eventually just left because they were not able to communicate with anyone. I expressed my extreme concern for her safety and reiterated that we would assist them in providing her with the necessary services until we could get her placed someplace where they had bilingual staff.[32]

After several more calls, the shelter finally agreed to take the woman. The woman called once more during the negotiation; however, after a plan was in place, the woman never called back. Said Campos, "After so many calls, we are now left to wonder if she is alive and well, and if she will ever have enough faith in our ability to help her to call us again the next time she is in crisis."[33]

Despite this woman's desperate need, she was unable to receive the protection afforded English-speaking women, due to the shelter's rigid commitment to exclusionary policies. Perhaps even more troubling than the shelter's lack of bilingual resources was its refusal to allow a friend or relative to translate for the woman. This story illustrates the absurdity of a feminist approach that would make the ability to attend a support group without a translator a more significant consideration in the distribution of resources than the risk of physical harm on the street. The point is not that the shelter's image of empowerment is empty, but rather that it was imposed without regard to the disempowering consequences for women who didn't match the kind of client the shelter's administrators imagined. And thus they failed to accomplish the basic priority of the shelter movement—to get the woman out of danger.

Here the woman in crisis was made to bear the burden of the shelter's refusal to anticipate and provide for the needs of non-English-speaking women. Said Campos, "It is unfair to impose more stress on victims by placing them in the position of having to demonstrate their proficiency in English in order to receive services that are readily available to other battered women."[34] The problem is not easily dismissed as one of well-intentioned ignorance. The specific issue of monolingualism and the monistic view of women's experience that set the stage for this tragedy were not new issues in New York. Indeed, several women of color reported that they had repeatedly struggled with the New York State Coalition Against Domestic Violence over language exclusion and other practices that marginalized the interests of women of color.[35] Yet despite repeated lobbying, the Coalition did not act to incorporate the specific needs of nonwhite women into its central organizing vision.

Some critics have linked the Coalition's failure to address these issues to the narrow vision of coalition that animated its interaction with women of color in the first place. The very location of the Coalition's headquarters in Woodstock, New York—an area where few people of color live—seemed to guarantee that women of color would play a limited role in formulating policy. Moreover, efforts to include women of color came, it seems, as something of an afterthought. Many were invited to participate only after the Coalition was awarded a grant by the state to recruit women of color. However, as one "recruit" said, "they were not really prepared to deal with us or our issues. They thought that they could simply incorporate us into their organization without rethinking any of their beliefs or priorities and that we would be happy."[36] Even the most formal gestures of inclusion were not to be taken for granted. On one occasion when several women of color attended a meeting to discuss a special task force on women of color, the group debated all day over including the issue on the agenda.[37]

The relationship between the white women and the women of color on the Board was a rocky one from beginning to end. Other conflicts developed over differing definitions of feminism. For example, the Board decided to hire a Latina staffperson to manage outreach programs to the Latino community, but the white members of the hiring committee rejected candidates favored by Latina committee members who did not have recognized feminist credentials. As Campos pointed out, by measuring Latinas against their own biographies, the white members of the Board failed to recognize the different circumstances under which feminist consciousness develops and manifests itself within minority communities. Many of the women who interviewed for the position were established activists and leaders within their own community, a fact in itself suggesting that these women were probably familiar with the specific gender dynamics in their communities and were accordingly better qualified to handle outreach than other candidates with more conventional feminist credentials.[38]

The Coalition ended a few months later when the women of color walked out.[39] Many of these women returned to community-based organizations, preferring to struggle over women's issues within their communities rather than struggle over race and class issues with white middle-class women. Yet as illustrated by the case of the Latina who could find no shelter, the dominance of a particular perspective and set of priorities within the shelter community continues to marginalize the needs of women of color.

The struggle over which differences matter and which do not is neither an abstract nor an insignificant debate among women. Indeed, these conflicts are about more than difference as such; they raise critical issues of power. The problem is not simply that women who dominate the antiviolence movement are different from women of color but that they frequently have power to determine, either through material or rhetorical resources, whether the intersectional differences of women of color will be incorporated at all into the basic formulation of policy. Thus, the struggle over incorporating these differences is not a petty or superficial conflict about who gets to sit at the head of the table. In the context of violence, it is sometimes a deadly serious matter of who will survive—and who will not. . . .

NOTES

1. During my research in Los Angeles, California, I visited Jenessee Battered Women's Shelter, the only shelter in the Western states primarily serving Black women, and Everywoman's Shelter, which primarily serves Asian women. I also visited Estelle Chueng at the Asian Pacific Law Foundation, and I spoke with a representative of La Casa, a shelter in the predominantly Latino community of East L.A.

2. One researcher has noted, in reference to a survey taken of battered women's shelters, that "many Caucasian women were probably excluded from the sample, since they are more likely to have available resources that enable them to avoid going to a shelter. Many shelters admit only women with few or no resources or alternatives." Mildred Daley Pagelow, *Woman-Battering: Victims and Their Experiences*, 97 (1981). On the other hand, many middle- and upper-class women are financially dependent upon their husbands and thus experience a diminution in their standard of living when they leave their husbands.

3. More specifically, African Americans suffer from high unemployment rates, low incomes, and high poverty rates. According to Dr. David Swinton, Dean of the School of Business at Jackson State University in Mississippi, African Americans "receive three-fifths as much income per person as whites and are three times as likely to have annual incomes below the federally defined poverty level of $12,675 for a family of four." Urban League Urges Action, *N.Y. Times*, Jan. 9, 1991, at A14. In fact, recent statistics indicate that racial economic inequality is "higher as we begin the 1990s than at any other time in the last 20 years." David Swinton, The Economic Status of African Americans: "Permanent" Poverty and Inequality, in *The State of Black America* 1991, 25 (1991).

The economic situation of minority women is, expectedly, worse than that of their male counterparts. Black women, who earn a median of $7,875 a year, make considerably less than Black men, who earn a median income of $12,609 a year, and white women, who earn a median income of $9,812 a year. *Id.* at 32 (Table 3). Additionally, the percentage of Black female-headed families living in poverty (46.5%) is almost twice that of white female-headed families (25.4%). *Id.* at 43 (Table 8). Latino households also earn considerably less than white households. In 1988, the median income of Latino households was $20,359 and for white households, $28,840—a difference of almost $8,000.

Hispanic Americans: A Statistical Sourcebook 149 (1991), Analyzing by origin, in 1988, Puerto Rican households were the worst off, with 34.1% earning below $10,000 a year and a median income for all Puerto Rican households of $15,447 per year. *Id.* at 155. 1989 statistics for Latino men and women show that women earned an average of $7,000 less than men. *Id.* at 169.

4. . . . Racial differences marked an interesting contrast between Jenessee's policies and those of other shelters situated outside the Black community. Unlike some other shelters in Los Angeles, Jenessee welcomed the assistance of men. According to the director, the shelter's policy was premised on a belief that given African Americans' need to maintain healthy relations to pursue a common struggle against racism, anti-violence programs within the African American community cannot afford to be antagonistic to men. For a discussion of the different needs of Black women who are battered, see Beth Richie, Battered Black Women: A Challenge for the Black Community, *Black Scholar* 40 (Mar./Apr. 1985).

5. §U.S.C. §1186a (1988), . . .

6. Immigration activists have pointed out that "[t]he 1986 Immigration Reform Act and the Immigration Marriage Fraud Amendment have combined to give the spouse applying for permanent residence a powerful tool to control his partner." Jorge Banales, Abuse Among Immigrants: As Their Numbers Grow So Does the Need for Services, *Washington Post*, Oct. 16, 1990, at E5. . . . In one egregious instance described by Beckie Masaki, executive director of the Asian Women's Shelter in San Francisco, the closer the Chinese bride came to getting her permanent residency in the United States, the more harshly her Asian-American husband beat her. Her husband, kicking her in the neck and face, warned her that she needed him, and if she did not do as he told her, he would call immigration officials. Deanna Hodgin, "Mail-Order" Brides Marry Pain to Get Green Cards, *Washington Times*, Apr. 16, 1991, at E1.

7. Immigration Act of 1990, Pub. L. No. 101–649, 104 Stat. 4978. . . .

8. H.R.Rep. No. 723(1). 101st Cong., 2d Sess. 79 (1990), *reprinted in* 1990 U.S.C.C.A.N. 6710, 6759.

9. Hodgin, *supra* note 6.

10. *Id.*

11. A citizen or permanent resident spouse can exercise power over an alien spouse by threatening not to file a petition for permanent residency. If he fails to file a petition for permanent residency, the alien spouse continues to be undocumented and is considered to be in the country illegally. These constraints often restrict an alien spouse from leaving. Dean Ito Taylor tells the story of "one client who has been hospitalized—she's had him arrested for beating her—but she keeps coming back to him because he promises he will file for her. . . . He holds that green card over her head." Hodgin, *supra* note 6. . . .

12. . . . To combat this lack of appropriate services for women of color at many shelters, special programs have been created specifically for women from particular communities. A few examples of such programs include the Victim Intervention Project in East Harlem for Latina women, Jenessee Shelter for African American women in Los Angeles, Apna Gar in Chicago for South Asian women, and, for Asian women generally, the Asian Women's Shelter in San Francisco, the New York Asian Women's Center, and the Center for the Pacific Asian Family in Los Angeles. Programs with hotlines include Sakhi for South Asian Women in New York, and Manavi in Jersey City, also for South Asian women, as well as programs for Korean women in Philadelphia and Chicago.

13. Most crime statistics are classified by sex or race but none are classified by sex and race. Because we know that most rape victims are women, the racial breakdown reveals, at best, rape rates for Black women. Yet, even given this head start, rates for other non-white women are difficult to collect. While there are some statistics for Latinas, statistics for Asian and Native American women are virtually nonexistent. Cf. G. Chezia Carraway, Violence Against Women of Color, *Stan. L. Rev.* 43 (1993); 1301.

14. Shahrazad Ali, *The Blackman's Guide to Understanding the Blackwoman* (1989). Ali's book sold quite well for an independently published title, an accomplishment no doubt due in part to her appearances on the Phil Donahue, Oprah Winfrey, and Sally Jesse Raphael television talk shows. For public and press reaction, see Dorothy Gilliam, Sick, Distorted Thinking, *Washington Post*, Oct. 11, 1990, at D3; Lena Williams, Black Woman's Book Starts a Predictable Storm, *New York Times*, Oct 2, 1990, at C11; see also Pearl Cleague, *Mad at Miles: A Black Women's Guide to Truth* (1990). The title clearly styled after Ali's, *Mad at Miles* responds not only to issues raised by Ali's book, but also to Miles Davis's admission in his autobiography, *Miles: The Autobiography* (1989), that he had physically abused, among other women, his former wife, actress Cicely Tyson.

15. Shahrazad Ali suggests that the "[Blackwoman] certainly does not believe that her disrespect for the Blackman is destructive, nor that her opposition to him has deteriorated the Black nation." S. Ali, *supra* note 14, at viii. Blaming the problems of the community on the failure of the Black woman to accept her "real definition," Ali explains that "[n]o nation can rise when the natural order of the behavior of the male and the female have been altered against their wishes by force. No species can survive if the female of the genus disturbs the balance of her nature by acting other than herself." *Id.* at 76.

16. Ali advises the Blackman to hit the Blackwoman in the mouth, "[b]ecause it is from that hole, in the lower part of her face, that all her rebellion culminates into words. Her unbridled tongue is a main reason she cannot get along with the Blackman. She often needs a reminder." *Id.* at 169.

Ali warns that "if [the Blackwoman] ignores the authority and superiority of the Blackman, there is a penalty. When she crosses this line and becomes viciously insulting, it is time for the Blackman to soundly slap her in the mouth." *Id.*

17. Ali explains that, "[r]egretfully some Blackwomen want to be physically controlled by the Blackman." *Id.* at 174. "The Blackwoman, deep inside her heart" Ali reveals, "wants to surrender but she wants to be coerced." *Id.* at 72. "[The Blackwoman] wants [the Blackman] to stand up and defend himself even if it means he has to knock her out of the way to do so. This is necessary whenever the Blackwoman steps out of the protection of womanly behavior and enters the dangerous domain of masculine challenge." *Id.* at 174.

18. [Women and Violence: Hearings Before the Senate Comm. on the Judiciary on Legislation to Reduce the Growing Problem of Violent Crime Against Women, 101st Cong., 2d Sess., pt. 2, at 142] (statement of Susan Kelly-Dreiss) (discussing several studies in Pennsylvania linking homelessness to domestic violence)

19. *Id.* at 143 (statement of Susan Kelly-Dreiss).

20. Alice Walker, *The Color Purple* (1982). The most severe criticism of Walker developed after the book was filmed as a movie. Donald Bogle, a film historian, argued that part of the criticism of the movie stemmed from the one-dimensional portrayal of Mister, the abusive man. See Jacqueline Trescott, Passions over Purple; Anger and Unease over Film's Depiction of Black Men, *Washington Post*, Feb. 5, 1986, at C1. Bogle argues that in the novel, Walker linked Mister's abusive conduct to his oppression in the white world—since Mister "can't be himself, he has to assert himself with the black woman." The movie failed to make any connection between Mister's abusive treatment of Black women and racism, and thereby presented Mister only as an "insensitive, callous man." *Id.*

21. See, e.g., Gerald Early, Her Picture in the Papers: Remembering Some Black Women, *Antaeus*, Spring 1988, at 9; Daryl Pickney, Black Victims, Black Villains, *New York Review of Books*, Jan. 29, 1987, at 17; Trescott, *supra* note 20.

22. Trudier Harris, On the Color Purple, Stereotypes, and Silence, *Black Am. Lit. F.* 18 (1984), 155.

23. The source of the resistance reveals an interesting difference between the Asian-American and African-American communities. In the African-American community, the resistance is usually grounded in efforts to avoid confirming negative stereotypes of African-Americans as violent; the concern of members in some Asian-American communities is to avoid tarnishing the model minority myth. Interview with Nilda Rimonte, Director of the Everywoman Shelter, in Los Angeles, California (April 19, 1991).

24. Nilda Rimonte, A Question of Culture: Cultural Approval of Violence Against Women in the Pacific-Asian Community and the Cultural Defense, *Stan. L. Rev.* 43 (1991), 1311; see also Nilda Rimonte, Domestic Violence Against Pacific

Asians, in Asian Women United of California ed., *Making Waves: An Anthology of Writings by and About Asian American Women*; 327, 328 (1989). . . .

When—or, more importantly, how—to take culture into account when addressing the needs of women of color is a complicated issue. Testimony as to the particularities of Asian "culture" has increasingly been used in trials to determine the culpability of both Asian immigrant women and men who are charged with crimes of interpersonal violence. A position on the use of the "cultural defense" in these instances depends on how "culture" is being defined as well as on whether and to what extent the "cultural defense" has been used differently for Asian men and Asian women. See Leti Volpp, (Mis) Identifying Culture: Asian Women and the "Cultural Defense," (unpublished manuscript).

25. See, e.g., Lenore F. Walker, *Terrifying Love: Why Battered Women Kill and How Society Responds*, 101–102 (1989). ("Battered women come from all types of economic, cultural, religious, and racial backgrounds. . . . They are women like you. Like me. Like those whom you know and love."); Murray A. Straus, Richard J. Gelles & Suzanne K. Steinmetz, *Behind Closed Doors: Violence in the American Family*, 31 (1980) ("Wife-beating is found in every class, at every income level."). . . .

26. For example, Susan Kelly-Dreiss states: "The public holds many myths about battered women—they are poor, they are women of color, they are uneducated, they are on welfare, they deserve to be beaten and they even like it. However, contrary to common misperceptions, domestic violence is not confined to any one socioeconomic, ethnic, religious, racial or age group." Hearings on Violent Crime Against Women, *supra* note 18, pt. 2, at 139 (testimony of Susan Kelly-Dreiss, Executive Director, Pennsylvania Coalition Against Domestic Violence). Kathleen Waits offers a possible explanation for this misperception: "It is true that battered women who are also poor are more likely to come to the attention of governmental officials than are their middle- and upper-class counterparts. However, this phenomenon is caused more by the lack of alternative resources and the intrusiveness of the welfare state than by any significantly higher incidence of violence among lower-class families." Kathleen Waits, The Criminal Justice System's Response to Battering: Understanding the Problem, Forging the Solutions, *Washington U.L. Rev.* 60 (1985), 267, 276–277.

27. However, no reliable statistics support such a claim. In fact, some statistics suggest that there is a greater frequency of violence among the working classes and the poor. See M. Straus, R. Gelles & S. Steinmetz, *supra* note 25, at 31. Yet these statistics are also unreliable because, to follow Waits's observation, violence in middle- and upper-class homes remains hidden from the view of statisticians and governmental officials alike. I would suggest that assertions that the problem is the same across race

and class are driven less by actual knowledge about the prevalence of domestic violence in different communities than by advocates' recognition that the image of domestic violence as an issue involving primarily the poor and minorities complicates efforts to mobilize against it.

28. 137 Cong. Rec. S611 (daily ed. Jan. 14, 1991) (statement of Sen. Boren). Senator William Cohen (D-Me.) followed with a similar statement. . . . *Id.* (statement of Sen. Cohen).

29. *48 Hours: Till Death Do Us Part* (CBS television broadcast, Feb. 6, 1991).

30. Letter of Diana M. Campos, Director of Human Services, PODER, to Joseph Semidei, Deputy Commissioner, New York State Department of Social Services (Mar. 26, 1992).

31. The woman had been slipping back into her home during the day when her husband was at work. She remained in a heightened state of anxiety because he was returning shortly and she would be forced to go back out into the streets for yet another night.

32. PODER Letter, *supra* note 30.

33. *Id.*

34. *Id.*

35. Roundtable Discussion on Racism and the Domestic Violence Movement (April 2, 1992). The participants in the discussion—Diana Campos, Director, Bilingual Outreach Project of the New York State Coalition Against Domestic Violence: Elsa A. Rios, Project Director, Victim Intervention Project (a community-based project in East Harlem, New York, serving battered women); and Haydee Rosario, a social worker with the East Harlem Council for Human Services and a Victim Intervention Project volunteer—recounted conflicts relating to race and culture during their association with the New York State Coalition Against Domestic Violence, a state oversight group that distributed resources to battered women's shelters throughout the state and generally set policy priorities for the shelters that were part of the Coalition.

36. *Id.*

37. *Id.*

38. *Id.*

39. Ironically, the specific dispute that led to the walk-out concerned the housing of the Spanish-language domestic violence hotline. The hotline was initially housed at the Coalition's headquarters, but languished after a succession of coordinators left the organization. Latinas on the Coalition board argued that the hotline should be housed at one of the community service agencies, while the board insisted on maintaining control of it. The hotline is now housed at PODER. *Id.*

PART FOUR
SOCIAL CHANGE

Thus far we have tended to emphasize the stability of gender inequality. We have examined how socialization, social definitions of gender, and the structure and content of all the major institutional arenas of social life converge to produce a world in which males and females are understood as essentially different and are differentially valued and rewarded. The forces that perpetuate gender inequality are so intricately interwoven into the social fabric and so deeply embedded in the identities of individuals that changing them is beyond the power of any one individual, no matter how well intentioned.

Yet societies can and do change, and signs of change are all around us. In earlier readings, we discussed some of the dynamic forces that have unintentionally recast gender consciousness and inequality, including new cultural meanings, technological innovations, demographic processes, and economic factors. To understand fully how systems of gender inequality change, we must also examine the ways that women have sought collectively and intentionally to reduce their disadvantage. Certainly, every society or group contains individuals who are nonconformists, but significant and lasting social change is ultimately the result of collective rather than individual action.

In Part Four, we turn our attention to struggles to transform culture and social institutions in two arenas. Section 10 focuses on the politicization of gender in the state and in global politics. Section 11 documents the rich history and diversity of women's movements and examines continuity and change in the history of American feminism. To understand the part that women themselves have played in improving their status, we focus, on the one hand, on women's actions "within the system" by conventional and orderly means and, on the other, on women's collective actions "outside the system" by unconventional and disorderly means.

Politics is generally thought to refer to the institutionalized or authoritative system by which a society makes decisions, allocates power, and distributes resources. According to the traditional view, voting, campaigning, lobbying, conducting organizational activities, holding office, and working in political parties are classified as politics because they take place in the context of formal governmental structure.

Feminist scholars have pointed out that the standard definition of politics is too narrow, however, for understanding women's political participation. It not only assumes a particular type of state and political system but ignores the fact that, until fairly recently in most industrialized societies, women have been denied access to the formal political process.

In the United States, women were not allowed to vote, hold office, or sit on juries until the early twentieth century. Even after women received the vote with the passage of the Nineteenth Amendment to the U.S. Constitution in 1920, their participation in electoral politics, involvement in major political parties, and election to public offices lagged significantly behind men's. African-American women, moreover, like African-American men, remained effectively disenfranchised in southern states by racist voter registration rules until the late 1960s.

It was not until a half century after women got the vote that the gap between men's and women's political party involvement and office holding began to shrink, and even today women fare better in local and state politics than in the national arena. Voting turnout differences between women and men finally disappeared in 1976. But it took until 1980 for women to use the electoral process to express their collective dissatisfaction by voting in line with their interests in women's equality, creating for the first time what has come to be known as the "gender gap." It is *striking, however, that women have ascended to the leadership of their countries in other parts of the world earlier than in the United States.*

Holding elections, participating in party politics, running for office, and lobbying are not, however, the only ways to express grievances, influence public policy, and achieve social change. Politics also include social movements, protests, union organizing, and other group actions intended to change cultural beliefs and influence the distribution of power and resources in a state or community. This definition is broad enough to encompass women's long history of participation in collective action on their own behalf through the feminist movement, as well as in pursuit of other human rights causes through female reform societies, women's church groups, alternative religious societies, women's clubs, and other social groups and movements.

Social movements are collective attempts to bring about change. They originate outside of the established political system, forge links between individuals and groups who share common concerns, and mobilize the people and resources necessary to pursue the goal of social change. In democratic societies, social movements and the tactics they employ—marches, boycotts, strikes, demonstrations, and protests—are a regular part of the democratic process. Movements act as pressure groups on behalf of people excluded from routine decision-making processes and the dominant power structure; they are a major source of new social patterns and cultural understandings.

In Part Four, we examine the many ways that women around the globe respond to local and global conditions and work to change the world. As you read these selections, think about the ways in which the efforts of women to transform gender have succeeded.

Global Politics and the State

National governments, international relations, and transnational economies and cultures exert wide-ranging influence on gender systems. Government-controlled economies shape differences in women's and men's wages and the prices of goods that women and men produce and consume. National and international policies on education, welfare, health, and various forms of violence against women affect women's daily lives in profound ways.

Because governmental policies frequently reflect dominant antiwoman ideologies, they often serve to reinforce the disadvantaged position of women. The state, in fact, plays a central part in maintaining a social structure of inequalities between women and men and between people of different social groups. That is, the state plays a crucial role in perpetuating inequalities of class (through regulation of the labor market or of minimum wages, for example) and of race and ethnicity and nationality (for example, through legislative policies regarding affirmative action or immigration).

Feminist scholars focus on the ways that state actions and policies create and perpetuate gender categories, ideologies of women's inferiority, and differential access of women and men to valued resources and power. The state's role in upholding gender stratification, of course, is inextricably linked to its role in reinforcing race and class stratification, as the articles in this section point out.

The increasing forces of globalization mean that women's lives are shaped not only by the governmental policies of their own countries but also by transnational politics and economics as well, as we have already seen in the case of Latina domestic workers in Los Angeles. A complex web of interrelationships among transnational corporations, states, transnational social movements, technology, and ideologies of gender, race, ethnicity, and religion shapes relations among women, states, and global politics. In this section, contributors examine the relationships among constructions of gender, the forces of globalization, women's lives and activism, and the state, both in the United States and transnationally.

We begin with Karen McCormack's discussion of how women on welfare think about motherhood. Popular images of "welfare mothers" in the United States paint them as women of color who, as McCormack says, are unfit, uncaring, and immoral. In 1996, passage of the Personal Responsibility and Work Opportunity Reconciliation Act, known as "welfare reform," enacted work requirements that forced poor single mothers into low-wage jobs—often into the domestic or home care work that Hondagneu-Sotelo and Klein and Boris discuss in Section 5—making it difficult for them to care for their own children. This is what McCormack means by "stratified reproduction," the representation and reality of class and racialized motherhood. As the new requirements for welfare recipients came into play in the 1990s, McCormack interviewed women on welfare about their identities as mothers. She found that they claim the identity of good mothers, accepting the mainstream definitions of prioritizing motherhood and protecting, disciplining, providing for, and spending time with their children. Of course, poverty and the requirement that they work make it extremely difficult to meet these standards.

By claiming the identity of good mothers and trying to do it all, they both resist dominant conceptions of women on welfare as bad mothers but at the same time set nearly impossible goals for themselves. How are the characteristics of a good mother shaped by dominant white middle-class ideals of motherhood? How do the situations of the women McCormack interviewed make it difficult to meet the demands of motherhood? How do they resist stereotypes of the bad welfare mother, and what does McCormack see as the limitations of this resistance? What might be a more fruitful way to think about mothering? How might government policies improve the situation of women on public assistance?

In the next article, Grace Chang draws connections between the new policies on welfare in the United States and Structural Adjustment Programs forced on countries of the global South. Such policies slash social services and undermine local economies, leaving many people no option for survival other than migration to the global North. Chang attends to the ways that women workers are fighting the forces of globalization by focusing on the activism of Filipina migrant workers in the United States and Canada. Her stories of Filipinas echo those of the Latin American nannies recounted by Hondagneu-Sotelo in Section 5.

How exactly do state policies shape the lives of women throughout the world? What strategies are women employing to resist the consequences of globalization? What kinds of policies and collective action could help to improve the lives of Filipina and other migrant workers?

Globalization is also central to the story that Marisa D'Mello tells in "Gendered Selves and Identities of Information Technology Professionals in Global Software Organizations in India." "Outsourcing," the sending of work abroad where it is performed by lower-paid workers, is a major issue in the United States, especially as unemployment continues to rise. The global software organizations D'Mello studies are an example of the kinds of firms that perform work for businesses across the globe. In this article, D'Mello looks at the way that gender and culture shape the work of Indian professionals working in global software firms. Here we see the local interacting with the global. Working in a male-dominated area of the economy, Indian women find their opportunities restricted because of the expectations for proper feminine behavior and, particularly, the demands of marriage and motherhood. Yet they also contribute a gendered style of work that is important to the success of their firms.

How does the nature of technology work affect women and men differently? How is the work gendered? How do Indian women manage the conflicting demands of marriage/motherhood and their professions? How are things changing? What would be different if D'Mello had studied a software firm in the United States? What does this research tell us about the relationship between the local and the global?

A different aspect of globalization emerges in Gwyn Kirk's "Contesting Militarization," a consideration of the connections between militarization and globalization and the impact of gender and race on globalized militarization. From Filipinas working in bars in South Korea to women in war-torn El Salvador to the ethnic cleansing in Bosnia, we see the impact of militarization on politics, the economy, the environment, and culture. Kirk draws connections between the obvious sign of militarization—the wars in Iraq and Afghanistan, the production of weapons—and less obvious ones, such as media portrayals of the plight of women in Afghanistan under the Taliban and the militarization of the English language. She names such things as the increase in domestic violence among military couples and environmental destruction through routine military training as costs of militarization. In the light of the pervasiveness of war and violence, Kirk proposes a variety of ways to contest militarization.

What connections does she draw between racialized gender and global militarization? Which of her proposals to fight militarization make the most sense to you? Are there examples on your campus of the struggle against what Kirk calls the "military-industrial-congressional-academic-media" complex?

As Kirk notes, when the United States went to war in Afghanistan after the attacks of September 11, one of the rationales was the need to liberate Afghan women. Lila Abu-Lughod addresses the question "Do Muslim Women Really Need Saving?" reminding us that Afghan women, like Filipinas and Latinas in North America, have their own history of activism. Critiquing the "missionary" notion of saving other women, Abu-Lughod calls for a serious appreciation of differences among women around the globe. Why do you think there is so much focus in the United States on the "oppression" of Muslim women? How does Abu-Lughod suggest that we deal with differences?

As the forces of globalization increase, the economic, political, and cultural power of the global North affects women everywhere. Yet we need to be respectful of difference, as Lila Abu-Lughod argues. Once again, this section returns to the question of the commonalities and differences among women. Given the disparities of wealth and power among women around the world, especially between the global North and South, do you think diverse women have anything in common by virtue of their gender?

Stratified Reproduction and Poor Women's Resistance

First published in 2005

The phrase "welfare mother" is one in which the adjective, "welfare," modifies the noun in such a way that it turns its meaning upside down. It is different from "working mother," "stay-at-home mother," or "soccer mom," all phrases that specify ways of doing motherhood and that suggest certain lifestyles, challenges, and benefits but do not fundamentally alter the meaning of the term "mother." "Welfare mother," as the term is currently used, obscures the mothering work involved. The stereotypical welfare mother is a symbol of the supposed irresponsible, sexually promiscuous, and immoral behavior of the poor. Embedded in the notion of the welfare mother are powerful ideologies of race, class, and gender that blame the poor for their own poverty; portray women, particularly Black and Hispanic women, as inadequate mothers; and view nontraditional family forms as pathological (Collins 2001; Fraser and Gordon 1994; Mullings 2001). Taken together, these ideological threads construct the notion of the welfare mother as a nonproductive citizen and a bad mother. My purpose in this article is to examine how poor mothers receiving welfare resist these dominant constructions through the appropriation of alternative discourses of motherhood and to examine the limits of this resistance.

The mid-1990s marked the apogee of recent anti-welfare rhetoric, culminating with the passage of the 1996 Personal Responsibility and Work Opportunity Reconciliation Act (PRA). While the passage of the

PRA has lessened the salience of the term "welfare mother," it has not weakened the system of stratified reproduction, an idea that "describe[s] the power relations by which some categories of people are empowered to nurture and reproduce, while others are disempowered" (Ginsberg and Rapp 1995, 3). Motherhood continues to be venerated when the mothers are middle and upper class, married, and white; the mothering done by poor, nonwhite women, however, is systematically devalued.

Stratified reproduction is created and reinforced through representation and public policy. Political debate in the 1990s increasingly characterized single mothers not only as a serious social problem but also as a threat to domestic stability (Hancock 2004; Sidel 1996). The 1994 Republican Contract with America claimed that "sky-rocketing out-of-wedlock births . . . [were] ripping apart our nation's social fabric" (Gingrich and Shelhas 1994, 65), and then-senator John Ashcroft called illegitimacy "a threat to the survival of our nation and our culture" (cited in Sidel 1996, 34). The welfare mother or "welfare queen" was the public face of poor women's mothering. While virtually equal numbers of white and Black women, and growing numbers of Hispanic women, were receiving welfare in the 1990s, the public face of the welfare mother was Black (Mink 1998; Neubeck and Cazenave 2001; Roberts 1999).

Racialized images of motherhood are central to the salience of the image of the welfare mother in the contemporary United States. "Dominant images have long depicted Black mothers as unfit, uncaring, and immoral. . . . Mammy, the sexually licentious Jezebel, the home-wrecking matriarch, the cheating welfare

AUTHOR'S NOTE: *I would like to thank Christine Williams, Patricia Ewick, Stephen Pfohl, Mike Osborn, Theresa McCormack. Joe Swingle, Dana Britton, and the anonymous reviewers at* Gender & Society *for their most helpful comments on earlier versions of this article.*

queen—were incredibly bad mothers" (Roberts 1999, 160). This racialization of welfare draws on myths of the pathology of the Black family as a single-parent family, a pathology capable of "infecting white women and causing a so-called epidemic of illegitimacy" (Thornton Dill, BacaZinn, and Patton 1999, 266). Many attempts by white liberals to understand the persistence of Black poverty have seen the Black family, particularly Black families living in poverty with single mothers, as a cultural deficit that causes poverty and community decline (Collins 1989). These myths allow for the figure of the public identity of the "welfare mother" to permeate political dialogue and consciousness (Hancock 2004; Sidel 1996). Bell Kaplan (1997) suggests that this view has become common within the Black community as well, targeting teenage parents as responsible for ongoing problems of crime and unemployment.

Political and cultural representations of motherhood form one component of stratified reproduction, but public policies buttressed these ideological positions by structuring the economic and political benefits of motherhood along class lines. For poor women, elements of the PRA create considerable difficulty. Work requirements in the PRA push poor mothers out of the home and into low-wage service work or community service, work that often involves caring for the children of others. The work requirements, however, apply only to single mothers; "the PRA's work provisions permit full-time care-giving where there are two parents, but forbid it when there is only one" (Mink 1998, 106).

Conversely, policies for middle-class families offer no such incentives for women to leave their children and work outside of the home. On the contrary, while welfare reform was being debated in the legislature, a new conservative family consensus was forming to suggest that the ideal arrangement for children was to have their mothers at home as primary caregivers. Mink (1998) contrasts the work requirements of welfare reform with proposals made during the 1997 White House Conference on Early Child Development to allow tax incentives for parents to stay at home to spend more time with their children. Mothers lacking economic resources and male support were not the targets of the proposed incentives, and "some experts buttressed this view with studies showing welfare mothers are least likely to positively effect their children's development" (Mink 1998, 121). With cutbacks in child care subsidies and increasing work requirements, the assumption behind the PRA appeared to be that children of welfare recipients did not deserve the care of their mothers or of trained caregivers yet that these same mothers were productive only when ministering to the needs of someone else's child (Roberts 1999).

While conservative critics lament women's move out of the home, suggesting a decreasing commitment to children, several recent empirical studies suggest that American mothers may actually spend more time with their children than they have in the past, even when they work outside of the home (Sandberg and Hofferth unpublished paper and Bianchi 2000, both cited in Crittenden 2001). An ideology of "intensive mothering" has become dominant, defined as a belief that (1) children require large investments of time and money, (2) the mother should be the central caregiver, and (3) motherhood is incomparable to paid work (Hays 1996). In her examination of mothers, Hays (1996) found a fairly consistent adoption of this ideology of "intensive mothering" across class lines and between working and nonworking mothers. Poor women are faced with a belief system that posits intensive mothering as central to their child's well-being yet marks them as inadequate to the task; at once they are told that they must work to be productive citizens and that motherhood is a full-time job.

In this article, I examine the discourse on mothering that is employed by poor women on welfare. Through in-depth interviews, I explore their commitment to the ideology of intensive mothering. I also discuss the contradictions and complications involved in promoting this set of beliefs. While adherence to the intensive mothering ideology protects them against the stereotype of the welfare mother, poverty and welfare policies limit their ability to conform to the strenuous expectations placed on mothers. While promoting this ideology is a form of resistance to the stereotype, it simultaneously and ironically constrains their practices and labels them bad mothers.

DISCURSIVE CATEGORIES AND EVERYDAY LIFE

The discursive categories of the welfare mother and of classed motherhood shape the way we think about and act in the world. Drawing from Foucault and ethnomethodology, I am using the term "discourse" to refer to a set of material and symbolic practices, a forceful field of restrictive communication rituals that positions both subjects and objects that operate within it. The welfare mother is a powerful material and symbolic category: material in that public policies and everyday treatment of poor women both reflect and construct the notion of the welfare mother (Hancock 2004; Mink 1998) and symbolic in the way that these categories shape our imaginings of the world and of ourselves. The discursive field that produces welfare mothers is restrictive: it marks boundaries that define what is acceptable and normative. The boundaries of the field of discourse are marked by powerful, taken-for-granted assumptions about the characteristics of moral citizens (as hardworking, independent, self-controlled, sexually monogamous) and about the economic and political structure (democratic, meritocratic). These assumptions shape the field of discourse in such a way that welfare recipients, along with a host of others who are unable to compete successfully in the economy, are located outside of the boundaries and are positioned as deviant others.

The welfare mother . . . erects boundaries around poor women's motherhood, defining a contradictory set of expectations. On one hand, as poor women, welfare recipients are supposed to dedicate themselves to hard work to overcome their impoverishment. On the other hand, as mothers, the ideology of intensive mothering suggests that they ought to dedicate their lives to the well-being of their children, necessitating full-time mothering. The presumptive race of the welfare mother further complicates mothering as Black women face additional barriers to attaining the label of the good mother given the effects of centuries of oppression and discrimination.

Foucault (1978, 101) suggests that while discourse can be an "instrument of power," it can also be "a stumbling-block, a point of resistance and a starting point for an opposing strategy." By naming the "welfare mother," might some form of resistance to these powerful ideologies of race, gender, and social class be made possible? For poor mothers to make sense of their own mothering, to avoid "being reduced to a shadow of themselves," they must actively challenge the dominant discursive practices (de Certeau 1984, xiv).

Resistance in everyday life is often "informal, often covert, and concerned largely with immediate, de facto gains" (Scott 1985, 33). For example, Bell Kaplan (1997) finds that Black teenage mothers in her sample "dressed up" to avoid some of the stigma associated with welfare receipt. Dressing up was a way of hiding welfare receipt and, while resisting the stigma of welfare, submitting to the construction of welfare itself as deviant. Impression management strategies functioned to protect an identity that would be tarnished by welfare receipt. Hondagneu-Sotelo and Avila (1997) found that Latina transnational mothers, women who live away from their children often for long periods of time, redefined motherhood as quality of time and emotional energy expended. Pelissier Kingfisher (1996) and Bell Kaplan (1997) both found that many welfare recipients adopt attitudes toward other welfare recipients that are consistent with the welfare mother ideology but make distinctions between good and bad welfare mothers. Transnational mothers applied this good mother/bad mother distinction to compare their own mothering with the practices of the white, middle- and upper-class mothers for whom they worked (Hondagneu-Sotelo and Avila 1997).

The mothers in this study employ some of the strategies described above to protect their identity as good mothers. Taken as a whole, the women express a great deal of agreement about the requirements of being a good mother, discussed at length below. This study extends earlier work in examining the contradictions poor women face as they attempt to enact the ideology of intensive mothering and the contradictions between various elements of this ideology as it plays out in the lives of women with few resources. Through an examination of the pieces of the good mother puzzle, I will also explore the irony of the situation wherein resistance to the welfare mother is constituted through partial adherence to the ideology of intensive mothering. In other words, it is through conformity with middle-class notions of motherhood that the women in this sample resist the dominant imagery of the welfare mother.

The tactics that disadvantaged mothers employ to negotiate dominant categories and meanings are often ignored; they do not produce immediate challenges to the organization of power and dominance. These tactics are critically important in forming identity and in foreshadowing the cracks within which future strategy may be devised. And yet Foucault also turns our attention to the limits of these tactics, to the limits of resistance. These alternative understandings always operate in relation to power and domination; "resistance is never in a position of exteriority in relation to power" (Foucault 1978, 95). Empirically, we must examine these discursive tactics employed by welfare mothers not only for the possibility of resistance but also with attention to the limits of such resistance.

METHOD

The data presented here are based on intensive interviews conducted with 34 women in Maryland in 1997, half of whom lived in the city of Baltimore and half in Frederick County, Maryland. To locate participants, I distributed fliers to educational and community centers in both locations asking for single women raising children and receiving aid who would be willing to share their experiences with welfare. I offered to compensate participants $15 for their time in participating in the interviews. After locating several volunteers from these sites, all other respondents were located using an informal snowball sample. I stratified the sample on the basis of location after finding that women living in the inner city experienced far less shame and stigma than the literature had led me to expect. Half of the women in the sample lived in very poor inner-city neighborhoods in Baltimore; the other half lived in a more rural county about 60 miles to the west of the city, an area where the poor, working, and middle classes lived in close proximity.

All of the women were receiving public assistance at the time of the interview and ranged in age from 16 to 43. Sixteen of the 34 women were receiving some form of formal education, most in the form of GED preparation. Furthermore, 23 respondents were involved in parenting classes offered either through educational or drug treatment programs. One cluster of women was also in a drug treatment program. None of the women in the sample were employed at the time of the interviews.

Twenty-eight of the 34 respondents were Black, and the remaining 6 were white, 1 of whom self-identified as Hispanic. Despite posting fliers in white, working-class neighborhoods, I was unable to locate a larger number of white recipients, as I will discuss below. While the imaginary welfare mother is Black, white recipients represented 39 percent of Aid to Families with Dependent Children recipients in 1993; Black recipients made up 37 percent, and Latinos (of any race) 18 percent (Albelda, Folbre, and Center for Popular Economics 1996).

For this article, I draw on tape-recorded and transcribed interviews with these 34 women. I talked with them about the daily problems that they faced as they interacted with other members of their communities and the representatives of the Department of Social Services. My questions to the respondents about mothering were largely focused on the material difficulties of raising children in poverty. I asked very few questions about the respondents' feelings or ideas about motherhood as I was primarily concerned with the management of stigma among welfare recipients. Despite my orientation to questions of stigma and welfare, the majority of women in the sample emphasized motherhood in describing themselves and their lives.

The data from these interviews suggest few clear differences between Black and white respondents in their discussions of motherhood or welfare receipt, although the difficulty of locating white women in the city points to the salience of racial classifications. Two Black women in the city did suggest that their welfare status was already assumed because of their skin color, which may mean that white women are able more often to "pass" as middle class (Goffman 1974). For Black women, race may be their master status, a designation far more powerful than welfare receipt. While white women may share the shame and stigma of welfare receipt that rest on racialized imagery, they are free from immediate identification by skin color (Thornton Dill, BacaZinn, and Patton 1999). White recipients may thus have more at stake in protecting their identity and concealing their welfare status as they are not already marked. As a white woman, my own skin color may have made it more difficult for respondents to fully share the racism and discrimination that they had faced in the welfare system, their communities, and the work force.

Despite differences in the experience of welfare stigma between women that I have explored elsewhere (McCormack 2004), what remained consistent between the urban and rural location, between Black and white women, teenagers through middle-aged women, was the importance of motherhood in their lives. In fact, without access to other sources of positive identity, motherhood appeared to hold the central place in identity formation for the women interviewed here. In the act of constituting themselves as good mothers, the respondents were able to separate themselves from the imagined welfare mother.

THE GOOD (WELFARE) MOTHER

To constitute themselves as good mothers, women relied on a variety of discursive strategies that often simultaneously challenged the dominant discursive practices and accommodated them. In the interviews, five criteria emerged to define a good mother; good mothers must (1) put children first, (2) spend time with children, (3) provide for children, (4) keep children out of trouble, and (5) keep children safe. Poverty makes each of these goals more difficult to accomplish. The women in this study articulate values consistent with the dominant ideology of mothering, with perhaps a greater emphasis on protecting and disciplining their children, understandable given the precariousness of their social and geographic locations. An examination of these five aspects of parenting highlights the ways that, at each juncture, these mothers define themselves as good mothers but face difficult structural barriers, both materially and discursively, in doing so.

Putting Children First

The criterion most frequently cited by my respondents as the mark of a good mother is that she puts her children first, a marker that seems consistent in the representations of mothers in all classes (Hays 1996; Hondagneu-Sotelo and Avila 1997). In contemporary middle-class debates between mothers who work in the home and those in the paid work force, for example, both sets of women must emphasize the best interests of the children. Working mothers justify their choices based on the best interests of their children, as they are acting as role models, ensuring independence, and bringing in money that can be spent to make lives better for children. On the other hand, mothers working in the home defend their choices based on what is best for children, valuing time spent above material values. In both cases, the language used to explain their situation suggests that children are at the forefront of decision making (Hays 1996).

Poor women face the same dilemmas in defining themselves as good mothers, yet they have markedly fewer choices to make regarding work and lifestyle, exacerbated by the imposition of work requirements on most welfare recipients as a component of the PRA (Mink 1998). The choices that the respondents were able to make were framed in terms of their children's best interest. Shantrise, a young Black mother whose parents' divorce changed her situation drastically at age 14, moved from a working-class town to a desperately poor inner-city neighborhood. At the time of our interview, she had an intense desire to move her own children outside of the city, even though it would mean moving away from her extended family. She explained her decision this way: "I'm doing it for my kids. That's what's most important to me." Shantrise, like many of the other women whom I interviewed, made it clear

that she was willing for her life to be made more difficult to make a better life for her children.

This better life was sometimes sought by sending children to live with relatives outside of the city or in areas with better school systems and less violence. Tricia Shephard, a Black woman in her 40s with two children and one grandson, sent her eight-year-old daughter lo live with her godmother during the week so that she could go to school in a nearby suburb instead of in the city. While this meant seeing her daughter only on the weekends, she was doing what she felt was best. "I'm doing the best for my child, It ain't like I don't have her. . . . A lot of other people do that too. 'Cause I feel like these schools ain't good enough. If they're not teaching them nothing, I don't want her to go there." The painful decisions to relocate or send a child away to school were made to produce the best outcome for the children.

Keeping children within the context of extended family, or even keeping them within the immediate family setting, sometimes conflicted with mothers' views of their long-term best interest. In the case of Tricia's younger daughter, separation during the week was made easier by the promise of better educational opportunities outside of the city but required her to spend most nights away from home. Tricia compensated for her daughter's absence by attending her chorus recitals and maintaining phone contact during the week. Hondagneu-Sotelo and Avila (1997) find that transnational mothers working in the United States with children in Mexico or Central America understood their absence as a sacrifice for their children and compensated with frequent calls and, if possible, visits home. Other conflicts arise between mothering and conformity to the demands of the new welfare regulations, nowhere more so than in the area of work requirements.

Spending Time with Children

All but the very youngest of the women whom I interviewed had worked during some part of their adult lives and identified more closely with working people than with welfare recipients. All recipients older than 17 had either worked until the birth of children or cycled from welfare to work, a phenomenon described clearly by Edin and Lein (1997). Most had held some type of job after having children, thereby experiencing the conflicting expectations of working and parenting. The ideology of intensive mothering suggests that good mothers spend large amounts of time with children and are primary caregivers for those children. Public assistance allowed some poor women the opportunity to do just that, but the conditions of the PRA now require that women work outside of the home to qualify for assistance. In 1997, at the time of the interviews, these new regulations were going into effect, and while the respondents were aware of the new rules, they had not yet been affected by them.

The jobs that welfare mothers were most frequently offered included factory work, warehouse positions, telemarketing, and janitorial/cleaning positions (Ehrenreich 2002; Riemer 2001). These jobs sometimes require shift work, oftentimes late at night or very early in the morning. Shifts can also rotate, changing hours with little notice, making it very difficult for single mothers to stay in these jobs. Donna Oakley, a 33-year-old Black mother of two boys who had managed to move out of the inner city and into an apartment building in a working-class community, describes this transition in this way: "First of all, I was on the 8 to 4 shift, they put me on the 12 to 8 shift, which really kind of put a damper on my lifestyle, 'cause I was a single parent. . . . It's like I'm not raising my kids. Somebody else is raising my kids." To be a good mother, Donna expresses her need to be with her children. While most mothers in this sample desired work, they were not willing to sacrifice being the primary caregivers for their children. They could not fulfill their role as good mothers, as they had defined it, if they left their children vulnerable to others. Hays (1996) finds that these dilemmas are shared by women of all social classes yet may be resolved more successfully for women for whom high-quality child care is available.

The desire to be involved in their children's activities and with schooling was also difficult to fulfill with the expectations of a low-skilled job. Annette Johnson, a young Black mother of two living in the housing projects of a small city, was faced with this decision the day before our interview: "I got offered a warehouse position yesterday, from 3 to 11. Now, I wanted to work, but what happens when my daughter starts school? . . . When I go to school in the morning, my daughter ain't gonna see me, and then when she get home from school she still not gonna see me. By the time I get home, she gonna be asleep." According to the dominant discourse, welfare mothers who turn down jobs do so because they are lazy, lack willpower, and would prefer to be on the dole (Fox Piven 1999).

Yet the motivations expressed in these interviews are far different. Rather than shun work, these women subscribe to the belief in "intensive mothering" and want to fulfill the role of the good mother (Hays 1996).

While some recipients refused these jobs outright, others tried to fulfill both obligations. Carolyn Barnes, a 24-year-old Black mother of two living in the city, began receiving public assistance when her grandmother passed away before her 18th birthday. Before becoming pregnant with her now four-year-old child, Carolyn was homeless and received some governmental aid. With her children now two and four, Carolyn was trying to get back into the work force: "When I had a job, I had called [social services] and they like cut me off for a couple of months until I quit the job . . . because I felt I had to take care of my kids. . . . I didn't have daycare, so it was like certain people was watchin' my kids, different people. . . . I had to let my kids know that I had time for them, too." Carolyn took the job offered to her, but without daycare she was forced to leave her young children with a variety of friends and family, offering no consistent caregivers from day to day. The "cultural contradictions of motherhood" (Hays 1996) left these women unable to fulfill the roles of both good mother and self-sufficient worker. The women whom I interviewed saw the role of mother as more fundamental than the role of worker to their purpose and sense of self.

This difficulty is exacerbated by the lack of social support available for the respondents. Most had occasionally relied on family members for assistance with child care and in economic crisis, but beyond immediate family members, there were few supports in place. Similarly, Jarrett (1994) finds that single African American mothers living in poverty extended domestic responsibilities by sharing child care with their mothers and other female relatives. Collins (1991) uses the term "other-mothers" to describe this extension of mothering. Stack (1974) also describes the extended family networks that help poor Black individuals survive within tightly knit communities. These sources of support appeared to be diminishing, however, as families lived farther apart and other family members had fewer resources to share (Bell Kaplan 1997). For most of the mothers I interviewed, their own mothers were the only outside source of support.

The irony of the work requirements coupled with a conservative push for women to remain at home with young children highlights the disparity of a system of stratified reproduction. Since the welfare mother, coded as a Black single mother, is identified publicly with bad mothering, the separation of mother and child in poor families does not appear to conflict with the goal of promoting healthy environments for children. For this group of women, resisting the identity of the welfare mother in fact meant embracing the identity of the self-sacrificing, child-defined mother so appealing to conservative legislators (Mink 1998). The means of their resistance, in fact, would be seen as conformity if embraced by middle-class, married women.

Providing for Children

Another criterion that must be met to claim the status of the good mother is providing for one's children. This necessary provision frequently includes not only food and clothes but also other material things that children desire. In a culture permeated with images of gift giving as a sign of affection, and with the constant bombardment of advertising, parents feel pressure to fulfill their child's material desires. Since these welfare recipients had virtually no disposable income, providing these extras for their children came at the expense of necessities (Bell Kaplan 1997; Edin and Lein 1997). Yet they felt the requirement of doing so. Mothers worried that if they did not provide their children with the right kinds of clothes and material goods, their children might turn to illegal means of attaining money, thereby putting themselves in danger.

Heather Davison, a 20-year-old Black mother of two living in the inner city had recently come up against the conflicting desires to satisfy her child's wants and meet her basic needs. She gave birth to a second child at the end of October, just two months before Christmas. Heather was forced to confront her preschool-aged daughter's long list to Santa Claus knowing that she would not be able to afford to please her and provide small gifts for the rest of her family. "My mother helped me out a little bit, you know, and my grandmother. They bought the little gifts and stuff. And then turn around, I had like a hundred and something [dollars to] spend on [presents]. . . . She wanted a doll baby that you fed. That thing costed 29 dollars, and I couldn't afford it. By the time I buy that, I couldn't afford to get her the rest of the stuff that she wanted. And she wanted that doll . . . and you know I couldn't even afford her a bike." Heather tried calling a local radio station, charities, and her social worker but in the end was unable to afford the doll that her daughter wanted. She told her daughter that Santa

"probably forgot" her doll when questioned and was terribly disappointed that she could not fulfill her daughter's Christmas wish.

Donna Oakley, a 33-year-old Black mother of two, described her first stint on welfare as quite difficult, recounting the two moments at which she knew that she wanted to leave the welfare rolls as quickly as possible.

> An ice cream truck came around, the end of the month. I didn't have no money. Ain't got no boyfriend, nobody to help you or nothing. My baby wanted ice cream, and I couldn't buy my baby ice cream. That thing, it hit me right there [pats chest]. And another thing . . . I had my own place and of course I had to pay the bills in my house, which meant, you know, that little $244, something's gonna be neglected, 'cause you gotta pay rent, telephone bill, gas and electric, and children. So something's gonna be neglected. My kid's shoes were kind of worn, and the shoe actually tore from the sole. Oh, that thing hurt me so bad.

Heather and Donna wanted more for their children than they were able to provide with a welfare check. These failings undercut their efforts at fulfilling the role of the good mother.

To bolster their identity as good mothers, recipients made every effort to provide their children with some of the markers of a middle-class upbringing, despite the obvious lack of money and access to resources like good schools, healthy food, and good housing. This was expressed in everyday practices such as dressing their children well and making sure that they had at least some of the luxuries that they desired. Putting children first required spending money on them first, preserving their image and ego before satisfying one's own. Among my respondents, this was a double-edged sword. Heather and Donna were not alone in wanting to give their children nice things, but other mothers were frequently criticized for spending their money foolishly, particularly if they spent money on themselves instead of their children. Joan Clark, a Black mother of two, offers one such criticism: "Some people that get it don't use it on their kids. Some of them don't even get high and they don't buy the kids no clothes. They buy themselves clothes, make themselves look nice, don't do nothin' for the kids." While spending money on children for unnecessary items could be understood and even lauded, spending it on oneself was the mark of a bad mother.

While most mothers on welfare need help in making ends meet (Edin and Lein 1997), some found it necessary to rely on illegal work to provide even the basic necessities for their children. Carmen Diego, for example, a 23-year-old white mother of three with a drug addiction that began in adolescence, described herself as putting her children first, even when she was actively addicted to heroin and cocaine. "Sometimes I even had to prostitute to get money for diapers, because I spent the other money in drugs. I'm pretty sure women do things just to support their family. You would do anything, you would go to any length to make sure your kids [have] whatever they need, you would go to any length. I mean that's what I would do." Even though Carmen's logic seems counterintuitive as she was using drugs at the time that she resorted to prostitution, she was telling us that she is a good mother. Despite her addiction, she was able to see her children's needs and do whatever it took to provide for them. At the time of the interview, Carmen had been free from drugs for nearly a year.

Carmen's story points clearly to the devastating effects of dominant economic and symbolic systems. On one hand, Carmen is able to keep the label of good mother in her toolkit for self-preservation. On the other, the life that she describes is a dismal, desperate one, where she is certainly reduced to a shadow of herself by poverty and drugs. While Carmen's story points clearly to the limits of resistance, it also points to another set of contradictory roles that mothers must fill. Along with the conflict between earning money and spending time with children, some forms of income procurement put children at risk. By prostituting herself, Carmen runs the risk of exposing her children to others who might harm them and to public scorn should her actions become widely known. She also risks losing her children should Child Protective Services become involved and charge her with endangerment. While Carmen was the only mother in this sample who described turning to prostitution for money, the conflict between providing financial support and protecting children was described by most mothers who did not want to leave children vulnerable to other adults while they went out to work.

Keeping Children out of Trouble

Providing consistent discipline for children is another central component of being a good mother, according to many of the women whom I interviewed. The form that this discipline should take most often involved setting consistent rules and rewarding good behavior. The first requirement of providing consistent discipline was time spent with children, to teach them and to enforce punishment when it was deemed necessary.

Tricia Shephard, a 36-year-old Black mother of two, took responsibility for her 13 nieces and nephews along with her 2 children and 1 grandchild during the summer months when school was out. She explained the need to keep her younger relatives out of trouble and provide discipline, something that her siblings were not able to do while they were at work. "Somebody's gotta be there for them, you know? Because if you just let them go here and go out there, then they'll be in trouble. . . . They get in trouble for certain things, but they're not bad children. . . . It's not nothing bad where you can't discipline it yourself." For Tricia, keeping the children in her family away from the police and the legal system, keeping them out of trouble, was her job since she had the time to do it. Hays (2003) and Newman (1999) both find that women on welfare often serve as daycare providers for other people's children. The guidelines for the PRA encourage this trend by counting child care work as work when done for others, while not recognizing the care of one's own children as work (Mink 1998).

Material factors made it more difficult to set consistent limits and enforce discipline. Poor mothers, for example, were much more likely to be "doubling up," living with other family members to reduce rent (Edin and Lein 1997). Many younger women still lived with their own mothers and younger siblings. In cases such as these, they benefited from the availability of babysitters in the form of grandparents, aunts, and friends. There can be negative consequences of doubling up, however. In addition to a lack of space, some young mothers in particular felt that their own authority and autonomy as mothers was undercut by the older women around them (Bell Kaplan 1997). Keisha, a 17-year-old Black mother of one, described her situation, living with her sister and her sister's children. Her sister's rules were much more flexible than her own, and because her sister was older, she often suggested to Lia, Keisha's two-year-old daughter, that she ignore her mother's punishments. "When I put Lia in time-out, [my sister says to me], 'Girl, she don't know nothing 'bout no time-out, let her get up.' And I be like, 'No, she know about it, that's what they do in school.' [Then my sister will contradict me and tell my daughter] 'Girl, Lia, get up.'" The constant negotiation between varying rules in the home was compounded by other rules at school, when children visited their fathers, and in the homes of other relatives. Providing discipline is more difficult then, on average, for women doubling up or living in the homes of their own mothers than for mothers raising their children in their own homes.

Another factor compounding the struggle to discipline children is the threat of the involvement of Child Protective Services if mothers use physical punishment. When I began an interview with Cheryl Phillips, a 26-year-old Black mother of four, she was visibly agitated and spent most of the hour and a half discussing her problems with discipline. Cheryl was newly living in a group home where she was recovering from a severe drug addiction. Her four children sat around the kitchen table eating bowls of cereal as we talked. They ate quietly as Cheryl described her problem: "I have a problem with putting my hands on [i.e., hitting] my youngest son, and I don't think it's that bad, but I guess other people do because . . . they don't allow any hitting, you know what I'm saying, and if I can't chastise my child, that mean when he get older he ain't gonna pay me no mind. But that's their rules, and I gotta follow them, but it burn me up on the inside. Because when we leave here, I ain't gonna have no structure with him." Cheryl had to decide whether to conform to the rules of the group home or to leave. She imagined that leaving would result in the resumption of her drug use. While she knew that her addiction was damaging to her children, she believed that her inability to "discipline" her youngest son was, perhaps, worse for him. "I know deep down in my heart that I'm not doing anything to hurt or harm my children, that I'm doing right, you know. And for them to call the people [Child Protective Services] in, that scares me because they been in and outta my life so much and now when I'm doing something right. . . ." The threat of involving Child Protective Services was very real to several of the women interviewed, particularly those with drug problems. Mink (1998) suggests that the requirements of the PRA intensify this risk for poor mothers as they may lose welfare benefits if they do not comply with work requirements, thereby exposing their children to worse conditions that could be seen as endangerment requiring the removal of a child from her or his home.

Interviewing Cheryl and deciding how her story fit in with the rest—none of which involved accounts of physical punishment—were difficult. Two aspects of her story seem worth noting. First, Cheryl was under nearly constant surveillance due to her involvement with a treatment facility. In addition, the amount of surveillance of poor mothers is much greater (through caseworkers, Housing Authority, etc.) than is the case for women with more resources, particularly those who own their own homes, pay market rents, or are otherwise uninvolved with the governmental relief programs. Child Protective Services workers are more frequently involved in the lives of poor families (Drake and Pandey 1996) and Black families (Fluke et al. 2003). Poor mothers have to be concerned about their disciplinary practices in a way that wealthier mothers do not. Second, all but 11 respondents were involved in parenting classes as a component of the educational or drug treatment programs to which they belong. They were taught strategies of discipline, such as time-outs and positive reinforcement, that were more palatable to their caseworkers, doctors, and, quite honestly, me. Yet some were not completely convinced that these newer methods would work. They were not sure that they were doing the right thing for their children by abandoning the strategies of their own parents for more socially acceptable forms of punishment.

Keeping Children Safe

The last piece in the good mother puzzle is protecting children from harm. This involves keeping them off of the streets but also keeping them out of the hands of adults who might harm them. The most common way that this shows up is the repeated refrain, "I won't let everybody watch my child." While a few close family members and friends might be appropriate caretakers for a child, daycare workers who are not known well, neighbors, and acquaintances are seen as potentially dangerous.

> I don't ask nobody to watch my children. If I can't take them, they have a cousin that lives straight up the street, they watch them. I don't let everybody watch my kids. (Carolyn Barnes, 26-year-old Black mother of two)
>
> I don't like nobody taking care of my kids. Nobody can take care of my kids but myself, especially nowadays with all the horrible stuff you hear about kids . . . and you might think, "Oh, this daycare worker is just fine." Yeah, put some cameras up and we'll see how fine she is, because I know people have their days, and

they're not abusive to kids, but they just might lash out that day to that kid and that can scar a kid for the rest of their life. (Carmen Diego, 23-year-old white mother of three)

Carmen, abused as a child, was particularly wary of others taking care of her children. Many of the women in this sample recounted abuse that they faced as children. The vulnerability of growing up in poverty, doubling up, living near drug dealers, and spending time in homeless shelters exposed some recipients to abuse in their own childhoods. Protecting their own children from harm, then, was seen as a high priority in their lives even if they had in the past exposed their own children to danger.

Mothers protected their identities by bracketing past experiences and events as anomalies in their otherwise good career as mothers. Recipients recovering from drug addictions frequently used this technique to explain away neglect that their children had suffered at their hands. Veronica Griffin, a 33-year-old Black mother of two, was getting ready to send her two-year-old son Mark back to his father at the time of our interview. She was distressed about the fact that he was "not being taken care of" and left to "fend for himself" in his father's house. Veronica had lost custody of Mark the year before when she "left him in the house by hisself" while she went to procure drugs. Veronica attributed the earlier neglect to her addiction, bracketing it off from her current mothering practices. Enos (2001) found similar strategies among mothers serving time in prison who were able to preserve their identities by setting aside moments in time as anomalous. The participation of a number of women in recovery groups such as Alcoholics Anonymous and Narcotics Anonymous gave them a medicalized language that supported this bracketing. By viewing their addictions as disease, those mothers could bolster their identities as good mothers as they fought the diseases that kept them from their children.

THE GOOD MOTHER AS STRATEGIC PRACTICE

The criteria that welfare recipients employed in claiming that they were good mothers reflect the intensive mothering ideology shared by mothers across class lines and advocated by child care experts (Hays 1996). In fact, the fulfillment of this role helps to minimize or render less powerful the stigma associated with welfare. Welfare stigma is powerful and demeaning, yet for many women, the need to provide for, protect, and spend time with their children allows them to overcome their own resistance to welfare receipt. It is the very act of prioritizing their children that may require them to rely on welfare while their children are little as it is the best of the options available to them. Connie Taylor, a 30-year-old Black mother of three, told a story that was common: "The first time I went [to the Department of Social Services], I was gonna leave because I was crying, and I was gonna leave 'cause I really didn't wanna be on public assistance. And I . . . thought about being pregnant and that my baby needed good medical care and my kids needed good medical care [in] case they got sick. And that's why I stayed." I was repeatedly told by recipients that they would not put up with the treatment that they received in the welfare office were it not for the fact that assistance allowed them to meet their children's basic needs.

To find evidence to support their claims that they have been good mothers, many women looked to their children. It is hardly unique to poor communities to find parents discussing the exceptionality of their children. For these women, with little external reinforcement, their children's success provided support for their self-identification with the image of a good mother. For example, Ayana Richards says of her son, "He talks very well for a two-year-old child; everybody tells me that. He knows how to hit a baseball if you throw it to him at two years of age. He's really smart, so I think coming [to this GED/family program] was the best for me, best for me and him" (Ayana Richards, 19-year-old Black mother of one). Like Ayana, Keisha claims that her daughter "just do[es] things that an average two-year-old wouldn't do. . . . She's more advanced than my niece, and my niece is five." Whether Ayana's and Keisha's daughters actually outperform other two-year-olds is inconsequential. What matters is their belief that their children are exceptional. While none of the women claim sole responsibility for their children's accomplishments, many do feel that this is evidence that they must have done something right.

Several of the mothers point more directly to the quality of their relationship with their children to demonstrate that they have fulfilled the expectations of motherhood. Alice Brown, a 40-year-old Black mother of two, described her children's ability to take care of themselves as well as their dedication to her. Alice had combined work and welfare through much of her life and had only in recent years become involved with drugs. The connection that she shared with her children became apparent when she was sent to jail:

> I wind up going to jail for 35 days in June of last year, and I think that was dying for me. But I raised them and I was so proud of that little man back there, my son, because he kept my house in order, my phone was off, my gas and electric was behind. My rent was, 'cause at the time I think I was paying about 58 dollars for rent and couldn't even pay that, you know. He got everything back up, he got the phone turned back on, he got the gas and electric bill back up to date, and, I just say, you know, I don't take all the credit, but like I was telling the judge when I did go to court, I said I had to do something right, you know?

The fact that her children took care of her house while she was gone, stayed out of trouble, and remained committed to their mother was proof that she had raised good children.

While never able to find a job that paid well enough to support the family without some assistance, Alice had succeeded in the most important, defining act of motherhood: raising strong, healthy children. Being a good mother mitigated her apparent failure in other arenas: establishing a successful career, maintaining a long-term partnership, or remaining independent of the welfare system. While these other goals may be reconcilable for middle-class women, they often are not for poor women, and motherhood takes priority. By defining themselves as good mothers, these women protected their identities as good people.

MOTHERHOOD AND IDENTITY: THE LIMITS OF RESISTANCE

Powerful ideologies of race, class, and gender underlie the image of the welfare mother, and while these respondents are able to partially counter the negative effects of this particular construct, they do so in ways that reinforce the dominant logic. These women simultaneously resist and support a system of stratified reproduction. The resistance can be seen in the ways in which this particular group of women created a space within which they could define themselves as good citizens. For their own survival and that of their children, women receiving public assistance must construct this safer space.

This is consistent with findings on other groups of women marked as outside of the discursive construction of good mothers, including lesbian mothers (Dunne 2000; Hequembourg and Farrell 1999), single mothers by choice (Bock 2000), and substance-abusing mothers (Baker and Carson 1999). While the logic of stratified reproduction casts these women as deviant others and bad mothers, they actively deploy and subvert these discursive practices to claim for themselves the identity of good mothers.

There are limits to this resistance, however, and while these women are able to mobilize discourses on motherhood, they often do so in ways that powerfully reinforce the logic of stratified reproduction. By relying so heavily on fulfilling traditional notions of motherhood, these mothers help to perpetuate a definition of motherhood that relies in part on traditional gender roles and the availability of adequate resources. By conforming to a middle-class definition of motherhood (coded as white), these women protect their identities but reinforce a system that by virtue of their class and race, is used to limit their power. In fact, one of the three elements of intensive mothering, as outlined by Hays (1996), is that mothering is incomparable and more valuable than paid work. None of the women in this sample claimed that their mothering was valuable for society or argued that mothers ought to be paid for raising children. They are left unable to formulate an argument that might unite mothers across class and race lines, an argument that mothering is work and that it ought to be respected and treated as such. This argument could challenge the underpinnings of the welfare mother and dismantle the myth that poor women are lazy and nonworking. Instead, they are left with a rationale that is quite personal and important but that is difficult to translate into a political argument that might appeal across class lines.

My findings suggest that this small group of women, interviewed just as the new welfare policies were being implemented, shared an ideology of mothering with mothers in other social classes. The importance of the time period during which these interviews were conducted cannot be overemphasized. In the late 1990s, welfare reform remained a central issue, frequently the subject of newspaper and television news stories. The visibility of welfare as a public issue and the welfare mother as a public identity has changed since that time with potentially significant results for welfare recipients. I am arguing here that my respondents are able to mobilize a discourse of motherhood as a resistance practice, however limited. In the current climate, perhaps recipients would require fewer strategies of resistance against dominant discourses on welfare but might need to engage more explicitly with ongoing debates about the family, marriage, and sexuality. Further research could explore the relationship between class, race, and motherhood in different cultural and political climates and further clarify the relationship between dominant ideologies, oppression, and resistance.

Foucault (1972, 1978) calls our attention to the interdependency of discourse practices, by which one discursive element must make sense in relation to others. Welfare discourse makes sense because it fits with dominant constructions of the economy, polity, family, and individual choice that create a dominant worldview in the United States, one that blames individuals for their own failings, particularly when they are unable to support themselves financially. It is vital to see welfare discourse as a critical component in this, for without the welfare mother and the stereotype of the poor as lazy, the existence of dire poverty in the midst of affluence creates doubt in the achievement ideology. Welfare mothers may protect their own identities and subvert the dominant welfare mother construct when they identify as good mothers, but the welfare mother is only one such discourse against which they must struggle. Procuring their basic necessities, working for a better life for their own children, and protecting their families from the most pernicious effects of poverty are daunting tasks. In demonstrating their ability to resist the welfare mother, we see that these women are not rendered docile. Yet while they are not passive victims of these dominant discourses, we can hear ample evidence in their stories of life on the margins that they are not free.

REFERENCES

Albelda, Randy, Nancy Folbre, and Center for Popular Economics. 1996. *The war on the poor: A defense manual.* New York: New Press.

Baker, Phyllis, and Amy Carson. 1999. "I take care of my kids": Mothering practices of substance-abusing women. *Gender & Society* 13:347–63.

Bell Kaplan, Elaine. 1997. *Not our kind of girl: Unraveling the myths of Black teenage motherhood.* Berkeley: University of California Press.

Bock, Jane. 2000. Doing the right thing: Single mothers by choice and the struggle for legitimacy. *Gender & Society* 14:62–86.

Collins, Patricia Hill. 1989. A comparison of two works on Black family life. *Signs: Journal of Women in Culture and Society* 14:875–84.

———. 1991. *Black feminist thought.* New York: HarperCollins.

———. 2001. Mammies, matriarchs, and other controlling images. In *Great divides,* edited by Thomas M. Shapiro. Mountain View, CA: Mayfield.

Crittenden, Ann. 2001. *The price of motherhood.* New York: Henry Holt.

de Certeau, Michel. 1984. *The practice of everyday life.* Berkeley: University of California Press.

Drake, Brett, and Shanta Pandey. 1996. Understanding the relationship between neighborhood poverty and specific types of child maltreatment. *Child Abuse & Neglect* 20:1003–18.

Dunne, Gillian. 2000. Opting into motherhood: Lesbians blurring the boundaries and transforming the meaning of parenthood and kinship. *Gender & Society* 14:11–35.

Edin, Kathryn, and Laura Lein. 1997. *Making ends meet.* New York: Russell Sage.

Ehrenreich, Barbara. 2002. *Nickel and dimed: On (not) getting by in America.* New York: Henry Holt.

Enos, Sandra. 2001. *Mothering from the inside.* Albany: State University of New York Press.

Fluke, John D., Ying-Ying Yuan, John Hedderson, and Patrick Curtis. 2003. Disproportionate representation of race and ethnicity in child maltreatment: Investigation and victimization. *Children and Youth Services Review* 25:359–73.

Foucault, Michel. 1972. *The archaeology of knowledge.* New York: Pantheon.

———. 1978. *The history of sexuality.* New York: Vintage.

Fox Piven, Frances. 1999. Welfare and work. In *Whose welfare,* edited by Gwendolyn Mink. Ithaca, NY: Cornell University Press.

Fraser, Nancy, and Linda Gordon. 1994. A genealogy of dependency: Tracing a key word of the welfare state. *Signs: Journal of Women in Culture and Society* 19 (2): 309–36.

Gingrich, Newt, and Bob Schelhas, eds. 1994. *Contract with America.* New York: New York Times Books.

Ginsberg, Faye, and Rayna Rapp, eds. 1995. *Conceiving the new world order: The global politics of reproduction.* Berkeley: University of California Press.

Goffman, Erving. 1974. *Stigma: Notes on the management of spoiled identity.* New York: Jason Aronson.

Hancock, Ange-Marie. 2004. *The politics of disgust: The public identity of the welfare queen.* New York: New York University Press.

Hays, Sharon. 1996. *The cultural contradictions of motherhood.* New Haven, CT: Yale University Press.

———. 2003. *Flat broke with children: Women in the age of welfare reform.* New York: Oxford University Press.

Hequembourg, Amy L., and Michael P. Farrell. 1999. Lesbian motherhood: Negotiating marginal-mainstream identities. *Gender & Society* 13:540–57.

Hondagneu-Sotelo, Pierette, and Ernestine Avila. 1997. "I'm here, but I'm there": The meanings of Latina transnational motherhood. *Gender & Society* 11:548–71.

Jarrett, Robin L. 1994. Living poor: Family life among single parent, African American women. *Social Problems* 41:30–49.

McCormack, Karen. 2004. Resisting the welfare mother: The power of welfare discourse and tactics of resistance. *Critical Sociology* 30:355–83.

Mink, Gwendolyn. 1998. *Welfare's end.* Ithaca, NY: Cornell University Press.

Mullings, Leith. 2001. Households headed by women: The politics of class, race, and gender. In *The new poverty studies,* edited by Judith Goode and Jeff Maskovsky. New York: New York University Press.

Neubeck, Kenneth, and Noel Cazenave. 2001. *Welfare racism: Playing the race card against America's poor.* New York: Routledge.

Newman, Katherine. 1999. *No shame in my game: The working poor in the inner city.* New York: Vantage Books.

Pelissier Kingfisher, Catherine, 1996. *Women in the American welfare trap.* Philadelphia: University of Pennsylvania Press.

Riemer, Frances Julia. 2001. *Working at the margins: Moving off welfare in America.* Albany, NY: State University of New York Press.

Roberts, Dorothy. 1999. Welfare's ban on poor motherhood. In *Whose welfare,* edited by Gwendolyn Mink. Ithaca, NY: Cornell University Press.

Scott, James C. 1985. *Weapons of the weak: Everyday forms of peasant resistance.* New Haven, CT: Yale University Press.

Sidel, Ruth. 1996. *Keeping women and children last.* New York: Penguin.

Stack, Carol. 1974. *All our kin.* New York: Harper and Row.

Thornton Dill, Bonnie, Maxine Baca Zinn, and Sandra Patton. 1999. Race, family values, and welfare reform. In *A new introduction to poverty,* edited by Louis Kushnick and James Jennings. New York: New York University Press.

R E A D I N G *45*   **Grace Chang**

From the Third World to the "Third World Within": Asian Women Workers Fighting Globalization

First published in 2004

The present form of globalization has not produced enough jobs for all those who seek them or in the places where they are most needed. This is probably its biggest failure.

—*Juan Somavia, Director-General, International Labor Organization*[1]

I want to begin to dispel the myths. It's not about mail-order brides. Hello, this is a global world. . . . We are a global population.

—*Mike Krosky, Owner, Cherry Blossoms*[2]

INTRODUCTION

These observations on globalization probably could not have come from more distant corners. Juan Somavia's comment, addressed to representatives from 175 International Labor Organization member countries was intended to be sobering. He warned that the failure of globalization to create new jobs in developing countries has fueled and will continue to fuel massive migration worldwide. He estimated that about 500 million jobs will have to be created over the next decade just to accommodate the young people and women now entering the labor market.

In contrast, Mike Krosky's comment from an interview about his Cherry Blossoms business is positively celebratory. Krosky's business lists over 6000 women available for order through print catalogs and a web site, half of whom are Filipina. The next largest group is Indonesian, and the group showing the greatest increase comes from Eastern European countries. Krosky celebrates globalization not only because of huge business profits, but also for his personal satisfaction as the happy husband of a Filipina more than 18 years his junior, whom he met through his own service.

Both these comments speak directly or otherwise to an important but often neglected aspect of globalization: migrations of Third World people from their homes as a result of the destruction wrought by globalization on their abilities to survive at home.

I want to address this dimension of globalization, particularly Third World women's migrations, and, like Mike Krosky, I want to begin to dispel the myths. I also want to address the reality that in today's globalized context, virtually all migration can be seen as coerced through economic means, through the institutionalized underdevelopment and impoverishment of Third World nations and people.

A few years ago I had the privilege of speaking on an International Women's Day radio program with Ethel Long Scott of the Women's Economic Agenda Project. Scott remarked that we must talk about globalization in its proper terms, as the *globalization of poverty*—that is, the creation, perpetuation, and exacerbation of poverty worldwide. Scott also cautioned listeners not to think that the ravages of globalization are confined "over there" in the Third World but to examine its impacts in our own communities of color.[3] Scott raised an important point missing from many debates surrounding globalization—that those in the Third World and those in the "Third World within" First World countries share these conditions and thus are central to the struggles against this globalization of poverty.[4]

I will examine how women of color and migrant women in First World host nations experience the impact of globalization on their lives and livelihoods daily and forge resistance to these impact daily. Specifically, I look at the struggles of Filipina migrant workers in the U.S. and Canada—women who suffer these impacts on both ends of the global "trade route."

I interviewed members of two migrant domestic worker organizations, one in Vancouver, Canada, and the other in Bronx, New York, who provide important models for critical gender analyses of globalization and organized resistance against it.

Many of us who attended the 1995 Non-Governmental Organizations (NGO) Forum on Women as members of the U.S. women of color delegation were humbled by our Third World sisters who danced circles around us in their analyses and first-hand knowledge of global economic restructuring and its impact. Poor women of color throughout the world suffer first and worst under globalization. They experience so-called "development" and "free trade" as losses in status, freedom, safety, education, access to basic needs of food, water, housing, and health care—indeed, as assaults on their very survival. As the first victims of globalization, poor women of color are also the primary leaders in fighting back, in resisting the so-called "New World Order" that they know is not new at all but a continuation of neo-imperialist activities into the twenty-first century.

GLOBAL ECONOMIC RESTRUCTURING

At the Fourth World NGO Forum on Women held in China in 1995, women from Africa, Latin America, the Middle East, and Asia echoed the same truth in their testimonies: Global economic restructuring embodied in Structural Adjustment Programs (SAPs) strikes poor women of color around the world the hardest, rendering them most vulnerable to exploitation both at home and in the global labor market. Since the 1980s, the World Bank, International Monetary Fund (IMF), and other international financial institutions based in the First World have routinely prescribed structural adjustment policies to the governments of indebted countries as preconditions for loans. These prescriptions included cutting government expenditures on social programs, slashing wages, liberalizing imports, opening markets to foreign investment, expanding exports, devaluing local currency, and privatizing state enterprises.

Women have consistently reported increasing poverty and rapidly deteriorating nutrition, health, and work conditions as a direct result of SAPs. When wages and food subsidies are cut, wives and mothers adjust household budgets often at the expense of their own and their children's nutrition. As public health care and education vanish, women suffer from lack of prenatal care and become nurses to ill family members at home; girls are the first family members to leave school to help at home or go to work. When export-oriented agriculture is encouraged—indeed, coerced—peasant families are evicted from their lands to make room for corporate farms, and women become seasonal workers in the fields or in processing areas instead of land-owning farmers.

Lands once used to raise staples like rice are used instead for raising shrimp, oranges, and orchids—all for export, not for local consumption—or for golf courses and luxury hotels for tourists. Essentially, SAPs lead to destruction of both subsistence and social service systems in Third World nations so that women have no viable options to sustain their families and leave them behind to migrate in search of work. Usually women go from villages to cities within their home countries first and then migrate to the First World to pursue service work, sex work, and manufacturing jobs.[5]

Since the 1995 NGO Forum, women of color around the world have spoken in no uncertain terms to these continuing trends that globalization imposes on their lives.[6] They report the persistence of the most devastating impact of globalization on their abilities to support their children and families in the form of increased assaults on their reproductive rights. In short, globalization threatens the very survival of people of color by hindering the ability of their women to reproduce and maintain their families and communities.

In 1999, before the Seattle protests against the World Trade Organization (WTO), the Northwest Labor and Employment Law Office (LELO), a multiracial community and labor organization, recognized the need for education to build awareness of these issues and the linkages between workers' struggles in the U.S. and abroad. LELO brought together several grassroots groups, including the Seattle Young People's Project, Committee Against Repression in Mexico, Community Coalition for Environmental Justice, and the Washington Alliance for Immigrant and Refugee Justice to form the Workers' Voices Coalition. The coalition sponsored the participation of eight women labor-rights organizers from Third World countries in the WTO protest activities and a post-WTO conference.

Cenen Bagon, a participant, responded to comments by Michael Moore, then WTO director-general, when he addressed the International Confederation of Free Trade Unions. Moore said, "There is also a darker side to the backlash against globalization. For some, the attacks on economic openness are part of a broader assault on internationalism, on foreigners, immigration, a more pluralistic and integrated world. . . ." Bagon, who works with Filipina and other immigrant women workers in Canada through the Vancouver Committee for Domestic Workers and Caregivers Rights, countered sharply:

> Moore and others like him, in his ideological dogma, forget to add, and I'm sure it's quite intentional, that what we are against are the realities brought about by trade authored by the backers of capitalist globalization. . . . And if these so-called leaders are really looking for indicators of whether their programs are truly creating economic improvements, they should look beyond the country's balance of payment and budget deficits and analyze how women are affected by these programs. . . . Supporters of structural adjustment programs should visit the night life in Japan, Hong Kong, and certain places in Canada and listen to the stories of Filipino and other women who unknowingly left their countries as entertainers and ended up being prostituted by their recruiters. They should also listen to the stories of domestic workers who left not only their countries . . . but their families and their own children, as well, to care for other women's children and households. . . . [7]

Bagon calls for world leaders to view the migration of women forced to leave their homelands and families because of the ravages of SAPs as true indicators of the impacts of global economic restructuring. Extending on this, the experiences of immigrant women workers can serve not only as measures of the effects, but as true indicators of the *intentions* of SAPs and other neoliberal economic policies. The sheer magnitude of women's migration urges us to examine this phenomenon and view it as both an effect of globalization and as a calculated feature of global economic restructuring.

In other words, it is important to understand the economic interventions in Third World nations embodied in SAPs and free-trade policies as deliberate. They facilitate the extraction of resources, especially labor and people, from the Third World and their importation into the First World. In effect, they support trade in and traffic of migrant women workers and their exploitation at both ends of the so-called trade route. This trade or forced migration is orchestrated through economic interventions compelling migration from the Third World coupled with welfare, labor, and immigration policies in the First World that channel these women into service work at poverty wages in host or receiving countries.

I have argued elsewhere that structural adjustment in the Third World and welfare reform in the First World are inextricably linked; indeed, they are two sides of the same coin. For example, in the U.S., domestic forms of structural adjustment, including privatization and cutbacks in health care and the continued lack of subsidized child care, contribute to expanded demand among dual-career middle-class households for child care, elder care, home health care, and housekeeping workers. The slashing of benefits and social services under "welfare reform" helps guarantee that this demand is met by a pool of migrant women readily available to serve as cheap labor. The dismantling of public support in the U.S. in general and the denial of benefits and services to immigrants in particular act in tandem with structural adjustment in the Third World to force migrant women into low-wage service work in the U.S.[8]

Migrant women workers from indebted nations are kept pliable by both the dependence of their families on remittances sent home and by the severe restrictions on immigrant access to almost all forms of assistance in the U.S. Their vulnerability is further reinforced by First World immigration policies explicitly designed to recruit migrant women as contract or temporary workers yet deny them the protections and rights afforded citizens. This phenomenon is readily apparent in the cases of both U.S. and Canadian immigration policies structured to ensure a ready supply of women workers available for nursing aide, home care, domestic care, child care, and elder care work at low wages and under conditions most citizens would not accept.

"FILIPINOS FOR THE WORLD"

The massive migration of women from the Philippines to all corners of the First World illustrates clearly how structural adjustments imposed on the Philippines and welfare and immigration policies in First World receiving countries combine to make the global traffic in Filipinas an explicit government practice and highly profitable industry on both ends of the trade route. Every day, an average of 2700 people are estimated to leave the Philippines in search of work. Currently,

more than 8 million Filipino migrant workers live in over 186 countries, and an estimated 65% are women.[9] Although the Philippine government denies that it has an official export policy now, an agency called the Philippine Overseas Employment Administration (POEA) was established in the 1970s to promote migrant labor with the stated goals of (1) earning foreign currency and (2) easing the Philippines' unemployment rate.[10]

Confining the analysis for the moment only to the benefits of this trade to the Philippine government and capital, the numbers are staggering. One woman migrating to Canada reported paying 1900 pesos at the embassy in the Philippines, 1500 pesos for a medical examination, and 5000 pesos to the POEA according to the research by the Philippine Women's Centre.[11] If we multiply this total 8400 pesos ($181 US) for typical bureaucratic expenses paid by one individual migrating from the Philippines by the average daily exodus of 2700 people leaving the country, the Philippine government receives the equivalent of almost half a million U.S. dollars in revenue daily for processing exports of people. Moreover, the remittances sent home to families by Filipino workers overseas infuse into the economy what amounts to the Philippines' largest source of foreign currency—far more than income from sugar and mineral exports.

Although the absolute numbers are remarkable, taken in context they are particularly telling. For example, in the year 2000, remittances from overseas workers were estimated at $6.23 billion officially, reported as channeled through the Central Bank of the Philippines. This does not include funds received through informal channels. The $6.23 billion represented 5.2% of the gross domestic product and exceeded the entire interest payment on the country's foreign debt that hovers around $5 billion a year.[12]

Philippine President Gloria Macapagal-Arroyo launched a program known as "Filipinos for the World" to celebrate and further institutionalize this exportation of workers for profit. Arroyo (unaffectionately referred to as GMA) persists in glorifying these migrant workers, following a long line of Philippines officials who once called women in particular the country's "modern heroes." In even more crass economic terms, GMA now calls them "overseas Philippines investors" and "internationally shared resources."[13] She is promoting her new labor export plan announced in June of 2002 as a push to have 100 million overseas Filipinos serving others across the globe. Arroyo's program will certainly serve her interests well. As one observer remarked, "Arroyo seeks not only the remittances from the migrant workers, but their absentee ballots to keep her in office and bolster her unstable position. She wants not only the dollars but the 8 million Filipinos abroad in her pocket at election time."[14]

It is particularly useful to examine the experiences of Filipinas trained as nurses who migrate to work in the U.S. and Canada. They provide cheap and highly skilled labor and also serve to further the neo-liberal agenda of privatizing health care. In both countries, immigration policy is structured to keep these trained workers underemployed and deskilled in exploitative situations closely resembling indentured servitude and debt bondage. Nursing schools graduating hundreds of thousands of registered nurses abound in the Philippines, but few graduates reside in their own country.

The Philippine Women Centre (PWC) of British Columbia, a group of Filipino–Canadian women working to educate, organize, and mobilize Filipina migrant workers in Canada, identifies this phenomenon as the "commodification of the nursing profession in the Philippines." The group observes that nursing training is promoted as "a quick route to work abroad," rather than as a means to serve the needs of Filipinos. As a result Filipina nurses are seen as exportable commodities.[15] A survey of members of the group revealed that 77% of participants studied nursing with the specific intention of going abroad, and 62% took entrance exams allowing foreigners to practice nursing in the U.S.[16]

Clearly, exclusion from both welfare benefits and workers' rights through immigration policy makes immigrant women workers available for—indeed, unable to refuse—low-wage service work in the U.S. In Canada, the connection between labor control and immigration policy is even more explicit because of the use of both immigration and nursing accreditation issues to prevent foreign-trained nurses from being able to practice nursing for several years after arrival in Canada. In tandem, the policies serve to exclude immigrant nurses from their professions and channel them into low-paid care work as nannies, domestics, and home support workers.

The Live-in Caregiver Program (LCP) is the immigration policy through which the vast majority of Filipina migrants enter Canada and become trapped in low-wage care work. Established in 1992 to facilitate the importation of primarily Filipino women, the program provides that a Canadian employer (individual or employment agency) may apply through the Canadian Employment Office for a prospective employee after showing that an attempt was made to find a Canadian to do the job. A job applicant must have 2 years of postsecondary education, 6 months of formal training or 12 months of experience in caregiving work, and be in good health. Once matched with an employer, she must notify the Ministry of Citizenship and Immigration if she wishes to change employers. After 2 years of live-in work, a nanny can apply for landed-immigrant status, but during those 2 years she is considered a temporary migrant. Three years after applying for landed-immigrant status, she can become a Canadian citizen.[17]

The PWC undertook a community-based participatory action research project, interviewing 30 Filipina nurses who entered Canada via the LCP and performed domestic work. According to Cecilia Diocson, founding chairperson of the PWC, the interviews revealed that women with up to 15 years of nursing experience in operating rooms, cancer units, and other facilities were becoming deskilled while working as nannies and home support workers.[18] Others were indeed using their skills, working around the clock and performing nursing tasks, but they were not recognized or compensated as such. Many of their tasks included heavy lifting; transferring; personal care duties; administering medications; and tube feeding for elderly, ill, and disabled clients. One nurse, Mary Jane reported:

> Because of the LCP requirements, we become responsible for our employers 24 hours a day, but we are only paid for 8 hours, with no overtime pay. For some of us, we accompany our employers to the hospital and even sleep at our employer's bedside at the hospital.[19]

Many of those interviewed did not realize when they migrated that they would not be doing nursing work after they entered Canada through the LCP. Many believed that they would perform nursing in private homes or care for disabled children. Moreover, many did not know that working as a nanny would mean so much labor demanded of them beyond caring for children. For example, Pamela, a registered nurse in the Philippines who left three children behind to seek work in Vancouver, said:

> I thought being a nanny, as the dictionary says, is child's nurse. In the Philippines, a yaya [Tagalog for nanny] works for the kids only, right? They don't do other jobs in the house. They just change the kids, feed them and put them to bed. . . . When I came here, I was shocked. I said, why is it a package? Three children in a big house, 5 bedrooms, 1½ baths, and 3 living rooms. . . . I feel like I'm going to die. My female employer didn't work. She stays at home. Then, she said that I'm not clean enough. I told her that I have to prioritize the work and I asked her, what's more important, the kids or cleaning? . . . It was so hard I quit.[20]

After Pamela quit, her former employer refused to give her a reference, nanny agencies would not accept her, and she decided to advertise for a job caring for the elderly. Several prospective employers who answered her ad sought caregivers willing to provide sexual services. After several such experiences and trying to work as a nanny for one more family, she found a job caring for a single woman.

Pamela supports her husband, who is a student, and her three children in the Philippines by sending a quarter of her wages home each month. She spoke of the hardships of separation from her family and her doubts and fears about reuniting:

> I'm confused whether I should get my family or not. The separation is really hard for me, but I also think if my family is here, my husband and I have to chip in. I fear that communication will be through messages on the refrigerator. We don't see each other any more. That's why sometimes I feel that maybe it's better for them to stay in the Philippines because they write to me and there's an attachment still. Here, it seems that you're not really intact.[21]

Mary Jane, another Filipina nurse working as a nanny, reflected on the pain of separation from her children and the great financial hardship of maintaining contact:

> My children are now 5 and 8. I spent so much money on the long distance because sometimes when I call, my child will say, "Mommy I still want to sing." You know, you didn't see your child for 4 years and she will tell you she wants to sing, you cannot say no. . . . I said I will call everyday so that [her youngest child] will not forget my voice. I only stopped calling because my phone bill is over $500.

For these women, the agony of separation from their own children is surely not diminished by caring for their employers' children. For many of the women interviewed, the hope of eventually being able to bring their families to join them in Canada influenced them to stay in unhappy and often abusive working situations in order to fulfill the 2-year live-in work requirement of the LCP as quickly as possible. The policy prohibits them from earning any extra income to supplement their low wages as caregivers and explicitly stipulates that working for anyone other than the employer named on the employment authorization is illegal, and unauthorized employment will not count toward satisfying the 2-year employment requirement to apply for permanent residence.[22] Thus, women are effectively kept bonded to the employers named on their original LCP employment authorizations at whatever wages and conditions the employer chooses to provide. As Pamela reports:

> Filipinos are abused because they are pressured to stay with the 24-month requirement. . . . You stay because it's not that easy to find an employer. And you get exploited and we are highly educated. . . . That's really racism.

In addition to these barriers that essentially lock trained nurses into nanny and home support work for at least 2 years, migrant Filipinas face more hurdles in trying to gain accreditation to practice nursing even after serving the 2-year live-in requirement. Applicants must take English tests that are irrelevant and extremely costly, about US $410. According to Leah Diana, a registered nurse and volunteer with the Filipino Nurses Support Group (FNSG) in Vancouver, Filipino nurses are usually educated in English, used English while employed in the Philippines and elsewhere, and passed mandatory English interviews before arrival in Canada. Diana says, "The English tests required are only based on the racist assumption that people of color can't speak English." These barriers are particularly outrageous when viewed in the context of Canada's recognized nursing shortage. A Canadian Nurses'

Association study showed an expected shortage of 59,000 to 113,000 registered nurses in Canada by the year 2011.[23]

Cecilia Diocson reports that the mainstream, predominantly white nursing unions in Canada have not been good allies. They have not supported allowing Filipina nurses to practice despite shortages. Diocson expressed outrage that the president of a nursing union tried to pass this off as concern that "the Philippines needs them." She said:

> We responded, "Don't give us that kind of rationalization. The nurses are already here, and in crisis, and we are seeking solidarity. Is the real issue that we are nonwhite, from the Third World, and foreign-trained? Are you threatened by our presence?" It's so clear that this is just racism. Otherwise, they would support and struggle with us.

Beyond the presence of women of color born and trained in the Third World, the existence of a surplus of low-wage workers and ostensible competitors is perhaps most threatening. Migrant women workers are well aware that the Canadian government can and does use their presence in the country and their exclusion through the LCP from the nursing profession to render them available to do other low-wage care and service work while keeping Canadian citizen nurses wary of competition. As Gemma Gambito, a member of FNSG who graduated from nursing school in the Philippines in 1993 and went to Canada in 1997 under the LCP, says:

> Our presence in Canada is used to drive down the wages of Canadian nurses and health care workers. Once completing our temporary work contract and becoming landed immigrants, many become home support workers, nursing aides, or continue to do domestic work for low wages. A pool of highly skilled yet low paid health workers has been created by the Canadian government's LCP.[24]

The LCP and its attendant racism facilitate the privatization of health care and help ensure the lack of movement or alliance building for subsidized child care, health care, and other staples of feminist and worker agendas. Dr. Lynn Farrales, a co-chair of the PWC, observes that the LCP functions simply to bring in women who are educated and trained nurses to do domestic work and provide live-in child care and private home care for the disabled and elderly for less than minimum wage. Farrales says:

> Canada, a country without a national day care program and a health care system moving towards increased privatization, has established in the LCP a means of importing highly educated and skilled workers to fulfill the need for flexible and cheap labor in the spheres of child care and health care. The economic and social consequences of the LCP have been devastating for Filipino women. They are highly exploited, oppressed, and de-skilled. Despite being highly educated, many are trapped in minimum wage jobs after completion of the LCP, and are effectively legislated into poverty.[25]

Moreover, Farrales notes that these negative consequences extend to the next generation of Filipino youth as well, including the effects of years of separation of mothers and children and the systemic racism in Canadian institutions that Filipino–Canadian youths encounter. Because Filipino youths drop out of high school at high rates, they join their mothers working for low wages in the service sector. Thus, the Canadian government achieves what Farrales calls the "commodification of the migration of the entire family as a package deal of cheap labor."[26] Meanwhile, ironically, with rapidly privatizing health care and the continuing nursing shortage in the public sector, health care becomes inaccessible for working-class Canadians, including Filipina nurses and their families. Thus, the Canadian government provides middle- and upper-class Canadian citizens with quality, low-cost, in-home child care and health care, literally at the expense of Filipina women workers and their families, who cannot afford these services for themselves.

Filipina migrant workers understand all too well how the Philippine government benefits and profits from this trade in women and thus plays a calculated role in ensuring its smooth functioning. The following statement of the PWC reflects this analysis of the past and current complicity of the Philippine government in this trade:

> The migration and commodification of Filipinos is sanctioned by official Philippine government policy. Known as the Labour Export Policy (LEP), this scheme of systematically exporting labour is part of the Structural Adjustment Programs (SAPs) imposed by the

IMF and World Bank as conditionalities for borrowing. Ultimately, the LEP and SAPs are part of the neoliberal policies of the globalization agenda. The LEP seeks to alleviate the continuing problems of massive unemployment, trade deficits, foreign debt and social unrest. . . . The government relies upon the remittances of these migrants to prop up the economy and pay off the massive foreign debt owed to the IMF and the World Bank. Instead of selling coconuts and sugar, the Philippine government is now engaged in the sophisticated practice of selling its own people to industrialized countries.[27]

This statement reflects these women's clear recognition that the official Philippine government labor export policy is part and parcel of structural adjustment programs that wreak havoc on their lives and force them to migrate in the first place. The LEP institutionalizes the exportation of Filipina women to other countries for cheap labor and effectively guarantees that remittances from these migrant women workers are used to pay off foreign debt.

TURNING THE "NEW WORLD ORDER" UPSIDE DOWN

Carol de Leon is now program director for the Women Workers Project at CAAAV (formerly Committee Against Anti-Asian Violence): Organizing Asian Communities in the Bronx, New York. She grew up in the Philippines, where she was a youth activist until she left in 1987 to work abroad as a nanny. She recalls that when she was in Hong Kong she applied to go to Canada, but it did not materialize, and this was probably fortunate. In the mid-1980s, the Canadian government was "very lenient, inviting people to come into the country, so at the time it was so easy to find an employer and go to Canada." In the 1990s, the Canadian government instituted requirements such as educational background checks for 2 to 3 years of college education. She comments:

It seems very appealing to go to Canada when you are in other countries . . . for a Third World woman to go there—but in reality that structure is not well implemented. When you go there, you'll end up working for a family for 2 or 3 years, and if you are being exploited, you can't leave while applying for a change in status. So the employer has all of the control, because the worker will end up staying anyway.[28]

De Leon knows that she is lucky not to be speaking from the experience of being trapped as a live-in caregiver in Canada. Although some aspects of her initial experiences in the U.S. were very similar, she not only was able to escape these exploitative situations, but is now organizing women like her to mobilize against the common abuses they face.

De Leon says that although the U.S. has no program like the Canadian LCP, it has a formal legal structure for au pairs who are usually young students from Europe. She says employers can hire them through agencies and arrange for them to have connections to church and school here. She also emphasizes that these "young students are treated very well and respected for what they do, compared to immigrant women who work as professional nannies." Third World women working for corporate executives do not get working permits. De Leon says, "You just get a visa that is tied to an employer." She had a contract to work as a live-in nanny for a family; her working papers described her as a "personal servant to American family." She added, "I really hated that because it sounded like back in the days when women and men are being brought here from Africa against their will and became enslaved. To me, *servant* means *slave*, and I'm certainly not one." She started working a few months after arrival in the New York City suburb of Ardsley. The people and weather appeared strange. Her job conditions were "a nightmare—I did everything from waking up the children, giving them breakfast, walking the dog, shoveling the snow, and cleaning the house." She worked from 6:30 A.M. to 9 P.M. 6 days a week. After a year, she asked for another day off after noting that others had 2 days off. Her employer, who worked for Philip Morris Corporation, said that he had seen that the common practice in Hong Kong was only one day off and refused her request on that basis.

She took the initiative to call the labor department to find out about the minimum wage and overtime pay and asked her employer to adjust her salary. Again, her employer said that the contract they signed was based on earnings in Hong Kong. De Leon pointed out that she could not support herself on those wages. When she asked for overtime, saying she understood the law limited the workday to 8 hours, her employers demanded to know where she got the information. After telling them that her source was the labor department, they still refused, then gave her a $25 raise. De Leon calculated that her earnings after the raise amounted to $2 an hour when the minimum wage was $4. After that, she decided that she wanted to leave, but met the typical tactics of exploitative household employers:

> When I told them that I'd rather leave, they said I couldn't break the contract. I said that in a contract, either party can break the contract if you are not happy, so I'm giving you 2 weeks' notice. They insisted that I couldn't do it, and tried to manipulate me, asking where I was going, if I was going back to my country. To me, that's an implication that I was going to starve! I told her that it's none of her business.

Ultimately de Leon decided to stay because she signed a contract to work for 2 years—"the reality is that I felt I was legally trafficked." She remarks that women who are brought here by executives or diplomats have no way to network with others and no assistance from employers to find a community. Instead, she observes, workers are discouraged from meeting others and deliberately isolated in the suburbs, where they had no contact with other nannies, not even in the park. She adds that, "Without other people giving me support, I decided to stay and finish my contract and just survive," recalling that this also happened to her in Hong Kong. She was finally able to leave and find a live-out job from 11 A.M. to 7 P.M. that allowed her to start going to the park:

> That's when I realized that in this industry the majority of workers are women from the Third World. I met other domestic workers from all over the Third World. I realized that these conditions were widespread, whether you were from Indonesia, Malaysia, Philippines, Barbados, Guyana, Trinidad, most domestic workers face long hours, low wages, and isolation, and lack of control of our living and working conditions. Labor laws are not enforced in this industry. And labor laws simply do not protect our basic human rights to decent housing, food, shelter, and livable wages. And many laws, like those protecting workers against discrimination in the workplace, including sexual harassment and racism, specifically exclude domestic workers.

De Leon recalls many accounts of women who were subject to abuse and exploitation, worked long hours even when they were sick, and were forced to terminate pregnancies. After 7 years, she met people from CAAAV when they were handing out fliers in the park. De Leon approached them, "they took my number, and the next week I met with them and ended up going to weekly meetings."

Now, de Leon leads the Women Workers Project, which holds monthly meetings to improve working and living conditions among women in the domestic work industry. The project members began drafting standard guidelines and a pay scale to make recommendations for how much should be paid per child, for housekeeping tasks, etc.:

> We started looking at the industry, and realized that we had to be strategic about it, doing outreach with women from other ethnicities, and women really embraced it. We did a survey in 2000 in parks, indoor playgrounds, train stations, to see the conditions of women—who gets minimum wage, overtime pay, sick days, holidays. One woman who was being sponsored was forced to work 6 days a week, over 65 hours. She wanted to have one day to go to church. She started asking and showing papers from the labor department, and her employers were furious. Employers will try all their ways to not follow the regulations.

De Leon remarks on the lack of regulation of the industry: "We're not even protected from sexual harassment or any other abuses." Moreover, she notes that employers try many different tactics, including using race to divide household workers. For example, they make comparisons and say women from the Philippines are "better than from other countries, to create tensions between workers." They also "discriminate against us because of race, language, and immigration status."

Domestic Workers United, a project sponsored by CAAAV and Andolan, a South Asian workers' group, is pushing now for legislation that de Leon's group drafted. Led by a steering committee composed mostly of women from the Caribbean, the group used their research to design a standard contract and approached the New York City Council to pass a new law regulating the industry. Essentially, the law will regulate the Department of Consumer Affairs, the agency that licenses employment agencies recruiting and placing domestic workers. Seventy-five percent of domestic workers get their jobs through such agencies. The agencies should serve to protect these workers' rights, yet, de Leon says, when a worker has an abusive employer and calls her agency, "they advise you to stay for at least 3 or 4 months because they want to receive their fees from the employers." Otherwise, the agency will have to give the money back to the employer or provide another employee without a fee. De Leon explains, "What we are asking for is a code of conduct, so that the agency provides a contract with your work conditions, including minimum wage, 2 weeks' paid vacation, etc. and the agency should enforce it."[29]

The group introduced the bill in March 2002 and provided supporting testimony at a hearing in May with the chair of the committee on labor. Supporters like Councilwoman Gail Brewer said the bill should have been easy to pass because it involved no cost to the city. The group staged a city-wide action on October 5, 2002, starting with a rally at Washington Square Park, followed by a march to City Hall. Participants wore yellow rubber gloves and aprons, just as they did when they introduced the bill. Media coverage surpassed their expectations: although the turnout for the action was strong at 500, the press coverage put the numbers above 1000.[30]

De Leon reflects on the Women Workers' Project and the demands of the bill. She also describes the nature of her organization's work and, more broadly, the movement she is helping build. The measure is in some ways modest and yet revolutionary:

The bill is very basic—how we should be treated, working conditions, minimum wage, overtime pay, legal holidays and sick days—but really, we want to turn the industry upside down and change the notions that immigrant workers are lazy and uneducated. Because it relates to history, because this country inherited this industry through American slavery and ideas that this is women's work, etc. We're calling for respect and recognition for women in this industry.

De Leon says the group continues to wait patiently for a meeting on the bill with the Department of Consumer Affairs but will stage another action if necessary. In the meantime, her project offers an immigrant rights law clinic through New York University students working with CAAAV to provide advice on negotiating with employers and maneuvering the health care system. The project also provides courses for nannies on child care, psychology, and cardiopulmonary resuscitation training leading to Red Cross certification.[31]

Similarly, while the PWC in Vancouver pursues its long-term campaign to dismantle the LCP, its members work to build the movement for immigrant workers' rights in Canada every day in myriad ways.

For example, the PWC has rented a house for use as a drop-in center for members who yearn for camaraderie and some comforting elements of Philippine culture. Cecilia Diocson, founding chairperson and director, describes how the center serves as a place for women to congregate, eat, and talk with women in similar situations:

The women started to educate each other, bringing their stories to discuss at the center. We have had a lot of successes in making these women more assertive in their employers' homes after gathering these stories over food. They report having to pay for their own room and board, sleeping in the garage without heat, and being "shared" by two employers. They say, "It's like being in prison from Monday through Friday." The majority work 14 to 16 hours and are underpaid. We found out that they are getting underfed too. They want rice at least twice a day, but lots of white employers don't eat rice, just pasta and potatoes. The regulars on Friday afternoon would be rushing to the kitchen, saying "I'm so hungry. I haven't had rice all week." They could hardly work because they were so hungry.

Clearly, the drop-in center provides more than a refuge for hungry workers. It serves as a space for these women to build a community base from which to organize. The effectiveness of the other work of the PWC is closely tied to this base, as much of it evolves from participatory research and is advanced through popular education including cultural events and political theater. The center has been able to conduct longitudinal studies, following women through 8- to 10-year time spans, to document the segregation and lack of mobility Filipinas face in the labor market in Canada.

The most recent research relates to the way the increasing number of Filipinas who enter Canada via the LCP led to growth over the past 20 years of the mail-order bride industry—"another category of slave," as Diocson says. The PWC also plans to launch a women's studies program with guest lecturers at the center for women who cannot afford to attend universities.[32]

At a recent international women's conference, Diocson presented an analysis of global migration and particularly the cases of Filipina women forced to migrate to Canada in the context of global capitalism. Her cogent analysis, both as a trained nurse who migrated from the Philippines and as a radical political organizer, is one of the most well-articulated analyses I have encountered in a variety of contexts. She commented about the LCP:

> Instead of instituting a universal day care system to address the needs of women who are leaving the home to join the workplace, the Canadian state's response to this economic restructuring is to import cheap but highly educated and relatively skilled foreign domestic workers. This confers several advantages both to the Canadian state and Canadians who can afford a foreign domestic worker. . . . [T]he Canadian state earns revenue through the processing of migration documents and taxation of these foreign domestic workers. . . . [F]oreign domestic workers help provide a stable base of cheap "reserve army of labor" that keeps wages down and ensures continuous accumulation of capital. . . . Thus, the foreign domestic worker is functional to the maintenance of the existing capitalist system in Canada. On the other side of the ledger, the

sending country also benefits much from its export of foreign domestic workers.[33]

In my experience, Third World women migrant workers have always been many steps ahead of us in formulating and articulating these analyses of globalization, perhaps because of its direct and dire impacts on the conditions of these women's lives. They have much at stake to develop strategies to resist these conditions effectively, and it is only fitting that those who have suffered first and worst under globalization will lead the way out from under its oppressive forces. The women of the Workers' Voices Coalition, the PWC, Domestic Workers United, and many other grassroots organizations are doing revolutionary work in the face of what they all know is surely not new under globalization. They remind us through their fierce struggles and sharp analyses that they will revolutionize not only their work force and their adopted societies, but the antiglobalization movement itself.

ACKNOWLEDGMENTS

Portions of this [reading] are reprinted from Chang, G., "The Global Trade in Filipina Workers," in *Dragon Ladies: Asian American Feminists Breathe Fire*, South End Press, Boston, 1997, p. 132; Chang, G., *Disposable Domestics: Immigrant Women Workers in the Global Economy*, South End Press, Boston, 2000, p. 123.

NOTES

1. "Globalization's Inability to Create Jobs Fuels Mass Migration: ILO Chief," *Tehran Times*, June 13, 2002.
2. Nishioka, J., "Marriage by Mail: The Internet Makes It Easier for Potential Mates to Connect Across Seas," *AsianWeek*, July 29, 1999. [Cherry Blossoms is identified by all but Krosky as an international mail-order bride business.]
3. KPFA Radio, Morning Show with host Andrea Lewis, International Women's Day Program, 2001, guests: Grace Chang and Ethel Long Scott.
4. See "Third World Within" cited in *CAAAV Voice*, Special Issue on Women, Race and Work, Vol. 10, Fall 2000, p. 17. Cindy Domingo, founder of the Workers' Voices Coalition, in her call for seizing the moment after the Battle at Seattle, 1999, said: "We saw the profound deterioration in the conditions of immigrant and women workers worldwide as a direct result of free trade policies, globalization and privatization. In the United States, immigrant workers have become scapegoats for the failures of the global economy because U.S. workers don't see their interests as one and the same with workers in Latin America, Asia or Africa. The WTO coming to our city gave us a once-in-a-lifetime opportunity to draw links between conditions faced by working people in developing countries and those faced by immigrants and people of color in the United States," cited by Joy, K., in "Gender, Immigration and the WTO," *Network News*, Winter 2000, p. 12.
5. Testimony of representative of the International Organization of Prostitutes, Gabriela Workshop, September 3, 1995.
6. See Sandrasagra, M. J., "Globalisation Heightening Gender Inequalities," IPS, October 10, 2000; Tauli-Corpuz, V., "Asia-Pacific Women Grapple with Financial Crisis and Globalisation," Roundtable Discussion on the Economic, Social, and Political Impacts of the Southeast Asian Financial Crisis, Manila, April 12–14, 1998, and Rural and Indigenous Women Speak Out on the Impact of Globalisation, Chiangmai, Thailand, May 22–25, 1998.

7. Testimony of Cenen Bagon, "Voices of Working Women," Proceedings of "Beyond the WTO: Conference on Women and Immigration the Global Economy" organized by North-west Labor and Employment Law Office (LELO) and Workers' Voice Coalition, Seattle, Washington, December 4, 1999, p. 16.

8. See Chang, G., "The Global Trade in Filipina Workers," in *Dragon Ladies: Asian American Feminists Breathe Fire*, South End Press, Boston, 1997, p 132; Chang, G., *Disposable Domestics: Immigrant Women Workers in the Global Economy*, South End Press, Boston, 2000, p. 123.

9. Filipino Nurses Support Group, "Contextualizing the Presence of Filipino Nurses in BC," in *Advancing the Rights and Welfare of Non-Practicing Filipino and Other Foreign-Trained Nurses*," proceedings of national consultation for Filipino and other foreign-trained nurses, December 7–9, 2001. The Philippines Department of Labor and Employment estimates that about 2748 Filipinos leave the country daily.

10. This number does not include women who are trafficked, illegally recruited, or migrate for marriage or students and tourists who eventually become undocumented workers. Data compiled by Kanlungan Center Foundation from Philippine Overseas Employment Administration and Department of Labor and Employment statistics, 1995; Vincent, I., "Canada Beckons Cream of Nannies: Much-Sought Filipinas Prefer Work Conditions," *Globe and Mail*, January 20, 1996, p. A1. Other authors more extensively address trafficking in women for the sex, entertainment, and mail-order bride industries. See Rosca, N., "The Philippines' Shameful Export," *Nation*, April 17, 1995, p. 523; Kim, E., "Sex Tourism in Asia: A Reflection of Political and Economic Equality," *Critical Perspectives of Third World America*, 2, Fall 1984, p. 215; Blitt, C., producer, "Sisters and Daughters Betrayed: The Trafficking of Women and Girls and the Fight to End It," Video, Global Fund for Women.

11. Testimony of Pamela, "Filipino Nurses Doing Domestic Work in Canada: A Stalled Development," Philippine Women Centre of British Columbia, March 2000, p. 20.

12. Philippine Overseas Employment Administration, 2000, bulatlat.com.

13. Presentation by Ethel Farrales, Filipino–Canadian Youth Alliance, Vancouver, "Link Arms, Raise Fists: U.S. Out of the Philippines Now!" North American Conference, July 6–7, 2002.

14. Comments of youth member of Overseas Filipino Workers' Organization, Vancouver, "Link Arms, Raise Fists: U.S. Out of the Philippines Now!" North American Conference, San Francisco, July 6–7, 2002.

15. Philippine Women Centre of British Columbia, "Filipino Nurses Doing Domestic Work in Canada: A Stalled Development," Vancouver, March 2000, p. 10.

16. Ibid., p. 16.

17. Ibid., p. 11.

18. Diocson, C., Philippine Women Centre of British Columbia, Vancouver, phone interview, August 2002.

19. Statement of Sheila Farrales, "The Use of Filipino Nurses in the Scheme to Privatize Health Care," Conference Proceedings: Advancing the Rights and Welfare of Non-Practicing Filipino and Other Foreign-Trained Nurses, Filipino Nurses' Support Group, Burnaby, British Columbia, December 7–9, 2001, p. 51.

20. Testimony of Pamela, "Filipino Nurses Doing Domestic Work in Canada: A Stalled Development," Philippine Women Centre of British Columbia, March 2000, p. 19.

21. Ibid., p. 20.

22. Ibid., p. 29.

23. Statement of Sheila Farrales, ibid.

24. Statement of Gemma Gambito, ibid., p. 61.

25. Statement of Lynn Farrales, ibid., p. 42.

26. Ibid.

27. Philippine Women Centre of British Columbia, "Filipino Nurses Doing Domestic Work in Canada: A Stalled Development," March 2000, p. 7.

28. De Leon, C., Women Workers Project, CAAAV, Bronx, NY, phone interview, September 2002.

29. De Leon, C., Women Workers Project, CAAAV, Bronx, NY, phone interviews, September 2002 and February 2003.

30. Alapo, L., "Bill to Protect Domestic Workers," *Newsday*, March 25, 2002; Greenhouse, S., "Wage Bill Would Protect Housekeepers and Nannies," *New York Times*, March 25, 2002; Richardson, L., "A Union Maid? Actually a Nanny, Organizing," *New York Times*, April 4, 2002; Ginsberg, A., "Nannies March for Fair Pay, OT," *Daily News*, October 6, 2002; Ramirez, M., "Domestic Workers Seek Wage, Personal Protection," *Newsday*, October 6, 2002; Geron, T., "All in a Day's Work," *AsianWeek*, July 11, 2002; Lee, C., "Revolt of the Nannies," *Village Voice*, March 9, 2002.

31. De Leon, C., Women Workers Project, CAAAV, Bronx, NY, phone interview, September 2002.

32. Diocson, C., Philippine Women Centre of British Columbia, phone interview, August 2002.

33. Diocson, C., "Forced Migration: Perpetuation of Underdevelopment," paper presented at Ninth International Forum, Association for Women's Rights in Development, Guadalajara, Mexico, October 3–6, 2002.

Gendered Selves and Identities of Information Technology Professionals in Global Software Organizations in India

First published in 2006

INTRODUCTION

The increased interconnection between globalizing influences and "personal dispositions" or identity-related aspects of individuals such as their beliefs, thoughts, and feelings is a distinctive feature of contemporary life (Castells, 1996; Giddens, 1991). In today's society, globalized work contexts, such as global software organizations (GSOs) are on the rise (Sahay, Nicholson, & Krishna, 2003). Engaged in knowledge/intensive software development work across boundaries of time, space, and place, GSOs employ programmers, designers, analysts, and managers, who are also called IT (information technology) professionals/knowledge workers who design, develop, test, and implement software (Nicholson & Sahay, 2004). In this way, GSOs include local "actors" as well as global elements and exemplify the interconnection between selves and identities of IT workers within volatile, turbulent technological and business market contexts (D'Mello, 2005; Sahay et al., 2003). (The term *local* broadly refers to the immediate context of one's sociocultural milieu within a particular geographical boundary. The term *global* refers to that which spans across diverse geographical boundaries as well as boundaries of time, space, and place. See D'Mello, 2005, for an elaboration of these concepts).

Viewed as "both a model of and a model for globalization" (Sahay et al., 2003, p. 2), the ever-changing "corporate ecology" of such contexts challenges traditional and stable self and identity constructs as well as sociocultural gendered norms and relations, influencing behavior of people in these settings. These aspects are important to analyze for several reasons.

First, while IT work is on the rise across the globe, there is an IT staff shortage, worldwide (Igbaria & Shayo, 2004). Global software organizations, for example, struggle daily with issues of attracting and retaining IT professionals. Second, women, in particular, while constituting 50% of the global population, constitute about 25% of the global IT workforce despite government- and industry-backed efforts to attract them into these fields (Klawe & Levenson, 1995; Panteli, Stack, & Ramsay, 1999; Trauth, Nielsen, & Von Hellens, 2003). These skewed percentages suggest that in terms of women's participation, the IT workforce is missing a significant number of potentially valuable human resources for the information age. Third, "feminine" or "relational" strengths such as intuition, empathy, relationship building, and collaboration skills are now assets in instrumental, "masculine" organizational contexts such as IT companies, for gaining a competitive edge in the global economy (Fletcher, 1994; Fletcher, 1998; D'Mello, 2005; Olsson & Walker, 2004). Such skills are particularly valuable in ICT-mediated distributed work teams or virtual teams involving "boundaryless collaboration" where work is increasingly coordinated through trust-based relationships (Sahay et al., 2003).

Finally, GSOs, like other global organizations, are locally situated and are sites that are embedded in " . . . relational hierarchies of gender, class, caste and other critical fault lines, which define identities and distribute power both symbolically and materially" (Rao & Kellner, 2003, p. 143). Offshore software development work is highly interactive, situated within broader social and organizational processes that shape and are shaped by human action (Nicholson & Sahay, 2004; Waterson, Clegg, & Axtell, 1997). Studying these processes within GSOs enables us to understand how *local* characteristics of a specific social context (e.g., gender relations) intersect with *global* imperatives to influence work as well as employees' sense of self and identity. . . .

Global software organizations in India are situated within a global capitalist economy, representing new forms of work contexts, while simultaneously incorporating local social structures and meanings. A micro-level analysis of how individual workers make personal interpretations in relation to social structures such as gender enables a deeper articulation of the global–local dialectic. There is a need for more micro-level analysis into local meanings and interpretations of larger social structures related to gender, and their interrelation with selves and identities of IT workers. . . .

Using a "gender lens," two questions in the context of GSOs are addressed in this article:

- How is gender expressed or played out in GSOs in India as a work setting?
- How do these expressions relate to self and identity constructions of male and female IT professionals employed in the GSO?. . .

SELF, IDENTITY, AND GENDER IN THE CONTEXT OF GLOBAL SOFTWARE ORGANIZATIONS

Gender-Related Processes in the Context of Global Software Organizations

Examining gender-related identity connections is relevant in the context of GSOs as work settings for several reasons: . . . underrepresentation of women in the IT workforce, mobility restrictions for women IT professionals in GSOs, and gendering of GSO-related work.

Underrepresentation of women in the IT workforce. Women account for 25% of technology workers in the European workforce and about 20% in the U.S. technology workforce —and these percentages are shrinking (Ahuja, 2002; Maitland, 2001; Nierderman & Mandviwalla, 2004). In India, within GSOs in the IT industry, women comprise 24% of the workforce (NASSCOM, 2005). Information technology professionals are typically drawn from engineering and computer science disciplines that are . . . male-dominated (Von Hellens, Nielsen, & Trauth, 2001). In the US and UK, the proportion of women in university computer studies courses is declining and this pattern carries over into organizations recruiting staff from these institutions (Ahuja, 2002; Von Hellens, Nielsen, & Beekhuyzen, 2004). Educational and training institutions in these disciplines exert a strong influence on gender-related constructions by gender segregation of courses, presence of role models or mentors for women, messages about IT as a "male domain" (Didio, 1996; Trauth, 2002; Turkle, 1988). . . . These influences and images, along with family and cultural messages reinforce, support, or resist the choice of IT as a career choice for women. They affect feelings of inclusion and exclusion, self-confidence or alienation among women as IT professionals, shaping their identities and impacting their participation in the industry (Ahuja, 2002; Trauth, 2002; Von Hellens et al., 2004).

Mobility of GSO work and mobility restrictions on women. A critical feature of GSOs as a work setting is its mobility. Individuals, teams, organizations, and nations with diverse social and cultural backgrounds and idiosyncratic styles of work, interact in a global setting across temporal and spatial boundaries (Sahay et al., 2003). Information technology employees are required to consistently work late hours because of diverse time zones, tight project schedules often in a crisis mode, rapidly switching between projects, technologies, and countries. Promotional and growth paths require experience in customer facing roles, relating to working and living overseas. Reflecting the volatile changes in technologies and platforms in the global marketplace, this work demands, on a constant basis, continuous updating of knowledge and skills, besides a formal education in engineering or IT fields. This puts pressure on IT workers to be in a continuous learning mode all the time to be "marketable," both within and outside the organization. These features are enormously stressful for all employees, often resulting in burnout and feelings of insecurity and anxiety (Igbaria & Shayo, 2004; Moore, 2000), impacting IT professionals at deep, existential levels (D'Mello, 2005).

The mobile nature of GSO work influences the participation of men and women differently (Kelkar et al., 2002; Suriya, 2003). Mobility restrictions for women are expressed in their inability to continuously work long hours, travel overseas on assignments, participate in informal networks that are important in career advancement or have a sustained career trajectory (Ahuja, 2002; Ragins & Cotton, 1991). In this profession, shifting between companies especially at lower levels is a means to progress one's career but women tend to stay longer in each job compared to men because of domestic responsibilities (Kelkar et al., 2002). While this is an advantage for them at the time of recruitment, it delays their promotion and their capacity to negotiate for a higher salary or benefits and stock options. The dominant model of career growth require linearity and continuity in work (Papanek, 1973) and career interruptions because of childcare commitments are found to disadvantage women (Sirianni & Negrey, 2000). Not surprisingly, internationally, the majority of women are employed in routine and specialist work while men are engaged in analytical and managerial activities (Ahuja, 2002). . . .

Gendering of GSO-related work. . . . Software development lies within a project-based competitive environment which is said to breed and reproduce a "masculine culture" (Knights & Murray, 1994). Similarly, . . . Panteli et al. (1999) propose that the It industry is not neutral and does little to promote or retain its female workforce. They highlight the following issues in IT companies: While women were underrepresented at managerial and technical levels, they predominated in support function roles; women were often assigned routine and monotonous tasks while their male colleagues engaged in more abstract and challenging computing work; women's earnings differential in relation to men increased with age; companies treated IT staff as homogenous with similar needs and career aspirations; gender stereotypes about men's and women's qualities persisted and home working and flexi-time arrangements for women were talked about but not implemented. They stated that women who may dislike masculine, "lad" or computing, "engineering" type cultures, may

decide to leave a company or exclude themselves from a technical field. . . .

Such experiences and barriers generate feelings relating directly to self-confidence, occupational worth, and self-esteem (Evetts, 1996). They marginalize not only women, but also reinforce entrenched gendered stereotypes about masculinity and femininity, even going against business interests. More and more, theories of organizational learning and management stress the value of affective and relational capacities such as empathy, sensitivity to emotional contexts, collaboration, also called "soft skills" to organizational productivity and efficiency (Gilleard & Gilleard, 2002; Senge, 1990). Research in intercultural adjustment and cross-cultural effectiveness (Kealey, 1990; Mendenhall & Oddou, 1985; Parker & McEvoy, 1993) support the view that empathy, relational and communication skills, associated with women and enacted in the private, home sphere, facilitate adjustment and interaction with host country nationals, the global actors in GSOs. Such skills are also increasingly critical in distributed software development work where knowledge demands are quite distinctive and embedded in social structures and relations (Kealey, 1990; Nicholson & Sahay, 2004; Sahay et al., 2003). In this way, the inclusion of women and the creation of gender-sensitive workspaces not only impact individual workers but also add value to the effectiveness of "faceless" teams.

In summary, GSOs, as ICT-mediated global work settings, embedded in local contexts, are not gender-neutral entities but actively reproduce sociocultural complexities of these contexts through their material practices and ideological constructions. These relate directly to individual workers' feelings of self-worth and esteem, their conceptions of masculine and feminine and their participation in the workforce. Women's underrepresentation and relative immobility as compared to male IT workers, point to masculinity and patriarchal norms underlying these settings. . . .

Sociocultural Context of Information Technology Professionals in India

India presents a valuable case of an economically developing country in the midst of globalization processes such as liberal economic reforms and changes in the mass media, among other dynamics, which has affected primarily the middle class (Singh,

2000). Globally considered a force to reckon with in the field of IT, this sector is the fastest growing industry within the country. The industry's contribution to India's gross domestic product (GDP) has nearly tripled, from 1.2% in 1998 to 3.5% in 2004 (NASSCOM, 2005). While there are over 1 million workers in the IT and IT-enabled services (ITES) industry today,[1] 345,000 IT professionals are employed in the software export sector (NASSCOM, 2005), which constitutes the work context for GSOs.

As in other countries, women are underrepresented in the IT industry in India (24% are women). Furthermore, most women in the Indian IT workforce are reported to be less than 30 years of age, overrepresented in lower-level jobs like programming and underrepresented in higher-level jobs like consulting and project management (Kelkar et al., 2002; Suriya, 2003). Reinforcing this pattern, the ratio of men to women dramatically shifts to 31:69 in the ITES, considered more "low-end" work in terms of skills and competence (NASSCOM, 2005).

Physical and career-related mobility restrictions exist for educated, women workers typically hailing from middle class families in India. Historically, education in India for girls was viewed as a potential liability in the marriage market as an agent that could "spoil a girl's character" (Chanana, 1994). While there are shifts, fears persist particularly in the field of science and engineering. For women particularly, marriage potential and social risks form key elements in family decisions about education as parents focus primarily on getting their daughters well-settled in a good marriage alliance (Mukhopadhyay, 1994). Social risks include traveling or living alone in hostels in urban areas and exposure to predominantly male peers where a girl's chastity may be jeopardized. Education, particularly in science and engineering, associated with critical and independent thinking and willingness to abandon outmoded traditions are the antithesis of the preferred stereotype of a "home-loving" patriarchal ideology for women (Mukhopadhyay, 1994). Family resources are invested more in the son's education as they are considered structurally and economically more central to the well-being of the family than daughters, who leave their natal family after marriage. Given these fears, bright and scientifically inclined daughters are encouraged to pursue medicine and pure sciences rather than engineering, reinforcing male dominance in these areas. In urban work settings, while desk jobs are considered more

reputable for women, their physical and social mobility is restricted (Arun & Arun, 2001). For example, in Mumbai city, a major base for software outsourcing, several IT companies are located at Santacruz Electronics Exports Processing Zone (SEEPZ[2]), in the north of the city. Here, transport connections are infrequent after office hours and the surrounding industrial area is considered unsafe for women after dark. The location of the office and commute time is a high priority for women who have domestic responsibilities in selecting a job, hence, the location restricts their options, unlike men. Finding it hard to juggle a myriad of job expectations and familial commitments, women often quit working, as part-time employment or telecommuting facilities in this industry are rare in Mumbai.

Typically, for Indian women, marriage and motherhood is most often assumed to have direct implications for their jobs and career (Aziz, 2004). A strong belief in India is that marriage and family forms the second stage of human existence in society, *grihasthashram*[3] (Chakraborty, 2000). Marriage rites symbolize the union of man and woman, two bodies in one soul, as opposed to the idea of a civil contract (Cormack, 1974). A married woman is expected to deeply identify with her husband and family. In Indian thought, wifehood and motherhood are seen as inseparable, sacred, and conferring social status and psychological security to women (Coomaraswamy, 1924). Some traditional terms for women such as *grihalakshmi*,[4] *dharmapatni*[5] are directly connected to the stage of *grihasthashram*. In the process of growth and development, the quality and meaning of relationships becomes a dominant anchor of the life-role of Indian women particularly when they take on prescriptive roles of daughter, wife, daughter-in-law, and mother (Parikh & Garg, 1989). For males, on the other hand, while marriage is important in *grihasthashram*, it is an event that typically does not effect a major shift in their domestic responsibilities, change of residence or location or job.

Indian feminists and scholars show how cultural and social values emphasizing female submissiveness and role-specific identities keep contemporary middle class, urban India families anchored in traditional patriarchal structures (Bagchi, 1995; Dube, 1988; Kakar, 1988). Studies also indicate that women experience the achievements of others such as their husband's good job or children's school success as their own (Kapadia, 1999), highlighting that for Indian women, the family and relationships with significant others are a critical source of self-worth and identity. The strong influence of family identity, where the "breadwinner" position of the man predominates and commands respect, makes it difficult for women to formulate a clear notion of her individual position or welfare (Sen, 1990, 2000).

Software development has been reported to offer a more relaxed and less discriminatory environment as compared to several other employment options in India (Heeks, 1998). Other jobs, such as mechanical or civil engineering involve outdoor, physical labor or commutes to relatively uninhabited localities are viewed as relatively unsuitable and unsafe for women, both physically and socially. Currently, working in the IT industry in India presents a possibility that lies at the intersection of the masculinized discipline of engineering and the "high-flying" world of global, international assignments similar, in some instances to knowledge-based work of the consulting service industry. Some structural changes are evident. Women's enrollment in undergraduate courses in engineering and technology has increased from 0.09% in 1971 to 10% in 1991 (Chanana, 2000). Unlike the figures in developed countries, the percentage of women's enrollment in science subjects in colleges and universities in India has increased from about 7% in 1950–1951 to about 34% in 1996–1997, and subsequently to 39.4% in 2001 (Chanana, 2000; Indian National Science Academy, 2004). This increase has been attributed to the prestige of science and engineering degrees and jobs in the country. The image of an IT person in India is very different from the "nerdy" image or fears of "gender inauthenticity" as mentioned in the literature. The risks of higher education are balanced by the social status associated with this profession. In social gatherings and family groups, IT people are often labeled as "smart," the "cream of society," "moneyed," and "well traveled." Also, spurred by rising housing costs in urban areas and middle class aspirations for an upward mobile lifestyle, there is an increased interest in having an earning-working woman as a wife. For urban middle class families in particular having an earning daughter or daughter-in-law doing a respectable job is seen as a positive asset. These shifts coexist with traditional norms such as fears about women's safety and sexuality, which are reportedly common in patriarchal societies like India (Sonpar & Kapur, 2001). Rather than a complete break with traditional restrictions on women's mobility, these changes

can be seen as a midpoint on a continuum ranging from extreme tradition to modern, Westernized notions of equality.

To summarize, gender relations are framed within distinctive sociocultural contexts, constituting integral elements of individuals' selves and identities. These relations and ideologies directly influence the participation of men and women IT professionals within work contexts of GSOs. Global software organization work is mobile and fluid, yet women experience many restrictions on their mobility in this workspace. While software work in the IT industry reflects a masculine culture, increasingly, the skills emphasized for business success in such global contexts, are feminine. In the Indian context, while traditional gendered norms still hold sway among the middle classes, globalization influences have triggered shifts not only in lifestyles but also challenged these norms and structures. Given the peculiar nature of social relations in the Indian context, we adopt the conceptualization of the "autonomous-relational" self (Kagitcibasi, 1996) as an analytic tool, to deepen our understanding of the relationship between gender and the self.

Kagitcibasi (1996) proposed that each individual has a relational (interdependent) as well as autonomous (independent) self in a "dialectic mutuality" or coexistence of opposites. These "selves" are embedded within gender role definitions internalized during socialization practices from childhood, impacting lifelong construction and enactment of women's and men's identities and organizing behavior and affecting self-esteem (Kapadia, 1999; Sonpar & Kapur, 2001). In most societies, women learn to define themselves in relation to and connection with others, in specific contexts, whereas men, socialized towards separation and individuation are encouraged to be rational, strong, and self-reliant (Chodorow, 1978; Gilligan, 1982; Miller, 1986). An emphasis on the role of mothering for women, places an "ethics of care" and nurturance deep in their "relational self" serving familial as well as social ends (Chodorow, 1978; Gilligan, 1982; Guzder & Krishna, 1991). For men, an emphasis on the provider role embeds an instrumental orientation and the "ethics of justice" in their "autonomous self." The coexistence of these selves within individuals implies that individuals can demonstrate both agency and relatedness (Kagitcibasi, 1996). In this article, I use the relational-autonomous self concept within the context of GSOs as a structuring device (Walsham, 2001) to provide a richer understanding of the linkages between gender norms and selves and identities of Indian IT professionals in GSOs.

METHODOLOGY

My case study InSync Ltd.[6] is a medium-sized GSO, headquartered in Mumbai, India, with offices in six different countries across the globe. InSync offers offshore software application outsourcing solutions and services to overseas clients. It has been accredited internationally at Level 5 for software processes as per the Capability Maturity Model (CMM). It employs around 2500 IT professionals. The men to women ratio among software staff is 82:18. Support functions, except for human relations (HR) and public relations (PR) are primarily staffed by male employees. The secretarial staff is 100% female.

The empirical material in this article is drawn from a larger research project on under-standing identity-related processes of IT professionals employed in GSOs in India. A case study method, based on an interpretative, ethnographic approach to information science (IS) research is used (Walsham, 1993). In stark contrast to positivist methods that look for regularities and causal relationships (Burrell & Morgan, 1979) the interpretive paradigm assumes that the social world is constructed and relativistic, understood as a subjective experience of those who are involved in its activities. An ethnographic approach seems appropriate to the study of identity processes because it remains close to ways people experience and make sense of themselves and others (Van Maanen, 1979). . . .

In-depth and semistructured interviews of 50 employees, between December 2002 and July 2004 were conducted. The respondents included 16 female and 34 males across the developer, module leader, project leader, project manager, and unit/function head job levels. Each interview typically lasted around 60–80 minutes. . . . Rather than a set interview protocol, a set of broad, open-ended questions relating to their career trajectory and their personal experiences at work and outside the work setting was used. Besides interview data, field notes, and observations from "hanging around" workstations, the cafeteria, commuting in the company bus to the office and back home, attending team and company gatherings, I reviewed some of the company's promotional material, Web site, intranet, in-house publication magazine, and annual reports. I also drew extensively on my experience in the various GSOs during my career as an HR professional for several years. . . .

Tape-recorded interviews were all transcribed verbatim. The empirical material, along with other data was read, reread, and analyzed for themes, subthemes, and patterns. Rather than some preconceived categorization, themes that emerged from the material were identified and data was manually sorted under these. Multiple perspectives from advisors, faculty, and interactions with others engaged in gender research, were solicited. Some of the interpretations were also informally discussed with select respondents. . . . The major themes are reported in the following section.

EMPIRICAL DATA AND ANALYSIS

In this section, the four themes that emerged from the empirical material are presented. . . .

The Marriage Mandate

The first theme relates to internalized norms and views on roles and responsibilities, particularly for married employees. Marriage is a critical event; it is a turning point in the lives of both Indian men and women but their salience differs. Echoing this, Soumya, a 26-year-old software developer, who quit InSync to join her husband who has a prestigious IT job in Europe, said in an e-mail interview:

> I was a girl from a moderately modern family. I never asked the question "Will I get married?" I realize that this point was certain. I WAS GOING TO GET MARRIED. I never saw anybody in my family/friend circle NOT MARRY except perhaps due to financial difficulty. As I grew up, I saw around me how important a man was, in order to live peacefully, to have certain "respectability" and social "acceptability" unlike a single woman. A single woman simply did not have enough means/outlets to go out and enjoy. So I got married. Similarly, I know I will have children some day.

Having been married for a year, and living in Europe, Soumya said,

> Initially, we were both very confident of me finding a job here. But jobs for foreigners are limited and I had to resign myself to be unemployed. Of course, it hurts . . . to have worked so hard at education, reading, practicing,

and updating knowledge all for cooking and cleaning? I now have to reconcile myself that I will never have the highflying career I dreamed of. . . . Whatever I do will be a supplement to my daily house keeping and the demands of my husband's job. Right now, I have not totally reconciled myself to this idea. But as things stand that is the only possibility.

Soumya's response suggests that marriage was experienced as culturally mandated. While it gave her social respectability and acceptability, the shifts it entailed generated strong emotions and a reconstruction of her professional identity to fit this relational choice.

Like Soumya there are other women in GSOs, often in their late 20s, from typically middle class backgrounds with computer science or engineering degrees or diplomas who marry and stop working partially or completely. During this time, they are fully immersed in household and family-related activities. When couples marry within the same company, the wife usually quits her job to join her husband at his location or shoulder family and childcare responsibilities, rather than the reverse. Their responses reflected ambivalence in these decisions, reflecting their dilemmas about domestic "bliss" that they aspired to as well as their compromise in relation to their professional achievement. Affirming this, Disha, one of the few senior women project managers in InSync said,

I have seen many young girls give up their career for marriage and babies. It is tough for women to manage both in this industry. One has to sacrifice a lot. I used to hold my baby in my hand and cry, thinking, how I will leave this baby and go to work after only 3 months maternity leave. It is a big challenge to manage because work pressures are tremendous. That is why many women fall back at senior levels. You can't be worrying about your babies when the customer is waiting at the other end for the system to be running.

While sharing about her responsibilities in her family comprising a husband in a senior job and young child, Leena, an assistant manager in the quality department said,

That is life—work and family. There are certain things that just don't bend. As an Indian, whoever's wife you are, whether it be the President's wife or peon's wife, there are certain activities you do like cooking food

for the family. You cannot put your feet up or buy food off the rack like the freedom that you have in Western countries. . . .

Organizing meals occupied a large share of domestic responsibilities of women respondents. Even though labor-saving devices and paid domestic help was available, it was still a time-consuming task. Several lunch table conversations with women employees often centered on issues of food preparation in the family. If men were present, they were silent on these matters as they said their wife or mother typically prepared their meals. Some women spoke about the help they received from their in-laws at home which enabled them to also have a career while married. Others spoke about the added responsibilities they had because they lived with their in-laws.

Having a spouse in the same company is common in GSOs. Maya, a project leader married to another project leader, Ramesh, in InSync, has two children. Living with his parents and unmarried brother, they were considering buying their own house. Responding to a question on managing household responsibility, Maya said,

We have the same educational qualifications and now are both project leaders. At one time, my salary was more than his. However, this does not change things at home, where I am responsible. Equality is somewhere in the air. I told my in-laws, that you have not trained your son to take up responsibility at home. It is the man's ego . . . if I expect him to serve food, for example, he will not do it everyday. Only when I say I am very much tired. They have grown up to think it is the woman. So even in the night he used to not get up to change the nappies of our son even though we both had similar work pressures. I used to feel bad and frustrated. I am now reconciled to dropping my expectations.

When responding to the same question, her husband, Ramesh said, "Yes, the mother surely has to take more responsibilities. I don't experience any conflict as the support of my parents and brother is always there." Several other respondents talked about their parents, unmarried siblings or in-laws as being available or willing to care for their children suggesting that while kinship support for family care is present, the primary responsibility is still with the wife.

From male respondents, and from conversations with IT employees, it appeared that men and women perceive work, marriage, and domestic responsibility differently. For many male respondents, the "bread-winner ideology" seemed to predominate, associated with a sense of certainty as reflected in the response of a project manager, Rakesh:

As an Indian male I am supposed to be the one earning the bread and butter. If I have to work for 12 hours a day I have to work, to earn the roti,[7] I have to work. If I am not able to come for your alana falana[8] stuff, I will not be apologetic about it or go back to my family and say, I am sorry I was not there, I was working.

The response of Isha, an unmarried woman in her late 20s and a module leader suggests that this provider role was seen as exclusive to males. Isha said,

In the UK, when I wanted to go bowling or play badminton which meant some expenditure, my male team members would say, "It is okay for you, you are a girl. You can spend money. You don't have to save for a family." This was upsetting. How do they know the real financial condition of my house? Luckily my dad is still working but I could well be the sole earning member.

When deeply internalized, the provider role can also be a source of stress among men. During the post September 11th period, when many lost their jobs in the US and returned back to India, feelings of low confidence and decreased self-worth were often clearly visible in the body language and limited salary negotiation of male candidates who interviewed with InSync suggesting the salience of work in the identity construction of males.

Field interviews, interviews of candidates, and informal conversations also revealed that while most men talked at length about their job responsibilities and their career aspirations, they were relatively silent on the organization of their domestic lives or duties. They would refer to "wanting to spend time playing with children or taking the family members out." Most women, on the other hand, spoke explicitly and at length about their husbands, children, and family responsibilities. The men's omission was not an effort to conceal their family life; it appears to reflect some taken-for-granted assumptions about domestic arrangements. The workspace also appeared to be a

space for expressing their masculinity. For example, Roshni, a software developer said,

In my project the initial period was very stressful. During this period, three teammates became fathers. On the face of it, they always complained about not being there for their wives. But I think, secretly they were very proud of the hard work they were doing. They wanted the fact recognized that they had put the project first, and were committed to on-time delivery of the project and were sitting night outs when their heavily pregnant wives waited at home. The team often boasted that we had tremendous difficulties during the delivery, and how the teammates put work first, etc. As a woman, I was often very troubled by this display because sometime in the vague future it could happen to me, i.e., my husband not being there for me.

Finally, presence of a supporting spouse is reported crucial for success and moving up the career ladder. Mohini, a senior project manager said, "Of course, the husband has to be supportive for women to succeed in this field. If both are running in different directions for their work, who is going to look after the family? One person's career would need to have more importance than the other."

A Woman's Place

This theme considers the relationship of gender with issues related to diverse mobilities and immobilities. One of the concerns of middle class parents was about job prospects for educated and particularly marriageable daughters. Soumya, a software developer stated, "I was allowed to study as much as I wanted but when it came to working . . . I would have to select something that my parents were reasonably comfortable with. It sounded safe and respectable to sit at the computer in an office." The concern with physical and social safety has been repeatedly mentioned by several respondents as why global, IT companies are preferred as work settings for women. . . .

Working late hours, often until midnight, as well as working on weekends, inevitable in this industry, emerged as very stressful for employees, especially given long commutes, humid weather, high pollution, bad roads, frequent traffic jams, and crowded public transport in Mumbai city. Commenting on this, Vanessa, a HR manager, said,

With women, the issue is magnified because of security and managing the home. Seniors, like project managers are generally protective and do not want women to sit late. In the project, the guys ensure the girls who are sitting late reach home safely. Some girls don't mind traveling alone. Facilities for transport for women working late, is pathetic. Only a few big companies provide it.

Sociocultural barriers to overseas travel are normal and, in the case of Zeenat, who is a Muslim, recently married, 26-year-old software developer, religious beliefs enter parental mandates. She said,

Nowadays many Muslim girls do go to colleges and schools so my parents were not too bothered about my late hours. But they raised a concern about me going onsite before marriage. It was not a personal concern. They were more concerned about what society would say. That if someone came with a proposal and came to know that I was onsite alone, they might object and that might be a problem to get married . . . My in-laws only concern is that I should not stay there alone if I am going long term. If I go, I must go with my husband. I don't want that he leaves a job for my sake and then he cannot find a job.

Zeenat expressed satisfaction with her current situation and said that she would tackle the issue about onsite postings when it came up.

Single women, who typically live with their parents, also report having domestic responsibilities, though they may not shoulder responsibilities of spouse and children. This can sometimes be experienced as a dilemma. For example, Deepali, an unmarried project manager in her mid-30s reported that she was seen by others as "footloose and fancy free" and available for work-related travels, as she was single. Although she had domestic responsibilities, it was hard to refuse onsite assignments that she did not want, as she did not have a valid excuse such as a spouse or children or in-law responsibilities, which many women her age have. Experiencing some feelings of guilt her responses suggest how strongly marriage and family is legitimized at the workplace.

Changes were also noted by respondents. Anita, a human resource manager at InSync said,

Earlier, women could not travel abroad because of their parents', husband's, or in-laws' disapproval.

Now, I see women wanting to go abroad, to make money, to be on par. This is more so in the younger generation and more so in single women. Those in their early 20s are now more go-getters, more trendy and westernized in their dress and behavior. And the money, opportunities, and success in this industry gives them a certain confidence.

The "Female Touch" at Work

This dimension relates to GSOs as a work setting, both socially and in terms of its family-related policies. Global software organizations reflect the gendered division of labor in some of their HR policies and practices. For example, maternity leave in GSOs in India is usually given only for 3 months as per statutory requirements. Human resource professionals report that GSOs with policies where such leave is officially longer are rare. In informal conversations, women stated that 3 months is too short and they usually seek an extension. The granting of such requests is handled on a case-to-case basis, depending upon the manager's discretion and the human resources department. This can be quite anxiety provoking for the woman employee who is then in a dilemma over losing her job versus not being available for her baby. Global software organizations typically do not have any official policy on paternity leave. Human resource personnel often receive appeals from new fathers to mandate paternity leave of some sort. They wanted to spend more time at home with their newborn but were unable to do so because of project pressures. One of the employees was upset because he was unable to witness the birth of his first child since he had been working in the office for a project "delivery." Policies like these (or lack of them) and such responses reinforce differential valuing by organizations of emotional and childcare labor and male instrumental labor. When there is less flexibility in policy implementation, the women employees are the most affected. . . .

Similarly, child-care facilities on or near office premises are most often absent, resulting in women quitting their jobs or take extended leave or depending on family support to tend to their children. . . .

Gender differences are also related to socialization and networking practices at InSync. In conversations with married women employees, they reported that while networking and socialization outside and within the office enhanced their career, they rarely did so as there was never enough time. Maya, a project leader said, "I don't network. I don't have time. My husband does it. I don't have a friends' group of my own. Sometimes, I don't call my mummy too. I get so focused on my work at home." Even while on the job, "there are some things that I just cannot do with my male colleagues," said Chitra, a project manager.

> For example, after some disagreement, one guy will come up to the next and slap him on the shoulder and say, 'let us go for a smoke.' *Jaise kandhe peh haath daal kar jaa sekte ho.*[9] It is amazing how many work-related matters are sorted out in chats in the 'smoking zone' and male banter. I can't do that and feel excluded as I don't smoke nor drink and I don't have that many female colleagues.

Affirming this another developer, Naina, who quit InSync and is now working in an IT company in Australia, said, "There is a disadvantage in terms of personal bonding with others since most of the men go out for Friday evening drinks here too, whereas women typically don't."

Managers, both male and female, said that overall, women software professionals are more committed, loyal, and sincere in their work. Women, they said, viewed things holistically "from all the stakeholders' perspectives." Furthermore, they made excellent project managers, even if their technical knowledge were lagging, as their interpersonal and team management skills were commendable. Because family was their major priority, they were not keen on job hopping or asking for onsite assignments. Also, they said that women employees added a "female touch" to the work environment, as women were more personal in their dealings as compared to men, who were seen as more professional. Another female manager while sharing her experience of this female touch working with an all-male team said, "While many interactions are easy, as a female boss I have to be careful about touch. With women, it is fine. With my male reportees, I feel awkward and hesitant and am very cautious not to give the wrong signal . . . like just wanting to put my hand on the arm of a team member who is feeling very low." Women have to negotiate these boundaries all the time. For example, jokes and humor is another arena where sexuality and masculinity can be expressed. Indu, a project leader said, "In teams 'non-veg' jokes ['dirty' jokes, derogatory to women] do get cracked but people see to it that you are not around especially if you are the boss. I get some of these jokes which are forwarded but just

delete them. It is easier to tell your junior about not talking about these jokes."

Making an observation about the different qualities women brought to her team, Sunaina, a developer said: "Women tend to behave a little gentler and often relax an atmosphere of stress. . . . Generally, during the end of a serious discussion, women often are instrumental in easing the tension a bit by cracking jokes or maybe just lightening up the mood. Men generally prefer discussing upcoming events with them. Team leaders generally allocate jobs like arranging for a birthday celebration, arranging a baby gift, chart-making for company competitions, articles for company magazine. . . . In all these women are actively encouraged." Her observation points to how the femininity of women is expressed and also reinforced by both men and women in work teams within the GSO.

At InSync, it was noted that male managers who were understanding and demonstrated good relational or "soft" skills were upheld as role models. Female managers, on the other hand, were expected to be automatically adept at this, suggesting that gender was produced by viewing these behaviors as intrinsic to female personhood. However, when these skills were not seen as embedded and appeared in a structured, quantifiable "hard" format within a competency framework for all employees, they were legitimized as neutral and made uniformly applicable, similar to technical skills. . . .

Overtime

This dimension related to how gender-related concerns shifted over the lifecycle of the individual worker. Emphasizing the different changes that marriage brings to male and female IT workers, Indu, a manager says,

> In IT, women concentrate on their work well especially in the first few years, in the 22 to 25 age range. After around 25, they get married. Then, the men start getting serious about work and women start getting serious about their household responsibilities and this can cause some unrest for women. Women are not free birds like men. As you grow in your career there are fewer options available for women because of the time constraints put on them.

The difference in perception of marriage and family, and their respective salience in social identity were reflected in how women and men talk in informal conversations at the workplace. For example, Rani, a 33-year-old unmarried project manager says, "Typically 90% of women at my level are married and their topics are around children, school, and studies. With males, these topics are rare. They speak of sports, politics, and what is happening in IT. I am more comfortable with these topics. On a one to one individual level, one male member might tell me "I applied for my daughter's passport today, let me see," etc. As a group, men discuss things differently."

In selection interviews, primarily women candidates were noted as specifically stating marriage, child-rearing and husband's job mobility as a cause of their career breaks. Interviewers in GSOs considered it normal to ask women candidates' direct questions about their family responsibilities, rather than male candidates. In a conversation with Kalpana, a HR manager, she said, "In interviews we assume a guy will be available 100% for work unlike a woman." Human resource managers were told to "keep their antennae up" if a female candidate was newly married and to check if she would follow her husband on his job posting. Interview notes were made of candidates' responses to such questions. These constitute some material practices by which gender issues are produced or expressed.

In selection interviews with male candidates, references to family were made in passing. If a male candidate made a city location shift, it was mostly because of his own planned career move or, in some instances, to responsibilities associated with his aging parents (who often relocated to where the son lived rather than vice versa). Caring for in-laws was stated as the prime responsibility of the wife. Women reported that this often took the form of medical support, ensuring that dietary regulations were maintained, observing duties related to religious rituals and festivals in the home. In salary discussions and promotion decisions women typically negotiated or bargained less than men and when asked, said they preferred to compromise on these aspects and negotiate on issues such as time off or long leave from the company, for domestic responsibilities. These responses and observations reinforce the differential salience of marriage and family responsibilities for men and women in the Indian context and these gendered notions are reproduced in the organization in the form of availability for work.

Anticipating the future changes that her marital status would entail, and also preparing for them in advance, Meena, a 23-year-old trainee, fresh from the IIT (Indian Institute of Technology, the most prestigious engineering college in India) said,

> I want to learn more and more since this is my first year. Maybe after 3 to 4 years when I am married I will look for stability. When you are getting married, you see, for a girl, it depends on your husband so one may relocate cities. . . . Before marriage is the main time to learn.

Women found different ways to find a balance and cope with the workload. For example, Tara, a module leader who was passionate about doing technical coding had this to say when asked how she kept up with these demands:

> I don't go out of my way to make friends at work. I do my work. Even while on maternity leave I bought books, I made sure I would spend 2 hours reading when my daughter was sleeping. It is lot of effort. Mornings, I pack tiffins [lunch packs], get my daughter ready for school. At night I just sit for my work.

When women found it hard to manage sustained work pressures, especially when their children were in school, they balanced both worlds by opting for less-demanding roles such as in quality control or training functions. At InSync for example, 82% of employees in software development were males and 18% females. In the quality control department, the ratios were slightly different with 60% men and 40%, women. While speaking with women in the quality control function at InSync, they acknowledged that this role enabled them to combine their work aspirations with family demands better than in a project role though it did not have the same "market currency" as working on "live" projects.

Employing cheap, paid domestic help or enrolling family members like in-laws or parents in child-care responsibilities were seen to be common strategies employed by women to manage the home front. One of the female managers at InSync reported that she had employed three maids to complete the household chores and this arrangement worked very well with her husband's erratic travel schedule and her long working hours. However, the responsibility for the supervision of the maids and the care of the household remained with her. So while she maintained equilibrium and avoided conflict, her response maintains the traditional gender order as the work just shifts to paid labor.

Recently, there have been some changes. Mohini said,

> Today in IT, the balance is tilting. Women in the age group 26 to 27 are prepared to leave everything at home to come to work. I find that men who are newly married or have small kids say, 'Oh my wife is saying this I need to go home, or I can't travel onsite my wife is alone, she has to look after the kids and my parents.' These were women's worries earlier, and now are men's worries.

One can attribute these changes in India as related to globalization, a decline in the availability of reliable domestic help in India particularly in Mumbai city, a shift towards couples preferring to live independently, and an exposure to mass media and overseas travel that promotes a shift towards "modern ideologies" of living and relating. Affirming this, Amrita says, "Women today are taking a lot of challenges. They forego marriages; they delay families. Especially in IT they rise faster, the money is good, they see the world much earlier in life and their expectations rise. Money gives women a lot of independence and is too good to be put aside. Part-time work is also coming to India which will benefit women.". . .

DISCUSSION

Gender and Global Software Organizations

Like other organizations, GSOs are sites where gender divisions of labor prevail in the boundaries between public and private, production and reproduction, family and work. Both socially and structurally, GSOs are not a "level playing field" for men and women IT workers but rather a site where traditional and stereotypical gendered norms and stereotypes are represented, explicitly and implicitly. However, unlike other organizations, they present a dialectic of the local and the global, not only geographically in terms of markets or in terms of locations but also socially and culturally. Global software organizations are a unique global work context, with immense possibilities to weaken or strengthen the division of labor and hegemonic status of local gendered ideological constructs. For example, the shifting market requirements of technical knowledge and skills, project-based work, diverse domain knowledge requirements and geographical customer locations, typical in GSO work make it a more flexible work setting, both structurally and socially than others like manufacturing or even global consulting firms. This quality of flexibility has the potential to weaken or eliminate mobility related restrictions and barriers for women. It also challenges the (male) dominant, linear trajectory of career growth by creating new and varied work possibilities for both men and women. GSOs provide an opportunity for skills to flow between the public and the private, giving them a competitive edge in global software work that is increasingly trust- and knowledge-based in the "Information Age" (Nicholson & Sahay, 2001; Sahay et al., 2003). . . . While it is true that GSOs often operate with a placeless logic, individual employees remain "historically and biographically place-dependent" (Sahay et al., p. 39) suggesting that such qualities are context-dependent or "spatially sticky" (Gertler, 2001). . . .

Gender, Self, and Identity

The data suggests beliefs in the sociocultural dimensions of femininity and family, masculinity, and career are powerful controlling forces in the working lives of both men and women in GSOs. These ideologies affect how they enter the IT profession, balance their paid and unpaid work roles, and their sense of satisfaction or ambivalence with themselves as professionals, parents, or single individuals. Resonating with the work of Gilligan (1982) women's voices spoke of an "ethics of care" that emerged from their social experience while men spoke of an "ethics of justice" in talking about their priorities and relationships. These different voices clearly demonstrate different gendered styles and different positioning of work in identity constructions of men and women. They also suggest how individuals are placed and place themselves in the Indian social system.

The empirical data suggests that the autonomous-relational self (Kagitcibasi, 1996) is operationalized among IT workers, in ways that are more dichotomous than dialectically mutual. The breadwinner ideology predominated as a central aspect of masculine identity constructs, while the relational self occupied center stage in feminine identity constructs. Individual responses as well as the coping means used by women, reinforces the view that the relational self was the predominant pathway of self-development (Kapadia, 1999), tied to the woman's sense of self. Such a self, legitimizing care giving by women and care receiving by men, binds women to this order even at the cost of their well-being (Kapadia, 1999; Sen, 2000). Negotiating for power and equality in the family system is a challenging task, threatening disintegration of family relationships impacting one's self-esteem, and many women in this study, found in-between solutions or compromised their own career aspirations.

The recent changes among younger women reflect new reality-defining social structures effected by flows of globalization and modernity in India. In addition to macro changes, these women also appear to assume a critical perspective on the present social relations, seeking self-fulfillment and success, and in this way, bringing in new elements into old contexts. At a self level, this implies a conscious kindling of their autonomous self to become successful, confident actors in a global work context where the nature of work offers abundant opportunities for personal and social accomplishment. Particularly, transnational opportunities for travel and living in such global work provides an opportunity for IT professionals to review traditional entrenched gender discourses and ideologies and be exposed to diverse possibilities of relating and being. The changes in the younger generation of IT professionals suggest a positive shift where both men and women seek to accommodate the influences of modernity in their gender-related identity constructions without threatening gender inauthenticity or increasing ghettoization for women, as earlier feared (Arun & Arun, 2001; Panteli et al., 1999). It appears that slowly but surely, there is a greater convergence of the relational and autonomous aspects of selves among IT professionals rather than a reinforcement of the existing dichotomy. Factors unique to the IT profession in GSOs such as high social status, high incomes, quick possibilities for success, and frequent overseas travel opportunities intersect with boundaries of gender and class to create possibilities for varied identity constructions and arenas where individuals can demonstrate increased agency as well as relatedness.

Theoretical and Practical Implications

. . . Theoretically, while macro-level concepts of globalization, modernity, gender, and identity provide us with relevant conceptual frameworks to understand people and processes, they often fail to explain how these dynamics are actually lived in the day-to-day life and experiences of people. It is only through micro-ethnographic studies like these that we can identify the push-pull aspects of sociocultural traditions that are enacted in the context of global workspaces and their source in local anchors. . . .

There are several practical implications. Women workers themselves can play a key role in bringing about changes in their workplace environments. They can pressure their organizations to establish day care centers near the organization or lobby for part-time work possibilities or working-from-home options. These options will provide them flexibility and enable a more sustained career trajectory even when their household responsibilities increase, preventing their disappearance or dropping out of the workforce. Given their relatively privileged social position in India, and as members of a limited pool of knowledge workers so critical for such work that is high on the national agenda, they can use this bargaining power to create such enabling possibilities for themselves.

Besides workers, GSOs would greatly benefit by the continued participation of women in the internal labor market pool and their work contributions with the added dimension of their female touch. Even though the gender ratios in GSOs are skewed, and women workers experience all kinds of mobility-related restrictions, their contributions have been noted as significant to organizational performance in this knowledge-work industry. Wider debates of female and male styles of relating or the feminine advantage (e.g., Fletcher, 1998; Kealey, 1990) have particular relevance for GSOs. . . .

This work also has implications for the IT export business in India, given its scorching growth rate. At one level, creating enabling opportunities for inclusion of more women into the IT workforce would contribute to increasing the overall labor pool of professionals in the country, where competent workers are always in short supply. These opportunities will also reduce attrition rates, so endemic to this volatile industry and so detrimental to the GSO (D'Mello, 2005). By participating in the IT sector, women can also actively contribute to technological development of the country. To this end, equal opportunity' task forces and their recommendations typically focus on increasing the number count of women in this industry (Suriya, 2003). However, structural transformations are certainly necessary but not sufficient to foster true empowerment and engagement of this group of knowledge workers. What is needed is a greater acceptance of the complicities between social norms and organizational practices that primarily constrain women's mobility and any attempts towards changing these mobility constraints. . . .

The notions of empowerment of both women and men or development as empowerment are also practically relevant (Sen, 2000). For women, where the relational self predominates, empowerment would mean kindling their autonomous self to enable them to question the patriarchal order and create a space for themselves. For men, empowerment would imply enabling them to develop and to express comfortably more relational qualities of nurturance, empathy, and care. For GSOs, it implies celebrating rather than stereotyping differences and finding holistic and creative settings for its employees to contribute and add value not only in terms of technical knowledge but also through a range of personal attributes. . . .

CONCLUSION

Gender is implicated in the daily working lives of IT professionals in GSOs in India. Contrary to beliefs about neutrality and professionalism, GSOs like other organizations, constitute a local as well as a global site where gender is enacted in its material practices and ideological constructions. Gender-related norms and beliefs frame selves and identities of IT workers, influencing their self-esteem and participation in the workforce. They also regulate behaviors of employees through their formal and informal processes. Particularities of GSO work make it a potential site for educated women in India to increase their agency and participation in the public sphere and disrupt traditional, mobility-related, and other restrictions. The persistence of the gender divide in GSOs has ramifications for not only the selves and identities of individual workers but also for the country's growth and development, given that IT is seen as a pivotal engine for national growth.

ACKNOWLEDGMENTS

I thank Professors Sundeep Sahay and Christina Mörtberg, Department of Informatics, University of Oslo (UIO), Turid Markussen, Centre for Women's Studies and Gender Research, UIO, and the anonymous reviewers for their valuable comments and feedback on earlier versions of this paper.

NOTES

1. With the recent burgeoning of the ITES industry which includes business process outsourcing and the call center industry NASSCOM, the apex body as well as the Chamber of Commerce for the IT industry in India, has combined the figures for software service and ITES, even though they are different businesses.
2. This is a special area in Mumbai set up by the government, offering a well-developed infrastructure, fiscal incentives, and quick approvals and clearances to firms developing and exporting IT-related products and services.
3. In Indian/Hindu thought, it is proposed that there are four stages of life. *Grihasthashram* is the second stage, that of a householder.

4. In Hindu thought, *Lakshmi* is the goddess of happiness and prosperity. The wife is the *Lakshmi* of the *griha*, i.e., the household.
5. This is similar to the above meaning. *Dharma* is duty and *patni* is wife.
6. The name of the company as well as respondents is kept confidential.
7. Hindi word for *bread*.
8. He is referring to social functions, mainly in the family circle.
9. This Hindi sentence means "to walk with another with your arm around that person's shoulder."

REFERENCES

Ahuja, M.K. (2002). Women in the information technology profession: A literature review, synthesis and research agenda. European Journal of Information Systems, 11, 20–34.

Arun, S., & Arun, T.G. (2001). Gender at work within the software industry: An Indian perspective. Journal of Women and Minorities in Science and Engineering, 7, 215–230.

Aziz, M. (2004). Role stress among women in the Indian information technology sector. Women in Management Review, 19(7), 356–363.

Bagchi, J. (Ed.). (1995). Indian women: Myth and reality. Hyderabad, India: Sangam Books Ltd.

Burrell, G., & Morgan, G. (1979). Sociological paradigms and organizational analysis: Elements of the sociology of corporate life. London: Heinemann.

Castells, M. (1996). The rise of the network society. Oxford & Malden, MA: Blackwell.

Chakraborty, S.K. (2000). The feminine dimension of human values: A journey with Tagore and others. Journal of Human Values, 6(1), 39–49.

Chanana, K. (1994). Social change or social reform: Women, education and family in pre-independence India. In C.C. Mukhopadhyay & S. Seymour (Eds.), Women, education and family structure in India (pp. 35–58). Boulder, CO: Westview Press.

Chanana, K. (2000). Treading the hallowed halls: Women in higher education. Economic and Political Weekly, 35(12), 1012–1022.

Chodorow, N. (1978). The reproduction of mothering: Psychoanalysis and the sociology of gender. Berkeley, CA: University of California Press.

Coomaraswamy, A.K. (1924). The dance of Shiva. New York: Sunwise Turn.

Cormack, M. (1974). The Hindu woman. Westport, CT: Greenwood Press.

D'Mello, M. (2005). "Thinking local, acting global": Issues of identity and related tensions in global software organizations in India. EJISDC, 22(2), 1–20.

Didio, L. (1996). Where the girls aren't. Computerworld, 30, 106.

Dube, L. (1988). Socialization of Hindu girls in partilineal India. In K. Chanana (Ed.), Socialization, education and women: Explorations in gender identity. New Delhi: Orient Longman Ltd.

Evetts, J. (1996). Gender and career in science and engineering. London: Taylor & Francis.

Fletcher, J. (1994). Castrating the female advantage: Feminist standpoint research and management science. Journal of Management Inquiry, 3(1), 74–82.

Fletcher, J.K. (1998). Relational practice: A feminist reconstruction of work. Journal of Management Inquiry, 7(2), 163–186.

Gertler, M. (2001, June). Tacit knowledge and the economic geography of context or the undefinable tacitness of being (there). Paper presented at the Nelson & Winter DRUID Summer Conference, Aalborg, Denmark.

Giddens, A. (1991). Modernity and self-identity: Self and society in the late modern age. Cambridge: Polity Press.

Gilleard, J., & Gilleard, J.D. (2002, October). Developing cross-cultural communication skills. Journal of Professional Issues in Engineering Education and Practice, 187–200.

Gilligan, C. (1982). In a different voice: Psychological theory and women's development. Cambridge: Harvard University Press.

Guzder, J., & Krishna, M. (1991). Sita-Shakti: Cultural paradigms for Indian women. Transcultural Research Review, 28, 257–301.

Heeks, R. (1998). The uneven profile of Indian software exports. Retrieved August 25, 2005, from http://www. sed. manchester.ac.uk/idpm/publications/wp/di/ di_wp03.pdf

Igbaria, M., & Shayo, C. (2004). Strategies for staffing the information systems department. In M. Igbaria & C. Shayo (Eds.), Strategies for managing IS/IT personnel (pp. 18–36). London: Idea Group Publishing.

Indian National Science Academy. (2004). Study and practice of science by Indian women. In Report: Science career for Indian women: An examination of Indian women's access to and retention in scientific careers. Retrieved August 25, 2005, from http://www.insaindia.org/Scienceservice/ science.htm

Kagitcibasi, C. (1996). The autonomous-relational self: A new synthesis. European Psychologist, 1(3), 180–186.

Kakar, S. (1988). Feminine identity in India. In R. Ghadially (Ed.), Women in Indian society. New Delhi: Sage.

Kapadia, S. (1999). Self, women and empowerment: A conceptual inquiry. In T.S. Saraswathi (Ed.), Culture, socialization and human development: The research and application in India (pp. 255–277). New Delhi: Sage.

Kealey, D.J. (1990). Cross-cultural effectiveness: A study of Canadian technical advisors overseas. Quebec: Canadian International Development Agency.

Kelkar, G., Shrestha, G., & Veena, N. (2002). IT industry and women's agency: Explorations in Bangalore and Delhi, India. Gender, Technology and Development, 6(1), 63–84.

Klawe, M., & Levenson, N. (1995). Women in computing: Where are we now? Communications of the ACM, 38, 29–44.

Knights, D., & Murray, F. (1994). Managers divided— Organizational politics and information technology management. Chicester, UK: Wiley.

Maitland, A. (2001, February). A long-term solution to the IT skill shortage. Financial Times, 22, 9.

Mendenhall, M., & Oddou, G. (1985). The dimensions of expatriate acculturation: A review. Academy of Management Review, 10, 39–47.

Miller, J.B. (1986). Towards a new psychology of women. Boston: Beacon Press.

Moore, J.E. (2000). One road to turnover: An examination of work exhaustion in technology professionals. MIS Quarterly, 24(1), 141–168.

Mukhopadhyay, C. (1994). Family structure and Indian women's participation in science and engineering. In C.C. Mukhopadhyay & S. Seymour (Eds.), Women, education and family structure in India (pp. 103–132). Boulder, CO: Westview Press.

NASSCOM. (2005). Strategic review: The IT industry in India. New Delhi: Author.

Nicholson, B., & Sahay, S. (2001). Some political and cultural issues in the globalization of software development: Case experience from Britain and India. Information and Organization, 11, 25–43.

Nicholson, B., & Sahay, S. (2004). Embedded knowledge and offshore software development. Information and Organization, 14(4), 329–365.

Nierderman, F., & Mandviwalla, M. (2004). Introduction to special issue on the evolution of IT (computer) personnel research: More theory, more understanding, more questions. The Database for Advances in Information Systems, 35(3), 6–8

Olsson, S., & Walker, R. (2004). "The wo-men and the boys": Patterns of identification and differentiation in senior women executives' representations of career identity. Women in Management Review, 19(5), 244–251.

Panteli, A., Stack, J., & Ramsay, H. (1999). Gender and professional ethics in the IT industry. Journal of Business Ethics, 22, 51–61.

Papanek, H. (1973). Men, women and work: Reflections on the two-person career. American Journal of Sociology, 78, 852–872.

Parikh, I., & Garg, P. (1989). Indian women: An inner dialogue. New Delhi: Sage.

Parker, B., & McEvoy, G. (1993). Model of intercultural adjustment. International Journal of Intercultural Relations, 17(3), 355–380.

Ragins, B.R., & Cotton, J.L. (1991). Easier said than done: Gender differences in perceived barriers to gaining a mentor. Academy of Management Journal, 34, 939–951.

Rao, A. , & Kellner, D. (2003). Institutions, organizations and gender equality in an era of globalization. Gender and Development, 11(1), 142–149.

Sahay, S., Nicholson, B., & Krishna, S. (2003). Global IT outsourcing: Software development across borders. Cambridge, UK: Cambridge University Press.

Sen, A.K. (1990). Gender and cooperative conflicts. In I. Tinker (Ed.), Persistent inequalities. New York: Oxford University Press.

Sen, A.K. (2000). Development as freedom. New Delhi: Oxford University Press.

Senge, P. (1990). The fifth discipline. New York: Doubleday.

Singh, Y. (2000). Culture change in India: Identity and globalization. Jaipur, India: Rawat Publications.

Sirianni, C., & Negrey, C. (2000). Working time as gendered time. Feminist Economics, 6(1), 59–76.

Sonpar, S., & Kapur, R. (2001, January 6). Non-conventional indicators: Gender disparities under structural reform. Economic and Political Weekly, 66–78.

Suriya, M. (2003). A gender perspective: Career development of IT professionals. Retrieved August 20, 2005, from http://www.i4donline.net/issue/sept-oct2003/career_full.htm

Trauth, E.M. (2002). Odd girl out: An individual differences perspective on women in the IT profession. Information Technology & People, 15(2), 98–118.

Trauth, E.M., Nielsen, S.H., & Von Hellens, L.A. (2003). Explaining the IT gender gap: Australian stories for the new millennium. Journal of Research and Practice in Information Technology, 35(1), 7–20.

Turkle, S. (1988). Computational reticence: Why women fear the intimate machine. In C. Kramarae (Ed.), Technology and women's voices. New York: Routledge & Keegan Paul.

Van Maanen, J. (1979). The fact of fiction in organizational ethnography. Administrative Science Quarterly, 24(4), 24, 539–550.

Von Hellens, L., Nielsen, S., & Trauth, E. (2001). Breaking and entering the male domain: Women in the IT industry. In M. Serva (Ed.), Proceedings of the ACM SIGCPR Special Interest Group on Computer Personnel Research (pp. 116–120). San Diego: Association for Computing Machinery.

Von Hellens, L., Nielsen, S.H., & Beekhuyzen, J. (2004). An exploration of dualisms in female perceptions of IT work. Journal of Information Technology Education, 3, 103–116.

Walsham, G. (1993). Interpreting information systems in organizations. Chicester, UK: Wiley.

Walsham, G. (2001). Making a world of difference: IT in a global context. Oxford: Oxford University Press.

Waterson, P., Clegg, C., & Axtell, C. (1997). The dynamics of work organization, knowledge and technology during software development. International Journal of Human—Computer Studies, 46, 79–101.

47 **Gwyn Kirk**

Contesting Militarization: Global Perspectives

First published in 2008

Currently, 80 percent of women working in bars and clubs near U.S. bases in South Korea are from the Philippines; Korean women have found other opportunities for making a living. In the Philippines, however, low wages, high unemployment, and no sustainable economic policy force roughly 10 percent of the country's workers to seek employment abroad. In 2005, these workers sent home $10.7 billion (or 12 percent of GNP) in official remittances. President Gloria Mapacalang Arroyo has proudly called these overseas workers "the backbone of the new global workforce" and "our greatest export" (Paddock 2006, A1).

Following the division of the Korean peninsula after World War II, the United States maintained approximately a hundred military bases and facilities in South Korea. Although the U.S. military is restructuring and reducing the number of its bases there, South Korea is still considered a war zone and a "hardship" posting, as no formal peace treaty has been signed between North and South Korea to conclude the Korean War (1950–1953). Typically, most U.S. service members based there are young, their tours of duty are short, and the military prefers them to be unencumbered by family members. They are usually posted to Korea after basic training, often en route to Iraq or Afghanistan.

Korean and U.S. officials' shared beliefs about the soldiers' sexuality have led to policies that ensure the availability of women in bars and clubs near U.S. bases. Racist and sexist assumptions about Asian women—as exotic, accommodating, and sexually compliant—are an integral part of these arrangements. Moreover, Filipinas have a reputation for friendliness, and many speak some English. They come to Korea on six-month entertainer visas to work as singers or dancers. They have varying expectations, but a major goal is to send money home. They arrive already indebted to club owners for their plane fare, passport costs, and agent's fees. In addition, their pay is often much lower than they were promised by recruiters, and they may be fined by owners for infractions of club rules. To pay off their debts they need to earn more, so they "go out" with U.S. soldiers. Thus, prostitution continues despite the U.S. military's declared "zero tolerance" policy.[1] Servicemen have privilege, as men and as buyers, in these encounters, whether the liaisons are one-night stands or longer-term live-in relationships. The servicemen's U.S. citizenship also privileges them and protects them from prosecution for many infringements of Korean law and customs. In class terms, many U.S. servicemen may be, like these women, part of a "poverty draft," But this analogous situation does not necessarily translate into sympathy or respect. Often the opposite is true, with some U.S. soldiers, notably white men, committing serious crimes of violence against bar women.

Nowadays soldiers prefer live-in relationships, and women often choose to live with them rather than be exploited in the clubs. If they leave the clubs, however, they lose both their work permits and residence permits, which are tied to the job. If caught by immigration officials, the women are fined and deported. They may get jobs in small Korean factories that employ undocumented workers. They may engage in street prostitution, usually for low fees, or rely on their military boyfriends for support. U.S. soldiers with live-in girlfriends are not, strictly speaking, engaging in prostitution or trafficking. Thus U.S. military authorities can talk about "zero tolerance" while, at the same time, their troops have sexual servicing (Kim 2006; Kirk 2006).

Approximately 2.5 million Salvadorans—out of a population of 6.5 million—live abroad, primarily in the United States, where they work in construction, gardening, child care, domestic work, restaurant service, and other areas of the service sector. They send remittances to relatives back home, estimated at $2. 8 billion a year (Aizenman 2006). Some have temporary protected status, a category negotiated between the two governments after a devastating earthquake wiped out homes, farms, and jobs in El Salvador in 2001. El Salvador took the dollar as its currency in 2001 and joined the Central America Free Trade Agreement (CAFTA) two years later. In August 2003, El Salvador reinforced its close ties to the United States by committing 360 soldiers to the war in Iraq (Garamone 2004).

As a colony of Spain for almost three hundred years, El Salvador developed an economy based on cash crops for export, especially sugar and coffee. A few families continue to control much of the nation's wealth, and most people are very poor. A third of the rural population survives thanks to remittances from abroad. For decades, peasants and workers organized to change the gross inequalities that have characterized the country since colonization. These efforts met with severe governmental repression. From 1980 to 1992, U.S.-backed government troops fought insurgents of the Frente Farabundo Martí para la Liberación Nacional (FMLN), who were struggling for land redistribution, genuine democracy, and an end to inequality and oppression. An estimated 80,000 people were killed and 7,000 more "disappeared" in this war (Ready, Stephen, and Cosgrove 2001, 184–185). Over a million were displaced. In many areas it was too dangerous to plant or tend crops, and people fled for their lives, some to Honduras or the United States.

Women were profoundly affected by the war in that they were usually the ones responsible for generating household income, caring for children, and finding medical help, food, and shelter for their families. During the war up to 51 percent of households were headed by women (Ready, Stephen, and Cosgrove 2001, 184–185). Some had to leave their children in the care of others or send them abroad for safety because government forces made a practice of abducting infants and young children. Thousands of women were killed. Thousands more lost family members and suffered from war trauma, including rape, abuse, and torture by the military, government security forces, and death squads.

A military stalemate brought the two sides to negotiate a peace settlement, finalized in 1992, which included political changes, downsizing of the military, demobilization of left-wing forces, and the legalization of the FMLN as a political party. There has been little improvement in the nation's persistent inequality, however. Economic policy has favored the financial sector and the *maquiladoras* surrounding San Salvador, rather than promoting land redistribution. The government is committed to "free market" principles, and hopes to stimulate the sluggish economy by opening new export markets and encouraging foreign investment. Remittances now make up 67 percent of El Salvador's foreign exchange, compared to the *maquila* sector (16 percent) and agro-exports (6 percent) (Rosa 2004). Before the civil war, coffee exports were the backbone of the economy, but from 1999 to 2001 world coffee prices slumped dramatically to an all-time low. A key factor was oversupply, mainly the result of a massive increase in production in Vietnam, as part of economic rebuilding in the aftermath of the Vietnam War (Greenfield 2002).

A United Nations truth commission that investigated human rights abuses perpetrated during the war in El Salvador found that the government and government-sponsored death squads had committed 90 percent of the atrocities; at the same time, it also condemned FMLN violence. The commission admonished the right-wing Nationalist Republican Alliance (ARENA) government to set up a legal process to deal with war crimes. Instead, the government pushed an amnesty law through parliament (Rubin 2004).

Reconstruction has been slow and uneven. Many elderly people, especially women whose husbands and children were killed, have no family support. During the war, adults and children witnessed—and committed—terrible atrocities. An "estimated 80 percent of government troops and 20 percent of FMLN recruits were under 18 years of age" (Hertvik 2006, n.p.) Unknown numbers suffer from injuries and war-related trauma. In many communities people report increasing gang-related violence—a manifestation of ongoing poverty, lack of opportunities, the disruptive effects of war, and culture of violence.

The former Federal People's Republic of Yugoslavia in the mountainous Balkan region of eastern Europe was created after World War II as a socialist state, with Bosnia-Herzegovina, Croatia, Macedonia, Montenegro, Serbia, and Slovenia as member republics. Vojvodina and Kosovo were autonomous provinces within Serbia. From 1991 to 2001, the member republics all experienced the devastation of war. Western media reports invariably emphasized aggressive nationalisms and age-old enmities among the many ethnic groups, suggesting that the Yugoslav federation was imploding from the inside. In addition to ethnic divisions and the political ambitions of Serbian president Slobodan Milosevic to create a Greater Serbia, economic factors and the role of Western governments and the International Monetary Fund (IMF) were also a major cause of bloodshed.

Yugoslavia declared autonomy from the Soviet Union in 1948. It developed a distinctive form of workers' self-management, with economic ties to western Europe and the United States. By the 1980s, however, the economy was in trouble, with high levels of inflation and mounting national debt. The IMF, dominated by Western powers, agreed to make loans on condition that a series of harsh austerity measures were enacted. Taken together, these led to a wage freeze, widespread unemployment, shortage of basic commodities, increased external debt, and the gradual dismantling of the welfare state (Chossudovsky 1996). People protested. Leaders of the republics argued among themselves and with federal officials. Federal funding that should have gone to the republics was diverted to debt repayment, which fueled "secessionist tendencies that fed on economic factors as well as ethnic divisions" (Chossudovsky 1996, 33).

In multiparty elections in 1990, separatist coalitions won in Croatia, Bosnia, and Slovenia. Croatia and Slovenia announced their secession from the federation in 1991 and were quickly recognized as independent states by the European Union. Serbian forces and the Yugoslav Army supported violent opposition to this move by the Serbian minority in Croatia. Bosnia, significant for its ethnic diversity and with considerable intermarriage among groups, held a referendum that called for independence in March 1992, and the Republic of Bosnia and Herzegovina was also recognized by European states. However, Bosnian Serb nationalists resisted secession. Bosnian Croats and Muslims fought together against Bosnian Serbs, but increasing polarization along ethnic lines, exacerbated by local media reporting, spiraled into a fury of violence and atrocity by armies and armed militias. Nationalist groups pursued "ethnic cleansing" by intimidation, forced expulsion or killing, and the destruction of cultural and historical buildings such as places of worship and cemeteries. Their practices included the systematic rape and forced impregnation of women by men from "other" groups.

War in Bosnia formally ended in 1995 with the Dayton Peace Accords, brokered by the United States. The new state of Bosnia and Herzegovina comprises two ethnic entities: the Federation of Bosnia and Herzegovina with a Bosnian Muslim and Croat majority, and the Republic Srpska with a Bosnian Serb majority. During the 1990s, Serbia took steps to reduce the autonomy of Kosovo, and Serb forces fought a secessionist movement in Kosovo. In March 1999, the United States and NATO (North Atlantic Treaty Organization) intervened with seventy-nine days of devastating air strikes against Serbia. This step was justified as necessary to stop Serbian brutality against ethnic Albanians and Muslims, who made up 85 percent of the population of Kosovo. Press reports, however, noted that these air strikes actually "precipitated a sharp escalation of ethnic cleansing and other atrocities" (Chomsky 1999, 37).

These wars redrew the map of the Balkans along ethnic lines. They resulted in shattered communities, people's acute distrust of "others," high unemployment, and poverty. Governments of the new states pledged themselves to "free market" principles, including extensive privatization of formerly state-owned enterprises and outside investment from Western companies. Economic recovery has been slow, and the multilayered process of healing and rebuilding will take many years.

These examples illustrate intersections between militarization and the globalization of the economy. They show how war and militarism uproot people and make them available, indeed force them, to look for livelihood elsewhere. They detail interlocking systems of inequality based on gender, race/ethnicity, class, and nation. I separate economic, political, and ideological dimensions of militarism briefly in what follows, but they must be understood as intersecting, as shown in these examples.

Virtually all nations make huge economic, political, and ideological investments in militaries and militarism—a broad system of institutions, practices, values, and cultures that take their meaning and value from war. By contrast, for everyday security, people need clean air and water, meaningful sources of livelihood, respectful systems of health care, community ties, and nourishment for body, mind, and spirit. To contest militarization and develop alternative views of security teachers, researchers, and activists need nuanced understandings. Although much is being done in this regard there is scope—and need—for very much more.

This (article) deals in generalizations and broad strokes, with a focus on intersections among gender, race, and militarization. Given the power of the dollar, the dominance of U.S.-based corporations, the United States' influence on World Bank and IMF policies, the worldwide reach of CNN and U.S. popular culture, and with more than seven hundred U.S. military bases spanning the globe, this account inevitably emphasizes U.S. militarism.

THE PERMANENT WAR ECONOMY

World military spending rose to a massive $1,118 billion in 2005 (Stockholm International Peace Research Institute 2006). Characterized as having a "permanent war economy" since World War II (Melman 1974, 2003), the United States spent 48 percent of this staggering total, almost as much as the rest of the world combined. In general, war is big business. A U.S. Department of Defense Web site describes the Pentagon as the "oldest," "largest," "busiest," and "most successful" U.S. company, boasting a budget bigger than ExxonMobil, Ford, or General Motors, and with wider geographical scope (U.S. Department of Defense 2002). Indeed, U.S. military policies and budget priorities are driving militarization worldwide. On leaving office in 1960, U.S. President Dwight Eisenhower warned against the power of the "military-industrial complex," now more accurately described as the "military-industrial-congressional-academic-media complex," to refer to institutional interconnections based on the overlapping goals, financial investments, and revolving-door job opportunities among top levels of government, the military, corporations, and academia.

Steven Staples, chair of the International Network on Disarmament and Globalization, argues that the large U.S. military budget "is for all practical purposes a corporate subsidy" siphoning public money into private hands and protected under article 21 of the General Agreement on Tariffs and Trade (GATT), which allows "governments free rein for actions taken in the interest of national security" (Staples 2000,19). He notes that

> globalization and militarism are two sides of the same coin. On the one side, globalization promotes the conditions that lead to unrest, inequality, conflict, and, ultimately war. On the other side, globalization fuels

the means to wage war by protecting and promoting the military industries needed to produce sophisticated weaponry. This weaponry, in turn, is used or is threatened to be used to protect the investments of transnational corporations and their shareholders. (18)

The U.S. military is both a state agency and a highly profitable sector that contracts with corporations like Lockheed Martin, Raytheon, Northrop Grumman, General Electric, and Boeing to produce weapons. Public funds underwrite the lengthy research and development process, and the government is the main customer for these weapons.

Nation-states, militaries, and corporations are intertwined through international trade in weapons, with the United States and Russia as the top weapons-exporting countries. The United States earned nearly $21 billion in overseas arms sales in fiscal year 2006 (Wayne 2006). Europe's main arms-manufacturing nations—Britain, France, and Germany—maintain a significant market share, whereas Israel and China seek to increase arms sales. Major bombing and missile strikes like the 1999 bombardment of Kosovo and more recent attacks on Afghanistan and Iraq serve as advertising campaigns for arms manufacturers. War-tested planes and weapons systems command a price double or triple that of those without such testing (Merle 2003; Pae 2003). Moreover, weapons must be used to justify continued production.

Worldwide, most people are killed by small arms that are cheap and easily available rather than by sophisticated weapons systems. The international trade in small arms is a central part of the global economy as an earner of hard currency and as a way for indebted nations to repay foreign loans. More than 1,135 companies in a hundred countries manufacture small arms, and nearly 60 percent of them are in civilian hands (Soto 2004). A good deal of the cross-border trade in small arms is illegal, but it is highly profitable for manufacturers, dealers, brokers, shippers, and financiers (Lumpe 2000). This trade sustains many of the conflicts currently going on, for example, in Burundi, Congo, Sudan, Myanmar, Nepal, the Philippines, Sri Lanka, Colombia, Peru, and Russia (Chechnya).

The outsourcing and privatization of U.S. military functions is a growing trend (Avant 2005; Ferguson and Turnbull 2004). Singer (2004) identifies provider firms (for example, Executive Outcomes) that offer direct, tactical military assistance; consulting firms (for example, Military Professional Resources Inc.) that provide strategic and administrative expertise; and support firms such as Halliburton's Kellogg Brown and Root that provide logistic and maintenance services to armed forces. Private military companies are active in the war in Iraq, with their own weapons supplies (Leigh 2004). Blackwater Security Consulting has engaged in full-scale battle, using its own helicopters, to resupply its commandos (Mokhiber and Weissman 2004). . . . Privatized soldiering is a cost-cutting measure using employees on short-term contracts, in contrast with regular troops who rely on the government to provide pensions and benefits, including medical insurance for their families. It shields military operations from congressional oversight and poaches troops who can earn much more from private companies. The practice also places employees in a legal grey area in which the military has no jurisdiction over them, as, for example, the private interrogators accused of abusing Iraqi prisoners, or the Dyncorp employees who were implicated in the trafficking of young women and other sex crimes in Bosnia (Singer 2004). If killed in war, such individuals do not appear on lists of official military deaths.

For centuries, colonial expansion and the quest for control of strategic locations and scarce resources have been motivating factors in military intervention. The economic reasons for contemporary wars are not always made clear in news reports, which often emphasize a conflict's ethnic, cultural, or religious aspects said to be based on old enmities and histories of aggression. Recent wars in the Balkans, the oppression of the Palestinians by Israel, and the sixty-year conflict between India and Pakistan over Kashmir all have strong cultural and religious elements. But in addition, Bosnia, Serbia, and Kosovo have valuable mineral and oil deposits; Israel wants control of land and water supplies; and the watershed region of Kashmir provides control of rivers flowing to the Indus. In Sierra Leone, the lucrative diamond trade has fueled and financed decades of civil war. In Colombia, coca and processed cocaine play a similar role.

The economic imperative to get business running again in the aftermath of war means that peace agreements rarely address the root causes of conflict or make provisions for meaningful reconciliation or reparations but instead focus on reconstruction and economic normalization (Lipschutz 1998). The rebuilding of destroyed factories, oil pipelines, dams, and bridges is highly lucrative. In the case of the bombing of Kosovo, Western corporations were maneuvering for

rebuilding contracts as soon as the bombing stopped; in the war against Iraq, this positioning began before the bombing started. Economic and military policies are not always a smooth fit, however. For example, John Feffer (2000) notes significant contradictions underlying U.S. policy in East Asia, where the United States seeks to open up new markets, especially in China with its more than one billion potential customers, but still pursues cold war foreign policy objectives in the region.

Some commentators argue that the nation-state is becoming weaker as a corollary of increased corporate power. Fifty-one of the world's top hundred economies are corporations. WalMart is bigger than Indonesia, and General Motors is roughly the size of Ireland, New Zealand, and Hungary combined (CorpWatch 2001). Under a market economy, a major role for the nation-state is to create and maintain conditions for business profitability. States also finance their militaries, buy from military contractors, and generate ideological support for militarization by invoking patriotism, ethnocentrism, nationalism, and national security.

NATIONAL SECURITY

A "realist" paradigm in international relations has dominated political, military, and academic thinking about state security for decades. It assumes "a hostile international environment" in which "sovereign, self-interested states" seek their own security through a balance of political and military power among them (Tickner 2001, 38). National security is thus equated with military security, which places militarism at the center of public policy, justifies vast military expenditures, and naturalizes military activities.

Many nations were founded as a result of military conquest or postwar territorial changes. In general, state violence is considered legitimate violence. War veterans are often highly respected and their sacrifices honored in national commemorations and ceremonies. Military cemeteries are important national symbols (Ferguson and Turnbull 1999). Military service and connections facilitate running for political office or gaining appointment to high-ranking government positions. Departments of Defense are key government ministries. Militaries can also be a source of organized political opposition. They may limit the political potential of fragile democratic regimes and, on occasion, may take power through coups d'etat. Armed struggle by popular forces, often characterized as rebels or insurgents, has been a key strategy in over-throwing colonial powers or achieving greater social and economic equality, and more democratic political institutions. Currently, more wars are being fought within nation-states than between states.

Serving in the military is considered a responsibility of citizenship. In the 1860s, African Americans wanted to fight in the American Civil War as part of their claim to equal citizenship. In the 1990s, gay men and lesbians in the United States also claimed this right. Nations where military service is compulsory for men include Austria, Chile, Egypt, Mexico, and South Korea, although with varying exemptions that include health and educational status. Peru, Libya, and Israel require military service from both men and women. In Britain, Germany, Greece, and the United States, women may volunteer for the military. Britain and the United States do not have conscription, but structural inequalities within these societies—based on race/ethnicity and class—constitute a "poverty draft." In many nations, job opportunities depend on military service and contacts. Much is made of military service as a rite of passage into manhood. Feminist scholars point to the construction of militarized masculinity in recruits, as well as the role of masculinity in national foreign policy, and argue that the nation-state, which the military is said to protect, is a patriarchal, heterosexist institution (Allen 2000; Enloe 2000b; Peterson 2000; Plumwood 1993).

Since the attacks on the World Trade Center and the Pentagon, the United States has pressed its allies especially throughout Europe and the Asia-Pacific region—by flattery, bribery, bullying, or coercion—to support its open-ended "war on terrorism. " In their adherence to U.S. foreign policy, allied governments trade national sovereignty for U.S. support and protection, real or imagined. They also jeopardize their own internal political processes in that their alignment with U S dominance is often at great cost to their citizens. Allied governments support this war despite their own people's opposition to their nation's involvement. In addition, taxpayers' resources and some citizens themselves are expropriated for it.

Within the United States the commonplace distinction between foreign and domestic policy masks the continuities between them. The U.S. government is pursuing an integrated imperial policy that affects communities at home and abroad. Since the collapse of the Soviet Union in the late 1980S, the United States

has been the sole superpower. On May 30, 2000, over a year before the attacks of September 11, 2001, the United States announced a policy of "full spectrum dominance" or "the ability of U.S. forces, operating alone or with allies, to defeat any adversary and control any situation across the range of military operations" on land, at sea, in the air, and in space (Garamone 2000). The United States has bases on every continent and has begun the militarization of space. In December 2006, NASA announced its intention to establish a permanent base on the moon by 2024.

EMBEDDED WITH THE MILITARY: INFORMATION, IDEOLOGIES, AND CULTURE

The term *embedded journalist,* referring to a reporter attached to a military unit involved in armed conflict, first came into use during the 2003 U.S. invasion of Iraq, when the U.S. military offered journalists the opportunity to undergo a period of boot camp-style training before allowing them into the combat zone. The much-repeated comment, "In war, truth is the first casualty," is attributed to the Greek dramatist Aeschylus (525–456 B.C.). Contemporary forms of this include press censorship, restricted access to war zones, one-sided reporting, highly conjectural "reports," and deliberate misinformation.

The mainstream U.S. media are owned and controlled by megacorporations like Disney/ABC and Time Warner/Turner, which Robert McChesney (2004) describes in terms of "hypercommercialism." When militarization plays a central role in the global economy and in government policies, one of the mainstream media's jobs is to enlist people's support for such a role and to convince us that military priorities are legitimate (Chomsky 1997; Herman and Chomsky 2002). Mainstream news media typically endorse militarism as the only feasible approach to security. After the attacks of September 11, 2001, "experts" brought in by U.S. television networks to discuss military and foreign policies were invariably high-ranking, middle-aged military men who supported military action. Since then, however, the picture has become more complicated. Only 35 percent of those members of the U.S military polled in 2006 said they approved of the way the president was handling the war in Iraq, and 41 percent said the United States should not have gone to war (Hodierne 2006). Senior military officers have also criticized the Bush administration's political agenda as preventing them from making properly reasoned choices regarding U.S. withdrawal. Nevertheless, television viewers rarely learn of alternative approaches to resolving conflicts. Presidents can simply declare that diplomacy has "failed." The development of nonmilitary forms of strength is assumed to be "unrealistic," and such notions are scorned as soft, wimpy, even laughable.

Feminist philosopher Val Plumwood (1993) highlights dualistic thinking as the methodology that underpins hierarchal systems such as militarism, colonialism, racism, sexism, and environmental destruction in that various attributes are thought of in terms of oppositions—culture/nature, mind/body, male/female, self/other, and so on. These systems all rely on the creation of "otherness," of enemies and inferiority, to justify superiority and domination. These dualisms are mutually reinforcing and should be viewed as an interlocking set. For members of dominant groups and nations, the construction of identity continually reinforces a belief in the group's superiority. This belief, in turn, involves the dehumanization of "others" and encourages ignorance of how policies of the dominant group or nation affect people outside its borders, and how citizens and residents benefit from such policies, including those who are otherwise marginalized by racism or class inequality.

Media reports use language and images, subtly or crudely, in service of these ends. In Israel, this practice includes gross dehumanization of Palestinian people as well as governments and citizens of Arab nations. In the Balkans, local media sowed distrust and hatred among people who had lived alongside each other for generations. The independent Rwandan radio station, Radio Télévision Libre des Milles Collines, broadcast hate propaganda against Tutsis, moderate Hutus, Belgians, and the UN mission (UNAMIR), greatly contributing to the racial hostilities that led to genocide. Since the attacks of September 11, 2001, U.S. government policies and news reporting have relied on explicit ideologies of racism in the demonization of very diverse peoples, conveniently lumped together as Arabs, Muslims, Arab Americans, and "people who look like Muslims." In an analysis of *New York Times* articles from 2000 to 2004, Suad Joseph and Benjamin D'Harlingue revealed "a predominantly negative representation of Islam. In article after article, Islam is presented as reactionary, violent, oppressive, anti-American, and incomprehensible to the 'Western

mind.' Muslim leaders are represented as dangerous fanatics rather than as respected spiritual leaders, and Muslim places of worship as sites of insurgencies rather than sites of the sacred" (2007, 464).

Drawing on such beliefs, U.S. president George W. Bush and British prime minister Tony Blair argued that the bombing of Afghanistan and Iraq would liberate Afghan and Iraqi women from domination by Muslim men. Their wives, Laura Bush and Cherie Blair, made public statements to this effect that were widely published by mainstream media: that is, the first ladies deployed gender arguments while their own gender was also being deployed. Anthropologists Lila Abu-Lughod (2002) and Charles Hirschkind and Saba Mahmood (2002) have critiqued the assumptions underlying this savior discourse as reminiscent of colonial and missionary rhetoric. Gayatri Spivak (1988, 297) notes that colonial ideology often seeks to justify domination as being in the interests of women and that arguments for intervention often are cast in terms of "white men saving brown women from brown men." By contrast, Afghan and Iraqi women argue that they desperately need military operations to stop. They need physical safety, resources to rebuild their homes and communities, genuine solidarity and support from feminists of other countries, and full involvement in peacemaking processes (Heyzer 2005; Kolhatkar 2004, 2005).

U.S. women were among the troops deployed ostensibly to "liberate" Muslim women. The differing experiences of three women who served in the U.S. Army 507th Maintenance Company unit ambushed after taking a "wrong turn in the desert" (Bragg 2003) are instructive in showing how news is created. Lori Piestewa, a single mother aged twenty-three, became the first Native American woman to die in combat as a U.S. soldier and the first female soldier killed in Iraq. Shoshanna Johnson, the first black female prisoner of war in the history of the United States, was shot in the legs and held prisoner for twenty-two days. Neither woman was given much attention, whereas Jessica Lynch, described as petite, pretty, blonde, and a plucky little fighter, made the front cover of *Time* magazine. Her story, which reverberated throughout the U.S. media, was cast in terms of a fairy-tale rescue narrative involving U.S. Marines flying Black Hawk helicopters. Lynch was alleged to have suffered multiple gunshot wounds. She was said to have fought to near death rather than be taken prisoner. These details turned out to be fiction—she survived partly due to the generosity and skills of Iraqi doctors—but they made a much better national story at a time when the war was going badly, and as a young white woman from Appalachia, Jessica Lynch made a better national hero than her colleagues of color.[2]

Whether or not women take part in combat, militaries need women's support and participation in many ways: as mothers who believe in heroism and patriotic duty and who support sons and daughters who enlist; as nurses who heal the wounded and the traumatized; as wives and girlfriends who anxiously wait to welcome soldiers home and help them adjust to civilian life; and as workers who produce food supplies, uniforms, and weapons (Enloe 2000a). Their experiences provide material for a steady stream of human-interest stories that affirm women's contribution to the war effort and the importance of the "home front."

The militarization of the English language includes commonplace usage in which ads "target" consumers and leaders "spearhead" reforms. The power of language is further co-opted to distract us from the reality of war: rocket-launched intercontinental ballistic missiles are code-named "Peacekeepers"; smaller surface-to-air missiles are "Patriots." A bloodless phrase such as "collateral damage" refers to the destruction of homes and hospitals, and to civilian casualties, an unfortunate side effect of bombing so-called military targets. The seemingly neutral term "national security" masks the fact that torture is an explicit part of U.S. national policy, even if its practice is defined as interrogation, for example.

The global "war on terrorism" is described as a "mission"—replete with religious overtones—by the Bush administration, part of its conflation of church and state. Forms of religious extremism and fundamentalism are one response to poverty and insecurity generated by the global economic system. U.S. responsibility for having promoted, supported, and armed Islamic fundamentalist groups to create a wedge against communism must be noted here. Religious fundamentalism—Christian, Hindu, Jewish, and Muslim—has increased intolerance and violence in many regions and reinforced "misogyny, homophobia, xenophobia and aggression, while narrowing secular space" (Global Fund for Women and Women of Color Resource Center n.d., 11). These developments have limited or closed down cultural and political spaces for critique and resistance, with significant impacts on antimilitary organizing.

CONSEQUENCES OF MILITARIZED SECURITY

Militarized national security undermines everyday human security and imposes vast personal, economic, political, cultural, and environmental costs. Indeed, the current international system of militarism, together with overconsumption in countries of the global North, is the main impediment to genuine security worldwide.

Killing, Trauma, Crisis, Destruction

Direct effects of wars include the killing of soldiers, mainly men, and of non-combatants—mainly women, children, and elders; the trauma of experiencing or witnessing destruction, torture, or rape; the chaos of everyday life, with hunger and loss of home, family, and livelihood; and the trauma of being forced to flee from home and live as refugees. Other effects are physical injuries and disabilities, post-traumatic stress disorders, loss of community, economic crisis, broken sewers, contaminated water, environmental devastation, and the prevalence of guns. War trauma greatly affects those in combat, particularly those who kill (Lifton 2005; MacNair 2002). Combatants experience brutalization as they learn to dehumanize others so as to be able to torture, rape, or kill. The proportion of civilians killed in war has leapt from 5 percent of casualties (after World War I) to over 90 percent by the end of the twentieth century. Over 80 percent of casualties of small arms are women and children. There are approximately 50 million uprooted people around the world—refugees who have sought safety in another country and people displaced within their own nation. About 75–80 percent of these are women and children, many of them war orphans (Fritz 2000; International Rescue Committee n.d.). Economic collapse resulting from war causes lack of food, water, and basic supplies; exorbitant prices; destruction of farms and gardens, factories, and other workplaces; and endless queuing for necessities. This situation impacts women severely as they try to care for children and sustain their families and communities.

Cultures of Violence

. . . The militarization of everyday culture, often unnoticed, is a critical tool of militarism. War toys, video games, movies, and television shows all teach children what it means to be a "real man." War movies are a Hollywood staple and screened worldwide, with heroes and adventure shown in military terms. As part of the "war on terrorism," the Bush administration called on the U.S. film industry to make more pro-war movies (Saunders 2001; Schneider and McDermott 2001). G.I. Jane Boot Camp exercise programs co-opt ideas of military strength and fitness. Toy manufacturer Ever Sparkle Inc. produced a bombed-out doll-house in which grenades replaced salt and pepper shakers, ammunition boxes littered the kitchen, and G.I. Joe, armed with a bazooka, was on the balcony ready for action. Fashion designers promote the "military look" and camouflage chic. Backpacks, cell-phone covers, baby clothes, and condoms all come in "camo" (Ahn and Kirk 2005).

Dynamics of dehumanization link violence against women by male family members, acquaintances, or strangers to state violence perpetrated by police officers, prison guards, immigration officers, and military personnel. The stress of war leads to increased violence against women, whether they are wives or girlfriends, or women who sexually service soldiers, in that they absorb the aggression and fear of men returning from training or from battle. Crisis and disruption invariably generate additional responsibilities for women to support their families as cultivators, breadwinners, or decision makers. Possibilities for greater authority and independence may emerge during such times, but in the aftermath, patriarchal relations are usually reinstated and many women say they are even less secure after the fighting stops, especially when men are armed and weapons remain in circulation (Rehn and Sirleaf 2002, 118).

In the United States, "rates of domestic violence are 3 to 5 times higher in military couples than in comparable civilian ones" (Lutz 2004, 17 . . .). Women in the U.S. military have reported sexual assault by their colleagues in the service academies, in basic training, and in Iraq. Peacekeeping forces also subject women to forced prostitution, sexual abuse, and rape (Rehn and Sirleaf 2002, 64). As a weapon of war, rape involves a complex intertwining of gender and race/ethnicity, and is a strategic and systematic way of dishonoring and attacking enemy men. Examples include Korean and Chinese "comfort women" forced to provide sexual services for the Japanese Imperial Army in World War II (Hicks 1994; Kim-Gibson 1999; Sajor 1998). In the 1990s, armies conducted systematic rapes

in the Balkans (Cockburn 1998; Kesic 2000; Walsh 2001) and in Rwanda (Newbury and Baldwin 2001; Rehn and Sirleaf 2002). More recently, pro-government militias have raped women and girls in the Darfur region of Sudan (Kristof 2005; Lacey 2004). Sexual abuse and torture committed by U.S. military personnel and contractors against Iraqi prisoners in Abu Ghraib prison illustrate a grim new twist on militarized violence, where race and nation "trumped" gender. White U.S. women were among the perpetrators (appropriating the masculinist role); Iraqi men were violated (forced into the feminized role).

Diverting Resources Needed for Everyday Security

Resources committed to war and militarization could provide for everyday security. In 2002, the Stockholm Peace Research Institute estimated that approximately $200 billion would allow nations to provide decent housing, health care, and education for everyone worldwide; this amount was one-quarter of the sum then invested in militaries (as quoted in Rehn and Sirleaf 2002, 123). A change in budget priorities could also provide resources for developing renewable energy and cleaning up environmental contamination as well as stopping global warming, easing the debt burden, disarming nuclear weapons, and ridding the world of landmines.

People's time, creativity, opportunities, and talents are valuable resources. In many countries it is much easier for young men to obtain and use guns than to hold a paying job or make a constructive contribution to their society. Militaries take capable young men and women from their home communities, in the process often depriving those communities of young people's energy and potential leadership. In industrial nations, especially the United States, a significant number of scientists, technologists, and researchers spend their professional lives creating ever more sophisticated ways of killing, with an increasing reliance on robotics. Scientists in fields like meteorology, cosmology, astrophysics, and complex chemistry must compete with military researchers for time on government-funded supercomputers.

Environmental Destruction and Effects on Human Health

Militarism and wars have serious long-term effects on the environment and human health (Kirk 2008). Take, for example, catastrophic wartime events such as the atomic bombing of Hiroshima and Nagasaki in 1945, use of the defoliant Agent Orange in the Vietnam War, the burning of oil fields and use of depleted uranium in the 1991 Persian Gulf War, and the bombing of Kosovo, Afghanistan, and Iraq. Environmental destruction for military ends occurs throughout the entire nuclear weapons cycle: from uranium mining, processing, development, and testing to disposal of weapons-grade plutonium and recirculation of depleted uranium in "conventional" weapons. Land mines in Bosnia-Herzegovina, Cambodia, Colombia, and Kosovo, for example, make the use of large areas a long-term danger. Mine removal is slow, expensive, and painstaking work. Routine military training also damages crops and agricultural land. Fuels, oils, solvents, and heavy metals used in the maintenance and repair of armored vehicles, ships, and planes contaminate land, water, and the ocean. Land used for bombing training is pulverized to dust and rubble. Unexploded ammunition and debris litter bombing ranges and live-fire artillery ranges as well as parts of the seabed.

Undermining Participatory Governance Structures and Processes

Increasing militarization happens through the accumulation of thousands of daily decisions taken by elected officials, political advisers and aides, voters, administrators, news editors, scientists, investors, corporate employees and executives, as well as members of the military. As nations move toward becoming more militarized, their decision-making processes become more centralized or autocratic. This change may involve the increasing use of presidential edicts, surveillance, secrecy, arbitrary arrests, military courts, extra-judicial killings, the "disappearance" of "suspects," or the shutdown of decision-making bodies. It may include outlawing opposition groups, closing down community newspapers, radio stations, and presses, banning books, or firing teachers. It invariably includes the demonization of enemy groups, as mentioned earlier. Governments may jettison citizens' rights to organize, to assemble lawfully, or to speak freely, for example, which they justify as necessary for national security. . . .

Socially and culturally, militarization requires and serves to enforce conformity, leading human rights law professor Zorica Mrsevic to comment: "The opposite of war is not peace—it is creativity" (2000, 41). Militarism operates through hierarchy and the

sacrosanct nature of the "chain of command." In civil wars, people with visions of an alternative society may be killed or forced to flee for their lives. The bloated budgets and distorted spending priorities required to sustain militarism take resources from many potential creative and generative projects.

CONTESTING MILITARIZATION

Contesting militarization means understanding and opposing this web of interconnected economic, political, and ideological factors and working for demilitarization along all these dimensions. It involves developing nonmilitary forms of strength to counteract military threats; expanding and disseminating knowledge and experiences of peaceful resolution to conflicts; and articulating visions of true security based on sustainable environmental and economic principles, participatory political systems, and sturdy connections among people that both acknowledge and go beyond narrow identities and territories.

The increasing integration of the world economy requires and has given rise to new political movements across national and regional boundaries. It is clear to many people that neither capitalism nor militarism can guarantee genuine security for the majority of the world's population or for the planet itself. Activists draw on various overlapping and diverging theoretical and political frameworks: feminisms, nationalisms, anti-imperialism, internationalism, critiques of neoliberal globalization, indigenous peoples' demands for sovereignty and reparations, and environmental justice. Given the centrality of militarization in the world economy, conventional thinking about international relations, and the imaginative hold of militarism in popular culture, creating genuine security is a huge undertaking involving four interconnected levels of analysis and action: the individual (micro), community (meso), institutional (macro), and transnational/global levels. . . .

[I draw here from] a feminist project originating in Switzerland and organized by an international coordinating group to recognize, honor, and make visible women's ongoing efforts to create peace and genuine security. . . .

At the Personal/Micro Level

Resistance to militarization at the microlevel includes thinking about how we are each affected by militarization and how we contribute to it, which varies greatly according to location and context. It may include individual decisions to turn in or destroy weapons, not to enlist in the military, to support or become a conscientious objector, or to undertake the personal work of healing from trauma after military service or experiencing military violence. Personal resistance to militarization may include joining antimilitary demonstrations, vigils, and organizations, supporting antimilitary candidates for political office, and urging them to promote sustainable development polices and projects. It may mean limiting our financial support for militarism through, for example, tax resistance; demilitarizing our knowledge by being more critical of what the mainstream media feed us; and seeking alternative sources of information.

On the positive side, it means using our personal resources—skills, talents, time, money, and imagination—to create ways of living that support everyday security and sustainability. Examples include teaching conflict resolution skills to children, cultivating gardens, supporting farmers' markets, making art, sharing in community events that affirm and celebrate nonviolence, and opening ourselves to connections and friendships across lines of race, class, religion, and culture.

At the Community/Meso Level

Women's peace work is most visible at the community level, where women draw on their skills and creativity to analyze their situation, define needs, and provide services. This work may include organizing workshops or rallies where women can speak about violence related to war, as has happened in Guatemala, Colombia, and Sierra Leone. It includes establishing women's centers to heal military violence (for example, Medica Women's Therapy Center in Bosnia-Herzegovina), helping women deal with the daily impact of Israeli occupation as well as the sexism of their society (Women's Center for Legal Aid and Counseling in Palestine), supporting Philippine women who work in bars and clubs around U.S. bases (My Sister's Place in South Korea), and providing health care and income-generating projects for women affected by war (Association of Widows of the Genocide of April 1994 in Rwanda). Organizations that support young men and women who oppose military service include the Central Committee for Conscientious Objectors (United States), Peace and Human Rights Solidarity (South Korea), and New Profile and Yesh Gvul (Israel).

Resisting militarization at the community level may include creating cultural spaces to explore the meaning of demilitarization and peace, such as the Center for Education for a Culture of Peace and Folk Art Museum (El Salvador), the Chicago Peace Museum (United States), Space Peace (South Korea), or the antimilitary fashion shows initiated by the Women of Color Resource Center (United States) to contest the militarization of everyday culture through camouflage "chic." It involves demonstrations and vigils. Women in Black stood in silent witness outside government offices in Belgrade and denounced Milosevic, their president. Dialogue projects—among Israeli and Palestinian people, across ethnic lines in the Balkans, or between Catholic and Protestant communities in Northern Ireland—have created spaces for listening and the deepening of understanding (Cockburn 1998). Community media projects that use street theater, comic books, storytelling, video, radio shows, alternative newspapers, or the Internet all distribute information and perspectives missing from mainstream media. Community resistance also includes music, poetry, writing, painting, theater, dance, and other cultural events that are healing and inspirational.

At the Institutional/Macro Level

Resistance at the institutional level involves lobbying governments, pushing them to uphold treaties, and holding them accountable to commitments made in ratifying international agreements such as the UN Charter, the 1993 Vienna Declaration on Human Rights, and the Platform for Action adopted by the 1995 UN Conference on women in Beijing. South Africa's postapartheid constitution is the first in the world to ban "speech that incites hatred of a person because of race, religions, gender, or sexual preference"—an example of demilitarizing the notion of free speech (Rehn and Sirleaf 2002, 107–108).

The demilitarization of education includes curriculum changes, as with the contentious debate over history textbooks used in Japanese classrooms and what students are taught about atrocities perpetrated by the Japanese Imperial Army before and during World War II, especially against China, Korea, and Okinawa. It also includes peace education in schools and community discussions in which people can assert their peacemaking traditions. In communities in Albania, Cambodia, and Niger, such discussions generated agreements to destroy knives and guns (Hague Appeal for Peace n.d.). In the United States, it means learning deeply about people from diverse communities and many nations, as well as about this nation's profound historic investment in colonialism, genocide, militarization, and imperialism. It includes creating an alternative curriculum to replace the JROTC presence in schools and fostering resistance to military recruiters in schools. The military is the only employer that systematically targets inner-city African American and Latino youth with promises of a disciplined lifestyle, enhanced pride and self-esteem, professional training, and money for college. For every college counselor at Roosevelt High School in East Los Angeles, for example, there are five military recruiters (Joiner 2003). Demilitarizing education includes refusing to undertake military-related research. It includes the actions of faculty, staff, students, and community members who opposed a proposed U.S. Navy University-Affiliated Research Center at the University of Hawai'i–Manoa. It means that feminist research and teaching must confront the centrality of militarism, a defining dimension of the nation-state and the articulation of state power.

In many nations, people are organizing to push for a larger share of public funds to be devoted to education rather than military operations. Closely related is the demilitarization of national budget priorities, which requires that people understand the relationship between military spending and socially useful government spending. Organizations in Britain, South Korea, and Sweden have started to do this. In the United States, the National Priorities Project, the War Resisters' League, and Women's Action for New Directions publish accessible materials on military spending.

Resistance to militarization at the institutional level means including women's meaningful participation in peace processes and efforts to demilitarize societies in the aftermath of war. In October 2000, the UN Security Council adopted Resolution 1325 on women, peace, and security. This is the first time the Security Council has addressed the disproportionate impact of armed conflict on women; recognized the undervalued contributions that women make to conflict prevention, conflict resolution, and peace building; and stressed the importance of women's equal and full participation as active agents in peace and security. Although not binding on governments, Resolution 1325 sets a new standard of inclusiveness and gender sensitivity in peace negotiations and

provides leverage for women's efforts to influence policy in postconflict reconstruction (Lynes and Torry 2005).

In June 2006, for example, women's organizations in Southern Sudan relied on this resolution in calling for UN support for women in conflict areas ("Message from the Women from Southern Sudan" 2006). They argued that women's rights violations, women's low social status, and continued gender-based discrimination are a result of high levels of poverty, twenty-one years of war, and a confluence of culture, religions, and traditions. They requested that the UN Security Council press the government of Southern Sudan for urgent reforms in the areas of family law, legal aid, psycho-social counseling, and health services for women; for increased participation of women in decision-making at all levels of conflict resolution, peace building, and development; for increased recruitment of female police who better understand the plight of women; and for support for women's organizations to undertake civic education, skills training, and consciousness raising on HIV/AIDS and gender issues. They also requested that the UN Security Council continue to support the parties to the Comprehensive Peace Agreement (CPA) in Southern Sudan; report on the protection of women and children from violence; and continue to provide necessary resources to UN agencies such as UNIFEM and UNFPA to ensure women's full participation in the implementation of the CPA.

At the Transnational/Global Level

Working across national borders builds on activities at other levels. This work needs guides and interpreters, opportunities to listen and learn, time, resources, organizational capacity, patience, perseverance, and the willingness to be uncomfortable at times. It includes networking at meetings and conferences, sharing information through journals and the Internet, and organizing coordinated activities.

The Pan-African Women's Conference on a Culture of Peace (Zanzibar, Tanzania, 1999), the International Women's Summit to Redefine Security (Okinawa, Japan, 2000), and international gatherings of Women in Black groups from North America, Europe, and the Middle East (Jerusalem, 2006) serve as examples of women organizing across borders. Such gatherings build on the work of networks like the Federation of African Women's Peace Networks, the Mano River

Union Women's Network for Peace, and the International Women's Network against Militarism. Women's groups in Croatia, Serbia, Bosnia, and Kosovo have done remarkable work across ethnic lines in supporting Serb, Croat, and Muslim women during war and in the aftermath to build bridges within their communities and between states. Long-standing organizations such as the Women's International League for Peace and Freedom (founded in 1915 and currently active in thirty-seven countries) can play an important role at this level, as can UN-sponsored gatherings, and other opportunities for dialogue and exchange such as the World Social Forum.

Transnational organizations that seek to prevent conflicts include Global Action to Prevent War and Armed Conflict, and Search for Common Ground, both of which work with partner organizations in various nations to find culturally appropriate ways for nations to strengthen their capacity to deal constructively with conflicts. These organizations use media production—radio, television, film, and print—mediation and facilitation, training, community organizing, sports, theater, and music to promote individual and institutional changes. The Nonviolent Peaceforce, with over ninety member organizations from around the world, works to build a trained, international civilian peace force able to intervene in conflicts. In December 2002, 130 delegates from forty-seven nations chose Sri Lanka as the site of the first pilot project. The goal is for field team members to contribute to protecting human rights, deterring violence, and creating space for local peacemakers to carry out their work. Peace Brigades International (PBI) has a similar mission, currently with volunteers in Colombia, Guatemala, Indonesia, and Mexico. Any kind of solidarity work needs clear understandings about whose needs, perspectives, and decisions are central to the task in order to avoid allowing individuals and groups with class or national privilege to define the direction in which projects should go, thereby reinforcing unequal relationships, even if this is not the intent. Many people working in transnational networks and solidarity organizations draw on what Chandra Talpade Mohanty (2003, 50) calls "a common context of struggle," with a shared framework opposing militarization.

Transnational work includes support for UN initiatives such as UNESCO's Culture of Peace, as well as the International Criminal Court (ICC), independent of the UN, which can try individuals accused of the most serious crimes of international concern: genocide, crimes against humanity, and war crimes. The ICC, based on a treaty that entered into force in 2002, has been joined by 105 countries so far.

Militarism's reach and power are vast. Increased intolerance and violence in many regions have reduced cultural and political spaces for critique and resistance, as mentioned earlier. Nevertheless, millions of people worldwide oppose and reject war, as shown on February 15, 2003, a day of unprecedented coordinated protest against the not-yet-begun U.S.- and British-led war on Iraq. Journalist Patrick Tyler (2003) wrote that "the huge anti-war demonstrations around the world this weekend are reminders that there may still be two superpowers on the planet: the United States and world public opinion." The "second superpower" has not yet stopped the war against Iraq, but it contests militarization in a myriad ways, including the examples mentioned in this chapter.

Betty Burkes, former president of Women's International League for Peace and Freedom (U.S. section) and among the thousand women nominated for the 2005 Nobel Peace Prize, comments: "We will succeed in building a strong base for transforming . . . power when together we weave a vision that in practice offers a way of life so *vital* it is impossible to resist."[3]

ACKNOWLEDGMENTS

An earlier version of this essay was given at the Gender, Race, and Militarization Conference, October 28, 2005, at the University of Oregon. I thank the editors of this volume for their insights and support, and also Margo Okazawa-Rey, long-time friend and colleague, with whom I shared and developed many of these ideas. This chapter's section "The Permanent War Economy" partly draws on ideas developed in *Social Justice* 27(4), a special issue on neoliberalism, militarism, and armed conflict, edited by Gwyn Kirk and Margo Okazawa-Rey (2000). Reprinted by permission; see www.socialjusticejournal.org.

NOTES

1. In January 2004, the U.S. Department of Defense issued a memorandum restating its opposition to "prostitution and any related activities that may contribute to the phenomenon of trafficking in persons as inherently harmful and dehumanizing" (as quoted in Equality Now 2006, n.p.). On October 14, 2005, President Bush signed Executive Order 13387, which makes "patronizing a prostitute" a violation of article 134 of the Uniform Code of Military Justice.
2. Margo Okazawa-Rey alerted me to the unequal treatment and visibility these women received.
3. Betty Burkes, pers. Comm.; this is a version of her statement in 1000 *Peace Women across the Globe* (1000 Women for the Nobel Peace Prize 2005, 718).

REFERENCES

Abu-Lughod, Lila. 2002. "Do Muslim Women Really Need Saving? Anthropological Reflections on Cultural Relativism and Its Others." *American Anthropologist* 104(3): 738–790.

Ahn, Christine, and Gwyn Kirk. 2005. "Why War Is All the Rage." *San Francisco Chronicle*, May 29, D5.

Aizenman, N. C. 2006. "Money Earned in U.S. Pushes up Prices in El Salvador." *Washington Post*, May 14, A17. http://www.washingtonpost.com/wp-dyn/content/article/2006/05/13/AR200605.I300879html?nav=rss_world/centralamerica (accessed December 12, 2006).

Allen, Holly. 2000. "Gender, Sexuality and the Military Model of U.S. National Community." In *Gender Ironies of Nationalism: Sexing the Nation*, ed. Tamar Mayer, 306–327. New York: Routledge.

Avant, Deborah. 2005. *The Market for Force: The Consequences of Privatizing Security*. New York: Cambridge University Press.

Bragg, Rick. 2003. "Wrong Turn in the Desert." *Time Magazine*, November 17. http://www time.com/time/magazine/article/0,9171,1213025-1,00.html (accessed December 26, 2006).

Chomsky, Noam. 1997. *Media Control: The Spectacular Achievements of Propaganda*. New York: Seven Stories Press.
———. 1999. "Kosovo Peace Accord." *Z Magazine* (July): 36–42.

Chossudovsky, Michel. 1996. "Dismantling Yugoslavia, Colonizing Bosnia." *Covert Action Quarterly* 56: 31–37.

Cockburn, Cynthia. 1998. *The Space between Us: Negotiating Gender and National Identities in Conflict*. London: Zed Books.

CorpWatch. 2001. "Corporate Globalization Fact Sheet." http://www.corpwatch.org/article.php?id=378 (accessed December 12, 2006).

Enloe, Cynthia. 2000a. *Maneuvers: The International Politics of Militarizing Women's Lives*. Berkeley: University of California Press.
———. 2000b. "Masculinity as a Foreign Policy Issue." *Foreign Policy in Focus* 5(36). http://www.fpif.org/fpiftxt/1502 (accessed February 13, 2007).

Equality Now. 2006. "United States: The Role of Military Forces in the Growth of the Commercial Sex Industry." Women's Action 23.2, March. http://www.equalitynow.org/english/actions/action_2302_en.html (accessed October 20, 2006).

Feffer, John. 2000. "Gunboat Diplomacy: The Intersection of Economics and Security in East Asia." *Social Justice* 27(4): 45–62.

Ferguson, Kathy, and Phyllis Turnbull. 1999. *Oh, Say, Can You See? The Semiotics of the Military in Hawai'i*. Minneapolis: University of Minnesota Press.
———. 2004. "Globalizing Militaries" In *Rethinking Globalism*, ed. Manfred B. Steger, 79–91. Lanham, MD: Rowman and Littlefield.

Fritz, Mark. 2000. *Lost on Earth: Nomads of the New World*. New York: Routledge.

Garamone, Jim. 2000. "Joint Vision 2020 Emphasizes Full-Spectrum Dominance." http://www.defenselink.mil/news/Jun2000/no6022000_20006025.html (accessed December 24, 2006).
———. 2004. "El Salvador to Continue Iraq Deployment." American Forces Press Service. http://www.defenselink.mil/news/Jul2004/no7222004_2004072207.html (accessed December 20, 2006).

Global Fund for Women and Women of Color Resource Center. N.d. *Building a 21st Century Transnational Women's Movement*. San Francisco: Global Fund for Women and Women of Color Resource Center.

Greenfield, Gerard. 2002. "Vietnam and the World Coffee Crisis: Local Coffee Riots in a Global Context." http://www.cb3rob.net/~merijn89/ARCH2/msg00037.html (accessed December 20, 2006).

Hague Appeal for Peace. N.d. *Peace and Disarmament Education: Changing Mindsets to Reduce Violence and Sustain the Removal of Small Arms*. New York: HAP.

Herman, Edward S., and Noam Chomsky. 2002. *Manufacturing Consent: The Political Economy of the Mass Media*. New York: Pantheon.

Hertvik, Nicole. 2006. "El Salvador: Effecting Change from Within." *UN Chronicle*. http://www.un.org/Pubs/chronicle/2002/issue3/0302p75_el_salvador.html (accessed December 12, 2006).

Heyzer, Noeleen. 2005. "Seating Women at the Peace Table." In *Stop the Next War Now*, ed. Medea Benjamin and Jodie Evans, 167–168. San Francisco: Inner Ocean Publishing.

Hicks, George. 1994. *The Comfort Women*. New York: Norton.

Hirschkind, Charles, and Saba Mahmood. 2002. "Feminism, the Taliban, and the Politics of Counterinsurgency." *Anthropological Quarterly* 75(2): 339–354.

Hodierne, Robert. 2006. "Down on the War. Poll: More Troops Unhappy with Bush's Course in Iraq." http://www.militarycity.com/polls/2006_main.php (accessed January 9, 2007).

International Rescue Committee. N.d. "Frequently Asked Questions about Refugees and Resettlement." http://www.theirc.org/what/frequently_asked_questions_about_refugees_and_resettlement.html (accessed February 13, 2007).

Joiner, Whitney. 2003. "The Army Be Thuggin' It—The New Black and Latino Recruitment Hustle." *Salon,* October 17. http://dir.salon.com/story/mwt/feature/2003/10/17/army/index.html (accessed December 13, 2006).

Joseph, Suad, and Benjamin D'Harlingue. 2007. "Media Representations and the Criminalization of Arab Americans and Muslim Americans." In *Women's Lives: Multicultural Perspectives,* 4th ed., ed. Gwyn Kirk and Margo Okazawa-Rey, 464–468. New York: McGraw-Hill.

Kesic, Vesna. 2000. "From Reverence to Rape: An Anthropology of Ethnic and Gendered Violence." In *Frontline Feminisms: Women, War, and Resistance,* ed. Marguerite R. Waller and Jennifer Rycenga, 23–36. New York: Garland.

Kim, D. S. 2006. "Human Rights Situation of Foreign Women in the Korean Sex Industry." In *Out of the Trap, Hope One Step: Case Studies of Prostitution and Sex Trafficking in Korea,* ed. Dasi Hamkke Center, 39–48. Seoul: Dasi Hamkke Center.

Kim-Gibson, Dai Sil. 1999. *Silence Broken: Korean Comfort Women.* Parkersburg, IA: Mid-Prairie Books.

Kirk, Gwyn. 2006. "Genuine Security for Women." Paper marking the twentieth anniversary of My Sister's Place, South Korea, including information from interviews with Yu Young Nim and Dong Shim Kim, July–September 2006.

———. 2008. "Environmental Effects of U.S. Military 'Security': Gendered Experiences from the Philippines, South Korea, and Japan." In *Gender and Globalization in Asia and the Pacific: Method, Practice, Theory,* ed. Kathy E. Ferguson and Monique Mironesco. Honolulu: University of Hawai'i Press.

Kirk, Gwyn, and Margo Okazawa-Rey, eds. 2000. "Neoliberalism, Militarism, and Armed Conflict." Special issue. *Social Justice* 27(4).

Kolhatkar, Sonali. 2004. "Afghan Women Continue to Fend for Themselves." *Foreign Policy in Focus,* March. http://www.fpif.org/papers/2004afghanwom.html (accessed February 13, 2007).

———. 2005. "Freedom through Solidarity—The Lie of 'Liberation.'" In *Stop the Next War Now,* ed. Medea Benjamin and Jodi Evans, 87–89. San Francisco: Inner Ocean Publishing.

Kristof, Nicholas. 2005. "A Policy of Rape." *New York Times,* June 5, D14.

Lacey, Marc. 2004. "Amnesty Says Sudan Militias Use Rape as Weapon" *New York Times,* July 19, A.

Leigh, David. 2004. "Who Commands the Private Soldiers?" *Guardian UK,* May 17. http://www.truthout.org/cgi-bin/artman/exec/view.cgi/9/4500/printer (accessed January 11, 2007).

Lifton, Robert J. 2005. *Home from the War: Learning from Vietnam Vets.* New York: Other Press.

Lipschutz, Ronnie D. 1998. "Beyond the Neoliberal Peace: From Conflict Resolution to Social Reconciliation." *Social Justice* 25(4): 5–19.

Lumpe, Lora. 2000. *Running Guns: The Global Black Market in Small Arms.* New York: Palgrave/St. Martins.

Lutz, Catherine. 2004. "Living Room Terrorists." *Women's Review of Books* 21(5): 17–18.

Lynes, Krista, and Gina Torry, eds. 2005. *From Local to Global: Making Peace Work for Women.* New York: NGO Working Group on Women, Peace and Security.

MacNair, Rachel. 2002. *Perpetration-Induced Traumatic Stress: The Psychological Consequences of Killing.* Westport, CT: Praeger.

McChesney, R. W. 2004. *The Problem of the Media: U.S. Communications Politics in the 21st-Century.* New York: Monthly Review Press.

Melman, Seymour. 1974. *Permanent War Economy: American Capitalism in Decline.* New York: Simon and Schuster.

———. 2003. "In the Grip of a Permanent War Economy." Counterpunch, March 15. http://www.counterpunch.org/melmano3152003.html (accessed December 13, 2006).

Merle, Renae. 2003. "Battlefield Is a Showcase for Defense Firms." *Washington Post,* April 1, E1.

"Message from the Women from Southern Sudan to the UN Security Council in Relation to UN Security Council Resolution No. 1325." 2006. June 8. http://www.peacewomen.org/campaigns/Sudan/Sudan.html (accessed January 5, 2007).

Mohanty, Chandra Talpade. 2003. *Feminism without Borders: Decolonizing Theory, Practicing Solidarity.* Durham, NC: Duke University Press.

Mokhiber, Russell, and Robert Weissman. 2004. "The Rising Corporate Military Monster." CommonDreams.org News Center, April 23. http://www.commondreams.org/views04/0423–12.htm (accessed February 13, 2007).

Mrsevic, Zorica. 2000. "The Opposite of War Is Not Peace—It Is Creativity." In *Frontline Feminisms: Women, War, and Resistance,* ed. Marguerite R. Waller and Jennifer Rycenga, 41–55. New York: Garland.

Newbury, Catharine, and Hannah Baldwin. 2001. "Profile: Rwanda." In *Women and Civil War: Impact, Organizations, and Action,* ed. Krishna Kumar, 29–38. Boulder, CO: Lynne Rienner.

1000 Women for the Nobel Peace Prize. 2005. *1000 Peacewomen across the Globe.* Zurich: Scalo.

Paddock, Richard G. 2006. "The Overseas Class." *Los Angeles Times,* April 20, A1, A20–22.

Pae, Peter. 2003. "Iraq a Proving Ground for Defense Firms." *Los Angeles Times*, April 1, C1.

Peterson, V. Spike. 2000. "Sexing Political Identities/ Nationalism as Heterosexism." In *Women, States, and Nationalism: At Home in the Nation?* ed. Sita Ranchod-Nilsson and Mary Ann Tétreault, 54–80. New York: Routledge.

Plumwood, Val. 1993. *Feminism and the Mastery of Nature.* New York: Routledge.

Ready, Kelley, Stephen, Lynn, and Cosgrove, Serena. 2001. "Women's Organizations in El Salvador: History, Accomplishments, and International Support." In *Women and Civil War: Impact, Organizations, and Action,* ed. Krishna Kumar, 183–204. Boulder, CO: Lynne Rienner.

Rehn, Elisabeth, and Ellen Johnson Sirleaf. 2002. *Women, War, Peace: The Independent Experts Assessment on the Impact of Armed Conflict on Women and Women's Role in Peace-Building.* New York: UNIFEM.

Rosa, Herman. 2004. *Economic Integration and the Environment in El Salvador.* San Salvador: PRISMA.

Rubin, Joe. 2004. "El Salvador: Payback." *Frontline World,* October 12. http://www.pbs.org/frontlineworld/elections/elsalvador/ (accessed January 11, 2007).

Sajor, Indai Lourdes, ed. 1998. *Common Grounds: Violence against Women in War and Armed Conflict Situations.* Quezon City, Philippines: Asian Center for Women's Human Rights.

Saunders, Doug. 2001. "Hollywood, D.C." *Toronto Globe and Mail,* November 17. http://www.theglobeandmail.com/series/hollywood/ (accessed February 19, 2007).

Schneider, Bill, and Anne McDermott. 2001. "Uncle Sam Wants Hollywood." CNN.com. http://archives.cnn.com/2001/SHOWBIZ/Movies/11/09/hollywood.war/ (accessed February 19, 2007).

Singer, P. W. 2004. *Corporate Warriors: The Rise of the Privatized Military Industry.* Ithaca, NY: Cornell University Press.

Soto, Jessica U. 2004. *Human Rights: A Cross-Cutting Issue in Peace and Conflict Situations and Violence against Women.* Report prepared for the International Meeting on Human Security and Development, November 21–28, Manila, Philippines.

Spivak, Gayatri Chakravorty. 1988. "Can the Subaltern Speak?" In *Marxism and the Interpretation of Culture,* ed. Cary Nelson and Lawrence Grossberg, 271–313. Urbana: University of Illinois Press.

Staples, Steven. 2000. "Globalization and Militarism." *Social Justice* 27(4): 18–22.

Stockholm International Peace Research Institute. 2006. *SIPRI Yearbook 2006.* Stockholm: SIPRI. http://yearbook2006.sipri.org/chap8 (accessed January 12, 2008).

Tickner, J. Ann. 2001. *Gendering World Politics: Issues and Approaches in the Post–Cold War Era.* New York: Columbia University Press.

Tyler, Patrick. 2003. "A New Power in the Streets: A Message to Bush Not to Rush to War." *New York Times,* February 17, A1.

U.S. Department of Defense. 2002. "DOD 101: An Introductory Overview of the Department of Defense." http://www.defenselink.mil/pubs/dod101/dod101_for_2002.html (accessed March 19, 2007).

Walsh, Martha. 2001. "Profile: Bosnia and Herzegovina." In *Women and Civil War: Impact, Organizations, and Action,* ed. Krishna Kumar, 57–67. Boulder, CO: Lynne Rienner.

Wayne, Leslie. 2006. "Foreign Sales by U.S. Arms Makers Doubled in a Year." *New York Times,* November 11, Business sec. http://www.nytimes.com/2006/11/11/business/11military.html?_r=1&scp=88&sq=Wayne%2C+Leslie&oref=slogin (accessed January 12, 2008).

Do Muslim Women Really Need Saving? Anthropological Reflections on Cultural Relativism and Its Others

First published in 2002

What are the ethics of the current "War on Terrorism," a war that justifies itself by purporting to liberate, or save, Afghan women? Does anthropology have anything to offer in our search for a viable position to take regarding this rationale for war?

I was led to pose the question of my title in part because of the way I personally experienced the response to the U.S. war in Afghanistan. Like many colleagues whose work has focused on women and gender in the Middle East, I was deluged with invitations to speak—not just on news programs but also to various departments at colleges and universities, especially women's studies programs. Why did this not please me, a scholar who has devoted more than 20 years of her life to this subject and who has some complicated personal connection to this identity? Here was an opportunity to spread the word, disseminate my knowledge, and correct misunderstandings. The urgent search for knowledge about our sister "women of cover" (as President George Bush so marvelously called them) is laudable and when it comes from women's studies programs where "transnational feminism" is now being taken seriously, it has a certain integrity (see Safire 2001).

My discomfort led me to reflect on why, as feminists in or from the West, or simply as people who have concerns about women's lives, we need to be wary of this response to the events and aftermath of September 11, 2001. I want to point out the minefields—a metaphor that is sadly too apt for a country like Afghanistan, with the world's highest number of mines per capita—of this obsession with the plight of Muslim women. I

hope to show some way through them using insights from anthropology, the discipline whose charge has been to understand and manage cultural difference. At the same time, I want to remain critical of anthropology's complicity in the reification of cultural difference.

CULTURAL EXPLANATIONS AND THE MOBILIZATION OF WOMEN

It is easier to see why one should be skeptical about the focus on the "Muslim woman" if one begins with the U.S. public response. I will analyze two manifestations of this response: some conversations I had with a reporter from the PBS *NewsHour with Jim Lehrer* and First Lady Laura Bush's radio address to the nation on November 17, 2001. The presenter from the *NewsHour* show first contacted me in October to see if I was willing to give some background for a segment on Women and Islam. I mischievously asked whether she had done segments on the women of Guatemala, Ireland, Palestine, or Bosnia when the show covered wars in those regions; but I finally agreed to look at the questions she was going to pose to panelists. The questions were hopelessly general. Do Muslim women believe "x"? Are Muslim women "y"? Does Islam allow "z" for women? I asked her: If you were to substitute Christian or Jewish wherever you have Muslim, would these questions make sense? I did not imagine she would call me back. But she did, twice, once with an idea for a segment on the meaning of Ramadan and another time on Muslim women in politics. One was in response to the bombing and the other to the speeches by Laura Bush and Cherie Blair, wife of the British Prime Minister.

What is striking about these three ideas for news programs is that there was a consistent resort to the cultural, as if knowing something about women and Islam or the meaning of a religious ritual would help one understand the tragic attack on New York's World Trade Center and the U.S. Pentagon, or how Afghanistan had come to be ruled by the Taliban, or what interests might have fueled U.S. and other interventions in the region over the past 25 years, or what the history of American support for conservative groups funded to undermine the Soviets might have been, or why the caves and bunkers out of which Bin Laden was to be smoked "dead or alive," as President Bush announced on television, were paid for and built by the CIA.

In other words, the question is why knowing about the "culture" of the region, and particularly its religious beliefs and treatment of women, was more urgent than exploring the history of the development of repressive regimes in the region and the U.S. role in this history. Such cultural framing, it seemed to me, prevented the serious exploration of the roots and nature of human suffering in this part of the world. Instead of political and historical explanations, experts were being asked to give religio-cultural ones. Instead of questions that might lead to the exploration of global interconnections, we were offered ones that worked to artificially divide the world into separate spheres—recreating an imaginative geography of West versus East, us versus Muslims, cultures in which First Ladies give speeches versus others where women shuffle around silently in burqas.

Most pressing for me was why the Muslim woman in general, and the Afghan woman in particular, were so crucial to this cultural mode of explanation, which ignored the complex entanglements in which we are all implicated, in sometimes surprising alignments. Why were these female symbols being mobilized in this "War against Terrorism" in a way they were not in other conflicts? Laura Bush's radio address on November 17 reveals the political work such mobilization accomplishes. On the one hand, her address collapsed important distinctions that should have been maintained. There was a constant slippage between the Taliban and the terrorists, so that they became almost one word—a kind of hyphenated monster identity: the Taliban-and-the-terrorists. Then there was the blurring of the very separate causes in Afghanistan of women's continuing malnutrition, poverty, and ill health, and their more recent exclusion under the Taliban from employment, schooling, and the joys of wearing nail polish. On the other hand, her speech reinforced chasmic divides, primarily between the "civilized people throughout the world" whose hearts break for the women and children of Afghanistan and the Taliban-and-the-terrorists, the cultural monsters who want to, as she put it, "impose their world on the rest of us."

Most revealingly, the speech enlisted women to justify American bombing and intervention in Afghanistan and to make a case for the "War on Terrorism" of which it was allegedly a part. As Laura Bush said, "Because of our recent military gains in much of Afghanistan, women are no longer imprisoned in their homes. They can listen to music and teach their daughters without fear of punishment. . . . The fight against terrorism is also a fight for the rights and dignity of women" (U.S. Government 2002).

These words have haunting resonances for anyone who has studied colonial history. Many who have worked on British colonialism in South Asia have noted the use of the woman question in colonial policies where intervention into sati (the practice of widows immolating themselves on their husbands' funeral pyres), child marriage, and other practices was used to justify rule. As Gayatri Chakravorty Spivak (1988) has cynically put it: white men saving brown women from brown men. The historical record is full of similar cases, including in the Middle East. In Turn of the Century Egypt, what Leila Ahmed (1992) has called "colonial feminism" was hard at work. This was a selective concern about the plight of Egyptian women that focused on the veil as a sign of oppression but gave no support to women's education and was professed loudly by the same Englishman, Lord Cromer, who opposed women's suffrage back home.

Sociologist Marnia Lazreg (1994) has offered some vivid examples of how French colonialism enlisted women to its cause in Algeria. She writes:

> Perhaps the most spectacular example of the colonial appropriation of women's voices, and the silencing of those among them who had begun to take women revolutionaries . . . as role models by not donning the veil, was the event of May 16, 1958 [just four years before Algeria finally gained its independence from France after a long bloody struggle and 130 years of French control—L.A.]. On that day a demonstration was organized by rebellious French generals in Algiers

to show their determination to keep Algeria French. To give the government of France evidence that Algerians were in agreement with them, the generals had a few thousand native men bused in from nearby villages, along with a few women who were solemnly unveiled by French women. . . . Rounding up Algerians and bringing them to demonstrations of loyalty to France was not in itself an unusual act during the colonial era. But to unveil women at a well-choreographed ceremony added to the event a symbolic dimension that dramatized the one constant feature of the Algerian occupation by France: its obsession with women. (Lazreg 1994:135)

Lazreg (1994) also gives memorable examples of the way in which the French had earlier sought to transform Arab women and girls. She describes skits at awards ceremonies at the Muslim Girls' School in Algiers in 1851 and 1852. In the first skit, written by "a French lady from Algiers," two Algerian Arab girls reminisced about their trip to France with words including the following:

> Oh! Protective France: Oh! Hospitable France! . . .
> Noble land, where I felt free
> Under Christian skies to pray to our God: . . .
> God bless you for the happiness you bring us!
> And you, adoptive mother, who taught us
> That we have a share of this world,
> We will cherish you forever! (Lazreg 1994:68–69)

These girls are made to invoke the gift of a share of this world, a world where freedom reigns under Christian skies. This is not the world the Taliban-and-the-terrorists would "like to impose on the rest of us."

Just as I argued above that we need to be suspicious when neat cultural icons are plastered over messier historical and political narratives, so we need to be wary when Lord Cromer in British-ruled Egypt, French ladies in Algeria, and Laura Bush, all with military troops behind them, claim to be saving or liberating Muslim women.

POLITICS OF THE VEIL

I want now to look more closely at those Afghan women Laura Bush claimed were "rejoicing" at their liberation by the Americans. This necessitates a discussion of the veil, or the burqa, because it is so central to contemporary concerns about Muslim women. This

will set the stage for a discussion of how anthropologists, feminist anthropologists in particular, contend with the problem of difference in a global world. In the conclusion, I will return to the rhetoric of saving Muslim women and offer an alternative.

It is common popular knowledge that the ultimate sign of the oppression of Afghan women under the Taliban-and-the-terrorists is that they were forced to wear the burqa. Liberals sometimes confess their surprise that even though Afghanistan has been liberated from the Taliban, women do not seem to be throwing off their burqas. Someone who has worked in Muslim regions must ask why this is so surprising. Did we expect that once "free" from the Taliban they would go "back" to belly shirts and blue jeans, or dust off their Chanel suits? We need to be more sensible about the clothing of "women of cover," and so there is perhaps a need to make some basic points about veiling.

First, it should be recalled that the Taliban did not invent the burqa. It was the local form of covering that Pashtun women in one region wore when they went out. The Pashtun are one of several ethnic groups in Afghanistan and the burqa was one of many forms of covering in the subcontinent and Southwest Asia that has developed as a convention for symbolizing women's modesty or respectability. The burqa, like some other forms of "cover" has, in many settings, marked the symbolic separation of men's and women's spheres, as part of the general association of women with family and home, not with public space where strangers mingled.

Twenty years ago the anthropologist Hanna Papanek (1982), who worked in Pakistan, described the burqa as "portable seclusion." She noted that many saw it as a liberating invention because it enabled women to move out of segregated living spaces while still observing the basic moral requirements of separating and protecting women from unrelated men. Ever since I came across her phrase "portable seclusion," I have thought of these enveloping robes as "mobile homes." Everywhere, such veiling signifies belonging to a particular community and participating in a moral way of life in which families are paramount in the organization of communities and the home is associated with the sanctity of women.

The obvious question that follows is this: If this were the case, why would women suddenly become immodest? Why would they suddenly throw off the markers of their respectability, markers, whether burqas or other forms of cover, which were supposed to assure their protection in the public sphere from the harassment of strange men by symbolically signaling to all that they were still in the inviolable space of their homes, even though moving in the public realm? Especially when these are forms of dress that had become so conventional that most women gave little thought to their meaning.

To draw some analogies, none of them perfect, why are we surprised that Afghan women do not throw off their burqas when we know perfectly well that it would not be appropriate to wear shorts to the opera? At the time these discussions of Afghan women's burqas were raging, a friend of mine was chided by her husband for suggesting she wanted to wear a pantsuit to a fancy wedding: "You know you don't wear pants to a WASP wedding," he reminded her. New Yorkers know that the beautifully coiffed Hasidic women, who look so fashionable next to their dour husbands in black coats and hats, are wearing wigs. This is because religious belief and community standards of propriety require the covering of the hair. They also alter boutique fashions to include high necks and long sleeves. As anthropologists know perfectly well, people wear the appropriate form of dress for their social communities and are guided by socially shared standards, religious beliefs, and moral ideals, unless they deliberately transgress to make a point or are unable to afford proper cover. If we think that U.S. women live in a world of choice regarding clothing, all we need to do is remind ourselves of the expression, "the tyranny of fashion."

What had happened in Afghanistan under the Taliban is that one regional style of covering or veiling, associated with a certain respectable but not elite class, was imposed on everyone as "religiously" appropriate, even though previously there had been many different styles, popular or traditional with different groups and classes—different ways to mark women's propriety, or, in more recent times, religious piety. Although I am not an expert on Afghanistan, I imagine that the majority of women left in Afghanistan by the time the Taliban took control were the rural or less educated, from nonelite families, since they were the only ones who could not emigrate to escape the hardship and violence that has marked Afghanistan's recent history. If liberated from the enforced wearing of burqas, most of these women would choose some other form of modest headcovering, like all those living nearby who were not under the Taliban—their rural Hindu counterparts in the North of India (who

cover their heads and veil their faces from affines [in-laws]) or their Muslim sisters in Pakistan.

Even *The New York Times* carried an article about Afghan women refugees in Pakistan that attempted to educate readers about this local variety (Fremson 2001). The article describes and pictures everything from the now-iconic burqa with the embroidered eyeholes, which a Pashtun woman explains is the proper dress for her community, to large scarves they call chadors, to the new Islamic modest dress that wearers refer to as *hijab*. Those in the new Islamic dress are characteristically students heading for professional careers, especially in medicine, just like their counterparts from Egypt to Malaysia. One wearing the large scarf was a school principal; the other was a poor street vendor. The telling quote from the young street vendor is, "If I did [wear the burqa] the refugees would tease me because the burqa is for 'good women' who stay inside the home" (Fremson 2001:14). Here you can see the local status associated with the burqa—it is for good respectable women from strong families who are not forced to make a living selling on the street.

The British newspaper *The Guardian* published an interview in January 2002 with Dr. Suheila Siddiqi, a respected surgeon in Afghanistan who holds the rank of lieutenant general in the Afghan medical corps (Goldenberg 2002). A woman in her sixties, she comes from an elite family and, like her sisters, was educated. Unlike most women of her class, she chose not to go into exile. She is presented in the article as "the woman who stood up to the Taliban" because she refused to wear the burqa. She had made it a condition of returning to her post as head of a major hospital when the Taliban came begging in 1996, just eight months after firing her along with other women. Siddiqi is described as thin, glamorous, and confident. But further into the article it is noted that her graying bouffant hair is covered in a gauzy veil. This is a reminder that though she refused the burqa, she had no question about wearing the chador or scarf.

Finally, I need to make a crucial point about veiling. Not only are there many forms of covering, which themselves have different meanings in the communities in which they are used, but also veiling itself must not be confused with, or made to stand for, lack of agency. As I have argued in my ethnography of a Bedouin community in Egypt in the late 1970s and 1980s (1986), pulling the black head cloth over the face in front of older respected men is considered a voluntary act by women who are deeply committed to being moral and have a sense of honor tied to family. One of the ways they show their standing is by covering their faces in certain contexts. They decide for whom they feel it is appropriate to veil.

To take a very different case, the modern Islamic modest dress that many educated women across the Muslim world have taken on since the mid-1970s now both publicly marks piety and can be read as a sign of educated urban sophistication, a sort of modernity (e.g., Abu-Lughod 1995, 1998; Brenner 1996; El Guindi 1999; MacLeod 1991; Ong 1990). As Saba Mahmood (2001) has so brilliantly shown in her ethnography of women in the mosque movement in Egypt, this new form of dress is also perceived by many of the women who adopt it as part of a bodily means to cultivate virtue, the outcome of their professed desire to be close to God.

Two points emerge from this fairly basic discussion of the meanings of veiling in the contemporary Muslim world. First, we need to work against the reductive interpretation of veiling as the quintessential sign of women's unfreedom, even if we object to state imposition of this form, as in Iran or with the Taliban. (It must be recalled that the modernizing states of Turkey and Iran had earlier in the century banned veiling and required men, except religious clerics, to adopt Western dress.) What does freedom mean if we accept the fundamental premise that humans are social beings, always raised in certain social and historical contexts and belonging to particular communities that shape their desires and understandings of the world? Is it not a gross violation of women's own understandings of what they are doing to simply denounce the burqa as a medieval imposition? Second, we must take care not to reduce the diverse situations and attitudes of millions of Muslim women to a single item of clothing. Perhaps it is time to give up the Western obsession with the veil and focus on some serious issues with which feminists and others should indeed be concerned.

Ultimately, the significant political-ethical problem the burqa raises is how to deal with cultural "others." How are we to deal with difference without accepting the passivity implied by the cultural relativism for which anthropologists are justly famous—a relativism that says it's their culture and it's not my business to judge or interfere, only to try to understand. Cultural relativism is certainly an improvement on ethnocentrism and the racism, cultural imperialism, and imperiousness that underlie it; the problem is that it is too late not to interfere. The forms of lives we find around the

world are already products of long histories of interactions.

I want to explore the issues of women, cultural relativism, and the problems of "difference" from three angles. First, I want to consider what feminist anthropologists (those stuck in that awkward relationship, as Strathern [1987] has claimed) are to do with strange political bedfellows. I used to feel torn when I received the e-mail petitions circulating for the last few years in defense of Afghan women under the Taliban. I was not sympathetic to the dogmatism of the Taliban; I do not support the oppression of women. But the provenance of the campaign worried me. I do not usually find myself in political company with the likes of Hollywood celebrities (see Hirschkind and Mahmood 2002). I had never received a petition from such women defending the right of Palestinian women to safety from Israeli bombing or daily harassment at checkpoints, asking the United States to reconsider its support for a government that had dispossessed them, closed them out from work and citizenship rights, refused them the most basic freedoms. Maybe some of these same people might be signing petitions to save African women from genital cutting, or Indian women from dowry deaths. However, I do not think that it would be as easy to mobilize so many of these American and European women if it were not a case of Muslim men oppressing Muslim women—women of cover for whom they can feel sorry and in relation to whom they can feel smugly superior. Would television diva Oprah Winfrey host the Women in Black, the women's peace group from Israel, as she did RAWA, the Revolutionary Association of Women of Afghanistan, who were also granted the *Glamour Magazine* Women of the Year Award? What are we to make of post-Taliban "Reality Tours" such as the one advertised on the internet by Global Exchange for March 2002 under the title "Courage and Tenacity: A Women's Delegation to Afghanistan"? The rationale for the $1,400 tour is that "with the removal of the Taliban government, Afghan women, for the first time in the past decade, have the opportunity to reclaim their basic human rights and establish their role as equal citizens by participating in the rebuilding of their nation." The tour's objective, to celebrate International Women's Week, is "to develop awareness of the concerns and issues the Afghan women are facing as well as to witness the changing political, economic, and social conditions which have created new opportunities for the women of Afghanistan" (Global Exchange 2002).

To be critical of this celebration of women's rights in Afghanistan is not to pass judgment on any local women's organizations, such as RAWA, whose members have courageously worked since 1977 for a democratic secular Afghanistan in which women's human rights are respected, against Soviet-backed regimes or U.S.-, Saudi-, and Pakistani-supported conservatives. Their documentation of abuse and their work through clinics and schools have been enormously important.

It is also not to fault the campaigns that exposed the dreadful conditions under which the Taliban placed women. The Feminist Majority campaign helped put a stop to a secret oil pipeline deal between the Taliban and the U.S. multinational Unocal that was going forward with U.S. administration support. Western feminist campaigns must not be confused with the hypocrisies of the new colonial feminism of a Republican president who was not elected for his progressive stance on feminist issues or of administrations that played down the terrible record of violations of women by the United States' allies in the Northern Alliance, as documented by Human Rights Watch and Amnesty International, among others. Rapes and assaults were widespread in the period of infighting that devastated Afghanistan before the Taliban came in to restore order.

It is, however, to suggest that we need to look closely at what we are supporting (and what we are not) and to think carefully about why. How should we manage the complicated politics and ethics of finding ourselves in agreement with those with whom we normally disagree? I do not know how many feminists who felt good about saving Afghan women from the Taliban are also asking for a global redistribution of wealth or contemplating sacrificing their own consumption radically so that African or Afghan women could have some chance of having what I do believe should be a universal human right—the right to freedom from the structural violence of global inequality and from the ravages of war, the everyday rights of having enough to eat, having homes for their families in which to live and thrive, having ways to make decent livings so their children can grow, and having the strength and security to work out, within their communities and with whatever alliances they want, how to live a good life, which might very well include changing the ways those communities are organized.

Suspicion about bedfellows is only a first step; it will not give us a way to think more positively about what to do or where to stand. For that, we need to confront two more big issues. First is the acceptance of the possibility of difference. Can we only free Afghan women to be like us or might we have to recognize that even after "liberation" from the Taliban, they might want different things than we would want for them? What do we do about that? Second, we need to be vigilant about the rhetoric of saving people because of what it implies about our attitudes.

Again, when I talk about accepting difference, I am not implying that we should resign ourselves to being cultural relativists who respect whatever goes on elsewhere as "just their culture." I have already discussed the dangers of "cultural" explanations; "their" cultures are just as much part of history and an interconnected world as ours are. What I am advocating is the hard work involved in recognizing and respecting differences—precisely as products of different histories, as expressions of different circumstances, and as manifestations of differently structured desires. We may want justice for women, but can we accept that there might be different ideas about justice and that different women might want, or choose, different futures from what we envision as best (see Ong 1988)? We must consider that they might be called to personhood, so to speak, in a different language.

Reports from the Bonn peace conference held in late November to discuss the rebuilding of Afghanistan revealed significant differences among the few Afghan women feminists and activists present. RAWA's position was to reject any conciliatory approach to Islamic governance. According to one report I read, most women activists, especially those based in Afghanistan who are aware of the realities on the ground, agreed that Islam had to be the starting point for reform. Fatima Gailani, a U.S.-based advisor to one of the delegations, is quoted as saying, "If I go to Afghanistan today and ask women for votes on the promise to bring them secularism, they are going to tell me to go to hell." Instead, according to one report, most of these women looked for inspiration on how to fight for equality to a place that might seem surprising. They looked to Iran as a country in which they saw women making significant gains within an Islamic framework—in part through an Islamically oriented feminist movement that is challenging injustices and reinterpreting the religious tradition.

The situation in Iran is itself the subject of heated debate within feminist circles, especially among Iranian feminists in the West (e.g., Mir-Hosseini 1999; Moghissi 1999; Najmabadi 1998, 2000). It is not clear whether and in what ways women have made gains and whether the great increases in literacy, decreases in birthrates, presence of women in the professions and government, and a feminist flourishing in cultural fields like writing and film-making are because of or despite the establishment of a so-called Islamic Republic. The concept of an Islamic feminism itself is also controversial. Is it an oxymoron or does it refer to a viable movement forged by brave women who want a third way?

One of the things we have to be most careful about in thinking about Third World feminisms, and feminism in different parts of the Muslim world, is how not to fall into polarizations that place feminism on the side of the West. I have written about the dilemmas faced by Arab feminists when Western feminists initiate campaigns that make them vulnerable to local denunciations by conservatives of various sorts, whether Islamist or nationalist, of being traitors (Abu-Lughod 2001). As some like Afsaneh Najmabadi are now arguing, not only is it wrong to see history simplistically in terms of a putative opposition between Islam and the West (as is happening in the United States now and has happened in parallel in the Muslim world), but it is also strategically dangerous to accept this cultural opposition between Islam and the West, between fundamentalism and feminism, because those many people within Muslim countries who are trying to find alternatives to present injustices, those who might want to refuse the divide and take from different histories and cultures, who do not accept that being feminist means being Western, will be under pressure to choose, just as we are: Are you with us or against us?

My point is to remind us to be aware of differences, respectful of other paths toward social change that might give women better lives. Can there be a liberation that is Islamic? And, beyond this, is liberation even a goal for which all women or people strive? Are emancipation, equality, and rights part of a universal language we must use? To quote Saba Mahmood, writing about the women in Egypt who are seeking to become pious Muslims, "The desire for freedom and liberation is a historically situated desire whose motivational force cannot be assumed a priori, but needs to be reconsidered in light of other desires aspirations, and capacities that inhere in a culturally and historically located subject" (2001:223). In other words, might other desires be more meaningful for different groups of people? Living in close families? Living in a godly way? Living without war? I have done fieldwork in Egypt over more than 20 years and I cannot think of a single woman I know, from the poorest rural to the most educated cosmopolitan, who has ever expressed envy of U.S. women, women they tend to perceive as bereft of community, vulnerable to sexual violence and social anomie, driven by individual success rather than morality, or strangely disrespectful of God.

Mahmood (2001) has pointed out a disturbing thing that happens when one argues for a respect for other traditions. She notes that there seems to be a difference in the political demands made on those who work on or are trying to understand Muslims and Islamists and those who work on secular-humanist projects. She, who studies the piety movement in Egypt, is consistently pressed to denounce all the harm done by Islamic movements around the world—otherwise she is accused of being an apologist. But there never seems to be a parallel demand for those who study secular humanism and its projects, despite the terrible violences that have been associated with it over the last couple of centuries, from world wars to colonialism, from genocides to slavery. We need to have as little dogmatic faith in secular humanism as in Islamism, and as open a mind to the complex possibilities of human projects undertaken in one tradition as the other.

BEYOND THE RHETORIC OF SALVATION

Let us return, finally, to my title, "Do Muslim Women Really Need Saving?" The discussion of culture, veiling, and how one can navigate the shoals of cultural difference should put Laura Bush's self-congratulation about the rejoicing of Afghan women liberated by American troops in a different light. It is deeply problematic to construct the Afghan woman as someone in need of saving. When you save someone, you imply that you are saving her from something. You are also saving her *to* something. What violences are entailed in this transformation, and what presumptions are being made about the superiority of that to which you are saving her? Projects of saving other women depend on and reinforce a sense of superiority by Westerners, a form of arrogance that deserves to be challenged. All one needs to do to appreciate the patronizing quality of the rhetoric of saving women is to imagine using it today in the United States about disadvantaged groups such as African American women or working-class women. We now understand them as suffering from structural violence. We have become politicized about race and class, but not culture.

As anthropologists, feminists, or concerned citizens, we should be wary of taking on the mantles of those nineteenth century Christian missionary women who devoted their lives to saving their Muslim sisters. One of my favorite documents from that period is a collection called *Our Moslem Sisters*, the proceedings of a conference of women missionaries held in Cairo in 1906 (U.S. Government 1907). The subtitle of the book is *A Cry of Need from the Lands of Darkness Interpreted by Those Who Heard It*. Speaking of the ignorance, seclusion, polygamy, and veiling that blighted women's lives across the Muslim world, the missionary women spoke of their responsibility to make these women's voices heard. As the introduction states, "They will never cry for themselves, for they are down under the yoke of centuries of oppression" (U.S. Government 1907:15). "This book," it begins, "with its sad, reiterated story of wrong and oppression is an indictment and an appeal. . . . It is an appeal to Christian womanhood to right these wrongs and enlighten this darkness by sacrifice and service" (U.S. Government 1907:5).

One can hear uncanny echoes of their virtuous goals today, even though the language is secular, the appeals not to Jesus but to human rights or the liberal West. The continuing currency of such imagery and sentiments can be seen in their deployment for perfectly good humanitarian causes. In February 2002, I received an invitation to a reception honoring an international medical humanitarian network called Médecins du Monde/Doctors of the World (MdM). Under the sponsorship of the French Ambassador to the United States, the Head of the delegation of the European Commission to the United Nations, and a member of the European Parliament, the cocktail reception was to feature an exhibition of photographs under the clichéd title "Afghan Women: Behind the Veil."

The invitation was remarkable not just for the colorful photograph of women in flowing burqas walking across the barren mountains of Afghanistan but also for the text, a portion of which I quote:

> For 20 years MdM has been ceaselessly struggling to help those who are most vulnerable. But increasingly, thick veils cover the victims of the war. When the Taliban came to power in 1996, Afghan Women became faceless. To unveil one's face while receiving medical care was to achieve a sort of intimacy, find a brief space for secret freedom and recover a little of one's dignity. In a country where women had no access to basic medical care because they did not have the right to appear in public, where women had no right to practice medicine, MdM's program stood as a stubborn reminder of human rights. . . . Please join us in helping to lift the veil.

Although I cannot take up here the fantasies of intimacy associated with unveiling, fantasies reminiscent of the French colonial obsessions so brilliantly unmasked by Alloula in *The Colonial Harem* (1986), I can ask why humanitarian projects and human rights discourse in the twenty-first century need rely on such constructions of Muslim women.

Could we not leave veils and vocations of saving others behind and instead train our sights on ways to make the world a more just place? The reason respect for difference should not be confused with cultural relativism is that it does not preclude asking how we, living in this privileged and powerful part of the world, might examine our own responsibilities for the situations in which others in distant places have found themselves. We do not stand outside the world, looking out over this sea of poor benighted people, living under the shadow—or veil—of oppressive cultures; we are part of that world. Islamic movements themselves have arisen in a world shaped by the intense engagements of Western powers in Middle Eastern lives.

A more productive approach, it seems to me, is to ask how we might contribute to making the world a more just place. A world not organized around strategic military and economic demands; a place where certain kinds of forces and values that we may still consider important could have an appeal and where there is the peace necessary for discussions, debates, and transformations to occur within communities. We need to ask ourselves what kinds of world conditions we could contribute to making such that popular desires will not be overdetermined by an overwhelming sense of helplessness in the face of forms of global injustice. Where we seek to be active in the affairs of distant places, can we do so in the spirit of support for those within those communities whose goals are to make women's (and men's) lives better (as Walley has argued in relation to practices of genital cutting in Africa [1997])? Can we use a more egalitarian language of alliances, coalitions, and solidarity, instead of salvation?

Even RAWA, the now celebrated Revolutionary Association of the Women of Afghanistan, which was so instrumental in bringing to U.S. women's attention the excesses of the Taliban, has opposed the U.S. bombing from the beginning. They do not see in it Afghan women's salvation but increased hardship and loss. They have long called for disarmament and for peacekeeping forces. Spokespersons point out the dangers of confusing governments with people, the Taliban with innocent Afghans who will be most harmed. They consistently remind audiences to take a close look at the ways policies are being organized around oil interests, the arms industry, and the international drug trade. They are not obsessed with the veil, even though they are the most radical feminists working for a

secular democratic Afghanistan. Unfortunately, only their messages about the excesses of the Taliban have been heard, even though their criticisms of those in power in Afghanistan have included previous regimes. A first step in hearing their wider message is to break with the language of alien cultures, whether to understand or eliminate them. Missionary work and colonial feminism belong in the past. Our task is to critically explore what we might do to help create a world in which those poor Afghan women, for whom "the hearts of those in the civilized world break," can have safety and decent lives.

ACKNOWLEDGMENTS

I want to thank Page Jackson, Fran Mascia-Lees, Tim Mitchell, Rosalind Morris, Anupama Rao, and members of the audience at the symposium "Responding to War," sponsored by Columbia University's Institute for Research on Women and Gender (where I presented an earlier version), for helpful comments, references, clippings, and encouragement.

REFERENCES

Abu-Lughod, Lila. 1986. *Veiled Sentiments: Honor and Poetry in a Bedouin Society.* Berkeley: University of California Press.

———. 1995. Movie Stars and Islamic Moralism in Egypt. *Social Text* 42:53–67.

———. 1998. *Remaking Women: Feminism and Modernity in the Middle East.* Princeton: Princeton University Press.

———. 2001. Orientalism and Middle East Feminist Studies. *Feminist Studies* 27(1):101–113.

Ahmed, Leila. 1992. *Women and Gender in Islam.* New Haven, CT: Yale University Press.

Alloula, Malek. 1986. *The Colonial Harem.* Minneapolis: University of Minnesota Press.

Brenner, Suzanne. 1996. Reconstructing Self and Society: Javanese Muslim Women and "the Veil." *American Ethnologist* 23(4):673–697.

El Guindi, Fadwa. 1999. *Veil: Modesty, Privacy and Resistance.* Oxford: Berg.

Fremson, Ruth. 2001. Allure Must Be Covered. Individuality Peeks Through. *New York Times* , November 4: 14.

Global Exchange. 2002. Courage and Tenacity: A Women's Delegation to Afghanistan. Electronic document, http://www.globalexchange.org/tours/auto/2002-03-05_Courageand-TenacityAWomensDele.html. Accessed February 11.

Goldenberg, Suzanne. 2002. The Woman Who Stood Up to the Taliban. *The Guardian*, January 24. Electronic document, http://222.guardian.co.ur/afghanistan/story/0,1284,63840.

Hirschkind, Charles, and Saba Mahmood. 2002. Feminism, the Taliban, and the Politics of Counter-Insurgency. *Anthropological Quarterly* 75(2):107–122.

Lazreg, Marnia. 1994. *The Eloquence of Silence: Algerian Women in Question.* New York: Routledge.

MacLeod, Arlene. 1991. *Accommodating Protest.* New York: Columbia University Press.

Mahmood, Saba. 2001. Feminist Theory, Embodiment, and the Docile Agent: Some Reflections on the Egyptian Islamic Revival. *Cultural Anthropology* 16(2):202–235.

Mir-Hosseini, Ziba. 1999. *Islam and Gender: The Religious Debate in Contemporary Iran.* Princeton: Princeton University Press.

Moghissi, Haideh. 1999. *Feminism and Islamic Fundamentalism.* London: Zed Books.

Najmabadi, Afsaneh. 1998. Feminism in an Islamic Republic. In *Islam, Gender and Social Change.* Yvonne Haddad and John Esposito, eds. Pp. 59–84. New York: Oxford University Press.

———. 2000. (Un)Veiling Feminism. *Social Text* 64:29–45.

Ong, Aihwa. 1988. Colonialism and Modernity: Feminist RePresentations of Women in Non-Western Societies. *Inscriptions* 3–4:79–93.

———. 1990. State Versus Islam: Malay Families, Women's Bodies, and the Body Politic in Malaysia. *American Ethnologist* 17(2):258–276.

Papanek, Hanna. 1982. Purdah in Pakistan: Seclusion and Modern Occupations for Women. In *Separate Worlds.*

Hanna Papanek and Gail Minault, eds. Pp. 190–216. Columbia, MO: South Asia Books.

Safire, William. 2001. "On Language." *New York Times Magazine* , October 28: 22.

Spivak, Gayatri Chakravorty. 1988. Can the Subaltern Speak? In *Marxism and the Interpretation of Culture*. Cary Nelson and Lawrence Grossberg, eds. Pp. 271–313. Urbana: University of Illinois Press.

Strathern, Marilyn. 1987. An Awkward Relationship: The Case of Feminism and Anthropology. *Signs* 12: 276–292.

U.S. Government. 1907. *Our Moslem Sisters: A Cry of Need from Lands of Darkness Interpreted by Those Who Heard It*. New York: Fleming H. Revell.

———. 2002. Electronic document, http://www. whitehouse. gov/news/releases/2001/11/20011117. Accessed January 10.

Walley, Christine. 1997. Searching for "Voices": Feminism, Anthropology, and the Global Debate over Female Genital Operations. *Cultural Anthropology* 12(3):405–438.

Social Protest and Feminist Movements

Throughout *Feminist Frontiers,* we have examined the breadth and magnitude of the social forces working to differentiate women and men and to disadvantage women. Socialization, the organization of social institutions, and social and economic policies all come together to hinder women's full political participation, self-determination, economic security, and even health and safety.

Despite the ubiquitous forms of inequality embedded in our social institutions, women resist. As we have seen, women often struggle against oppression in individual ways. Women also come together to take collective action to pursue social change. This section explores contemporary forms of social protest, noting how feminist movements attract different constituencies, develop different ideas, articulate different goals, and utilize different tactics and strategies across time and place.

In the first article, Alison Crossley, Verta Taylor, Nancy Whittier, and Cynthia Fabrizio Pelak present an overview of the multiple ideologies and forms of the feminist movement in the United States from its resurgence in the 1960s to the present. "Forever Feminism" considers the larger social and economic conditions responsible for the rise of women's movements in the Western world, the organizational structures and locations of feminist organizations, diverse strategies and tactics, antifeminism, and the global context of feminist movements, and describes the transnational

context of feminism. In line with our interest throughout *Feminist Frontiers* in the ways that new technologies shape women's lives, the authors consider the role of online activity in contemporary feminism. They focus on the way feminist movements have changed over time as a result of activists' own ideas and goals.

Based on the analysis presented in this article, what do you think might be the future of feminism? Why do you think feminism is so persistent? How would you explain to someone who asked what it means to be a feminist?

Feminism, as this article demonstrates, has a long and vibrant history and strong prospects for the future. Yet a great deal of attention has been devoted to the generational divisions in feminism. Some see a "third wave" of feminism; others see the death of feminism in the "postfeminist" generation. Pamela Aronson, in "Feminists or 'Postfeminists'? Young Women's Attitudes Toward Feminism and Gender Relations," explores attitudes toward feminism through interviews with a diverse sample of young women. She shows that the majority of her sample is aware that the women's movement increased opportunity and that inequality remains, but that young women embrace a range of positions on the question of whether they identify as feminists. What difference do class, race, and life experience make in shaping young women's perspectives? Where would you fit on a spectrum of attitudes toward feminism?

Picking up on the theme of online activism from "Forever Feminism," Anita Harris, in "Young Women, Late Modern Politics, and the Participatory Possibilities of Online Cultures," considers young women's use of online DIY culture and social networking sites as a potential form of political activism. As we have already noted, conventional definitions of politics often exclude the activities of women, and this is certainly true about women's use of new technologies. Web sites created by young women that express political points of view or even discuss art and music have political potential. Harris argues that they are examples of women acting as cultural producers rather than simply consumers, the role the dominant culture is apt to assign them. Even social networking sites such as Facebook give young women a way, in Harris's words, of "generating public selves." In this way, she asks us to think more creatively about what it means to be political.

What does Harris conclude about whether young women's use of these new technologies qualifies as political? Do you agree with her? How does online activity create a "public self" and what does that mean for thinking of oneself as a citizen? Are there ways that your own online activity, whether you are male or female, might be considered political?

Turning to a different kind of activism in "Punks, Bulldaggers, and Welfare Queens: The Radical Potential of Queer Politics?" Cathy Cohen calls for a new form of progressive and transformative coalition building. She embraces queer activists' in-your-face strategies intended to challenge the invisibility of gay,

lesbian, bisexual, and transgendered people and to embrace sexual difference. But she criticizes the narrowness of queer politics for its overemphasis on deconstructing the historically and culturally recognized categories of homosexual and heterosexual. Such a strategy, she argues, exaggerates the similarities among individuals categorized under the label of "heterosexual" and ignores the way other systems of oppression regulate the lives of women and men of all races, classes, and sexualities. A truly queer politics, she suggests, would bring together those, like punks, bulldaggers, and welfare queens, who live outside not heterosexuality, but heteronormativity. What might the kinds of coalitions Cohen envisages look like? What kind of differences might they make in U.S. society?

We end with two short pieces that reveal both the diversity and the promise of contemporary feminism. Moya Bailey and Alexis Pauline Gumbs describe their online activism as young black feminists, pointing to their connections to "the rich tapestry of Black feminism that has come before us." And Nikki Ayanna Stewart addresses the question so many women's students are asked: "What can you do with a degree in women's studies?" She answers simply: transform the world. Women's movements in the twenty-first century are becoming more diverse than ever and hold great promise for transforming for the better the lives of both women and men. As you finish reading *Feminist Frontiers*, think about what changes you would like to see in your world. How do you propose to work for these changes?

Alison Dahl Crossley
Verta Taylor
Nancy Whittier
Cynthia Fabrizio Pelak

Forever Feminism: The Persistence of the U.S. Women's Movement, 1960–2011

First published in 2011

INTRODUCTION

Today, you may find feminists in Manhattan protesting BP and the catastrophic oil spill, in Los Angeles organizing their garment worker colleagues for increased wages and improved working conditions, or in St. Paul being arrested for marching against the war in Iraq. You may also find feminists online debating the impact of race on the campaign for same-sex marriage, blogging about the extreme airbrushing of models in advertisements, or raising money via PayPal to support women's groups in Haiti. In fact, feminism is one of the most persistent and continuous social movements in modern history. Although the vibrancy of the feminist movement has undoubtedly ebbed and flowed over time, the movement itself remains relevant and influential. Feminism and the injustices that produced it have not vanished. Rather, feminism and its strategies have evolved to accommodate changes in society. Today, we have to look in new settings to see the varied forms of feminism. Whether in formal organizations, informal networks, online communities, or the institutions of education, church or the military, feminism persists. To recognize the abundance of feminist forums in the U.S. today requires an understanding of the historical trajectory of feminism as well as an expanded notion of its strategies and tactics.

We explore here continuity and change in the U.S. women's movement from the 1960s to the present. We highlight important historical events in the movement and demonstrate the continued impact of feminism on contemporary U.S. society. First we consider the structural preconditions of women's movements in the Western world. Then we focus on the changing ideologies, structures, political contexts, strategies, and tactics of the women's movement in the United States. Next we address the increasing significance of online feminism and the challenge of antifeminism. Finally, we discuss the women's movement from a global perspective.

STRUCTURAL PRECONDITIONS OF U.S. FEMINIST MOVEMENTS

As this chapter will demonstrate, the specific contours of feminist ideology and identity are complex and not monolithic. However, we may understand a feminist community to "encompass those who see gender as a main category of analysis, who critique female disadvantage, and who work to improve women's situations" (Rupp and Taylor 1999). Indeed, women have always had sufficient grievances to propel feminist activity, and women's collective action abounds throughout history. However, collective activity on the part of women directed toward improving their own status has flourished primarily in periods of generalized social upheaval, when sensitivity to moral injustice, discrimination, and social inequality has been widespread in the society as a whole (Chafe 1977; Staggenborg 1998a). The first wave of feminism in the United States grew out of the abolitionist struggle of the 1830s and peaked with the suffrage victory in 1920, and the second wave emerged out of the general social discontent of the 1960s. The third wave of feminism emerged in the 1990s, but its ideology and identity are more contested than previous waves (Walker 1992; Henry 2004). Although the women's movement did not die between these periods of heightened activism, it declined sharply in the 1930s, 1940s, 1950s and 1980s.

While the wave framework correctly identifies time periods of heightened feminist collective action, scholars challenge the concept of distinct feminist waves because it obscures the persistence of feminism in a variety of political, social, and cultural climates (Naples 2005; Rupp and Taylor 2005; Reger 2005). Instead of disappearing between waves, the women's movement went into abeyance (Taylor 1989) in order to survive in hostile political climates such as in the 1950s (Rupp and Taylor 1987). Movements in abeyance are in a holding pattern, during which activists from an earlier period maintain the ideology and structural base of the movement but few new recruits join. A movement in abeyance is primarily oriented toward maintaining itself rather than confronting the established order directly. Focusing on building an alternative culture, for example, is a means of surviving when external resources are not available and the political structure is not amenable to challenge. The concept of abeyance has since been used to analyze contemporary women's movements in a variety of countries and national contexts, including Britain, Australia, South Korea, and Japan (Grey and Sawer 2008; Bagguley 2002). Abeyance encourages a close examination of the women's movement in a variety of contexts and a consideration of how movements change over time and in relationship to larger social processes.

Despite temporal and geographical differences in feminist movements, scholars identify certain basic structural conditions that have contributed to the emergence of feminist protest in most parts of the Western world (Oppenheimer 1973; Huber and Spitze 1983; Chafetz and Dworkin 1986). Broad societal changes in the patterns of women's participation in the paid labor force, increases in women's formal educational attainment, and shifts in women's fertility rates and reproductive roles disrupt traditional social arrangements and set the stage for women's movements. As industrialization and urbanization bring greater education for women, expanding public roles create role and status conflicts for middle-class women, who then develop the discontent and gender consciousness necessary for political action. Specifically,

when women enter the paid labor force, their gender consciousness increases because they are more likely to use men as a reference group when assessing their access to societal rewards. Similarly, women often experience strains and discrepancies in their lives as their gender consciousness is raised through formal education (Klein 1984).

Other important structural factors that serve as preconditions for feminist mobilization include changes in family relationships, marriage, fertility, and sexual mores (Ferree and Hess 2000). Declines in women's childbearing and increases in their age at first marriage can improve women's educational attainment and participation in the paid labor force—which, in turn, raise their gender consciousness (Klein 1984). Moreover, changes in the traditional relationships between women and men in marriage and in sexual mores, such as the shift from authoritarian marriages to romantic or companionate marriages at the turn of the last century in the U.S. and the "sexual revolution" of the 1960s, can politicize gender relations and create the motivations for feminist mobilization.

Such structural changes are partial, as exhibited by women's continued unequal status in the workforce (Williams 1995), by persistent debates over the institution of marriage (Taylor et al. 2009), and by inequalities at the intersection of sex and power (Price-Glynn 2010). New structural conditions have also arisen, shifting and expanding feminist mobilization. Disenchantment with transnational relations, immigration policies, and the economic, penal, and health care systems in the U.S. has mobilized new feminist action. For example, feminist scholars have turned their attention to inequalities in transnational feminism (Thayer 2010), access to health care and social services (Taylor 1996, Whittier 2009), "intimate labor" (Hondagneu-Sotelo 2001; Boris and Parreñas 2010), women's health movements (Dubel 2010, Bell 2009), global flows of gendered labor (Ehrenreich and Hochschild 2004), the surveillance of inner city girls (Jones 2010), and shifting family formations (Gerson 2010).

The structural preconditions underlying the genesis and continuation of feminist collective mobilization not only vary with historical and geographic context, but are also perpetually evolving. Demographic, economic, and cultural processes that spur feminist movements in the U.S. are different from those in other countries. Even within the U.S., political and cultural variations in feminism are reflected in differences in the ways women define their collective interests, whether by national, regional, cultural, ethnic, or community identities. These differences are manifested in the distinct ideologies, organizational forms, and strategies adopted by feminist movements in different times and places.

FEMINIST IDEOLOGIES

Ideology, or a set of beliefs, goals, and worldviews, is a central component in the life of any social movement (Morris and Mueller 1992). The modern feminist movement, like most social movements, is not ideologically monolithic. Feminist ideologies encompass numerous strands that differ in the scope of change sought, the extent to which gender inequality is linked to other systems of domination—especially class, race, ethnicity, and sexuality—and the significance attributed to gender differences. We focus here on the evolution of the dominant ideologies that have motivated participants in the two major branches of the feminist movement from its inception: *liberal feminism* and *radical feminism.*

The first wave of the women's movement in the nineteenth century was, by and large, a liberal feminist reform movement. It sought equality within the existing social structure and, indeed, in many ways functioned like other reform movements to reaffirm existing values within the society (Ferree and Hess 2000). Nineteenth-century feminists believed that if they obtained the right to an education, the right to own property, the right to vote, employment rights— in other words, equal civil rights under the law—they would attain equality with men. Scholars have labeled this thinking "individualist" or "equity" feminism, linking the goal of equal rights to gender assumptions about women's basic sameness with men (Offen 1988; Black 1989).

The basic ideas identified with contemporary liberal or "mainstream" feminism have changed little since their formulation in the nineteenth century, when they seemed progressive, even radical (Eisenstein 1981). Contemporary liberal feminist ideology holds that women lack power simply because we are not, as women, allowed equal opportunity to compete and succeed in the male-dominated economic and political arenas but, instead, are relegated to the subordinate world of home, domestic labor, motherhood, and family. The major strategy for change is to gain legal and economic equalities and to obtain access to elite positions in the workplace and in politics. Thus, liberal

feminists tend to place as much emphasis on changing individual women as they do on changing society. For instance, establishing an engineering degree program at an all-women's college or instructing rape victims in "survival" strategies strikes a blow at social definitions that channel women into traditionally feminine occupations or passive behaviors that make them easy targets of aggression from men.

Throughout the 1970s and 1980s, liberal feminists both initiated and supported the massive transformation in work and family life occurring as the U.S. underwent the transition to a postindustrial order (Mitchell 1986; Stacey 1987). Some writers contend that by urging women to enter the workplace and adopt a male orientation, the equal opportunity approach to feminism unwittingly contributed to a host of problems that further disadvantaged women, especially working-class women and women of color. These problems included the rise in divorce rates, the "feminization" of working-class occupations, and the devaluation of motherhood and traditionally female characteristics (Gordon 1991).

In contrast, radical feminist ideology dates to Simone de Beauvoir's early 1950s theory of "sex class," which was developed further in the late 1960s among small groups of radical women who fought the subordination of women's liberation within the New Left (Beauvoir 1952; Firestone 1970; Millett 1971; Atkinson 1974; Rubin 1975; Rich 1976, 1980; Griffin 1978; Daly 1978; Eisenstein 1981; Hartmann 1981; Frye 1983; Hartsock 1983; MacKinnon 1983). The radical approach recognizes women's identity and subordination as a "sex class," emphasizes women's fundamental difference from men, views gender as the primary contradiction and foundation for the unequal distribution of a society's rewards and privileges, and recasts relations between women and men in political terms (Echols 1989). Defining women as a "sex class" means no longer treating patriarchy in individual terms but acknowledging the social and structural nature of women's subordination. Radical feminists hold that in all societies, institutions and social patterns are structured to maintain and perpetuate gender inequality and female disadvantage permeates virtually all aspects of sociocultural and personal life. Further, through the gender division of labor, social institutions are linked so that male superiority depends upon female subordination (Hartmann 1981). In the U.S., as in most industrialized societies, power, prestige, and wealth accrue to those who control the distribution of resources outside the home, in the economic and political spheres. The sexual division of labor that assigns child care and domestic responsibilities to women not only ensures gender inequality in the family system but perpetuates male advantage in political and economic institutions as well.

To unravel the complex structure on which gender inequality rests, requires, from a radical feminist perspective, a fundamental transformation of all institutions in society. To meet this challenge, radical feminists formulated influential critiques of the family, marriage, love, motherhood, heterosexuality, sexual violence, capitalism, reproductive policies, the media, science, language and culture, the beauty industry, sports, politics, the law, technology, and more. Radical feminism's ultimate vision is revolutionary in scope: a fundamentally new social order that eliminates the sex-class system and replaces it with new ways—based on women's difference—of defining and structuring experience. Central to the development of radical feminist ideology was the strategy of forming small groups for the purpose of "consciousness-raising." Pioneered initially among New Left women, consciousness-raising can be understood as a kind of conversion in which women come to view experiences previously thought of as personal and individual, such as sexual exploitation or employment discrimination, as social problems that are the result of gender inequality.

By 1971, major segments of feminism had crystallized: liberal feminism, embodied in the formation of groups such as NOW, the Women's Equity Action League (WEAL) in 1967, and the National Women's Political Caucus (NWPC) in 1971; radical feminism and socialist feminism, emerging from consciousness-raising groups, theory groups, and small action groups such as Redstockings and the Feminists in 1969; and lesbian feminism, organized in such groups as Radicalesbians in 1970 and the Furies (initially called "Those Women") in 1971 (Echols 1989).

By the late 1970s, the distinction between liberal and radical feminism was becoming less clear (Carden 1978; Whittier 1995). Ideological shifts took place at both the individual and organizational levels. Participation in liberal feminist reform and service organizations working on such issues as rape, battering, abortion, legal and employment discrimination, and women's health problems raised women's consciousness, increased their feminist activism, and contributed to their radicalization as they came to see connections between these issues and the larger system of gender inequality (Schlesinger and Bart 1983; Whittier 1995). Women were also radicalized by working through their own personal experiences of sexual harassment, divorce, rape, abortion, and incest (Huber 1973; Klein 1984; Whittier 2009). Radicalization occurred at the group level as well. By the end of the 1970s, liberal feminist organizations such as NOW, the Women's Legal Defense Fund, and the National Abortion Rights Action League (NARAL), which had been pursuing equality within the law, began to adopt strategies and goals consistent with a more radical stance. NOW included in its 1979 objectives not only such legal strategies as the ERA and reproductive choice, but broader issues such as the threat of nuclear energy, lesbian and gay rights, homemakers' rights, the exploitation of women in the home, and sex segregation in the workplace (Eisenstein 1981). Even the ERA, which sought equality for women within the existing legal and economic structure, was based on the fact that women are discriminated against as a "sex class" (Mansbridge 1986).

Beginning in the mid-1980s, with the defeat of the unifying issue of the ERA and the growing diversification of the movement, feminist ideology deemphasized the question of women's similarity to or difference from men in favor of "deconstructing" the term *woman*. Women of color, Jewish women, lesbians, and working-class women challenged radical feminists' idea of a "sex class" that implied a distinctive and essential female condition. Since women are distributed throughout all social classes, racial and ethnic groupings, sexual communities, cultures, and religions, disadvantage for women varies and is multidimensional (Spelman 1988). The recognition that the circumstances of women's oppression differ has given way to a new intersectional feminist paradigm that views race, class, gender, ethnicity, and sexuality as interlocking systems of oppression, forming what Patricia Hill Collins (1990) refers to as a "matrix of domination."

Many people view the women's movement as the territory of white middle-class women, and indeed some arms of the women's movement attracted primarily these women. When we examine the wide variety of feminist organizing in the U.S., however, the integral role of Black, Chicana and White women in the development of feminism emerges (Roth 2004). Many Black and Chicana feminists prioritized working within their own racial and ethnic communities, advancing feminist goals and visions different from the white feminist communities (Barnett 1993; Robnett 1996). Distinct and vibrant Black, Latina, Asian-American, and Native feminist organizations developed, along with a feminist ideology that emphasized the intersection of race, class, sexuality and gender (Roth 2004; Springer 2005). When we expand our perspective of feminism to include a multiplicity of feminist ideologies and organizations, a fuller picture of feminism emerges that counters the historical inaccuracies and oversimplification of the U.S. feminist movement. Historians have called our attention to this erroneous discourse, describing it as the "whitewashing" of feminism (Roth 2004), or the suspension of the women's movement in "ahistorical amber" (Gilmore 2008, 2). In reality, feminism has never been monolithic, and women from all backgrounds have both gained from and contributed to its successes.

Although discussions focusing on women's differences from one another sometimes result in vehement arguments, some scholars see these tensions over women's differences as a sign of life (Taylor and Rupp 1993). Modern feminist movements often have developed around women's commonalities, but differences of race, class, ethnicity, and nationality are also expressed in the collective identities deployed by feminists (Moraga and Anzaldúa 1981; Mohanty, Russo, and Torres 1991). African-American women have organized around interlocking structures of oppression that affect women differently depending on their ethnicity, class, or sexual identities (Collins 1990; Springer 2005). For example, African-American and Latina women from low-income urban neighborhoods have struggled for quality education, affordable and safe housing, and expanded child care services for their families and communities (Naples 1992).

These themes continue in the third wave of feminism, which emphasizes intersectionality of race, class, gender, sexuality, ability and the complex nature of identity (Walker 1995; Reger 2005; Bobel 2010). Third wave feminists highlight the diversity of participants, ideologies and tactics (Walker 1995; Drake 1997; Henry 2005; Zita 1997; Springer 2002; Reger 2005). Many third wave feminists question the notion that there is a unified "woman," reject the gender binary and rigid gender roles, embrace sexuality, and seek to include men in the movement. The term third wave is now used to include a wide range of feminist strategies, tactics, grievances, identities, and participants from diverse generations. Unlike the second wave of feminism, which continues to be active, the third wave is more

nebulous in both its definition and mobilization. However, there is dissension over the term "third wave," with some scholars preferring the term "contemporary feminism" to avoid using the wave framework (Reger 2005).

Common ideological themes do recur throughout the history of the U.S. women's movement. However, ideology alone is an incomplete explanation of either the direction or the consequences of a social movement (Marx and Wood 1975; McCarthy and Zald 1977). Much depends on a movement's structures and strategies, as well as on the larger political and cultural context. We now turn to a discussion of the 1960s, a formative time for the feminist movement.

FEMINIST ORGANIZATIONS AND HABITATS

Social movements do not generally have a single central organization or unified direction. Rather, the structure of any general, broad-based social movement is more diffuse—composed typically of a number of relatively independent organizations that differ in ideology, structure, goals, and tactics (Gerlach and Hine 1970). The organizational structure of the modern feminist movement has been decentralized from its beginnings, while feminist organizations have varied widely in structure (Freeman 1975; Cassell 1977; Ferree and Martin 1995; Staggenborg 1989). The diversity of feminist organizational forms reflects both ideological differences and the movement's diverse membership base (Freeman 1979).

There have been two main types of organizational structure in the modern feminist movement since its resurgence, reflecting the two sources of feminist organizing in the late 1960s: bureaucratically structured movement organizations with hierarchical leadership and democratic decision-making procedures, such as the National Organization for Women; and smaller, collectively structured groups that formed a more diffuse social movement community held together by a feminist political culture. Collectively organized groups, at least in theory, strove to exemplify a better way of structuring society by constructing a distinctive women's culture that valorized egalitarianism, the expression of emotion, and the sharing of personal experience (Cassell 1977, Taylor and Rupp 1993, Taylor 1995). It is important to recognize, however, that while the two strands of the women's movement emerged separately, they have not remained distinct or opposed to each other. Most women's movement organizations are mixed in form from the outset (Staggenborg 1988, 1989; Martin 1990; Ryan 1992; Ferree and Martin 1995; Whittier 1995). The bureaucratically structured and professionalized movement organizations initially adopted by liberal groups such as NOW were well suited to work within the similarly structured political arena and to members' previous experience in professional organizations. The structures that radical feminist groups initially adopted, on the other hand, built on their prior involvement in the New Left (Evans 1979). Collectivist organizations grew from radical feminists' attempts to structure relations among members, processes of decision making, and group leadership in a way that reflected or prefigured the values and goals of the movement (Rothschild-Whitt 1979; Breines 1982). Feminist collective organizations made decisions by consensus, rotated leadership and other tasks among members, and shared skills to avoid hierarchy and specialization. Such groups often failed to meet their ideals and did, in fact, spawn unacknowledged hierarchies (Freeman 1972/3). Nevertheless, the conscious effort to build a feminist collective structure has had a lasting impact on the women's movement and has led to the growth of a social movement community (Buechler 1990).

The collectivist branch of the women's movement initially sparked the growth of a feminist social movement community in which alternative structures guided by a distinctively feminist women's culture flourished—including bookstores, theater groups, music and art collectives, poetry groups, publishing and recording companies, spirituality groups, vacation resorts, self-help groups, and a variety of feminist-run businesses. This "women's culture," though it included feminists of diverse political persuasions, was largely maintained by lesbian feminists. It nurtured a feminist collective identity that was important to the survival of the women's movement as a whole (Taylor and Whittier 1992; Taylor and Rupp 1993; Staggenborg and Lecomte 2009).

Both bureaucratic organizations working within mainstream politics and the alternative feminist culture have expanded and converged since the movement's emergence in the 1960s. Organizations such as NOW and NARAL incorporated some of the innovations of collectivism, including consciousness-raising groups, modified consensus decision making, and the use of direct-action tactics and civil disobedience. A host of structural variations emerged, including formally structured groups that use consensus decision making, organizations with deliberately democratic structures, and groups that officially operate by majority-rule democracy but in practice make most decisions by consensus (Staggenborg 1988, 1989; Martin 1990; Ryan 1992; Taylor 1996). At the same time, feminist collectives shifted their focus from consciousness-raising and radical feminist critique to the development of feminist self-help and service organizations such as rape crisis centers, shelters for battered women, women's health centers, job training programs for displaced homemakers, and lesbian peer counseling groups (Whittier 2009, Gagné 1998, Morgen 2002).

Organizing by women of color grew during the 1970s, and when African-American activists in the women's movement formed the National Black Feminist Organization in 1973 it grew to a membership of 1,000 within its first year (Deckard 1983). In the 1980s and 1990s, independent feminist organizations and networks of women of color such as the National Black Women's Health Project and the National Coalition of 100 Black Women emerged. Women of color also formed active caucuses within predominantly white feminist organizations, such as the National Women's Studies Association, to work against racism within the women's movement (Leidner 1993). Likewise, Jewish women, who had historically played important roles within the women's movement, organized their own groups in the 1980s and spoke out against anti-Semitism within the movement (Beck 1980; Bulkin, Pratt, and Smith 1984).

While women had little opportunities for leadership in most of the public sector, women in the labor movement were able to secure positions of leadership and "were instrumental in state and federal campaigns for equal pay and fair labor standards" (Stansell 2010, 191). Union women have played a significant role in contemporary feminism, from their involvement in the formation of NOW to the feminist activism in the United Steelworkers Union. Women steelworkers in the U.S. and Canada made significant strides in challenging racism and sexism on the job, and through consciousness-raising, conferences, and multi-racial organizing, the women fostered feminist communities in the union (Fonow 2003). Moreover, in making connections between issues of labor, gender, race, and class, feminist union organizing highlights the multidimensional nature of feminism and the potential for feminist ideology and collective action to contribute to a variety of sectors.

Feminism has flourished in disparate social contexts because of a variety of feminist collective actions, including within institutions and organizations. Traditional social movement scholars understood social movements in narrow terms by focusing on the state as a primary target of movement activity, but scholars are also highlighting the wide range of collective action beyond the state (Taylor and Van Dyke 2004; Raeburn 2004; Taylor and Zald 2010; Taylor 2010; Taft 2010; Whittier 2009). Gender and social movement scholars have also sought to expand notions of the targets and goals of social movements in order to recognize the variety of ways that feminism is practiced, including in everyday life (Whittier 1995), in self-help groups (Taylor 1989, 1996), and in institutions such as the church and military (Katzenstein 1998b). In her research on contemporary US feminism, Jo Reger (forthcoming) finds evidence of the significance of everyday actions in the continuation of the feminist movement. The continued vitality of feminism in the U.S. is exhibited by the continuity of feminist organizations, the expansion and creativity of feminist protest tactics, and the existence of feminist culture and collective identity (Staggenborg and Taylor 2005).

The term "feminist habitat" describes the institutional contexts of feminist mobilization (Katzenstein 1998a). Ideologically conservative institutions such as the military and Catholic church are assumed to be harmful environments for feminist organizing. While this is true in many respects, such institutions also provide fertile ground for the development of "feminist habitats" and subsequent feminist successes, such as opening employment positions in the military to women that were previously only open to men (Katzenstein 1998a). Institutional activists are important actors in social movements, and may establish flourishing "feminist habitats" in otherwise unwelcoming settings. When we expand our notion of feminism to consider a variety of organizational contexts, the diversity of relationships, networks, and settings that are sites of feminist collective action is illuminated (Staggenborg 1998; Taft 2010).

Collective action by the women's movement has moved into almost every major institution of society and has been shaped by women of all racial, ethnic and class backgrounds. Now, we turn to a discussion of strategies and tactics for social change.

MULTIPLE STRATEGIES AND TACTICS

Gender resistance, challenge, and change can occur at three levels: the individual level of consciousness and interactions, the social structural level, and the cultural level (Collins 1990). Applying this conceptualization to feminist activism allows us to recognize that movements adopt many strategies and tactics. It also acknowledges the important role of women's movements in the reconstruction of gender.

Resisting Gender Practices

At the level of consciousness and social interactions, individual women may resist norms and expectations of the dominant gender system (Thorne 1994, 1995). It is, however, social movements or collectives, rather than isolated individuals, who perform the critical role of refashioning the gender code and calling institutions to account for gender inequality (Chafetz 1990; Connell 1987). One of the primary goals of the modern feminist movement has been to change the unequal power relations between women and men. A general strategy used by feminists to achieve this goal has been to resist and challenge sexist practices within a diverse set of social contexts, ranging from the institution of marriage and the gender division of labor in rearing and nurturing children to the gendered workplace and the male-dominated medical establishment.

The formation of consciousness-raising groups facilitated the process of resisting and challenging gender practices and of politicizing everyday life. Because consciousness-raising enables women to view the "personal as political," for most women it is an identity-altering experience. Becoming a feminist can transform a woman's entire self-concept and way of life: her biography, appearance, beliefs, behavior, and relationships (Cassell 1977; Esterberg 1997, Reger 2005). As women's consciousness changes through personalized political strategies, women individually and collectively defy traditionally feminine role expectations for women and, in so doing, reconstruct the meanings of women, femininity, and interpersonal relationships between women and men. For example, in addition to problematizing the consumer-driven nature of "pink ribbon culture," some breast cancer activists have chosen to resist the pre-occupation with breasts in contemporary society by refusing to wear prostheses or by displaying mastectomy scars following breast surgery

(Sulik 2010). Some feminist blogs serve a consciousness-raising function, bringing together posters and commenters to discuss issues such as beauty norms and practices, personal experiences with sexism or racism, work experiences, and interpersonal relationships.

Feminists may organize their lives around feminist beliefs, even when they are not involved in organized feminist activity. They may choose leisure and cultural activities, significant relationships, dress, and presentation of self consistent with feminist ideology (Whittier 1995). Many hold jobs in government, social service organizations, or women's studies departments and other academic programs that allow them to incorporate their political goals into their work.

Another example of women resisting gender practices at the interactional level is found among young African-American women involved in little sister fraternity programs on college campuses. Such women embrace a collective identity built on notions of sisterhood and womanly strength to challenge the sexist practices of fraternities (Stombler and Padavic 1997). Also in the educational realm, young women are forming robotics clubs across the U.S. to provide a forum for girls to develop their skills and talents in the male-dominated fields of science, technology, engineering and math. Even within the most traditional male-dominated organizations and fields, gender relations are not immutable and women employ diverse strategies to resist gender inequality.

Challenging the Structure of Gender Inequality

The challenge to gender inequality and the dominant gender order is also waged at the social structural level. As we have seen, the liberal bureaucratic strand of the modern feminist movement has employed legal reform strategies and engaged in street protests to counter sex discrimination in the economic, education, political, and domestic spheres. Legislative campaigns for equal pay for work of comparable worth and for maternity leave policies in the workplace challenge institutions that essentialize differences between women and men and rank "masculine" values and attributes above those identified as "feminine" (Vogel 1993). The women's movement has also created a feminist policy network of elected officials, lobbying organizations, social movement organizations, and individuals who have mobilized to address issues ranging from abortion rights, domestic violence, childhood sexual abuse, and pregnancy discrimination to day care, sexual harassment, and welfare rights (Ferree and Hess 1994; Gagné 1998; Luker 1984; Staggenborg 1996; Whittier 2009).

In the last thirty years, feminist activism has also moved into diverse institutional settings. As an indication of the success and influence of feminist mobilization in earlier years, women found niches from which to challenge and transform institutional policies and structures, from pay equity to sexual harassment to occupational sex segregation (Blum 1991). In major corporations, feminists and GLBT activists campaign successfully for domestic partnership benefits for lesbian and gay employees (Raeburn 2004). Although the form and location of feminist protest have changed, the radical power of feminism has continued, as seen in the transformative potential of feminism inside institutions not generally considered amenable to feminist goals and ideologies, such as the Catholic church, the military, and the medical establishment.

As part of its legislative or legal strategies, the modern feminist movement has engaged in street protests such as picketing, mass demonstrations, and civil disobedience. Even in conservative political contexts, the feminist movement sparked some of the largest feminist demonstrations and actions in years. In 2004, during the presidency of George W. Bush, a coalition of feminist organizations organized the March for Women's Lives in Washington D.C., with an estimated one million participants marching in support of women's rights and reproductive freedom. Prochoice activists have organized electoral lobbying, defended abortion clinics, held conferences, and attempted to form coalitions across racial and ethnic lines and among women of different ages (Staggenborg 1991; Ryan 1992).

Reconstructing the Culture of Gender

The feminist social movement community has challenged cultural values, beliefs, and norms related to gender and the gender order by building alternative social and cultural institutions for women outside mainstream institutions. The strategy of creating autonomous institutions is rooted in radical feminist ideology, which emphasizes that women need places and experiences apart from patriarchal society in order to develop their strength. Feminist communities contribute to the reconstruction of the culture of gender by resisting the devaluation of the feminine and undermining androcentric values and beliefs. At the same time they rearticulate alternative femininities and woman-centered values and beliefs (Taylor and Rupp 1993; Staggenborg and Lecomte 2009).

Another example of resistance on the cultural level is the emergence of women's self-help groups, which sprang directly out of the early women's health movement and continue to model support groups on feminist consciousness-raising (Rapping 1996; Simonds 1996). Some feminist writers contend that women's self-help diverts the feminist agenda away from social and political change and directs women, instead, to change themselves (Kaminer 1992). Others argue that explicitly feminist self-help movements, such as strands of the postpartum depression and breast cancer movements, are contributing to the reconstruction of gender through the collective redefinition of womanhood and the cultural articulation of alternative femininities (Taylor 1996; Taylor and Van Willigen 1996; Klawiter 1999). These self-help movements are not depoliticized and purely individually focused; they perform a critical role of challenging institutional gender biases and refashioning the dominant gender code (Taylor 1996, 1999).

Zines, or low-budget, do-it-yourself photocopied pamphlets distributed through the mail and independent bookstores, emerged as an important cultural tactic of young feminists in the 1990s. With the rise of the Internet, blogs and websites now fill the same niche. An avenue for young women to express their opinions, share their experiences, and connect with other feminists, blog or zine topics include gender oppression, connecting the personal and the political, and sexism in everyday life (Bates and McHugh 2005). Blogs and zines represent continued feminist vitality and novel forms of resistance (Piepmeier 2009).

All of these diverse strategies, operating at different levels, challenge traditional societal definitions of femininity and the dominant gender order. From the individual to the social structural to the cultural plane, we can see the continuous impact of the women's movement.

FEMINISM ONLINE

In order to fully recognize the numerous forms of contemporary feminism, we must also expand our understandings of feminism to include online activity. Feminism online incorporates individual, social-cultural and cultural elements of feminism, and has emerged as a valuable resource for individual feminists, feminist networks, feminist communities, and feminist organizations. Scholars point to the vibrant feminist communities on the Internet as evidence that feminism is flourishing, and not in abeyance (Ferree 2007; Rowe 2008; Grey and Sawer 2008, McCaughey and Ayers 2003). Feminists across the world, of all ages and backgrounds, use the Internet as a resource to further feminist goals and make feminist connections. Online feminism includes numerous strategies, tactics, goals and outcomes. Since the mid-1990s, feminists have used the Internet to circulate news and information related to women and feminism, to connect feminists across the world, to create and sustain feminist communities, to empower women through sharing gendered experiences, and to broaden the scope of organizations that operate primarily offline (Ferree 2007; Gittler 1999; Duncan 2005).

Much of the power of feminism online lies in its global dissemination of feminist information and resources, which would have been virtually impossible before the widespread use of the Internet. Although an international women's movement existed prior to the development of Internet technologies (Rupp 1997; Ferree and Mueller 2007), the Internet has shifted both the potential and trajectory of contemporary feminism, particularly related to the creation and sustenance of transnational feminist networks (Ferree 2007; Gittler 1999; Huyer 1999; Moghadam 2005). The Association for Women's Right in Development (AWID) is an organization that seeks to strengthen "movements to advance women's rights and gender equality worldwide" (www.awid.org). Their website can be viewed in English, French or Spanish. AWID has thousands of members throughout the world, with offices in Toronto, Cape Town, and Mexico City, and other support staff located "everywhere from Lomé to Rosario and from Shanghai to Bangalore" (www.awid.org/about-AWID/Staff; Evans 2005, 168). The success of their projects and campaigns, such as a web-based feminist analysis of the global crisis and their offline international forums, relies on the connections and speed that Internet technology affords.

Online feminism has not only shaped an international feminist movement, but it has also allowed for the rapid dissemination of information and dialogue between feminists within the U.S. For example, www.feminist.com is a U.S.-based general information website that has attracted a high volume of traffic since its launch in 1995. The extensive site includes feminist news; a variety of resources such as book excerpts, articles, links and organizational referrals; opportunities to get involved in activism and e-mail lists; and "Ask Amy," a feminist advice column. Because of its easily searchable web address, feminist.com draws a wide range of users and connects and educates millions of people on feminist topics. Other U.S.-based websites have more specialized topics and audiences, but provide similar breadth of information. For example, INCITE! Women of Color Against Violence has an extensive website, with resources for organizing, a blog, and invitations to connect offline to chapters across the U.S.

In contrast to large websites such as www.feminist. com, blogs detailing women's everyday experiences provide an individual feminist perspective and connect personal experiences to a broad social network of women. Although blogs are frequently written by only one person, many receive significant media attention and web traffic. For example, a number of bloggers recently documented their abortion experiences. They provided details about the decision to have an abortion, the procedure itself, as well as general reflections. One such blog called "Un-Expecting" featured daily updates, including suggestions for before, during and after the abortion procedure (http://myabortionblog. tumblr.com). Another blog about abortion, written by a "forty year old feminist who works a little to change the world every day," features a title banner that reads: "One in three women in the United States has an abortion by the age of 45. Still the experience remains shrouded in silence, and for some women, shame. This is a pro-choice abortion blog based on my personal experience" (http://1outof3.blogspot.com). This demonstrates how blogs can be an outlet for "politicized actions in every day life," a significant element of social movements (Whittier 1995, 118). Blogs may also have the power to connect women to each other and lead to the understanding of their individual experiences within a larger social context. Although the content of feminist blogs runs the gamut, the common potential of blogs is the empowerment of women through shared personal experiences and the provision of a voice to marginalized communities or stigmatized experiences.

While feminism on the Internet may seem starkly different from offline feminism, it does reconfigure elements of traditional feminist modes such as self-help and consciousness-raising groups. Although in very different settings, the process of politicization may be similar. For example, feminist websites develop communities of readers who get to know each other by posting comments on a regular basis or by participating in a discussion board. Commentators or participants may become aware of the connections between their individual lives and broader social inequalities through the online sharing of knowledge, experiences, and news. While consciousness-raising groups required face to face connections between feminists in the same geographical area, online communities may be established across a variety of boundaries, and are open to feminists who may not know any feminists in their day-to-day, offline lives. Although differences between offline and online relationships may be vast, similar issues are discussed in both contexts, including sharing experiences of and reactions to sexism in everyday life, and supporting each other through difficult life experiences.

Like consciousness-raising groups, involvement in feminist websites may lead to organizational affiliations, additional feminist activism, and/or the maintenance of feminist networks (Cassell 1977). For example, the website www.feministing.com allows users to import lists of offline feminist events into the iCalendar program on their smart phone or computer, facilitating the transformation from online feminism to offline feminism. Another example is a recent Feminists for Choice "tweetup" in New York City, a face-to-face meeting for people who twitter together about issues of reproductive rights, but who may have never met in person.

Online feminism is best analyzed and understood as complementary to other forms of feminism. Brick and mortar feminist organizations have amended their tactics and organizational structures to accommodate the growing influence of the Internet. For example, NOW currently has a "media hall of shame" on their website devoted to objectionable images of women in media, including a "misogyny meter," detailed media analyses, and links to take action. The website of NARAL Pro-Choice America not only provides up-to-date news about abortion rights in the U.S., but also has an option to sign up to receive text messages with pro-choice news. "Our Bodies Ourselves" has an online health information and resource center with extensive information ranging from nutrition to sexual health, to menopause, to the politics of women's health. The websites of existing feminist organizations provide access to information as well as an outlet for feminist action, allowing a broad scope of influence and a collaboration of constituents. Sometimes the boundary between online and offline activism is murky, as in the Hollaback project, in which women who are harassed on the street text an account of the experience, which is then posted to the Hollaback website.

The influence of the Internet on feminist organizing and networks is not fully understood, in large part due to the nebulous and continually changing nature of the Internet. Because online feminism remains, for the most part, unanalyzed, there is a perception that feminist organizing may not be happening on the web. The widespread belief that young women are disinterested in feminism is fueled by the lack of understanding of the changes in forms of feminist organizing and strategies. This phenomenon was highlighted in a recent online article: "Young Feminists to Old Feminists: If You Can't Find Us, It's Because We're Online" (Herold 2010). This article was one of many written in response to remarks made in *Newsweek* by Nancy Keenan, Executive Director of NARAL, questioning the devotion of young women to issues of reproductive freedom. The author of "Young Feminist to Old Feminists" highlights how young feminists are using social networking sites, blogs, Twitter, and other forms of new media to advance feminist claims. Herold writes: "Whether we tweet feminism or blog about it, young feminists use the Internet to expand and explore what it means to be involved in the feminist movement. We usually do it in addition to other feminist work, using the Internet to launch campaigns, reach new audiences with our message, and create a sense of feminist community" (Herold 2010, paragraph 4). Just as online feminism can only be fully understood within the larger context of face-to-face feminism, contemporary offline feminism can only be fully understood with a consideration of the Internet.

Although the Internet has changed the way feminists communicate across boundaries, we must avoid overestimating the power of online feminism *on its own*. Women across the world are still without access to computers or reliable Internet technology (Farwell et. al. 1999), and the Internet cannot replace offline feminism. Romanticized views of the power of Internet communities lead us to believe that the act of tweeting a fact about domestic violence, of "liking" a feminist cause on Facebook, or of participating in an online feminist forum is feminism in and of itself. In truth, the offline implications of online activism are not fully understood (Ayers 2003; McLaine 2003). Both

online and offline feminism are significant in the future of feminism, but they must be understood in tandem, and not separately. Online feminism pushes feminism in new directions, speeds up the processes of organizing and network building, creates and sustains communities across geographic divides, destabilizes identity categories, and combines and introduces new tactics and strategies. The Internet may also provide a forum for feminist communities to flourish in inhospitable political climates, a topic to which we now turn.

ANTIFEMINISM

As this chapter has demonstrated, the U.S. women's movement has been in varying degrees of motion throughout modern history. However, the interaction between social movements and oppositional movements is a prominent feature of contemporary social movements (Fetner 2008; Meyer and Staggenborg 1996). Any social movement analysis is incomplete without a consideration of the interdependence of movements and countermovements. We cannot fully understand the tactics, strategies, organizational forms, and feminist identities characteristic of the contemporary feminist movement without considering the effects of antifeminist mobilization (Marshall 1984; 1985; Klatch 1987; Schreiber 2008).

Politically conservative times, such as during the Ronald Reagan, George H.W. Bush and George W. Bush presidencies, saw a rapid decrease in the number of feminist organizations and a transformation in the form and activities of the women's movement. Federal funds and grants to feminist service organizations were severely cut. Because other social service organizations were also hard hit by budget cuts, competition increased for relatively scarce money from private foundations. As a result, many feminist programs such as rape crisis centers, shelters for battered women, abortion clinics, women's health clinics, and job training programs were forced to close or limit their services.

Abortion rights, won in 1973 with the Supreme Court's *Roe v. Wade* decision, have continuously eroded since the 1989 Supreme Court decision in *Webster v. Reproductive Services* that permitted states to enact restrictions on abortion (Staggenborg 1991, 137–38). Following the *Webster* decision, state governments set increasingly tight restrictions on abortion, ranging from "informed consent" laws that required a waiting period before women could obtain abortion surgery, to parental consent laws for underage women, to outright bans on abortion unless the woman's life was in danger. Such restrictions, including the implementation of parental consent and mandatory counseling laws continue on a state-by-state basis. The antiabortion movement has continued to escalate and harden its tactics, culminating in the 2009 killing of physician George Tiller. The antiabortion movement continues to threaten physicians who perform abortions, harass women entering clinics, and influence federal and state lawmakers (Staggenborg 1991; Simonds 1996).

Antifeminism is also produced by the mainstream print and news media, which rely on fabricated stereotypes and clichés when referencing feminism. The media is responsible for the "false feminist death syndrome," or the widespread declaration of the death of feminism, despite evidence to its continued vitality (Pozner 2003). Such discourse declares that since women have achieved equality with men, they no longer need a protest movement. It also perpetuates the widespread popular opinion that the U.S. is a gender egalitarian nation, despite data to the contrary (Charles and Bradley 2009). In this antifeminist context, those who continue to press for gender equality are described in negative terms, illustrated in a variety of contexts including mainstream news sources (Lind and Salo 2002). These depictions of feminism reduce a complex set of ideologies and strategies into an outdated trope that leads to perceptions of feminism as unnecessary, at best. The consequences of such antifeminism include women's distancing from feminism and the undercutting of continued struggles for gender equality.

The prevalence of antifeminist resistance throughout history highlights the significance of the family, sexuality, reproduction, and traditional gendered arrangements for the maintenance of the dominant social order. Antifeminism, however, does not imply that the women's movement has failed or run its course. On the contrary, it attests to feminism's successful challenge to the status quo. While feminism is certainly susceptible to the ramifications of challenging political and social environments, feminism has persevered over time in a variety of hospitable and inhospitable political environments. In contrast to oversimplifications of the feminist movement by antifeminists, feminism has a heterogeneous constituency, nuanced ideologies, and complex organizational structures. However, a hostile political climate in the U.S. during the 1980s, 1990s, and early twenty-first century did not succeed in halting feminist progress. In response, many U.S. feminists turned their attention to a growing global network of women's movements (Stansell 2010, 356), to which we now turn.

FEMINIST MOVEMENTS IN A GLOBAL CONTEXT

Situating U.S. feminism in a global context highlights both the interconnectedness and tensions among feminists worldwide. Throughout modern history, women in all regions of the world have organized collectively against the injustice and oppression in their lives and communities (Basu 1995). They mobilize around a constellation of oppressions, including gender, class, race and ethnicity (Banaszak 2006). Feminist mobilization in diverse political, cultural, and historical contexts has varied widely in organization, strategy, ideology, and structure. Ideological, organizational, and strategic differences in women's movements may lie in differences in the political culture of a region (Ray 1999) or in relationships to global feminist networks (Thayer 2010).

Although the origins of international women's organizations date back to the closing decades of the nineteenth century (Rupp 1997), it is only since the 1970s that there has been a phenomenal growth in regional, sub-regional, interregional, international and transnational networking among feminist groups (Miles 1996). The global stage of feminism has changed dramatically in recent history. Basu (2010) identifies three key elements of changes in international and transnational organizing: "the growth of transnational networks and advocacy groups…the growth of international funding for nongovernmental organizations…and international conferences, particularly under the aegis of the United Nations" (5). Each of these changes has led to a significant shift in the context of women's movements in the global sphere and has also brought women's lives and experiences to the discussions of globalization and transnational politics (Desai 2009).

The United Nations has spearheaded numerous campaigns for women and has created and dramatically shifted global feminist networks and organizing (Snyder 2006). UN efforts include International Women's Year (1975), the Decade for Women (1975–1985), and the fourth world conference on women (1995). Each has fostered global feminist dialogues and stimulated local and transnational feminist activities. Although these conferences have been sites of considerable debate and conflict over the meaning of "women's issues" and the definition of feminism, their forums facilitated the development of networks and strategies that positioned the language of gender equality and human rights at the forefront of the UN.

The UN set the stage for unprecedented social change regarding women in the global context, and it also highlighted tensions between feminists. Because the UN Conferences convened feminists from across the world, they became stages for the drama of conflicting feminist ideologies. They also foreshadowed the challenges many feminists would face when building coalitions across metaphorical and physical borders. These tensions included disagreement over the use of terminology such as "feminist," "first world," "third world," and "post-colonial" (Ferree and Pudrovska 2006; Naples 2002), the prioritization of "equality and sexuality issues versus economic and political issues" (Moghadam 2005, 6), and the perpetuation of inequalities between feminists of the global and economic North and South (Desai 2009; Tripp 2006).

The institutional landscape of global feminism was forever altered by the policies and actions of the UN, but these changes happened alongside other feminist efforts, including NGOs, transnational networks, and grassroots organizing (Moghadam 2005; Basu 2010). Grassroots feminist organizing effectively incorporated voices and experiences of women from a variety of communities, educational backgrounds, and socioeconomic statuses. The Huairou Commission, a network of grassroots partnerships, was formed in 1995 in response to the absence of grassroots women organizers at the UN conferences (Desai 2009, 40–41). Other successful grassroots feminist organizations include DAWN (Development Alternatives with Women for a New Era) and SEWA (Self Employed Women's Association), which have not only created change at the individual and policy levels, but have also commanded attention to women's agency in development and globalization (Swider 2006; Bhavnani et. al 2003).

Women from governmental organizations, non governmental organizations, and those not associated with formal organizations are actively working to eradicate sexism and other interrelated forms of inequality on local, regional and global scales. Although these networks are not without struggles over difference and power inequalities, feminists are forging global relations around a diverse set of issues. Analyzing feminism from a global context provides an important perspective from which to understand the trajectory of U.S. feminism and further demonstrates the continued vibrancy of the feminist movement around the globe.

CONCLUSION: FEMINISM SHIFTING, NEVER STOPPING

Social movement scholars understand the myriad ways that social movements affect one another. The abolitionist movement in the mid-nineteenth century influenced the first wave of the women's movement in the United States, and the civil rights and New Left movements of the 1960s shaped the course of the second wave (Buechler 1990). In turn, the women's movement has had a substantial impact on other social movements. Meyer and Whittier (1994) argue that "the ideas, tactics, style, participants, and organizations of one movement often *spill over* its boundaries to affect other social movements" (277, emphasis in the original). The gay and lesbian, transgender, AIDS, addiction recovery, New Age, environment, anti-globalization, peace, postpartum depression, immigrant-rights and animal-rights movements have been profoundly influenced by feminist values and ideology, including the emphasis on collective structure and consensus, the notion of the personal as political, and the critique of patriarchy extended to the mistreatment of animals and ecological resources (Jasper and Poulsen 1995; Einwohner 1999).

Although the women's movement has changed form and location, the level of mass mobilization and the movement's confrontation with the social structural system has declined since the 1980s. Because feminism has come to focus more on consciousness and culture, has established roots in other social movements of the period, and mobilizes to a large extent through the Internet, feminist protest is less visible than it was during the heyday of the women's movement. Although the meaning of feminist identity is a point of contestation for some women (Aronson 2003; Hercus 2005), social movement scholars suggest that feminist identities can be placed on a continuum (Taylor 1996), or that they fluctuate depending on the context (Reger 2008). Despite ongoing tensions around feminist identity, support for feminist goals remain consistent, suggesting the importance of expanding definitions and understandings of feminism (Aronson 2003).

The need for feminist responses to social inequality has never faded. Although feminists in the U.S. have gained ground and improved the status of women in many respects, scholars have found widespread evidence of an "unfinished revolution" or an "uneven and stalled" gender revolution, due to a lack of institutional and cultural changes in gender arrangements (Gerson 2010; England 2010). For example, women of all race and class backgrounds continue to struggle to balance work and family obligations (Maume, Sebastian, Bardo 2010; Hondagneu-Sotelo 2001). As one of the richest countries in the world, the U.S. is one of only two countries that does not require paid parental leave (Gerson 2010, 222), and the U.S. has fallen behind in areas such as welfare benefits, health care benefits, and other important policy areas that inevitably hurt women disproportionately (Tripp 2006). Inequalities continue to shape the experiences of women in the workforce, in educational institutions, and in women's representations in cultural realms such as music and film. Although the status of women in the U.S. has undoubtedly improved because of the achievements of feminism, the continued relevance of feminism for women's lives is undeniable.

In response to these inequalities, many younger women have embraced a feminist identity and feminist practices. As one generation of feminists fades from the scene with its ultimate goals unrealized, another takes up the challenge. But each new generation of feminists does not simply carry on where the previous generation left off. Rather, it speaks for itself and defines its own objectives and strategies, often to the dismay and disapproval of feminists from earlier generations (Whittier 1995; Henry 2004).

A new generation of feminists continues to work in tandem with previous generations. They may write a blog focusing on feminist analysis of corporate greed, may "girlcott" clothing stores selling shirts displaying sexist messages or made in sweatshops, may write and direct an independent film documenting the history of Chicana feminists, or may use Facebook to organize a feminist protest in their community. They may be employed as a political lobbyist to fight for women's policies, they may put on "drag king" performances to challenge the restrictions placed on expressions of womwn's sexuality, may distribute condoms and dental dams to promote women's sexual health. While feminists may disagree about what constitutes feminist ideology and identity, feminism has never been monolithic and will continue to develop and evolve. Just as the women's movement of the twentieth century persisted through transformation, feminism of the twenty-first century will endure through diversity, continuity and change.

REFERENCES

Aronson, Pamela. (2003.) Feminists or 'Postfeminists'? Young Women's Attitudes toward Feminism and Gender Relations. *Gender and Society* 17: 903–922.

Atkinson, T. G. (1974). *Amazon Odyssey*. New York: Links.

Ayers, Michael D. (2003). "Comparing Collective Identity in Online and Offline Feminist Activists." In *Cyberactivism: Online Activism in Theory and Practice*. Pps 145–164. ed. Martha McCaughey and Michael D. Ayers. New York: Routledge.

Bagguley, Paul. (2002). "Contemporary British Feminism: A Social Movement in Abeyance?" *Social Movement Studies* 1, 169–185.

Banaszak, Lee Ann. (2006.) *The U.S. Women's Movement in Global Perspective*. Lanham, Maryland: Rowman and Littlefield.

Barnett, Bernice McNair. (1993). Invisible southern black men leaders in the civil rights movement: The triple constraints of gender, race, and class. *Gender & Society*, 7, 162–182.

Basu, Amrita, ed. (1995). *The Challenge of Local Feminisms: Women's Movements in Global Perspective*. Boulder, CO: Westview Press.

———, ed. (2010). *Women's Movements in the Global Era: The Power of Local Feminisms*. Boulder, CO: Westview Press.

Bates, Dawn and Maureen C. McHugh. (2005). Zines: Voices of Third Wave Feminists. In Jo Reger, ed., *Different Wavelengths: Studies of the Contemporary Women's Movement*. (Pp. 179–194.) New York: Routledge.

Beauvoir, S. de. (1952). *The Second Sex*. New York: Bantam.

Beck, E. T. (1980). *Nice Jewish Girls: A Lesbian Anthology*. Watertown, MA: Persephone.

Bell, Susan. (2009). *DES Daughters: Embodied Knowledge, and the Transformation of Women's Health Politics in the Late Twentieth Century*. Philadelphia: Temple University Press.

Bhavnani, Kum Kum, John Foran, and Priya Kurian, eds. (2003). *Feminist Futures: Reimagining Women, Culture and Development*. London: Zed.

Black, Naomi. (1989). *Social Feminism*. Ithaca, NY: Cornell University Press.

Blum, Linda M. (1991). *Between Feminism and Labor: The Significance of the Comparable Worth Movement*, Berkeley: University of California Press.

Bobel, Chris. (2010.) *New Blood: Third Wave Feminism and the Politics of Menstruation*. New Brunswick, NJ: Rutgers.

Boris, Eileen and Rhacel Parreñas, eds. (2010). *Intimate Labors: Cultures, Technologies, and the Politics of Care*. Palo Alto: Stanford.

Breines, W. (1982). *Community and Organization in the New Left, 1962–68*. New York: Praeger.

Buechler, Steven M. (1990). *Women's Movements in the United States*. New Brunswick, NJ: Rutgers.

Bulkin, Elly, Minnie Bruce Pratt, & Barbara Smith. (1984). *Yours in Struggle: Three Feminist Perspectives on Anti-Semitism and Racism*. New York: Long Haul Press.

Carden, Maren. (1978). The proliferation of a social movement. In Louis Kriesberg, ed., *Research in Social Movements, Conflict, and Change*, vol. 1 (pp. 179–196). Greenwich, CT: JAI Press.

Cassell, J. (1977). *A Group Called Women: Sisterhood and Symbolism in the Feminist Movement*. New York: David McKay.

Chafe, W. H. (1977). *Women and Equality: Changing Patterns in American Culture*. New York: Oxford University Press.

Chafetz, Janet. (1990). *Gender Equity: An Integrated Theory of Stability and Change*. Newbury Park, CA: Sage.

Chafetz, Janet, & Gary Dworkin. (1986). *Female Revolt*. Totowa, NJ: Rowman Allanheld.

———. (1987). In the face of threat: Organized antifeminism in comparative perspective. *Gender & Society*, 1, 33–60.

Charles, Maria and Karen Bradley. (2009). Indulging our Gendered Selves? Sex Segregation by Field of Study in 44 Countries. *American Journal of Sociology*, 114, 4: 924–976.

Collins, Patricia Hill. (1990). *Black Feminist Thought*. New York: Routledge.

Connell, R. W. (1987). *Gender and Power*. Stanford, CA: Stanford University Press.

Daly, Mary. (1978). *Gyn/ecology*. Boston: Beacon.

Deckard, Barbara Sinclair. (1983). *The Women's Movement*. New York: Harper & Row.

Desai, Manisha. (2009). *Gender and the Politics of Possibilities: Rethinking Globalization*. Boulder, CO: Rowman and Littlefield.

Drake, Jennifer. (1997). "Third Wave Feminisms." *Feminist Studies* 23, 1: 30–39.

Duncan, Barbara. (2005). "Searching for a Home Place: On-Line in the Third Wave" In Jo Reger ed., *Different Wavelengths: Studies of the Contemporary Women's Movement*. (Pp. 161–178). New York: Routledge.

Echols, Alice. (1989). *Daring to Be Bad: Radical Feminism in America 1967–1975*. Minneapolis: University of Minnesota Press.

Ehrenreich, Barbara and Hochschild, Arlie Russell, eds. (2004). *Global Women: Nannies, Maids and Sex Workers in the New Economy*. New York: Holt.

Einwohner, Rachel L. (1999). Gender, class, and social movement outcomes: Identity and effectiveness in two animal rights campaigns. *Gender & Society* 13, 56–76.

Eisenstein, Z. (1981). *The Radical Future of Liberal Feminism*. New York: Longman.

England, Paula. (2010). The Gender Revolution: Uneven and Stalled. *Gender and Society* 24, 2149–166.

Esterberg, Kristin G. (1997). *Lesbian and Bisexual Identities: Constructing Communities, Constructing Selves*. Philadelphia: Temple University Press.

Evans, Sarah. (1979). *Personal Politics*. New York: Knopf.

Evans, Kristy. (2005). Cyber girls . . . Hello are you out there? In Shamillah Wilson, Anasuya Sengupta, and Kristy Evans, eds. *Defending our Dreams: Global Feminist Voices for a New Generation* (Pp. 167–178). London: Zed.

Farwell, Edie, Peregrine Wood, Maureen James, and Karen Banks. (1999). "Global Networking for Change: Experiences from the APC Women's Programme." In Wendy Harcourt, ed. *Women @ internet: Creating New Cultures in Cyberspace*. (Pp. 102–113). New York: Zed Books.

Ferree, Myra Marx. 2007. "On-line Identities and Organizational Connections: Networks of Transnational Feminist Websites" Pp. 141–166 in *Gender Orders Unbound? Globalization, Restructuring and Reciprocity*. Edited by Ilse Lenz, Charlotte Ullrich, Barbara Fersch. Barbara Budrich Publishers.

Ferree, Myra Marx and Beth B. Hess. [1985] (1994) (2000). *Controversy and Coalition: The New Feminist Movement*. Boston: Twayne.

Ferree, Myra Marx and Patricia Yancey Martin. (1995). *Feminist Organizations: Harvest of the New Women's Movement*. Philadelphia: Temple University Press.

Ferree, Myra Marx and Carol McClurg Mueller. (2004) [2007]. Feminism and the Women's Movement: A Global Perspective. Pp. 576–607 in *The Blackwell Companion to Social Movements*. Edited by David A. Snow, Sarah A. Soule, and Hanspeter Kriesi. Oxford: Blackwell.

Ferree, Myra Marx and Tetyana Pudrovska. (2006). "Transnational Feminist NGOs on the Web: Networks and Identities in the Global North and South." In Myra Marx Ferree and Aili Mari Tripp, eds, in *Global Feminism: Transnational Women's Activism, Organizing, and Human Rights* (Pp. 247–272). New York: NYU Press.

Fetner, Tina. (2008). *How the Religious Right Shaped Lesbian and Gay Activism*. Minneapolis: University of Minnesota Press.

Firestone, S. (1970). *The Dialectic of Sex*. New York: William Morrow.

Fonow, Mary Margaret. (2003). *Union Women: Forging Feminism in the United Steelworkers of America*. Minneapolis: University of Minnesota Press.

Freeman, Jo. (1972/3). The tyranny of structurelessness. *Berkeley Journal of Sociology*, 17, 151–164.

———. (1975). *The Politics of Women's Liberation*. New York: David McKay.

———. (1979). Resource mobilization and strategy: A model for analyzing social movement organization actions. In M. N. Zald & J. D. McCarthy, eds. *The Dynamics of Social Movements* (pp. 167–89). Cambridge, MA: Winthrop.

Frye, Marilyn. (1983). *The Politics of Reality: Essays in Feminist Theory*. Trumansburg, NY: Crossing Press.

Gagné, Patricia. (1998). *Battered Women's Justice: The Movement for Democracy and the Politics of Self-defense.* New York: Twayne Publishers.

Gerlach, L. P., & V. H. Hine. (1970). *People, Power, Change: Movements of Social Transformation.* Indianapolis: Bobbs-Merrill.

Gerson, Kathleen. (2010). *The Unfinished Revolution: How a New Generation is Reshaping Family, Work, and Gender in America.* Oxford: Oxford University Press.

Gilmore, Stephanie, ed. (2008). *Feminist Coalitions: Historical Perspectives on Second-Wave Feminism in the United States.* Urbana and Chicago: University of Illinois Press.

Gittler, Alice Mastrangelo. (1999). Mapping women's Global Communications and Networking. In Wendy Harcourt, ed. *Women @ internet: Creating New Cultures in Cyberspace.* (Pp. 91–101). New York: Zed Books.

Giugni, Marco, Doug McAdam, and Charles Tilly, eds. (1999). *How Social Movements Matter.* Minneapolis: University of Minnesota Press.

Gordon, Suzanne. (1991). *Prisoners of Men's Dreams.* New York: Little, Brown.

Grey, Sandra and Marian Sawer, eds. (2008). *Women's Movements: Flourishing or in Abeyance?* London: Routledge.

Griffin, Susan. (1978). *Women and Nature.* New York: Harper and Row.

Hartmann, Heidi. (1981). The family as the locus of gender, class, and political struggle: The example of housework. *Signs*, 6, 366–394.

Hartsock, Nancy. (1983). *Money, Sex, and Power: Toward a Feminist Historical Materialism.* New York: Longman.

Henry, Astrid. (2004). Not My Mother's Sister: Generational Conflict and Third Wave Feminism. Bloomington, Indiana: Indiana University Press.

Henry, Astrid. (2005). "Solitary Sisterhood: Individualism Meets Collectivity in Feminism's Third Wave." In Jo Reger, ed. *Different Wavelengths:Studies of the Contemporary Women's Movement* (Pp. 81–96). New York: Routledge.

Hercus, Cheryl. (2005). *Stepping Out of Line: Becoming and Being Feminist.* New York: Routledge.

Herold, Stephanie. (2010). "Young feminists to Older feminists: if you can't find us it's because we're on-line" Campus Progress. July 19, 2010

Hill Collins, Patricia. (1990). *Black Feminist Thought: Knowledge, Consciousness, and the Politics of Empowerment.* Boston, MA: UnwinHyman.

Hondagneu-Sotelo, Pierrette. (2001). *Domestica: Immigrant Workers Cleaning and Caring in the Shadows of Affluence.* Berkeley: University of California Press.

Huber, Joan. (1973). From sugar and spice to professor. In A.S. Rossi & A. Calderwood, *Academic Women on the Move.* New York: Russell Sage Foundation.

Huber, Joan, & Glenna Spitze. (1983). *Sex Stratification: Children, Housework, and Jobs.* New York: Academic.

Huyer, Sophia. (1999). "Shifting Agendas at GK97. Women and International Policy on Information and Communication Technologies." In Wendy Harcourt, ed.

Women @ internet: Creating New Cultures in Cyberspace. (Pp. 114–130).New York: Zed Books.

Jasper, James M., & Jane D. Poulsen. (1995). Recruiting strangers and friends: Moral shocks and social networks in animal rights and anti-nuclear protests. *Social Problems* 42, 493–512.

Jones, Nikki. (2010). *Between Good and Ghetto: Apican American Girls and Inner-City Violence.* New Brunswick: Rutgers University Press.

Kaminer, Wendy. (1992). *I'm Dysfunctional, You're Dysfunctional: The Recovery Movement and Other Self-help Fashions.* Reading, MA: Addison-Wesley.

Katzenstein, Mary Fainsod (1998a) Stepsisters: Feminist movement activism in different institutional spaces. In David Meyer & Sidney Tarrow, eds., *A Movement Society? Contentious Politics for a New Century.* Boulder, CO: Rowman & Littlefield.

———. (1998b). *Faithful and Fearless: Moving Feminist Protest Inside the Church and Military.* Princeton, NJ: Princeton University Press.

Klatch, Rebecca. (1987). *Women of the New Right.* Philadelphia: Temple University Press.

Klawiter, Maren. (1999). Racing for the Cure, walking women, and toxic touring: Mapping cultures of action within the Bay Area terrain of breast cancer. *Social Problems*, 46, 104–126.

Klein, Ethel. (1984). *Gender Politics.* Cambridge, MA: Harvard University Press.

Leidner, Robin. (1993). Constituency, accountability, and deliberation: Reshaping democracy in the National Women's Studies Association. *NWSA Journal*, 5, 4–27.

Lind, Rebecca Ann and Salo, Colleen. (2002.) The Framing of Feminists and Feminism in News and Public Affairs Programs in U.S. Electronic Media. *The Journal of Communication*, 52, 1 : 211–228.

Luker, Kristin. (1984). *Abortion and the Politics of Motherhood.* Berkeley: University of California Press.

MacKinnon, C. A. (1983). Feminism, Marxism, method, and the state: Toward feminist jurisprudence. *Signs*, 8, 635–668.

Mansbridge, Jane. (1986). *Why We Lost the ERA.* Chicago: University of Chicago Press.

Marshall, Susan E. (1984). Keep us on the pedestal: Women against feminism in twentieth-century America. In Jo Freeman, ed., *Women: A Feminist Perspective* (pp. 568–581). Palo Alto: Mayfield.

———. (1985). Ladies against women: Mobilization dilemmas of antifeminist movements. *Social Problems*, 32, 348–362.

Martin, Patricia Yancey. (1990). Rethinking feminist organizations. *Gender & Society*, 4, 182–206.

Marx, G. T., & J. L. Wood. (1975). Strands of theory and research in collective behavior. *Annual Review of Sociology*, 1, 363–428.

Maume, David J., Rachel A. Sebastian and Anthony Bardo. (2010). Gender, Work-Family Responsibility, and Sleep. *Gender and Society* 24, 6: 746–768.

McCaughey, Martha and Michael D. Ayers. (2003). *Cyberactivism: On-Line Activism in Theory and Practice.* New York: Routledge.

McCarthy, J. D., & M. N. Zald. (1977). Resource mobilization and social movements: A partial theory. *American Journal of Sociology,* 82, 1212–1239.

McLaine, Steven. (2003). "Ethnic Online Communities." In Martha McCaughey and Michael D. Ayers, eds. *Cyberactivism: Online Activism in Theory and Practice* (Pps 233–254). New York: Routledge.

Meyer, David S. and Nancy Whittier. (1994). Social movement spillover. *Social Problems,* 41, 277–298.

Meyer, David S., and Suzanne Staggenborg. (1996). "Movements, Countermovements and the Structure of Political Opportunity." *American Journal of Sociology,* vol. 101(6), pp. 1628–1660.

Miles, Angela. (1996). *Integrative Feminisms: Building Global Visions, 1960s–1990s.* New York: Routledge.

Millett, K. (1971). *Sexual Politics.* New York: Avon.

Mitchell, Juliet. (1986). Reflections on twenty years of feminism. In Juliet Mitchell & Ann Oakley, eds., *What Is Feminism?* (pp. 34–48). Oxford: Basil Blackwell.

Moghadam, Valentine. (2005). *Globalizing Women: Transnational Feminist Networks.* Baltimore: Johns Hopkins.

Mohanty, Chandra Talpade, Ann Russo, & Lordes Torres, eds. (1991). *Third World Women and the Politics of Feminism.* Bloomington: Indiana University Press.

Moraga, Cherríe & Gloria Anzaldúa. (1981). *This Bridge Called My Back: Writings by Radical Women of Color.* Watertown, MA: Persephone.

Morgen, Sandra. *Into Our Own Hands: The Women's Health Movement in the United States, 1969–1990.* New Brunswick: Rutgers University Press, 2002.

Morris, Aldon D., & Carol McClurg Mueller, eds. (1992). *Frontiers in Social Movement Theory.* New Haven, CT: Yale University Press.

Naples, Nancy A. (1992). Activist mothering: Cross-generational continuity in the community work of women from low-income neighborhoods. *Gender & Society,* 6, 441–463.

———. (2002). Community Activism, Globalization, and the Dilemmas of Transnational Feminist Praxis. In Nancy Naples and Manisha Desai, eds. *Women's Activism and Globalization: Linking Local Struggles and Transnational Politics* (pp. 3–14). New York: Routledge.

———. (2005). Confronting the Future, Learning from the Past: Feminist Praxis in the Twenty-First Century. In Jo Reger, ed., *Different Wavelengths: Studies of the Contemporary Women's Movement* (pp. 215–235). New York: Routledge.

Offen, Karen. (1988). Defining feminism: A comparative historical approach. *Signs,* 14, 119–157.

Oppenheimer, Valerie Kincade. (1973). Demographic influence on female employment and the status of women. In Joan Huber, ed., *Changing Women in a Changing Society* (pp. 184–199). Chicago: University of Chicago Press.

Piepmeier, Alison. (2009). *Girl Zines: Making Media, Doing Feminism.* New York: New York University Press.

Pozner, Jennifer. (2003). The 'Big Lie': False Feminist Death Syndrome, Profit, and the Media. In Rory Dicker and Alison Piepmeier, eds. *Catching a Wave: Reclaiming Feminism for the 21st Century* (pp. 31–56). Boston: Northeastern University Press.

Price-Glynn, Kim. (2010). *Strip Club: Gender, Power and Sex Work.* New York: NYU Press.

Rapping Elayne. (1996). *The Culture of Recovery: Making Sense of the Recovery Movement in Women's Lives.* Boston: Beacon Press.

Raeburn, Nicole. (2004) *Changing Corporate America from the Inside Out.* Minneapolis, University of Minnesota Press.

Ray, Raka. (1999). *Fields of Protest: Women's Movements in India.* Minneapolis: University of Minnesota Press.

Reger, Jo, ed. (2005). *Different Wavelengths: Studies of the Contemporary Women's Movement.* New York: Routledge.

———. (2008). Drawing Identity Boundaries: The Creation of Contemporary Feminism. In Jo Reger, Daniel J. Myers, and Rachel Einwohner, eds. *Identity Work in Social Movements.* (Pp. 101–120.) Minneapolis: University of Minnesota Press.

———. (forthcoming). *Generation Fluoride: Community, Identity, and the Continuity of US Contemporary Feminism.*

———. (1980). Compulsory heterosexuality and lesbian existence. *Signs,* 5, 631–660.

Rich, Adrienne. (1976). *Of Woman Born.* New York: Norton.

Robnett, Belinda. (1996). African-American women in the civil rights movement, 1954–1965: Gender, leadership, and micromobilization. *American Journal of Sociology,* 101, 1661–1693.

Roth, Benita. (2004). *Separate Roads to Feminism: Black, Chicana, and White feminist Movements in America's Second Wave.* Cambridge, UK: Cambridge University Press.

Rothschild-Whitt, Joyce. (1979). The collectivist organization: An alternative to rational-bureaucratic models. *American Sociological Review,* 44, 509–527.

Rowe, CJ. (2008). "Cyberfeminism in Action: Claiming Women's Space in Cyberspace." In Grey, Sandra and Marian Sawer, eds. Pp. 128–139. *Women's Movements: Flourishing or in Abeyance?* London: Routledge.

Rubin, G. (1975). Traffic in women: Notes on the "political economy" of sex. In Rayne Reiter, ed., *Toward an Anthropology of Women,* New York: Monthly Review Press.

Rupp, Leila J. (1997). *Worlds of Women: The Making of an International Women's Movement.* Princeton, NJ: Princeton University Press.

Rupp, Leila J., & Verta Taylor. (1987). *Survival in the Doldrums: The American Women's Rights Movement, 1945 to 1960s.* New York: Oxford University Press.

———. 1999. "Forging Feminist Identity in an International Movement: A Collective Identity Approach to Twentieth-Century Feminism." *Signs* 24(2): 363–386.

———. (2005). Foreword. In Jo Reger, ed., *Different Wavelengths: Studies of the Contemporary Women's Movement* (pp. xi-xiv) New York: Routledge.

Ryan, Barbara. (1989). Ideological purity and feminism: The U.S. women's movement from 1966 to 1975. *Gender & Society*, 3, 239–257.

———. (1992). *Feminism and the Women's Movement.* New York: Routledge.

Schlesinger, M. B., & P. Bart. (1983). Collective work and self-identity: The effect of working in a feminist illegal abortion collective. In L. Richardson & V. Taylor, eds., *Feminist Frontiers.* Reading, MA: Addison-Wesley.

Schreiber, Ronnee. (2008). *Righting Feminism: Conservative Women and American Politics.* New York: Oxford University Press.

Simonds, Wendy. (1996). *Abortion at Work: Ideology and Practice in a Feminist Clinic.* New Brunswick, NJ: Rutgers University Press.

Snyder, Margaret. 2006. "Unlikely Godmother: The UN and the Global Women's Movement." In Myra Marx Ferree and Aili Mari Tripp, eds. in *Global Feminism: Transnational Women's Activism, Organizing, and Human Rights.* (Pp. 24–50). New York: NYU Press.

Spelman, Elizabeth. (1988). *Inessential Woman: Problems of Exclusion in Feminist Thought.* Boston: Beacon Press.

Springer, Kimberly. (2002). "Third Wave Black Feminism." *Signs* 27 (4): 1059–82.

———. (2005). *Living for the Revolution: Black Feminist Organizations, 1968–1980.* Durham, NC: Duke University Press.

Stacey, Judith. (1987). Sexism by a subtler name? Postindustrial conditions and postfeminist consciousness. *Socialist Review*, 17, 7–28.

Stansell, Christine. (2010). *The Feminist Promise: 1792 to the Present.* New York: Modern Library.

Staggenborg, Suzanne. (1988). The consequences of professionalization and formalization in the pro-choice movement. *American Sociological Review*, 53, 585–606.

———. (1989). Stability and Innovation in the Women's Movement: A Comparison of Two Movement Organizations. *Social Problems* 36: 1, 75–92.

———. (1991). *The Pro-choice Movement.* New York: Oxford University Press.

———. (1996). The survival of the women's movement: Turnover and continuity in Bloomington, Indiana. *Mobilization*, 1, 143–158.

———. (1998). *Gender, Family, and Social Movements.* Thousand Oaks, CA: Pine Forge Press.

Staggenborg Suzanne, and Lecomte, Josee. (2009). Social Movement Campaigns: Mobilization and Outcomes in the Montreal Women's Movement Community. *Mobilization* 14:405–427.

Staggenborg, Suzanne, and Verta Taylor. (2005.) "Whatever Happened to the Women's Movement?" *Mobilization* 10 (1): 37–52.

Stombler, Mindy, & Irene Padavic. (1997). Sister acts: Resisting men's domination in black and white fraternity little sister programs. *Social Problems*, 44, 257–275.

Sulik, Gayle. (2010). *Pink Ribbon Blues: How Breast Cancer Culture Undermines Women's Health.* New York: Oxford University Press.

Swider, Sarah. (2006). Working Women of the World Unite? Labor Organizing and Transnational Gender Solidarity among Domestic Workers in Hong Kong. In Myra Marx Ferree and Aili Mari Tripp, eds. in *Global Feminism: Transnational Women's Activism, Organizing, and Human Rights.* (Pp. 110–140). New York: NYU Press.

Taft, Jessica. (2010). *Rebel Girls: Youth Activism and Social Change Across the Americas.* New York: New York University Press.

Taylor, Verta. (1989). Social movement continuity: The women's movement in abeyance. *American Sociological Review*, 54, 761–775.

———. (1995). "Watching for Vibes: Bringing Emotions into the Study of Feminist Organizations." Pp. 223–233 in *Feminist Organizations: Harvest of the New Women's Movement*, ed. Myra Marx Ferree and Patricia Yancey Martin. Philadelphia: Temple University Press.

———. (1996). *Rock-a-by Baby: Feminism, Self-help, and Postpartum Depression.* New York: Routledge.

———. (1999). Gender and social movements: Gender processes and women's self-help movements. *Gender & Society*, 13, 8–33.

———. 2010. "Culture, Identity, and Social Movements: Studying Protest as If People Really Matter." *Mobilization* (15) 2: 113–134.

Taylor, Verta and Leila J. Rupp. (1993). Women's culture and lesbian feminist activism: A reconsideration of cultural feminism. *Signs*, 19, 32–61.

Taylor, Verta, & Marieke Van Willigen. (1996). Women's self-help and the reconstruction of gender: The postpartum support and breast cancer movements. *Mobilization: An International Journal*, 2, 123–142.

Taylor, Verta, & Nancy Whittier. (1992). Collective identity in social movement communities: Lesbian feminist mobilization. In Aldon Morris & Carol Mueller, eds., *Frontiers of Social Movement Theory.* New Haven, CT: Yale University Press.

Taylor, Verta and Nella Van Dyke. (2004). [2007]. "'Get up, Stand up': Tactical Repertoires of Social Movements." Pp. 262–293 in *The Blackwell Companion to Social Movements.* Edited by David A. Snow, Sarah A. Soule, and Hanspeter Kriesi. Oxford: Blackwell.

Taylor, Verta, Katrina Kimport, Nella Van Dyke and Ellen Ann Andersen. (2009). Culture and Mobilization: Tactical Repertoires, Same-Sex Weddings, and the Impact on Same-Sex Activism. *American Sociological Review* 74.

Taylor, Verta and Mayer N. Zald, (2010.) "Conclusion: The Shape of Collective Action in the U.S. Health Sector." Pp. 300–317 in *Social Movements and the Transformation of American Health Care.* Jane Banaszak-Holl, Sandra Levitsky, and Mayer N. Zald, eds. New York: Oxford University Press.

Thayer, Millie. (2010). *Making Transnational Feminism: Rural Women, NGO Activists, and Northern Donors in Brazil* New York: Routledge.

Thorne, Barrie. (1994). *Gender Play: Girls and Boys in School.* New Brunswick, NJ: Rutgers University Press.

———. (1995). Symposium on West and Fenstermaker's "Doing Difference." *Gender & Society* 9, 498–499.

Tripp, Aili Mari. (2006). "The Evolution of Transnational Feminism: Consensus, Conflict, and New Dynamics." In Myra Marx Ferree and Aili Mari Tripp, eds. *Global Feminism: Transnational Women's Activism, Organizing, and Human Rights.* (Pp. 51–75). New York: NYU Press.

Vogel, Lisa. (1993). *Mothers on the Job: Maternity Policy in the U.S. Workplace.* New Brunswick, NJ: Rutgers University Press.

Walker, Rebecca. (1992). Becoming the third wave. *Ms.,* 2 (January/February), 39–41.

———. (1995.) *To Be Real: Telling the Truth and Changing the Face of Feminism.* New York: Anchor Books.

Whittier, Nancy E. (1995). *Feminist Generations: The Persistence of the Radical Women's Movement.* Philadelphia: Temple University Press.

———. (2009). *The Politics of Child Sexual Abuse: Emotion, Social Movements, and the State.* New York: Oxford University Press.

Williams, Christine L. (1995). *Still A Man's World: Men Who Do Women's Work.* Berkeley: University of California Press.

Zita, Jacquelyn N., ed. (1997.) "Third Wave Feminisms." Special issue, *Hypatia* 12 (3).

READING *50*   **Pamela Aronson**

Feminists or "Postfeminists"? Young Women's Attitudes Toward Feminism and Gender Relations

First published in 2003

A late 1990s cover of *Time* magazine with the caption "Is feminism dead?" featured photos of prominent feminist activists, including one of the flighty television lawyer character, Ally McBeal (Bellafante 1998). Such media pronouncements of the "death" of feminism rest on widespread presumptions that young women do not appreciate gains made by the women's movement, are not concerned about discrimination, and do not support feminism. These suppositions have rarely been tested.

How do young women view their own opportunities and obstacles, particularly when compared to those faced by women of their mothers' generation? How do they perceive and experience gender discrimination? How do they identify themselves with respect to feminism, and how can we make sense of their seemingly contradictory perspectives? Finally, what are the impacts of racial and class background and life experience on attitudes toward feminism? Although prior studies have considered aspects of these questions, my research examines them through interviews with a diverse sample. This diversity reveals the importance not only of race and class, but also life experience, in the development of attitudes toward feminism. Furthermore, by not imposing a set definition of feminism but letting it emerge from the interviewees themselves, my study reveals great ambiguity in the meanings of feminism today and suggests that we need to rethink some of the assumptions about young women's identities.

GROWING UP IN THE SHADOW OF THE WOMEN'S MOVEMENT[1]

Since the mid-1980s, 30 to 40 percent of women have called themselves feminists, and by 1990, nearly 80 percent favored efforts to "strengthen and change women's status in society" (Marx Ferree and Hess 1995, 88). Although the media often question why so few women call themselves feminists, Marx Ferree and Hess (1995) pointed out that the number of women who do so represents the same percentage of people who label themselves as Republicans or Democrats. Addressing the same concerns, Gurin (1985, 1987) distinguished between four components of gender consciousness: identification (recognizing women's shared interests), discontent (recognizing women's lack of power), assessment of legitimacy (seeing gender disparities as illegitimate), and collective orientation (believing in collective action). Although women historically have become more critical of men's claims to power, women's gender consciousness has been weaker than the group consciousness of African Americans, the working class, and the elderly. At the same time, women, especially employed women, are often conscious of women's structural disadvantage in the labor market (Gurin 1985). However, an average woman may have somewhat vague understandings of political labels such as "feminism," as activists and political elites are generally more consistent and coherent in their positions (Converse 1964; Unger 1989).

In the early 1980s, the media began to label women in their teens and twenties as the "postfeminist" generation[2] (Bellafante 1998; Bolotin 1982; Whittier 1995). Twenty years later, the term continues to be applied to young women, who are thought to benefit from the women's movement through expanded access to employment and education and new family arrangements but at the same time do not push for further political change. Postfeminism has been the subject of considerable debate, since its usage connotes the "death" of feminism and because the equality it assumes is largely a myth (Coppock, Haydon, and Richter 1995; Overholser 1986; Rosenfelt and Stacey 1987; Whittier 1995). The term has been used by researchers to reflect the current cycle and stage of the women's movement (Taylor 1989; Taylor and Rupp 1993; Whittier 1995). Indeed, Rossi (1982) has written of a cyclical generational pattern in the women's movement, with each feminist wave separated by roughly fifty years, or two generations. "Quiet periods" (Rossi 1982, 9) see diminished political action, but continued progress in private arenas, such as education and employment. Because movement stages greatly influence how women identify with the movement (Taylor 1989; Taylor and Rupp 1993; Whittier 1995), women's individual attitudes toward feminism are likely to vary.

The second-wave women's movement has simultaneously experienced great successes and backlash. Successes include the maintenance of movement organizations (Marx Ferree and Yancey Martin 1995; Whittier 1995), as well as a "broadly institutionalized and effective interest group," with an institutional base in academia, particularly women's studies programs (Brenner 1996, 24). Backlash is evident in a decline in grassroots mobilization and negative public discourse by antifeminist organizations and media figures (Faludi 1991; Marx Ferree and Hess 1995; Schneider 1988).

Scholars have found that young women tend to be depoliticized and individualistic and that few identify as feminists (Rupp 1988; Stacey 1987)—they typically focus on individual solutions (Budgeon and Currie 1995) and express feminist ideas without labeling them as such (Henderson-King and Stewart 1994; Morgan 1995; Percy and Kremer 1995; Renzetti 1987; Rupp 1988; Stacey 1987; Weis 1990). Many of these apolitical women assume that discrimination will not happen to them (Sigel 1996). The lack of grassroots mobilization results in no framework for understanding individual experiences in politicized terms (Aronson 2000; Taylor 1996) and limits "postfeminists" to viewing gender disparities as illegitimate, rather than in collective terms or in terms of women's shared interests (Gurin 1985, 1987). Their attitudes are also influenced by the media, which have supported the antifeminist backlash (Faludi 1991; Marx Ferree and Hess 1995) and have implied that "no further feminist action is needed" (Schneider 1988, 11).

This generally negative picture of contemporary feminist consciousness is occasionally countered by researchers who have been discovering a "third wave." They point to more than one micro cohort within the postfeminist generation, noting that women who came of age in the 1990s more frequently support feminist goals and are more politically active to achieve these goals (e.g., abortion rights activism) than women who came of age in the 1980s (Whittier 1995). From activists who seek to represent a diversity of young women's experiences (Walker 1995), to the Riot Grrrl movement in music (Rosenberg and Garofalo 1998; Wald 1998), third-wave feminism is said to explicitly embrace hybridity, contradiction, and multiple identities (particularly "connections between racial, sexual and gender identities," Heywood and Drake 1997, 7, 8, 15). However, this new emphasis is questioned by scholars arguing that African American and Chicana feminists have focused historically, and continue to focus, on organizing not only in terms of gender but also along racial lines (Hurtado 1998; Springer 2002). In addition, the third wave is sometimes perceived as nonactivist in nature (Heywood and Drake 1997).

Although not explicitly defining themselves as feminists, other women are said to have the "potential for feminist critique" (Weis 1990, 179). Stacey (1991, 262) argued that young women have "semiconsciously incorporated feminist principles into their gender and kinship expectations and practices." This approach includes "taking for granted" many recent gains: women's work opportunities, combining work with family, sexual autonomy and freedom, and male participation in domestic work and child rearing (Stacey 1991, 1987). This "simultaneous incorporation, revision and depoliticization" (Stacey 1987, 8) of feminism indicates that worldviews include more feminist principles while being less explicitly feminist.

The negative as well as the positive prognosis of these studies should be taken with a grain of salt. They tend to operate with uniform definitions of feminism, ignore generational differences, and/or study groups that are too homogeneous to provide conclusions about the full diversity of today's young women. My study seeks to correct each of these limitations and hopes to provide insights that are more nuanced, complex, and attentive to diversity. . . .

This [reading] explores young women's attitudes toward feminism in relation to differences in background and life experience. In contrast to prior research, I recognize the ambivalent and sometimes contradictory orientations of the women who have grown up in the shadow of the women's movement. While prior research has given some attention to the contexts within which feminist attitudes develop (Sigel 1996; Stacey 1987; Taylor 1996; Whittier 1995), many studies have not directly considered women's perceptions of some key goals of feminist organizing,

such as advancing women's opportunities, and the obstacles and discrimination that feminism addresses. To discern the context of young women's attitudes toward gender relations, I begin my analysis with an examination of perceptions of women's opportunities, obstacles, and discrimination. I continue the analysis by considering young women's attitudes toward feminism and the impact of race, class, and life experience on these attitudes. Taken together, this article reveals support for feminist goals and complexity in attitudes toward the term *feminism*.

METHOD[3]

This study is based on in-depth interviews with members of a panel study of young people, the Youth Development Study, an ongoing longitudinal study of adolescent development and the transition to adulthood (Jeylan Mortimer is the principal investigator). The larger survey sample ($N = 1,000$) was randomly chosen from a list of enrolled ninth-grade students in St. Paul, Minnesota. Respondents completed surveys annually, with the first year (ninth grade) in 1988. Of the original 1,000 panel members who took part in the first year of data collection, the Youth Development Study retained 77.5 percent through 1995, the last year of the survey before my interview study.

For my in-depth interviews, I followed Glaser and Strauss's (1967) suggestions for theoretical sampling and interviewed women with varying trajectories of life experience and background, as reported in surveys during the four years following high school (1991 to 1995). I focused on differences in education, parenthood, and careers and interviewed nearly equal proportions of women in each group. . . . A "school" group had attended a four-year college or university for at least eight months annually in three of the four years following high school. A "parent" group had become mothers by the eighth year of the study and could also be engaged in school and/or work. A "labor force" group did not have an extensive school trajectory, nor had they become mothers. Instead, they typically worked full-time or moved between postsecondary school and work after high school. . . .

. . . The women were aged twenty-three or twenty-four at the time of my interviews. Among them, 33 percent were women of color (11.9 percent African American, 9.5 percent Asian American, 9.5 percent biracial and multiracial, and 2.4 percent Latina). Their socioeconomic backgrounds included 31 percent from working-class families, 48 percent from the middle class, and 21 percent from upper-middle-class backgrounds.[4] At the time of the interviews, two-thirds of the women were working full-time (28), 3 were working part-time, 7 were in school full-time (and not working), and 4 were out of the labor force for other reasons (2 were caring for their young children, 1 was not working as a result of a severe disability, and 1 was in prison). Slightly more than one-third had completed a bachelor's degree.

Half of the interviewees were involved in committed relationships: 10 were married, 3 were engaged, 8 were in exclusive relationships, and 1 was divorced and involved in a new relationship. Although none of the women directly labeled themselves as lesbians, 2 suggested this possibility. . . . Although it would be interesting to examine whether young lesbian and bisexual women would report different perceptions of feminism than heterosexual young women, this issue cannot be adequately addressed with my sample.

One-third (14) of the interviewees had become mothers by the time of the interviews. Ten of these women were single parents, while 4 of them were married. However, nearly all had previously been single parents; only 1 woman was married prior to becoming a parent.

. . . In the analysis that follows, using pseudonyms for my respondents, I examine several key issues that emerged during the interviews. First, to provide a context for attitudes toward feminism, I consider two themes about women's treatment by society: perceptions of opportunities and obstacles, and experiences with gender discrimination. I then explicate the five approaches to feminist identification that came out of my analysis of the interviews.

PERCEPTIONS OF OPPORTUNITIES AND OBSTACLES

My interviews revealed a general optimism about women's expanded opportunities, coupled with a realization that older women have struggled to create these new opportunities. At the same time, most (35 out of 42) of the interviewees were quite aware that gender-based obstacles still remained. These perspectives were shared by women of all racial and class backgrounds and life experiences.

A majority (36) of the interviewees discussed women's current opportunities in terms of expanded educational and career choices, which have in turn led to women's independence from men and new family arrangements. For example, Hoa, a middle-class Vietnamese American woman who was in law school at the time of the interview, said that women used to think "'I will *marry* a doctor. I will *marry* a lawyer.' It was never: 'I will *become* one.'" Nora, a working-class Hispanic woman, saw this issue in generational terms:

> When my mom was growing up, *men* pretty much *ruled* it. . . . [Men] decided what would happen *when* and where you were going to go and where you're going to live. Nowadays men have an opinion, but that's all it is. . . . Women have their opinions and can go with what they want to do. . . . They can make their own decisions without men.

There was widespread awareness that changes resulted from the struggles of older women, who helped to create new opportunities. Although most of the interviewees attributed these changes to an aggregate of individuals who became "fed up" or "got sick and tired" of gender inequalities, a number credited the women's movement directly.

At the same time, 35 of the interviewees also observed that women continue to face many obstacles, including sexism, difficulty balancing conflicting work and family demands, greater responsibility than men for child rearing and domestic work, and violence against women. For example, Esther, a working-class white woman, said, "Although it's changing, I think that there's a lot of things that are still real male dominated." Nine of the interviewees mentioned that new opportunities have produced new strains, particularly balancing work and family. As Linda, a middle-class white woman working in a traditionally male field, put it, "Companies aren't supportive yet of working mothers."

This recognition of the need for further social change diverges from prior research on the postfeminist generation in two ways. While the micro cohort of women I interviewed here may be more aware of obstacles than prior postfeminist micro cohorts (Whittier 1995), my respondents were more diverse in background than prior studies and thus may have been more apt to perceive obstacles. At the same time that this recognition of inequalities and their illegitimacy suggests significant gender consciousness, my interviewees stopped short of a collective orientation focused on women's movement activism (Gurin 1985, 1987).

EXPERIENCES WITH GENDER DISCRIMINATION

Have these young women experienced discrimination? Although only 6 (14 percent) of the 42 interviewees felt they had experienced blatant instances of gender discrimination, nearly all had experienced what they considered to be minor instances of discrimination or were aware of its possibility in the future. Specifically, a third (14) were concerned about workplace inequality and discrimination. Nearly a quarter (10) approached discrimination somewhat paradoxically: They did not expect that gender discrimination would have an impact on their lives, despite the subtle instances of discrimination that they had experienced. The final quarter (12 out of 42) of interviewees focused on individual solutions to discrimination, such as confronting their perpetrator. In all, these findings reveal a substantial awareness of gender discrimination.

Of the six women who recounted instances of blatant gender discrimination, the main problem was workplace discrimination and sexual harassment. For example, Shonda, a working-class African American woman, experienced both gender and racial discrimination on the job. Although she was aware that she could have filed a lawsuit, her more immediate concern of financially supporting her two children took precedence.

One-third of the women were concerned about future discrimination, including pay equity, hitting a "glass ceiling," and career advancement. Reflecting the career trajectories that these women anticipated, most of those with this approach were middle-class white women with college educations. For example, Linda, a middle-class white woman who worked in the field of accounting, said, "I can see being a woman coming in the way. I work for a company that does still have a little bit of the old boy's club at the upper management."

Nearly a quarter of the interviewees did not originally label their own experiences "discrimination" but realized through telling their stories that gender inequalities were, in fact, part of their life experience. For example, when I asked Sherri, an upper-middle-class white woman who worked in a hospital, whether she had experienced discrimination, she said, "I never thought about it. Probably because in my field it's mostly women." She went on to say the following:

The highest paid people around here are *men*. I *do* think that's a big obstacle for women—that it's a male, white, male-dominated world, and they're the ones who make the rules. . . . It's not something that I worry about, but I think that's a big obstacle for women.

Similarly, Hillary, a working-class Korean American woman, never felt less "capable" as a result of being a woman, yet she described women's second shift with regard to household responsibilities and her anger at feeling afraid to walk alone at night. Illustrating both an awareness, and the minimizing, of gender discrimination, she said, "Other than the constraints that I felt being a woman, I really don't think that I've . . . missed out on opportunities . . . because I'm a woman, luckily." This paradoxical approach indicates that some women are reluctant to label their experiences with inequality as "discrimination" because they define discrimination narrowly in terms of blatant workplace harassment.

The remaining quarter of the women in this study focused on individual solutions to the problem of discrimination, such as confronting the perpetrator. For example, Felicia, a middle-class white woman, said she wouldn't "tolerate" discrimination: "I feel . . . like I can take care of myself. Some man might want to put me back in my place, but I think I'm a tough little bitch . . . ! Take some karate classes!" Here, individual resistance to discrimination resulted in feelings of personal strength, yet it is important to note that this approach is based on an assumption that individuals must be strong enough to defend themselves against discriminatory actions. Other women focused on the impact of their own choices, particularly choosing female-dominated careers. For example, Kelly, a middle-class white woman who worked in female-dominated retail, said that discrimination "*definitely* hasn't affected me. . . . I haven't been in a situation where it's been more of a man's field. . . . I've never, *ever* felt discriminated [against]."[5]

In sum, although only a small proportion of the interviewees felt that they had experienced blatant gender discrimination, most of the women had known it in minor ways and expressed some concern about it in the future. These findings run contrary to past studies, which imply that young women are unrealistic about the forces that have the potential to hold them back (Coppock, Haydon, and Richter 1995; Sigel 1996; Stacey 1987).[6] At the same time, the term *discrimination* was itself often defined in a narrow way, to include only blatant instances of workplace inequality. This low level of awareness may result from the successes of the women's movement, which have made discrimination less pronounced than in the past. It may also reflect arguments made by other scholars: Women partially accept discrimination as a given because they try to protect themselves from its negative effects (Sigel 1996), or they may feel helpless when thinking of themselves as victims (Gurin 1987). The extent of gender consciousness observed here does not include a collective orientation (Gurin 1985, 1987) since the emphasis was on individual responsibility rather than a broader framework of inequality. It may be that such a political vision, based on social movement involvement, is not available to these women.

ATTITUDES TOWARD FEMINISM

When asked about their attitudes toward feminism, nearly half of these women's responses could be categorized on the continuums developed in previous studies (e.g., Kamen 1991; Taylor 1996) including those who identified as feminists, those who called themselves feminists but qualified their support, and those who said they were not feminists but supported a range of feminist issues. However, suggesting ambiguity in the term *feminism* and its negative connotations, more than half of these women did not want to explicitly define themselves in relation to feminism at all. Most of these interviewees were, in the words of one woman, "fence-sitters": They embraced a number of feminist principles yet rejected others and failed to classify themselves as either feminists or nonfeminists. In addition, nearly a quarter had never thought about feminism as a concept and were unable to articulate an opinion altogether. Despite this ambiguity, nearly all of the interviewees were supportive of feminist issues.

Racial and Class Background and Life Experience

Attitudes toward feminism were differentiated by racial and class background and life experience. . . . In the interviews, nearly a quarter of the women (10 out of 42) identified themselves as feminists. Among this group, 6 defined themselves as feminists without qualifying what they meant by the term *feminist*, while 4 qualified their support by outlining the specific aspects of feminism with which they agreed and disagreed. Those who did not qualify their support were nearly

all white or middle class; all were college educated and came to feminism as a result of their experiences with women's studies courses. The women who qualified their feminist identities were women of color or white working-class women who had nearly all attended college but had no experience with women's studies courses.

As young women are most commonly characterized in other research, eight of the interviewees (19 percent) defined themselves as not being feminists but agreed with many of the principles of feminist ideology. Nearly all of these interviewees were from quite privileged backgrounds—close to 90 percent were white and middle to upper-middle class. However, unlike the nearly all-white and middle-class group who called themselves feminists, only two of these women had attended college and neither had taken women's studies courses.

One-third of the interview sample (13 out of 42 interviewees) were what one woman called "fence-sitters" since they would not position themselves in relation to feminism as an identity. These women were evenly divided in their life experiences and proportionally divided along racial lines, although a greater proportion were from working-class backgrounds.

One-quarter of the interviewees (11 out of 42) were uncertain about their attitudes toward feminism yet endorsed an ideology of equality. Among these women who never thought about feminism, the majority (7 out of 11) were young parents—typically single parents—while the others were focused on the full-time labor force; none had completed a four-year college degree. In addition, a disproportionate number of these interviewees were women of color. A number of these women experienced great stress in daily living, leaving little time for reflection about such issues. This suggests that not only racial and class background but also life paths and life experience in early adulthood may be linked to attitudes toward feminism. I will now consider each of these approaches in turn.

"I'm a Feminist"

Among those who identified as feminists without qualifying their support, feminism was viewed primarily as an ideology of equality. The women in this group were supportive of equal opportunity, abortion rights, equality in childhood socialization, and "social justice" and were concerned about issues such as sexual assault. These interviewees largely came to see themselves as feminists as a result of taking women's studies courses. Tina, a working-class white woman, said that a woman's studies course "started the whole movement for *me*. . . . If I hadn't taken that class . . . I could be married with 6 children right now!" Involvement in women's studies courses reveals that young feminists are not only highly educated but also exposed to feminist ideologies through an institutional location that supports and legitimates feminist perspectives.

"I'm a Feminist, but . . ."

Those who defined themselves as feminists but qualified their support came to their views not through women's studies courses but through assumptions of equality inherent in the attitudes of their families when they were growing up. Although they called themselves feminists, they also distanced themselves from certain negative associations of feminism. For example, Esther, a working-class white woman, said, "Feminism has gotten a bad rap . . . that it's sort of this *angry, radical* [view-point]. . . . I consider myself a feminist, definitely. I consider myself a *strong* feminist, but I'm not someone who is always needing to assert it." Although she endorsed an ideology of equality and supported diversity in men's and women's work and family arrangements, Esther distanced herself from two negative associations with feminism: those who "always assert" their viewpoints and those who "want to alienate men."

These women grew up with an assumption of equality in their families, yet this may itself explain why they qualify their feminist identities. As Esther put it,

> Feminism isn't something that I've had to *discover* on my own. . . . People who *just* discover . . . *activism* or *feminism* . . . are . . . more vocal about it and . . . *champion* it because it's new and different. And I feel like it's just a *given* that everyone should be treated equally. It's just a *given* that . . . because I'm a woman, that doesn't stop me from doing whatever I want to do.

"I'm Not a Feminist, but . . ."

Nineteen percent of the interviewees distanced themselves from feminism while endorsing many of the principles of feminist ideology. One example of this perspective comes from Betsy, a middle-class white woman, who said, "I'm *not* a feminist, I would say.

Probably a lot of feminists wouldn't like me. But, well, I mean I guess it depends on what feminism. . . . I think everybody should be treated equally at the base." These women gave several reasons for distancing themselves from the identity of "feminist." A number of interviewees felt that feminism goes "too far." Whitney, a middle-class Korean American woman, said that "a lot of feminism goes overboard," yet she suspected that she had this view because she herself had never faced discrimination: "Maybe people who are a little bit older or have been discriminated against [call themselves feminists] and I haven't really experienced that. So, I mean if I had, maybe I would become a feminist, but I either don't *see* it [or] haven't *been*" discriminated against. Here, feminism is seen as a place where grievances against discrimination can be voiced, rather than a perspective that sees power inequalities influencing every domain of gender relations.

Other interviewees distanced themselves from activism and political engagement. Dawn, an upper-middle-class white woman, appreciated the benefits of the women's movement, particularly educational and occupational opportunities, and was supportive of equality more generally. At the same time, she said, "I *don't* believe that *I* would consider *myself* a feminist." Implying that it was activism from which she distanced herself, she said, "I don't go out every day and say 'women's rights and more opportunities for women. . . . I don't think about it on a day-to-day basis." Similarly, Linda, a middle-class white woman, said of feminism: "Folks should just live their lives and not get so caught up in everything." Clearly, these women's gender consciousness does not include a collective orientation (Gurin 1985, 1987).

These women also distanced themselves from feminism as a result of negative perceptions of feminists, particularly lesbianism and separatism from men. For example, although Alice, a middle-class white woman, said, "I just think that everybody is *equal*," she did not want to distance herself from men: "I don't go around bashing men. . . . I *like* men." Linda thought that being a feminist meant that she could not live the type of life she wanted to lead:

> I have a couple of feminist friends that have *very* different views than I do. . . . My boyfriend's sister is a feminist, and she will *never* have children. She will probably *never* get married. And that's fine, but that's not what I want to do. That's not the life that I want to lead. I want to raise a family.

This perspective reflects the antifeminist movement and the media's construction of feminists as lesbians and militants (Faludi 1991; Marx Ferree and Hess 1995). As was also the case in previous eras (e.g., Marshall 1997), the media have perpetuated "the social climate of antifeminism and thwart[ed] the possibility of mobilizing discontented women" (Rupp and Taylor 1987).

"I'm a Fence-Sitter"

The fence-sitting approach (taken by one-third of the women) reveals a paradox: support for feminist issues, as well as the ambiguous connotations of "feminism" today. Rather than identifying themselves in relation to feminist identity, these women focused on evaluating the ideologies and stereotypes associated with feminism. This group is distinct from the others because they would not classify themselves as either feminists or nonfeminists. In embracing ambiguity, they truly remained "on the fence." In some respects, they evaded the interview questions and chose instead to support and critique aspects of the term *feminism*.

One woman who took this approach was Ann, who is working class and white. When I asked her thoughts about feminism, she said, "I'd be supportive," yet she stopped short of calling herself a feminist. She went on to call herself a fence-sitter and said, "I would still be reserved about some things." When asked to elaborate, she discussed only her support of feminist issues: eradicating the "perpetuation" of stereotypes about women, violence against women, governmental cuts in welfare, and sexual harassment and favoring comparable worth and gay rights. Likewise, Susan, a middle-class white woman, said that "a lot of feminism is lesbianism" and she did not want to "go hate men." She also recognized this stereotype as a "big generalization" about feminists. In fact, she had enjoyed taking women's studies courses in college: "As far as identifying similar experiences and . . . feeling like you're not alone, that's what I *like* about feminism."

Other studies have also found that some women reject feminism because they are worried about creating "male antagonism" (Sigel 1996, 114). These views may reflect a general reluctance to express anger over discrimination because some women accept unfairness, see discrimination as realistic, or want to protect themselves from recognizing inequality (Sigel 1996). Stereotypes against feminists have been powerfully advanced by the antifeminist movement and the media, which may have influenced these women's views.

"I Never Thought About Feminism"

The remaining quarter (11 out of 42) of the interviewees expressed a great deal of uncertainty about their attitudes toward feminism, had no opinion on the topic, or had substantial difficulty defining the term itself. Of these women, most felt that they were unable to comment because they did not know enough about feminism or had never thought about it in enough depth to express an opinion. One interviewee who was unable to articulate an opinion was Kelly, a middle-class white woman. Although she felt that "women should have the same rights as a man does," she said that she had "never been a real *strong* activist." Kelly went on to explain her view as follows: "I don't really have a lot of feelings on that because I kind of take it as it is. . . . I don't really think about that kind of stuff." Kim, a middle-class white woman, said, "I don't even really know what [feminism] *is*."

Why were these women unable or unwilling to articulate an opinion of feminism? Some of the interviewees were simply confused over the definition of feminism. For others, feminism was implicitly defined as an activist approach that addressed discrimination and thus did not have personal relevance. For example, when I asked Caroline, an upper-middle-class white woman, about her view of feminism, she said that "nothing has *happened* to me that I would have to be that way." Here, being "that way" connotes that feminist perspectives go along with discrimination: without it, there was no need to think about feminism. Other women also saw feminism as irrelevant to their everyday lives. Jill, a middle-class, white, single parent of two children, was explicit that she had more pressing daily issues to worry about than feminism:

> I don't care. No big thing. I've never been treated unfairly by a man. I don't think I have. . . . I blow off things, because I'm an easy come, easy go [person]. I'm already stressed out with kids and a job. . . . I don't need to be stressed out about things like that. So [in terms of] *feminism*, I don't *care*. Who *cares*?

To Jill, feminism is irrelevant, perhaps even frivolous, when compared with the struggles of combining work and single motherhood. Feminism is primarily a way to redress workplace discrimination, in contrast to confronting issues that are central to basic survival as a woman. Ironically, both Caroline and Jill (in another part of the interview) also recounted their own experiences with domestic violence, suggesting that some of the women who would benefit the most from a feminist political perspective or agenda see it as the least relevant to their own lives.

At the same time, these women were supportive of equality between men and women. For example, Yolanda, a working-class biracial (African American and white) single parent said,

> I can change a tire. I can change oil . . . and I don't have a problem with it. And I can move my *own* furniture, *pregnant* or *not,* you know?! . . . When a guy tells me I can't do something, I'll tell him to *prove* it. . . . I'll tell a guy off real quick if he tells *me* that [I can't do something] because of my gender.

As I explore elsewhere (Aronson 1999, 2001), the young women in this study (even the engaged and married women) emphasized the importance of their own independence from men in many areas of their lives—career, finances, childbearing and child rearing, and self-development. In fact, marital status does not seem to make any difference in attitudes toward feminism, as women with different relationships to men were evenly dispersed among the groups examined here.

CONCLUSIONS

My findings about the widespread awareness of the extent of gender inequality run contrary to prior studies of the postfeminist generation (Renzetti 1987; Rupp 1988; Sigel 1996; Stacey 1987, 1991). And while many of the interviewees fit on a continuum of feminist identification previously defined by other researchers (Kamen 1991; Sigel 1996; Taylor 1989), more than half of the young women in this study approached feminism even more ambiguously than previously reported, especially the fence-sitters who embrace some aspects of feminism while rejecting others and avoid defining themselves in relation to the identity of feminist.

My findings also extend prior research by illustrating that attitudes toward feminism are shaped by racial and class background, and also by life experience. No prior studies have examined the role of diverse types of life experience in developing particular attitudes

toward feminism. I have shown that the feminist identification without qualification and the "I'm not a feminist, but . . ." approach are associated with more privileged racial and class backgrounds. The feminists were more likely to be college educated, and most had taken women's studies courses. Those who qualified their feminist identities and those who had never thought about feminism were disproportionately from less privileged racial and class backgrounds, but their life experience differentiates them from the other groups as well. The "qualified" feminists were college-educated, working-class women and/or women of color who came to feminism as a result of assumptions of equality when growing up. Among the women who had never thought about feminism, two-thirds had become parents early in life, and none had pursued a college degree.

My findings also indicate that young women's development of a feminist perspective and identity is tied closely with institutions that support and nurture such a perspective—particularly women's studies programs. This institutionalization of feminism has occurred at the same time as antifeminist organizations and media figures have advanced negative stereotypes that have become incorporated in some young women's conceptions of feminism. In addition, although the women of color that I interviewed were supportive of equality, most distanced themselves from the identity of feminist, suggesting that the institutional supports for feminism may be more appealing or available to white women.

This study also suggests that having the space to think about political issues such as feminism may be a luxury that some young women, especially single mothers, cannot afford. For these women, feminism was seen as lacking personal relevance and viewed primarily as a place to redress workplace discrimination. Many of these women had never thought about their positions on feminism or saw it as frivolous when compared with the struggles of supporting and raising their children. Obviously, this is a broader problem than simply creating better public relations within feminist organizations, as it involves developing new initiatives and expanding institutional power. A new wave of political organizing might in turn lead to new personal understandings of feminism at later points in the life course (Aronson 2000).

Most important, whether or not young women call themselves feminists, they support feminist goals. In fact, the young women I interviewed were more supportive of feminism than had been found in past research, and none expressed antifeminist sentiments. The fence-sitting stance, while not as politicized as in previous generations, is not entirely individualized and apolitical either. Although most researchers and the media have painted a pessimistic view of young women's ambivalence, I believe that my results offer some promise for feminism. Many of these young women may be passive supporters rather than agents of change, but they are supporters nonetheless. Their endorsement may represent the seeds of change, which, under the right historical conditions, and in interaction with the growth of grassroots feminist organizing, could blossom into the next wave of the women's movement.

ACKNOWLEDGMENTS

This research was supported by a National Research Service Award from the National Institute of Mental Health (Training Program in Identity, Self, Role, and Mental Health—PHST 32 MH 14588), the National Institute of Mental Health (MH 42843, Jeylan T. Mortimer, principal investigator), the Personal Narratives Award from the Center for Advanced Feminist Studies, University of Minnesota, and a Graduate School Block Grant Stipend Award from the Department of Sociology, University of Minnesota. The author would like to thank a number of people who provided comments and suggestions on earlier versions of this article: Ronald Aronson, Christine Bose, Donna Eder, Debbie Engelen-Eigles, Amy Kaler, Barbara Laslett, Jane McLeod, Jeylan T. Mortimer, Irene Padavic, Katie See, Beth Schneider, and Kim Simmons, as well as the social psychology seminar members at Indiana University and several anonymous reviewers.

NOTES

1. I would like to thank Karen Lutfey for the origination of this phrase.
2. This term had also been used after the first-wave women's movement (Taylor 1996).
3. For details about methodology, see the original article from which this selection is excerpted.
4. Social class background was based on parents' income and education as reported in the parent surveys in the first year of the study (1988). "Working class" includes those whose parents had less than a bachelor's degree and earned less than $30,000 per year in 1988. "Middle class" includes four subgroups: parents who had high educational attainment (at least a bachelor's degree) and low income (less than $30,000 per year in 1988), low educational attainment (less than a bachelor's degree) but high income (at least $50,000 per year in 1988), high education (at least a bachelor's degree) and middle income (between $30,000 and $50,000 per year in 1988), and low education (less than a bachelor's degree) and middle income. "Upper-middle class" includes those parents who had high educational attainment (at least a bachelor's degree) and earned a middle to high income (more than $50,000 per year in 1988).
5. This lack of salience of gender discrimination within female-dominated occupations is supported by Slevin and Wingrove's (1998) findings that African American women do not find race to be extremely salient when working in African American organizations.
6. It is possible that the differences between my study and prior findings result from historical shifts—that this micro cohort of young women is more aware of inequalities than prior micro cohorts of the postfeminist generation (Whittier 1995).

REFERENCES

Aronson, Pamela. 1999. The balancing act: Young women's expectations and experiences of work and family. In *Research in the sociology of work,* vol. 7, edited by Toby Parcel. Stamford, CT: JAI.

——. 2000. The development and transformation of feminist identities under changing historical conditions. In *Advances in life course research: Identity across the life course in cross-cultural perspective,* vol. 5, edited by Timothy J. Owens. Stamford, CT: JAI.

——. 2001. The markers and meanings of growing up: Contemporary young women's transition to adulthood. Paper presented at the annual meeting of the American Sociological Association, Anaheim, CA.

Bellafante, Ginia. 1998. Is feminism dead? *Time Magazine,* 29 June, 25.

Bolotin, Susan. 1982. Views from the post-feminist generation. *New York Times Magazine,* 17 October, 29–31, 103–16.

Brenner, Johanna. 1996. The best of times, the worst of times: Feminism in the United States. In *Mapping the women's movement: Feminist politics and social transformation in the North,* edited by Monica Threlfall. London: Verso.

Budgeon, Shelley, and Dawn Currie. 1995. From feminism to postfeminism: Women's liberation in fashion magazines. *Women's Studies International Forum* 18 (2): 173–86.

Converse, Philip E. 1964. The nature of belief systems in mass publics. In *Ideology and Discontent,* edited by David E. Apter. London: Free Press of Glencoe.

Coppock, Vicki, Deena Haydon, and Ingrid Richter. 1995. *The illusions of "post-feminism": New women, old myths.* London: Taylor and Francis.

Faludi, Susan. 1991. *Backlash: The undeclared war against American women.* New York: Crown.

Glaser, Barney, and Anselm Strauss. 1967. *The discovery of grounded theory.* Chicago: Aldine.

Gurin, Patricia. 1985. Women's gender consciousness. *Public Opinion Quarterly* 49 (2): 143–63.

———. 1987. The political implications of women's statuses. In *Spouse, parent, worker: On gender and multiple roles,* edited by Faye J. Crosby. New Haven, CT: Yale University Press.

Henderson-King, Donna, and Abigail Stewart. 1994. Women or feminists? Assessing women's group consciousness. *Sex Roles* 31 (9–10): 505–16.

Heywood, Leslie, and Jennifer Drake. 1997. Introduction. *Third wave agenda: Being feminist, doing feminism,* edited by Leslie Heywood and Jennifer Drake. Minneapolis: University of Minnesota Press.

Hurtado, Aida. 1998. Sitios y lenguas: Chicanas theorize feminisms. *Hypatia* 13 (2): 134–61.

Kamen, Paula. 1991. *Feminist fatale: Voices from the "twenty-something" generation explore the future of the "women's movement."* New York: Donald I. Fine.

Marshall, Susan. 1997. *Splintered sisterhood: Gender and class in the campaign against woman suffrage.* Madison: University of Wisconsin Press.

Marx Ferree, Myra, and Beth B. Hess. 1995. *Controversy and coalition: The new feminist movement across four decades of change.* 3d ed. New York: Routledge.

Marx Ferree, Myra, and Patricia Yancey Martin. 1995. *Feminist organizations: Harvest of the new women's movement.* Philadelphia: Temple University Press.

Morgan, Debi. 1995. Invisible women: Young women and feminism. In *Feminist activism in the 1990s,* edited by Gabriele Griffin. London: Taylor and Francis.

Overholser, Geneva. 1986. What "post-feminism" really means. *New York Times,* 19 September, 30.

Percy, Carol, and John Kremer. 1995. Feminist identifications in a troubled society. *Feminism and Psychology* 5 (2): 201–22.

Renzetti, Claire. 1987. New wave or second stage? Attitudes of college women toward feminism. *Sex Roles* 16 (5/6): 265–77.

Rosenberg, Jessica, and Gitana Garofalo. 1998. Riot grrrl: Revolutions from within. *Signs: Journal of Women in Culture and Society* 23 (3): 809–41.

Rosenfelt, Deborah, and Judith Stacey. 1987. Second thoughts on the second wave. *Feminist Studies* 13 (2): 341–61.

Rossi, Alice. 1982. *Feminists in politics.* New York: Academic.

Rupp, Lelia, and Verta Taylor. 1987. *Survival in the doldrums: The American women's rights movement, 1945 to the 1960s.* New York: Oxford University Press.

Rupp, Rayna. 1988. Is the legacy of second-wave feminism postfeminism? *Socialist Review* (January–March): 52–57.

Schneider, Beth. 1988. Political generations and the contemporary women's movement. *Sociological Inquiry* 58: 4–21.

Sigel, Roberta. 1996. *Ambition and accommodation: How women view gender relations.* Chicago: University of Chicago Press.

Slevin, Kathleen F., and C. Ray Wingrove. 1998. *From stumbling blocks to stepping stones: The life experiences of fifty professional African American women.* New York: New York University Press.

Springer, Kimberly. 2002. Third wave Black feminism? *Signs: Journal of Women in Culture and Society* 27 (4): 1059–82.

Stacey, Judith. 1987. Sexism by a subtler name? Postindustrial conditions and postfeminist consciousness in the Silicon Valley. *Socialist Review* 17 (6): 7–28.

———. 1991. *Brave new families: Stories of domestic upheaval in late twentieth century America.* New York Basic Books.

Taylor, Verta. 1996. *Rock-a-by baby: Feminism, self-help, and postpartum depression.* New York: Routledge.

———. 1989. Social movement continuity: The women's movement in abeyance. *American Sociological Review* 54:761–75.

Taylor, Verta, and Lelia Rupp. 1993. Women's culture and lesbian feminist activism: A reconsideration of cultural feminism. *Signs: Journal of Women in Culture and Society* 19 (1): 32–61.

Unger, Rhoda. 1989. Explorations in feminist ideology: Surprising consistencies and unexamined conflicts. In *Representations: Social constructions of gender,* edited by Rhoda Unger. Amityville, NY: Baywood.

Wald, Gayle. 1998. Just a girl? Rock music, feminism, and the cultural construction of female youth. *Signs: Journal of Women in Culture and Society* 23 (3): 585–610.

Walker, Rebecca. 1995. *To be real: Telling the truth and changing the face of feminism.* New York: Anchor.

Weis, Lois. 1990. *Working class without work: High school students in a de-industrializing economy.* New York: Routledge.

Whittier, Nancy. 1995. *Feminist generations: The persistence of the radical women's movement.* Philadelphia: Temple University Press.

Young Women, Late Modern Politics, and the Participatory Possibilities of Online Cultures

First published in 2008

INTRODUCTION

This article examines some of the ways young women use new technologies in order to open up debates about young people and political participation. Young women are under-represented in many conventional forms of political practice and often use new technologies in under-valued ways. It is widely acknowledged that they feel more alienated from, and less entitled to participate in, formal political activities than young men, but are more likely to be engaged in informal, localized politics or social-conscience-style activism (Vromen 2006, Roker 2008). Similarly, some research suggests that young women have less access to new technologies and experience lower usage of the Internet (Livingstone et al. 2005), and that their enjoyment and confidence in using technologies diminishes as they reach post-primary age (Haas et al. 2002, Christensen et al. 2005). This picture is complicated by other findings that young women are among the fastest growing group of Internet users (Mazzarella 2005, p. 2), but there is a general consensus that young women and young men use new technologies differently. While it is critical to enquire *which* young women and *which* young men, the fact remains that youth participation in both politics and technology continues to be structured by gender, alongside other dimensions of social experience, such that even when equivalence of participation can be achieved, different value is attached to modes of participation. From the point of view of those seeking to increase young women's participation in technology-enabled political practice, the objective often becomes to attempt to recruit young women to conventional (masculinist) practice, and/or highlight those who are already involved. In doing so,

however, we can fail to see the political possibilities in young women's current engagements with new technologies. Thus, the purpose of this article is to consider the ways that many young women currently use technology, and then to reflect on what might be political about these uses, rather than to designate political uses of technology and look for young women within these. In particular (although not exclusively), I focus on young women's use of the Internet.

New technologies are often perceived as an important way to get young people to connect with politics, but the kinds of politics and political activities that are typically imagined in this process can be fairly narrowly defined. For example, technologies such as mobile phones and the Internet have been seen as especially important resources in facilitating young people's involvement in conventional politics, as in assisting them to retrieve information about formal political or civic matters, to learn about and engage with election campaigns and politicians, and to develop political knowledge and foster activism (see Kann et al. 2007). At the same time, it is acknowledged that young people are disenchanted with formal politics and that until traditional political institutions and processes respond to their needs and interests, even imaginative efforts to enhance young people's engagement with the present structures are likely to have limited effect (Harris et al. 2008). This perspective focuses on the destabilising effects of globalisation, deindustrialisation and individualisation that have made traditional forms of participation and citizenship less viable for young people, as the state loses its authority and the public sphere contracts. Accordingly, there is also a certain amount of academic and practitioner interest in other kinds of technology-enabled activity that could be described as socially and politically aware, but not conventionally political. One important example of this is what can be described as 'online DIY [Do It Yourself] cultures,' which refers to young people's blogs, e-zines and websites that operate as spaces for expression and dialogue about political and social issues in light of youth marginalisation from and disenchantment with formal politics. . . . Finally, those who research youth also attend to their participation in social and personal uses of new technologies. It is widely acknowledged that this is a much more common way for young people, and young women in particular, to engage with new technologies than either of the above. There is a considerable amount written about why young people construct personal home pages, how they use mobile phones, and what risks face them in their social networking online. Typically, however, these activities are not considered in the context of political participation because they are seen as personal, if not exactly private.

In this article I want to explore these last two kinds of activities—online DIY culture and social/personal uses of new technologies—from a gendered perspective. In doing so, I hope to open up some questions about what counts as politics, and what is possible as politics for young people, and young women in particular, at the present moment. I argue that it is important to look at less conventional, technology-enabled political and social activity in order to understand how these are operating as emergent modes of participation in a new political environment. I suggest that we need to take seriously young women's styles of technology-enabled social and political engagement, as they represent new directions in activism, the construction of new participatory communities, and the development of new kinds of public selves. The enthusiastic take-up of these practices by young women in particular tells us important things about the limits of the kinds of conventional citizen subject positions offered to young women at this time. In particular, it suggests that some young women are seeking alternative modes and spaces to engage in activism, especially in relation to feminist and anti-racist agendas, in light of the contraction of the conventional public sphere and the encroachment of corporate and government interests on to youth political cultures. It also indicates that some young women are keen to create unregulated, albeit *public* spaces for peer communities where they can express their personal interests and concerns away from adult intervention. At the same time, it reveals

the challenges for young women of constructing public selves at a time when young female citizenship is operationalised through consumption and display rather than political agency. As argued elsewhere (Harris 2004a), young women have been targeted as ideal neoliberal citizens, primarily as individual consumers with no collective orientation, and I suggest here that their use of new technologies indicates their active negotiation of this interpellation. . . .

ONLINE DIY CULTURES

. . . Online DIY cultures constitute technology-enabled practices that are socially and politically aware, but not conventionally political. These include websites that are created by young women and express political points of view on topics of relevance to young women. These often set out key ideas about girl-centred feminism and anti-racism, and direct readers to off-line activities that may be activist or cultural. These sites are often, although not always, inspired by the early 1990s riotgrrrl or grrrlpower movement, which saw punk and feminism come together in a new young women-oriented scene focused on music, left-wing politics, art and writing (see Harris 2004a). Many bear the hallmarks of the original medium of riotgrrrl culture: zines (a comprehensive inventory of e-zines and blogs and other grrrl media can be found at Elke Zobl's site, http://www.grrrlzines.net/). They include websites that combine personal points of view, political analysis, strategies for activism, artwork, links to other relevant sites and information about 'real-life' activities that relate to the focus of the site. These are sometimes collectively constructed and represent a loose affiliation of young women or can be individually authored, in which case they are usually known as blogs; that is, websites that are individually written and narrative based. (Here I am using the term 'blog' in a fairly specific sense, to refer to self-published, regularly updated, online narratives that include socially and politically engaged content. I discuss personal journals later.)

While it is difficult to measure, mainly due to definitional challenges, some researchers have claimed that young women are the largest group of creators and readers of blogs (Orlowski 2003, Bortree 2006), while others contend that both women and youth are represented at least as frequently as adult men, but that young women outnumber young men (Herring et al. 2004). However, unlike blogs authored by male political pundits, women's blogs are taken less seriously, are valued less within blogging culture and in the mainstream, and are less likely to be ranked highly or linked to (Ratliff 2004, Gregg 2006). Similarly, girl-centred websites created by and for young women have been a significant subgenre of personal websites since the early 1990s, but have not generally received attention as a politics outside feminism. I would suggest, however, that both girl-centred websites and blogs are important practices of 'counter-public' construction in that they are forums for debate and exchange of politically and socially engaged ideas by those who are marginalised within mainstream political debate. However, what is sometimes frustrating for analysts is that these forums are not necessarily outcome-oriented, or rather their end function is often simply to exist as a space for expression and debate. They tend to operate for information sharing, dialogue, consciousness-raising and community-building, but can also be playful and leisure-oriented and mix up personal and political material. They often focus on having a voice and building a place for speaking rather than agitating for change through appeals to political institutions, the state and its actors (see Melucci 1996). In this regard, they can be seen as just one manifestation of a wholesale shift in activism from the traditional social movements of the 1960s to a postmodern style of glocalised, decentralised and individualised politics. There is of course overlap, and some blogs, e-zines and websites connect with more conventional political campaigns, activism or advocacy. However, they often advocate individual strategies, political practices based on youth cultural experiences and culture-industry-oriented activism. These include practices such as culture jamming (altering an advertising slogan or image to undermine its message), examples of which can be found on the website of the Jammin' Ladies at http://jamming.wordpress.com/, or radical cheerleading (groups gathering in public with pom-poms calling out political 'cheers'), exemplified on the website of the Dutch grrrl collective, Bunnies on Strike at http://bunniesonstrike.cjb.net/.

Young women who are involved in these kinds of activities often articulate a need to act as cultural producers at a time when they feel overwhelmingly interpellated as consumers (see Stasko 2008). Many talk about the need for a new kind of feminist practice that takes into account the encroachment of the culture industry into every aspect of their lives, including politics (Harris 2004b). Using the Internet as a space that

exists between the public and the private enables them to negotiate a desire to organise and communicate with others with a need to avoid surveillance and appropriation of their cultures and politics. It also operates as a safer and more welcoming space for young women than traditional political forums.

However, it must be acknowledged that participation in online DIY culture, especially the creation of politically and socially engaged websites, occurs among only a minority of young women. Most do not have the resources, time or subcultural capital to engage with these kinds of activities. Moreover, the feminism that is drawn upon in the specifically 'grrrl' online cultures is of a specific kind that has its roots in what is often seen to be an elite, white, US-based scene. This is in spite of its international take-up. However, what is also worthy of note is the popularity with young women of youth-led Internet sites that do not necessarily focus on feminist or women's issues. For example, two important Australian-based websites run for and by young people are Reach Out! and Vibewire, which focus on social services and media, respectively, and are overwhelmingly used by young women (Vromen 2007). Vromen's (2008) research shows that sites such as Vibewire are valued because they offer a place in the media, which is perceived as *the* site of power in an information society, for young voices to be heard and for young people to be engaged. She has also found that participants appreciate the more open kinds of youth communities that are created through these sites, and that, in contrast to the usual argument, these are perceived to actually bring together diverse groups of youth who hold different opinions on issues rather than simply cater to the like-minded.

However, while online DIY cultures are an important, albeit minor practice in young women's technologically enabled political activities, the fact remains that if we want to talk about where the girls are in terms of uses of new technologies, we have to turn to much less intentionally political practices; that is, social networking.

SOCIAL NETWORKING

'Social networking' has a specific meaning related to the creation of personal profiles on sites such as MySpace and Facebook and the engagement in online interaction with others who also have profiles. These sites feature profiles, friends and a public commenting component. . . . However, social networking can also be used as a catch-all phrase to mean the various ways that technology is used by people to meet up with others, often peers, and communicate about personal issues. This can include the use of organised, commercial social networking sites, the construction of independent personal websites and journals, the use of Internet chat rooms or bulletin boards, photo- and video-sharing websites, and texting and image sharing via mobile phones. In both its broad and specific definition, social networking is a very popular use of new technology by young women (Boyd 2007b). Even before the phenomena of Friendster, MySpace, Bebo, Facebook, LiveJournal, YouTube and so on, research has shown that girls have tended to use new technologies more frequently for social purposes through email, chatting facilities and Instant Messaging, whereas boys have been more likely to play and download games and music (Lenhart et al. 2001, Tufte 2003, quoted in Mazzarella 2005, p. 2). Young women have also been well established as heavy users of text messaging since the early take-up of mobile phones among youth in pioneer countries such as Finland (Kasesniemi 2001).

Social networking technologies are often perceived as frivolous or problematic because of their association with youth and femininity, as illustrated by a current debate within blogging communities about gender difference in journal-style uses of the Internet (see Herring et al. 2004, Gregg 2006). Nowhere is this more evident, however, than in the broader public debate about the risks facing young women in their use of the Internet. There is a growing body of literature on the dangers of social networking, wherein young women's own perspectives are not always prominent, and there is little regard for what Gregg and Driscoll (forthcoming, p. 14) describe as 'the forms of literacy involved in being able to control and realise "what you're being" in online spaces'. Current approaches to social networking are heavily weighted towards addressing the risks that face young people, and often young women in particular, by revealing personal information that might become embarrassing, by exposing themselves to online predators, and by spending too much time away from 'real life' (see, for example, Dewey 2002, Wolak et al. 2003, and for a critique, Gregg 2007). Young women's social networking is perceived as a risky behaviour that needs to be managed by responsible adults.

When their own points of view are solicited, young women tend to demonstrate significant competencies in regard to risk (Gregg and Driscoll forthcoming 2008,

p. 14), and widely report that they use these social networking technologies simply to stay in touch and communicate with their friends (Schofield Clark 2005, Boyd 2007b). Very early research on young women's use of bulletin boards (Kaplan and Farrell 1994) notes that these are activities perceived by young women as an extension of their immediate, off-line social worlds. Australian research on young women's use of online chat rooms has found that they use chatting facilities for social interaction and to maintain connection with friends in ways that are outside adult monitoring and freer of some of the social mores they feel constrain their off-line lives (Gibian 2003). UK research on mobile phones (Henderson et al. 2002, p. 508) supports this perspective that young women enjoy the opportunities that are offered by communication technology 'to claim greater personal and sexual freedom in a movement from the domestic to more public spheres'. Early research with young women who create personal websites (Takayoshi et al. 1999, p. 99) has found that this activity is valued because, in their words, 'it allows [girls] to speak out and no one can stop them.' In summary, research with young female users of social networking technologies shows that they enjoy creating and using a space where they can engage with friends, sometimes meet new people, and express themselves in a public forum where they are not under parental or other authoritarian control.

Profiles on social networking sites and personal web pages and blogs often reflect this peer orientation strongly through their design and discursive style. To adults, they are often hard to 'read', and can appear aesthetically messy and full of banal, inconclusive exchanges. As Kaplan and Farrell (1994, p. 8) note in relation to bulletin boards, 'the sociability of [the] exchange seems its sole reason for being', and this is primarily a peer-to-peer sociability that confounds those it excludes. In this respect, there is a case that social networking is a way for young women to create new participatory communities for and by their peers. As Barnes (2007, p. 2) suggests, 'teenagers are learning how to use social networks by interacting with their friends, rather than learning these behaviours from their parents or teachers.' This capacity to bypass adults in the construction of public communication communities is seeing young people generating public selves in their own ways. This is qualitatively different from the traditional constitution of youth cultures or subcultures, which have also operated to allow young people to create identities and spaces of their own, because of the reach offered by the global stage and the large-scale participation on the part of 'ordinary' youth that characterise online social networks.

This in turn has implications for young people's political participation in two significant ways. First, theorists such as Boyd (2007b) suggest that these kinds of youth communities ought be understood as counter-publics, even though the content of the sites is usually personal rather than related to matters of the public good. She suggests that social network sites are places where young people 'write themselves and their community into being' (pp. 13 14) in view of an audience, and that they do this online because they have very little access to real public spaces (p. 19). She says 'their participation is deeply rooted in their desire to engage publicly' (p. 21). Social network sites are therefore an important way for young women in particular to participate in a public sphere, regardless of the fact that the nature of their public expressions is not necessarily political. Second, others have argued that social networking facilitates or can be a precursor to 'real' participation. That is, it is valued insofar as it can lead to the formation of communities or collective activities focused on civic or political practices (see, for example, Burgess et al. 2006, p. 2). This kind of analysis of social networks sits within a larger body of work on the political significance of virtual communities, where claims and counter-claims are made about their capacity to empower the marginalised and to deliver more democratic modes of communication. In the next section, I explore these and other arguments about the political possibilities of both social networking and online DIY culture in depth.

DO ONLINE DIY CULTURES AND SOCIAL NETWORKING CONSTITUTE POLITICAL PARTICIPATION?

I would suggest that there are several ways in which both online DIY cultures and, more controversially, social networking, ought be included in the conversation about young women's political participation, but there are some important arguments that qualify these interpretations. First, I would argue that these activities are about creating a public self, which is the first step in seeing oneself as a citizen. They give young women an opportunity to bring the private into the public in ways that were unprecedented prior to new technologies. Whether or not these private matters can

then be worked into joined-up, publicly deliberated public issues is an open question, but it is clear that many young women are attempting the work of public self-making in the counter-publics of online DIY cultures, while others are simply engaged in creating public identities that can connect with others, a process that may be valuable in itself. Moreover, literature that looks at social networking as a technique for young women's identity construction work demonstrates that the kinds of public selves they create can undermine gender expectations. New technologies facilitate young women's capacity to play with gender and to resist feminine stereotypes—for example, by acting more confidently than they might be face to face, and by feeling less constrained by gendered norms about appearance, especially in the cases of pre-video mobile phones, instant messaging and chat rooms (Henderson et al. 2002, Gibian 2003, Thiel 2005).

However, many would claim, along the lines of Bauman (2001, pp. 106–107), that these young women are merely filling what is left of public space with personal stories and troubles, without any capacity for these to be, as he says, 'translated as public issues [such that] public solutions are sought, negotiated and agreed'. From this perspective, the kinds of communities and dialogues that occur in online DIY cultures and social networking cannot be political because they infrequently move beyond personal sharing. In other words, as Vromen (2007, p. 52) points out, it is questionable whether this kind of use of the Internet 'can progress from fostering individualised participation into more collectively oriented participation with the capacity to foster deliberation'. This is most clearly a problem in social networking, for online DIY cultures often explicitly attempt to make this move beyond the personal to a structural critique, and sometimes work towards public solutions. It can appear, though, that even the structures of the messaging tools of social networking (emphasis on expression rather than listening, lack of closure or resolution, absence of moderators) seem to work against the conventions of democratic deliberation, as does the style of much interaction (see Davis 2005, p. 130). For example, as Kaplan and Farrell (1994, p. 8) note in relation to bulletin boards (bboards), 'the conversations among these young women and their contacts on the bboards often seem, at least to an outsider, driven more by the desire of the participants to keep the conversation going than by their desire to achieve understanding of or consensus about some topic or issue'.

Even so, I would argue that there is much to be gained from understanding how young women interact online. Feminists have noted that traditional ideas about deliberation and how public conversations should look are gender biased (Tannen 1995). Sociability and the capacity for deliberation are not necessarily inconsistent, and in fact the former may even expand the conventions of the latter. Coleman (2006, p. 258) has written that it is 'random sociability that makes the internet such an attractive place for young people', and to learn from this, 'policy designed to promote democratic online interaction must resist the anxieties of managed communication and take its chances within networks of autonomous and acephalous interaction.' In other words, online deliberative democracy and random social networks of unmanaged participation are not mutually exclusive, and to draw young people into deliberative democratic practices online requires adaptation to their preferred modes of interaction.

Social networking activities are also not cut and dried in terms of their relationship with conventional politics or activism. They do not always sit easily on the 'private' side of the divide, but negotiate this very border. For example, there is a considerable amount of activism and social justice campaigning that occurs on these sites. MySpace, for example, has over 33,000 'government and politics' groups. Kann et al. (2007, p. 4) suggest that 'this merging of social networking and online politics has the potential to integrate political discourse into youths' everyday lives.' Perhaps an indication of this is that in defiance of the stereotype, research has found that a majority of polled MySpace participants had voted for a candidate for public office, while only 21% had voted for a contestant on an Idol show (Jenkins 2006). There are many examples of online DIY cultures and social networking sites using public space to debate matters of the common good: just one small illustration is a current political campaign established by young women on Facebook regarding new policy about government management of Indigenous Australian communities.

Notwithstanding this issue of what kind of public conversation counts as politics, there is perhaps a thornier one of what kinds of public selves are being constructed in these sites by young women. The very project of making a self that is publicly visible is contained within the new discourses of femininity for young women that link success to image, style, and visible work on oneself rather than a more robust con-cept of citizenship (McRobbie 2000, Harris 2004a). Hopkins (2002) argues that young women have become the stars of a postmodern contemporary culture obsessed with omnipresence of identity, image and celebrity. She says (2002, p. 4) that 'the new hero is a girl in pursuit of media visibility, public recognition and notoriety. She wants to be somebody and "live large".' Being 'somebody,' however, means living a celebrity life: looking good, having a watched and envied persona, and engaging with leisure and consumption rather than politics. Thus, the public selves that young women are encouraged to create are not political subjectivities, but self-inventing celebrity selves that gain status from their take up of consumer culture. . . . For young women creating public identities online, the goals of self-expression and peer connection are bound up with being on display as a consumer citizen.

What seems indisputable, though, is that these activities allow young women to take up virtual public space at a time when physical public space for young people is diminishing. . . . If young people have few free spaces left to them, then these online activities indicate a desire to create and occupy new public spaces beyond these constraints. . . . The rise of the shopping mall as *the* 'public' space for youth and for young female consumers in particular (Harris 2004a) and its demand on participants that if they wish to enjoy this space they must spend money, also increases the appeal of non-commercial spaces of sociality and community for young women.

Thus, both online DIY cultures and social networking signify a desire to be a cultural producer; that is, to actively engage in the construction of one's cultural world, rather than simply consume. There is considerable pleasure to be taken in the design and upkeep of personal websites and blogs, especially when youth culture artefacts are used creatively and playfully in order to attribute new meaning to them (see, for example, Reid-Walsh and Mitchell 2004). Young women have been the primary targets of a shift to consumer citizenship for youth, and these creative uses of new technologies demonstrate how they play with, negotiate and sometimes resist the encroachment of the consumer imperative on their everyday lives. The idea of talking back to youth consumer culture is an explicit political agenda of many girl-centred websites, but even the engagement with the products of this culture, as evident in the profiles and conversations on social network sites, often reveals a critical agency rather than passive consumption.

However, there are concerns raised about the potential for such practices to remain free from corporate or government interests; that is, for young people to craft out truly public spaces, given the encroachment of interested parties, including corporate media, the advertising industry and mainstream politics, upon them (see Castells 2007). There is some evidence that young people are moving away from the sites taken over by major corporations (for example, MySpace's purchase by NewsCorp and YouTube by Google), and towards less commercial networking sites (see Boyd 2007b, Castells 2007—with Microsoft's recent negotiations to buy a stake in Facebook, its fate will be interesting to watch). However, the fact remains that the Internet and mobile phones have been an enormous boon for those seeking to capture the youth market, and at best young people who use them are engaged in a constant negotiation of advertising interests (Barnes 2007). But even if corporate and government interests are advancing on youth online spaces, parents and other authority figures are some way behind, and in this regard, these activities allow young women to connect with their peers away from the prying eyes of the adults in their lives. In this sense, they contribute to the making of a whole lot of admittedly 'thin' youth communities to which their members feel a commitment and in which they actively participate.

CONCLUSION

In order to situate young women in the debate about youth, new technologies and political participation, it is important to expand definitions of participatory practice and to take account of the new socio-economic landscape which has radically changed the meaning of citizenship, politics and participation. Online DIY cultures and social networking are important examples of the ways that young women are negotiating the absence of traditional citizenship identities and the emergence of new, somewhat problematic ones in their place. Young women engage in these activities at times to develop new modes of activism and political subjectivity, but more often to create unregulated, public spaces for peer communities and to construct public selves. These practices reveal the challenges for young women in positioning themselves within a regulatory culture that rewards them for their capacity as ideal neoliberal consumer subjects.

I have suggested that the ways in which young women are using new technologies demonstrate that, in the light of the so-called crisis of youth political engagement, and in concert with the pressures to perform as particular kinds of consumer citizens, many are already doing their own kinds of participation. This is a different argument from the idea that an emergent collectivist politics or conventional civic or political activity will flow out of such practices. It is not always or even predominantly the case that conventional or activist off-line participation emerges out of these. The work of Livingstone and her colleagues (2007, p. 307) from the UK Children Go Online project suggests that we must be cautious about the assumption that once young people are online in some capacity they will be drawn to ever more civic or political uses of the Internet. But it is important to recognise the ways that simply participating in online cultures and networking is a form of developing citizenship skills, regardless of any specific involvement in political causes. Kann et al. (2007, p. 2) argue that this kind of 'participatory culture has the potential to enhance youth participation in politics (in part because) it promotes the key democratic values of involvement and openness'. More than this, though, I would suggest that we need to consider the value of these practices in themselves, rather than only looking towards what 'better' or more conventional participatory practices they might turn into. It is important to acknowledge in the face of the widespread youth citizenship panic that young people, and young women in particular, are participating in their own communities and are expressing a desire to occupy public space on their own terms. . . .

For young women especially, these activities may provide less intimidating, more familiar modes for doing politics and for acting as citizens. They also provide opportunities for placing matters on a public agenda that are not formally political, but are at the heart of contemporary issues in the lives of young people: for example, school and study, sexuality, mental health and family relations. These constitute an everyday politics for young people and need to be taken seriously as the kinds of issues in which they are deeply engaged.

I have argued that it is vital to talk about online DIY cultures and social networking when we discuss young people, and young women in particular, in relation to new technologies and political participation.

I would suggest that conventional recruitment strategies to get them into conventional participation are misdirected, even when new technologies are utilised, because young women are grappling with a new political environment. Its features include a contracted public sphere, an increasingly impotent state, a blurring of private and public, and a hyperregulation of young people, and young women in particular, as good consumer citizens. This article has offered some ways that *we* can grapple with the meaning of participation in spaces created by and for other young people that are being forged by young women in response.

ACKNOWLEDGEMENTS

I thank Rachel Brooks, Paul Hodkinson and the two anonymous reviewers. I also thank Ariadne Vromen and Melissa Gregg for very helpful conversations, and Lesley Pruitt for research assistance.

REFERENCES

Barnes, S., 2007. A privacy paradox: social networking in the United States [online]. *First Monday*, 11 (9). Available from: http://www.firstmonday.org/issues/issue11_9/barnes/index.html [Accessed 28 September 2007].

Bauman, Z., 2001. *The individualised society*. Cambridge: Polity.

Boyd, D., 2007b. Identity production in a networked culture: why youth (heart) social network sites: the role of networked publics in teenage social life. *In:* D. Buckingham, ed. *Youth, identity and digital media* [online]. MacArthur Foundation Series on Digital Learning. Cambridge, MA: MIT Press. Available from: http://www.danah.org/papers/AAAS2006.html [Accessed 23 October 2007].

Bortree, D., 2006. Review of *Girl wide Web. New media and society*, 8(5), 851–856.

Burgess, J., Foth, M., and Klaebe, H., 2006. *Everyday creativity as civic engagement: a cultural citizenship view of new media*. Communications Policy and Research Forum, 25–26 September 2006, Sydney. Unpublished paper.

Castells, M., 2007. Communication, power and counter-power in the network society. *International journal of communication*, 1, 238–266.

Christensen, R., Knezek, G., and Overall, T., 2005. Transition points for the gender gap in computer enjoyment. *Journal of research on technology in education*, 38 (1), 23–37.

Coleman, S., 2006. Digital voices and analogue citizenship: bridging the gap between young people and the democratic process. *Public policy research*, 13 (4), 257–261.

Davis, R., 2005. *Politics online: blogs, chatrooms, and discussion groups in American democracy*. New York: Routledge.

Dewey, L., 2002. Girls online feeling out of bounds. *Camping magazine*, 75 (5), 48–50.

Gibian, J., 2003. 'They're all wog rooms': the online chat of culturally diverse teenage girls in Western Sydney. *In:* M. Butcher and M. Thomas, eds. *Ingenious: emerging youth cultures in Australia*. North Melbourne: Pluto Press, 47–65.

Gregg, M., 2006. Posting with passion: blogs and the politics of gender. *In:* J. Jacobs and A. Bruns, eds. *Uses of blogs*. New York: Peter Lang, 151–160.

Gregg, M., 2007. *Thanks for the ad(d): neolibernlism's compulsory friendship*. Presentation at Goldsmiths College, July 2007, London. Unpublished paper.

Gregg, M. and Driscoll, C., 2008 (forthcoming). The YouTube generation: moral panic, youth culture and Internet studies. *In:* U. Rodrigues, ed. *Youth and media in the Asia-Pacific region*. Cambridge: Cambridge Scholars Press.

Haas, A., Tulley, C., and Blair, K., 2002. Mentors versus masters: women's and girls' narratives of (re)negotiation in Web-based writing space. *Computers and composition*, 19 (3), 231–249.

Hahn, C.L., 1998. *Becoming political*. Albany, NY: State University of New York Press.

Harris, A., 2004a. *Future girl: young women in the twenty-first century*. New York and London: Routledge.

Harris, A., 2004b. Jamming girl culture: young women and consumer citizenship. *In:* A. Harris, ed. *All about the girl: culture, power and identity*. New York and London: Routledge, 163–172.

Harris, A., Wyn, J., and Younes, S., 2008. *Rethinking youth citizenship; identity and connection*. Research Report, Melbourne: Youth Research Centre.

Henderson, S., Taylor, R., and Thomson, R., 2002. In touch: young people, communication and technologies. *Information, communication and society*, 5 (4), 494–512.

Herring, S., *et al.*, 2004. Women and children last: the discursive construction of weblogs [online]. *In:* L.J. Gurak, *et al.*, eds. *Into the blogosphere: rhetoric, community and culture of weblogs*. Available from: http://blog.lib.umn.edu/blogosphere/women_and_children.html [Accessed 17 April 2007].

Hopkins, S., 2002. *Girl heroes: the new force in popular culture*. Annandale: Pluto Press.

Jenkins, H., 2006. *Tracking the MySpace generation* [online]. Confessions of an Aca-Fan: the Official Weblog of Henry Jenkins. 29 August 2006, §3. Available from: http://www.henryjenkins.org/2006/08/tracking_the_MySpace_generatio.html [Accessed 26 September 2007].

Kann, M.E., *et al.*, 2007. *The Internet and youth political participation* [online]. *First Monday*, 12 (8). Available from: http://www.firstmonday.org/issues/issue12_8/kann/index.html [Accessed 18 September 2007].

Kaplan, N. and Farrell, E., 1994. Weavers of webs: a portrait of young women on the net [online]. *Arachnet journal on virtual culture*, 2 (3). Available from: www.ftp_byrd.mu.wvnet.edu/pub/ejvc/Kaplan.v2n3 [Accessed 17 October 2007].

Kasesniemi, E., 2001. Finnish teenagers and mobile communication: chatting and storytelling in text messages *In:* A. Furlong and I. Guidikova, eds. *Transitions of youth citizenship in Europe: culture, subculture and identity.* Strasbourg: Council of Europe Publishing, 157–179.

Lenhart, A., Rainie, L., and Lewis, O., 2001. *Teenage life online: the rise of the instant message generation and the Internet's impact on friendships and family relationships* [online]. Washington, DC: Pew Internet and American Life Project. Available from: http://www.pewinternet.org/pdfs/PIP_Teens_Report.pdf [Accessed 17 October 2007].

Livingstone, S., Bober, M., and Helsper, E.J., 2005. *Internet literacy among children and young people* [online]. London: LSE Report, February 2005. Available from: http://www.children-go-online.net. [Accessed 25 March 2008].

Livingstone, S., Bobel; M., and Helsper, E.J., 2007. Active participation or just more information? Young people's take up of opportunities to act and interact on the Internet. *Information, communication and society*, 8 (3), 287–314.

Mazzarella, S.R., 2005. It's a girl wide Web. *In:* S.R. Mazzarella, ed. *Girl wide Web: girls, the Internet and the negotiation of identity.* New York: Peter Lang, 1–12.

McRobbie, A., 2000. *Feminism and youth culture.* London: Macmillan.

Melucci, A., 1996. *Challenging codes: collective action in the information age.* Cambridge: Cambridge University Press.

Orlowski, A., 2003. Most bloggers 'are teenage girls' — survey [online]. *The register.* Available from: http://www.theregister.co.uk/2003/05/30/most_bloggers_are_teenage_girls/ [Accessed 17 April 2007].

Ratliff, C., 2004. Whose voices get heard? Gender politics in the blogosphere [online]. CultureCat. Available from: http://culturecat.net/ [Accessed 17 April 2007].

Reid-Walsh, J. and Mitchell, C., 2004. Girls' websites: a virtual 'room of one's own'? *In:* A. Harris, ed. *All about the girl: culture, power and identity.* New York: Routledge, 173–184.

Roker, D., 2008. Young women and social action in the UK. *In:* A. Harris, ed. *Next wave cultures: feminism, subcultures, activism.* New York: Routledge, 243–260.

Schofield Clark, L., 2005. The constant contact generation: exploring teen friendship networks online. *In:* S.R. Mazzarella, ed. *Girl wide Web: girls, the Internet and the negotiation of identity.* New York: Peter Lang, 203–222.

Stasko, C., 2008. (r)Evolutionary healing: jamming with culture and shifting the power. *In:* A. Harris, ed. *Next wave cultures: feminism, subcultures, activism.* New York: Routledge, 193–219.

Takayoshi, P., Huot, E., and Huot, M., 1999. No boys allowed: the World Wide Web as a clubhouse for girls. *Computers and consumption*, 16, 89–106.

Tannen, D., 1995. *Gender and discourse.* Oxford: Oxford University Press.

Thiel, S.M., 2005. IM ME: identity construction and gender negotiation in the world of adolescent girls and instant messaging. *In:* S.R. Mazzarella, ed. *Girl wide Web: girls, the Internet and the negotiation of identity.* New York: Peter Lang, 179–202.

Vromen, A., 2006. *Gendering generations: young people's participatory citizenship.* ESRC Research Seminar Series: Gender, Participation and Citizenship, University of the West of England, June 2006. Unpublished paper.

Vromen, A., 2007. Australian young people's participatory practices and Internet use. *Information, communication and society*, 10 (1), 48–68.

Vromen, A., 2008. Building virtual spaces: young people, participation and the Internet. *Australian journal of political science*, 43 (1), 79–97.

Wolak, J., Mitchell, K.J., and Finkelhor, D., 2003. Escaping or connecting? Characteristics of youth who form close online relationships. *Journal of adolescence*, 26 (1), 105–119.

Punks, Bulldaggers, and Welfare Queens: The Radical Potential of Queer Politics?

First published in 1997

On the eve of finishing this essay my attention is focused not on how to rework the conclusion (as it should be) but instead on news stories of alleged racism at Gay Men's Health Crisis (GMHC). It seems that three black board members of this largest and oldest AIDS organization in the world have resigned over their perceived subservient position on the GMHC board. Billy E. Jones, former head of the New York City Health and Hospitals Corporation and one of the board members to quit, was quoted in the *New York Times* as saying, "Much work needs to be done at GMHC to make it truly inclusive and welcoming of diversity. . . . It is also clear that such work will be a great struggle. I am resigning because I do not choose to engage in such struggle at GMHC, but rather prefer to fight for the needs of those ravaged by HIV" (Dunlap).

This incident raises mixed emotions for me, for it points to the continuing practice of racism many of us experience on a daily basis in lesbian and gay communities. But just as disturbingly it also highlights the limits of a lesbian and gay political agenda based on a civil rights strategy, where assimilation into, and replication of, dominant institutions are the goals. Many of us continue to search for a new political direction and agenda, one that does not focus on integration into dominant structures but instead seeks to transform the basic fabric and hierarchies that allow systems of oppression to persist and operate efficiently. For some of us, such a challenge to traditional gay and lesbian politics was offered by the idea of queer politics. Here we had a potential movement of young antiassimilationist activists committed to challenging the very way people understand and respond to sexuality. These activists promised to engage in struggles that would disrupt dominant norms of sexuality, radically transforming politics in lesbian, gay, bisexual, and transgendered communities.

Despite the possibility invested in the idea of queerness and the practice of queer politics, I argue that a truly radical or transformative politics has not resulted from queer activism. In many instances, instead of destabilizing the assumed categories and binaries of sexual identity, queer politics has served to reinforce simple dichotomies between heterosexual and everything "queer." An understanding of the ways in which power informs and constitutes privileged and marginalized subjects on both sides of this dichotomy has been left unexamined.

I query in this essay whether there are lessons to be learned from queer activism that can help us construct a new politics. I envision a politics where one's relation to power, and not some homogenized identity, is privileged in determining one's political comrades. I'm talking about a politics where the *nonnormative* and *marginal* position of punks, bulldaggers, and welfare queens, for example, is the basis for progressive transformative coalition work. Thus, if there is any truly radical potential to be found in the idea of queerness and the practice of queer politics, it would seem to be located in its ability to create a space in opposition to dominant norms, a space where transformational political work can begin.

EMERGENCE OF QUEER POLITICS AND A NEW POLITICS OF TRANSFORMATION

Theorists and activists alike generally agree that it was in the early 1990s that we began to see, with any regularity, the use of the term "queer."[1] This term would come to denote not only an emerging politics, but also a new cohort of academics working in programs primarily in the humanities centered around social and cultural criticism (Morton 121). Individuals such as Judith Butler, Eve Sedgwick, Teresa de Lauretis, Diana Fuss, and Michael Warner produced what are now thought of as the first canonical works of "queer theory." Working from a variety of postmodernist and poststructuralist theoretical perspectives, these scholars focused on identifying and contesting the discursive and cultural markers found within both dominant and marginal identities and institutions which prescribe and reify "heterogendered" understandings and behavior.[2] These theorists presented a different conceptualization of sexuality, one which sought to replace socially named and presumably stable categories of sexual expression with a new fluid movement among and between forms of sexual behavior (Stein and Plummer 182).

Through its conception of a wide continuum of sexual possibilities, queer theory stands in direct contrast to the normalizing tendencies of hegemonic sexuality rooted in ideas of static, stable sexual identities and behaviors. In queer theorizing the sexual subject is understood to be constructed and contained by multiple practices of categorization and regulation that systematically marginalize and oppress those subjects thereby defined as deviant and "other." And, at its best, queer theory focuses on and makes central not only the socially constructed nature of sexuality and sexual categories, but also the varying degrees and multiple sites of power distributed within all categories of sexuality, including the normative category of heterosexuality.

It was in the early 1990s, however, that the postmodern theory being produced in the academy (later to be recategorized as queer theory) found its most direct interaction with the real-life politics of lesbian, gay, bisexual, and transgendered activists. Frustrated with what was perceived to be the scientific "degaying" and assimilationist tendencies of AIDS activism, with their invisibility in the more traditional civil rights politics of lesbian and gay organizations, and with increasing legal and physical attacks against lesbian and gay community members, a new generation of activists began the process of building a more confrontational political formation—labeling it queer politics (Bérubé and Escoffier 12). Queer politics, represented most notoriously in the actions of Queer Nation, is understood as an "in your face" politics of a younger generation. Through action and analysis these individuals seek to make "queer" function as more than just an abbreviation for lesbian, gay, bisexual, and transgendered. Similar to queer theory, the queer politics articulated and pursued by these activists first and foremost recognizes and encourages the fluidity and movement of people's sexual lives. In queer politics sexual expression is something that always entails the possibility of change, movement, redefinition, and subversive performance—from year to year, from partner to partner, from day to day, even from act to act. In addition to highlighting the instability of sexual categories and sexual subjects, queer activists also directly challenge the multiple practices and vehicles of power which render them invisible and at risk. However, what seems to make queer activists unique, at this particular moment, is their willingness to confront normalizing power by emphasizing and exaggerating their own antinormative characteristics and nonstable behavior. Joshua Gamson, in "Must Identity Movements Self-Destruct? A Queer Dilemma," writes that

> queer activism and theory pose the challenge of a form of organizing in which, far from inhibiting accomplishments, the *destabilization* of collective identity is itself a goal and accomplishment of collective action.
>
> The assumption that stable collective identities are necessary for collective action is turned on its head by queerness, and the question becomes: *When and how are stable collective identities necessary for social action and social change?* Secure boundaries and stabilized identities are necessary not in general, but in the specific, a point social movement theory seems currently to miss. (403, original emphasis)

Thus queer politics, much like queer theory, is often perceived as standing in opposition, or in contrast, to the category-based identity politics of traditional lesbian and gay activism. And for those of us who find ourselves on the margins, operating through multiple identities and thus not fully served or recognized through traditional single-identity-based politics, *theoretical conceptualizations* of queerness hold great political promise. For many of us, the label "queer" symbolizes an acknowledgment that through our existence and everyday survival we embody sustained and multisited resistance to systems (based on dominant constructions of race and gender) that seek to normalize our sexuality, exploit our labor, and constrain our visibility. At the intersection of oppression and resistance lies the radical potential of queerness to challenge and bring together all those deemed marginal and all those committed to liberatory politics.

The problem, however, with such a conceptualization and expectation of queer identity and politics is that in its present form queer politics has not emerged as an encompassing challenge to systems of domination and oppression, especially those normalizing processes embedded in heteronormativity. By "heteronormativity" I mean both those localized practices and those centralized institutions which legitimize and privilege heterosexuality and heterosexual relationships as fundamental and "natural" within society. I raise the subject of heteronormativity because it is this normalizing practice/power that has most often been the focus of queer politics (Blasius 19–20; Warner xxi–xxv).

The inability of queer politics to effectively challenge heteronormativity rests, in part, on the fact that despite a surrounding discourse which highlights the destabilization and even deconstruction of sexual categories, queer politics has often been built around a simple dichotomy between those deemed queer and those deemed heterosexual. Whether in the infamous "I Hate Straights" publication or queer kiss-ins at malls and straight dance clubs, very near the surface in queer political action is an uncomplicated understanding of power as it is encoded in sexual categories: all heterosexuals are represented as dominant and controlling and all queers are understood as marginalized and invisible. Thus, even in the name of destabilization, some queer activists have begun to prioritize sexuality as the primary frame through which they pursue their politics.[3] Undoubtedly, within different contexts various characteristics of our total being—for example, race, gender, class, sexuality—are highlighted or called upon to make sense of a particular situation. However, my concern is centered on those individuals who consistently activate only one characteristic of their identity, or a single perspective of consciousness, to organize their politics, rejecting any recognition of the multiple and intersecting systems of power that largely dictate our life chances.

It is the disjuncture, evident in queer politics, between an articulated commitment to promoting an understanding of sexuality that rejects the idea of static, monolithic, bounded categories, on the one hand, and political practices structured around binary conceptions of sexuality and power, on the other hand, that is the focus of this article. Specifically, I am concerned with those manifestations of queer politics in which the capital and

advantage invested in a range of sexual categories are disregarded and, as a result, narrow and homogenized political identities are reproduced that inhibit the radical potential of queer politics. It is my contention that queer activists who evoke a single-oppression framework misrepresent the distribution of power within and outside of gay, lesbian, bisexual, and transgendered communities, and therefore limit the comprehensive and transformational character of queer politics.

Recognizing the limits of current conceptions of queer identities and queer politics, I am interested in examining the concept of "queer" in order to think about how we might construct a new political identity that is truly liberating, transformative, and inclusive of all those who stand on the outside of the dominant constructed norm of state-sanctioned white middle- and upper-class heterosexuality.[4] Such a broadened understanding of queerness must be based on an intersectional analysis that recognizes how numerous systems of oppression interact to regulate and police the lives of most people. Black lesbian, bisexual, and heterosexual feminist authors such as Kimberle Crenshaw, Barbara Ransby, Angela Davis, Cheryl Clarke, and Audre Lorde have repeatedly emphasized in their writing the intersectional workings of oppression. And it is just such an understanding of the interlocking systems of domination that is noted in the opening paragraph of the now famous black feminist statement by the Combahee River Collective:

> The most general statement of our politics at the present time would be that we are actively committed to struggling against racial, sexual, heterosexual, and class oppression and see as our particular task the development of *integrated* analysis and practice based upon the fact that the major systems of oppression are interlocking. The synthesis of these oppressions creates the conditions of our lives. As Black women we see Black feminism as the logical political movement to combat the manifold and simultaneous oppressions that all women of color face. (272)

This analysis of one's place in the world which focuses on the intersection of systems of oppression is informed by a consciousness that undoubtedly grows from the lived experience of existing within and resisting multiple and connected practices of domination and normalization. Just such a lived experience and analysis have determined much of the progressive and expansive nature of the politics emanating from people of color, people who are both inside and outside of lesbian and gay communities.

However, beyond a mere recognition of the intersection of oppressions, there must also be an understanding of the ways our multiple identities work to limit the entitlement and status some receive from obeying a heterosexual imperative. For instance, how would queer activists understand politically the lives of women—in particular women of color—on welfare, who may fit into the category of heterosexual, but whose sexual choices are not perceived as normal, moral, or worthy of state support? Further, how do queer activists understand and relate politically to those whose same-sex sexual identities position them within the category of queer, but who hold other identities based on class, race and/or gender categories which provide them with membership in and the resources of dominant institutions and groups?

Thus, inherent in our new politics must be a commitment to left analysis and left politics. Black feminists as well as other marginalized and progressive scholars and activists have long argued that any political response to the multilayered oppression that most of us experience must be rooted in a left understanding of our political, economic, social, and cultural institutions. Fundamentally, a left framework makes central the interdependency among multiple systems of domination. Such a perspective also ensures that while activists should rightly be concerned with forms of discursive and cultural coercion, we also recognize and confront the more direct and concrete forms of exploitation and violence rooted in state-regulated institutions and economic systems. The Statement of Purpose from the first Dialogue on the Lesbian and Gay Left comments specifically on the role of interlocking systems of oppression in the lives of gays and lesbians. "By leftist we mean people who understand the struggle for lesbian and gay liberation to be integrally tied to struggles against class oppression, racism, and sexism. While we might use different political labels, we share a commitment to a fundamental transformation of the economic, political and social structures of society."

A left framework of politics, unlike civil rights or liberal frameworks, brings into focus the systematic relationship among forms of domination, where the creation and maintenance of exploited, subservient, marginalized classes is a necessary part of, at the very least, the economic configuration. Urvashi Vaid, in *Virtual Equality,* for example, writes of the limits of civil rights strategies in confronting systemic homophobia:

Civil rights do not change the social order in dramatic ways; they change only the privileges of the group asserting those rights. Civil rights strategies do not challenge the moral and antisexual underpinnings of homophobia, because homophobia does not originate in our lack of full civil equality. Rather, homophobia arises from the nature and construction of the political, legal, economic, sexual, racial and family systems within which we live. (183)

Proceeding from the starting point of a system-based left analysis, strategies built upon the possibility of incorporation and assimilation are exposed as simply expanding and making accessible the status quo for more privileged members of marginal groups, while the most vulnerable in our communities continue to be stigmatized and oppressed.

It is important to note, however, that while left theorists tend to provide a more structural analysis of oppression and exploitation, many of these theorists and activists have also been homophobic and heterosexist in their approach to or avoidance of the topics of sexuality and heteronormativity. For example, Robin Podolsky, in "Sacrificing Queers and other 'Proletarian' Artifacts," writes that quite often on the left lesbian and gay sexuality and desire have been characterized as "more to do with personal happiness and sexual pleasure than with the 'material basis' of procreation—we were considered self-indulgent distractions from struggle . . . [an example of] 'bourgeois decadence'" (54).

This contradiction between a stated left analysis and an adherence to heteronormativity has probably been most dramatically identified in the writing of some feminist authors. I need only refer to Adrienne Rich's well-known article, "Compulsory Heterosexuality and Lesbian Existence," as a poignant critique of the white, middle-class heterosexual standard running through significant parts of feminist analysis and actions. The same adherence to a heterosexual norm can be found in the writing of self-identified black left intellectuals such as Cornel West and Michael Eric Dyson. Thus, while these writers have learned to make reference to lesbian, gay, bisexual, and transgendered segments of black communities—sparingly—they continue to foreground black heterosexuality and masculinity as the central unit of analysis in their writing—and most recently in their politics, witness their participation in the Million Man March.

This history of left organizing and the left's visible absence from any serious and sustained response to the AIDS epidemic have provoked many lesbian, gay, bisexual and transgendered people to question the relevance of this political configuration to the needs of our communities. Recognizing that reservations of this type are real and should be noted, I still hold that a left-rooted analysis which emphasizes economic exploitation and class structure, culture, and the systemic nature of power provides a framework of politics that is especially effective in representing and challenging the numerous sites and systems of oppression. Further, the left-centered approach that I embrace is one that designates sexuality and struggles against sexual normalization as central to the politics of all marginal communities.

THE ROOT OF QUEER POLITICS: CHALLENGING HETERONORMATIVITY?

In the introduction to the edited volume *Fear of a Queer Planet: Queer Politics and Social Theory*, Michael Warner asks the question: "What do queers want?" (vii). He suggests that the goals of queers and their politics extend beyond the sexual arena. Warner contends that what queers want is acknowledgment of their lives, struggles, and complete existence; queers want to be represented and included fully in left political analysis and American culture. Thus what queers want is to be a part of the social, economic, and political restructuring of this society; as Warner writes, queers want to have queer experience and politics "taken as starting points rather than as footnotes" in the social theories and political agendas of the left (vii). He contends that it has been the absence or invisibility of lived queer experience that has marked or constrained much of left social and political theories and "has posited and naturalized a heterosexual society" in such theories (vii).

The concerns and emerging politics of queer activists, as formulated by Warner and others interested in understanding the implications of the idea of queerness, are focused on highlighting queer presence and destroying heteronormativity not only in the larger dominant society but also in extant spaces, theories, and sites of resistance, presumably on the left. He suggests that those embracing the label of "queer" understand the need to challenge the

assumption of heteronormativity in every aspect of their existence:

> Every person who comes to a queer self-understanding knows in one way or another that her stigmatization is connected with gender, the family, notions of individual freedom, the state, public speech, consumption and desire, nature and culture, maturation, reproductive politics, racial and national fantasy, class identity, truth and trust, censorship, intimate life and social display, terror and violence, health care, and deep cultural norms about the bearing of the body. Being queer means fighting about these issues all the time, locally and piecemeal but always with consequences. (xiii)

Now, independent of the fact that few of us could find ourselves in such a grandiose description of queer consciousness, I believe that Warner's description points to the fact that in the roots of a lived "queer" existence are experiences with domination and in particular heteronormativity that form the basis for genuine transformational politics. By transformational, again, I mean a politics that does not search for opportunities to integrate into dominant institutions and normative social relationships, but instead pursues a political agenda that seeks to change values, definitions, and laws which make these institutions and relationships oppressive.

Queer activists experiencing displacement both within and outside of lesbian and gay communities rebuff what they deem the assimilationist practices and policies of more established lesbian and gay organizations. These organizers and activists reject cultural norms of acceptable sexual behavior and identification and instead embrace political strategies which promote self-definition and full expression. Members of the Chicago-based group Queers United Against Straight-acting Homosexuals (QUASH) state just such a position in the article "Assimilation Is Killing Us: Fight for a Queer United Front" published in their newsletter, WHY I HATED THE MARCH ON WASHINGTON:

> Assimilation is killing us. We are falling into a trap. Some of us adopt an apologetic stance, stating "that's just the way I am" (read: "I'd be straight if I could."). Others pattern their behavior in such a way as to mimic heterosexual society so as to minimize the glaring differences between us and them. No matter how

much [money] you make, fucking your lover is still illegal in nearly half of the states. Getting a corporate job, a fierce car and a condo does not protect you from dying of AIDS or getting your head bashed in by neo-Nazis. The myth of assimilation must be shattered.

. . . Fuck the heterosexual, nuclear family. Let's make families which promote sexual choices and liberation rather than sexual oppression. We must learn from the legacy of resistance that is ours: a legacy which shows that empowerment comes through grassroots activism, not mainstream politics, a legacy which shows that real change occurs when we are inclusive, not exclusive. (4)

At the very heart of queer politics, at least as it is formulated by QUASH, is a fundamental challenge to the heteronormativity—the privilege, power, and normative status invested in heterosexuality—of the dominant society.

It is in their fundamental challenge to a systemic process of domination and exclusion, with a specific focus on heteronormativity, that queer activists and queer theorists are tied to and rooted in a tradition of political struggle most often identified with people of color and other marginal groups. For example, activists of color have, through many historical periods, questioned their formal and informal inclusion and power in prevailing social categories. Through just such a process of challenging their centrality to lesbian and gay politics in particular, and lesbian and gay communities more generally, lesbian, gay, bisexual, and transgendered people of color advanced debates over who and what would be represented as "truly gay." As Steven Seidman reminds us in "Identity and Politics in a 'Postmodern' Gay Culture: Some Historical and Conceptual Notes," beyond the general framing provided by postmodern queer theory, gay and lesbian—and now queer—politics owes much of its impetus to the politics of people of color and other marginalized members of lesbian and gay communities.

Specifically, I make the case that postmodern strains in gay thinking and politics have their immediate social origin in recent developments in the gay culture. In the reaction by people of color, third-world-identified gays, poor and working-class gays, and sex rebels to the ethnic/essentialist model of identity and community that achieved dominance in the lesbian and gay cultures of the 1970s, I locate the social basis for a rethinking of identity and politics. (106)

Through the demands of lesbian, gay, bisexual, and transgendered people of color as well as others who did not see themselves or their numerous communities in the more narrowly constructed politics of white gays and lesbians, the contestation took shape over who and what type of issues would be represented in lesbian and gay politics and in larger community discourse.

While similarities and connections between the politics of lesbians, gay men, bisexuals, and transgendered people of color during the 1970s and 1980s and queer activists of today clearly exist, the present-day rendition of this politics has deviated significantly from its legacy. Specifically, while both political efforts include as a focus of their work the radicalization and/or expansion of traditional lesbian and gay politics, the politics of lesbian, gay, bisexual, and transgendered people of color have been and continue to be much broader in its understanding of transformational politics.

The politics of lesbian, gay, bisexual, and transgendered people of color has often been guided by the type of radical intersectional left analysis I detailed earlier. Thus, while the politics of lesbian, gay, bisexual, and transgendered activists of color might recognize heteronormativity as a primary system of power structuring our lives, it understands that heteronormativity interacts with institutional racism, patriarchy, and class exploitation to define us in numerous ways as marginal and oppressed subjects.[5] And it is this constructed subservient position that allows our sisters and brothers to be used either as surplus labor in an advanced capitalist structure and/or seen as expendable, denied resources, and thus locked into correctional institutions across the country. While heterosexual privilege negatively impacts and constrains the lived experience of "queers" of color, so too do racism, classism, and sexism.

In contrast to the left intersectional analysis that has structured much of the politics of "queers" of color, the basis of the politics of some white queer activists and organizations has come dangerously close to a single-oppression model. Experiencing "deviant" sexuality as the prominent characteristic of their marginalization, these activists begin to envision the world in terms of a "hetero/queer" divide. Using the framework of queer theory in which heteronormativity is identified as a system of regulation and normalization, some queer activists map the power and entitlement of normative heterosexuality onto the bodies of all heterosexuals. Further, these activists naively characterize all those who exist under the category of "queer" as powerless. Thus, in the process of conceptualizing a decentered identity of queerness, meant to embrace all those who stand on the outside of heteronormativity, a monolithic understanding of heterosexuality and queerness has come to dominate the political imagination and actions of many queer activists.

This reconstruction of a binary divide between heterosexuals and queers, while discernible in many of the actions of Queer Nation, is probably most evident in the manifesto "I Hate Straights." Distributed at gay pride parades in New York and Chicago in 1990, the declaration written by an anonymous group of queers begins,

I have friends. Some of them are straight.

Year after year, I see my straight friends. I want to see how they are doing, to add newness to our long and complicated histories, to experience some continuity.

Year after year I continue to realize that the facts of my life are irrelevant to them and that I am only half listened to, that I am an appendage to the doings of a greater world, a world of power and privilege, of the laws of installation, a world of exclusion. "That's not true," argue my straight friends. There is the one certainty in the politics of power; those left out of it beg for inclusion, while the insiders claim that they already are. Men do it to women, whites do it to blacks, *and everyone does it to queers.*

. . . *The main dividing line, both conscious and unconscious, is procreation . . . and that magic word—Family.* (emphasis added)

Screaming out from this manifesto is an analysis which places not heteronormativity, but heterosexuality, as the central "dividing line" between those who would be dominant and those who are oppressed. Nowhere in this essay is there recognition that "nonnormative" procreation patterns and family structures of people who are labeled heterosexual have also been used to regulate and exclude *them.* Instead, the authors declare. "Go tell them [straights] to go away until they have spent a month walking hand in hand in public with someone of the same sex. After they survive that, then you'll hear what they have to say about queer anger. Otherwise, tell them to shut up and listen." For these activists, the power of heterosexuality is the focus, and queer anger the means of queer politics. Missing from this equation is any attention to, or acknowledgment of, the ways in which identities of

race, class, and/or gender either enhance or mute the marginalization of queers, on the one hand, and the power of heterosexuals, on the other.

The fact that this essay is written about and out of queer anger is undoubtedly part of the rationale for its defense (Berlant and Freeman 200). But I question the degree to which we should read this piece as just an aberrational diatribe against straights motivated by intense queer anger. While anger is clearly a motivating factor for such writing, we should also understand this action to represent an analysis and politics structured around the simple dichotomy of straight and queer. We know, for instance, that similar positions have been put forth in other anonymously published, publicly distributed manifestos. For example, in the document *Queers Read This,* the authors write, "Don't be fooled, straight people own the world and the only reason you have been spared is you're smart, lucky or a fighter. Straight people have a privilege that allows them to do whatever they please and fuck without fear." They continue by stating: "Straight people are your enemy."

Even within this document, which seems to exemplify the narrowness of queer conceptions, there is a surprising glimpse at a more enlightened left intersectional understanding of what queerness might mean. For instance, the authors continue, "being queer is not about a right to privacy; it is about the freedom to be public, to just be who we are. It means everyday fighting oppression; homophobia, racism, misogyny, the bigotry of religious hypocrites and our own self-hatred." Evident in this one document are the inherent tensions and dilemmas many queer activists currently encounter: how does one implement in real political struggle a decentered political identity that is not constituted by a process of seemingly reductive "othering"?

The process of ignoring or at least downplaying queers' varying relationships to power is evident not only in the writing of queer activists, but also in the political actions pursued by queer organizations. I question the ability of political actions such as mall invasions (pursued by groups such as the Queer Shopping Network in New York and the Suburban Homosexual Outreach Program [SHOP] in San Francisco), to address the fact that queers exist in different social locations. Lauren Berlant and Elizabeth Freeman describe mall invasion projects as

[an attempt to take] the relatively bounded spectacle of the urban pride parade to the ambient pleasures of the shopping mall. "Mall visibility actions" thus conjoin the spectacular lure of the parade with Hare Krishna-style conversion and proselytizing techniques. Stepping into malls in hair-gelled splendor, holding hands and handing out fliers, the queer auxiliaries produce an "invasion" that conveys a different message. "We're here, we're queer, *you're* going shopping." (210)

The activity of entering or "invading" the shopping mall on the part of queer nationals is clearly one of attempted subversion. Intended by their visible presence in this clearly coded heterosexual family economic mecca is a disruption of the agreed-upon segregation between the allowable spaces for queer "deviant" culture and the rest of the "naturalized" world. Left unchallenged in such an action, however, are the myriad ways, besides the enforcement of normative sexuality, in which some queers feel alienated and excluded from the space of the mall. Where does the mall as an institution of consumer culture and relative economic privilege play into this analysis? How does this action account for the varying economic relationships queers have to consumer culture? If you are a poor or working-class queer the exclusion and alienation you experience when entering the mall may not be limited to the normative sexual codes associated with the mall, but may also be centered on the assumed economic status of those shopping in suburban malls. If you are a queer of color your exclusion from the mall may, in part, be rooted in racial norms and stereotypes which construct you as a threatening subject every time you enter this economic institution. Queer activists must confront a question that haunts most political organizing: How do we put into politics a broad and inclusive left analysis that can actually engage and mobilize individuals with intersecting identities?

Clearly, there will be those critics who will claim that I am asking too much from any political organization. Demands that every aspect of oppression and regulation be addressed in each political act seem, and are indeed, unreasonable. However, I make the critique of queer mall invasions neither to stop such events nor to suggest that every oppression be dealt with by this one political action. Instead, I raise these concerns to emphasize the ways in which varying relation to power exist not only among heterosexuals, but also among those who label themselves queer.

In its current rendition, queer politics is coded with class, gender, and race privilege, and may have lost its potential to be a politically expedient organizing tool for addressing the needs—and mobilizing the bodies—of people of color. As some queer theorists and activists call for the destruction of stable sexual categories, for example, moving instead toward a more fluid understanding of sexual behavior, left unspoken is the class privilege which allows for such fluidity. Class or material privilege is a cornerstone of much of queer politics and theory as they exist today. Queer theorizing which calls for the elimination of fixed categories of sexual identity seems to ignore the ways in which some traditional social identities and communal ties can, in fact, be important to one's survival. Further, a queer politics which demonizes all heterosexuals discounts the relationships—especially those based on shared experiences of marginalization—that exist between gays and straights, particularly in communities of color.

Queers who operate out of a political culture of individualism assume a material independence that allows them to disregard historically or culturally recognized categories and communities or at the very least to move fluidly among them without ever establishing permanent relationships or identities within them. However, I and many other lesbian and gay people of color, as well as poor and working-class lesbians and gay men, do not have such material independence. Because of my multiple identities, which locate me and other "queer" people of color at the margins in this country, my material advancement, my physical protection and my emotional well-being are constantly threatened. In those stable categories and named communities whose histories have been structured by shared resistance to oppression, I find relative degrees of safety and security.

Let me emphasize again that the safety I feel is relative to other threats and is clearly not static or constant. For in those named communities I also find versions of domination and normalization being replicated and employed as more privileged/assimilated marshal group members use their associations with dominant institutions and resources to regulate and police the activities of other marginal group members. Any lesbian, gay, bisexual, or transgendered person of color who has experienced exclusion from indigenous institutions, such as the exclusion many out black gay men have encountered from some black churches responding to AIDS, recognizes that even within marginal groups there are normative rules determining community membership and power (Cohen). However, in spite of the unequal power relationships located in marginal communities, I am still not interested in disassociating politically from those communities, for queerness, as it is currently constructed, offers no viable political alternative, since it invites us to put forth a political agenda that makes invisible the prominence of race, class, and to varying degrees gender in determining the life chances of those on both sides of the hetero/queer divide.

So despite the roots of queer politics in the struggles of "queer" people of color, despite the calls for highlighting categories which have sought to regulate and control black bodies like my own, and despite the attempts at decentralized grassroots activism in some queer political organizations, there still exist—for some, like myself—great misgivings about current constructions of the term "queer." Personally speaking, I do not consider myself a "queer" activist or, for that matter, a "queer" anything. This is not because I do not consider myself an activist; in fact I hold my political work to be one of my most important contributions to all of my communities. But like other lesbian, gay, bisexual, and transgendered activists of color, I find the label "queer" fraught with unspoken assumptions which inhibit the radical political potential of this category.

The alienation, or at least discomfort, many activists and theorists of color have with current conceptions of queerness is evidenced, in part, by the minimal numbers of theorists of color who engage in the process of theorizing about the concept. Further, the sparse numbers of people of color who participate in "queer" political organizations might also be read as a sign of discomfort with the term. Most important, my confidence in making such a claim of distance and uneasiness with the term "queer" on the part of many people of color comes from my interactions with other lesbian, gay, bisexual, and transgendered people of color who repeatedly express their interpretation of "queer" as a term rooted in class, race, and gender privilege. For us, "queer" is a politics based on narrow sexual dichotomies which make no room either for the analysis of oppression of those we might categorize as heterosexual, or for the privilege of those who operate as "queer." As black lesbian activist and writer Barbara Smith argues in "Queer Politics: Where's the Revolution?":

Unlike the early lesbian and gay movement, which had both ideological and practical links to the left, black activism and feminism, today's "queer" politicos seem to operate in a historical and ideological vacuum. "Queer" activists focus on "queer" issues, and racism, sexual oppression and economic exploitation do not

qualify, despite the fact that the majority of "queers" are people of color, female or working class. . . . Building unified, ongoing coalitions that challenge the system and ultimately prepare a way for revolutionary change simply isn't what "queer" activists have in mind. (13–14)

It is this narrow understanding of the idea of queer that negates its use in fundamentally reorienting the politics and privilege of lesbian and gay politics as well as more generally moving or transforming the politics of the left. Despite its liberatory claim to stand in opposition to static categories of oppression, queer politics and much of queer theory seem in fact to be static in the understanding of race, class, and gender and their roles in how heteronormativity regulates sexual behavior and identities. Distinctions between the status and the acceptance of different individuals categorized under the label of "heterosexual" go unexplored.

I emphasize the marginalized position of some who embrace heterosexual identities not because I want to lead any great crusade to understand more fully the plight of "the heterosexual." Rather, I recognize the potential for shared resistance with such individuals. This potential not only for coalitional work but for a shared analysis is especially relevant, from my vantage point, to "queer" people of color. Again, in my call for coalition work across sexual categories, I do not want to suggest that same-sex political struggles have not, independently, played an essential and distinct role in the liberatory politics and social movements of marginal people. My concern, instead, is with any political analysis or theory which collapses our understanding of power into a single continuum of evaluation.

Through a brief review of some of the ways in which nonnormative heterosexuality has been controlled and regulated through the state and systems of marginalization we may be reminded that differentials in power exist within all socially named categories. And through such recognition we may begin to envision a new political formation in which one's relation to dominant power serves as the basis of unity for radical coalition work in the twenty-first century.

HETEROSEXUALS ON THE (OUT)SIDE OF HETERONORMATIVITY

In this section I want to return to the question of a monolithic understanding of heterosexuality. I believe that through this issue we can begin to think critically about the components of a radical politics built not exclusively on identities, but on identities as they are invested with varying degrees of normative power. Thus, fundamental to my concern about the current structure and future agenda of queer politics is the unchallenged assumption of a uniform heteronormativity from which all heterosexuals benefit. I want again to be clear that there are, in fact, some who identify themselves as queer activists who do acknowledge relative degrees of power, and heterosexual access to that power, even evoking the term "straight queers." "Queer means to fuck with gender. There are straight queers, bi queers, tranny queers, lez queers, fag queers, SM queers, fisting queers in every single street in this apathetic country of ours" (anonymous, qtd. McIntosh 31).

Despite such sporadic insight, much of the politics of queer activists has been structured around the dichotomy of straight versus everything else, assuming a monolithic experience of heterosexual privilege for all those identified publicly with heterosexuality. A similar reductive dichotomy between men and women has consistently reemerged in the writing and actions of some feminists. And only through the demands, the actions, and the writing of many "feminists" and/or lesbians of color have those women who stand outside the norm of white, middle-class, legalized heterosexuality begun to see their lives, needs, and bodies represented in feminist theory (Carby; Collins; hooks). In a similar manner lesbian, gay, bisexual, and transgendered people of color have increasingly taken on the responsibility for at the very least complicating and most often challenging reductive notions of heteronormativity articulated by queer activists and scholars (Alexander; Farajaje-Jones; Lorde; Moraga and Anzaldúa; B. Smith).

If we follow such examples, complicating our understanding of both heteronormativity and queerness, we move one step closer to building the progressive coalition politics many of us desire. Specifically, if we pay attention to both historical and current examples of heterosexual relationships which have been prohibited, stigmatized, and generally repressed, we may begin to identify those spaces of shared or similar oppression and resistance that provide a basis for radical coalition work. Further, we may begin to answer certain questions: In narrowly positing a dichotomy of heterosexual privilege and queer oppression under which we all exist, are we negating a basis of political unity that could serve to strengthen many communities

and movements seeking justice and societal transformation? How do we use the relative degrees of ostracization all sexual/cultural "deviants" experience to build a basis of unity for broader coalition and movement work?

A little history (as a political scientist a little history is all I can offer) might be helpful in trying to sort out the various ways heterosexuality, especially as it has intersected with race, has been defined and experienced by different groups of people. It should also help to underscore the fact that many of the roots of heteronormativity are in white supremacist ideologies which sought (and continue) to use the state and its regulation of sexuality, in particular through the institution of heterosexual marriage, to designate which individuals were truly "fit" for full rights and privileges of citizenship. For example, the prohibition of marriages between black women and men imprisoned in the slave system was a component of many slave codes enacted during the seventeenth and eighteenth centuries. M. G. Smith, in his article on the structure of slave economic systems, succinctly states, "As property slaves were prohibited from forming legal relationships or marriages which would interfere with and restrict their owner's property rights" (71–72). Herbert G. Gutman, in *The Black Family in Slavery and Freedom, 1750–1925*, elaborates on the ideology of slave societies which denied the legal sanctioning of marriages between slaves and further reasoned that Blacks had no conception of family.

> The *Nation* identified sexual restraint, civil marriage, and family "stability" with "civilization" itself.
>
> Such mid-nineteenth-century class and sexual beliefs reinforced racial beliefs about Afro-Americans. As slaves, after all, their marriages had not been sanctioned by the civil laws and therefore "the sexual passion" went unrestrained. . . . Many white abolitionists denied the slaves a family life or even, often, a family consciousness because for them [whites] the family had its origins in and had to be upheld by the civil law. (295)

Thus it was not the promotion of marriage or heterosexuality per se that served as the standard or motivation of most slave societies. Instead, marriage and heterosexuality, as viewed through the lenses of profit and domination, and the ideology of white supremacy, were reconfigured to justify the exploitation and regulation of black bodies, even those presumably engaged in heterosexual behavior. It was this system of state-sanctioned, white male, upper-class, heterosexual domination that forced these presumably black *heterosexual* men and women to endure a history of rape, lynching, and other forms of physical and mental terrorism. In this way, marginal group members, lacking power and privilege although engaged in heterosexual behavior, have often found themselves defined as outside the norms and values of dominant society. This position has most often resulted in the suppression or negation of their legal, social, and physical relationships and rights.

In addition to the prohibition of marriage between slaves, A. Leon Higginbotham, Jr., in *The Matter* of *Color—Race and the American Legal Process: The Colonial Period,* writes of the legal restrictions barring interracial marriages. He reminds us that the essential core of the American legal tradition was the preservation of the white race. The "mixing" of the races was to be strictly prohibited in early colonial laws. The regulation of interracial heterosexual relationships, however, should not be understood as exclusively relegated to the seventeenth, eighteenth and nineteenth centuries. In fact, Higginbotham informs us that the final law prohibiting miscegenation (the "interbreeding" or marrying of individuals from different "races"—actually meant to inhibit the "tainting" of the white race) was not repealed until 1967:

Colonial anxiety about interracial sexual activity cannot be attributed solely to seventeenth-century values, for it was not until 1967 that the United States Supreme Court finally declared unconstitutional those statutes prohibiting interracial marriages. The Supreme Court waited thirteen years after its *Brown* decision dealing with desegregation of schools before, in *Loving v. Virginia,* it agreed to consider the issue of interracial marriages. (41)

It is this pattern of regulating the behavior and denigrating the identities of those heterosexuals on the outside of heteronormative privilege, in particular those perceived as threatening systems of white supremacy, male domination, and capitalist advancement, that I want to highlight. An understanding of the ways in which heteronormativity works to support and reinforce institutional racism, patriarchy, and class exploitation must therefore be a part of how we problematize current constructions of heterosexuality. As I stated previously, I am not suggesting that those

involved in publicly identifiable heterosexual behavior do not receive political, economic, and social advantage, especially in comparison to the experiences of some lesbian, transgendered, gay, and bisexual individuals. But the equation linking identity and behavior to power is not as linear and clear as some queer theorists and activists would have us believe.

A more recent example of regulated nonnormative heterosexuality is located in current debates and rhetoric regarding the "underclass" and the destruction of the welfare system. The stigmatization and demonization of single mothers, teen mothers, and, primarily, poor women of color dependent on state assistance has had a long and suspicious presence in American "intellectual" and political history. It was in 1965 that Daniel Patrick Moynihan released his "study" entitled *The Negro Family: The Case for National Action.* In this report, which would eventually come to be known as the Moynihan Report, the author points to the "pathologies" increasingly evident in so-called Negro families. In this document were allegations of the destructive nature of Negro family formations. The document's introduction argues that

the fundamental problem, in which this is most clearly the case, is that of family structure. The evidence—not final, but powerfully persuasive—is that the Negro family in urban ghettos is crumbling. A middle-class group has managed to save itself, but for vast numbers of the unskilled, poorly educated city working class the fabric of conventional social relationships has all but disintegrated.

Moynihan, later in the document, goes on to describe the crisis and pathologies facing Negro family structure as being generated by the increasing number of single-female-headed households, the increasing number of "illegitimate" births and, of course, increasing welfare dependency:

In essence, the Negro community has been forced into a matriarchal structure which, because it is so out of line with the rest of the American society, seriously retards the progress of the group as a whole, and imposes a crushing burden on the Negro male and, in consequence, on a great many Negro women as well. . . . In a word, most Negro youth are in danger of being caught up in the tangle of pathology that affects their world, and probably a majority are so entrapped. . . . Obviously, not every instance of social pathology afflicting the Negro community can be traced to the weakness of family structure. . . . Nonetheless, at the center of the tangle of pathology is the weakness of the family structure. (29–30)

It is not the nonheterosexist behavior of these black men and women that is under fire, but rather the perceived nonnormative sexual behavior and family structures of these individuals, whom many queer activists—without regard to the impact of race, class, or gender—would designate as part of the heterosexist establishment or those mighty "straights they hate."

Over the last thirty years the demonization of poor women, engaged in nonnormative heterosexual relationships, has continued under the auspices of scholarship on the "underclass." Adolph L. Reed, in "The 'Underclass' as Myth and Symbol: The Poverty of Discourse About Poverty," discusses the gendered and racist nature of much of this literature, in which poor, often black and Latina women are portrayed as unable to control their sexual impulses and eventual reproductive decisions, unable to raise their children with the right moral fiber, unable to find "gainful" employment to support themselves and their "illegitimate children," and of course unable to manage "effectively" the minimal assistance provided by the state. Reed writes:

> The underclass notion may receive the greatest ideological boost from its gendered imagery and relation to gender politics. As I noted in a critique of Wilson's *The Truly Disadvantaged*, "family" is an intrinsically ideological category. The rhetoric of "disorganization," "disintegration," "deterioration" reifies one type of living arrangement—the ideal type of the bourgeois nuclear family—as outside history, nearly as though it were decreed by natural law. But—as I asked earlier—why exactly is out-of-wedlock birth pathological? Why is the female-headed household an indicator of disorganization and pathology? Does that stigma attach to *all* such households—even, say, a divorced executive who is a custodial mother? If not, what are the criteria for assigning it? The short answer is race and class bias inflected through a distinctively gendered view of the world. (33–34)

In this same discourse of the "underclass," young black men engaged in "reckless" heterosexual behavior are represented as irresponsible baby factories, unable to control or restrain their "sexual passion"

(to borrow a term from the seventeenth century). And unfortunately, often it has been the work of professed liberals like William Julius Wilson, in his book *The Truly Disadvantaged,* that, while not using the word "pathologies," has substantiated in its own tentative way the conservative dichotomy between the deserving working poor and the lazy, Cadillac-driving, steak-eating welfare queens of Ronald Reagan's imagination. Again, I raise this point to remind us of the numerous ways that sexuality and sexual deviance from a prescribed norm have been used to demonize and to oppress various segments of the population, even some classified under the label "heterosexual."

The policies of politicians and the actions of law enforcement officials have reinforced, in much more devastating ways, the distinctions between acceptable forms of heterosexual expression and those to be regulated—increasingly through incarceration. This move toward the disallowance of some forms of heterosexual expression and reproductive choice can be seen in the practice of prosecuting pregnant women suspected of using drugs—nearly 80 percent of all women prosecuted are women of color; through the forced sterilization of Puerto Rican and Native American women; and through the state-dictated use of Norplant by women answering to the criminal justice system and by women receiving state assistance.[6] Further, it is the "nonnormative" children of many of these nonnormative women that Newt Gingrich would place in orphanages. This is the same Newt Gingrich who, despite his clear disdain for gay and lesbian "lifestyles," has invited lesbians and gay men into the Republican party. I need not remind you that he made no such offer to the women on welfare discussed above. Who, we might ask, is truly on the outside of heteronormative power—maybe *most* of us?

CONCLUSION: DESTABILIZATION AND RADICAL COALITION WORK

While all this may, in fact, seem interesting or troubling or both, you may be wondering: What does it have to do with the question of the future of queer politics? It is my argument, as I stated earlier, that one of the great failings of queer theory and especially queer politics has been their inability to incorporate into analysis of the world and strategies for political mobilization the roles that race, class, and gender play in defining people's differing relations to dominant and normalizing power. I present this essay as the beginning of a much longer and protracted struggle to acknowledge and delineate the distribution of power within and outside of queer communities. This is a discussion of how to build a politics organized not merely by reductive categories of straight and queer, but organized instead around a more intersectional analysis of who and what the enemy is and where our potential allies can be found. This analysis seeks to make clear the privilege and power embedded in the categorizations of, on the one hand, an upstanding, "morally correct," white, state-authorized, middle-class, male *heterosexual,* and on the other, a culturally deficient, materially bankrupt, state-dependent, *heterosexual* woman of color, the latter found most often in our urban centers (those that haven't been gentrified), on magazine covers, and on the evening news.

I contend, therefore, that the radical potential of queer politics, or any liberatory movement, rests on its ability to advance strategically oriented political identities arising from a more nuanced understanding of power. One of the most difficult tasks in such an endeavor (and there are many) is not to forsake the complexities of both how power is structured and how we might think about the coalitions we create. Far too often movements revert to a position in which membership and joint political work are based upon a necessarily similar history of oppression—but this is too much like identity politics (Phelan). Instead, I am suggesting that the process of movement building be rooted not in our shared history or identity, but in our shared marginal relationship to dominant power which normalizes, legitimizes, and privileges.

We must, therefore, start our political work from the recognition that multiple systems of oppression are in operation and that these systems use institutionalized categories and identities to regulate and socialize. We must also understand that power and access to dominant resources are distributed across the boundaries of "het" and "queer" that we construct. A model of queer politics that simply pits the grand "heterosexuals" against all those oppressed "queers" is ineffectual as the basis for action in a political environment dominated by Newt Gingrich, the Christian Right, and the recurring ideology of white supremacy. As we stand on the verge of watching those in power dismantle the welfare system through a process of demonizing poor and young, primarily poor and young women of color—many of whom have existed for their entire

lives outside the white, middle-class, heterosexual norm—we have to ask if these women do not fit into society's categories of marginal, deviant, and "queer." As we watch the explosion of prison construction and the disproportionate incarceration rates of young men and women of color, often as part of the economic development of poor white rural communities, we have to ask if these individuals do not fit society's definition of "queer" and expendable.

I am not proposing a political strategy that homogenizes and glorifies the experience of poor heterosexual people of color. In fact, in calling for a more expansive left political identity and formation I do not seek to erase the specific historical relation between the stigma of "queer" and the sexual activity of gay men, lesbians, bisexual, and transgendered individuals. And in no way do I mean to, or want to, equate the experiences of marginal heterosexual women and men to the lived experiences of queers. There is no doubt that heterosexuality, even for those heterosexuals who stand outside the norms of heteronormativity, results in some form of privilege and feelings of supremacy. I need only recount the times when other women of color, more economically vulnerable than myself, expressed superiority and some feelings of disgust when they realized that the nice young professor (me) was "that way."

However, in recognizing the distinct history of oppression lesbian, gay, bisexual, and transgendered people have confronted and challenged, I am not willing to embrace every queer as my marginalized political ally. In the same way, I do not assume that shared racial, gender, and/or class position or identity guarantees or produces similar political commitments. Thus, identities and communities, while important to this strategy, must be complicated and destabilized through a recognition of the multiple social positions and relations to dominant power found *within* any one category or identity. Kimberlé Crenshaw, in "Mapping the Margins: Intersectionality, Identity Politics, and Violence Against Women of Color," suggests that such a project use the idea of intersectionality to reconceptualize or problematize the identities and communities that are "home" to us. She demands that we challenge those identities that seem like home by acknowledging the other parts of our identities that are excluded:

With identity thus reconceptualized [through a recognition of intersectionality], it may be easier to understand the need to summon up the courage to challenge groups that are after all, in one sense, "home" to us, in the name of the parts of us that are not made at home. . . . The most one could expect is that we will dare to speak against internal exclusions and marginalizations, that we might call attention to how the identity of "the group" has been centered on the intersectional identities of a few. . . . Through an awareness of intersectionality, we can better acknowledge and ground the differences among us and negotiate the means by which these differences will find expression in constructing group politics. (1299)

In the same ways that we account for the varying privilege to be gained by a heterosexual identity, we must also pay attention to the privilege some queers receive from being white, male, and upper class. Only through recognizing the many manifestations of power, across and within categories, can we truly begin to build a movement based on one's politics and not exclusively on one's identity.

I want to be clear that what I and others are calling for is the destabilization, and not the destruction or abandonment, of identity categories.[7] We must reject a queer politics which seems to ignore, in its analysis of the usefulness of traditionally named categories, the roles of identity and community as paths to survival, using shared experiences of oppression and resistance to build indigenous resources, shape consciousness, and act collectively. Instead, I would suggest that it is the multiplicity and interconnectedness of our identities which provide the most promising avenue for the *destabilization and radical politicalization* of these same categories.

This is not an easy path to pursue because most often this will mean building a political analysis and political strategies around the most marginal in our society, some of whom look like us, many of whom do not. Most often, this will mean rooting our struggle in, and addressing the needs of, communities of color. Most often this will mean highlighting the intersectionality of one's race, class, gender, and sexuality and the relative power and privilege that one receives from being a man and/or being white and/or being middle class and/or being heterosexual. This, in particular, is a daunting challenge because so much of our political consciousness has been built around simple dichotomies such as powerful/powerless; oppressor/victim; enemy/comrade. It is difficult to feel safe and secure in those spaces where both your relative privilege and your experiences with marginalization are understood to shape your commitment to radical politics. How-

ever, as Bernice Johnson Reagon so aptly put it in her essay, "Coalition Politics: Turning the Century," "if you feel the strain, you may be doing some good work" (362).

And while this is a daunting challenge and uncomfortable position, those who have taken it up have not only survived, but succeeded in their efforts. For example, both the needle exchange and prison projects pursued through the auspices of ACT UP New York point to the possibilities and difficulties involved in principled transformative coalition work. In each project individuals from numerous identities—heterosexual, gay, poor, wealthy, white, black, Latino—came together to challenge dominant constructions of who should be allowed and who deserved care. No particular identity exclusively determined the shared political commitments of these activists; instead their similar positions, as marginalized subjects relative to the state—made clear through the government's lack of response to AIDS—formed the basis of this political unity.

In the prison project, it was the contention of activists that the government which denied even wealthy gay men access to drugs to combat this disease must be regarded as the same source of power that denied incarcerated men and women access to basic health care, including those drugs and conditions needed to combat HIV and AIDS. The coalition work this group engaged in involved a range of people, from formerly incarcerated individuals, to heterosexual men and women of color, to those we might deem privileged white lesbians and gay men. And this same group of people who came together to protest the conditions of incarcerated people with AIDS also showed up to public events challenging the homophobia that guided the government's and biomedical industries' response to this epidemic. The political work of this group of individuals was undoubtedly informed by the public identities they embraced, but these were identities that they further acknowledged as complicated by intersectionality and placed within a political framework where their shared experience as marginal, nonnormative subjects could be foregrounded. Douglas Crimp, in his article "Right On, Girlfriend!" suggests that through political work our identities become remade and must therefore be understood as *relational*. Describing such a transformation in the identities of queer activists engaged in, and prosecuted for, needle exchange work, Crimp writes:

> But once engaged in the struggle to end the crisis, these queers' identities were no longer the same. It's not that

"queer" doesn't any longer encompass their sexual practices; it does, but it also entails a *relation* between those practices and other circumstances that make very different people vulnerable both to HIV infection and to the stigma, discrimination, and neglect that have characterized the societal and governmental response to the constituencies most affected by the AIDS epidemic. (317–18)

The radical potential of those of us on the outside of heteronormativity rests in our understanding that we need not base our politics in the dissolution of all categories and communities, but we need instead to work toward the destabilization and remaking of our identities. Difference, in and of itself—even that difference designated through named categories—is not the problem. Instead it is the power invested in certain identity categories and the idea that bounded categories are not to be transgressed that serve as the basis of domination and control. The reconceptualization not only of the content of identity categories, but the intersectional nature of identities themselves, must become part of our political practice.

We must thus begin to link our intersectional analysis of power with concrete coalitional work. In real terms this means identifying political struggles such as the needle exchange and prison projects of ACT UP that transgress the boundaries of identity to highlight, in this case, both the repressive power of the state and the normalizing power evident within both dominant and marginal communities. This type of principled coalition work is also being pursued in a more modest fashion by the Policy Institute of the National Gay and Lesbian Task Force. Recently, the staff at the Task Force distributed position papers not only on the topics of gay marriages and gays in the military, but also on right-wing attacks against welfare and affirmative action. Here we have political work based in the knowledge that the rhetoric and accusations of nonnormativity that Newt Gingrich and other right-wingers launch against women on welfare closely resemble the attacks of nonnormativity mounted against gays, lesbians, bisexuals, and transgendered individuals. Again it is the marginalized relation to power, experienced by both of these groups—and I do not mean to suggest that the groups are mutually exclusive—that frames the possibility for transformative coalition work. This prospect diminishes when we do not recognize and deal with the reality that the intersecting identities that gay people embody—in terms of race, class, and gender privilege—put some of us on Gingrich's side of the welfare struggle (e.g., Log Cabin Republicans). And in a similar manner a woman's dependence on state financial assistance in no way secures her position as one supportive of gay rights and/or liberation. While a marginal identity undoubtedly increases the prospects of shared consciousness, only an articulation and commitment to mutual support can truly be the test of unity when pursuing transformational politics.

Finally, I realize that I have been short on specifics when trying to describe how we move concretely toward a transformational coalition politics among marginalized subjects. The best I can do is offer this discussion as a starting point for reassessing the shape of queer/lesbian/gay/bisexual/transgendered politics as we approach the twenty-first century. A reconceptualization of the politics of marginal groups allows us not only to privilege the specific lived experience of distinct communities, but also to search for those interconnected sites of resistance from which we can wage broader political struggles. Only by recognizing the link *between* the ideological, social, political, and economic marginalization of punks, bulldaggers, and welfare queens can we begin to develop political analyses and political strategies effective in confronting the linked yet varied sites of power in this country. Such a project is important because it provides a framework from which the difficult work of coalition politics can begin. And it is in these complicated and contradictory spaces that the liberatory and left politics that so many of us work for is located.

ACKNOWLEDGMENTS

The author would like to thank Mark Blasius, Nan Boyd, Ed Cohen, Carolyn Dinshaw, Jeff Edwards, Licia Fiol-Matta, Joshua Gamson, Lynne Huffer, Tamara Jones, Carla Kaplan, Ntanya Lee, Ira Livingston, and Barbara Ransby for their comments on various versions of this paper. All shortcomings are of course the fault of the author.

NOTES

1. The very general chronology of queer theory and queer politics referred to throughout this article is not meant to write the definitive historical development of each phenomenon. Instead, the dates are used to provide the reader with a general frame of reference. See Epstein for a similar genealogy of queer theory and queer politics.

2. See Ingraham for a discussion of the heterogendered imaginary.

3. I want to be clear that in this essay I am including the destruction of sexual categories as part of the agenda of queer politics. While a substantial segment of queer activists and theorists call for the *destabilization* of sexual categories, there are also those self-avowed queers who embrace a politics built around the *deconstruction* and/or elimination of sexual categories. For example, a number of my self-identified queer students engage in sexual behavior that most people would interpret as *transgressive* of sexual identities and categories. However, these students have repeatedly articulated a different interpretation of their sexual behavior. They put forth an understanding that does not highlight their transgression of categories, but one which instead represents them as individuals who operate outside of categories and sexual identities altogether. They are sexual beings, given purely to desire, truly living sexual fluidity, and not constrained by any form of sexual categorization or identification. This interpretation seems at least one step removed from that held by people who embrace the fluidity of sexuality while still recognizing the political usefulness of categories or labels for certain sexual behavior and communities. One example of such people might be those women who identify as lesbians and who also acknowledge that sometimes they choose to sleep with men. These individuals exemplify the process of destabilization that I try to articulate within this essay. Even further removed from the queers who would do away with all sexual categories are those who also transgress what many consider to be categories of sexual behaviors while they publicly embrace one stable sexual identity (for example, those self-identified heterosexual men who sleep with other men sporadically and secretly).

4. I want to thank Mark Blasius for raising the argument that standing on the outside of heteronormativity is a bit of a misnomer, since as a dominant normalizing process it is a practice of regulation in which we are all implicated. However, despite this insight I will on occasion continue to use this phrasing, understanding the limits of its meaning.

5. See Hennessy for a discussion of left analysis and the limits of queer theory.

6. For an insightful discussion of the numerous methods used to regulate and control the sexual and reproductive choices of women, see Shende.

7. See Jones for an articulation of differences between the destabilization and the destruction of identity categories.

REFERENCES

Alexander, Jacqui. "Redrafting Morality: The Postcolonial State and the Sexual Offences Bill of Trinidad and Tobago." *Third World Women and the Politics of Feminism*, ed. C. T. Mohanty, A. Russo, and L. Torres. Bloomington: Indiana UP, 1991. 133–52.

Berlant, Lauren, and Elizabeth Freeman. "Queer Nationality." Warner 193–229.

Bérubé, Allan, and Jeffrey Escoffier "Queer/Nation." *Out/Look: National Lesbian and Gay Quarterly* II (Winter 1991): 12–14.

Blasius, Mark. *Gay and Lesbian Politics: Sexuality and the Emergence of a New Ethic*. Philadelphia: Temple UP, 1994.

Butler, Judith. *Gender Trouble*. New York Routledge, 1990.

Carby, Hazel. *Reconstructing Womanhood: The Emergence of the Afro-American Woman Novelist*. New York: Oxford UP, 1987.

Clarke, Cheryl. "The Failure to Transform: Homophobia in the Black Community." Smith, *Home Girls* 197–208.

Cohen, Cathy J. "Contested Membership: Black Gay Identities and the Politics of AIDS." *Queer Theory/Sociology*, ed. S. Seidman. Oxford: Blackwell, 1996. 362–94.

Collins, Patricia Hill. *Black Feminist Thought: Knowledge, Consciousness, and the Politics of Sociology Empowerment*. New York: Harper, 1990.

Combahee River Collective. "The Combahee River Collective Statement." Smith, *Home Girls* 272–82.

Crenshaw, Kimberle. "Mapping the Margins: Intersectionality, Identity Politics, and Violence Against Women of Color." *Stanford Law Review* 43 (1991): 1241–99.

Crimp, Douglas. "Right On, Girlfriend!" Warner 300–20.

Davis, Angela Y. *Women, Race and Class*. New York Vintage, 1983.

de Lauretis, Teresa. "Queer Theory: Lesbian and Gay Sexualities." *Differences* 3.2 (Summer 1991): iii–xviii.

Dunlap, David W. "Three Black Members Quit AIDS Organization Board." *New York Times* 11 Jan. 1996: B2.

Dyson, Michael Eric. *Between God and Gangsta Rap*. New York: Oxford UP, 1996.

Epstein, Steven. "A Queer Encounter: Sociology and the Study of Sexuality." *Sociological Theory* 12 (1994): 188–202.

Farajaje-Jones, Elias. "Ain't I a Queer." Creating Change Conference, National Gay and Lesbian Task Force, Detroit, Michigan, 8–12 Nov. 1995.

Fuss, Diana, ed. *Inside/Outside*. New York: Routledge, 1991.

Gamson, Joshua. "Must Identity Movements Self-Destruct? A Queer Dilemma." *Social Problems* 42 (1995): 390–407.

Gutman, Herbert G. *The Black Family in Slavery and Freedom, 1750–1925*. New York: Vintage, 1976.

Hennessy, Rosemary. "Queer Theory, Left Politics," *Rethinking MARXISM* 7.3 (1994): 85–111.

Higginbotham, A. Leon, Jr. *In the Matter of Color—Race and the American Legal Process: The Colonial Period.* New York: Oxford UP, 1978.

hooks, bell. *Feminist Theory: From Margin to Center.* Boston: South End, 1984.

Ingraham, Chrys. "The Heterosexual Imaginary: Feminist Sociology and Theories of Gender." *Sociological Theory* 12 (1994): 203–19.

Jones, Tamara. "Inside the Kaleidoscope: How the Construction of Black Gay and Lesbian Identities Inform Political Strategies." Unpublished. Yale University, 1995.

Lorde, Audre. *Sister Outsider: Essays and Speeches by Audre Lorde.* New York: The Crossing P. 1984.

McIntosh, Mary. "Queer Theory and the War of the Sexes." *Activating Theory: Lesbian, Gay, Bisexual Politics,* ed. J. Bristow and A. R. Wilson. London: Lawrence and Wishart, 1993. 33–52.

Moraga, Cherríe, and Gloria Anzaldúa, eds. *This Bridge Called My Back: Writings by Radical Women of Color.* New York: Kitchen Table/Women of Color, 1981.

Morton, Donald. "The Politics of Queer Theory in the (Post) Modern Moment," *Genders* 17 (Fall 1993): 121–15.

Moynihan, Daniel Patrick. *The Negro Family: The Case for National Action.* Washington D.C.: Office of Policy Planning and Research, U.S. Department of Labor, 1965.

Phelan, Shane. *Identity Politics: Lesbian Feminism and the Limits of Community.* Philadelphia: Temple UP, 1989.

Podolsky, Robin. "Sacrificing Queer and other 'Proletarian' Artifacts." *Radical America* 25.1 (January 1991): 53–60.

Queer Nation. "I Hate Straights" manifesto. New York, 1990.

Queers United Against Straight-Acting Homosexuals. "Assimilation Is Killing Us: Fight for a Queer United Front." WHY I HATED THE MARCH ON WASHINGTON (1993): 4.

Ransby, Barbara, and Tracye Matthews. "Black Popular Culture and the Transcendence of Patriarchical Illusions." *Race & Class* 35.1 (July–September 1993): 57–70.

Reagon, Bernice Johnson. "Coalition Politics: Turning the Century." Smith, *Home Girls* 356–68.

Reed, Adolph L., Jr. "The 'Underclass' as Myth and Symbol: The Poverty of Discourse About Poverty." *Radical America* 24.1 (January 1990): 21–40.

Rich, Adrienne. "Compulsory Heterosexuality and Lesbian Existence." *Powers of Desire: The Politics of Sexuality,* ed. A. Snitow, C. Stansell and S. Thompson. New York: Monthly Review, 1983. 177–206.

Sedgwick, Eve. *The Epistemology of the Closet.* Berkeley: U of California P, 1990.

Seidman, Steven. "Identity and Politics in a 'Postmodern' Gay Culture." Warner 105–42.

Shende, Suzanne. "Fighting the Violence Against Our Sisters: Prosecution of Pregnant Women and the Coercive Use of Norplant." *Women Transforming Politics: An Alternative Reader,* ed. C. Cohen, K. Jones, and J. Tronto, New York: New York UP, 1997.

Smith, Barbara. "Queer Politics: Where's the Revolution?" *The Nation* 257.1 (July 5, 1993): 12–16.

——, ed. *Home Girls: A Black Feminist Anthology.* New York: Kitchen Table/Women of Color, 1983.

Smith, M. G. "Social Structure in the British Caribbean About 1820." *Social and Economic Studies* 1.4 (August 1953): 55–79.

"Statement of Purpose." Dialogue on the Lesbian and Gay Left. Duncan Conference Center in Del Ray Beach, Florida. 1–4 April 1993.

Stein, Arlene, and Ken Plummer. "'I Can't Even Think Straight': 'Queer' Theory and the Missing Sexual Revolution in Sociology." *Sociological Theory* 12 (1994): 178–87.

Vaid, Urvashi. *Virtual Equality: The Mainstreaming of Gay & Lesbian Liberation.* New York: Anchor, 1995.

Warner, Michael, ed. *Fear of a Queer Planet: Queer Politics and Social Theory.* Minneapolis: U of Minnesota P, 1993.

West, Cornel. *Race Matters.* Boston: Beacon, 1993.

Wilson, William Julius. *The Truly Disadvantaged: The Inner City, the Underclass, and Public Policy.* Chicago: U of Chicago P, 1987.

Moya Bailey
Alexis Pauline Gumbs

We Are the Ones We've Been Waiting For: Young Black Feminists Take Their Research and Activism Online

First published in 2010

For black feminists in the U.S., it has always been uncertain whether and how our words will survive. Who would have thought that the line "We are the ones we've been waiting for," from June Jordan's 1980 "Poem for South African Women," would have ended up in a speech by a successful presidential candidate—Barack Obama—and then dispersed, unattributed, on countless mugs, T-shirts, key chains and posters? Who would have thought that classic literary devices such as dramatic irony, used by enslaved eighteenth century poet Phillis Wheatley to ensure her words would be published despite unspeakable odds, would be the same devices that convinced Black literary critics her work was "not black enough" for more than a century?

When Black feminism's words do live on, it is not by accident, default or simple popularity: It is often because Black feminists scraped coins together to publish them, as when Black women's social clubs raised the funds for Ida B. Wells to put out her 1890s anti-lynching and anti-rape pamphlets. Similarly, nearly a century later, in the late 1980s, Barbara Smith risked bankruptcy to continue funding Kitchen Table, an autonomous press for writing by women of color.

We—the 1980s babies who authored this article—treasure this grassroots legacy, while knowing that Black feminism still lives on unstable ground. So from these roots, a new(er) generation of Black feminist voices coming out of academia are using free and direct means of publication—the Internet and its social media—to spread our visions and provoke an ongoing dialogue.

The Black feminist blogosphere that we are connected to includes more than 100 sites. To name just a couple created by Black feminist Ph.D. students at the University of Maryland, there are women's studies student Renina Jarmon's blog Model Minority: Thugs + Feminists + Boom Bap, which takes Black feminist theory to the streets, and Jessica M. Johnson's blog African Diaspora, Ph.D., which "honors the activists, artists, teachers, researchers, librarians, bloggers and others who bring depth to our work."

These sites defy the voices of cynics who have lamented since before we were born that when Black feminism moved into the academy it moved away from its activist roots. We know that the work of Black feminist critical practice has never been contained within the walls of universities, and has consistently lived in popular media outlets, including pamphlets, stickers and open letters. Thus, we work with interactive modes of inquiry that challenge the ownership of knowledge within the university.

For instance, we're involved with Eternal Summer of the Black Feminist Mind, a blog that hosts a series of virtual and in-person "potlucks" that brings together participants from Durham, N.C., to Washington, D.C., and from Chicago to Nairobi, Kenya, to discuss Black feminist theory. In this way, we can take the research we've gained on the university's dime and use it to fortify and inform popular conversations based in activist communities.

Then there's the blog FireWalkers, a list-serv-linked network of African Diaspora women who do feminist activism and research both within and outside of the academy. Taking our name from Beverly Guy-Sheftall's *Words of Fire*, we cross the artificial line between the politics of Black liberation and women's liberation, sometimes catching fire from both sides yet continuing to move forward with purpose. With our scholarship we hope to evolve the conversations in the Black and feminist communities into a more holistic understanding of each other.

Our websites also challenge the dominance of mainstream publishing. For instance, when the mainstream media gave little attention to a series of violent acts against Black women in the fall of 2007, Black feminist University of Chicago graduate student Fallon Wilson and activist Izetta Mobley used the Web to launch the Be Bold Be Red Be Brave: Ending Violence Against Women of Color campaign. Students, faculty, community organizers and other concerned individuals nationwide posted photos of rallies and vigils in which they wore red to protest a media that seemed only able to see racist and gendered violence as separate issues, not linked, and occurring only one sensationalist moment at a time. The site quotes Audre Lorde's words, "When we speak we are afraid our words will not be heard or welcomed. But when we are silent, we are still afraid. So it is better to speak."

Another important aspect of these networking endeavors is the social— long a key part of Black feminist movements. Black feminists have created alternative rituals and understandings of beauty, love, friendship, celebration and mourning as a way to critique, reject and replace dominant norms. We're inspired by the 1977 statement by the Combahee River Collective, a Black feminist socialist collective in the Boston area, which wrote about how valuable it was to have "found each other."

So we, Alexis and Moya, decided to create a social network called Quirky Black Girls, which allows a diverse group of self-identified QBGs to post our own videos, music and imagery, all the while building bravery and challenging each other's thinking. We maintain a blog, a site on social networking service Ning, a Facebook group and a Black speculative fiction reading group, and we organize regular in-person arcade nights, jam sessions, cookouts and more. We put the network in an explicitly Black feminist frame by reflecting weekly with the group on specific quotes from the

Combahee River Collective Statement and Audre Lorde's journals.

The two of us have found that our Web activism carries into our very relationships and the way we speak. When the Black women's blogosphere grieved over the brutal multiple rape of a 20-year-old who was in her apartment and went unaided by neighbors who listened for four hours, we communicated through listservs and blogs to create action plans in our neighborhoods. We discussed our desire for responses that didn't involve the police and instead affirmed our faith in each other. Many ideas were spawned, including baking cupcakes in our apartment buildings and sharing them with fellow renters in order to dissolve the culture of anonymity and ambivalence an apartment complex can create.

In another action, after noticing the absence of children and their parents from activist events, Black feminists—along with other folks of color and white allies—felt the need to create child-care collectives. Online tools like Google groups and riseup.net helped us create a network of volunteers to provide this child care.

And finally, out of our desire to see, hear and feel Black women artists who create work that resonates in our souls, we are using Google Wave technology to plan a Quirky Black Girl Festival for 2012. The power of connecting people who might otherwise feel isolated and alone, but for that song that gets them through the day or tha!t painting that rejuvenates the spirit, is a magic that the Internet seems born to do.

Our projects to create online and in-person spaces for Black feminist conversation honor and supplement the rich tapestry of Black feminism that has come before us. We are the new thread connecting patches in a well-worn quilt, both tactile and virtual. We believe that our ancestors knew we were coming, and that our elders, communities, students and future comrades have demands on us that require a fully interactive frame. We are the ones we've been waiting for.

Transform The World: What You Can Do with a Degree in Women's Studies

First published in 2007

A. Become the first woman president of Harvard University
B. Win a Rhodes Scholarship to study sexual civil rights
C. Advocate for domestic-violence survivors while starring on TV's *Survivor*
D. Teach the next generation
E. All of the above, and more

It's a typical question from parents, fellow students and even faculty: What can you do with your college degree? In an era of conservative impediments to progressive liberal arts education, a field such as women's studies seems a particularly common target for that query.

Recently, we have had at least one excellent role model to point to: Drew Gilpin Faust, the first woman president of Harvard. She may have earned her Ph.D. in American civilization, but she was formerly chair of the women's studies program at the University of Pennsylvania and founding dean of the Radcliffe Institute for Advanced Study. Under her leadership, Radcliffe—Harvard's former women's college—has become an interdisciplinary research center supporting "transformative works," with a special commitment to studying women, gender and society. In a similar fashion, many women's studies majors tend to intermix their fields of concentration in order to craft distinctive careers aimed at transforming our world.

How many women's studies grads are we talking about? According to the National Center for Education Statistics, in the 2003–2004 academic year U.S. institutions of higher education granted 1,024 bachelor's degrees, 135 master's degrees and five doctoral degrees

in women's studies. These statistics, however, are suspect, given that the National Women's Studies Association (NWSA) has documented 750 active undergraduate and graduate women's studies programs in U.S. colleges and universities.

"It is very difficult to get a picture of women's studies as a field," says Allison Kimmich, executive director of the NWSA and a Ph.D. in women's studies from Emory University, "particularly the number of graduates now out in the workforce and the kinds of career paths those graduates have taken. Women's studies has not historically collected that data on itself." A clearer picture of women's studies programs should begin to emerge, however, as NWSA has embarked on a Ford Foundation–funded project to map women's and gender studies in the U.S. In the future, the association hopes to collect data on graduates' career paths.

Earlier studies of women's studies graduates, such as that by Barbara F. Luebke and Mary Ellen Reilly in their 1995 book *Women's Studies Graduates: The First Generation* (Teachers College Press), were similarly concerned with documenting the value of such degrees. They found that the fact that women's studies majors and graduates were persistently asked what could be done with their degrees reflected a continuing ignorance about women's studies as an academic discipline. In their study, Luebke and Reilly were also able to document a unique set of skills learned through women's studies programs: empowerment, self-confidence, critical thinking, building community, and understanding differences and intersections among racism, homophobia, sexism, classism, ableism, anti-Semitism and other types of oppression.

Moya Bailey, a B.A. in comparative women's studies at Spelman College (the first historically black U.S. college to offer a women's studies major) and now a Ph.D. student in women's studies at Emory University, has already been able to use some of her women's studies skills in community action. While at Spelman, Bailey participated in "The Nelly Protest," a nationally publicized demonstration against misogyny in hip-hop music and videos.

That and other protest actions were so meaningful to her that, as a doctoral student at Emory, she has studied how "intentional communities"—like the nurturing spaces often created by women's studies programs—assist marginalized groups to develop much-needed critical and political perspectives. Within 10 years, she hopes to be teaching women's studies at a historically black college or university, "adding gender, class and sexuality as important pieces of the conversation within an African American community context."

Similarly, Harvard undergraduate Ryan Thoreson hopes to develop a career focused on the intersection of multiple concerns. As a dual major in government and women/gender/sexuality studies, Thoreson believes that women's studies will enrich his planned practice of international sexual civil-rights law. "In my government courses I learned about political theory, but I found the political theory I learned in my women's studies curriculum to be much more broadly applicable," says Thoreson, a Rhodes Scholarship winner. "If I had only majored in government, I would not come to legal and policy questions as thoughtfully, wanting to understand the social and cultural context of groups affected by the law."

Maria Bevacqua, associate professor and chair of the Department of Women's Studies at Minnesota State University, Mankato, believes that women's studies has carved out a niche in the area of applied theory and practice. Like many programs, Mankato's women's studies curriculum includes internships in feminist organizations and collective action projects for course credit. Bevacqua—who has her own women's studies Ph.D. from Emory—has seen her program's graduates do everything from working in human service agencies to opening feminist businesses. Moreover, women's studies graduates act as "ambassadors of feminism, bringing the women's studies perspective into the rest of the world."

Beverly Guy-Sheftall, founding director of the Women's Research and Resource Center and professor of women's studies at Spelman, has increasingly seen students' take women's studies into the public sphere. "In the early years, women's studies graduates tended to work on gender-specific issues, getting jobs in battered-women's shelters and rape crisis centers," she says. "But more and more we have students going into public health, international policy, journalism, electoral politics, filmmaking, K–12 education and other careers that allow them to effect large-scale change."

Guy-Sheftall has also seen students increasingly desire to be public intellectuals and media producers, so much so that Spelman has incorporated digital media production into its women's studies curriculum. "I think we are going to see many more women's studies graduates going into film and television, and many of our students already produce documentaries—even if they choose to do something else as a career."

Deborah Siegel, author of the 2007 book *Sisterhood, Interrupted: From Radical Women to Grrls Gone Wild* (Palgrave Macmillan), has noticed the same thing. She observes that in the 1970s, "women's studies was about bridging the divide between scholarship and activism. This current generation is bridging scholarship, activism and *media*."

Becky Lee is representative of this new generation. After acquiring a B.A. in women's studies from the University of Michigan in 2000, Lee went on to law school and then worked as an advocate for domestic-violence survivors. While doing this work, she was approached to audition for the popular reality TV show *Survivor*. Thinking it could serve as a good platform for her cause, she joined the cast, and while she found that most of her statements on domestic violence got left on the editing floor, she has used the *Survivor* experience to expand her advocacy.

"I came in third and used my $75,000 prize to found a fund for domestic-violence prevention with a special focus on immigrant women from marginalized communities," she says. "Now when I make public appearances for the show, I talk about the fund as a way to raise the issue of domestic violence for mainstream audiences."

So what can *you* do with a degree in women's studies? Perhaps transform enough minds through feminist education that this question is no longer asked.

ACKNOWLEDGMENTS

Lila Abu-Lughod, "Do Muslim Women Really Need Saving? Anthropological Reflections on Cultural Relativism and Its Others" from *American Anthropologist* 104, no. 3 (2002). Copyright © 2002 by the American Anthropological Association. Reprinted with permission.

Paula Gunn Allen, "Where I Come From Is Like This" from *The Sacred Hoop: Recovering the Feminine Side in American Indian Traditions*. Copyright © 1986 by Paula Gunn Allen. Reprinted with the permission of Beacon Press, Boston.

Elizabeth A. Armstrong, Laura Hamilton, and Paula England, "Is Hooking Up Bad for Young Women?" from *Contexts* 9, no. 3 (Summer 2010): 22–27. Copyright © 2010 by the American Sociological Association. Reprinted with the permission of the University of California Press Journals c/o Copyright Clearance Center.

Pamela Aronson, "Feminists or 'Postfeminists?' Young Women's Attitudes toward Feminism and Gender Relations" from *Gender & Society* 17, no. 6 (December 2003). Copyright © 2003 by Sociologists for Women in Society. Reprinted with the permission of Sage Publications, Inc. c/o Copyright Clearance Center.

Moya Bailey and Alexis Pauline Gumbs, "We Are the Ones We've Been Waiting For: Young Black feminists take their research and activism online" from *Ms.* (Winter 2010). Copyright © 2010. Reprinted with permission.

Ingrid Banks, "Hair Still Matters." Reprinted with the permission of the author.

Christine E. Bose and Rachel Bridges Whaley, "Sex Segregation in the U.S. Labor Force" from *Gender Mosaics: Social Perspectives*, edited by Dana Vannoy. Copyright © 2001 by Roxbury Publishing Company. Reprinted with the permission of Oxford University Press, Ltd.

danah boyd, "Sexing the Internet: Reflections on the role of identification in online communities." Reprinted with the permission of the author.

Grace Chang, "From the Third World to the 'Third World Within': Asian Women Workers Fighting Globalization" from *Labor Versus Empire: Race, Gender, and Migration*, edited by Gilbert G. Gonzalez, Raul Fernandez, Vivian Price, David Smith, and Linda Trinh Vo. Copyright © 2004 by Taylor &

Francis Books, Inc. Reprinted with the permission of Routledge/Taylor & Francis Group, LLC.

Eli Clare, "The Mountain" from *Exile and Public Disability, Queerness, and Liberation*. Copyright © 1999 by Eli Clare. Reprinted with the permission of South End Press.

Cathy Cohen, "Punks, Bulldaggers, and Welfare Queens: The Radical Potential of Queer Politics?" from *GLQ: A Journal of Lesbian and Gay Studies* 3, no. 4 (1997): 437–65. Copyright © 1997 by Duke University Press. All rights reserved. Reprinted by permission of the publisher.

R. W. Connell, "Masculinities and Globalization" from *Men and Masculinities* 1 (1999). Copyright © 1999 by Sage Publications, Inc. Reprinted with the permission of Sage Publications, Inc. c/o Copyright Clearance Center.

Kimberlé Crenshaw, "Mapping the Margins: Intersectionality, Identity Politics, and Violence Against Women of Color" from *Stanford Law Review* 1241 (1991). Reprinted with the permission of the author and the *Stanford Law Review*, Stanford University School of Law.

Alison Dahl Crossley, Verta Taylor, Nancy Whittier, and Cynthia Fabrizio Pelak, "Forever Feminism: The Persistence of the U.S. Women's Movement, 1960–2011." Reprinted by permission.

Simone Weil Davis, "Loose Lips Sink Ships" from *Feminist Studies* 28, no. 1 (Spring 2002). Reprinted with the permission of the publisher, *Feminist Studies*, Inc.

Sophia DeMasi, "Shopping for Love: Online dating and the making of a cyber culture of romance" from *Handbook of the New Sexuality Studies*, edited by Steven Seidman, Nancy Fischer and Chet Meeks. Copyright © 2006 by Routledge. Reprinted with the permission of Routledge/Taylor & Francis Group, Ltd.

Marisa D'Mello, "Gendered selves and identities of information technology professionals in global software organizations in India" from *Information Technology for Development* 12, no. 2 (April 2006). Copyright © 2006 by the Commonwealth Secretariat. Reprinted with the permission of Taylor & Francis Ltd, http://www.tandf.co.uk/journals on behalf of Commonwealth Secretariat.

Yen Le Espiritu, "'We Don't Sleep Around Like White Girls Do': Family, Culture, and Gender in Filipina American Lives"

Copyright © 2005. Reprinted with the permission of Seal Press, a member of Perseus Books Group c/o Copyright Clearance Center.

Laurel Richardson, "Gender Stereotyping in the English Language" adapted from *The Dynamics of Sex and Gender: A Sociological Perspective, Third Edition* (New York: Harper & Row, 1987). Copyright © 1981 by Houghton Mifflin Company. Copyright © 1987 by Harper & Row, Publishers, Inc. Reprinted with the permission of the author.

Leila J. Rupp and Verta Taylor, "Straight Girls Kissing" from *Contexts* 9, no. 3 (Summer 2010): 28–32. Copyright © 2010 by the American Sociological Association. Reprinted with the permission of the University of California Press.

Denise Segura and Patricia Zavella, "Gender in the Borderlands" (previously unpublished). Copyright © 2011 by Denise Segura and Patricia Zavella. Reprinted with the permission of the authors.

Laurie Schaffner, "Violence Against Girls Provokes Girls' Violence" from *Violence Against Women*, Volume 13, Issue 12 (December 2007): 1229–1248. Copyright © 2007 by Sage Publications, Inc. Reprinted with the permission of the author and Sage Publications, Inc. c/o Copyright Clearance Center.

Kristen Schilt and Laurel Westbrook, "'Gender Normals,' Transgender People, and the Social Maintenance of Heterosexuality" (originally titles "Doing Gender, Doing Heteronormativity: 'Gender Normals,' Transgender People, and the Social Maintenance of Heterosexuality") from *Gender & Society* 23, no. 4 (August 2009): 440–464. Copyright © 2009. Reprinted with the permission of the author and Sage Publications, Inc. c/o Copyright Clearance Center.

Andrea Smith, "Beyond Pro-Choice versus Pro-Life: Women of Color and Reproductive Justice" from *NWSA Journal* 17.1 (2005): 119–140. Copyright © 2005. Reprinted with the permission of The Johns Hopkins University Press.

Kimberly Springer, "Being the Bridge: A Solitary Black Woman's Position in the Women's Studies Classroom as a Feminist Student and Professor" from *This Bridge We Call Home: Radical Visions for Transformation*, edited by Gloria Anzaldua and AnaLouise Keating. Copyright © 2002 by Gloria Anzaldua and AnaLouise Keating. Reprinted with the permission of Routledge/Taylor & Francis, Inc. c/o Copyright Clearance Center.

Anne Fausto Sterling, "The Bare Bones of Sex" from *Signs: Journal of Women in Culture and Society* 30, no. 2 (2005). Copyright © 2005 by The University of Chicago. All rights reserved.

Reprinted with the permission of The University of Chicago Press.

Nikki Ayanna Stewart, "Transform the World: What You Can Do with a Degree in Women's Studies" from *Ms.* (Spring 2007). Copyright © 2007. Reprinted with permission.

Susan Stryker, "Transgender Feminism: Queering the Woman Question" from *Third Wave Feminism and Post-Feminism: A Critical Explanation*, Second Revised Edition, edited by Stacy Gillis, Gillian Howe, and Rebecca Munford. Reprinted with the permission of Palgrave.

Judith Taylor and Josée Johnston, "Feminist Consumerism and Fat Activists: A Comparative Study of Grassroots Activism and the Dove 'Real Beauty' Campaign" from *Signs: Journal of Women in Culture and Society* (Summer 2008). Copyright © 2008 by The University of Chicago. Reprinted with the permission of The University of Chicago Press.

Becky Wangsgaard Thompson, "'A Way Outa No Way': Eating Problems among African American, Latina, and White Women" from *Gender & Society* 6, no. 4 (December 1992). Copyright © 1994 by Sociologists for Women in Society. Reprinted with the permission of the author.

Barrie Thorne, "Girls and Boys Together … But Mostly Apart: Gender Arrangements in Elementary Schools" from *Relationships and Development*, edited by Willard W. Hartup and Zick. Volume sponsored by the Social Science Research Council. Copyright © 1986 by Lawrence Erlbaum Associates. Reprinted with the permission of the author and publisher c/o Copyright Clearance Center.

Deborah L. Tolman, "Doing Desire: Adolescent Girls' Struggles for/with Sexuality" from *Gender & Society* 8, no. 3 (September 1994). Copyright © 1994 by Sociologists for Women in Society. Reprinted with the permission of Sage Publications, Inc. c/o Copyright Clearance Center.

France Winddance Twine, "Google Babies: Race, Class, and Gestational Surrogacy" from *Outsourcing the Womb: Race, Class and Gestational Surrogacy in a Global Market*. Copyright © 2011 by Taylor & Francis Books, Inc. Reprinted with the permission of Routledge/Taylor & Francis Group, LLC.

Nancy Whittier, "Median Annual Earnings." Reprinted by permission of the author.

Maxine Baca Zinn and Bonnie Thornton Dill, "Theorizing Difference from Multiracial Feminism" from *Feminist Studies* 22, no. 2 (Summer 1996). Reprinted with the permission of the publisher, *Feminist Studies*, Inc.